THE COMPLETE PAPERS AND WRITINGS OF ABRAHAM LINCOLN

Works of the Public Domain

TABLE OF CONTENTS

VOLUME 1.

INTRODUCTORY

INTRODUCTORY NOTE

ABRAHAM LINCOLN: AN ESSAY BY CARL SHURZ

ABRAHAM LINCOLN, BY JOSEPH H. CHOATE

THE WRITINGS OF ABRAHAM LINCOLN, 1832-1843

1832

ADDRESS TO THE PEOPLE OF SANGAMON COUNTY.

1833

TO E. C. BLANKENSHIP.

RESPONSE TO REQUEST FOR POSTAGE RECEIPT

1836

ANNOUNCEMENT OF POLITICAL VIEWS.

RESPONSE TO POLITICAL SMEAR

TO MISS MARY OWENS.

1837

SPEECH IN ILLINOIS LEGISLATURE.

OPPOSITION TO MOB-RULE

PROTEST IN THE ILLINOIS LEGISLATURE ON THE SUBJECT OF SLAVERY.

TO MISS MARY OWENS.

TO JOHN BENNETT.

TO MARY OWENS.

LEGAL SUIT OF WIDOW v.s. Gen. ADAMS

LINCOLN AND TALBOTT IN REPLY TO GEN. ADAMS.

Gen. ADAMS CONTROVERSY—CONTINUED

1838

TO Mrs. O. H. BROWNING—A FARCE

1839

REMARKS ON SALE OF PUBLIC LANDS

TO ―――― ROW.

SPEECH ON NATIONAL BANK

TO JOHN T. STUART.

1840

CIRCULAR FROM WHIG COMMITTEE.

TO JOHN T. STUART.

RESOLUTION IN THE ILLINOIS LEGISLATURE.

RESOLUTION IN THE ILLINOIS LEGISLATURE.

REMARKS IN THE ILLINOIS LEGISLATURE.

REMARKS IN THE ILLINOIS LEGISLATURE.

1841

TO JOHN T. STUART—ON DEPRESSION

REMARKS IN THE ILLINOIS LEGISLATURE.

CIRCULAR FROM WHIG COMMITTEE.

AGAINST THE REORGANIZATION OF THE JUDICIARY.

TO JOSHUA F. SPEED—MURDER CASE

STATEMENT ABOUT HARRY WILTON.

TO MISS MARY SPEED—PRACTICAL SLAVERY

1842

TO JOSHUA F. SPEED—ON MARRIAGE

TO JOSHUA F. SPEED.

TO JOSHUA F. SPEED—ON DEPRESSION

TO G. B. SHELEDY.

TO GEORGE E. PICKETT—ADVICE TO YOUTH

ADDRESS BEFORE THE SPRINGFIELD WASHINGTONIAN TEMPERANCE SOCIETY,

TO JOSHUA F. SPEED.

TO JOSHUA F. SPEED—ON MARRIAGE CONCERNS

TO JOSHUA F. SPEED.

TO JOSHUA F. SPEED.

A LETTER FROM THE LOST TOWNSHIPS

LOST TOWNSHIPS

INVITATION TO HENRY CLAY.

CORRESPONDENCE ABOUT THE LINCOLN-SHIELDS DUEL.

TO J. SHIELDS.

TO A. LINCOLN FROM JAS. SHIELDS

MEMORANDUM OF INSTRUCTIONS TO E. H. MERRYMAN,

TO JOSHUA F. SPEED.

TO JAMES S. IRWIN.

1843

RESOLUTIONS AT A WHIG MEETING AT SPRINGFIELD, ILLINOIS, MARCH 1, 1843.

CIRCULAR FROM WHIG COMMITTEE.

TO JOHN BENNETT.

JOSHUA F. SPEED.

TO MARTIN M. MORRIS.

TO MARTIN M. MORRIS.

TO GEN. J. J. HARDIN.

VOLUME II., 1843-1858

1843

FIRST CHILD

1844

TO Gen. J. J. HARDIN.

1845

SELECTION OF CONGRESSIONAL CANDIDATES

TO ——— WILLIAMS,

ABOLITION MOVEMENT

1846

REQUEST FOR POLITICAL SUPPORT

TO JOHN BENNETT.

TO N. J. ROCKWELL.

TO JAMES BERDAN.

TO JAMES BERDAN.

VERSES WRITTEN BY LINCOLN AFTER A VISIT TO HIS OLD HOME IN INDIANA

SECOND CHILD

TO MORRIS AND BROWN

TO WILLIAM H. HERNDON

TO WILLIAM H. HERNDON.

RESOLUTIONS IN THE UNITED STATES HOUSE OF REPRESENTATIVES,

REMARKS IN THE UNITED STATES HOUSE OF REPRESENTATIVES,

1848

DESIRE FOR SECOND TERM IN CONGRESS

SPEECH ON DECLARATION OF WAR ON MEXICO

REPORT IN THE HOUSE OF REPRESENTATIVES, JANUARY 19, 1848.

TO WILLIAM H. HERNDON—LEGAL WORK

REGARDING SPEECH ON MEXICAN WAR

TO WILLIAM H. HERNDON.

ON THE MEXICAN WAR

REPORT IN THE HOUSE OF REPRESENTATIVES,

REPORT IN THE HOUSE OF REPRESENTATIVES,

REMARKS IN THE UNITED STATES HOUSE OF REPRESENTATIVES, MARCH 29, 1848.

TO ARCHIBALD WILLIAMS.

REMARKS IN THE HOUSE OF REPRESENTATIVES,

ON TAYLOR'S NOMINATION

DEFENSE OF MEXICAN WAR POSITION

ON ZACHARY TAYLOR NOMINATION

SPEECH IN THE HOUSE OF REPRESENTATIVES,

OPPORTUNITIES FOR YOUNG POLITICIANS

SALARY OF JUDGE IN WESTERN VIRGINIA

NATIONAL BANK

YOUNG v.s. OLD—POLITICAL JEALOUSY

GENERAL TAYLOR AND THE VETO

SPEECH DELIVERED AT WORCESTER, MASS., ON SEPT. 12, 1848.

HIS FATHER'S REQUEST FOR MONEY

1849

BILL GRANTING LANDS TO THE STATES TO MAKE RAILWAYS AND CANALS

ON FEDERAL POLITICAL APPOINTMENTS

MORE POLITICAL PATRONAGE REQUESTS

TO THE SECRETARY OF THE INTERIOR

TO THE SECRETARY OF THE INTERIOR.

TO THE POSTMASTER-GENERAL.

TO THE SECRETARY OF THE INTERIOR.

TO THOMPSON.

TO THE SECRETARY OF THE INTERIOR.

TO J. GILLESPIE.

REQUEST FOR GENERAL LAND-OFFICE APPPOINTMENT

REQUEST FOR A PATENT

TO THE SECRETARY OF INTERIOR.
TO W. H. HERNDON.

TO J. GILLESPIE.

RESOLUTIONS OF SYMPATHY WITH THE
CAUSE OF HUNGARIAN FREEDOM,

TO Dr. WILLIAM FITHIAN.

SPRINGFIELD, Dec. 15, 1849.

1850

RESOLUTIONS ON THE DEATH OF JUDGE
NATHANIEL POPE.

NOTES FOR LAW LECTURE

1851

LETTERS TO FAMILY MEMBERS

TO JOHN D. JOHNSTON.

TO C. HOYT.

TO JOHN D. JOHNSTON.

PETITION ON BEHALF OF ONE JOSHUA
GIPSON

TO J. D. JOHNSTON.

TO J. D. JOHNSTON.

Nov. 4, 1851

TO JOHN D. JOHNSTON.

TO JOHN D. JOHNSTON.

1852

EULOGY ON HENRY CLAY,

CHALLENGED VOTERS

1853

LEGAL OFFICE WORK

TO JOSHUA R. STANFORD.

1854

NEBRASKA MEASURE

TO A. B. MOREAU.

REPLY TO SENATOR DOUGLAS—PEORIA
SPEECH

REQUEST FOR SENATE SUPPORT

TO T. J. HENDERSON.

TO J. GILLESPIE.

POLITICAL REFERENCES

TO T. J. HENDERSON.

1855

LOSS OF PRIMARY FOR SENATOR

RETURN TO LAW PROFESSION

TO O. H. BROWNING.

TO H. C. WHITNEY.

RESPONSE TO A PRO-SLAVERY FRIEND

1856

REQUEST FOR A RAILWAY PASS

SPEECH DELIVERED BEFORE THE FIRST
REPUBLICAN STATE CONVENTION

POLITICAL CORRESPONDENCE

ON OUT-OF-STATE CAMPAIGNERS

REPUBLICAN CAMPAIGN SPEECH

ON THE DANGER OF THIRD-PARTIES

TO JESSE K. DUBOIS.

TO HARRISON MALTBY.

TO Dr. R. BOAL.

TO HENRY O'CONNER, MUSCATINE, IOWA.

AFTER THE DEMOCRATIC VICTORY OF
BUCHANAN

TO Dr. R. BOAL.

1857

RESPONSE TO A DOUGLAS SPEECH

TO WILLIAM GRIMES.

ARGUMENT IN THE ROCK ISLAND BRIDGE
CASE.

TO JESSE K. DUBOIS.

TO JOSEPH GILLESPIE.

TO J. GILLESPIE.

TO H. C. WHITNEY.

| ANOTHER POLITICAL PATRONAGE REFERENCE | 1858 |
| BRIEF AUTOBIOGRAPHY, | |

VOLUME 3 THE LINCOLN-DOUGLAS

THE LINCOLN-DOUGLAS DEBATES I

SPEECH AT CHICAGO, JULY 10, 1858.

SPEECH AT SPRINGFIELD, JULY 17, 1858.

CORRESPONDENCE BETWEEN LINCOLN AND DOUGLAS

MR. LINCOLN TO MR. DOUGLAS.

Mr. DOUGLAS TO Mr. LINCOLN.

Mr. LINCOLN TO Mr. DOUGLAS.

FIRST JOINT DEBATE, AT OTTAWA,

SECOND JOINT DEBATE, AT FREEPORT,

Mr. LINCOLN'S REJOINDER.

THIRD JOINT DEBATE, AT JONESBORO,

INTERROGATORIES:

CAMPBELL'S REPLY.

VOLUME 4 THE LINCOLN-DOUGLAS

THE LINCOLN-DOUGLAS DEBATES II

LINCOLN AND DOUGLAS FOURTH DEBATE, AT CHARLESTON, SEPTEMBER 18, 1858.

Mr. LINCOLN'S REJOINDER.

FIFTH JOINT DEBATE, AT GALESBURGH, OCTOBER 7, 1858

SIXTH JOINT DEBATE, AT QUINCY, OCTOBER 13, 1858.

Mr. LINCOLN'S REJOINDER.

LAST DEBATE, AT ALTON, OCTOBER 15, 1858

Mr. LINCOLN'S REPLY

THE WRITINGS OF ABRAHAM LINCOLN,
VOLUME FIVE, 1858-1862

1858

TO SYDNEY SPRING, GRAYVILLE, ILL.

TO H. C. WHITNEY.

TO J. W. SOMERS.

TO A. CAMPBELL.

TO J. GILLESPIE.

TO JOHN MATHERS, JACKSONVILLE, ILL.

TO JOSEPH GILLESPIE.

TO B. C. COOK.

TO HON. J. M. PALMER.

TO ALEXANDER SYMPSON.

TO J. O. CUNNINGHAM.

ON SLAVERY IN A DEMOCRACY.

TO B. C. COOK.

TO DR. WILLIAM FITHIAN, DANVILLE, ILL.

FRAGMENT OF SPEECH AT PARIS, ILL.,

SPEECH AT CLINTON, ILLINOIS,

FRAGMENT OF SPEECH AT EDWARDSVILLE, ILL.,

VERSE TO "LINNIE"

NEGROES ARE MEN

TO A. SYMPSON.

SENATORIAL ELECTION LOST AND OUT OF MONEY

THE FIGHT MUST GO ON

REALIZATION THAT DEBATES MUST BE SAVED

TO H. C. WHITNEY.

TO H. D. SHARPE.

TO A. SYMPSON.

ON BANKRUPTCY

NOTES OF AN ARGUMENT.

A LEGAL OPINION BY ABRAHAM LINCOLN.

TO M. W. DELAHAY.

TO W. M. MORRIS.

TO H. L. PIERCE AND OTHERS.

TO T. CANISIUS.

TO THE GOVERNOR, AUDITOR, AND TREASURER OF THE STATE OF ILLINOIS.

ON LINCOLN'S SCRAP BOOK

1859

FIRST SUGGESTION OF A PRESIDENTIAL OFFER.

TO S. GALLOWAY.

IT IS BAD TO BE POOR.

SPEECH AT COLUMBUS, OHIO.

SPEECH AT CINCINNATI OHIO, SEPTEMBER 17, 1859

ON PROTECTIVE TARIFFS

ON MORTGAGES

FRAGMENT OF SPEECH AT LEAVENWORTH, KANSAS,

TO G. W. DOLE, G. S. HUBBARD, AND W. H. BROWN.

TO G. M. PARSONS AND OTHERS.

AUTOBIOGRAPHICAL SKETCH

ON NOMINATION TO THE NATIONAL TICKET

1860

SPEECH AT NEW HAVEN, CONNECTICUT, MARCH 6, 1860

RESPONSE TO AN ELECTOR'S REQUEST FOR MONEY

TO J. W. SOMERS.

ACCUSATION OF HAVING BEEN PAID FOR A POLITICAL SPEECH

TO H. TAYLOR.

TELEGRAM TO A MEMBER OF THE ILLINOIS DELEGATION

REPLY TO THE COMMITTEE SENT BY THE CHICAGO CONVENTION TO INFORM

ACCEPTANCE OF NOMINATION AS REPUBLICAN CANDIDATE FOR PRESIDENT

To C. B. SMITH.

FORM OF REPLY PREPARED BY MR. LINCOLN,

TO E. B. WASHBURNE.

TO S. HAYCRAFT.

ABRAHAM OR "ABRAM"

UNAUTHORIZED BIOGRAPHY

TO HANNIBAL HAMLIN.

TO A. JONAS.

TO JOHN B. FRY.

TO THURLOW WEED

SLOW TO LISTEN TO CRIMINATIONS

TO HANNIBAL HAMLIN

TO E. B. WASHBURNE.

TO W. H. HERNDON.

TO L. M. BOND.

LETTER SUGGESTING A BEARD

EARLY INFORMATION ON ARMY DEFECTION IN SOUTH

TO HANNIBAL HAMLIN

TO SAMUEL HAYCRAFT.

TO ALEXANDER H. STEPHENS

TO HANNIBAL HAMLIN

BLOCKING "COMPROMISE" ON SLAVERY ISSUE

OPINION ON SECESSION

SOME FORTS SURRENDERED TO THE SOUTH

TO A. H. STEPHENS.

SUPPORT OF THE FUGITIVE SLAVE CLAUSE

TO D. HUNTER.

TO I. N. MORRIS

ATTEMPT TO FORM A COALITION CABINET

1861

TO W. H. SEWARD.

TO E. D. MORGAN

PATRONAGE CLAIMS

FAREWELL ADDRESS AT SPRINGFIELD, ILLINOIS,

REMARKS AT TOLONO, ILLINOIS, FEBRUARY 11, 1861

REPLY TO ADDRESS OF WELCOME, INDIANAPOLIS,

ADDRESS TO THE LEGISLATURE OF INDIANA, AT INDIANAPOLIS,

INTENTIONS TOWARD THE SOUTH

ADDRESS TO THE GERMAN CLUB OF CINCINNATI, OHIO,

ADDRESS TO THE LEGISLATURE OF OHIO AT COLUMBUS

ADDRESS AT STEUBENVILLE, OHIO,

ADDRESS AT PITTSBURGH, PENNSYLVANIA

ADDRESS AT CLEVELAND, OHIO,

ADDRESS AT BUFFALO, NEW YORK,

ADDRESS AT ROCHESTER, NEW YORK,

ADDRESS AT SYRACUSE, NEW YORK,

ADDRESS AT UTICA, NEW YORK,

REPLY TO THE MAYOR OF ALBANY, NEW YORK

REPLY TO GOVERNOR MORGAN OF NEW YORK, AT ALBANY,

ADDRESS TO THE LEGISLATURE OF NEW YORK, AT ALBANY,

ADDRESS AT TROY, NEW YORK,

ADDRESS AT POUGHKEEPSIE, NEW YORK,

ADDRESS AT HUDSON, NEW YORK.

ADDRESS AT PEEKSKILL, NEW YORK,

ADDRESS AT FISHKILL LANDING

REMARKS AT THE ASTOR HOUSE, NEW YORK CITY, FEBRUARY 19, 1861

ADDRESS AT NEW YORK CITY,

REPLY TO THE MAYOR OF NEW YORK CITY,

ADDRESS AT JERSEY CITY, NEW JERSEY

REPLY TO THE MAYOR OF NEWARK, NEW JERSEY,

ADDRESS IN TRENTON AT THE TRENTON HOUSE,

ADDRESS TO THE SENATE OF NEW JERSEY

ADDRESS TO THE ASSEMBLY OF NEW JERSEY,

REPLY TO THE MAYOR OF PHILADELPHIA, PENNSYLVANIA,

ADDRESS IN THE HALL OF INDEPENDENCE, PHILADELPHIA,

REPLY TO THE WILMINGTON DELEGATION,

ADDRESS AT LANCASTER, PENNSYLVANIA,

ADDRESS TO THE LEGISLATURE OF PENNSYLVANIA, AT HARRISBURG,

REPLY TO THE MAYOR OF WASHINGTON, D.C.,

REPLY TO A SERENADE AT WASHINGTON, D.C.,

WASHINGTON, SUNDAY, MARCH 3, 1861

FIRST INAUGURAL ADDRESS, MARCH 4, 1861

REFUSAL OF SEWARD RESIGNATION

REPLY TO THE PENNSYLVANIA DELEGATION,

REPLY TO THE MASSACHUSETTS DELEGATION,

TO SECRETARY SEWARD

REPLY TO THE DIPLOMATIC CORPS

TO SECRETARY SEWARD

TO J. COLLAMER

TO THE POSTMASTER-GENERAL.

NOTE ASKING CABINET OPINIONS ON FORT SUMTER.

ON ROYAL ARBITRATION OF AMERICAN BOUNDARY LINE

AMBASSADORIAL APPOINTMENTS

TO G. E. PATTEN.

RESPONSE TO SENATE INQUIRY RE. FORT SUMTER

PREPARATION OF FIRST NAVAL ACTION

TO ——— STUART.

TO THE COMMANDANT OF THE NEW YORK NAVY-YARD.

TO LIEUTENANT D. D. PORTER

RELIEF EXPEDITION FOR FORT SUMTER

ORDER TO CAPTAIN SAMUEL MERCER.

SECRETARY SEWARD'S BID FOR POWER

REPLY TO SECRETARY SEWARD'S MEMORANDUM

REPLY TO A COMMITTEE FROM THE VIRGINIA CONVENTION, APRIL 13, 1861

PROCLAMATION CALLING FOR 75,000 MILITIA,

PROCLAMATION OF BLOCKADE, APRIL 19, 1861

TO GOVERNOR HICKS AND MAYOR BROWN.

xii

TO GOVERNOR HICKS.

ORDER TO DEFEND FROM A MARYLAND INSURRECTION

PROCLAMATION OF BLOCKADE, APRIL 27, 1861

REMARKS TO A MILITARY COMPANY, WASHINGTON, APRIL 27, 1861

LOCALIZED REPEAL OF WRIT OF HABEAS CORPUS

MILITARY ENROLLMENT OF ST. LOUIS CITIZENS

CONDOLENCE OVER FAILURE OF FT. SUMTER RELIEF

PROCLAMATION CALLING FOR 42,034 VOLUNTEERS,

COMMUNICATION WITH VICE-PRESIDENT

ORDER TO COLONEL ANDERSON,

PROCLAMATION SUSPENDING THE WRIT OF HABEAS CORPUS IN FLORIDA,

TO SECRETARY WELLES.

PRESIDENT LINCOLN'S CORRECTIONS OF A DIPLOMATIC DESPATCH

TO THE SECRETARY OF WAR,

TO GOVERNOR MORGAN.

TO CAPTAIN DAHLGREEN.

LETTER OF CONDOLENCE TO ONE OF FIRST CASUALTIES

TO COLONEL BARTLETT.

MEMORANDUM ABOUT INDIANA REGIMENTS.

TO THE SECRETARY OF WAR.

TO THE SECRETARY OF WAR.

TO THE SECRETARY OF WAR.

TO THE SECRETARY OF WAR.

TO N. W. EDWARDS

TO SECRETARY CAMERON.

HON. SECRETARY OF WAR.

TO THE KENTUCKY DELEGATION.

August 5, 1861.

ORDER AUTHORIZING GENERAL SCOTT TO SUSPEND THE WRIT OF HABEAS CORPUS, JULY

TO SECRETARY SEWARD.

MESSAGE TO CONGRESS IN SPECIAL SESSION,

TO THE SECRETARY OF THE INTERIOR.

MESSAGE TO THE HOUSE OF REPRESENTATIVES.

MESSAGE TO CONGRESS.

MESSAGE TO CONGRESS.

TO THE ADJUTANT-GENERAL

MEMORANDA OF MILITARY POLICY SUGGESTED BY THE BULL RUN DEFEAT. JULY 23,

TO THE GOVERNOR OF NEW JERSEY.

MESSAGE TO THE HOUSE OF REPRESENTATIVES.

MESSAGE TO THE HOUSE OF REPRESENTATIVES.

TO SECRETARY CHASE.

MESSAGE TO THE HOUSE OF REPRESENTATIVES.

MESSAGE TO THE SENATE.

MESSAGE TO THE SENATE.

ORDER TO UNITED STATES MARSHALS.

MESSAGE TO THE HOUSE OF REPRESENTATIVES.

MESSAGE TO THE SENATE.

TO SECRETARY CAMERON.

PROCLAMATION OF A NATIONAL FAST-DAY, AUGUST 12, 1861.

TO JAMES POLLOCK.

TELEGRAM TO GOVERNOR O. P. MORTON.

TELEGRAM TO GENERAL FREMONT,

PROCLAMATION FORBIDDING INTERCOURSE WITH REBEL STATES, AUGUST 16, 1861.

TO SECRETARY CAMERON.

TO GOVERNOR MAGOFFIN,

TO GENERAL FREMONT.

TELEGRAM TO GOVERNORS

TO GENERAL FREMONT.

TO MRS. FREMONT.

TO JOSEPH HOLT,

TO GENERAL SCOTT

TO SECRETARY CAMERON.

TO GENERAL FREMONT,

To O. H. BROWNING.

MEMORANDUM FOR A PLAN OF CAMPAIGN

TO THE SECRETARY OF STATE.

TO THE VICEROY OF EGYPT.

ORDER AUTHORIZING SUSPENSION OF THE WRIT OF HABEAS CORPUS.

TO SECRETARY OF INTERIOR.

TWO SONS WHO WANT TO WORK

TO GENERAL THOMAS W. SHERMAN.

TO GENERAL CURTIS, WITH INCLOSURES.

WASHINGTON, October 24, 1861

WASHINGTON, October 24, 1861

ORDER RETIRING GENERAL SCOTT AND APPOINTING

EXECUTIVE MANSION, WASHINGTON.

ORDER APPROVING THE PLAN OF GOVERNOR GAMBLE OF MISSOURI.

REPLY TO THE MINISTER FROM SWEDEN.

INDORSEMENT AUTHORIZING MARTIAL LAW IN SAINT LOUIS.

OFFER TO COOPERATE AND GIVE SPECIAL LINE OF INFORMATION TO HORACE GREELEY

ORDER AUTHORIZING GENERAL HALLECK TO SUSPEND THE WRIT OF HABEAS CORPUS,

ANNUAL MESSAGE TO CONGRESS.

MESSAGE TO CONGRESS.

LETTER OF REPRIMAND TO GENERAL HUNTER

TELEGRAM TO GENERAL HALLECK.

1862

TELEGRAM TO GENERAL D. C. BUELL.

TO GENERAL H. W. HALLECK.

TO THE PEOPLE OF MARYLAND,

MESSAGE TO CONGRESS.

MESSAGES OF DISAPPOINTMENT WITH HIS GENERALS

TO GENERAL D. C. BUELL.

TELEGRAM TO GENERAL BUELL.

MESSAGE TO CONGRESS.

INDORSEMENT ON LETTER FROM GENERAL HALLECK,

TELEGRAM TO GOVERNOR ANDREW.

TO GENERAL D. C. BUELL.

TO GENERAL H. W. HALLECK.

MESSAGE TO CONGRESS.

TO GENERAL McCLELLAN.

PRESIDENT'S GENERAL WAR ORDER NO. 1

TO SECRETARY STANTON,

PRESIDENT'S SPECIAL WAR ORDER NO. 1.

OPPOSITION TO McCLELLAN'S PLANS

TO WM. H. HERNDON.

RESPITE FOR NATHANIEL GORDON

MESSAGE TO THE SENATE.

TO GENERALS D. HUNTER AND J. H. LANE.

EXECUTIVE ORDER NO. 1, RELATING TO POLITICAL PRISONERS.

MESSAGE TO CONGRESS. WASHINGTON CITY, February 15, 1862

FIRST WRITTEN NOTICE OF GRANT

EXECUTIVE ORDER NO. 2.—IN RELATION TO STATE PRISONERS.

ORDER RELATING TO COMMERCIAL INTERCOURSE.

SPEECH TO THE PERUVIAN MINISTER,

MESSAGE TO CONGRESS RECOMMENDING COMPENSATED EMANCIPATION.

INDORSEMENT ON LETTER FROM GOVERNOR YATES.

PRESIDENT'S GENERAL WAR ORDER NO.2.

PRESIDENT'S GENERAL WAR ORDER NO.3.

INTERVIEW BETWEEN THE PRESIDENT AND SOME BORDER SLAVE STATE

PRESIDENT'S SPECIAL WAR ORDER NO.3.

FROM SECRETARY STANTON TO GENERAL MCCLELLAN.

SPEECH TO A PARTY OF MASSACHUSETTS GENTLEMAN

MESSAGE TO CONGRESS.

TO GENERAL G. B. McCLELLAN.

GIFT OF SOME RABBITS

INSTRUCTION TO SECRETARY STANTON.

TELEGRAM TO GENERAL McCLELLAN.

TO GENERAL G. B. McCLELLAN.

TO GENERAL H. W. HALLECK.

PROCLAMATION RECOMMENDING THANKSGIVING FOR VICTORIES,

ABOLISHING SLAVERY IN WASHINGTON, D.C.

TELEGRAM TO GENERAL G. B. McCLELLAN.

TO POSTMASTER-GENERAL

TELEGRAM TO GENERAL G. B. McCLELLAN.

MESSAGE TO THE SENATE, MAY 1, 1862.

TELEGRAM TO GENERAL McCLELLAN

TELEGRAM TO GENERAL H. W. HALLECK.

RESPONSE TO EVANGELICAL LUTHERANS, MAY 6, 1862

TELEGRAM TO FLAG-OFFICER L. M. GOLDSBOROUGH.

FURTHER REPRIMAND OF McCLELLAN

TO FLAG-OFFICER L. M. GOLDSBOROUGH,

PROCLAMATION RAISING THE BLOCKADE OF CERTAIN PORTS

THE WRITINGS OF A. LINCOLN, VOLUME SIX, 1862-1863

1862

RECOMMENDATION OF NAVAL OFFICERS

TO THE SENATE AND HOUSE OF REPRESENTATIVES:

TELEGRAM TO GENERAL G. B. McCLELLAN.

SPEECH TO THE 12TH INDIANA REGIMENT, MAY [15?] 1862

TELEGRAM TO GENERAL I. McDOWELL.

MEMORANDUM OF PROPOSED ADDITIONS TO INSTRUCTIONS OF ABOVE DATE

MILITARY EMANCIPATION

FROM SECRETARY STANTON TO GENERAL McCLELLAN.

PROCLAMATION REVOKING GENERAL HUNTER'S ORDER OF MILITARY EMANCIPATION,

TELEGRAM TO GENERAL G. E. McCLELLAN.

TELEGRAM TO GENERAL G. B. McCLELLAN.

TELEGRAM TO GENERAL McCLELLAN.

TELEGRAM TO GENERAL McCLELLAN

TELEGRAM TO GENERAL RUFUS SAXTON.

TELEGRAM TO COLONEL D. S. MILES.

TELEGRAM TO GENERAL J. C. FREMONT.

TELEGRAM TO GENERAL J. C. FREMONT.

TELEGRAM TO GENERAL H. W. HALLECK.

TELEGRAM TO GENERAL McDOWELL.

TELEGRAM TO GENERAL J. W. GEARY.

TELEGRAM TO GENERAL G. B. McCLELLAN.

ORDER TAKING MILITARY POSSESSION OF RAILROADS.

TELEGRAM TO SECRETARY CHASE.

TELEGRAM TO GENERAL R. SAXTON.

TELEGRAM TO GENERAL R. SAXTON.

TELEGRAM TO GENERAL R. SAXTON.

TELEGRAM TO GENERAL G. B. McCLELLAN.

HISTORY OF CONSPIRACY OF REBELLION

TELEGRAM TO GENERAL G. B. McCLELLAN.

TELEGRAM TO GENERAL I. McDOWELL.

TELEGRAM TO GENERAL McCLELLAN.

TELEGRAM TO GENERAL J. C. FREMONT.

TELEGRAM FROM SECRETARY STANTON TO GOVERNOR ANDREW.

TELEGRAM FROM SECRETARY STANTON TO GENERAL J. C. FREMONT,

TELEGRAM TO GENERAL I. McDOWELL.

TELEGRAM TO GENERAL G. B. McCLELLAN.

TELEGRAM TO GENERAL I. McDOWELL.

TELEGRAM TO GENERAL I. McDOWELL.

TELEGRAM TO GENERAL G. B. McCLELLAN

TELEGRAM FROM SECRETARY STANTON TO GENERAL FREMONT.

TELEGRAM TO GENERAL MARCY.

TELEGRAM TO GENERAL G. B. McCLELLAN.

TELEGRAM TO GENERAL N. P. BANKS.

TELEGRAM TO GENERAL FREMONT

TELEGRAM TO GENERAL I. McDOWELL.

TELEGRAM TO GENERAL MARCY.

TELEGRAM TO GENERAL I. McDOWELL.

TELEGRAM TO GENERAL N. P. BANKS.

TELEGRAM TO GENERAL I. McDOWELL.

TELEGRAM TO GENERAL FREMONT.

TELEGRAM TO GENERAL I. McDOWELL.

TELEGRAM TO GENERAL G. B. McCLELLAN.

TELEGRAM FROM SECRETARY STANTON

TELEGRAM TO GENERAL G. B. McCLELLAN.

TELEGRAM TO GENERAL G. B. McCLELLAN.

TELEGRAM TO GENERAL I. McDOWELL.

TELEGRAM TO GENERAL H. W. HALLECK.

TELEGRAM TO GOVERNOR JOHNSON.

TO GENERAL G. B. McCLELLAN.

TELEGRAM TO GENERAL H. W. HALLECK.

TELEGRAM TO GENERAL N. P. BANKS.

TELEGRAM TO GENERAL J. C. FREMONT.

TELEGRAM TO GOVERNOR JOHNSON.

TO GENERAL J. C. FREMONT. WASHINGTON, June 12, 1862.

MESSAGE TO CONGRESS.

TO GENERAL J. C. FREMONT.

TO GENERAL J. C. FREMONT.

TO GENERAL C. SCHURZ.

TELEGRAM TO GENERAL H. W. HALLECK.

TELEGRAM TO GENERAL G. B. McCLELLAN.

TELEGRAM TO GENERAL G. B. McCLELLAN.

TELEGRAM TO GENERAL G. B. McCLELLAN.

TELEGRAM TO GENERAL G. B. McCLELLAN.

TELEGRAM TO GENERAL G. B. McCLELLAN.

TELEGRAM TO GENERAL N. P. BANKS.

TREATY WITH MEXICO

VETO OF A CURRENCY BILL

SPEECH AT JERSEY CITY, JUNE 24, 1862.

TO GENERAL G. B. McCLELLAN.

ORDER CONSTITUTING THE ARMY OF VIRGINIA.

TELEGRAM FROM SECRETARY STANTON TO GENERAL H. W. HALLECK.

TELEGRAMS TO GENERAL A. E. BURNSIDE.

WAR DEPARTMENT, June, 28, 1862

TELEGRAM TO GENERAL G. B. McCLELLAN.

TO SECRETARY SEWARD.

TELEGRAM TO GENERAL J. A. DIX.

TELEGRAM TO FLAG-OFFICER L. M. GOLDSBOROUGH.

To GOVERNOR MORTON.

TELEGRAM TO SECRETARY SEWARD.

TELEGRAM TO SECRETARY SEWARD. WAR DEPARTMENT, June 30, 1862.

CALL FOR TROOPS. NEW YORK, June 30, 1862.

TELEGRAM TO GENERAL J. A. DIX.

TELEGRAMS TO GENERAL H. W. HALLECK.

WASHINGTON, D.C., June 30, 1862.

CALL FOR 300,000 VOLUNTEERS, JULY 1, 1862.

EXECUTIVE MANSION, WASHINGTON, July 1, 1862

PROCLAMATION CONCERNING TAXES IN REBELLIOUS STATES, JULY 1, 1862.

MESSAGE TO CONGRESS, JULY 1, 1862.

TELEGRAM TO GENERAL McCLELLAN.

TO GENERAL G. B. McCLELLAN.

TELEGRAM TO GENERAL H. W. HALLECK.

MESSAGE TO THE SENATE.

CIRCULAR LETTER TO THE GOVERNORS.

TO GENERAL G. B. McCLELLAN.

TO GENERAL G. B. McCLELLAN.

TELEGRAM TO GENERAL H. W. HALLECK.

TELEGRAM TO GENERAL J. A. DIX.

TELEGRAM TO GENERAL G. B. McCLELLAN.

TO GENERAL H. W. HALLECK.

MEMORANDUM OF AN INTERVIEW BETWEEN THE PRESIDENT AND GENERAL McCLELLAN

xvii

ORDER MAKING HALLECK GENERAL-IN-CHIEF.

ORDER CONCERNING THE SOUTHWEST BRANCH OF THE PACIFIC RAILROAD.

MESSAGE TO CONGRESS.

TELEGRAM TO GOVERNOR JOHNSON. WAR DEPARTMENT, July 11, 1862.

TELEGRAM TO GENERAL H. W. HALLECK. WAR DEPARTMENT, July 11, 1862.

APPEAL TO BORDER-STATES IN FAVOR OF COMPENSATED EMANCIPATION.

TO GENERAL G. B. McCLELLAN.

TELEGRAM TO GENERAL H. W. HALLECK.

TELEGRAM TO GENERAL J. T. BOYLE.

TELEGRAM TO GENERAL J. T. BOYLE.

ACT OF COMPENSATED EMANCIPATION

TELEGRAM TO GENERAL H. W. HALLECK.

TELEGRAM TO GENERAL G. B. McCLELLAN.

TO SOLOMON FOOT.

MESSAGE TO CONGRESS. July 17, 1862.

MESSAGE TO CONGRESS. July 17, 1862.

FELLOW-CITIZENS OF THE HOUSE OF REPRESENTATIVES:

TELEGRAM TO GENERAL G. B. McCLELLAN.

ORDER IN REGARD TO BEHAVIOR OF ALIENS

ORDER AUTHORIZING EMPLOYMENT OF "CONTRABANDS."

WARNING TO REBEL SYMPATHIZERS

HOLD MY HAND WHILST THE ENEMY STABS ME

TO CUTHBERT BULLITT.

TO LOYAL GOVERNORS.

BROKEN EGGS CANNOT BE MENDED

TO COUNT GASPARIN.

SPEECH AT A WAR MEETING, WASHINGTON, AUGUST 6, 1862

TELEGRAM TO GOVERNOR ANDREW. August 12, 1862.

TELEGRAM TO GOVERNOR CURTIN. August 12, 1862.

TELEGRAM TO GENERAL S. R. CURTIS. August 12, 1862.

ADDRESS ON COLONIZATION TO A DEPUTATION OF COLORED MEN.

TELEGRAM TO OFFICER AT CAMP CHASE, OHIO.

TO HIRAM BARNEY.

NOTE OF INTRODUCTION.

TO Mrs. PRESTON.

TELEGRAM TO GENERAL BURNSIDE OR GENERAL PARKE.

TO G. P. WATSON.

TO HORACE GREELEY.

TELEGRAM TO GOVERNOR YATES.

TELEGRAM TO GOVERNOR RAMSEY.

TELEGRAM TO GENERAL G. B. McCLELLAN.

TELEGRAM TO GENERAL A. E. BURNSIDE.

TELEGRAM TO GENERAL A. E. BURNSIDE.

TELEGRAM TO COLONEL HAUPT.

TELEGRAM TO GENERAL A. E. BURNSIDE.

TELEGRAM TO GENERAL G. B. McCLELLAN.

TELEGRAM TO GENERAL G. B. McCLELLAN.

TELEGRAM TO COLONEL HAUPT.

TELEGRAM TO COLONEL HAUPT.

TELEGRAM TO GENERAL BANKS.

TELEGRAM TO GENERAL J. T. BOYLE.

ORDER TO GENERAL H. W. HALLECK.

TELEGRAM TO GENERAL H. G. WRIGHT.

TELEGRAM TO GENERAL J. T. BOYLE.

TELEGRAM TO GENERAL J. E. WOOL.

TELEGRAM TO GENERAL G. B. McCLELLAN.

TELEGRAM TO GENERAL D. C. BUELL.

TELEGRAM TO T. WEBSTER.

TELEGRAM TO GENERAL G. B. McCLELLAN.

TO GOVERNOR CURTIN. September 11, 1862.

TELEGRAM TO GOVERNOR CURTIN.

TELEGRAM TO GENERAL C. B. McCLELLAN.

TELEGRAM TO GENERAL G. B. McCLELLAN.

TELEGRAM TO GOVERNOR CURTIN.

TELEGRAM TO GENERAL H. G. WRIGHT.

TELEGRAM TO GENERAL J. T. BOYLE.

TELEGRAM TO A. HENRY.

TELEGRAM TO GENERAL G. B. McCLELLAN.

REPLY TO REQUEST THE PRESIDENT ISSUE A PROCLAMATION OF EMANCIPATION.

TELEGRAM TO GENERAL H. G. WRIGHT.

TELEGRAM TO GENERAL G. B. McCLELLAN.

TELEGRAM TO J. K. DUBOIS. WASHINGTON, D.C.,

TELEGRAM TO GOVERNOR CURTIN,

TELEGRAM TO GOVERNOR MORTON.

TELEGRAM TO GENERAL KETCHUM.

PRELIMINARY EMANCIPATION PROCLAMATION, SEPTEMBER 22, 1862.

PROCLAMATION SUSPENDING THE WRIT OF HABEAS CORPUS,

REPLY TO SERENADE, SEPTEMBER 24, 1862.

RECORD EXPLAINING THE DISMISSAL OF MAJOR JOHN J. KEY

TO HANNIBAL HAMLIN.

TO GENERAL HALLECK.

REMARKS TO THE ARMY OF THE POTOMAC AT FREDERICK, MARYLAND,

TELEGRAM FROM GENERAL HALLECK

TELEGRAM TO GENERAL McCLELLAN.

TO T. H. CLAY.

TELEGRAM TO GENERAL U. S. GRANT.

TELEGRAM TO GENERAL J. T. BOYLE.

TELEGRAM TO GENERAL J. T. BOYLE.

TELEGRAM TO GENERAL CURTIS.

TO GENERAL G. B. McCLELLAN.

TELEGRAM TO GOVERNOR PIERPOINT.

EXECUTIVE ORDER ESTABLISHING A PROVISIONAL COURT IN LOUISIANA.

TO GENERAL U.S. GRANT.

TELEGRAM TO GENERAL JAMESON.

GENERAL McCLELLAN'S TIRED HORSES

TELEGRAM TO GENERAL G. B. McCLELLAN.

TO GENERAL DIX.

TELEGRAM TO GENERAL G. B. McCLELLAN.

TELEGRAM TO GENERAL G. B. McCLELLAN.

TELEGRAM TO GENERAL G. B. McCLELLAN.

TELEGRAM TO GOVERNOR CURTIN.

TELEGRAM TO GOVERNOR JOHNSON.

MEMORANDUM.

ORDER RELIEVING GENERAL G. B. McCLELLAN

TELEGRAM TO M. F. ODELL.

TELEGRAM TO COLONEL LOWE.

TELEGRAM TO GENERAL J. POPE.

TO COMMODORE FARRAGUT.

ORDER CONCERNING BLOCKADE.

ORDER CONCERNING THE CONFISCATION ACT.

TELEGRAM TO GOVERNOR JOHNSON.

GENERAL ORDER RESPECTING THE OBSERVANCE OF THE SABBATH DAY

TELEGRAM TO GENERAL BLAIR

TELEGRAM TO GENERAL J. A. DIX.

TO GOVERNOR SHEPLEY.

ORDER PROHIBITING THE EXPORT OF ARMS AND MUNITIONS OF WAR.

DELAYING TACTICS OF GENERALS

TO CARL SCHURZ.

TELEGRAM TO GENERAL A. E. BURNSIDE.

TO ATTORNEY-GENERAL BATES.

TELEGRAM TO GENERAL CURTIS.

ON EXECUTING 300 INDIANS

ANNUAL MESSAGE TO CONGRESS, DECEMBER 1, 1862.

MESSAGE TO CONGRESS.

TELEGRAM TO H. J. RAYMOND.

TELEGRAM TO B. G. BROWN.

TELEGRAM TO GOVERNOR JOHNSON.

MESSAGE TO CONGRESS. December 8, 1862.

TO GENERAL S. R. CURTIS.

TO J. K. DUBOIS.

MESSAGE TO THE SENATE.

MESSAGE TO CONGRESS.

TO FERNANDO WOOD.

TELEGRAM TO GENERAL CURTIS.

TELEGRAM TO GENERAL H. H. SIBLEY.

TELEGRAM TO GENERAL CURTIS.

TELEGRAM TO GENERAL BURNSIDE.

TELEGRAM TO GENERAL CURTIS.

TELEGRAM TO GENERAL BURNSIDE.

TELEGRAM TO GOVERNOR GAMBLE.

TELEGRAM TO GENERAL CURTIS.

TELEGRAM TO GENERAL A. E. BURNSIDE.

TO SECRETARIES SEWARD AND CHASE.

TELEGRAM TO GOVERNOR ANDREW.

TO T. J. HENDERSON.

CONGRATULATIONS TO THE ARMY OF THE POTOMAC

LETTER OF CONDOLENCE

TO SECRETARY OF WAR.

TELEGRAM TO GENERAL CURTIS.

TELEGRAM TO GOVERNOR GAMBLE.

TELEGRAM TO GENERAL A. E. BURNSIDE.

TELEGRAM TO GENERAL DIX.

TELEGRAM TO H. J. RAYMOND.

1863

EMANCIPATION PROCLAMATION, JANUARY 1, 1863.

TO GENERAL H. W. HALLECK.

MESSAGE TO CONGRESS

TO GENERAL S. R. CURTIS.

TO SECRETARY WELLES.

TO GENERAL S. L CURTIS.

TO CALEB RUSSELL AND SALLIE A. FENTON.

TELEGRAM TO GENERAL ROSECRANS.

TELEGRAM TO GENERAL DIX.

TO GENERAL H. W. HALLECK.

TELEGRAM TO B. G. BROWN.

CORRESPONDENCE WITH GENERAL A. E. BURNSIDE, JANUARY 8, 1863.

HEADQUARTERS OF THE ARMY, WASHINGTON, January 7, 1863.

TELEGRAM TO GOVERNOR JOHNSON.

TELEGRAM TO GENERAL S. R. CURTIS.

TELEGRAM TO GOVERNOR JOHNSON.

INSTRUCTION TO THE JUDGE-ADVOCATE-GENERAL.

MESSAGE TO THE HOUSE OF REPRESENTATIVES. JANUARY 14, 1863.

TO SECRETARY OF WAR.

PRINTING MONEY

TO THE WORKING-MEN OF MANCHESTER, ENGLAND.

MESSAGE TO CONGRESS.

FITZ-JOHN PORTER COURT-MARTIAL.

FROM GENERAL HALLECK TO GENERAL U. S. GRANT.

TELEGRAM TO GENERAL BURNSIDE.

ORDER RELIEVING GENERAL A. E. BURNSIDE AND MAKING OTHER CHANGES.

TO GENERAL J. HOOKER.

MESSAGE TO CONGRESS.

TELEGRAM TO GENERAL BUTLER

TELEGRAM TO GENERAL DIX.

TO THURLOW WEED.

TELEGRAM TO GENERAL DIX.

TELEGRAM TO GENERAL DIX.

TELEGRAM TO GENERAL SCHENCK.

TO THE WORKING-MEN OF LONDON, ENGLAND.

TELEGRAM TO GENERAL SCHENCK. [Cipher.] WAR DEPARTMENT, WASHINGTON, D. C.,

MESSAGE TO THE SENATE.

MESSAGE TO THE SENATE.

TELEGRAM TO GENERAL W. S. ROSECRANS.

TELEGRAM TO SIMON CAMERON.

TO ALEXANDER REED.

TELEGRAM TO J. K. DUBOIS.

TELEGRAM TO GENERAL HOOKER

PROCLAMATION CONVENING THE SENATE, FEBRUARY 28, 1863

TO SECRETARY SEWARD.

TELEGRAM TO GOVERNOR TOD,

PROCLAMATION RECALLING SOLDIERS TO THEIR REGIMENTS, MARCH 10, 1863

TELEGRAM TO GENERAL HOOKER.

TO SECRETARY SEWARD.

TELEGRAM TO J. O. MORTON.

GRANT'S EXCLUSION OF A NEWSPAPER REPORTER

TO BENJAMIN GRATZ.

TELEGRAM TO GENERAL ROSECRANS.

TELEGRAM TO GENERAL S. A. HURLBUT.

QUESTION OF RAISING NEGRO TROOPS

PROCLAMATION APPOINTING A NATIONAL FAST-DAY.

LICENSE OF COMMERCIAL INTERCOURSE.

TO GENERAL D. HUNTER.

PROCLAMATION ABOUT COMMERCIAL INTERCOURSE, APRIL 2, 1863

TELEGRAM TO GENERAL HOOKER.

OPINION ON HARBOR DEFENSE.

TELEGRAM TO THE SECRETARY OF THE NAVY.

TELEGRAM TO OFFICER IN COMMAND AT NASHVILLE.

TELEGRAM TO GENERAL HOOKER.

TELEGRAM TO ADMIRAL S. P. DUPONT.

TO GENERAL D. HUNTER AND ADMIRAL S. F. DUPONT.

TELEGRAM TO GENERAL S. HOOKER.

ON COLONIZATION ARRANGEMENTS

STATEHOOD FOR WEST VIRGINIA, APRIL 20, 1863.

TELEGRAM TO GENERAL W. S. ROSECRANS.

TELEGRAM TO GENERAL J. HOOKER.

TELEGRAM TO GOVERNOR CURTIN.

TELEGRAM TO W. A. NEWELL.

TELEGRAM TO GOVERNOR CURTIN,

TELEGRAM TO GOVERNOR CURTIN

xxi

TELEGRAM TO GENERAL D. BUTTERFIELD.

GENERALS LOST

TELEGRAM TO GENERAL J. HOOKER.

TELEGRAM TO GENERAL BURNSIDE.

TELEGRAM TO GENERAL HOOKER.

TELEGRAM TO GENERAL HOOKER

TELEGRAM TO COLONEL R. INGALLS.

TO GENERAL J. HOOKER.

DRAFTING OF ALIENS

TELEGRAM TO GENERAL J. HOOKER.

TELEGRAM TO GENERAL J. A. DIX.

TO SECRETARY SEWARD.

TO SECRETARY STANTON.

TELEGRAM TO GENERAL DIX.

TELEGRAM TO GENERAL BUTTERFIELD.

TELEGRAM TO GOVERNOR SEYMOUR

TELEGRAM TO A. G. HENRY.

TO GENERAL J. HOOKER.

FACTIONAL QUARRELS

TELEGRAM TO JAMES GUTHRIE.

TO SECRETARY OF WAR.

ORDERS SENDING C. L. VALLANDIGHAM BEYOND MILITARY LINES.

WAR DEPARTMENT, May 20, 1863.

TELEGRAM TO GENERAL W. S. ROSECRANS.

TELEGRAM TO GENERAL W. S. ROSECRANS.

TELEGRAM TO GENERAL S. A. HURLBUT.

TELEGRAM TO ANSON STAGER.

TELEGRAM TO COLONEL HAGGARD.

TELEGRAM TO GENERAL BURNSIDE.

TELEGRAM TO GENERAL SCHENCK.

TELEGRAM TO GOVERNOR BUCKINGHAM.

TELEGRAM TO GENERAL W. S. ROSECRANS.

TO GENERAL SCHOFIELD.

TELEGRAM TO GENERAL HOOKER.

TO ERASTUS CORNING.

TELEGRAM TO GENERAL W. S. ROSECRANS.

TELEGRAM TO GOVERNOR JOHNSON.

TO J. K. DUBOIS AND OTHERS.

TELEGRAM TO GENERAL A. E. BURNSIDE.

TELEGRAM TO COLONEL LUDLOW.

TELEGRAM TO GENERAL HOOKER.

TELEGRAM TO GENERAL U.S. GRANT.

TELEGRAM TO MAJOR-GENERAL HOOKER. [Cipher.] EXECUTIVE MANSION, WASHINGTON,

TELEGRAM TO GENERAL BUTTERFIELD.

TO SECRETARY STANTON.

TELEGRAM TO GENERAL HOOKER.

TELEGRAM TO MRS. GRIMSLEY.

TELEGRAM TO GENERAL DIX,

TELEGRAM TO GENERAL DIX.

TELEGRAM TO GENERAL DIX.

TELEGRAM TO J. P. HALE.

TELEGRAM TO MRS. LINCOLN.

TELEGRAM TO GENERAL HOOKER.

TELEGRAM TO GENERAL HOOKER.

TELEGRAM TO MRS. LINCOLN.

TELEGRAM TO GENERAL HOOKER.

TO ERASTUS CORNING AND OTHERS.

TO THE SECRETARY OF THE TREASURY.

TELEGRAM TO GENERAL TYLER.

RESPONSE TO A "BESIEGED" GENERAL

TELEGRAM TO GENERAL KELLEY.

TELEGRAM TO GENERAL HOOKER.

TELEGRAM TO GENERAL R. C. SCHENCK.

NEEDS NEW TIRES ON HIS CARRIAGE

CALL FOR 100,000 MILITIA TO SERVE FOR SIX MONTHS, JUNE 15, 1863.

TELEGRAM TO P. KAPP AND OTHERS.

TELEGRAM TO GENERAL MEAGHER.

TELEGRAM TO MRS. LINCOLN.

TELEGRAM TO COLONEL BLISS.

TELEGRAM TO GENERAL HOOKER.

TELEGRAM TO GENERAL HOOKER.

TELEGRAM TO JOSHUA TEVIS.

TELEGRAM TO GOVERNOR TOD.

TELEGRAM TO GENERAL DINGMAN.

TO B. B. MALHIOT AND OTHERS.

TO GENERAL J. M. SCHOFIELD.

TELEGRAM TO GENERAL J. HOOKER.

TO SECRETARY OF WAR.

TELEGRAM TO MAJOR VAN VLIET.

TELEGRAM TO GENERAL COUCH.

TELEGRAM TO GENERAL DIX.

TELEGRAM TO GENERAL PECK.

TELEGRAM TO GENERAL SLOCUM.

TELEGRAM TO GENERAL HOOKER.

TELEGRAM TO GENERAL BURNSIDE.

TELEGRAM TO GOVERNOR BOYLE.

TELEGRAM TO GENERAL SCHENCK.

FURTHER DEMOCRATIC PARTY CRITICISM

TELEGRAM TO GOVERNOR PARKER.

TELEGRAM TO A. K. McCLURE.

TELEGRAM TO GENERAL COUCH. [Cipher] WASHINGTON CITY, June 30, 1863. 3.23

TO GENERAL D. HUNTER.

TELEGRAM TO GENERAL BURNSIDE.

REASSURING SON IN COLLEGE

ANNOUNCEMENT OF NEWS FROM GETTYSBURG.

TELEGRAM TO GENERAL FRENCH. [Cipher] WAR DEPARTMENT, WASHINGTON, D. C.,

CONTINUED FAILURE TO PURSUE ENEMY

RESPONSE TO A SERENADE,

SURRENDER OF VICKSBURG TO GENERAL GRANT

TELEGRAM FROM GENERAL HALLECK TO GENERAL G. C. MEADE.

TELEGRAM TO GENERAL THOMAS.

NEWS OF GRANT'S CAPTURE OF VICKSBURG

TELEGRAM TO F. F. LOWE.

TELEGRAM TO L. SWETT AND P. F. LOWE.

TELEGRAM TO J. K. DUBOIS.

TELEGRAM TO GENERAL SCHENCK.

TO GENERAL GRANT.

TELEGRAM TO GENERAL J. M. SCHOFIELD.

SON IN COLLEGE DOES NOT WRITE HIS PARENTS

INTIMATION OF ARMISTICE PROPOSALS

PROCLAMATION FOR THANKSGIVING, JULY 15, 1863

TELEGRAM TO L. SWETT.

TELEGRAM TO SIMON CAMERON.

TELEGRAM TO J. O. BROADHEAD.

TO GENERAL LANE.

TELEGRAM TO GOVERNOR MORTON.

TO GOVERNOR PARKER

TO GENERAL SCHOFIELD.

TELEGRAM TO GENERAL J. M. SCHOFIELD

TO POSTMASTER-GENERAL BLAIR

TO SECRETARY OF THE NAVY.

LETTER TO GOVERNOR PARKER.

To GENERAL G. G. MEADE. (Private.)

xxiii

TELEGRAM TO GENERAL A. B. BURNSIDE.

TO GENERAL H. W. HALLECK.

TO SECRETARY STANTON.

ORDER OF RETALIATION.

TO GENERAL S. A. HURLBUT.

TELEGRAM FROM GOVERNOR SEYMOUR.

TELEGRAM TO GOVERNOR SEYMOUR

TELEGRAM TO GENERAL FOSTER.

TO GENERAL N. P. BANKS.

TO GOVERNOR SEYMOUR.

TO GENERAL U.S. GRANT.

TO GENERAL W. S. ROSECRANS.

TO GOVERNOR SEYMOUR.

TO GENERAL J. A. McCLERNAND.

TELEGRAM TO GOVERNOR SEYMOUR.

To J. H. HACKETT.

TO F. F. LOWE.

TELEGRAM TO GENERAL MEADE.

TELEGRAM TO GENERAL SCHOFIELD.

TELEGRAM TO MRS. GRIMSLEY.

TO CRITICS OF EMANCIPATION

TO JAMES CONKLING.

TO SECRETARY STANTON.

TO GOVERNOR SEYMOUR.

TELEGRAM TO GENERAL J. M. SCHOFIELD.

TELEGRAM TO GENERAL G. G. MEADE.

TELEGRAM TO F. C. SHERMAN AND J. S. HAYES.

TELEGRAM TO GENERAL FOSTER.

TELEGRAM TO GENERAL CRAWFORD.

TELEGRAM TO L. SWETT.

TELEGRAM TO MRS. LINCOLN.

TELEGRAM TO J. C. CONKLING.

TO GENERAL W. S. ROSECRANS.

TO GENERAL H. W. HALLECK.

POLITICAL MOTIVATED MISQUOTATION IN NEWSPAPER

ORDER CONCERNING COMMERCIAL REGULATIONS.

TELEGRAM TO J. SEGAR.

TELEGRAM TO MRS. LINCOLN.

TELEGRAM TO SECRETARY STANTON.

TELEGRAM TO F. C. SHERMAN AND J. S. HAYES.

TELEGRAM TO GOVERNOR JOHNSON.

TELEGRAM TO GENERAL MEADE.

TELEGRAM TO GENERAL WHEATON.

TO GOVERNOR JOHNSON.

TELEGRAM TO GENERAL A. E. BURNSIDE.

TELEGRAM TO GENERAL MEADE.

TELEGRAM TO GENERAL MEADE.

TELEGRAM TO H. H. SCOTT.

TELEGRAM TO J. G. BLAINE.

PROCLAMATION SUSPENDING WRIT OF HABEAS CORPUS, SEPTEMBER 15, 1863.

TO GENERAL H. W. HALLECK.

TELEGRAM TO MRS. SPEED.

TELEGRAM TO GENERAL MEADE.

TELEGRAM TO GENERAL SCHENCK.

TELEGRAM TO GENERAL MEADE.

REQUEST TO SUGGEST NAME FOR A BABY

TELEGRAM TO MRS. ARMSTRONG.

TO GOVERNOR JOHNSON.

MILITARY STRATEGY

TELEGRAM TO MRS. LINCOLN.

TELEGRAM TO MRS. LINCOLN.

TO GENERAL H. W. HALLECK.

TELEGRAM TO GENERAL A. E. BURNSIDE

TELEGRAM TO GENERAL A. E. BURNSIDE

TELEGRAM TO GENERAL W. S. ROSECRANS

TELEGRAM TO GENERAL W. S. ROSECRANS.

TELEGRAM TO O. M. HATCH AND J. K. DUBOIS.

TELEGRAM TO MRS. LINCOLN.

TELEGRAM TO GENERAL W. S. ROSECRANS.

PROCLAMATION OPENING THE PORT OF ALEXANDRIA, VIRGINIA,

TELEGRAM TO GENERAL W. S. ROSECRANS.

MRS. LINCOLN'S REBEL BROTHER-IN-LAW KILLED

TELEGRAM TO GENERAL McCALLUM.

TELEGRAM TO GENERAL MEADE.

TO GENERAL W. S. ROSECRANS.

TELEGRAM TO GENERAL W. S. ROSECRANS.

TELEGRAM TO GENERAL SCHOFIELD.

TELEGRAM TO F. S. CORKRAN.

TELEGRAM TO GENERAL TYLER

TO GENERAL SCHOFIELD.

TELEGRAM TO GENERAL S. M. SCHOFIELD.

PROCLAMATION FOR THANKSGIVING, OCTOBER 3, 1863.

TELEGRAM TO GENERAL J. M. SCHOFIELD.

TELEGRAM TO GENERAL W. S. ROSECRANS.

TO C. D. DRAKE AND OTHERS.

THE CASE OF DR. DAVID M. WRIGHT

TELEGRAM TO GENERAL MEADE.

TELEGRAM TO GENERAL MEADE.

TELEGRAM TO GENERAL MEADE.

TELEGRAM TO W. S. ROSECRANS.

TELEGRAM TO GENERAL G. G. MEADE.

TELEGRAM TO WAYNE McVEIGH.

TO THURLOW WEED.

TO L. B. TODD.

AID TO MRS. HELM, MRS. LINCOLN'S SISTER

TELEGRAM TO GENERAL FOSTER.

TELEGRAM TO GENERAL MEADE.

TELEGRAM TO T. W. SWEENEY.

TELEGRAM TO T. C. DURANT.

COMMENT ON A NOTE.

TO GENERAL H. W. HALLECK.

CALL FOR 300,000 VOLUNTEERS, OCTOBER 17, 1863.

TELEGRAM TO GENERAL FOSTER.

TELEGRAM TO W. B. THOMAS

TELEGRAM TO J. WILLIAMS AND N. G. TAYLOR.

TELEGRAM TO T. C. DURANT.

TELEGRAM TO GENERAL W. S. ROSECRANS.

TELEGRAM TO GENERAL R. C. SCHENCK.

TELEGRAM TO GENERAL R. C. SCHENCK.

TO GENERAL H. W. HALLECK.

TO E. B. WASHBURNE.

TO SECRETARY CHASE.

xxv

THE WRITINGS OF A. LINCOLN, VOLUME SEVEN, 1863-1865

1863

TO GENERAL SCHOFIELD.

TELEGRAM TO GOVERNOR JOHNSON.

TO VICE-PRESIDENT HAMLIN.

TO J. W. GRIMES.

TELEGRAM TO P. F. LOWE.

TELEGRAM TO GENERAL MEADE.

MEMORANDUM.

TELEGRAM TO W. H. SEWARD.

TO POSTMASTER-GENERAL BLAIR.

TO GOVERNOR BRADFORD.

TO J. H. HACKETT

TELEGRAM TO W. H. SEWARD.

TELEGRAM TO GENERAL MEADE EXECUTIVE MANSION, WASHINGTON, November 3, 1863.

TELEGRAM TO GENERAL MEADE.

TELEGRAM TO GENERAL A. E. BURNSIDE. WAR DEPARTMENT, WASHINGTON, November

TELEGRAM TO GENERAL G. G. MEADE.

ORDER CONCERNING THE EXPORT OF TOBACCO PURCHASED BY FOREIGN NATIONS.

TELEGRAM TO GENERAL SCHOFIELD.

TELEGRAM TO GENERAL SCHOFIELD.

TELEGRAM TO HIRAM BARNEY.

TELEGRAM TO J. MILDERBORGER.

TELEGRAM to E. H. AND E. JAMESON.

TELEGRAM TO GENERAL W. S. ROSECRANS.

TELEGRAM TO GENERAL BURNSIDE.

TO SECRETARY CHASE

ADDRESS AT GETTYSBURG

TELEGRAM TO GENERAL MEADE.

TELEGRAM TO GENERAL MEADE.

TELEGRAM TO E. P. EVANS.

TO SECRETARY SEWARD.

TELEGRAM TO GENERAL GRANT.

TO C. P. KIRKLAND.

ANNOUNCEMENT OF UNION SUCCESS IN EAST TENNESSEE.

PROCLAMATION OF AMNESTY AND RECONSTRUCTION. DECEMBER 8, 1863.

ANNUAL MESSAGE TO CONGRESS, DECEMBER 8, 1863.

MESSAGE TO CONGRESS. WASHINGTON D. C., December 8, 1863.

MESSAGE TO THE SENATE. WASHINGTON, D. C., December 8, 1863.

TELEGRAM TO GENERAL U. S. GRANT.

TO GOVERNOR CURTIN.

TELEGRAM TO GENERAL BUTLER.

TELEGRAM TO GENERAL MEADE.

TO JUDGE HOFFMAN.

TELEGRAM TO MARY GONYEAG.

PROCLAMATION CONCERNING DISCRIMINATING DUTIES, DECEMBER 16, 1863.

MESSAGE TO CONGRESS,

TELEGRAM TO GENERAL HURLBUT.

TELEGRAM TO GENERAL U.S. GRANT.

TO SECRETARY STANTON.

TO O. D. FILLEY.

TELEGRAM TO MILITARY COMMANDER AT POINT LOOKOUT.

TELEGRAM TO MILITARY COMMANDER AT POINT LOOKOUT.

TELEGRAM TO U. F. LINDER.

TO GENERAL N. P. BANKS.

TELEGRAM TO GENERAL BUTLER.

TO SECRETARY STANTON.

1864

TELEGRAM TO GOVERNOR PIERPOINT.

TELEGRAM TO GENERAL BUTLER.

TELEGRAM TO GENERAL MEADE.

MESSAGE TO CONGRESS,

TELEGRAM TO GOVERNOR BRAMLETTE.

TO GENERAL Q. A. GILLMORE.

TELEGRAM TO GOVERNOR BROUGH. EXECUTIVE MANSION, WASHINGTON, January 15,

TO CROSBY AND NICHOLS.

TO GENERAL P. STEELE.

MESSAGE TO CONGRESS, JANUARY 20, 1864

ORDER APPROVING TRADE REGULATIONS.

TELEGRAM TO GENERAL FOSTER.

TELEGRAM TO E. STANLEY.

TO GENERAL H. W. HALLECK.

TELEGRAM TO GENERAL SICKLES.

TELEGRAM TO GOVERNOR BRAMLETTE.

COLONIZATION EXPERIMENT

ORDER FOR A DRAFT OF FIVE HUNDRED THOUSAND MEN.

TELEGRAM TO GOVERNOR YATES.

TELEGRAM TO GOVERNOR MURPHY.

THE STORY OF THE EMANCIPATION PROCLAMATION

TELEGRAM TO GENERAL SEDGWICK.

TELEGRAM TO HORACE MAYNARD.

TO W. M. FISHBACK.

TELEGRAM TO GENERAL STEELE.

TELEGRAM TO A. ROBINSON.

PROCLAMATION CONCERNING BLOCKADE, FEBRUARY 18, 1864.

TELEGRAM TO COMMANDER BLAKE.

TELEGRAM FROM WARREN JORDAN.

TELEGRAM TO GENERAL ROSECRANS.

TELEGRAM TO GENERAL STEELE.

TO GENERAL F. STEELE.

DESERTERS DEATH SENTENCES REMITTED

FEMALE SPY

TO W. JAYNE.

TO E. H. EAST.

TO SECRETARY STANTON.

TO SECRETARY CHASE.

TO GENERAL THOMAS.

TELEGRAM TO GENERAL STEELE.

TELEGRAM TO GENERAL BUTLER.

ORDER IN REGARD TO THE EXPORTATION OF TOBACCO BELONGING TO THE FRENCH

TELEGRAM TO UNITED STATES MARSHAL, LOUISVILLE.

TELEGRAM TO GENERAL MEADE.

MESSAGE TO SENATE.

ADDRESS TO GENERAL GRANT,

ORDER ASSIGNING U. S. GRANT COMMAND OF THE ARMIES OF THE UNITED STATES.

TELEGRAM TO GOVERNOR MURPHY.

TO GENERAL HAHN. (Private.)

CALL FOR TWO HUNDRED THOUSAND MEN.

TELEGRAM TO GENERAL U. S. GRANT.

PASS FOR GENERAL D. E. SICKLES.

ORDER TO GOVERNOR HAHN.

REMARKS AT A FAIR IN THE PATENT OFFICE,

REPLY TO A COMMITTEE FROM THE WORKINGMEN'S ASSOCIATION OF NEW YORK,

TELEGRAM TO GENERAL BUTLER.

CORRESPONDENCE WITH GENERAL C. SCHURZ.

PROCLAMATION ABOUT AMNESTY,

TO SECRETARY STANTON.

TO GENERAL G. G. MEADE.

TELEGRAM TO GENERAL U. S. GRANT.

TO A. G. HODGES.

TO MRS. HORACE MANN.

TELEGRAM TO GENERAL BUTLER.

TELEGRAM TO GENERAL MEADE.

LECTURE ON LIBERTY

TO CALVIN TRUESDALE.

TELEGRAM TO OFFICER COMMANDING AT FORT WARREN.

TELEGRAM TO OFFICER COMMANDING AT FORT WARREN.

TELEGRAM TO GENERAL DIX.

TELEGRAM TO GENERAL BUTLER.

INDORSEMENT ON OFFER OF TROOPS, APRIL 23, 1864.

TO SECRETARY STANTON.

TELEGRAM TO JOHN WILLIAMS.

TELEGRAM TO GENERAL MEADE.

TELEGRAM TO GENERAL THOMAS.

TO GOVERNOR MURPHY.

MESSAGE TO CONGRESS, APRIL 28, 1864.

MESSAGE TO THE HOUSE OF REPRESENTATIVES,

TO GENERAL U. S. GRANT.

MESSAGE TO THE HOUSE OF REPRESENTATIVES

TELEGRAM TO GENERAL W. T. SHERMAN.

TELEGRAM TO GENERAL ROSECRANS.

TO MRS. S. B. McCONKEY.

RECOMMENDATION OF THANKSGIVING.

RESPONSE TO A SERENADE,

TELEGRAM TO GENERAL LEW WALLACE.

TELEGRAM TO GENERAL W. S. ROSECRANS,

TO P. B. LOOMIS.

RESPONSE TO A METHODIST DELEGATION, MAY 14, 1864.

TELEGRAM TO GOVERNOR YATES. EXECUTIVE MANSION, WASHINGTON, May 18, 1864.

ARREST AND IMPRISONMENT OF IRRESPONSIBLE NEWSPAPER REPORTERS AND EDITORS

TELEGRAM TO GENERAL B. P. BUTLER.

ORDER CONCERNING THE EXEMPTION OF AMERICAN CONSULS FROM MILITARY SERVICE

TELEGRAM TO GOVERNOR MORTON AND OTHERS. EXECUTIVE MANSION, May 21, 1864

TELEGRAM TO CHRISTIANA A. SACK. WAR DEPARTMENT WASHINGTON, D. C., May 21,

TELEGRAM TO GOVERNOR BROUGH. WASHINGTON CITY, May 24, 1864.

TELEGRAM TO GENERAL MEADE. EXECUTIVE MANSION, WASHINGTON, May 25,1864.

MEMORANDUM CONCERNING THE TRANSPORTATION OF THE NEW YORK NAVAL BRIGADE.

TO P. A. CONKLING AND OTHERS.

INDORSEMENT ON A LETTER TOUCHING THE REPUBLICAN NATIONAL CONVENTION.

TELEGRAM TO GENERAL MEADE. EXECUTIVE MANSION, WASHINGTON, June 6, 1864.

TELEGRAM TO GENERAL W. S. ROSECRANS. WASHINGTON, June 8, 1864.

REPLY TO THE COMMITTEE NOTIFYING PRESIDENT LINCOLN OF HIS RENOMINATION,

PLATFORM OF THE UNION NATIONAL CONVENTION HELD IN BALTIMORE, MD., JUNE 7

REPLY TO A DELEGATION FROM THE NATIONAL UNION LEAGUE,

REPLY TO A DELEGATION FROM OHIO,

ADDRESS TO THE ENVOY FROM THE HAWAIIAN ISLANDS,

REMARKS TO AN OHIO REGIMENT,

TELEGRAM TO GENERAL L. THOMAS. EXECUTIVE MANSION, WASHINGTON, June 13,

TELEGRAM TO THOMAS WEBSTER. WASHINGTON, D. C., June 13, 1864.

TELEGRAM TO GENERAL U. S. GRANT. WASHINGTON, June 15, 1864. 7 A.M.

ADDRESS AT A SANITARY FAIR IN PHILADELPHIA,

TO ATTORNEY-GENERAL BATES.

TELEGRAM TO MRS. LINCOLN.

TELEGRAM TO GENERAL W. S. ROSECRANS. WASHINGTON, June 24, 1864.

LETTER ACCEPTING THE NOMINATION FOR PRESIDENT.

TO GENERAL P. STEELE.

TELEGRAM TO GENERAL GRANT. EXECUTIVE MANSION, WASHINGTON, June 29, 1864.

TELEGRAM TO DAVID TOD.

TO J. L. SCRIPPS.

FROM SECRETARY STANTON TO GOVERNOR SEYMOUR.

PROCLAMATION SUSPENDING THE WRIT OF HABEAS CORPUS,

PROCLAMATION FOR A DAY OF PRAYER, JULY 7, 1864.

PROCLAMATION CONCERNING A BILL "TO GUARANTEE TO CERTAIN STATES,

TO HORACE GREELEY.

TELEGRAM TO J. W. GARRETT. WASHINGTON, D. C., July 9, 1864

TELEGRAM FROM GENERAL HALLECK TO GENERAL WALLACE.

TELEGRAM TO T. SWAN AND OTHERS. WASHINGTON, D. C., July 10, 1864. 9.20

TELEGRAM TO GENERAL U.S. GRANT. WASHINGTON CITY, July TO, 1864.2 P.M.

TELEGRAM TO GENERAL U.S. GRANT. WASHINGTON, July 11, 1864. 8 A.M.

TELEGRAM TO GENERAL U.S. GRANT. WASHINGTON, D. C., July 12, 1864. 11.30

TELEGRAM AND LETTER TO HORACE GREELEY. EXECUTIVE MANSION, WASHINGTON, July

EXECUTIVE MANSION, WASHINGTON, JULY 15, 1864.

SAFE CONDUCT FOR CLEMENT C. CLAY AND OTHERS,

TELEGRAM TO GENERAL U. S. GRANT. [WASHINGTON] July 17. 1864. 11.25 A.M.

TELEGRAM TO GENERAL D. HUNTER WASHINGTON JULY 17, 1864.

TELEGRAM TO GENERAL W. T. SHERMAN.

ANNOUNCEMENT CONCERNING TERMS OF PEACE.

xxix

PROCLAMATION CALLING FOR FIVE HUNDRED THOUSAND VOLUNTEERS,

TELEGRAM TO GENERAL U.S. GRANT.

TELEGRAM TO J. L. WRIGHT.

TELEGRAM TO GENERAL D. HUNTER. (Cipher.)

TO GOVERNOR CURTIN, ENCLOSING A LETTER TO WILLIAM O. SNIDER.

PRESENTATION OF A CANE

FROM JOHN HAY TO J. C. WELLING.

TO COLONEL, FIRST N. Y. VETERAN CAVALRY.

TELEGRAM TO GENERAL W. T. SHERMAN.

FROM SECRETARY STANTON TO GENERAL HALLECK.

TELEGRAM TO GOVERNOR JOHNSON. WASHINGTON, July 27, 1864.

TO Mrs. ANNE WILLIAMSON,

TELEGRAM TO GENERAL U, S. GRANT.

TELEGRAM TO HORACE GREELEY.

TELEGRAM TO HORACE GREELEY.

ON DISLOYAL FAMILY MEMBER

TELEGRAM TO GENERAL U. S. GRANT.

TELEGRAM TO GENERAL W. T. SHERMAN.

INTERVIEW WITH JOHN T. MILLS,

ENDORSEMENT OF APPLICATION FOR EMPLOYMENT, AUGUST 15, 1864.

TO H. J. RAYMOND.

TELEGRAM TO GENERAL U. S. GRANT.

PROCLAMATION CONCERNING COMMERCIAL REGULATIONS, AUGUST 18, 1864.

INDORSEMENT CONCERNING AN EXCHANGE OF PRISONERS, AUGUST 18, 1864.

ADDRESS TO THE 164TH OHIO REGIMENT,

TELEGRAM TO GENERAL BUTLER. EXECUTIVE MANSION, WASHINGTON, D. C., August

ADDRESS TO THE 166TH OHIO REGIMENT,

MEMORANDUM.

TELEGRAM TO GOVERNOR JOHNSON. EXECUTIVE MANSION, WASHINGTON, August 26,

TELEGRAM TO B. H. BREWSTER. EXECUTIVE MANSION, WASHINGTON, D. C., August

ORDER CONCERNING COTTON.

TO COLONEL HUIDEKOPER.

PROCLAMATION OF THANKSGIVING,

ORDERS OF GRATITUDE AND REJOICING.

EXECUTIVE MANSION, September 3, 1864.

EXECUTIVE MANSION, September 3, 1864.

TO MRS. GURNEY.

REPLY TO A COMMITTEE OF COLORED PEOPLE FROM BALTIMORE

TELEGRAM TO GOVERNOR PICKERING.

ORDER OF THANKS TO HUNDRED-DAY TROOPS FROM OHIO.

TO GENERAL U.S. GRANT.

TELEGRAM TO JAMES G. BLAINE. WAR DEPARTMENT, WASHINGTON, D. C., September

TELEGRAM TO GENERAL SLOUGH.

TELEGRAM TO GENERAL W. T. SHERMAN. WASHINGTON, D. C., September 17,1864.

TO GENERAL W. T. SHERMAN.

INDORSEMENT CONCERNING AN EXCHANGE OF PRISONERS, SEPTEMBER 1864.

TELEGRAM TO GENERAL P. SHERIDAN. EXECUTIVE MANSION, WASHINGTON, September

TO GENERAL HITCHCOCK,

TO GENERAL U.S. GRANT.

TO POSTMASTER-GENERAL BLAIR.

ORDER CONCERNING THE PURCHASE OF PRODUCTS IN INSURRECTIONARY STATES.

TELEGRAM TO GENERAL W. T. SHERMAN. WASHINGTON, D. C., September 27, 1864.

TELEGRAM TO GENERAL U. S. GRANT. WASHINGTON, D.C., September 29,1864.

INDORSEMENT.

ORDER RETURNING THANKS TO THE VOLUNTEERS FOR ONE HUNDRED DAYS

TO GENERAL U.S. GRANT.

INDORSEMENT ON A MEMORANDUM BY GENERAL McDOWELL, OCTOBER 7, 1864

TO H. W. HOFFMAN.

TELEGRAM TO GOVERNOR CURTIN.

TELEGRAM TO ROBERT T. LINCOLN, Cambridge, Mass.:

TELEGRAM TO GENERAL U. S. GRANT. WASHINGTON, D. C., October 12, 1864.

RESPONSE TO A SERENADE,

PROCLAMATION OF THANKSGIVING, OCTOBER 20, 1864.

TELEGRAM To J. G. NICOLAY. WASHINGTON, D. C., October 21, 1864. 9.45 P.M.

TO WILLIAM B. CAMPBELL AND OTHERS.

TELEGRAM TO GENERAL G. H. THOMAS. WASHINGTON, D. C., October 23, 1864 5

TELEGRAM TO T. T. DAVIS. EXECUTIVE MANSION, WASHINGTON, D.C., October 31,

PROCLAMATION ADMITTING NEVADA INTO THE UNION

TELEGRAM TO GENERAL BURBRIDGE.

TELEGRAM TO NAVAL OFFICER AT MOBILE BAY.

TELEGRAM TO SAILORS' FAIR, BOSTON, MASSACHUSETTS.

TELEGRAM TO A. H. RICE.

TELEGRAM TO SECRETARY SEWARD. WASHINGTON, November 8, 1864.

RESPONSE TO A SERENADE, NOVEMBER 9, 1864.

TELEGRAM TO H. W. HOFFMAN. WAR DEPARTMENT, WASHINGTON, D. C. November 10,

ON DEMOCRATIC GOVERNMENT

TELEGRAM TO GENERAL S. O. BURBRIDGE. WASHINGTON, D.C., November 10, 1864.

WASHINGTON, D.C., November 10, 1864. GOVERNOR BRAMLETTE, Frankfort, Ky.:

TO GENERAL S. A. HURLBUT.

REPLY TO MARYLAND UNION COMMITTEE, NOVEMBER 17, 1864.

PROCLAMATION CONCERNING BLOCKADE, NOVEMBER 19, 1864

FIVE-STAR MOTHER

TO J. PHILLIPS.

TELEGRAM TO GOVERNOR BRAMLETTE. WASHINGTON, D. C. NOVEMBER 22, 1864.

TELEGRAM TO GOVERNOR CURTIN, WASHINGTON, D.C., NOVEMBER 25, 1864

TELEGRAM TO GENERAL ROSECRANS. EXECUTIVE MANSION, WASHINGTON D.C., NOV.

MEMORANDUM,

ORDER CONCERNING THE STEAMER "FUNAYMA SOLACE."

MESSAGE TO CONGRESS.

ANNUAL MESSAGE TO CONGRESS,

RESPONSE TO A SERENADE, DECEMBER 6, 1864.

TELEGRAM TO GOVERNOR HALL.

TELEGRAM TO COLONEL FASLEIGH.

ORDER APPOINTING COMMISSIONERS

TELEGRAM TO GENERAL G, H. THOMAS.
WASHINGTON, D.C., December 16, 1864.

ORIGIN OF THE "GREENBACK" CURRENCY

TELEGRAM TO OFFICER IN COMMAND AT
CHATTANOOGA. EXECUTIVE MANSION,

CALL FOR 300,000 VOLUNTEERS,
DECEMBER 19, 1864.

SHERMAN'S MARCH TO THE SEA

TELEGRAM TO OFFICER IN COMMAND AT
LEXINGTON.

TO J. MACLEAN.

TELEGRAM TO OFFICER IN COMMAND AT
NASHVILLE.

TELEGRAM TO GENERAL U. S. GRANT.

TELEGRAM TO GENERAL BUTLER.

TELEGRAM TO COLONEL WARNER.

1865

TELEGRAM TO J. WILLIAMS.

MESSAGE TO THE HOUSE OF
REPRESENTATIVES.

TO GENERAL U. S. GRANT.

TELEGRAM TO GENERAL GRANT.

MESSAGE TO CONGRESS,

TO SCHUYLER COLFAX.

PROCLAMATION CONCERNING
COMMERCE, JANUARY 10, 1865.

TELEGRAM TO GENERAL B. F. BUTLER.

TELEGRAM TO GENERAL B. F. BUTLER.

TELEGRAM TO GOVERNOR JOHNSON.

TELEGRAM TO GENERAL G. M. DODGE.
EXECUTIVE MANSION, WASHINGTON,
January

FIRST OVERTURES FOR SURRENDER FROM
DAVIS

EXECUTIVE MANSION,

TELEGRAM TO GENERAL DODGE.

TELEGRAM TO GENERAL ORD.

TELEGRAM TO GENERAL G. M. DODGE.

TELEGRAM TO GOVERNOR JOHNSON.

REPLY TO A COMMITTEE, JANUARY 24,
1865.

TELEGRAM TO GENERAL GRANT.

TELEGRAM TO GENERAL GRANT.

EARLY CONSULTATIONS WITH REBELS

TELEGRAM FROM SECRETARY OF WAR TO
GENERAL ORD.

INDORSEMENT ON A LETTER FROM J. M.
ASHLEY.

TELEGRAM TO GENERAL U.S. GRANT.

INSTRUCTIONS TO SECRETARY SEWARD.

CONSTITUTIONAL AMENDMENT FOR THE
ABOLISHING OF SLAVERY

TELEGRAM TO GENERAL U. S. GRANT.
WASHINGTON, February 1, 1865

TELEGRAM TO MAJOR ECKERT.
WASHINGTON, D. C., February 1, 1865.

TELEGRAM TO GENERAL U. S. GRANT.
WASHINGTON, D. C., February 2, 1865

TELEGRAM TO SECRETARY SEWARD,
WASHINGTON, D. C., February 2, 1865.

ORDER TO MAKE CORRECTIONS IN THE
DRAFT.

TO PROVOST-MARSHAL-GENERAL.

TELEGRAM TO LIEUTENANT-COLONEL
GLENN.

TO GOVERNOR SMITH.

MESSAGE TO CONGRESS.

TELEGRAM TO GENERAL U. S. GRANT.
EXECUTIVE MANSION, WASHINGTON,
February

RESULT OF THE ELECTORAL COUNT

CHRONOLOGIC REVIEW OF PEACE PROPOSALS

Afterwards Mr. Blair dictated for and authorized me to make an entry on

Afterwards the Secretary of War placed in my hands the following telegram,

MESSAGE TO THE SENATE. WASHINGTON, February 10, 1865

MR. SEWARD TO MR. ADAMS.

TO ADMIRAL DAVID D. PORTER.

TELEGRAM TO GENERAL S. POPE.

TO THE COMMANDING OFFICERS IN WEST TENNESSEE

TELEGRAM TO GENERAL J. POPE.

TELEGRAM TO GENERAL POPE.

PROCLAMATION CONVENING THE SENATE IN EXTRA SESSION,

TELEGRAM TO OFFICER IN COMMAND AT HARPER'S FERRY.

TELEGRAM TO GENERAL U.S. GRANT.

TELEGRAM TO GENERAL POPE.

TELEGRAM TO GENERAL U. S. GRANT. WASHINGTON, February 25, 1865

TELEGRAM TO GENERAL U. S. GRANT. WASHINGTON, D. C., February 27, 1865.

TO T. W. CONWAY.

TELEGRAM TO GENERAL U.S. GRANT. WASHINGTON, D. C., March 2, 1865.

TELEGRAM FROM SECRETARY STANTON TO GENERAL GRANT.

SECOND INAUGURAL ADDRESS, MARCH 4, 1865.

TELEGRAM TO GENERAL JOHN POPE.

TO GENERAL U.S. GRANT. WASHINGTON, D. C., March 8, 1865.

PROCLAMATION OFFERING PARDON TO DESERTERS,

TELEGRAM TO H. T. BLOW.

LETTER TO THURLOW WEED,

TELEGRAM TO COLONEL ROUGH AND OTHERS.

ADDRESS TO AN INDIANA REGIMENT,

PROCLAMATION CONCERNING INDIANS,

ORDER ANNULLING THE SENTENCE

TELEGRAM TO GENERAL J. POPE.

TELEGRAM TO GENERAL ORD.

TELEGRAM TO JUDGE SCATES.

TELEGRAM TO GENERAL W. S. HANCOCK.

ANOTHER FEMALE SPY

TELEGRAM TO SECRETARY STANTON.

TELEGRAM TO SECRETARY STANTON.

TELEGRAM TO SECRETARY STANTON.

TELEGRAM TO SECRETARY STANTON.

TELEGRAM TO SECRETARY STANTON.

TELEGRAM TO SECRETARY STANTON.

TELEGRAM TO SECRETARY STANTON.

TELEGRAM TO GENERAL U. S. GRANT.

TELEGRAM TO SECRETARY STANTON.

TELEGRAM TO GENERAL U.S. GRANT. CITY POINT, April 1, 1865.

TELEGRAM TO MRS. LINCOLN.

TELEGRAMS TO SECRETARY STANTON. CITY POINT, VIRGINIA, April 2, 1865. 8.30

TELEGRAM TO MRS. LINCOLN. CITY POINT, VA., April 1, 1865.

TELEGRAM TO GENERAL U. S. GRANT.

TELEGRAM TO SECRETARY STANTON.

TELEGRAM TO SECRETARY STANTON.

TELEGRAM TO SECRETARY STANTON.

TELEGRAM TO SECRETARY SEWARD.

TELEGRAM TO GENERAL U. S. GRANT.

TELEGRAM TO GENERAL G. WEITZEL.

TELEGRAM TO SECRETARY STANTON.

LET THE THING BE PRESSED.

NOTE ON A CARD TO SECRETARY STANTON.

RESPONSE TO A CALL,

TELEGRAM TO GENERAL G. H. GORDON.

PROCLAMATION CLOSING CERTAIN PORTS, APRIL 11, 1865.

PROCLAMATION OPENING THE PORT OF KEY WEST,

PROCLAMATION CLAIMING EQUALITY OF RIGHTS WITH ALL MARITIME NATIONS,

LAST PUBLIC ADDRESS,

TELEGRAM TO GENERAL G. WEITZEL.

TELEGRAM TO GENERAL G. WEITZEL. WASHINGTON, D.C., April 12, 1865.

INTERVIEW WITH SCHUYLER COLFAX ON THE MORNING OF APRIL 14, 1865.

TO GENERAL VAN ALLEN.

LINCOLN'S LAST WRITTEN WORDS

VOLUME 1.

INTRODUCTORY

Immediately after Lincoln's re-election to the Presidency, in an off-hand speech, delivered in response to a serenade by some of his admirers on the evening of November 10, 1864, he spoke as follows:
"It has long been a grave question whether any government not too strong for the liberties of its people can be strong enough to maintain its existence in great emergencies. On this point, the present rebellion brought our republic to a severe test, and the Presidential election, occurring in regular course during the rebellion, added not a little to the strain.... The strife of the election is but human nature practically applied to the facts in the case. What has occurred in this case must ever occur in similar cases. Human nature will not change. In any future great national trial, compared with the men of this, we shall have as weak and as strong, as silly and as wise, as bad and as good. Let us therefore study the incidents in this as philosophy to learn wisdom from and none of them as wrongs to be avenged.... Now that the election is over, may not all having a common interest reunite in a common fort to save our common country? For my own part, I have striven and shall strive to avoid placing any obstacle in the way. So long as I have been here, I have not willingly planted a thorn in any man's bosom. While I am deeply sensible to the high compliment of a re-election and duly grateful, as I trust, to Almighty God for having directed my countrymen to a right conclusion, as I think for their own good, it adds nothing to my satisfaction that any other man may be disappointed or pained by the result."
This speech has not attracted much general attention, yet it is in a peculiar degree both illustrative and typical of the great statesman who made it, alike in its strong common-sense and in its lofty standard of morality. Lincoln's life, Lincoln's deeds and words, are not only of consuming interest to the historian, but should be intimately known to every man engaged in the hard practical work of American political life. It is difficult to overstate how much it means to a nation to have as the two foremost figures in its history men like Washington and Lincoln. It is good for every man in any way concerned in public life to feel that the highest ambition any American can possibly have will be gratified just in proportion as he raises himself toward the standards set by these two men.
It is a very poor thing, whether for nations or individuals, to advance the history of great deeds done in the past as an excuse for doing poorly in the present; but it is an excellent thing to study the history of the great deeds of the past, and of the great men who did them, with an earnest desire to profit thereby so as to render better service in the present. In their essentials, the men of the present day are much like the men of the past, and the live issues of the present can be faced to better advantage by men who have in good faith studied how the leaders of the nation faced the dead issues of the past. Such a study of Lincoln's life will enable us to avoid the twin gulfs of immorality and inefficiency—the gulfs which always lie one on each side of the careers alike of man and of nation. It helps nothing to have avoided one if shipwreck is encountered in the other. The fanatic, the well-meaning moralist of unbalanced mind, the parlor critic who condemns others but has no power himself to do good and but little power to do ill—all these were as alien to Lincoln as the vicious and unpatriotic themselves. His life teaches our people that they must act with wisdom, because otherwise adherence to right will be mere sound and fury without substance; and that they must also act high-mindedly, or else what seems to be wisdom will in the end turn out to be the most destructive kind of folly.
Throughout his entire life, and especially after he rose to leadership in his party, Lincoln was stirred to his depths by the sense of fealty to a lofty ideal; but throughout his entire life, he also accepted human nature as it is, and worked with keen, practical good sense to achieve results with the instruments at hand. It is impossible to conceive of a man farther removed from baseness, farther removed from corruption, from mere self-seeking; but it is also impossible to conceive of a man of more sane and healthy mind—a man less under the influence of that fantastic and diseased morality (so fantastic and diseased as to be in reality profoundly immoral) which makes a man in this work-a-day world refuse to do what is possible because he cannot accomplish the impossible.
In the fifth volume of Lecky's History of England, the historian draws an interesting distinction between the qualities needed for a successful political career in modern society and those which lead to eminence in the spheres of pure intellect or pure moral effort. He says:
"....the moral qualities that are required in the higher spheres of statesmanship [are not] those of a hero or a saint. Passionate earnestness and self-devotion, complete concentration of every faculty on an unselfish aim, uncalculating daring, a delicacy of conscience and a loftiness of aim far exceeding those of the average of men, are here likely to prove rather a hindrance than an assistance. The politician deals very largely with the superficial and the commonplace; his art is in a great measure that of skilful compromise, and in the conditions of modern life, the statesman is likely to succeed best who possesses secondary qualities to an unusual degree, who is in the closest intellectual and moral sympathy with the average of the intelligent men of his time, and who pursues common ideals with more than common ability.... Tact, business talent, knowledge of men, resolution, promptitude and sagacity in dealing with immediate emergencies, a character which lends itself easily to conciliation, diminishes friction and inspires confidence, are especially needed, and they are more likely to be found among shrewd and enlightened men of the world than among men of great original genius or of an heroic type of character."

The American people should feel profoundly grateful that the greatest American statesman since Washington, the statesman who in this absolutely democratic republic succeeded best, was the very man who actually combined the two sets of qualities which the historian thus puts in antithesis. Abraham Lincoln, the rail-splitter, the Western country lawyer, was one of the shrewdest and most enlightened men of the world, and he had all the practical qualities which enable such a man to guide his countrymen; and yet he was also a genius of the heroic type, a leader who rose level to the greatest crisis through which this nation or any other nation had to pass in the nineteenth century.
THEODORE ROOSEVELT
SAGAMORE HILL, OYSTER BAY, N. Y., September 22, 1905.

INTRODUCTORY NOTE

"I have endured," wrote Lincoln not long before his death, "a great deal of ridicule without much malice, and have received a great deal of kindness not quite free from ridicule." On Easter Day, 1865, the world knew how little this ridicule, how much this kindness, had really signified. Thereafter, Lincoln the man became Lincoln the hero, year by year more heroic, until to-day, with the swift passing of those who knew him, his figure grows ever dimmer, less real. This should not be. For Lincoln the man, patient, wise, set in a high resolve, is worth far more than Lincoln the hero, vaguely glorious. Invaluable is the example of the man, intangible that of the hero.

And, though it is not for us, as for those who in awed stillness listened at Gettysburg with inspired perception, to know Abraham Lincoln, yet there is for us another way whereby we may attain such knowledge—through his words—uttered in all sincerity to those who loved or hated him. Cold, unsatisfying they may seem, these printed words, while we can yet speak with those who knew him, and look into eyes that once looked into his. But in truth it is here that we find his simple greatness, his great simplicity, and though no man tried less so to show his power, no man has so shown it more clearly.

Thus these writings of Abraham Lincoln are associated with those of Washington, Hamilton, Franklin, and of the other "Founders of the Republic," not that Lincoln should become still more of the past, but, rather, that he with them should become still more of the present. However faint and mythical may grow the story of that Great Struggle, the leader, Lincoln, at least should remain a real, living American. No matter how clearly, how directly, Lincoln has shown himself in his writings, we yet should not forget those men whose minds, from their various view-points, have illumined for us his character. As this nation owes a great debt to Lincoln, so, also, Lincoln's memory owes a great debt to a nation which, as no other nation could have done, has been able to appreciate his full worth. Among the many who have brought about this appreciation, those only whose estimates have been placed in these volumes may be mentioned here. To President Roosevelt, to Mr. Schurz and to Mr. Choate, the editor, for himself, for the publishers, and on behalf of the readers, wishes to offer his sincere acknowledgments.

Thanks are also due, for valuable and sympathetic assistance rendered in the preparation of this work, to Mr. Gilbert A. Tracy, of Putnam, Conn., Major William H. Lambert, of Philadelphia, and Mr. C. F. Gunther, of Chicago, to the Chicago Historical Association and personally to its capable Secretary, Miss McIlvaine, to Major Henry S. Burrage, of Portland, Me., and to General Thomas J. Henderson, of Illinois.

For various courtesies received, the editor is furthermore indebted to the Librarian of the Library of Congress; to Messrs. McClure, Phillips & Co., D. Appleton & Co., Macmillan & Co., Dodd, Mead & Co., and Harper Brothers, of New York; to Houghton, Mifflin & Co., Dana, Estes & Co., and L. C. Page & Co., of Boston; to A. C. McClure & Co., of Chicago; to The Robert Clarke Co., of Cincinnati, and to the J. B. Lippincott Co., of Philadelphia.

It is hardly necessary to add that every effort has been made by the editor to bring into these volumes whatever material may there properly belong, material much of which is widely scattered in public libraries and in private collections. He has been fortunate in securing certain interesting correspondence and papers which had not before come into print in book form. Information concerning some of these papers had reached him too late to enable the papers to find place in their proper chronological order in the set. Rather, however, than not to present these papers to the readers they have been included in the seventh volume of the set, which concludes the "Writings."

[These later papers are, in this etext, re-arranged into chronologic
   order. D.W.]
October, 1905, A. B. L.

ABRAHAM LINCOLN: AN ESSAY BY CARL SHURZ

No American can study the character and career of Abraham Lincoln without being carried away by sentimental emotions. We are always inclined to idealize that which we love,—a state of mind very unfavorable to the exercise of sober critical judgment. It is therefore not surprising that most of those who have written or spoken on that extraordinary man, even while conscientiously endeavoring to draw a lifelike portraiture of his being, and to form a just estimate of his public conduct, should have drifted into more or less indiscriminating eulogy, painting his great features in the most glowing colors, and covering with tender shadings whatever might look like a blemish.

But his standing before posterity will not be exalted by mere praise of his virtues and abilities, nor by any concealment of his limitations and faults. The stature of the great man, one of whose peculiar charms consisted in his being so unlike all other great men, will rather lose than gain by the idealization which so easily runs into the commonplace. For it was distinctly the weird mixture of qualities and forces in him, of the lofty with the common, the ideal with the uncouth, of that which he had become with that which he had not ceased to be, that made him so fascinating a character among his fellow-men, gave him his singular power over their minds and hearts, and fitted him to be the greatest leader in the greatest crisis of our national life.

His was indeed a marvellous growth. The statesman or the military hero born and reared in a log cabin is a familiar figure in American history; but we may search in vain among our celebrities for one whose origin and early life equalled Abraham Lincoln's in wretchedness. He first saw the light in a miserable hovel in Kentucky, on a farm consisting of a few barren acres in a dreary neighborhood; his father a typical "poor Southern white," shiftless and without ambition for himself or his children, constantly looking for a new piece of land on which he might make a living without much work; his mother, in her youth handsome and bright, grown prematurely coarse in feature and soured in mind by daily toil and care; the whole household squalid, cheerless, and utterly void of elevating inspirations... Only when the family had "moved" into the malarious backwoods of Indiana, the mother had died, and a stepmother, a woman of thrift and energy, had taken charge of the children, the shaggy-headed, ragged, barefooted, forlorn boy, then seven years old, "began to feel like a human being." Hard work was his early lot. When a mere boy he had to help in supporting the family, either on his father's clearing, or hired out to other farmers to plough, or dig ditches, or chop wood, or drive ox teams; occasionally also to "tend the baby," when the farmer's wife was otherwise engaged. He could regard it as an advancement to a higher sphere of activity when he obtained work in a "crossroads store," where he amused the customers by his talk over the counter; for he soon distinguished himself among the backwoods folk as one who had something to say worth listening to. To win that distinction, he had to draw mainly upon his wits; for, while his thirst for knowledge was great, his opportunities for satisfying that thirst were wofully slender.

In the log schoolhouse, which he could visit but little, he was taught only reading, writing, and elementary arithmetic. Among the people of the settlement, bush farmers and small tradesmen, he found none of uncommon intelligence or education; but some of them had a few books, which he borrowed eagerly. Thus he read and reread, Æsop's Fables, learning to tell stories with a point and to argue by parables; he read Robinson Crusoe, The Pilgrim's Progress, a short history of the United States, and Weems's Life of Washington. To the town constable's he went to read the Revised Statutes of Indiana. Every printed page that fell into his hands he would greedily devour, and his family and friends watched him with wonder, as the uncouth boy, after his daily work, crouched in a corner of the log cabin or outside under a tree, absorbed in a book while munching his supper of corn bread. In this manner he began to gather some knowledge, and sometimes he would astonish the girls with such startling remarks as that the earth was moving around the sun, and not the sun around the earth, and they marvelled where "Abe" could have got such queer notions. Soon he also felt the impulse to write; not only making extracts from books he wished to remember, but also composing little essays of his own. First he sketched these with charcoal on a wooden shovel scraped white with a drawing-knife, or on basswood shingles. Then he transferred them to paper, which was a scarce commodity in the Lincoln household; taking care to cut his expressions close, so that they might not cover too much space,—a style-forming method greatly to be commended. Seeing boys put a burning coal on the back of a wood turtle, he was moved to write on cruelty to animals. Seeing men intoxicated with whiskey, he wrote on temperance. In verse-making, too, he tried himself, and in satire on persons offensive to him or others,—satire the rustic wit of which was not always fit for ears polite. Also political thoughts he put upon paper, and some of his pieces were even deemed good enough for publication in the county weekly.

Thus he won a neighborhood reputation as a clever young man, which he increased by his performances as a speaker, not seldom drawing upon himself the dissatisfaction of his employers by mounting a stump in the field, and keeping the farm hands from their work by little speeches in a jocose and sometimes also a serious vein. At the rude social frolics of the settlement he became an important person, telling funny, stories, mimicking the itinerant preachers who had happened to pass by, and making his mark at wrestling matches, too; for at the age of seventeen he had attained his full height, six feet four inches in his stockings, if he had any, and a terribly muscular clodhopper he was. But he was known never to use his extraordinary strength to the injury or humiliation of others; rather to do them a kindly turn, or to enforce justice and fair dealing between them. All this made him a favorite in backwoods society, although in some things he appeared a little odd, to his friends. Far more than any of them, he was given not only to reading, but to fits of abstraction, to quiet musing with himself, and also to strange spells of melancholy, from which he often would pass in a moment to rollicking outbursts of droll humor. But on the whole he was one of the people among whom he lived; in appearance perhaps even a little more uncouth than most of them,—a very tall, rawboned youth, with large features, dark, shrivelled skin, and rebellious hair; his arms and legs long, out of proportion; clad in deerskin trousers, which from frequent exposure to the rain had shrunk so as to sit tightly on his limbs, leaving several inches of bluish shin exposed between their lower end and the heavy tan-colored shoes; the nether garment held usually by only one suspender, that was strung over a coarse homemade shirt; the head covered in winter with a coonskin cap, in summer with a rough straw hat of uncertain shape, without a band.

It is doubtful whether he felt himself much superior to his surroundings, although he confessed to a yearning for some knowledge of the world outside of the circle in which he lived. This wish was gratified; but how? At the age of nineteen he went down the Mississippi to New Orleans as a flatboat hand, temporarily joining a trade many members of which at that time still took pride in being called "half horse and half alligator." After his return he worked and lived in the old way until the spring of 1830, when his father "moved again," this time to Illinois; and on the journey of fifteen days "Abe" had to drive the ox wagon which carried the household goods. Another log cabin was built, and then, fencing a field, Abraham Lincoln split those historic rails which were destined to play so picturesque a part in the Presidential campaign twenty-eight years later.

Having come of age, Lincoln left the family, and "struck out for himself." He had to "take jobs whenever he could get them." The first of these carried him again as a flatboat hand to New Orleans. There something happened that made a lasting impression upon his soul: he witnessed a slave auction. "His heart bled," wrote one of his companions; "said nothing much; was silent; looked bad. I can say, knowing it, that it was on this trip that he formed his opinion on slavery. It run its iron in him then and there, May, 1831. I have heard him say so often." Then he lived several years at New Salem, in Illinois, a small mushroom village, with a mill, some "stores" and whiskey shops, that rose quickly, and soon disappeared again. It was a desolate, disjointed, half-working and half-loitering life, without any other aim than to gain food and shelter from day to day. He served as pilot on a steamboat trip, then as clerk in a store and a mill; business failing, he was adrift for some time. Being compelled to measure his strength with the chief bully of the neighborhood, and overcoming him, he became a noted person in that muscular community, and won the esteem and friendship of the ruling gang of ruffians to such a degree that, when the Black Hawk war broke out, they elected him, a young man of twenty-three, captain of a volunteer company, composed mainly of roughs of their kind. He took the field, and his most noteworthy deed of valor consisted, not in killing an Indian, but in protecting against his own men, at the peril of his own life, the life of an old savage who had strayed into his camp.

The Black Hawk war over, he turned to politics. The step from the captaincy of a volunteer company to a candidacy for a seat in the Legislature seemed a natural one. But his popularity, although great in New Salem, had not spread far enough over the district, and he was defeated. Then the wretched hand-to-mouth struggle began again. He "set up in store-business" with a dissolute partner, who drank whiskey while Lincoln was reading books. The result was a disastrous failure and a load of debt. Thereupon he became a deputy surveyor, and was appointed postmaster of New Salem, the business of the post-office being so small that he could carry the incoming and outgoing mail in his hat. All this could not lift him from poverty, and his surveying instruments and horse and saddle were sold by the sheriff for debt.

But while all this misery was upon him his ambition rose to higher aims. He walked many miles to borrow from a schoolmaster a grammar with which to improve his language. A lawyer lent him a copy of Blackstone, and he began to study law.

People would look wonderingly at the grotesque figure lying in the grass, "with his feet up a tree," or sitting on a fence, as, absorbed in a book, he learned to construct correct sentences and made himself a jurist. At once he gained a little practice, pettifogging before a justice of the peace for friends, without expecting a fee. Judicial functions, too, were thrust upon him, but only at horse-races or wrestling matches, where his acknowledged honesty and fairness gave his verdicts undisputed authority. His popularity grew apace, and soon he could be a candidate for the Legislature again. Although he called himself a Whig, an ardent admirer of Henry Clay, his clever stump speeches won him the election in the strongly Democratic district. Then for the first time, perhaps, he thought seriously of his outward appearance. So far he had been content with a garb of "Kentucky jeans," not seldom ragged, usually patched, and always shabby. Now, he borrowed some money from a friend to buy a new suit of clothes—"store clothes" fit for a Sangamon County statesman; and thus adorned he set out for the state capital, Vandalia, to take his seat among the lawmakers.

His legislative career, which stretched over several sessions—for he was thrice re-elected, in 1836, 1838, and 1840—was not remarkably brilliant. He did, indeed, not lack ambition. He dreamed even of making himself "the De Witt Clinton of Illinois," and he actually distinguished himself by zealous and effective work in those "log-rolling" operations by which the young State received "a general system of internal improvements" in the shape of railroads, canals, and banks,—a reckless policy, burdening the State with debt, and producing the usual crop of political demoralization, but a policy characteristic of the time and the impatiently enterprising spirit of the Western people. Lincoln, no doubt with the best intentions, but with little knowledge of the subject, simply followed the popular current. The achievement in which, perhaps, he gloried most was the removal of the State government from Vandalia to Springfield; one of those triumphs of political management which are apt to be the pride of the small politician's statesmanship. One thing, however, he did in which his true nature asserted itself, and which gave distinct promise of the future pursuit of high aims. Against an overwhelming preponderance of sentiment in the Legislature, followed by only one other member, he recorded his protest against a proslavery resolution,—that protest declaring "the institution of slavery to be founded on both injustice and bad policy." This was not only the irrepressible voice of his conscience; it was true moral valor, too; for at that time, in many parts of the West, an abolitionist was regarded as little better than a horse-thief, and even "Abe Lincoln" would hardly have been forgiven his antislavery principles, had he not been known as such an "uncommon good fellow." But here, in obedience to the great conviction of his life, he manifested his courage to stand alone, that courage which is the first requisite of leadership in a great cause.

Together with his reputation and influence as a politician grew his law practice, especially after he had removed from New Salem to Springfield, and associated himself with a practitioner of good standing. He had now at last won a fixed position in society. He became a successful lawyer, less, indeed, by his learning as a jurist than by his effectiveness as an advocate and by the striking uprightness of his character; and it may truly be said that his vivid sense of truth and justice had much to do with his effectiveness as an advocate. He would refuse to act as the attorney even of personal friends when he saw the right on the other side. He would abandon cases, even during trial, when the testimony convinced him that his client was in the wrong. He would dissuade those who sought his service from pursuing an obtainable advantage when their claims seemed to him unfair. Presenting his very first case in the United States Circuit Court, the only question being one of authority, he declared that, upon careful examination, he found all the authorities on the other side, and none on his. Persons accused of crime, when he thought them guilty, he would not defend at all, or, attempting their defence, he was unable to put forth his powers. One notable exception is on record, when his personal sympathies had been strongly aroused. But when he felt himself to be the protector of innocence, the defender of justice, or the prosecutor of wrong, he frequently disclosed such unexpected resources of reasoning, such depth of feeling, and rose to such fervor of appeal as to astonish and overwhelm his hearers, and make him fairly irresistible. Even an ordinary law argument, coming from him, seldom failed to produce the impression that he was profoundly convinced of the soundness of his position. It is not surprising that the mere appearance of so conscientious an attorney in any case should have carried, not only to juries, but even to judges, almost a presumption of right on his side, and that the people began to call him, sincerely meaning it, "honest Abe Lincoln."

In the meantime he had private sorrows and trials of a painfully afflicting nature. He had loved and been loved by a fair and estimable girl, Ann Rutledge, who died in the flower of her youth and beauty, and he mourned her loss with such intensity of grief that his friends feared for his reason. Recovering from his morbid depression, he bestowed what he thought a new affection upon another lady, who refused him. And finally, moderately prosperous in his worldly affairs, and having prospects of political distinction before him, he paid his addresses to Mary Todd, of Kentucky, and was accepted. But then tormenting doubts of the genuineness of his own affection for her, of the compatibility of their characters, and of their future happiness came upon him. His distress was so great that he felt himself in danger of suicide, and feared to carry a pocket-knife with him; and he gave mortal offence to his bride by not appearing on the appointed wedding day. Now the torturing consciousness of the wrong he had done her grew unendurable. He won back her affection, ended the agony by marrying her, and became a faithful and patient husband and a good father. But it was no secret to those who knew the family well that his domestic life was full of trials. The erratic temper of his wife not seldom put the gentleness of his nature to the severest tests; and these troubles and struggles, which accompanied him through all the vicissitudes of his life from the modest home in Springfield to the White House at Washington, adding untold bitterness to his public cares, and sometimes precipitating upon him incredible embarrassments in the discharge of his public duties, form one of the most pathetic features of his career.

He continued to "ride the circuit," read books while travelling in his buggy, told funny stories to his fellow-lawyers in the tavern, chatted familiarly with his neighbors around the stove in the store and at the post-office, had his hours of melancholy brooding as of old, and became more and more widely known and trusted and beloved among the people of his State for his ability as a lawyer and politician, for the uprightness of his character and the overflowing spring of sympathetic kindness in his heart. His main ambition was confessedly that of political distinction; but hardly any one would at that time have seen in him the man destined to lead the nation through the greatest crisis of the century.

His time had not yet come when, in 1846, he was elected to Congress. In a clever speech in the House of Representatives he denounced President Polk for having unjustly forced war upon Mexico, and he amused the Committee of the Whole by a witty attack upon General Cass. More important was the expression he gave to his antislavery impulses by offering a bill looking to the emancipation of the slaves in the District of Columbia, and by his repeated votes for the famous Wilmot Proviso, intended to exclude slavery from the Territories acquired from Mexico. But when, at the expiration of his term, in March, 1849, he left his seat, he gloomily despaired of ever seeing the day when the cause nearest to his heart would be rightly grasped by the people, and when he would be able to render any service to his country in solving the great problem. Nor had his career as a member of Congress in any sense been such as to gratify his ambition. Indeed, if he ever had any belief in a great destiny for himself, it must have been weak at that period; for he actually sought to obtain from the new Whig President, General Taylor, the place of Commissioner of the General Land Office; willing to bury himself in one of the administrative bureaus of the government. Fortunately for the country, he failed; and no less fortunately, when, later, the territorial governorship of Oregon was offered to him, Mrs. Lincoln's protest induced him to decline it. Returning to Springfield, he gave himself with renewed zest to his law practice, acquiesced in the Compromise of 1850 with reluctance and a mental reservation, supported in the Presidential campaign of 1852 the Whig candidate in some spiritless speeches, and took but a languid interest in the politics of the day. But just then his time was drawing near.

The peace promised, and apparently inaugurated, by the Compromise of 1850 was rudely broken by the introduction of the Kansas-Nebraska Bill in 1854. The repeal of the Missouri Compromise, opening the Territories of the United States, the heritage of coming generations, to the invasion of slavery, suddenly revealed the whole significance of the slavery question to the people of the free States, and thrust itself into the politics of the country as the paramount issue. Something like an electric shock flashed through the North. Men who but a short time before had been absorbed by their business pursuits, and deprecated all political agitation, were startled out of their security by a sudden alarm, and excitedly took sides. That restless trouble of conscience about slavery, which even in times of apparent repose had secretly disturbed the souls of Northern people, broke forth in an utterance louder than ever. The bonds of accustomed party allegiance gave way. Antislavery Democrats and antislavery Whigs felt themselves drawn together by a common overpowering sentiment, and soon they began to rally in a new organization. The Republican party sprang into being to meet the overruling call of the hour. Then Abraham Lincoln's time was come. He rapidly advanced to a position of conspicuous championship in the struggle. This, however, was not owing to his virtues and abilities alone. Indeed, the slavery question stirred his soul in its profoundest depths; it was, as one of his intimate friends said, "the only one on which he would become excited"; it called forth all his faculties and energies. Yet there were many others who, having long and arduously fought the antislavery battle in the popular assembly, or in the press, or in the halls of Congress, far surpassed him in prestige, and compared with whom he was still an obscure and untried man. His reputation, although highly honorable and well earned, had so far been essentially local. As a stump-speaker in Whig canvasses outside of his State he had attracted comparatively little attention; but in Illinois he had been recognized as one of the foremost men of the Whig party. Among the opponents of the Nebraska Bill he occupied in his State so important a position, that in 1856 he was the choice of a large majority of the "Anti-Nebraska men" in the Legislature for a seat in the Senate of the United States which then became vacant; and when he, an old Whig, could not obtain the votes of the Anti-Nebraska Democrats necessary to make a majority, he generously urged his friends to transfer their votes to Lyman Trumbull, who was then elected. Two years later, in the first national convention of the Republican party, the delegation from Illinois brought him forward as a candidate for the vice-presidency, and he received respectable support. Still, the name of Abraham Lincoln was not widely known beyond the boundaries of his own State. But now it was this local prominence in Illinois that put him in a position of peculiar advantage on the battlefield of national politics. In the assault on the Missouri Compromise which broke down all legal barriers to the spread of slavery Stephen Arnold Douglas was the ostensible leader and central figure; and Douglas was a Senator from Illinois, Lincoln's State. Douglas's national theatre of action was the Senate, but in his constituency in Illinois were the roots of his official position and power. What he did in the Senate he had to justify before the people of Illinois, in order to maintain himself in place; and in Illinois all eyes turned to Lincoln as Douglas's natural antagonist.

As very young men they had come to Illinois, Lincoln from Indiana, Douglas from Vermont, and had grown up together in public life, Douglas as a Democrat, Lincoln as a Whig. They had met first in Vandalia, in 1834, when Lincoln was in the Legislature and Douglas in the lobby; and again in 1836, both as members of the Legislature. Douglas, a very able politician, of the agile, combative, audacious, "pushing" sort, rose in political distinction with remarkable rapidity. In quick succession he became a member of the Legislature, a State's attorney, secretary of state, a judge on the supreme bench of Illinois, three times a Representative in Congress, and a Senator of the United States when only thirty-nine years old. In the National Democratic convention of 1852 he appeared even as an aspirant to the nomination for the Presidency, as the favorite of "young America," and received a respectable vote. He had far outstripped Lincoln in what is commonly called political success and in reputation. But it had frequently happened that in political campaigns Lincoln felt himself impelled, or was selected by his Whig friends, to answer Douglas's speeches; and thus the two were looked upon, in a large part of the State at least, as the representative combatants of their respective parties in the debates before popular meetings. As soon, therefore, as, after the passage of his Kansas-Nebraska Bill, Douglas returned to Illinois to defend his cause before his constituents, Lincoln, obeying not only his own impulse, but also general expectation, stepped forward as his principal opponent. Thus the struggle about the principles involved in the Kansas-Nebraska Bill, or, in a broader sense, the struggle between freedom and slavery, assumed in Illinois the outward form of a personal contest between Lincoln and Douglas; and, as it continued and became more animated, that personal contest in Illinois was watched with constantly increasing interest by the whole country. When, in 1858, Douglas's senatorial term being about to expire, Lincoln was formally designated by the Republican convention of Illinois as their candidate for the Senate, to take Douglas's place, and the two contestants agreed to debate the questions at issue face to face in a series of public meetings, the eyes of the whole American people were turned eagerly to that one point: and the spectacle reminded one of those lays of ancient times telling of two armies, in battle array, standing still to see their two principal champions fight out the contested cause between the lines in single combat.

Lincoln had then reached the full maturity of his powers. His equipment as a statesman did not embrace a comprehensive knowledge of public affairs. What he had studied he had indeed made his own, with the eager craving and that zealous tenacity characteristic of superior minds learning under difficulties. But his narrow opportunities and the unsteady life he had led during his younger years had not permitted the accumulation of large stores in his mind. It is true, in political campaigns he had occasionally spoken on the ostensible issues between the Whigs and the Democrats, the tariff, internal improvements, banks, and so on, but only in a perfunctory manner. Had he ever given much serious thought and study to these subjects, it is safe to assume that a mind so prolific of original conceits as his would certainly have produced some utterance upon them worth remembering. His soul had evidently never been deeply stirred by such topics. But when his moral nature was aroused, his brain developed an untiring activity until it had mastered all the knowledge within reach. As soon as the repeal of the Missouri Compromise had thrust the slavery question into politics as the paramount issue, Lincoln plunged into an arduous study of all its legal, historical, and moral aspects, and then his mind became a complete arsenal of argument. His rich natural gifts, trained by long and varied practice, had made him an orator of rare persuasiveness. In his immature days, he had pleased himself for a short period with that inflated, high-flown style which, among the uncultivated, passes for "beautiful speaking." His inborn truthfulness and his artistic instinct soon overcame that aberration and revealed to him the noble beauty and strength of simplicity. He possessed an uncommon power of clear and compact statement, which might have reminded those who knew the story of his early youth of the efforts of the poor boy, when he copied his compositions from the scraped wooden shovel, carefully to trim his expressions in order to save paper. His language had the energy of honest directness and he was a master of logical lucidity. He loved to point and enliven his reasoning by humorous illustrations, usually anecdotes of Western life, of which he had an inexhaustible store at his command. These anecdotes had not seldom a flavor of rustic robustness about them, but he used them with great effect, while amusing the audience, to give life to an abstraction, to explode an absurdity, to clinch an argument, to drive home an admonition. The natural kindliness of his tone, softening prejudice and disarming partisan rancor, would often open to his reasoning a way into minds most unwilling to receive it.

Yet his greatest power consisted in the charm of his individuality. That charm did not, in the ordinary way, appeal to the ear or to the eye. His voice was not melodious; rather shrill and piercing, especially when it rose to its high treble in moments of great animation. His figure was unhandsome, and the action of his unwieldy limbs awkward. He commanded none of the outward graces of oratory as they are commonly understood. His charm was of a different kind. It flowed from the rare depth and genuineness of his convictions and his sympathetic feelings. Sympathy was the strongest element in his nature. One of his biographers, who knew him before he became President, says: "Lincoln's compassion might be stirred deeply by an object present, but never by an object absent and unseen. In the former case he would most likely extend relief, with little inquiry into the merits of the case, because, as he expressed it himself, it 'took a pain out of his own heart.'" Only half of this is correct. It is certainly true that he could not witness any individual distress or oppression, or any kind of suffering, without feeling a pang of pain himself, and that by relieving as much as he could the suffering of others he put an end to his own. This compassionate impulse to help he felt not only for human beings, but for every living creature. As in his boyhood he angrily reproved the boys who tormented a wood turtle by putting a burning coal on its back, so, we are told, he would, when a mature man, on a journey, dismount from his buggy and wade waist-deep in mire to rescue a pig struggling in a swamp. Indeed, appeals to his compassion were so irresistible to him, and he felt it so difficult to refuse anything when his refusal could give pain, that he himself sometimes spoke of his inability to say "no" as a positive weakness. But that certainly does not prove that his compassionate feeling was confined to individual cases of suffering witnessed with his own eyes. As the boy was moved by the aspect of the tortured wood turtle to compose an essay against cruelty to animals in general, so the aspect of other cases of suffering and wrong wrought up his moral nature, and set his mind to work against cruelty, injustice, and oppression in general.

As his sympathy went forth to others, it attracted others to him. Especially those whom he called the "plain people" felt themselves drawn to him by the instinctive feeling that he understood, esteemed, and appreciated them. He had grown up among the poor, the lowly, the ignorant. He never ceased to remember the good souls he had met among them, and the many kindnesses they had done him. Although in his mental development he had risen far above them, he never looked down upon them. How they felt and how they reasoned he knew, for so he had once felt and reasoned himself. How they could be moved he knew, for so he had once been moved himself and practised moving others. His mind was much larger than theirs, but it thoroughly comprehended theirs; and while he thought much farther than they, their thoughts were ever present to him. Nor had the visible distance between them grown as wide as his rise in the world would seem to have warranted. Much of his backwoods speech and manners still clung to him. Although he had become "Mr. Lincoln" to his later acquaintances, he was still "Abe" to the "Nats" and "Billys" and "Daves" of his youth; and their familiarity neither appeared unnatural to them, nor was it in the least awkward to him. He still told and enjoyed stories similar to those he had told and enjoyed in the Indiana settlement and at New Salem. His wants remained as modest as they had ever been; his domestic habits had by no means completely accommodated themselves to those of his more highborn wife; and though the "Kentucky jeans" apparel had long been dropped, his clothes of better material and better make would sit ill sorted on his gigantic limbs. His cotton umbrella, without a handle, and tied together with a coarse string to keep it from flapping, which he carried on his circuit rides, is said to be remembered still by some of his surviving neighbors. This rusticity of habit was utterly free from that affected contempt of refinement and comfort which self-made men sometimes carry into their more affluent circumstances. To Abraham Lincoln it was entirely natural, and all those who came into contact with him knew it to be so. In his ways of thinking and feeling he had become a gentleman in the highest sense, but the refining process had polished but little the outward form. The plain people, therefore, still considered "honest Abe Lincoln" one of themselves; and when they felt, which they no doubt frequently did, that his thoughts and aspirations moved in a sphere above their own, they were all the more proud of him, without any diminution of fellow-feeling. It was this relation of mutual sympathy and understanding between Lincoln and the plain people that gave him his peculiar power as a public man, and singularly fitted him, as we shall see, for that leadership which was preeminently required in the great crisis then coming on,—the leadership which indeed thinks and moves ahead of the masses, but always remains within sight and sympathetic touch of them.

He entered upon the campaign of 1858 better equipped than he had ever been before. He not only instinctively felt, but he had convinced himself by arduous study, that in this struggle against the spread of slavery he had right, justice, philosophy, the enlightened opinion of mankind, history, the Constitution, and good policy on his side. It was observed that after he began to discuss the slavery question his speeches were pitched in a much loftier key than his former oratorical efforts. While he remained fond of telling funny stories in private conversation, they disappeared more and more from his public discourse. He would still now and then point his argument with expressions of inimitable quaintness, and flash out rays of kindly humor and witty irony; but his general tone was serious, and rose sometimes to genuine solemnity. His masterly skill in dialectical thrust and parry, his wealth of knowledge, his power of reasoning and elevation of sentiment, disclosed in language of rare precision, strength, and beauty, not seldom astonished his old friends.

Neither of the two champions could have found a more formidable antagonist than each now met in the other. Douglas was by far the most conspicuous member of his party. His admirers had dubbed him "the Little Giant," contrasting in that nickname the greatness of his mind with the smallness of his body. But though of low stature, his broad-shouldered figure appeared uncommonly sturdy, and there was something lion-like in the squareness of his brow and jaw, and in the defiant shake of his long hair. His loud and persistent advocacy of territorial expansion, in the name of patriotism and "manifest destiny," had given him an enthusiastic following among the young and ardent. Great natural parts, a highly combative temperament, and long training had made him a debater unsurpassed in a Senate filled with able men. He could be as forceful in his appeals to patriotic feelings as he was fierce in denunciation and thoroughly skilled in all the baser tricks of parliamentary pugilism. While genial and rollicking in his social intercourse—the idol of the "boys" he felt himself one of the most renowned statesmen of his time, and would frequently meet his opponents with an overbearing haughtiness, as persons more to be pitied than to be feared. In his speech opening the campaign of 1858, he spoke of Lincoln, whom the Republicans had dared to advance as their candidate for "his" place in the Senate, with an air of patronizing if not contemptuous condescension, as "a kind, amiable, and intelligent gentleman and a good citizen." The Little Giant would have been pleased to pass off his antagonist as a tall dwarf. He knew Lincoln too well, however, to indulge himself seriously in such a delusion. But the political situation was at that moment in a curious tangle, and Douglas could expect to derive from the confusion great advantage over his opponent.

By the repeal of the Missouri Compromise, opening the Territories to the ingress of slavery, Douglas had pleased the South, but greatly alarmed the North. He had sought to conciliate Northern sentiment by appending to his Kansas-Nebraska Bill the declaration that its intent was "not to legislate slavery into any State or Territory, nor to exclude it therefrom, but to leave the people thereof perfectly free to form and regulate their institutions in their own way, subject only to the Constitution of the United States." This he called "the great principle of popular sovereignty." When asked whether, under this act, the people of a Territory, before its admission as a State, would have the right to exclude slavery, he answered, "That is a question for the courts to decide." Then came the famous "Dred Scott decision," in which the Supreme Court held substantially that the right to hold slaves as property existed in the Territories by virtue of the Federal Constitution, and that this right could not be denied by any act of a territorial government. This, of course, denied the right of the people of any Territory to exclude slavery while they were in a territorial condition, and it alarmed the Northern people still more. Douglas recognized the binding force of the decision of the Supreme Court, at the same time maintaining, most illogically, that his great principle of popular sovereignty remained in force nevertheless. Meanwhile, the proslavery people of western Missouri, the so-called "border ruffians," had invaded Kansas, set up a constitutional convention, made a constitution of an extreme pro-slavery type, the "Lecompton Constitution," refused to submit it fairly to a vote of the people of Kansas, and then referred it to Congress for acceptance,—seeking thus to accomplish the admission of Kansas as a slave State. Had Douglas supported such a scheme, he would have lost all foothold in the North. In the name of popular sovereignty he loudly declared his opposition to the acceptance of any constitution not sanctioned by a formal popular vote. He "did not care," he said, "whether slavery be voted up or down," but there must be a fair vote of the people. Thus he drew upon himself the hostility of the Buchanan administration, which was controlled by the proslavery interest, but he saved his Northern following. More than this, not only did his Democratic admirers now call him "the true champion of freedom," but even some Republicans of large influence, prominent among them Horace Greeley, sympathizing with Douglas in his fight against the Lecompton Constitution, and hoping to detach him permanently from the proslavery interest and to force a lasting breach in the Democratic party, seriously advised the Republicans of Illinois to give up their opposition to Douglas, and to help re-elect him to the Senate. Lincoln was not of that opinion. He believed that great popular movements can succeed only when guided by their faithful friends, and that the antislavery cause could not safely be entrusted to the keeping of one who "did not care whether slavery be voted up or down." This opinion prevailed in Illinois; but the influences within the Republican party over which it prevailed yielded only a reluctant acquiescence, if they acquiesced at all, after having materially strengthened Douglas's position. Such was the situation of things when the campaign of 1858 between Lincoln and Douglas began.

Lincoln opened the campaign on his side at the convention which nominated him as the Republican candidate for the senatorship, with a memorable saying which sounded like a shout from the watchtower of history: "A house divided against itself cannot stand. I believe this government cannot endure permanently half slave and half free. I do not expect the Union to be dissolved. I do not expect the house to fall, but I expect it will cease to be divided. It will become all one thing or all the other. Either the opponents of slavery will arrest the further spread of it, and place it where the public mind shall rest in the belief that it is in the course of ultimate extinction, or its advocates will push it forward, till it shall become alike lawful in all the States,—old as well as new, North as well as South." Then he proceeded to point out that the Nebraska doctrine combined with the Dred Scott decision worked in the direction of making the nation "all slave." Here was the "irrepressible conflict" spoken of by Seward a short time later, in a speech made famous mainly by that phrase. If there was any new discovery in it, the right of priority was Lincoln's. This utterance proved not only his statesmanlike conception of the issue, but also, in his situation as a candidate, the firmness of his moral courage. The friends to whom he had read the draught of this speech before he delivered it warned him anxiously that its delivery might be fatal to his success in the election. This was shrewd advice, in the ordinary sense. While a slaveholder could threaten disunion with impunity, the mere suggestion that the existence of slavery was incompatible with freedom in the Union would hazard the political chances of any public man in the North. But Lincoln was inflexible. "It is true," said he, "and I will deliver it as written.... I would rather be defeated with these expressions in my speech held up and discussed before the people than be victorious without them." The statesman was right in his far-seeing judgment and his conscientious statement of the truth, but the practical politicians were also right in their prediction of the immediate effect. Douglas instantly seized upon the declaration that a house divided against itself cannot stand as the main objective point of his attack, interpreting it as an incitement to a "relentless sectional war," and there is no doubt that the persistent reiteration of this charge served to frighten not a few timid souls.

Lincoln constantly endeavored to bring the moral and philosophical side of the subject to the foreground. "Slavery is wrong" was the keynote of all his speeches. To Douglas's glittering sophism that the right of the people of a Territory to have slavery or not, as they might desire, was in accordance with the principle of true popular sovereignty, he made the pointed answer: "Then true popular sovereignty, according to Senator Douglas, means that, when one man makes another man his slave, no third man shall be allowed to object." To Douglas's argument that the principle which demanded that the people of a Territory should be permitted to choose whether they would have slavery or not "originated when God made man, and placed good and evil before him, allowing him to choose upon his own responsibility," Lincoln solemnly replied: "No; God—did not place good and evil before man, telling him to make his choice. On the contrary, God did tell him there was one tree of the fruit of which he should not eat, upon pain of death." He did not, however, place himself on the most advanced ground taken by the radical anti-slavery men. He admitted that, under the Constitution, "the Southern people were entitled to a Congressional fugitive slave law," although he did not approve the fugitive slave law then existing. He declared also that, if slavery were kept out of the Territories during their territorial existence, as it should be, and if then the people of any Territory, having a fair chance and a clear field, should do such an extraordinary thing as to adopt a slave constitution, uninfluenced by the actual presence of the institution among them, he saw no alternative but to admit such a Territory into the Union. He declared further that, while he should be exceedingly glad to see slavery abolished in the District of Columbia, he would, as a member of Congress, with his present views, not endeavor to bring on that abolition except on condition that emancipation be gradual, that it be approved by the decision of a majority of voters in the District, and that compensation be made to unwilling owners. On every available occasion, he pronounced himself in favor of the deportation and colonization of the blacks, of course with their consent. He repeatedly disavowed any wish on his part to have social and political equality established between whites and blacks. On this point he summed up his views in a reply to Douglas's assertion that the Declaration of Independence, in speaking of all men as being created equal, did not include the negroes, saying: "I do not understand the Declaration of Independence to mean that all men were created equal in all respects. They are not equal in color. But I believe that it does mean to declare that all men are equal in some respects; they are equal in their right to life, liberty, and the pursuit of happiness."

With regard to some of these subjects Lincoln modified his position at a later period, and it has been suggested that he would have professed more advanced principles in his debates with Douglas, had he not feared thereby to lose votes. This view can hardly be sustained. Lincoln had the courage of his opinions, but he was not a radical. The man who risked his election by delivering, against the urgent protest of his friends, the speech about "the house divided against itself" would not have shrunk from the expression of more extreme views, had he really entertained them. It is only fair to assume that he said what at the time he really thought, and that if, subsequently, his opinions changed, it was owing to new conceptions of good policy and of duty brought forth by an entirely new set of circumstances and exigencies. It is characteristic that he continued to adhere to the impracticable colonization plan even after the Emancipation Proclamation had already been issued.

But in this contest Lincoln proved himself not only a debater, but also a political strategist of the first order. The "kind, amiable, and intelligent gentleman," as Douglas had been pleased to call him, was by no means as harmless as a dove. He possessed an uncommon share of that worldly shrewdness which not seldom goes with genuine simplicity of character; and the political experience gathered in the Legislature and in Congress, and in many election campaigns, added to his keen intuitions, had made him as far-sighted a judge of the probable effects of a public man's sayings or doings upon the popular mind, and as accurate a calculator in estimating political chances and forecasting results, as could be found among the party managers in Illinois. And now he perceived keenly the ugly dilemma in which Douglas found himself, between the Dred Scott decision, which declared the right to hold slaves to exist in the Territories by virtue of the Federal Constitution, and his "great principle of popular sovereignty," according to which the people of a Territory, if they saw fit, were to have the right to exclude slavery therefrom. Douglas was twisting and squirming to the best of his ability to avoid the admission that the two were incompatible. The question then presented itself if it would be good policy for Lincoln to force Douglas to a clear expression of his opinion as to whether, the Dred Scott decision notwithstanding, "the people of a Territory could in any lawful way exclude slavery from its limits prior to the formation of a State constitution." Lincoln foresaw and predicted what Douglas would answer: that slavery could not exist in a Territory unless the people desired it and gave it protection by territorial legislation. In an improvised caucus the policy of pressing the interrogatory on Douglas was discussed. Lincoln's friends unanimously advised against it, because the answer foreseen would sufficiently commend Douglas to the people of Illinois to insure his re-election to the Senate. But Lincoln persisted. "I am after larger game," said he. "If Douglas so answers, he can never be President, and the battle of 1860 is worth a hundred of this." The interrogatory was pressed upon Douglas, and Douglas did answer that, no matter what the decision of the Supreme Court might be on the abstract question, the people of a Territory had the lawful means to introduce or exclude slavery by territorial legislation friendly or unfriendly to the institution. Lincoln found it easy to show the absurdity of the proposition that, if slavery were admitted to exist of right in the Territories by virtue of the supreme law, the Federal Constitution, it could be kept out or expelled by an inferior law, one made by a territorial Legislature. Again the judgment of the politicians, having only the nearest object in view, proved correct: Douglas was reelected to the Senate. But Lincoln's judgment proved correct also: Douglas, by resorting to the expedient of his "unfriendly legislation doctrine," forfeited his last chance of becoming President of the United States. He might have hoped to win, by sufficient atonement, his pardon from the South for his opposition to the Lecompton Constitution; but that he taught the people of the Territories a trick by which they could defeat what the proslavery men considered a constitutional right, and that he called that trick lawful, this the slave power would never forgive. The breach between the Southern and the Northern Democracy was thenceforth irremediable and fatal.

The Presidential election of 1860 approached. The struggle in Kansas, and the debates in Congress which accompanied it, and which not unfrequently provoked violent outbursts, continually stirred the popular excitement. Within the Democratic party raged the war of factions. The national Democratic convention met at Charleston on the 23d of April, 1860. After a struggle of ten days between the adherents and the opponents of Douglas, during which the delegates from the cotton States had withdrawn, the convention adjourned without having nominated any candidates, to meet again in Baltimore on the 18th of June. There was no prospect, however, of reconciling the hostile elements. It appeared very probable that the Baltimore convention would nominate Douglas, while the seceding Southern Democrats would set up a candidate of their own, representing extreme proslavery principles.

Meanwhile, the national Republican convention assembled at Chicago on the 16th of May, full of enthusiasm and hope. The situation was easily understood. The Democrats would have the South. In order to succeed in the election, the Republicans had to win, in addition to the States carried by Fremont in 1856, those that were classed as "doubtful,"— New Jersey, Pennsylvania, and Indiana, or Illinois in the place of either New Jersey or Indiana. The most eminent Republican statesmen and leaders of the time thought of for the Presidency were Seward and Chase, both regarded as belonging to the more advanced order of antislavery men. Of the two, Seward had the largest following, mainly from New York, New England, and the Northwest. Cautious politicians doubted seriously whether Seward, to whom some phrases in his speeches had undeservedly given the reputation of a reckless radical, would be able to command the whole Republican vote in the doubtful States. Besides, during his long public career he had made enemies. It was evident that those who thought Seward's nomination too hazardous an experiment would consider Chase unavailable for the same reason. They would then look round for an "available" man; and among the "available" men Abraham Lincoln was easily discovered to stand foremost. His great debate with Douglas had given him a national reputation. The people of the East being eager to see the hero of so dramatic a contest, he had been induced to visit several Eastern cities, and had astonished and delighted large and distinguished audiences with speeches of singular power and originality. An address delivered by him in the Cooper Institute in New York, before an audience containing a large number of important persons, was then, and has ever since been, especially praised as one of the most logical and convincing political speeches ever made in this country. The people of the West had grown proud of him as a distinctively Western great man, and his popularity at home had some peculiar features which could be expected to exercise a potent charm. Nor was Lincoln's name as that of an available candidate left to the chance of accidental discovery. It is indeed not probable that he thought of himself as a Presidential possibility, during his contest with Douglas for the senatorship. As late as April, 1859, he had written to a friend who had approached him on the subject that he did not think himself fit for the Presidency. The Vice-Presidency was then the limit of his ambition. But some of his friends in Illinois took the matter seriously in hand, and Lincoln, after some hesitation, then formally authorized "the use of his name." The matter was managed with such energy and excellent judgment that, in the convention, he had not only the whole vote of Illinois to start with, but won votes on all sides without offending any rival. A large majority of the opponents of Seward went over to Abraham Lincoln, and gave him the nomination on the third ballot.

As had been foreseen, Douglas was nominated by one wing of the Democratic party at Baltimore, while the extreme proslavery wing put Breckinridge into the field as its candidate. After a campaign conducted with the energy of genuine enthusiasm on the antislavery side the united Republicans defeated the divided Democrats, and Lincoln was elected President by a majority of fifty-seven votes in the electoral colleges.

The result of the election had hardly been declared when the disunion movement in the South, long threatened and carefully planned and prepared, broke out in the shape of open revolt, and nearly a month before Lincoln could be inaugurated as President of the United States seven Southern States had adopted ordinances of secession, formed an independent confederacy, framed a constitution for it, and elected Jefferson Davis its president, expecting the other slaveholding States soon to join them. On the 11th of February, 1861, Lincoln left Springfield for Washington; having, with characteristic simplicity, asked his law partner not to change the sign of the firm "Lincoln and Herndon" during the four years unavoidable absence of the senior partner, and having taken an affectionate and touching leave of his neighbors.

The situation which confronted the new President was appalling: the larger part of the South in open rebellion, the rest of the slaveholding States wavering preparing to follow; the revolt guided by determined, daring, and skillful leaders; the Southern people, apparently full of enthusiasm and military spirit, rushing to arms, some of the forts and arsenals already in their possession; the government of the Union, before the accession of the new President, in the hands of men some of whom actively sympathized with the revolt, while others were hampered by their traditional doctrines in dealing with it, and really gave it aid and comfort by their irresolute attitude; all the departments full of "Southern sympathizers" and honeycombed with disloyalty; the treasury empty, and the public credit at the lowest ebb; the arsenals ill supplied with arms, if not emptied by treacherous practices; the regular army of insignificant strength, dispersed over an immense surface, and deprived of some of its best officers by defection; the navy small and antiquated. But that was not all. The threat of disunion had so often been resorted to by the slave power in years gone by that most Northern people had ceased to believe in its seriousness. But, when disunion actually appeared as a stern reality, something like a chill swept through the whole Northern country. A cry for union and peace at any price rose on all sides. Democratic partisanship reiterated this cry with vociferous vehemence, and even many Republicans grew afraid of the victory they had just achieved at the ballot-box, and spoke of compromise. The country fairly resounded with the noise of "anticoercion meetings." Expressions of firm resolution from determined antislavery men were indeed not wanting, but they were for a while almost drowned by a bewildering confusion of discordant voices. Even this was not all. Potent influences in Europe, with an ill-concealed desire for the permanent disruption of the American Union, eagerly espoused the cause of the Southern seceders, and the two principal maritime powers of the Old World seemed only to be waiting for a favorable opportunity to lend them a helping hand.

This was the state of things to be mastered by "honest Abe Lincoln" when he took his seat in the Presidential chair,—"honest Abe Lincoln," who was so good-natured that he could not say "no"; the greatest achievement in whose life had been a debate on the slavery question; who had never been in any position of power; who was without the slightest experience of high executive duties, and who had only a speaking acquaintance with the men upon whose counsel and cooperation he was to depend. Nor was his accession to power under such circumstances greeted with general confidence even by the members of his party. While he had indeed won much popularity, many Republicans, especially among those who had advocated Seward's nomination for the Presidency, saw the simple "Illinois lawyer" take the reins of government with a feeling little short of dismay. The orators and journals of the opposition were ridiculing and lampooning him without measure. Many people actually wondered how such a man could dare to undertake a task which, as he himself had said to his neighbors in his parting speech, was "more difficult than that of Washington himself had been."

But Lincoln brought to that task, aside from other uncommon qualities, the first requisite,—an intuitive comprehension of its nature. While he did not indulge in the delusion that the Union could be maintained or restored without a conflict of arms, he could indeed not foresee all the problems he would have to solve. He instinctively understood, however, by what means that conflict would have to be conducted by the government of a democracy. He knew that the impending war, whether great or small, would not be like a foreign war, exciting a united national enthusiasm, but a civil war, likely to fan to uncommon heat the animosities of party even in the localities controlled by the government; that this war would have to be carried on not by means of a ready-made machinery, ruled by an undisputed, absolute will, but by means to be furnished by the voluntary action of the people:—armies to be formed by voluntary enlistments; large sums of money to be raised by the people, through representatives, voluntarily taxing themselves; trust of extraordinary power to be voluntarily granted; and war measures, not seldom restricting the rights and liberties to which the citizen was accustomed, to be voluntarily accepted and submitted to by the people, or at least a large majority of them; and that this would have to be kept up not merely during a short period of enthusiastic excitement; but possibly through weary years of alternating success and disaster, hope and despondency. He knew that in order to steer this government by public opinion successfully through all the confusion created by the prejudices and doubts and differences of sentiment distracting the popular mind, and so to propitiate, inspire, mould, organize, unite, and guide the popular will that it might give forth all the means required for the performance of his great task, he would have to take into account all the influences strongly affecting the current of popular thought and feeling, and to direct while appearing to obey.

This was the kind of leadership he intuitively conceived to be needed when a free people were to be led forward en masse to overcome a great common danger under circumstances of appalling difficulty, the leadership which does not dash ahead with brilliant daring, no matter who follows, but which is intent upon rallying all the available forces, gathering in the stragglers, closing up the column, so that the front may advance well supported. For this leadership Abraham Lincoln was admirably fitted, better than any other American statesman of his day; for he understood the plain people, with all their loves and hates, their prejudices and their noble impulses, their weaknesses and their strength, as he understood himself, and his sympathetic nature was apt to draw their sympathy to him.

His inaugural address foreshadowed his official course in characteristic manner. Although yielding nothing in point of principle, it was by no means a flaming antislavery manifesto, such as would have pleased the more ardent Republicans. It was rather the entreaty of a sorrowing father speaking to his wayward children. In the kindliest language he pointed out to the secessionists how ill advised their attempt at disunion was, and why, for their own sakes, they should desist. Almost plaintively, he told them that, while it was not their duty to destroy the Union, it was his sworn duty to preserve it; that the least he could do, under the obligations of his oath, was to possess and hold the property of the United States; that he hoped to do this peaceably; that he abhorred war for any purpose, and that they would have none unless they themselves were the aggressors. It was a masterpiece of persuasiveness, and while Lincoln had accepted many valuable amendments suggested by Seward, it was essentially his own. Probably Lincoln himself did not expect his inaugural address to have any effect upon the secessionists, for he must have known them to be resolved upon disunion at any cost. But it was an appeal to the wavering minds in the North, and upon them it made a profound impression. Every candid man, however timid and halting, had to admit that the President was bound by his oath to do his duty; that under that oath he could do no less than he said he would do; that if the secessionists resisted such an appeal as the President had made, they were bent upon mischief, and that the government must be supported against them. The partisan sympathy with the Southern insurrection which still existed in the North did indeed not disappear, but it diminished perceptibly under the influence of such reasoning. Those who still resisted it did so at the risk of appearing unpatriotic.

It must not be supposed, however, that Lincoln at once succeeded in pleasing everybody, even among his friends,—even among those nearest to him. In selecting his cabinet, which he did substantially before he left Springfield for Washington, he thought it wise to call to his assistance the strong men of his party, especially those who had given evidence of the support they commanded as his competitors in the Chicago convention. In them he found at the same time representatives of the different shades of opinion within the party, and of the different elements—former Whigs and former Democrats—from which the party had recruited itself. This was sound policy under the circumstances. It might indeed have been foreseen that among the members of a cabinet so composed, troublesome disagreements and rivalries would break out. But it was better for the President to have these strong and ambitious men near him as his co-operators than to have them as his critics in Congress, where their differences might have been composed in a common opposition to him. As members of his cabinet he could hope to control them, and to keep them busily employed in the service of a common purpose, if he had the strength to do so. Whether he did possess this strength was soon tested by a singularly rude trial.

There can be no doubt that the foremost members of his cabinet, Seward and Chase, the most eminent Republican statesmen, had felt themselves wronged by their party when in its national convention it preferred to them for the Presidency a man whom, not unnaturally, they thought greatly their inferior in ability and experience as well as in service. The soreness of that disappointment was intensified when they saw this Western man in the White House, with so much of rustic manner and speech as still clung to him, meeting his fellow-citizens, high and low, on a footing of equality, with the simplicity of his good nature unburdened by any conventional dignity of deportment, and dealing with the great business of state in an easy-going, unmethodical, and apparently somewhat irreverent way. They did not understand such a man. Especially Seward, who, as Secretary of State, considered himself next to the Chief Executive, and who quickly accustomed himself to giving orders and making arrangements upon his own motion, thought it necessary that he should rescue the direction of public affairs from hands so unskilled, and take full charge of them himself. At the end of the first month of the administration he submitted a "memorandum" to President Lincoln, which has been first brought to light by Nicolay and Hay, and is one of their most valuable contributions to the history of those days. In that paper Seward actually told the President that at the end of a month's administration the government was still without a policy, either domestic or foreign; that the slavery question should be eliminated from the struggle about the Union; that the matter of the maintenance of the forts and other possessions in the South should be decided with that view; that explanations should be demanded categorically from the governments of Spain and France, which were then preparing, one for the annexation of San Domingo, and both for the invasion of Mexico; that if no satisfactory explanations were received war should be declared against Spain and France by the United States; that explanations should also be sought from Russia and Great Britain, and a vigorous continental spirit of independence against European intervention be aroused all over the American continent; that this policy should be incessantly pursued and directed by somebody; that either the President should devote himself entirely to it, or devolve the direction on some member of his cabinet, whereupon all debate on this policy must end.

This could be understood only as a formal demand that the President should acknowledge his own incompetency to perform his duties, content himself with the amusement of distributing post-offices, and resign his power as to all important affairs into the hands of his Secretary of State. It seems to-day incomprehensible how a statesman of Seward's calibre could at that period conceive a plan of policy in which the slavery question had no place; a policy which rested upon the utterly delusive assumption that the secessionists, who had already formed their Southern Confederacy and were with stern resolution preparing to fight for its independence, could be hoodwinked back into the Union by some sentimental demonstration against European interference; a policy which, at that critical moment, would have involved the Union in a foreign war, thus inviting foreign intervention in favor of the Southern Confederacy, and increasing tenfold its chances in the struggle for independence. But it is equally incomprehensible how Seward could fail to see that this demand of an unconditional surrender was a mortal insult to the head of the government, and that by putting his proposition on paper he delivered himself into the hands of the very man he had insulted; for, had Lincoln, as most Presidents would have done, instantly dismissed Seward, and published the true reason for that dismissal, it would inevitably have been the end of Seward's career. But Lincoln did what not many of the noblest and greatest men in history would have been noble and great enough to do. He considered that Seward was still capable of rendering great service to his country in the place in which he was, if rightly controlled. He ignored the insult, but firmly established his superiority. In his reply, which he forthwith despatched, he told Seward that the administration had a domestic policy as laid down in the inaugural address with Seward's approval; that it had a foreign policy as traced in Seward's despatches with the President's approval; that if any policy was to be maintained or changed, he, the President, was to direct that on his responsibility; and that in performing that duty the President had a right to the advice of his secretaries. Seward's fantastic schemes of foreign war and continental policies Lincoln brushed aside by passing them over in silence. Nothing more was said. Seward must have felt that he was at the mercy of a superior man; that his offensive proposition had been generously pardoned as a temporary aberration of a great mind, and that he could atone for it only by devoted personal loyalty. This he did. He was thoroughly subdued, and thenceforth submitted to Lincoln his despatches for revision and amendment without a murmur. The war with European nations was no longer thought of; the slavery question found in due time its proper place in the struggle for the Union; and when, at a later period, the dismissal of Seward was demanded by dissatisfied senators, who attributed to him the shortcomings of the administration, Lincoln stood stoutly by his faithful Secretary of State.

Chase, the Secretary of the Treasury, a man of superb presence, of eminent ability and ardent patriotism, of great natural dignity and a certain outward coldness of manner, which made him appear more difficult of approach than he really was, did not permit his disappointment to burst out in such extravagant demonstrations. But Lincoln's ways were so essentially different from his that they never became quite intelligible, and certainly not congenial to him. It might, perhaps, have been better had there been, at the beginning of the administration, some decided clash between Lincoln and Chase, as there was between Lincoln and Seward, to bring on a full mutual explanation, and to make Chase appreciate the real seriousness of Lincoln's nature. But, as it was, their relations always remained somewhat formal, and Chase never felt quite at ease under a chief whom he could not understand, and whose character and powers he never learned to esteem at their true value. At the same time, he devoted himself zealously to the duties of his department, and did the country arduous service under circumstances of extreme difficulty. Nobody recognized this more heartily than Lincoln himself, and they managed to work together until near the end of Lincoln's first Presidential term, when Chase, after some disagreements concerning appointments to office, resigned from the treasury; and, after Taney's death, the President made him Chief Justice.

The rest of the cabinet consisted of men of less eminence, who subordinated themselves more easily. In January, 1862, Lincoln found it necessary to bow Cameron out of the war office, and to put in his place Edwin M. Stanton, a man of intensely practical mind, vehement impulses, fierce positiveness, ruthless energy, immense working power, lofty patriotism, and severest devotion to duty. He accepted the war office not as a partisan, for he had never been a Republican, but only to do all he could in "helping to save the country." The manner in which Lincoln succeeded in taming this lion to his will, by frankly recognizing his great qualities, by giving him the most generous confidence, by aiding him in his work to the full of his power, by kindly concession or affectionate persuasiveness in cases of differing opinions, or, when it was necessary, by firm assertions of superior authority, bears the highest testimony to his skill in the management of men. Stanton, who had entered the service with rather a mean opinion of Lincoln's character and capacity, became one of his warmest, most devoted, and most admiring friends, and with none of his secretaries was Lincoln's intercourse more intimate. To take advice with candid readiness, and to weigh it without any pride of his own opinion, was one of Lincoln's preeminent virtues; but he had not long presided over his cabinet council when his was felt by all its members to be the ruling mind.

The cautious policy foreshadowed in his inaugural address, and pursued during the first period of the civil war, was far from satisfying all his party friends. The ardent spirits among the Union men thought that the whole North should at once be called to arms, to crush the rebellion by one powerful blow. The ardent spirits among the antislavery men insisted that, slavery having brought forth the rebellion, this powerful blow should at once be aimed at slavery. Both complained that the administration was spiritless, undecided, and lamentably slow in its proceedings. Lincoln reasoned otherwise. The ways of thinking and feeling of the masses, of the plain people, were constantly present to his mind. The masses, the plain people, had to furnish the men for the fighting, if fighting was to be done. He believed that the plain people would be ready to fight when it clearly appeared necessary, and that they would feel that necessity when they felt themselves attacked. He therefore waited until the enemies of the Union struck the first blow. As soon as, on the 12th of April, 1861, the first gun was fired in Charleston harbor on the Union flag upon Fort Sumter, the call was sounded, and the Northern people rushed to arms.

Lincoln knew that the plain people were now indeed ready to fight in defence of the Union, but not yet ready to fight for the destruction of slavery. He declared openly that he had a right to summon the people to fight for the Union, but not to summon them to fight for the abolition of slavery as a primary object; and this declaration gave him numberless soldiers for the Union who at that period would have hesitated to do battle against the institution of slavery. For a time he succeeded in rendering harmless the cry of the partisan opposition that the Republican administration were perverting the war for the Union into an "abolition war." But when he went so far as to countermand the acts of some generals in the field, looking to the emancipation of the slaves in the districts covered by their commands, loud complaints arose from earnest antislavery men, who accused the President of turning his back upon the antislavery cause. Many of these antislavery men will now, after a calm retrospect, be willing to admit that it would have been a hazardous policy to endanger, by precipitating a demonstrative fight against slavery, the success of the struggle for the Union.

Lincoln's views and feelings concerning slavery had not changed. Those who conversed with him intimately upon the subject at that period know that he did not expect slavery long to survive the triumph of the Union, even if it were not immediately destroyed by the war. In this he was right. Had the Union armies achieved a decisive victory in an early period of the conflict, and had the seceded States been received back with slavery, the "slave power" would then have been a defeated power, defeated in an attempt to carry out its most effective threat. It would have lost its prestige. Its menaces would have been hollow sound, and ceased to make any one afraid. It could no longer have hoped to expand, to maintain an equilibrium in any branch of Congress, and to control the government. The victorious free States would have largely overbalanced it. It would no longer have been able to withstand the onset of a hostile age. It could no longer have ruled,—and slavery had to rule in order to live. It would have lingered for a while, but it would surely have been "in the course of ultimate extinction." A prolonged war precipitated the destruction of slavery; a short war might only have prolonged its death struggle. Lincoln saw this clearly; but he saw also that, in a protracted death struggle, it might still have kept disloyal sentiments alive, bred distracting commotions, and caused great mischief to the country. He therefore hoped that slavery would not survive the war.

But the question how he could rightfully employ his power to bring on its speedy destruction was to him not a question of mere sentiment. He himself set forth his reasoning upon it, at a later period, in one of his inimitable letters. "I am naturally antislavery," said he. "If slavery is not wrong, nothing is wrong. I cannot remember the time when I did not so think and feel. And yet I have never understood that the Presidency conferred upon me an unrestricted right to act upon that judgment and feeling. It was in the oath I took that I would, to the best of my ability, preserve, protect, and defend the Constitution of the United States. I could not take the office without taking the oath. Nor was it my view that I might take an oath to get power, and break the oath in using that power. I understood, too, that, in ordinary civil administration, this oath even forbade me practically to indulge my private abstract judgment on the moral question of slavery. I did understand, however, also, that my oath imposed upon me the duty of preserving, to the best of my ability, by every indispensable means, that government, that nation, of which the Constitution was the organic law. I could not feel that, to the best of my ability, I had even tied to preserve the Constitution—if, to save slavery, or any minor matter, I should permit the wreck of government, country, and Constitution all together." In other words, if the salvation of the government, the Constitution, and the Union demanded the destruction of slavery, he felt it to be not only his right, but his sworn duty to destroy it. Its destruction became a necessity of the war for the Union.

As the war dragged on and disaster followed disaster, the sense of that necessity steadily grew upon him. Early in 1862, as some of his friends well remember, he saw, what Seward seemed not to see, that to give the war for the Union an antislavery character was the surest means to prevent the recognition of the Southern Confederacy as an independent nation by European powers; that, slavery being abhorred by the moral sense of civilized mankind, no European government would dare to offer so gross an insult to the public opinion of its people as openly to favor the creation of a state founded upon slavery to the prejudice of an existing nation fighting against slavery. He saw also that slavery untouched was to the rebellion an element of power, and that in order to overcome that power it was necessary to turn it into an element of weakness. Still, he felt no assurance that the plain people were prepared for so radical a measure as the emancipation of the slaves by act of the government, and he anxiously considered that, if they were not, this great step might, by exciting dissension at the North, injure the cause of the Union in one quarter more than it would help it in another. He heartily welcomed an effort made in New York to mould and stimulate public sentiment on the slavery question by public meetings boldly pronouncing for emancipation. At the same time he himself cautiously advanced with a recommendation, expressed in a special message to Congress, that the United States should co-operate with any State which might adopt the gradual abolishment of slavery, giving such State pecuniary aid to compensate the former owners of emancipated slaves. The discussion was started, and spread rapidly. Congress adopted the resolution recommended, and soon went a step farther in passing a bill to abolish slavery in the District of Columbia. The plain people began to look at emancipation on a larger scale as a thing to be considered seriously by patriotic citizens; and soon Lincoln thought that the time was ripe, and that the edict of freedom could be ventured upon without danger of serious confusion in the Union ranks.

The failure of McClellan's movement upon Richmond increased immensely the prestige of the enemy. The need of some great act to stimulate the vitality of the Union cause seemed to grow daily more pressing. On July 21, 1862, Lincoln surprised his cabinet with the draught of a proclamation declaring free the slaves in all the States that should be still in rebellion against the United States on the 1st of January,1863. As to the matter itself he announced that he had fully made up his mind; he invited advice only concerning the form and the time of publication. Seward suggested that the proclamation, if then brought out, amidst disaster and distress, would sound like the last shriek of a perishing cause. Lincoln accepted the suggestion, and the proclamation was postponed. Another defeat followed, the second at Bull Run. But when, after that battle, the Confederate army, under Lee, crossed the Potomac and invaded Maryland, Lincoln vowed in his heart that, if the Union army were now blessed with success, the decree of freedom should surely be issued. The victory of Antietam was won on September 17, and the preliminary Emancipation Proclamation came forth on the a 22d. It was Lincoln's own resolution and act; but practically it bound the nation, and permitted no step backward. In spite of its limitations, it was the actual abolition of slavery. Thus he wrote his name upon the books of history with the title dearest to his heart, the liberator of the slave.

It is true, the great proclamation, which stamped the war as one for "union and freedom," did not at once mark the turning of the tide on the field of military operations. There were more disasters, Fredericksburg and Chancellorsville. But with Gettysburg and Vicksburg the whole aspect of the war changed. Step by step, now more slowly, then more rapidly, but with increasing steadiness, the flag of the Union advanced from field to field toward the final consummation. The decree of emancipation was naturally followed by the enlistment of emancipated negroes in the Union armies. This measure had a anther reaching effect than merely giving the Union armies an increased supply of men. The laboring force of the rebellion was hopelessly disorganized. The war became like a problem of arithmetic. As the Union armies pushed forward, the area from which the Southern Confederacy could draw recruits and supplies constantly grew smaller, while the area from which the Union recruited its strength constantly grew larger; and everywhere, even within the Southern lines, the Union had its allies. The fate of the rebellion was then virtually decided; but it still required much bloody work to convince the brave warriors who fought for it that they were really beaten.

Neither did the Emancipation Proclamation forthwith command universal assent among the people who were loyal to the Union. There were even signs of a reaction against the administration in the fall elections of 1862, seemingly justifying the opinion, entertained by many, that the President had really anticipated the development of popular feeling. The cry that the war for the Union had been turned into an "abolition war" was raised again by the opposition, and more loudly than ever. But the good sense and patriotic instincts of the plain people gradually marshalled themselves on Lincoln's side, and he lost no opportunity to help on this process by personal argument and admonition. There never has been a President in such constant and active contact with the public opinion of the country, as there never has been a President who, while at the head of the government, remained so near to the people. Beyond the circle of those who had long known him the feeling steadily grew that the man in the White House was "honest Abe Lincoln" still, and that every citizen might approach him with complaint, expostulation, or advice, without danger of meeting a rebuff from power-proud authority, or humiliating condescension; and this privilege was used by so many and with such unsparing freedom that only superhuman patience could have endured it all. There are men now living who would to-day read with amazement, if not regret, what they ventured to say or write to him. But Lincoln repelled no one whom he believed to speak to him in good faith and with patriotic purpose. No good advice would go unheeded. No candid criticism would offend him. No honest opposition, while it might pain him, would produce a lasting alienation of feeling between him and the opponent. It may truly be said that few men in power have ever been exposed to more daring attempts to direct their course, to severer censure of their acts, and to more cruel misrepresentation of their motives: And all this he met with that good-natured humor peculiarly his own, and with untiring effort to see the right and to impress it upon those who differed from him. The conversations he had and the correspondence he carried on upon matters of public interest, not only with men in official position, but with private citizens, were almost unceasing, and in a large number of public letters, written ostensibly to meetings, or committees, or persons of importance, he addressed himself directly to the popular mind. Most of these letters stand among the finest monuments of our political literature. Thus he presented the singular spectacle of a President who, in the midst of a great civil war, with unprecedented duties weighing upon him, was constantly in person debating the great features of his policy with the people.

While in this manner he exercised an ever-increasing influence upon the popular understanding, his sympathetic nature endeared him more and more to the popular heart. In vain did journals and speakers of the opposition represent him as a lightminded trifler, who amused himself with frivolous story-telling and coarse jokes, while the blood of the people was flowing in streams. The people knew that the man at the head of affairs, on whose haggard face the twinkle of humor so frequently changed into an expression of profoundest sadness, was more than any other deeply distressed by the suffering he witnessed; that he felt the pain of every wound that was inflicted on the battlefield, and the anguish of every woman or child who had lost husband or father; that whenever he could he was eager to alleviate sorrow, and that his mercy was never implored in vain. They looked to him as one who was with them and of them in all their hopes and fears, their joys and sorrows, who laughed with them and wept with them; and as his heart was theirs; so their hearts turned to him. His popularity was far different from that of Washington, who was revered with awe, or that of Jackson, the unconquerable hero, for whom party enthusiasm never grew weary of shouting. To Abraham Lincoln the people became bound by a genuine sentimental attachment. It was not a matter of respect, or confidence, or party pride, for this feeling spread far beyond the boundary lines of his party; it was an affair of the heart, independent of mere reasoning. When the soldiers in the field or their folks at home spoke of "Father Abraham," there was no cant in it. They felt that their President was really caring for them as a father would, and that they could go to him, every one of them, as they would go to a father, and talk to him of what troubled them, sure to find a willing ear and tender sympathy. Thus, their President, and his cause, and his endeavors, and his success gradually became to them almost matters of family concern. And this popularity carried him triumphantly through the Presidential election of 1864, in spite of an opposition within his own party which at first seemed very formidable.

Many of the radical antislavery men were never quite satisfied with Lincoln's ways of meeting the problems of the time. They were very earnest and mostly very able men, who had positive ideas as to "how this rebellion should be put down." They would not recognize the necessity of measuring the steps of the government according to the progress of opinion among the plain people. They criticised Lincoln's cautious management as irresolute, halting, lacking in definite purpose and in energy; he should not have delayed emancipation so long; he should not have confided important commands to men of doubtful views as to slavery; he should have authorized military commanders to set the slaves free as they went on; he dealt too leniently with unsuccessful generals; he should have put down all factious opposition with a strong hand instead of trying to pacify it; he should have given the people accomplished facts instead of arguing with them, and so on. It is true, these criticisms were not always entirely unfounded. Lincoln's policy had, with the virtues of democratic government, some of its weaknesses, which in the presence of pressing exigencies were apt to deprive governmental action of the necessary vigor; and his kindness of heart, his disposition always to respect the feelings of others, frequently made him recoil from anything like severity, even when severity was urgently called for. But many of his radical critics have since then revised their judgment sufficiently to admit that Lincoln's policy was, on the whole, the wisest and safest; that a policy of heroic methods, while it has sometimes accomplished great results, could in a democracy like ours be maintained only by constant success; that it would have quickly broken down under the weight of disaster; that it might have been successful from the start, had the Union, at the beginning of the conflict, had its Grants and Shermans and Sheridans, its Farraguts and Porters, fully matured at the head of its forces; but that, as the great commanders had to be evolved slowly from the developments of the war, constant success could not be counted upon, and it was best to follow a policy which was in friendly contact with the popular force, and therefore more fit to stand trial of misfortune on the battlefield. But at that period they thought differently, and their dissatisfaction with Lincoln's doings was greatly increased by the steps he took toward the reconstruction of rebel States then partially in possession of the Union forces.

In December, 1863, Lincoln issued an amnesty proclamation, offering pardon to all implicated in the rebellion, with certain specified exceptions, on condition of their taking and maintaining an oath to support the Constitution and obey the laws of the United States and the proclamations of the President with regard to slaves; and also promising that when, in any of the rebel States, a number of citizens equal to one tenth of the voters in 1860 should re-establish a state government in conformity with the oath above mentioned, such should be recognized by the Executive as the true government of the State. The proclamation seemed at first to be received with general favor. But soon another scheme of reconstruction, much more stringent in its provisions, was put forward in the House of Representatives by Henry Winter Davis. Benjamin Wade championed it in the Senate. It passed in the closing moments of the session in July, 1864, and Lincoln, instead of making it a law by his signature, embodied the text of it in a proclamation as a plan of reconstruction worthy of being earnestly considered. The differences of opinion concerning this subject had only intensified the feeling against Lincoln which had long been nursed among the radicals, and some of them openly declared their purpose of resisting his re-election to the Presidency. Similar sentiments were manifested by the advanced antislavery men of Missouri, who, in their hot faction-fight with the "conservatives" of that State, had not received from Lincoln the active support they demanded. Still another class of Union men, mainly in the East, gravely shook their heads when considering the question whether Lincoln should be re-elected. They were those who cherished in their minds an ideal of statesmanship and of personal bearing in high office with which, in their opinion, Lincoln's individuality was much out of accord. They were shocked when they heard him cap an argument upon grave affairs of state with a story about "a man out in Sangamon County,"—a story, to be sure, strikingly clinching his point, but sadly lacking in dignity. They could not understand the man who was capable, in opening a cabinet meeting, of reading to his secretaries a funny chapter from a recent book of Artemus Ward, with which in an unoccupied moment he had relieved his care-burdened mind, and who then solemnly informed the executive council that he had vowed in his heart to issue a proclamation emancipating the slaves as soon as God blessed the Union arms with another victory. They were alarmed at the weakness of a President who would indeed resist the urgent remonstrances of statesmen against his policy, but could not resist the prayer of an old woman for the pardon of a soldier who was sentenced to be shot for desertion. Such men, mostly sincere and ardent patriots, not only wished, but earnestly set to work, to prevent Lincoln's renomination. Not a few of them actually believed, in 1863, that, if the national convention of the Union party were held then, Lincoln would not be supported by the delegation of a single State. But when the convention met at Baltimore, in June, 1864, the voice of the people was heard. On the first ballot Lincoln received the votes of the delegations from all the States except Missouri; and even the Missourians turned over their votes to him before the result of the ballot was declared.

But even after his renomination the opposition to Lincoln within the ranks of the Union party did not subside. A convention, called by the dissatisfied radicals in Missouri, and favored by men of a similar way of thinking in other States, had been held already in May, and had nominated as its candidate for the Presidency General Fremont. He, indeed, did not attract a strong following, but opposition movements from different quarters appeared more formidable. Henry Winter Davis and Benjamin Wade assailed Lincoln in a flaming manifesto. Other Union men, of undoubted patriotism and high standing, persuaded themselves, and sought to persuade the people, that Lincoln's renomination was ill advised and dangerous to the Union cause. As the Democrats had put off their convention until the 29th of August, the Union party had, during the larger part of the summer, no opposing candidate and platform to attack, and the political campaign languished. Neither were the tidings from the theatre of war of a cheering character. The terrible losses suffered by Grant's army in the battles of the Wilderness spread general gloom. Sherman seemed for a while to be in a precarious position before Atlanta. The opposition to Lincoln within the Union party grew louder in its complaints and discouraging predictions. Earnest demands were heard that his candidacy should be withdrawn. Lincoln himself, not knowing how strongly the masses were attached to him, was haunted by dark forebodings of defeat. Then the scene suddenly changed as if by magic.

The Democrats, in their national convention, declared the war a failure, demanded, substantially, peace at any price, and nominated on such a platform General McClellan as their candidate. Their convention had hardly adjourned when the capture of Atlanta gave a new aspect to the military situation. It was like a sun-ray bursting through a dark cloud. The rank and file of the Union party rose with rapidly growing enthusiasm. The song "We are coming, Father Abraham, three hundred thousand strong," resounded all over the land. Long before the decisive day arrived, the result was beyond doubt, and Lincoln was re-elected President by overwhelming majorities. The election over even his severest critics found themselves forced to admit that Lincoln was the only possible candidate for the Union party in 1864, and that neither political combinations nor campaign speeches, nor even victories in the field, were needed to insure his success. The plain people had all the while been satisfied with Abraham Lincoln: they confided in him; they loved him; they felt themselves near to him; they saw personified in him the cause of Union and freedom; and they went to the ballot-box for him in their strength.

The hour of triumph called out the characteristic impulses of his nature. The opposition within the Union party had stung him to the quick. Now he had his opponents before him, baffled and humiliated. Not a moment did he lose to stretch out the hand of friendship to all. "Now that the election is over," he said, in response to a serenade, "may not all, having a common interest, reunite in a common effort to save our common country? For my own part, I have striven, and will strive, to place no obstacle in the way. So long as I have been here I have not willingly planted a thorn in any man's bosom. While I am deeply sensible to the high compliment of a re-election, it adds nothing to my satisfaction that any other man may be pained or disappointed by the result. May I ask those who were with me to join with me in the same spirit toward those who were against me?" This was Abraham Lincoln's character as tested in the furnace of prosperity.

The war was virtually decided, but not yet ended. Sherman was irresistibly carrying the Union flag through the South. Grant had his iron hand upon the ramparts of Richmond. The days of the Confederacy were evidently numbered. Only the last blow remained to be struck. Then Lincoln's second inauguration came, and with it his second inaugural address. Lincoln's famous "Gettysburg speech" has been much and justly admired. But far greater, as well as far more characteristic, was that inaugural in which he poured out the whole devotion and tenderness of his great soul. It had all the solemnity of a father's last admonition and blessing to his children before he lay down to die. These were its closing words: "Fondly do we hope, fervently do we pray, that this mighty scourge of war may speedily pass away. Yet if God wills that it continue until all the wealth piled up by the bondman's two hundred and fifty years of unrequited toil shall be sunk, and until every drop of blood drawn with the lash shall be paid by another drawn with the sword, as was said three thousand years ago, so still it must be said, 'The judgments of the Lord are true and righteous altogether.' With malice toward none, with charity for all, with firmness in the right as God gives us to see the right, let us strive to finish the work we are in; to bind up the nation's wounds; to care for him who shall have borne the battle, and for his widow and his orphan; to do all which may achieve and cherish a just and lasting peace among ourselves and with all nations." This was like a sacred poem. No American President had ever spoken words like these to the American people. America never had a President who found such words in the depth of his heart.

Now followed the closing scenes of the war. The Southern armies fought bravely to the last, but all in vain. Richmond fell. Lincoln himself entered the city on foot, accompanied only by a few officers and a squad of sailors who had rowed him ashore from the flotilla in the James River, a negro picked up on the way serving as a guide. Never had the world seen a more modest conqueror and a more characteristic triumphal procession, no army with banners and drums, only a throng of those who had been slaves, hastily run together, escorting the victorious chief into the capital of the vanquished foe. We are told that they pressed around him, kissed his hands and his garments, and shouted and danced for joy, while tears ran down the President's care-furrowed cheeks.

A few days more brought the surrender of Lee's army, and peace was assured. The people of the North were wild with joy. Everywhere festive guns were booming, bells pealing, the churches ringing with thanksgivings, and jubilant multitudes thronging the thoroughfares, when suddenly the news flashed over the land that Abraham Lincoln had been murdered. The people were stunned by the blow. Then a wail of sorrow went up such as America had never heard before. Thousands of Northern households grieved as if they had lost their dearest member. Many a Southern man cried out in his heart that his people had been robbed of their best friend in their humiliation and distress, when Abraham Lincoln was struck down. It was as if the tender affection which his countrymen bore him had inspired all nations with a common sentiment. All civilized mankind stood mourning around the coffin of the dead President. Many of those, here and abroad, who not long before had ridiculed and reviled him were among the first to hasten on with their flowers of eulogy, and in that universal chorus of lamentation and praise there was not a voice that did not tremble with genuine emotion. Never since Washington's death had there been such unanimity of judgment as to a man's virtues and greatness; and even Washington's death, although his name was held in greater reverence, did not touch so sympathetic a chord in the people's hearts.

Nor can it be said that this was owing to the tragic character of Lincoln's end. It is true, the death of this gentlest and most merciful of rulers by the hand of a mad fanatic was well apt to exalt him beyond his merits in the estimation of those who loved him, and to make his renown the object of peculiarly tender solicitude. But it is also true that the verdict pronounced upon him in those days has been affected little by time, and that historical inquiry has served rather to increase than to lessen the appreciation of his virtues, his abilities, his services. Giving the fullest measure of credit to his great ministers,—to Seward for his conduct of foreign affairs, to Chase for the management of the finances under terrible difficulties, to Stanton for the performance of his tremendous task as war secretary,—and readily acknowledging that without the skill and fortitude of the great commanders, and the heroism of the soldiers and sailors under them, success could not have been achieved, the historian still finds that Lincoln's judgment and will were by no means governed by those around him; that the most important steps were owing to his initiative; that his was the deciding and directing mind; and that it was pre-eminently he whose sagacity and whose character enlisted for the administration in its struggles the countenance, the sympathy, and the support of the people. It is found, even, that his judgment on military matters was astonishingly acute, and that the advice and instructions he gave to the generals commanding in the field would not seldom have done honor to the ablest of them. History, therefore, without overlooking, or palliating, or excusing any of his shortcomings or mistakes, continues to place him foremost among the saviours of the Union and the liberators of the slave. More than that, it awards to him the merit of having accomplished what but few political philosophers would have recognized as possible,—of leading the republic through four years of furious civil conflict without any serious detriment to its free institutions.

He was, indeed, while President, violently denounced by the opposition as a tyrant and a usurper, for having gone beyond his constitutional powers in authorizing or permitting the temporary suppression of newspapers, and in wantonly suspending the writ of habeas corpus and resorting to arbitrary arrests. Nobody should be blamed who, when such things are done, in good faith and from patriotic motives protests against them. In a republic, arbitrary stretches of power, even when demanded by necessity, should never be permitted to pass without a protest on the one hand, and without an apology on the other. It is well they did not so pass during our civil war. That arbitrary measures were resorted to is true. That they were resorted to most sparingly, and only when the government thought them absolutely required by the safety of the republic, will now hardly be denied. But certain it is that the history of the world does not furnish a single example of a government passing through so tremendous a crisis as our civil war was with so small a record of arbitrary acts, and so little interference with the ordinary course of law outside the field of military operations. No American President ever wielded such power as that which was thrust into Lincoln's hands. It is to be hoped that no American President ever will have to be entrusted with such power again. But no man was ever entrusted with it to whom its seductions were less dangerous than they proved to be to Abraham Lincoln. With scrupulous care he endeavored, even under the most trying circumstances, to remain strictly within the constitutional limitations of his authority; and whenever the boundary became indistinct, or when the dangers of the situation forced him to cross it, he was equally careful to mark his acts as exceptional measures, justifiable only by the imperative necessities of the civil war, so that they might not pass into history as precedents for similar acts in time of peace. It is an unquestionable fact that during the reconstruction period which followed the war, more things were done capable of serving as dangerous precedents than during the war itself. Thus it may truly be said of him not only that under his guidance the republic was saved from disruption and the country was purified of the blot of slavery, but that, during the stormiest and most perilous crisis in our history, he so conducted the government and so wielded his almost dictatorial power as to leave essentially intact our free institutions in all things that concern the rights and liberties of the citizens. He understood well the nature of the problem. In his first message to Congress he defined it in admirably pointed language: "Must a government be of necessity too strong for the liberties of its own people, or too weak to maintain its own existence? Is there in all republics this inherent weakness?" This question he answered in the name of the great American republic, as no man could have answered it better, with a triumphant "No...."

It has been said that Abraham Lincoln died at the right moment for his fame. However that may be, he had, at the time of his death, certainly not exhausted his usefulness to his country. He was probably the only man who could have guided the nation through the perplexities of the reconstruction period in such a manner as to prevent in the work of peace the revival of the passions of the war. He would indeed not have escaped serious controversy as to details of policy; but he could have weathered it far better than any other statesman of his time, for his prestige with the active politicians had been immensely strengthened by his triumphant re-election; and, what is more important, he would have been supported by the confidence of the victorious Northern people that he would do all to secure the safety of the Union and the rights of the emancipated negro, and at the same time by the confidence of the defeated Southern people that nothing would be done by him from motives of vindictiveness, or of unreasoning fanaticism, or of a selfish party spirit. "With malice toward none, with charity for all," the foremost of the victors would have personified in himself the genius of reconciliation.

He might have rendered the country a great service in another direction. A few days after the fall of Richmond, he pointed out to a friend the crowd of office-seekers besieging his door. "Look at that," said he. "Now we have conquered the rebellion, but here you see something that may become more dangerous to this republic than the rebellion itself." It is true, Lincoln as President did not profess what we now call civil service reform principles. He used the patronage of the government in many cases avowedly to reward party work, in many others to form combinations and to produce political effects advantageous to the Union cause, and in still others simply to put the right man into the right place. But in his endeavors to strengthen the Union cause, and in his search for able and useful men for public duties, he frequently went beyond the limits of his party, and gradually accustomed himself to the thought that, while party service had its value, considerations of the public interest were, as to appointments to office, of far greater consequence. Moreover, there had been such a mingling of different political elements in support of the Union during the civil war that Lincoln, standing at the head of that temporarily united motley mass, hardly felt himself, in the narrow sense of the term, a party man. And as he became strongly impressed with the dangers brought upon the republic by the use of public offices as party spoils, it is by no means improbable that, had he survived the all-absorbing crisis and found time to turn to other objects, one of the most important reforms of later days would have been pioneered by his powerful authority. This was not to be. But the measure of his achievements was full enough for immortality.

To the younger generation Abraham Lincoln has already become a half-mythical figure, which, in the haze of historic distance, grows to more and more heroic proportions, but also loses in distinctness of outline and feature. This is indeed the common lot of popular heroes; but the Lincoln legend will be more than ordinarily apt to become fanciful, as his individuality, assembling seemingly incongruous qualities and forces in a character at the same time grand and most lovable, was so unique, and his career so abounding in startling contrasts. As the state of society in which Abraham Lincoln grew up passes away, the world will read with increasing wonder of the man who, not only of the humblest origin, but remaining the simplest and most unpretending of citizens, was raised to a position of power unprecedented in our history; who was the gentlest and most peace-loving of mortals, unable to see any creature suffer without a pang in his own breast, and suddenly found himself called to conduct the greatest and bloodiest of our wars; who wielded the power of government when stern resolution and relentless force were the order of the day and then won and ruled the popular mind and heart by the tender sympathies of his nature; who was a cautious conservative by temperament and mental habit, and led the most sudden and sweeping social revolution of our time; who, preserving his homely speech and rustic manner even in the most conspicuous position of that period, drew upon himself the scoffs of polite society, and then thrilled the soul of mankind with utterances of wonderful beauty and grandeur; who, in his heart the best friend of the defeated South, was murdered because a crazy fanatic took him for its most cruel enemy; who, while in power, was beyond measure lampooned and maligned by sectional passion and an excited party spirit, and around whose bier friend and foe gathered to praise him which they have since never ceased to do—as one of the greatest of Americans and the best of men.

ABRAHAM LINCOLN, BY JOSEPH H. CHOATE

[This Address was delivered before the Edinburgh Philosophical Institution, November 13, 1900. It is included in this set with the courteous permission of the author and of Messrs. Thomas Y. Crowell & Company.]
ABRAHAM LINCOLN.
When you asked me to deliver the Inaugural Address on this occasion, I recognized that I owed this compliment to the fact that I was the official representative of America, and in selecting a subject I ventured to think that I might interest you for an hour in a brief study in popular government, as illustrated by the life of the most American of all Americans. I therefore offer no apology for asking your attention to Abraham Lincoln—to his unique character and the part he

bore in two important achievements of modern history: the preservation of the integrity of the American Union and the emancipation of the colored race.

During his brief term of power he was probably the object of more abuse, vilification, and ridicule than any other man in the world; but when he fell by the hand of an assassin, at the very moment of his stupendous victory, all the nations of the earth vied with one another in paying homage to his character, and the thirty-five years that have since elapsed have established his place in history as one of the great benefactors not of his own country alone, but of the human race.

One of many noble utterances upon the occasion of his death was that in which 'Punch' made its magnanimous recantation of the spirit with which it had pursued him:

"Beside this corpse that bears for winding sheet
The stars and stripes he lived to rear anew,
Between the mourners at his head and feet,
Say, scurrile jester, is there room for you?

....

"Yes, he had lived to shame me from my sneer,
To lame my pencil, and confute my pen
To make me own this hind—of princes peer,
This rail-splitter—a true born king of men."

Fiction can furnish no match for the romance of his life, and biography will be searched in vain for such startling vicissitudes of fortune, so great power and glory won out of such humble beginnings and adverse circumstances.

Doubtless you are all familiar with the salient points of his extraordinary career. In the zenith of his fame he was the wise, patient, courageous, successful ruler of men; exercising more power than any monarch of his time, not for himself, but for the good of the people who had placed it in his hands; commander-in-chief of a vast military power, which waged with ultimate success the greatest war of the century; the triumphant champion of popular government, the deliverer of four millions of his fellowmen from bondage; honored by mankind as Statesman, President, and Liberator. Let us glance now at the first half of the brief life of which this was the glorious and happy consummation. Nothing could be more squalid and miserable than the home in which Abraham Lincoln was born—a one-roomed cabin without floor or window in what was then the wilderness of Kentucky, in the heart of that frontier life which swiftly moved westward from the Alleghanies to the Mississippi, always in advance of schools and churches, of books and money, of railroads and newspapers, of all things which are generally regarded as the comforts and even necessaries of life. His father, ignorant, needy, and thriftless, content if he could keep soul and body together for himself and his family, was ever seeking, without success, to better his unhappy condition by moving on from one such scene of dreary desolation to another. The rude society which surrounded them was not much better. The struggle for existence was hard, and absorbed all their energies. They were fighting the forest, the wild beast, and the retreating savage. From the time when he could barely handle tools until he attained his majority, Lincoln's life was that of a simple farm laborer, poorly clad, housed, and fed, at work either on his father's wretched farm or hired out to neighboring farmers. But in spite, or perhaps by means, of this rude environment, he grew to be a stalwart giant, reaching six feet four at nineteen, and fabulous stories are told of his feats of strength. With the growth of this mighty frame began that strange education which in his ripening years was to qualify him for the great destiny that awaited him, and the development of those mental faculties and moral endowments which, by the time he reached middle life, were to make him the sagacious, patient, and triumphant leader of a great nation in the crisis of its fate. His whole schooling, obtained during such odd times as could be spared from grinding labor, did not amount in all to as much as one year, and the quality of the teaching was of the lowest possible grade, including only the elements of reading, writing, and ciphering. But out of these simple elements, when rightly used by the right man, education is achieved, and Lincoln knew how to use them. As so often happens, he seemed to take warning from his father's unfortunate example. Untiring industry, an insatiable thirst for knowledge, and an ever-growing desire to rise above his surroundings, were early manifestations of his character.

Books were almost unknown in that community, but the Bible was in every house, and somehow or other Pilgrim's Progress, AEsop's Fables, a History of the United States, and a Life of Washington fell into his hands. He trudged on foot many miles through the wilderness to borrow an English Grammar, and is said to have devoured greedily the contents of the Statutes of Indiana that fell in his way. These few volumes he read and reread—and his power of assimilation was great. To be shut in with a few books and to master them thoroughly sometimes does more for the development of character than freedom to range at large, in a cursory and indiscriminate way, through wide domains of literature. This youth's mind, at any rate, was thoroughly saturated with Biblical knowledge and Biblical language, which, in after life, he used with great readiness and effect. But it was the constant use of the little knowledge which he had that developed and exercised his mental powers. After the hard day's work was done, while others slept, he toiled on, always reading or writing. From an early age he did his own thinking and made up his own mind—invaluable traits in the future President. Paper was such a scarce commodity that, by the evening firelight, he would write and cipher on the back of a wooden shovel, and then shave it off to make room for more. By and by, as he approached manhood, he began speaking in the rude gatherings of the neighborhood, and so laid the foundation of that art of persuading his fellow-men which was one rich result of his education, and one great secret of his subsequent success.

Accustomed as we are in these days of steam and telegraphs to have every intelligent boy survey the whole world each morning before breakfast, and inform himself as to what is going on in every nation, it is hardly possible to conceive how benighted and isolated was the condition of the community at Pigeon Creek in Indiana, of which the family of Lincoln's father formed a part, or how eagerly an ambitious and high-spirited boy, such as he, must have yearned to escape. The first glimpse that he ever got of any world beyond the narrow confines of his home was in 1828, at the age of nineteen, when a neighbor employed him to accompany his son down the river to New Orleans to dispose of a flatboat of produce—a commission which he discharged with great success.

Shortly after his return from this his first excursion into the outer world, his father, tired of failure in Indiana, packed his family and all his worldly goods into a single wagon drawn by two yoke of oxen, and after a fourteen days' tramp through the wilderness, pitched his camp once more, in Illinois. Here Abraham, having come of age and being now his own master, rendered the last service of his minority by ploughing the fifteen-acre lot and splitting from the tall walnut trees of the primeval forest enough rails to surround the little clearing with a fence. Such was the meagre outfit of this coming leader of men, at the age when the future British Prime Minister or statesman emerges from the university as a double first or senior wrangler, with every advantage that high training and broad culture and association with the wisest and the best of men and women can give, and enters upon some form of public service on the road to usefulness and honor, the University course being only the first stage of the public training. So Lincoln, at twenty-one, had just begun his preparation for the public life to which he soon began to aspire. For some years yet he must continue to earn his daily bread by the sweat of his brow, having absolutely no means, no home, no friend to consult. More farm work as a hired hand, a clerkship in a village store, the running of a mill, another trip to New Orleans on a flatboat of his own contriving, a pilot's berth on the river—these were the means by which he subsisted until, in the summer of 1832, when he was twenty-three years of age, an event occurred which gave him public recognition.

The Black Hawk war broke out, and, the Governor of Illinois calling for volunteers to repel the band of savages whose leader bore that name, Lincoln enlisted and was elected captain by his comrades, among whom he had already established his supremacy by signal feats of strength and more than one successful single combat. During the brief hostilities he was engaged in no battle and won no military glory, but his local leadership was established. The same year he offered himself as a candidate for the Legislature of Illinois, but failed at the polls. Yet his vast popularity with those who knew him was manifest. The district consisted of several counties, but the unanimous vote of the people of his own county was for Lincoln. Another unsuccessful attempt at store-keeping was followed by better luck at surveying, until his horse and instruments were levied upon under execution for the debts of his business adventure.

I have been thus detailed in sketching his early years because upon these strange foundations the structure of his great fame and service was built. In the place of a school and university training fortune substituted these trials, hardships, and struggles as a preparation for the great work which he had to do. It turned out to be exactly what the emergency required. Ten years instead at the public school and the university certainly never could have fitted this man for the unique work which was to be thrown upon him. Some other Moses would have had to lead us to our Jordan, to the sight of our promised land of liberty.

At the age of twenty-five he became a member of the Legislature of Illinois, and so continued for eight years, and, in the meantime, qualified himself by reading such law books as he could borrow at random—for he was too poor to buy any to be called to the Bar. For his second quarter of a century—during which a single term in Congress introduced him into the arena of national questions—he gave himself up to law and politics. In spite of his soaring ambition, his two years in Congress gave him no premonition of the great destiny that awaited him,—and at its close, in 1849, we find him an unsuccessful applicant to the President for appointment as Commissioner of the General Land Office—a purely administrative bureau; a fortunate escape for himself and for his country. Year by year his knowledge and power, his experience and reputation extended, and his mental faculties seemed to grow by what they fed on. His power of persuasion, which had always been marked, was developed to an extraordinary degree, now that he became engaged in congenial questions and subjects. Little by little he rose to prominence at the Bar, and became the most effective public speaker in the West. Not that he possessed any of the graces of the orator; but his logic was invincible, and his clearness and force of statement impressed upon his hearers the convictions of his honest mind, while his broad sympathies and sparkling and genial humor made him a universal favorite as far and as fast as his acquaintance extended.

These twenty years that elapsed from the time of his establishment as a lawyer and legislator in Springfield, the new capital of Illinois, furnished a fitting theatre for the development and display of his great faculties, and, with his new and enlarged opportunities, he obviously grew in mental stature in this second period of his career, as if to compensate for the absolute lack of advantages under which he had suffered in youth. As his powers enlarged, his reputation extended, for he was always before the people, felt a warm sympathy with all that concerned them, took a zealous part in the discussion of every public question, and made his personal influence ever more widely and deeply felt.

My brethren of the legal profession will naturally ask me, how could this rough backwoodsman, whose youth had been spent in the forest or on the farm and the flatboat, without culture or training, education or study, by the random reading, on the wing, of a few miscellaneous law books, become a learned and accomplished lawyer? Well, he never did. He never would have earned his salt as a 'Writer' for the 'Signet', nor have won a place as advocate in the Court of Session, where the technique of the profession has reached its highest perfection, and centuries of learning and precedent are involved in the equipment of a lawyer. Dr. Holmes, when asked by an anxious young mother, "When should the education of a child begin?" replied, "Madam, at least two centuries before it is born!" and so I am sure it is with the Scots lawyer.

But not so in Illinois in 1840. Between 1830 and 1880 its population increased twenty-fold, and when Lincoln began practising law in Springfield in 1837, life in Illinois was very crude and simple, and so were the courts and the administration of justice. Books and libraries were scarce. But the people loved justice, upheld the law, and followed the courts, and soon found their favorites among the advocates. The fundamental principles of the common law, as set forth by Blackstone and Chitty, were not so difficult to acquire; and brains, common sense, force of character, tenacity of purpose, ready wit and power of speech did the rest, and supplied all the deficiencies of learning.

The lawsuits of those days were extremely simple, and the principles of natural justice were mainly relied on to dispose of them at the Bar and on the Bench, without resort to technical learning. Railroads, corporations absorbing the chief business of the community, combined and inherited wealth, with all the subtle and intricate questions they breed, had not yet come in—and so the professional agents and the equipment which they require were not needed. But there were many highly educated and powerful men at the Bar of Illinois, even in those early days, whom the spirit of enterprise had carried there in search of fame and fortune. It was by constant contact and conflict with these that Lincoln acquired professional strength and skill. Every community and every age creates its own Bar, entirely adequate for its present uses and necessities. So in Illinois, as the population and wealth of the State kept on doubling and quadrupling, its Bar presented a growing abundance of learning and science and technical skill. The early practitioners grew with its growth and mastered the requisite knowledge. Chicago soon grew to be one of the largest and richest and certainly the most intensely active city on the continent, and if any of my professional friends here had gone there in Lincoln's later years, to try or argue a cause, or transact other business, with any idea that Edinburgh or London had a monopoly of legal learning, science, or subtlety, they would certainly have found their mistake.

In those early days in the West, every lawyer, especially every court lawyer, was necessarily a politician, constantly engaged in the public discussion of the many questions evolved from the rapid development of town, county, State, and Federal affairs. Then and there, in this regard, public discussion supplied the place which the universal activity of the press has since monopolized, and the public speaker who, by clearness, force, earnestness, and wit; could make himself felt on the questions of the day would rapidly come to the front. In the absence of that immense variety of popular entertainments which now feed the public taste and appetite, the people found their chief amusement in frequenting the courts and public and political assemblies. In either place, he who impressed, entertained, and amused them most was the hero of the hour. They did not discriminate very carefully between the eloquence of the forum and the eloquence of the hustings. Human nature ruled in both alike, and he who was the most effective speaker in a political harangue was often retained as most likely to win in a cause to be tried or argued. And I have no doubt in this way many retainers came to Lincoln. Fees, money in any form, had no charms for him—in his eager pursuit of fame he could not afford to make money. He was ambitious to distinguish himself by some great service to mankind, and this ambition for fame and real public service left no room for avarice in his composition. However much he earned, he seems to have ended every year hardly richer than he began it, and yet, as the years passed, fees came to him freely. One of L 1,000 is recorded—a very large professional fee at that time, even in any part of America, the paradise of lawyers. I lay great stress on Lincoln's career as a lawyer—much more than his biographers do because in America a state of things exists wholly different from that which prevails in Great Britain. The profession of the law always has been and is to this day the principal avenue to public life; and I am sure that his training and experience in the courts had much to do with the development of those forces of intellect and character which he soon displayed on a broader arena.

It was in political controversy, of course, that he acquired his wide reputation, and made his deep and lasting impression upon the people of what had now become the powerful State of Illinois, and upon the people of the Great West, to whom the political power and control of the United States were already surely and swiftly passing from the older Eastern States. It was this reputation and this impression, and the familiar knowledge of his character which had come to them from his local leadership, that happily inspired the people of the West to present him as their candidate, and to press him upon the Republican convention of 1860 as the fit and necessary leader in the struggle for life which was before the nation.

That struggle, as you all know, arose out of the terrible question of slavery—and I must trust to your general knowledge of the history of that question to make intelligible the attitude and leadership of Lincoln as the champion of the hosts of freedom in the final contest. Negro slavery had been firmly established in the Southern States from an early period of their history. In 1619, the year before the Mayflower landed our Pilgrim Fathers upon Plymouth Rock, a Dutch ship had discharged a cargo of African slaves at Jamestown in Virginia: All through the colonial period their importation had continued. A few had found their way into the Northern States, but none of them in sufficient numbers to constitute danger or to afford a basis for political power. At the time of the adoption of the Federal Constitution, there is no doubt that the principal members of the convention not only condemned slavery as a moral, social, and political evil, but believed that by the suppression of the slave trade it was in the course of gradual extinction in the South, as it certainly was in the North. Washington, in his will, provided for the emancipation of his own slaves, and said to Jefferson that it "was among his first wishes to see some plan adopted by which slavery in his country might be abolished." Jefferson said, referring to the institution: "I tremble for my country when I think that God is just; that His justice cannot sleep forever,"—and Franklin, Adams, Hamilton, and Patrick Henry were all utterly opposed to it. But it was made the subject of a fatal compromise in the Federal Constitution, whereby its existence was recognized in the States as a basis of representation, the prohibition of the importation of slaves was postponed for twenty years, and the return of fugitive slaves provided for. But no imminent danger was apprehended from it till, by the invention of the cotton gin in 1792, cotton culture by negro labor became at once and forever the leading industry of the South, and gave a new impetus to the importation of slaves, so that in 1808, when the constitutional prohibition took effect, their numbers had vastly increased. From that time forward slavery became the basis of a great political power, and the Southern States, under all circumstances and at every opportunity, carried on a brave and unrelenting struggle for its maintenance and extension.

The conscience of the North was slow to rise against it, though bitter controversies from time to time took place. The Southern leaders threatened disunion if their demands were not complied with. To save the Union, compromise after compromise was made, but each one in the end was broken. The Missouri Compromise, made in 1820 upon the occasion of the admission of Missouri into the Union as a slave State, whereby, in consideration of such admission, slavery was forever excluded from the Northwest Territory, was ruthlessly repealed in 1854, by a Congress elected in the interests of the slave power, the intent being to force slavery into that vast territory which had so long been dedicated to freedom. This challenge at last aroused the slumbering conscience and passion of the North, and led to the formation of the Republican party for the avowed purpose of preventing, by constitutional methods, the further extension of slavery.

In its first campaign, in 1856, though it failed to elect its candidates; it received a surprising vote and carried many of the States. No one could any longer doubt that the North had made up its mind that no threats of disunion should deter it from pressing its cherished purpose and performing its long neglected duty. From the outset, Lincoln was one of the most active and effective leaders and speakers of the new party, and the great debates between Lincoln and Douglas in 1858, as the respective champions of the restriction and extension of slavery, attracted the attention of the whole country. Lincoln's powerful arguments carried conviction everywhere. His moral nature was thoroughly aroused his conscience was stirred to the quick. Unless slavery was wrong, nothing was wrong. Was each man, of whatever color, entitled to the fruits of his own labor, or could one man live in idle luxury by the sweat of another's brow, whose skin was darker? He was an implicit believer in that principle of the Declaration of Independence that all men are vested with certain inalienable rights the equal rights to life, liberty, and the pursuit of happiness. On this doctrine he staked his case and carried it. We have time only for one or two sentences in which he struck the keynote of the contest.

"The real issue in this country is the eternal struggle between these two principles—right and wrong—throughout the world. They are the two principles that have stood face to face from the beginning of time, and will ever continue to struggle. The one is the common right of humanity, and the other the divine right of kings. It is the same principle in whatever shape it develops itself. It is the same spirit that says, 'You work and toil and earn bread and I'll eat it.'"

He foresaw with unerring vision that the conflict was inevitable and irrepressible—that one or the other, the right or the wrong, freedom or slavery, must ultimately prevail and wholly prevail, throughout the country; and this was the principle that carried the war, once begun, to a finish.

One sentence of his is immortal:

"Under the operation of the policy of compromise, the slavery agitation has not only not ceased, but has constantly augmented. In my opinion it will not cease until a crisis shall have been reached and passed. 'A house divided against itself cannot stand.' I believe this government cannot endure permanently half slave and half free. I do not expect the Union to be dissolved. I do not expect the house to fall, but I do expect it will cease to be divided. It will become all one thing or all the other; either the opponents of slavery will arrest the further spread of it, and place it where the public mind shall rest in the belief that it is in the course of ultimate extinction, or its advocates will push it forward till it shall become alike lawful in all the States, old as well as new, North as well as South."

During the entire decade from 1850 to 1860 the agitation of the slavery question was at the boiling point, and events which have become historical continually indicated the near approach of the overwhelming storm. No sooner had the Compromise Acts of 1850 resulted in a temporary peace, which everybody said must be final and perpetual, than new outbreaks came. The forcible carrying away of fugitive slaves by Federal troops from Boston agitated that ancient stronghold of freedom to its foundations. The publication of Uncle Tom's Cabin, which truly exposed the frightful possibilities of the slave system; the reckless attempts by force and fraud to establish it in Kansas against the will of the vast majority of the settlers; the beating of Summer in the Senate Chamber for words spoken in debate; the Dred Scott decision in the Supreme Court, which made the nation realize that the slave power had at last reached the fountain of Federal justice; and finally the execution of John Brown, for his wild raid into Virginia, to invite the slaves to rally to the standard of freedom which he unfurled:—all these events tend to illustrate and confirm Lincoln's contention that the nation could not permanently continue half slave and half free, but must become all one thing or all the other. When John Brown lay under sentence of death he declared that now he was sure that slavery must be wiped out in blood; but neither he nor his executioners dreamt that within four years a million soldiers would be marching across the country for its final extirpation, to the music of the war-song of the great conflict:

"John Brown's body lies a-mouldering in the grave,
But his soul is marching on."

And now, at the age of fifty-one, this child of the wilderness, this farm laborer, rail-splitter, flatboatman, this surveyor, lawyer, orator, statesman, and patriot, found himself elected by the great party which was pledged to prevent at all hazards the further extension of slavery, as the chief magistrate of the Republic, bound to carry out that purpose, to be the leader and ruler of the nation in its most trying hour.

Those who believe that there is a living Providence that overrules and conducts the affairs of nations, find in the elevation of this plain man to this extraordinary fortune and to this great duty, which he so fitly discharged, a signal vindication of their faith. Perhaps to this philosophical institution the judgment of our philosopher Emerson will commend itself as a just estimate of Lincoln's historical place.

"His occupying the chair of state was a triumph of the good sense of mankind and of the public conscience. He grew according to the need; his mind mastered the problem of the day: and as the problem grew, so did his comprehension of it. In the war there was no place for holiday magistrate, nor fair-weather sailor. The new pilot was hurried to the helm in a tornado. In four years—four years of battle days—his endurance, his fertility of resource, his magnanimity, were sorely tried, and never found wanting. There, by his courage, his justice, his even temper, his fertile counsel, his humanity, he stood a heroic figure in the centre of a heroic epoch. He is the true history of the American people in his time, the true representative of this continent—father of his country, the pulse of twenty millions throbbing in his heart, the thought of their mind—articulated in his tongue."

He was born great, as distinguished from those who achieve greatness or have it thrust upon them, and his inherent capacity, mental, moral, and physical, having been recognized by the educated intelligence of a free people, they happily chose him for their ruler in a day of deadly peril.

It is now forty years since I first saw and heard Abraham Lincoln, but the impression which he left on my mind is ineffaceable. After his great successes in the West he came to New York to make a political address. He appeared in every sense of the word like one of the plain people among whom he loved to be counted. At first sight there was nothing impressive or imposing about him—except that his great stature singled him out from the crowd: his clothes hung awkwardly on his giant frame; his face was of a dark pallor, without the slightest tinge of color; his seamed and rugged features bore the furrows of hardship and struggle; his deep-set eyes looked sad and anxious; his countenance in repose gave little evidence of that brain power which had raised him from the lowest to the highest station among his countrymen; as he talked to me before the meeting, he seemed ill at ease, with that sort of apprehension which a young man might feel before presenting himself to a new and strange audience, whose critical disposition he dreaded. It was a great audience, including all the noted men—all the learned and cultured of his party in New York editors, clergymen, statesmen, lawyers, merchants, critics. They were all very curious to hear him. His fame as a powerful speaker had preceded him, and exaggerated rumor of his wit—the worst forerunner of an orator—had reached the East. When Mr. Bryant presented him, on the high platform of the Cooper Institute, a vast sea of eager upturned faces greeted him, full of intense curiosity to see what this rude child of the people was like. He was equal to the occasion. When he spoke he was transformed; his eye kindled, his voice rang, his face shone and seemed to light up the whole assembly. For an hour and a half he held his audience in the hollow of his hand. His style of speech and manner of delivery were severely simple. What Lowell called "the grand simplicities of the Bible," with which he was so familiar, were reflected in his discourse. With no attempt at ornament or rhetoric, without parade or pretence, he spoke straight to the point. If any came expecting the turgid eloquence or the ribaldry of the frontier, they must have been startled at the earnest and sincere purity of his utterances. It was marvellous to see how this untutored man, by mere self-discipline and the chastening of his own spirit, had outgrown all meretricious arts, and found his own way to the grandeur and strength of absolute simplicity.

He spoke upon the theme which he had mastered so thoroughly. He demonstrated by copious historical proofs and masterly logic that the fathers who created the Constitution in order to form a more perfect union, to establish justice, and to secure the blessings of liberty to themselves and their posterity, intended to empower the Federal Government to exclude slavery from the Territories. In the kindliest spirit he protested against the avowed threat of the Southern States to destroy the Union if, in order to secure freedom in those vast regions out of which future States were to be carved, a Republican President were elected. He closed with an appeal to his audience, spoken with all the fire of his aroused and kindling conscience, with a full outpouring of his love of justice and liberty, to maintain their political purpose on that lofty and unassailable issue of right and wrong which alone could justify it, and not to be intimidated from their high resolve and sacred duty by any threats of destruction to the government or of ruin to themselves. He concluded with this telling sentence, which drove the whole argument home to all our hearts: "Let us have faith that right makes might, and in that faith let us to the end dare to do our duty as we understand it." That night the great hall, and the next day the whole city, rang with delighted applause and congratulations, and he who had come as a stranger departed with the laurels of great triumph.

Alas! in five years from that exulting night I saw him again, for the last time, in the same city, borne in his coffin through its draped streets. With tears and lamentations a heart-broken people accompanied him from Washington, the scene of his martyrdom, to his last resting-place in the young city of the West where he had worked his way to fame.

Never was a new ruler in a more desperate plight than Lincoln when he entered office on the fourth of March, 1861, four months after his election, and took his oath to support the Constitution and the Union. The intervening time had been busily employed by the Southern States in carrying out their threat of disunion in the event of his election. As soon as the fact was ascertained, seven of them had seceded and had seized upon the forts, arsenals, navy yards, and other public property of the United States within their boundaries, and were making every preparation for war. In the meantime the retiring President, who had been elected by the slave power, and who thought the seceding States could not lawfully be coerced, had done absolutely nothing. Lincoln found himself, by the Constitution, Commander-in-Chief of the Army and Navy of the United States, but with only a remnant of either at hand. Each was to be created on a great scale out of the unknown resources of a nation untried in war.

In his mild and conciliatory inaugural address, while appealing to the seceding States to return to their allegiance, he avowed his purpose to keep the solemn oath he had taken that day, to see that the laws of the Union were faithfully executed, and to use the troops to recover the forts, navy yards, and other property belonging to the government. It is probable, however, that neither side actually realized that war was inevitable, and that the other was determined to fight, until the assault on Fort Sumter presented the South as the first aggressor and roused the North to use every possible resource to maintain the government and the imperilled Union, and to vindicate the supremacy of the flag over every inch of the territory of the United States. The fact that Lincoln's first proclamation called for only 75,000 troops, to serve for three months, shows how inadequate was even his idea of what the future had in store. But from that moment Lincoln and his loyal supporters never faltered in their purpose. They knew they could win, that it was their duty to win, and that for America the whole hope of the future depended upon their winning; for now by the acts of the seceding States the issue of the election to secure or prevent the extension of slavery—stood transformed into a struggle to preserve or to destroy the Union.

We cannot follow this contest. You know its gigantic proportions; that it lasted four years instead of three months; that in its progress, instead of 75,000 men, more than 2,000,000 were enrolled on the side of the government alone; that the aggregate cost and loss to the nation approximated to 1,000,000,000 pounds sterling, and that not less than 300,000 brave and precious lives were sacrificed on each side. History has recorded how Lincoln bore himself during these four frightful years; that he was the real President, the responsible and actual head of the government, through it all; that he listened to all advice, heard all parties, and then, always realizing his responsibility to God and the nation, decided every great executive question for himself. His absolute honesty had become proverbial long before he was President. "Honest Abe Lincoln" was the name by which he had been known for years. His every act attested it.

In all the grandeur of the vast power that he wielded, he never ceased to be one of the plain people, as he always called them, never lost or impaired his perfect sympathy with them, was always in perfect touch with them and open to their appeals; and here lay the very secret of his personality and of his power, for the people in turn gave him their absolute confidence. His courage, his fortitude, his patience, his hopefulness, were sorely tried but never exhausted.

He was true as steel to his generals, but had frequent occasion to change them, as he found them inadequate. This serious and painful duty rested wholly upon him, and was perhaps his most important function as Commander-in-Chief; but when, at last, he recognized in General Grant the master of the situation, the man who could and would bring the war to a triumphant end, he gave it all over to him and upheld him with all his might. Amid all the pressure and distress that the burdens of office brought upon him, his unfailing sense of humor saved him; probably it made it possible for him to live under the burden. He had always been the great story-teller of the West, and he used and cultivated this faculty to relieve the weight of the load he bore.

It enabled him to keep the wonderful record of never having lost his temper, no matter what agony he had to bear. A whole night might be spent in recounting the stories of his wit, humor, and harmless sarcasm. But I will recall only two of his sayings, both about General Grant, who always found plenty of enemies and critics to urge the President to oust him from his command. One, I am sure, will interest all Scotchmen. They repeated with malicious intent the gossip that Grant drank. "What does he drink?" asked Lincoln. "Whiskey," was, of course, the answer; doubtless you can guess the brand. "Well," said the President, "just find out what particular kind he uses and I'll send a barrel to each of my other generals." The other must be as pleasing to the British as to the American ear. When pressed again on other grounds to get rid of Grant, he declared, "I can't spare that man, he fights!"

He was tender-hearted to a fault, and never could resist the appeals of wives and mothers of soldiers who had got into trouble and were under sentence of death for their offences. His Secretary of War and other officials complained that they never could get deserters shot. As surely as the women of the culprit's family could get at him he always gave way. Certainly you will all appreciate his exquisite sympathy with the suffering relatives of those who had fallen in battle. His heart bled with theirs. Never was there a more gentle and tender utterance than his letter to a mother who had given all her sons to her country, written at a time when the angel of death had visited almost every household in the land, and was already hovering over him.

"I have been shown," he says, "in the files of the War Department a statement that you are the mother of five sons who have died gloriously on the field of battle. I feel how weak and fruitless must be any words of mine which should attempt to beguile you from your grief for a loss so overwhelming but I cannot refrain from tendering to you the consolation which may be found in the thanks of the Republic they died to save. I pray that our Heavenly Father may assuage the anguish of your bereavement and leave you only the cherished memory of the loved and the lost, and the solemn pride that must be yours to have laid so costly a sacrifice upon the altar of freedom."

Hardly could your illustrious sovereign, from the depths of her queenly and womanly heart, have spoken words more touching and tender to soothe the stricken mothers of her own soldiers.

The Emancipation Proclamation, with which Mr. Lincoln delighted the country and the world on the first of January, 1863, will doubtless secure for him a foremost place in history among the philanthropists and benefactors of the race, as it rescued, from hopeless and degrading slavery, so many millions of his fellow-beings described in the law and existing in fact as "chattels-personal, in the hands of their owners and possessors, to all intents, constructions, and purposes whatsoever." Rarely does the happy fortune come to one man to render such a service to his kind—to proclaim liberty throughout the land unto all the inhabitants thereof.

Ideas rule the world, and never was there a more signal instance of this triumph of an idea than here. William Lloyd Garrison, who thirty years before had begun his crusade for the abolition of slavery, and had lived to see this glorious and unexpected consummation of the hopeless cause to which he had devoted his life, well described the proclamation as a "great historic event, sublime in its magnitude, momentous and beneficent in its far-reaching consequences, and eminently just and right alike to the oppressor and the oppressed."

Lincoln had always been heart and soul opposed to slavery. Tradition says that on the trip on the flatboat to New Orleans he formed his first and last opinion of slavery at the sight of negroes chained and scourged, and that then and there the iron entered into his soul. No boy could grow to manhood in those days as a poor white in Kentucky and

Indiana, in close contact with slavery or in its neighborhood, without a growing consciousness of its blighting effects on free labor, as well as of its frightful injustice and cruelty. In the Legislature of Illinois, where the public sentiment was all for upholding the institution and violently against every movement for its abolition or restriction, upon the passage of resolutions to that effect he had the courage with one companion to put on record his protest, "believing that the institution of slavery is founded both in injustice and bad policy." No great demonstration of courage, you will say; but that was at a time when Garrison, for his abolition utterances, had been dragged by an angry mob through the streets of Boston with a rope around his body, and in the very year that Lovejoy in the same State of Illinois was slain by rioters while defending his press, from which he had printed antislavery appeals.

In Congress he brought in a bill for gradual abolition in the District of Columbia, with compensation to the owners, for until they raised treasonable hands against the life of the nation he always maintained that the property of the slaveholders, into which they had come by two centuries of descent, without fault on their part, ought not to be taken away from them without just compensation. He used to say that, one way or another, he had voted forty-two times for the Wilmot Proviso, which Mr. Wilmot of Pennsylvania moved as an addition to every bill which affected United States territory, "that neither slavery nor involuntary servitude shall ever exist in any part of the said territory," and it is evident that his condemnation of the system, on moral grounds as a crime against the human race, and on political grounds as a cancer that was sapping the vitals of the nation, and must master its whole being or be itself extirpated, grew steadily upon him until it culminated in his great speeches in the Illinois debate.

By the mere election of Lincoln to the Presidency, the further extension of slavery into the Territories was rendered forever impossible—Vox populi, vox Dei. Revolutions never go backward, and when founded on a great moral sentiment stirring the heart of an indignant people their edicts are irresistible and final. Had the slave power acquiesced in that election, had the Southern States remained under the Constitution and within the Union, and relied upon their constitutional and legal rights, their favorite institution, immoral as it was, blighting and fatal as it was, might have endured for another century. The great party that had elected him, unalterably determined against its extension, was nevertheless pledged not to interfere with its continuance in the States where it already existed. Of course, when new regions were forever closed against it, from its very nature it must have begun to shrink and to dwindle; and probably gradual and compensated emancipation, which appealed very strongly to the new President's sense of justice and expediency, would, in the progress of time, by a reversion to the ideas of the founders of the Republic, have found a safe outlet for both masters and slaves. But whom the gods wish to destroy they first make mad, and when seven States, afterwards increased to eleven, openly seceded from the Union, when they declared and began the war upon the nation, and challenged its mighty power to the desperate and protracted struggle for its life, and for the maintenance of its authority as a nation over its territory, they gave to Lincoln and to freedom the sublime opportunity of history.

In his first inaugural address, when as yet not a drop of precious blood had been shed, while he held out to them the olive branch in one hand, in the other he presented the guarantees of the Constitution, and after reciting the emphatic resolution of the convention that nominated him, that the maintenance inviolate of the "rights of the States, and especially the right of each State to order and control its own domestic institutions according to its own judgment exclusively, is essential to that balance of power on which the perfection and endurance of our political fabric depend," he reiterated this sentiment, and declared, with no mental reservation, "that all the protection which, consistently with the Constitution and the laws, can be given, will be cheerfully given to all the States when lawfully demanded for whatever cause as cheerfully to one section as to another."

When, however, these magnanimous overtures for peace and reunion were rejected; when the seceding States defied the Constitution and every clause and principle of it; when they persisted in staying out of the Union from which they had seceded, and proceeded to carve out of its territory a new and hostile empire based on slavery; when they flew at the throat of the nation and plunged it into the bloodiest war of the nineteenth century the tables were turned, and the belief gradually came to the mind of the President that if the Rebellion was not soon subdued by force of arms, if the war must be fought out to the bitter end, then to reach that end the salvation of the nation itself might require the destruction of slavery wherever it existed; that if the war was to continue on one side for Disunion, for no other purpose than to preserve slavery, it must continue on the other side for the Union, to destroy slavery.

As he said, "Events control me; I cannot control events," and as the dreadful war progressed and became more deadly and dangerous, the unalterable conviction was forced upon him that, in order that the frightful sacrifice of life and treasure on both sides might not be all in vain, it had become his duty as Commander-in-Chief of the Army, as a necessary war measure, to strike a blow at the Rebellion which, all others failing, would inevitably lead to its annihilation, by annihilating the very thing for which it was contending. His own words are the best:

"I understood that my oath to preserve the Constitution to the best of my ability imposed upon me the duty of preserving by every indispensable means that government—that nation—of which that Constitution was the organic law. Was it possible to lose the nation and yet preserve the Constitution? By general law, life and limb must be protected, yet often a limb must be amputated to save a life; but a life is never wisely given to save a limb. I felt that measures otherwise unconstitutional might become lawful by becoming indispensable to the preservation of the Constitution through the preservation of the nation. Right or wrong, I assumed this ground and now avow it. I could not feel that to the best of my ability I had ever tried to preserve the Constitution if to save slavery or any minor matter I should permit the wreck of government, country, and Constitution all together."

And so, at last, when in his judgment the indispensable necessity had come, he struck the fatal blow, and signed the proclamation which has made his name immortal. By it, the President, as Commander-in-Chief in time of actual armed rebellion, and as a fit and necessary war measure for suppressing the rebellion, proclaimed all persons held as slaves in the States and parts of States then in rebellion to be thenceforward free, and declared that the executive, with the army and navy, would recognize and maintain their freedom.

In the other great steps of the government, which led to the triumphant prosecution of the war, he necessarily shared the responsibility and the credit with the great statesmen who stayed up his hands in his cabinet, with Seward, Chase and Stanton, and the rest,—and with his generals and admirals, his soldiers and sailors, but this great act was absolutely his own. The conception and execution were exclusively his. He laid it before his cabinet as a measure on which his mind was made up and could not be changed, asking them only for suggestions as to details. He chose the time and the circumstances under which the Emancipation should be proclaimed and when it should take effect.

It came not an hour too soon; but public opinion in the North would not have sustained it earlier. In the first eighteen months of the war its ravages had extended from the Atlantic to beyond the Mississippi. Many victories in the West had been balanced and paralyzed by inaction and disasters in Virginia, only partially redeemed by the bloody and indecisive battle of Antietam; a reaction had set in from the general enthusiasm which had swept the Northern States after the assault upon Sumter. It could not truly be said that they had lost heart, but faction was raising its head. Heard through the land like the blast of a bugle, the proclamation rallied the patriotism of the country to fresh sacrifices and renewed ardor. It was a step that could not be revoked. It relieved the conscience of the nation from an incubus that had oppressed it from its birth. The United States were rescued from the false predicament in which they had been from the beginning, and the great popular heart leaped with new enthusiasm for "Liberty and Union, henceforth and forever, one and inseparable." It brought not only moral but material support to the cause of the government, for within two years 120,000 colored troops were enlisted in the military service and following the national flag, supported by all the loyalty of the North, and led by its choicest spirits. One mother said, when her son was offered the command of the first colored regiment, "If he accepts it I shall be as proud as if I had heard that he was shot." He was shot heading a gallant charge of his regiment.... The Confederates replied to a request of his friends for his body that they had "buried him under a layer of his niggers...;" but that mother has lived to enjoy thirty-six years of his glory, and Boston has erected its noblest monument to his memory.

The effect of the proclamation upon the actual progress of the war was not immediate, but wherever the Federal armies advanced they carried freedom with them, and when the summer came round the new spirit and force which had animated the heart of the government and people were manifest. In the first week of July the decisive battle of Gettysburg turned the tide of war, and the fall of Vicksburg made the great river free from its source to the Gulf.

On foreign nations the influence of the proclamation and of these new victories was of great importance. In those days, when there was no cable, it was not easy for foreign observers to appreciate what was really going on; they could not see clearly the true state of affairs, as in the last year of the nineteenth century we have been able, by our new electric vision, to watch every event at the antipodes and observe its effect. The Rebel emissaries, sent over to solicit intervention, spared no pains to impress upon the minds of public and private men and upon the press their own views of the character of the contest. The prospects of the Confederacy were always better abroad than at home. The stock markets of the world gambled upon its chances, and its bonds at one time were high in favor.

Such ideas as these were seriously held: that the North was fighting for empire and the South for independence; that the Southern States, instead of being the grossest oligarchies, essentially despotisms, founded on the right of one man to appropriate the fruit of other men's toil and to exclude them from equal rights, were real republics, feebler to be sure than their Northern rivals, but representing the same idea of freedom, and that the mighty strength of the nation was being put forth to crush them; that Jefferson Davis and the Southern leaders had created a nation; that the republican experiment had failed and the Union had ceased to exist. But the crowning argument to foreign minds was that it was an utter impossibility for the government to win in the contest; that the success of the Southern States, so far as separation was concerned, was as certain as any event yet future and contingent could be; that the subjugation of the South by the North, even if it could be accomplished, would prove a calamity to the United States and the world, and especially calamitous to the negro race; and that such a victory would necessarily leave the people of the South for many generations cherishing deadly hostility against the government and the North, and plotting always to recover their independence.

When Lincoln issued his proclamation he knew that all these ideas were founded in error; that the national resources were inexhaustible; that the government could and would win, and that if slavery were once finally disposed of, the only cause of difference being out of the way, the North and South would come together again, and by and by be as good friends as ever. In many quarters abroad the proclamation was welcomed with enthusiasm by the friends of America; but I think the demonstrations in its favor that brought more gladness to Lincoln's heart than any other were the meetings held in the manufacturing centres, by the very operatives upon whom the war bore the hardest, expressing the most enthusiastic sympathy with the proclamation, while they bore with heroic fortitude the grievous privations which the war entailed upon them. Mr. Lincoln's expectation when he announced to the world that all slaves in all States then in rebellion were set free must have been that the avowed position of his government, that the continuance of the war now meant the annihilation of slavery, would make intervention impossible for any foreign nation whose people were lovers of liberty—and so the result proved.

The growth and development of Lincoln's mental power and moral force, of his intense and magnetic personality, after the vast responsibilities of government were thrown upon him at the age of fifty-two, furnish a rare and striking illustration of the marvellous capacity and adaptability of the human intellect—of the sound mind in the sound body. He came to the discharge of the great duties of the Presidency with absolutely no experience in the administration of government, or of the vastly varied and complicated questions of foreign and domestic policy which immediately arose, and continued to press upon him during the rest of his life; but he mastered each as it came, apparently with the facility of a trained and experienced ruler. As Clarendon said of Cromwell, "His parts seemed to be raised by the demands of great station." His life through it all was one of intense labor, anxiety, and distress, without one hour of peaceful repose from first to last. But he rose to every occasion. He led public opinion, but did not march so far in advance of it as to fail of its effective support in every great emergency. He knew the heart and thought of the people, as no man not in constant and absolute sympathy with them could have known it, and so holding their confidence, he triumphed through and with them. Not only was there this steady growth of intellect, but the infinite delicacy of his nature and its capacity for refinement developed also, as exhibited in the purity and perfection of his language and style of speech. The rough backwoodsman, who had never seen the inside of a university, became in the end, by self-training and the exercise of his own powers of mind, heart, and soul, a master of style, and some of his utterances will rank with the best, the most perfectly adapted to the occasion which produced them.

Have you time to listen to his two-minutes speech at Gettysburg, at the dedication of the Soldiers' Cemetery? His whole soul was in it:

"Four score and seven years ago our fathers brought forth on this continent a new nation, conceived in liberty and dedicated to the proposition that all men are created equal. Now we are engaged in a great civil war, testing whether that nation, or any nation so conceived and so dedicated, can long endure. We are met on a great battlefield of that war. We have come to dedicate a portion of that field as a final resting-place for those who here gave their lives that that nation might live. It is altogether fitting and proper that we should do this. But in a larger sense we cannot dedicate—we cannot consecrate—we cannot hallow this ground. The brave men, living and dead, who struggled here have consecrated it far above our poor power to add or detract. The world will little note, nor long remember, what we say here but it can never forget what they did here. It is for us, the living, rather, to be dedicated here to the unfinished work which they who fought here have thus far so nobly advanced. It is rather for us to be here dedicated to the great task remaining before us that from these honored dead we take increased devotion to that cause for which they gave the last full measure of devotion—that we here highly resolve that these dead shall not have died in vain—that this nation under God shall have a new birth of freedom—and that government of the people, by the people, and for the people shall not perish from the earth."

He lived to see his work indorsed by an overwhelming majority of his countrymen. In his second inaugural address, pronounced just forty days before his death, there is a single passage which well displays his indomitable will and at the same time his deep religious feeling, his sublime charity to the enemies of his country, and his broad and catholic humanity:

"If we shall suppose that American slavery is one of those offences which in the Providence of God must needs come, but which, having continued through the appointed time, He now wills to remove, and that He gives to both North and South this terrible war, as the woe due to those by whom the offence came, shall we discern therein any departure from those divine attributes which the believers in a living God always ascribe to Him? Fondly do we hope, fervently do we pray, that this mighty scourge of war may speedily pass away. Yet, if God wills that it continue until all the wealth piled by the bondsmen's two hundred and fifty years of unrequited toil shall be sunk, and until every drop of blood drawn with the lash shall be paid with another drawn by the sword, as was said three thousand years ago, so still it must be said, 'the judgments of the Lord are true and righteous altogether.'

"With malice toward none, with charity for all, with firmness in the right as God gives us to see the right let us strive on to finish the work we are in to bind up the nation's wounds; to care for him who shall have borne the battle and for his widow and his orphan to do all which may achieve, and cherish a just and lasting peace among ourselves, and with all nations."

His prayer was answered. The forty days of life that remained to him were crowned with great historic events. He lived to see his Proclamation of Emancipation embodied in an amendment of the Constitution, adopted by Congress, and submitted to the States for ratification. The mighty scourge of war did speedily pass away, for it was given him to witness the surrender of the Rebel army and the fall of their capital, and the starry flag that he loved waving in triumph over the national soil. When he died by the madman's hand in the supreme hour of victory, the vanquished lost their best friend, and the human race one of its noblest examples; and all the friends of freedom and justice, in whose cause he lived and died, joined hands as mourners at his grave.

THE WRITINGS OF ABRAHAM LINCOLN, 1832-1843

1832

ADDRESS TO THE PEOPLE OF SANGAMON COUNTY.

March 9, 1832.

FELLOW CITIZENS:—Having become a candidate for the honorable office of one of your Representatives in the next General Assembly of this State, in according with an established custom and the principles of true Republicanism it becomes my duty to make known to you, the people whom I propose to represent, my sentiments with regard to local affairs.
Time and experience have verified to a demonstration the public utility of internal improvements. That the poorest and most thinly populated countries would be greatly benefited by the opening of good roads, and in the clearing of navigable streams within their limits, is what no person will deny. Yet it is folly to undertake works of this or any other without first knowing that we are able to finish them—as half-finished work generally proves to be labor lost. There cannot justly be any objection to having railroads and canals, any more than to other good things, provided they cost nothing. The only objection is to paying for them; and the objection arises from the want of ability to pay.
With respect to the County of Sangamon, some....
Yet, however desirable an object the construction of a railroad through our country may be, however high our imaginations may be heated at thoughts of it,—there is always a heart-appalling shock accompanying the amount of its cost, which forces us to shrink from our pleasing anticipations. The probable cost of this contemplated railroad is estimated at $290,000; the bare statement of which, in my opinion, is sufficient to justify the belief that the improvement of the Sangamon River is an object much better suited to our infant resources.......
What the cost of this work would be, I am unable to say. It is probable, however, that it would not be greater than is common to streams of the same length. Finally, I believe the improvement of the Sangamon River to be vastly important and highly desirable to the people of the county; and, if elected, any measure in the Legislature having this for its object, which may appear judicious, will meet my approbation and receive my support.
It appears that the practice of loaning money at exorbitant rates of interest has already been opened as a field for discussion; so I suppose I may enter upon it without claiming the honor or risking the danger which may await its first explorer. It seems as though we are never to have an end to this baneful and corroding system, acting almost as prejudicially to the general interests of the community as a direct tax of several thousand dollars annually laid on each county for the benefit of a few individuals only, unless there be a law made fixing the limits of usury. A law for this purpose, I am of opinion, may be made without materially injuring any class of people. In cases of extreme necessity, there could always be means found to cheat the law; while in all other cases it would have its intended effect. I would favor the passage of a law on this subject which might not be very easily evaded. Let it be such that the labor and difficulty of evading it could only be justified in cases of greatest necessity.
Upon the subject of education, not presuming to dictate any plan or system respecting it, I can only say that I view it as the most important subject which we as a people can be engaged in. That every man may receive at least a moderate education, and thereby be enabled to read the histories of his own and other countries, by which he may duly appreciate the value of our free institutions, appears to be an object of vital importance, even on this account alone, to say nothing of the advantages and satisfaction to be derived from all being able to read the Scriptures, and other works both of a religious and moral nature, for themselves.
For my part, I desire to see the time when education—and by its means, morality, sobriety, enterprise, and industry—shall become much more general than at present, and should be gratified to have it in my power to contribute something to the advancement of any measure which might have a tendency to accelerate that happy period.
With regard to existing laws, some alterations are thought to be necessary. Many respectable men have suggested that our estray laws, the law respecting the issuing of executions, the road law, and some others, are deficient in their present form, and require alterations. But, considering the great probability that the framers of those laws were wiser than myself, I should prefer not meddling with them, unless they were first attacked by others; in which case I should feel it both a privilege and a duty to take that stand which, in my view, might tend most to the advancement of justice.
But, fellow-citizens, I shall conclude. Considering the great degree of modesty which should always attend youth, it is probable I have already been more presuming than becomes me. However, upon the subjects of which I have treated, I have spoken as I have thought. I may be wrong in regard to any or all of them; but, holding it a sound maxim that it is better only sometimes to be right than at all times to be wrong, so soon as I discover my opinions to be erroneous, I shall be ready to renounce them.
Every man is said to have his peculiar ambition. Whether it be true or not, I can say, for one, that I have no other so great as that of being truly esteemed of my fellow-men, by rendering myself worthy of their esteem. How far I shall succeed in gratifying this ambition is yet to be developed. I am young, and unknown to many of you. I was born, and have ever remained, in the most humble walks of life. I have no wealthy or popular relations or friends to recommend me. My case is thrown exclusively upon the independent voters of the county; and, if elected, they will have conferred a favor upon me for which I shall be unremitting in my labors to compensate. But, if the good people in their wisdom shall see fit to keep me in the background, I have been too familiar with disappointments to be very much chagrined.
Your friend and fellow-citizen, A. LINCOLN.
New Salem, March 9, 1832.

1833

TO E. C. BLANKENSHIP.

NEW SALEM, Aug. 10, 1833

E. C. BLANKENSHIP.
Dear Sir:—In regard to the time David Rankin served the enclosed discharge shows correctly—as well as I can recollect—having no writing to refer. The transfer of Rankin from my company occurred as follows: Rankin having lost his horse at Dixon's ferry and having acquaintance in one of the foot companies who were going down the river was desirous to go with them, and one Galishen being an acquaintance of mine and belonging to the company in which Rankin wished to go wished to leave it and join mine, this being the case it was agreed that they should exchange places and answer to each other's names—as it was expected we all would be discharged in very few days. As to a blanket—I have no knowledge of Rankin ever getting any. The above embraces all the facts now in my recollection which are pertinent to the case.
I shall take pleasure in giving any further information in my power should you call on me.
Your friend, A. LINCOLN.

RESPONSE TO REQUEST FOR POSTAGE RECEIPT

TO Mr. SPEARS.

Mr. SPEARS:
At your request I send you a receipt for the postage on your paper. I am somewhat surprised at your request. I will, however, comply with it. The law requires newspaper postage to be paid in advance, and now that I have waited a full year you choose to wound my feelings by insinuating that unless you get a receipt I will probably make you pay it again.
Respectfully, A. LINCOLN.

1836

ANNOUNCEMENT OF POLITICAL VIEWS.

New Salem, June 13, 1836.

TO THE EDITOR OF THE "JOURNAL"—In your paper of last Saturday I see a communication, over the signature of "Many Voters," in which the candidates who are announced in the Journal are called upon to "show their hands." Agreed. Here's mine.
I go for all sharing the privileges of the government who assist in bearing its burdens. Consequently, I go for admitting all whites to the right of suffrage who pay taxes or bear arms (by no means excluding females).
If elected, I shall consider the whole people of Sangamon my constituents, as well those that oppose as those that support me.
While acting as their representative, I shall be governed by their will on all subjects upon which I have the means of knowing what their will is; and upon all others I shall do what my own judgment teaches me will best advance their interests. Whether elected or not, I go for distributing the proceeds of the sales of the public lands to the several States,

to enable our State, in common with others, to dig canals and construct railroads without borrowing money and paying the interest on it. If alive on the first Monday in November, I shall vote for Hugh L. White for President.
Very respectfully, A. LINCOLN.

RESPONSE TO POLITICAL SMEAR

TO ROBERT ALLEN

New Salem, June 21, 1836
DEAR COLONEL:—I am told that during my absence last week you passed through this place, and stated publicly that you were in possession of a fact or facts which, if known to the public, would entirely destroy the prospects of N. W. Edwards and myself at the ensuing election; but that, through favor to us, you should forbear to divulge them. No one has needed favors more than I, and, generally, few have been less unwilling to accept them; but in this case favor to me would be injustice to the public, and therefore I must beg your pardon for declining it. That I once had the confidence of the people of Sangamon, is sufficiently evident; and if I have since done anything, either by design or misadventure, which if known would subject me to a forfeiture of that confidence, he that knows of that thing, and conceals it, is a traitor to his country's interest.
I find myself wholly unable to form any conjecture of what fact or facts, real or supposed, you spoke; but my opinion of your veracity will not permit me for a moment to doubt that you at least believed what you said. I am flattered with the personal regard you manifested for me; but I do hope that, on more mature reflection, you will view the public interest as a paramount consideration, and therefore determine to let the worst come. I here assure you that the candid statement of facts on your part, however low it may sink me, shall never break the tie of personal friendship between us. I wish an answer to this, and you are at liberty to publish both, if you choose.
Very respectfully, A. LINCOLN.

TO MISS MARY OWENS.

VANDALIA, December 13, 1836.

MARY:—I have been sick ever since my arrival, or I should have written sooner. It is but little difference, however, as I have very little even yet to write. And more, the longer I can avoid the mortification of looking in the post-office for your letter and not finding it, the better. You see I am mad about that old letter yet. I don't like very well to risk you again. I'll try you once more, anyhow.
The new State House is not yet finished, and consequently the Legislature is doing little or nothing. The governor delivered an inflammatory political message, and it is expected there will be some sparring between the parties about it as soon as the two Houses get to business. Taylor delivered up his petition for the new county to one of our members this morning. I am told he despairs of its success, on account of all the members from Morgan County opposing it. There are names enough on the petition, I think, to justify the members from our county in going for it; but if the members from Morgan oppose it, which they say they will, the chance will be bad.
Our chance to take the seat of government to Springfield is better than I expected. An internal-improvement convention was held there since we met, which recommended a loan of several millions of dollars, on the faith of the State, to construct railroads. Some of the Legislature are for it, and some against it; which has the majority I cannot tell. There is great strife and struggling for the office of the United States Senator here at this time. It is probable we shall ease their pains in a few days. The opposition men have no candidate of their own, and consequently they will smile as complacently at the angry snarl of the contending Van Buren candidates and their respective friends as the Christian does at Satan's rage. You recollect that I mentioned at the outset of this letter that I had been unwell. That is the fact, though I believe I am about well now; but that, with other things I cannot account for, have conspired, and have gotten my spirits so low that I feel that I would rather be any place in the world than here. I really cannot endure the thought of staying here ten weeks. Write back as soon as you get this, and, if possible, say something that will please me, for really I have not been pleased since I left you. This letter is so dry and stupid that I am ashamed to send it, but with my present feelings I cannot do any better.
Give my best respects to Mr. and Mrs. Able and family.
Your friend, LINCOLN

SPEECH IN ILLINOIS LEGISLATURE.

January [?], 1837

Mr. CHAIRMAN:—Lest I should fall into the too common error of being mistaken in regard to which side I design to be upon, I shall make it my first care to remove all doubt on that point, by declaring that I am opposed to the resolution under consideration, in toto. Before I proceed to the body of the subject, I will further remark, that it is not without a considerable degree of apprehension that I venture to cross the track of the gentleman from Coles [Mr. Linder]. Indeed, I do not believe I could muster a sufficiency of courage to come in contact with that gentleman, were it not for the fact that he, some days since, most graciously condescended to assure us that he would never be found wasting ammunition on small game. On the same fortunate occasion, he further gave us to understand, that he regarded himself as being decidedly the superior of our common friend from Randolph [Mr. Shields]; and feeling, as I really do, that I, to say the most of myself, am nothing more than the peer of our friend from Randolph, I shall regard the gentleman from Coles as decidedly my superior also, and consequently, in the course of what I shall have to say, whenever I shall have occasion to allude to that gentleman, I shall endeavor to adopt that kind of court language which I understand to be due to decided superiority. In one faculty, at least, there can be no dispute of the gentleman's superiority over me and most other men, and that is, the faculty of entangling a subject, so that neither himself, or any other man, can find head or tail to it. Here he has introduced a resolution embracing ninety-nine printed lines across common writing paper, and yet more than one half of his opening speech has been made upon subjects about which there is not one word said in his resolution.

Though his resolution embraces nothing in regard to the constitutionality of the Bank, much of what he has said has been with a view to make the impression that it was unconstitutional in its inception. Now, although I am satisfied that an ample field may be found within the pale of the resolution, at least for small game, yet, as the gentleman has traveled out of it, I feel that I may, with all due humility, venture to follow him. The gentleman has discovered that some gentleman at Washington city has been upon the very eve of deciding our Bank unconstitutional, and that he would probably have completed his very authentic decision, had not some one of the Bank officers placed his hand upon his mouth, and begged him to withhold it. The fact that the individuals composing our Supreme Court have, in an official capacity, decided in favor of the constitutionality of the Bank, would, in my mind, seem a sufficient answer to this. It is a fact known to all, that the members of the Supreme Court, together with the Governor, form a Council of Revision, and that this Council approved this Bank charter. I ask, then, if the extra-judicial decision not quite but almost made by the gentleman at Washington, before whom, by the way, the question of the constitutionality of our Bank never has, nor never can come—is to be taken as paramount to a decision officially made by that tribunal, by which, and which alone, the constitutionality of the Bank can ever be settled? But, aside from this view of the subject, I would ask, if the committee which this resolution proposes to appoint are to examine into the Constitutionality of the Bank? Are they to be clothed with power to send for persons and papers, for this object? And after they have found the bank to be unconstitutional, and decided it so, how are they to enforce their decision? What will their decision amount to? They cannot compel the Bank to cease operations, or to change the course of its operations. What good, then, can their labors result in? Certainly none.

The gentleman asks, if we, without an examination, shall, by giving the State deposits to the Bank, and by taking the stock reserved for the State, legalize its former misconduct. Now I do not pretend to possess sufficient legal knowledge to decide whether a legislative enactment proposing to, and accepting from, the Bank, certain terms, would have the effect to legalize or wipe out its former errors, or not; but I can assure the gentleman, if such should be the effect, he has already got behind the settlement of accounts; for it is well known to all, that the Legislature, at its last session, passed a supplemental Bank charter, which the Bank has since accepted, and which, according to his doctrine, has legalized all the alleged violations of its original charter in the distribution of its stock.

I now proceed to the resolution. By examination it will be found that the first thirty-three lines, being precisely one third of the whole, relate exclusively to the distribution of the stock by the commissioners appointed by the State. Now, Sir, it is clear that no question can arise on this portion of the resolution, except a question between capitalists in regard to the ownership of stock. Some gentlemen have their stock in their hands, while others, who have more money than they know what to do with, want it; and this, and this alone, is the question, to settle which we are called on to squander thousands of the people's money. What interest, let me ask, have the people in the settlement of this question? What difference is it to them whether the stock is owned by Judge Smith or Sam Wiggins? If any gentleman be entitled to stock in the Bank, which he is kept out of possession of by others, let him assert his right in the Supreme Court, and let him or his antagonist, whichever may be found in the wrong, pay the costs of suit. It is an old maxim, and a very sound one, that he that dances should always pay the fiddler. Now, Sir, in the present case, if any gentlemen, whose money is a burden to them, choose to lead off a dance, I am decidedly opposed to the people's money being used to pay the fiddler. No one can doubt that the examination proposed by this resolution must cost the State some ten or twelve thousand dollars; and all this to settle a question in which the people have no interest, and about which they care nothing. These capitalists generally act harmoniously and in concert, to fleece the people, and now that they have got into a quarrel with themselves we are called upon to appropriate the people's money to settle the quarrel.

I leave this part of the resolution and proceed to the remainder. It will be found that no charge in the remaining part of the resolution, if true, amounts to the violation of the Bank charter, except one, which I will notice in due time. It might seem quite sufficient to say no more upon any of these charges or insinuations than enough to show they are not violations of the charter; yet, as they are ingeniously framed and handled, with a view to deceive and mislead, I will notice in their order all the most prominent of them. The first of these is in relation to a connection between our Bank and several banking institutions in other States. Admitting this connection to exist, I should like to see the gentleman from Coles, or any other gentleman, undertake to show that there is any harm in it. What can there be in such a connection, that the people of Illinois are willing to pay their money to get a peep into? By a reference to the tenth section of the Bank charter, any gentleman can see that the framers of the act contemplated the holding of stock in the institutions of other corporations. Why, then, is it, when neither law nor justice forbids it, that we are asked to spend our time and money in inquiring into its truth?

The next charge, in the order of time, is, that some officer, director, clerk or servant of the Bank, has been required to take an oath of secrecy in relation to the affairs of said Bank. Now, I do not know whether this be true or false—neither do I believe any honest man cares. I know that the seventh section of the charter expressly guarantees to the Bank the right of making, under certain restrictions, such by-laws as it may think fit; and I further know that the requiring an oath of secrecy would not transcend those restrictions. What, then, if the Bank has chosen to exercise this right? Whom can it injure? Does not every merchant have his secret mark? and who is ever silly enough to complain of it? I presume if the Bank does require any such oath of secrecy, it is done through a motive of delicacy to those individuals who deal with it. Why, Sir, not many days since, one gentleman upon this floor, who, by the way, I have no doubt is now ready to join this hue and cry against the Bank, indulged in a philippic against one of the Bank officials, because, as he said, he had divulged a secret.

Immediately following this last charge, there are several insinuations in the resolution, which are too silly to require any sort of notice, were it not for the fact that they conclude by saying, "to the great injury of the people at large." In answer to this I would say that it is strange enough, that the people are suffering these "great injuries," and yet are not sensible of it! Singular indeed that the people should be writhing under oppression and injury, and yet not one among them to be found to raise the voice of complaint. If the Bank be inflicting injury upon the people, why is it that not a single petition is presented to this body on the subject? If the Bank really be a grievance, why is it that no one of the real people is found to ask redress of it? The truth is, no such oppression exists. If it did, our people would groan with memorials and petitions, and we would not be permitted to rest day or night, till we had put it down. The people know their rights, and they are never slow to assert and maintain them, when they are invaded. Let them call for an investigation, and I shall ever stand ready to respond to the call. But they have made no such call. I make the assertion boldly, and without fear of contradiction, that no man, who does not hold an office, or does not aspire to one, has ever found any fault of the Bank. It has doubled the prices of the products of their farms, and filled their pockets with a sound circulating medium, and they are all well pleased with its operations. No, Sir, it is the politician who is the first to sound the alarm (which, by the way, is a false one.) It is he, who, by these unholy means, is endeavoring to blow up a storm that he may ride upon and direct. It is he, and he alone, that here proposes to spend thousands of the people's public treasure, for no other advantage to them than to make valueless in their pockets the reward of their industry. Mr. Chairman, this work is exclusively the work of politicians; a set of men who have interests aside from the interests of the people, and who, to say the most of them, are, taken as a mass, at least one long step removed from honest men. I say this with the greater freedom, because, being a politician myself, none can regard it as personal.

Again, it is charged, or rather insinuated, that officers of the Bank have loaned money at usurious rates of interest. Suppose this to be true, are we to send a committee of this House to inquire into it? Suppose the committee should find it true, can they redress the injured individuals? Assuredly not. If any individual had been injured in this way, is there not an ample remedy to be found in the laws of the land? Does the gentleman from Coles know that there is a statute standing in full force making it highly penal for an individual to loan money at a higher rate of interest than twelve per cent? If he does not he is too ignorant to be placed at the head of the committee which his resolution purposes and if he does, his neglect to mention it shows him to be too uncandid to merit the respect or confidence of any one.

But besides all this, if the Bank were struck from existence, could not the owners of the capital still loan it usuriously, as well as now? whatever the Bank, or its officers, may have done, I know that usurious transactions were much more frequent and enormous before the commencement of its operations than they have ever been since.

The next insinuation is, that the Bank has refused specie payments. This, if true is a violation of the charter. But there is not the least probability of its truth; because, if such had been the fact, the individual to whom payment was refused would have had an interest in making it public, by suing for the damages to which the charter entitles him. Yet no such thing has been done; and the strong presumption is, that the insinuation is false and groundless.

From this to the end of the resolution, there is nothing that merits attention—I therefore drop the particular examination of it.

By a general view of the resolution, it will be seen that a principal object of the committee is to examine into, and ferret out, a mass of corruption supposed to have been committed by the commissioners who apportioned the stock of the Bank. I believe it is universally understood and acknowledged that all men will ever act correctly unless they have a motive to do otherwise. If this be true, we can only suppose that the commissioners acted corruptly by also supposing that they were bribed to do so. Taking this view of the subject, I would ask if the Bank is likely to find it more difficult to bribe the committee of seven, which, we are about to appoint, than it may have found it to bribe the commissioners? (Here Mr. Linder called to order. The Chair decided that Mr. Lincoln was not out of order. Mr. Linder appealed to the House, but, before the question was put, withdrew his appeal, saying he preferred to let the gentleman go on; he thought he would break his own neck. Mr. Lincoln proceeded:)

Another gracious condescension! I acknowledge it with gratitude. I know I was not out of order; and I know every sensible man in the House knows it. I was not saying that the gentleman from Coles could be bribed, nor, on the other hand, will I say he could not. In that particular I leave him where I found him. I was only endeavoring to show that there was at least as great a probability of any seven members that could be selected from this House being bribed to act corruptly, as there was that the twenty-four commissioners had been so bribed. By a reference to the ninth section of the Bank charter, it will be seen that those commissioners were John Tilson, Robert K. McLaughlin, Daniel Warm, A.G. S. Wight, John C. Riley, W. H. Davidson, Edward M. Wilson, Edward L. Pierson, Robert R. Green, Ezra Baker, Aquilla Wren, John Taylor, Samuel C. Christy, Edmund Roberts, Benjamin Godfrey, Thomas Mather, A. M. Jenkins, W. Linn, W. S. Gilman, Charles Prentice, Richard I. Hamilton, A.H. Buckner, W. F. Thornton, and Edmund D. Taylor. These are twenty-four of the most respectable men in the State. Probably no twenty-four men could be selected in the State with whom the people are better acquainted, or in whose honor and integrity they would more readily place confidence. And I now repeat, that there is less probability that those men have been bribed and corrupted, than that any seven men, or rather any six men, that could be selected from the members of this House, might be so bribed and corrupted, even though they were headed and led on by "decided superiority" himself.

In all seriousness, I ask every reasonable man, if an issue be joined by these twenty-four commissioners, on the one part, and any other seven men, on the other part, and the whole depend upon the honor and integrity of the contending parties, to which party would the greatest degree of credit be due? Again: Another consideration is, that we have no right to make the examination. What I shall say upon this head I design exclusively for the law-loving and law-abiding part of the House. To those who claim omnipotence for the Legislature, and who in the plenitude of their assumed powers are disposed to disregard the Constitution, law, good faith, moral right, and everything else, I have not a word to say. But to the law-abiding part I say, examine the Bank charter, examine the Constitution, go examine the acts that the General Assembly of this State has passed, and you will find just as much authority given in each and every of them to compel the Bank to bring its coffers to this hall and to pour their contents upon this floor, as to compel it to submit to this examination which this resolution proposes. Why, Sir, the gentleman from Coles, the mover of this resolution, very lately denied on this floor that the Legislature had any right to repeal or otherwise meddle with its own acts, when those acts were made in the nature of contracts, and had been accepted and acted on by other parties. Now I ask if this resolution does not propose, for this House alone, to do what he, but the other day, denied the right of the whole Legislature to do? He must either abandon the position he then took, or he must now vote against his own resolution. It is no difference to me, and I presume but little to any one else, which he does.

I am by no means the special advocate of the Bank. I have long thought that it would be well for it to report its condition to the General Assembly, and that cases might occur, when it might be proper to make an examination of its affairs by a committee. Accordingly, during the last session, while a bill supplemental to the Bank charter was pending before the House, I offered an amendment to the same, in these words: "The said corporation shall, at the next session of the General Assembly, and at each subsequent General Session, during the existence of its charter, report to the same the amount of debts due from said corporation; the amount of debts due to the same; the amount of specie in its vaults, and an account of all lands then owned by the same, and the amount for which such lands have been taken; and moreover, if said corporation shall at any time neglect or refuse to submit its books, papers, and all and everything necessary for a full and fair examination of its affairs, to any person or persons appointed by the General Assembly, for the purpose of making such examination, the said corporation shall forfeit its charter."

This amendment was negatived by a vote of 34 to 15. Eleven of the 34 who voted against it are now members of this House; and though it would be out of order to call their names, I hope they will all recollect themselves, and not vote for this examination to be made without authority, inasmuch as they refused to receive the authority when it was in their power to do so.

I have said that cases might occur, when an examination might be proper; but I do not believe any such case has now occurred; and if it has, I should still be opposed to making an examination without legal authority. I am opposed to encouraging that lawless and mobocratic spirit, whether in relation to the Bank or anything else, which is already abroad in the land and is spreading with rapid and fearful impetuosity, to the ultimate overthrow of every institution, of every moral principle, in which persons and property have hitherto found security.

But supposing we had the authority, I would ask what good can result from the examination? Can we declare the Bank unconstitutional, and compel it to desist from the abuses of its power, provided we find such abuses to exist? Can we repair the injuries which it may have done to individuals? Most certainly we can do none of these things. Why then shall we spend the public money in such employment? Oh, say the examiners, we can injure the credit of the Bank, if nothing else, Please tell me, gentlemen, who will suffer most by that? You cannot injure, to any extent, the stockholders. They are men of wealth—of large capital; and consequently, beyond the power of malice. But by injuring the credit of the Bank, you will depreciate the value of its paper in the hands of the honest and unsuspecting farmer and mechanic, and that is all you can do. But suppose you could effect your whole purpose; suppose you could wipe the Bank from existence, which is the grand ultimatum of the project, what would be the consequence? why, Sir, we should spend several thousand dollars of the public treasure in the operation, annihilate the currency of the State, render valueless in the hands of our people that reward of their former labors, and finally be once more under the comfortable obligation of paying the Wiggins loan, principal and interest.

OPPOSITION TO MOB-RULE

ADDRESS BEFORE THE YOUNG MEN'S LYCEUM OF SPRINGFIELD, ILLINOIS.

January 27, 1837.
As a subject for the remarks of the evening, "The Perpetuation of our Political Institutions" is selected.
In the great journal of things happening under the sun, we, the American people, find our account running under date of the nineteenth century of the Christian era. We find ourselves in the peaceful possession of the fairest portion of the earth as regards extent of territory, fertility of soil, and salubrity of climate. We find ourselves under the government of a system of political institutions conducing more essentially to the ends of civil and religious liberty than any of which the history of former times tells us. We, when mounting the stage of existence, found ourselves the legal inheritors of these fundamental blessings. We toiled not in the acquirement or establishment of them; they are a legacy bequeathed us by a once hardy, brave, and patriotic, but now lamented and departed, race of ancestors. Theirs was the task (and nobly they performed it) to possess themselves, and through themselves us, of this goodly land, and to uprear upon its hills and its valleys a political edifice of liberty and equal rights; it is ours only to transmit these—the former unprofaned by the foot of an invader, the latter undecayed by the lapse of time and untorn by usurpation—to the latest generation that fate shall permit the world to know. This task gratitude to our fathers, justice to ourselves, duty to posterity, and love for our species in general, all imperatively require us faithfully to perform.
How then shall we perform it? At what point shall we expect the approach of danger? By what means shall we fortify against it? Shall we expect some transatlantic military giant to step the ocean and crush us at a blow? Never! All the armies of Europe, Asia, and Africa combined, with all the treasure of the earth (our own excepted) in their military chest, with a Bonaparte for a commander, could not by force take a drink from the Ohio or make a track on the Blue Ridge in a trial of a thousand years.
At what point then is the approach of danger to be expected? I answer: If it ever reach us it must spring up amongst us; it cannot come from abroad. If destruction be our lot we must ourselves be its author and finisher. As a nation of freemen we must live through all time, or die by suicide.
I hope I am over-wary; but if I am not, there is even now something of ill omen amongst us. I mean the increasing disregard for law which pervades the country—the growing disposition to substitute the wild and furious passions in lieu of the sober judgment of courts, and the worse than savage mobs for the executive ministers of justice. This disposition is awfully fearful in any community; and that it now exists in ours, though grating to our feelings to admit, it would be a violation of truth and an insult to our intelligence to deny. Accounts of outrages committed by mobs form the everyday news of the times. They have pervaded the country from New England to Louisiana; they are neither peculiar to the eternal snows of the former nor the burning suns of the latter; they are not the creature of climate, neither are they confined to the slave holding or the non-slave holding States. Alike they spring up among the pleasure-hunting masters of Southern slaves, and the order-loving citizens of the land of steady habits. Whatever then their cause may be, it is common to the whole country.
It would be tedious as well as useless to recount the horrors of all of them. Those happening in the State of Mississippi and at St. Louis are perhaps the most dangerous in example and revolting to humanity. In the Mississippi case they first commenced by hanging the regular gamblers—a set of men certainly not following for a livelihood a very useful or very honest occupation, but one which, so far from being forbidden by the laws, was actually licensed by an act of the Legislature passed but a single year before. Next, negroes suspected of conspiring to raise an insurrection were caught up and hanged in all parts of the State; then, white men supposed to be leagued with the negroes; and finally, strangers from neighboring States, going thither on business, were in many instances subjected to the same fate. Thus went on this process of hanging, from gamblers to negroes, from negroes to white citizens, and from these to strangers, till dead men were seen literally dangling from the boughs of trees upon every roadside, and in numbers almost sufficient to rival the native Spanish moss of the country as a drapery of the forest.
Turn then to that horror-striking scene at St. Louis. A single victim only was sacrificed there. This story is very short, and is perhaps the most highly tragic of anything of its length that has ever been witnessed in real life. A mulatto man by the name of McIntosh was seized in the street, dragged to the suburbs of the city, chained to a tree, and actually burned to death; and all within a single hour from the time he had been a freeman attending to his own business and at peace with the world.
Such are the effects of mob law, and such are the scenes becoming more and more frequent in this land so lately famed for love of law and order, and the stories of which have even now grown too familiar to attract anything more than an idle remark.
But you are perhaps ready to ask, "What has this to do with the perpetuation of our political institutions?" I answer, It has much to do with it. Its direct consequences are, comparatively speaking, but a small evil, and much of its danger

consists in the proneness of our minds to regard its direct as its only consequences. Abstractly considered, the hanging of the gamblers at Vicksburg was of but little consequence. They constitute a portion of population that is worse than useless in any community; and their death, if no pernicious example be set by it, is never matter of reasonable regret with any one. If they were annually swept from the stage of existence by the plague or smallpox, honest men would perhaps be much profited by the operation. Similar too is the correct reasoning in regard to the burning of the negro at St. Louis. He had forfeited his life by the perpetration of an outrageous murder upon one of the most worthy and respectable citizens of the city, and had he not died as he did, he must have died by the sentence of the law in a very short time afterwards. As to him alone, it was as well the way it was as it could otherwise have been. But the example in either case was fearful. When men take it in their heads to-day to hang gamblers or burn murderers, they should recollect that in the confusion usually attending such transactions they will be as likely to hang or burn some one who is neither a gambler nor a murderer as one who is, and that, acting upon the example they set, the mob of to-morrow may, and probably will, hang or burn some of them by the very same mistake. And not only so: the innocent, those who have ever set their faces against violations of law in every shape, alike with the guilty fall victims to the ravages of mob law; and thus it goes on, step by step, till all the walls erected for the defense of the persons and property of individuals are trodden down and disregarded. But all this, even, is not the full extent of the evil. By such examples, by instances of the perpetrators of such acts going unpunished, the lawless in spirit are encouraged to become lawless in practice; and having been used to no restraint but dread of punishment, they thus become absolutely unrestrained. Having ever regarded government as their deadliest bane, they make a jubilee of the suspension of its operations, and pray for nothing so much as its total annihilation. While, on the other hand, good men, men who love tranquillity, who desire to abide by the laws and enjoy their benefits, who would gladly spill their blood in the defense of their country, seeing their property destroyed, their families insulted, and their lives endangered, their persons injured, and seeing nothing in prospect that forebodes a change for the better, become tired of and disgusted with a government that offers them no protection, and are not much averse to a change in which they imagine they have nothing to lose. Thus, then, by the operation of this mobocratic spirit which all must admit is now abroad in the land, the strongest bulwark of any government, and particularly of those constituted like ours, may effectually be broken down and destroyed—I mean the attachment of the people. Whenever this effect shall be produced among us; whenever the vicious portion of population shall be permitted to gather in bands of hundreds and thousands, and burn churches, ravage and rob provision-stores, throw printing presses into rivers, shoot editors, and hang and burn obnoxious persons at pleasure and with impunity, depend on it, this government cannot last. By such things the feelings of the best citizens will become more or less alienated from it, and thus it will be left without friends, or with too few, and those few too weak to make their friendship effectual. At such a time, and under such circumstances, men of sufficient talent and ambition will not be wanting to seize the opportunity, strike the blow, and overturn that fair fabric which for the last half century has been the fondest hope of the lovers of freedom throughout the world.

I know the American people are much attached to their government; I know they would suffer much for its sake; I know they would endure evils long and patiently before they would ever think of exchanging it for another,—yet, notwithstanding all this, if the laws be continually despised and disregarded, if their rights to be secure in their persons and property are held by no better tenure than the caprice of a mob, the alienation of their affections from the government is the natural consequence; and to that, sooner or later, it must come.

Here, then, is one point at which danger may be expected.

The question recurs, How shall we fortify against it? The answer is simple. Let every American, every lover of liberty, every well-wisher to his posterity swear by the blood of the Revolution never to violate in the least particular the laws of the country, and never to tolerate their violation by others. As the patriots of seventy-six did to the support of the Declaration of Independence, so to the support of the Constitution and laws let every American pledge his life, his property, and his sacred honor. Let every man remember that to violate the law is to trample on the blood of his father, and to tear the charter of his own and his children's liberty. Let reverence for the laws be breathed by every American mother to the lisping babe that prattles on her lap; let it be taught in schools, in seminaries, and in colleges; let it be written in primers, spelling books, and in almanacs; let it be preached from the pulpit, proclaimed in legislative halls, and enforced in courts of justice. And, in short, let it become the political religion of the nation; and let the old and the young, the rich and the poor, the grave and the gay of all sexes and tongues and colors and conditions, sacrifice unceasingly upon its altars.

While ever a state of feeling such as this shall universally or even very generally prevail throughout the nation, vain will be every effort, and fruitless every attempt, to subvert our national freedom.

When, I so pressingly urge a strict observance of all the laws, let me not be understood as saying there are no bad laws, or that grievances may not arise for the redress of which no legal provisions have been made. I mean to say no such thing. But I do mean to say that although bad laws, if they exist, should be repealed as soon as possible, still, while they continue in force, for the sake of example they should be religiously observed. So also in unprovided cases. If such arise, let proper legal provisions be made for them with the least possible delay, but till then let them, if not too intolerable, be borne with.

There is no grievance that is a fit object of redress by mob law. In any case that may arise, as, for instance, the promulgation of abolitionism, one of two positions is necessarily true—that is, the thing is right within itself, and therefore deserves the protection of all law and all good citizens, or it is wrong, and therefore proper to be prohibited by legal enactments; and in neither case is the interposition of mob law either necessary, justifiable, or excusable.

But it may be asked, Why suppose danger to our political institutions? Have we not preserved them for more than fifty years? And why may we not for fifty times as long?

We hope there is no sufficient reason. We hope all danger may be overcome; but to conclude that no danger may ever arise would itself be extremely dangerous. There are now, and will hereafter be, many causes, dangerous in their tendency, which have not existed heretofore, and which are not too insignificant to merit attention. That our government should have been maintained in its original form, from its establishment until now, is not much to be wondered at. It had many props to support it through that period, which now are decayed and crumbled away. Through that period it was felt by all to be an undecided experiment; now it is understood to be a successful one. Then, all that sought celebrity and fame and distinction expected to find them in the success of that experiment. Their all was staked upon it; their destiny was inseparably linked with it. Their ambition aspired to display before an admiring world a practical demonstration of the truth of a proposition which had hitherto been considered at best no better than problematical—namely, the capability of a people to govern themselves. If they succeeded they were to be immortalized; their names were to be transferred to counties, and cities, and rivers, and mountains; and to be revered and sung, toasted through all time. If they failed, they were to be called knaves and fools, and fanatics for a fleeting hour; then to sink and be forgotten. They succeeded. The experiment is successful, and thousands have won their deathless names in making it so. But the game is caught; and I believe it is true that with the catching end the pleasures of the chase. This field of glory is harvested, and the crop is already appropriated. But new reapers will arise, and they too will seek a field. It is to deny what the history of the world tells us is true, to suppose that men of ambition and talents will not continue to spring up amongst us. And when they do, they will as naturally seek the gratification of their ruling passion as others have done before them. The question then is, Can that gratification be found in supporting and in maintaining an edifice that has been erected by others? Most certainly it cannot. Many great and good men, sufficiently qualified for any task they should undertake, may ever be found whose ambition would aspire to nothing beyond a seat in Congress, a Gubernatorial or a Presidential chair; but such belong not to the family of the lion, or the tribe of the eagle. What! think you these places would satisfy an Alexander, a Caesar, or a Napoleon? Never! Towering genius disdains a beaten path. It seeks regions hitherto unexplored. It sees no distinction in adding story to story upon the monuments of fame erected to the memory of others. It denies that it is glory enough to serve under any chief. It scorns to tread in the footsteps of any predecessor, however illustrious. It thirsts and burns for distinction; and if possible, it will have it, whether at the expense of emancipating slaves or enslaving freemen. Is it unreasonable, then, to expect that some man possessed of the loftiest genius, coupled with ambition sufficient to push it to its utmost stretch, will at some time spring up among us? And when such an one does it will require the people to be united with each other, attached to the government and laws, and generally intelligent, to successfully frustrate his designs.

Distinction will be his paramount object, and although he would as willingly, perhaps more so, acquire it by doing good as harm, yet, that opportunity being past, and nothing left to be done in the way of building up, he would set boldly to the task of pulling down.

Here then is a probable case, highly dangerous, and such an one as could not have well existed heretofore.

Another reason which once was, but which, to the same extent, is now no more, has done much in maintaining our institutions thus far. I mean the powerful influence which the interesting scenes of the Revolution had upon the passions of the people as distinguished from their judgment. By this influence, the jealousy, envy, and avarice incident to our nature, and so common to a state of peace, prosperity, and conscious strength, were for the time in a great measure smothered and rendered inactive, while the deep-rooted principles of hate, and the powerful motive of revenge, instead of being turned against each other, were directed exclusively against the British nation. And thus, from the force of circumstances, the basest principles of our nature were either made to lie dormant, or to become the active agents in the advancement of the noblest of causes—that of establishing and maintaining civil and religious liberty.

But this state of feeling must fade, is fading, has faded, with the circumstances that produced it.

I do not mean to say that the scenes of the Revolution are now or ever will be entirely forgotten, but that, like everything else, they must fade upon the memory of the world, and grow more and more dim by the lapse of time. In history, we hope, they will be read of, and recounted, so long as the Bible shall be read; but even granting that they will, their influence cannot be what it heretofore has been. Even then they cannot be so universally known nor so vividly felt as they were by the generation just gone to rest. At the close of that struggle, nearly every adult male had been a participator in some of its scenes. The consequence was that of those scenes, in the form of a husband, a father, a son, or a brother, a living history was to be found in every family—a history bearing the indubitable testimonies of its own authenticity, in the limbs mangled, in the scars of wounds received, in the midst of the very scenes related—a history, too, that could be read and understood alike by all, the wise and the ignorant, the learned and the unlearned. But those histories are gone. They can be read no more forever. They were a fortress of strength; but what invading foeman could never do the silent artillery of time has done—the leveling of its walls. They are gone. They were a forest of giant oaks; but the all-restless hurricane has swept over them, and left only here and there a lonely trunk, despoiled of its verdure, shorn of its foliage, unshading and unshaded, to murmur in a few more gentle breezes, and to combat with its mutilated limbs a few more ruder storms, then to sink and be no more.

They were pillars of the temple of liberty; and now that they have crumbled away that temple must fall unless we, their descendants, supply their places with other pillars, hewn from the solid quarry of sober reason. Passion has helped us, but can do so no more. It will in future be our enemy. Reason cold, calculating, unimpassioned reason—must furnish all the materials for our future support and defense. Let those materials be moulded into general intelligence, sound morality, and in particular, a reverence for the Constitution and laws; and that we improved to the last, that we remained free to the last, that we revered his name to the last, that during his long sleep we permitted no hostile foot to pass over or desecrate his resting place, shall be that which to learn the last trump shall awaken our Washington.

Upon these let the proud fabric of freedom rest, as the rock of its basis; and as truly as has been said of the only greater institution, "the gates of hell shall not prevail against it."

PROTEST IN THE ILLINOIS LEGISLATURE ON THE SUBJECT OF SLAVERY.

March 3, 1837.

The following protest was presented to the House, which was read and ordered to be spread in the journals, to wit:
"Resolutions upon the subject of domestic slavery having passed both branches of the General Assembly at its present session, the undersigned hereby protest against the passage of the same.
"They believe that the institution of slavery is founded on both injustice and bad policy, but that the promulgation of abolition doctrines tends rather to increase than abate its evils.
"They believe that the Congress of the United States has no power under the Constitution to interfere with the institution of slavery in the different States.
"They believe that the Congress of the United States has the power, under the Constitution, to abolish slavery in the District of Columbia, but that the power ought not to be exercised, unless at the request of the people of the District.
"The difference between these opinions and those contained in the said resolutions is their reason for entering this protest.
"DAN STONE, "A. LINCOLN,
"Representatives from the County of Sangamon."

TO MISS MARY OWENS.

SPRINGFIELD, May 7, 1837.

MISS MARY S. OWENS.
FRIEND MARY:—I have commenced two letters to send you before this, both of which displeased me before I got half done, and so I tore them up. The first I thought was not serious enough, and the second was on the other extreme. I shall send this, turn out as it may.
This thing of living in Springfield is rather a dull business, after all; at least it is so to me. I am quite as lonesome here as I ever was anywhere in my life. I have been spoken to by but one woman since I have been here, and should not have been by her if she could have avoided it. I've never been to church yet, and probably shall not be soon. I stay away because I am conscious I should not know how to behave myself.
I am often thinking of what we said about your coming to live at Springfield. I am afraid you would not be satisfied. There is a great deal of flourishing about in carriages here, which it would be your doom to see without sharing it. You would have to be poor, without the means of hiding your poverty. Do you believe you could bear that patiently? Whatever woman may cast her lot with mine, should any ever do so, it is my intention to do all in my power to make her happy and contented; and there is nothing I can imagine that would make me more unhappy than to fail in the effort. I know I should be much happier with you than the way I am, provided I saw no signs of discontent in you. What you have said to me may have been in the way of jest, or I may have misunderstood you. If so, then let it be forgotten; if otherwise, I much wish you would think seriously before you decide. What I have said I will most positively abide by, provided you wish it. My opinion is that you had better not do it. You have not been accustomed to hardship, and it may be more severe than you now imagine. I know you are capable of thinking correctly on any subject, and if you deliberate maturely upon this subject before you decide, then I am willing to abide your decision.
You must write me a good long letter after you get this. You have nothing else to do, and though it might not seem interesting to you after you had written it, it would be a good deal of company to me in this "busy wilderness." Tell your sister I don't want to hear any more about selling out and moving. That gives me the "hypo" whenever I think of it.
Yours, etc., LINCOLN.

TO JOHN BENNETT.

SPRINGFIELD, ILL., Aug. 5, 1837. JOHN BENNETT, ESQ.

DEAR SIR:-Mr. Edwards tells me you wish to know whether the act to which your own incorporation provision was attached passed into a law. It did. You can organize under the general incorporation law as soon as you choose.
I also tacked a provision onto a fellow's bill to authorize the relocation of the road from Salem down to your town, but I am not certain whether or not the bill passed, neither do I suppose I can ascertain before the law will be published, if it is a law. Bowling Greene, Bennette Abe? and yourself are appointed to make the change. No news. No excitement except a little about the election of Monday next.
I suppose, of course, our friend Dr. Heney stands no chance in your diggings.
Your friend and humble servant, A. LINCOLN.

TO MARY OWENS.

SPRINGFIELD, Aug. 16, 1837

FRIEND MARY: You will no doubt think it rather strange that I should write you a letter on the same day on which we parted, and I can only account for it by supposing that seeing you lately makes me think of you more than usual; while at our late meeting we had but few expressions of thoughts. You must know that I cannot see you, or think of you, with entire indifference; and yet it may be that you are mistaken in regard to what my real feelings toward you are. If I knew you were not, I should not have troubled you with this letter. Perhaps any other man would know enough without information; but I consider it my peculiar right to plead ignorance, and your bounden duty to allow the plea. I want in all cases to do right; and most particularly so in all cases with women.
I want, at this particular time, more than any thing else to do right with you; and if I knew it would be doing right, as I rather suspect it would, to let you alone I would do it. And, for the purpose of making the matter as plain as possible, I now say that you can drop the subject, dismiss your thoughts (if you ever had any) from me for ever and leave this letter unanswered without calling forth one accusing murmur from me. And I will even go further and say that, if it will add anything to your comfort or peace of mind to do so, it is my sincere wish that you should. Do not understand by this that I wish to cut your acquaintance. I mean no such thing. What I do wish is that our further acquaintance shall depend upon yourself. If such further acquaintance would contribute nothing to your happiness, I am sure it would not to mine. If you feel yourself in any degree bound to me, I am now willing to release you, provided you wish it; while on the other hand I am willing and even anxious to bind you faster if I can be convinced that it will, in any considerable degree, add to your happiness. This, indeed, is the whole question with me. Nothing would make me more miserable than to believe you miserable, nothing more happy than to know you were so.
In what I have now said, I think I cannot be misunderstood; and to make myself understood is the only object of this letter.
If it suits you best not to answer this, farewell. A long life and a merry one attend you. But, if you conclude to write back, speak as plainly as I do. There can neither be harm nor danger in saying to me anything you think, just in the manner you think it. My respects to your sister.
Your friend, LINCOLN.

LEGAL SUIT OF WIDOW v.s. Gen. ADAMS

TO THE PEOPLE.

"SANGAMON JOURNAL," SPRINGFIELD, ILL., Aug. 19, 1837.
In accordance with our determination, as expressed last week, we present to the reader the articles which were published in hand-bill form, in reference to the case of the heirs of Joseph Anderson vs. James Adams. These articles can now be read uninfluenced by personal or party feeling, and with the sole motive of learning the truth. When that is done, the reader can pass his own judgment on the matters at issue.
We only regret in this case, that the publications were not made some weeks before the election. Such a course might have prevented the expressions of regret, which have often been heard since, from different individuals, on account of the disposition they made of their votes.
To the Public:
It is well known to most of you, that there is existing at this time considerable excitement in regard to Gen. Adams's titles to certain tracts of land, and the manner in which he acquired them. As I understand, the Gen. charges that the whole has been gotten up by a knot of lawyers to injure his election; and as I am one of the knot to which he refers,

and as I happen to be in possession of facts connected with the matter, I will, in as brief a manner as possible, make a statement of them, together with the means by which I arrived at the knowledge of them.

Sometime in May or June last, a widow woman, by the name of Anderson, and her son, who resides in Fulton county, came to Springfield, for the purpose as they said of selling a ten acre lot of ground lying near town, which they claimed as the property of the deceased husband and father.

When they reached town they found the land was claimed by Gen. Adams. John T. Stuart and myself were employed to look into the matter, and if it was thought we could do so with any prospect of success, to commence a suit for the land. I went immediately to the recorder's office to examine Adams's title, and found that the land had been entered by one Dixon, deeded by Dixon to Thomas, by Thomas to one Miller, and by Miller to Gen. Adams. The oldest of these three deeds was about ten or eleven years old, and the latest more than five, all recorded at the same time, and that within less than one year. This I thought a suspicious circumstance, and I was thereby induced to examine the deeds very closely, with a view to the discovery of some defect by which to overturn the title, being almost convinced then it was founded in fraud. I discovered that in the deed from Thomas to Miller, although Miller's name stood in a sort of marginal note on the record book, it was nowhere in the deed itself. I told the fact to Talbott, the recorder, and proposed to him that he should go to Gen. Adams's and get the original deed, and compare it with the record, and thereby ascertain whether the defect was in the original or there was merely an error in the recording. As Talbott afterwards told me, he went to the General's, but not finding him at home, got the deed from his son, which, when compared with the record, proved what we had discovered was merely an error of the recorder. After Mr. Talbott corrected the record, he brought the original to our office, as I then thought and think yet, to show us that it was right. When he came into the room he handed the deed to me, remarking that the fault was all his own. On opening it, another paper fell out of it, which on examination proved to be an assignment of a judgment in the Circuit Court of Sangamon County from Joseph Anderson, the late husband of the widow above named, to James Adams, the judgment being in favor of said Anderson against one Joseph Miller. Knowing that this judgment had some connection with the land affair, I immediately took a copy of it, which is word for word, letter for letter and cross for cross as follows:

Joseph Anderson, vs. Joseph Miller.

Judgment in Sangamon Circuit Court against Joseph Miller obtained on a note originally 25 dolls and interest thereon accrued. I assign all my right, title and interest to James Adams which is in consideration of a debt I owe said Adams.
his JOSEPH x ANDERSON. mark.

As the copy shows, it bore date May 10, 1827; although the judgment assigned by it was not obtained until the October afterwards, as may be seen by any one on the records of the Circuit Court. Two other strange circumstances attended it which cannot be represented by a copy. One of them was, that the date "1827" had first been made "1837" and, without the figure "3," being fully obliterated, the figure "2" had afterwards been made on top of it; the other was that, although the date was ten years old, the writing on it, from the freshness of its appearance, was thought by many, and I believe by all who saw it, not to be more than a week old. The paper on which it was written had a very old appearance; and there were some old figures on the back of it which made the freshness of the writing on the face of it much more striking than I suppose it otherwise might have been. The reader's curiosity is no doubt excited to know what connection this assignment had with the land in question. The story is this: Dixon sold and deeded the land to Thomas; Thomas sold it to Anderson; but before he gave a deed, Anderson sold it to Miller, and took Miller's note for the purchase money. When this note became due, Anderson sued Miller on it, and Miller procured an injunction from the Court of Chancery to stay the collection of the money until he should get a deed for the land. Gen. Adams was employed as an attorney by Anderson in this chancery suit, and at the October term, 1827, the injunction was dissolved, and a judgment given in favor of Anderson against Miller; and it was provided that Thomas was to execute a deed for the land in favor of Miller and deliver it to Gen. Adams, to be held up by him till Miller paid the judgment, and then to deliver it to him. Miller left the county without paying the judgment. Anderson moved to Fulton county, where he has since died When the widow came to Springfield last May or June, as before mentioned, and found the land deeded to Gen. Adams by Miller, she was naturally led to inquire why the money due upon the judgment had not been sent to them, inasmuch as he, Gen. Adams, had no authority to deliver Thomas's deed to Miller until the money was paid. Then it was the General told her, or perhaps her son, who came with her, that Anderson, in his lifetime, had assigned the judgment to him, Gen. Adams. I am now told that the General is exhibiting an assignment of the same judgment bearing date "1828" and in other respects differing from the one described; and that he is asserting that no such assignment as the one copied by me ever existed; or if there did, it was forged between Talbott and the lawyers, and slipped into his papers for the purpose of injuring him. Now, I can only say that I know precisely such a one did exist, and that Ben. Talbott, Wm. Butler, C.R. Matheny, John T. Stuart, Judge Logan, Robert Irwin, P. C. Canedy and S. M. Tinsley, all saw and examined it, and that at least one half of them will swear that IT WAS IN GENERAL ADAMS'S HANDWRITING!! And further, I know that Talbott will swear that he got it out of the General's possession, and returned it into his possession again. The assignment which the General is now exhibiting purports to have been by Anderson in writing. The one I copied was signed with a cross.

I am told that Gen. Neale says that he will swear that he heard Gen. Adams tell young Anderson that the assignment made by his father was signed with a cross.

The above are 'facts,' as stated. I leave them without comment. I have given the names of persons who have knowledge of these facts, in order that any one who chooses may call on them and ascertain how far they will corroborate my statements. I have only made these statements because I am known by many to be one of the individuals against whom the charge of forging the assignment and slipping it into the General's papers has been made, and because our silence might be construed into a confession of its truth. I shall not subscribe my name; but I hereby authorize the editor of the Journal to give it up to any one that may call for it.

LINCOLN AND TALBOTT IN REPLY TO GEN. ADAMS.

"SANGAMON JOURNAL," SPRINGFIELD, ILL., Oct. 28, 1837.

In the Republican of this morning a publication of Gen. Adams's appears, in which my name is used quite unreservedly. For this I thank the General. I thank him because it gives me an opportunity, without appearing obtrusive, of explaining a part of a former publication of mine, which appears to me to have been misunderstood by many.
In the former publication alluded to, I stated, in substance, that Mr. Talbott got a deed from a son of Gen. Adams's for the purpose of correcting a mistake that had occurred on the record of the said deed in the recorder's office; that he corrected the record, and brought the deed and handed it to me, and that on opening the deed, another paper, being the assignment of a judgment, fell out of it. This statement Gen. Adams and the editor of the Republican have seized upon as a most palpable evidence of fabrication and falsehood. They set themselves gravely about proving that the assignment could not have been in the deed when Talbott got it from young Adams, as he, Talbott, would have seen it when he opened the deed to correct the record. Now, the truth is, Talbott did see the assignment when he opened the deed, or at least he told me he did on the same day; and I only omitted to say so, in my former publication, because it was a matter of such palpable and necessary inference. I had stated that Talbott had corrected the record by the deed; and of course he must have opened it; and, just as the General and his friends argue, must have seen the assignment. I omitted to state the fact of Talbott's seeing the assignment, because its existence was so necessarily connected with other facts which I did state, that I thought the greatest dunce could not but understand it. Did I say Talbott had not seen it? Did I say anything that was inconsistent with his having seen it before? Most certainly I did neither; and if I did not, what becomes of the argument? These logical gentlemen can sustain their argument only by assuming that I did say negatively everything that I did not say affirmatively; and upon the same assumption, we may expect to find the General, if a little harder pressed for argument, saying that I said Talbott came to our office with his head downward, not that I actually said so, but because I omitted to say he came feet downward.
In his publication to-day, the General produces the affidavit of Reuben Radford, in which it is said that Talbott told Radford that he did not find the assignment in the deed, in the recording of which the error was committed, but that he found it wrapped in another paper in the recorder's office, upon which statement the Genl. comments as follows, to wit: "If it be true as stated by Talbott to Radford, that he found the assignment wrapped up in another paper at his office, that contradicts the statement of Lincoln that it fell out of the deed."
Is common sense to be abused with such sophistry? Did I say what Talbott found it in? If Talbott did find it in another paper at his office, is that any reason why he could not have folded it in a deed and brought it to my office? Can any one be so far duped as to be made believe that what may have happened at Talbot's office at one time is inconsistent with what happened at my office at another time?
Now Talbott's statement of the case as he makes it to me is this, that he got a bunch of deeds from young Adams, and that he knows he found the assignment in the bunch, but he is not certain which particular deed it was in, nor is he certain whether it was folded in the same deed out of which it was taken, or another one, when it was brought to my office. Is this a mysterious story? Is there anything suspicious about it?
"But it is useless to dwell longer on this point. Any man who is not wilfully blind can see at a flash, that there is no discrepancy, and Lincoln has shown that they are not only inconsistent with truth, but each other"—I can only say, that I have shown that he has done no such thing; and if the reader is disposed to require any other evidence than the General's assertion, he will be of my opinion.
Excepting the General's most flimsy attempt at mystification, in regard to a discrepance between Talbott and myself, he has not denied a single statement that I made in my hand-bill. Every material statement that I made has been sworn to by men who, in former times, were thought as respectable as General Adams. I stated that an assignment of a judgment, a copy of which I gave, had existed—Benj. Talbott, C. R. Matheny, Wm. Butler, and Judge Logan swore to its existence. I stated that it was said to be in Gen. Adams's handwriting—the same men swore it was in his handwriting. I stated that Talbott would swear that he got it out of Gen. Adams's possession—Talbott came forward and did swear it.
Bidding adieu to the former publication, I now propose to examine the General's last gigantic production. I now propose to point out some discrepancies in the General's address; and such, too, as he shall not be able to escape from. Speaking of the famous assignment, the General says: "This last charge, which was their last resort, their dying effort to render my character infamous among my fellow citizens, was manufactured at a certain lawyer's office in the town, printed at the office of the Sangamon Journal, and found its way into the world some time between two days just before the last election." Now turn to Mr. Keys' affidavit, in which you will find the following, viz.: "I certify that some time in May or the early part of June, 1837, I saw at Williams's corner a paper purporting to be an assignment from Joseph Anderson to James Adams, which assignment was signed by a mark to Anderson's name," etc. Now mark, if Keys saw the assignment on the last of May or first of June, Gen. Adams tells a falsehood when he says it was manufactured just

before the election, which was on the 7th of August; and if it was manufactured just before the election, Keys tells a falsehood when he says he saw it on the last of May or first of June. Either Keys or the General is irretrievably in for it; and in the General's very condescending language, I say "Let them settle it between them."

Now again, let the reader, bearing in mind that General Adams has unequivocally said, in one part of his address, that the charge in relation to the assignment was manufactured just before the election, turn to the affidavit of Peter S. Weber, where the following will be found viz.: "I, Peter S. Weber, do certify that from the best of my recollection, on the day or day after Gen. Adams started for the Illinois Rapids, in May last, that I was at the house of Gen. Adams, sitting in the kitchen, situated on the back part of the house, it being in the afternoon, and that Benjamin Talbott came around the house, back into the kitchen, and appeared wild and confused, and that he laid a package of papers on the kitchen table and requested that they should be handed to Lucian. He made no apology for coming to the kitchen, nor for not handing them to Lucian himself, but showed the token of being frightened and confused both in demeanor and speech and for what cause I could not apprehend."

Commenting on Weber's affidavit, Gen. Adams asks, "Why this fright and confusion?" I reply that this is a question for the General himself. Weber says that it was in May, and if so, it is most clear that Talbott was not frightened on account of the assignment, unless the General lies when he says the assignment charge was manufactured just before the election. Is it not a strong evidence, that the General is not traveling with the pole-star of truth in his front, to see him in one part of his address roundly asserting that the assignment was manufactured just before the election, and then, forgetting that position, procuring Weber's most foolish affidavit, to prove that Talbott had been engaged in manufacturing it two months before?

In another part of his address, Gen. Adams says: "That I hold an assignment of said judgment, dated the 20th of May, 1828, and signed by said Anderson, I have never pretended to deny or conceal, but stated that fact in one of my circulars previous to the election, and also in answer to a bill in chancery." Now I pronounce this statement unqualifiedly false, and shall not rely on the word or oath of any man to sustain me in what I say; but will let the whole be decided by reference to the circular and answer in chancery of which the General speaks. In his circular he did speak of an assignment; but he did not say it bore date 20th of May, 1828; nor did he say it bore any date. In his answer in chancery, he did say that he had an assignment; but he did not say that it bore date the 20th May, 1828; but so far from it, he said on oath (for he swore to the answer) that as well as recollected, he obtained it in 1827. If any one doubts, let him examine the circular and answer for himself. They are both accessible.

It will readily be observed that the principal part of Adams's defense rests upon the argument that if he had been base enough to forge an assignment he would not have been fool enough to forge one that would not cover the case. This argument he used in his circular before the election. The Republican has used it at least once, since then; and Adams uses it again in his publication of to-day. Now I pledge myself to show that he is just such a fool that he and his friends have contended it was impossible for him to be. Recollect—he says he has a genuine assignment; and that he got Joseph Klein's affidavit, stating that he had seen it, and that he believed the signature to have been executed by the same hand that signed Anderson's name to the answer in chancery. Luckily Klein took a copy of this genuine assignment, which I have been permitted to see; and hence I know it does not cover the case. In the first place it is headed "Joseph Anderson vs. Joseph Miller," and heads off "Judgment in Sangamon Circuit Court." Now, mark, there never was a case in Sangamon Circuit Court entitled Joseph Anderson vs. Joseph Miller. The case mentioned in my former publication, and the only one between these parties that ever existed in the Circuit Court, was entitled Joseph Miller vs. Joseph Anderson, Miller being the plaintiff. What then becomes of all their sophistry about Adams not being fool enough to forge an assignment that would not cover the case? It is certain that the present one does not cover the case; and if he got it honestly, it is still clear that he was fool enough to pay for an assignment that does not cover the case.

The General asks for the proof of disinterested witnesses. Whom does he consider disinterested? None can be more so than those who have already testified against him. No one of them had the least interest on earth, so far as I can learn, to injure him. True, he says they had conspired against him; but if the testimony of an angel from Heaven were introduced against him, he would make the same charge of conspiracy. And now I put the question to every reflecting man, Do you believe that Benjamin Talbott, Chas. R. Matheny, William Butler and Stephen T. Logan, all sustaining high and spotless characters, and justly proud of them, would deliberately perjure themselves, without any motive whatever, except to injure a man's election; and that, too, a man who had been a candidate, time out of mind, and yet who had never been elected to any office?

Adams's assurance, in demanding disinterested testimony, is surpassing. He brings in the affidavit of his own son, and even of Peter S. Weber, with whom I am not acquainted, but who, I suppose, is some black or mulatto boy, from his being kept in the kitchen, to prove his points; but when such a man as Talbott, a man who, but two years ago, ran against Gen. Adams for the office of Recorder and beat him more than four votes to one, is introduced against him, he asks the community, with all the consequence of a lord, to reject his testimony.

I might easily write a volume, pointing out inconsistencies between the statements in Adams's last address with one another, and with other known facts; but I am aware the reader must already be tired with the length of this article. His opening statements, that he was first accused of being a Tory, and that he refuted that; that then the Sampson's ghost story was got up, and he refuted that; that as a last resort, a dying effort, the assignment charge was got up is all as false as hell, as all this community must know. Sampson's ghost first made its appearance in print, and that, too, after Keys swears he saw the assignment, as any one may see by reference to the files of papers; and Gen. Adams himself, in reply to the Sampson's ghost story, was the first man that raised the cry of toryism, and it was only by way of set-off, and never in seriousness, that it was bandied back at him. His effort is to make the impression that his enemies first made

the charge of toryism and he drove them from that, then Sampson's ghost, he drove them from that, then finally the assignment charge was manufactured just before election. Now, the only general reply he ever made to the Sampson's ghost and tory charges he made at one and the same time, and not in succession as he states; and the date of that reply will show, that it was made at least a month after the date on which Keys swears he saw the Anderson assignment. But enough. In conclusion I will only say that I have a character to defend as well as Gen. Adams, but I disdain to whine about it as he does. It is true I have no children nor kitchen boys; and if I had, I should scorn to lug them in to make affidavits for me.
A. LINCOLN, September 6, 1837.

Gen. ADAMS CONTROVERSY—CONTINUED

TO THE PUBLIC.

"SANGAMON JOURNAL," Springfield, Ill, Oct.28, 1837.
Such is the turn which things have taken lately, that when Gen. Adams writes a book, I am expected to write a commentary on it. In the Republican of this morning he has presented the world with a new work of six columns in length; in consequence of which I must beg the room of one column in the Journal. It is obvious that a minute reply cannot be made in one column to everything that can be said in six; and, consequently, I hope that expectation will be answered if I reply to such parts of the General's publication as are worth replying to.
It may not be improper to remind the reader that in his publication of Sept. 6th General Adams said that the assignment charge was manufactured just before the election; and that in reply I proved that statement to be false by Keys, his own witness. Now, without attempting to explain, he furnishes me with another witness (Tinsley) by which the same thing is proved, to wit, that the assignment was not manufactured just before the election; but that it was some weeks before. Let it be borne in mind that Adams made this statement—has himself furnished two witnesses to prove its falsehood, and does not attempt to deny or explain it. Before going farther, let a pin be stuck here, labeled "One lie proved and confessed." On the 6th of September he said he had before stated in the hand-bill that he held an assignment dated May 20th, 1828, which in reply I pronounced to be false, and referred to the hand-bill for the truth of what I said. This week he forgets to make any explanation of this. Let another pin be stuck here, labelled as before. I mention these things because, if, when I convict him in one falsehood, he is permitted to shift his ground and pass it by in silence, there can be no end to this controversy.
The first thing that attracts my attention in the General's present production is the information he is pleased to give to "those who are made to suffer at his (my) hands."
Under present circumstances, this cannot apply to me, for I am not a widow nor an orphan: nor have I a wife or children who might by possibility become such. Such, however, I have no doubt, have been, and will again be made to suffer at his hands! Hands! Yes, they are the mischievous agents. The next thing I shall notice is his favorite expression, "not of lawyers, doctors and others," which he is so fond of applying to all who dare expose his rascality. Now, let it be remembered that when he first came to this country he attempted to impose himself upon the community as a lawyer, and actually carried the attempt so far as to induce a man who was under a charge of murder to entrust the defence of his life in his hands, and finally took his money and got him hanged. Is this the man that is to raise a breeze in his favor by abusing lawyers? If he is not himself a lawyer, it is for the lack of sense, and not of inclination. If he is not a lawyer, he is a liar, for he proclaimed himself a lawyer, and got a man hanged by depending on him.
Passing over such parts of the article as have neither fact nor argument in them, I come to the question asked by Adams whether any person ever saw the assignment in his possession. This is an insult to common sense. Talbott has sworn once and repeated time and again, that he got it out of Adams's possession and returned it into the same possession. Still, as though he was addressing fools, he has assurance to ask if any person ever saw it in his possession.
Next I quote a sentence, "Now my son Lucian swears that when Talbott called for the deed, that he, Talbott, opened it and pointed out the error." True. His son Lucian did swear as he says; and in doing so, he swore what I will prove by his own affidavit to be a falsehood. Turn to Lucian's affidavit, and you will there see that Talbott called for the deed by which to correct an error on the record. Thus it appears that the error in question was on the record, and not in the deed. How then could Talbott open the deed and point out the error? Where a thing is not, it cannot be pointed out. The error was not in the deed, and of course could not be pointed out there. This does not merely prove that the error could not be pointed out, as Lucian swore it was; but it proves, too, that the deed was not opened in his presence with a special view to the error, for if it had been, he could not have failed to see that there was no error in it. It is easy enough to see why Lucian swore this. His object was to prove that the assignment was not in the deed when Talbott got it: but it was discovered he could not swear this safely, without first swearing the deed was opened—and if he swore it was opened, he must show a motive for opening it, and the conclusion with him and his father was that the pointing out the error would appear the most plausible.
For the purpose of showing that the assignment was not in the bundle when Talbott got it, is the story introduced into Lucian's affidavit that the deeds were counted. It is a remarkable fact, and one that should stand as a warning to all liars and fabricators, that in this short affidavit of Lucian's he only attempted to depart from the truth, so far as I have the

means of knowing, in two points, to wit, in the opening the deed and pointing out the error and the counting of the deeds,—and in both of these he caught himself. About the counting, he caught himself thus—after saying the bundle contained five deeds and a lease, he proceeds, "and I saw no other papers than the said deed and lease." First he has six papers, and then he saw none but two; for "my son Lucian's" benefit, let a pin be stuck here.

Adams again adduces the argument, that he could not have forged the assignment, for the reason that he could have had no motive for it. With those that know the facts there is no absence of motive. Admitting the paper which he has filed in the suit to be genuine, it is clear that it cannot answer the purpose for which he designs it. Hence his motive for making one that he supposed would answer is obvious. His making the date too old is also easily enough accounted for. The records were not in his hands, and then, there being some considerable talk upon this particular subject, he knew he could not examine the records to ascertain the precise dates without subjecting himself to suspicion; and hence he concluded to try it by guess, and, as it turned out, missed it a little. About Miller's deposition I have a word to say. In the first place, Miller's answer to the first question shows upon its face that he had been tampered with, and the answer dictated to him. He was asked if he knew Joel Wright and James Adams; and above three-fourths of his answer consists of what he knew about Joseph Anderson, a man about whom nothing had been asked, nor a word said in the question—a fact that can only be accounted for upon the supposition that Adams had secretly told him what he wished him to swear to.

Another of Miller's answers I will prove both by common sense and the Court of Record is untrue. To one question he answers, "Anderson brought a suit against me before James Adams, then an acting justice of the peace in Sangamon County, before whom he obtained a judgment.

"Q.—Did you remove the same by injunction to the Sangamon Circuit Court? Ans.—I did remove it."

Now mark—it is said he removed it by injunction. The word "injunction" in common language imports a command that some person or thing shall not move or be removed; in law it has the same meaning. An injunction issuing out of chancery to a justice of the peace is a command to him to stop all proceedings in a named case until further orders. It is not an order to remove but to stop or stay something that is already moving. Besides this, the records of the Sangamon Circuit Court show that the judgment of which Miller swore was never removed into said Court by injunction or otherwise.

I have now to take notice of a part of Adams's address which in the order of time should have been noticed before. It is in these words: "I have now shown, in the opinion of two competent judges, that the handwriting of the forged assignment differed from mine, and by one of them that it could not be mistaken for mine." That is false. Tinsley no doubt is the judge referred to; and by reference to his certificate it will be seen that he did not say the handwriting of the assignment could not be mistaken for Adams's—nor did he use any other expression substantially, or anything near substantially, the same. But if Tinsley had said the handwriting could not be mistaken for Adams's, it would have been equally unfortunate for Adams: for it then would have contradicted Keys, who says, "I looked at the writing and judged it the said Adams's or a good imitation."

Adams speaks with much apparent confidence of his success on attending lawsuits, and the ultimate maintenance of his title to the land in question. Without wishing to disturb the pleasure of his dream, I would say to him that it is not impossible that he may yet be taught to sing a different song in relation to the matter.

At the end of Miller's deposition, Adams asks, "Will Mr. Lincoln now say that he is almost convinced my title to this ten acre tract of land is founded in fraud?" I answer, I will not. I will now change the phraseology so as to make it run—I am quite convinced, &c. I cannot pass in silence Adams's assertion that he has proved that the forged assignment was not in the deed when it came from his house by Talbott, the recorder. In this, although Talbott has sworn that the assignment was in the bundle of deeds when it came from his house, Adams has the unaccountable assurance to say that he has proved the contrary by Talbott. Let him or his friends attempt to show wherein he proved any such thing by Talbott.

In his publication of the 6th of September he hinted to Talbott, that he might be mistaken. In his present, speaking of Talbott and me he says "They may have been imposed upon." Can any man of the least penetration fail to see the object of this? After he has stormed and raged till his hopes and imagines he has got us a little scared he wishes to softly whisper in our ears, "If you'll quit I will." If he could get us to say that some unknown, undefined being had slipped the assignment into our hands without our knowledge, not a doubt remains but that he would immediately discover that we were the purest men on earth. This is the ground he evidently wishes us to understand he is willing to compromise upon. But we ask no such charity at his hands. We are neither mistaken nor imposed upon. We have made the statements we have because we know them to be true and we choose to live or die by them.

Esq. Carter, who is Adams's friend, personal and political, will recollect, that, on the 5th of this month, he (Adams), with a great affectation of modesty, declared that he would never introduce his own child as a witness. Notwithstanding this affectation of modesty, he has in his present publication introduced his child as witness; and as if to show with how much contempt he could treat his own declaration, he has had this same Esq. Carter to administer the oath to him. And so important a witness does he consider him, and so entirely does the whole of his entire present production depend upon the testimony of his child, that in it he has mentioned "my son," "my son Lucian," "Lucian, my son," and the like expressions no less than fifteen different times. Let it be remembered here, that I have shown the affidavit of "my darling son Lucian" to be false by the evidence apparent on its own face; and I now ask if that affidavit be taken away what foundation will the fabric have left to stand upon?

General Adams's publications and out-door maneuvering, taken in connection with the editorial articles of the Republican, are not more foolish and contradictory than they are ludicrous and amusing. One week the Republican

43

notifies the public that Gen. Adams is preparing an instrument that will tear, rend, split, rive, blow up, confound, overwhelm, annihilate, extinguish, exterminate, burst asunder, and grind to powder all its slanderers, and particularly Talbott and Lincoln—all of which is to be done in due time.

Then for two or three weeks all is calm—not a word said. Again the Republican comes forth with a mere passing remark that "public" opinion has decided in favor of Gen. Adams, and intimates that he will give himself no more trouble about the matter. In the meantime Adams himself is prowling about and, as Burns says of the devil, "For prey, and holes and corners tryin'," and in one instance goes so far as to take an old acquaintance of mine several steps from a crowd and, apparently weighed down with the importance of his business, gravely and solemnly asks him if "he ever heard Lincoln say he was a deist."

Anon the Republican comes again. "We invite the attention of the public to General Adams's communication," &c. "The victory is a great one, the triumph is overwhelming." I really believe the editor of the Illinois Republican is fool enough to think General Adams leads off—"Authors most egregiously mistaken &c. Most woefully shall their presumption be punished," &c. (Lord have mercy on us.) "The hour is yet to come, yea, nigh at hand—(how long first do you reckon?)—when the Journal and its junto shall say, I have appeared too early." "Their infamy shall be laid bare to the public gaze." Suddenly the General appears to relent at the severity with which he is treating us and he exclaims: "The condemnation of my enemies is the inevitable result of my own defense." For your health's sake, dear Gen., do not permit your tenderness of heart to afflict you so much on our account. For some reason (perhaps because we are killed so quickly) we shall never be sensible of our suffering.

Farewell, General. I will see you again at court if not before—when and where we will settle the question whether you or the widow shall have the land.

A. LINCOLN. October 18, 1837.

1838

TO Mrs. O. H. BROWNING—A FARCE

SPRINGFIELD, April 1, 1838.

DEAR MADAM:—Without apologizing for being egotistical, I shall make the history of so much of my life as has elapsed since I saw you the subject of this letter. And, by the way, I now discover that, in order to give a full and intelligible account of the things I have done and suffered since I saw you, I shall necessarily have to relate some that happened before.

It was, then, in the autumn of 1836 that a married lady of my acquaintance, and who was a great friend of mine, being about to pay a visit to her father and other relatives residing in Kentucky, proposed to me that on her return she would bring a sister of hers with her on condition that I would engage to become her brother-in-law with all convenient despatch. I, of course, accepted the proposal, for you know I could not have done otherwise had I really been averse to it; but privately, between you and me, I was most confoundedly well pleased with the project. I had seen the said sister some three years before, thought her intelligent and agreeable, and saw no good objection to plodding life through hand in hand with her. Time passed on; the lady took her journey and in due time returned, sister in company, sure enough. This astonished me a little, for it appeared to me that her coming so readily showed that she was a trifle too willing, but on reflection it occurred to me that she might have been prevailed on by her married sister to come without anything concerning me ever having been mentioned to her, and so I concluded that if no other objection presented itself, I would consent to waive this. All this occurred to me on hearing of her arrival in the neighborhood—for, be it remembered, I had not yet seen her, except about three years previous, as above mentioned. In a few days we had an interview, and, although I had seen her before, she did not look as my imagination had pictured her. I knew she was over-size, but she now appeared a fair match for Falstaff. I knew she was called an "old maid," and I felt no doubt of the truth of at least half of the appellation, but now, when I beheld her, I could not for my life avoid thinking of my mother; and this, not from withered features,—for her skin was too full of fat to permit of its contracting into wrinkles,—but from her want of teeth, weather-beaten appearance in general, and from a kind of notion that ran in my head that nothing could have commenced at the size of infancy and reached her present bulk in less than thirty-five or forty years; and in short, I was not at all pleased with her. But what could I do? I had told her sister that I would take her for better or for worse, and I made a point of honor and conscience in all things to stick to my word especially if others had been induced to act on it which in this case I had no doubt they had, for I was now fairly convinced that no other man on earth would have her, and hence the conclusion that they were bent on holding me to my bargain.

"Well," thought I, "I have said it, and, be the consequences what they may, it shall not be my fault if I fail to do it." At once I determined to consider her my wife; and, this done, all my powers of discovery were put to work in search of perfections in her which might be fairly set off against her defects. I tried to imagine her handsome, which, but for her unfortunate corpulency, was actually true. Exclusive of this no woman that I have ever seen has a finer face. I also tried to convince myself that the mind was much more to be valued than the person; and in this she was not inferior, as I could discover, to any with whom I had been acquainted.

Shortly after this, without coming to any positive understanding with her, I set out for Vandalia, when and where you first saw me. During my stay there I had letters from her which did not change my opinion of either her intellect or intention, but on the contrary confirmed it in both.

All this while, although I was fixed, "firm as the surge-repelling rock," in my resolution, I found I was continually repenting the rashness which had led me to make it. Through life, I have been in no bondage, either real or imaginary, from the thraldom of which I so much desired to be free. After my return home, I saw nothing to change my opinions of her in any particular. She was the same, and so was I. I now spent my time in planning how I might get along through life after my contemplated change of circumstances should have taken place, and how I might procrastinate the evil day for a time, which I really dreaded as much, perhaps more, than an Irishman does the halter.

After all my suffering upon this deeply interesting subject, here I am, wholly, unexpectedly, completely, out of the "scrape"; and now I want to know if you can guess how I got out of it——out, clear, in every sense of the term; no violation of word, honor, or conscience. I don't believe you can guess, and so I might as well tell you at once. As the lawyer says, it was done in the manner following, to wit: After I had delayed the matter as long as I thought I could in honor do (which, by the way, had brought me round into the last fall), I concluded I might as well bring it to a consummation without further delay; and so I mustered my resolution, and made the proposal to her direct; but, shocking to relate, she answered, No. At first I supposed she did it through an affectation of modesty, which I thought but ill became her under the peculiar circumstances of her case; but on my renewal of the charge, I found she repelled it with greater firmness than before. I tried it again and again but with the same success, or rather with the same want of success.

I finally was forced to give it up; at which I very unexpectedly found myself mortified almost beyond endurance. I was mortified, it seemed to me, in a hundred different ways. My vanity was deeply wounded by the reflection that I had been too stupid to discover her intentions, and at the same time never doubting that I understood them perfectly, and also that she, whom I had taught myself to believe nobody else would have, had actually rejected me with all my fancied greatness. And, to cap the whole, I then for the first time began to suspect that I was really a little in love with her. But let it all go. I'll try and outlive it. Others have been made fools of by the girls, but this can never with truth be said of me. I most emphatically in this instance, made a fool of myself. I have now come to the conclusion never again to think of marrying, and for this reason: I can never be satisfied with any one who would be blockhead enough to have me. When you receive this, write me a long yarn about something to amuse me. Give my respects to Mr. Browning.

Your sincere friend, A. LINCOLN.

1839

REMARKS ON SALE OF PUBLIC LANDS

IN THE HOUSE OF REPRESENTATIVES, January 17, 1839.

Mr. Lincoln, from Committee on Finance, to which the subject was referred, made a report on the subject of purchasing of the United States all the unsold lands lying within the limits of the State of Illinois, accompanied by resolutions that this State propose to purchase all unsold lands at twenty-five cents per acre, and pledging the faith of the State to carry the proposal into effect if the government accept the same within two years.

Mr. Lincoln thought the resolutions ought to be seriously considered. In reply to the gentleman from Adams, he said that it was not to enrich the State. The price of the lands may be raised, it was thought by some; by others, that it would be reduced. The conclusion in his mind was that the representatives in this Legislature from the country in which the lands lie would be opposed to raising the price, because it would operate against the settlement of the lands. He referred to the lands in the military tract. They had fallen into the hands of large speculators in consequence of the low price. He was opposed to a low price of land. He thought it was adverse to the interests of the poor settler, because speculators buy them up. He was opposed to a reduction of the price of public lands.

Mr. Lincoln referred to some official documents emanating from Indiana, and compared the progressive population of the two States. Illinois had gained upon that State under the public land system as it is. His conclusion was that ten years from this time Illinois would have no more public land unsold than Indiana now has. He referred also to Ohio. That State had sold nearly all her public lands. She was but twenty years ahead of us, and as our lands were equally salable—more so, as he maintained—we should have no more twenty years from now than she has at present.

Mr. Lincoln referred to the canal lands, and supposed that the policy of the State would be different in regard to them, if the representatives from that section of country could themselves choose the policy; but the representatives from other parts of the State had a veto upon it, and regulated the policy. He thought that if the State had all the lands, the policy of the Legislature would be more liberal to all sections.

He referred to the policy of the General Government. He thought that if the national debt had not been paid, the expenses of the government would not have doubled, as they had done since that debt was paid.

TO ——— ROW.

SPRINGFIELD, June 11, 1839 DEAR ROW:

Mr. Redman informs me that you wish me to write you the particulars of a conversation between Dr. Felix and myself relative to you. The Dr. overtook me between Rushville and Beardstown.

He, after learning that I had lived at Springfield, asked if I was acquainted with you. I told him I was. He said you had lately been elected constable in Adams, but that you never would be again. I asked him why. He said the people there had found out that you had been sheriff or deputy sheriff in Sangamon County, and that you came off and left your securities to suffer. He then asked me if I did not know such to be the fact. I told him I did not think you had ever been sheriff or deputy sheriff in Sangamon, but that I thought you had been constable. I further told him that if you had left your securities to suffer in that or any other case, I had never heard of it, and that if it had been so, I thought I would have heard of it.

If the Dr. is telling that I told him anything against you whatever, I authorize you to contradict it flatly. We have no news here.

Your friend, as ever, A. LINCOLN.

SPEECH ON NATIONAL BANK

IN THE HALL OF THE HOUSE OF REPRESENTATIVES

SPRINGFIELD, ILLINOIS, December 20, 1839.

FELLOW-CITIZENS:—It is peculiarly embarrassing to me to attempt a continuance of the discussion, on this evening, which has been conducted in this hall on several preceding ones. It is so because on each of those evenings there was a much fuller attendance than now, without any reason for its being so, except the greater interest the community feel in the speakers who addressed them then than they do in him who is to do so now. I am, indeed, apprehensive that the few who have attended have done so more to spare me mortification than in the hope of being interested in anything I may be able to say. This circumstance casts a damp upon my spirits, which I am sure I shall be unable to overcome during the evening. But enough of preface.

The subject heretofore and now to be discussed is the subtreasury scheme of the present administration, as a means of collecting, safe-keeping, transferring, and disbursing, the revenues of the nation, as contrasted with a national bank for the same purposes. Mr. Douglas has said that we (the Whigs) have not dared to meet them (the Locos) in argument on this question. I protest against this assertion. I assert that we have again and again, during this discussion, urged facts and arguments against the subtreasury which they have neither dared to deny nor attempted to answer. But lest some may be led to believe that we really wish to avoid the question, I now propose, in my humble way, to urge those arguments again; at the same time begging the audience to mark well the positions I shall take and the proof I shall offer to sustain them, and that they will not again permit Mr. Douglas or his friends to escape the force of them by a round and groundless assertion that we "dare not meet them in argument."

Of the subtreasury, then, as contrasted with a national bank for the before-enumerated purposes, I lay down the following propositions, to wit: (1) It will injuriously affect the community by its operation on the circulating medium. (2) It will be a more expensive fiscal agent. (3) It will be a less secure depository of the public money. To show the truth of the first proposition, let us take a short review of our condition under the operation of a national bank. It was the depository of the public revenues. Between the collection of those revenues and the disbursement of them by the government, the bank was permitted to and did actually loan them out to individuals, and hence the large amount of money actually collected for revenue purposes, which by any other plan would have been idle a great portion of the time, was kept almost constantly in circulation. Any person who will reflect that money is only valuable while in circulation will readily perceive that any device which will keep the government revenues in constant circulation, instead of being locked up in idleness, is no inconsiderable advantage. By the subtreasury the revenue is to be collected and kept in iron boxes until the government wants it for disbursement; thus robbing the people of the use of it, while the government does not itself need it, and while the money is performing no nobler office than that of rusting in iron

46

boxes. The natural effect of this change of policy, every one will see, is to reduce the quantity of money in circulation. But, again, by the subtreasury scheme the revenue is to be collected in specie. I anticipate that this will be disputed. I expect to hear it said that it is not the policy of the administration to collect the revenue in specie. If it shall, I reply that Mr. Van Buren, in his message recommending the subtreasury, expended nearly a column of that document in an attempt to persuade Congress to provide for the collection of the revenue in specie exclusively; and he concludes with these words:
"It may be safely assumed that no motive of convenience to the citizens requires the reception of bank paper." In addition to this, Mr. Silas Wright, Senator from New York, and the political, personal and confidential friend of Mr. Van Buren, drafted and introduced into the Senate the first subtreasury bill, and that bill provided for ultimately collecting the revenue in specie. It is true, I know, that that clause was stricken from the bill, but it was done by the votes of the Whigs, aided by a portion only of the Van Buren senators. No subtreasury bill has yet become a law, though two or three have been considered by Congress, some with and some without the specie clause; so that I admit there is room for quibbling upon the question of whether the administration favor the exclusive specie doctrine or not; but I take it that the fact that the President at first urged the specie doctrine, and that under his recommendation the first bill introduced embraced it, warrants us in charging it as the policy of the party until their head as publicly recants it as he at first espoused it. I repeat, then, that by the subtreasury the revenue is to be collected in specie. Now mark what the effect of this must be. By all estimates ever made there are but between sixty and eighty millions of specie in the United States. The expenditures of the Government for the year 1838—the last for which we have had the report—were forty millions. Thus it is seen that if the whole revenue be collected in specie, it will take more than half of all the specie in the nation to do it. By this means more than half of all the specie belonging to the fifteen millions of souls who compose the whole population of the country is thrown into the hands of the public office-holders, and other public creditors comprising in number perhaps not more than one quarter of a million, leaving the other fourteen millions and three quarters to get along as they best can, with less than one half of the specie of the country, and whatever rags and shinplasters they may be able to put, and keep, in circulation. By this means, every office-holder and other public creditor may, and most likely will, set up shaver; and a most glorious harvest will the specie-men have of it,—each specie-man, upon a fair division, having to his share the fleecing of about fifty-nine rag-men. In all candor let me ask, was such a system for benefiting the few at the expense of the many ever before devised? And was the sacred name of Democracy ever before made to indorse such an enormity against the rights of the people?
I have already said that the subtreasury will reduce the quantity of money in circulation. This position is strengthened by the recollection that the revenue is to be collected in Specie, so that the mere amount of revenue is not all that is withdrawn, but the amount of paper circulation that the forty millions would serve as a basis to is withdrawn, which would be in a sound state at least one hundred millions. When one hundred millions, or more, of the circulation we now have shall be withdrawn, who can contemplate without terror the distress, ruin, bankruptcy, and beggary that must follow? The man who has purchased any article—say a horse—on credit, at one hundred dollars, when there are two hundred millions circulating in the country, if the quantity be reduced to one hundred millions by the arrival of pay-day, will find the horse but sufficient to pay half the debt; and the other half must either be paid out of his other means, and thereby become a clear loss to him, or go unpaid, and thereby become a clear loss to his creditor. What I have here said of a single case of the purchase of a horse will hold good in every case of a debt existing at the time a reduction in the quantity of money occurs, by whomsoever, and for whatsoever, it may have been contracted. It may be said that what the debtor loses the creditor gains by this operation; but on examination this will be found true only to a very limited extent. It is more generally true that all lose by it—the creditor by losing more of his debts than he gains by the increased value of those he collects; the debtor by either parting with more of his property to pay his debts than he received in contracting them, or by entirely breaking up his business, and thereby being thrown upon the world in idleness.
The general distress thus created will, to be sure, be temporary, because, whatever change may occur in the quantity of money in any community, time will adjust the derangement produced; but while that adjustment is progressing, all suffer more or less, and very many lose everything that renders life desirable. Why, then, shall we suffer a severe difficulty, even though it be but temporary, unless we receive some equivalent for it?
What I have been saying as to the effect produced by a reduction of the quantity of money relates to the whole country. I now propose to show that it would produce a peculiar and permanent hardship upon the citizens of those States and Territories in which the public lands lie. The land-offices in those States and Territories, as all know, form the great gulf by which all, or nearly all, the money in them is swallowed up. When the quantity of money shall be reduced, and consequently everything under individual control brought down in proportion, the price of those lands, being fixed by law, will remain as now. Of necessity it will follow that the produce or labor that now raises money sufficient to purchase eighty acres will then raise but sufficient to purchase forty, or perhaps not that much; and this difficulty and hardship will last as long, in some degree, as any portion of these lands shall remain undisposed of. Knowing, as I well do, the difficulty that poor people now encounter in procuring homes, I hesitate not to say that when the price of the public lands shall be doubled or trebled, or, which is the same thing, produce and labor cut down to one half or one third of their present prices, it will be little less than impossible for them to procure those homes at all....
Well, then, what did become of him? (Postmaster General Barry) Why, the President immediately expressed his high disapprobation of his almost unequaled incapacity and corruption by appointing him to a foreign mission, with a salary and outfit of $18,000 a year! The party now attempt to throw Barry off, and to avoid the responsibility of his sins. Did not the President indorse those sins when, on the very heel of their commission, he appointed their author to the very

highest and most honorable office in his gift, and which is but a single step behind the very goal of American political ambition?

I return to another of Mr. Douglas's excuses for the expenditures of 1838, at the same time announcing the pleasing intelligence that this is the last one. He says that ten millions of that year's expenditure was a contingent appropriation, to prosecute an anticipated war with Great Britain on the Maine boundary question. Few words will settle this. First, that the ten millions appropriated was not made till 1839, and consequently could not have been expended in 1838; second, although it was appropriated, it has never been expended at all. Those who heard Mr. Douglas recollect that he indulged himself in a contemptuous expression of pity for me. "Now he's got me," thought I. But when he went on to say that five millions of the expenditure of 1838 were payments of the French indemnities, which I knew to be untrue; that five millions had been for the post-office, which I knew to be untrue; that ten millions had been for the Maine boundary war, which I not only knew to be untrue, but supremely ridiculous also; and when I saw that he was stupid enough to hope that I would permit such groundless and audacious assertions to go unexposed,—I readily consented that, on the score both of veracity and sagacity, the audience should judge whether he or I were the more deserving of the world's contempt.

Mr. Lamborn insists that the difference between the Van Buren party and the Whigs is that, although the former sometimes err in practice, they are always correct in principle, whereas the latter are wrong in principle; and, better to impress this proposition, he uses a figurative expression in these words: "The Democrats are vulnerable in the heel, but they are sound in the head and the heart." The first branch of the figure—that is, that the Democrats are vulnerable in the heel—I admit is not merely figuratively, but literally true. Who that looks but for a moment at their Swartwouts, their Prices, their Harringtons, and their hundreds of others, scampering away with the public money to Texas, to Europe, and to every spot of the earth where a villain may hope to find refuge from justice, can at all doubt that they are most distressingly affected in their heels with a species of "running itch"? It seems that this malady of their heels operates on these sound-headed and honest-hearted creatures very much like the cork leg in the comic song did on its owner: which, when he had once got started on it, the more he tried to stop it, the more it would run away. At the hazard of wearing this point threadbare, I will relate an anecdote which seems too strikingly in point to be omitted. A witty Irish soldier, who was always boasting of his bravery when no danger was near, but who invariably retreated without orders at the first charge of an engagement, being asked by his captain why he did so, replied: "Captain, I have as brave a heart as Julius Caesar ever had; but, somehow or other, whenever danger approaches, my cowardly legs will run away with it." So with Mr. Lamborn's party. They take the public money into their hand for the most laudable purpose that wise heads and honest hearts can dictate; but before they can possibly get it out again, their rascally "vulnerable heels" will run away with them.

Seriously this proposition of Mr. Lamborn is nothing more or less than a request that his party may be tried by their professions instead of their practices. Perhaps no position that the party assumes is more liable to or more deserving of exposure than this very modest request; and nothing but the unwarrantable length to which I have already extended these remarks forbids me now attempting to expose it. For the reason given, I pass it by.

I shall advert to but one more point. Mr. Lamborn refers to the late elections in the States, and from their results confidently predicts that every State in the Union will vote for Mr. Van Buren at the next Presidential election. Address that argument to cowards and to knaves; with the free and the brave it will effect nothing. It may be true; if it must, let it. Many free countries have lost their liberty, and ours may lose hers; but if she shall, be it my proudest plume, not that I was the last to desert, but that I never deserted her. I know that the great volcano at Washington, aroused and directed by the evil spirit that reigns there, is belching forth the lava of political corruption in a current broad and deep, which is sweeping with frightful velocity over the whole length and breadth of the land, bidding fair to leave unscathed no green spot or living thing; while on its bosom are riding, like demons on the waves of hell, the imps of that evil spirit, and fiendishly taunting all those who dare resist its destroying course with the hopelessness of their effort; and, knowing this, I cannot deny that all may be swept away. Broken by it I, too, may be; bow to it I never will. The probability that we may fall in the struggle ought not to deter us from the support of a cause we believe to be just; it shall not deter me. If ever I feel the soul within me elevate and expand to those dimensions not wholly unworthy of its almighty Architect, it is when I contemplate the cause of my country deserted by all the world beside, and I standing up boldly and alone, and hurling defiance at her victorious oppressors. Here, without contemplating consequences, before high heaven and in the face of the world, I swear eternal fidelity to the just cause, as I deem it, of the land of my life, my liberty, and my love. And who that thinks with me will not fearlessly adopt the oath that I take? Let none falter who thinks he is right, and we may succeed. But if, after all, we shall fail, be it so. We still shall have the proud consolation of saying to our consciences, and to the departed shade of our country's freedom, that the cause approved of our judgment, and adored of our hearts, in disaster, in chains, in torture, in death, we never faltered in defending.

TO JOHN T. STUART.

SPRINGFIELD, December 23, 1839.

DEAR STUART:

Dr. Henry will write you all the political news. I write this about some little matters of business. You recollect you told me you had drawn the Chicago Masark money, and sent it to the claimants. A hawk-billed Yankee is here besetting me at every turn I take, saying that Robert Kinzie never received the eighty dollars to which he was entitled. Can you tell me anything about the matter? Again, old Mr. Wright, who lives up South Fork somewhere, is teasing me continually about some deeds which he says he left with you, but which I can find nothing of. Can you tell me where they are? The Legislature is in session and has suffered the bank to forfeit its charter without benefit of clergy. There seems to be little disposition to resuscitate it.

Whenever a letter comes from you to Mrs._____ I carry it to her, and then I see Betty; she is a tolerable nice "fellow" now. Maybe I will write again when I get more time.

Your friend as ever, A. LINCOLN

P. S.—The Democratic giant is here, but he is not much worth talking about. A.L.

1840

CIRCULAR FROM WHIG COMMITTEE.

Confidential.

January [1?], 1840.
To MESSRS ———
GENTLEMEN:—In obedience to a resolution of the Whig State convention, we have appointed you the Central Whig Committee of your county. The trust confided to you will be one of watchfulness and labor; but we hope the glory of having contributed to the overthrow of the corrupt powers that now control our beloved country will be a sufficient reward for the time and labor you will devote to it. Our Whig brethren throughout the Union have met in convention, and after due deliberation and mutual concessions have elected candidates for the Presidency and Vice-Presidency not only worthy of our cause, but worthy of the support of every true patriot who would have our country redeemed, and her institutions honestly and faithfully administered. To overthrow the trained bands that are opposed to us whose salaried officers are ever on the watch, and whose misguided followers are ever ready to obey their smallest commands, every Whig must not only know his duty, but must firmly resolve, whatever of time and labor it may cost, boldly and faithfully to do it. Our intention is to organize the whole State, so that every Whig can be brought to the polls in the coming Presidential contest. We cannot do this, however, without your co-operation; and as we do our duty, so we shall expect you to do yours. After due deliberation, the following is the plan of organization, and the duties required of each county committee:

(1) To divide their county into small districts, and to appoint in each a subcommittee, whose duty it shall be to make a perfect list of all the voters in their respective districts, and to ascertain with certainty for whom they will vote. If they meet with men who are doubtful as to the man they will support, such voters should be designated in separate lines, with the name of the man they will probably support.

(2) It will be the duty of said subcommittee to keep a constant watch on the doubtful voters, and from time to time have them talked to by those in whom they have the most confidence, and also to place in their hands such documents as will enlighten and influence them.

(3) It will also be their duty to report to you, at least once a month, the progress they are making, and on election days see that every Whig is brought to the polls.

(4) The subcommittees should be appointed immediately; and by the last of April, at least, they should make their first report.

(5) On the first of each month hereafter we shall expect to hear from you. After the first report of your subcommittees, unless there should be found a great many doubtful voters, you can tell pretty accurately the manner in which your county will vote. In each of your letters to us, you will state the number of certain votes both for and against us, as well as the number of doubtful votes, with your opinion of the manner in which they will be cast.

(6) When we have heard from all the counties, we shall be able to tell with similar accuracy the political complexion of the State. This information will be forwarded to you as soon as received.

(7) Inclosed is a prospectus for a newspaper to be continued until after the Presidential election. It will be superintended by ourselves, and every Whig in the State must take it. It will be published so low that every one can afford it. You must raise a fund and forward us for extra copies,—every county ought to send—fifty or one hundred dollars,—and the copies will be forwarded to you for distribution among our political opponents. The paper will be devoted exclusively to the great cause in which we are engaged. Procure subscriptions, and forward them to us immediately.

(8) Immediately after any election in your county, you must inform us of its results; and as early as possible after any general election we will give you the like information.

(9) A senator in Congress is to be elected by our next Legislature. Let no local interests divide you, but select candidates that can succeed.

(10) Our plan of operations will of course be concealed from every one except our good friends who of right ought to know them.

Trusting much in our good cause, the strength of our candidates, and the determination of the Whigs everywhere to do their duty, we go to the work of organization in this State confident of success. We have the numbers, and if properly organized and exerted, with the gallant Harrison at our head, we shall meet our foes and conquer them in all parts of the Union.

Address your letters to Dr. A. G. Henry, R. F, Barrett; A. Lincoln, E. D. Baker, J. F. Speed.

TO JOHN T. STUART.

SPRINGFIELD, March 1, 1840

DEAR STUART:

I have never seen the prospects of our party so bright in these parts as they are now. We shall carry this county by a larger majority than we did in 1836, when you ran against May. I do not think my prospects, individually, are very flattering, for I think it probable I shall not be permitted to be a candidate; but the party ticket will succeed triumphantly. Subscriptions to the "Old Soldier" pour in without abatement. This morning I took from the post office a letter from Dubois enclosing the names of sixty subscribers, and on carrying it to Francis I found he had received one hundred and forty more from other quarters by the same day's mail. That is but an average specimen of every day's receipts. Yesterday Douglas, having chosen to consider himself insulted by something in the Journal, undertook to cane Francis in the street. Francis caught him by the hair and jammed him back against a market cart where the matter ended by Francis being pulled away from him. The whole affair was so ludicrous that Francis and everybody else (Douglass excepted) have been laughing about it ever since.

I send you the names of some of the V.B. men who have come out for Harrison about town, and suggest that you send them some documents.

Moses Coffman (he let us appoint him a delegate yesterday), Aaron Coffman, George Gregory, H. M. Briggs, Johnson (at Birchall's Bookstore), Michael Glyn, Armstrong (not Hosea nor Hugh, but a carpenter), Thomas Hunter, Moses Pilcher (he was always a Whig and deserves attention), Matthew Crowder Jr., Greenberry Smith; John Fagan, George Fagan, William Fagan (these three fell out with us about Early, and are doubtful now), John M. Cartmel, Noah Rickard, John Rickard, Walter Marsh.

The foregoing should be addressed at Springfield.

Also send some to Solomon Miller and John Auth at Salisbury. Also to Charles Harper, Samuel Harper, and B. C. Harper, and T. J. Scroggins, John Scroggins at Pulaski, Logan County.

Speed says he wrote you what Jo Smith said about you as he passed here. We will procure the names of some of his people here, and send them to you before long. Speed also says you must not fail to send us the New York Journal he wrote for some time since.

Evan Butler is jealous that you never send your compliments to him. You must not neglect him next time.

Your friend, as ever, A. LINCOLN

RESOLUTION IN THE ILLINOIS LEGISLATURE.

November 28, 1840.

In the Illinois House of Representatives, November 28, 1840, Mr. Lincoln offered the following:

Resolved, That so much of the governor's message as relates to fraudulent voting, and other fraudulent practices at elections, be referred to the Committee on Elections, with instructions to said committee to prepare and report to the House a bill for such an act as may in their judgment afford the greatest possible protection of the elective franchise against all frauds of all sorts whatever.

RESOLUTION IN THE ILLINOIS LEGISLATURE.

December 2, 1840.

Resolved, That the Committee on Education be instructed to inquire into the expediency of providing by law for the examination as to the qualification of persons offering themselves as school teachers, that no teacher shall receive any part of the public school fund who shall not have successfully passed such examination, and that they report by bill or otherwise.

REMARKS IN THE ILLINOIS LEGISLATURE.

December 4, 1840

In the House of Representatives, Illinois, December 4, 1840, on presentation of a report respecting petition of H. N. Purple, claiming the seat of Mr. Phelps from Peoria, Mr. Lincoln moved that the House resolve itself into Committee of the Whole on the question, and take it up immediately. Mr. Lincoln considered the question of the highest importance whether an individual had a right to sit in this House or not. The course he should propose would be to take up the evidence and decide upon the facts seriatim.
Mr. Drummond wanted time; they could not decide in the heat of debate, etc.
Mr. Lincoln thought that the question had better be gone into now. In courts of law jurors were required to decide on evidence, without previous study or examination. They were required to know nothing of the subject until the evidence was laid before them for their immediate decision. He thought that the heat of party would be augmented by delay.
The Speaker called Mr. Lincoln to order as being irrelevant; no mention had been made of party heat.
Mr. Drummond said he had only spoken of debate. Mr. Lincoln asked what caused the heat, if it was not party? Mr. Lincoln concluded by urging that the question would be decided now better than hereafter, and he thought with less heat and excitement.
(Further debate, in which Lincoln participated.)

REMARKS IN THE ILLINOIS LEGISLATURE.

December 4, 1840.

In the Illinois House of Representatives, December 4, 1840, House in Committee of the Whole on the bill providing for payment of interest on the State debt,—Mr. Lincoln moved to strike out the body and amendments of the bill, and insert in lieu thereof an amendment which in substance was that the governor be authorized to issue bonds for the payment of the interest; that these be called "interest bonds"; that the taxes accruing on Congress lands as they become taxable be irrevocably set aside and devoted as a fund to the payment of the interest bonds. Mr. Lincoln went into the reasons which appeared to him to render this plan preferable to that of hypothecating the State bonds. By this course we could get along till the next meeting of the Legislature, which was of great importance. To the objection which might be urged that these interest bonds could not be cashed, he replied that if our other bonds could, much more could these, which offered a perfect security, a fund being irrevocably set aside to provide for their redemption. To another objection, that we should be paying compound interest, he would reply that the rapid growth and increase of our resources was in so great a ratio as to outstrip the difficulty; that his object was to do the best that could be done in the present emergency. All agreed that the faith of the State must be preserved; this plan appeared to him preferable to a hypothecation of bonds, which would have to be redeemed and the interest paid. How this was to be done, he could not see; therefore he had, after turning the matter over in every way, devised this measure, which would carry us on till the next Legislature.
(Mr. Lincoln spoke at some length, advocating his measure.)
Lincoln advocated his measure, December 11, 1840.
December 12, 1840, he had thought some permanent provision ought to be made for the bonds to be hypothecated, but was satisfied taxation and revenue could not be connected with it now.

1841

TO JOHN T. STUART—ON DEPRESSION

SPRINGFIELD, Jan 23, 1841

DEAR STUART: I am now the most miserable man living. If what I feel were equally distributed to the whole human family, there would not be one cheerful face on earth. Whether I shall ever be better, I cannot tell; I awfully forbode I shall not. To remain as I am is impossible. I must die or be better, as it appears to me.... I fear I shall be unable to attend any business here, and a change of scene might help me. If I could be myself, I would rather remain at home with Judge Logan. I can write no more.

REMARKS IN THE ILLINOIS LEGISLATURE.

January 23, 1841

In the House of Representatives January 23, 1841, while discussing the continuation of the Illinois and Michigan Canal, Mr. Moore was afraid the holders of the "scrip" would lose.
Mr. Napier thought there was no danger of that; and Mr. Lincoln said he had not examined to see what amount of scrip would probably be needed. The principal point in his mind was this, that nobody was obliged to take these certificates. It is altogether voluntary on their part, and if they apprehend it will fall in their hands they will not take it. Further the loss, if any there be, will fall on the citizens of that section of the country.
This scrip is not going to circulate over an extensive range of country, but will be confined chiefly to the vicinity of the canal. Now, we find the representatives of that section of the country are all in favor of the bill.
When we propose to protect their interests, they say to us: Leave us to take care of ourselves; we are willing to run the risk. And this is reasonable; we must suppose they are competent to protect their own interests, and it is only fair to let them do it.

CIRCULAR FROM WHIG COMMITTEE.

February 9, 1841.

Appeal to the People of the State of Illinois.
FELLOW-CITIZENS:—When the General Assembly, now about adjourning, assembled in November last, from the bankrupt state of the public treasury, the pecuniary embarrassments prevailing in every department of society, the dilapidated state of the public works, and the impending danger of the degradation of the State, you had a right to expect that your representatives would lose no time in devising and adopting measures to avert threatened calamities, alleviate the distresses of the people, and allay the fearful apprehensions in regard to the future prosperity of the State. It was not expected by you that the spirit of party would take the lead in the councils of the State, and make every interest bend to its demands. Nor was it expected that any party would assume to itself the entire control of legislation, and convert the means and offices of the State, and the substance of the people, into aliment for party subsistence. Neither could it have been expected by you that party spirit, however strong its desires and unreasonable its demands, would have passed the sanctuary of the Constitution, and entered with its unhallowed and hideous form into the formation of the judiciary system.
At the early period of the session, measures were adopted by the dominant party to take possession of the State, to fill all public offices with party men, and make every measure affecting the interests of the people and the credit of the State operate in furtherance of their party views. The merits of men and measures therefore became the subject of discussion in caucus, instead of the halls of legislation, and decisions there made by a minority of the Legislature have been executed and carried into effect by the force of party discipline, without any regard whatever to the rights of the people or the interests of the State. The Supreme Court of the State was organized, and judges appointed, according to the provisions of the Constitution, in 1824. The people have never complained of the organization of that court; no attempt has ever before been made to change that department. Respect for public opinion, and regard for the rights and liberties of the people, have hitherto restrained the spirit of party from attacks upon the independence and integrity of the judiciary. The same judges have continued in office since 1824; their decisions have not been the subject of complaint among the people; the integrity and honesty of the court have not been questioned, and it has never been supposed that the court has ever permitted party prejudice or party considerations to operate upon their decisions. The

court was made to consist of four judges, and by the Constitution two form a quorum for the transaction of business. With this tribunal, thus constituted, the people have been satisfied for near sixteen years. The same law which organized the Supreme Court in 1824 also established and organized circuit courts to be held in each county in the State, and five circuit judges were appointed to hold those courts. In 1826 the Legislature abolished these circuit courts, repealed the judges out of office, and required the judges of the Supreme Court to hold the circuit courts. The reasons assigned for this change were, first, that the business of the country could be better attended to by the four judges of the Supreme Court than by the two sets of judges; and, second, the state of the public treasury forbade the employment of unnecessary officers. In 1828 a circuit was established north of the Illinois River, in order to meet the wants of the people, and a circuit judge was appointed to hold the courts in that circuit.

In 1834 the circuit-court system was again established throughout the State, circuit judges appointed to hold the courts, and the judges of the Supreme Court were relieved from the performance of circuit court duties. The change was recommended by the then acting governor of the State, General W. L. D. Ewing, in the following terms:

"The augmented population of the State, the multiplied number of organized counties, as well as the increase of business in all, has long since convinced every one conversant with this department of our government of the indispensable necessity of an alteration in our judiciary system, and the subject is therefore recommended to the earnest patriotic consideration of the Legislature. The present system has never been exempt from serious and weighty objections. The idea of appealing from the circuit court to the same judges in the Supreme Court is recommended by little hopes of redress to the injured party below. The duties of the circuit, too, it may be added, consume one half of the year, leaving a small and inadequate portion of time (when that required for domestic purposes is deducted) to erect, in the decisions of the Supreme Court, a judicial monument of legal learning and research, which the talent and ability of the court might otherwise be entirely competent to."

With this organization of circuit courts the people have never complained. The only complaints which we have heard have come from circuits which were so large that the judges could not dispose of the business, and the circuits in which Judges Pearson and Ralston lately presided.

Whilst the honor and credit of the State demanded legislation upon the subject of the public debt, the canal, the unfinished public works, and the embarrassments of the people, the judiciary stood upon a basis which required no change—no legislative action. Yet the party in power, neglecting every interest requiring legislative action, and wholly disregarding the rights, wishes, and interests of the people, has, for the unholy purpose of providing places for its partisans and supplying them with large salaries, disorganized that department of the government. Provision is made for the election of five party judges of the Supreme Court, the proscription of four circuit judges, and the appointment of party clerks in more than half the counties of the State. Men professing respect for public opinion, and acknowledged to be leaders of the party, have avowed in the halls of legislation that the change in the judiciary was intended to produce political results favorable to their party and party friends. The immutable principles of justice are to make way for party interests, and the bonds of social order are to be rent in twain, in order that a desperate faction may be sustained at the expense of the people. The change proposed in the judiciary was supported upon grounds so destructive to the institutions of the country, and so entirely at war with the rights and liberties of the people, that the party could not secure entire unanimity in its support, three Democrats of the Senate and five of the House voting against the measure. They were unwilling to see the temples of justice and the seats of independent judges occupied by the tools of faction. The declarations of the party leaders, the selection of party men for judges, and the total disregard for the public will in the adoption of the measure, prove conclusively that the object has been not reform, but destruction; not the advancement of the highest interests of the State, but the predominance of party.

We cannot in this manner undertake to point out all the objections to this party measure; we present you with those stated by the Council of Revision upon returning the bill, and we ask for them a candid consideration.

Believing that the independence of the judiciary has been destroyed, that hereafter our courts will be independent of the people, and entirely dependent upon the Legislature; that our rights of property and liberty of conscience can no longer be regarded as safe from the encroachments of unconstitutional legislation; and knowing of no other remedy which can be adopted consistently with the peace and good order of society, we call upon you to avail yourselves of the opportunity afforded, and, at the next general election, vote for a convention of the people.

S. H. LITTLE,
E. D. BAKER,
J. J. HARDIN,
E. B. WEBS,
A. LINCOLN,
J. GILLESPIE,

Committee on behalf of the Whig members of the Legislature.

AGAINST THE REORGANIZATION OF THE JUDICIARY.

EXTRACT FROM A PROTEST IN THE ILLINOIS LEGISLATURE

February 26, 1841

For the reasons thus presented, and for others no less apparent, the undersigned cannot assent to the passage of the bill, or permit it to become a law, without this evidence of their disapprobation; and they now protest against the reorganization of the judiciary, because—(1) It violates the great principles of free government by subjecting the judiciary to the Legislature. (2) It is a fatal blow at the independence of the judges and the constitutional term of their office. (3) It is a measure not asked for, or wished for, by the people. (4) It will greatly increase the expense of our courts, or else greatly diminish their utility. (5) It will give our courts a political and partisan character, thereby impairing public confidence in their decisions. (6) It will impair our standing with other States and the world. (7) It is a party measure for party purposes, from which no practical good to the people can possibly arise, but which may be the source of immeasurable evils.

The undersigned are well aware that this protest will be altogether unavailing with the majority of this body. The blow has already fallen, and we are compelled to stand by, the mournful spectators of the ruin it will cause.

[Signed by 35 members, among whom was Abraham Lincoln.]

TO JOSHUA F. SPEED—MURDER CASE

SPRINGFIELD June 19, 1841.

DEAR SPEED:—We have had the highest state of excitement here for a week past that our community has ever witnessed; and, although the public feeling is somewhat allayed, the curious affair which aroused it is very far from being even yet cleared of mystery. It would take a quire of paper to give you anything like a full account of it, and I therefore only propose a brief outline. The chief personages in the drama are Archibald Fisher, supposed to be murdered, and Archibald Trailor, Henry Trailor, and William Trailor, supposed to have murdered him. The three Trailors are brothers: the first, Arch., as you know, lives in town; the second, Henry, in Clary's Grove; and the third, William, in Warren County; and Fisher, the supposed murdered, being without a family, had made his home with William. On Saturday evening, being the 29th of May, Fisher and William came to Henry's in a one-horse dearborn, and there stayed over Sunday; and on Monday all three came to Springfield (Henry on horseback) and joined Archibald at Myers's, the Dutch carpenter. That evening at supper Fisher was missing, and so next morning some ineffectual search was made for him; and on Tuesday, at one o'clock P.M., William and Henry started home without him. In a day or two Henry and one or two of his Clary-Grove neighbors came back for him again, and advertised his disappearance in the papers. The knowledge of the matter thus far had not been general, and here it dropped entirely, till about the 10th instant, when Keys received a letter from the postmaster in Warren County, that William had arrived at home, and was telling a very mysterious and improbable story about the disappearance of Fisher, which induced the community there to suppose he had been disposed of unfairly. Keys made this letter public, which immediately set the whole town and adjoining county agog. And so it has continued until yesterday. The mass of the people commenced a systematic search for the dead body, while Wickersham was despatched to arrest Henry Trailor at the Grove, and Jim Maxcy to Warren to arrest William. On Monday last, Henry was brought in, and showed an evident inclination to insinuate that he knew Fisher to be dead, and that Arch. and William had killed him. He said he guessed the body could be found in Spring Creek, between the Beardstown road and Hickox's mill. Away the people swept like a herd of buffalo, and cut down Hickox's mill-dam nolens volens, to draw the water out of the pond, and then went up and down and up the creek, fishing and raking, and raking and ducking and diving for two days, and, after all, no dead body found.

In the meantime a sort of scuffling-ground had been found in the brush in the angle, or point, where the road leading into the woods past the brewery and the one leading in past the brick-yard meet. From the scuffle-ground was the sign of something about the size of a man having been dragged to the edge of the thicket, where it joined the track of some small-wheeled carriage drawn by one horse, as shown by the road-tracks. The carriage-track led off toward Spring Creek. Near this drag-trail Dr. Merryman found two hairs, which, after a long scientific examination, he pronounced to be triangular human hairs, which term, he says, includes within it the whiskers, the hair growing under the arms and on other parts of the body; and he judged that these two were of the whiskers, because the ends were cut, showing that they had flourished in the neighborhood of the razor's operations. On Thursday last Jim Maxcy brought in William Trailor from Warren. On the same day Arch. was arrested and put in jail. Yesterday (Friday) William was put upon his examining trial before May and Lovely. Archibald and Henry were both present. Lamborn prosecuted, and Logan, Baker, and your humble servant defended. A great many witnesses were introduced and examined, but I shall only mention those whose testimony seemed most important. The first of these was Captain Ransdell. He swore that when William and Henry left Springfield for home on Tuesday before mentioned they did not take the direct route,—which, you know, leads by the butcher shop,—but that they followed the street north until they got opposite, or nearly opposite, May's new house, after which he could not see them from where he stood; and it was afterwards proved that in about an hour after they started, they came into the street by the butcher shop from toward the brickyard. Dr. Merryman and others swore to what is stated about the scuffle-ground, drag-trail, whiskers, and carriage tracks. Henry was then introduced by the prosecution. He swore that when they started for home they went out north, as Ransdell stated, and turned down west by the brick-yard into the woods, and there met Archibald; that they proceeded a small distance farther, when he was placed as a sentinel to watch for and announce the approach of any one that might happen that way; that William and Arch. took the dearborn out of the road a small distance to the edge of the thicket, where they stopped, and he saw them lift the body of a man into it; that they then moved off with the carriage in the direction of Hickox's mill, and he loitered about for something like an hour, when William returned with the carriage, but without Arch., and said they had put him in a safe place; that they went somehow he did not know exactly how—into the road close to the brewery, and proceeded on to Clary's Grove. He also stated that some time during the day William told him that he and Arch. had killed Fisher the evening before; that the way they did it was by him William knocking him down with a club, and Arch. then choking him to death.

An old man from Warren, called Dr. Gilmore, was then introduced on the part of the defense. He swore that he had known Fisher for several years; that Fisher had resided at his house a long time at each of two different spells—once while he built a barn for him, and once while he was doctored for some chronic disease; that two or three years ago Fisher had a serious hurt in his head by the bursting of a gun, since which he had been subject to continued bad health and occasional aberration of mind. He also stated that on last Tuesday, being the same day that Maxcy arrested William Trailor, he (the doctor) was from home in the early part of the day, and on his return, about eleven o'clock, found Fisher at his house in bed, and apparently very unwell; that he asked him how he came from Springfield; that Fisher said he had come by Peoria, and also told of several other places he had been at more in the direction of Peoria, which showed that he at the time of speaking did not know where he had been wandering about in a state of derangement. He further stated that in about two hours he received a note from one of Trailor's friends, advising him of his arrest, and requesting him to go on to Springfield as a witness, to testify as to the state of Fisher's health in former times; that he immediately set off, calling up two of his neighbors as company, and, riding all evening and all night, overtook Maxcy and William at Lewiston in Fulton County; that Maxcy refusing to discharge Trailor upon his statement, his two neighbors returned and he came on to Springfield. Some question being made as to whether the doctor's story was not a fabrication, several acquaintances of his (among whom was the same postmaster who wrote Keys, as before mentioned) were introduced as sort of compurgators, who swore that they knew the doctor to be of good character for truth and veracity, and generally of good character in every way.

Here the testimony ended, and the Trailors were discharged, Arch. and William expressing both in word and manner their entire confidence that Fisher would be found alive at the doctor's by Galloway, Mallory, and Myers, who a day before had been despatched for that purpose; which Henry still protested that no power on earth could ever show Fisher alive. Thus stands this curious affair. When the doctor's story was first made public, it was amusing to scan and contemplate the countenances and hear the remarks of those who had been actively in search for the dead body: some looked quizzical, some melancholy, and some furiously angry. Porter, who had been very active, swore he always knew the man was not dead, and that he had not stirred an inch to hunt for him; Langford, who had taken the lead in cutting down Hickox's mill-dam, and wanted to hang Hickox for objecting, looked most awfully woebegone: he seemed the "victim of unrequited affection," as represented in the comic almanacs we used to laugh over; and Hart, the little drayman that hauled Molly home once, said it was too damned bad to have so much trouble, and no hanging after all.

I commenced this letter on yesterday, since which I received yours of the 13th. I stick to my promise to come to Louisville. Nothing new here except what I have written. I have not seen _____ since my last trip, and I am going out there as soon as I mail this letter.

Yours forever, LINCOLN.

STATEMENT ABOUT HARRY WILTON.

June 25, 1841

It having been charged in some of the public prints that Harry Wilton, late United States marshal for the district of Illinois, had used his office for political effect, in the appointment of deputies for the taking of the census for the year 1840, we, the undersigned, were called upon by Mr. Wilton to examine the papers in his possession relative to these appointments, and to ascertain therefrom the correctness or incorrectness of such charge. We accompanied Mr. Wilton to a room, and examined the matter as fully as we could with the means afforded us. The only sources of information bearing on the subject which were submitted to us were the letters, etc., recommending and opposing the various appointments made, and Mr. Wilton's verbal statements concerning the same. From these letters, etc., it appears that in some instances appointments were made in accordance with the recommendations of leading Whigs, and in opposition to those of leading Democrats; among which instances the appointments at Scott, Wayne, Madison, and Lawrence are the strongest. According to Mr. Wilton's statement of the seventy-six appointments we examined, fifty-four were of Democrats, eleven of Whigs, and eleven of unknown politics.

The chief ground of complaint against Mr. Wilton, as we had understood it, was because of his appointment of so many Democratic candidates for the Legislature, thus giving them a decided advantage over their Whig opponents; and consequently our attention was directed rather particularly to that point. We found that there were many such appointments, among which were those in Tazewell, McLean, Iroquois, Coles, Menard, Wayne, Washington, Fayette,

etc.; and we did not learn that there was one instance in which a Whig candidate for the Legislature had been appointed. There was no written evidence before us showing us at what time those appointments were made; but Mr. Wilton stated that they all with one exception were made before those appointed became candidates for the Legislature, and the letters, etc., recommending them all bear date before, and most of them long before, those appointed were publicly announced candidates.
We give the foregoing naked facts and draw no conclusions from them.
BEND. S. EDWARDS, A. LINCOLN.

TO MISS MARY SPEED—PRACTICAL SLAVERY

BLOOMINGTON, ILL., September 27, 1841.

Miss Mary Speed, Louisville, Ky.
MY FRIEND: By the way, a fine example was presented on board the boat for contemplating the effect of condition upon human happiness. A gentleman had purchased twelve negroes in different parts of Kentucky, and was taking them to a farm in the South. They were chained six and six together. A small iron clevis was around the left wrist of each, and this fastened to the main chain by a shorter one, at a convenient distance from the others, so that the negroes were strung together precisely like so many fish upon a trotline. In this condition they were being separated forever from the scenes of their childhood, their friends, their fathers and mothers, and brothers and sisters, and many of them from their wives and children, and going into perpetual slavery where the lash of the master is proverbially more ruthless and unrelenting than any other; and yet amid all these distressing circumstances, as we would think them, they were the most cheerful and apparently happy creatures on board. One, whose offence for which he had been sold was an overfondness for his wife, played the fiddle almost continually, and the others danced, sang, cracked jokes, and played various games with cards from day to day. How true it is that 'God tempers the wind to the shorn lamb,' or in other words, that he renders the worst of human conditions tolerable, while he permits the best to be nothing better than tolerable. To return to the narrative: When we reached Springfield I stayed but one day, when I started on this tedious circuit where I now am. Do you remember my going to the city, while I was in Kentucky, to have a tooth extracted, and making a failure of it? Well, that same old tooth got to paining me so much that about a week since I had it torn out, bringing with it a bit of the jawbone, the consequence of which is that my mouth is now so sore that I can neither talk nor eat.
Your sincere friend, A. LINCOLN.

1842

TO JOSHUA F. SPEED—ON MARRIAGE

January 30, 1842.

MY DEAR SPEED:—Feeling, as you know I do, the deepest solicitude for the success of the enterprise you are engaged in, I adopt this as the last method I can adopt to aid you, in case (which God forbid!) you shall need any aid. I do not place what I am going to say on paper because I can say it better that way than I could by word of mouth, but, were I to say it orally before we part, most likely you would forget it at the very time when it might do you some good. As I think it reasonable that you will feel very badly some time between this and the final consummation of your purpose, it is intended that you shall read this just at such a time. Why I say it is reasonable that you will feel very badly yet, is because of three special causes added to the general one which I shall mention.
The general cause is, that you are naturally of a nervous temperament; and this I say from what I have seen of you personally, and what you have told me concerning your mother at various times, and concerning your brother William at the time his wife died. The first special cause is your exposure to bad weather on your journey, which my experience clearly proves to be very severe on defective nerves. The second is the absence of all business and conversation of friends, which might divert your mind, give it occasional rest from the intensity of thought which will sometimes wear the sweetest idea threadbare and turn it to the bitterness of death. The third is the rapid and near approach of that crisis on which all your thoughts and feelings concentrate.

If from all these causes you shall escape and go through triumphantly, without another "twinge of the soul," I shall be most happily but most egregiously deceived. If, on the contrary, you shall, as I expect you will at sometime, be agonized and distressed, let me, who have some reason to speak with judgment on such a subject, beseech you to ascribe it to the causes I have mentioned, and not to some false and ruinous suggestion of the Devil.

"But," you will say, "do not your causes apply to every one engaged in a like undertaking?" By no means. The particular causes, to a greater or less extent, perhaps do apply in all cases; but the general one,—nervous debility, which is the key and conductor of all the particular ones, and without which they would be utterly harmless,—though it does pertain to you, does not pertain to one in a thousand. It is out of this that the painful difference between you and the mass of the world springs.

I know what the painful point with you is at all times when you are unhappy; it is an apprehension that you do not love her as you should. What nonsense! How came you to court her? Was it because you thought she deserved it, and that you had given her reason to expect it? If it was for that why did not the same reason make you court Ann Todd, and at least twenty others of whom you can think, and to whom it would apply with greater force than to her? Did you court her for her wealth? Why, you know she had none. But you say you reasoned yourself into it. What do you mean by that? Was it not that you found yourself unable to reason yourself out of it? Did you not think, and partly form the purpose, of courting her the first time you ever saw her or heard of her? What had reason to do with it at that early stage? There was nothing at that time for reason to work upon. Whether she was moral, amiable, sensible, or even of good character, you did not, nor could then know, except, perhaps, you might infer the last from the company you found her in.

All you then did or could know of her was her personal appearance and deportment; and these, if they impress at all, impress the heart, and not the head.

Say candidly, were not those heavenly black eyes the whole basis of all your early reasoning on the subject? After you and I had once been at the residence, did you not go and take me all the way to Lexington and back, for no other purpose but to get to see her again, on our return on that evening to take a trip for that express object? What earthly consideration would you take to find her scouting and despising you, and giving herself up to another? But of this you have no apprehension; and therefore you cannot bring it home to your feelings.

I shall be so anxious about you that I shall want you to write by every mail.

Your friend, LINCOLN.

TO JOSHUA F. SPEED.

SPRINGFIELD, ILLINOIS, February 3, 1842.

DEAR SPEED:—Your letter of the 25th January came to hand to-day. You well know that I do not feel my own sorrows much more keenly than I do yours, when I know of them; and yet I assure you I was not much hurt by what you wrote me of your excessively bad feeling at the time you wrote. Not that I am less capable of sympathizing with you now than ever, not that I am less your friend than ever, but because I hope and believe that your present anxiety and distress about her health and her life must and will forever banish those horrid doubts which I know you sometimes felt as to the truth of your affection for her. If they can once and forever be removed (and I almost feel a presentiment that the Almighty has sent your present affliction expressly for that object), surely nothing can come in their stead to fill their immeasurable measure of misery. The death-scenes of those we love are surely painful enough; but these we are prepared for and expect to see: they happen to all, and all know they must happen. Painful as they are, they are not an unlooked for sorrow. Should she, as you fear, be destined to an early grave, it is indeed a great consolation to know that she is so well prepared to meet it. Her religion, which you once disliked so much, I will venture you now prize most highly. But I hope your melancholy bodings as to her early death are not well founded. I even hope that ere this reaches you she will have returned with improved and still improving health, and that you will have met her, and forgotten the sorrows of the past in the enjoyments of the present. I would say more if I could, but it seems that I have said enough. It really appears to me that you yourself ought to rejoice, and not sorrow, at this indubitable evidence of your undying affection for her. Why, Speed, if you did not love her although you might not wish her death, you would most certainly be resigned to it. Perhaps this point is no longer a question with you, and my pertinacious dwelling upon it is a rude intrusion upon your feelings. If so, you must pardon me. You know the hell I have suffered on that point, and how tender I am upon it. You know I do not mean wrong. I have been quite clear of "hypo" since you left, even better than I was along in the fall. I have seen _____ but once. She seemed very cheerful, and so I said nothing to her about what we spoke of.

Old Uncle Billy Herndon is dead, and it is said this evening that Uncle Ben Ferguson will not live. This, I believe, is all the news, and enough at that unless it were better. Write me immediately on the receipt of this.

Your friend, as ever, LINCOLN.

TO JOSHUA F. SPEED—ON DEPRESSION

SPRINGFIELD, ILLINOIS, February 13, 1842.

DEAR SPEED:—Yours of the 1st instant came to hand three or four days ago. When this shall reach you, you will have been Fanny's husband several days. You know my desire to befriend you is everlasting; that I will never cease while I know how to do anything. But you will always hereafter be on ground that I have never occupied, and consequently, if advice were needed, I might advise wrong. I do fondly hope, however, that you will never again need any comfort from abroad. But should I be mistaken in this, should excessive pleasure still be accompanied with a painful counterpart at times, still let me urge you, as I have ever done, to remember, in the depth and even agony of despondency, that very shortly you are to feel well again. I am now fully convinced that you love her as ardently as you are capable of loving. Your ever being happy in her presence, and your intense anxiety about her health, if there were nothing else, would place this beyond all dispute in my mind. I incline to think it probable that your nerves will fail you occasionally for a while; but once you get them firmly guarded now that trouble is over forever. I think, if I were you, in case my mind were not exactly right, I would avoid being idle. I would immediately engage in some business, or go to making preparations for it, which would be the same thing. If you went through the ceremony calmly, or even with sufficient composure not to excite alarm in any present, you are safe beyond question, and in two or three months, to say the most, will be the happiest of men.

I would desire you to give my particular respects to Fanny; but perhaps you will not wish her to know you have received this, lest she should desire to see it. Make her write me an answer to my last letter to her; at any rate I would set great value upon a note or letter from her. Write me whenever you have leisure. Yours forever, A. LINCOLN. P. S.—I have been quite a man since you left.

TO G. B. SHELEDY.

SPRINGFIELD, ILL., Feb. 16, 1842.

G. B. SHELEDY, ESQ.:

Yours of the 10th is duly received. Judge Logan and myself are doing business together now, and we are willing to attend to your cases as you propose. As to the terms, we are willing to attend each case you prepare and send us for $10 (when there shall be no opposition) to be sent in advance, or you to know that it is safe. It takes $5.75 of cost to start upon, that is, $1.75 to clerk, and $2 to each of two publishers of papers. Judge Logan thinks it will take the balance of $20 to carry a case through. This must be advanced from time to time as the services are performed, as the officers will not act without. I do not know whether you can be admitted an attorney of the Federal court in your absence or not; nor is it material, as the business can be done in our names.

Thinking it may aid you a little, I send you one of our blank forms of Petitions. It, you will see, is framed to be sworn to before the Federal court clerk, and, in your cases, will have [to] be so far changed as to be sworn to before the clerk of your circuit court; and his certificate must be accompanied with his official seal. The schedules, too, must be attended to. Be sure that they contain the creditors' names, their residences, the amounts due each, the debtors' names, their residences, and the amounts they owe, also all property and where located.

Also be sure that the schedules are all signed by the applicants as well as the Petition. Publication will have to be made here in one paper, and in one nearest the residence of the applicant. Write us in each case where the last advertisement is to be sent, whether to you or to what paper.

I believe I have now said everything that can be of any advantage. Your friend as ever, A. LINCOLN.

TO GEORGE E. PICKETT—ADVICE TO YOUTH

February 22, 1842.

I never encourage deceit, and falsehood, especially if you have got a bad memory, is the worst enemy a fellow can have. The fact is truth is your truest friend, no matter what the circumstances are. Notwithstanding this copy-book preamble, my boy, I am inclined to suggest a little prudence on your part. You see I have a congenital aversion to failure, and the sudden announcement to your Uncle Andrew of the success of your "lamp rubbing" might possibly prevent your passing the severe physical examination to which you will be subjected in order to enter the Military Academy. You see I should like to have a perfect soldier credited to dear old Illinois—no broken bones, scalp wounds, etc. So I think it might be wise to hand this letter from me in to your good uncle through his room-window after he has had a comfortable dinner, and watch its effect from the top of the pigeon-house.

I have just told the folks here in Springfield on this 111th anniversary of the birth of him whose name, mightiest in the cause of civil liberty, still mightiest in the cause of moral reformation, we mention in solemn awe, in naked, deathless splendor, that the one victory we can ever call complete will be that one which proclaims that there is not one slave or one drunkard on the face of God's green earth. Recruit for this victory.

Now, boy, on your march, don't you go and forget the old maxim that "one drop of honey catches more flies than a half-gallon of gall." Load your musket with this maxim, and smoke it in your pipe.

ADDRESS BEFORE THE SPRINGFIELD WASHINGTONIAN TEMPERANCE SOCIETY,

FEBRUARY 22, 1842.

Although the temperance cause has been in progress for near twenty years, it is apparent to all that it is just now being crowned with a degree of success hitherto unparalleled.

The list of its friends is daily swelled by the additions of fifties, of hundreds, and of thousands. The cause itself seems suddenly transformed from a cold abstract theory to a living, breathing, active, and powerful chieftain, going forth "conquering and to conquer." The citadels of his great adversary are daily being stormed and dismantled; his temple and his altars, where the rites of his idolatrous worship have long been performed, and where human sacrifices have long been wont to be made, are daily desecrated and deserted. The triumph of the conqueror's fame is sounding from hill to hill, from sea to sea, and from land to land, and calling millions to his standard at a blast.

For this new and splendid success we heartily rejoice. That that success is so much greater now than heretofore is doubtless owing to rational causes; and if we would have it continue, we shall do well to inquire what those causes are. The warfare heretofore waged against the demon intemperance has somehow or other been erroneous. Either the champions engaged or the tactics they adopted have not been the most proper. These champions for the most part have been preachers, lawyers, and hired agents. Between these and the mass of mankind there is a want of approachability, if the term be admissible, partially, at least, fatal to their success. They are supposed to have no sympathy of feeling or interest with those very persons whom it is their object to convince and persuade.

And again, it is so common and so easy to ascribe motives to men of these classes other than those they profess to act upon. The preacher, it is said, advocates temperance because he is a fanatic, and desires a union of the Church and State; the lawyer from his pride and vanity of hearing himself speak; and the hired agent for his salary. But when one who has long been known as a victim of intemperance bursts the fetters that have bound him, and appears before his neighbors "clothed and in his right mind," a redeemed specimen of long-lost humanity, and stands up, with tears of joy trembling in his eyes, to tell of the miseries once endured, now to be endured no more forever; of his once naked and starving children, now clad and fed comfortably; of a wife long weighed down with woe, weeping, and a broken heart, now restored to health, happiness, and a renewed affection; and how easily it is all done, once it is resolved to be done; how simple his language! there is a logic and an eloquence in it that few with human feelings can resist. They cannot say that he desires a union of Church and State, for he is not a church member; they cannot say he is vain of hearing himself speak, for his whole demeanor shows he would gladly avoid speaking at all; they cannot say he speaks for pay, for he receives none, and asks for none. Nor can his sincerity in any way be doubted, or his sympathy for those he would persuade to imitate his example be denied.

In my judgment, it is to the battles of this new class of champions that our late success is greatly, perhaps chiefly, owing. But, had the old-school champions themselves been of the most wise selecting, was their system of tactics the most judicious? It seems to me it was not. Too much denunciation against dram-sellers and dram-drinkers was indulged in. This I think was both impolitic and unjust. It was impolitic, because it is not much in the nature of man to be driven to anything; still less to be driven about that which is exclusively his own business; and least of all where such driving is to be submitted to at the expense of pecuniary interest or burning appetite. When the dram-seller and drinker were incessantly told not in accents of entreaty and persuasion, diffidently addressed by erring man to an erring brother, but in the thundering tones of anathema and denunciation with which the lordly judge often groups together all the crimes of the felon's life, and thrusts them in his face just ere he passes sentence of death upon him that they were the authors of all the vice and misery and crime in the land; that they were the manufacturers and material of all the thieves and robbers and murderers that infest the earth; that their houses were the workshops of the devil; and that their persons should be shunned by all the good and virtuous, as moral pestilences—I say, when they were told all this, and in this way, it is not wonderful that they were slow to acknowledge the truth of such denunciations, and to join the ranks of their denouncers in a hue and cry against themselves.

To have expected them to do otherwise than they did to have expected them not to meet denunciation with denunciation, crimination with crimination, and anathema with anathema—was to expect a reversal of human nature, which is God's decree and can never be reversed.

When the conduct of men is designed to be influenced, persuasion, kind, unassuming persuasion, should ever be adopted. It is an old and a true maxim that "a drop of honey catches more flies than a gallon of gall." So with men. If you would win a man to your cause, first convince him that you are his sincere friend. Therein is a drop of honey that catches his heart, which, say what he will, is the great highroad to his reason; and which, when once gained, you will find but little trouble in convincing his judgment of the justice of your cause, if indeed that cause really be a just one. On the contrary, assume to dictate to his judgment, or to command his action, or to mark him as one to be shunned and despised, and he will retreat within himself, close all the avenues to his head and his heart; and though your cause be naked truth itself, transformed to the heaviest lance, harder than steel, and sharper than steel can be made, and though you throw it with more than herculean force and precision, you shall be no more able to pierce him than to penetrate the hard shell of a tortoise with a rye straw. Such is man, and so must he be understood by those who would lead him, even to his own best interests.

On this point the Washingtonians greatly excel the temperance advocates of former times. Those whom they desire to convince and persuade are their old friends and companions. They know they are not demons, nor even the worst of men; they know that generally they are kind, generous, and charitable even beyond the example of their more staid and sober neighbors. They are practical philanthropists; and they glow with a generous and brotherly zeal that mere theorizers are incapable of feeling. Benevolence and charity possess their hearts entirely; and out of the abundance of their hearts their tongues give utterance; "love through all their actions runs, and all their words are mild." In this spirit they speak and act, and in the same they are heard and regarded. And when such is the temper of the advocate, and such of the audience, no good cause can be unsuccessful. But I have said that denunciations against dramsellers and dram-drinkers are unjust, as well as impolitic. Let us see. I have not inquired at what period of time the use of intoxicating liquors commenced; nor is it important to know. It is sufficient that, to all of us who now inhabit the world, the practice of drinking them is just as old as the world itself that is, we have seen the one just as long as we have seen the other. When all such of us as have now reached the years of maturity first opened our eyes upon the stage of existence, we found intoxicating liquor recognized by everybody, used by everybody, repudiated by nobody. It commonly entered into the first draught of the infant and the last draught of the dying man. From the sideboard of the parson down to the ragged pocket of the houseless loafer, it was constantly found. Physicians proscribed it in this, that, and the other disease; government provided it for soldiers and sailors; and to have a rolling or raising, a husking or "hoedown," anywhere about without it was positively insufferable. So, too, it was everywhere a respectable article of manufacture and merchandise. The making of it was regarded as an honorable livelihood, and he who could make most was the most enterprising and respectable. Large and small manufactories of it were everywhere erected, in which all the earthly goods of their owners were invested. Wagons drew it from town to town; boats bore it from clime to clime, and the winds wafted it from nation to nation; and merchants bought and sold it, by wholesale and retail, with precisely the same feelings on the part of the seller, buyer, and bystander as are felt at the selling and buying of ploughs, beef, bacon, or any other of the real necessaries of life. Universal public opinion not only tolerated but recognized and adopted its use.

It is true that even then it was known and acknowledged that many were greatly injured by it; but none seemed to think the injury arose from the use of a bad thing, but from the abuse of a very good thing. The victims of it were to be pitied and compassionated, just as are the heirs of consumption and other hereditary diseases. Their failing was treated as a misfortune, and not as a crime, or even as a disgrace. If, then, what I have been saying is true, is it wonderful that some should think and act now as all thought and acted twenty years ago? and is it just to assail, condemn, or despise them for doing so? The universal sense of mankind on any subject is an argument, or at least an influence, not easily overcome. The success of the argument in favor of the existence of an overruling Providence mainly depends upon that sense; and men ought not in justice to be denounced for yielding to it in any case, or giving it up slowly, especially when they are backed by interest, fixed habits, or burning appetites.

Another error, as it seems to me, into which the old reformers fell, was the position that all habitual drunkards were utterly incorrigible, and therefore must be turned adrift and damned without remedy in order that the grace of temperance might abound, to the temperate then, and to all mankind some hundreds of years thereafter. There is in this some thing so repugnant to humanity, so uncharitable, so cold-blooded and feelingless, that it, never did nor ever can enlist the enthusiasm of a popular cause. We could not love the man who taught it we could not hear him with patience. The heart could not throw open its portals to it, the generous man could not adopt it—it could not mix with his blood. It looked so fiendishly selfish, so like throwing fathers and brothers overboard to lighten the boat for our security, that the noble-minded shrank from the manifest meanness of the thing. And besides this, the benefits of a reformation to be effected by such a system were too remote in point of time to warmly engage many in its behalf. Few can be induced to labor exclusively for posterity, and none will do it enthusiastically. —Posterity has done nothing for us; and, theorize on it as we may, practically we shall do very little for it, unless we are made to think we are at the same time doing something for ourselves.

What an ignorance of human nature does it exhibit to ask or to expect a whole community to rise up and labor for the temporal happiness of others, after themselves shall be consigned to the dust, a majority of which community take no pains whatever to secure their own eternal welfare at no more distant day! Great distance in either time or space has wonderful power to lull and render quiescent the human mind. Pleasures to be enjoyed, or pains to be endured, after we shall be dead and gone are but little regarded even in our own cases, and much less in the cases of others. Still, in addition to this there is something so ludicrous in promises of good or threats of evil a great way off as to render the whole subject with which they are connected easily turned into ridicule. "Better lay down that spade you are stealing, Paddy; if you don't you'll pay for it at the day of judgment." "Be the powers, if ye'll credit me so long I'll take another jist."

By the Washingtonians this system of consigning the habitual drunkard to hopeless ruin is repudiated. They adopt a more enlarged philanthropy; they go for present as well as future good. They labor for all now living, as well as hereafter to live. They teach hope to all-despair to none. As applying to their cause, they deny the doctrine of unpardonable sin; as in Christianity it is taught, so in this they teach—"While—While the lamp holds out to burn, The vilest sinner may return." And, what is a matter of more profound congratulation, they, by experiment upon experiment and example upon example, prove the maxim to be no less true in the one case than in the other. On every hand we behold those who but yesterday were the chief of sinners, now the chief apostles of the cause. Drunken devils are cast out by ones, by sevens, by legions; and their unfortunate victims, like the poor possessed who were redeemed from their long and lonely wanderings in the tombs, are publishing to the ends of the earth how great things have been done for them.

To these new champions and this new system of tactics our late success is mainly owing, and to them we must mainly look for the final consummation. The ball is now rolling gloriously on, and none are so able as they to increase its speed and its bulk, to add to its momentum and its magnitude—even though unlearned in letters, for this task none are so well educated. To fit them for this work they have been taught in the true school. They have been in that gulf from which they would teach others the means of escape. They have passed that prison wall which others have long declared impassable; and who that has not shall dare to weigh opinions with them as to the mode of passing?

But if it be true, as I have insisted, that those who have suffered by intemperance personally, and have reformed, are the most powerful and efficient instruments to push the reformation to ultimate success, it does not follow that those who have not suffered have no part left them to perform. Whether or not the world would be vastly benefited by a total and final banishment from it of all intoxicating drinks seems to me not now an open question. Three fourths of mankind confess the affirmative with their tongues, and, I believe, all the rest acknowledge it in their hearts.

Ought any, then, to refuse their aid in doing what good the good of the whole demands? Shall he who cannot do much be for that reason excused if he do nothing? "But," says one, "what good can I do by signing the pledge? I never drank, even without signing." This question has already been asked and answered more than a million of times. Let it be answered once more. For the man suddenly or in any other way to break off from the use of drams, who has indulged in them for a long course of years and until his appetite for them has grown ten or a hundredfold stronger and more craving than any natural appetite can be, requires a most powerful moral effort. In such an undertaking he needs every moral support and influence that can possibly be brought to his aid and thrown around him. And not only so, but every moral prop should be taken from whatever argument might rise in his mind to lure him to his backsliding. When he casts his eyes around him, he should be able to see all that he respects, all that he admires, all that he loves, kindly and anxiously pointing him onward, and none beckoning him back to his former miserable "wallowing in the mire."

But it is said by some that men will think and act for themselves; that none will disuse spirits or anything else because his neighbors do; and that moral influence is not that powerful engine contended for. Let us examine this. Let me ask the man who could maintain this position most stiffly, what compensation he will accept to go to church some Sunday and sit during the sermon with his wife's bonnet upon his head? Not a trifle, I'll venture. And why not? There would be nothing irreligious in it, nothing immoral, nothing uncomfortable—then why not? Is it not because there would be something egregiously unfashionable in it? Then it is the influence of fashion; and what is the influence of fashion but the influence that other people's actions have on our actions—the strong inclination each of us feels to do as we see all our neighbors do? Nor is the influence of fashion confined to any particular thing or class of things; it is just as strong on one subject as another. Let us make it as unfashionable to withhold our names from the temperance cause as for husbands to wear their wives' bonnets to church, and instances will be just as rare in the one case as the other.

"But," say some, "we are no drunkards, and we shall not acknowledge ourselves such by joining a reformed drunkard's society, whatever our influence might be." Surely no Christian will adhere to this objection. If they believe as they profess, that Omnipotence condescended to take on himself the form of sinful man, and as such to die an ignominious death for their sakes, surely they will not refuse submission to the infinitely lesser condescension, for the temporal, and perhaps eternal, salvation of a large, erring, and unfortunate class of their fellow-creatures. Nor is the condescension very great. In my judgment such of us as have never fallen victims have been spared more by the absence of appetite than from any mental or moral superiority over those who have. Indeed, I believe if we take habitual drunkards as a class, their heads and their hearts will bear an advantageous comparison with those of any other class. There seems ever to have been a proneness in the brilliant and warm-blooded to fall into this vice—the demon of intemperance ever seems to have delighted in sucking the blood of genius and of generosity. What one of us but can call to mind some relative, more promising in youth than all his fellows, who has fallen a sacrifice to his rapacity? He ever seems to have gone forth like the Egyptian angel of death, commissioned to slay, if not the first, the fairest born of every family. Shall he now be arrested in his desolating career? In that arrest all can give aid that will; and who shall be excused that can and will not? Far around as human breath has ever blown he keeps our fathers, our brothers, our sons, and our friends prostrate in the chains of moral death. To all the living everywhere we cry, "Come sound the moral trump, that these may rise and stand up an exceeding great army." "Come from the four winds, O breath! and breathe upon these slain that they may live." If the relative grandeur of revolutions shall be estimated by the great amount of human misery they alleviate, and the small amount they inflict, then indeed will this be the grandest the world shall ever have seen.

Of our political revolution of '76 we are all justly proud. It has given us a degree of political freedom far exceeding that of any other nation of the earth. In it the world has found a solution of the long-mooted problem as to the capability of man to govern himself. In it was the germ which has vegetated, and still is to grow and expand into the universal liberty of mankind. But, with all these glorious results, past, present, and to come, it had its evils too. It breathed forth famine, swam in blood, and rode in fire; and long, long after, the orphan's cry and the widow's wail continued to break the sad silence that ensued. These were the price, the inevitable price, paid for the blessings it bought.

Turn now to the temperance revolution. In it we shall find a stronger bondage broken, a viler slavery manumitted, a greater tyrant deposed; in it, more of want supplied, more disease healed, more sorrow assuaged. By it no Orphans starving, no widows weeping. By it none wounded in feeling, none injured in interest; even the drammaker and dramseller will have glided into other occupations so gradually as never to have felt the change, and will stand ready to join all others in the universal song of gladness. And what a noble ally this to the cause of political freedom, with such an aid its march cannot fail to be on and on, till every son of earth shall drink in rich fruition the sorrow-quenching draughts of perfect liberty. Happy day when-all appetites controlled, all poisons subdued, all matter subjected-mind, all-conquering mind, shall live and move, the monarch of the world. Glorious consummation! Hail, fall of fury! Reign of reason, all hail!

And when the victory shall be complete, when there shall be neither a slave nor a drunkard on the earth, how proud the title of that land which may truly claim to be the birthplace and the cradle of both those revolutions that shall have ended in that victory. How nobly distinguished that people who shall have planted and nurtured to maturity both the political and moral freedom of their species.

This is the one hundred and tenth anniversary of the birthday of Washington; we are met to celebrate this day. Washington is the mightiest name of earth long since mightiest in the cause of civil liberty, still mightiest in moral reformation. On that name no eulogy is expected. It cannot be. To add brightness to the sun or glory to the name of Washington is alike impossible. Let none attempt it. In solemn awe pronounce the name, and in its naked deathless splendor leave it shining on.

TO JOSHUA F. SPEED.

SPRINGFIELD, February 25, 1842.

DEAR SPEED:—Yours of the 16th instant, announcing that Miss Fanny and you are "no more twain, but one flesh," reached me this morning. I have no way of telling you how much happiness I wish you both, though I believe you both can conceive it. I feel somewhat jealous of both of you now: you will be so exclusively concerned for one another, that I shall be forgotten entirely. My acquaintance with Miss Fanny (I call her this, lest you should think I am speaking of your mother) was too short for me to reasonably hope to long be remembered by her; and still I am sure I shall not forget her soon. Try if you cannot remind her of that debt she owes me—and be sure you do not interfere to prevent her paying it.

I regret to learn that you have resolved to not return to Illinois. I shall be very lonesome without you. How miserably things seem to be arranged in this world! If we have no friends, we have no pleasure; and if we have them, we are sure to lose them, and be doubly pained by the loss. I did hope she and you would make your home here; but I own I have no right to insist. You owe obligations to her ten thousand times more sacred than you can owe to others, and in that light let them be respected and observed. It is natural that she should desire to remain with her relatives and friends. As to friends, however, she could not need them anywhere: she would have them in abundance here.

Give my kind remembrance to Mr. Williamson and his family, particularly Miss Elizabeth; also to your mother, brother, and sisters. Ask little Eliza Davis if she will ride to town with me if I come there again. And finally, give Fanny a double reciprocation of all the love she sent me. Write me often, and believe me

Yours forever, LINCOLN.

P. S. Poor Easthouse is gone at last. He died awhile before day this morning. They say he was very loath to die....

L.

TO JOSHUA F. SPEED—ON MARRIAGE CONCERNS

SPRINGFIELD, February 25, 1842.

DEAR SPEED:—I received yours of the 12th written the day you went down to William's place, some days since, but delayed answering it till I should receive the promised one of the 16th, which came last night. I opened the letter with intense anxiety and trepidation; so much so, that, although it turned out better than I expected, I have hardly yet, at a distance of ten hours, become calm.

I tell you, Speed, our forebodings (for which you and I are peculiar) are all the worst sort of nonsense. I fancied, from the time I received your letter of Saturday, that the one of Wednesday was never to come, and yet it did come, and what is more, it is perfectly clear, both from its tone and handwriting, that you were much happier, or, if you think the term preferable, less miserable, when you wrote it than when you wrote the last one before. You had so obviously improved at the very time I so much fancied you would have grown worse. You say that something indescribably horrible and alarming still haunts you. You will not say that three months from now, I will venture. When your nerves once get steady now, the whole trouble will be over forever. Nor should you become impatient at their being even very slow in becoming steady. Again you say, you much fear that that Elysium of which you have dreamed so much is never to be realized. Well, if it shall not, I dare swear it will not be the fault of her who is now your wife. I now have no doubt that it is the peculiar misfortune of both you and me to dream dreams of Elysium far exceeding all that anything earthly can realize. Far short of your dreams as you may be, no woman could do more to realize them than that same black-eyed Fanny. If you could but contemplate her through my imagination, it would appear ridiculous to you that any one should for a moment think of being unhappy with her. My old father used to have a saying that "If you make a bad bargain, hug it all the tighter"; and it occurs to me that if the bargain you have just closed can possibly be called a bad one, it is certainly the most pleasant one for applying that maxim to which my fancy can by any effort picture.

I write another letter, enclosing this, which you can show her, if she desires it. I do this because she would think strangely, perhaps, should you tell her that you received no letters from me, or, telling her you do, refuse to let her see them. I close this, entertaining the confident hope that every successive letter I shall have from you (which I here pray may not be few, nor far between) may show you possessing a more steady hand and cheerful heart than the last preceding it. As ever, your friend, LINCOLN.

TO JOSHUA F. SPEED.

SPRINGFIELD, March 27, 1842

DEAR SPEED:—Yours of the 10th instant was received three or four days since. You know I am sincere when I tell you the pleasure its contents gave me was, and is, inexpressible. As to your farm matter, I have no sympathy with you. I have no farm, nor ever expect to have, and consequently have not studied the subject enough to be much interested with it. I can only say that I am glad you are satisfied and pleased with it. But on that other subject, to me of the most intense interest whether in joy or sorrow, I never had the power to withhold my sympathy from you. It cannot be told how it now thrills me with joy to hear you say you are "far happier than you ever expected to be." That much I know is enough. I know you too well to suppose your expectations were not, at least, sometimes extravagant, and if the reality exceeds them all, I say, Enough, dear Lord. I am not going beyond the truth when I tell you that the short space it took me to read your last letter gave me more pleasure than the total sum of all I have enjoyed since the fatal 1st of January, 1841. Since then it seems to me I should have been entirely happy, but for the never-absent idea that there is one still unhappy whom I have contributed to make so. That still kills my soul. I cannot but reproach myself for even wishing to be happy while she is otherwise. She accompanied a large party on the railroad cars to Jacksonville last Monday, and on her return spoke, so that I heard of it, of having enjoyed the trip exceedingly. God be praised for that.

You know with what sleepless vigilance I have watched you ever since the commencement of your affair; and although I am almost confident it is useless, I cannot forbear once more to say that I think it is even yet possible for your spirits to flag down and leave you miserable. If they should, don't fail to remember that they cannot long remain so. One thing I can tell you which I know you will be glad to hear, and that is that I have seen—and scrutinized her feelings as well as I could, and am fully convinced she is far happier now than she has been for the last fifteen months past.

You will see by the last Sangamon Journal, that I made a temperance speech on the 22d of February, which I claim that Fanny and you shall read as an act of charity to me; for I cannot learn that anybody else has read it, or is likely to. Fortunately it is not very long, and I shall deem it a sufficient compliance with my request if one of you listens while the other reads it.

As to your Lockridge matter, it is only necessary to say that there has been no court since you left, and that the next commences to-morrow morning, during which I suppose we cannot fail to get a judgment.

I wish you would learn of Everett what he would take, over and above a discharge for all the trouble we have been at, to take his business out of our hands and give it to somebody else. It is impossible to collect money on that or any other claim here now; and although you know I am not a very petulant man, I declare I am almost out of patience with Mr. Everett's importunity. It seems like he not only writes all the letters he can himself, but gets everybody else in Louisville and vicinity to be constantly writing to us about his claim. I have always said that Mr. Everett is a very clever fellow, and I am very sorry he cannot be obliged; but it does seem to me he ought to know we are interested to collect his claim, and therefore would do it if we could.

I am neither joking nor in a pet when I say we would thank him to transfer his business to some other, without any compensation for what we have done, provided he will see the court cost paid, for which we are security.

The sweet violet you inclosed came safely to hand, but it was so dry, and mashed so flat, that it crumbled to dust at the first attempt to handle it. The juice that mashed out of it stained a place in the letter, which I mean to preserve and cherish for the sake of her who procured it to be sent. My renewed good wishes to her in particular, and generally to all such of your relations who know me.

As ever,
LINCOLN.

TO JOSHUA F. SPEED.

SPRINGFIELD, ILLINOIS, July 4, 1842.

DEAR SPEED:—Yours of the 16th June was received only a day or two since. It was not mailed at Louisville till the 25th. You speak of the great time that has elapsed since I wrote you. Let me explain that. Your letter reached here a day or two after I started on the circuit. I was gone five or six weeks, so that I got the letters only a few weeks before Butler started to your country. I thought it scarcely worth while to write you the news which he could and would tell you more in detail. On his return he told me you would write me soon, and so I waited for your letter. As to my having been displeased with your advice, surely you know better than that. I know you do, and therefore will not labor to convince you. True, that subject is painful to me; but it is not your silence, or the silence of all the world, that can make me forget it. I acknowledge the correctness of your advice too; but before I resolve to do the one thing or the other, I must gain my confidence in my own ability to keep my resolves when they are made. In that ability you know I once prided myself as the only or chief gem of my character; that gem I lost—how and where you know too well. I have not yet regained it; and until I do, I cannot trust myself in any matter of much importance. I believe now that had you understood my case at the time as well as I understand yours afterward, by the aid you would have given me I should have sailed through clear, but that does not now afford me sufficient confidence to begin that or the like of that again. You make a kind acknowledgment of your obligations to me for your present happiness. I am pleased with that acknowledgment. But a thousand times more am I pleased to know that you enjoy a degree of happiness worthy of an acknowledgment. The truth is, I am not sure that there was any merit with me in the part I took in your difficulty; I was drawn to it by a fate. If I would I could not have done less than I did. I always was superstitious; I believe God made me one of the instruments of bringing your Fanny and you together, which union I have no doubt He had fore-ordained. Whatever He designs He will do for me yet. "Stand still, and see the salvation of the Lord" is my text just now. If, as you say, you have told Fanny all, I should have no objection to her seeing this letter, but for its reference to our friend here: let her seeing it depend upon whether she has ever known anything of my affairs; and if she has not, do not let her.
I do not think I can come to Kentucky this season. I am so poor and make so little headway in the world, that I drop back in a month of idleness as much as I gain in a year's sowing. I should like to visit you again. I should like to see that "sis" of yours that was absent when I was there, though I suppose she would run away again if she were to hear I was coming.
My respects and esteem to all your friends there, and, by your permission, my love to your Fanny.
Ever yours,
LINCOLN.

A LETTER FROM THE LOST TOWNSHIPS

Article written by Lincoln for the Sangamon Journal in ridicule of James Shields, who, as State Auditor, had declined to receive State Bank notes in payment of taxes. The above letter purported to come from a poor widow who, though supplied with State Bank paper, could not obtain a receipt for her tax bill. This, and another subsequent letter by Mary Todd, brought about the "Lincoln-Shields Duel."

LOST TOWNSHIPS

August 27, 1842.

DEAR Mr. PRINTER:
I see you printed that long letter I sent you a spell ago. I 'm quite encouraged by it, and can't keep from writing again. I think the printing of my letters will be a good thing all round—it will give me the benefit of being known by the world, and give the world the advantage of knowing what's going on in the Lost Townships, and give your paper respectability besides. So here comes another. Yesterday afternoon I hurried through cleaning up the dinner dishes and stepped over to neighbor S—— to see if his wife Peggy was as well as mout be expected, and hear what they called the baby. Well, when I got there and just turned round the corner of his log cabin, there he was, setting on the doorstep reading a newspaper. "How are you, Jeff?" says I. He sorter started when he heard me, for he hadn't seen me before.

"Why," says he, "I'm mad as the devil, Aunt 'Becca!" "What about?" says I; "ain't its hair the right color? None of that nonsense, Jeff; there ain't an honester woman in the Lost Townships than..."—"Than who?" says he; "what the mischief are you about?" I began to see I was running the wrong trail, and so says I, "Oh! nothing: I guess I was mistaken a little, that's all. But what is it you're mad about?"

"Why," says he, "I've been tugging ever since harvest, getting out wheat and hauling it to the river to raise State Bank paper enough to pay my tax this year and a little school debt I owe; and now, just as I've got it, here I open this infernal Extra Register, expecting to find it full of 'Glorious Democratic Victories' and 'High Comb'd Cocks,' when, lo and behold! I find a set of fellows, calling themselves officers of the State, have forbidden the tax collectors, and school commissioners to receive State paper at all; and so here it is dead on my hands. I don't now believe all the plunder I've got will fetch ready cash enough to pay my taxes and that school debt."

I was a good deal thunderstruck myself; for that was the first I had heard of the proclamation, and my old man was pretty much in the same fix with Jeff. We both stood a moment staring at one another without knowing what to say. At last says I, "Mr. S—— let me look at that paper." He handed it to me, when I read the proclamation over.

"There now," says he, "did you ever see such a piece of impudence and imposition as that?" I saw Jeff was in a good tune for saying some ill-natured things, and so I tho't I would just argue a little on the contrary side, and make him rant a spell if I could. "Why," says I, looking as dignified and thoughtful as I could, "it seems pretty tough, to be sure, to have to raise silver where there's none to be raised; but then, you say, 'there will be danger of loss' if it ain't done."

"Loss! damnation!" says he. "I defy Daniel Webster, I defy King Solomon, I defy the world—I defy—I defy—yes, I defy even you, Aunt 'Becca, to show how the people can lose anything by paying their taxes in State paper."

"Well," says I, "you see what the officers of State say about it, and they are a desarnin' set of men. But," says I, "I guess you're mistaken about what the proclamation says. It don't say the people will lose anything by the paper money being taken for taxes. It only says 'there will be danger of loss'; and though it is tolerable plain that the people can't lose by paying their taxes in something they can get easier than silver, instead of having to pay silver; and though it's just as plain that the State can't lose by taking State Bank paper, however low it may be, while she owes the bank more than the whole revenue, and can pay that paper over on her debt, dollar for dollar;—still there is danger of loss to the 'officers of State'; and you know, Jeff, we can't get along without officers of State."

"Damn officers of State!" says he; "that's what Whigs are always hurrahing for."

"Now, don't swear so, Jeff," says I, "you know I belong to the meetin', and swearin' hurts my feelings."

"Beg pardon, Aunt 'Becca," says he; "but I do say it's enough to make Dr. Goddard swear, to have tax to pay in silver, for nothing only that Ford may get his two thousand a year, and Shields his twenty-four hundred a year, and Carpenter his sixteen hundred a year, and all without 'danger of loss' by taking it in State paper. Yes, yes: it's plain enough now what these officers of State mean by 'danger of loss.' Wash, I s'pose, actually lost fifteen hundred dollars out of the three thousand that two of these 'officers of State' let him steal from the treasury, by being compelled to take it in State paper. Wonder if we don't have a proclamation before long, commanding us to make up this loss to Wash in silver."

And so he went on till his breath run out, and he had to stop. I couldn't think of anything to say just then, and so I begun to look over the paper again. "Ay! here's another proclamation, or something like it."

"Another?" says Jeff; "and whose egg is it, pray?"

I looked to the bottom of it, and read aloud, "Your obedient servant, James Shields, Auditor."

"Aha!" says Jeff, "one of them same three fellows again. Well read it, and let's hear what of it."

I read on till I came to where it says, "The object of this measure is to suspend the collection of the revenue for the current year."

"Now stop, now stop!" says he; "that's a lie a'ready, and I don't want to hear of it."

"Oh, maybe not," says I.

"I say it-is-a-lie. Suspend the collection, indeed! Will the collectors, that have taken their oaths to make the collection, dare to end it? Is there anything in law requiring them to perjure themselves at the bidding of James Shields?

"Will the greedy gullet of the penitentiary be satisfied with swallowing him instead of all of them, if they should venture to obey him? And would he not discover some 'danger of loss,' and be off about the time it came to taking their places?

"And suppose the people attempt to suspend, by refusing to pay; what then? The collectors would just jerk up their horses and cows, and the like, and sell them to the highest bidder for silver in hand, without valuation or redemption. Why, Shields didn't believe that story himself; it was never meant for the truth. If it was true, why was it not writ till five days after the proclamation? Why did n't Carlin and Carpenter sign it as well as Shields? Answer me that, Aunt 'Becca. I say it's a lie, and not a well told one at that. It grins out like a copper dollar. Shields is a fool as well as a liar. With him truth is out of the question; and as for getting a good, bright, passable lie out of him, you might as well try to strike fire from a cake of tallow. I stick to it, it's all an infernal Whig lie!"

"A Whig lie! Highty tighty!"

"Yes, a Whig lie; and it's just like everything the cursed British Whigs do. First they'll do some divilment, and then they'll tell a lie to hide it. And they don't care how plain a lie it is; they think they can cram any sort of a one down the throats of the ignorant Locofocos, as they call the Democrats."

"Why, Jeff, you're crazy: you don't mean to say Shields is a Whig!"

"Yes, I do."

"Why, look here! the proclamation is in your own Democratic paper, as you call it."

"I know it; and what of that? They only printed it to let us Democrats see the deviltry the Whigs are at."

"Well, but Shields is the auditor of this Loco—I mean this Democratic State."

65

"So he is, and Tyler appointed him to office."

"Tyler appointed him?"

"Yes (if you must chaw it over), Tyler appointed him; or, if it was n't him, it was old Granny Harrison, and that's all one. I tell you, Aunt 'Becca, there's no mistake about his being a Whig. Why, his very looks shows it; everything about him shows it: if I was deaf and blind, I could tell him by the smell. I seed him when I was down in Springfield last winter. They had a sort of a gatherin' there one night among the grandees, they called a fair. All the gals about town was there, and all the handsome widows and married women, finickin' about trying to look like gals, tied as tight in the middle, and puffed out at both ends, like bundles of fodder that had n't been stacked yet, but wanted stackin' pretty bad. And then they had tables all around the house kivered over with [———] caps and pincushions and ten thousand such little knick-knacks, tryin' to sell 'em to the fellows that were bowin', and scrapin' and kungeerin' about 'em. They would n't let no Democrats in, for fear they'd disgust the ladies, or scare the little gals, or dirty the floor. I looked in at the window, and there was this same fellow Shields floatin' about on the air, without heft or earthly substances, just like a lock of cat fur where cats had been fighting.

"He was paying his money to this one, and that one, and t' other one, and sufferin' great loss because it was n't silver instead of State paper; and the sweet distress he seemed to be in,—his very features, in the ecstatic agony of his soul, spoke audibly and distinctly, 'Dear girls, it is distressing, but I cannot marry you all. Too well I know how much you suffer; but do, do remember, it is not my fault that I am so handsome and so interesting.'

"As this last was expressed by a most exquisite contortion of his face, he seized hold of one of their hands, and squeezed, and held on to it about a quarter of an hour. 'Oh, my good fellow!' says I to myself, 'if that was one of our Democratic gals in the Lost Townships, the way you 'd get a brass pin let into you would be about up to the head.' He a Democrat! Fiddlesticks! I tell you, Aunt 'Becca, he's a Whig, and no mistake; nobody but a Whig could make such a conceity dunce of himself."

"Well," says I, "maybe he is; but, if he is, I 'm mistaken the worst sort. Maybe so, maybe so; but, if I am, I'll suffer by it; I'll be a Democrat if it turns out that Shields is a Whig, considerin' you shall be a Whig if he turns out a Democrat."

"A bargain, by jingoes!" says he; "but how will we find out?"

"Why," says I, "we'll just write and ax the printer."

"Agreed again!" says he; "and by thunder! if it does turn out that Shields is a Democrat, I never will——"

"Jefferson! Jefferson!"

"What do you want, Peggy?"

"Do get through your everlasting clatter some time, and bring me a gourd of water; the child's been crying for a drink this livelong hour."

"Let it die, then; it may as well die for water as to be taxed to death to fatten officers of State."

Jeff run off to get the water, though, just like he hadn't been saying anything spiteful, for he's a raal good-hearted fellow, after all, once you get at the foundation of him.

I walked into the house, and, "Why, Peggy," says I, "I declare we like to forgot you altogether."

"Oh, yes," says she, "when a body can't help themselves, everybody soon forgets 'em; but, thank God! by day after to-morrow I shall be well enough to milk the cows, and pen the calves, and wring the contrary ones' tails for 'em, and no thanks to nobody."

"Good evening, Peggy," says I, and so I sloped, for I seed she was mad at me for making Jeff neglect her so long.

And now, Mr. Printer, will you be sure to let us know in your next paper whether this Shields is a Whig or a Democrat? I don't care about it for myself, for I know well enough how it is already; but I want to convince Jeff. It may do some good to let him, and others like him, know who and what these officers of State are. It may help to send the present hypocritical set to where they belong, and to fill the places they now disgrace with men who will do more work for less pay, and take fewer airs while they are doing it. It ain't sensible to think that the same men who get us in trouble will change their course; and yet it's pretty plain if some change for the better is not made, it's not long that either Peggy or I or any of us will have a cow left to milk, or a calf's tail to wring.

Yours truly,

REBECCA ———.

INVITATION TO HENRY CLAY.

SPRINGFIELD, ILL., Aug 29, 1842.

HON. HENRY CLAY, Lexington, Ky.

DEAR SIR:—We hear you are to visit Indianapolis, Indiana, on the 5th Of October next. If our information in this is correct we hope you will not deny us the pleasure of seeing you in our State. We are aware of the toil necessarily incident to a journey by one circumstanced as you are; but once you have embarked, as you have already determined to do, the toil would not be greatly augmented by extending the journey to our capital. The season of the year will be most favorable for good roads, and pleasant weather; and although we cannot but believe you would be highly gratified with such a visit to the prairie-land, the pleasure it would give us and thousands such as we is beyond all question. You have never visited Illinois, or at least this portion of it; and should you now yield to our request, we promise you such a reception as shall be worthy of the man on whom are now turned the fondest hopes of a great and suffering nation. Please inform us at the earliest convenience whether we may expect you.

Very respectfully your obedient servants,

A. G. HENRY, A. T. BLEDSOE,
C. BIRCHALL, A. LINCOLN,
G. M. CABANNISS, ROB'T IRWIN,
P. A. SAUNDERS, J. M. ALLEN,
F. N. FRANCIS.
Executive Committee "Clay Club."
(Clay's answer, September 6, 1842, declines with thanks.)

CORRESPONDENCE ABOUT THE LINCOLN-SHIELDS DUEL.

TREMONT, September 17, 1842.

ABRA. LINCOLN, ESQ.:—I regret that my absence on public business compelled me to postpone a matter of private consideration a little longer than I could have desired. It will only be necessary, however, to account for it by informing you that I have been to Quincy on business that would not admit of delay. I will now state briefly the reasons of my troubling you with this communication, the disagreeable nature of which I regret, as I had hoped to avoid any difficulty with any one in Springfield while residing there, by endeavoring to conduct myself in such a way amongst both my political friends and opponents as to escape the necessity of any. Whilst thus abstaining from giving provocation, I have become the object of slander, vituperation, and personal abuse, which were I capable of submitting to, I would prove myself worthy of the whole of it.

In two or three of the last numbers of the Sangamon Journal, articles of the most personal nature and calculated to degrade me have made their appearance. On inquiring, I was informed by the editor of that paper, through the medium of my friend General Whitesides, that you are the author of those articles. This information satisfies me that I have become by some means or other the object of your secret hostility. I will not take the trouble of inquiring into the reason of all this; but I will take the liberty of requiring a full, positive, and absolute retraction of all offensive allusions used by you in these communications, in relation to my private character and standing as a man, as an apology for the insults conveyed in them.

This may prevent consequences which no one will regret more than myself.

Your obedient servant, JAS. SHIELDS.

TO J. SHIELDS.

TREMONT, September 17, 1842

JAS. SHIELDS, ESQ.:—Your note of to-day was handed me by General Whitesides. In that note you say you have been informed, through the medium of the editor of the Journal, that I am the author of certain articles in that paper which you deem personally abusive of you; and without stopping to inquire whether I really am the author, or to point out what is offensive in them, you demand an unqualified retraction of all that is offensive, and then proceed to hint at consequences.

Now, sir, there is in this so much assumption of facts and so much of menace as to consequences, that I cannot submit to answer that note any further than I have, and to add that the consequences to which I suppose you allude would be matter of as great regret to me as it possibly could to you.

Respectfully,
A. LINCOLN.

TO A. LINCOLN FROM JAS. SHIELDS

TREMONT, September 17, 1842.

ABRA. LINCOLN, ESQ.:—In reply to my note of this date, you intimate that I assume facts and menace consequences, and that you cannot submit to answer it further. As now, sir, you desire it, I will be a little more particular. The editor of the Sangamon Journal gave me to understand that you are the author of an article which appeared, I think, in that paper of the 2d September instant, headed "The Lost Townships," and signed Rebecca or 'Becca. I would therefore take the liberty of asking whether you are the author of said article, or any other over the same signature which has appeared in any of the late numbers of that paper. If so, I repeat my request of an absolute retraction of all offensive allusions contained therein in relation to my private character and standing. If you are not the author of any of these articles, your denial will be sufficient. I will say further, it is not my intention to menace, but to do myself justice.

Your obedient servant, JAS. SHIELDS.

MEMORANDUM OF INSTRUCTIONS TO E. H. MERRYMAN,

Lincoln's Second,

September 19, 1842.
In case Whitesides shall signify a wish to adjust this affair without further difficulty, let him know that if the present papers be withdrawn, and a note from Mr. Shields asking to know if I am the author of the articles of which he complains, and asking that I shall make him gentlemanly satisfaction if I am the author, and this without menace, or dictation as to what that satisfaction shall be, a pledge is made that the following answer shall be given:
"I did write the 'Lost Townships' letter which appeared in the Journal of the 2d instant, but had no participation in any form in any other article alluding to you. I wrote that wholly for political effect—I had no intention of injuring your personal or private character or standing as a man or a gentleman; and I did not then think, and do not now think, that that article could produce or has produced that effect against you; and had I anticipated such an effect I would have forborne to write it. And I will add that your conduct toward me, so far as I know, had always been gentlemanly; and that I had no personal pique against you, and no cause for any."
If this should be done, I leave it with you to arrange what shall and what shall not be published. If nothing like this is done, the preliminaries of the fight are to be—
First. Weapons: Cavalry broadswords of the largest size, precisely equal in all respects, and such as now used by the cavalry company at Jacksonville.
Second. Position: A plank ten feet long, and from nine to twelve inches broad, to be firmly fixed on edge, on the ground, as the line between us, which neither is to pass his foot over upon forfeit of his life. Next a line drawn on the ground on either side of said plank and parallel with it, each at the distance of the whole length of the sword and three feet additional from the plank; and the passing of his own such line by either party during the fight shall be deemed a surrender of the contest.
Third. Time: On Thursday evening at five o'clock, if you can get it so; but in no case to be at a greater distance of time than Friday evening at five o'clock.
Fourth. Place: Within three miles of Alton, on the opposite side of the river, the particular spot to be agreed on by you. Any preliminary details coming within the above rules you are at liberty to make at your discretion; but you are in no case to swerve from these rules, or to pass beyond their limits.

TO JOSHUA F. SPEED.

SPRINGFIELD, October 4, 1842.

DEAR SPEED:—You have heard of my duel with Shields, and I have now to inform you that the dueling business still rages in this city. Day before yesterday Shields challenged Butler, who accepted, and proposed fighting next morning at sunrise in Bob Allen's meadow, one hundred yards' distance, with rifles. To this Whitesides, Shields's second, said "No," because of the law. Thus ended duel No. 2. Yesterday Whitesides chose to consider himself insulted by Dr. Merryman, so sent him a kind of quasi-challenge, inviting him to meet him at the Planter's House in St. Louis on the next Friday, to settle their difficulty. Merryman made me his friend, and sent Whitesides a note, inquiring to know if he meant his note as a challenge, and if so, that he would, according to the law in such case made and provided, prescribe the terms of the meeting. Whitesides returned for answer that if Merryman would meet him at the Planter's House as desired, he would challenge him. Merryman replied in a note that he denied Whitesides's right to dictate time and place, but that he (Merryman) would waive the question of time, and meet him at Louisiana, Missouri. Upon my presenting this note to Whitesides and stating verbally its contents, he declined receiving it, saying he had business in St. Louis, and it was as near as Louisiana. Merryman then directed me to notify Whitesides that he should publish the correspondence between them, with such comments as he thought fit. This I did. Thus it stood at bedtime last night. This morning Whitesides, by his friend Shields, is praying for a new trial, on the ground that he was mistaken in Merryman's proposition to meet him at Louisiana, Missouri, thinking it was the State of Louisiana. This Merryman hoots at, and is preparing his publication; while the town is in a ferment, and a street fight somewhat anticipated.

But I began this letter not for what I have been writing, but to say something on that subject which you know to be of such infinite solicitude to me. The immense sufferings you endured from the first days of September till the middle of February you never tried to conceal from me, and I well understood. You have now been the husband of a lovely woman nearly eight months. That you are happier now than the day you married her I well know, for without you could not be living. But I have your word for it, too, and the returning elasticity of spirits which is manifested in your letters. But I want to ask a close question, "Are you now in feeling as well as judgment glad that you are married as you are?" From anybody but me this would be an impudent question, not to be tolerated; but I know you will pardon it in me. Please answer it quickly, as I am impatient to know. I have sent my love to your Fanny so often, I fear she is getting tired of it. However, I venture to tender it again.

Yours forever,
LINCOLN.

TO JAMES S. IRWIN.

SPRINGFIELD, November 2, 1842.

JAS. S. IRWIN ESQ.:

Owing to my absence, yours of the 22nd ult. was not received till this moment. Judge Logan and myself are willing to attend to any business in the Supreme Court you may send us. As to fees, it is impossible to establish a rule that will apply in all, or even a great many cases. We believe we are never accused of being very unreasonable in this particular; and we would always be easily satisfied, provided we could see the money—but whatever fees we earn at a distance, if not paid before, we have noticed, we never hear of after the work is done. We, therefore, are growing a little sensitive on that point.

Yours etc.,
A. LINCOLN.

1843

RESOLUTIONS AT A WHIG MEETING AT SPRINGFIELD, ILLINOIS, MARCH 1, 1843.

The object of the meeting was stated by Mr. Lincoln of Springfield, who offered the following resolutions, which were unanimously adopted:

Resolved, That a tariff of duties on imported goods, producing sufficient revenue for the payment of the necessary expenditures of the National Government, and so adjusted as to protect American industry, is indispensably necessary to the prosperity of the American people.

Resolved, That we are opposed to direct taxation for the support of the National Government.

Resolved, That a national bank, properly restricted, is highly necessary and proper to the establishment and maintenance of a sound currency, and for the cheap and safe collection, keeping, and disbursing of the public revenue.

Resolved, That the distribution of the proceeds of the sales of the public lands, upon the principles of Mr. Clay's bill, accords with the best interests of the nation, and particularly with those of the State of Illinois.

Resolved, That we recommend to the Whigs of each Congressional district of the State to nominate and support at the approaching election a candidate of their own principles, regardless of the chances of success.

Resolved, That we recommend to the Whigs of all portions of the State to adopt and rigidly adhere to the convention system of nominating candidates.

Resolved, That we recommend to the Whigs of each Congressional district to hold a district convention on or before the first Monday of May next, to be composed of a number of delegates from each county equal to double the number of its representatives in the General Assembly, provided, each county shall have at least one delegate. Said delegates to be chosen by primary meetings of the Whigs, at such times and places as they in their respective counties may see fit. Said district conventions each to nominate one candidate for Congress, and one delegate to a national convention for

the purpose of nominating candidates for President and Vice-President of the United States. The seven delegates so nominated to a national convention to have power to add two delegates to their own number, and to fill all vacancies.
Resolved, That A. T. Bledsoe, S. T. Logan, and A. Lincoln be appointed a committee to prepare an address to the people of the State.
Resolved, That N. W. Edwards, A. G. Henry, James H. Matheny, John C. Doremus, and James C. Conkling be appointed a Whig Central State Committee, with authority to fill any vacancy that may occur in the committee.

CIRCULAR FROM WHIG COMMITTEE.

Address to the People of Illinois.

FELLOW-CITIZENS:-By a resolution of a meeting of such of the Whigs of the State as are now at Springfield, we, the undersigned, were appointed to prepare an address to you. The performance of that task we now undertake.
Several resolutions were adopted by the meeting; and the chief object of this address is to show briefly the reasons for their adoption.
The first of those resolutions declares a tariff of duties upon foreign importations, producing sufficient revenue for the support of the General Government, and so adjusted as to protect American industry, to be indispensably necessary to the prosperity of the American people; and the second declares direct taxation for a national revenue to be improper. Those two resolutions are kindred in their nature, and therefore proper and convenient to be considered together. The question of protection is a subject entirely too broad to be crowded into a few pages only, together with several other subjects. On that point we therefore content ourselves with giving the following extracts from the writings of Mr. Jefferson, General Jackson, and the speech of Mr. Calhoun:
"To be independent for the comforts of life, we must fabricate them ourselves. We must now place the manufacturer by the side of the agriculturalist. The grand inquiry now is, Shall we make our own comforts, or go without them at the will of a foreign nation? He, therefore, who is now against domestic manufactures must be for reducing us either to dependence on that foreign nation, or to be clothed in skins and to live like wild beasts in dens and caverns. I am not one of those; experience has taught me that manufactures are now as necessary to our independence as to our comfort." Letter of Mr. Jefferson to Benjamin Austin.
"I ask, What is the real situation of the agriculturalist? Where has the American farmer a market for his surplus produce? Except for cotton, he has neither a foreign nor a home market. Does not this clearly prove, when there is no market at home or abroad, that there [is] too much labor employed in agriculture? Common sense at once points out the remedy. Take from agriculture six hundred thousand men, women, and children, and you will at once give a market for more breadstuffs than all Europe now furnishes. In short, we have been too long subject to the policy of British merchants. It is time we should become a little more Americanized, and instead of feeding the paupers and laborers of England, feed our own; or else in a short time, by continuing our present policy, we shall all be rendered paupers ourselves."—General Jackson's Letter to Dr. Coleman.
"When our manufactures are grown to a certain perfection, as they soon will be, under the fostering care of government, the farmer will find a ready market for his surplus produce, and,—what is of equal consequence—a certain and cheap supply of all he wants; his prosperity will diffuse itself to every class of the community." Speech of Hon. J. C. Calhoun on the Tariff.
The question of revenue we will now briefly consider. For several years past the revenues of the government have been unequal to its expenditures, and consequently loan after loan, sometimes direct and sometimes indirect in form, has been resorted to. By this means a new national debt has been created, and is still growing on us with a rapidity fearful to contemplate—a rapidity only reasonably to be expected in time of war. This state of things has been produced by a prevailing unwillingness either to increase the tariff or resort to direct taxation. But the one or the other must come. Coming expenditures must be met, and the present debt must be paid; and money cannot always be borrowed for these objects. The system of loans is but temporary in its nature, and must soon explode. It is a system not only ruinous while it lasts, but one that must soon fail and leave us destitute. As an individual who undertakes to live by borrowing soon finds his original means devoured by interest, and, next, no one left to borrow from, so must it be with a government. We repeat, then, that a tariff sufficient for revenue, or a direct tax, must soon be resorted to; and, indeed, we believe this alternative is now denied by no one. But which system shall be adopted? Some of our opponents, in theory, admit the propriety of a tariff sufficient for a revenue, but even they will not in practice vote for such a tariff; while others boldly advocate direct taxation. Inasmuch, therefore, as some of them boldly advocate direct taxation, and all the rest—or so nearly all as to make exceptions needless—refuse to adopt the tariff, we think it is doing them no injustice to class them all as advocates of direct taxation. Indeed, we believe they are only delaying an open avowal of the system till they can assure themselves that the people will tolerate it. Let us, then, briefly compare the two systems. The tariff is the cheaper system, because the duties, being collected in large parcels at a few commercial points, will require comparatively few officers in their collection; while by the direct-tax system the land must be literally covered with assessors and collectors, going forth like swarms of Egyptian locusts, devouring every blade of grass and other green thing. And, again, by the tariff system the whole revenue is paid by the consumers of foreign goods, and those chiefly

the luxuries, and not the necessaries, of life. By this system the man who contents himself to live upon the products of his own country pays nothing at all. And surely that country is extensive enough, and its products abundant and varied enough, to answer all the real wants of its people. In short, by this system the burthen of revenue falls almost entirely on the wealthy and luxurious few, while the substantial and laboring many who live at home, and upon home products, go entirely free. By the direct-tax system none can escape. However strictly the citizen may exclude from his premises all foreign luxuries,—fine cloths, fine silks, rich wines, golden chains, and diamond rings,—still, for the possession of his house, his barn, and his homespun, he is to be perpetually haunted and harassed by the tax-gatherer. With these views we leave it to be determined whether we or our opponents are the more truly democratic on the subject.

The third resolution declares the necessity and propriety of a national bank. During the last fifty years so much has been said and written both as to the constitutionality and expediency of such an institution, that we could not hope to improve in the least on former discussions of the subject, were we to undertake it. We, therefore, upon the question of constitutionality content ourselves with remarking the facts that the first national bank was established chiefly by the same men who formed the Constitution, at a time when that instrument was but two years old, and receiving the sanction, as President, of the immortal Washington; that the second received the sanction, as President, of Mr. Madison, to whom common consent has awarded the proud title of "Father of the Constitution"; and subsequently the sanction of the Supreme Court, the most enlightened judicial tribunal in the world. Upon the question of expediency, we only ask you to examine the history of the times during the existence of the two banks, and compare those times with the miserable present.

The fourth resolution declares the expediency of Mr. Clay's land bill. Much incomprehensible jargon is often used against the constitutionality of this measure. We forbear, in this place, attempting an answer to it, simply because, in our opinion, those who urge it are through party zeal resolved not to see or acknowledge the truth. The question of expediency, at least so far as Illinois is concerned, seems to us the clearest imaginable. By the bill we are to receive annually a large sum of money, no part of which we otherwise receive. The precise annual sum cannot be known in advance; it doubtless will vary in different years. Still it is something to know that in the last year—a year of almost unparalleled pecuniary pressure—it amounted to more than forty thousand dollars. This annual income, in the midst of our almost insupportable difficulties, in the days of our severest necessity, our political opponents are furiously resolving to take and keep from us. And for what? Many silly reasons are given, as is usual in cases where a single good one is not to be found. One is that by giving us the proceeds of the lands we impoverish the national treasury, and thereby render necessary an increase of the tariff. This may be true; but if so, the amount of it only is that those whose pride, whose abundance of means, prompt them to spurn the manufactures of our country, and to strut in British cloaks and coats and pantaloons, may have to pay a few cents more on the yard for the cloth that makes them. A terrible evil, truly, to the Illinois farmer, who never wore, nor ever expects to wear, a single yard of British goods in his whole life. Another of their reasons is that by the passage and continuance of Mr. Clay's bill, we prevent the passage of a bill which would give us more. This, if it were sound in itself, is waging destructive war with the former position; for if Mr. Clay's bill impoverishes the treasury too much, what shall be said of one that impoverishes it still more? But it is not sound in itself. It is not true that Mr. Clay's bill prevents the passage of one more favorable to us of the new States. Considering the strength and opposite interest of the old States, the wonder is that they ever permitted one to pass so favorable as Mr. Clay's. The last twenty-odd years' efforts to reduce the price of the lands, and to pass graduation bills and cession bills, prove the assertion to be true; and if there were no experience in support of it, the reason itself is plain. The States in which none, or few, of the public lands lie, and those consequently interested against parting with them except for the best price, are the majority; and a moment's reflection will show that they must ever continue the majority, because by the time one of the original new States (Ohio, for example) becomes populous and gets weight in Congress, the public lands in her limits are so nearly sold out that in every point material to this question she becomes an old State. She does not wish the price reduced, because there is none left for her citizens to buy; she does not wish them ceded to the States in which they lie, because they no longer lie in her limits, and she will get nothing by the cession. In the nature of things, the States interested in the reduction of price, in graduation, in cession, and in all similar projects, never can be the majority. Nor is there reason to hope that any of them can ever succeed as a Democratic party measure, because we have heretofore seen that party in full power, year after year, with many of their leaders making loud professions in favor of these projects, and yet doing nothing. What reason, then, is there to believe they will hereafter do better? In every light in which we can view this question, it amounts simply to this: Shall we accept our share of the proceeds under Mr. Clay's bill, or shall we rather reject that and get nothing?

The fifth resolution recommends that a Whig candidate for Congress be run in every district, regardless of the chances of success. We are aware that it is sometimes a temporary gratification, when a friend cannot succeed, to be able to choose between opponents; but we believe that that gratification is the seed-time which never fails to be followed by a most abundant harvest of bitterness. By this policy we entangle ourselves. By voting for our opponents, such of us as do it in some measure estop ourselves to complain of their acts, however glaringly wrong we may believe them to be. By this policy no one portion of our friends can ever be certain as to what course another portion may adopt; and by this want of mutual and perfect understanding our political identity is partially frittered away and lost. And, again, those who are thus elected by our aid ever become our bitterest persecutors. Take a few prominent examples. In 1830 Reynolds was elected Governor; in 1835 we exerted our whole strength to elect Judge Young to the United States Senate, which effort, though failing, gave him the prominence that subsequently elected him; in 1836 General Ewing, was so elected to the United States Senate; and yet let us ask what three men have been more perseveringly vindictive in their assaults upon all our men and measures than they? During the last summer the whole State was covered with pamphlet editions of misrepresentations against us, methodized into chapters and verses, written by two of these same men,—Reynolds and Young, in which they did not stop at charging us with error merely, but roundly denounced us as the designing enemies of human liberty, itself. If it be the will of Heaven that such men shall politically live, be it so; but never, never again permit them to draw a particle of their sustenance from us.

The sixth resolution recommends the adoption of the convention system for the nomination of candidates. This we believe to be of the very first importance. Whether the system is right in itself we do not stop to inquire; contenting ourselves with trying to show that, while our opponents use it, it is madness in us not to defend ourselves with it. Experience has shown that we cannot successfully defend ourselves without it. For examples, look at the elections of last year. Our candidate for governor, with the approbation of a large portion of the party, took the field without a nomination, and in open opposition to the system. Wherever in the counties the Whigs had held conventions and nominated candidates for the Legislature, the aspirants who were not nominated were induced to rebel against the nominations, and to become candidates, as is said, "on their own hook." And, go where you would into a large Whig county, you were sure to find the Whigs not contending shoulder to shoulder against the common enemy, but divided into factions, and fighting furiously with one another. The election came, and what was the result? The governor beaten, the Whig vote being decreased many thousands since 1840, although the Democratic vote had not increased any. Beaten almost everywhere for members of the Legislature,—Tazewell, with her four hundred Whig majority, sending a delegation half Democratic; Vermillion, with her five hundred, doing the same; Coles, with her four hundred, sending two out of three; and Morgan, with her two hundred and fifty, sending three out of four,—and this to say nothing of the numerous other less glaring examples; the whole winding up with the aggregate number of twenty-seven Democratic representatives sent from Whig counties. As to the senators, too, the result was of the same character. And it is most worthy to be remembered that of all the Whigs in the State who ran against the regular nominees, a single one only was elected. Although they succeeded in defeating the nominees almost by scores, they too were defeated, and the spoils chucklingly borne off by the common enemy.

We do not mention the fact of many of the Whigs opposing the convention system heretofore for the purpose of censuring them. Far from it. We expressly protest against such a conclusion. We know they were generally, perhaps universally, as good and true Whigs as we ourselves claim to be.

We mention it merely to draw attention to the disastrous result it produced, as an example forever hereafter to be avoided. That "union is strength" is a truth that has been known, illustrated, and declared in various ways and forms in all ages of the world. That great fabulist and philosopher Aesop illustrated it by his fable of the bundle of sticks; and he whose wisdom surpasses that of all philosophers has declared that "a house divided against itself cannot stand." It is to induce our friends to act upon this important and universally acknowledged truth that we urge the adoption of the convention system. Reflection will prove that there is no other way of practically applying it. In its application we know there will be incidents temporarily painful; but, after all, those incidents will be fewer and less intense with than without the system. If two friends aspire to the same office it is certain that both cannot succeed. Would it not, then, be much less painful to have the question decided by mutual friends some time before, than to snarl and quarrel until the day of election, and then both be beaten by the common enemy?

Before leaving this subject, we think proper to remark that we do not understand the resolution as intended to recommend the application of the convention system to the nomination of candidates for the small offices no way connected with politics; though we must say we do not perceive that such an application of it would be wrong.

The seventh resolution recommends the holding of district conventions in May next, for the purpose of nominating candidates for Congress. The propriety of this rests upon the same reasons with that of the sixth, and therefore needs no further discussion.

The eighth and ninth also relate merely to the practical application of the foregoing, and therefore need no discussion. Before closing, permit us to add a few reflections on the present condition and future prospects of the Whig party. In almost all the States we have fallen into the minority, and despondency seems to prevail universally among us. Is there just cause for this? In 1840 we carried the nation by more than a hundred and forty thousand majority. Our opponents charged that we did it by fraudulent voting; but whatever they may have believed, we know the charge to be untrue. Where, now, is that mighty host? Have they gone over to the enemy? Let the results of the late elections answer. Every State which has fallen off from the Whig cause since 1840 has done so not by giving more Democratic votes than they did then, but by giving fewer Whig. Bouck, who was elected Democratic Governor of New York last fall by more than 15,000 majority, had not then as many votes as he had in 1840, when he was beaten by seven or eight thousand. And so has it been in all the other States which have fallen away from our cause. From this it is evident that tens of thousands in the late elections have not voted at all. Who and what are they? is an important question, as respects the future. They can come forward and give us the victory again. That all, or nearly all, of them are Whigs is most apparent. Our opponents, stung to madness by the defeat of 1840, have ever since rallied with more than their usual unanimity. It has not been they that have been kept from the polls. These facts show what the result must be, once the people again rally in their entire strength. Proclaim these facts, and predict this result; and although unthinking opponents may smile at us, the sagacious ones will "believe and tremble." And why shall the Whigs not all rally again? Are their principles less dear now than in 1840? Have any of their doctrines since then been discovered to be untrue? It is true, the victory of 1840 did not produce the happy results anticipated; but it is equally true, as we believe, that the unfortunate death of General Harrison was the cause of the failure. It was not the election of General Harrison that was expected to produce happy effects, but the measures to be adopted by his administration. By means of his death, and the unexpected course of his successor, those measures were never adopted. How could the fruits follow? The consequences we always predicted would follow the failure of those measures have followed, and are now upon us in all their horrors. By the course of Mr. Tyler the policy of our opponents has continued in operation, still leaving them with the advantage of charging all its evils upon us as the results of a Whig administration. Let none be deceived by this somewhat plausible, though entirely false charge. If they ask us for the sufficient and sound currency we promised, let them be answered that we only promised it through the medium of a national bank, which they, aided by Mr. Tyler, prevented our establishing. And let them be reminded, too, that their own policy in relation to the currency has all the time been, and still is, in full operation. Let us then again come forth in our might, and by a second victory accomplish that which death prevented in the first. We can do it. When did the Whigs ever fail if they were fully aroused and united? Even in single States, under such circumstances, defeat seldom overtakes them. Call to mind the contested elections within the last few years, and particularly those of Moore and Letcher from Kentucky, Newland and Graham from North Carolina, and the famous New Jersey case. In all these districts Locofocoism had stalked omnipotent before; but when the whole people were aroused by its enormities on those occasions, they put it down, never to rise again.

We declare it to be our solemn conviction, that the Whigs are always a majority of this nation; and that to make them always successful needs but to get them all to the polls and to vote unitedly. This is the great desideratum. Let us make every effort to attain it. At every election, let every Whig act as though he knew the result to depend upon his action. In the great contest of 1840 some more than twenty one hundred thousand votes were cast, and so surely as there shall be that many, with the ordinary increase added, cast in 1844 that surely will a Whig be elected President of the United States.

A. LINCOLN. S. T. LOGAN. A. T. BLEDSOE.
March 4, 1843.

TO JOHN BENNETT.

SPRINGFIELD, March 7, 1843.

FRIEND BENNETT:
Your letter of this day was handed me by Mr. Miles. It is too late now to effect the object you desire. On yesterday morning the most of the Whig members from this district got together and agreed to hold the convention at Tremont in Tazewell County. I am sorry to hear that any of the Whigs of your county, or indeed of any county, should longer be against conventions. On last Wednesday evening a meeting of all the Whigs then here from all parts of the State was held, and the question of the propriety of conventions was brought up and fully discussed, and at the end of the discussion a resolution recommending the system of conventions to all the Whigs of the State was unanimously adopted. Other resolutions were also passed, all of which will appear in the next Journal. The meeting also appointed a committee to draft an address to the people of the State, which address will also appear in the next journal.

In it you will find a brief argument in favor of conventions—and although I wrote it myself I will say to you that it is conclusive upon the point and can not be reasonably answered. The right way for you to do is hold your meeting and appoint delegates any how, and if there be any who will not take part, let it be so. The matter will work so well this time that even they who now oppose will come in next time.

The convention is to be held at Tremont on the 5th of April and according to the rule we have adopted your county is to have delegates—being double your representation.

If there be any good Whig who is disposed to stick out against conventions get him at least to read the arguement in their favor in the address.
Yours as ever,
A. LINCOLN.

JOSHUA F. SPEED.

SPRINGFIELD, March 24, 1843.

DEAR SPEED:—We had a meeting of the Whigs of the county here on last Monday to appoint delegates to a district convention; and Baker beat me, and got the delegation instructed to go for him. The meeting, in spite of my attempt to decline it, appointed me one of the delegates; so that in getting Baker the nomination I shall be fixed a good deal like a fellow who is made a groomsman to a man that has cut him out and is marrying his own dear "gal." About the prospects of your having a namesake at our town, can't say exactly yet.
A. LINCOLN.

TO MARTIN M. MORRIS.

SPRINGFIELD, ILL., March 26, 1843.

FRIEND MORRIS:
Your letter of the a 3 d, was received on yesterday morning, and for which (instead of an excuse, which you thought proper to ask) I tender you my sincere thanks. It is truly gratifying to me to learn that, while the people of Sangamon have cast me off, my old friends of Menard, who have known me longest and best, stick to me. It would astonish, if not amuse, the older citizens to learn that I (a stranger, friendless, uneducated, penniless boy, working on a flatboat at ten dollars per month) have been put down here as the candidate of pride, wealth, and aristocratic family distinction. Yet so, chiefly, it was. There was, too, the strangest combination of church influence against me. Baker is a Campbellite; and therefore, as I suppose, with few exceptions got all that church. My wife has some relations in the Presbyterian churches, and some with the Episcopal churches; and therefore, wherever it would tell, I was set down as either the one or the other, while it was everywhere contended that no Christian ought to go for me, because I belonged to no church, was suspected of being a deist, and had talked about fighting a duel. With all these things, Baker, of course, had nothing to do. Nor do I complain of them. As to his own church going for him, I think that was right enough, and as to the influences I have spoken of in the other, though they were very strong, it would be grossly untrue and unjust to charge that they acted upon them in a body or were very near so. I only mean that those influences levied a tax of a considerable per cent. upon my strength throughout the religious controversy. But enough of this.
You say that in choosing a candidate for Congress you have an equal right with Sangamon, and in this you are undoubtedly correct. In agreeing to withdraw if the Whigs of Sangamon should go against me, I did not mean that they alone were worth consulting, but that if she, with her heavy delegation, should be against me, it would be impossible for me to succeed, and therefore I had as well decline. And in relation to Menard having rights, permit me fully to recognize them, and to express the opinion that, if she and Mason act circumspectly, they will in the convention be able so far to enforce their rights as to decide absolutely which one of the candidates shall be successful. Let me show the reason of this. Hardin, or some other Morgan candidate, will get Putnam, Marshall, Woodford, Tazewell, and Logan—making sixteen. Then you and Mason, having three, can give the victory to either side.
You say you shall instruct your delegates for me, unless I object. I certainly shall not object. That would be too pleasant a compliment for me to tread in the dust. And besides, if anything should happen (which, however, is not probable) by which Baker should be thrown out of the fight, I would be at liberty to accept the nomination if I could get it. I do, however, feel myself bound not to hinder him in any way from getting the nomination. I should despise myself were I to attempt it. I think, then, it would be proper for your meeting to appoint three delegates and to instruct them to go for some one as the first choice, some one else as a second, and perhaps some one as a third; and if in those instructions I were named as the first choice, it would gratify me very much. If you wish to hold the balance of power, it is important for you to attend to and secure the vote of Mason also: You should be sure to have men appointed delegates that you know you can safely confide in. If yourself and James Short were appointed from your county, all would be safe; but whether Jim's woman affair a year ago might not be in the way of his appointment is a question. I don't know whether you know it, but I know him to be as honorable a man as there is in the world. You have my permission, and even request, to show this letter to Short; but to no one else, unless it be a very particular friend who you know will not speak of it.
Yours as ever, A. LINCOLN.
P. S Will you write me again?

TO MARTIN M. MORRIS.

April 14, 1843.

FRIEND MORRIS:
I have heard it intimated that Baker has been attempting to get you or Miles, or both of you, to violate the instructions of the meeting that appointed you, and to go for him. I have insisted, and still insist, that this cannot be true. Surely Baker would not do the like. As well might Hardin ask me to vote for him in the convention. Again, it is said there will be an attempt to get up instructions in your county requiring you to go for Baker. This is all wrong. Upon the same rule, Why might not I fly from the decision against me in Sangamon, and get up instructions to their delegates to go for me? There are at least twelve hundred Whigs in the county that took no part, and yet I would as soon put my head in the fire as to attempt it. Besides, if any one should get the nomination by such extraordinary means, all harmony in the district would inevitably be lost. Honest Whigs (and very nearly all of them are honest) would not quietly abide such enormities. I repeat, such an attempt on Baker's part cannot be true. Write me at Springfield how the matter is. Don't show or speak of this letter.

A. LINCOLN

TO GEN. J. J. HARDIN.

SPRINGFIELD, May 11, 1843.

FRIEND HARDIN:
Butler informs me that he received a letter from you, in which you expressed some doubt whether the Whigs of Sangamon will support you cordially. You may, at once, dismiss all fears on that subject. We have already resolved to make a particular effort to give you the very largest majority possible in our county. From this, no Whig of the county dissents. We have many objects for doing it. We make it a matter of honor and pride to do it; we do it because we love the Whig cause; we do it because we like you personally; and last, we wish to convince you that we do not bear that hatred to Morgan County that you people have so long seemed to imagine. You will see by the journals of this week that we propose, upon pain of losing a barbecue, to give you twice as great a majority in this county as you shall receive in your own. I got up the proposal.

Who of the five appointed is to write the district address? I did the labor of writing one address this year, and got thunder for my reward. Nothing new here.

Yours as ever, A. LINCOLN.

P. S.—I wish you would measure one of the largest of those swords we took to Alton and write me the length of it, from tip of the point to tip of the hilt, in feet and inches. I have a dispute about the length.

A. L.

VOLUME II., 1843-1858

1843

FIRST CHILD

TO JOSHUA F. SPEED. SPRINGFIELD, May 18, 1843.

DEAR SPEED:—Yours of the 9th instant is duly received, which I do not meet as a "bore," but as a most welcome visitor. I will answer the business part of it first.

In relation to our Congress matter here, you were right in supposing I would support the nominee. Neither Baker nor I, however, is the man, but Hardin, so far as I can judge from present appearances. We shall have no split or trouble about the matter; all will be harmony. In relation to the "coming events" about which Butler wrote you, I had not heard one word before I got your letter; but I have so much confidence in the judgment of Butler on such a subject that I incline to think there may be some reality in it. What day does Butler appoint? By the way, how do "events" of the same sort come on in your family? Are you possessing houses and lands, and oxen and asses, and men-servants and maid-servants, and begetting sons and daughters? We are not keeping house, but boarding at the Globe Tavern, which is very well kept now by a widow lady of the name of Beck. Our room (the same that Dr. Wallace occupied there) and boarding only costs us four dollars a week. Ann Todd was married something more than a year since to a fellow by the name of Campbell, and who, Mary says, is pretty much of a "dunce," though he has a little money and property. They live in Boonville, Missouri, and have not been heard from lately enough for me to say anything about her health. I reckon it will scarcely be in our power to visit Kentucky this year. Besides poverty and the necessity of attending to business, those "coming events," I suspect, would be somewhat in the way. I most heartily wish you and your Fanny would not fail to come. Just let us know the time, and we will have a room provided for you at our house, and all be merry together for a while. Be sure to give my respects to your mother and family; assure her that if ever I come near her, I will not fail to call and see her. Mary joins in sending love to your Fanny and you.

Yours as ever,

A. LINCOLN.

1844

TO Gen. J. J. HARDIN.

SPRINGFIELD, May 21, 1844.

DEAR HARDIN: Knowing that you have correspondents enough, I have forborne to trouble you heretofore; and I now only do so to get you to set a matter right which has got wrong with one of our best friends. It is old Uncle Thomas Campbell of Spring Creek—(Berlin P.O.). He has received several documents from you, and he says they are old newspapers and documents, having no sort of interest in them. He is, therefore, getting a strong impression that you treat him with disrespect. This, I know, is a mistaken impression; and you must correct it. The way, I leave to yourself. Rob't W. Canfield says he would like to have a document or two from you.

The Locos (Democrats) here are in considerable trouble about Van Buren's letter on Texas, and the Virginia electors. They are growing sick of the Tariff question; and consequently are much confounded at V.B.'s cutting them off from the new Texas question. Nearly half the leaders swear they won't stand it. Of those are Ford, T. Campbell, Ewing, Calhoun and others. They don't exactly say they won't vote for V.B., but they say he will not be the candidate, and that they are for Texas anyhow.

As ever yours,

A. LINCOLN.

1845

SELECTION OF CONGRESSIONAL CANDIDATES

TO Gen. J. J. HARDIN, SPRINGFIELD, Jany. 19, 1845.

DEAR GENERAL:

I do not wish to join in your proposal of a new plan for the selection of a Whig candidate for Congress because:

1st. I am entirely satisfied with the old system under which you and Baker were successively nominated and elected to Congress; and because the Whigs of the district are well acquainted with the system, and, so far as I know or believe, are well satisfied with it. If the old system be thought to be vague, as to all the delegates of the county voting the same way, or as to instructions to them as to whom they are to vote for, or as to filling vacancies, I am willing to join in a provision to make these matters certain.

2d. As to your proposals that a poll shall be opened in every precinct, and that the whole shall take place on the same day, I do not personally object. They seem to me to be not unfair; and I forbear to join in proposing them only because I choose to leave the decision in each county to the Whigs of the county, to be made as their own judgment and convenience may dictate.

3d. As to your proposed stipulation that all the candidates shall remain in their own counties, and restrain their friends in the same it seems to me that on reflection you will see the fact of your having been in Congress has, in various ways, so spread your name in the district as to give you a decided advantage in such a stipulation. I appreciate your desire to keep down excitement; and I promise you to "keep cool" under all circumstances.

4th. I have already said I am satisfied with the old system under which such good men have triumphed and that I desire no departure from its principles. But if there must be a departure from it, I shall insist upon a more accurate and just apportionment of delegates, or representative votes, to the constituent body, than exists by the old, and which you propose to retain in your new plan. If we take the entire population of the counties as shown by the late census, we shall see by the old plan, and by your proposed new plan,

Morgan County, with a population 16,541, has but .... 8 votes

While Sangamon with 18,697—2156 greater has but .... 8 "

So Scott with 6553 has 4   "

While Tazewell with 7615 1062 greater has but 4   "

So Mason with 3135 has .... 1 vote

While Logan with 3907, 772 greater, has but 1   "

And so on in a less degree the matter runs through all the counties, being not only wrong in principle, but the advantage of it being all manifestly in your favor with one slight exception, in the comparison of two counties not here mentioned.

Again, if we take the Whig votes of the counties as shown by the late Presidential election as a basis, the thing is still worse.

It seems to me most obvious that the old system needs adjustment in nothing so much as in this; and still, by your proposal, no notice is taken of it. I have always been in the habit of acceding to almost any proposal that a friend would make and I am truly sorry that I cannot in this. I perhaps ought to mention that some friends at different places are endeavoring to secure the honor of the sitting of the convention at their towns respectively, and I fear that they would not feel much complimented if we shall make a bargain that it should sit nowhere.

Yours as ever,

A. LINCOLN.

TO ———— WILLIAMS,

SPRINGFIELD, March 1, 1845.

FRIEND WILLIAMS:

The Supreme Court adjourned this morning for the term. Your cases of Reinhardt vs. Schuyler, Bunce vs. Schuyler, Dickhut vs. Dunell, and Sullivan vs. Andrews are continued. Hinman vs. Pope I wrote you concerning some time ago. McNutt et al. vs. Bean and Thompson is reversed and remanded.

Fitzpatrick vs. Brady et al. is reversed and remanded with leave to complainant to amend his bill so as to show the real consideration given for the land.

Bunce against Graves the court confirmed, wherefore, in accordance with your directions, I moved to have the case remanded to enable you to take a new trial in the court below. The court allowed the motion; of which I am glad, and I guess you are.

This, I believe, is all as to court business. The canal men have got their measure through the Legislature pretty much or quite in the shape they desired. Nothing else now.

Yours as ever,

A. LINCOLN.

ABOLITION MOVEMENT

TO WILLIAMSON DURLEY.

SPRINGFIELD, October 3, 1845

When I saw you at home, it was agreed that I should write to you and your brother Madison. Until I then saw you I was not aware of your being what is generally called an abolitionist, or, as you call yourself, a Liberty man, though I well knew there were many such in your country.

I was glad to hear that you intended to attempt to bring about, at the next election in Putnam, a Union of the Whigs proper and such of the Liberty men as are Whigs in principle on all questions save only that of slavery. So far as I can perceive, by such union neither party need yield anything on the point in difference between them. If the Whig abolitionists of New York had voted with us last fall, Mr. Clay would now be President, Whig principles in the ascendant, and Texas not annexed; whereas, by the division, all that either had at stake in the contest was lost. And, indeed, it was extremely probable, beforehand, that such would be the result. As I always understood, the Liberty men deprecated the annexation of Texas extremely; and this being so, why they should refuse to cast their votes [so] as to prevent it, even to me seemed wonderful. What was their process of reasoning, I can only judge from what a single one of them told me. It was this: "We are not to do evil that good may come." This general proposition is doubtless correct; but did it apply? If by your votes you could have prevented the extension, etc., of slavery would it not have been good, and not evil, so to have used your votes, even though it involved the casting of them for a slaveholder? By the fruit the tree is to be known. An evil tree cannot bring forth good fruit. If the fruit of electing Mr. Clay would have been to prevent the extension of slavery, could the act of electing have been evil?

But I will not argue further. I perhaps ought to say that individually I never was much interested in the Texas question. I never could see much good to come of annexation, inasmuch as they were already a free republican people on our own model. On the other hand, I never could very clearly see how the annexation would augment the evil of slavery. It always seemed to me that slaves would be taken there in about equal numbers, with or without annexation. And if more were taken because of annexation, still there would be just so many the fewer left where they were taken from. It is possibly true, to some extent, that, with annexation, some slaves may be sent to Texas and continued in slavery that otherwise might have been liberated. To whatever extent this may be true, I think annexation an evil. I hold it to be a paramount duty of us in the free States, due to the Union of the States, and perhaps to liberty itself (paradox though it may seem), to let the slavery of the other States alone; while, on the other hand, I hold it to be equally clear that we should never knowingly lend ourselves, directly or indirectly, to prevent that slavery from dying a natural death—to find new places for it to live in when it can no longer exist in the old. Of course I am not now considering what would be our duty in cases of insurrection among the slaves. To recur to the Texas question, I understand the Liberty men to have viewed annexation as a much greater evil than ever I did; and I would like to convince you, if I could, that they could have prevented it, if they had chosen. I intend this letter for you and Madison together; and if you and he or either shall think fit to drop me a line, I shall be pleased.

Yours with respect,

A. LINCOLN.

1846

REQUEST FOR POLITICAL SUPPORT

TO Dr. ROBERT BOAL. SPRINGFIELD, January 7, 1846.

Dr. ROBERT BOAL, Lacon, Ill.

DEAR DOCTOR:—Since I saw you last fall, I have often thought of writing to you, as it was then understood I would, but, on reflection, I have always found that I had nothing new to tell you. All has happened as I then told you I expected it would—Baker's declining, Hardin's taking the track, and so on.

If Hardin and I stood precisely equal, if neither of us had been to Congress, or if we both had, it would only accord with what I have always done, for the sake of peace, to give way to him; and I expect I should do it. That I can voluntarily postpone my pretensions, when they are no more than equal to those to which they are postponed, you have yourself seen. But to yield to Hardin under present circumstances seems to me as nothing else than yielding to one who would gladly sacrifice me altogether. This I would rather not submit to. That Hardin is talented, energetic, usually generous and magnanimous, I have before this affirmed to you and do not deny. You know that my only argument is that "turn about is fair play." This he, practically at least, denies.

If it would not be taxing you too much, I wish you would write me, telling the aspect of things in your country, or rather your district; and also, send the names of some of your Whig neighbors, to whom I might, with propriety, write. Unless I can get some one to do this, Hardin, with his old franking list, will have the advantage of me. My reliance for a fair shake (and I want nothing more) in your country is chiefly on you, because of your position and standing, and because I am acquainted with so few others. Let me hear from you soon.

Yours truly,

A. LINCOLN.

TO JOHN BENNETT.

SPRINGFIELD, Jan. 15, 1846.

JOHN BENNETT. FRIEND JOHN:

Nathan Dresser is here, and speaks as though the contest between Hardin and me is to be doubtful in Menard County. I know he is candid and this alarms me some. I asked him to tell me the names of the men that were going strong for Hardin, he said Morris was about as strong as any-now tell me, is Morris going it openly? You remember you wrote me that he would be neutral. Nathan also said that some man, whom he could not remember, had said lately that Menard County was going to decide the contest and that made the contest very doubtful. Do you know who that was? Don't fail to write me instantly on receiving this, telling me all—particularly the names of those who are going strong against me.

Yours as ever,

A. LINCOLN.

TO N. J. ROCKWELL.

SPRINGFIELD, January 21, 1846.

DEAR SIR:—You perhaps know that General Hardin and I have a contest for the Whig nomination for Congress for this district.

He has had a turn and my argument is "turn about is fair play."

I shall be pleased if this strikes you as a sufficient argument.

Yours truly,

A. LINCOLN.

TO JAMES BERDAN.

SPRINGFIELD, April 26, 1846.

DEAR SIR:—I thank you for the promptness with which you answered my letter from Bloomington. I also thank you for the frankness with which you comment upon a certain part of my letter; because that comment affords me an opportunity of trying to express myself better than I did before, seeing, as I do, that in that part of my letter, you have not understood me as I intended to be understood.

In speaking of the "dissatisfaction" of men who yet mean to do no wrong, etc., I mean no special application of what I said to the Whigs of Morgan, or of Morgan & Scott. I only had in my mind the fact that previous to General Hardin's withdrawal some of his friends and some of mine had become a little warm; and I felt, and meant to say, that for them now to meet face to face and converse together was the best way to efface any remnant of unpleasant feeling, if any such existed.

I did not suppose that General Hardin's friends were in any greater need of having their feelings corrected than mine were. Since I saw you at Jacksonville, I have had no more suspicion of the Whigs of Morgan than of those of any other part of the district. I write this only to try to remove any impression that I distrust you and the other Whigs of your country.

Yours truly,

A. LINCOLN.

TO JAMES BERDAN.

SPRINGFIELD, May 7, 1866.

DEAR SIR:—It is a matter of high moral obligation, if not of necessity, for me to attend the Coles and Edwards courts. I have some cases in both of them, in which the parties have my promise, and are depending upon me. The court commences in Coles on the second Monday, and in Edgar on the third. Your court in Morgan commences on the fourth Monday; and it is my purpose to be with you then, and make a speech. I mention the Coles and Edgar courts in order that if I should not reach Jacksonville at the time named you may understand the reason why. I do not, however, think there is much danger of my being detained; as I shall go with a purpose not to be, and consequently shall engage in no new cases that might delay me.

Yours truly,

A. LINCOLN.

VERSES WRITTEN BY LINCOLN AFTER A VISIT TO HIS OLD HOME IN INDIANA

(A FRAGMENT).

[In December, 1847, when Lincoln was stumping for Clay, he crossed into Indiana and revisited his old home. He writes: "That part of the country is within itself as unpoetical as any spot on earth; but still seeing it and its objects and inhabitants aroused feelings in me which were certainly poetry; though whether my expression of these feelings is poetry, is quite another question."]

  Near twenty years have passed away

  Since here I bid farewell

  To woods and fields, and scenes of play,

And playmates loved so well.

Where many were, but few remain

Of old familiar things;

But seeing them to mind again

The lost and absent brings.

The friends I left that parting day,

How changed, as time has sped!

Young childhood grown, strong manhood gray,

And half of all are dead.

I hear the loved survivors tell

How naught from death could save,

Till every sound appears a knell,

And every spot a grave.

I range the fields with pensive tread,

And pace the hollow rooms,

And feel (companion of the dead)

I 'm living in the tombs.

VERSES WRITTEN BY LINCOLN CONCERNING A SCHOOL-FELLOW

WHO BECAME INSANE—(A FRAGMENT).

And when at length the drear and long

Time soothed thy fiercer woes,

How plaintively thy mournful song

Upon the still night rose

I've heard it oft as if I dreamed,

Far distant, sweet and lone;

The funeral dirge it ever seemed

Of reason dead and gone.

Air held her breath; trees with the spell

Seemed sorrowing angels round,

Whose swelling tears in dewdrops fell

Upon the listening ground.

But this is past, and naught remains

That raised thee o'er the brute;

Thy piercing shrieks and soothing strains

Are like, forever mute.

Now fare thee well! More thou the cause

Than subject now of woe.

All mental pangs by time's kind laws

Hast lost the power to know.

O Death! thou awe-inspiring prince

That keepst the world in fear,

Why dost thou tear more blest ones hence,

And leave him lingering here?

SECOND CHILD

TO JOSHUA P. SPEED

SPRINGFIELD, October 22, 1846.

DEAR SPEED:—You, no doubt, assign the suspension of our correspondence to the true philosophic cause; though it must be confessed by both of us that this is rather a cold reason for allowing a friendship such as ours to die out by degrees. I propose now that, upon receipt of this, you shall be considered in my debt, and under obligations to pay soon, and that neither shall remain long in arrears hereafter. Are you agreed?

Being elected to Congress, though I am very grateful to our friends for having done it, has not pleased me as much as I expected.

We have another boy, born the 10th of March. He is very much such a child as Bob was at his age, rather of a longer order. Bob is "short and low," and I expect always will be. He talks very plainly,—almost as plainly as anybody. He is quite smart enough. I sometimes fear that he is one of the little rare-ripe sort that are smarter at about five than ever after. He has a great deal of that sort of mischief that is the offspring of such animal spirits. Since I began this letter, a messenger came to tell me Bob was lost; but by the time I reached the house his mother had found him and had him whipped, and by now, very likely, he is run away again. Mary has read your letter, and wishes to be remembered to Mrs. Speed and you, in which I most sincerely join her.

As ever yours,

A. LINCOLN.

TO MORRIS AND BROWN

SPRINGFIELD, October 21, 1847.

MESSRS. MORRIS AND BROWN.

GENTLEMEN:—Your second letter on the matter of Thornton and others, came to hand this morning. I went at once to see Logan, and found that he is not engaged against you, and that he has so sent you word by Mr. Butterfield, as he says. He says that some time ago, a young man (who he knows not) came to him, with a copy of the affidavit, to engage him to aid in getting the Governor to grant the warrant; and that he, Logan, told the man, that in his opinion, the affidavit was clearly insufficient, upon which the young man left, without making any engagement with him. If the Governor shall arrive before I leave, Logan and I will both attend to the matter, and he will attend to it, if he does not come till after I leave; all upon the condition that the Governor shall not have acted upon the matter, before his arrival here. I mention this condition because, I learned this morning from the Secretary of State, that he is forwarding to the Governor, at Palestine, all papers he receives in the case, as fast as he receives them. Among the papers forwarded will be your letter to the Governor or Secretary of, I believe, the same date and about the same contents of your last letter to me; so that the Governor will, at all events have your points and authorities. The case is a clear one on our side; but whether the Governor will view it so is another thing.

Yours as ever,

A. LINCOLN.

TO WILLIAM H. HERNDON

WASHINGTON, December 5, 1847.

DEAR WILLIAM:—You may remember that about a year ago a man by the name of Wilson (James Wilson, I think) paid us twenty dollars as an advance fee to attend to a case in the Supreme Court for him, against a Mr. Campbell, the record of which case was in the hands of Mr. Dixon of St. Louis, who never furnished it to us. When I was at Bloomington last fall I met a friend of Wilson, who mentioned the subject to me, and induced me to write to Wilson, telling him I would leave the ten dollars with you which had been left with me to pay for making abstracts in the case, so that the case may go on this winter; but I came away, and forgot to do it. What I want now is to send you the money, to be used accordingly, if any one comes on to start the case, or to be retained by you if no one does.

There is nothing of consequence new here. Congress is to organize to-morrow. Last night we held a Whig caucus for the House, and nominated Winthrop of Massachusetts for speaker, Sargent of Pennsylvania for sergeant-at-arms, Homer of New Jersey door-keeper, and McCormick of District of Columbia postmaster. The Whig majority in the House is so small that, together with some little dissatisfaction, [it] leaves it doubtful whether we will elect them all.

This paper is too thick to fold, which is the reason I send only a half-sheet.

Yours as ever, A. LINCOLN.

TO WILLIAM H. HERNDON.

WASHINGTON, December 13, 1847

DEAR WILLIAM:—Your letter, advising me of the receipt of our fee in the bank case, is just received, and I don't expect to hear another as good a piece of news from Springfield while I am away. I am under no obligations to the bank; and I therefore wish you to buy bank certificates, and pay my debt there, so as to pay it with the least money possible. I would as soon you should buy them of Mr. Ridgely, or any other person at the bank, as of any one else, provided you can get them as cheaply. I suppose, after the bank debt shall be paid, there will be some money left, out of which I would like to have you pay Lavely and Stout twenty dollars, and Priest and somebody (oil-makers) ten dollars, for materials got for house-painting. If there shall still be any left, keep it till you see or hear from me.

I shall begin sending documents so soon as I can get them. I wrote you yesterday about a "Congressional Globe." As you are all so anxious for me to distinguish myself, I have concluded to do so before long.

Yours truly,

A. LINCOLN.

RESOLUTIONS IN THE UNITED STATES HOUSE OF REPRESENTATIVES,

DECEMBER 22, 1847

Whereas, The President of the United States, in his message of May 11, 1846, has declared that "the Mexican Government not only refused to receive him [the envoy of the United States], or to listen to his propositions, but, after a long-continued series of menaces, has at last invaded our territory and shed the blood of our fellow-citizens on our own soil";

And again, in his message of December 8, 1846, that "we had ample cause of war against Mexico long before the breaking out of hostilities; but even then we forbore to take redress into our own hands until Mexico herself became the aggressor, by invading our soil in hostile array, and shedding the blood of our citizens";

And yet again, in his message of December 7, 1847, that "the Mexican Government refused even to hear the terms of adjustment which he [our minister of peace] was authorized to propose, and finally, under wholly unjustifiable pretexts, involved the two countries in war, by invading the territory of the State of Texas, striking the first blow, and shedding the blood of our citizens on our own soil";

And whereas, This House is desirous to obtain a full knowledge of all the facts which go to establish whether the particular spot on which the blood of our citizens was so shed was or was not at that time our own soil: therefore,

Resolved, By the House of Representatives, that the President of the United States be respectfully requested to inform this House:

First. Whether the spot on which the blood of our citizens was shed, as in his message declared, was or was not within the territory of Spain, at least after the treaty of 1819, until the Mexican revolution.

Second. Whether that spot is or is not within the territory which was wrested from Spain by the revolutionary government of Mexico.

Third. Whether that spot is or is not within a settlement of people, which settlement has existed ever since long before the Texas revolution, and until its inhabitants fled before the approach of the United States army.

Fourth. Whether that settlement is or is not isolated from any and all other settlements by the Gulf and the Rio Grande on the south and west, and by wide uninhabited regions on the north and east.

Fifth. Whether the people of that settlement, or a majority of them, or any of them, have ever submitted themselves to the government or laws of Texas or of the United States, by consent or by compulsion, either by accepting office, or voting at elections, or paying tax, or serving on juries, or having process served upon them, or in any other way.

Sixth. Whether the people of that settlement did or did not flee from the approach of the United States army, leaving unprotected their homes and their growing crops, before the blood was shed, as in the message stated; and whether the first blood, so shed, was or was not shed within the inclosure of one of the people who had thus fled from it.

Seventh. Whether our citizens, whose blood was shed, as in his message declared, were or were not, at that time, armed officers and soldiers, sent into that settlement by the military order of the President, through the Secretary of War.

Eighth. Whether the military force of the United States was or was not so sent into that settlement after General Taylor had more than once intimated to the War Department that, in his opinion, no such movement was necessary to the defence or protection of Texas.

REMARKS IN THE UNITED STATES HOUSE OF REPRESENTATIVES,

JANUARY 5, 1848.

Mr. Lincoln said he had made an effort, some few days since, to obtain the floor in relation to this measure [resolution to direct Postmaster-General to make arrangements with railroad for carrying the mails—in Committee of the Whole], but had failed. One of the objects he had then had in view was now in a great measure superseded by what had fallen from the gentleman from Virginia who had just taken his seat. He begged to assure his friends on the other side of the House that no assault whatever was meant upon the Postmaster-General, and he was glad that what the gentleman had now said modified to a great extent the impression which might have been created by the language he had used on a previous occasion. He wanted to state to gentlemen who might have entertained such impressions, that the Committee on the Post-office was composed of five Whigs and four Democrats, and their report was understood as sustaining, not impugning, the position taken by the Postmaster-General. That report had met with the approbation of all the Whigs, and of all the Democrats also, with the exception of one, and he wanted to go even further than this. [Intimation was informally given Mr. Lincoln that it was not in order to mention on the floor what had taken place in committee.] He then observed that if he had been out of order in what he had said he took it all back so far as he could. He had no desire, he could assure gentlemen, ever to be out of order—though he never could keep long in order.

Mr. Lincoln went on to observe that he differed in opinion, in the present case, from his honorable friend from Richmond [Mr. Botts]. That gentleman, had begun his remarks by saying that if all prepossessions in this matter could be removed out of the way, but little difficulty would be experienced in coming to an agreement. Now, he could assure that gentleman that he had himself begun the examination of the subject with prepossessions all in his favor. He had long and often heard of him, and, from what he had heard, was prepossessed in his favor. Of the Postmaster-General he had also heard, but had no prepossessions in his favor, though certainly none of an opposite kind. He differed, however, with that gentleman in politics, while in this respect he agreed with the gentleman from Virginia [Mr. Botts], whom he wished to oblige whenever it was in his power. That gentleman had referred to the report made to the House by the Postmaster-General, and had intimated an apprehension that gentlemen would be disposed to rely, on that report alone, and derive their views of the case from that document alone. Now it so happened that a pamphlet had been slipped into his [Mr. Lincoln's] hand before he read the report of the Postmaster-General; so that, even in this, he had begun with prepossessions in favor of the gentleman from Virginia.

As to the report, he had but one remark to make: he had carefully examined it, and he did not understand that there was any dispute as to the facts therein stated the dispute, if he understood it, was confined altogether to the inferences to be drawn from those facts. It was a difference not about facts, but about conclusions. The facts were not disputed. If he was right in this, he supposed the House might assume the facts to be as they were stated, and thence proceed to draw their own conclusions.

The gentleman had said that the Postmaster-General had got into a personal squabble with the railroad company. Of this Mr. Lincoln knew nothing, nor did he need or desire to know anything, because it had nothing whatever to do with a just conclusion from the premises. But the gentleman had gone on to ask whether so great a grievance as the present detention of the Southern mail ought not to be remedied. Mr. Lincoln would assure the gentleman that if there was a proper way of doing it, no man was more anxious than he that it should be done. The report made by the committee had been intended to yield much for the sake of removing that grievance. That the grievance was very great there was no dispute in any quarter. He supposed that the statements made by the gentleman from Virginia to show this were all entirely correct in point of fact. He did suppose that the interruptions of regular intercourse, and all the other inconveniences growing out of it, were all as that gentleman had stated them to be; and certainly, if redress could be rendered, it was proper it should be rendered as soon as possible. The gentleman said that in order to effect this no new legislative action was needed; all that was necessary was that the Postmaster-General should be required to do what the law, as it stood, authorized and required him to do.

We come then, said Mr. Lincoln, to the law. Now the Postmaster-General says he cannot give to this company more than two hundred and thirty-seven dollars and fifty cents per railroad mile of transportation, and twelve and a half per cent. less for transportation by steamboats. He considers himself as restricted by law to this amount; and he says, further, that he would not give more if he could, because in his apprehension it would not be fair and just.

1848

DESIRE FOR SECOND TERM IN CONGRESS

TO WILLIAM H. HERNDON.

WASHINGTON, January 8, 1848.

DEAR WILLIAM:—Your letter of December 27 was received a day or two ago. I am much obliged to you for the trouble you have taken, and promise to take in my little business there. As to speech making, by way of getting the hang of the House I made a little speech two or three days ago on a post-office question of no general interest. I find speaking here and elsewhere about the same thing. I was about as badly scared, and no worse as I am when I speak in court. I expect to make one within a week or two, in which I hope to succeed well enough to wish you to see it.

It is very pleasant to learn from you that there are some who desire that I should be reelected. I most heartily thank them for their kind partiality; and I can say, as Mr. Clay said of the annexation of Texas, that "personally I would not object" to a reelection, although I thought at the time, and still think, it would be quite as well for me to return to the law at the end of a single term. I made the declaration that I would not be a candidate again, more from a wish to deal fairly with others, to keep peace among our friends, and to keep the district from going to the enemy, than for any cause personal to myself; so that if it should so happen that nobody else wishes to be elected, I could not refuse the people the right of sending me again. But to enter myself as a competitor of others, or to authorize any one so to enter me is what my word and honor forbid.

I got some letters intimating a probability of so much difficulty amongst our friends as to lose us the district; but I remember such letters were written to Baker when my own case was under consideration, and I trust there is no more ground for such apprehension now than there was then. Remember I am always glad to receive a letter from you.

Most truly your friend,

A. LINCOLN.

SPEECH ON DECLARATION OF WAR ON MEXICO

SPEECH IN THE UNITED STATES HOUSE OF REPRESENTATIVES,

JANUARY 12, 1848.

MR CHAIRMAN:—Some if not all the gentlemen on the other side of the House who have addressed the committee within the last two days have spoken rather complainingly, if I have rightly understood them, of the vote given a week or ten days ago declaring that the war with Mexico was unnecessarily and unconstitutionally commenced by the President. I admit that such a vote should not be given in mere party wantonness, and that the one given is justly censurable if it have no other or better foundation. I am one of those who joined in that vote; and I did so under my best impression of the truth of the case. How I got this impression, and how it may possibly be remedied, I will now try to show. When the war began, it was my opinion that all those who because of knowing too little, or because of knowing too much, could not conscientiously approve the conduct of the President in the beginning of it should nevertheless, as good citizens and patriots, remain silent on that point, at least till the war should be ended. Some leading Democrats, including ex-President Van Buren, have taken this same view, as I understand them; and I adhered to it and acted upon it, until since I took my seat here; and I think I should still adhere to it were it not that the President and his friends will not allow it to be so. Besides the continual effort of the President to argue every silent vote given for supplies into an indorsement of the justice and wisdom of his conduct; besides that singularly candid paragraph in his late message in which he tells us that Congress with great unanimity had declared that "by the act of the Republic of Mexico, a state of war exists between that government and the United States," when the same journals that informed him of this also informed him that when that declaration stood disconnected from the question of supplies sixty-seven in the House, and not fourteen merely, voted against it; besides this open attempt to prove by telling the truth what he could not prove by telling the whole truth-demanding of all who will not submit to be misrepresented, in justice to themselves, to speak out, besides all this, one of my colleagues [Mr. Richardson] at a very early day in the session brought in a set of resolutions expressly indorsing the original justice of the war on the part of the President. Upon these resolutions when they shall be put on their passage I shall be compelled to vote; so that I cannot be silent if I would. Seeing this, I went about preparing myself to give the vote understandingly when it should come. I carefully examined the President's message, to ascertain what he himself had said and proved upon the point. The result of this examination was to make the impression that, taking for true all the President states as facts, he falls far short of proving his justification; and that the President would have gone further with his proof if it had not been for the small matter that the truth would not permit him. Under the impression thus made I gave the vote before mentioned. I propose now to give concisely the process of the examination I made, and how I reached the conclusion I did. The President, in his first war message of May, 1846, declares that the soil was ours on which hostilities were commenced by Mexico, and he repeats that declaration almost in the same language in each successive annual message, thus showing that he deems that point a highly essential one. In the importance of that point I entirely agree with the President. To my judgment it is the very point upon which he should be justified, or condemned. In his message of December, 1846, it seems to have occurred to him, as is certainly true, that title-ownership-to soil or anything else is not a simple fact, but is a conclusion following on one or more simple facts; and that it was incumbent upon him to present the facts from which he concluded the soil was ours on which the first blood of the war was shed.

Accordingly, a little below the middle of page twelve in the message last referred to, he enters upon that task; forming an issue and introducing testimony, extending the whole to a little below the middle of page fourteen. Now, I propose to try to show that the whole of this—issue and evidence—is from beginning to end the sheerest deception. The issue, as he presents it, is in these words: "But there are those who, conceding all this to be true, assume the ground that the true western boundary of Texas is the Nueces, instead of the Rio Grande; and that, therefore, in marching our army to the east bank of the latter river, we passed the Texas line and invaded the territory of Mexico." Now this issue is made up of two affirmatives and no negative. The main deception of it is that it assumes as true that one river or the other is necessarily the boundary; and cheats the superficial thinker entirely out of the idea that possibly the boundary is somewhere between the two, and not actually at either. A further deception is that it will let in evidence which a true issue would exclude. A true issue made by the President would be about as follows: "I say the soil was ours, on which the first blood was shed; there are those who say it was not."

I now proceed to examine the President's evidence as applicable to such an issue. When that evidence is analyzed, it is all included in the following propositions:

(1) That the Rio Grande was the western boundary of Louisiana as we purchased it of France in 1803.

(2) That the Republic of Texas always claimed the Rio Grande as her eastern boundary.

(3) That by various acts she had claimed it on paper.

(4) That Santa Anna in his treaty with Texas recognized the Rio Grande as her boundary.

(5) That Texas before, and the United States after, annexation had exercised jurisdiction beyond the Nueces—between the two rivers.

(6) That our Congress understood the boundary of Texas to extend beyond the Nueces.

Now for each of these in its turn. His first item is that the Rio Grande was the western boundary of Louisiana, as we purchased it of France in 1803; and seeming to expect this to be disputed, he argues over the amount of nearly a page to prove it true, at the end of which he lets us know that by the treaty of 1803 we sold to Spain the whole country from the Rio Grande eastward to the Sabine. Now, admitting for the present that the Rio Grande was the boundary of Louisiana, what under heaven had that to do with the present boundary between us and Mexico? How, Mr. Chairman, the line that once divided your land from mine can still be the boundary between us after I have sold my land to you is to me beyond all comprehension. And how any man, with an honest purpose only of proving the truth, could ever have thought of introducing such a fact to prove such an issue is equally incomprehensible. His next piece of evidence is that "the Republic of Texas always claimed this river [Rio Grande] as her western boundary." That is not true, in fact. Texas has claimed it, but she has not always claimed it. There is at least one distinguished exception. Her State constitution the republic's most solemn and well-considered act, that which may, without impropriety, be called her last will and testament, revoking all others-makes no such claim. But suppose she had always claimed it. Has not Mexico always claimed the contrary? So that there is but claim against claim, leaving nothing proved until we get back of the claims and find which has the better foundation. Though not in the order in which the President presents his evidence, I now consider that class of his statements which are in substance nothing more than that Texas has, by various acts of her Convention and Congress, claimed the Rio Grande as her boundary, on paper. I mean here what he says about the fixing of the Rio Grande as her boundary in her old constitution (not her State constitution), about forming Congressional districts, counties, etc. Now all of this is but naked claim; and what I have already said about claims is strictly applicable to this. If I should claim your land by word of mouth, that certainly would not make it mine; and if I were to claim it by a deed which I had made myself, and with which you had had nothing to do, the claim would be quite the same in substance—or rather, in utter nothingness. I next consider the President's statement that Santa Anna in his treaty with Texas recognized the Rio Grande as the western boundary of Texas. Besides the position so often taken, that Santa Anna while a prisoner of war, a captive, could not bind Mexico by a treaty, which I deem conclusive—besides this, I wish to say something in relation to this treaty, so called by the President, with Santa Anna. If any man would like to be amused by a sight of that little thing which the President calls by that big name, he can have it by turning to Niles's Register, vol. 1, p. 336. And if any one should suppose that Niles's Register is a curious repository of so mighty a document as a solemn treaty between nations, I can only say that I learned to a tolerable degree of certainty, by inquiry at the State Department, that the President himself never saw it anywhere else. By the way, I believe I should not err if I were to declare that during the first ten years of the existence of that document it was never by anybody called a treaty—that it was never so called till the President, in his extremity, attempted by so calling it to wring something from it in justification of himself in connection with the Mexican War. It has none of the distinguishing features of a treaty. It does not call itself a treaty. Santa Anna does not therein assume to bind Mexico; he assumes only to act as the President—Commander-in-Chief of the Mexican army and navy; stipulates that the then present hostilities should cease, and that he would not himself take up arms, nor influence the Mexican people to take up arms, against Texas during the existence of the war of independence. He did not recognize the independence of Texas; he did not assume to put an end to the war, but clearly indicated his expectation of its continuance; he did not say one word about boundary, and, most probably, never thought of it. It is stipulated therein that the Mexican forces should evacuate the territory of Texas, passing to the other side of the Rio Grande; and in another article it is stipulated that, to prevent collisions between the armies, the Texas army should not approach nearer than within five leagues—of what is not said, but clearly, from the object stated, it is of the Rio Grande. Now, if this is a treaty recognizing the Rio Grande as the boundary of Texas, it contains the singular feature of stipulating that Texas shall not go within five leagues of her own boundary.

Next comes the evidence of Texas before annexation, and the United States afterwards, exercising jurisdiction beyond the Nueces and between the two rivers. This actual exercise of jurisdiction is the very class or quality of evidence we want. It is excellent so far as it goes; but does it go far enough? He tells us it went beyond the Nueces, but he does not tell us it went to the Rio Grande. He tells us jurisdiction was exercised between the two rivers, but he does not tell us it was exercised over all the territory between them. Some simple-minded people think it is possible to cross one river and go beyond it without going all the way to the next, that jurisdiction may be exercised between two rivers without covering all the country between them. I know a man, not very unlike myself, who exercises jurisdiction over a piece of land between the Wabash and the Mississippi; and yet so far is this from being all there is between those rivers that it is just one hundred and fifty-two feet long by fifty feet wide, and no part of it much within a hundred miles of either. He has a neighbor between him and the Mississippi—that is, just across the street, in that direction—whom I am sure he could neither persuade nor force to give up his habitation; but which nevertheless he could certainly annex, if it were to be done by merely standing on his own side of the street and claiming it, or even sitting down and writing a deed for it.

But next the President tells us the Congress of the United States understood the State of Texas they admitted into the Union to extend beyond the Nueces. Well, I suppose they did. I certainly so understood it. But how far beyond? That Congress did not understand it to extend clear to the Rio Grande is quite certain, by the fact of their joint resolutions for admission expressly leaving all questions of boundary to future adjustment. And it may be added that Texas herself is proven to have had the same understanding of it that our Congress had, by the fact of the exact conformity of her new constitution to those resolutions.

I am now through the whole of the President's evidence; and it is a singular fact that if any one should declare the President sent the army into the midst of a settlement of Mexican people who had never submitted, by consent or by force, to the authority of Texas or of the United States, and that there and thereby the first blood of the war was shed, there is not one word in all the which would either admit or deny the declaration. This strange omission it does seem to me could not have occurred but by design. My way of living leads me to be about the courts of justice; and there I have sometimes seen a good lawyer, struggling for his client's neck in a desperate case, employing every artifice to work round, befog, and cover up with many words some point arising in the case which he dared not admit and yet could not deny. Party bias may help to make it appear so, but with all the allowance I can make for such bias, it still does appear to me that just such, and from just such necessity, is the President's struggle in this case.

Sometime after my colleague [Mr. Richardson] introduced the resolutions I have mentioned, I introduced a preamble, resolution, and interrogations, intended to draw the President out, if possible, on this hitherto untrodden ground. To show their relevancy, I propose to state my understanding of the true rule for ascertaining the boundary between Texas and Mexico. It is that wherever Texas was exercising jurisdiction was hers; and wherever Mexico was exercising jurisdiction was hers; and that whatever separated the actual exercise of jurisdiction of the one from that of the other was the true boundary between them. If, as is probably true, Texas was exercising jurisdiction along the western bank of the Nueces, and Mexico was exercising it along the eastern bank of the Rio Grande, then neither river was the boundary: but the uninhabited country between the two was. The extent of our territory in that region depended not on any treaty-fixed boundary (for no treaty had attempted it), but on revolution. Any people anywhere being inclined and having the power have the right to rise up and shake off the existing government, and form a new one that suits them better. This is a most valuable, a most sacred right—a right which we hope and believe is to liberate the world. Nor is this right confined to cases in which the whole people of an existing government may choose to exercise it. Any portion of such people that can may revolutionize and make their own of so much of the territory as they inhabit. More than this, a majority of any portion of such people may revolutionize, putting down a minority, intermingled with or near about them, who may oppose this movement. Such minority was precisely the case of the Tories of our own revolution. It is a quality of revolutions not to go by old lines or old laws, but to break up both, and make new ones.

As to the country now in question, we bought it of France in 1803, and sold it to Spain in 1819, according to the President's statements. After this, all Mexico, including Texas, revolutionized against Spain; and still later Texas revolutionized against Mexico. In my view, just so far as she carried her resolution by obtaining the actual, willing or unwilling, submission of the people, so far the country was hers, and no farther. Now, sir, for the purpose of obtaining the very best evidence as to whether Texas had actually carried her revolution to the place where the hostilities of the present war commenced, let the President answer the interrogatories I proposed, as before mentioned, or some other similar ones. Let him answer fully, fairly, and candidly. Let him answer with facts and not with arguments. Let him remember he sits where Washington sat, and so remembering, let him answer as Washington would answer. As a nation should not, and the Almighty will not, be evaded, so let him attempt no evasion—no equivocation. And if, so answering, he can show that the soil was ours where the first blood of the war was shed,—that it was not within an inhabited country, or, if within such, that the inhabitants had submitted themselves to the civil authority of Texas or of the United States, and that the same is true of the site of Fort Brown, then I am with him for his justification. In that case I shall be most happy to reverse the vote I gave the other day. I have a selfish motive for desiring that the President may do this—I expect to gain some votes, in connection with the war, which, without his so doing, will be of doubtful propriety in my own judgment, but which will be free from the doubt if he does so. But if he can not or will not do this,—if on any pretence or no pretence he shall refuse or omit it then I shall be fully convinced of what I more than suspect already that he is deeply conscious of being in the wrong; that he feels the blood of this war, like the blood of Abel, is crying to heaven against him; that originally having some strong motive—what, I will not stop now to give my opinion concerning to involve the two countries in a war, and trusting to escape scrutiny by fixing the public gaze upon the exceeding brightness of military glory,—that attractive rainbow that rises in showers of blood, that serpent's eye that charms to destroy,—he plunged into it, and was swept on and on till, disappointed in his calculation of the ease with which Mexico might be subdued, he now finds himself he knows not where. How like the half insane mumbling of a fever dream is the whole war part of his late message! At one time telling us that Mexico has nothing whatever that we can get—but territory; at another showing us how we can support the war by levying contributions on Mexico. At one time urging the national honor, the security of the future, the prevention of foreign interference, and even the good of Mexico herself as among the objects of the war; at another telling us that "to reject indemnity, by refusing to accept a cession of territory, would be to abandon all our just demands, and to wage the war, bearing all its expenses, without a purpose or definite object." So then this national honor, security of the future, and everything but territorial indemnity may be considered the no-purposes and indefinite objects of the war! But, having it now settled that territorial indemnity is the only object, we are urged to seize, by legislation here, all that he was content to take a few months ago, and the whole province of Lower California to boot, and to still carry on the war to take all we are fighting for, and still fight on. Again, the President is resolved under all circumstances to have full territorial indemnity for the expenses of the war; but he forgets to tell us how we are to get the excess after those expenses shall have surpassed the value of the whole of the Mexican territory. So again, he insists that the separate national existence of Mexico shall be maintained; but he does not tell us how this can be done, after we shall have taken all her territory. Lest the questions I have suggested be considered speculative merely, let me be indulged a moment in trying to show they are not. The war has gone on some twenty months; for the expenses of which, together with an inconsiderable old score, the President now claims about one half of the Mexican territory, and that by far the better half, so far as concerns our ability to make anything out of it. It is comparatively uninhabited; so that we could establish land-offices in it, and raise some money in that way. But the other half is already inhabited, as I understand it, tolerably densely for the nature of the country, and all its lands, or all that are valuable, already appropriated as private property. How then are we to make anything out of these lands with this encumbrance on them? or how remove the encumbrance? I suppose no one would say we should kill the people, or drive them out, or make slaves of them, or confiscate their property. How, then, can we make much out of this part of the territory? If the prosecution of the war has in expenses already equalled the better half of the country, how long its future prosecution will be in equalling the less valuable half is not a speculative, but a practical, question, pressing closely upon us. And yet it is a question which the President seems never to have thought of. As to the mode of terminating the war and securing peace, the President is equally wandering and indefinite. First, it is to be done by a more vigorous prosecution of the war in the vital parts of the enemy's country; and after apparently talking himself tired on this point, the President drops down into a half-despairing tone, and tells us that "with a people distracted and divided by contending factions, and a government subject to constant changes by successive revolutions, the continued success of our arms may fail to secure a satisfactory peace." Then he suggests the propriety of wheedling the Mexican people to desert the counsels of their own leaders, and, trusting in our protestations, to set up a government from which we can secure a satisfactory peace; telling us that "this may become the only mode of obtaining such a peace." But soon he falls into doubt of this too; and then drops back on to the already half-abandoned ground of "more vigorous prosecution." All this shows that the President is in nowise satisfied with his own positions. First he takes up one, and in attempting to argue us into it he argues himself out of it, then seizes another and goes through the same process, and then, confused at being able to think of nothing new, he snatches up the old one again, which he has some time before cast off. His mind, taxed beyond its power, is running hither and thither, like some tortured creature on a burning surface, finding no position on which it can settle down and be at ease.

Again, it is a singular omission in this message that it nowhere intimates when the President expects the war to terminate. At its beginning, General Scott was by this same President driven into disfavor if not disgrace, for intimating that peace could not be conquered in less than three or four months. But now, at the end of about twenty months, during which time our arms have given us the most splendid successes, every department and every part, land and water, officers and privates, regulars and volunteers, doing all that men could do, and hundreds of things which it had ever before been thought men could not do—after all this, this same President gives a long message, without showing us that as to the end he himself has even an imaginary conception. As I have before said, he knows not where he is. He is a bewildered, confounded, and miserably perplexed man. God grant he may be able to show there is not something about his conscience more painful than his mental perplexity.

The following is a copy of the so-called "treaty" referred to in the speech:

"Articles of Agreement entered into between his Excellency

David G. Burnet, President of the Republic of Texas, of the one part,

and his Excellency General Santa Anna, President-General-in-Chief of the

Mexican army, of the other part:

"Article I. General Antonio Lopez de Santa Anna agrees that

he will not take up arms, nor will he exercise his influence to cause

them to be taken up, against the people of Texas during the present war of

independence.

"Article II. All hostilities between the Mexican and Texan

troops will cease immediately, both by land and water.

"Article III. The Mexican troops will evacuate the territory of Texas, passing to the other side of the Rio Grande Del Norte.

"Article IV. The Mexican army, in its retreat, shall not take the property of any person without his consent and just indemnification, using only such articles as may be necessary for its subsistence, in cases when the owner may not be present, and remitting to the commander of the army of Texas, or to the commissioners to be appointed for the adjustment of such matters, an account of the value of the property consumed, the place where taken, and the name of the owner, if it can be ascertained.

"Article V. That all private property, including cattle, horses, negro slaves, or indentured persons, of whatever denomination, that may have been captured by any portion of the Mexican army, or may have taken refuge in the said army, since the commencement of the late invasion, shall be restored to the commander of the Texan army, or to such other persons as may be appointed by the Government of Texas to receive them.

"Article VI. The troops of both armies will refrain from coming in contact with each other; and to this end the commander of the army of Texas will be careful not to approach within a shorter distance than five leagues.

"Article VII. The Mexican army shall not make any other delay on its march than that which is necessary to take up their hospitals, baggage, etc., and to cross the rivers; any delay not necessary to these purposes to be considered an infraction of this agreement.

"Article VIII. By an express, to be immediately despatched, this agreement shall be sent to General Vincente Filisola and to General T. J. Rusk, commander of the Texan army, in order that they may be apprised of its stipulations; and to this end they will exchange engagements to comply with the same.

"Article IX. That all Texan prisoners now in the possession of the Mexican army, or its authorities, be forthwith released, and furnished with free passports to return to their homes; in consideration of which a corresponding number of Mexican prisoners, rank and file, now in possession of the Government of Texas shall be immediately released; the remainder of the Mexican prisoners that continue in the possession of the Government of Texas to be treated with due humanity,—any extraordinary comforts that may be furnished them to be at the charge of the Government of Mexico.

"Article X. General Antonio Lopez de Santa Anna will be sent to Vera Cruz as soon as it shall be deemed proper.

"The contracting parties sign this instrument for the abovementioned purposes, in duplicate, at the port of Velasco, this fourteenth day of May, 1836.

"DAVID G. BURNET, President,

"JAS. COLLINGSWORTH, Secretary of State,

"ANTONIO LOPEZ DE SANTA ANNA,

"B. HARDIMAN, Secretary of the Treasury,

"P. W. GRAYSON, Attorney-General."

REPORT IN THE HOUSE OF REPRESENTATIVES, JANUARY 19, 1848.

Mr. Lincoln, from the Committee on the Post-office and Post Roads, made the following report:

The Committee on the Post-office and Post Roads, to whom was referred the petition of Messrs. Saltmarsh and Fuller, report: That, as proved to their satisfaction, the mail routes from Milledgeville to Athens, and from Warrenton to Decatur, in the State of Georgia (numbered 2366 and 2380), were let to Reeside and Avery at $1300 per annum for the former and $1500 for the latter, for the term of four years, to commence on the first day of January, 1835; that, previous to the time for commencing the service, Reeside sold his interest therein to Avery; that on the 5th of May, 1835, Avery sold the whole to these petitioners, Saltmarsh and Fuller, to take effect from the beginning, January a 1835; that at this time, the Assistant Postmaster-General, being called on for that purpose, consented to the transfer of the contracts from Reeside and Avery to these petitioners, and promised to have proper entries of the transfer made on the books of the department, which, however, was neglected to be done; that the petitioners, supposing all was right, in good faith commenced the transportation of the mail on these routes, and after difficulty arose, still trusting that all would be made right, continued the service till December a 1837; that they performed the service to the entire satisfaction of the department, and have never been paid anything for it except $——; that the difficulty occurred as follows:

Mr. Barry was Postmaster-General at the times of making the contracts and the attempted transfer of them; Mr. Kendall succeeded Mr. Barry, and finding Reeside apparently in debt to the department, and these contracts still standing in the names of Reeside and Avery, refused to pay for the services under them, otherwise than by credits to Reeside; afterward, however, he divided the compensation, still crediting one half to Reeside, and directing the other to be paid to the order of Avery, who disclaimed all right to it. After discontinuing the service, these petitioners, supposing they might have legal redress against Avery, brought suit against him in New Orleans; in which suit they failed, on the ground that Avery had complied with his contract, having done so much toward the transfer as they had accepted and been satisfied with. Still later the department sued Reeside on his supposed indebtedness, and by a verdict of the jury it was determined that the department was indebted to him in a sum much beyond all the credits given him on the account above stated. Under these circumstances, the committee consider the petitioners clearly entitled to relief, and they report a bill accordingly; lest, however, there should be some mistake as to the amount which they have already received, we so frame it as that, by adjustment at the department, they may be paid so much as remains unpaid for services actually performed by them not charging them with the credits given to Reeside. The committee think it not improbable that the petitioners purchased the right of Avery to be paid for the service from the 1st of January, till their purchase on May 11, 1835; but, the evidence on this point being very vague, they forbear to report in favor of allowing it.

TO WILLIAM H. HERNDON—LEGAL WORK

WASHINGTON, January 19, 1848.

DEAR WILLIAM:—Inclosed you find a letter of Louis W. Chandler. What is wanted is that you shall ascertain whether the claim upon the note described has received any dividend in the Probate Court of Christian County, where the estate of Mr. Overbon Williams has been administered on. If nothing is paid on it, withdraw the note and send it to me, so that Chandler can see the indorser of it. At all events write me all about it, till I can somehow get it off my hands. I have already been bored more than enough about it; not the least of which annoyance is his cursed, unreadable, and ungodly handwriting.

I have made a speech, a copy of which I will send you by next mail.

Yours as ever,

A. LINCOLN.

REGARDING SPEECH ON MEXICAN WAR

TO WILLIAM H. HERNDON.

WASHINGTON, February 1, 1848.

DEAR WILLIAM:—Your letter of the 19th ultimo was received last night, and for which I am much obliged. The only thing in it that I wish to talk to you at once about is that because of my vote for Ashmun's amendment you fear that you and I disagree about the war. I regret this, not because of any fear we shall remain disagreed after you have read this letter, but because if you misunderstand I fear other good friends may also. That vote affirms that the war was unnecessarily and unconstitutionally commenced by the President; and I will stake my life that if you had been in my place you would have voted just as I did. Would you have voted what you felt and knew to be a lie? I know you would not. Would you have gone out of the House—skulked the vote? I expect not. If you had skulked one vote, you would have had to skulk many more before the end of the session. Richardson's resolutions, introduced before I made any move or gave any vote upon the subject, make the direct question of the justice of the war; so that no man can be silent if he would. You are compelled to speak; and your only alternative is to tell the truth or a lie. I cannot doubt which you would do.

This vote has nothing to do in determining my votes on the questions of supplies. I have always intended, and still intend, to vote supplies; perhaps not in the precise form recommended by the President, but in a better form for all purposes, except Locofoco party purposes. It is in this particular you seem mistaken. The Locos are untiring in their efforts to make the impression that all who vote supplies or take part in the war do of necessity approve the President's conduct in the beginning of it; but the Whigs have from the beginning made and kept the distinction between the two. In the very first act nearly all the Whigs voted against the preamble declaring that war existed by the act of Mexico; and yet nearly all of them voted for the supplies. As to the Whig men who have participated in the war, so far as they have spoken in my hearing they do not hesitate to denounce as unjust the President's conduct in the beginning of the war. They do not suppose that such denunciation is directed by undying hatred to him, as The Register would have it believed. There are two such Whigs on this floor (Colonel Haskell and Major James) The former fought as a colonel by the side of Colonel Baker at Cerro Gordo, and stands side by side with me in the vote that you seem dissatisfied with. The latter, the history of whose capture with Cassius Clay you well know, had not arrived here when that vote was given; but, as I understand, he stands ready to give just such a vote whenever an occasion shall present. Baker, too, who is now here, says the truth is undoubtedly that way; and whenever he shall speak out, he will say so. Colonel Doniphan, too, the favorite Whig of Missouri, and who overran all Northern Mexico, on his return home in a public speech at St. Louis condemned the administration in relation to the war. If I remember, G. T. M. Davis, who has been through almost the whole war, declares in favor of Mr. Clay; from which I infer that he adopts the sentiments of Mr. Clay, generally at least. On the other hand, I have heard of but one Whig who has been to the war attempting to justify the President's conduct. That one was Captain Bishop, editor of the Charleston Courier, and a very clever fellow. I do not mean this letter for the public, but for you. Before it reaches you, you will have seen and read my pamphlet speech, and perhaps been scared anew by it. After you get over your scare, read it over again, sentence by sentence, and tell me honestly what you think of it. I condensed all I could for fear of being cut off by the hour rule, and when I got through I had spoken but forty-five minutes.

Yours forever,

A. LINCOLN.

TO WILLIAM H. HERNDON.

WASHINGTON, February 2, 1848

DEAR WILLIAM:—I just take my pen to say that Mr. Stephens, of Georgia, a little, slim, pale-faced, consumptive man, with a voice like Logan's, has just concluded the very best speech of an hour's length I ever heard. My old withered dry eyes are full of tears yet.

If he writes it out anything like he delivered it, our people shall see a good many copies of it.

Yours truly,

A. LINCOLN.

ON THE MEXICAN WAR

TO WILLIAM H. HERNDON.

WASHINGTON, February 15, 1848.

DEAR WILLIAM:—Your letter of the 29th January was received last night. Being exclusively a constitutional argument, I wish to submit some reflections upon it in the same spirit of kindness that I know actuates you. Let me first state what I understand to be your position. It is that if it shall become necessary to repel invasion, the President may, without violation of the Constitution, cross the line and invade the territory of another country, and that whether such necessity exists in any given case the President is the sole judge.

Before going further consider well whether this is or is not your position. If it is, it is a position that neither the President himself, nor any friend of his, so far as I know, has ever taken. Their only positions are—first, that the soil was ours when the hostilities commenced; and second, that whether it was rightfully ours or not, Congress had annexed it, and the President for that reason was bound to defend it; both of which are as clearly proved to be false in fact as you can prove that your house is mine. The soil was not ours, and Congress did not annex or attempt to annex it. But to return to your position. Allow the President to invade a neighboring nation whenever he shall deem it necessary to repel an invasion, and you allow him to do so whenever he may choose to say he deems it necessary for such purpose, and you allow him to make war at pleasure. Study to see if you can fix any limit to his power in this respect, after having given him so much as you propose. If to-day he should choose to say he thinks it necessary to invade Canada to prevent the British from invading us, how could you stop him? You may say to him,—"I see no probability of the British invading us"; but he will say to you, "Be silent: I see it, if you don't."

The provision of the Constitution giving the war making power to Congress was dictated, as I understand it, by the following reasons: kings had always been involving and impoverishing their people in wars, pretending generally, if not always, that the good of the people was the object. This our convention understood to be the most oppressive of all kingly oppressions, and they resolved to so frame the Constitution that no one man should hold the power of bringing this oppression upon us. But your view destroys the whole matter, and places our President where kings have always stood. Write soon again.

Yours truly,

A. LINCOLN.

REPORT IN THE HOUSE OF REPRESENTATIVES,

MARCH 9, 1848.

Mr. Lincoln, from the Committee on the Postoffice and Post Roads, made the following report:

The Committee on the Post-office and Post Roads, to whom was referred the resolution of the House of Representatives entitled "An Act authorizing postmasters at county seats of justice to receive subscriptions for newspapers and periodicals, to be paid through the agency of the Post-office Department, and for other purposes," beg leave to submit the following report:

The committee have reason to believe that a general wish pervades the community at large that some such facility as the proposed measure should be granted by express law, for subscribing, through the agency of the Post-office Department, to newspapers and periodicals which diffuse daily, weekly, or monthly intelligence of passing events. Compliance with this general wish is deemed to be in accordance with our republican institutions, which can be best sustained by the diffusion of knowledge and the due encouragement of a universal, national spirit of inquiry and discussion of public events through the medium of the public press. The committee, however, has not been insensible to its duty of guarding the Post-office Department against injurious sacrifices for the accomplishment of this object, whereby its ordinary efficacy might be impaired or embarrassed. It has therefore been a subject of much consideration; but it is now confidently hoped that the bill herewith submitted effectually obviates all objections which might exist with regard to a less matured proposition.

The committee learned, upon inquiry, that the Post-office Department, in view of meeting the general wish on this subject, made the experiment through one if its own internal regulations, when the new postage system went into operation on the first of July, 1845, and that it was continued until the thirtieth of September, 1847. But this experiment, for reasons hereafter stated, proved unsatisfactory, and it was discontinued by order of the Postmaster-General. As far as the committee can at present ascertain, the following seem to have been the principal grounds of dissatisfaction in this experiment:

(1) The legal responsibility of postmasters receiving newspaper subscriptions, or of their sureties, was not defined.

(2) The authority was open to all postmasters instead of being limited to those of specific offices.

(3) The consequence of this extension of authority was that, in innumerable instances, the money, without the previous knowledge or control of the officers of the department who are responsible for the good management of its finances, was deposited in offices where it was improper such funds should be placed; and the repayment was ordered, not by the financial officers, but by the postmasters, at points where it was inconvenient to the department so to disburse its funds.

(4) The inconvenience of accumulating uncertain and fluctuating sums at small offices was felt seriously in consequent overpayments to contractors on their quarterly collecting orders; and, in case of private mail routes, in litigation concerning the misapplication of such funds to the special service of supplying mails.

(5) The accumulation of such funds on draft offices could not be known to the financial clerks of the department in time to control it, and too often this rendered uncertain all their calculations of funds in hand.

(6) The orders of payment were for the most part issued upon the principal offices, such as New York, Philadelphia, Boston, Baltimore, etc., where the large offices of publishers are located, causing an illimitable and uncontrollable drain of the department funds from those points where it was essential to husband them for its own regular disbursements. In Philadelphia alone this drain averaged $5000 per quarter; and in other cities of the seaboard it was proportionate.

(7) The embarrassment of the department was increased by the illimitable, uncontrollable, and irresponsible scattering of its funds from concentrated points suitable for its distributions, to remote, unsafe, and inconvenient offices, where they could not be again made available till collected by special agents, or were transferred at considerable expense into the principal disbursing offices again.

(8) There was a vast increase of duties thrown upon the limited force before necessary to conduct the business of the department; and from the delay of obtaining vouchers impediments arose to the speedy settlement of accounts with present or retired post-masters, causing postponements which endangered the liability of sureties under the act of limitations, and causing much danger of an increase of such cases.

(9) The most responsible postmasters (at the large offices) were ordered by the least responsible (at small offices) to make payments upon their vouchers, without having the means of ascertaining whether these vouchers were genuine or forged, or if genuine, whether the signers were in or out of office, or solvent or defaulters.

(10) The transaction of this business for subscribers and publishers at the public expense, an the embarrassment, inconvenience, and delay of the department's own business occasioned by it, were not justified by any sufficient remuneration of revenue to sustain the department, as required in every other respect with regard to its agency.

The committee, in view of these objections, has been solicitous to frame a bill which would not be obnoxious to them in principle or in practical effect.

It is confidently believed that by limiting the offices for receiving subscriptions to less than one tenth of the number authorized by the experiment already tried, and designating the county seat in each county for the purpose, the control of the department will be rendered satisfactory; particularly as it will be in the power of the Auditor, who is the officer required by law to check the accounts, to approve or disapprove of the deposits, and to sanction not only the payments, but to point out the place of payment. If these payments should cause a drain on the principal offices of the seaboard, it will be compensated by the accumulation of funds at county seats, where the contractors on those routes can be paid to that extent by the department's drafts, with more local convenience to themselves than by drafts on the seaboard offices.

The legal responsibility for these deposits is defined, and the accumulation of funds at the point of deposit, and the repayment at points drawn upon, being known to and controlled by the Auditor, will not occasion any such embarrassments as were before felt; the record kept by the Auditor on the passing of the certificates through his hands will enable him to settle accounts without the delay occasioned by vouchers being withheld; all doubt or uncertainty as to the genuineness of certificates, or the propriety of their issue, will be removed by the Auditor's examination and approval; and there can be no risk of loss of funds by transmission, as the certificate will not be payable till sanctioned by the Auditor, and after his sanction the payor need not pay it unless it is presented by the publisher or his known clerk or agent.

The main principle of equivalent for the agency of the department is secured by the postage required to be paid upon the transmission of the certificates, augmenting adequately the post-office revenue.

The committee, conceiving that in this report all the difficulties of the subject have been fully and fairly stated, and that these difficulties have been obviated by the plan proposed in the accompanying bill, and believing that the measure will satisfactorily meet the wants and wishes of a very large portion of the community, beg leave to recommend its adoption.

REPORT IN THE HOUSE OF REPRESENTATIVES,

MARCH 9, 1848.

Mr. Lincoln, from the Committee on the Postoffice and Post Roads, made the following report:

The Committee on the Post-office and Post Roads, to whom was referred the petition of H. M. Barney, postmaster at Brimfield, Peoria County, Illinois, report: That they have been satisfied by evidence, that on the 15th of December, 1847, said petitioner had his store, with some fifteen hundred dollars' worth of goods, together with all the papers of the post-office, entirely destroyed by fire; and that the specie funds of the office were melted down, partially lost and partially destroyed; that this large individual loss entirely precludes the idea of embezzlement; that the balances due the department of former quarters had been only about twenty-five dollars; and that owing to the destruction of papers, the exact amount due for the quarter ending December 31, 1847, cannot be ascertained. They therefore report a joint resolution, releasing said petitioner from paying anything for the quarter last mentioned.

REMARKS IN THE UNITED STATES HOUSE OF REPRESENTATIVES, MARCH 29, 1848.

The bill for raising additional military force for limited time, etc., was reported from Committee on judiciary; similar bills had been reported from Committee on, Public Lands and Military Committee.

Mr. Lincoln said if there was a general desire on the part of the House to pass the bill now he should be glad to have it done—concurring, as he did generally, with the gentleman from Arkansas [Mr. Johnson] that the postponement might jeopard the safety of the proposition. If, however, a reference was to be made, he wished to make a very few remarks in relation to the several subjects desired by the gentlemen to be embraced in amendments to the ninth section of the act of the last session of Congress. The first amendment desired by members of this House had for its only object to give bounty lands to such persons as had served for a time as privates, but had never been discharged as such, because promoted to office. That subject, and no other, was embraced in this bill. There were some others who desired, while they were legislating on this subject, that they should also give bounty lands to the volunteers of the War of 1812. His friend from Maryland said there were no such men. He [Mr. L.] did not say there were many, but he was very confident there were some. His friend from Kentucky near him, [Mr. Gaines] told him he himself was one.

There was still another proposition touching this matter; that was, that persons entitled to bounty lands should by law be entitled to locate these lands in parcels, and not be required to locate them in one body, as was provided by the existing law.

Now he had carefully drawn up a bill embracing these three separate propositions, which he intended to propose as a substitute for all these bills in the House, or in Committee of the Whole on the State of the Union, at some suitable time. If there was a disposition on the part of the House to act at once on this separate proposition, he repeated that, with the gentlemen from Arkansas, he should prefer it lest they should lose all. But if there was to be a reference, he desired to introduce his bill embracing the three propositions, thus enabling the committee and the House to act at the same time, whether favorably or unfavorably, upon all. He inquired whether an amendment was now in order.

The Speaker replied in the negative.

TO ARCHIBALD WILLIAMS.

WASHINGTON, April 30, 1848.

DEAR WILLIAMS:—I have not seen in the papers any evidence of a movement to send a delegate from your circuit to the June convention. I wish to say that I think it all-important that a delegate should be sent. Mr. Clay's chance for an election is just no chance at all. He might get New York, and that would have elected in 1844, but it will not now, because he must now, at the least, lose Tennessee, which he had then, and in addition the fifteen new votes of Florida, Texas, Iowa, and Wisconsin. I know our good friend Browning is a great admirer of Mr. Clay, and I therefore fear he is favoring his nomination. If he is, ask him to discard feeling, and try if he can possibly, as a matter of judgment, count the votes necessary to elect him.

In my judgment we can elect nobody but General Taylor; and we cannot elect him without a nomination. Therefore don't fail to send a delegate.

Your friend as ever,

A. LINCOLN.

REMARKS IN THE HOUSE OF REPRESENTATIVES,

MAY 11, 1848.

A bill for the admission of Wisconsin into the Union had been passed.

Mr. Lincoln moved to reconsider the vote by which the bill was passed. He stated to the House that he had made this motion for the purpose of obtaining an opportunity to say a few words in relation to a point raised in the course of the debate on this bill, which he would now proceed to make if in order. The point in the case to which he referred arose on the amendment that was submitted by the gentleman from Vermont [Mr. Collamer] in Committee of the Whole on the State of the Union, and which was afterward renewed in the House, in relation to the question whether the reserved sections, which, by some bills heretofore passed, by which an appropriation of land had been made to Wisconsin, had been enhanced in value, should be reduced to the minimum price of the public lands. The question of the reduction in value of those sections was to him at this time a matter very nearly of indifference. He was inclined to desire that Wisconsin should be obliged by having it reduced. But the gentleman from Indiana [Mr. C. B. Smith], the chairman of the Committee on Territories, yesterday associated that question with the general question, which is now to some extent agitated in Congress, of making appropriations of alternate sections of land to aid the States in making internal improvements, and enhancing the price of the sections reserved, and the gentleman from Indiana took ground against that policy. He did not make any special argument in favor of Wisconsin, but he took ground generally against the policy of giving alternate sections of land, and enhancing the price of the reserved sections. Now he [Mr. Lincoln] did not at this time take the floor for the purpose of attempting to make an argument on the general subject. He rose simply to protest against the doctrine which the gentleman from Indiana had avowed in the course of what he [Mr. Lincoln] could not but consider an unsound argument.

It might, however, be true, for anything he knew, that the gentleman from Indiana might convince him that his argument was sound; but he [Mr. Lincoln] feared that gentleman would not be able to convince a majority in Congress that it was sound. It was true the question appeared in a different aspect to persons in consequence of a difference in the point from which they looked at it. It did not look to persons residing east of the mountains as it did to those who lived among the public lands. But, for his part, he would state that if Congress would make a donation of alternate sections of public land for the purpose of internal improvements in his State, and forbid the reserved sections being sold at $1.25, he should be glad to see the appropriation made; though he should prefer it if the reserved sections were not enhanced in price. He repeated, he should be glad to have such appropriations made, even though the reserved sections should be enhanced in price. He did not wish to be understood as concurring in any intimation that they would refuse to receive such an appropriation of alternate sections of land because a condition enhancing the price of the reserved sections should be attached thereto. He believed his position would now be understood: if not, he feared he should not be able to make himself understood.

But, before he took his seat, he would remark that the Senate during the present session had passed a bill making appropriations of land on that principle for the benefit of the State in which he resided the State of Illinois. The alternate sections were to be given for the purpose of constructing roads, and the reserved sections were to be enhanced in value in consequence. When that bill came here for the action of this House—it had been received, and was now before the Committee on Public Lands—he desired much to see it passed as it was, if it could be put in no more favorable form for the State of Illinois. When it should be before this House, if any member from a section of the Union in which these lands did not lie, whose interest might be less than that which he felt, should propose a reduction of the price of the reserved sections to $1.25, he should be much obliged; but he did not think it would be well for those who came from the section of the Union in which the lands lay to do so.—He wished it, then, to be understood that he did not join in the warfare against the principle which had engaged the minds of some members of Congress who were favorable to the improvements in the western country. There was a good deal of force, he admitted, in what fell from the chairman of the Committee on Territories. It might be that there was no precise justice in raising the price of the reserved sections to $2.50 per acre. It might be proper that the price should be enhanced to some extent, though not to double the usual price; but he should be glad to have such an appropriation with the reserved sections at $2.50; he should be better pleased to have the price of those sections at something less; and he should be still better pleased to have them without any enhancement at all.

There was one portion of the argument of the gentleman from Indiana, the chairman of the Committee on Territories [Mr. Smith], which he wished to take occasion to say that he did not view as unsound. He alluded to the statement that the General Government was interested in these internal improvements being made, inasmuch as they increased the value of the lands that were unsold, and they enabled the government to sell the lands which could not be sold without them. Thus, then, the government gained by internal improvements as well as by the general good which the people derived from them, and it might be, therefore, that the lands should not be sold for more than $1.50 instead of the price being doubled. He, however, merely mentioned this in passing, for he only rose to state, as the principle of giving these lands for the purposes which he had mentioned had been laid hold of and considered favorably, and as there were some gentlemen who had constitutional scruples about giving money for these purchases who would not hesitate to give land, that he was not willing to have it understood that he was one of those who made war against that principle. This was all he desired to say, and having accomplished the object with which he rose, he withdrew his motion to reconsider.

ON TAYLOR'S NOMINATION

TO E. B. WASHBURNE.

WASHINGTON, April 30,1848.

DEAR WASHBURNE:

I have this moment received your very short note asking me if old Taylor is to be used up, and who will be the nominee. My hope of Taylor's nomination is as high—a little higher than it was when you left. Still, the case is by no means out of doubt. Mr. Clay's letter has not advanced his interests any here. Several who were against Taylor, but not for anybody particularly, before, are since taking ground, some for Scott and some for McLean. Who will be nominated neither I nor any one else can tell. Now, let me pray to you in turn. My prayer is that you let nothing discourage or baffle you, but that, in spite of every difficulty, you send us a good Taylor delegate from your circuit. Make Baker, who is now with you, I suppose, help about it. He is a good hand to raise a breeze.

General Ashley, in the Senate from Arkansas, died yesterday. Nothing else new beyond what you see in the papers.

Yours truly,

A. LINCOLN

DEFENSE OF MEXICAN WAR POSITION

TO REV. J. M. PECK

WASHINGTON, May 21, 1848. DEAR SIR:

....Not in view of all the facts. There are facts which you have kept out of view. It is a fact that the United States army in marching to the Rio Grande marched into a peaceful Mexican settlement, and frightened the inhabitants away from their homes and their growing crops. It is a fact that Fort Brown, opposite Matamoras, was built by that army within a Mexican cotton-field, on which at the time the army reached it a young cotton crop was growing, and which crop was wholly destroyed and the field itself greatly and permanently injured by ditches, embankments, and the like. It is a fact that when the Mexicans captured Captain Thornton and his command, they found and captured them within another Mexican field.

Now I wish to bring these facts to your notice, and to ascertain what is the result of your reflections upon them. If you deny that they are facts, I think I can furnish proofs which shall convince you that you are mistaken. If you admit that they are facts, then I shall be obliged for a reference to any law of language, law of States, law of nations, law of morals, law of religions, any law, human or divine, in which an authority can be found for saying those facts constitute "no aggression."

Possibly you consider those acts too small for notice. Would you venture to so consider them had they been committed by any nation on earth against the humblest of our people? I know you would not. Then I ask, is the precept "Whatsoever ye would that men should do to you, do ye even so to them" obsolete? of no force? of no application?

Yours truly,

A. LINCOLN.

ON ZACHARY TAYLOR NOMINATION

TO ARCHIBALD WILLIAMS.

WASHINGTON, June 12, 1848.

DEAR WILLIAMS:—On my return from Philadelphia, where I had been attending the nomination of "Old Rough," (Zachary Taylor) I found your letter in a mass of others which had accumulated in my absence. By many, and often, it had been said they would not abide the nomination of Taylor; but since the deed has been done, they are fast falling in, and in my opinion we shall have a most overwhelming, glorious triumph. One unmistakable sign is that all the odds and ends are with us—Barnburners, Native Americans, Tyler men, disappointed office-seeking Locofocos, and the Lord knows what. This is important, if in nothing else, in showing which way the wind blows. Some of the sanguine men have set down all the States as certain for Taylor but Illinois, and it as doubtful. Cannot something be done even in Illinois? Taylor's nomination takes the Locos on the blind side. It turns the war thunder against them. The war is now to them the gallows of Haman, which they built for us, and on which they are doomed to be hanged themselves.

Excuse this short letter. I have so many to write that I cannot devote much time to any one.

Yours as ever,

A. LINCOLN.

SPEECH IN THE HOUSE OF REPRESENTATIVES,

JUNE 20, 1848.

In Committee of the Whole on the State of the Union, on the Civil and Diplomatic Appropriation Bill:

Mr. CHAIRMAN:—I wish at all times in no way to practise any fraud upon the House or the committee, and I also desire to do nothing which may be very disagreeable to any of the members. I therefore state in advance that my object in taking the floor is to make a speech on the general subject of internal improvements; and if I am out of order in doing so, I give the chair an opportunity of so deciding, and I will take my seat.

The Chair: I will not undertake to anticipate what the gentleman may say on the subject of internal improvements. He will, therefore, proceed in his remarks, and if any question of order shall be made, the chair will then decide it.

Mr. Lincoln: At an early day of this session the President sent us what may properly be called an internal improvement veto message. The late Democratic convention, which sat at Baltimore, and which nominated General Cass for the Presidency, adopted a set of resolutions, now called the Democratic platform, among which is one in these words:

"That the Constitution does not confer upon the General Government the power to commence and carry on a general system of internal improvements."

General Cass, in his letter accepting the nomination, holds this language:

"I have carefully read the resolutions of the Democratic national convention, laying down the platform of our political faith, and I adhere to them as firmly as I approve them cordially."

These things, taken together, show that the question of internal improvements is now more distinctly made—has become more intense—than at any former period. The veto message and the Baltimore resolution I understand to be, in substance, the same thing; the latter being the more general statement, of which the former is the amplification the bill of particulars. While I know there are many Democrats, on this floor and elsewhere, who disapprove that message, I understand that all who voted for General Cass will thereafter be counted as having approved it, as having indorsed all its doctrines.

I suppose all, or nearly all, the Democrats will vote for him. Many of them will do so not because they like his position on this question, but because they prefer him, being wrong on this, to another whom they consider farther wrong on other questions. In this way the internal improvement Democrats are to be, by a sort of forced consent, carried over and arrayed against themselves on this measure of policy. General Cass, once elected, will not trouble himself to make a constitutional argument, or perhaps any argument at all, when he shall veto a river or harbor bill; he will consider it a sufficient answer to all Democratic murmurs to point to Mr. Polk's message, and to the Democratic platform. This being the case, the question of improvements is verging to a final crisis; and the friends of this policy must now battle, and battle manfully, or surrender all. In this view, humble as I am, I wish to review, and contest as well as I may, the general positions of this veto message. When I say general positions, I mean to exclude from consideration so much as relates to the present embarrassed state of the treasury in consequence of the Mexican War.

Those general positions are: that internal improvements ought not to be made by the General Government—First. Because they would overwhelm the treasury Second. Because, while their burdens would be general, their benefits would be local and partial, involving an obnoxious inequality; and Third. Because they would be unconstitutional. Fourth. Because the States may do enough by the levy and collection of tonnage duties; or if not—Fifth. That the Constitution may be amended. "Do nothing at all, lest you do something wrong," is the sum of these positions is the sum of this message. And this, with the exception of what is said about constitutionality, applying as forcibly to what is said about making improvements by State authority as by the national authority; so that we must abandon the improvements of the country altogether, by any and every authority, or we must resist and repudiate the doctrines of this message. Let us attempt the latter.

The first position is, that a system of internal improvements would overwhelm the treasury. That in such a system there is a tendency to undue expansion, is not to be denied. Such tendency is founded in the nature of the subject. A member of Congress will prefer voting for a bill which contains an appropriation for his district, to voting for one which does not; and when a bill shall be expanded till every district shall be provided for, that it will be too greatly expanded is obvious. But is this any more true in Congress than in a State Legislature? If a member of Congress must have an appropriation for his district, so a member of a Legislature must have one for his county. And if one will overwhelm the national treasury, so the other will overwhelm the State treasury. Go where we will, the difficulty is the same. Allow it to drive us from the halls of Congress, and it will, just as easily, drive us from the State Legislatures. Let us, then, grapple with it, and test its strength. Let us, judging of the future by the past, ascertain whether there may not be, in the discretion of Congress, a sufficient power to limit and restrain this expansive tendency within reasonable and proper bounds. The President himself values the evidence of the past. He tells us that at a certain point of our history more than two hundred millions of dollars had been applied to make improvements; and this he does to prove that the treasury would be overwhelmed by such a system. Why did he not tell us how much was granted? Would not that have been better evidence? Let us turn to it, and see what it proves. In the message the President tells us that "during the four succeeding years embraced by the administration of President Adams, the power not only to appropriate money, but to apply it, under the direction and authority of the General Government, as well to the construction of roads as to the improvement of harbors and rivers, was fully asserted and exercised." This, then, was the period of greatest enormity. These, if any, must have been the days of the two hundred millions. And how much do you suppose was really expended for improvements during that four years? Two hundred millions? One hundred? Fifty? Ten? Five? No, sir; less than two millions. As shown by authentic documents, the expenditures on improvements during 1825, 1826, 1827, and 1828 amounted to one million eight hundred and seventy-nine thousand six hundred and twenty-seven dollars and one cent. These four years were the period of Mr. Adams's administration, nearly and substantially. This fact shows that when the power to make improvements "was fully asserted and exercised," the Congress did keep within reasonable limits; and what has been done, it seems to me, can be done again.

Now for the second portion of the message—namely, that the burdens of improvements would be general, while their benefits would be local and partial, involving an obnoxious inequality. That there is some degree of truth in this position, I shall not deny. No commercial object of government patronage can be so exclusively general as to not be of some peculiar local advantage. The navy, as I understand it, was established, and is maintained at a great annual expense, partly to be ready for war when war shall come, and partly also, and perhaps chiefly, for the protection of our commerce on the high seas. This latter object is, for all I can see, in principle the same as internal improvements. The driving a pirate from the track of commerce on the broad ocean, and the removing of a snag from its more narrow path in the Mississippi River, cannot, I think, be distinguished in principle. Each is done to save life and property, and for nothing else.

The navy, then, is the most general in its benefits of all this class of objects; and yet even the navy is of some peculiar advantage to Charleston, Baltimore, Philadelphia, New York, and Boston, beyond what it is to the interior towns of Illinois. The next most general object I can think of would be improvements on the Mississippi River and its tributaries. They touch thirteen of our States-Pennsylvania, Virginia, Kentucky, Tennessee, Mississippi, Louisiana, Arkansas, Missouri, Illinois, Indiana, Ohio, Wisconsin, and Iowa. Now I suppose it will not be denied that these thirteen States are a little more interested in improvements on that great river than are the remaining seventeen. These instances of the navy and the Mississippi River show clearly that there is something of local advantage in the most general objects. But the converse is also true. Nothing is so local as to not be of some general benefit. Take, for instance, the Illinois and Michigan Canal. Considered apart from its effects, it is perfectly local. Every inch of it is within the State of Illinois. That canal was first opened for business last April. In a very few days we were all gratified to learn, among other things, that sugar had been carried from New Orleans through this canal to Buffalo in New York. This sugar took this route, doubtless, because it was cheaper than the old route. Supposing benefit of the reduction in the cost of carriage to be shared between seller and the buyer, result is that the New Orleans merchant sold his sugar a little dearer, and the people of Buffalo sweetened their coffee a little cheaper, than before,—a benefit resulting from the canal, not to Illinois, where the canal is, but to Louisiana and New York, where it is not. In other transactions Illinois will, of course, have her share, and perhaps the larger share too, of the benefits of the canal; but this instance of the sugar clearly shows that the benefits of an improvement are by no means confined to the particular locality of the improvement itself. The just conclusion from all this is that if the nation refuse to make improvements of the more general kind because their benefits may be somewhat local, a State may for the same reason refuse to make an improvement of a local kind because its benefits may be somewhat general. A State may well say to the nation, "If you will do nothing for me, I will do nothing for you." Thus it is seen that if this argument of "inequality" is sufficient anywhere, it is sufficient everywhere, and puts an end to improvements altogether. I hope and believe that if both the nation and the States would, in good faith, in their respective spheres do what they could in the way of improvements, what of inequality might be produced in one place might be compensated in another, and the sum of the whole might not be very unequal.

But suppose, after all, there should be some degree of inequality. Inequality is certainly never to be embraced for its own sake; but is every good thing to be discarded which may be inseparably connected with some degree of it? If so, we must discard all government. This Capitol is built at the public expense, for the public benefit; but does any one doubt that it is of some peculiar local advantage to the property-holders and business people of Washington? Shall we remove it for this reason? And if so, where shall we set it down, and be free from the difficulty? To make sure of our object, shall we locate it nowhere, and have Congress hereafter to hold its sessions, as the loafer lodged, "in spots about"? I make no allusion to the present President when I say there are few stronger cases in this world of "burden to the many and benefit to the few," of "inequality," than the Presidency itself is by some thought to be. An honest laborer digs coal at about seventy cents a day, while the President digs abstractions at about seventy dollars a day. The coal is clearly worth more than the abstractions, and yet what a monstrous inequality in the prices! Does the President, for this reason, propose to abolish the Presidency? He does not, and he ought not. The true rule, in determining to embrace or reject anything, is not whether it have any evil in it, but whether it have more of evil than of good. There are few things wholly evil or wholly good. Almost everything, especially of government policy, is an inseparable compound of the two; so that our best judgment of the preponderance between them is continually demanded. On this principle the President, his friends, and the world generally act on most subjects. Why not apply it, then, upon this question? Why, as to improvements, magnify the evil, and stoutly refuse to see any good in them?

Mr. Chairman, on the third position of the message the constitutional question—I have not much to say. Being the man I am, and speaking, where I do, I feel that in any attempt at an original constitutional argument I should not be and ought not to be listened to patiently. The ablest and the best of men have gone over the whole ground long ago. I shall attempt but little more than a brief notice of what some of them have said. In relation to Mr. Jefferson's views, I read from Mr. Polk's veto message:

"President Jefferson, in his message to Congress in 1806, recommended an amendment of the Constitution, with a view to apply an anticipated surplus in the treasury 'to the great purposes of the public education, roads, rivers, canals, and such other objects of public improvement as it may be thought proper to add to the constitutional enumeration of the federal powers'; and he adds: 'I suppose an amendment to the Constitution, by consent of the States, necessary, because the objects now recommended are not among those enumerated in the Constitution, and to which it permits the public moneys to be applied.' In 1825, he repeated in his published letters the opinion that no such power has been conferred upon Congress."

I introduce this not to controvert just now the constitutional opinion, but to show that, on the question of expediency, Mr. Jefferson's opinion was against the present President; that this opinion of Mr. Jefferson, in one branch at least, is in the hands of Mr. Polk like McFingal's gun—"bears wide and kicks the owner over."

But to the constitutional question. In 1826 Chancellor Kent first published his Commentaries on American law. He devoted a portion of one of the lectures to the question of the authority of Congress to appropriate public moneys for internal improvements. He mentions that the subject had never been brought under judicial consideration, and proceeds to give a brief summary of the discussion it had undergone between the legislative and executive branches of the government. He shows that the legislative branch had usually been for, and the executive against, the power, till the period of Mr. J.Q. Adams's administration, at which point he considers the executive influence as withdrawn from opposition, and added to the support of the power. In 1844 the chancellor published a new edition of his Commentaries, in which he adds some notes of what had transpired on the question since 1826. I have not time to read the original text on the notes; but the whole may be found on page 267, and the two or three following pages, of the first volume of the edition of 1844. As to what Chancellor Kent seems to consider the sum of the whole, I read from one of the notes:

"Mr. Justice Story, in his Commentaries on the Constitution of the United States, Vol. II., pp. 429-440, and again pp. 519-538, has stated at large the arguments for and against the proposition that Congress have a constitutional authority to lay taxes and to apply the power to regulate commerce as a means directly to encourage and protect domestic manufactures; and without giving any opinion of his own on the contested doctrine, he has left the reader to draw his own conclusions. I should think, however, from the arguments as stated, that every mind which has taken no part in the discussion, and felt no prejudice or territorial bias on either side of the question, would deem the arguments in favor of the Congressional power vastly superior."

It will be seen that in this extract the power to make improvements is not directly mentioned; but by examining the context, both of Kent and Story, it will be seen that the power mentioned in the extract and the power to make improvements are regarded as identical. It is not to be denied that many great and good men have been against the power; but it is insisted that quite as many, as great and as good, have been for it; and it is shown that, on a full survey of the whole, Chancellor Kent was of opinion that the arguments of the latter were vastly superior. This is but the opinion of a man; but who was that man? He was one of the ablest and most learned lawyers of his age, or of any age. It is no disparagement to Mr. Polk, nor indeed to any one who devotes much time to politics, to be placed far behind Chancellor Kent as a lawyer. His attitude was most favorable to correct conclusions. He wrote coolly, and in retirement. He was struggling to rear a durable monument of fame; and he well knew that truth and thoroughly sound reasoning were the only sure foundations. Can the party opinion of a party President on a law question, as this purely is, be at all compared or set in opposition to that of such a man, in such an attitude, as Chancellor Kent? This constitutional question will probably never be better settled than it is, until it shall pass under judicial consideration; but I do think no man who is clear on the questions of expediency need feel his conscience much pricked upon this.

Mr. Chairman, the President seems to think that enough may be done, in the way of improvements, by means of tonnage duties under State authority, with the consent of the General Government. Now I suppose this matter of tonnage duties is well enough in its own sphere. I suppose it may be efficient, and perhaps sufficient, to make slight improvements and repairs in harbors already in use and not much out of repair. But if I have any correct general idea of it, it must be wholly inefficient for any general beneficent purposes of improvement. I know very little, or rather nothing at all, of the practical matter of levying and collecting tonnage duties; but I suppose one of its principles must be to lay a duty for the improvement of any particular harbor upon the tonnage coming into that harbor; to do otherwise—to collect money in one harbor, to be expended on improvements in another—would be an extremely aggravated form of that inequality which the President so much deprecates. If I be right in this, how could we make any entirely new improvement by means of tonnage duties? How make a road, a canal, or clear a greatly obstructed river? The idea that we could involves the same absurdity as the Irish bull about the new boots. "I shall niver git 'em on," says Patrick, "till I wear 'em a day or two, and stretch 'em a little." We shall never make a canal by tonnage duties until it shall already have been made awhile, so the tonnage can get into it.

After all, the President concludes that possibly there may be some great objects of improvement which cannot be effected by tonnage duties, and which it therefore may be expedient for the General Government to take in hand. Accordingly he suggests, in case any such be discovered, the propriety of amending the Constitution. Amend it for what? If, like Mr. Jefferson, the President thought improvements expedient, but not constitutional, it would be natural enough for him to recommend such an amendment. But hear what he says in this very message:

"In view of these portentous consequences, I cannot but think that this course of legislation should be arrested, even were there nothing to forbid it in the fundamental laws of our Union."

For what, then, would he have the Constitution amended? With him it is a proposition to remove one impediment merely to be met by others which, in his opinion, cannot be removed, to enable Congress to do what, in his opinion, they ought not to do if they could.

Here Mr. Meade of Virginia inquired if Mr. Lincoln understood the President to be opposed, on grounds of expediency, to any and every improvement.

Mr. Lincoln answered: In the very part of his message of which I am speaking, I understand him as giving some vague expression in favor of some possible objects of improvement; but in doing so I understand him to be directly on the teeth of his own arguments in other parts of it. Neither the President nor any one can possibly specify an improvement which shall not be clearly liable to one or another of the objections he has urged on the score of expediency. I have shown, and might show again, that no work—no object—can be so general as to dispense its benefits with precise equality; and this inequality is chief among the "portentous consequences" for which he declares that improvements should be arrested. No, sir. When the President intimates that something in the way of improvements may properly be done by the General Government, he is shrinking from the conclusions to which his own arguments would force him. He feels that the improvements of this broad and goodly land are a mighty interest; and he is unwilling to confess to the people, or perhaps to himself, that he has built an argument which, when pressed to its conclusions, entirely annihilates this interest.

I have already said that no one who is satisfied of the expediency of making improvements needs be much uneasy in his conscience about its constitutionality. I wish now to submit a few remarks on the general proposition of amending the Constitution. As a general rule, I think we would much better let it alone. No slight occasion should tempt us to touch it. Better not take the first step, which may lead to a habit of altering it. Better, rather, habituate ourselves to think of it as unalterable. It can scarcely be made better than it is. New provisions would introduce new difficulties, and thus create and increase appetite for further change. No, sir; let it stand as it is. New hands have never touched it. The men who made it have done their work, and have passed away. Who shall improve on what they did?

Mr. Chairman, for the purpose of reviewing this message in the least possible time, as well as for the sake of distinctness, I have analyzed its arguments as well as I could, and reduced them to the propositions I have stated. I have now examined them in detail. I wish to detain the committee only a little while longer with some general remarks upon the subject of improvements. That the subject is a difficult one, cannot be denied. Still it is no more difficult in Congress than in the State Legislatures, in the counties, or in the smallest municipal districts which anywhere exist. All can recur to instances of this difficulty in the case of county roads, bridges, and the like. One man is offended because a road passes over his land, and another is offended because it does not pass over his; one is dissatisfied because the bridge for which he is taxed crosses the river on a different road from that which leads from his house to town; another cannot bear that the county should be got in debt for these same roads and bridges; while not a few struggle hard to have roads located over their lands, and then stoutly refuse to let them be opened until they are first paid the damages. Even between the different wards and streets of towns and cities we find this same wrangling and difficulty. Now these are no other than the very difficulties against which, and out of which, the President constructs his objections of "inequality," "speculation," and "crushing the treasury." There is but a single alternative about them: they are sufficient, or they are not. If sufficient, they are sufficient out of Congress as well as in it, and there is the end. We must reject them as insufficient, or lie down and do nothing by any authority. Then, difficulty though there be, let us meet and encounter it. "Attempt the end, and never stand to doubt; nothing so hard, but search will find it out." Determine that the thing can and shall be done, and then we shall find the way. The tendency to undue expansion is unquestionably the chief difficulty.

How to do something, and still not do too much, is the desideratum. Let each contribute his mite in the way of suggestion. The late Silas Wright, in a letter to the Chicago convention, contributed his, which was worth something; and I now contribute mine, which may be worth nothing. At all events, it will mislead nobody, and therefore will do no harm. I would not borrow money. I am against an overwhelming, crushing system. Suppose that, at each session, Congress shall first determine how much money can, for that year, be spared for improvements; then apportion that sum to the most important objects. So far all is easy; but how shall we determine which are the most important? On this question comes the collision of interests. I shall be slow to acknowledge that your harbor or your river is more important than mine, and vice versa. To clear this difficulty, let us have that same statistical information which the gentleman from Ohio [Mr. Vinton] suggested at the beginning of this session. In that information we shall have a stern, unbending basis of facts—a basis in no wise subject to whim, caprice, or local interest. The prelimited amount of means will save us from doing too much, and the statistics will save us from doing what we do in wrong places. Adopt and adhere to this course, and, it seems to me, the difficulty is cleared.

One of the gentlemen from South Carolina [Mr. Rhett] very much deprecates these statistics. He particularly objects, as I understand him, to counting all the pigs and chickens in the land. I do not perceive much force in the objection. It is true that if everything be enumerated, a portion of such statistics may not be very useful to this object. Such products of the country as are to be consumed where they are produced need no roads or rivers, no means of transportation, and have no very proper connection with this subject. The surplus—that which is produced in one place to be consumed in another; the capacity of each locality for producing a greater surplus; the natural means of transportation, and their susceptibility of improvement; the hindrances, delays, and losses of life and property during transportation, and the causes of each, would be among the most valuable statistics in this connection. From these it would readily appear where a given amount of expenditure would do the most good. These statistics might be equally accessible, as they would be equally useful, to both the nation and the States. In this way, and by these means, let the nation take hold of the larger works, and the States the smaller ones; and thus, working in a meeting direction, discreetly, but steadily and firmly, what is made unequal in one place may be equalized in another, extravagance avoided, and the whole country put on that career of prosperity which shall correspond with its extent of territory, its natural resources, and the intelligence and enterprise of its people.

OPPORTUNITIES FOR YOUNG POLITICIANS

TO WILLIAM H. HERNDON.

WASHINGTON, June 22, 1848.

DEAR WILLIAM:—Last night I was attending a sort of caucus of the Whig members, held in relation to the coming Presidential election. The whole field of the nation was scanned, and all is high hope and confidence. Illinois is expected to better her condition in this race. Under these circumstances, judge how heartrending it was to come to my room and find and read your discouraging letter of the 15th. We have made no gains, but have lost "H. R. Robinson, Turner, Campbell, and four or five more." Tell Arney to reconsider, if he would be saved. Baker and I used to do something, but I think you attach more importance to our absence than is just. There is another cause. In 1840, for instance, we had two senators and five representatives in Sangamon; now we have part of one senator and two representatives. With quite one third more people than we had then, we have only half the sort of offices which are sought by men of the speaking sort of talent. This, I think, is the chief cause. Now, as to the young men. You must not wait to be brought forward by the older men. For instance, do you suppose that I should ever have got into notice if I had waited to be hunted up and pushed forward by older men? You young men get together and form a "Rough and Ready Club," and have regular meetings and speeches. Take in everybody you can get. Harrison Grimsley, L. A. Enos, Lee Kimball, and C. W. Matheny will do to begin the thing; but as you go along gather up all the shrewd, wild boys about town, whether just of age, or a little under age, Chris. Logan, Reddick Ridgely, Lewis Zwizler, and hundreds such. Let every one play the part he can play best,—some speak, some sing, and all "holler." Your meetings will be of evenings; the older men, and the women, will go to hear you; so that it will not only contribute to the election of "Old Zach," but will be an interesting pastime, and improving to the intellectual faculties of all engaged. Don't fail to do this.

You ask me to send you all the speeches made about "Old Zach," the war, etc. Now this makes me a little impatient. I have regularly sent you the Congressional Globe and Appendix, and you cannot have examined them, or you would have discovered that they contain every speech made by every man in both houses of Congress, on every subject, during the session. Can I send any more? Can I send speeches that nobody has made? Thinking it would be most natural that the newspapers would feel interested to give at least some of the speeches to their readers, I at the beginning of the session made arrangements to have one copy of the Globe and Appendix regularly sent to each Whig paper of the district. And yet, with the exception of my own little speech, which was published in two only of the then five, now four, Whig papers, I do not remember having seen a single speech, or even extract from one, in any single one of those papers. With equal and full means on both sides, I will venture that the State Register has thrown before its readers more of Locofoco speeches in a month than all the Whig papers of the district have done of Whig speeches during the session.

If you wish a full understanding of the war, I repeat what I believe I said to you in a letter once before, that the whole, or nearly so, is to be found in the speech of Dixon of Connecticut. This I sent you in pamphlet as well as in the Globe. Examine and study every sentence of that speech thoroughly, and you will understand the whole subject. You ask how Congress came to declare that war had existed by the act of Mexico. Is it possible you don't understand that yet? You have at least twenty speeches in your possession that fully explain it. I will, however, try it once more. The news reached Washington of the commencement of hostilities on the Rio Grande, and of the great peril of General Taylor's army. Everybody, Whigs and Democrats, was for sending them aid, in men and money. It was necessary to pass a bill for this. The Locos had a majority in both houses, and they brought in a bill with a preamble saying: Whereas, War exists by the act of Mexico, therefore we send General Taylor money. The Whigs moved to strike out the preamble, so that they could vote to send the men and money, without saying anything about how the war commenced; but being in the minority, they were voted down, and the preamble was retained. Then, on the passage of the bill, the question came upon them, Shall we vote for preamble and bill together, or against both together? They did not want to vote against sending help to General Taylor, and therefore they voted for both together. Is there any difficulty in understanding this? Even my little speech shows how this was; and if you will go to the library, you may get the Journal of 1845-46, in which you will find the whole for yourself.

We have nothing published yet with special reference to the Taylor race; but we soon will have, and then I will send them to everybody. I made an internal-improvement speech day before yesterday, which I shall send home as soon as I can get it written out and printed,—and which I suppose nobody will read.

Your friend as ever,

A. LINCOLN.

SALARY OF JUDGE IN WESTERN VIRGINIA

REMARKS IN THE HOUSE OF REPRESENTATIVES, JUNE 28, 1848.

Discussion as to salary of judge of western Virginia:—Wishing to increase it from $1800 to $2500.

Mr. Lincoln said he felt unwilling to be either unjust or ungenerous, and he wanted to understand the real case of this judicial officer. The gentleman from Virginia had stated that he had to hold eleven courts. Now everybody knew that it was not the habit of the district judges of the United States in other States to hold anything like that number of courts; and he therefore took it for granted that this must happen under a peculiar law which required that large number of courts to be holden every year; and these laws, he further supposed, were passed at the request of the people of that judicial district. It came, then, to this: that the people in the western district of Virginia had got eleven courts to be held among them in one year, for their own accommodation; and being thus better accommodated than neighbors elsewhere, they wanted their judge to be a little better paid. In Illinois there had been until the present season but one district court held in the year. There were now to be two. Could it be that the western district of Virginia furnished more business for a judge than the whole State of Illinois?

NATIONAL BANK

JULY, 1848,

[FRAGMENT]

The question of a national bank is at rest. Were I President, I should not urge its reagitation upon Congress; but should Congress see fit to pass an act to establish such an institution, I should not arrest it by the veto, unless I should consider it subject to some constitutional objection from which I believe the two former banks to have been free.

YOUNG v.s. OLD—POLITICAL JEALOUSY

TO W. H. HERNDON.

WASHINGTON, July 10, 1848.

DEAR WILLIAM:

Your letter covering the newspaper slips was received last night. The subject of that letter is exceedingly painful to me, and I cannot but think there is some mistake in your impression of the motives of the old men. I suppose I am now one of the old men; and I declare on my veracity, which I think is good with you, that nothing could afford me more satisfaction than to learn that you and others of my young friends at home were doing battle in the contest and endearing themselves to the people and taking a stand far above any I have ever been able to reach in their admiration. I cannot conceive that other men feel differently. Of course I cannot demonstrate what I say; but I was young once, and I am sure I was never ungenerously thrust back. I hardly know what to say. The way for a young man to rise is to improve himself every way he can, never suspecting that anybody wishes to hinder him. Allow me to assure you that suspicion and jealousy never did help any man in any situation. There may sometimes be ungenerous attempts to keep a young man down; and they will succeed, too, if he allows his mind to be diverted from its true channel to brood over the attempted injury. Cast about and see if this feeling has not injured every person you have ever known to fall into it.

Now, in what I have said I am sure you will suspect nothing but sincere friendship. I would save you from a fatal error. You have been a studious young man. You are far better informed on almost all subjects than I ever have been. You cannot fail in any laudable object unless you allow your mind to be improperly directed. I have some the advantage of you in the world's experience, merely by being older; and it is this that induces me to advise. You still seem to be a little mistaken about the Congressional Globe and Appendix. They contain all of the speeches that are published in any way. My speech and Dayton's speech which you say you got in pamphlet form are both word for word in the Appendix. I repeat again, all are there.

Your friend, as ever,

A. LINCOLN.

GENERAL TAYLOR AND THE VETO

SPEECH IN THE HOUSE OF REPRESENTATIVES, JULY 27, 1848.

Mr. SPEAKER, our Democratic friends seem to be in a great distress because they think our candidate for the Presidency don't suit us. Most of them cannot find out that General Taylor has any principles at all; some, however, have discovered that he has one, but that one is entirely wrong. This one principle is his position on the veto power. The gentleman from Tennessee [Mr. Stanton] who has just taken his seat, indeed, has said there is very little, if any, difference on this question between General Taylor and all the Presidents; and he seems to think it sufficient detraction from General Taylor's position on it that it has nothing new in it. But all others whom I have heard speak assail it furiously. A new member from Kentucky [Mr. Clark], of very considerable ability, was in particular concerned about it. He thought it altogether novel and unprecedented for a President or a Presidential candidate to think of approving bills whose constitutionality may not be entirely clear to his own mind. He thinks the ark of our safety is gone unless Presidents shall always veto such bills as in their judgment may be of doubtful constitutionality. However clear Congress may be on their authority to pass any particular act, the gentleman from Kentucky thinks the President must veto it if he has doubts about it. Now I have neither time nor inclination to argue with the gentleman on the veto power as an original question; but I wish to show that General Taylor, and not he, agrees with the earlier statesmen on this question. When the bill chartering the first Bank of the United States passed Congress, its constitutionality was questioned. Mr. Madison, then in the House of Representatives, as well as others, had opposed it on that ground. General Washington, as President, was called on to approve or reject it. He sought and obtained on the constitutionality question the separate written opinions of Jefferson, Hamilton, and Edmund Randolph,—they then being respectively Secretary of State, Secretary of the Treasury, and Attorney general. Hamilton's opinion was for the power; while Randolph's and Jefferson's were both against it. Mr. Jefferson, after giving his opinion deciding only against the constitutionality of the bill, closes his letter with the paragraph which I now read:

"It must be admitted, however, that unless the President's mind, on a view of everything which is urged for and against this bill, is tolerably clear that it is unauthorized by the Constitution,—if the pro and con hang so even as to balance his judgment, a just respect for the wisdom of the legislature would naturally decide the balance in favor of their opinion. It is chiefly for cases where they are clearly misled by error, ambition, or interest, that the Constitution has placed a check in the negative of the President.

"THOMAS JEFFERSON.

"February 15, 1791."

General Taylor's opinion, as expressed in his Allison letter, is as I now read:

"The power given by the veto is a high conservative power; but, in my opinion, should never be exercised except in cases of clear violation of the Constitution, or manifest haste and want of consideration by Congress."

It is here seen that, in Mr. Jefferson's opinion, if on the constitutionality of any given bill the President doubts, he is not to veto it, as the gentleman from Kentucky would have him do, but is to defer to Congress and approve it. And if we compare the opinion of Jefferson and Taylor, as expressed in these paragraphs, we shall find them more exactly alike than we can often find any two expressions having any literal difference. None but interested faultfinders, I think, can discover any substantial variation.

But gentlemen on the other side are unanimously agreed that General Taylor has no other principles. They are in utter darkness as to his opinions on any of the questions of policy which occupy the public attention. But is there any doubt as to what he will do on the prominent questions if elected? Not the least. It is not possible to know what he will or would do in every imaginable case, because many questions have passed away, and others doubtless will arise which none of us have yet thought of; but on the prominent questions of currency, tariff, internal improvements, and Wilmot Proviso, General Taylor's course is at least as well defined as is General Cass's. Why, in their eagerness to get at General

Taylor, several Democratic members here have desired to know whether, in case of his election, a bankrupt law is to be established. Can they tell us General Cass's opinion on this question?

[Some member answered, "He is against it."]

Aye, how do you know he is? There is nothing about it in the platform, nor elsewhere, that I have seen. If the gentleman knows of anything which I do not know he can show it. But to return. General Taylor, in his Allison letter, says:

"Upon the subject of the tariff, the currency, the improvement of our great highways, rivers, lakes, and harbors, the will of the people, as expressed through their representatives in Congress, ought to be respected and carried out by the executive."

Now this is the whole matter. In substance, it is this: The people say to General Taylor, "If you are elected, shall we have a national bank?" He answers, "Your will, gentlemen, not mine." "What about the tariff?" "Say yourselves." "Shall our rivers and harbors be improved?" "Just as you please. If you desire a bank, an alteration of the tariff, internal improvements, any or all, I will not hinder you. If you do not desire them, I will not attempt to force them on you. Send up your members of Congress from the various districts, with opinions according to your own, and if they are for these measures, or any of them, I shall have nothing to oppose; if they are not for them, I shall not, by any appliances whatever, attempt to dragoon them into their adoption."

Now can there be any difficulty in understanding this? To you Democrats it may not seem like principle; but surely you cannot fail to perceive the position plainly enough. The distinction between it and the position of your candidate is broad and obvious, and I admit you have a clear right to show it is wrong if you can; but you have no right to pretend you cannot see it at all. We see it, and to us it appears like principle, and the best sort of principle at that—the principle of allowing the people to do as they please with their own business. My friend from Indiana (C. B. Smith) has aptly asked, "Are you willing to trust the people?" Some of you answered substantially, "We are willing to trust the people; but the President is as much the representative of the people as Congress." In a certain sense, and to a certain extent, he is the representative of the people. He is elected by them, as well as Congress is; but can he, in the nature of things know the wants of the people as well as three hundred other men, coming from all the various localities of the nation? If so, where is the propriety of having a Congress? That the Constitution gives the President a negative on legislation, all know; but that this negative should be so combined with platforms and other appliances as to enable him, and in fact almost compel him, to take the whole of legislation into his own hands, is what we object to, is what General Taylor objects to, and is what constitutes the broad distinction between you and us. To thus transfer legislation is clearly to take it from those who understand with minuteness the interests of the people, and give it to one who does not and cannot so well understand it. I understand your idea that if a Presidential candidate avow his opinion upon a given question, or rather upon all questions, and the people, with full knowledge of this, elect him, they thereby distinctly approve all those opinions. By means of it, measures are adopted or rejected contrary to the wishes of the whole of one party, and often nearly half of the other. Three, four, or half a dozen questions are prominent at a given time; the party selects its candidate, and he takes his position on each of these questions. On all but one his positions have already been indorsed at former elections, and his party fully committed to them; but that one is new, and a large portion of them are against it. But what are they to do? The whole was strung together; and they must take all, or reject all. They cannot take what they like, and leave the rest. What they are already committed to being the majority, they shut their eyes, and gulp the whole. Next election, still another is introduced in the same way. If we run our eyes along the line of the past, we shall see that almost if not quite all the articles of the present Democratic creed have been at first forced upon the party in this very way. And just now, and just so, opposition to internal improvements is to be established if General Cass shall be elected. Almost half the Democrats here are for improvements; but they will vote for Cass, and if he succeeds, their vote will have aided in closing the doors against improvements. Now this is a process which we think is wrong. We prefer a candidate who, like General Taylor, will allow the people to have their own way, regardless of his private opinions; and I should think the internal-improvement Democrats, at least, ought to prefer such a candidate. He would force nothing on them which they don't want, and he would allow them to have improvements which their own candidate, if elected, will not.

Mr. Speaker, I have said General Taylor's position is as well defined as is that of General Cass. In saying this, I admit I do not certainly know what he would do on the Wilmot Proviso. I am a Northern man or rather a Western Free-State man, with a constituency I believe to be, and with personal feelings I know to be, against the extension of slavery. As such, and with what information I have, I hope and believe General Taylor, if elected, would not veto the proviso. But I do not know it. Yet if I knew he would, I still would vote for him. I should do so because, in my judgment, his election alone can defeat General Cass; and because, should slavery thereby go to the territory we now have, just so much will certainly happen by the election of Cass, and in addition a course of policy leading to new wars, new acquisitions of territory and still further extensions of slavery. One of the two is to be President. Which is preferable?

But there is as much doubt of Cass on improvements as there is of Taylor on the proviso. I have no doubt myself of General Cass on this question; but I know the Democrats differ among themselves as to his position. My internal-improvement colleague [Mr. Wentworth] stated on this floor the other day that he was satisfied Cass was for improvements, because he had voted for all the bills that he [Mr. Wentworth] had. So far so good. But Mr. Polk vetoed some of these very bills. The Baltimore convention passed a set of resolutions, among other things, approving these vetoes, and General Cass declares, in his letter accepting the nomination, that he has carefully read these resolutions, and that he adheres to them as firmly as he approves them cordially. In other words, General Cass voted for the bills, and thinks the President did right to veto them; and his friends here are amiable enough to consider him as being on one side or the other, just as one or the other may correspond with their own respective inclinations. My colleague admits that the platform declares against the constitutionality of a general system of improvements, and that General Cass indorses the platform; but he still thinks General Cass is in favor of some sort of improvements. Well, what are they? As he is against general objects, those he is for must be particular and local. Now this is taking the subject precisely by the wrong end. Particularity expending the money of the whole people for an object which will benefit only a portion of them—is the greatest real objection to improvements, and has been so held by General Jackson, Mr. Polk, and all others, I believe, till now. But now, behold, the objects most general—nearest free from this objection—are to be rejected, while those most liable to it are to be embraced. To return: I cannot help believing that General Cass, when he wrote his letter of acceptance, well understood he was to be claimed by the advocates of both sides of this question, and that he then closed the door against all further expressions of opinion purposely to retain the benefits of that double position. His subsequent equivocation at Cleveland, to my mind, proves such to have been the case.

One word more, and I shall have done with this branch of the subject. You Democrats, and your candidate, in the main are in favor of laying down in advance a platform—a set of party positions—as a unit, and then of forcing the people, by every sort of appliance, to ratify them, however unpalatable some of them may be. We and our candidate are in favor of making Presidential elections and the legislation of the country distinct matters; so that the people can elect whom they please, and afterward legislate just as they please, without any hindrance, save only so much as may guard against infractions of the Constitution, undue haste, and want of consideration. The difference between us is clear as noonday. That we are right we cannot doubt. We hold the true Republican position. In leaving the people's business in their hands, we cannot be wrong. We are willing, and even anxious, to go to the people on this issue.

But I suppose I cannot reasonably hope to convince you that we have any principles. The most I can expect is to assure you that we think we have and are quite contented with them. The other day one of the gentlemen from Georgia [Mr. Iverson], an eloquent man, and a man of learning, so far as I can judge, not being learned myself, came down upon us astonishingly. He spoke in what the 'Baltimore American' calls the "scathing and withering style." At the end of his second severe flash I was struck blind, and found myself feeling with my fingers for an assurance of my continued existence. A little of the bone was left, and I gradually revived. He eulogized Mr. Clay in high and beautiful terms, and then declared that we had deserted all our principles, and had turned Henry Clay out, like an old horse, to root. This is terribly severe. It cannot be answered by argument—at least I cannot so answer it. I merely wish to ask the gentleman if the Whigs are the only party he can think of who sometimes turn old horses out to root. Is not a certain Martin Van Buren an old horse which your own party have turned out to root? and is he not rooting a little to your discomfort about now? But in not nominating Mr. Clay we deserted our principles, you say. Ah! In what? Tell us, ye men of principle, what principle we violated. We say you did violate principle in discarding Van Buren, and we can tell you how. You violated the primary, the cardinal, the one great living principle of all democratic representative government—the principle that the representative is bound to carry out the known will of his constituents. A large majority of the Baltimore convention of 1844 were, by their constituents, instructed to procure Van Buren's nomination if they could. In violation—in utter glaring contempt of this, you rejected him; rejected him, as the gentleman from New York [Mr. Birdsall] the other day expressly admitted, for availability—that same "general availability" which you charge upon us, and daily chew over here, as something exceedingly odious and unprincipled. But the gentleman from Georgia [Mr. Iverson] gave us a second speech yesterday, all well considered and put down in writing, in which Van Buren was scathed and withered a "few" for his present position and movements. I cannot remember the gentleman's precise language; but I do remember he put Van Buren down, down, till he got him where he was finally to "stink" and "rot."

Mr. Speaker, it is no business or inclination of mine to defend Martin Van Buren in the war of extermination now waging between him and his old admirers. I say, "Devil take the hindmost"—and the foremost. But there is no mistaking the origin of the breach; and if the curse of "stinking" and "rotting" is to fall on the first and greatest violators of principle in the matter, I disinterestedly suggest that the gentleman from Georgia and his present co-workers are bound to take it upon themselves. But the gentleman from Georgia further says we have deserted all our principles, and taken shelter under General Taylor's military coat-tail, and he seems to think this is exceedingly degrading. Well, as his faith is, so be it unto him. But can he remember no other military coat-tail under which a certain other party have been sheltering for near a quarter of a century? Has he no acquaintance with the ample military coat tail of General Jackson? Does he not know that his own party have run the five last Presidential races under that coat-tail, and that they are now running the sixth under the same cover? Yes, sir, that coat-tail was used not only for General Jackson himself, but has been clung to, with the grip of death, by every Democratic candidate since. You have never ventured, and dare not now venture, from under it. Your campaign papers have constantly been "Old Hickories," with rude likenesses of the old general upon them; hickory poles and hickory brooms your never-ending emblems; Mr. Polk himself was "Young Hickory," or something so; and even now your campaign paper here is proclaiming that Cass and Butler are of the true "Hickory stripe." Now, sir, you dare not give it up. Like a horde of hungry ticks you have stuck to the tail of the Hermitage Lion to the end of his life; and you are still sticking to it, and drawing a loathsome sustenance from it, after he is dead. A fellow once advertised that he had made a discovery by which he could make a new man out of an old one, and have enough of the stuff left to make a little yellow dog. Just such a discovery has General Jackson's popularity been to you. You not only twice made President of him out of it, but you have had enough of the stuff left to make Presidents of several comparatively small men since; and it is your chief reliance now to make still another.

Mr. Speaker, old horses and military coat-tails, or tails of any sort, are not figures of speech such as I would be the first to introduce into discussions here; but as the gentleman from Georgia has thought fit to introduce them, he and you are welcome to all you have made, or can make by them. If you have any more old horses, trot them out; any more tails, just cock them and come at us. I repeat, I would not introduce this mode of discussion here; but I wish gentlemen on the other side to understand that the use of degrading figures is a game at which they may not find themselves able to take all the winnings.

["We give it up!"]

Aye, you give it up, and well you may; but for a very different reason from that which you would have us understand. The point—the power to hurt—of all figures consists in the truthfulness of their application; and, understanding this, you may well give it up. They are weapons which hit you, but miss us.

But in my hurry I was very near closing this subject of military tails before I was done with it. There is one entire article of the sort I have not discussed yet,—I mean the military tail you Democrats are now engaged in dovetailing into the great Michigander [Cass]. Yes, sir; all his biographies (and they are legion) have him in hand, tying him to a military tail, like so many mischievous boys tying a dog to a bladder of beans. True, the material they have is very limited, but they drive at it might and main. He invaded Canada without resistance, and he outvaded it without pursuit. As he did both under orders, I suppose there was to him neither credit nor discredit in them; but they constitute a large part of the tail. He was not at Hull's surrender, but he was close by; he was volunteer aid to General Harrison on the day of the battle of the Thames; and as you said in 1840 Harrison was picking huckleberries two miles off while the battle was fought, I suppose it is a just conclusion with you to say Cass was aiding Harrison to pick huckleberries. This is about all, except the mooted question of the broken sword. Some authors say he broke it, some say he threw it away, and some others, who ought to know, say nothing about it. Perhaps it would be a fair historical compromise to say, if he did not break it, he did not do anything else with it.

By the way, Mr. Speaker, did you know I am a military hero? Yes, sir; in the days of the Black Hawk war I fought, bled, and came away. Speaking of General Cass's career reminds me of my own. I was not at Stiliman's defeat, but I was about as near it as Cass was to Hull's surrender; and, like him, I saw the place very soon afterward. It is quite certain I did not break my sword, for I had none to break; but I bent a musket pretty badly on one occasion. If Cass broke his sword, the idea is he broke it in desperation; I bent the musket by accident. If General Cass went in advance of me in picking huckleberries, I guess I surpassed him in charges upon the wild onions. If he saw any live, fighting Indians, it was more than I did; but I had a good many bloody struggles with the mosquitoes, and although I never fainted from the loss of blood, I can truly say I was often very hungry. Mr. Speaker, if I should ever conclude to doff whatever our Democratic friends may suppose there is of black-cockade federalism about me, and therefore they shall take me up as their candidate for the Presidency, I protest they shall not make fun of me, as they have of General Cass, by attempting to write me into a military hero.

While I have General Cass in hand, I wish to say a word about his political principles. As a specimen, I take the record of his progress in the Wilmot Proviso. In the Washington Union of March 2, 1847, there is a report of a speech of General Cass, made the day before in the Senate, on the Wilmot Proviso, during the delivery of which Mr. Miller of New Jersey is reported to have interrupted him as follows, to wit:

"Mr. Miller expressed his great surprise at the change in the sentiments of the Senator from Michigan, who had been regarded as the great champion of freedom in the Northwest, of which he was a distinguished ornament. Last year the Senator from Michigan was understood to be decidedly in favor of the Wilmot Proviso; and as no reason had been stated for the change, he [Mr. Miller] could not refrain from the expression of his extreme surprise."

To this General Cass is reported to have replied as follows, to wit:

"Mr. Cass said that the course of the Senator from New Jersey was most extraordinary. Last year he [Mr. Cass] should have voted for the proposition, had it come up. But circumstances had altogether changed. The honorable Senator then read several passages from the remarks, as given above, which he had committed to writing, in order to refute such a charge as that of the Senator from New Jersey."

In the "remarks above reduced to writing" is one numbered four, as follows, to wit:

"Fourth. Legislation now would be wholly inoperative, because no territory hereafter to be acquired can be governed without an act of Congress providing for its government; and such an act, on its passage, would open the whole subject, and leave the Congress called on to pass it free to exercise its own discretion, entirely uncontrolled by any declaration found on the statute-book."

In Niles's Register, vol. lxxiii., p. 293, there is a letter of General Cass to ——— Nicholson, of Nashville, Tennessee, dated December 24, 1847, from which the following are correct extracts:

"The Wilmot Proviso has been before the country some time. It has been repeatedly discussed in Congress and by the public press. I am strongly impressed with the opinion that a great change has been going on in the public mind upon this subject,—in my own as well as others',—and that doubts are resolving themselves into convictions that the principle it involves should be kept out of the national legislature, and left to the people of the confederacy in their respective local governments.... Briefly, then, I am opposed to the exercise of any jurisdiction by Congress over this matter; and I am in favor of leaving the people of any territory which may be hereafter acquired the right to regulate it themselves, under the general principles of the Constitution. Because—'First. I do not see in the Constitution any grant of the requisite power to Congress; and I am not disposed to extend a doubtful precedent beyond its necessity,—the establishment of territorial governments when needed,—leaving to the inhabitants all the right compatible with the relations they bear to the confederation."

These extracts show that in 1846 General Cass was for the proviso at once; that in March, 1847, he was still for it, but not just then; and that in December, 1847, he was against it altogether. This is a true index to the whole man. When the question was raised in 1846, he was in a blustering hurry to take ground for it. He sought to be in advance, and to avoid the uninteresting position of a mere follower; but soon he began to see glimpses of the great Democratic ox-goad waving in his face, and to hear indistinctly a voice saying, "Back! Back, sir! Back a little!" He shakes his head, and bats his eyes, and blunders back to his position of March, 1847; but still the goad waves, and the voice grows more distinct and sharper still, "Back, sir! Back, I say! Further back!"—and back he goes to the position of December, 1847, at which the goad is still, and the voice soothingly says, "So! Stand at that!"

Have no fears, gentlemen, of your candidate. He exactly suits you, and we congratulate you upon it. However much you may be distressed about our candidate, you have all cause to be contented and happy with your own. If elected, he may not maintain all or even any of his positions previously taken; but he will be sure to do whatever the party exigency for the time being may require; and that is precisely what you want. He and Van Buren are the same "manner of men"; and, like Van Buren, he will never desert you till you first desert him.

Mr. Speaker, I adopt the suggestion of a friend, that General Cass is a general of splendidly successful charges—charges, to be sure, not upon the public enemy, but upon the public treasury. He was Governor of Michigan territory, and ex-officio Superintendent of Indian Affairs, from the 9th of October, 1813, till the 31st of July, 1831—a period of seventeen years, nine months, and twenty-two days. During this period he received from the United States treasury, for personal services and personal expenses, the aggregate sum of ninety-six thousand and twenty eight dollars, being an average of fourteen dollars and seventy-nine cents per day for every day of the time. This large sum was reached by assuming that he was doing service at several different places, and in several different capacities in the same place, all at the same time. By a correct analysis of his accounts during that period, the following propositions may be deduced:

First. He was paid in three different capacities during the whole of the time: that is to say—(1) As governor a salary at the rate per year of $2000. (2) As estimated for office rent, clerk hire, fuel, etc., in superintendence of Indian affairs in Michigan, at the rate per year of $1500. (3) As compensation and expenses for various miscellaneous items of Indian service out of Michigan, an average per year of $625.

Second. During part of the time—that is, from the 9th of October, 1813, to the 29th of May, 1822 he was paid in four different capacities; that is to say, the three as above, and, in addition thereto, the commutation of ten rations per day, amounting per year to $730.

Third. During another part of the time—that is, from the beginning of 1822 to the 31st of July, '83 he was also paid in four different capacities; that is to say, the first three, as above (the rations being dropped after the 29th of May, 1822), and, in addition thereto, for superintending Indian Agencies at Piqua, Ohio; Fort Wayne, Indiana; and Chicago, Illinois, at the rate per year of $1500. It should be observed here that the last item, commencing at the beginning of 1822, and the item of rations, ending on the 29th of May, 1822, lap on each other during so much of the time as lies between those two dates.

Fourth. Still another part of the time—that is, from the 31st of October, 1821, to the 29th of May, 1822—he was paid in six different capacities; that is to say, the three first, as above; the item of rations, as above; and, in addition thereto, another item of ten rations per day while at Washington settling his accounts, being at the rate per year of $730; and also an allowance for expenses traveling to and from Washington, and while there, of $1022, being at the rate per year of $1793.

Fifth. And yet during the little portion of the time which lies between the 1st of January, 1822, and the 29th of May, 1822, he was paid in seven different capacities; that is to say, the six last mentioned, and also, at the rate of $1500 per year, for the Piqua, Fort Wayne, and Chicago service, as mentioned above.

These accounts have already been discussed some here; but when we are amongst them, as when we are in the Patent Office, we must peep about a good deal before we can see all the curiosities. I shall not be tedious with them. As to the large item of $1500 per year—amounting in the aggregate to $26,715 for office rent, clerk hire, fuel, etc., I barely wish to remark that, so far as I can discover in the public documents, there is no evidence, by word or inference, either from any disinterested witness or of General Cass himself, that he ever rented or kept a separate office, ever hired or kept a clerk, or even used any extra amount of fuel, etc., in consequence of his Indian services. Indeed, General Cass's entire silence in regard to these items, in his two long letters urging his claims upon the government, is, to my mind, almost conclusive that no such claims had any real existence.

But I have introduced General Cass's accounts here chiefly to show the wonderful physical capacities of the man. They show that he not only did the labor of several men at the same time, but that he often did it at several places, many hundreds of miles apart, at the same time. And at eating, too, his capacities are shown to be quite as wonderful. From October, 1821, to May, 1822, he eat ten rations a day in Michigan, ten rations a day here in Washington, and near five dollars' worth a day on the road between the two places! And then there is an important discovery in his example—the art of being paid for what one eats, instead of having to pay for it. Hereafter if any nice young man should owe a bill which he cannot pay in any other way, he can just board it out. Mr. Speaker, we have all heard of the animal standing in doubt between two stacks of hay and starving to death. The like of that would never happen to General Cass. Place the stacks a thousand miles apart, he would stand stock-still midway between them, and eat them both at once, and the green grass along the line would be apt to suffer some, too, at the same time. By all means make him President, gentlemen. He will feed you bounteously—if—if there is any left after he shall have helped himself.

But, as General Taylor is, par excellence, the hero of the Mexican War, and as you Democrats say we Whigs have always opposed the war, you think it must be very awkward and embarrassing for us to go for General Taylor. The declaration that we have always opposed the war is true or false, according as one may understand the term "oppose the war." If to say "the war was unnecessarily and unconstitutionally commenced by the President" by opposing the war, then the Whigs have very generally opposed it. Whenever they have spoken at all, they have said this; and they have said it on what has appeared good reason to them. The marching an army into the midst of a peaceful Mexican settlement, frightening the inhabitants away, leaving their growing crops and other property to destruction, to you may appear a perfectly amiable, peaceful, unprovoking procedure; but it does not appear so to us. So to call such an act, to us appears no other than a naked, impudent absurdity, and we speak of it accordingly. But if, when the war had begun, and had become the cause of the country, the giving of our money and our blood, in common with yours, was support of the war, then it is not true that we have always opposed the war. With few individual exceptions, you have constantly had our votes here for all the necessary supplies. And, more than this, you have had the services, the blood, and the lives of our political brethren in every trial and on every field. The beardless boy and the mature man, the humble and the distinguished—you have had them. Through suffering and death, by disease and in battle they have endured and fought and fell with you. Clay and Webster each gave a son, never to be returned. From the State of my own residence, besides other worthy but less known Whig names, we sent Marshall, Morrison, Baker, and Hardin; they all fought, and one fell, and in the fall of that one we lost our best Whig man. Nor were the Whigs few in number, or laggard in the day of danger. In that fearful, bloody, breathless struggle at Buena Vista, where each man's hard task was to beat back five foes or die himself, of the five high officers who perished, four were Whigs.

In speaking of this, I mean no odious comparison between the lion-hearted Whigs and the Democrats who fought there. On other occasions, and among the lower officers and privates on that occasion, I doubt not the proportion was different. I wish to do justice to all. I think of all those brave men as Americans, in whose proud fame, as an American, I too have a share. Many of them, Whigs and Democrats are my constituents and personal friends; and I thank them,—more than thank them,—one and all, for the high imperishable honor they have conferred on our common State.

But the distinction between the cause of the President in beginning the war, and the cause of the country after it was begun, is a distinction which you cannot perceive. To you the President and the country seem to be all one. You are interested to see no distinction between them; and I venture to suggest that probably your interest blinds you a little. We see the distinction, as we think, clearly enough; and our friends who have fought in the war have no difficulty in seeing it also. What those who have fallen would say, were they alive and here, of course we can never know; but with those who have returned there is no difficulty. Colonel Haskell and Major Gaines, members here, both fought in the war, and both of them underwent extraordinary perils and hardships; still they, like all other Whigs here, vote, on the record, that the war was unnecessarily and unconstitutionally commenced by the President. And even General Taylor himself, the noblest Roman of them all, has declared that as a citizen, and particularly as a soldier, it is sufficient for him to know that his country is at war with a foreign nation, to do all in his power to bring it to a speedy and honorable termination by the most vigorous and energetic operations, without inquiry about its justice, or anything else connected with it.

Mr. Speaker, let our Democratic friends be comforted with the assurance that we are content with our position, content with our company, and content with our candidate; and that although they, in their generous sympathy, think we ought to be miserable, we really are not, and that they may dismiss the great anxiety they have on our account.

Mr. Speaker, I see I have but three minutes left, and this forces me to throw out one whole branch of my subject. A single word on still another. The Democrats are keen enough to frequently remind us that we have some dissensions in our ranks. Our good friend from Baltimore immediately before me [Mr. McLane] expressed some doubt the other day as to which branch of our party General Taylor would ultimately fall into the hands of. That was a new idea to me. I knew we had dissenters, but I did not know they were trying to get our candidate away from us. I would like to say a word to our dissenters, but I have not the time. Some such we certainly have; have you none, gentlemen Democrats? Is it all union and harmony in your ranks? no bickerings? no divisions? If there be doubt as to which of our divisions will get our candidate, is there no doubt as to which of your candidates will get your party? I have heard some things from New York; and if they are true, one might well say of your party there, as a drunken fellow once said when he heard the reading of an indictment for hog-stealing. The clerk read on till he got to and through the words, "did steal, take, and carry away ten boars, ten sows, ten shoats, and ten pigs," at which he exclaimed, "Well, by golly, that is the most equally divided gang of hogs I ever did hear of!" If there is any other gang of hogs more equally divided than the Democrats of New York are about this time, I have not heard of it.

SPEECH DELIVERED AT WORCESTER, MASS., ON SEPT. 12, 1848.

(From the Boston Advertiser.)

Mr. Kellogg then introduced to the meeting the Hon. Abram Lincoln, Whig member of Congress from Illinois, a representative of free soil.

Mr. Lincoln has a very tall and thin figure, with an intellectual face, showing a searching mind, and a cool judgment. He spoke in a clear and cool and very eloquent manner, for an hour and a half, carrying the audience with him in his able arguments and brilliant illustrations—only interrupted by warm and frequent applause. He began by expressing a real feeling of modesty in addressing an audience "this side of the mountains," a part of the country where, in the opinion of the people of his section, everybody was supposed to be instructed and wise. But he had devoted his attention to the question of the coming Presidential election, and was not unwilling to exchange with all whom he might the ideas to which he had arrived. He then began to show the fallacy of some of the arguments against Gen. Taylor, making his chief theme the fashionable statement of all those who oppose him ("the old Locofocos as well as the new") that he has no principles, and that the Whig party have abandoned their principles by adopting him as their candidate. He maintained that Gen. Taylor occupied a high and unexceptionable Whig ground, and took for his first instance and proof of this the statement in the Allison letter—with regard to the bank, tariff, rivers and harbors, etc.—that the will of the people should produce its own results, without executive influence. The principle that the people should do what—under the Constitution—as they please, is a Whig principle. All that Gen. Taylor is not only to consent to, but appeal to the people to judge and act for themselves. And this was no new doctrine for Whigs. It was the "platform" on which they had fought all their battles, the resistance of executive influence, and the principle of enabling the people to frame the government according to their will. Gen. Taylor consents to be the candidate, and to assist the people to do what they think to be their duty, and think to be best in their national affairs, but because he don't want to tell what we ought to do, he is accused of having no principles. The Whigs here maintained for years that neither the influence, the duress, or the prohibition of the executive should control the legitimately expressed will of the people; and now that, on that very ground, Gen. Taylor says that he should use the power given him by the people to do, to the best of his judgment, the will of the people, he is accused of want of principle, and of inconsistency in position.

Mr. Lincoln proceeded to examine the absurdity of an attempt to make a platform or creed for a national party, to all parts of which all must consent and agree, when it was clearly the intention and the true philosophy of our government, that in Congress all opinions and principles should be represented, and that when the wisdom of all had been compared and united, the will of the majority should be carried out. On this ground he conceived (and the audience seemed to go with him) that Gen. Taylor held correct, sound republican principles.

Mr. Lincoln then passed to the subject of slavery in the States, saying that the people of Illinois agreed entirely with the people of Massachusetts on this subject, except perhaps that they did not keep so constantly thinking about it. All agreed that slavery was an evil, but that we were not responsible for it and cannot affect it in States of this Union where we do not live. But the question of the extension of slavery to new territories of this country is a part of our responsibility and care, and is under our control. In opposition to this Mr. L. believed that the self-named "Free Soil" party was far behind the Whigs. Both parties opposed the extension. As he understood it the new party had no principle except this opposition. If their platform held any other, it was in such a general way that it was like the pair of pantaloons the Yankee pedlar offered for sale, "large enough for any man, small enough for any boy." They therefore had taken a position calculated to break down their single important declared object. They were working for the election of either Gen. Cass or Gen. Taylor. The speaker then went on to show, clearly and eloquently, the danger of extension of slavery, likely to result from the election of Gen. Cass. To unite with those who annexed the new territory to prevent the extension of slavery in that territory seemed to him to be in the highest degree absurd and ridiculous. Suppose these gentlemen succeed in electing Mr. Van Buren, they had no specific means to prevent the extension of slavery to New Mexico and California, and Gen. Taylor, he confidently believed, would not encourage it, and would not prohibit its restriction. But if Gen. Cass was elected, he felt certain that the plans of farther extension of territory would be encouraged, and those of the extension of slavery would meet no check. The "Free Soil" mart in claiming that name indirectly attempts a deception, by implying that Whigs were not Free Soil men. Declaring that they would "do their duty and leave the consequences to God" merely gave an excuse for taking a course they were not able to maintain by a fair and full argument. To make this declaration did not show what their duty was. If it did we should have no use for judgment, we might as well be made without intellect; and when divine or human law does not clearly point out what is our duty, we have no means of finding out what it is but by using our most intelligent judgment of the consequences. If there were divine law or human law for voting for Martin Van Buren, or if a fair examination of the consequences and just reasoning would show that voting for him would bring about the ends they pretended to wish—then he would give up the argument. But since there was no fixed law on the subject, and since the whole probable result of their action would be an assistance in electing Gen. Cass, he must say that they were behind the Whigs in their advocacy of the freedom of the soil.

Mr. Lincoln proceeded to rally the Buffalo convention for forbearing to say anything—after all the previous declarations of those members who were formerly Whigs—on the subject of the Mexican War, because the Van Burens had been known to have supported it. He declared that of all the parties asking the confidence of the country, this new one had less of principle than any other.

He wondered whether it was still the opinion of these Free Soil gentlemen, as declared in the "whereas" at Buffalo, that the Whig and Democratic parties were both entirely dissolved and absorbed into their own body. Had the Vermont election given them any light? They had calculated on making as great an impression in that State as in any part of the Union, and there their attempts had been wholly ineffectual. Their failure was a greater success than they would find in any other part of the Union.

Mr. Lincoln went on to say that he honestly believed that all those who wished to keep up the character of the Union; who did not believe in enlarging our field, but in keeping our fences where they are and cultivating our present possessions, making it a garden, improving the morals and education of the people, devoting the administrations to this purpose; all real Whigs, friends of good honest government—the race was ours. He had opportunities of hearing from almost every part of the Union from reliable sources and had not heard of a county in which we had not received accessions from other parties. If the true Whigs come forward and join these new friends, they need not have a doubt. We had a candidate whose personal character and principles he had already described, whom he could not eulogize if he would. Gen. Taylor had been constantly, perseveringly, quietly standing up, doing his duty and asking no praise or reward for it. He was and must be just the man to whom the interests, principles, and prosperity of the country might be safely intrusted. He had never failed in anything he had undertaken, although many of his duties had been considered almost impossible.

Mr. Lincoln then went into a terse though rapid review of the origin of the Mexican War and the connection of the administration and General Taylor with it, from which he deduced a strong appeal to the Whigs present to do their duty in the support of General Taylor, and closed with the warmest aspirations for and confidence in a deserved success.

At the close of his truly masterly and convincing speech, the audience gave three enthusiastic cheers for Illinois, and three more for the eloquent Whig member from the State.

HIS FATHER'S REQUEST FOR MONEY

TO THOMAS LINCOLN

WASHINGTON, Dec. 24, 1848.

MY DEAR FATHER:—Your letter of the 7th was received night before last. I very cheerfully send you the twenty dollars, which sum you say is necessary to save your land from sale. It is singular that you should have forgotten a judgment against you; and it is more singular that the plaintiff should have let you forget it so long; particularly as I suppose you always had property enough to satisfy a judgment of that amount. Before you pay it, it would be well to be sure you have not paid, or at least, that you cannot prove you have paid it.

Give my love to mother and all the connections. Affectionately your son,

A. LINCOLN.

1849

BILL TO ABOLISH SLAVERY IN THE DISTRICT OF COLUMBIA

Resolved, That the Committee on the District of Columbia be instructed to report a bill in substance as follows:

Sec. 1. Be it enacted by the Senate and House of Representatives of the United States, in Congress assembled, That no person not now within the District of Columbia, nor now owned by any person or persons now resident within it, nor hereafter born within it, shall ever be held in slavery within said District.

Sec. 2. That no person now within said District, or now owned by any person or persons now resident within the same, or hereafter born within it, shall ever be held in slavery without the limits of said District: Provided, That officers of the Government of the United States, being citizens of the slaveholding States, coming into said District on public business, and remaining only so long as may be reasonably necessary for that object, may be attended into and out of said District, and while there, by the necessary servants of themselves and their families, without their right to hold such servants in service being thereby impaired.

Sec. 3. That all children born of slave mothers within said District, on or after the first day of January, in the year of our Lord eighteen hundred and fifty, shall be free; but shall be reasonably supported and educated by the respective owners of their mothers, or by their heirs or representatives, and shall owe reasonable service as apprentices to such owners, heirs, or representatives, until they respectively arrive at the age of __ years, when they shall be entirely free; and the municipal authorities of Washington and Georgetown, within their respective jurisdictional limits, are hereby empowered and required to make all suitable and necessary provision for enforcing obedience to this section, on the part of both masters and apprentices.

Sec. 4. That all persons now within this District, lawfully held as slaves, or now owned by any person or persons now resident within said District, shall remain such at the will of their respective owners, their heirs, and legal representatives: Provided, That such owner, or his legal representative, may at any time receive from the Treasury of the United States the full value of his or her slave, of the class in this section mentioned, upon which such slave shall be forthwith and forever free: And provided further, That the President of the United States, the Secretary of State, and the Secretary of the Treasury shall be a board for determining the value of such slaves as their owners may desire to emancipate under this section, and whose duty it shall be to hold a session for the purpose on the first Monday of each calendar month, to receive all applications, and, on satisfactory evidence in each case that the person presented for valuation is a slave, and of the class in this section mentioned, and is owned by the applicant, shall value such slave at his or her full cash value, and give to the applicant an order on the Treasury for the amount, and also to such slave a certificate of freedom.

Sec. 5. That the municipal authorities of Washington and Georgetown, within their respective jurisdictional limits, are hereby empowered and required to provide active and efficient means to arrest and deliver up to their owners all fugitive slaves escaping into said District.

Sec. 6. That the election officers within said District of Columbia are hereby empowered and required to open polls, at all the usual places of holding elections, on the first Monday of April next, and receive the vote of every free white male citizen above the age of twenty-one years, having resided within said District for the period of one year or more next preceding the time of such voting for or against this act, to proceed in taking said votes, in all respects not herein specified, as at elections under the municipal laws, and with as little delay as possible to transmit correct statements of the votes so cast to the President of the United States; and it shall be the duty of the President to canvass said votes immediately, and if a majority of them be found to be for this act, to forthwith issue his proclamation giving notice of the fact; and this act shall only be in full force and effect on and after the day of such proclamation.

Sec. 7. That involuntary servitude for the punishment of crime, whereof the party shall have been duly convicted, shall in no wise be prohibited by this act.

Sec. 8. That for all the purposes of this act, the jurisdictional limits of Washington are extended to all parts of the District of Columbia not now included within the present limits of Georgetown.

BILL GRANTING LANDS TO THE STATES TO MAKE RAILWAYS AND CANALS

REMARKS IN THE HOUSE OF REPRESENTATIVES, FEBRUARY 13, 1849.

Mr. Lincoln said he had not risen for the purpose of making a speech, but only for the purpose of meeting some of the objections to the bill. If he understood those objections, the first was that if the bill were to become a law, it would be used to lock large portions of the public lands from sale, without at last effecting the ostensible object of the bill—the construction of railroads in the new States; and secondly, that Congress would be forced to the abandonment of large portions of the public lands to the States for which they might be reserved, without their paying for them. This he understood to be the substance of the objections of the gentleman from Ohio to the passage of the bill.

If he could get the attention of the House for a few minutes, he would ask gentlemen to tell us what motive could induce any State Legislature, or individual, or company of individuals, of the new States, to expend money in surveying roads which they might know they could not make.

(A voice: They are not required to make the road.)

Mr. Lincoln continued: That was not the case he was making. What motive would tempt any set of men to go into an extensive survey of a railroad which they did not intend to make? What good would it do? Did men act without motive? Did business men commonly go into an expenditure of money which could be of no account to them? He generally found that men who have money were disposed to hold on to it, unless they could see something to be made by its investment. He could not see what motive of advantage to the new States could be subserved by merely keeping the public lands out of market, and preventing their settlement. As far as he could see, the new States were wholly without any motive to do such a thing. This, then, he took to be a good answer to the first objection.

In relation to the fact assumed, that after a while, the new States having got hold of the public lands to a certain extent, they would turn round and compel Congress to relinquish all claim to them, he had a word to say, by way of recurring to the history of the past. When was the time to come (he asked) when the States in which the public lands were situated would compose a majority of the representation in Congress, or anything like it? A majority of Representatives would very soon reside west of the mountains, he admitted; but would they all come from States in which the public lands were situated? They certainly would not; for, as these Western States grew strong in Congress, the public lands passed away from them, and they got on the other side of the question; and the gentleman from Ohio [Mr. Vinton] was an example attesting that fact.

Mr. Vinton interrupted here to say that he had stood on this question just where he was now, for five and twenty years.

Mr. Lincoln was not making an argument for the purpose of convicting the gentleman of any impropriety at all. He was speaking of a fact in history, of which his State was an example. He was referring to a plain principle in the nature of things. The State of Ohio had now grown to be a giant. She had a large delegation on that floor; but was she now in favor of granting lands to the new States, as she used to be? The New England States, New York, and the Old Thirteen were all rather quiet upon the subject; and it was seen just now that a member from one of the new States was the first man to rise up in opposition. And such would be with the history of this question for the future. There never would come a time when the people residing in the States embracing the public lands would have the entire control of this subject; and so it was a matter of certainty that Congress would never do more in this respect than what would be dictated by a just liberality. The apprehension, therefore, that the public lands were in danger of being wrested from the General Government by the strength of the delegation in Congress from the new States, was utterly futile. There never could be such a thing. If we take these lands (said he) it will not be without your consent. We can never outnumber you. The result is that all fear of the new States turning against the right of Congress to the public domain must be effectually quelled, as those who are opposed to that interest must always hold a vast majority here, and they will never surrender the whole or any part of the public lands unless they themselves choose to do so. That was all he desired to say.

ON FEDERAL POLITICAL APPOINTMENTS

TO THE SECRETARY OF THE TREASURY.

WASHINGTON, March 9, 1849.

HON. SECRETARY OF THE TREASURY.

DEAR SIR: Colonel R. D. Baker and myself are the only Whig members of Congress from Illinois of the Thirtieth, and he of the Thirty-first. We have reason to think the Whigs of that State hold us responsible, to some extent, for the appointments which may be made of our citizens. We do not know you personally, and our efforts to you have so far been unavailing. I therefore hope I am not obtrusive in saying in this way, for him and myself, that when a citizen of Illinois is to be appointed in your department, to an office either in or out of the State, we most respectfully ask to be heard.

Your obedient servant,

A. LINCOLN.

MORE POLITICAL PATRONAGE REQUESTS

TO THE SECRETARY OF STATE.

WASHINGTON, March 10, 1849.

HON. SECRETARY OF STATE.

SIR:—There are several applicants for the office of United States Marshal for the District of Illinois. Among the most prominent of them are Benjamin Bond, Esq., of Carlyle, and Thomas, Esq., of Galena. Mr. Bond I know to be personally every way worthy of the office; and he is very numerously and most respectably recommended. His papers I send to you; and I solicit for his claims a full and fair consideration.

Having said this much, I add that in my individual judgment the appointment of Mr. Thomas would be the better.

Your obedient servant,

A. LINCOLN.

(Indorsed on Mr. Bond's papers.)

In this and the accompanying envelope are the recommendations of about two hundred good citizens of all parts of Illinois, that Benjamin Bond be appointed marshal for that district. They include the names of nearly all our Whigs who now are, or have ever been, members of the State Legislature, besides forty-six of the Democratic members of the present Legislature, and many other good citizens. I add that from personal knowledge I consider Mr. Bond every way worthy of the office, and qualified to fill it. Holding the individual opinion that the appointment of a different gentleman would be better, I ask especial attention and consideration for his claims, and for the opinions expressed in his favor by those over whom I can claim no superiority.

A. LINCOLN.

TO THE SECRETARY OF THE INTERIOR

SPRINGFIELD, ILLINOIS, April 7, 1849

HON. SECRETARY OF THE HOME DEPARTMENT.

DEAR SIR:—I recommend that Walter Davis be appointed receiver of the land-office at this place, whenever there shall be a vacancy. I cannot say that Mr. Herndon, the present incumbent, has failed in the proper discharge of any of the duties of the office. He is a very warm partisan, and openly and actively opposed to the election of General Taylor. I also understand that since General Taylor's election he has received a reappointment from Mr. Polk, his old commission not having expired. Whether this is true the records of the department will show. I may add that the Whigs here almost universally desire his removal.

I give no opinion of my own, but state the facts, and express the hope that the department will act in this as in all other cases on some proper general rule.

Your obedient servant,

A. LINCOLN.

P. S.—The land district to which this office belongs is very nearly if not entirely within my district; so that Colonel Baker, the other Whig representative, claims no voice in the appointment. A. L.

TO THE SECRETARY OF THE INTERIOR.

SPRINGFIELD, ILLINOIS, April 7, 1849.

HON. SECRETARY OF THE HOME DEPARTMENT.

DEAR SIR:—I recommend that Turner R. King, now of Pekin, Illinois, be appointed register of the land-office at this place whenever there shall be a vacancy.

I do not know that Mr. Barret, the present incumbent, has failed in the proper discharge of any of his duties in the office. He is a decided partisan, and openly and actively opposed the election of General Taylor. I understand, too, that since the election of General Taylor, Mr. Barret has received a reappointment from Mr. Polk, his old commission not having expired. Whether this be true, the records of the department will show.

Whether he should be removed I give no opinion, but merely express the wish that the department may act upon some proper general rule, and that Mr. Barret's case may not be made an exception to it.

Your obedient servant,

A. LINCOLN.

P. S.-The land district to which this office belongs is very nearly if not entirely within my district; so that Colonel Baker, the other Whig representative, claims no voice in the appointment. A. L.

TO THE POSTMASTER-GENERAL.

SPRINGFIELD, ILLINOIS, April 7,1849.

HON. POSTMASTER-GENERAL.

DEAR Sir:—I recommend that Abner Y. Ellis be appointed postmaster at this place, whenever there shall be a vacancy. J. R. Diller, the present incumbent, I cannot say has failed in the proper discharge of any of the duties of the office. He, however, has been an active partisan in opposition to us.

Located at the seat of government of the State, he has been, for part if not the whole of the time he has held the office, a member of the Democratic State Central Committee, signing his name to their addresses and manifestoes; and has been, as I understand, reappointed by Mr. Polk since General Taylor's election. These are the facts of the case as I understand them, and I give no opinion of mine as to whether he should or should not be removed. My wish is that the department may adopt some proper general rule for such cases, and that Mr. Diller may not be made an exception to it, one way or the other.

Your obedient servant,

A. LINCOLN.

P. S.—This office, with its delivery, is entirely within my district; so that Colonel Baker, the other Whig representative, claims no voice in the appointment.L.

TO THE SECRETARY OF THE INTERIOR.

SPRINGFIELD, ILLINOIS, April 7, 1849.

HON. SECRETARY OF THE HOME DEPARTMENT.

DEAR SIR:—I recommend that William Butler be appointed pension agent for the Illinois agency, when the place shall be vacant. Mr. Hurst, the present incumbent, I believe has performed the duties very well. He is a decided partisan, and I believe expects to be removed. Whether he shall, I submit to the department. This office is not confined to my district, but pertains to the whole State; so that Colonel Baker has an equal right with myself to be heard concerning it. However, the office is located here; and I think it is not probable that any one would desire to remove from a distance to take it.

Your obedient servant,

A. LINCOLN.

TO THOMPSON.

SPRINGFIELD, April 25, 1849.

DEAR THOMPSON: A tirade is still kept up against me here for recommending T. R. King. This morning it is openly avowed that my supposed influence at Washington shall be broken down generally, and King's prospects defeated in particular. Now, what I have done in this matter I have done at the request of you and some other friends in Tazewell; and I therefore ask you to either admit it is wrong or come forward and sustain me. If the truth will permit, I propose that you sustain me in the following manner: copy the inclosed scrap in your own handwriting and get everybody (not three or four, but three or four hundred) to sign it, and then send it to me. Also, have six, eight or ten of our best known Whig friends there write to me individual letters, stating the truth in this matter as they understand it. Don't neglect or delay in the matter. I understand information of an indictment having been found against him about three years ago, for gaming or keeping a gaming house, has been sent to the department. I shall try to take care of it at the department till your action can be had and forwarded on.

Yours as ever,

A. LINCOLN.

TO THE SECRETARY OF THE INTERIOR.

SPRINGFIELD ILLINOIS. May 10, 1849.

HON. SECRETARY OF THE INTERIOR.

DEAR SIR:—I regret troubling you so often in relation to the land-offices here, but I hope you will perceive the necessity of it, and excuse me. On the 7th of April I wrote you recommending Turner R. King for register, and Walter Davis for receiver. Subsequently I wrote you that, for a private reason, I had concluded to transpose them. That private reason was the request of an old personal friend who himself desired to be receiver, but whom I felt it my duty to refuse a recommendation. He said if I would transpose King and Davis he would be satisfied. I thought it a whim, but, anxious to oblige him, I consented. Immediately he commenced an assault upon King's character, intending, as I suppose, to defeat his appointment, and thereby secure another chance for himself. This double offence of bad faith to me and slander upon a good man is so totally outrageous that I now ask to have King and Davis placed as I originally recommended,—that is, King for register and Davis for receiver.

An effort is being made now to have Mr. Barret, the present register, retained. I have already said he has done the duties of the office well, and I now add he is a gentleman in the true sense. Still, he submits to be the instrument of his party to injure us. His high character enables him to do it more effectually. Last year he presided at the convention which nominated the Democratic candidate for Congress in this district, and afterward ran for the State Senate himself, not desiring the seat, but avowedly to aid and strengthen his party. He made speech after speech with a degree of fierceness and coarseness against General Taylor not quite consistent with his habitually gentlemanly deportment. At least one (and I think more) of those who are now trying to have him retained was himself an applicant for this very office, and, failing to get my recommendation, now takes this turn.

In writing you a third time in relation to these offices, I stated that I supposed charges had been forwarded to you against King, and that I would inquire into the truth of them. I now send you herewith what I suppose will be an ample defense against any such charges. I ask attention to all the papers, but particularly to the letters of Mr. David Mack, and the paper with the long list of names. There is no mistake about King's being a good man. After the unjust assault upon him, and considering the just claims of Tazewell County, as indicated in the letters I inclose you, it would in my opinion be injustice, and withal a blunder, not to appoint him, at least as soon as any one is appointed to either of the offices here.

Your obedient servant,

A. LINCOLN.

TO J. GILLESPIE.

SPRINGFIELD, ILL., May 19, 1849.

DEAR GILLESPIE:

Butterfield will be commissioner of the Gen'l Land Office, unless prevented by strong and speedy efforts. Ewing is for him, and he is only not appointed yet because Old Zach. hangs fire.

I have reliable information of this. Now, if you agree with me that this appointment would dissatisfy rather than gratify the Whigs of this State, that it would slacken their energies in future contests, that his appointment in '41 is an old sore with them which they will not patiently have reopened,—in a word that his appointment now would be a fatal blunder to the administration and our political men here in Illinois, write Crittenden to that effect. He can control the matter. Were you to write Ewing I fear the President would never hear of your letter. This may be mere suspicion. You might write directly to Old Zach. You will be the best judge of the propriety of that. Not a moment's time is to be lost.

Let this be confidential except with Mr. Edwards and a few others whom you know I would trust just as I do you.

Yours as ever,

A. LINCOLN.

REQUEST FOR GENERAL LAND-OFFICE APPPOINTMENT

TO E. EMBREE.

[Confidential]

SPRINGFIELD, ILLINOIS, May 25, 1849.

HON. E. EMBREE

DEAR SIR:—I am about to ask a favor of you, one which I hope will not cost you much. I understand the General Land-Office is about to be given to Illinois, and that Mr. Ewing desires Justin Butterfield, of Chicago, to be the man. I give you my word, the appointment of Mr. Butterfield will be an egregious political blunder. It will give offence to the whole Whig party here, and be worse than a dead loss to the administration of so much of its patronage. Now, if you can conscientiously do so, I wish you to write General Taylor at once, saying that either I or the man I recommend should in your opinion be appointed to that office, if any one from Illinois shall be. I restrict my request to Illinois because you may have a man from your own State, and I do not ask to interfere with that.

Your friend as ever,

A. LINCOLN.

REQUEST FOR A PATENT

IMPROVED METHOD OF LIFTING VESSELS OVER SHOALS.

Application for Patent:

What I claim as my invention, and desire to secure by letters patent, is the combination of expansible buoyant chambers placed at the sides of a vessel with the main shaft or shafts by means of the sliding spars, which pass down through the buoyant chambers and are made fast to their bottoms and the series of ropes and pulleys or their equivalents in such a manner that by turning the main shaft or shafts in one direction the buoyant chambers will be forced downward into the water, and at the same time expanded and filled with air for buoying up the vessel by the displacement of water, and by turning the shafts in an opposite direction the buoyant chambers will be contracted into a small space and secured against injury.

A. LINCOLN.

TO THE SECRETARY OF INTERIOR.

SPRINGFIELD, ILL., June 3, 1849

HON. SECRETARY OF INTERIOR.

DEAR SIR:—Vandalia, the receiver's office at which place is the subject of the within, is not in my district; and I have been much perplexed to express any preference between Dr. Stapp and Mr. Remann. If any one man is better qualified for such an office than all others, Dr. Stapp is that man; still, I believe a large majority of the Whigs of the district prefer Mr. Remann, who also is a good man. Perhaps the papers on file will enable you to judge better than I can. The writers of the within are good men, residing within the land district.

Your obt. servant,

A. LINCOLN.

TO W. H. HERNDON.

SPRINGFIELD, June 5, 1849.

DEAR WILLIAM:—Your two letters were received last night. I have a great many letters to write, and so cannot write very long ones. There must be some mistake about Walter Davis saying I promised him the post-office. I did not so promise him. I did tell him that if the distribution of the offices should fall into my hands, he should have something; and if I shall be convinced he has said any more than this, I shall be disappointed. I said this much to him because, as I understand, he is of good character, is one of the young men, is of the mechanics, and always faithful and never troublesome; a Whig, and is poor, with the support of a widow mother thrown almost exclusively on him by the death of his brother. If these are wrong reasons, then I have been wrong; but I have certainly not been selfish in it, because in my greatest need of friends he was against me, and for Baker.

Yours as ever,

A. LINCOLN.

P. S. Let the above be confidential.

TO J. GILLESPIE.

DEAR GILLESPIE:

Mr. Edwards is unquestionably offended with me in connection with the matter of the General Land-Office. He wrote a letter against me which was filed at the department.

The better part of one's life consists of his friendships; and, of them, mine with Mr. Edwards was one of the most cherished. I have not been false to it. At a word I could have had the office any time before the department was committed to Mr. Butterfield, at least Mr. Ewing and the President say as much. That word I forbore to speak, partly for other reasons, but chiefly for Mr. Edwards' sake, losing the office (that he might gain it) I was always for; but to lose his friendship, by the effort for him, would oppress me very much, were I not sustained by the utmost consciousness of rectitude. I first determined to be an applicant, unconditionally, on the 2nd of June; and I did so then upon being informed by a telegraphic despatch that the question was narrowed down to Mr. B and myself, and that the Cabinet had postponed the appointment three weeks, for my benefit. Not doubting that Mr. Edwards was wholly out of the question I, nevertheless, would not then have become an applicant had I supposed he would thereby be brought to suspect me of treachery to him. Two or three days afterwards a conversation with Levi Davis convinced me Mr. Edwards was dissatisfied; but I was then too far in to get out. His own letter, written on the 25th of April, after I had fully informed him of all that had passed, up to within a few days of that time, gave assurance I had that entire confidence from him which I felt my uniform and strong friendship for him entitled me to. Among other things it says, "Whatever course your judgment may dictate as proper to be pursued, shall never be excepted to by me." I also had had a letter from Washington, saying Chambers, of the Republic, had brought a rumor then, that Mr. E had declined in my favor, which rumor I judged came from Mr. E himself, as I had not then breathed of his letter to any living creature. In saying I had never, before the 2nd of June, determined to be an applicant, unconditionally, I mean to admit that, before then, I had said substantially I would take the office rather than it should be lost to the State, or given to one in the State whom the Whigs did not want; but I aver that in every instance in which I spoke of myself, I intended to keep, and now believe I did keep, Mr. E above myself. Mr. Edwards' first suspicion was that I had allowed Baker to overreach me, as his friend, in behalf of Don Morrison. I knew this was a mistake; and the result has proved it. I understand his view now is, that if I had gone to open war with Baker I could have ridden him down, and had the thing all my own way. I believe no such thing. With Baker and some strong man from the Military tract & elsewhere for Morrison, and we and some strong man from the Wabash & elsewhere for Mr. E, it was not possible for either to succeed. I believed this in March, and I know it now. The only thing which gave either any chance was the very thing Baker & I proposed,—an adjustment with themselves.

You may wish to know how Butterfield finally beat me. I can not tell you particulars now, but will when I see you. In the meantime let it be understood I am not greatly dissatisfied,—I wish the offer had been so bestowed as to encourage our friends in future contests, and I regret exceedingly Mr. Edwards' feelings towards me. These two things away, I should have no regrets,—at least I think I would not.

Write me soon.

Your friend, as ever,

A. LINCOLN.

RESOLUTIONS OF SYMPATHY WITH THE CAUSE OF HUNGARIAN FREEDOM,

SEPTEMBER [1??], 1849.

At a meeting to express sympathy with the cause of Hungarian freedom, Dr. Todd, Thos. Lewis, Hon. A. Lincoln, and Wm. Carpenter were appointed a committee to present appropriate resolutions, which reported through Hon. A. Lincoln the following:

Resolved, That, in their present glorious struggle for liberty, the Hungarians command our highest admiration and have our warmest sympathy.

Resolved, That they have our most ardent prayers for their speedy triumph and final success.

Resolved, That the Government of the United States should acknowledge the independence of Hungary as a nation of freemen at the very earliest moment consistent with our amicable relations with the government against which they are contending.

Resolved, That, in the opinion of this meeting, the immediate acknowledgment of the independence of Hungary by our government is due from American freemen to their struggling brethren, to the general cause of republican liberty, and not violative of the just rights of any nation or people.

TO Dr. WILLIAM FITHIAN.

SPRINGFIELD, Sept. 14, 1849.

Dr. WILLIAM FITHIAN, Danville, Ill.

DEAR DOCTOR:—Your letter of the 9th was received a day or two ago. The notes and mortgages you enclosed me were duly received. I also got the original Blanchard mortgage from Antrim Campbell, with whom Blanchard had left it for you. I got a decree of foreclosure on the whole; but, owing to there being no redemption on the sale to be under the Blanchard mortgage, the court allowed Mobley till the first of March to pay the money, before advertising for sale. Stuart was empowered by Mobley to appear for him, and I had to take such decree as he would consent to, or none at all. I cast the matter about in my mind and concluded that as I could not get a decree we would put the accrued interest at interest, and thereby more than match the fact of throwing the Blanchard debt back from twelve to six per cent., it was better to do it. This is the present state of the case.

I can well enough understand and appreciate your suggestions about the Land-Office at Danville; but in my present condition, I can do nothing.

Yours, as ever,

A. LINCOLN.

SPRINGFIELD, Dec. 15, 1849.

——— ESQ.

DEAR SIR:—On my return from Kentucky I found your letter of the 7th of November, and have delayed answering it till now for the reason I now briefly state. From the beginning of our acquaintance I had felt the greatest kindness for you and had supposed it was reciprocated on your part. Last summer, under circumstances which I mentioned to you, I was painfully constrained to withhold a recommendation which you desired, and shortly afterwards I learned, in such a way as to believe it, that you were indulging in open abuse of me. Of course my feelings were wounded. On receiving your last letter the question occurred whether you were attempting to use me at the same time you would injure me, or whether you might not have been misrepresented to me. If the former, I ought not to answer you; if the latter, I ought, and so I have remained in suspense. I now enclose you the letter, which you may use if you see fit.

Yours, etc.,

A. LINCOLN.

1850

RESOLUTIONS ON THE DEATH OF JUDGE NATHANIEL POPE.

Circuit and District Court of the U. S. in and for the State and District of Illinois. Monday, June 3, 1850.

On the opening of the Court this morning, the Hon. A. Lincoln, a member of the Bar of this Court, suggested the death of the Hon. Nathaniel Pope, late a judge of this Court, since the adjournment of the last term; whereupon, in token of respect for the memory of the deceased, it is ordered that the Court do now adjourn until to-morrow morning at ten o'clock.

The Hon. Stephen T. Logan, the Hon. Norman H. Purple, the Hon. David L. Gregg, the Hon. A. Lincoln, and George W. Meeker, Esq., were appointed a Committee to prepare resolutions.

Whereupon, the Hon. Stephen T. Logan, in behalf of the Committee, presented the following preamble and resolutions:

Whereas The Hon. Nathaniel Pope, District Judge of the United States Court for the District of Illinois, having departed this life during the last vacation of said Court, and the members of the Bar of said Court, entertaining the highest veneration for his memory, a profound respect for his ability, great experience, and learning as a judge, and cherishing for his many virtues, public and private, his earnest simplicity of character and unostentatious deportment, both in his public and private relations, the most lively and affectionate recollections, have

Resolved, That, as a manifestation of their deep sense of the loss which has been sustained in his death, they will wear the usual badge of mourning during the residue of the term.

Resolved, That the Chairman communicate to the family of the deceased a copy of these proceedings, with an assurance of our sincere condolence on account of their heavy bereavement.

Resolved, That the Hon. A. Williams, District Attorney of this Court, be requested in behalf of the meeting to present these proceedings to the Circuit Court, and respectfully to ask that they may be entered on the records.

E. N. POWELL, Sec'y. SAMUEL H. TREAT, Ch'n.

NOTES FOR LAW LECTURE

(fragments)

JULY 1, 1850

DISCOURAGE LITIGATION. Persuade your neighbors to compromise whenever you can. Point out to them how the nominal winner is often a real loser—in fees, expenses, and waste of time. As a peace-maker the lawyer has a superior opportunity of being a good man. There will still be business enough.

Never stir up litigation. A worse man can scarcely be found than one who does this. Who can be more nearly a fiend than he who habitually over-hauls the register of deeds in search of defects in titles, whereon to stir up strife, and put money in his pocket? A moral tone ought to be infused into the profession which should drive such men out of it.

The matter of fees is important, far beyond the mere question of bread and butter involved. Properly attended to, fuller justice is done to both lawyer and client. An exorbitant fee should never be claimed. As a general rule never take your whole fee in advance, nor any more than a small retainer. When fully paid beforehand, you are more than a common mortal if you can feel the same interest in the case as if something was still in prospect for you, as well as for your client. And when you lack interest in the case the job will very likely lack skill and diligence in the performance. Settle the amount of fee and take a note in advance. Then you will feel that you are working for something, and you are sure to do your work faithfully and well. Never sell a fee note—at least not before the consideration service is performed. It leads to negligence and dishonesty—negligence by losing interest in the case, and dishonesty in refusing to refund when you have allowed the consideration to fail.

This idea of a refund or reduction of charges from the lawyer in a failed case is a new one to me—but not a bad one.

1851

LETTERS TO FAMILY MEMBERS

TO JOHN D. JOHNSTON.

January 2, 1851

DEAR JOHNSTON:—Your request for eighty dollars I do not think it best to comply with now. At the various times when I have helped you a little you have said to me, "We can get along very well now"; but in a very short time I find you in the same difficulty again. Now, this can only happen by some defect in your conduct. What that defect is, I think I know. You are not lazy, and still you are an idler. I doubt whether, since I saw you, you have done a good whole day's work in any one day. You do not very much dislike to work, and still you do not work much merely because it does not seem to you that you could get much for it. This habit of uselessly wasting time is the whole difficulty; it is vastly important to you, and still more so to your children, that you should break the habit. It is more important to them, because they have longer to live, and can keep out of an idle habit before they are in it, easier than they can get out after they are in.

You are now in need of some money; and what I propose is, that you shall go to work, "tooth and nail," for somebody who will give you money for it. Let father and your boys take charge of your things at home, prepare for a crop, and make the crop, and you go to work for the best money wages, or in discharge of any debt you owe, that you can get; and, to secure you a fair reward for your labor, I now promise you, that for every dollar you will, between this and the first of May, get for your own labor, either in money or as your own indebtedness, I will then give you one other dollar. By this, if you hire yourself at ten dollars a month, from me you will get ten more, making twenty dollars a month for your work. In this I do not mean you shall go off to St. Louis, or the lead mines, or the gold mines in California, but I mean for you to go at it for the best wages you can get close to home in Coles County. Now, if you will do this, you will be soon out of debt, and, what is better, you will have a habit that will keep you from getting in debt again. But, if I should now clear you out of debt, next year you would be just as deep in as ever. You say you would almost give your place in heaven for seventy or eighty dollars. Then you value your place in heaven very cheap, for I am sure you can, with the offer I make, get the seventy or eighty dollars for four or five months' work. You say if I will furnish you the money you will deed me the land, and, if you don't pay the money back, you will deliver possession. Nonsense! If you can't now live with the land, how will you then live without it? You have always been kind to me, and I do not mean to be unkind to you. On the contrary, if you will but follow my advice, you will find it worth more than eighty times eighty dollars to you.

Affectionately your brother,

A. LINCOLN.

TO C. HOYT.

SPRINGFIELD, Jan. 11, 1851.

C. HOYT, ESQ.

MY DEAR SIR:—Our case is decided against us. The decision was announced this morning. Very sorry, but there is no help. The history of the case since it came here is this. On Friday morning last, Mr. Joy filed his papers, and entered his motion for a mandamus, and urged me to take up the motion as soon as possible. I already had the points and authority sent me by you and by Mr. Goodrich, but had not studied them. I began preparing as fast as possible.

The evening of the same day I was again urged to take up the case. I refused on the ground that I was not ready, and on which plea I also got off over Saturday. But on Monday (the 14th) I had to go into it. We occupied the whole day, I using the large part. I made every point and used every authority sent me by yourself and by Mr. Goodrich; and in addition all the points I could think of and all the authorities I could find myself. When I closed the argument on my part, a large package was handed me, which proved to be the plat you sent me.

The court received it of me, but it was not different from the plat already on the record. I do not think I could ever have argued the case better than I did. I did nothing else, but prepare to argue and argue this case, from Friday morning till Monday evening. Very sorry for the result; but I do not think it could have been prevented.

Your friend, as ever,

A. LINCOLN.

TO JOHN D. JOHNSTON.

SPRINGFIELD, January 12, 1851

DEAR BROTHER:—On the day before yesterday I received a letter from Harriet, written at Greenup. She says she has just returned from your house, and that father is very low and will hardly recover. She also says you have written me two letters, and that, although you do not expect me to come now, you wonder that I do not write.

I received both your letters, and although I have not answered them it is not because I have forgotten them, or been uninterested about them, but because it appeared to me that I could write nothing which would do any good. You already know I desire that neither father nor mother shall be in want of any comfort, either in health or sickness, while they live; and I feel sure you have not failed to use my name, if necessary, to procure a doctor, or anything else for father in his present sickness. My business is such that I could hardly leave home now, if it was not as it is, that my own wife is sick abed. (It is a case of baby-sickness, and I suppose is not dangerous.) I sincerely hope father may recover his health, but at all events, tell him to remember to call upon and confide in our great and good and merciful Maker, who will not turn away from him in any extremity. He notes the fall of a sparrow, and numbers the hairs of our heads, and He will not forget the dying man who puts his trust in Him. Say to him that if we could meet now it is doubtful whether it would not be more painful than pleasant, but that if it be his lot to go now, he will soon have a joyous meeting with many loved ones gone before, and where the rest of us, through the help of God, hope ere long to join them.

Write to me again when you receive this.

Affectionately,

A. LINCOLN.

PETITION ON BEHALF OF ONE JOSHUA GIPSON

TO THE JUDGE OF THE SANGAMON COUNTY COURT,

MAY 13, 1851. TO THE HONORABLE, THE JUDGE OF THE COUNTY COURT IN AND FOR THE COUNTY OF SANGAMON AND STATE OF ILLINOIS:

Your Petitioner, Joshua Gipson, respectfully represents that on or about the 21st day of December, 1850, a judgment was rendered against your Petitioner for costs, by J. C. Spugg, one of the Justices of the Peace in and for said County of Sangamon, in a suit wherein your Petitioner was plaintiff and James L. and C. B. Gerard were defendants; that said judgment was not the result of negligence on the part of your Petitioner; that said judgment, in his opinion, is unjust and erroneous in this, that the defendants were at that time and are indebted to this Petitioner in the full amount of the principal and interest of the note sued on, the principal being, as affiant remembers and believes, thirty-one dollars and eighty two cents; and that, as affiant is informed and believes, the defendants succeeded in the trial of said cause by proving old claims against your petitioner, in set-off against said note, which claims had been settled, adjusted and paid before said note was executed. Your Petitioner further states that the reasons of his not being present at said trial, as he was not, and of its not being in his power to take an appeal in the ordinary way, as it was not, were that your Petitioner then resided in Edgar County about one hundred and twenty miles from where defendants resided; that a very short time before the suit was commenced your Petitioner was in Sangamon County for the purpose of collecting debts due him, and with the rest, the note in question, which note had then been given more than a year, that your Petitioner then saw the defendant J. L. Gerard who is the principal in said note, and solicited payment of the same; that said defendant then made no pretense that he did not owe the same, but on the contrary expressly promised that he would come into Springfield, in a very few days and either pay the money, or give a new note, payable by the then next Christmas; that your Petitioner accordingly left said note with said J. C. Spugg, with directions to give defendant full time to pay the money or give the new note as above, and if he did neither to sue; and then affiant came home to Edgar County, not having the slightest suspicion that if suit should be brought, the defendants would make any defense whatever; and your Petitioner never did in any way learn that said suit had been commenced until more than twenty days after it had been decided against him. He therefore prays for a writ of Certiorari.

HIS

JOSHUA x GIPSON

MARK

TO J. D. JOHNSTON.

SPRINGFIELD, Aug. 31, 1851

DEAR BROTHER: Inclosed is the deed for the land. We are all well, and have nothing in the way of news. We have had no Cholera here for about two weeks.

Give my love to all, and especially to Mother.

Yours as ever,

A. LINCOLN.

TO J. D. JOHNSTON.

SHELBYVILLE, Nov. 4, 1851

DEAR BROTHER:

When I came into Charleston day before yesterday I learned that you are anxious to sell the land where you live, and move to Missouri. I have been thinking of this ever since, and cannot but think such a notion is utterly foolish. What can you do in Missouri better than here? Is the land richer? Can you there, any more than here, raise corn and wheat and oats without work? Will anybody there, any more than here, do your work for you? If you intend to go to work, there is no better place than right where you are; if you do not intend to go to work you cannot get along anywhere. Squirming and crawling about from place to place can do no good. You have raised no crop this year, and what you really want is to sell the land, get the money and spend it. Part with the land you have, and, my life upon it, you will never after own a spot big enough to bury you in. Half you will get for the land you spend in moving to Missouri, and the other half you will eat and drink and wear out, and no foot of land will be bought. Now I feel it is my duty to have no hand in such a piece of foolery. I feel that it is so even on your own account, and particularly on Mother's account. The eastern forty acres I intend to keep for Mother while she lives; if you will not cultivate it, it will rent for enough to support her; at least it will rent for something. Her dower in the other two forties she can let you have, and no thanks to me.

Now do not misunderstand this letter. I do not write it in any unkindness. I write it in order, if possible, to get you to face the truth, which truth is, you are destitute because you have idled away all your time. Your thousand pretenses for not getting along better are all nonsense; they deceive nobody but yourself. Go to work is the only cure for your case.

A word for Mother: Chapman tells me he wants you to go and live with him. If I were you I would try it awhile. If you get tired of it (as I think you will not) you can return to your own home. Chapman feels very kindly to you; and I have no doubt he will make your situation very pleasant.

Sincerely yours,

A. LINCOLN.

Nov. 4, 1851

DEAR MOTHER:

Chapman tells me he wants you to go and live with him. If I were you I would try it awhile. If you get tired of it (as I think you will not) you can return to your own home. Chapman feels very kindly to you; and I have no doubt he will make your situation very pleasant.

Sincerely your son,

A. LINCOLN.

TO JOHN D. JOHNSTON.

SHELBYVILLE, November 9, 1851

DEAR BROTHER:—When I wrote you before, I had not received your letter. I still think as I did, but if the land can be sold so that I get three hundred dollars to put to interest for Mother, I will not object, if she does not. But before I will make a deed, the money must be had, or secured beyond all doubt, at ten per cent.

As to Abram, I do not want him, on my own account; but I understand he wants to live with me, so that he can go to school and get a fair start in the world, which I very much wish him to have. When I reach home, if I can make it convenient to take, I will take him, provided there is no mistake between us as to the object and terms of my taking him. In haste, as ever,

A. LINCOLN.

TO JOHN D. JOHNSTON.

SPRINGFIELD, November 25, 1851.

DEAR BROTHER:—Your letter of the 22d is just received. Your proposal about selling the east forty acres of land is all that I want or could claim for myself; but I am not satisfied with it on Mother's account—I want her to have her living, and I feel that it is my duty, to some extent, to see that she is not wronged. She had a right of dower (that is, the use of one-third for life) in the other two forties; but, it seems, she has already let you take that, hook and line. She now has the use of the whole of the east forty, as long as she lives; and if it be sold, of course she is entitled to the interest on all the money it brings, as long as she lives; but you propose to sell it for three hundred dollars, take one hundred away with you, and leave her two hundred at 8 per cent., making her the enormous sum of 16 dollars a year. Now, if you are satisfied with treating her in that way, I am not. It is true that you are to have that forty for two hundred dollars, at Mother's death, but you are not to have it before. I am confident that land can be made to produce for Mother at least $30 a year, and I can not, to oblige any living person, consent that she shall be put on an allowance of sixteen dollars a year.

Yours, etc.,

A. LINCOLN.

1852

EULOGY ON HENRY CLAY,

DELIVERED IN THE STATE HOUSE AT SPRINGFIELD, ILLINOIS, JULY 16, 1852.

On the fourth day of July, 1776, the people of a few feeble and oppressed colonies of Great Britain, inhabiting a portion of the Atlantic coast of North America, publicly declared their national independence, and made their appeal to the justice of their cause and to the God of battles for the maintenance of that declaration. That people were few in number and without resources, save only their wise heads and stout hearts. Within the first year of that declared independence, and while its maintenance was yet problematical, while the bloody struggle between those resolute rebels and their haughty would-be masters was still waging,—of undistinguished parents and in an obscure district of one of those colonies Henry Clay was born. The infant nation and the infant child began the race of life together. For three quarters of a century they have travelled hand in hand. They have been companions ever. The nation has passed its perils, and it is free, prosperous, and powerful. The child has reached his manhood, his middle age, his old age, and is dead. In all that has concerned the nation the man ever sympathized; and now the nation mourns the man.

The day after his death one of the public journals, opposed to him politically, held the following pathetic and beautiful language, which I adopt partly because such high and exclusive eulogy, originating with a political friend, might offend good taste, but chiefly because I could not in any language of my own so well express my thoughts:

"Alas, who can realize that Henry Clay is dead! Who can realize that never again that majestic form shall rise in the council-chambers of his country to beat back the storms of anarchy which may threaten, or pour the oil of peace upon the troubled billows as they rage and menace around! Who can realize that the workings of that mighty mind have ceased, that the throbbings of that gallant heart are stilled, that the mighty sweep of that graceful arm will be felt no more, and the magic of that eloquent tongue, which spake as spake no other tongue besides, is hushed hushed for ever! Who can realize that freedom's champion, the champion of a civilized world and of all tongues and kindreds of people, has indeed fallen! Alas, in those dark hours of peril and dread which our land has experienced, and which she may be called to experience again, to whom now may her people look up for that counsel and advice which only wisdom and experience and patriotism can give, and which only the undoubting confidence of a nation will receive? Perchance in the whole circle of the great and gifted of our land there remains but one on whose shoulders the mighty mantle of the departed statesman may fall; one who while we now write is doubtless pouring his tears over the bier of his brother and friend brother, friend, ever, yet in political sentiment as far apart as party could make them. Ah, it is at times like these that the petty distinctions of mere party disappear. We see only the great, the grand, the noble features of the departed statesman; and we do not even beg permission to bow at his feet and mingle our tears with those who have ever been his political adherents—we do [not] beg this permission, we claim it as a right, though we feel it as a privilege. Henry Clay belonged to his country—to the world; mere party cannot claim men like him. His career has been national, his fame has filled the earth, his memory will endure to the last syllable of recorded time.

"Henry Clay is dead! He breathed his last on yesterday, at twenty minutes after eleven, in his chamber at Washington. To those who followed his lead in public affairs, it more appropriately belongs to pronounce his eulogy and pay specific honors to the memory of the illustrious dead. But all Americans may show the grief which his death inspires, for his character and fame are national property. As on a question of liberty he knew no North, no South, no East, no West, but only the Union which held them all in its sacred circle, so now his countrymen will know no grief that is not as wide-spread as the bounds of the confederacy. The career of Henry Clay was a public career. From his youth he has been devoted to the public service, at a period, too, in the world's history justly regarded as a remarkable era in human affairs. He witnessed in the beginning the throes of the French Revolution. He saw the rise and fall of Napoleon. He was called upon to legislate for America and direct her policy when all Europe was the battlefield of contending dynasties, and when the struggle for supremacy imperilled the rights of all neutral nations. His voice spoke war and peace in the contest with Great Britain.

"When Greece rose against the Turks and struck for liberty, his name was mingled with the battle-cry of freedom. When South America threw off the thraldom of Spain, his speeches were read at the head of her armies by Bolivar. His name has been, and will continue to be, hallowed in two hemispheres, for it is

"'One of the few, the immortal names

That were not born to die!'

"'To the ardent patriot and profound statesman he added a quality possessed by few of the gifted on earth. His eloquence has not been surpassed. In the effective power to move the heart of man, Clay was without an equal, and the heaven-born endowment, in the spirit of its origin, has been most conspicuously exhibited against intestine feud. On at least three important occasions he has quelled our civil commotions by a power and influence which belonged to no other statesman of his age and times. And in our last internal discord, when this Union trembled to its centre, in old age he left the shades of private life, and gave the death-blow to fraternal strife, with the vigor of his earlier years, in a series of senatorial efforts which in themselves would bring immortality by challenging comparison with the efforts of any statesman in any age. He exorcised the demon which possessed the body politic, and gave peace to a distracted land. Alas! the achievement cost him his life. He sank day by day to the tomb his pale but noble brow bound with a triple wreath, put there by a grateful country. May his ashes rest in peace, while his spirit goes to take its station among the great and good men who preceded him."

While it is customary and proper upon occasions like the present to give a brief sketch of the life of the deceased, in the case of Mr. Clay it is less necessary than most others; for his biography has been written and rewritten and read and reread for the last twenty-five years; so that, with the exception of a few of the latest incidents of his life, all is as well known as it can be. The short sketch which I give is, therefore, merely to maintain the connection of this discourse.

Henry Clay was born on the twelfth day of April, 1777, in Hanover County, Virginia. Of his father, who died in the fourth or fifth year of Henry's age, little seems to be known, except that he was a respectable man and a preacher of the Baptist persuasion. Mr. Clay's education to the end of life was comparatively limited. I say "to the end of life," because I have understood that from time to time he added something to his education during the greater part of his whole life. Mr. Clay's lack of a more perfect early education, however it may be regretted generally, teaches at least one profitable lesson: it teaches that in this country one can scarcely be so poor but that, if he will, he can acquire sufficient education to get through the world respectably. In his twenty-third year Mr. Clay was licensed to practise law, and emigrated to Lexington, Kentucky. Here he commenced and continued the practice till the year 1803, when he was first elected to the Kentucky Legislature. By successive elections he was continued in the Legislature till the latter part of 1806, when he was elected to fill a vacancy of a single session in the United States Senate. In 1807 he was again elected to the Kentucky House of Representatives, and by that body chosen Speaker. In 1808 he was re-elected to the same body. In 1809 he was again chosen to fill a vacancy of two years in the United States Senate. In 1811 he was elected to the United States House of Representatives, and on the first day of taking his seat in that body he was chosen its Speaker. In 1813 he was again elected Speaker. Early in 1814, being the period of our last British war, Mr. Clay was sent as commissioner, with others, to negotiate a treaty of peace, which treaty was concluded in the latter part of the same year. On his return from Europe he was again elected to the lower branch of Congress, and on taking his seat in December, 1815, was called to his old post-the Speaker's chair, a position in which he was retained by successive elections, with one brief intermission, till the inauguration of John Quincy Adams, in March, 1825. He was then appointed Secretary of State, and occupied that important station till the inauguration of General Jackson, in March, 1829. After this he returned to Kentucky, resumed the practice of law, and continued it till the autumn of 1831, when he was by the Legislature of Kentucky again placed in the United States Senate. By a reelection he was continued in the Senate till he resigned his seat and retired, in March, 1848. In December, 1849, he again took his seat in the Senate, which he again resigned only a few months before his death.

By the foregoing it is perceived that the period from the beginning of Mr. Clay's official life in 1803 to the end of 1852 is but one year short of half a century, and that the sum of all the intervals in it will not amount to ten years. But mere duration of time in office constitutes the smallest part of Mr. Clay's history. Throughout that long period he has constantly been the most loved and most implicitly followed by friends, and the most dreaded by opponents, of all living American politicians. In all the great questions which have agitated the country, and particularly in those fearful crises, the Missouri question, the nullification question, and the late slavery question, as connected with the newly acquired territory, involving and endangering the stability of the Union, his has been the leading and most conspicuous part. In 1824 he was first a candidate for the Presidency, and was defeated; and, although he was successively defeated for the same office in 1832 and in 1844, there has never been a moment since 1824 till after 1848 when a very large portion of the American people did not cling to him with an enthusiastic hope and purpose of still elevating him to the Presidency. With other men, to be defeated was to be forgotten; but with him defeat was but a trifling incident, neither changing him nor the world's estimate of him. Even those of both political parties who have been preferred to him for the highest office have run far briefer courses than he, and left him still shining high in the heavens of the political world. Jackson, Van Buren, Harrison, Polk, and Taylor all rose after, and set long before him. The spell—the long-enduring spell—with which the souls of men were bound to him is a miracle. Who can compass it? It is probably true he owed his pre-eminence to no one quality, but to a fortunate combination of several. He was surpassingly eloquent; but many eloquent men fail utterly, and they are not, as a class, generally successful. His judgment was excellent; but many men of good judgment live and die unnoticed. His will was indomitable; but this quality often secures to its owner nothing better than a character for useless obstinacy. These, then, were Mr. Clay's leading qualities. No one of them is very uncommon; but all together are rarely combined in a single individual, and this is probably the reason why such men as Henry Clay are so rare in the world.

Mr. Clay's eloquence did not consist, as many fine specimens of eloquence do, of types and figures, of antithesis and elegant arrangement of words and sentences, but rather of that deeply earnest and impassioned tone and manner which can proceed only from great sincerity, and a thorough conviction in the speaker of the justice and importance of his cause. This it is that truly touches the chords of sympathy; and those who heard Mr. Clay never failed to be moved by it, or ever afterward forgot the impression. All his efforts were made for practical effect. He never spoke merely to be heard. He never delivered a Fourth of July oration, or a eulogy on an occasion like this. As a politician or statesman, no one was so habitually careful to avoid all sectional ground. Whatever he did he did for the whole country. In the construction of his measures, he ever carefully surveyed every part of the field, and duly weighed every conflicting interest. Feeling as he did, and as the truth surely is, that the world's best hope depended on the continued union of these States, he was ever jealous of and watchful for whatever might have the slightest tendency to separate them.

Mr. Clay's predominant sentiment, from first to last, was a deep devotion to the cause of human liberty—a strong sympathy with the oppressed everywhere, and an ardent wish for their elevation. With him this was a primary and all-controlling passion. Subsidiary to this was the conduct of his whole life. He loved his country partly because it was his own country, and mostly because it was a free country; and he burned with a zeal for its advancement, prosperity, and glory, because he saw in such the advancement, prosperity, and glory of human liberty, human right, and human nature. He desired the prosperity of his countrymen, partly because they were his countrymen, but chiefly to show to the world that free men could be prosperous.

That his views and measures were always the wisest needs not to be affirmed; nor should it be on this occasion, where so many thinking differently join in doing honor to his memory. A free people in times of peace and quiet when pressed by no common danger-naturally divide into parties. At such times the man who is of neither party is not, cannot be, of any consequence. Mr. Clay therefore was of a party. Taking a prominent part, as he did, in all the great political questions of his country for the last half century, the wisdom of his course on many is doubted and denied by a large portion of his countrymen; and of such it is not now proper to speak particularly. But there are many others, about his course upon which there is little or no disagreement amongst intelligent and patriotic Americans. Of these last are the War of 1812, the Missouri question, nullification, and the now recent compromise measures. In 1812 Mr. Clay, though not unknown, was still a young man. Whether we should go to war with Great Britain being the question of the day, a minority opposed the declaration of war by Congress, while the majority, though apparently inclined to war, had for years wavered, and hesitated to act decisively. Meanwhile British aggressions multiplied, and grew more daring and aggravated. By Mr. Clay more than any other man the struggle was brought to a decision in Congress. The question, being now fully before Congress, came up in a variety of ways in rapid succession, on most of which occasions Mr. Clay spoke. Adding to all the logic of which the subject was susceptible that noble inspiration which came to him as it came to no other, he aroused and nerved and inspired his friends, and confounded and bore down all opposition. Several of his speeches on these occasions were reported and are still extant, but the best of them all never was. During its delivery the reporters forgot their vocation, dropped their pens, and sat enchanted from near the beginning to quite the close. The speech now lives only in the memory of a few old men, and the enthusiasm with which they cherish their recollection of it is absolutely astonishing. The precise language of this speech we shall never know; but we do know we cannot help knowing—that with deep pathos it pleaded the cause of the injured sailor, that it invoked the genius of the Revolution, that it apostrophized the names of Otis, of Henry, and of Washington, that it appealed to the interests, the pride, the honor, and the glory of the nation, that it shamed and taunted the timidity of friends, that it scorned and scouted and withered the temerity of domestic foes, that it bearded and defied the British lion, and, rising and swelling and maddening in its course, it sounded the onset, till the charge, the shock, the steady struggle, and the glorious victory all passed in vivid review before the entranced hearers.

Important and exciting as was the war question of 1812, it never so alarmed the sagacious statesmen of the country for the safety of the Republic as afterward did the Missouri question. This sprang from that unfortunate source of discord—negro slavery. When our Federal Constitution was adopted, we owned no territory beyond the limits or ownership of the States, except the territory northwest of the River Ohio and east of the Mississippi. What has since been formed into the States of Maine, Kentucky and Tennessee, was, I believe, within the limits of or owned by Massachusetts, Virginia, and North Carolina. As to the Northwestern Territory, provision had been made even before the adoption of the Constitution that slavery should never go there. On the admission of States into the Union, carved from the territory we owned before the Constitution, no question, or at most no considerable question, arose about slavery—those which were within the limits of or owned by the old States following respectively the condition of the parent State, and those within the Northwest Territory following the previously made provision. But in 1803 we purchased Louisiana of the French, and it included with much more what has since been formed into the State of Missouri. With regard to it, nothing had been done to forestall the question of slavery. When, therefore, in 1819, Missouri, having formed a State constitution without excluding slavery, and with slavery already actually existing within its limits, knocked at the door of the Union for admission, almost the entire representation of the non-slaveholding States objected. A fearful and angry struggle instantly followed. This alarmed thinking men more than any previous question, because, unlike all the former, it divided the country by geographical lines. Other questions had their opposing partisans in all localities of the country and in almost every family, so that no division of the Union could follow such without a separation of friends to quite as great an extent as that of opponents. Not so with the Missouri question. On this a geographical line could be traced, which in the main would separate opponents only. This was the danger. Mr. Jefferson, then in retirement, wrote:

"I had for a long time ceased to read newspapers or to pay any attention to public affairs, confident they were in good hands and content to be a passenger in our bark to the shore from which I am not distant. But this momentous question, like a firebell in the night, awakened and filled me with terror. I considered it at once as the knell of the Union. It is hushed, indeed, for the moment. But this is a reprieve only, not a final sentence. A geographical line coinciding with a marked principle, moral and political, once conceived and held up to the angry passions of men, will never be obliterated, and every irritation will mark it deeper and deeper. I can say with conscious truth that there is not a man on earth who would sacrifice more than I would to relieve us from this heavy reproach in any practicable way.

"The cession of that kind of property—for it is so misnamed—is a bagatelle which would not cost me a second thought if in that way a general emancipation and expatriation could be effected, and gradually and with due sacrifices I think it might be. But as it is, we have the wolf by the ears, and we can neither hold him nor safely let him go. Justice is in one scale, and self-preservation in the other."

Mr. Clay was in Congress, and, perceiving the danger, at once engaged his whole energies to avert it. It began, as I have said, in 1819; and it did not terminate till 1821. Missouri would not yield the point; and Congress that is, a majority in Congress—by repeated votes showed a determination not to admit the State unless it should yield. After several failures, and great labor on the part of Mr. Clay to so present the question that a majority could consent to the admission, it was by a vote rejected, and, as all seemed to think, finally. A sullen gloom hung over the nation. All felt that the rejection of Missouri was equivalent to a dissolution of the Union, because those States which already had what Missouri was rejected for refusing to relinquish would go with Missouri. All deprecated and deplored this, but none saw how to avert it. For the judgment of members to be convinced of the necessity of yielding was not the whole difficulty; each had a constituency to meet and to answer to. Mr. Clay, though worn down and exhausted, was appealed to by members to renew his efforts at compromise. He did so, and by some judicious modifications of his plan, coupled with laborious efforts with individual members and his own overmastering eloquence upon that floor, he finally secured the admission of the State. Brightly and captivating as it had previously shown, it was now perceived that his great eloquence was a mere embellishment, or at most but a helping hand to his inventive genius and his devotion to his country in the day of her extreme peril.

After the settlement of the Missouri question, although a portion of the American people have differed with Mr. Clay, and a majority even appear generally to have been opposed to him on questions of ordinary administration, he seems constantly to have been regarded by all as the man for the crisis. Accordingly, in the days of nullification, and more recently in the reappearance of the slavery question connected with our territory newly acquired of Mexico, the task of devising a mode of adjustment seems to have been cast upon Mr. Clay by common consent—and his performance of the task in each case was little else than a literal fulfilment of the public expectation.

Mr. Clay's efforts in behalf of the South Americans, and afterward in behalf of the Greeks, in the times of their respective struggles for civil liberty, are among the finest on record, upon the noblest of all themes, and bear ample corroboration of what I have said was his ruling passion—a love of liberty and right, unselfishly, and for their own sakes.

Having been led to allude to domestic slavery so frequently already, I am unwilling to close without referring more particularly to Mr. Clay's views and conduct in regard to it. He ever was on principle and in feeling opposed to slavery. The very earliest, and one of the latest, public efforts of his life, separated by a period of more than fifty years, were both made in favor of gradual emancipation. He did not perceive that on a question of human right the negroes were to be excepted from the human race. And yet Mr. Clay was the owner of slaves. Cast into life when slavery was already widely spread and deeply seated, he did not perceive, as I think no wise man has perceived, how it could be at once eradicated without producing a greater evil even to the cause of human liberty itself. His feeling and his judgment, therefore, ever led him to oppose both extremes of opinion on the subject. Those who would shiver into fragments the Union of these States, tear to tatters its now venerated Constitution, and even burn the last copy of the Bible, rather than slavery should continue a single hour, together with all their more halting sympathizers, have received, and are receiving, their just execration; and the name and opinions and influence of Mr. Clay are fully and, as I trust, effectually and enduringly arrayed against them. But I would also, if I could, array his name, opinions, and influence against the opposite extreme—against a few but an increasing number of men who, for the sake of perpetuating slavery, are beginning to assail and to ridicule the white man's charter of freedom, the declaration that "all men are created free and equal." So far as I have learned, the first American of any note to do or attempt this was the late John C. Calhoun; and if I mistake not, it soon after found its way into some of the messages of the Governor of South Carolina. We, however, look for and are not much shocked by political eccentricities and heresies in South Carolina. But only last year I saw with astonishment what purported to be a letter of a very distinguished and influential clergyman of Virginia, copied, with apparent approbation, into a St. Louis newspaper, containing the following to me very unsatisfactory language:

"I am fully aware that there is a text in some Bibles that is not in mine. Professional abolitionists have made more use of it than of any passage in the Bible. It came, however, as I trace it, from Saint Voltaire, and was baptized by Thomas Jefferson, and since almost universally regarded as canonical authority 'All men are born free and equal.'

"This is a genuine coin in the political currency of our generation. I am sorry to say that I have never seen two men of whom it is true. But I must admit I never saw the Siamese Twins, and therefore will not dogmatically say that no man ever saw a proof of this sage aphorism."

This sounds strangely in republican America. The like was not heard in the fresher days of the republic. Let us contrast with it the language of that truly national man whose life and death we now commemorate and lament: I quote from a speech of Mr. Clay delivered before the American Colonization Society in 1827:

"We are reproached with doing mischief by the agitation of this question. The society goes into no household to disturb its domestic tranquillity. It addresses itself to no slaves to weaken their obligations of obedience. It seeks to affect no man's property. It neither has the power nor the will to affect the property of any one contrary to his consent. The execution of its scheme would augment instead of diminishing the value of property left behind. The society, composed of free men, conceals itself only with the free. Collateral consequences we are not responsible for. It is not this society which has produced the great moral revolution which the age exhibits. What would they who thus reproach us have done? If they would repress all tendencies toward liberty and ultimate emancipation, they must do more than put down the benevolent efforts of this society. They must go back to the era of our liberty and independence, and muzzle the cannon which thunders its annual joyous return. They must renew the slave trade, with all its train of atrocities. They must suppress the workings of British philanthropy, seeking to meliorate the condition of the unfortunate West Indian slave. They must arrest the career of South American deliverance from thraldom. They must blow out the moral lights around us and extinguish that greatest torch of all which America presents to a benighted world—pointing the way to their rights, their liberties, and their happiness. And when they have achieved all those purposes their work will be yet incomplete. They must penetrate the human soul, and eradicate the light of reason and the love of liberty. Then, and not till then, when universal darkness and despair prevail, can you perpetuate slavery and repress all sympathy and all humane and benevolent efforts among free men in behalf of the unhappy portion of our race doomed to bondage."

The American Colonization Society was organized in 1816. Mr. Clay, though not its projector, was one of its earliest members; and he died, as for many preceding years he had been, its president. It was one of the most cherished objects of his direct care and consideration, and the association of his name with it has probably been its very greatest collateral support. He considered it no demerit in the society that it tended to relieve the slave-holders from the troublesome presence of the free negroes; but this was far from being its whole merit in his estimation. In the same speech from which we have quoted he says:

"There is a moral fitness in the idea of returning to Africa her children, whose ancestors have been torn from her by the ruthless hand of fraud and violence. Transplanted in a foreign land, they will carry back to their native soil the rich fruits of religion, civilization, law, and liberty. May it not be one of the great designs of the Ruler of the universe, whose ways are often inscrutable by short-sighted mortals, thus to transform an original crime into a signal blessing to that most unfortunate portion of the globe?"

This suggestion of the possible ultimate redemption of the African race and African continent was made twenty-five years ago. Every succeeding year has added strength to the hope of its realization. May it indeed be realized. Pharaoh's country was cursed with plagues, and his hosts were lost in the Red Sea, for striving to retain a captive people who had already served them more than four hundred years. May like disasters never befall us! If, as the friends of colonization hope, the present and coming generations of our countrymen shall by any means succeed in freeing our land from the dangerous presence of slavery, and at the same time in restoring a captive people to their long-lost fatherland with bright prospects for the future, and this too so gradually that neither races nor individuals shall have suffered by the change, it will indeed be a glorious consummation. And if to such a consummation the efforts of Mr. Clay shall have contributed, it will be what he most ardently wished, and none of his labors will have been more valuable to his country and his kind.

But Henry Clay is dead. His long and eventful life is closed. Our country is prosperous and powerful; but could it have been quite all it has been, and is, and is to be, without Henry Clay? Such a man the times have demanded, and such in the providence of God was given us. But he is gone. Let us strive to deserve, as far as mortals may, the continued care of Divine Providence, trusting that in future national emergencies He will not fail to provide us the instruments of safety and security.

NOTE. We are indebted for a copy of this speech to the courtesy of Major Wm. H. Bailhache, formerly one of the proprietors of the Illinois State Journal.

CHALLENGED VOTERS

OPINION ON THE ILLINOIS ELECTION LAW.

SPRINGFIELD, November 1, 1852

A leading article in the Daily Register of this morning has induced some of our friends to request our opinion on the election laws as applicable to challenged voters. We have examined the present constitution of the State, the election law of 1849, and the unrepealed parts of the election law in the revised code of 1845; and we are of the opinion that any person taking the oath prescribed in the act of 1849 is entitled to vote unless counter-proof be made satisfactory to a majority of the judges that such oath is untrue; and that for the purpose of obtaining such counter-proof, the proposed voter may be asked questions in the way of cross-examination, and other independent testimony may be received. We base our opinion as to receiving counter-proof upon the unrepealed Section nineteen of the election law in the revised code.

A. LINCOLN,

B. S. EDWARDS

S. T. LOGAN.

S. H. TREAT

1853

LEGAL OFFICE WORK

TO JOSHUA R. STANFORD.

PEKIN, MAY 12, 1853

Mr. JOSHUA R. STANFORD.

SIR:—I hope the subject-matter of this letter will appear a sufficient apology to you for the liberty I, a total stranger, take in addressing you. The persons here holding two lots under a conveyance made by you, as the attorney of Daniel M. Baily, now nearly twenty-two years ago, are in great danger of losing the lots, and very much, perhaps all, is to depend on the testimony you give as to whether you did or did not account to Baily for the proceeds received by you on this sale of the lots. I, therefore, as one of the counsel, beg of you to fully refresh your recollection by any means in your power before the time you may be called on to testify. If persons should come about you, and show a disposition to pump you on the subject, it may be no more than prudent to remember that it may be possible they design to misrepresent you and embarrass the real testimony you may ultimately give. It may be six months or a year before you are called on to testify.

Respectfully,

A. LINCOLN.

1854

TO O. L. DAVIS.

SPRINGFIELD, June 22, 1854.

O. L. DAVIS, ESQ.

DEAR SIR:—You, no doubt, remember the enclosed memorandum being handed me in your office. I have just made the desired search, and find that no such deed has ever been here. Campbell, the auditor, says that if it were here, it would be in his office, and that he has hunted for it a dozen times, and could never find it. He says that one time and another, he has heard much about the matter, that it was not a deed for Right of Way, but a deed, outright, for Depot-ground—at least, a sale for Depot-ground, and there may never have been a deed. He says, if there is a deed, it is most probable General Alexander, of Paris, has it.

Yours truly,

A. LINCOLN.

NEBRASKA MEASURE

TO J. M. PALMER

[Confidential]

SPRINGFIELD, Sept. 7, 1854.

HON. J. M. PALMER.

DEAR SIR:—You know how anxious I am that this Nebraska measure shall be rebuked and condemned everywhere. Of course I hope something from your position; yet I do not expect you to do anything which may be wrong in your own judgment; nor would I have you do anything personally injurious to yourself. You are, and always have been, honestly and sincerely a Democrat; and I know how painful it must be to an honest, sincere man to be urged by his party to the support of a measure which in his conscience he believes to be wrong. You have had a severe struggle with yourself, and you have determined not to swallow the wrong. Is it not just to yourself that you should, in a few public speeches, state your reasons, and thus justify yourself? I wish you would; and yet I say, don't do it, if you think it will injure you. You may have given your word to vote for Major Harris; and if so, of course you will stick to it. But allow me to suggest that you should avoid speaking of this; for it probably would induce some of your friends in like manner to cast their votes. You understand. And now let me beg your pardon for obtruding this letter upon you, to whom I have ever been opposed in politics. Had your party omitted to make Nebraska a test of party fidelity, you probably would have been the Democratic candidate for Congress in the district. You deserved it, and I believe it would have been given you. In that case I should have been quite happy that Nebraska was to be rebuked at all events. I still should have voted for the Whig candidate; but I should have made no speeches, written no letters; and you would have been elected by at least a thousand majority.

Yours truly,

A. LINCOLN.

TO A. B. MOREAU.

SPRINGFIELD, September 7, 1854

A. B. MOREAU, ESQ.

SIR:—Stranger though I am, personally, being a brother in the faith, I venture to write you. Yates can not come to your court next week. He is obliged to be at Pike court where he has a case, with a fee of five hundred dollars, two hundred dollars already paid. To neglect it would be unjust to himself, and dishonest to his client. Harris will be with you, head up and tail up, for Nebraska. You must have some one to make an anti-Nebraska speech. Palmer is the best, if you can get him, I think. Jo. Gillespie, if you can not get Palmer, and somebody anyhow, if you can get neither. But press Palmer hard. It is in his Senatorial district, I believe.

Yours etc.,

A. LINCOLN.

REPLY TO SENATOR DOUGLAS—PEORIA SPEECH

SPEECH AT PEORIA, ILLINOIS, IN REPLY TO SENATOR DOUGLAS,

OCTOBER 16, 1854.

I do not rise to speak now, if I can stipulate with the audience to meet me here at half-past six or at seven o'clock. It is now several minutes past five, and Judge Douglas has spoken over three hours. If you hear me at all, I wish you to hear me through. It will take me as long as it has taken him. That will carry us beyond eight o'clock at night. Now, every one of you who can remain that long can just as well get his supper, meet me at seven, and remain an hour or two later. The Judge has already informed you that he is to have an hour to reply to me. I doubt not but you have been a little surprised to learn that I have consented to give one of his high reputation and known ability this advantage of me. Indeed, my consenting to it, though reluctant, was not wholly unselfish, for I suspected, if it were understood that the Judge was entirely done, you Democrats would leave and not hear me; but by giving him the close, I felt confident you would stay for the fun of hearing him skin me.

The audience signified their assent to the arrangement, and adjourned to seven o'clock P.M., at which time they reassembled, and Mr. Lincoln spoke substantially as follows:

The repeal of the Missouri Compromise, and the propriety of its restoration, constitute the subject of what I am about to say. As I desire to present my own connected view of this subject, my remarks will not be specifically an answer to Judge Douglas; yet, as I proceed, the main points he has presented will arise, and will receive such respectful attention as I may be able to give them. I wish further to say that I do not propose to question the patriotism or to assail the motives of any man or class of men, but rather to confine myself strictly to the naked merits of the question. I also wish to be no less than national in all the positions I may take, and whenever I take ground which others have thought, or may think, narrow, sectional, and dangerous to the Union, I hope to give a reason which will appear sufficient, at least to some, why I think differently.

And as this subject is no other than part and parcel of the larger general question of domestic slavery, I wish to make and to keep the distinction between the existing institution and the extension of it so broad and so clear that no honest man can misunderstand me, and no dishonest one successfully misrepresent me.

In order to a clear understanding of what the Missouri Compromise is, a short history of the preceding kindred subjects will perhaps be proper.

When we established our independence, we did not own or claim the country to which this compromise applies. Indeed, strictly speaking, the Confederacy then owned no country at all; the States respectively owned the country within their limits, and some of them owned territory beyond their strict State limits. Virginia thus owned the Northwestern Territory—the country out of which the principal part of Ohio, all Indiana, all Illinois, all Michigan, and all Wisconsin have since been formed. She also owned (perhaps within her then limits) what has since been formed into the State of Kentucky. North Carolina thus owned what is now the State of Tennessee; and South Carolina and Georgia owned, in separate parts, what are now Mississippi and Alabama. Connecticut, I think, owned the little remaining part of Ohio, being the same where they now send Giddings to Congress and beat all creation in making cheese.

These territories, together with the States themselves, constitute all the country over which the Confederacy then claimed any sort of jurisdiction. We were then living under the Articles of Confederation, which were superseded by the Constitution several years afterward. The question of ceding the territories to the General Government was set on foot. Mr. Jefferson,—the author of the Declaration of Independence, and otherwise a chief actor in the Revolution; then a delegate in Congress; afterward, twice President; who was, is, and perhaps will continue to be, the most distinguished politician of our history; a Virginian by birth and continued residence, and withal a slaveholder,—conceived the idea of taking that occasion to prevent slavery ever going into the Northwestern Territory. He prevailed on the Virginia Legislature to adopt his views, and to cede the Territory, making the prohibition of slavery therein a condition of the deed. (Jefferson got only an understanding, not a condition of the deed to this wish.) Congress accepted the cession with the condition; and the first ordinance (which the acts of Congress were then called) for the government of the Territory provided that slavery should never be permitted therein. This is the famed "Ordinance of '87," so often spoken of.

Thenceforward for sixty-one years, and until, in 1848, the last scrap of this Territory came into the Union as the State of Wisconsin, all parties acted in quiet obedience to this ordinance. It is now what Jefferson foresaw and intended—the happy home of teeming millions of free, white, prosperous people, and no slave among them.

Thus, with the author of the Declaration of Independence, the policy of prohibiting slavery in new territory originated. Thus, away back to the Constitution, in the pure, fresh, free breath of the Revolution, the State of Virginia and the national Congress put that policy into practice. Thus, through more than sixty of the best years of the republic, did that policy steadily work to its great and beneficent end. And thus, in those five States, and in five millions of free, enterprising people, we have before us the rich fruits of this policy.

But now new light breaks upon us. Now Congress declares this ought never to have been, and the like of it must never be again. The sacred right of self-government is grossly violated by it. We even find some men who drew their first breath—and every other breath of their lives—under this very restriction, now live in dread of absolute suffocation if they should be restricted in the "sacred right" of taking slaves to Nebraska. That perfect liberty they sigh for—the liberty of making slaves of other people, Jefferson never thought of, their own fathers never thought of, they never thought of themselves, a year ago. How fortunate for them they did not sooner become sensible of their great misery! Oh, how difficult it is to treat with respect such assaults upon all we have ever really held sacred!

But to return to history. In 1803 we purchased what was then called Louisiana, of France. It included the present States of Louisiana, Arkansas, Missouri, and Iowa; also the Territory of Minnesota, and the present bone of contention, Kansas and Nebraska. Slavery already existed among the French at New Orleans, and to some extent at St. Louis. In 1812 Louisiana came into the Union as a slave State, without controversy. In 1818 or '19, Missouri showed signs of a wish to come in with slavery. This was resisted by Northern members of Congress; and thus began the first great slavery agitation in the nation. This controversy lasted several months, and became very angry and exciting—the House of Representatives voting steadily for the prohibition of slavery in Missouri, and the Senate voting as steadily against it. Threats of the breaking up of the Union were freely made, and the ablest public men of the day became seriously alarmed. At length a compromise was made, in which, as in all compromises, both sides yielded something. It was a law, passed on the 6th of March, 1820, providing that Missouri might come into the Union with slavery, but that in all the remaining part of the territory purchased of France which lies north of thirty-six degrees and thirty minutes north latitude, slavery should never be permitted. This provision of law is the "Missouri Compromise." In excluding slavery north of the line, the same language is employed as in the Ordinance of 1787. It directly applied to Iowa, Minnesota, and to the present bone of contention, Kansas and Nebraska. Whether there should or should not be slavery south of that line, nothing was said in the law. But Arkansas constituted the principal remaining part south of the line; and it has since been admitted as a slave State, without serious controversy. More recently, Iowa, north of the line, came in as a free State without controversy. Still later, Minnesota, north of the line, had a territorial organization without controversy. Texas, principally south of the line, and west of Arkansas, though originally within the purchase from France, had, in 1819, been traded off to Spain in our treaty for the acquisition of Florida. It had thus become a part of

Mexico. Mexico revolutionized and became independent of Spain. American citizens began settling rapidly with their slaves in the southern part of Texas. Soon they revolutionized against Mexico, and established an independent government of their own, adopting a constitution with slavery, strongly resembling the constitutions of our slave States. By still another rapid move, Texas, claiming a boundary much farther west than when we parted with her in 1819, was brought back to the United States, and admitted into the Union as a slave State. Then there was little or no settlement in the northern part of Texas, a considerable portion of which lay north of the Missouri line; and in the resolutions admitting her into the Union, the Missouri restriction was expressly extended westward across her territory. This was in 1845, only nine years ago.

Thus originated the Missouri Compromise; and thus has it been respected down to 1845. And even four years later, in 1849, our distinguished Senator, in a public address, held the following language in relation to it:

"The Missouri Compromise has been in practical operation for about a quarter of a century, and has received the sanction and approbation of men of all parties in every section of the Union. It has allayed all sectional jealousies and irritations growing out of this vexed question, and harmonized and tranquillized the whole country. It has given to Henry Clay, as its prominent champion, the proud sobriquet of the 'Great Pacificator,' and by that title, and for that service, his political friends had repeatedly appealed to the people to rally under his standard as a Presidential candidate, as the man who had exhibited the patriotism and power to suppress an unholy and treasonable agitation, and preserve the Union. He was not aware that any man or any party, from any section of the Union, had ever urged as an objection to Mr. Clay that he was the great champion of the Missouri Compromise. On the contrary, the effort was made by the opponents of Mr. Clay to prove that he was not entitled to the exclusive merit of that great patriotic measure, and that the honor was equally due to others, as well as to him, for securing its adoption; that it had its origin in the hearts of all patriotic men, who desired to preserve and perpetuate the blessings of our glorious Union—an origin akin to that of the Constitution of the United States, conceived in the same spirit of fraternal affection, and calculated to remove forever the only danger which seemed to threaten, at some distant day, to sever the social bond of union. All the evidences of public opinion at that day seemed to indicate that this compromise had been canonized in the hearts of the American people, as a sacred thing which no ruthless hand would ever be reckless enough to disturb."

I do not read this extract to involve Judge Douglas in an inconsistency. If he afterward thought he had been wrong, it was right for him to change. I bring this forward merely to show the high estimate placed on the Missouri Compromise by all parties up to so late as the year 1849.

But going back a little in point of time. Our war with Mexico broke out in 1846. When Congress was about adjourning that session, President Polk asked them to place two millions of dollars under his control, to be used by him in the recess, if found practicable and expedient, in negotiating a treaty of peace with Mexico, and acquiring some part of her territory. A bill was duly gotten up for the purpose, and was progressing swimmingly in the House of Representatives, when a member by the name of David Wilmot, a Democrat from Pennsylvania, moved as an amendment, "Provided, that in any territory thus acquired there never shall be slavery."

This is the origin of the far-famed Wilmot Proviso. It created a great flutter; but it stuck like wax, was voted into the bill, and the bill passed with it through the House. The Senate, however, adjourned without final action on it, and so both appropriation and proviso were lost for the time. The war continued, and at the next session the President renewed his request for the appropriation, enlarging the amount, I think, to three millions. Again came the proviso, and defeated the measure. Congress adjourned again, and the war went on. In December, 1847, the new Congress assembled. I was in the lower House that term. The Wilmot Proviso, or the principle of it, was constantly coming up in some shape or other, and I think I may venture to say I voted for it at least forty times during the short time I was there. The Senate, however, held it in check, and it never became a law. In the spring of 1848 a treaty of peace was made with Mexico, by which we obtained that portion of her country which now constitutes the Territories of New Mexico and Utah and the present State of California. By this treaty the Wilmot Proviso was defeated, in so far as it was intended to be a condition of the acquisition of territory. Its friends, however, were still determined to find some way to restrain slavery from getting into the new country. This new acquisition lay directly west of our old purchase from France, and extended west to the Pacific Ocean, and was so situated that if the Missouri line should be extended straight west, the new country would be divided by such extended line, leaving some north and some south of it. On Judge Douglas's motion, a bill, or provision of a bill, passed the Senate to so extend the Missouri line. The proviso men in the House, including myself, voted it down, because, by implication, it gave up the southern part to slavery, while we were bent on having it all free.

In the fall of 1848 the gold-mines were discovered in California. This attracted people to it with unprecedented rapidity, so that on, or soon after, the meeting of the new Congress in December, 1849, she already had a population of nearly a hundred thousand, had called a convention, formed a State constitution excluding slavery, and was knocking for admission into the Union. The proviso men, of course, were for letting her in, but the Senate, always true to the other side, would not consent to her admission, and there California stood, kept out of the Union because she would not let slavery into her borders. Under all the circumstances, perhaps, this was not wrong. There were other points of dispute connected with the general question of Slavery, which equally needed adjustment. The South clamored for a more efficient fugitive slave law. The North clamored for the abolition of a peculiar species of slave trade in the District of Columbia, in connection with which, in view from the windows of the Capitol, a sort of negro livery-stable, where droves of negroes were collected, temporarily kept, and finally taken to Southern markets, precisely like droves of horses, had been openly maintained for fifty years. Utah and New Mexico needed territorial governments; and whether slavery should or should not be prohibited within them was another question. The indefinite western boundary of Texas was to be settled. She was a slave State, and consequently the farther west the slavery men could push her boundary, the more slave country they secured; and the farther east the slavery opponents could thrust the boundary back, the less slave ground was secured. Thus this was just as clearly a slavery question as any of the others.

These points all needed adjustment, and they were held up, perhaps wisely, to make them help adjust one another. The Union now, as in 1820, was thought to be in danger, and devotion to the Union rightfully inclined men to yield somewhat in points where nothing else could have so inclined them. A compromise was finally effected. The South got their new fugitive slave law, and the North got California, (by far the best part of our acquisition from Mexico) as a free State. The South got a provision that New Mexico and Utah, when admitted as States, may come in with or without slavery as they may then choose; and the North got the slave trade abolished in the District of Columbia.. The North got the western boundary of Texas thrown farther back eastward than the South desired; but, in turn, they gave Texas ten millions of dollars with which to pay her old debts. This is the Compromise of 1850.

Preceding the Presidential election of 1852, each of the great political parties, Democrats and Whigs, met in convention and adopted resolutions indorsing the Compromise of '50, as a "finality," a final settlement, so far as these parties could make it so, of all slavery agitation. Previous to this, in 1851, the Illinois Legislature had indorsed it.

During this long period of time, Nebraska (the Nebraska Territory, not the State of as we know it now) had remained substantially an uninhabited country, but now emigration to and settlement within it began to take place. It is about one third as large as the present United States, and its importance, so long overlooked, begins to come into view. The restriction of slavery by the Missouri Compromise directly applies to it—in fact was first made, and has since been maintained expressly for it. In 1853, a bill to give it a territorial government passed the House of Representatives, and, in the hands of Judge Douglas, failed of passing only for want of time. This bill contained no repeal of the Missouri Compromise. Indeed, when it was assailed because it did not contain such repeal, Judge Douglas defended it in its existing form. On January 4, 1854, Judge Douglas introduces a new bill to give Nebraska territorial government. He accompanies this bill with a report, in which last he expressly recommends that the Missouri Compromise shall neither be affirmed nor repealed. Before long the bill is so modified as to make two territories instead of one, calling the southern one Kansas.

Also, about a month after the introduction of the bill, on the Judge's own motion it is so amended as to declare the Missouri Compromise inoperative and void; and, substantially, that the people who go and settle there may establish slavery, or exclude it, as they may see fit. In this shape the bill passed both branches of Congress and became a law.

This is the repeal of the Missouri Compromise. The foregoing history may not be precisely accurate in every particular, but I am sure it is sufficiently so for all the use I shall attempt to make of it, and in it we have before us the chief material enabling us to judge correctly whether the repeal of the Missouri Compromise is right or wrong. I think, and shall try to show, that it is wrong—wrong in its direct effect, letting slavery into Kansas and Nebraska, and wrong in its prospective principle, allowing it to spread to every other part of the wide world where men can be found inclined to take it.

This declared indifference, but, as I must think, covert real zeal, for the spread of slavery, I cannot but hate. I hate it because of the monstrous injustice of slavery itself. I hate it because it deprives our republican example of its just influence in the world; enables the enemies of free institutions with plausibility to taunt us as hypocrites; causes the real friends of freedom to doubt our sincerity; and especially because it forces so many good men among ourselves into an open war with the very fundamental principles of civil liberty, criticizing the Declaration of Independence, and insisting that there is no right principle of action but self-interest.

Before proceeding let me say that I think I have no prejudice against the Southern people. They are just what we would be in their situation. If slavery did not now exist among them, they would not introduce it. If it did now exist among us, we should not instantly give it up. This I believe of the masses North and South. Doubtless there are individuals on both sides who would not hold slaves under any circumstances, and others who would gladly introduce slavery anew if it were out of existence. We know that some Southern men do free their slaves, go North and become tip-top abolitionists, while some Northern ones go South and become most cruel slave masters.

When Southern people tell us that they are no more responsible for the origin of slavery than we are, I acknowledge the fact. When it is said that the institution exists, and that it is very difficult to get rid of it in any satisfactory way, I can understand and appreciate the saying. I surely will not blame them for not doing what I should not know how to do myself. If all earthly power were given me, I should not know what to do as to the existing institution. My first impulse would be to free all the slaves, and send them to Liberia, to their own native land. But a moment's reflection would convince me that whatever of high hope (as I think there is) there may be in this in the long run, its sudden execution is impossible. If they were all landed there in a day, they would all perish in the next ten days; and there are not surplus shipping and surplus money enough to carry them there in many times ten days. What then? Free them all, and keep them among us as underlings? Is it quite certain that this betters their condition? I think I would not hold one in slavery at any rate, yet the point is not clear enough for me to denounce people upon. What next? Free them, and make them politically and socially our equals? My own feelings will not admit of this, and if mine would, we well know that those of the great mass of whites will not. Whether this feeling accords with justice and sound judgment is not the sole question, if indeed it is any part of it. A universal feeling, whether well or ill founded, cannot be safely disregarded. We cannot then make them equals. It does seem to me that systems of gradual emancipation might be adopted, but for their tardiness in this I will not undertake to judge our brethren of the South.

When they remind us of their constitutional rights, I acknowledge them—not grudgingly, but fully and fairly; and I would give them any legislation for the reclaiming of their fugitives which should not in its stringency be more likely to carry a free man into slavery than our ordinary criminal laws are to hang an innocent one.

But all this, to my judgment, furnishes no more excuse for permitting slavery to go into our own free territory than it would for reviving the African slave trade by law. The law which forbids the bringing of slaves from Africa, and that which has so long forbidden the taking of them into Nebraska, can hardy be distinguished on any moral principle, and the repeal of the former could find quite as plausible excuses as that of the latter.

The arguments by which the repeal of the Missouri Compromise is sought to be justified are these:

First. That the Nebraska country needed a territorial government.

Second. That in various ways the public had repudiated that compromise and

demanded the repeal, and therefore should not now complain of it.

And, lastly, That the repeal establishes a principle which is

intrinsically right.

I will attempt an answer to each of them in its turn.

First, then: If that country was in need of a territorial organization, could it not have had it as well without as with a repeal? Iowa and Minnesota, to both of which the Missouri restriction applied, had, without its repeal, each in succession, territorial organizations. And even the year before, a bill for Nebraska itself was within an ace of passing without the repealing clause, and this in the hands of the same men who are now the champions of repeal. Why no necessity then for repeal? But still later, when this very bill was first brought in, it contained no repeal. But, say they, because the people had demanded, or rather commanded, the repeal, the repeal was to accompany the organization whenever that should occur.

Now, I deny that the public ever demanded any such thing—ever repudiated the Missouri Compromise, ever commanded its repeal. I deny it, and call for the proof. It is not contended, I believe, that any such command has ever been given in express terms. It is only said that it was done in principle. The support of the Wilmot Proviso is the first fact mentioned to prove that the Missouri restriction was repudiated in principle, and the second is the refusal to extend the Missouri line over the country acquired from Mexico. These are near enough alike to be treated together. The one was to exclude the chances of slavery from the whole new acquisition by the lump, and the other was to reject a division of it, by which one half was to be given up to those chances. Now, whether this was a repudiation of the Missouri line in principle depends upon whether the Missouri law contained any principle requiring the line to be extended over the country acquired from Mexico. I contend it did not. I insist that it contained no general principle, but that it was, in every sense, specific. That its terms limit it to the country purchased from France is undenied and undeniable. It could have no principle beyond the intention of those who made it. They did not intend to extend the line to country which they did not own. If they intended to extend it in the event of acquiring additional territory, why did they not say so? It was just as easy to say that "in all the country west of the Mississippi which we now own, or may hereafter acquire, there shall never be slavery," as to say what they did say; and they would have said it if they had meant it. An intention to extend the law is not only not mentioned in the law, but is not mentioned in any contemporaneous history. Both the law itself, and the history of the times, are a blank as to any principle of extension; and by neither the known rules of construing statutes and contracts, nor by common sense, can any such principle be inferred.

Another fact showing the specific character of the Missouri law—showing that it intended no more than it expressed, showing that the line was not intended as a universal dividing line between Free and Slave territory, present and prospective, north of which slavery could never go—is the fact that by that very law Missouri came in as a slave State, north of the line. If that law contained any prospective principle, the whole law must be looked to in order to ascertain what the principle was. And by this rule the South could fairly contend that, inasmuch as they got one slave State north of the line at the inception of the law, they have the right to have another given them north of it occasionally, now and then, in the indefinite westward extension of the line. This demonstrates the absurdity of attempting to deduce a prospective principle from the Missouri Compromise line.

When we voted for the Wilmot Proviso we were voting to keep slavery out of the whole Mexican acquisition, and little did we think we were thereby voting to let it into Nebraska lying several hundred miles distant. When we voted against extending the Missouri line, little did we think we were voting to destroy the old line, then of near thirty years' standing.

To argue that we thus repudiated the Missouri Compromise is no less absurd than it would be to argue that because we have so far forborne to acquire Cuba, we have thereby, in principle, repudiated our former acquisitions and determined to throw them out of the Union. No less absurd than it would be to say that because I may have refused to build an addition to my house, I thereby have decided to destroy the existing house! And if I catch you setting fire to my house, you will turn upon me and say I instructed you to do it!

The most conclusive argument, however, that while for the Wilmot Proviso, and while voting against the extension of the Missouri line, we never thought of disturbing the original Missouri Compromise, is found in the fact that there was then, and still is, an unorganized tract of fine country, nearly as large as the State of Missouri, lying immediately west of Arkansas and south of the Missouri Compromise line, and that we never attempted to prohibit slavery as to it. I wish particular attention to this. It adjoins the original Missouri Compromise line by its northern boundary, and consequently is part of the country into which by implication slavery was permitted to go by that compromise. There it has lain open ever s, and there it still lies, and yet no effort has been made at any time to wrest it from the South. In all our struggles to prohibit slavery within our Mexican acquisitions, we never so much as lifted a finger to prohibit it as to this tract. Is not this entirely conclusive that at all times we have held the Missouri Compromise as a sacred thing, even when against ourselves as well as when for us?

Senator Douglas sometimes says the Missouri line itself was in principle only an extension of the line of the Ordinance of '87—that is to say, an extension of the Ohio River. I think this is weak enough on its face. I will remark, however, that, as a glance at the map will show, the Missouri line is a long way farther south than the Ohio, and that if our Senator in proposing his extension had stuck to the principle of jogging southward, perhaps it might not have been voted down so readily.

But next it is said that the compromises of '50, and the ratification of them by both political parties in '52, established a new principle which required the repeal of the Missouri Compromise. This again I deny. I deny it, and demand the proof. I have already stated fully what the compromises of '50 are. That particular part of those measures from which the virtual repeal of the Missouri Compromise is sought to be inferred (for it is admitted they contain nothing about it in express terms) is the provision in the Utah and New Mexico laws which permits them when they seek admission into the Union as States to come in with or without slavery, as they shall then see fit. Now I insist this provision was made for Utah and New Mexico, and for no other place whatever. It had no more direct reference to Nebraska than it had to the territories of the moon. But, say they, it had reference to Nebraska in principle. Let us see. The North consented to this provision, not because they considered it right in itself, but because they were compensated—paid for it.

They at the same time got California into the Union as a free State. This was far the best part of all they had struggled for by the Wilmot Proviso. They also got the area of slavery somewhat narrowed in the settlement of the boundary of Texas. Also they got the slave trade abolished in the District of Columbia.

For all these desirable objects the North could afford to yield something; and they did yield to the South the Utah and New Mexico provision. I do not mean that the whole North, or even a majority, yielded, when the law passed; but enough yielded—when added to the vote of the South, to carry the measure. Nor can it be pretended that the principle of this arrangement requires us to permit the same provision to be applied to Nebraska, without any equivalent at all. Give us another free State; press the boundary of Texas still farther back; give us another step toward the destruction of slavery in the District, and you present us a similar case. But ask us not to repeat, for nothing, what you paid for in the first instance. If you wish the thing again, pay again. That is the principle of the compromises of '50, if, indeed, they had any principles beyond their specific terms—it was the system of equivalents.

Again, if Congress, at that time, intended that all future Territories should, when admitted as States, come in with or without slavery at their own option, why did it not say so? With such a universal provision, all know the bills could not have passed. Did they, then—could they-establish a principle contrary to their own intention? Still further, if they intended to establish the principle that, whenever Congress had control, it should be left to the people to do as they thought fit with slavery, why did they not authorize the people of the District of Columbia, at their option, to abolish slavery within their limits?

I personally know that this has not been left undone because it was unthought of. It was frequently spoken of by members of Congress, and by citizens of Washington, six years ago; and I heard no one express a doubt that a system of gradual emancipation, with compensation to owners, would meet the approbation of a large majority of the white people of the District. But without the action of Congress they could say nothing; and Congress said "No." In the measures of 1850, Congress had the subject of slavery in the District expressly on hand. If they were then establishing the principle of allowing the people to do as they please with slavery, why did they not apply the principle to that people?

Again it is claimed that by the resolutions of the Illinois Legislature, passed in 1851, the repeal of the Missouri Compromise was demanded. This I deny also. Whatever may be worked out by a criticism of the language of those resolutions, the people have never understood them as being any more than an indorsement of the compromises of 1850, and a release of our senators from voting for the Wilmot Proviso. The whole people are living witnesses that this only was their view. Finally, it is asked, "If we did not mean to apply the Utah and New Mexico provision to all future territories, what did we mean when we, in 1852, indorsed the compromises of 1850?"

For myself I can answer this question most easily. I meant not to ask a repeal or modification of the Fugitive Slave law. I meant not to ask for the abolition of slavery in the District of Columbia. I meant not to resist the admission of Utah and New Mexico, even should they ask to come in as slave States. I meant nothing about additional Territories, because, as I understood, we then had no Territory whose character as to slavery was not already settled. As to Nebraska, I regarded its character as being fixed by the Missouri Compromise for thirty years—as unalterably fixed as that of my own home in Illinois. As to new acquisitions, I said, "Sufficient unto the day is the evil thereof." When we make new acquisitions, we will, as heretofore, try to manage them somehow. That is my answer; that is what I meant and said; and I appeal to the people to say each for himself whether that is not also the universal meaning of the free States.

And now, in turn, let me ask a few questions. If, by any or all these matters, the repeal of the Missouri Compromise was commanded, why was not the command sooner obeyed? Why was the repeal omitted in the Nebraska Bill of 1853? Why was it omitted in the original bill of 1854? Why in the accompanying report was such a repeal characterized as a departure from the course pursued in 1850 and its continued omission recommended?

I am aware Judge Douglas now argues that the subsequent express repeal is no substantial alteration of the bill. This argument seems wonderful to me. It is as if one should argue that white and black are not different. He admits, however, that there is a literal change in the bill, and that he made the change in deference to other senators who would not support the bill without. This proves that those other senators thought the change a substantial one, and that the Judge thought their opinions worth deferring to. His own opinions, therefore, seem not to rest on a very firm basis, even in his own mind; and I suppose the world believes, and will continue to believe, that precisely on the substance of that change this whole agitation has arisen.

I conclude, then, that the public never demanded the repeal of the Missouri Compromise.

I now come to consider whether the appeal with its avowed principles, is intrinsically right. I insist that it is not. Take the particular case. A controversy had arisen between the advocates and opponents of slavery, in relation to its establishment within the country we had purchased of France. The southern, and then best, part of the purchase was already in as a slave State. The controversy was settled by also letting Missouri in as a slave State; but with the agreement that within all the remaining part of the purchase, north of a certain line, there should never be slavery. As to what was to be done with the remaining part, south of the line, nothing was said; but perhaps the fair implication was, it should come in with slavery if it should so choose. The southern part, except a portion heretofore mentioned, afterward did come in with slavery, as the State of Arkansas. All these many years, since 1820, the northern part had remained a wilderness. At length settlements began in it also. In due course Iowa came in as a free State, and Minnesota was given a territorial government, without removing the slavery restriction. Finally, the sole remaining part north of the line—Kansas and Nebraska—was to be organized; and it is proposed, and carried, to blot out the old dividing line of thirty-four years' standing, and to open the whole of that country to the introduction of slavery. Now this, to my mind, is manifestly unjust. After an angry and dangerous controversy, the parties made friends by dividing the bone of contention. The one party first appropriates her own share, beyond all power to be disturbed in the possession of it, and then seizes the share of the other party. It is as if two starving men had divided their only loaf, the one had hastily swallowed his half, and then grabbed the other's half just as he was putting it to his mouth.

Let me here drop the main argument, to notice what I consider rather an inferior matter. It is argued that slavery will not go to Kansas and Nebraska, in any event. This is a palliation, a lullaby. I have some hope that it will not; but let us not be too confident. As to climate, a glance at the map shows that there are five slave States—Delaware, Maryland, Virginia, Kentucky, and Missouri, and also the District of Columbia, all north of the Missouri Compromise line. The census returns of 1850 show that within these there are eight hundred and sixty-seven thousand two hundred and seventy-six slaves, being more than one fourth of all the slaves in the nation.

It is not climate, then, that will keep slavery out of these Territories. Is there anything in the peculiar nature of the country? Missouri adjoins these Territories by her entire western boundary, and slavery is already within every one of her western counties. I have even heard it said that there are more slaves in proportion to whites in the northwestern county of Missouri than within any other county in the State. Slavery pressed entirely up to the old western boundary of the State, and when rather recently a part of that boundary at the northwest was moved out a little farther west, slavery followed on quite up to the new line. Now, when the restriction is removed, what is to prevent it from going still farther? Climate will not, no peculiarity of the country will, nothing in nature will. Will the disposition of the people prevent it? Those nearest the scene are all in favor of the extension. The Yankees who are opposed to it may be most flumerous; but, in military phrase, the battlefield is too far from their base of operations.

But it is said there now is no law in Nebraska on the subject of slavery, and that, in such case, taking a slave there operates his freedom. That is good book-law, but it is not the rule of actual practice. Wherever slavery is it has been first introduced without law. The oldest laws we find concerning it are not laws introducing it, but regulating it as an already existing thing. A white man takes his slave to Nebraska now. Who will inform the negro that he is free? Who will take him before court to test the question of his freedom? In ignorance of his legal emancipation he is kept chopping, splitting, and plowing. Others are brought, and move on in the same track. At last, if ever the time for voting comes on the question of slavery the institution already, in fact, exists in the country, and cannot well be removed. The fact of its presence, and the difficulty of its removal, will carry the vote in its favor. Keep it out until a vote is taken, and a vote in favor of it cannot be got in any population of forty thousand on earth, who have been drawn together by the ordinary motives of emigration and settlement. To get slaves into the Territory simultaneously with the whites in the incipient stages of settlement is the precise stake played for and won in this Nebraska measure.

The question is asked us: "If slaves will go in notwithstanding the general principle of law liberates them, why would they not equally go in against positive statute law—go in, even if the Missouri restriction were maintained!" I answer, because it takes a much bolder man to venture in with his property in the latter case than in the former; because the positive Congressional enactment is known to and respected by all, or nearly all, whereas the negative principle that no law is free law is not much known except among lawyers. We have some experience of this practical difference. In spite of the Ordinance of '87, a few negroes were brought into Illinois, and held in a state of quasi-slavery, not enough, however, to carry a vote of the people in favor of the institution when they came to form a constitution. But into the adjoining Missouri country, where there was no Ordinance of '87,—was no restriction,—they were carried ten times, nay, a hundred times, as fast, and actually made a slave State. This is fact-naked fact.

Another lullaby argument is that taking slaves to new countries does not increase their number, does not make any one slave who would otherwise be free. There is some truth in this, and I am glad of it; but it is not wholly true. The African slave trade is not yet effectually suppressed; and, if we make a reasonable deduction for the white people among us who are foreigners and the descendants of foreigners arriving here since 1808, we shall find the increase of the black population outrunning that of the white to an extent unaccountable, except by supposing that some of them, too, have been coming from Africa. If this be so, the opening of new countries to the institution increases the demand for and augments the price of slaves, and so does, in fact, make slaves of freemen, by causing them to be brought from Africa and sold into bondage.

But however this may be, we know the opening of new countries to slavery tends to the perpetuation of the institution, and so does keep men in slavery who would otherwise be free. This result we do not feel like favoring, and we are under no legal obligation to suppress our feelings in this respect.

Equal justice to the South, it is said, requires us to consent to the extension of slavery to new countries. That is to say, inasmuch as you do not object to my taking my hog to Nebraska, therefore I must not object to your taking your slave. Now, I admit that this is perfectly logical if there is no difference between hogs and negroes. But while you thus require me to deny the humanity of the negro, I wish to ask whether you of the South, yourselves, have ever been willing to do as much? It is kindly provided that of all those who come into the world only a small percentage are natural tyrants. That percentage is no larger in the slave States than in the free. The great majority South, as well as North, have human sympathies, of which they can no more divest themselves than they can of their sensibility to physical pain. These sympathies in the bosoms of the Southern people manifest, in many ways, their sense of the wrong of slavery, and their consciousness that, after all, there is humanity in the negro. If they deny this, let me address them a few plain questions. In 1820 you (the South) joined the North, almost unanimously, in declaring the African slave trade piracy, and in annexing to it the punishment of death. Why did you do this? If you did not feel that it was wrong, why did you join in providing that men should be hung for it? The practice was no more than bringing wild negroes from Africa to such as would buy them. But you never thought of hanging men for catching and selling wild horses, wild buffaloes, or wild bears.

Again, you have among you a sneaking individual of the class of native tyrants known as the "slavedealer." He watches your necessities, and crawls up to buy your slave, at a speculating price. If you cannot help it, you sell to him; but if you can help it, you drive him from your door. You despise him utterly. You do not recognize him as a friend, or even as an honest man. Your children must not play with his; they may rollick freely with the little negroes, but not with the slave-dealer's children. If you are obliged to deal with him, you try to get through the job without so much as touching him. It is common with you to join hands with the men you meet, but with the slave-dealer you avoid the ceremony—instinctively shrinking from the snaky contact. If he grows rich and retires from business, you still remember him, and still keep up the ban of non-intercourse upon him and his family. Now, why is this? You do not so treat the man who deals in corn, cotton, or tobacco.

And yet again: There are in the United States and Territories, including the District of Columbia, 433,643 free blacks. At five hundred dollars per head they are worth over two hundred millions of dollars. How comes this vast amount of property to be running about without owners? We do not see free horses or free cattle running at large. How is this? All these free blacks are the descendants of slaves, or have been slaves themselves; and they would be slaves now but for something which has operated on their white owners, inducing them at vast pecuniary sacrifice to liberate them. What is that something? Is there any mistaking it? In all these cases it is your sense of justice and human sympathy continually telling you that the poor negro has some natural right to himself—that those who deny it and make mere merchandise of him deserve kickings, contempt, and death.

And now why will you ask us to deny the humanity of the slave, and estimate him as only the equal of the hog? Why ask us to do what you will not do yourselves? Why ask us to do for nothing what two hundred millions of dollars could not induce you to do?

But one great argument in support of the repeal of the Missouri Compromise is still to come. That argument is "the sacred right of self-government." It seems our distinguished Senator has found great difficulty in getting his antagonists, even in the Senate, to meet him fairly on this argument. Some poet has said:

"Fools rush in where angels fear to tread."

At the hazard of being thought one of the fools of this quotation, I meet that argument—I rush in—I take that bull by the horns. I trust I understand and truly estimate the right of self-government. My faith in the proposition that each man should do precisely as he pleases with all which is exclusively his own lies at the foundation of the sense of justice there is in me. I extend the principle to communities of men as well as to individuals. I so extend it because it is politically wise, as well as naturally just; politically wise in saving us from broils about matters which do not concern us. Here, or at Washington, I would not trouble myself with the oyster laws of Virginia, or the cranberry laws of Indiana. The doctrine of self-government is right,—absolutely and eternally right,—but it has no just application as here attempted. Or perhaps I should rather say that whether it has such application depends upon whether a negro is or is not a man. If he is not a man, in that case he who is a man may as a matter of self-government do just what he pleases with him. But if the negro is a man, is it not to that extent a total destruction of self-government to say that he too shall not govern himself? When the white man governs himself, that is self-government; but when he governs himself and also governs another man, that is more than self-government—that is despotism. If the negro is a man, why, then, my ancient faith teaches me that "all men are created equal," and that there can be no moral right in connection with one man's making a slave of another.

Judge Douglas frequently, with bitter irony and sarcasm, paraphrases our argument by saying: "The white people of Nebraska are good enough to govern themselves, but they are not good enough to govern a few miserable negroes!"

Well, I doubt not that the people of Nebraska are and will continue to be as good as the average of people elsewhere. I do not say the contrary. What I do say is that no man is good enough to govern another man without that other's consent. I say this is the leading principle, the sheet-anchor of American republicanism. Our Declaration of Independence says:

"We hold these truths to be self-evident: That all men are created equal; that they are endowed by their Creator with certain inalienable rights; that among these are life, liberty, and the pursuit of happiness. That to secure these rights, governments are instituted among men, DERIVING THEIR JUST POWERS PROM THE CONSENT OF THE GOVERNED."

I have quoted so much at this time merely to show that, according to our ancient faith, the just powers of government are derived from the consent of the governed. Now the relation of master and slave is pro tanto a total violation of this principle. The master not only governs the slave without his consent, but he governs him by a set of rules altogether different from those which he prescribes for himself. Allow all the governed an equal voice in the government, and that, and that only, is self-government.

Let it not be said that I am contending for the establishment of political and social equality between the whites and blacks. I have already said the contrary. I am not combating the argument of necessity, arising from the fact that the blacks are already among us; but I am combating what is set up as moral argument for allowing them to be taken where they have never yet been—arguing against the extension of a bad thing, which, where it already exists, we must of necessity manage as we best can.

In support of his application of the doctrine of self-government, Senator Douglas has sought to bring to his aid the opinions and examples of our Revolutionary fathers. I am glad he has done this. I love the sentiments of those old-time men, and shall be most happy to abide by their opinions. He shows us that when it was in contemplation for the colonies to break off from Great Britain, and set up a new government for themselves, several of the States instructed their delegates to go for the measure, provided each State should be allowed to regulate its domestic concerns in its own way. I do not quote; but this in substance. This was right; I see nothing objectionable in it. I also think it probable that it had some reference to the existence of slavery among them. I will not deny that it had. But had it any reference to the carrying of slavery into new countries? That is the question, and we will let the fathers themselves answer it.

This same generation of men, and mostly the same individuals of the generation who declared this principle, who declared independence, who fought the war of the Revolution through, who afterward made the Constitution under which we still live—these same men passed the Ordinance of '87, declaring that slavery should never go to the Northwest Territory.

I have no doubt Judge Douglas thinks they were very inconsistent in this. It is a question of discrimination between them and him. But there is not an inch of ground left for his claiming that their opinions, their example, their authority, are on his side in the controversy.

Again, is not Nebraska, while a Territory, a part of us? Do we not own the country? And if we surrender the control of it, do we not surrender the right of self-government? It is part of ourselves. If you say we shall not control it, because it is only part, the same is true of every other part; and when all the parts are gone, what has become of the whole? What is then left of us? What use for the General Government, when there is nothing left for it to govern?

But you say this question should be left to the people of Nebraska, because they are more particularly interested. If this be the rule, you must leave it to each individual to say for himself whether he will have slaves. What better moral right have thirty-one citizens of Nebraska to say that the thirty-second shall not hold slaves than the people of the thirty-one States have to say that slavery shall not go into the thirty-second State at all?

But if it is a sacred right for the people of Nebraska to take and hold slaves there, it is equally their sacred right to buy them where they can buy them cheapest; and that, undoubtedly, will be on the coast of Africa, provided you will consent not to hang them for going there to buy them. You must remove this restriction, too, from the sacred right of self-government. I am aware you say that taking slaves from the States to Nebraska does not make slaves of freemen; but the African slave-trader can say just as much. He does not catch free negroes and bring them here. He finds them already slaves in the hands of their black captors, and he honestly buys them at the rate of a red cotton handkerchief a head. This is very cheap, and it is a great abridgment of the sacred right of self-government to hang men for engaging in this profitable trade.

Another important objection to this application of the right of self-government is that it enables the first few to deprive the succeeding many of a free exercise of the right of self-government. The first few may get slavery in, and the subsequent many cannot easily get it out. How common is the remark now in the slave States, "If we were only clear of our slaves, how much better it would be for us." They are actually deprived of the privilege of governing themselves as they would, by the action of a very few in the beginning. The same thing was true of the whole nation at the time our Constitution was formed.

Whether slavery shall go into Nebraska, or other new Territories, is not a matter of exclusive concern to the people who may go there. The whole nation is interested that the best use shall be made of these Territories. We want them for homes of free white people. This they cannot be, to any considerable extent, if slavery shall be planted within them. Slave States are places for poor white people to remove from, not to remove to. New free States are the places for poor people to go to, and better their condition. For this use the nation needs these Territories.

Still further: there are constitutional relations between the slave and free States which are degrading to the latter. We are under legal obligations to catch and return their runaway slaves to them: a sort of dirty, disagreeable job, which, I believe, as a general rule, the slaveholders will not perform for one another. Then again, in the control of the government—the management of the partnership affairs—they have greatly the advantage of us. By the Constitution each State has two senators, each has a number of representatives in proportion to the number of its people, and each has a number of Presidential electors equal to the whole number of its senators and representatives together. But in ascertaining the number of the people for this purpose, five slaves are counted as being equal to three whites. The slaves do not vote; they are only counted and so used as to swell the influence of the white people's votes. The practical effect of this is more aptly shown by a comparison of the States of South Carolina and Maine. South Carolina has six representatives, and so has Maine; South Carolina has eight Presidential electors, and so has Maine. This is precise equality so far; and of course they are equal in senators, each having two. Thus in the control of the government the two States are equals precisely. But how are they in the number of their white people? Maine has 581,813, while South Carolina has 274,567; Maine has twice as many as South Carolina, and 32,679 over. Thus, each white man in South Carolina is more than the double of any man in Maine. This is all because South Carolina, besides her free people, has 384,984 slaves. The South Carolinian has precisely the same advantage over the white man in every other free State as well as in Maine. He is more than the double of any one of us in this crowd. The same advantage, but not to the same extent, is held by all the citizens of the slave States over those of the free; and it is an absolute truth, without an exception, that there is no voter in any slave State but who has more legal power in the government than any voter in any free State. There is no instance of exact equality; and the disadvantage is against us the whole chapter through. This principle, in the aggregate, gives the slave States in the present Congress twenty additional representatives, being seven more than the whole majority by which they passed the Nebraska Bill.

Now all this is manifestly unfair; yet I do not mention it to complain of it, in so far as it is already settled. It is in the Constitution, and I do not for that cause, or any other cause, propose to destroy, or alter, or disregard the Constitution. I stand to it, fairly, fully, and firmly.

But when I am told I must leave it altogether to other people to say whether new partners are to be bred up and brought into the firm, on the same degrading terms against me, I respectfully demur. I insist that whether I shall be a whole man or only the half of one, in comparison with others is a question in which I am somewhat concerned, and one which no other man can have a sacred right of deciding for me. If I am wrong in this, if it really be a sacred right of self-government in the man who shall go to Nebraska to decide whether he will be the equal of me or the double of me, then, after he shall have exercised that right, and thereby shall have reduced me to a still smaller fraction of a man than I already am, I should like for some gentleman, deeply skilled in the mysteries of sacred rights, to provide himself with a microscope, and peep about, and find out, if he can, what has become of my sacred rights. They will surely be too small for detection with the naked eye.

Finally, I insist that if there is anything which it is the duty of the whole people to never intrust to any hands but their own, that thing is the preservation and perpetuity of their own liberties and institutions. And if they shall think as I do, that the extension of slavery endangers them more than any or all other causes, how recreant to themselves if they submit The question, and with it the fate of their country, to a mere handful of men bent only on self-interest. If this question of slavery extension were an insignificant one, one having no power to do harm—it might be shuffled aside in this way; and being, as it is, the great Behemoth of danger, shall the strong grip of the nation be loosened upon him, to intrust him to the hands of such feeble keepers?

I have done with this mighty argument of self-government. Go, sacred thing! Go in peace.

But Nebraska is urged as a great Union-saving measure. Well, I too go for saving the Union. Much as I hate slavery, I would consent to the extension of it rather than see the Union dissolved, just as I would consent to any great evil to avoid a greater one. But when I go to Union-saving, I must believe, at least, that the means I employ have some adaptation to the end. To my mind, Nebraska has no such adaptation.

"It hath no relish of salvation in it."

It is an aggravation, rather, of the only one thing which ever endangers the Union. When it came upon us, all was peace and quiet. The nation was looking to the forming of new bends of union, and a long course of peace and prosperity seemed to lie before us. In the whole range of possibility, there scarcely appears to me to have been anything out of which the slavery agitation could have been revived, except the very project of repealing the Missouri Compromise. Every inch of territory we owned already had a definite settlement of the slavery question, by which all parties were pledged to abide. Indeed, there was no uninhabited country on the continent which we could acquire, if we except some extreme northern regions which are wholly out of the question.

In this state of affairs the Genius of Discord himself could scarcely have invented a way of again setting us by the ears but by turning back and destroying the peace measures of the past. The counsels of that Genius seem to have prevailed. The Missouri Compromise was repealed; and here we are in the midst of a new slavery agitation, such, I think, as we have never seen before. Who is responsible for this? Is it those who resist the measure, or those who causelessly brought it forward, and pressed it through, having reason to know, and in fact knowing, it must and would be so resisted? It could not but be expected by its author that it would be looked upon as a measure for the extension of slavery, aggravated by a gross breach of faith.

Argue as you will and long as you will, this is the naked front and aspect of the measure. And in this aspect it could not but produce agitation. Slavery is founded in the selfishness of man's nature—opposition to it in his love of justice. These principles are at eternal antagonism, and when brought into collision so fiercely as slavery extension brings them, shocks and throes and convulsions must ceaselessly follow. Repeal the Missouri Compromise, repeal all compromises, repeal the Declaration of Independence, repeal all past history, you still cannot repeal human nature. It still will be the abundance of man's heart that slavery extension is wrong, and out of the abundance of his heart his mouth will continue to speak.

The structure, too, of the Nebraska Bill is very peculiar. The people are to decide the question of slavery for themselves; but when they are to decide, or how they are to decide, or whether, when the question is once decided, it is to remain so or is to be subject to an indefinite succession of new trials, the law does not say. Is it to be decided by the first dozen settlers who arrive there, or is it to await the arrival of a hundred? Is it to be decided by a vote of the people or a vote of the Legislature, or, indeed, by a vote of any sort? To these questions the law gives no answer. There is a mystery about this; for when a member proposed to give the Legislature express authority to exclude slavery, it was hooted down by the friends of the bill. This fact is worth remembering. Some Yankees in the East are sending emigrants to Nebraska to exclude slavery from it; and, so far as I can judge, they expect the question to be decided by voting in some way or other. But the Missourians are awake, too. They are within a stone's-throw of the contested ground. They hold meetings and pass resolutions, in which not the slightest allusion to voting is made. They resolve that slavery already exists in the Territory; that more shall go there; that they, remaining in Missouri, will protect it, and that abolitionists shall be hung or driven away. Through all this bowie knives and six-shooters are seen plainly enough, but never a glimpse of the ballot-box.

And, really, what is the result of all this? Each party within having numerous and determined backers without, is it not probable that the contest will come to blows and bloodshed? Could there be a more apt invention to bring about collision and violence on the slavery question than this Nebraska project is? I do not charge or believe that such was intended by Congress; but if they had literally formed a ring and placed champions within it to fight out the controversy, the fight could be no more likely to come off than it is. And if this fight should begin, is it likely to take a very peaceful, Union-saving turn? Will not the first drop of blood so shed be the real knell of the Union?

The Missouri Compromise ought to be restored. For the sake of the Union, it ought to be restored. We ought to elect a House of Representatives which will vote its restoration. If by any means we omit to do this, what follows? Slavery may or may not be established in Nebraska. But whether it be or not, we shall have repudiated—discarded from the councils of the nation—the spirit of compromise; for who, after this, will ever trust in a national compromise? The spirit of mutual concession—that spirit which first gave us the Constitution, and which has thrice saved the Union— we shall have strangled and cast from us forever. And what shall we have in lieu of it? The South flushed with triumph and tempted to excess; the North, betrayed as they believe, brooding on wrong and burning for revenge. One side will provoke, the other resent. The one will taunt, the other defy; one aggresses, the other retaliates. Already a few in the North defy all constitutional restraints, resist the execution of the Fugitive Slave law, and even menace the institution of slavery in the States where it exists. Already a few in the South claim the constitutional right to take and to hold slaves in the free States, demand the revival of the slave trade, and demand a treaty with Great Britain by which fugitive slaves may be reclaimed from Canada. As yet they are but few on either side. It is a grave question for lovers of the union whether the final destruction of the Missouri Compromise, and with it the spirit of all compromise, will or will not embolden and embitter each of these, and fatally increase the number of both.

But restore the compromise, and what then? We thereby restore the national faith, the national confidence, the national feeling of brotherhood. We thereby reinstate the spirit of concession and compromise, that spirit which has never failed us in past perils, and which may be safely trusted for all the future. The South ought to join in doing this. The peace of the nation is as dear to them as to us. In memories of the past and hopes of the future, they share as largely as we. It would be on their part a great act—great in its spirit, and great in its effect. It would be worth to the nation a hundred years purchase of peace and prosperity. And what of sacrifice would they make? They only surrender to us what they gave us for a consideration long, long ago; what they have not now asked for, struggled or cared for; what has been thrust upon them, not less to their astonishment than to ours.

But it is said we cannot restore it; that though we elect every member of the lower House, the Senate is still against us. It is quite true that of the senators who passed the Nebraska Bill a majority of the whole Senate will retain their seats in spite of the elections of this and the next year. But if at these elections their several constituencies shall clearly express their will against Nebraska, will these senators disregard their will? Will they neither obey nor make room for those who will?

But even if we fail to technically restore the compromise, it is still a great point to carry a popular vote in favor of the restoration. The moral weight of such a vote cannot be estimated too highly. The authors of Nebraska are not at all satisfied with the destruction of the compromise—an indorsement of this principle they proclaim to be the great object. With them, Nebraska alone is a small matter—to establish a principle for future use is what they particularly desire.

The future use is to be the planting of slavery wherever in the wide world local and unorganized opposition cannot prevent it. Now, if you wish to give them this indorsement, if you wish to establish this principle, do so. I shall regret it, but it is your right. On the contrary, if you are opposed to the principle,—intend to give it no such indorsement, let no wheedling, no sophistry, divert you from throwing a direct vote against it.

Some men, mostly Whigs, who condemn the repeal of the Missouri Compromise, nevertheless hesitate to go for its restoration, lest they be thrown in company with the abolitionists. Will they allow me, as an old Whig, to tell them, good-humoredly, that I think this is very silly? Stand with anybody that stands right. Stand with him while he is right, and part with him when he goes wrong. Stand with the abolitionist in restoring the Missouri Compromise, and stand against him when he attempts to repeal the Fugitive Slave law. In the latter case you stand with the Southern disunionist. What of that? You are still right. In both cases you are right. In both cases you oppose the dangerous extremes. In both you stand on middle ground, and hold the ship level and steady. In both you are national, and nothing less than national. This is the good old Whig ground. To desert such ground because of any company is to be less than a Whig—less than a man—less than an American.

I particularly object to the new position which the avowed principle of this Nebraska law gives to slavery in the body politic. I object to it because it assumes that there can be moral right in the enslaving of one man by another. I object to it as a dangerous dalliance for a free people—a sad evidence that, feeling prosperity, we forget right; that liberty, as a principle, we have ceased to revere. I object to it because the fathers of the republic eschewed and rejected it. The argument of "necessity" was the only argument they ever admitted in favor of slavery; and so far, and so far only, as it carried them did they ever go. They found the institution existing among us, which they could not help, and they cast blame upon the British king for having permitted its introduction.

The royally appointed Governor of Georgia in the early 1700's was threatened by the King with removal if he continued to oppose slavery in his colony—at that time the King of England made a small profit on every slave imported to the colonies. The later British criticism of the United States for not eradicating slavery in the early 1800's, combined with their tacit support of the 'Confederacy' during the Civil War is a prime example of the irony and hypocrisy of politics: that self-interest will ever overpower right.

Before the Constitution they prohibited its introduction into the Northwestern Territory, the only country we owned then free from it. At the framing and adoption of the Constitution, they forbore to so much as mention the word "slave" or "slavery" in the whole instrument. In the provision for the recovery of fugitives, the slave is spoken of as a "person held to service or labor." In that prohibiting the abolition of the African slave trade for twenty years, that trade is spoken of as "the migration or importation of such persons as any of the States now existing shall think proper to admit," etc. These are the only provisions alluding to slavery. Thus the thing is hid away in the Constitution, just as an afflicted man hides away a wen or cancer which he dares not cut out at once, lest he bleed to death,—with the promise, nevertheless, that the cutting may begin at a certain time. Less than this our fathers could not do, and more they would not do. Necessity drove them so far, and farther they would not go. But this is not all. The earliest Congress under the Constitution took the same view of slavery. They hedged and hemmed it in to the narrowest limits of necessity.

In 1794 they prohibited an outgoing slave trade—that is, the taking of slaves from the United States to sell. In 1798 they prohibited the bringing of slaves from Africa into the Mississippi Territory, this Territory then comprising what are now the States of Mississippi and Alabama. This was ten years before they had the authority to do the same thing as to the States existing at the adoption of the Constitution. In 1800 they prohibited American citizens from trading in slaves between foreign countries, as, for instance, from Africa to Brazil. In 1803 they passed a law in aid of one or two slave-State laws in restraint of the internal slave trade. In 1807, in apparent hot haste, they passed the law, nearly a year in advance,—to take effect the first day of 1808, the very first day the Constitution would permit, prohibiting the African slave trade by heavy pecuniary and corporal penalties. In 1820, finding these provisions ineffectual, they declared the slave trade piracy, and annexed to it the extreme penalty of death. While all this was passing in the General Government, five or six of the original slave States had adopted systems of gradual emancipation, by which the institution was rapidly becoming extinct within their limits. Thus we see that the plain, unmistakable spirit of that age toward slavery was hostility to the principle and toleration only by necessity.

But now it is to be transformed into a "sacred right." Nebraska brings it forth, places it on the highroad to extension and perpetuity, and with a pat on its back says to it, "Go, and God speed you." Henceforth it is to be the chief jewel of the nation the very figure-head of the ship of state. Little by little, but steadily as man's march to the grave, we have been giving up the old for the new faith. Near eighty years ago we began by declaring that all men are created equal; but now from that beginning we have run down to the other declaration, that for some men to enslave others is a "sacred right of self-government." These principles cannot stand together. They are as opposite as God and Mammon; and who ever holds to the one must despise the other. When Pettit, in connection with his support of the Nebraska Bill, called the Declaration of Independence "a self-evident lie," he only did what consistency and candor require all other Nebraska men to do. Of the forty-odd Nebraska senators who sat present and heard him, no one rebuked him. Nor am I apprised that any Nebraska newspaper, or any Nebraska orator, in the whole nation has ever yet rebuked him. If this had been said among Marion's men, Southerners though they were, what would have become of the man who said it? If this had been said to the men who captured Andre, the man who said it would probably have been hung sooner than Andre was. If it had been said in old Independence Hall seventy-eight years ago, the very doorkeeper would have throttled the man and thrust him into the street. Let no one be deceived. The spirit of seventy-six and the spirit of Nebraska are utter antagonisms; and the former is being rapidly displaced by the latter.

Fellow-countrymen, Americans, South as well as North, shall we make no effort to arrest this? Already the liberal party throughout the world express the apprehension that "the one retrograde institution in America is undermining the principles of progress, and fatally violating the noblest political system the world ever saw." This is not the taunt of enemies, but the warning of friends. Is it quite safe to disregard it—to despise it? Is there no danger to liberty itself in discarding the earliest practice and first precept of our ancient faith? In our greedy chase to make profit of the negro, let us beware lest we "cancel and tear in pieces" even the white man's charter of freedom.

Our republican robe is soiled and trailed in the dust. Let us repurify it. Let us turn and wash it white in the spirit, if not the blood, of the Revolution. Let us turn slavery from its claims of "moral right," back upon its existing legal rights and its arguments of "necessity." Let us return it to the position our fathers gave it, and there let it rest in peace. Let us readopt the Declaration of Independence, and with it the practices and policy which harmonize with it. Let North and South, let all Americans—let all lovers of liberty everywhere join in the great and good work. If we do this, we shall not only have saved the Union, but we shall have so saved it as to make and to keep it forever worthy of the saving. We shall have so saved it that the succeeding millions of free happy people the world over shall rise up and call us blessed to the latest generations.

At Springfield, twelve days ago, where I had spoken substantially as I have here, Judge Douglas replied to me; and as he is to reply to me here, I shall attempt to anticipate him by noticing some of the points he made there. He commenced by stating I had assumed all the way through that the principle of the Nebraska Bill would have the effect of extending slavery. He denied that this was intended or that this effect would follow.

I will not reopen the argument upon this point. That such was the intention the world believed at the start, and will continue to believe. This was the countenance of the thing, and both friends and enemies instantly recognized it as such. That countenance cannot now be changed by argument. You can as easily argue the color out of the negro's skin. Like the "bloody hand," you may wash it and wash it, the red witness of guilt still sticks and stares horribly at you.

Next he says that Congressional intervention never prevented slavery anywhere; that it did not prevent it in the Northwestern Territory, nor in Illinois; that, in fact, Illinois came into the Union as a slave State; that the principle of the Nebraska Bill expelled it from Illinois, from several old States, from everywhere.

Now this is mere quibbling all the way through. If the Ordinance of '87 did not keep slavery out of the Northwest Territory, how happens it that the northwest shore of the Ohio River is entirely free from it, while the southeast shore, less than a mile distant, along nearly the whole length of the river, is entirely covered with it?

If that ordinance did not keep it out of Illinois, what was it that made the difference between Illinois and Missouri? They lie side by side, the Mississippi River only dividing them, while their early settlements were within the same latitude. Between 1810 and 1820 the number of slaves in Missouri increased 7211, while in Illinois in the same ten years they decreased 51. This appears by the census returns. During nearly all of that ten years both were Territories, not States. During this time the ordinance forbade slavery to go into Illinois, and nothing forbade it to go into Missouri. It did go into Missouri, and did not go into Illinois. That is the fact. Can any one doubt as to the reason of it? But he says Illinois came into the Union as a slave State. Silence, perhaps, would be the best answer to this flat contradiction of the known history of the country. What are the facts upon which this bold assertion is based? When we first acquired the country, as far back as 1787, there were some slaves within it held by the French inhabitants of Kaskaskia. The territorial legislation admitted a few negroes from the slave States as indentured servants. One year after the adoption of the first State constitution, the whole number of them was—what do you think? Just one hundred and seventeen, while the aggregate free population was 55,094,—about four hundred and seventy to one. Upon this state of facts the people framed their constitution prohibiting the further introduction of slavery, with a sort of guaranty to the owners of the few indentured servants, giving freedom to their children to be born thereafter, and making no mention whatever of any supposed slave for life. Out of this small matter the Judge manufactures his argument that Illinois came into the Union as a slave State. Let the facts be the answer to the argument.

The principles of the Nebraska Bill, he says, expelled slavery from Illinois. The principle of that bill first planted it here—that is, it first came because there was no law to prevent it, first came before we owned the country; and finding it here, and having the Ordinance of '87 to prevent its increasing, our people struggled along, and finally got rid of it as best they could.

But the principle of the Nebraska Bill abolished slavery in several of the old States. Well, it is true that several of the old States, in the last quarter of the last century, did adopt systems of gradual emancipation by which the institution has finally become extinct within their limits; but it may or may not be true that the principle of the Nebraska Bill was the cause that led to the adoption of these measures. It is now more than fifty years since the last of these States adopted its system of emancipation.

If the Nebraska Bill is the real author of the benevolent works, it is rather deplorable that it has for so long a time ceased working altogether. Is there not some reason to suspect that it was the principle of the Revolution, and not the principle of the Nebraska Bill, that led to emancipation in these old States? Leave it to the people of these old emancipating States, and I am quite certain they will decide that neither that nor any other good thing ever did or ever will come of the Nebraska Bill.

In the course of my main argument, Judge Douglas interrupted me to say that the principle of the Nebraska Bill was very old; that it originated when God made man, and placed good and evil before him, allowing him to choose for himself, being responsible for the choice he should make. At the time I thought this was merely playful, and I answered it accordingly. But in his reply to me he renewed it as a serious argument. In seriousness, then, the facts of this proposition are not true as stated. God did not place good and evil before man, telling him to make his choice. On the contrary, he did tell him there was one tree of the fruit of which he should not eat, upon pain of certain death. I should scarcely wish so strong a prohibition against slavery in Nebraska.

But this argument strikes me as not a little remarkable in another particular—in its strong resemblance to the old argument for the "divine right of kings." By the latter, the king is to do just as he pleases with his white subjects, being responsible to God alone. By the former, the white man is to do just as he pleases with his black slaves, being responsible to God alone. The two things are precisely alike, and it is but natural that they should find similar arguments to sustain them.

I had argued that the application of the principle of self-government, as contended for, would require the revival of the African slave trade; that no argument could be made in favor of a man's right to take slaves to Nebraska which could not be equally well made in favor of his right to bring them from the coast of Africa. The Judge replied that the Constitution requires the suppression of the foreign slave trade, but does not require the prohibition of slavery in the Territories. That is a mistake in point of fact. The Constitution does not require the action of Congress in either case, and it does authorize it in both. And so there is still no difference between the cases.

In regard to what I have said of the advantage the slave States have over the free in the matter of representation, the Judge replied that we in the free States count five free negroes as five white people, while in the slave States they count five slaves as three whites only; and that the advantage, at last, was on the side of the free States.

Now, in the slave States they count free negroes just as we do; and it so happens that, besides their slaves, they have as many free negroes as we have, and thirty thousand over. Thus, their free negroes more than balance ours; and their advantage over us, in consequence of their slaves, still remains as I stated it.

In reply to my argument that the compromise measures of 1850 were a system of equivalents, and that the provisions of no one of them could fairly be carried to other subjects without its corresponding equivalent being carried with it, the Judge denied outright that these measures had any connection with or dependence upon each other. This is mere desperation. If they had no connection, why are they always spoken of in connection? Why has he so spoken of them a thousand times? Why has he constantly called them a series of measures? Why does everybody call them a compromise? Why was California kept out of the Union six or seven months, if it was not because of its connection with the other measures? Webster's leading definition of the verb "to compromise" is "to adjust and settle a difference, by mutual agreement, with concessions of claims by the parties." This conveys precisely the popular understanding of the word "compromise."

We knew, before the Judge told us, that these measures passed separately, and in distinct bills, and that no two of them were passed by the votes of precisely the same members. But we also know, and so does he know, that no one of them could have passed both branches of Congress but for the understanding that the others were to pass also. Upon this understanding, each got votes which it could have got in no other way. It is this fact which gives to the measures their true character; and it is the universal knowledge of this fact that has given them the name of "compromises," so expressive of that true character.

I had asked: "If, in carrying the Utah and New Mexico laws to Nebraska, you could clear away other objection, how could you leave Nebraska 'perfectly free' to introduce slavery before she forms a constitution, during her territorial government, while the Utah and New Mexico laws only authorize it when they form constitutions and are admitted into the Union?" To this Judge Douglas answered that the Utah and New Mexico laws also authorized it before; and to prove this he read from one of their laws, as follows: "That the legislative power of said Territory shall extend to all rightful subjects of legislation, consistent with the Constitution of the United States and the provisions of this act."

Now it is perceived from the reading of this that there is nothing express upon the subject, but that the authority is sought to be implied merely for the general provision of "all rightful subjects of legislation." In reply to this I insist, as a legal rule of construction, as well as the plain, popular view of the matter, that the express provision for Utah and New Mexico coming in with slavery, if they choose, when they shall form constitutions, is an exclusion of all implied authority on the same subject; that Congress having the subject distinctly in their minds when they made the express provision, they therein expressed their whole meaning on that subject.

The Judge rather insinuated that I had found it convenient to forget the Washington territorial law passed in 1853. This was a division of Oregon, organizing the northern part as the Territory of Washington. He asserted that by this act the Ordinance of '87, theretofore existing in Oregon, was repealed; that nearly all the members of Congress voted for it, beginning in the House of Representatives with Charles Allen of Massachusetts, and ending with Richard Yates of Illinois; and that he could not understand how those who now opposed the Nebraska Bill so voted there, unless it was because it was then too soon after both the great political parties had ratified the compromises of 1850, and the ratification therefore was too fresh to be then repudiated.

Now I had seen the Washington act before, and I have carefully examined it since; and I aver that there is no repeal of the Ordinance of '87, or of any prohibition of slavery, in it. In express terms, there is absolutely nothing in the whole

177

law upon the subject—in fact, nothing to lead a reader to think of the subject. To my judgment it is equally free from everything from which repeal can be legally implied; but, however this may be, are men now to be entrapped by a legal implication, extracted from covert language, introduced perhaps for the very purpose of entrapping them? I sincerely wish every man could read this law quite through, carefully watching every sentence and every line for a repeal of the Ordinance of '87, or anything equivalent to it.

Another point on the Washington act: If it was intended to be modeled after the Utah and New Mexico acts, as Judge Douglas insists, why was it not inserted in it, as in them, that Washington was to come in with or without slavery as she may choose at the adoption of her constitution? It has no such provision in it; and I defy the ingenuity of man to give a reason for the omission, other than that it was not intended to follow the Utah and New Mexico laws in regard to the question of slavery.

The Washington act not only differs vitally from the Utah and New Mexico acts, but the Nebraska act differs vitally from both. By the latter act the people are left "perfectly free" to regulate their own domestic concerns, etc.; but in all the former, all their laws are to be submitted to Congress, and if disapproved are to be null. The Washington act goes even further; it absolutely prohibits the territorial Legislature, by very strong and guarded language, from establishing banks or borrowing money on the faith of the Territory. Is this the sacred right of self-government we hear vaunted so much? No, sir; the Nebraska Bill finds no model in the acts of '50 or the Washington act. It finds no model in any law from Adam till to-day. As Phillips says of Napoleon, the Nebraska act is grand, gloomy and peculiar, wrapped in the solitude of its own originality, without a model and without a shadow upon the earth.

In the course of his reply Senator Douglas remarked in substance that he had always considered this government was made for the white people and not for the negroes. Why, in point of mere fact, I think so too. But in this remark of the Judge there is a significance which I think is the key to the great mistake (if there is any such mistake) which he has made in this Nebraska measure. It shows that the Judge has no very vivid impression that the negro is human, and consequently has no idea that there can be any moral question in legislating about him. In his view the question of whether a new country shall be slave or free is a matter of as utter indifference as it is whether his neighbor shall plant his farm with tobacco or stock it with horned cattle. Now, whether this view is right or wrong, it is very certain that the great mass of mankind take a totally different view. They consider slavery a great moral wrong, and their feeling against it is not evanescent, but eternal. It lies at the very foundation of their sense of justice, and it cannot be trifled with. It is a great and durable element of popular action, and I think no statesman can safely disregard it.

Our Senator also objects that those who oppose him in this matter do not entirely agree with one another. He reminds me that in my firm adherence to the constitutional rights of the slave States I differ widely from others who are cooperating with me in opposing the Nebraska Bill, and he says it is not quite fair to oppose him in this variety of ways. He should remember that he took us by surprise—astounded us by this measure. We were thunderstruck and stunned, and we reeled and fell in utter confusion. But we rose, each fighting, grasping whatever he could first reach—a scythe, a pitchfork, a chopping-ax, or a butcher's cleaver. We struck in the direction of the sound, and we were rapidly closing in upon him. He must not think to divert us from our purpose by showing us that our drill, our dress, and our weapons are not entirely perfect and uniform. When the storm shall be past he shall find us still Americans, no less devoted to the continued union and prosperity of the country than heretofore.

Finally, the Judge invokes against me the memory of Clay and Webster. They were great men, and men of great deeds. But where have I assailed them? For what is it that their lifelong enemy shall now make profit by assuming to defend them against me, their lifelong friend? I go against the repeal of the Missouri Compromise; did they ever go for it? They went for the Compromise of 1850; did I ever go against them? They were greatly devoted to the Union; to the small measure of my ability was I ever less so? Clay and Webster were dead before this question arose; by what authority shall our Senator say they would espouse his side of it if alive? Mr. Clay was the leading spirit in making the Missouri Compromise; is it very credible that if now alive he would take the lead in the breaking of it? The truth is that some support from Whigs is now a necessity with the Judge, and for this it is that the names of Clay and Webster are invoked. His old friends have deserted him in such numbers as to leave too few to live by. He came to his own, and his own received him not; and lo! he turns unto the Gentiles.

A word now as to the Judge's desperate assumption that the compromises of 1850 had no connection with one another; that Illinois came into the Union as a slave State, and some other similar ones. This is no other than a bold denial of the history of the country. If we do not know that the compromises of 1850 were dependent on each other; if we do not know that Illinois came into the Union as a free State,—we do not know anything. If we do not know these things, we do not know that we ever had a Revolutionary War or such a chief as Washington. To deny these things is to deny our national axioms,—or dogmas, at least,—and it puts an end to all argument. If a man will stand up and assert, and repeat and reassert, that two and two do not make four, I know nothing in the power of argument that can stop him. I think I can answer the Judge so long as he sticks to the premises; but when he flies from them, I cannot work any argument into the consistency of a mental gag and actually close his mouth with it. In such a case I can only commend him to the seventy thousand answers just in from Pennsylvania, Ohio, and Indiana.

REQUEST FOR SENATE SUPPORT

TO CHARLES HOYT

CLINTON, De WITT Co., Nov. 10, 1854

DEAR SIR:—You used to express a good deal of partiality for me, and if you are still so, now is the time. Some friends here are really for me for the U.S. Senate, and I should be very grateful if you could make a mark for me among your members. Please write me at all events, giving me the names, post-offices, and "political position" of members round about you. Direct to Springfield.

Let this be confidential.

Yours truly,

A. LINCOLN.

TO T. J. HENDERSON.

SPRINGFIELD,

November 27, 1854 T. J. HENDERSON, ESQ.

MY DEAR SIR:—It has come round that a whig may, by possibility, be elected to the United States Senate, and I want the chance of being the man. You are a member of the Legislature, and have a vote to give. Think it over, and see whether you can do better than to go for me.

Write me, at all events; and let this be confidential.

Yours truly,

A. LINCOLN.

TO J. GILLESPIE.

SPRINGFIELD, Dec. 1, 1854.

DEAR SIR:—I have really got it into my head to try to be United States Senator, and, if I could have your support, my chances would be reasonably good. But I know, and acknowledge, that you have as just claims to the place as I have; and therefore I cannot ask you to yield to me, if you are thinking of becoming a candidate, yourself. If, however, you are not, then I should like to be remembered affectionately by you; and also to have you make a mark for me with the Anti-Nebraska members down your way.

If you know, and have no objection to tell, let me know whether Trumbull intends to make a push. If he does, I suppose the two men in St. Clair, and one, or both, in Madison, will be for him. We have the Legislature, clearly enough, on joint ballot, but the Senate is very close, and Cullom told me to-day that the Nebraska men will stave off the election, if they can. Even if we get into joint vote, we shall have difficulty to unite our forces. Please write me, and let this be confidential.

Your friend, as ever,

A. LINCOLN.

POLITICAL REFERENCES

TO JUSTICE MCLEAN.

SPRINGFIELD, ILL., December 6, 1854.

SIR:—I understand it is in contemplation to displace the present clerk and appoint a new one for the Circuit and District Courts of Illinois. I am very friendly to the present incumbent, and, both for his own sake and that of his family, I wish him to be retained so long as it is possible for the court to do so.

In the contingency of his removal, however, I have recommended William Butler as his successor, and I do not wish what I write now to be taken as any abatement of that recommendation.

William J. Black is also an applicant for the appointment, and I write this at the solicitation of his friends to say that he is every way worthy of the office, and that I doubt not the conferring it upon him will give great satisfaction.

Your ob't servant,

A. LINCOLN.

TO T. J. HENDERSON.

SPRINGFIELD, December 15. 1854

HON. T. J. HENDERSON.

DEAR SIR:—Yours of the 11th was received last night, and for which I thank you. Of course I prefer myself to all others; yet it is neither in my heart nor my conscience to say I am any better man than Mr. Williams. We shall have a terrible struggle with our adversaries. They are desperate and bent on desperate deeds. I accidentally learned of one of the leaders here writing to a member south of here, in about the following language:

We are beaten. They have a clean majority of at least nine, on joint ballot. They outnumber us, but we must outmanage them. Douglas must be sustained. We must elect the Speaker; and we must elect a Nebraska United States Senator, or "elect none at all." Similar letters, no doubt, are written to every Nebraska member. Be considering how we can best meet, and foil, and beat them. I send you, by mail, a copy of my Peoria speech. You may have seen it before, or you may not think it worth seeing now.

Do not speak of the Nebraska letter mentioned above; I do not wish it to become public, that I received such information.

Yours truly,

A. LINCOLN.

1855

LOSS OF PRIMARY FOR SENATOR

TO E. B. WASHBURNE.

SPRINGFIELD, February 9, 1855 MY DEAR SIR:

I began with 44 votes, Shields 41, and Trumbull 5,—yet Trumbull was elected. In fact 47 different members voted for me,—getting three new ones on the second ballot, and losing four old ones. How came my 47 to yield to Trumbull's 5? It was Governor Matteson's work. He has been secretly a candidate ever since (before, even) the fall election.

All the members round about the canal were Anti-Nebraska, but were nevertheless nearly all Democrats and old personal friends of his. His plan was to privately impress them with the belief that he was as good Anti-Nebraska as any one else—at least could be secured to be so by instructions, which could be easily passed.

The Nebraska men, of course, were not for Matteson; but when they found they could elect no avowed Nebraska man, they tardily determined to let him get whomever of our men he could, by whatever means he could, and ask him no questions.

The Nebraska men were very confident of the election of Matteson, though denying that he was a candidate, and we very much believing also that they would elect him. But they wanted first to make a show of good faith to Shields by voting for him a few times, and our secret Matteson men also wanted to make a show of good faith by voting with us a few times. So we led off. On the seventh ballot, I think, the signal was given to the Nebraska men to turn to Matteson, which they acted on to a man, with one exception. . . Next ballot the remaining Nebraska man and one pretended Anti went over to him, giving him 46. The next still another, giving him 47, wanting only three of an election. In the meantime our friends, with a view of detaining our expected bolters, had been turning from me to Trumbull till he had risen to 35 and I had been reduced to 15. These would never desert me except by my direction; but I became satisfied that if we could prevent Matteson's election one or two ballots more, we could not possibly do so a single ballot after my friends should begin to return to me from Trumbull. So I determined to strike at once, and accordingly advised my remaining friends to go for him, which they did and elected him on the tenth ballot.

Such is the way the thing was done. I think you would have done the same under the circumstances.

I could have headed off every combination and been elected, had it not been for Matteson's double game—and his defeat now gives me more pleasure than my own gives me pain. On the whole, it is perhaps as well for our general cause that Trumbull is elected. The Nebraska men confess that they hate it worse than anything that could have happened. It is a great consolation to see them worse whipped than I am.

Yours forever,

A. LINCOLN.

RETURN TO LAW PROFESSION

TO SANFORD, PORTER, AND STRIKER, NEW YORK.

SPRINGFIELD, MARCH 10, 1855

GENTLEMEN:—Yours of the 5th is received, as also was that of 15th Dec, last, inclosing bond of Clift to Pray. When I received the bond I was dabbling in politics, and of course neglecting business. Having since been beaten out I have gone to work again.

As I do not practice in Rushville, I to-day open a correspondence with Henry E. Dummer, Esq., of Beardstown, Ill., with the view of getting the job into his hands. He is a good man if he will undertake it.

Write me whether I shall do this or return the bond to you.

Yours respectfully,

A. LINCOLN.

TO O. H. BROWNING.

SPRINGFIELD, March 23, 1855.

HON. O. H. BROWNING.

MY DEAR SIR:—Your letter to Judge Logan has been shown to us by him; and, with his consent, we answer it. When it became probable that there would be a vacancy on the Supreme Bench, public opinion, on this side of the river, seemed to be universally directed to Logan as the proper man to fill it. I mean public opinion on our side in politics, with very small manifestation in any different direction by the other side. The result is, that he has been a good deal pressed to allow his name to be used, and he has consented to it, provided it can be done with perfect cordiality and good feeling on the part of all our own friends. We, the undersigned, are very anxious for it; and the more so now that he has been urged, until his mind is turned upon the matter. We, therefore are very glad of your letter, with the information it brings us, mixed only with a regret that we can not elect Logan and Walker both. We shall be glad, if you will hoist Logan's name, in your Quincy papers.

Very truly your friends,

A. LINCOLN, B. S. EWARDS, JOHN T. STUART.

TO H. C. WHITNEY.

SPRINGFIELD, June 7, 1855.

H. C. WHITNEY, ESQ.

MY DEAR SIR:—Your note containing election news is received; and for which I thank you. It is all of no use, however. Logan is worse beaten than any other man ever was since elections were invented—beaten more than twelve hundred in this county. It is conceded on all hands that the Prohibitory law is also beaten.

184

Yours truly,

A. LINCOLN.

RESPONSE TO A PRO-SLAVERY FRIEND

TO JOSHUA. F. SPEED.

SPRINGFIELD, August 24, 1855

DEAR SPEED:—You know what a poor correspondent I am. Ever since I received your very agreeable letter of the 22d of May, I have been intending to write you an answer to it. You suggest that in political action, now, you and I would differ. I suppose we would; not quite as much, however, as you may think. You know I dislike slavery, and you fully admit the abstract wrong of it. So far there is no cause of difference. But you say that sooner than yield your legal right to the slave, especially at the bidding of those who are not themselves interested, you would see the Union dissolved. I am not aware that any one is bidding you yield that right; very certainly I am not. I leave that matter entirely to yourself. I also acknowledge your rights and my obligations under the Constitution in regard to your slaves. I confess I hate to see the poor creatures hunted down and caught and carried back to their stripes and unrequited toil; but I bite my lips and keep quiet. In 1841 you and I had together a tedious low-water trip on a steamboat from Louisville to St. Louis. You may remember, as I well do, that from Louisville to the mouth of the Ohio there were on board ten or a dozen slaves shackled together with irons. That sight was a continued torment to me, and I see something like it every time I touch the Ohio or any other slave border. It is not fair for you to assume that I have no interest in a thing which has, and continually exercises, the power of making me miserable. You ought rather to appreciate how much the great body of the Northern people do crucify their feelings, in order to maintain their loyalty to the Constitution and the Union. I do oppose the extension of slavery because my judgment and feeling so prompt me, and I am under no obligations to the contrary. If for this you and I must differ, differ we must. You say, if you were President, you would send an army and hang the leaders of the Missouri outrages upon the Kansas elections; still, if Kansas fairly votes herself a slave State she must be admitted or the Union must be dissolved. But how if she votes herself a slave State unfairly, that is, by the very means for which you say you would hang men? Must she still be admitted, or the Union dissolved? That will be the phase of the question when it first becomes a practical one. In your assumption that there may be a fair decision of the slavery question in Kansas, I plainly see you and I would differ about the Nebraska law. I look upon that enactment not as a law, but as a violence from the beginning. It was conceived in violence, is maintained in violence, and is being executed in violence. I say it was conceived in violence, because the destruction of the Missouri Compromise, under the circumstances, was nothing less than violence. It was passed in violence because it could not have passed at all but for the votes of many members in violence of the known will of their constituents. It is maintained in violence, because the elections since clearly demand its repeal; and the demand is openly disregarded.

You say men ought to be hung for the way they are executing the law; I say the way it is being executed is quite as good as any of its antecedents. It is being executed in the precise way which was intended from the first, else why does no Nebraska man express astonishment or condemnation? Poor Reeder is the only public man who has been silly enough to believe that anything like fairness was ever intended, and he has been bravely undeceived.

That Kansas will form a slave constitution, and with it will ask to be admitted into the Union, I take to be already a settled question, and so settled by the very means you so pointedly condemn. By every principle of law ever held by any court North or South, every negro taken to Kansas is free; yet, in utter disregard of this,—in the spirit of violence merely,—that beautiful Legislature gravely passes a law to hang any man who shall venture to inform a negro of his legal rights. This is the subject and real object of the law. If, like Haman, they should hang upon the gallows of their own building, I shall not be among the mourners for their fate. In my humble sphere, I shall advocate the restoration of the Missouri Compromise so long as Kansas remains a Territory, and when, by all these foul means, it seeks to come into the Union as a slave State, I shall oppose it. I am very loath in any case to withhold my assent to the enjoyment of property acquired or located in good faith; but I do not admit that good faith in taking a negro to Kansas to be held in slavery is a probability with any man. Any man who has sense enough to be the controller of his own property has too much sense to misunderstand the outrageous character of the whole Nebraska business. But I digress. In my opposition to the admission of Kansas I shall have some company, but we may be beaten. If we are, I shall not on that account attempt to dissolve the Union. I think it probable, however, we shall be beaten. Standing as a unit among yourselves, You can, directly and indirectly, bribe enough of our men to carry the day, as you could on the open proposition to establish a monarchy. Get hold of some man in the North whose position and ability is such that he can make the support of your measure, whatever it may be, a Democratic party necessity, and the thing is done. Apropos of this, let me tell you an anecdote. Douglas introduced the Nebraska Bill in January. In February afterward there was a called session of the Illinois Legislature. Of the one hundred members composing the two branches of that body, about seventy were Democrats. These latter held a caucus in which the Nebraska Bill was talked of, if not formally discussed. It was thereby discovered that just three, and no more, were in favor of the measure. In a day or two Douglas's orders came on to have resolutions passed approving the bill; and they were passed by large majorities!!!! The truth of this is vouched for by a bolting Democratic member. The masses, too, Democratic as well as Whig, were even nearer unanimous against it; but, as soon as the party necessity of supporting it became apparent, the way the Democrats began to see the wisdom and justice of it was perfectly astonishing.

You say that if Kansas fairly votes herself a free State, as a Christian you will rejoice at it. All decent slaveholders talk that way, and I do not doubt their candor. But they never vote that way. Although in a private letter or conversation you will express your preference that Kansas shall be free, you would vote for no man for Congress who would say the same thing publicly. No such man could be elected from any district in a slave State. You think Stringfellow and company ought to be hung; and yet at the next Presidential election you will vote for the exact type and representative of Stringfellow. The slave-breeders and slave-traders are a small, odious, and detested class among you; and yet in politics they dictate the course of all of you, and are as completely your masters as you are the master of your own negroes. You inquire where I now stand. That is a disputed point. I think I am a Whig; but others say there are no Whigs, and that I am an Abolitionist. When I was at Washington, I voted for the Wilmot Proviso as good as forty times; and I never heard of any one attempting to un-Whig me for that. I now do no more than oppose the extension of slavery. I am not a Know-Nothing; that is certain. How could I be? How can any one who abhors the oppression of negroes be in favor of degrading classes of white people? Our progress in degeneracy appears to me to be pretty rapid. As a nation we began by declaring that "all men are created equal." We now practically read it "all men are created equal, except negroes." When the Know-Nothings get control, it will read "all men are created equal, except negroes and foreigners and Catholics." When it comes to this, I shall prefer emigrating to some country where they make no pretense of loving liberty,—to Russia, for instance, where despotism can be taken pure, and without the base alloy of hypocrisy.

Mary will probably pass a day or two in Louisville in October. My kindest regards to Mrs. Speed. On the leading subject of this letter I have more of her sympathy than I have of yours; and yet let me say I am,

Your friend forever,

A. LINCOLN.

1856

REQUEST FOR A RAILWAY PASS

TO R. P. MORGAN

SPRINGFIELD, February 13, 1856.

R. P. MORGAN, ESQ.:

Says Tom to John, "Here's your old rotten wheelbarrow. I've broke it usin' on it. I wish you would mend it, 'case I shall want to borrow it this afternoon." Acting on this as a precedent, I say, "Here's your old 'chalked hat,—I wish you would take it and send me a new one, 'case I shall want to use it the first of March."

Yours truly,

A. LINCOLN.

(A 'chalked hat' was the common term, at that time, for a railroad pass.)

SPEECH DELIVERED BEFORE THE FIRST REPUBLICAN STATE CONVENTION

OF ILLINOIS, HELD AT BLOOMINGTON, ON MAY 29, 1856.

[From the Report by William C. Whitney.]

(Mr. Whitney's notes were made at the time, but not written out until 1896. He does not claim that the speech, as here reported, is literally correct only that he has followed the argument, and that in many cases the sentences are as Mr. Lincoln spoke them.)

Mr. CHAIRMAN AND GENTLEMEN: I was over at [Cries of "Platform!" "Take the platform!"]—I say, that while I was at Danville Court, some of our friends of Anti-Nebraska got together in Springfield and elected me as one delegate to represent old Sangamon with them in this convention, and I am here certainly as a sympathizer in this movement and by virtue of that meeting and selection. But we can hardly be called delegates strictly, inasmuch as, properly speaking, we represent nobody but ourselves. I think it altogether fair to say that we have no Anti-Nebraska party in Sangamon, although there is a good deal of Anti-Nebraska feeling there; but I say for myself, and I think I may speak also for my colleagues, that we who are here fully approve of the platform and of all that has been done [A voice, "Yes!"], and even if we are not regularly delegates, it will be right for me to answer your call to speak. I suppose we truly stand for the public sentiment of Sangamon on the great question of the repeal, although we do not yet represent many numbers who have taken a distinct position on the question.

We are in a trying time—it ranges above mere party—and this movement to call a halt and turn our steps backward needs all the help and good counsels it can get; for unless popular opinion makes itself very strongly felt, and a change is made in our present course, blood will flow on account of Nebraska, and brother's hands will be raised against brother!

[The last sentence was uttered in such an earnest, impressive, if not, indeed, tragic, manner, as to make a cold chill creep over me. Others gave a similar experience.]

I have listened with great interest to the earnest appeal made to Illinois men by the gentleman from Lawrence [James S. Emery] who has just addressed us so eloquently and forcibly. I was deeply moved by his statement of the wrongs done to free-State men out there. I think it just to say that all true men North should sympathize with them, and ought to be willing to do any possible and needful thing to right their wrongs. But we must not promise what we ought not, lest we be called on to perform what we cannot; we must be calm and moderate, and consider the whole difficulty, and determine what is possible and just. We must not be led by excitement and passion to do that which our sober judgments would not approve in our cooler moments. We have higher aims; we will have more serious business than to dally with temporary measures.

We are here to stand firmly for a principle—to stand firmly for a right. We know that great political and moral wrongs are done, and outrages committed, and we denounce those wrongs and outrages, although we cannot, at present, do much more. But we desire to reach out beyond those personal outrages and establish a rule that will apply to all, and so prevent any future outrages.

We have seen to-day that every shade of popular opinion is represented here, with Freedom, or rather Free Soil, as the basis. We have come together as in some sort representatives of popular opinion against the extension of slavery into territory now free in fact as well as by law, and the pledged word of the statesmen of the nation who are now no more. We come—we are here assembled together—to protest as well as we can against a great wrong, and to take measures, as well as we now can, to make that wrong right; to place the nation, as far as it may be possible now, as it was before the repeal of the Missouri Compromise; and the plain way to do this is to restore the Compromise, and to demand and determine that Kansas shall be free! [Immense applause.] While we affirm, and reaffirm, if necessary, our devotion to the principles of the Declaration of Independence, let our practical work here be limited to the above. We know that there is not a perfect agreement of sentiment here on the public questions which might be rightfully considered in this convention, and that the indignation which we all must feel cannot be helped; but all of us must give up something for the good of the cause. There is one desire which is uppermost in the mind, one wish common to us all, to which no dissent will be made; and I counsel you earnestly to bury all resentment, to sink all personal feeling, make all things work to a common purpose in which we are united and agreed about, and which all present will agree is absolutely necessary—which must be done by any rightful mode if there be such: Slavery must be kept out of Kansas! [Applause.] The test—the pinch—is right there. If we lose Kansas to freedom, an example will be set which will prove fatal to freedom in the end. We, therefore, in the language of the Bible, must "lay the axe to the root of the tree." Temporizing will not do longer; now is the time for decision—for firm, persistent, resolute action. [Applause.]

The Nebraska Bill, or rather Nebraska law, is not one of wholesome legislation, but was and is an act of legislative usurpation, whose result, if not indeed intention, is to make slavery national; and unless headed off in some effective way, we are in a fair way to see this land of boasted freedom converted into a land of slavery in fact. [Sensation.] Just open your two eyes, and see if this be not so. I need do no more than state, to command universal approval, that almost the entire North, as well as a large following in the border States, is radically opposed to the planting of slavery in free territory. Probably in a popular vote throughout the nation nine tenths of the voters in the free States, and at least one-half in the border States, if they could express their sentiments freely, would vote NO on such an issue; and it is safe to say that two thirds of the votes of the entire nation would be opposed to it. And yet, in spite of this overbalancing of sentiment in this free country, we are in a fair way to see Kansas present itself for admission as a slave State. Indeed, it is a felony, by the local law of Kansas, to deny that slavery exists there even now. By every principle of law, a negro in Kansas is free; yet the bogus Legislature makes it an infamous crime to tell him that he is free!

Statutes of Kansas, 1555, chapter 151, Sec. 12: If any free person, by speaking or by writing, assert or maintain that persons have not the right to hold slaves in this Territory, or shall introduce into this Territory, print, publish, write, circulate . . . any book, paper, magazine, pamphlet, or circular containing any denial of the right of persons to hold slaves in this Territory such person shall be deemed guilty of felony, and punished by imprisonment at hard labor for a term of not less than two years. Sec. 13. No person who is conscientiously opposed to holding slaves, or who does not admit the right to hold slaves in this Territory, shall sit as a juror on the trial of any prosecution for any violation of any Sections of this Act.

The party lash and the fear of ridicule will overawe justice and liberty; for it is a singular fact, but none the less a fact, and well known by the most common experience, that men will do things under the terror of the party lash that they would not on any account or for any consideration do otherwise; while men who will march up to the mouth of a loaded cannon without shrinking will run from the terrible name of "Abolitionist," even when pronounced by a worthless creature whom they, with good reason, despise. For instance—to press this point a little—Judge Douglas introduced his Nebraska Bill in January; and we had an extra session of our Legislature in the succeeding February, in which were seventy-five Democrats; and at a party caucus, fully attended, there were just three votes, out of the whole seventy-five, for the measure. But in a few days orders came on from Washington, commanding them to approve the measure; the party lash was applied, and it was brought up again in caucus, and passed by a large majority. The masses were against it, but party necessity carried it; and it was passed through the lower house of Congress against the will of the people, for the same reason. Here is where the greatest danger lies that, while we profess to be a government of law and reason, law will give way to violence on demand of this awful and crushing power. Like the great Juggernaut— I think that is the name—the great idol, it crushes everything that comes in its way, and makes a [?]—or, as I read once, in a blackletter law book, "a slave is a human being who is legally not a person but a thing." And if the safeguards to liberty are broken down, as is now attempted, when they have made things of all the free negroes, how long, think you, before they will begin to make things of poor white men? [Applause.] Be not deceived. Revolutions do not go backward. The founder of the Democratic party declared that all men were created equal. His successor in the leadership has written the word "white" before men, making it read "all white men are created equal." Pray, will or may not the Know-Nothings, if they should get in power, add the word "Protestant," making it read "all Protestant white men...?"

Meanwhile the hapless negro is the fruitful subject of reprisals in other quarters. John Pettit, whom Tom Benton paid his respects to, you will recollect, calls the immortal Declaration "a self-evident lie"; while at the birthplace of freedom— in the shadow of Bunker Hill and of the "cradle of liberty," at the home of the Adamses and Warren and Otis—Choate, from our side of the house, dares to fritter away the birthday promise of liberty by proclaiming the Declaration to be "a string of glittering generalities"; and the Southern Whigs, working hand in hand with proslavery Democrats, are making Choate's theories practical. Thomas Jefferson, a slaveholder, mindful of the moral element in slavery, solemnly declared that he trembled for his country when he remembered that God is just; while Judge Douglas, with an insignificant wave of the hand, "don't care whether slavery is voted up or voted down." Now, if slavery is right, or even negative, he has a right to treat it in this trifling manner. But if it is a moral and political wrong, as all Christendom considers it to be, how can he answer to God for this attempt to spread and fortify it? [Applause.]

But no man, and Judge Douglas no more than any other, can maintain a negative, or merely neutral, position on this question; and, accordingly, he avows that the Union was made by white men and for white men and their descendants. As matter of fact, the first branch of the proposition is historically true; the government was made by white men, and they were and are the superior race. This I admit. But the corner-stone of the government, so to speak, was the declaration that "all men are created equal," and all entitled to "life, liberty, and the pursuit of happiness." [Applause.]

And not only so, but the framers of the Constitution were particular to keep out of that instrument the word "slave," the reason being that slavery would ultimately come to an end, and they did not wish to have any reminder that in this free country human beings were ever prostituted to slavery. [Applause.] Nor is it any argument that we are superior and the negro inferior—that he has but one talent while we have ten. Let the negro possess the little he has in independence; if he has but one talent, he should be permitted to keep the little he has. [Applause:] But slavery will endure no test of reason or logic; and yet its advocates, like Douglas, use a sort of bastard logic, or noisy assumption it might better be termed, like the above, in order to prepare the mind for the gradual, but none the less certain, encroachments of the Moloch of slavery upon the fair domain of freedom. But however much you may argue upon it, or smother it in soft phrase, slavery can only be maintained by force—by violence. The repeal of the Missouri Compromise was by violence. It was a violation of both law and the sacred obligations of honor, to overthrow and trample under foot a solemn compromise, obtained by the fearful loss to freedom of one of the fairest of our Western domains. Congress violated the will and confidence of its constituents in voting for the bill; and while public sentiment, as shown by the elections of 1854, demanded the restoration of this compromise, Congress violated its trust by refusing simply because it had the force of numbers to hold on to it. And murderous violence is being used now, in order to force slavery on to Kansas; for it cannot be done in any other way. [Sensation.]

The necessary result was to establish the rule of violence—force, instead of the rule of law and reason; to perpetuate and spread slavery, and in time to make it general. We see it at both ends of the line. In Washington, on the very spot where the outrage was started, the fearless Sumner is beaten to insensibility, and is now slowly dying; while senators who claim to be gentlemen and Christians stood by, countenancing the act, and even applauding it afterward in their places in the Senate. Even Douglas, our man, saw it all and was within helping distance, yet let the murderous blows fall unopposed. Then, at the other end of the line, at the very time Sumner was being murdered, Lawrence was being destroyed for the crime of freedom. It was the most prominent stronghold of liberty in Kansas, and must give way to the all-dominating power of slavery. Only two days ago, Judge Trumbull found it necessary to propose a bill in the Senate to prevent a general civil war and to restore peace in Kansas.

We live in the midst of alarms; anxiety beclouds the future; we expect some new disaster with each newspaper we read. Are we in a healthful political state? Are not the tendencies plain? Do not the signs of the times point plainly the way in which we are going? [Sensation.]

In the early days of the Constitution slavery was recognized, by South and North alike, as an evil, and the division of sentiment about it was not controlled by geographical lines or considerations of climate, but by moral and philanthropic views. Petitions for the abolition of slavery were presented to the very first Congress by Virginia and Massachusetts alike. To show the harmony which prevailed, I will state that a fugitive slave law was passed in 1793, with no dissenting voice in the Senate, and but seven dissenting votes in the House. It was, however, a wise law, moderate, and, under the Constitution, a just one. Twenty-five years later, a more stringent law was proposed and defeated; and thirty-five years after that, the present law, drafted by Mason of Virginia, was passed by Northern votes. I am not, just now, complaining of this law, but I am trying to show how the current sets; for the proposed law of 1817 was far less offensive than the present one. In 1774 the Continental Congress pledged itself, without a dissenting vote, to wholly discontinue the slave trade, and to neither purchase nor import any slave; and less than three months before the passage of the Declaration of Independence, the same Congress which adopted that declaration unanimously resolved "that no slave be imported into any of the thirteen United Colonies." [Great applause.]

On the second day of July, 1776, the draft of a Declaration of Independence was reported to Congress by the committee, and in it the slave trade was characterized as "an execrable commerce," as "a piratical warfare," as the "opprobrium of infidel powers," and as "a cruel war against human nature." [Applause.] All agreed on this except South Carolina and Georgia, and in order to preserve harmony, and from the necessity of the case, these expressions were omitted. Indeed, abolition societies existed as far south as Virginia; and it is a well-known fact that Washington, Jefferson, Madison, Lee, Henry, Mason, and Pendleton were qualified abolitionists, and much more radical on that subject than we of the Whig and Democratic parties claim to be to-day. On March 1, 1784, Virginia ceded to the confederation all its lands lying northwest of the Ohio River. Jefferson, Chase of Maryland, and Howell of Rhode Island, as a committee on that and territory thereafter to be ceded, reported that no slavery should exist after the year 1800. Had this report been adopted, not only the Northwest, but Kentucky, Tennessee, Alabama, and Mississippi also would have been free; but it required the assent of nine States to ratify it. North Carolina was divided, and thus its vote was lost; and Delaware, Georgia, and New Jersey refused to vote. In point of fact, as it was, it was assented to by six States. Three years later on a square vote to exclude slavery from the Northwest, only one vote, and that from New York, was against it. And yet, thirty-seven years later, five thousand citizens of Illinois, out of a voting mass of less than twelve thousand, deliberately, after a long and heated contest, voted to introduce slavery in Illinois; and, to-day, a large party in the free State of Illinois are willing to vote to fasten the shackles of slavery on the fair domain of Kansas, notwithstanding it received the dowry of freedom long before its birth as a political community. I repeat, therefore, the question: Is it not plain in what direction we are tending? [Sensation.] In the colonial time, Mason, Pendleton, and Jefferson were as hostile to slavery in Virginia as Otis, Ames, and the Adamses were in Massachusetts; and Virginia made as earnest an effort to get rid of it as old Massachusetts did. But circumstances were against them and they failed; but not that the good will of its leading men was lacking. Yet within less than fifty years Virginia changed its tune, and made negro-breeding for the cotton and sugar States one of its leading industries. [Laughter and applause.]

In the Constitutional Convention, George Mason of Virginia made a more violent abolition speech than my friends Lovejoy or Codding would desire to make here to-day—a speech which could not be safely repeated anywhere on Southern soil in this enlightened year. But, while there were some differences of opinion on this subject even then, discussion was allowed; but as you see by the Kansas slave code, which, as you know, is the Missouri slave code, merely ferried across the river, it is a felony to even express an opinion hostile to that foul blot in the land of Washington and the Declaration of Independence. [Sensation.]

In Kentucky—my State—in 1849, on a test vote, the mighty influence of Henry Clay and many other good then there could not get a symptom of expression in favor of gradual emancipation on a plain issue of marching toward the light of civilization with Ohio and Illinois; but the State of Boone and Hardin and Henry Clay, with a nigger under each arm, took the black trail toward the deadly swamps of barbarism. Is there—can there be—any doubt about this thing? And is there any doubt that we must all lay aside our prejudices and march, shoulder to shoulder, in the great army of Freedom? [Applause.]

Every Fourth of July our young orators all proclaim this to be "the land of the free and the home of the brave!" Well, now, when you orators get that off next year, and, may be, this very year, how would you like some old grizzled farmer to get up in the grove and deny it? [Laughter.] How would you like that? But suppose Kansas comes in as a slave State, and all the "border ruffians" have barbecues about it, and free-State men come trailing back to the dishonored North, like whipped dogs with their tails between their legs, it is—ain't it?—evident that this is no more the "land of the free"; and if we let it go so, we won't dare to say "home of the brave" out loud. [Sensation and confusion.]

Can any man doubt that, even in spite of the people's will, slavery will triumph through violence, unless that will be made manifest and enforced? Even Governor Reeder claimed at the outset that the contest in Kansas was to be fair, but he got his eyes open at last; and I believe that, as a result of this moral and physical violence, Kansas will soon apply for admission as a slave State. And yet we can't mistake that the people don't want it so, and that it is a land which is free both by natural and political law. No law, is free law! Such is the understanding of all Christendom. In the Somerset case, decided nearly a century ago, the great Lord Mansfield held that slavery was of such a nature that it must take its rise in positive (as distinguished from natural) law; and that in no country or age could it be traced back to any other source. Will some one please tell me where is the positive law that establishes slavery in Kansas? [A voice: "The bogus laws."] Aye, the bogus laws! And, on the same principle, a gang of Missouri horse-thieves could come into Illinois and declare horse-stealing to be legal [Laughter], and it would be just as legal as slavery is in Kansas. But by express statute, in the land of Washington and Jefferson, we may soon be brought face to face with the discreditable fact of showing to the world by our acts that we prefer slavery to freedom—darkness to light! [Sensation.]

It is, I believe, a principle in law that when one party to a contract violates it so grossly as to chiefly destroy the object for which it is made, the other party may rescind it. I will ask Browning if that ain't good law. [Voices: "Yes!"] Well, now if that be right, I go for rescinding the whole, entire Missouri Compromise and thus turning Missouri into a free State; and I should like to know the difference—should like for any one to point out the difference—between our making a free State of Missouri and their making a slave State of Kansas. [Great applause.] There ain't one bit of difference, except that our way would be a great mercy to humanity. But I have never said, and the Whig party has never said, and those who oppose the Nebraska Bill do not as a body say, that they have any intention of interfering with slavery in the slave States. Our platform says just the contrary. We allow slavery to exist in the slave States, not because slavery is right or good, but from the necessities of our Union. We grant a fugitive slave law because it is so "nominated in the bond"; because our fathers so stipulated—had to—and we are bound to carry out this agreement. But they did not agree to introduce slavery in regions where it did not previously exist. On the contrary, they said by their example and teachings that they did not deem it expedient—did n't consider it right—to do so; and it is wise and right to do just as they did about it. [Voices: "Good!"] And that it what we propose—not to interfere with slavery where it exists (we have never tried to do it), and to give them a reasonable and efficient fugitive slave law. [A voice: "No!"] I say YES! [Applause.] It was part of the bargain, and I'm for living up to it; but I go no further; I'm not bound to do more, and I won't agree any further. [Great applause.]

We, here in Illinois, should feel especially proud of the provision of the Missouri Compromise excluding slavery from what is now Kansas; for an Illinois man, Jesse B. Thomas, was its father. Henry Clay, who is credited with the authorship of the Compromise in general terms, did not even vote for that provision, but only advocated the ultimate admission by a second compromise; and Thomas was, beyond all controversy, the real author of the "slavery restriction" branch of the Compromise. To show the generosity of the Northern members toward the Southern side: on a test vote to exclude slavery from Missouri, ninety voted not to exclude, and eighty-seven to exclude, every vote from the slave States being ranged with the former and fourteen votes from the free States, of whom seven were from New England alone; while on a vote to exclude slavery from what is now Kansas, the vote was one hundred and thirty-four for, to forty-two against. The scheme, as a whole, was, of course, a Southern triumph. It is idle to contend otherwise, as is now being done by the Nebraskites; it was so shown by the votes and quite as emphatically by the expressions of representative men. Mr. Lowndes of South Carolina was never known to commit a political mistake; his was the great judgment of that section; and he declared that this measure "would restore tranquillity to the country—a result demanded by every consideration of discretion, of moderation, of wisdom, and of virtue." When the measure came before President Monroe for his approval, he put to each member of his cabinet this question: "Has Congress the constitutional power to prohibit slavery in a Territory?" And John C. Calhoun and William H. Crawford from the South, equally with John Quincy Adams, Benjamin Rush, and Smith Thompson from the North, alike answered, "Yes!" without qualification or equivocation; and this measure, of so great consequence to the South, was passed; and Missouri was, by means of it, finally enabled to knock at the door of the Republic for an open passage to its brood of slaves. And, in spite of this, Freedom's share is about to be taken by violence—by the force of misrepresentative votes, not called for by the popular will. What name can I, in common decency, give to this wicked transaction? [Sensation.]

But even then the contest was not over; for when the Missouri constitution came before Congress for its approval, it forbade any free negro or mulatto from entering the State. In short, our Illinois "black laws" were hidden away in their constitution [Laughter], and the controversy was thus revived. Then it was that Mr. Clay's talents shone out conspicuously, and the controversy that shook the union to its foundation was finally settled to the satisfaction of the conservative parties on both sides of the line, though not to the extremists on either, and Missouri was admitted by the small majority of six in the lower House. How great a majority, do you think, would have been given had Kansas also been secured for slavery? [A voice: "A majority the other way."] "A majority the other way," is answered. Do you think it would have been safe for a Northern man to have confronted his constituents after having voted to consign both Missouri and Kansas to hopeless slavery? And yet this man Douglas, who misrepresents his constituents and who has exerted his highest talents in that direction, will be carried in triumph through the State and hailed with honor while applauding that act. [Three groans for "Dug!"] And this shows whither we are tending. This thing of slavery is more powerful than its supporters—even than the high priests that minister at its altar. It debauches even our greatest men. It gathers strength, like a rolling snowball, by its own infamy. Monstrous crimes are committed in its name by persons collectively which they would not dare to commit as individuals. Its aggressions and encroachments almost surpass belief. In a despotism, one might not wonder to see slavery advance steadily and remorselessly into new dominions; but is it not wonderful, is it not even alarming, to see its steady advance in a land dedicated to the proposition that "all men are created equal"? [Sensation.]

It yields nothing itself; it keeps all it has, and gets all it can besides. It really came dangerously near securing Illinois in 1824; it did get Missouri in 1821. The first proposition was to admit what is now Arkansas and Missouri as one slave State. But the territory was divided and Arkansas came in, without serious question, as a slave State; and afterwards Missouri, not, as a sort of equality, free, but also as a slave State. Then we had Florida and Texas; and now Kansas is about to be forced into the dismal procession. [Sensation.] And so it is wherever you look. We have not forgotten—it is but six years since—how dangerously near California came to being a slave State. Texas is a slave State, and four other slave States may be carved from its vast domain. And yet, in the year 1829, slavery was abolished throughout that vast region by a royal decree of the then sovereign of Mexico. Will you please tell me by what right slavery exists in Texas to-day? By the same right as, and no higher or greater than, slavery is seeking dominion in Kansas: by political force—peaceful, if that will suffice; by the torch (as in Kansas) and the bludgeon (as in the Senate chamber), if required. And so history repeats itself; and even as slavery has kept its course by craft, intimidation, and violence in the past, so it will persist, in my judgment, until met and dominated by the will of a people bent on its restriction.

We have, this very afternoon, heard bitter denunciations of Brooks in Washington, and Titus, Stringfellow, Atchison, Jones, and Shannon in Kansas—the battle-ground of slavery. I certainly am not going to advocate or shield them; but they and their acts are but the necessary outcome of the Nebraska law. We should reserve our highest censure for the authors of the mischief, and not for the catspaws which they use. I believe it was Shakespeare who said, "Where the offence lies, there let the axe fall"; and, in my opinion, this man Douglas and the Northern men in Congress who advocate "Nebraska" are more guilty than a thousand Joneses and Stringfellows, with all their murderous practices, can be. [Applause.]

We have made a good beginning here to-day. As our Methodist friends would say, "I feel it is good to be here." While extremists may find some fault with the moderation of our platform, they should recollect that "the battle is not always to the strong, nor the race to the swift." In grave emergencies, moderation is generally safer than radicalism; and as this struggle is likely to be long and earnest, we must not, by our action, repel any who are in sympathy with us in the main, but rather win all that we can to our standard. We must not belittle nor overlook the facts of our condition—that we are new and comparatively weak, while our enemies are entrenched and relatively strong. They have the administration and the political power; and, right or wrong, at present they have the numbers. Our friends who urge an appeal to arms with so much force and eloquence should recollect that the government is arrayed against us, and that the numbers are now arrayed against us as well; or, to state it nearer to the truth, they are not yet expressly and affirmatively for us; and we should repel friends rather than gain them by anything savoring of revolutionary methods. As it now stands, we must appeal to the sober sense and patriotism of the people. We will make converts day by day; we will grow strong by calmness and moderation; we will grow strong by the violence and injustice of our adversaries. And, unless truth be a mockery and justice a hollow lie, we will be in the majority after a while, and then the revolution which we will accomplish will be none the less radical from being the result of pacific measures. The battle of freedom is to be fought out on principle. Slavery is a violation of the eternal right. We have temporized with it from the necessities of our condition; but as sure as God reigns and school children read, THAT BLACK FOUL LIE CAN NEVER BE CONSECRATED INTO GOD'S HALLOWED TRUTH! [Immense applause lasting some time.]

One of our greatest difficulties is, that men who know that slavery is a detestable crime and ruinous to the nation are compelled, by our peculiar condition and other circumstances, to advocate it concretely, though damning it in the raw. Henry Clay was a brilliant example of this tendency; others of our purest statesmen are compelled to do so; and thus slavery secures actual support from those who detest it at heart. Yet Henry Clay perfected and forced through the compromise which secured to slavery a great State as well as a political advantage. Not that he hated slavery less, but that he loved the whole Union more. As long as slavery profited by his great compromise, the hosts of proslavery could not sufficiently cover him with praise; but now that this compromise stands in their way—

"....they never mention him,

His name is never heard:

Their lips are now forbid to speak

That once familiar word."

They have slaughtered one of his most cherished measures, and his ghost would arise to rebuke them. [Great applause.]

Now, let us harmonize, my friends, and appeal to the moderation and patriotism of the people: to the sober second thought; to the awakened public conscience. The repeal of the sacred Missouri Compromise has installed the weapons of violence: the bludgeon, the incendiary torch, the death-dealing rifle, the bristling cannon—the weapons of kingcraft, of the inquisition, of ignorance, of barbarism, of oppression. We see its fruits in the dying bed of the heroic Sumner; in the ruins of the "Free State" hotel; in the smoking embers of the Herald of Freedom; in the free-State Governor of Kansas chained to a stake on freedom's soil like a horse-thief, for the crime of freedom. [Applause.] We see it in Christian statesmen, and Christian newspapers, and Christian pulpits applauding the cowardly act of a low bully, WHO CRAWLED UPON HIS VICTIM BEHIND HIS BACK AND DEALT THE DEADLY BLOW. [Sensation and applause.] We note our political demoralization in the catch-words that are coming into such common use; on the one hand, "freedom-shriekers," and sometimes "freedom-screechers" [Laughter], and, on the other hand, "border-ruffians," and that fully deserved. And the significance of catch-words cannot pass unheeded, for they constitute a sign of the times. Everything in this world "jibes" in with everything else, and all the fruits of this Nebraska Bill are like the poisoned source from which they come. I will not say that we may not sooner or later be compelled to meet force by force; but the time has not yet come, and, if we are true to ourselves, may never come. Do not mistake that the ballot is stronger than the bullet. Therefore let the legions of slavery use bullets; but let us wait patiently till November and fire ballots at them in return; and by that peaceful policy I believe we shall ultimately win. [Applause.]

It was by that policy that here in Illinois the early fathers fought the good fight and gained the victory. In 1824 the free men of our State, led by Governor Coles (who was a native of Maryland and President Madison's private secretary), determined that those beautiful groves should never re-echo the dirge of one who has no title to himself. By their resolute determination, the winds that sweep across our broad prairies shall never cool the parched brow, nor shall the unfettered streams that bring joy and gladness to our free soil water the tired feet, of a slave; but so long as those heavenly breezes and sparkling streams bless the land, or the groves and their fragrance or memory remain, the humanity to which they minister SHALL BE FOREVER FREE! [Great applause] Palmer, Yates, Williams, Browning, and some more in this convention came from Kentucky to Illinois (instead of going to Missouri), not only to better their conditions, but also to get away from slavery. They have said so to me, and it is understood among us Kentuckians that we don't like it one bit. Now, can we, mindful of the blessings of liberty which the early men of Illinois left to us, refuse a like privilege to the free men who seek to plant Freedom's banner on our Western outposts? ["No!" "No!"] Should we not stand by our neighbors who seek to better their conditions in Kansas and Nebraska? ["Yes!" "Yes!"] Can we as Christian men, and strong and free ourselves, wield the sledge or hold the iron which is to manacle anew an already oppressed race? ["No!" "No!"] "Woe unto them," it is written, "that decree unrighteous decrees and that write grievousness which they have prescribed." Can we afford to sin any more deeply against human liberty? ["No!" "No!"]

One great trouble in the matter is, that slavery is an insidious and crafty power, and gains equally by open violence of the brutal as well as by sly management of the peaceful. Even after the Ordinance of 1787, the settlers in Indiana and Illinois (it was all one government then) tried to get Congress to allow slavery temporarily, and petitions to that end were sent from Kaskaskia, and General Harrison, the Governor, urged it from Vincennes, the capital. If that had succeeded, good-bye to liberty here. But John Randolph of Virginia made a vigorous report against it; and although they persevered so well as to get three favorable reports for it, yet the United States Senate, with the aid of some slave States, finally squelched if for good. [Applause.] And that is why this hall is to-day a temple for free men instead of a negro livery-stable. [Great applause and laughter.] Once let slavery get planted in a locality, by ever so weak or doubtful a title, and in ever so small numbers, and it is like the Canada thistle or Bermuda grass—you can't root it out. You yourself may detest slavery; but your neighbor has five or six slaves, and he is an excellent neighbor, or your son has married his daughter, and they beg you to help save their property, and you vote against your interests and principle to accommodate a neighbor, hoping that your vote will be on the losing side. And others do the same; and in those ways slavery gets a sure foothold. And when that is done the whole mighty Union—the force of the nation—is committed to its support. And that very process is working in Kansas to-day. And you must recollect that the slave property is worth a billion of dollars; while free-State men must work for sentiment alone. Then there are "blue lodges"—as they call them—everywhere doing their secret and deadly work.

It is a very strange thing, and not solvable by any moral law that I know of, that if a man loses his horse, the whole country will turn out to help hang the thief; but if a man but a shade or two darker than I am is himself stolen, the same crowd will hang one who aids in restoring him to liberty. Such are the inconsistencies of slavery, where a horse is more sacred than a man; and the essence of squatter or popular sovereignty—I don't care how you call it—is that if one man chooses to make a slave of another, no third man shall be allowed to object. And if you can do this in free Kansas, and it is allowed to stand, the next thing you will see is shiploads of negroes from Africa at the wharf at Charleston, for one thing is as truly lawful as the other; and these are the bastard notions we have got to stamp out, else they will stamp us out. [Sensation and applause.]

Two years ago, at Springfield, Judge Douglas avowed that Illinois came into the Union as a slave State, and that slavery was weeded out by the operation of his great, patent, everlasting principle of "popular sovereignty." [Laughter.] Well, now, that argument must be answered, for it has a little grain of truth at the bottom. I do not mean that it is true in essence, as he would have us believe. It could not be essentially true if the Ordinance of '87 was valid. But, in point of fact, there were some degraded beings called slaves in Kaskaskia and the other French settlements when our first State constitution was adopted; that is a fact, and I don't deny it. Slaves were brought here as early as 1720, and were kept here in spite of the Ordinance of 1787 against it. But slavery did not thrive here. On the contrary, under the influence of the ordinance the number decreased fifty-one from 1810 to 1820; while under the influence of squatter sovereignty, right across the river in Missouri, they increased seven thousand two hundred and eleven in the same time; and slavery finally faded out in Illinois, under the influence of the law of freedom, while it grew stronger and stronger in Missouri, under the law or practice of "popular sovereignty." In point of fact there were but one hundred and seventeen slaves in Illinois one year after its admission, or one to every four hundred and seventy of its population; or, to state it in another way, if Illinois was a slave State in 1820, so were New York and New Jersey much greater slave States from having had greater numbers, slavery having been established there in very early times. But there is this vital difference between all these States and the Judge's Kansas experiment: that they sought to disestablish slavery which had been already established, while the Judge seeks, so far as he can, to disestablish freedom, which had been established there by the Missouri Compromise. [Voices: "Good!"]

The Union is under-going a fearful strain; but it is a stout old ship, and has weathered many a hard blow, and "the stars in their courses," aye, an invisible Power, greater than the puny efforts of men, will fight for us. But we ourselves must not decline the burden of responsibility, nor take counsel of unworthy passions. Whatever duty urges us to do or to omit must be done or omitted; and the recklessness with which our adversaries break the laws, or counsel their violation, should afford no example for us. Therefore, let us revere the Declaration of Independence; let us continue to obey the Constitution and the laws; let us keep step to the music of the Union. Let us draw a cordon, so to speak, around the slave States, and the hateful institution, like a reptile poisoning itself, will perish by its own infamy. [Applause.]

But we cannot be free men if this is, by our national choice, to be a land of slavery. Those who deny freedom to others deserve it not for themselves; and, under the rule of a just God, cannot long retain it.[Loud applause.]

Did you ever, my friends, seriously reflect upon the speed with which we are tending downwards? Within the memory of men now present the leading statesman of Virginia could make genuine, red-hot abolitionist speeches in old Virginia! and, as I have said, now even in "free Kansas" it is a crime to declare that it is "free Kansas." The very sentiments that I and others have just uttered would entitle us, and each of us, to the ignominy and seclusion of a dungeon; and yet I suppose that, like Paul, we were "free born." But if this thing is allowed to continue, it will be but one step further to impress the same rule in Illinois. [Sensation.]

The conclusion of all is, that we must restore the Missouri Compromise. We must highly resolve that Kansas must be free! [Great applause.] We must reinstate the birthday promise of the Republic; we must reaffirm the Declaration of Independence; we must make good in essence as well as in form Madison's avowal that "the word slave ought not to appear in the Constitution"; and we must even go further, and decree that only local law, and not that time-honored instrument, shall shelter a slaveholder. We must make this a land of liberty in fact, as it is in name. But in seeking to attain these results—so indispensable if the liberty which is our pride and boast shall endure—we will be loyal to the Constitution and to the "flag of our Union," and no matter what our grievance—even though Kansas shall come in as a slave State; and no matter what theirs—even if we shall restore the compromise—WE WILL SAY TO THE SOUTHERN DISUNIONISTS, WE WON'T GO OUT OF THE UNION, AND YOU SHAN'T!

[This was the climax; the audience rose to its feet en masse, applauded, stamped, waved handkerchiefs, threw hats in the air, and ran riot for several minutes. The arch-enchanter who wrought this transformation looked, meanwhile, like the personification of political justice.]

But let us, meanwhile, appeal to the sense and patriotism of the people, and not to their prejudices; let us spread the floods of enthusiasm here aroused all over these vast prairies, so suggestive of freedom. Let us commence by electing the gallant soldier Governor (Colonel) Bissell who stood for the honor of our State alike on the plains and amidst the chaparral of Mexico and on the floor of Congress, while he defied the Southern Hotspur; and that will have a greater moral effect than all the border ruffians can accomplish in all their raids on Kansas. There is both a power and a magic in popular opinion. To that let us now appeal; and while, in all probability, no resort to force will be needed, our moderation and forbearance will stand US in good stead when, if ever, WE MUST MAKE AN APPEAL TO BATTLE AND TO THE GOD OF HOSTS! [Immense applause and a rush for the orator.]

One can realize with this ability to move people's minds that the Southern Conspiracy were right to hate this man. He, better than any at the time was able to uncover their stratagems and tear down their sophisms and contradictions.

POLITICAL CORRESPONDENCE

TO W. C. WHITNEY.

SPRINGFIELD, July 9, 1856.

DEAR WHITNEY:—I now expect to go to Chicago on the 15th, and I probably shall remain there or thereabouts for about two weeks.

It turned me blind when I first heard Swett was beaten and Lovejoy nominated; but, after much reflection, I really believe it is best to let it stand. This, of course, I wish to be confidential.

Lamon did get your deeds. I went with him to the office, got them, and put them in his hands myself.

Yours very truly,

A. LINCOLN.

ON OUT-OF-STATE CAMPAIGNERS

TO WILLIAM GRIMES.

SPRINGFIELD, ILLINOIS, July 12, 1856

Your's of the 29th of June was duly received. I did not answer it because it plagued me. This morning I received another from Judd and Peck, written by consultation with you. Now let me tell you why I am plagued:

1. I can hardly spare the time.

2. I am superstitious. I have scarcely known a party preceding an election to call in help from the neighboring States but they lost the State. Last fall, our friends had Wade, of Ohio, and others, in Maine; and they lost the State. Last spring our adversaries had New Hampshire full of South Carolinians, and they lost the State. And so, generally, it seems to stir up more enemies than friends.

Have the enemy called in any foreign help? If they have a foreign champion there I should have no objection to drive a nail in his track. I shall reach Chicago on the night of the 15th, to attend to a little business in court. Consider the things I have suggested, and write me at Chicago. Especially write me whether Browning consents to visit you.

Your obedient servant,

A. LINCOLN.

REPUBLICAN CAMPAIGN SPEECH

FRAGMENT OF SPEECH AT GALENA, ILLINOIS, IN THE FREMONT CAMPAIGN,

AUGUST 1, 1856.

You further charge us with being disunionists. If you mean that it is our aim to dissolve the Union, I for myself answer that it is untrue; for those who act with me I answer that it is untrue. Have you heard us assert that as our aim? Do you really believe that such is our aim? Do you find it in our platform, our speeches, our conventions, or anywhere? If not, withdraw the charge.

But you may say that, though it is not our aim, it will be the result if we succeed, and that we are therefore disunionists in fact. This is a grave charge you make against us, and we certainly have a right to demand that you specify in what way we are to dissolve the Union. How are we to effect this?

The only specification offered is volunteered by Mr. Fillmore in his Albany speech. His charge is that if we elect a President and Vice-President both from the free States, it will dissolve the Union. This is open folly. The Constitution provides that the President and Vice-President of the United States shall be of different States, but says nothing as to the latitude and longitude of those States. In 1828 Andrew Jackson, of Tennessee, and John C. Calhoun, of South Carolina, were elected President and Vice-President, both from slave States; but no one thought of dissolving the Union then on that account. In 1840 Harrison, of Ohio, and Tyler, of Virginia, were elected. In 1841 Harrison died and John Tyler succeeded to the Presidency, and William R. King, of Alabama, was elected acting Vice-President by the Senate; but no one supposed that the Union was in danger. In fact, at the very time Mr. Fillmore uttered this idle charge, the state of things in the United States disproved it. Mr. Pierce, of New Hampshire, and Mr. Bright, of Indiana, both from free States, are President and Vice-President, and the Union stands and will stand. You do not pretend that it ought to dissolve the Union, and the facts show that it won't; therefore the charge may be dismissed without further consideration.

No other specification is made, and the only one that could be made is that the restoration of the restriction of 1820, making the United States territory free territory, would dissolve the Union. Gentlemen, it will require a decided majority to pass such an act. We, the majority, being able constitutionally to do all that we purpose, would have no desire to dissolve the Union. Do you say that such restriction of slavery would be unconstitutional, and that some of the States would not submit to its enforcement? I grant you that an unconstitutional act is not a law; but I do not ask and will not take your construction of the Constitution. The Supreme Court of the United States is the tribunal to decide such a question, and we will submit to its decisions; and if you do also, there will be an end of the matter. Will you? If not, who are the disunionists—you or we? We, the majority, would not strive to dissolve the Union; and if any attempt is made, it must be by you, who so loudly stigmatize us as disunionists. But the Union, in any event, will not be dissolved. We don't want to dissolve it, and if you attempt it we won't let you. With the purse and sword, the army and navy and treasury, in our hands and at our command, you could not do it. This government would be very weak indeed if a majority with a disciplined army and navy and a well-filled treasury could not preserve itself when attacked by an unarmed, undisciplined, unorganized minority. All this talk about the dissolution of the Union is humbug, nothing but folly. We do not want to dissolve the Union; you shall not.

ON THE DANGER OF THIRD-PARTIES

TO JOHN BENNETT.

SPRINGFIELD, AUG. 4, 1856

DEAR SIR:—I understand you are a Fillmore man. If, as between Fremont and Buchanan, you really prefer the election of Buchanan, then burn this without reading a line further. But if you would like to defeat Buchanan and his gang, allow me a word with you: Does any one pretend that Fillmore can carry the vote of this State? I have not heard a single man pretend so. Every vote taken from Fremont and given to Fillmore is just so much in favor of Buchanan. The Buchanan men see this; and hence their great anxiety in favor of the Fillmore movement. They know where the shoe pinches. They now greatly prefer having a man of your character go for Fillmore than for Buchanan because they expect several to go with you, who would go for Fremont if you were to go directly for Buchanan.

I think I now understand the relative strength of the three parties in this State as well as any one man does, and my opinion is that to-day Buchanan has alone 85,000, Fremont 78,000, and Fillmore 21,000.

This gives B. the State by 7000 and leaves him in the minority of the whole 14,000.

Fremont and Fillmore men being united on Bissell, as they already are, he cannot be beaten. This is not a long letter, but it contains the whole story.

Yours as ever,

A. LINCOLN.

TO JESSE K. DUBOIS.

SPRINGFIELD, Aug. 19, 1856.

DEAR DUBOIS: Your letter on the same sheet with Mr. Miller's is just received. I have been absent four days. I do not know when your court sits.

Trumbull has written the committee here to have a set of appointments made for him commencing here in Springfield, on the 11th of Sept., and to extend throughout the south half of the State. When he goes to Lawrenceville, as he will, I will strain every nerve to be with you and him. More than that I cannot promise now.

Yours as truly as ever,

A. LINCOLN.

TO HARRISON MALTBY.

[Confidential]

SPRINGFIELD, September 8, 1856.

DEAR SIR:—I understand you are a Fillmore man. Let me prove to you that every vote withheld from Fremont and given to Fillmore in this State actually lessens Fillmore's chance of being President. Suppose Buchanan gets all the slave States and Pennsylvania, and any other one State besides; then he is elected, no matter who gets all the rest. But suppose Fillmore gets the two slave States of Maryland and Kentucky; then Buchanan is not elected; Fillmore goes into the House of Representatives, and may be made President by a compromise. But suppose, again, Fillmore's friends throw away a few thousand votes on him in Indiana and Illinois; it will inevitably give these States to Buchanan, which will more than compensate him for the loss of Maryland and Kentucky, will elect him, and leave Fillmore no chance in the House of Representatives or out of it.

This is as plain as adding up the weight of three small hogs. As Mr. Fillmore has no possible chance to carry Illinois for himself, it is plainly to his interest to let Fremont take it, and thus keep it out of the hands of Buchanan. Be not deceived. Buchanan is the hard horse to beat in this race. Let him have Illinois, and nothing can beat him; and he will get Illinois if men persist in throwing away votes upon Mr. Fillmore. Does some one persuade you that Mr. Fillmore can carry

Illinois? Nonsense! There are over seventy newspapers in Illinois opposing Buchanan, only three or four of which support Mr. Fillmore, all the rest going for Fremont. Are not these newspapers a fair index of the proportion of the votes? If not, tell me why.

Again, of these three or four Fillmore newspapers, two, at least, are supported in part by the Buchanan men, as I understand. Do not they know where the shoe pinches? They know the Fillmore movement helps them, and therefore they help it. Do think these things over, and then act according to your judgment.

Yours very truly,

A. LINCOLN.

TO Dr. R. BOAL.

Sept. 14, 1856.

Dr. R. BOAL, Lacon, Ill.

MY DEAR SIR:—Yours of the 8th inviting me to be with [you] at Lacon on the 30th is received. I feel that I owe you and our friends of Marshall a good deal, and I will come if I can; and if I do not get there, it will be because I shall think my efforts are now needed farther south.

Present my regards to Mrs. Boal, and believe [me], as ever,

Your friend,

A. LINCOLN.

TO HENRY O'CONNER, MUSCATINE, IOWA.

SPRINGFIELD, Sept. 14, 1856.

DEAR SIR:—Yours, inviting me to attend a mass-meeting on the 23d inst., is received. It would be very pleasant to strike hands with the Fremonters of Iowa, who have led the van so splendidly, in this grand charge which we hope and believe will end in a most glorious victory. All thanks, all honor to Iowa! But Iowa is out of all danger, and it is no time for us, when the battle still rages, to pay holiday visits to Iowa. I am sure you will excuse me for remaining in Illinois, where much hard work is still to be done.

Yours very truly,

A. LINCOLN.

AFTER THE DEMOCRATIC VICTORY OF BUCHANAN

FRAGMENT OF SPEECH AT A REPUBLICAN BANQUET IN CHICAGO, DECEMBER 10, 1856.

We have another annual Presidential message. Like a rejected lover making merry at the wedding of his rival, the President felicitates himself hugely over the late Presidential election. He considers the result a signal triumph of good principles and good men, and a very pointed rebuke of bad ones. He says the people did it. He forgets that the "people," as he complacently calls only those who voted for Buchanan, are in a minority of the whole people by about four hundred thousand votes—one full tenth of all the votes. Remembering this, he might perceive that the "rebuke" may not be quite as durable as he seems to think—that the majority may not choose to remain permanently rebuked by that minority.

The President thinks the great body of us Fremonters, being ardently attached to liberty, in the abstract, were duped by a few wicked and designing men. There is a slight difference of opinion on this. We think he, being ardently attached to the hope of a second term, in the concrete, was duped by men who had liberty every way. He is the cat's-paw. By much dragging of chestnuts from the fire for others to eat, his claws are burnt off to the gristle, and he is thrown aside as unfit for further use. As the fool said of King Lear, when his daughters had turned him out of doors, "He 's a shelled peascod" ("That 's a sheal'd peascod").

So far as the President charges us "with a desire to change the domestic institutions of existing States," and of "doing everything in our power to deprive the Constitution and the laws of moral authority," for the whole party on belief, and for myself on knowledge, I pronounce the charge an unmixed and unmitigated falsehood.

Our government rests in public opinion. Whoever can change public opinion can change the government practically just so much. Public opinion, on any subject, always has a "central idea," from which all its minor thoughts radiate. That "central idea" in our political public opinion at the beginning was, and until recently has continued to be, "the equality of men." And although it has always submitted patiently to whatever of inequality there seemed to be as matter of actual necessity, its constant working has been a steady progress toward the practical equality of all men. The late Presidential election was a struggle by one party to discard that central idea and to substitute for it the opposite idea that slavery is right in the abstract, the workings of which as a central idea may be the perpetuity of human slavery and its extension to all countries and colors. Less than a year ago the Richmond Enquirer, an avowed advocate of slavery, regardless of color, in order to favor his views, invented the phrase "State equality," and now the President, in his message, adopts the Enquirer's catch-phrase, telling us the people "have asserted the constitutional equality of each and all of the States of the Union as States." The President flatters himself that the new central idea is completely inaugurated; and so indeed it is, so far as the mere fact of a Presidential election can inaugurate it. To us it is left to know that the majority of the people have not yet declared for it, and to hope that they never will.

All of us who did not vote for Mr. Buchanan, taken together, are a majority of four hundred thousand. But in the late contest we were divided between Fremont and Fillmore. Can we not come together for the future? Let every one who really believes and is resolved that free society is not and shall not be a failure, and who can conscientiously declare that in the last contest he has done only what he thought best—let every such one have charity to believe that every other one can say as much. Thus let bygones be bygones; let past differences as nothing be; and with steady eye on the real issue let us reinaugurate the good old "central idea" of the republic. We can do it. The human heart is with us; God is with us. We shall again be able, not to declare that "all States as States are equal," nor yet that "all citizens as citizens are equal," but to renew the broader, better declaration, including both these and much more, that "all men are created equal."

TO Dr. R. BOAL.

SPRINGFIELD, Dec. 25, 1856.

DEAR SIR:-When I was at Chicago two weeks ago I saw Mr. Arnold, and from a remark of his I inferred he was thinking of the speakership, though I think he was not anxious about it. He seemed most anxious for harmony generally, and particularly that the contested seats from Peoria and McDonough might be rightly determined. Since I came home I had a talk with Cullom, one of our American representatives here, and he says he is for you for Speaker and also that he thinks all the Americans will be for you, unless it be Gorin, of Macon, of whom he cannot speak. If you would like to be Speaker go right up and see Arnold. He is talented, a practised debater, and, I think, would do himself more credit on the floor than in the Speaker's seat. Go and see him; and if you think fit, show him this letter.

Your friend as ever,

A. LINCOLN.

1857

TO JOHN E. ROSETTE. Private.

SPRINGFIELD, ILL., February 10, 1857.

DEAR SIR:—Your note about the little paragraph in the Republican was received yesterday, since which time I have been too unwell to notice it. I had not supposed you wrote or approved it. The whole originated in mistake. You know by the conversation with me that I thought the establishment of the paper unfortunate, but I always expected to throw no obstacle in its way, and to patronize it to the extent of taking and paying for one copy. When the paper was brought to my house, my wife said to me, "Now are you going to take another worthless little paper?" I said to her evasively, "I have not directed the paper to be left." From this, in my absence, she sent the message to the carrier. This is the whole story.

Yours truly,

A. LINCOLN.

RESPONSE TO A DOUGLAS SPEECH

SPEECH IN SPRINGFIELD, ILLINOIS, JUNE 26, 1857.

FELLOW-CITIZENS:—I am here to-night partly by the invitation of some of you, and partly by my own inclination. Two weeks ago Judge Douglas spoke here on the several subjects of Kansas, the Dred Scott decision, and Utah. I listened to the speech at the time, and have the report of it since. It was intended to controvert opinions which I think just, and to assail (politically, not personally) those men who, in common with me, entertain those opinions. For this reason I wished then, and still wish, to make some answer to it, which I now take the opportunity of doing.

I begin with Utah. If it prove to be true, as is probable, that the people of Utah are in open rebellion to the United States, then Judge Douglas is in favor of repealing their territorial organization, and attaching them to the adjoining States for judicial purposes. I say, too, if they are in rebellion, they ought to be somehow coerced to obedience; and I am not now prepared to admit or deny that the Judge's mode of coercing them is not as good as any. The Republicans can fall in with it without taking back anything they have ever said. To be sure, it would be a considerable backing down by Judge Douglas from his much-vaunted doctrine of self-government for the Territories; but this is only additional proof of what was very plain from the beginning, that that doctrine was a mere deceitful pretense for the benefit of slavery. Those who could not see that much in the Nebraska act itself, which forced governors, and secretaries, and judges on the people of the Territories without their choice or consent, could not be made to see, though one should rise from the dead.

But in all this it is very plain the Judge evades the only question the Republicans have ever pressed upon the Democracy in regard to Utah. That question the Judge well knew to be this: "If the people of Utah peacefully form a State constitution tolerating polygamy, will the Democracy admit them into the Union?" There is nothing in the United States Constitution or law against polygamy; and why is it not a part of the Judge's "sacred right of self-government" for the people to have it, or rather to keep it, if they choose? These questions, so far as I know, the Judge never answers. It might involve the Democracy to answer them either way, and they go unanswered.

As to Kansas. The substance of the Judge's speech on Kansas is an effort to put the free-State men in the wrong for not voting at the election of delegates to the constitutional convention. He says:

"There is every reason to hope and believe that the law will be fairly interpreted and impartially executed, so as to insure to every bona fide inhabitant the free and quiet exercise of the elective franchise."

It appears extraordinary that Judge Douglas should make such a statement.

He knows that, by the law, no one can vote who has not been registered;

and he knows that the free-State men place their refusal to vote on the

ground that but few of them have been registered. It is possible that this

is not true, but Judge Douglas knows it is asserted to be true in letters,

newspapers, and public speeches, and borne by every mail and blown by

every breeze to the eyes and ears of the world. He knows it is boldly

declared that the people of many whole counties, and many whole

neighborhoods in others, are left unregistered; yet he does not venture

to contradict the declaration, or to point out how they can vote without

being registered; but he just slips along, not seeming to know there is

any such question of fact, and complacently declares:

"There is every reason to hope and believe that the law will be

fairly and impartially executed, so as to insure to every bona fide

inhabitant the free and quiet exercise of the elective franchise."

I readily agree that if all had a chance to vote they ought to have voted. If, on the contrary, as they allege, and Judge Douglas ventures not to particularly contradict, few only of the free-State men had a chance to vote, they were perfectly right in staying from the polls in a body.

By the way, since the Judge spoke, the Kansas election has come off. The Judge expressed his confidence that all the Democrats in Kansas would do their duty-including "free-State Democrats," of course. The returns received here as yet are very incomplete; but so far as they go, they indicate that only about one sixth of the registered voters have really voted; and this, too, when not more, perhaps, than one half of the rightful voters have been registered, thus showing the thing to have been altogether the most exquisite farce ever enacted. I am watching with considerable interest to ascertain what figure "the free-State Democrats" cut in the concern. Of course they voted,—all Democrats do their duty,—and of course they did not vote for slave-State candidates. We soon shall know how many delegates they elected, how many candidates they had pledged to a free State, and how many votes were cast for them.

Allow me to barely whisper my suspicion that there were no such things in Kansas as "free-State Democrats"—that they were altogether mythical, good only to figure in newspapers and speeches in the free States. If there should prove to be one real living free-State Democrat in Kansas, I suggest that it might be well to catch him, and stuff and preserve his skin as an interesting specimen of that soon-to-be extinct variety of the genus Democrat.

And now as to the Dred Scott decision. That decision declares two propositions—first, that a negro cannot sue in the United States courts; and secondly, that Congress cannot prohibit slavery in the Territories. It was made by a divided court dividing differently on the different points. Judge Douglas does not discuss the merits of the decision, and in that respect I shall follow his example, believing I could no more improve on McLean and Curtis than he could on Taney.

He denounces all who question the correctness of that decision, as offering violent resistance to it. But who resists it? Who has, in spite of the decision, declared Dred Scott free, and resisted the authority of his master over him?

Judicial decisions have two uses—first, to absolutely determine the case decided, and secondly, to indicate to the public how other similar cases will be decided when they arise. For the latter use, they are called "precedents" and "authorities."

We believe as much as Judge Douglas (perhaps more) in obedience to, and respect for, the judicial department of government. We think its decisions on constitutional questions, when fully settled, should control not only the particular cases decided, but the general policy of the country, subject to be disturbed only by amendments of the Constitution as provided in that instrument itself. More than this would be revolution. But we think the Dred Scott decision is erroneous. We know the court that made it has often overruled its own decisions, and we shall do what we can to have it to overrule this. We offer no resistance to it.

Judicial decisions are of greater or less authority as precedents according to circumstances. That this should be so accords both with common sense and the customary understanding of the legal profession.

If this important decision had been made by the unanimous concurrence of the judges, and without any apparent partisan bias, and in accordance with legal public expectation and with the steady practice of the departments throughout our history, and had been in no part based on assumed historical facts which are not really true; or, if wanting in some of these, it had been before the court more than once, and had there been affirmed and reaffirmed through a course of years, it then might be, perhaps would be, factious, nay, even revolutionary, not to acquiesce in it as a precedent.

But when, as is true, we find it wanting in all these claims to the public confidence, it is not resistance, it is not factious, it is not even disrespectful, to treat it as not having yet quite established a settled doctrine for the country. But Judge Douglas considers this view awful. Hear him:

"The courts are the tribunals prescribed by the Constitution and created by the authority of the people to determine, expound, and enforce the law. Hence, whoever resists the final decision of the highest judicial tribunal aims a deadly blow at our whole republican system of government—a blow which, if successful, would place all our rights and liberties at the mercy of passion, anarchy, and violence. I repeat, therefore, that if resistance to the decisions of the Supreme Court of the United States, in a matter like the points decided in the Dred Scott case, clearly within their jurisdiction as defined by the Constitution, shall be forced upon the country as a political issue, it will become a distinct and naked issue between the friends and enemies of the Constitution—the friends and the enemies of the supremacy of the laws."

Why, this same Supreme Court once decided a national bank to be constitutional; but General Jackson, as President of the United States, disregarded the decision, and vetoed a bill for a recharter, partly on constitutional ground, declaring that each public functionary must support the Constitution "as he understands it." But hear the General's own words. Here they are, taken from his veto message:

"It is maintained by the advocates of the bank that its constitutionality, in all its features, ought to be considered as settled by precedent, and by the decision of the Supreme Court. To this conclusion I cannot assent. Mere precedent is a dangerous source of authority, and should not be regarded as deciding questions of constitutional power, except where the acquiescence of the people and the States can be considered as well settled. So far from this being the case on this subject, an argument against the bank might be based on precedent. One Congress, in 1791, decided in favor of a bank; another, in 1811, decided against it. One Congress, in 1815, decided against a bank; another, in 1816, decided in its favor. Prior to the present Congress, therefore, the precedents drawn from that course were equal. If we resort to the States, the expressions of legislative, judicial, and executive opinions against the bank have been probably to those in its favor as four to one. There is nothing in precedent, therefore, which, if its authority were admitted, ought to weigh in favor of the act before me."

I drop the quotations merely to remark that all there ever was in the way of precedent up to the Dred Scott decision, on the points therein decided, had been against that decision. But hear General Jackson further:

"If the opinion of the Supreme Court covered the whole ground of this act, it ought not to control the coordinate authorities of this government. The Congress, the executive, and the courts must, each for itself, be guided by its own opinion of the Constitution. Each public officer who takes an oath to support the Constitution swears that he will support it as he understands it, and not as it is understood by others."

Again and again have I heard Judge Douglas denounce that bank decision and applaud General Jackson for disregarding it. It would be interesting for him to look over his recent speech, and see how exactly his fierce philippics against us for resisting Supreme Court decisions fall upon his own head. It will call to mind a long and fierce political war in this country, upon an issue which, in his own language, and, of course, in his own changeless estimation, "was a distinct issue between the friends and the enemies of the Constitution," and in which war he fought in the ranks of the enemies of the Constitution.

I have said, in substance, that the Dred Scott decision was in part based on assumed historical facts which were not really true, and I ought not to leave the subject without giving some reasons for saying this; I therefore give an instance or two, which I think fully sustain me. Chief Justice Taney, in delivering the opinion of the majority of the court, insists at great length that negroes were no part of the people who made, or for whom was made, the Declaration of Independence, or the Constitution of the United States.

On the contrary, Judge Curtis, in his dissenting opinion, shows that in five of the then thirteen States—to wit, New Hampshire, Massachusetts, New York, New Jersey, and North Carolina—free negroes were voters, and in proportion to their numbers had the same part in making the Constitution that the white people had. He shows this with so much particularity as to leave no doubt of its truth; and as a sort of conclusion on that point, holds the following language:

"The Constitution was ordained and established by the people of the United States, through the action, in each State, of those persons who were qualified by its laws to act thereon in behalf of themselves and all other citizens of the State. In some of the States, as we have seen, colored persons were among those qualified by law to act on the subject. These colored persons were not only included in the body of 'the people of the United States' by whom the Constitution was ordained and established; but in at least five of the States they had the power to act, and doubtless did act, by their suffrages, upon the question of its adoption."

Again, Chief Justice Taney says:

"It is difficult at this day to realize the state of public opinion, in relation to that unfortunate race, which prevailed in the civilized and enlightened portions of the world at the time of the Declaration of Independence, and when the Constitution of the United States was framed and adopted."

And again, after quoting from the Declaration, he says:

"The general words above quoted would seem to include the whole human family, and if they were used in a similar instrument at this day, would be so understood."

In these the Chief Justice does not directly assert, but plainly assumes as a fact, that the public estimate of the black man is more favorable now than it was in the days of the Revolution. This assumption is a mistake. In some trifling particulars the condition of that race has been ameliorated; but as a whole, in this country, the change between then and now is decidedly the other way, and their ultimate destiny has never appeared so hopeless as in the last three or four years. In two of the five States—New Jersey and North Carolina—that then gave the free negro the right of voting, the right has since been taken away, and in a third—New York—it has been greatly abridged; while it has not been extended, so far as I know, to a single additional State, though the number of the States has more than doubled. In those days, as I understand, masters could, at their own pleasure, emancipate their slaves; but since then such legal restraints have been made upon emancipation as to amount almost to prohibition. In those days Legislatures held the unquestioned power to abolish slavery in their respective States, but now it is becoming quite fashionable for State constitutions to withhold that power from the Legislatures. In those days, by common consent, the spread of the black man's bondage to the new countries was prohibited, but now Congress decides that it will not continue the prohibition, and the Supreme Court decides that it could not if it would. In those days our Declaration of Independence was held sacred by all, and thought to include all; but now, to aid in making the bondage of the negro universal and eternal, it is assailed and sneered at and construed and hawked at and torn, till, if its framers could rise from their graves, they could not at all recognize it. All the powers of earth seem rapidly combining against him. Mammon is after him, ambition follows, philosophy follows, and the theology of the day fast joining the cry. They have him in his prison house; they have searched his person, and left no prying instrument with him. One after another they have closed the heavy iron doors upon him; and now they have him, as it were, bolted in with a lock of hundred keys, which can never be unlocked without the concurrence of every key—the keys in the hands of a hundred different men, and they scattered to hundred different and distant places; and they stand musing as to what invention, in all the dominions of mind and matter, can be produced to make the impossibility of his escape more complete than it is.

It is grossly incorrect to say or assume that the public estimate of the negro is more favorable now than it was at the origin of the government.

Three years and a half ago, Judge Douglas brought forward his famous Nebraska Bill. The country was at once in a blaze. He scorned all opposition, and carried it through Congress. Since then he has seen himself superseded in a Presidential nomination by one indorsing the general doctrine of his measure, but at the same time standing clear of the odium of its untimely agitation and its gross breach of national faith; and he has seen that successful rival constitutionally elected, not by the strength of friends, but by the division of adversaries, being in a popular minority of nearly four hundred thousand votes. He has seen his chief aids in his own State, Shields and Richardson, politically speaking, successively tried, convicted, and executed for an offence not their own but his. And now he sees his own case standing next on the docket for trial.

There is a natural disgust in the minds of nearly all white people at the idea of an indiscriminate amalgamation of the white and black races; and Judge Douglas evidently is basing his chief hope upon the chances of his being able to appropriate the benefit of this disgust to himself. If he can, by much drumming and repeating, fasten the odium of that idea upon his adversaries, he thinks he can struggle through the storm. He therefore clings to this hope, as a drowning man to the last plank. He makes an occasion for lugging it in from the opposition to the Dred Scott decision. He finds the Republicans insisting that the Declaration of Independence includes all men, black as well as white, and forthwith he boldly denies that it includes negroes at all, and proceeds to argue gravely that all who contend it does, do so only because they want to vote, and eat, and sleep, and marry with negroes. He will have it that they cannot be consistent else. Now I protest against the counterfeit logic which concludes that, because I do not want a black woman for a slave I must necessarily want her for a wife. I need not have her for either. I can just leave her alone. In some respects she certainly is not my equal; but in her natural right to eat the bread she earns with her own hands, without asking leave of any one else, she is my equal and the equal of all others.

Chief Justice Taney, in his opinion in the Dred Scott case, admits that the language of the Declaration is broad enough to include the whole human family, but he and Judge Douglas argue that the authors of that instrument did not intend to include negroes, by the fact that they did not at once actually place them on an equality with the whites. Now this grave argument comes to just nothing at all, by the other fact that they did not at once, or ever afterward, actually place all white people on an equality with one another. And this is the staple argument of both the Chief Justice and the Senator for doing this obvious violence to the plain, unmistakable language of the Declaration.

I think the authors of that notable instrument intended to include all men, but they did not intend to declare all men equal in all respects. They did not mean to say all were equal in color, size, intellect, moral developments, or social capacity. They defined with tolerable distinctness in what respects they did consider all men created equal—equal with "certain inalienable rights, among which are life, liberty, and the pursuit of happiness." This they said, and this they meant. They did not mean to assert the obvious untruth that all were then actually enjoying that equality, nor yet that they were about to confer it immediately upon them. In fact, they had no power to confer such a boon. They meant simply to declare the right, so that enforcement of it might follow as fast as circumstances should permit.

They meant to set up a standard maxim for free society, which should be familiar to all, and revered by all; constantly looked to, constantly labored for, and, even though never perfectly attained, constantly approximated, and thereby constantly spreading and deepening its influence and augmenting the happiness and value of life to all people of all colors everywhere. The assertion that "all men are created equal" was of no practical use in effecting our separation from Great Britain; and it was placed in the Declaration not for that, but for future use. Its authors meant it to be—as thank God, it is now proving itself—stumbling-block to all those who in after times might seek to turn a free people back into the hateful paths of despotism. They knew the proneness of prosperity to breed tyrants, and they meant when such should reappear in this fair land and commence their vocation, they should find left for them at least one hard nut to crack.

I have now briefly expressed my view of the meaning and object of that part of the Declaration of Independence which declares that "all men are created equal."

Now let us hear Judge Douglas's view of the same subject, as I find it in the printed report of his late speech. Here it is:

"No man can vindicate the character, motives, and conduct of the signers of the Declaration of Independence, except upon the hypothesis that they referred to the white race alone, and not to the African, when they declared all men to have been created equal; that they were speaking of British subjects on this continent being equal to British subjects born and residing in Great Britain; that they were entitled to the same inalienable rights, and among them were enumerated life, liberty, and the pursuit of happiness. The Declaration was adopted for the purpose of justifying the colonists in the eyes of the civilized world in withdrawing their allegiance from the British crown, and dissolving their connection with the mother country."

My good friends, read that carefully over some leisure hour, and ponder well upon it; see what a mere wreck—mangled ruin—it makes of our once glorious Declaration.

"They were speaking of British subjects on this continent being equal to British subjects born and residing in Great Britain"! Why, according to this, not only negroes but white people outside of Great Britain and America were not spoken of in that instrument. The English, Irish, and Scotch, along with white Americans, were included, to be sure, but the French, Germans, and other white people of the world are all gone to pot along with the Judge's inferior races!

I had thought the Declaration promised something better than the condition of British subjects; but no, it only meant that we should be equal to them in their own oppressed and unequal condition. According to that, it gave no promise that, having kicked off the king and lords of Great Britain, we should not at once be saddled with a king and lords of our own.

I had thought the Declaration contemplated the progressive improvement in the condition of all men everywhere; but no, it merely "was adopted for the purpose of justifying the colonists in the eyes of the civilized world in withdrawing their allegiance from the British crown, and dissolving their connection with the mother country." Why, that object having been effected some eighty years ago, the Declaration is of no practical use now—mere rubbish—old wadding left to rot on the battlefield after the victory is won.

I understand you are preparing to celebrate the "Fourth," to-morrow week. What for? The doings of that day had no reference to the present; and quite half of you are not even descendants of those who were referred to at that day. But I suppose you will celebrate, and will even go so far as to read the Declaration. Suppose, after you read it once in the old-fashioned way, you read it once more with Judge Douglas's version. It will then run thus:

"We hold these truths to be self-evident, that all British subjects who were on this continent eighty-one years ago were created equal to all British subjects born and then residing in Great Britain."

And now I appeal to all—to Democrats as well as others—are you really willing that the Declaration shall thus be frittered away?—thus left no more, at most, than an interesting memorial of the dead past?—thus shorn of its vitality and practical value, and left without the germ or even the suggestion of the individual rights of man in it?

But Judge Douglas is especially horrified at the thought of the mixing of blood by the white and black races. Agreed for once—a thousand times agreed. There are white men enough to marry all the white women and black men enough to marry all the black women; and so let them be married. On this point we fully agree with the Judge, and when he shall show that his policy is better adapted to prevent amalgamation than ours, we shall drop ours and adopt his. Let us see. In 1850 there were in the United States 405,751 mulattoes. Very few of these are the offspring of whites and free blacks; nearly all have sprung from black slaves and white masters. A separation of the races is the only perfect preventive of amalgamation; but as an immediate separation is impossible, the next best thing is to keep them apart where they are not already together. If white and black people never get together in Kansas, they will never mix blood in Kansas. That is at least one self-evident truth. A few free colored persons may get into the free States, in any event; but their number is too insignificant to amount to much in the way of mixing blood. In 1850 there were in the free States 56,649 mulattoes; but for the most part they were not born there—they came from the slave States, ready made up. In the same year the slave States had 348,874 mulattoes, all of home production. The proportion of free mulattoes to free blacks—the only colored classes in the free States is much greater in the slave than in the free States. It is worthy of note, too, that among the free States those which make the colored man the nearest equal to the white have proportionably the fewest mulattoes, the least of amalgamation. In New Hampshire, the State which goes farthest toward equality between the races, there are just 184 mulattoes, while there are in Virginia—how many do you think?—79,775, being 23,126 more than in all the free States together.

These statistics show that slavery is the greatest source of amalgamation, and next to it, not the elevation, but the degradation of the free blacks. Yet Judge Douglas dreads the slightest restraints on the spread of slavery, and the slightest human recognition of the negro, as tending horribly to amalgamation!

The very Dred Scott case affords a strong test as to which party most favors amalgamation, the Republicans or the dear Union-saving Democracy. Dred Scott, his wife, and two daughters were all involved in the suit. We desired the court to have held that they were citizens so far at least as to entitle them to a hearing as to whether they were free or not; and then, also, that they were in fact and in law really free. Could we have had our way, the chances of these black girls ever mixing their blood with that of white people would have been diminished at least to the extent that it could not have been without their consent. But Judge Douglas is delighted to have them decided to be slaves, and not human enough to have a hearing, even if they were free, and thus left subject to the forced concubinage of their masters, and liable to become the mothers of mulattoes in spite of themselves: the very state of case that produces nine tenths of all the mulattoes all the mixing of blood in the nation.

Of course, I state this case as an illustration only, not meaning to say or intimate that the master of Dred Scott and his family, or any more than a percentage of masters generally, are inclined to exercise this particular power which they hold over their female slaves.

I have said that the separation of the races is the only perfect preventive of amalgamation. I have no right to say all the members of the Republican party are in favor of this, nor to say that as a party they are in favor of it. There is nothing in their platform directly on the subject. But I can say a very large proportion of its members are for it, and that the chief plank in their platform—opposition to the spread of slavery—is most favorable to that separation.

Such separation, if ever effected at all, must be effected by colonization; and no political party, as such, is now doing anything directly for colonization. Party operations at present only favor or retard colonization incidentally. The enterprise is a difficult one; but "where there is a will there is a way," and what colonization needs most is a hearty will.

Will springs from the two elements of moral sense and self-interest. Let us be brought to believe it is morally right, and at the same time favorable to, or at least not against, our interest to transfer the African to his native clime, and we shall find a way to do it, however great the task may be. The children of Israel, to such numbers as to include four hundred thousand fighting men, went out of Egyptian bondage in a body.

How differently the respective courses of the Democratic and Republican parties incidentally, bear on the question of forming a will—a public sentiment—for colonization, is easy to see. The Republicans inculcate, with whatever of ability they can, that the negro is a man, that his bondage is cruelly wrong, and that the field of his oppression ought not to be enlarged. The Democrats deny his manhood; deny, or dwarf to insignificance, the wrong of his bondage; so far as possible crush all sympathy for him, and cultivate and excite hatred and disgust against him; compliment themselves as Union-savers for doing so; and call the indefinite outspreading of his bondage "a sacred right of self-government."

The plainest print cannot be read through a gold eagle; and it will be ever hard to find many men who will send a slave to Liberia, and pay his passage, while they can send him to a new country—Kansas, for instance—and sell him for fifteen hundred dollars, and the rise.

TO WILLIAM GRIMES.

SPRINGFIELD, ILLINOIS, August, 1857

DEAR SIR:—Yours of the 14th is received, and I am much obliged for the legal information you give.

You can scarcely be more anxious than I that the next election in Iowa should result in favor of the Republicans. I lost nearly all the working part of last year, giving my time to the canvass; and I am altogether too poor to lose two years together. I am engaged in a suit in the United States Court at Chicago, in which the Rock Island Bridge Company is a party. The trial is to commence on the 8th of September, and probably will last two or three weeks. During the trial it is not improbable that all hands may come over and take a look at the bridge, and, if it were possible to make it hit right, I could then speak at Davenport. My courts go right on without cessation till late in November. Write me again, pointing out the more striking points of difference between your old and new constitutions, and also whether Democratic and Republican party lines were drawn in the adoption of it, and which were for and which were against it. If, by possibility, I could get over among you it might be of some advantage to know these things in advance.

Yours very truly,

A. LINCOLN.

ARGUMENT IN THE ROCK ISLAND BRIDGE CASE.

(From the Daily Press of Chicago, Sept. 24, 1857.)

Hurd et al. vs Railroad Bridge Co.

United States Circuit Court, Hon. John McLean, Presiding Judge.

13th day, Tuesday, Sept. 22, 1857.

Mr. A. Lincoln addressed the jury. He said he did not purpose to assail anybody, that he expected to grow earnest as he proceeded but not ill-natured. "There is some conflict of testimony in the case," he said, "but one quarter of such a number of witnesses seldom agree, and even if all were on one side some discrepancy might be expected. We are to try and reconcile them, and to believe that they are not intentionally erroneous as long as we can." He had no prejudice, he said, against steamboats or steamboat men nor any against St. Louis, for he supposed they went about this matter as other people would do in their situation. "St. Louis," he continued, "as a commercial place may desire that this bridge should not stand, as it is adverse to her commerce, diverting a portion of it from the river; and it may be that she supposes that the additional cost of railroad transportation upon the productions of Iowa will force them to go to St. Louis if this bridge is removed. The meetings in St. Louis are connected with this case only as some witnesses are in it, and thus has some prejudice added color to their testimony." The last thing that would be pleasing to him, Mr. Lincoln said, would be to have one of these great channels, extending almost from where it never freezes to where it never thaws, blocked up, but there is a travel from east to west whose demands are not less important than those of the river. It is growing larger and larger, building up new countries with a rapidity never before seen in the history of the world. He alluded to the astonishing growth of Illinois, having grown within his memory to a population of a million and a half; to Iowa and the other young rising communities of the Northwest.

"This current of travel," said he, "has its rights as well as that of north and south. If the river had not the advantage in priority and legislation we could enter into free competition with it and we could surpass it. This particular railroad line has a great importance and the statement of its business during a little less than a year shows this importance. It is in evidence that from September 8, 1856, to August 8, 1857, 12,586 freight cars and 74,179 passengers passed over this bridge. Navigation was closed four days short of four months last year, and during this time while the river was of no use this road and bridge were valuable. There is, too, a considerable portion of time when floating or thin ice makes the river useless while the bridge is as useful as ever. This shows that this bridge must be treated with respect in this court and is not to be kicked about with contempt. The other day Judge Wead alluded to the strike of the contending interest and even a dissolution of the Union. The proper mode for all parties in this affair is to 'live and let live,' and then we will find a cessation of this trouble about the bridge. What mood were the steamboat men in when this bridge was burned? Why, there was a shouting and ringing of bells and whistling on all the boats as it fell. It was a jubilee, a greater celebration than follows an excited election. The first thing I will proceed to is the record of Mr. Gurney and the complaint of Judge Wead that the record did not extend back over all the time from the completion of the bridge. The principal part of the navigation after the bridge was burned passed through the span. When the bridge was repaired and the boats were a second time confined to the draw it was provided that this record should be kept. That is the simple history of that book.

"From April 19th, 1856, to May 6th—seventeen days—there were twenty accidents and all the time since then there have been but twenty hits, including seven accidents, so that the dangers of this place are tapering off and as the boatmen get cool the accidents get less. We may soon expect if this ratio is kept up that there will be no accidents at all.

"Judge Wead said, while admitting that the floats went straight through, there was a difference between a float and a boat, but I do not remember that he indulged us with an argument in support of this statement. Is it because there is a difference in size? Will not a small body and a large one float the same way under the same influence? True a flatboat will float faster than an egg shell and the egg shell might be blown away by the wind, but if under the same influence they would go the same way. Logs, floats, boards, various things the witnesses say all show the same current. Then is not this test reliable? At all depths too the direction of the current is the same. A series of these floats would make a line as long as a boat and would show any influence upon any part and all parts of the boat.

"I will now speak of the angular position of the piers. What is the amount of the angle? The course of the river is a curve and the pier is straight. If a line is produced from the upper end of the long pier straight with the pier to a distance of 350 feet, and a line is drawn from a point in the channel opposite this point to the head of the pier, Colonel Nason says they will form an angle of twenty degrees. But the angle if measured at the pier is seven degrees; that is, we would have to move the pier seven degrees to make it exactly straight with the current. Would that make the navigation better or worse? The witnesses of the plaintiff seem to think it was only necessary to say that the pier formed an angle with the current and that settled the matter. Our more careful and accurate witnesses say that, though they had been accustomed to seeing the piers placed straight with the current, yet they could see that here the current had been made straight by us in having made this slight angle; that the water now runs just right, that it is straight and cannot be improved. They think that if the pier was changed the eddy would be divided and the navigation improved.

"I am not now going to discuss the question what is a material obstruction. We do not greatly differ about the law. The cases produced here are, I suppose, proper to be taken into consideration by the court in instructing a jury. Some of them I think are not exactly in point, but I am still willing to trust his honor, Judge McLean, and take his instructions as law. What is reasonable skill and care? This is a thing of which the jury are to judge. I differ from the other side when it says that they are bound to exercise no more care than was taken before the building of the bridge. If we are allowed by the Legislature to build the bridge which will require them to do more than before, when a pilot comes along, it is unreasonable for him to dash on heedless of this structure which has been legally put there. The Afton came there on the 5th and lay at Rock Island until next morning. When a boat lies up the pilot has a holiday, and would not any of these jurors have then gone around to the bridge and gotten acquainted with the place? Pilot Parker has shown here that he does not understand the draw. I heard him say that the fall from the head to the foot of the pier was four feet; he needs information. He could have gone there that day and seen there was no such fall. He should have discarded passion and the chances are that he would have had no disaster at all. He was bound to make himself acquainted with the place.

"McCammon says that the current and the swell coming from the long pier drove her against the long pier. In other words drove her toward the very pier from which the current came! It is an absurdity, an impossibility. The only recollection I can find for this contradiction is in a current which White says strikes out from the long pier and then like a ram's horn turns back, and this might have acted somehow in this manner.

"It is agreed by all that the plaintiff's boat was destroyed and that it was destroyed upon the head of the short pier; that she moved from the channel where she was with her bow above the head of the long pier, till she struck the short one, swung around under the bridge and there was crowded and destroyed.

"I shall try to prove that the average velocity of the current through the draw with the boat in it should be five and a half miles an hour; that it is slowest at the head of the pier and swiftest at the foot of the pier. Their lowest estimate in evidence is six miles an hour, their highest twelve miles. This was the testimony of men who had made no experiment, only conjecture. We have adopted the most exact means. The water runs swiftest in high water and we have taken the point of nine feet above low water. The water when the Afton was lost was seven feet above low water, or at least a foot lower than our time. Brayton and his assistants timed the instruments, the best instruments known in measuring currents. They timed them under various circumstances and they found the current five miles an hour and no more. They found that the water at the upper end ran slower than five miles; that below it was swifter than five miles, but that the average was five miles. Shall men who have taken no care, who conjecture, some of whom speak of twenty miles an hour, be believed against those who have had such a favorable and well improved opportunity? They should not even qualify the result. Several men have given their opinion as to the distance of the steamboat Carson, and I suppose if one should go and measure that distance you would believe him in preference to all of them.

"These measurements were made when the boat was not in the draw. It has been ascertained what is the area of the cross section of this stream and the area of the face of the piers, and the engineers say that the piers being put there will increase the current proportionally as the space is decreased. So with the boat in the draw. The depth of the channel was twenty-two feet, the width one hundred and sixteen feet; multiply these and you have the square-feet across the water of the draw, viz.: 2552 feet. The Afton was 35 feet wide and drew 5 feet, making a fourteenth of the sum. Now, one-fourteenth of five miles is five-fourteenths of one mile—about one third of a mile—the increase of the current. We will call the current five and a half miles per hour. The next thing I will try to prove is that the plaintiff's (?) boat had power to run six miles an hour in that current. It had been testified that she was a strong, swift boat, able to run eight miles an hour up stream in a current of four miles an hour, and fifteen miles down stream. Strike the average and you will find what is her average—about eleven and a half miles. Take the five and a half miles which is the speed of the current in the draw and it leaves the power of that boat in that draw at six miles an hour, 528 feet per minute and 8 4/5 feet to the second.

"Next I propose to show that there are no cross currents. I know their witnesses say that there are cross currents—that, as one witness says, there were three cross currents and two eddies; so far as mere statement, without experiment, and mingled with mistakes, can go, they have proved. But can these men's testimony be compared with the nice, exact, thorough experiments of our witnesses? Can you believe that these floats go across the currents? It is inconceivable that they could not have discovered every possible current. How do boats find currents that floats cannot discover? We assume the position then that those cross currents are not there. My next proposition is that the Afton passed between the S. B. Carson and the Iowa shore. That is undisputed.

"Next I shall show that she struck first the short pier, then the long pier, then the short one again and there she stopped." Mr. Lincoln then cited the testimony of eighteen witnesses on this point.

"How did the boat strike when she went in? Here is an endless variety of opinion. But ten of them say what pier she struck; three of them testify that she struck first the short, then the long and then the short for the last time. None of the rest substantially contradict this. I assume that these men have got the truth because I believe it an established fact. My next proposition is that after she struck the short and long pier and before she got back to the short pier the boat got right with her bow up. So says the pilot Parker—that he got her through until her starboard wheel passed the short pier. This would make her head about even with the head of the long pier. He says her head was as high or higher than the head of the long pier. Other witnesses confirmed this one. The final stroke was in the splash door aft the wheel. Witnesses differ, but the majority say that she struck thus."

Court adjourned.

14th day, Wednesday, Sept. 23, 1857.

Mr. A. LINCOLN resumed. He said he should conclude as soon as possible. He said the colored map of the plaintiff which was brought in during one stage of the trial showed itself that the cross currents alleged did not exist. That the current as represented would drive an ascending boat to the long pier but not to the short pier, as they urge. He explained from a model of a boat where the splash door is, just behind the wheel. The boat struck on the lower shoulder of the short pier as she swung around in the splash door; then as she went on around she struck the point or end of the pier, where she rested. "Her engineers," said Mr. Lincoln, "say the starboard wheel then was rushing around rapidly. Then the boat must have struck the upper point of the pier so far back as not to disturb the wheel. It is forty feet from the stern of the Afton to the splash door, and thus it appears that she had but forty feet to go to clear the pier. How was it that the Afton with all her power flanked over from the channel to the short pier without moving one foot ahead? Suppose she was in the middle of the draw, her wheel would have been 31 feet from the short pier. The reason she went over thus is her starboard wheel was not working. I shall try to establish the fact that the wheel was not running and that after she struck she went ahead strong on this same wheel. Upon the last point the witnesses agree, that the starboard wheel was running after she struck, and no witnesses say that it was running while she was out in the draw flanking over."

Mr. Lincoln read from the testimonies of various witnesses to prove that the starboard wheel was not working while the Afton was out in the stream.

"Other witnesses show that the captain said something of the machinery of the wheel, and the inference is that he knew the wheel was not working. The fact is undisputed that she did not move one inch ahead while she was moving this 31 feet sideways. There is evidence proving that the current there is only five miles an hour, and the only explanation is that her power was not all used—that only one wheel was working. The pilot says he ordered the engineers to back her up. The engineers differ from him and said they kept on going ahead. The bow was so swung that the current pressed it over; the pilot pressed the stern over with the rudder, though not so fast but that the bow gained on it, and only one wheel being in motion the boat nearly stood still so far as motion up and down is concerned, and thus she was thrown upon this pier. The Afton came into the draw after she had just passed the Carson, and as the Carson no doubt kept the true course the Afton going around her got out of the proper way, got across the current into the eddy which is west of a straight line drawn down from the long pier, was compelled to resort to these changes of wheels, which she did not do with sufficient adroitness to save her. Was it not her own fault that she entered wrong, so far wrong that she never got right? Is the defence to blame for that?

"For several days we were entertained with depositions about boats 'smelling a bar.' Why did the Afton then, after she had come up smelling so close to the long pier sheer off so strangely. When she got to the centre of the very nose she was smelling she seemed suddenly to have lost her sense of smell and to have flanked over to the short pier."

Mr. Lincoln said there was no practicability in the project of building a tunnel under the river, for there "is not a tunnel that is a successful project in this world. A suspension bridge cannot be built so high but that the chimneys of the boats will grow up till they cannot pass. The steamboat men will take pains to make them grow. The cars of a railroad cannot without immense expense rise high enough to get even with a suspension bridge or go low enough to get through a tunnel; such expense is unreasonable.

"The plaintiffs have to establish that the bridge is a material obstruction and that they have managed their boat with reasonable care and skill. As to the last point high winds have nothing to do with it, for it was not a windy day. They must show due skill and care. Difficulties going down stream will not do, for they were going up stream. Difficulties with barges in tow have nothing to do with the accident, for they had no barge." Mr. Lincoln said he had much more to say, many things he could suggest to the jury, but he wished to close to save time.

TO JESSE K. DUBOIS.

DEAR DUBOIS:

BLOOMINGTON, Dec. 19, 1857.

J. M. Douglas of the I. C. R. R. Co. is here and will carry this letter. He says they have a large sum (near $90,000) which they will pay into the treasury now, if they have an assurance that they shall not be sued before Jan., 1859—otherwise not. I really wish you could consent to this. Douglas says they cannot pay more, and I believe him.

I do not write this as a lawyer seeking an advantage for a client; but only as a friend, only urging you to do what I think I would do if I were in your situation. I mean this as private and confidential only, but I feel a good deal of anxiety about it.

Yours as ever,

A. LINCOLN.

TO JOSEPH GILLESPIE.

SPRINGFIELD, Jan. 19, 1858.

MY DEAR SIR: This morning Col. McClernand showed me a petition for a mandamus against the Secretary of State to compel him to certify the apportionment act of last session; and he says it will be presented to the court to-morrow morning. We shall be allowed three or four days to get up a return, and I, for one, want the benefit of consultation with you.

Please come right up.

Yours as ever,

A. LINCOLN.

TO J. GILLESPIE.

SPRINGFIELD, Feb 7, 1858

MY DEAR SIR: Yesterday morning the court overruled the demurrer to Hatches return in the mandamus case. McClernand was present; said nothing about pleading over; and so I suppose the matter is ended.

The court gave no reason for the decision; but Peck tells me confidentially that they were unanimous in the opinion that even if the Gov'r had signed the bill purposely, he had the right to scratch his name off so long as the bill remained in his custody and control.

Yours as ever,

A. LINCOLN.

TO H. C. WHITNEY.

SPRINGFIELD, December 18, 1857.

HENRY C. WHITNEY, ESQ.

MY DEAR SIR:—Coming home from Bloomington last night I found your letter of the 15th.

I know of no express statute or decisions as to what a J. P. upon the expiration of his term shall do with his docket books, papers, unfinished business, etc., but so far as I know, the practice has been to hand over to the successor, and to cease to do anything further whatever, in perfect analogy to Sections 110 and 112, and I have supposed and do suppose this is the law. I think the successor may forthwith do whatever the retiring J. P. might have done. As to the proviso to Section 114 I think it was put in to cover possible cases, by way of caution, and not to authorize the J. P. to go forward and finish up whatever might have been begun by him.

The view I take, I believe, is the Common law principle, as to retiring officers and their successors, to which I remember but one exception, which is the case of Sheriff and ministerial officers of that class.

I have not had time to examine this subject fully, but I have great confidence I am right. You must not think of offering me pay for this.

Mr. John O. Johnson is my friend; I gave your name to him. He is doing the work of trying to get up a Republican organization. I do not suppose "Long John" ever saw or heard of him. Let me say to you confidentially, that I do not entirely appreciate what the Republican papers of Chicago are so constantly saying against "Long John." I consider those papers truly devoted to the Republican cause, and not unfriendly to me; but I do think that more of what they say against "Long John" is dictated by personal malice than themselves are conscious of. We can not afford to lose the services of "Long John" and I do believe the unrelenting warfare made upon him is injuring our cause. I mean this to be confidential.

If you quietly co-operate with Mr. J. O. Johnson on getting up an organization, I think it will be right.

Your friend as ever,

A. LINCOLN.

1858

ANOTHER POLITICAL PATRONAGE REFERENCE

TO EDWARD G. MINER.

SPRINGFIELD, Feb.19, 1858.

MY DEAR SIR:

Mr. G. A. Sutton is an applicant for superintendent of the addition of the Insane Asylum, and I understand it partly depends on you whether he gets it.

Sutton is my fellow-townsman and friend, and I therefore wish to say for him that he is a man of sterling integrity and as a master mechanic and builder not surpassed by any in our city, or any I have known anywhere, as far as I can judge. I hope you will consider me as being really interested for Mr. Sutton and not as writing merely to relieve myself of importunity. Please show this to Col. William Ross and let him consider it as much intended for him as for yourself.

Your friend as ever,

A. LINCOLN.

POLITICAL COMMUNICATION

TO W. H. LAMON, ESQ.

SPRINGFIELD, JUNE 11, 1858

DEAR SIR:—Yours of the 9th written at Joliet is just received. Two or three days ago I learned that McLean had appointed delegates in favor of Lovejoy, and thenceforward I have considered his renomination a fixed fact. My opinion—if my opinion is of any consequence in this case, in which it is no business of mine to interfere—remains unchanged, that running an independent candidate against Lovejoy will not do; that it will result in nothing but disaster all round. In the first place, whosoever so runs will be beaten and will be spotted for life; in the second place, while the race is in progress, he will be under the strongest temptation to trade with the Democrats, and to favor the election of certain of their friends to the Legislature; thirdly, I shall be held responsible for it, and Republican members of the Legislature who are partial to Lovejoy will for that purpose oppose us; and lastly, it will in the end lose us the district altogether. There is no safe way but a convention; and if in that convention, upon a common platform which all are willing to stand upon, one who has been known as an abolitionist, but who is now occupying none but common ground, can get the majority of the votes to which all look for an election, there is no safe way but to submit.

As to the inclination of some Republicans to favor Douglas, that is one of the chances I have to run, and which I intend to run with patience.

I write in the court room. Court has opened, and I must close.

Yours as ever,

A. LINCOLN.

BRIEF AUTOBIOGRAPHY,

JUNE 15, 1858.

The compiler of the Dictionary of Congress states that while preparing that work for publication, in 1858, he sent to Mr. Lincoln the usual request for a sketch of his life, and received the following reply:

Born February 12, 1809, in Hardin County, Kentucky.

Education, defective.

Profession, a lawyer.

Have been a captain of volunteers in Black Hawk war.

Postmaster at a very small office.

Four times a member of the Illinois Legislature and was a member of the lower house of Congress.

Yours, etc.,

A. LINCOLN.

THE LINCOLN-DOUGLAS DEBATES I

POLITICAL SPEECHES & DEBATES of LINCOLN WITH DOUGLAS In the Senatorial Campaign of 1858 in Illinois SPEECH AT SPRINGFIELD, JUNE 17, 1858

[The following speech was delivered at Springfield, Ill., at the close of the Republican State Convention held at that time and place, and by which Convention Mr. LINCOLN had been named as their candidate for United States Senator. Mr. DOUGLAS was not present.]

Mr. PRESIDENT AND GENTLEMEN OF THE CONVENTION:—If we could first know where we are, and whither we are tending, we could better judge what to do, and how to do it. We are now far into the fifth year since a policy was initiated with the avowed object and confident promise of putting an end to slavery agitation. Under the operation of that policy, that agitation has not only not ceased, but has constantly augmented. In my opinion, it will not cease until a crisis shall have been reached and passed. "A house divided against itself cannot stand." I believe this government cannot endure permanently half slave and half free. I do not expect the Union to be dissolved; I do not expect the house to fall; but I do expect it will cease to be divided. It will become all one thing, or all the other. Either the opponents of slavery will arrest the further spread of it, and place it where the public mind shall rest in the belief that it is in the course of ultimate extinction, or its advocates will push it forward till it shall become alike lawful in all the States, old as well as new, North as well as South.

Have we no tendency to the latter condition?

Let any one who doubts, carefully contemplate that now almost complete legal combination-piece of machinery, so to speak compounded of the Nebraska doctrine and the Dred Scott decision. Let him consider, not only what work the machinery is adapted to do, and how well adapted, but also let him study the history of its construction, and trace, if he can, or rather fail, if he can, to trace the evidences of design, and concert of action, among its chief architects, from the beginning.

The new year of 1854 found slavery excluded from more than half the States by State Constitutions, and from most of the National territory by Congressional prohibition. Four days later, commenced the struggle which ended in repealing that Congressional prohibition. This opened all the National territory to slavery, and was the first point gained.

But, so far, Congress only had acted, and an indorsement by the people, real or apparent, was indispensable to save the point already gained, and give chance for more.

This necessity had not been overlooked, but had been provided for, as well as might be, in the notable argument of "squatter sovereignty," otherwise called "sacred right of self-government," which latter phrase, though expressive of the only rightful basis of any government, was so perverted in this attempted use of it as to amount to just this: That if any one man choose to enslave another, no third man shall be allowed to object. That argument was incorporated into the Nebraska Bill itself, in the language which follows:

"It being the true intent and meaning of this Act not to legislate slavery into any Territory or State, nor to exclude it therefrom, but to leave the people thereof perfectly free to form and regulate their domestic institutions in their own way, subject only to the Constitution of the United States."

Then opened the roar of loose declamation in favor of "squatter sovereignty," and "sacred right of self-government." "But," said opposition members, "let us amend the bill so as to expressly declare that the people of the Territory may exclude slavery." "Not we," said the friends of the measure, and down they voted the amendment.

While the Nebraska Bill was passing through Congress, a law case, involving the question of a negro's freedom, by reason of his owner having voluntarily taken him first into a free State, and then into a territory covered by the Congressional Prohibition, and held him as a slave for a long time in each, was passing through the United States Circuit Court for the District of Missouri; and both Nebraska Bill and lawsuit were brought to a decision in the same month of May, 1854. The negro's name was "Dred Scott," which name now designates the decision finally made in the case. Before the then next Presidential election, the law case came to, and was argued in, the Supreme Court of the United States; but the decision of it was deferred until after the election. Still, before the election, Senator Trumbull, on the floor of the Senate, requested the leading advocate of the Nebraska Bill to state his opinion whether the people of a territory can constitutionally exclude slavery from their limits; and the latter answers: "That is a question for the Supreme Court."

The election came. Mr. Buchanan was elected, and the indorsement, such as it was, secured. That was the second point gained. The indorsement, however, fell short of a clear popular majority by nearly four hundred thousand votes,(approximately 10% of the vote) and so, perhaps, was not overwhelmingly reliable and satisfactory. The outgoing President, in his last annual message, as impressively as possible echoed back upon the people the weight and authority of the indorsement. The Supreme Court met again, did not announce their decision, but ordered a reargument. The Presidential inauguration came, and still no decision of the court; but the incoming President, in his inaugural address, fervently exhorted the people to abide by the forth-coming decision, whatever it might be. Then, in a few days, came the decision.

The reputed author of the Nebraska Bill finds an early occasion to make a speech at this capital indorsing the Dred Scott decision, and vehemently denouncing all opposition to it. The new President, too, seizes the early occasion of the Silliman letter to indorse and strongly construe that decision, and to express his astonishment that any different view had ever been entertained!

At length a squabble springs up between the President and the author of the Nebraska Bill, on the mere question of fact, whether the Lecompton Constitution was or was not in any just sense made by the people of Kansas; and in that quarrel the latter declares that all he wants is a fair vote for the people, and that he cares not whether slavery be voted down or voted up. I do not understand his declaration, that he cares not whether slavery be voted down or voted up, to be intended by him other than as an apt definition of the policy he would impress upon the public mind,—the principle for which he declares he has suffered so much, and is ready to suffer to the end. And well may he cling to that principle! If he has any parental feeling, well may he cling to it. That principle is the only shred left of his original Nebraska doctrine. Under the Dred Scott decision "squatter sovereignty" squatted out of existence, tumbled down like temporary scaffolding; like the mould at the foundry, served through one blast, and fell back into loose sand; helped to carry an election, and then was kicked to the winds. His late joint struggle with the Republicans, against the Lecompton Constitution, involves nothing of the original Nebraska doctrine. That struggle was made on a point—the right of a people to make their own constitution—upon which he and the Republicans have never differed.

The several points of the Dred Scott decision, in connection with Senator Douglas's "care not" policy, constitute the piece of machinery, in its present state of advancement. This was the third point gained. The working points of that machinery are:

Firstly, That no negro slave, imported as such from Africa, and no descendant of such slave, can ever be a citizen of any State, in the sense of that term as used in the Constitution of the United States. This point is made in order to deprive the negro, in every possible event, of the benefit of that provision of the United States Constitution which declares that "The citizens of each State shall be entitled to all privileges and immunities of citizens in the several States."

Secondly, That, "subject to the Constitution of the United States," neither Congress nor a Territorial Legislature can exclude slavery from any United States Territory. This point is made in order that individual men may fill up the Territories with slaves, without danger of losing them as property, and thus to enhance the chances of permanency to the institution through all the future.

Thirdly, That whether the holding a negro in actual slavery in a free State makes him free, as against the holder, the United States courts will not decide, but will leave to be decided by the courts of any slave State the negro may be forced into by the master. This point is made, not to be pressed immediately; but, if acquiesced in for a while, and apparently indorsed by the people at an election, then to sustain the logical conclusion that what Dred Scott's master might lawfully do with Dred Scott, in the free State of Illinois, every other master may lawfully do with any other one, or one thousand slaves, in Illinois, or in any other free State.

Auxiliary to all this, and working hand in hand with it, the Nebraska doctrine, or what is left of it, is to educate and mould public opinion, at least Northern public opinion, not to care whether slavery is voted down or voted up. This shows exactly where we now are; and partially, also, wither we are tending.

It will throw additional light on the latter, to go back and run the mind over the string of historical facts already stated. Several things will now appear less dark and mysterious than they did when they were transpiring. The people were to be left "perfectly free," "subject only to the Constitution." What the Constitution had to do with it, outsiders could not then see. Plainly enough now,—it was an exactly fitted niche, for the Dred Scott decision to afterward come in, and declare the perfect freedom of the people to be just no freedom at all. Why was the amendment, expressly declaring the right of the people, voted down? Plainly enough now,—the adoption of it would have spoiled the niche for the Dred Scott decision. Why was the court decision held up? Why even a Senator's individual opinion withheld, till after the Presidential election? Plainly enough now,—the speaking out then would have damaged the "perfectly free" argument upon which the election was to be carried. Why the outgoing President's felicitation on the indorsement? Why the delay of a reargument? Why the incoming President's advance exhortation in favor of the decision? These things look like the cautious patting and petting of a spirited horse preparatory to mounting him, when it is dreaded that he may give the rider a fall. And why the hasty after-indorsement of the decision by the President and others?

We cannot absolutely know that all these exact adaptations are the result of preconcert. But when we see a lot of framed timbers, different portions of which we know have been gotten out at different times and places and by different workmen, Stephen, Franklin, Roger, and James, for instance, and when we see these timbers joined together, and see they exactly make the frame of a house or a mill, all the tenons and mortises exactly fitting, and all the lengths and proportions of the different pieces exactly adapted to their respective places, and not a piece too many or too few,—not omitting even scaffolding,—or, if a single piece be lacking, we see the place in the frame exactly fitted and prepared yet to bring such piece in,—in such a case, we find it impossible not to believe that Stephen and Franklin and Roger and James all understood one another from the beginning, and all worked upon a common plan or draft drawn up before the first blow was struck.

It should not be overlooked that by the Nebraska Bill the people of a State as well as Territory were to be left "perfectly free," "subject only to the Constitution." Why mention a State? They were legislating for Territories, and not for or about States. Certainly the people of a State are and ought to be subject to the Constitution of the United States; but why is mention of this lugged into this merely Territorial law? Why are the people of a Territory and the people of a State therein lumped together, and their relation to the Constitution therefore treated as being precisely the same? While the opinion of the court, by Chief Justice Taney, in the Dred Scott case, and the separate opinions of all the concurring Judges, expressly declare that the Constitution of the United States neither permits Congress nor a Territorial Legislature to exclude slavery from any United States Territory, they all omit to declare whether or not the same Constitution permits a State, or the people of a State, to exclude it. Possibly, this is a mere omission; but who can be quite sure, if McLean or Curtis had sought to get into the opinion a declaration of unlimited power in the people of a State to exclude slavery from their limits, just as Chase and Mace sought to get such declaration, in behalf of the people of a Territory, into the Nebraska Bill,—I ask, who can be quite sure that it would not have been voted down in the one case as it had been in the other? The nearest approach to the point of declaring the power of a State over slavery is made by Judge Nelson. He approaches it more than once, Using the precise idea, and almost the language, too, of the Nebraska Act. On one occasion, his exact language is, "Except in cases where the power is restrained by the Constitution of the United States, the law of the State is supreme over the subject of slavery within its jurisdiction." In what cases the power of the States is so restrained by the United States Constitution, is left an open question, precisely as the same question, as to the restraint on the power of the Territories, was left open in the Nebraska Act. Put this and that together, and we have another nice little niche, which we may, ere long, see filled with another Supreme Court decision, declaring that the Constitution of the United States does not permit a State to exclude slavery from its limits. And this may especially be expected if the doctrine of "care not whether slavery be voted down or voted up" shall gain upon the public mind sufficiently to give promise that such a decision can be maintained when made.

Such a decision is all that slavery now lacks of being alike lawful in all the States. Welcome or unwelcome, such decision is probably coming, and will soon be upon us, unless the power of the present political dynasty shall be met and overthrown. We shall lie down pleasantly dreaming that the people of Missouri are on the verge of making their State free, and we shall awake to the reality instead that the Supreme Court has made Illinois a slave State. To meet and overthrow the power of that dynasty is the work now before all those who would prevent that consummation. That is what we have to do. How can we best do it?

There are those who denounce us openly to their friends, and yet whisper to us softly that Senator Douglas is the aptest instrument there is with which to effect that object. They wish us to infer all, from the fact that he now has a little quarrel with the present head of the dynasty, and that he has regularly voted with us on a single point, upon which he and we have never differed. They remind us that he is a great man, and that the largest of us are very small ones. Let this be granted. But "a living dog is better than a dead lion." Judge Douglas, if not a dead lion, for this work is at least a caged and toothless one. How can he oppose the advances of slavery? He don't care anything about it. His avowed mission is impressing the "public heart" to care nothing about it. A leading Douglas Democratic newspaper thinks Douglas's superior talent will be needed to resist the revival of the African slave trade. Does Douglas believe an effort to revive that trade is approaching? He has not said so. Does he really think so? But if it is, how can he resist it? For years he has labored to prove it a sacred right of white men to take negro slaves into the new Territories. Can he possibly show that it is less a sacred right to buy them where they can be bought cheapest? And unquestionably they can be bought cheaper in Africa than in Virginia. He has done all in his power to reduce the whole question of slavery to one of a mere right of property; and, as such, how can he oppose the foreign slave trade, how can he refuse that trade in that "property" shall be "perfectly free,"—unless he does it as a protection to the home production? And as the home producers will probably not ask the protection, he will be wholly without a ground of opposition.

Senator Douglas holds, we know, that a man may rightfully be wiser to-day than he was yesterday; that he may rightfully change when he finds himself wrong. But can we, for that reason, run ahead, and infer that he will make any particular change, of which he himself has given no intimation? Can we safely base our action upon any such vague inference? Now, as ever, I wish not to misrepresent Judge Douglas's position, question his motives, or do aught that can be personally offensive to him. Whenever, if ever, he and we can come together on principle so that our cause may have assistance from his great ability, I hope to have interposed no adventitious obstacles. But clearly he is not now with us; he does not pretend to be,—he does not promise ever to be.

Our cause, then, must be intrusted to, and conducted by, its own undoubted friends,—those whose hands are free, whose hearts are in the work, who do care for the result. Two years ago the Republicans of the nation mustered over thirteen hundred thousand strong. We did this under the single impulse of resistance to a common danger, with every external circumstance against us. Of strange, discordant, and even hostile elements we gathered from the four winds, and formed and fought the battle through, under the constant hot fire of a disciplined, proud, and pampered enemy. Did we brave all then to falter now,—now, when that same enemy is wavering, dissevered, and belligerent? The result is not doubtful. We shall not fail; if we stand firm, we shall not fail. Wise counsels may accelerate, or mistakes delay it, but, sooner or later, the victory is sure to come.

SPEECH AT CHICAGO, JULY 10, 1858.

IN REPLY TO SENATOR DOUGLAS

DELIVERED AT CHICAGO, SATURDAY EVENING, JULY 10, 1858.

(Mr. DOUGLAS WAS NOT PRESENT.)

[Mr. LINCOLN was introduced by C. L. Wilson, Esq., and as he made his appearance he was greeted with a perfect storm of applause. For some moments the enthusiasm continued unabated. At last, when by a wave of his hand partial silence was restored, Mr. LINCOLN said,]

MY FELLOW-CITIZENS:—On yesterday evening, upon the occasion of the reception given to Senator Douglas, I was furnished with a seat very convenient for hearing him, and was otherwise very courteously treated by him and his friends, and for which I thank him and them. During the course of his remarks my name was mentioned in such a way as, I suppose, renders it at least not improper that I should make some sort of reply to him. I shall not attempt to follow him in the precise order in which he addressed the assembled multitude upon that occasion, though I shall perhaps do so in the main.

There was one question to which he asked the attention of the crowd, which I deem of somewhat less importance— at least of propriety—for me to dwell upon than the others, which he brought in near the close of his speech, and which I think it would not be entirely proper for me to omit attending to, and yet if I were not to give some attention to it now, I should probably forget it altogether. While I am upon this subject, allow me to say that I do not intend to indulge in that inconvenient mode sometimes adopted in public speaking, of reading from documents; but I shall depart from that rule so far as to read a little scrap from his speech, which notices this first topic of which I shall speak,—that is, provided I can find it in the paper:

"I have made up my mind to appeal to the people against the combination that has been made against me; the Republican leaders having formed an alliance, an unholy and unnatural alliance, with a portion of unscrupulous Federal office-holders. I intend to fight that allied army wherever I meet them. I know they deny the alliance; but yet these men who are trying to divide the Democratic party for the purpose of electing a Republican Senator in my place are just as much the agents and tools of the supporters of Mr. Lincoln. Hence I shall deal with this allied army just as the Russians dealt with the Allies at Sebastopol,—that is, the Russians did not stop to inquire, when they fired a broadside, whether it hit an Englishman, a Frenchman, or a Turk. Nor will I stop to inquire, nor shall I hesitate, whether my blows shall hit the Republican leaders or their allies, who are holding the Federal offices, and yet acting in concert with them."

Well, now, gentlemen, is not that very alarming? Just to think of it! right at the outset of his canvass, I, a poor, kind, amiable, intelligent gentleman,—I am to be slain in this way! Why, my friend the Judge is not only, as it turns out, not a dead lion, nor even a living one,—he is the rugged Russian Bear!

But if they will have it—for he says that we deny it—that there is any such alliance, as he says there is,—and I don't propose hanging very much upon this question of veracity,—but if he will have it that there is such an alliance, that the Administration men and we are allied, and we stand in the attitude of English, French, and Turk, he occupying the position of the Russian, in that case I beg that he will indulge us while we barely suggest to him that these allies took Sebastopol.

Gentlemen, only a few more words as to this alliance. For my part, I have to say that whether there be such an alliance depends, so far as I know, upon what may be a right definition of the term alliance. If for the Republican party to see the other great party to which they are opposed divided among themselves, and not try to stop the division, and rather be glad of it,—if that is an alliance, I confess I am in; but if it is meant to be said that the Republicans had formed an alliance going beyond that, by which there is contribution of money or sacrifice of principle on the one side or the other, so far as the Republican party is concerned,—if there be any such thing, I protest that I neither know anything of it, nor do I believe it. I will, however, say,—as I think this branch of the argument is lugged in,—I would before I leave it state, for the benefit of those concerned, that one of those same Buchanan men did once tell me of an argument that he made for his opposition to Judge Douglas. He said that a friend of our Senator Douglas had been talking to him, and had, among other things, said to him:

"...why, you don't want to beat Douglas?" "Yes," said he, "I do want to beat him, and I will tell you why. I believe his original Nebraska Bill was right in the abstract, but it was wrong in the time that it was brought forward. It was wrong in the application to a Territory in regard to which the question had been settled; it was brought forward at a time when nobody asked him; it was tendered to the South when the South had not asked for it, but when they could not well refuse it; and for this same reason he forced that question upon our party. It has sunk the best men all over the nation, everywhere; and now, when our President, struggling with the difficulties of this man's getting up, has reached the very hardest point to turn in the case, he deserts him and I am for putting him where he will trouble us no more."

Now, gentlemen, that is not my argument; that is not my argument at all. I have only been stating to you the argument of a Buchanan man. You will judge if there is any force in it.

Popular sovereignty! Everlasting popular sovereignty! Let us for a moment inquire into this vast matter of popular sovereignty. What is popular sovereignty? We recollect that at an early period in the history of this struggle there was another name for the same thing,—"squatter sovereignty." It was not exactly popular sovereignty, but squatter sovereignty. What do those terms mean? What do those terms mean when used now? And vast credit is taken by our friend the Judge in regard to his support of it, when he declares the last years of his life have been, and all the future years of his life shall be, devoted to this matter of popular sovereignty. What is it? Why, it is the sovereignty of the people! What was squatter sovereignty? I suppose, if it had any significance at all, it was the right of the people to govern themselves, to be sovereign in their own affairs while they were squatted down in a country not their own, while they had squatted on a Territory that did not belong to them, in the sense that a State belongs to the people who inhabit it, when it belonged to the nation; such right to govern themselves was called "squatter sovereignty."

Now, I wish you to mark: What has become of that squatter sovereignty? what has become of it? Can you get anybody to tell you now that the people of a Territory have any authority to govern themselves, in regard to this mooted question of slavery, before they form a State constitution? No such thing at all; although there is a general running fire, and although there has been a hurrah made in every speech on that side, assuming that policy had given the people of a Territory the right to govern themselves upon this question, yet the point is dodged. To-day it has been decided—no more than a year ago it was decided—by the Supreme Court of the United States, and is insisted upon to-day that the people of a Territory have no right to exclude slavery from a Territory; that if any one man chooses to take slaves into a Territory, all the rest of the people have no right to keep them out. This being so, and this decision being made one of the points that the Judge approved, and one in the approval of which he says he means to keep me down,—put me down I should not say, for I have never been up,—he says he is in favor of it, and sticks to it, and expects to win his battle on that decision, which says that there is no such thing as squatter sovereignty, but that any one man may take slaves into a Territory, and all the other men in the Territory may be opposed to it, and yet by reason of the Constitution they cannot prohibit it. When that is so, how much is left of this vast matter of squatter sovereignty, I should like to know?

When we get back, we get to the point of the right of the people to make a constitution. Kansas was settled, for example, in 1854. It was a Territory yet, without having formed a constitution, in a very regular way, for three years. All this time negro slavery could be taken in by any few individuals, and by that decision of the Supreme Court, which the Judge approves, all the rest of the people cannot keep it out; but when they come to make a constitution, they may say they will not have slavery. But it is there; they are obliged to tolerate it some way, and all experience shows it will be so, for they will not take the negro slaves and absolutely deprive the owners of them. All experience shows this to be so. All that space of time that runs from the beginning of the settlement of the Territory until there is sufficiency of people to make a State constitution,—all that portion of time popular sovereignty is given up. The seal is absolutely put down upon it by the court decision, and Judge Douglas puts his own upon the top of that; yet he is appealing to the people to give him vast credit for his devotion to popular sovereignty.

Again, when we get to the question of the right of the people to form a State constitution as they please, to form it with slavery or without slavery, if that is anything new, I confess I don't know it. Has there ever been a time when anybody said that any other than the people of a Territory itself should form a constitution? What is now in it that Judge Douglas should have fought several years of his life, and pledge himself to fight all the remaining years of his life for? Can Judge Douglas find anybody on earth that said that anybody else should form a constitution for a people? [A voice, "Yes."] Well, I should like you to name him; I should like to know who he was. [Same voice, "John Calhoun."]

No, sir, I never heard of even John Calhoun saying such a thing. He insisted on the same principle as Judge Douglas; but his mode of applying it, in fact, was wrong. It is enough for my purpose to ask this crowd whenever a Republican said anything against it. They never said anything against it, but they have constantly spoken for it; and whoever will undertake to examine the platform, and the speeches of responsible men of the party, and of irresponsible men, too, if you please, will be unable to find one word from anybody in the Republican ranks opposed to that popular sovereignty which Judge Douglas thinks that he has invented. I suppose that Judge Douglas will claim, in a little while, that he is the inventor of the idea that the people should govern themselves; that nobody ever thought of such a thing until he brought it forward. We do not remember that in that old Declaration of Independence it is said that:

"We hold these truths to be self-evident, that all men are created equal; that they are endowed by their Creator with certain inalienable rights; that among these are life, liberty, and the pursuit of happiness; that to secure these rights, governments are instituted among men, deriving their just powers from the consent of the governed."

There is the origin of popular sovereignty. Who, then, shall come in at this day and claim that he invented it?

The Lecompton Constitution connects itself with this question, for it is in this matter of the Lecompton Constitution that our friend Judge Douglas claims such vast credit. I agree that in opposing the Lecompton Constitution, so far as I can perceive, he was right. I do not deny that at all; and, gentlemen, you will readily see why I could not deny it, even if I wanted to. But I do not wish to; for all the Republicans in the nation opposed it, and they would have opposed it just as much without Judge Douglas's aid as with it. They had all taken ground against it long before he did. Why, the reason that he urges against that constitution I urged against him a year before. I have the printed speech in my hand. The argument that he makes, why that constitution should not be adopted, that the people were not fairly represented nor allowed to vote, I pointed out in a speech a year ago, which I hold in my hand now, that no fair chance was to be given to the people. ["Read it, Read it."] I shall not waste your time by trying to read it. ["Read it, Read it."] Gentlemen, reading from speeches is a very tedious business, particularly for an old man that has to put on spectacles, and more so if the man be so tall that he has to bend over to the light.

A little more, now, as to this matter of popular sovereignty and the Lecompton Constitution. The Lecompton Constitution, as the Judge tells us, was defeated. The defeat of it was a good thing or it was not. He thinks the defeat of it was a good thing, and so do I, and we agree in that. Who defeated it?

[A voice: Judge Douglas.]

Yes, he furnished himself, and if you suppose he controlled the other Democrats that went with him, he furnished three votes; while the Republicans furnished twenty.

That is what he did to defeat it. In the House of Representatives he and his friends furnished some twenty votes, and the Republicans furnished ninety odd. Now, who was it that did the work?

[A voice: Douglas.]

Why, yes, Douglas did it! To be sure he did.

Let us, however, put that proposition another way. The Republicans could not have done it without Judge Douglas. Could he have done it without them? Which could have come the nearest to doing it without the other?

[A voice: Who killed the bill?]

[Another voice: Douglas.]

Ground was taken against it by the Republicans long before Douglas did it. The proportion of opposition to that measure is about five to one.

[A voice: Why don't they come out on it?]

You don't know what you are talking about, my friend. I am quite willing to answer any gentleman in the crowd who asks an intelligent question.

Now, who in all this country has ever found any of our friends of Judge Douglas's way of thinking, and who have acted upon this main question, that has ever thought of uttering a word in behalf of Judge Trumbull?

[A voice: We have.]

I defy you to show a printed resolution passed in a Democratic meeting—I take it upon myself to defy any man to show a printed resolution of a Democratic meeting, large or small—in favor of Judge Trumbull, or any of the five to one Republicans who beat that bill. Everything must be for the Democrats! They did everything, and the five to the one that really did the thing they snub over, and they do not seem to remember that they have an existence upon the face of the earth.

Gentlemen, I fear that I shall become tedious. I leave this branch of the subject to take hold of another. I take up that part of Judge Douglas's speech in which he respectfully attended to me.

Judge Douglas made two points upon my recent speech at Springfield. He says they are to be the issues of this campaign. The first one of these points he bases upon the language in a speech which I delivered at Springfield, which I believe I can quote correctly from memory. I said there that "we are now far into the fifth year since a policy was instituted for the avowed object, and with the confident promise, of putting an end to slavery agitation; under the operation of that policy, that agitation has not only not ceased, but has constantly augmented." "I believe it will not cease until a crisis shall have been reached and passed. 'A house divided against itself cannot stand.' I believe this government cannot endure permanently half slave and half free." "I do not expect the Union to be dissolved,"—I am quoting from my speech, "—I do not expect the house to fall, but I do expect it will cease to be divided. It will become all one thing or all the other. Either the opponents of slavery will arrest the spread of it and place it where the public mind shall rest in the belief that it is in the course of ultimate extinction, or its advocates will push it forward until it shall become alike lawful in all the States, north as well as south."

What is the paragraph? In this paragraph, which I have quoted in your hearing, and to which I ask the attention of all, Judge Douglas thinks he discovers great political heresy. I want your attention particularly to what he has inferred from it. He says I am in favor of making all the States of this Union uniform in all their internal regulations; that in all their domestic concerns I am in favor of making them entirely uniform. He draws this inference from the language I have quoted to you. He says that I am in favor of making war by the North upon the South for the extinction of slavery; that I am also in favor of inviting (as he expresses it) the South to a war upon the North for the purpose of nationalizing slavery. Now, it is singular enough, if you will carefully read that passage over, that I did not say that I was in favor of anything in it. I only said what I expected would take place. I made a prediction only,—it may have been a foolish one, perhaps. I did not even say that I desired that slavery should be put in course of ultimate extinction. I do say so now, however, so there need be no longer any difficulty about that. It may be written down in the great speech.

Gentlemen, Judge Douglas informed you that this speech of mine was probably carefully prepared. I admit that it was. I am not master of language; I have not a fine education; I am not capable of entering into a disquisition upon dialectics, as I believe you call it; but I do not believe the language I employed bears any such construction as Judge Douglas puts upon it. But I don't care about a quibble in regard to words. I know what I meant, and I will not leave this crowd in doubt, if I can explain it to them, what I really meant in the use of that paragraph.

I am not, in the first place, unaware that this government has endured eighty-two years half slave and half free. I know that. I am tolerably well acquainted with the history of the country, and I know that it has endured eighty-two years half slave and half free. I believe—and that is what I meant to allude to there—I believe it has endured because during all that time, until the introduction of the Nebraska Bill, the public mind did rest all the time in the belief that slavery was in course of ultimate extinction. That was what gave us the rest that we had through that period of eighty-two years,—at least, so I believe. I have always hated slavery, I think, as much as any Abolitionist,—I have been an Old Line Whig,—I have always hated it; but I have always been quiet about it until this new era of the introduction of the Nebraska Bill began. I always believed that everybody was against it, and that it was in course of ultimate extinction. [Pointing to Mr. Browning, who stood near by.] Browning thought so; the great mass of the nation have rested in the belief that slavery was in course of ultimate extinction. They had reason so to believe.

The adoption of the Constitution and its attendant history led the people to believe so; and that such was the belief of the framers of the Constitution itself, why did those old men, about the time of the adoption of the Constitution, decree that slavery should not go into the new Territory, where it had not already gone? Why declare that within twenty years the African slave trade, by which slaves are supplied, might be cut off by Congress? Why were all these acts? I might enumerate more of these acts; but enough. What were they but a clear indication that the framers of the Constitution intended and expected the ultimate extinction of that institution? And now, when I say, as I said in my speech that Judge Douglas has quoted from, when I say that I think the opponents of slavery will resist the farther spread of it, and place it where the public mind shall rest with the belief that it is in course of ultimate extinction, I only mean to say that they will place it where the founders of this government originally placed it.

I have said a hundred times, and I have now no inclination to take it back, that I believe there is no right, and ought to be no inclination, in the people of the free States to enter into the slave States and interfere with the question of slavery at all. I have said that always; Judge Douglas has heard me say it, if not quite a hundred times, at least as good as a hundred times; and when it is said that I am in favor of interfering with slavery where it exists, I know it is unwarranted by anything I have ever intended, and, as I believe, by anything I have ever said. If, by any means, I have ever used language which could fairly be so construed (as, however, I believe I never have), I now correct it.

So much, then, for the inference that Judge Douglas draws, that I am in favor of setting the sections at war with one another. I know that I never meant any such thing, and I believe that no fair mind can infer any such thing from anything I have ever said.

Now, in relation to his inference that I am in favor of a general consolidation of all the local institutions of the various States. I will attend to that for a little while, and try to inquire, if I can, how on earth it could be that any man could draw such an inference from anything I said. I have said, very many times, in Judge Douglas's hearing, that no man believed more than I in the principle of self-government; that it lies at the bottom of all my ideas of just government, from beginning to end. I have denied that his use of that term applies properly. But for the thing itself, I deny that any man has ever gone ahead of me in his devotion to the principle, whatever he may have done in efficiency in advocating it. I think that I have said it in your hearing, that I believe each individual is naturally entitled to do as he pleases with himself and the fruit of his labor, so far as it in no wise interferes with any other man's rights; that each community as a State has a right to do exactly as it pleases with all the concerns within that State that interfere with the right of no other State; and that the General Government, upon principle, has no right to interfere with anything other than that general class of things that does concern the whole. I have said that at all times. I have said, as illustrations, that I do not believe in the right of Illinois to interfere with the cranberry laws of Indiana, the oyster laws of Virginia, or the liquor laws of Maine. I have said these things over and over again, and I repeat them here as my sentiments.

How is it, then, that Judge Douglas infers, because I hope to see slavery put where the public mind shall rest in the belief that it is in the course of ultimate extinction, that I am in favor of Illinois going over and interfering with the cranberry laws of Indiana? What can authorize him to draw any such inference?

I suppose there might be one thing that at least enabled him to draw such an inference that would not be true with me or many others: that is, because he looks upon all this matter of slavery as an exceedingly little thing,—this matter of keeping one sixth of the population of the whole nation in a state of oppression and tyranny unequaled in the world. He looks upon it as being an exceedingly little thing,—only equal to the question of the cranberry laws of Indiana; as something having no moral question in it; as something on a par with the question of whether a man shall pasture his land with cattle, or plant it with tobacco; so little and so small a thing that he concludes, if I could desire that anything should be done to bring about the ultimate extinction of that little thing, I must be in favor of bringing about an amalgamation of all the other little things in the Union. Now, it so happens—and there, I presume, is the foundation of this mistake—that the Judge thinks thus; and it so happens that there is a vast portion of the American people that do not look upon that matter as being this very little thing. They look upon it as a vast moral evil; they can prove it as such by the writings of those who gave us the blessings of liberty which we enjoy, and that they so looked upon it, and not as an evil merely confining itself to the States where it is situated; and while we agree that, by the Constitution we assented to, in the States where it exists, we have no right to interfere with it, because it is in the Constitution; and we are by both duty and inclination to stick by that Constitution, in all its letter and spirit, from beginning to end.

So much, then, as to my disposition—my wish to have all the State legislatures blotted out, and to have one consolidated government, and a uniformity of domestic regulations in all the States, by which I suppose it is meant, if we raise corn here, we must make sugar-cane grow here too, and we must make those which grow North grow in the South. All this I suppose he understands I am in favor of doing. Now, so much for all this nonsense; for I must call it so. The Judge can have no issue with me on a question of establishing uniformity in the domestic regulations of the States.

A little now on the other point,—the Dred Scott decision. Another of the issues he says that is to be made with me is upon his devotion to the Dred Scott decision, and my opposition to it.

I have expressed heretofore, and I now repeat, my opposition to the Dred Scott decision; but I should be allowed to state the nature of that opposition, and I ask your indulgence while I do so. What is fairly implied by the term Judge Douglas has used, "resistance to the decision"? I do not resist it. If I wanted to take Dred Scott from his master, I would be interfering with property, and that terrible difficulty that Judge Douglas speaks of, of interfering with property, would arise. But I am doing no such thing as that, but all that I am doing is refusing to obey it as a political rule. If I were in Congress, and a vote should come up on a question whether slavery should be prohibited in a new Territory, in spite of the Dred Scott decision, I would vote that it should.

That is what I should do. Judge Douglas said last night that before the decision he might advance his opinion, and it might be contrary to the decision when it was made; but after it was made he would abide by it until it was reversed. Just so! We let this property abide by the decision, but we will try to reverse that decision. We will try to put it where Judge Douglas would not object, for he says he will obey it until it is reversed. Somebody has to reverse that decision, since it is made, and we mean to reverse it, and we mean to do it peaceably.

What are the uses of decisions of courts? They have two uses. As rules of property they have two uses. First, they decide upon the question before the court. They decide in this case that Dred Scott is a slave. Nobody resists that, not only that, but they say to everybody else that persons standing just as Dred Scott stands are as he is. That is, they say that when a question comes up upon another person, it will be so decided again, unless the court decides in another way, unless the court overrules its decision. Well, we mean to do what we can to have the court decide the other way. That is one thing we mean to try to do.

The sacredness that Judge Douglas throws around this decision is a degree of sacredness that has never been before thrown around any other decision. I have never heard of such a thing. Why, decisions apparently contrary to that decision, or that good lawyers thought were contrary to that decision, have been made by that very court before. It is the first of its kind; it is an astonisher in legal history. It is a new wonder of the world. It is based upon falsehood in the main as to the facts; allegations of facts upon which it stands are not facts at all in many instances, and no decision made on any question—the first instance of a decision made under so many unfavorable circumstances—thus placed, has ever been held by the profession as law, and it has always needed confirmation before the lawyers regarded it as settled law. But Judge Douglas will have it that all hands must take this extraordinary decision, made under these extraordinary circumstances, and give their vote in Congress in accordance with it, yield to it, and obey it in every possible sense. Circumstances alter cases. Do not gentlemen here remember the case of that same Supreme Court some twenty-five or thirty years ago deciding that a National Bank was constitutional? I ask, if somebody does not remember that a National Bank was declared to be constitutional? Such is the truth, whether it be remembered or not. The Bank charter ran out, and a recharter was granted by Congress. That recharter was laid before General Jackson. It was urged upon him, when he denied the constitutionality of the Bank, that the Supreme Court had decided that it was constitutional; and General Jackson then said that the Supreme Court had no right to lay down a rule to govern a coordinate branch of the government, the members of which had sworn to support the Constitution; that each member had sworn to support that Constitution as he understood it. I will venture here to say that I have heard Judge Douglas say that he approved of General Jackson for that act. What has now become of all his tirade about "resistance of the Supreme Court"?

My fellow-citizens, getting back a little,—for I pass from these points,—when Judge Douglas makes his threat of annihilation upon the "alliance," he is cautious to say that that warfare of his is to fall upon the leaders of the Republican party. Almost every word he utters, and every distinction he makes, has its significance. He means for the Republicans who do not count themselves as leaders, to be his friends; he makes no fuss over them; it is the leaders that he is making war upon. He wants it understood that the mass of the Republican party are really his friends. It is only the leaders that are doing something that are intolerant, and that require extermination at his hands. As this is clearly and unquestionably the light in which he presents that matter, I want to ask your attention, addressing myself to the Republicans here, that I may ask you some questions as to where you, as the Republican party, would be placed if you sustained Judge Douglas in his present position by a re-election? I do not claim, gentlemen, to be unselfish; I do not pretend that I would not like to go to the United States Senate,—I make no such hypocritical pretense; but I do say to you that in this mighty issue it is nothing to you—nothing to the mass of the people of the nation,—whether or not Judge Douglas or myself shall ever be heard of after this night; it may be a trifle to either of us, but in connection with this mighty question, upon which hang the destinies of the nation, perhaps, it is absolutely nothing: but where will you be placed if you reindorse Judge Douglas? Don't you know how apt he is, how exceedingly anxious he is at all times, to seize upon anything and everything to persuade you that something he has done you did yourselves? Why, he tried to persuade you last night that our Illinois Legislature instructed him to introduce the Nebraska Bill. There was nobody in that Legislature ever thought of such a thing; and when he first introduced the bill, he never thought of it; but still he fights furiously for the proposition, and that he did it because there was a standing instruction to our Senators to be always introducing Nebraska bills. He tells you he is for the Cincinnati platform, he tells you he is for the Dred Scott decision. He tells you, not in his speech last night, but substantially in a former speech, that he cares not if slavery is voted up or down; he tells you the struggle on Lecompton is past; it may come up again or not, and if it does, he stands where he stood when, in spite of him and his opposition, you built up the Republican party. If you indorse him, you tell him you do not care whether slavery be voted up or down, and he will close or try to close your mouths with his declaration, repeated by the day, the week, the month, and the year. Is that what you mean? [Cries of "No," one voice "Yes."] Yes, I have no doubt you who have always been for him, if you mean that. No doubt of that, soberly I have said, and I repeat it. I think, in the position in which Judge Douglas stood in opposing the Lecompton Constitution, he was right; he does not know that it will return, but if it does we may know where to find him, and if it does not, we may know where to look for him, and that is on the Cincinnati platform. Now, I could ask the Republican party, after all the hard names that Judge Douglas has called them by all his repeated charges of their inclination to marry with and hug negroes; all his declarations of Black Republicanism,—by the way, we are improving, the black has got rubbed off,—but with all that, if he be indorsed by Republican votes, where do you stand? Plainly, you stand ready saddled, bridled, and harnessed, and waiting to be driven over to the slavery extension camp of the nation,—just ready to be driven over, tied together in a lot, to be driven over, every man with a rope around his neck, that halter being held by Judge Douglas. That is the question. If Republican men have been in earnest in what they have done, I think they had better not do it; but I think that the Republican party is made up of those who, as far as they can peaceably, will oppose the extension of slavery, and who will hope for its ultimate extinction. If they believe it is wrong in grasping up the new lands of the continent and keeping them from the settlement of free white laborers, who want the land to bring up their families upon; if they are in earnest, although they may make a mistake, they will grow restless, and the time will come when they will come back again and reorganize, if not by the same name, at least upon the same principles as their party now has. It is better, then, to save the work while it is begun. You have done the labor; maintain it, keep it. If men choose to serve you, go with them; but as you have made up your organization upon principle, stand by it; for, as surely as God reigns over you, and has inspired your mind, and given you a sense of propriety, and continues to give you hope, so surely will you still cling to these ideas, and you will at last come back again after your wanderings, merely to do your work over again.

We were often,—more than once, at least,—in the course of Judge Douglas's speech last night, reminded that this government was made for white men; that he believed it was made for white men. Well, that is putting it into a shape in which no one wants to deny it; but the Judge then goes into his passion for drawing inferences that are not warranted. I protest, now and forever, against that counterfeit logic which presumes that because I did not want a negro woman for a slave, I do necessarily want her for a wife. My understanding is that I need not have her for either, but, as God made us separate, we can leave one another alone, and do one another much good thereby. There are white men enough to marry all the white women, and enough black men to marry all the black women; and in God's name let them be so married. The Judge regales us with the terrible enormities that take place by the mixture of races; that the inferior race bears the superior down. Why, Judge, if we do not let them get together in the Territories, they won't mix there.

[A voice: "Three cheers for Lincoln".—The cheers were given with a hearty good-will.]

I should say at least that that is a self-evident truth.

Now, it happens that we meet together once every year, sometimes about the 4th of July, for some reason or other. These 4th of July gatherings I suppose have their uses. If you will indulge me, I will state what I suppose to be some of them.

We are now a mighty nation; we are thirty or about thirty millions of people, and we own and inhabit about one fifteenth part of the dry land of the whole earth. We run our memory back over the pages of history for about eighty-two years, and we discover that we were then a very small people in point of numbers, vastly inferior to what we are now, with a vastly less extent of country, with vastly less of everything we deem desirable among men; we look upon the change as exceedingly advantageous to us and to our posterity, and we fix upon something that happened away back, as in some way or other being connected with this rise of prosperity. We find a race of men living in that day whom we claim as our fathers and grandfathers; they were iron men; they fought for the principle that they were contending for; and we understood that by what they then did it has followed that the degree of prosperity which we now enjoy has come to us. We hold this annual celebration to remind ourselves of all the good done in this process of time, of how it was done and who did it, and how we are historically connected with it; and we go from these meetings in better humor with ourselves, we feel more attached the one to the other, and more firmly bound to the country we inhabit. In every way we are better men in the age and race and country in which we live, for these celebrations. But after we have done all this we have not yet reached the whole. There is something else connected with it. We have—besides these, men descended by blood from our ancestors—among us perhaps half our people who are not descendants at all of these men; they are men who have come from Europe, German, Irish, French, and Scandinavian,—men that have come from Europe themselves, or whose ancestors have come hither and settled here, finding themselves our equals in all things. If they look back through this history to trace their connection with those days by blood, they find they have none, they cannot carry themselves back into that glorious epoch and make themselves feel that they are part of us; but when they look through that old Declaration of Independence, they find that those old men say that "We hold these truths to be self-evident, that all men are created equal"; and then they feel that that moral sentiment, taught in that day, evidences their relation to those men, that it is the father of all moral principle in them, and that they have a right to claim it as though they were blood of the blood, and flesh of the flesh, of the men who wrote that Declaration; and so they are. That is the electric cord in that Declaration that links the hearts of patriotic and liberty-loving men together, that will link those patriotic hearts as long as the love of freedom exists in the minds of men throughout the world.

Now, sirs, for the purpose of squaring things with this idea of "don't care if slavery is voted up or voted down," for sustaining the Dred Scott decision, for holding that the Declaration of Independence did not mean anything at all, we have Judge Douglas giving his exposition of what the Declaration of Independence means, and we have him saying that the people of America are equal to the people of England. According to his construction, you Germans are not connected with it. Now, I ask you in all soberness if all these things, if indulged in, if ratified, if confirmed and indorsed, if taught to our children, and repeated to them, do not tend to rub out the sentiment of liberty in the country, and to transform this government into a government of some other form. Those arguments that are made, that the inferior race are to be treated with as much allowance as they are capable of enjoying; that as much is to be done for them as their condition will allow,—what are these arguments? They are the arguments that kings have made for enslaving the people in all ages of the world. You will find that all the arguments in favor of kingcraft were of this class; they always bestrode the necks of the people not that they wanted to do it, but because the people were better off for being ridden. That is their argument, and this argument of the Judge is the same old serpent that says, You work, and I eat; you toil, and I will enjoy the fruits of it. Turn in whatever way you will, whether it come from the mouth of a king, an excuse for enslaving the people of his country, or from the mouth of men of one race as a reason for enslaving the men of another race, it is all the same old serpent; and I hold, if that course of argumentation that is made for the purpose of convincing the public mind that we should not care about this should be granted, it does not stop with the negro. I should like to know, if taking this old Declaration of Independence, which declares that all men are equal upon principle, and making exceptions to it, where will it stop? If one man says it does not mean a negro, why not another say it does not mean some other man? If that Declaration is not the truth, let us get the statute book, in which we find it, and tear it out! Who is so bold as to do it? If it is not true, let us tear it out! [Cries of "No, no."] Let us stick to it, then; let us stand firmly by it, then.

It may be argued that there are certain conditions that make necessities and impose them upon us; and to the extent that a necessity is imposed upon a man, he must submit to it. I think that was the condition in which we found ourselves when we established this government. We had slavery among us, we could not get our Constitution unless we permitted them to remain in slavery, we could not secure the good we did secure if we grasped for more; and having by necessity submitted to that much, it does not destroy the principle that is the charter of our liberties. Let that charter stand as our standard.

My friend has said to me that I am a poor hand to quote Scripture. I will try it again, however. It is said in one of the admonitions of our Lord, "As your Father in heaven is perfect, be ye also perfect." The Savior, I suppose, did not expect that any human creature could be perfect as the Father in heaven; but he said, "As your Father in heaven is perfect, be ye also perfect." He set that up as a standard; and he who did most towards reaching that standard attained the highest degree of moral perfection. So I say in relation to the principle that all men are created equal, let it be as nearly reached as we can. If we cannot give freedom to every creature, let us do nothing that will impose slavery upon any other creature. Let us then turn this government back into the channel in which the framers of the Constitution originally placed it. Let us stand firmly by each other. If we do not do so, we are turning in the contrary direction, that our friend Judge Douglas proposes—not intentionally—as working in the traces tends to make this one universal slave nation. He is one that runs in that direction, and as such I resist him.

My friends, I have detained you about as long as I desired to do, and I have only to say: Let us discard all this quibbling about this man and the other man, this race and that race and the other race being inferior, and therefore they must be placed in an inferior position; discarding our standard that we have left us. Let us discard all these things, and unite as one people throughout this land, until we shall once more stand up declaring that all men are created equal.

My friends, I could not, without launching off upon some new topic, which would detain you too long, continue to-night. I thank you for this most extensive audience that you have furnished me to-night. I leave you, hoping that the lamp of liberty will burn in your bosoms until there shall no longer be a doubt that all men are created free and equal.

SPEECH AT SPRINGFIELD, JULY 17, 1858.

DELIVERED SATURDAY EVENING

(Mr. Douglas was not present.)

FELLOW-CITIZENS:—Another election, which is deemed an important one, is approaching, and, as I suppose, the Republican party will, without much difficulty, elect their State ticket. But in regard to the Legislature, we, the Republicans, labor under some disadvantages. In the first place, we have a Legislature to elect upon an apportionment of the representation made several years ago, when the proportion of the population was far greater in the South (as compared with the North) than it now is; and inasmuch as our opponents hold almost entire sway in the South, and we a correspondingly large majority in the North, the fact that we are now to be represented as we were years ago, when the population was different, is to us a very great disadvantage. We had in the year 1855, according to law, a census, or enumeration of the inhabitants, taken for the purpose of a new apportionment of representation. We know what a fair apportionment of representation upon that census would give us. We know that it could not, if fairly made, fail to give the Republican party from six to ten more members of the Legislature than they can probably get as the law now stands. It so happened at the last session of the Legislature that our opponents, holding the control of both branches of the Legislature, steadily refused to give us such an apportionment as we were rightly entitled to have upon the census already taken. The Legislature steadily refused to give us such an apportionment as we were rightfully entitled to have upon the census taken of the population of the State. The Legislature would pass no bill upon that subject, except such as was at least as unfair to us as the old one, and in which, in some instances, two men in the Democratic regions were allowed to go as far toward sending a member to the Legislature as three were in the Republican regions. Comparison was made at the time as to representative and senatorial districts, which completely demonstrated that such was the fact. Such a bill was passed and tendered to the Republican Governor for his signature; but, principally for the reasons I have stated, he withheld his approval, and the bill fell without becoming a law.

Another disadvantage under which we labor is that there are one or two Democratic Senators who will be members of the next Legislature, and will vote for the election of Senator, who are holding over in districts in which we could, on all reasonable calculation, elect men of our own, if we only had the chance of an election. When we consider that there are but twenty-five Senators in the Senate, taking two from the side where they rightfully belong, and adding them to the other, is to us a disadvantage not to be lightly regarded. Still, so it is; we have this to contend with. Perhaps there is no ground of complaint on our part. In attending to the many things involved in the last general election for President, Governor, Auditor, Treasurer, Superintendent of Public Instruction, Members of Congress, of the Legislature, County Officers, and so on, we allowed these things to happen by want of sufficient attention, and we have no cause to complain of our adversaries, so far as this matter is concerned. But we have some cause to complain of the refusal to give us a fair apportionment.

There is still another disadvantage under which we labor, and to which I will ask your attention. It arises out of the relative positions of the two persons who stand before the State as candidates for the Senate. Senator Douglas is of world-wide renown. All the anxious politicians of his party, or who have been of his party for years past, have been looking upon him as certainly, at no distant day, to be the President of the United States. They have seen in his round, jolly, fruitful face post-offices, land-offices, marshalships, and cabinet appointments, charge-ships and foreign missions bursting and sprouting out in wonderful exuberance, ready to be laid hold of by their greedy hands. And as they have been gazing upon this attractive picture so long, they cannot, in the little distraction that has taken place in the party, bring themselves to give up the charming hope; but with greedier anxiety they rush about him, sustain him, and give him marches, triumphal entries, and receptions beyond what even in the days of his highest prosperity they could have brought about in his favor. On the contrary, nobody has ever expected me to be President. In my poor, lean, lank face, nobody has ever seen that any cabbages were sprouting out. These are disadvantages all, taken together, that the Republicans labor under. We have to fight this battle upon principle, and upon principle alone. I am, in a certain sense, made the standard-bearer in behalf of the Republicans. I was made so merely because there had to be some one so placed,—I being in nowise preferable to any other one of twenty-five, perhaps a hundred, we have in the Republican ranks. Then I say I wish it to be distinctly understood and borne in mind that we have to fight this battle without many—perhaps without any of the external aids which are brought to bear against us. So I hope those with whom I am surrounded have principle enough to nerve themselves for the task, and leave nothing undone that can be fairly done to bring about the right result.

After Senator Douglas left Washington, as his movements were made known by the public prints, he tarried a considerable time in the city of New York; and it was heralded that, like another Napoleon, he was lying by and framing the plan of his campaign. It was telegraphed to Washington City, and published in the Union, that he was framing his plan for the purpose of going to Illinois to pounce upon and annihilate the treasonable and disunion speech which Lincoln had made here on the 16th of June. Now, I do suppose that the Judge really spent some time in New York maturing the plan of the campaign, as his friends heralded for him. I have been able, by noting his movements since his arrival in Illinois, to discover evidences confirmatory of that allegation. I think I have been able to see what are the material points of that plan. I will, for a little while, ask your attention to some of them. What I shall point out, though not showing the whole plan, are, nevertheless, the main points, as I suppose.

They are not very numerous. The first is popular sovereignty. The second and third are attacks upon my speech made on the 16th of June. Out of these three points—drawing within the range of popular sovereignty the question of the Lecompton Constitution—he makes his principal assault. Upon these his successive speeches are substantially one and the same. On this matter of popular sovereignty I wish to be a little careful. Auxiliary to these main points, to be sure, are their thunderings of cannon, their marching and music, their fizzlegigs and fireworks; but I will not waste time with them. They are but the little trappings of the campaign.

Coming to the substance,—the first point, "popular sovereignty." It is to be labeled upon the cars in which he travels; put upon the hacks he rides in; to be flaunted upon the arches he passes under, and the banners which wave over him. It is to be dished up in as many varieties as a French cook can produce soups from potatoes. Now, as this is so great a staple of the plan of the campaign, it is worth while to examine it carefully; and if we examine only a very little, and do not allow ourselves to be misled, we shall be able to see that the whole thing is the most arrant Quixotism that was ever enacted before a community. What is the matter of popular sovereignty? The first thing, in order to understand it, is to get a good definition of what it is, and after that to see how it is applied.

I suppose almost every one knows that, in this controversy, whatever has been said has had reference to the question of negro slavery. We have not been in a controversy about the right of the people to govern themselves in the ordinary matters of domestic concern in the States and Territories. Mr. Buchanan, in one of his late messages (I think when he sent up the Lecompton Constitution) urged that the main point to which the public attention had been directed was not in regard to the great variety of small domestic matters, but was directed to the question of negro slavery; and he asserts that if the people had had a fair chance to vote on that question there was no reasonable ground of objection in regard to minor questions. Now, while I think that the people had not had given, or offered, them a fair chance upon that slavery question, still, if there had been a fair submission to a vote upon that main question, the President's proposition would have been true to the utmost. Hence, when hereafter I speak of popular sovereignty, I wish to be understood as applying what I say to the question of slavery only, not to other minor domestic matters of a Territory or a State.

Does Judge Douglas, when he says that several of the past years of his life have been devoted to the question of "popular sovereignty," and that all the remainder of his life shall be devoted to it, does he mean to say that he has been devoting his life to securing to the people of the Territories the right to exclude slavery from the Territories? If he means so to say he means to deceive; because he and every one knows that the decision of the Supreme Court, which he approves and makes especial ground of attack upon me for disapproving, forbids the people of a Territory to exclude slavery. This covers the whole ground, from the settlement of a Territory till it reaches the degree of maturity entitling it to form a State Constitution. So far as all that ground is concerned, the Judge is not sustaining popular sovereignty, but absolutely opposing it. He sustains the decision which declares that the popular will of the Territory has no constitutional power to exclude slavery during their territorial existence. This being so, the period of time from the first settlement of a Territory till it reaches the point of forming a State Constitution is not the thing that the Judge has fought for or is fighting for, but, on the contrary, he has fought for, and is fighting for, the thing that annihilates and crushes out that same popular sovereignty.

Well, so much being disposed of, what is left? Why, he is contending for the right of the people, when they come to make a State Constitution, to make it for themselves, and precisely as best suits themselves. I say again, that is quixotic. I defy contradiction when I declare that the Judge can find no one to oppose him on that proposition. I repeat, there is nobody opposing that proposition on principle. Let me not be misunderstood. I know that, with reference to the Lecompton Constitution, I may be misunderstood; but when you understand me correctly, my proposition will be true and accurate. Nobody is opposing, or has opposed, the right of the people, when they form a constitution, to form it for themselves. Mr. Buchanan and his friends have not done it; they, too, as well as the Republicans and the Anti-Lecompton Democrats, have not done it; but on the contrary, they together have insisted on the right of the people to form a constitution for themselves. The difference between the Buchanan men on the one hand, and the Douglas men and the Republicans on the other, has not been on a question of principle, but on a question of fact.

The dispute was upon the question of fact, whether the Lecompton Constitution had been fairly formed by the people or not. Mr. Buchanan and his friends have not contended for the contrary principle any more than the Douglas men or the Republicans. They have insisted that whatever of small irregularities existed in getting up the Lecompton Constitution were such as happen in the settlement of all new Territories. The question was, Was it a fair emanation of the people? It was a question of fact, and not of principle. As to the principle, all were agreed. Judge Douglas voted with the Republicans upon that matter of fact.

He and they, by their voices and votes, denied that it was a fair emanation of the people. The Administration affirmed that it was. With respect to the evidence bearing upon that question of fact, I readily agree that Judge Douglas and the Republicans had the right on their side, and that the Administration was wrong. But I state again that, as a matter of principle, there is no dispute upon the right of a people in a Territory, merging into a State, to form a constitution for themselves without outside interference from any quarter. This being so, what is Judge Douglas going to spend his life for? Is he going to spend his life in maintaining a principle that nobody on earth opposes? Does he expect to stand up in majestic dignity, and go through his apotheosis and become a god in the maintaining of a principle which neither man nor mouse in all God's creation is opposing? Now something in regard to the Lecompton Constitution more specially; for I pass from this other question of popular sovereignty as the most arrant humbug that has ever been attempted on an intelligent community.

As to the Lecompton Constitution, I have already said that on the question of fact, as to whether it was a fair emanation of the people or not, Judge Douglas, with the Republicans and some Americans, had greatly the argument against the Administration; and while I repeat this, I wish to know what there is in the opposition of Judge Douglas to the Lecompton Constitution that entitles him to be considered the only opponent to it,—as being par excellence the very quintessence of that opposition. I agree to the rightfulness of his opposition. He in the Senate and his class of men there formed the number three and no more. In the House of Representatives his class of men—the Anti-Lecompton Democrats—formed a number of about twenty. It took one hundred and twenty to defeat the measure, against one hundred and twelve. Of the votes of that one hundred and twenty, Judge Douglas's friends furnished twenty, to add to which there were six Americans and ninety-four Republicans. I do not say that I am precisely accurate in their numbers, but I am sufficiently so for any use I am making of it.

Why is it that twenty shall be entitled to all the credit of doing that work, and the hundred none of it? Why, if, as Judge Douglas says, the honor is to be divided and due credit is to be given to other parties, why is just so much given as is consonant with the wishes, the interests, and advancement of the twenty? My understanding is, when a common job is done, or a common enterprise prosecuted, if I put in five dollars to your one, I have a right to take out five dollars to your one. But he does not so understand it. He declares the dividend of credit for defeating Lecompton upon a basis which seems unprecedented and incomprehensible.

Let us see. Lecompton in the raw was defeated. It afterward took a sort of cooked-up shape, and was passed in the English bill. It is said by the Judge that the defeat was a good and proper thing. If it was a good thing, why is he entitled to more credit than others for the performance of that good act, unless there was something in the antecedents of the Republicans that might induce every one to expect them to join in that good work, and at the same time something leading them to doubt that he would? Does he place his superior claim to credit on the ground that he performed a good act which was never expected of him? He says I have a proneness for quoting Scripture. If I should do so now, it occurs that perhaps he places himself somewhat upon the ground of the parable of the lost sheep which went astray upon the mountains, and when the owner of the hundred sheep found the one that was lost, and threw it upon his shoulders and came home rejoicing, it was said that there was more rejoicing over the one sheep that was lost and had been found than over the ninety and nine in the fold. The application is made by the Saviour in this parable, thus: "Verily, I say unto you, there is more rejoicing in heaven over one sinner that repenteth, than over ninety and nine just persons that need no repentance."

And now, if the Judge claims the benefit of this parable, let him repent. Let him not come up here and say: "I am the only just person; and you are the ninety-nine sinners!" Repentance before forgiveness is a provision of the Christian system, and on that condition alone will the Republicans grant his forgiveness.

How will he prove that we have ever occupied a different position in regard to the Lecompton Constitution or any principle in it? He says he did not make his opposition on the ground as to whether it was a free or slave constitution, and he would have you understand that the Republicans made their opposition because it ultimately became a slave constitution. To make proof in favor of himself on this point, he reminds us that he opposed Lecompton before the vote was taken declaring whether the State was to be free or slave. But he forgets to say that our Republican Senator, Trumbull, made a speech against Lecompton even before he did.

Why did he oppose it? Partly, as he declares, because the members of the convention who framed it were not fairly elected by the people; that the people were not allowed to vote unless they had been registered; and that the people of whole counties, some instances, were not registered. For these reasons he declares the Constitution was not an emanation, in any true sense, from the people. He also has an additional objection as to the mode of submitting the Constitution back to the people. But bearing on the question of whether the delegates were fairly elected, a speech of his, made something more than twelve months ago, from this stand, becomes important. It was made a little while before the election of the delegates who made Lecompton. In that speech he declared there was every reason to hope and believe the election would be fair; and if any one failed to vote, it would be his own culpable fault.

I, a few days after, made a sort of answer to that speech. In that answer I made, substantially, the very argument with which he combated his Lecompton adversaries in the Senate last winter. I pointed to the facts that the people could not vote without being registered, and that the time for registering had gone by. I commented on it as wonderful that Judge Douglas could be ignorant of these facts which every one else in the nation so well knew.

I now pass from popular sovereignty and Lecompton. I may have occasion to refer to one or both.

When he was preparing his plan of campaign, Napoleon-like, in New York, as appears by two speeches I have heard him deliver since his arrival in Illinois, he gave special attention to a speech of mine, delivered here on the 16th of June last. He says that he carefully read that speech. He told us that at Chicago a week ago last night and he repeated it at Bloomington last night. Doubtless, he repeated it again to-day, though I did not hear him. In the first two places— Chicago and Bloomington I heard him; to-day I did not. He said he had carefully examined that speech,—when, he did not say; but there is no reasonable doubt it was when he was in New York preparing his plan of campaign. I am glad he did read it carefully. He says it was evidently prepared with great care. I freely admit it was prepared with care. I claim not to be more free from errors than others,—perhaps scarcely so much; but I was very careful not to put anything in that speech as a matter of fact, or make any inferences, which did not appear to me to be true and fully warrantable. If I had made any mistake, I was willing to be corrected; if I had drawn any inference in regard to Judge Douglas or any one else which was not warranted, I was fully prepared to modify it as soon as discovered. I planted myself upon the truth and the truth only, so far as I knew it, or could be brought to know it.

Having made that speech with the most kindly feelings toward Judge Douglas, as manifested therein, I was gratified when I found that he had carefully examined it, and had detected no error of fact, nor any inference against him, nor any misrepresentations of which he thought fit to complain. In neither of the two speeches I have mentioned did he make any such complaint. I will thank any one who will inform me that he, in his speech to-day, pointed out anything I had stated respecting him as being erroneous. I presume there is no such thing. I have reason to be gratified that the care and caution used in that speech left it so that he, most of all others interested in discovering error, has not been able to point out one thing against him which he could say was wrong. He seizes upon the doctrines he supposes to be included in that speech, and declares that upon them will turn the issues of this campaign. He then quotes, or attempts to quote, from my speech. I will not say that he wilfully misquotes, but he does fail to quote accurately. His attempt at quoting is from a passage which I believe I can quote accurately from memory. I shall make the quotation now, with some comments upon it, as I have already said, in order that the Judge shall be left entirely without excuse for misrepresenting me. I do so now, as I hope, for the last time. I do this in great caution, in order that if he repeats his misrepresentation it shall be plain to all that he does so wilfully. If, after all, he still persists, I shall be compelled to reconstruct the course I have marked out for myself, and draw upon such humble resources, as I have, for a new course, better suited to the real exigencies of the case. I set out in this campaign with the intention of conducting it strictly as a gentleman, in substance at least, if not in the outside polish. The latter I shall never be; but that which constitutes the inside of a gentleman I hope I understand, and am not less inclined to practice than others. It was my purpose and expectation that this canvass would be conducted upon principle, and with fairness on both sides, and it shall not be my fault if this purpose and expectation shall be given up.

He charges, in substance, that I invite a war of sections; that I propose all the local institutions of the different States shall become consolidated and uniform. What is there in the language of that speech which expresses such purpose or bears such construction? I have again and again said that I would not enter into any of the States to disturb the institution of slavery. Judge Douglas said, at Bloomington, that I used language most able and ingenious for concealing what I really meant; and that while I had protested against entering into the slave States, I nevertheless did mean to go on the banks of the Ohio and throw missiles into Kentucky, to disturb them in their domestic institutions.

I said in that speech, and I meant no more, that the institution of slavery ought to be placed in the very attitude where the framers of this government placed it and left it. I do not understand that the framers of our Constitution left the people of the free States in the attitude of firing bombs or shells into the slave States. I was not using that passage for the purpose for which he infers I did use it. I said:

"We are now far advanced into the fifth year since a policy was created for the avowed object and with the confident promise of putting an end to slavery agitation. Under the operation of that policy that agitation has not only not ceased, but has constantly augmented. In my opinion it will not cease till a crisis shall have been reached and passed. 'A house divided against itself cannot stand.' I believe that this government cannot endure permanently half slave and half free; it will become all one thing or all the other. Either the opponents of slavery will arrest the further spread of it, and place it where the public mind shall rest in the belief that it is in the course of ultimate extinction, or its advocates will push it forward till it shall become alike lawful in all the States, old as well as new, North as well as South."

Now, you all see, from that quotation, I did not express my wish on anything. In that passage I indicated no wish or purpose of my own; I simply expressed my expectation. Cannot the Judge perceive a distinction between a purpose and an expectation? I have often expressed an expectation to die, but I have never expressed a wish to die. I said at Chicago, and now repeat, that I am quite aware this government has endured, half slave and half free, for eighty-two years. I understand that little bit of history. I expressed the opinion I did because I perceived—or thought I perceived—a new set of causes introduced. I did say at Chicago, in my speech there, that I do wish to see the spread of slavery arrested, and to see it placed where the public mind shall rest in the belief that it is in the course of ultimate extinction. I said that because I supposed, when the public mind shall rest in that belief, we shall have peace on the slavery question. I have believed—and now believe—the public mind did rest on that belief up to the introduction of the Nebraska Bill.

Although I have ever been opposed to slavery, so far I rested in the hope and belief that it was in the course of ultimate extinction. For that reason it had been a minor question with me. I might have been mistaken; but I had believed, and now believe, that the whole public mind, that is, the mind of the great majority, had rested in that belief up to the repeal of the Missouri Compromise. But upon that event I became convinced that either I had been resting in a delusion, or the institution was being placed on a new basis, a basis for making it perpetual, national, and universal. Subsequent events have greatly confirmed me in that belief. I believe that bill to be the beginning of a conspiracy for that purpose. So believing, I have since then considered that question a paramount one. So believing, I thought the public mind will never rest till the power of Congress to restrict the spread of it shall again be acknowledged and exercised on the one hand or, on the other, all resistance be entirely crushed out. I have expressed that opinion, and I entertain it to-night. It is denied that there is any tendency to the nationalization of slavery in these States.

Mr. Brooks, of South Carolina, in one of his speeches, when they were presenting him canes, silver plate, gold pitchers, and the like, for assaulting Senator Sumner, distinctly affirmed his opinion that when this Constitution was formed it was the belief of no man that slavery would last to the present day. He said, what I think, that the framers of our Constitution placed the institution of slavery where the public mind rested in the hope that it was in the course of ultimate extinction. But he went on to say that the men of the present age, by their experience, have become wiser than the framers of the Constitution, and the invention of the cotton gin had made the perpetuity of slavery a necessity in this country.

As another piece of evidence tending to this same point: Quite recently in Virginia, a man—the owner of slaves—made a will providing that after his death certain of his slaves should have their freedom if they should so choose, and go to Liberia, rather than remain in slavery. They chose to be liberated. But the persons to whom they would descend as property claimed them as slaves. A suit was instituted, which finally came to the Supreme Court of Virginia, and was therein decided against the slaves upon the ground that a negro cannot make a choice; that they had no legal power to choose, could not perform the condition upon which their freedom depended.

I do not mention this with any purpose of criticizing it, but to connect it with the arguments as affording additional evidence of the change of sentiment upon this question of slavery in the direction of making it perpetual and national. I argue now as I did before, that there is such a tendency; and I am backed, not merely by the facts, but by the open confession in the slave States.

And now as to the Judge's inference that because I wish to see slavery placed in the course of ultimate extinction,—placed where our fathers originally placed it,—I wish to annihilate the State Legislatures, to force cotton to grow upon the tops of the Green Mountains, to freeze ice in Florida, to cut lumber on the broad Illinois prairie,—that I am in favor of all these ridiculous and impossible things.

It seems to me it is a complete answer to all this to ask if, when Congress did have the fashion of restricting slavery from free territory; when courts did have the fashion of deciding that taking a slave into a free country made him free,—I say it is a sufficient answer to ask if any of this ridiculous nonsense about consolidation and uniformity did actually follow. Who heard of any such thing because of the Ordinance of '87? because of the Missouri restriction? because of the numerous court decisions of that character?

Now, as to the Dred Scott decision; for upon that he makes his last point at me. He boldly takes ground in favor of that decision.

This is one half the onslaught, and one third of the entire plan of the campaign. I am opposed to that decision in a certain sense, but not in the sense which he puts it. I say that in so far as it decided in favor of Dred Scott's master, and against Dred Scott and his family, I do not propose to disturb or resist the decision.

I never have proposed to do any such thing. I think that in respect for judicial authority my humble history would not suffer in comparison with that of Judge Douglas. He would have the citizen conform his vote to that decision; the member of Congress, his; the President, his use of the veto power. He would make it a rule of political action for the people and all the departments of the government. I would not. By resisting it as a political rule, I disturb no right of property, create no disorder, excite no mobs.

When he spoke at Chicago, on Friday evening of last week, he made this same point upon me. On Saturday evening I replied, and reminded him of a Supreme Court decision which he opposed for at least several years. Last night, at Bloomington, he took some notice of that reply, but entirely forgot to remember that part of it.

He renews his onslaught upon me, forgetting to remember that I have turned the tables against himself on that very point. I renew the effort to draw his attention to it. I wish to stand erect before the country, as well as Judge Douglas, on this question of judicial authority; and therefore I add something to the authority in favor of my own position. I wish to show that I am sustained by authority, in addition to that heretofore presented. I do not expect to convince the Judge. It is part of the plan of his campaign, and he will cling to it with a desperate grip. Even turn it upon him,—the sharp point against him, and gaff him through,—he will still cling to it till he can invent some new dodge to take the place of it.

In public speaking it is tedious reading from documents; but I must beg to indulge the practice to a limited extent. I shall read from a letter written by Mr. Jefferson in 1820, and now to be found in the seventh volume of his correspondence, at page 177. It seems he had been presented by a gentleman of the name of Jarvis with a book, or essay, or periodical, called the Republican, and he was writing in acknowledgment of the present, and noting some of its contents. After expressing the hope that the work will produce a favorable effect upon the minds of the young, he proceeds to say:

"That it will have this tendency may be expected, and for that reason I feel an urgency to note what I deem an error in it, the more requiring notice as your opinion is strengthened by that of many others. You seem, in pages 84 and 148, to consider the judges as the ultimate arbiters of all constitutional questions,—a very dangerous doctrine indeed, and one which would place us under the despotism of an oligarchy. Our judges are as honest as other men, and not more so. They have, with others, the same passions for party, for power, and the privilege of their corps. Their maxim is, 'Boni judicis est ampliare jurisdictionem'; and their power is the more dangerous as they are in office for life, and not responsible, as the other functionaries are, to the elective control. The Constitution has erected no such single tribunal, knowing that, to whatever hands confided, with the corruptions of time and party, its members would become despots. It has more wisely made all the departments co-equal and co-sovereign with themselves."

Thus we see the power claimed for the Supreme Court by Judge Douglas, Mr. Jefferson holds, would reduce us to the despotism of an oligarchy.

Now, I have said no more than this,—in fact, never quite so much as this; at least I am sustained by Mr. Jefferson.

Let us go a little further. You remember we once had a National Bank. Some one owed the bank a debt; he was sued, and sought to avoid payment on the ground that the bank was unconstitutional. The case went to the Supreme Court, and therein it was decided that the bank was constitutional. The whole Democratic party revolted against that decision. General Jackson himself asserted that he, as President, would not be bound to hold a National Bank to be constitutional, even though the court had decided it to be so. He fell in precisely with the view of Mr. Jefferson, and acted upon it under his official oath, in vetoing a charter for a National Bank. The declaration that Congress does not possess this constitutional power to charter a bank has gone into the Democratic platform, at their National Conventions, and was brought forward and reaffirmed in their last Convention at Cincinnati. They have contended for that declaration, in the very teeth of the Supreme Court, for more than a quarter of a century. In fact, they have reduced the decision to an absolute nullity. That decision, I repeat, is repudiated in the Cincinnati platform; and still, as if to show that effrontery can go no further, Judge Douglas vaunts in the very speeches in which he denounces me for opposing the Dred Scott decision that he stands on the Cincinnati platform.

Now, I wish to know what the Judge can charge upon me, with respect to decisions of the Supreme Court, which does not lie in all its length, breadth, and proportions at his own door. The plain truth is simply this: Judge Douglas is for Supreme Court decisions when he likes and against them when he does not like them. He is for the Dred Scott decision because it tends to nationalize slavery; because it is part of the original combination for that object. It so happens, singularly enough, that I never stood opposed to a decision of the Supreme Court till this, on the contrary, I have no recollection that he was ever particularly in favor of one till this. He never was in favor of any nor opposed to any, till the present one, which helps to nationalize slavery.

Free men of Sangamon, free men of Illinois, free men everywhere, judge ye between him and me upon this issue.

He says this Dred Scott case is a very small matter at most,—that it has no practical effect; that at best, or rather, I suppose, at worst, it is but an abstraction. I submit that the proposition that the thing which determines whether a man is free or a slave is rather concrete than abstract. I think you would conclude that it was, if your liberty depended upon it, and so would Judge Douglas, if his liberty depended upon it. But suppose it was on the question of spreading slavery over the new Territories that he considers it as being merely an abstract matter, and one of no practical importance. How has the planting of slavery in new countries always been effected? It has now been decided that slavery cannot be kept out of our new Territories by any legal means. In what do our new Territories now differ in this respect from the old Colonies when slavery was first planted within them? It was planted, as Mr. Clay once declared, and as history proves true, by individual men, in spite of the wishes of the people; the Mother Government refusing to prohibit it, and withholding from the people of the Colonies the authority to prohibit it for themselves. Mr. Clay says this was one of the great and just causes of complaint against Great Britain by the Colonies, and the best apology we can now make for having the institution amongst us. In that precise condition our Nebraska politicians have at last succeeded in placing our own new Territories; the government will not prohibit slavery within them, nor allow the people to prohibit it.

I defy any man to find any difference between the policy which originally planted slavery in these Colonies and that policy which now prevails in our new Territories. If it does not go into them, it is only because no individual wishes it to go. The Judge indulged himself doubtless to-day with the question as to what I am going to do with or about the Dred Scott decision. Well, Judge, will you please tell me what you did about the bank decision? Will you not graciously allow us to do with the Dred Scott decision precisely as you did with the bank decision? You succeeded in breaking down the moral effect of that decision: did you find it necessary to amend the Constitution, or to set up a court of negroes in order to do it?

There is one other point. Judge Douglas has a very affectionate leaning toward the Americans and Old Whigs. Last evening, in a sort of weeping tone, he described to us a death-bed scene. He had been called to the side of Mr. Clay, in his last moments, in order that the genius of "popular sovereignty" might duly descend from the dying man and settle upon him, the living and most worthy successor. He could do no less than promise that he would devote the remainder of his life to "popular sovereignty"; and then the great statesman departs in peace. By this part of the "plan of the campaign" the Judge has evidently promised himself that tears shall be drawn down the cheeks of all Old Whigs, as large as half-grown apples.

Mr. Webster, too, was mentioned; but it did not quite come to a death-bed scene as to him. It would be amusing, if it were not disgusting, to see how quick these compromise-breakers administer on the political effects of their dead adversaries, trumping up claims never before heard of, and dividing the assets among themselves. If I should be found dead to-morrow morning, nothing but my insignificance could prevent a speech being made on my authority, before the end of next week. It so happens that in that "popular sovereignty" with which Mr. Clay was identified, the Missouri Compromise was expressly reversed; and it was a little singular if Mr. Clay cast his mantle upon Judge Douglas on purpose to have that compromise repealed.

Again, the Judge did not keep faith with Mr. Clay when he first brought in his Nebraska Bill. He left the Missouri Compromise unrepealed, and in his report accompanying the bill he told the world he did it on purpose. The manes of Mr. Clay must have been in great agony till thirty days later, when "popular sovereignty" stood forth in all its glory.

One more thing. Last night Judge Douglas tormented himself with horrors about my disposition to make negroes perfectly equal with white men in social and political relations. He did not stop to show that I have said any such thing, or that it legitimately follows from anything I have said, but he rushes on with his assertions. I adhere to the Declaration of Independence. If Judge Douglas and his friends are not willing to stand by it, let them come up and amend it. Let them make it read that all men are created equal except negroes. Let us have it decided whether the Declaration of Independence, in this blessed year of 1858, shall be thus amended. In his construction of the Declaration last year, he said it only meant that Americans in America were equal to Englishmen in England. Then, when I pointed out to him that by that rule he excludes the Germans, the Irish, the Portuguese, and all the other people who have come among us since the revolution, he reconstructs his construction. In his last speech he tells us it meant Europeans.

I press him a little further, and ask if it meant to include the Russians in Asia; or does he mean to exclude that vast population from the principles of our Declaration of Independence? I expect ere long he will introduce another amendment to his definition. He is not at all particular. He is satisfied with anything which does not endanger the nationalizing of negro slavery. It may draw white men down, but it must not lift negroes up.

Who shall say, "I am the superior, and you are the inferior"?

My declarations upon this subject of negro slavery may be misrepresented, but cannot be misunderstood. I have said that I do not understand the Declaration to mean that all men were created equal in all respects. They are not our equal in color; but I suppose that it does mean to declare that all men are equal in some respects; they are equal in their right to "life, liberty, and the pursuit of happiness." Certainly the negro is not our equal in color, perhaps not in many other respects; still, in the right to put into his mouth the bread that his own hands have earned, he is the equal of every other man, white or black. In pointing out that more has been given you, you cannot be justified in taking away the little which has been given him. All I ask for the negro is that if you do not like him, let him alone. If God gave him but little, that little let him enjoy.

When our government was established we had the institution of slavery among us. We were in a certain sense compelled to tolerate its existence. It was a sort of necessity. We had gone through our struggle and secured our own independence. The framers of the Constitution found the institution of slavery amongst their own institutions at the time. They found that by an effort to eradicate it they might lose much of what they had already gained. They were obliged to bow to the necessity. They gave power to Congress to abolish the slave trade at the end of twenty years. They also prohibited it in the Territories where it did not exist. They did what they could, and yielded to the necessity for the rest. I also yield to all which follows from that necessity. What I would most desire would be the separation of the white and black races.

One more point on this Springfield speech which Judge Douglas says he has read so carefully. I expressed my belief in the existence of a conspiracy to perpetuate and nationalize slavery. I did not profess to know it, nor do I now. I showed the part Judge Douglas had played in the string of facts constituting to my mind the proof of that conspiracy. I showed the parts played by others.

I charged that the people had been deceived into carrying the last Presidential election, by the impression that the people of the Territories might exclude slavery if they chose, when it was known in advance by the conspirators that the court was to decide that neither Congress nor the people could so exclude slavery. These charges are more distinctly made than anything else in the speech.

Judge Douglas has carefully read and reread that speech. He has not, so far as I know, contradicted those charges. In the two speeches which I heard he certainly did not. On this own tacit admission, I renew that charge. I charge him with having been a party to that conspiracy and to that deception for the sole purpose of nationalizing slavery.

CORRESPONDENCE BETWEEN LINCOLN AND DOUGLAS

[The following is the correspondence between the two rival candidates for the United States Senate]

MR. LINCOLN TO MR. DOUGLAS.

CHICAGO, ILL., July 24, 1558.

HON. S. A. DOUGLAS:

My dear Sir,—Will it be agreeable to you to make an arrangement for you and myself to divide time, and address the same audiences the present canvass? Mr. Judd, who will hand you this, is authorized to receive your answer; and, if agreeable to you, to enter into the terms of such arrangement.

Your obedient servant,

A. LINCOLN.

Mr. DOUGLAS TO Mr. LINCOLN.

BEMENT, PLATT Co., ILL., July 30, 1858.

Dear Sir,—Your letter dated yesterday, accepting my proposition for a joint discussion at one prominent point in each Congressional District, as stated in my previous letter, was received this morning.

The times and places designated are as follows:

Ottawa, La Salle County   August 21st, 1858.

Freeport, Stephenson County   "   27th,

Jonesboro, Union County, September 15th,

Charleston, Coles County   "   18th,

Galesburgh, Knox County October 7th,

Quincy, Adams County   "   13th,

Alton, Madison County " 15th,

I agree to your suggestion that we shall alternately open and close the discussion. I will speak at Ottawa one hour, you can reply, occupying an hour and a half, and I will then follow for half an hour. At Freeport, you shall open the discussion and speak one hour; I will follow for an hour and a half, and you can then reply for half an hour. We will alternate in like manner in each successive place.

Very respectfully, your obedient servant,

S. A. DOUGLAS.

Mr. LINCOLN TO Mr. DOUGLAS.

SPRINGFIELD, July 31, 1858. HON. S. A. DOUGLAS:

Dear Sir,—Yours of yesterday, naming places, times, and terms for joint discussions between us, was received this morning. Although, by the terms, as you propose, you take four openings and closes, to my three, I accede, and thus close the arrangement. I direct this to you at Hillsborough, and shall try to have both your letter and this appear in the Journal and Register of Monday morning.

Your obedient servant,

A. LINCOLN.

FIRST JOINT DEBATE, AT OTTAWA,

AUGUST 21, 1858

Mr. LINCOLN'S REPLY

MY FELLOW-CITIZENS:—When a man hears himself somewhat misrepresented, it provokes him, at least, I find it so with myself; but when misrepresentation becomes very gross and palpable, it is more apt to amuse him. The first thing I see fit to notice is the fact that Judge Douglas alleges, after running through the history of the old Democratic and the old Whig parties, that Judge Trumbull and myself made an arrangement in 1854, by which I was to have the place of General Shields in the United States Senate, and Judge Trumbull was to have the place of Judge Douglas. Now, all I have to say upon that subject is that I think no man not even Judge Douglas can prove it, because it is not true. I have no doubt he is "conscientious" in saying it. As to those resolutions that he took such a length of time to read, as being the platform of the Republican party in 1854, I say I never had anything to do with them, and I think Trumbull never had. Judge Douglas cannot show that either of us ever did have anything to do with them.

I believe this is true about those resolutions: There was a call for a convention to form a Republican party at Springfield, and I think that my friend Mr. Lovejoy, who is here upon this stand, had a hand in it. I think this is true, and I think if he will remember accurately he will be able to recollect that he tried to get me into it, and I would not go in. I believe it is also true that I went away from Springfield when the convention was in session, to attend court in Tazewell county. It is true they did place my name, though without authority, upon the committee, and afterward wrote me to attend the meeting of the committee; but I refused to do so, and I never had anything to do with that organization. This is the plain truth about all that matter of the resolutions.

Now, about this story that Judge Douglas tells of Trumbull bargaining to sell out the old Democratic party, and Lincoln agreeing to sell out the old Whig party, I have the means of knowing about that: Judge Douglas cannot have; and I know there is no substance to it whatever. Yet I have no doubt he is "conscientious" about it. I know that after Mr. Lovejoy got into the Legislature that winter, he complained of me that I had told all the old Whigs of his district that the old Whig party was good enough for them, and some of them voted against him because I told them so. Now, I have no means of totally disproving such charges as this which the Judge makes. A man cannot prove a negative; but he has a right to claim that when a man makes an affirmative charge, he must offer some proof to show the truth of what he says. I certainly cannot introduce testimony to show the negative about things, but I have a right to claim that if a man says he knows a thing, then he must show how he knows it. I always have a right to claim this, and it is not satisfactory to me that he may be "conscientious" on the subject.

Now, gentlemen, I hate to waste my time on such things; but in regard to that general Abolition tilt that Judge Douglas makes, when he says that I was engaged at that time in selling out and Abolitionizing the old Whig party, I hope you will permit me to read a part of a printed speech that I made then at Peoria, which will show altogether a different view of the position I took in that contest of 1854.

[Voice: "Put on your specs."]

Mr. LINCOLN: Yes, sir, I am obliged to do so; I am no longer a young man.

"This is the repeal of the Missouri Compromise. The foregoing history may not be precisely accurate in every particular, but I am sure it is sufficiently so for all the uses I shall attempt to make of it, and in it we have before us the chief materials enabling us to correctly judge whether the repeal of the Missouri Compromise is right or wrong.

"I think, and shall try to show, that it is wrong—wrong in its direct effect, letting slavery into Kansas and Nebraska, and wrong in its prospective principle, allowing it to spread to every other part of the wide world where men can be found inclined to take it.

"This declared indifference, but, as I must think, covert real zeal for the spread of slavery, I cannot but hate. I hate it because of the monstrous injustice of slavery itself. I hate it because it deprives our republican example of its just influence in the world,—enables the enemies of free institutions, with plausibility, to taunt us as hypocrites; causes the real friends of freedom to doubt our sincerity, and especially because it forces so many really good men amongst ourselves into an open war with the very fundamental principles of civil liberty, criticizing the Declaration of Independence, and insisting that there is no right principle of action but self-interest.

"Before proceeding, let me say I think I have no prejudice against the Southern people. They are just what we would be in their situation. If slavery did not now exist among them, they would not introduce it. If it did now exist among us, we should not instantly give it up. This I believe of the masses north and south. Doubtless there are individuals on both sides who would not hold slaves under any circumstances; and others who would gladly introduce slavery anew, if it were out of existence. We know that some Southern men do free their slaves, go north, and become tip-top Abolitionists; while some Northern ones go south and become most cruel slave-masters.

"When Southern people tell us they are no more responsible for the origin of slavery than we, I acknowledge the fact. When it is said that the institution exists, and that it is very difficult to get rid of it, in any satisfactory way, I can understand and appreciate the saying. I will not blame them for not doing what I should not know how to do myself. If all earthly power were given me, I should not know what to do, as to the existing institution. My first impulse would be to free all the slaves and send them to Liberia,—to their own native land. But a moment's reflection would convince me that whatever of high hope (as I think there is) there may be in this in the long term, its sudden execution is impossible. If they were all landed there in a day, they would all perish in the next ten days; and there are not surplus shipping and surplus money enough in the world to carry them there in many times ten days. What then? Free them all and keep them among us as underlings? Is it quite certain that this betters their condition? I think I would not hold one in slavery, at any rate; yet the point is not clear enough to me to denounce people upon. What next? Free them, and make them politically and socially our equals? My own feelings will not admit of this; and if mine would, we well know that those of the great mass of white people will not. Whether this feeling accords with justice and sound judgment, is not the sole question, if, indeed, it is any part of it. A universal feeling, whether well or ill founded, cannot be safely disregarded. We cannot, then, make them equals. It does seem to me that systems of gradual emancipation might be adopted; but for their tardiness in this I will not undertake to judge our brethren of the South.

"When they remind us of their constitutional rights, I acknowledge them, not grudgingly, but fully and fairly; and I would give them any legislation for the reclaiming of their fugitives, which should not, in its stringency, be more likely to carry a free man into slavery than Our ordinary criminal laws are to hang an innocent one.

"But all this, to my judgment, furnishes no more excuse for permitting slavery to go into our own free territory than it would for reviving the African slave-trade by law. The law which forbids the bringing of slaves from Africa, and that which has so long forbid the taking of them to Nebraska, can hardly be distinguished on any moral principle; and the repeal of the former could find quite as plausible excuses as that of the latter."

I have reason to know that Judge Douglas knows that I said this. I think he has the answer here to one of the questions he put to me. I do not mean to allow him to catechize me unless he pays back for it in kind. I will not answer questions one after another, unless he reciprocates; but as he has made this inquiry, and I have answered it before, he has got it without my getting anything in return. He has got my answer on the Fugitive Slave law.

Now, gentlemen, I don't want to read at any greater length; but this is the true complexion of all I have ever said in regard to the institution of slavery and the black race. This is the whole of it; and anything that argues me into his idea of perfect social and political equality with the negro is but a specious and fantastic arrangement of words, by which a man can prove a horse-chestnut to be a chestnut horse. I will say here, while upon this subject, that I have no purpose, directly or indirectly, to interfere with the institution of slavery in the States where it exists. I believe I have no lawful right to do so, and I have no inclination to do so. I have no purpose to introduce political and social equality between the white and the black races. There is a physical difference between the two which, in my judgment, will probably forever forbid their living together upon the footing of perfect equality; and inasmuch as it becomes a necessity that there must be a difference, I, as well as Judge Douglas, am in favor of the race to which I belong having the superior position. I have never said anything to the contrary, but I hold that, notwithstanding all this, there is no reason in the world why the negro is not entitled to all the natural rights enumerated in the Declaration of Independence, the right to life, liberty, and the pursuit of happiness. I hold that he is as much entitled to these as the white man. I agree with Judge Douglas he is not my equal in many respects, certainly not in color, perhaps not in moral or intellectual endowment. But in the right to eat the bread, without the leave of anybody else, which his own hand earns, he is my equal, and the equal of Judge Douglas, and the equal of every living man.

Now I pass on to consider one or two more of these little follies. The Judge is woefully at fault about his early friend Lincoln being a "grocery-keeper." I don't know as it would be a great sin, if I had been; but he is mistaken. Lincoln never kept a grocery anywhere in the world. It is true that Lincoln did work the latter part of one winter in a little stillhouse, up at the head of a hollow. And so I think my friend the Judge is equally at fault when he charges me at the time when I was in Congress of having opposed our soldiers who were fighting in the Mexican war. The Judge did not make his charge very distinctly, but I can tell you what he can prove, by referring to the record. You remember I was an old Whig, and whenever the Democratic party tried to get me to vote that the war had been righteously begun by the President, I would not do it. But whenever they asked for any money, or landwarrants, or anything to pay the soldiers there, during all that time, I gave the same vote that Judge Douglas did. You can think as you please as to whether that was consistent. Such is the truth, and the Judge has the right to make all he can out of it. But when he, by a general charge, conveys the idea that I withheld supplies from the soldiers who were fighting in the Mexican war, or did anything else to hinder the soldiers, he is, to say the least, grossly and altogether mistaken, as a consultation of the records will prove to him.

As I have not used up so much of my time as I had supposed, I will dwell a little longer upon one or two of these minor topics upon which the Judge has spoken. He has read from my speech in Springfield, in which I say that "a house divided against itself cannot stand." Does the Judge say it can stand? I don't know whether he does or not. The Judge does not seem to be attending to me just now, but I would like to know if it is his opinion that a house divided against itself can stand. If he does, then there is a question of veracity, not between him and me, but between the Judge and an Authority of a somewhat higher character.

Now, my friends, I ask your attention to this matter for the purpose of saying something seriously. I know that the Judge may readily enough agree with me that the maxim which was put forth by the Savior is true, but he may allege that I misapply it; and the Judge has a right to urge that, in my application, I do misapply it, and then I have a right to show that I do not misapply it, When he undertakes to say that because I think this nation, so far as the question of slavery is concerned, will all become one thing or all the other, I am in favor of bringing about a dead uniformity in the various States, in all their institutions, he argues erroneously. The great variety of the local institutions in the States, springing from differences in the soil, differences in the face of the country, and in the climate, are bonds of Union. They do not make "a house divided against itself," but they make a house united. If they produce in one section of the country what is called for, by the wants of another section, and this other section can supply the wants of the first, they are not matters of discord, but bonds of union, true bonds of union. But can this question of slavery be considered as among these varieties in the institutions of the country? I leave it to you to say whether, in the history of our government, this institution of slavery has not always failed to be a bond of union, and, on the contrary, been an apple of discord and an element of division in the house. I ask you to consider whether, so long as the moral constitution of men's minds shall continue to be the same, after this generation and assemblage shall sink into the grave, and another race shall arise, with the same moral and intellectual development we have, whether, if that institution is standing in the same irritating position in which it now is, it will not continue an element of division? If so, then I have a right to say that, in regard to this question, the Union is a house divided against itself; and when the Judge reminds me that I have often said to him that the institution of slavery has existed for eighty years in some States, and yet it does not exist in some others, I agree to the fact, and I account for it by looking at the position in which our fathers originally placed it—restricting it from the new Territories where it had not gone, and legislating to cut off its source by the abrogation of the slave trade, thus putting the seal of legislation against its spread. The public mind did rest in the belief that it was in the course of ultimate extinction. But lately, I think—and in this I charge nothing on the Judge's motives—lately, I think that he, and those acting with him, have placed that institution on a new basis, which looks to the perpetuity and nationalization of slavery. And while it is placed upon this new basis, I say, and I have said, that I believe we shall not have peace upon the question until the opponents of slavery arrest the further spread of it, and place it where the public mind shall rest in the belief that it is in the course of ultimate extinction; or, on the other hand, that its advocates will push it forward until it shall become alike lawful in all the States, old as well as new, North as well as South. Now, I believe if we could arrest the spread, and place it where Washington and Jefferson and Madison placed it, it would be in the course of ultimate extinction, and the public mind would, as for eighty years past, believe that it was in the course of ultimate extinction. The crisis would be past, and the institution might be let alone for a hundred years, if it should live so long, in the States where it exists; yet it would be going out of existence in the way best for both the black and the white races.

[A voice: "Then do you repudiate popular sovereignty?"]

Well, then, let us talk about popular sovereignty! what is popular sovereignty? Is it the right of the people to have slavery or not have it, as they see fit, in the Territories? I will state—and I have an able man to watch me—my understanding is that popular sovereignty, as now applied to the question of slavery, does allow the people of a Territory to have slavery if they want to, but does not allow them not to have it if they do not want it. I do not mean that if this vast concourse of people were in a Territory of the United States, any one of them would be obliged to have a slave if he did not want one; but I do say that, as I understand the Dred Scott decision, if any one man wants slaves, all the rest have no way of keeping that one man from holding them.

When I made my speech at Springfield, of which the Judge complains, and from which he quotes, I really was not thinking of the things which he ascribes to me at all. I had no thought in the world that I was doing anything to bring about a war between the free and slave states. I had no thought in the world that I was doing anything to bring about a political and social equality of the black and white races. It never occurred to me that I was doing anything or favoring anything to reduce to a dead uniformity all the local institutions of the various States. But I must say, in all fairness to him, if he thinks I am doing something which leads to these bad results, it is none the better that I did not mean it. It is just as fatal to the country, if I have any influence in producing it, whether I intend it or not. But can it be true that placing this institution upon the original basis—the basis upon which our fathers placed it—can have any tendency to set the Northern and the Southern States at war with one another, or that it can have any tendency to make the people of Vermont raise sugar-cane, because they raise it in Louisiana, or that it can compel the people of Illinois to cut pine logs on the Grand Prairie, where they will not grow, because they cut pine logs in Maine, where they do grow? The Judge says this is a new principle started in regard to this question. Does the Judge claim that he is working on the plan of the founders of government? I think he says in some of his speeches indeed, I have one here now—that he saw evidence of a policy to allow slavery to be south of a certain line, while north of it it should be excluded, and he saw an indisposition on the part of the country to stand upon that policy, and therefore he set about studying the subject upon original principles, and upon original principles he got up the Nebraska Bill! I am fighting it upon these "original principles," fighting it in the Jeffersonian, Washingtonian, and Madisonian fashion.

Now, my friends, I wish you to attend for a little while to one or two other things in that Springfield speech. My main object was to show, so far as my humble ability was capable of showing, to the people of this country what I believed was the truth,—that there was a tendency, if not a conspiracy, among those who have engineered this slavery question for the last four or five years, to make slavery perpetual and universal in this nation. Having made that speech principally for that object, after arranging the evidences that I thought tended to prove my proposition, I concluded with this bit of comment:

"We cannot absolutely know that these exact adaptations are the result of preconcert; but when we see a lot of framed timbers, different portions of which we know have been gotten out at different times and places, and by different workmen—Stephen, Franklin, Roger, and James, for instance,—and when we see these timbers joined together, and see they exactly make the frame of a house or a mill, all the tenons and mortises exactly fitting, and all the lengths and proportions of the different pieces exactly adapted to their respective places, and not a piece too many or too few,—not omitting even the scaffolding,—or if a single piece be lacking, we see the place in the frame exactly fitted and prepared yet to bring such piece in,—in such a case we feel it impossible not to believe that Stephen and Franklin and Roger and James all understood one another from the beginning, and all worked upon a common plan or draft drawn before the first blow was struck."

When my friend Judge Douglas came to Chicago on the 9th of July, this speech having been delivered on the 16th of June, he made an harangue there, in which he took hold of this speech of mine, showing that he had carefully read it; and while he paid no attention to this matter at all, but complimented me as being a "kind, amiable, and intelligent gentleman," notwithstanding I had said this, he goes on and eliminates, or draws out, from my speech this tendency of mine to set the States at war with one another, to make all the institutions uniform, and set the niggers and white people to marrying together. Then, as the Judge had complimented me with these pleasant titles (I must confess to my weakness), I was a little "taken," for it came from a great man. I was not very much accustomed to flattery, and it came the sweeter to me. I was rather like the Hoosier, with the gingerbread, when he said he reckoned he loved it better than any other man, and got less of it. As the Judge had so flattered me, I could not make up my mind that he meant to deal unfairly with me; so I went to work to show him that he misunderstood the whole scope of my speech, and that I really never intended to set the people at war with one another. As an illustration, the next time I met him, which was at Springfield, I used this expression, that I claimed no right under the Constitution, nor had I any inclination, to enter into the slave States and interfere with the institutions of slavery. He says upon that: Lincoln will not enter into the slave States, but will go to the banks of the Ohio, on this side, and shoot over! He runs on, step by step, in the horse-chestnut style of argument, until in the Springfield speech he says: "Unless he shall be successful in firing his batteries until he shall have extinguished slavery in all the States the Union shall be dissolved." Now, I don't think that was exactly the way to treat "a kind, amiable, intelligent gentleman." I know if I had asked the Judge to show when or where it was I had said that, if I didn't succeed in firing into the slave States until slavery should be extinguished, the Union should be dissolved, he could not have shown it. I understand what he would do. He would say: I don't mean to quote

246

from you, but this was the result of what you say. But I have the right to ask, and I do ask now, Did you not put it in such a form that an ordinary reader or listener would take it as an expression from me?

In a speech at Springfield, on the night of the 17th, I thought I might as well attend to my own business a little, and I recalled his attention as well as I could to this charge of conspiracy to nationalize slavery. I called his attention to the fact that he had acknowledged in my hearing twice that he had carefully read the speech, and, in the language of the lawyers, as he had twice read the speech, and still had put in no plea or answer, I took a default on him. I insisted that I had a right then to renew that charge of conspiracy. Ten days afterward I met the Judge at Clinton,—that is to say, I was on the ground, but not in the discussion,—and heard him make a speech. Then he comes in with his plea to this charge, for the first time; and his plea when put in, as well as I can recollect it, amounted to this: that he never had any talk with Judge Taney or the President of the United States with regard to the Dred Scott decision before it was made. I (Lincoln) ought to know that the man who makes a charge without knowing it to be true falsifies as much as he who knowingly tells a falsehood; and, lastly, that he would pronounce the whole thing a falsehood; but, he would make no personal application of the charge of falsehood, not because of any regard for the "kind, amiable, intelligent gentleman," but because of his own personal self-respect! I have understood since then (but [turning to Judge Douglas] will not hold the Judge to it if he is not willing) that he has broken through the "self-respect," and has got to saying the thing out. The Judge nods to me that it is so. It is fortunate for me that I can keep as good-humored as I do, when the Judge acknowledges that he has been trying to make a question of veracity with me. I know the Judge is a great man, while I am only a small man, but I feel that I have got him. I demur to that plea. I waive all objections that it was not filed till after default was taken, and demur to it upon the merits. What if Judge Douglas never did talk with Chief Justice Taney and the President before the Dred Scott decision was made, does it follow that he could not have had as perfect an understanding without talking as with it? I am not disposed to stand upon my legal advantage. I am disposed to take his denial as being like an answer in chancery, that he neither had any knowledge, information, or belief in the existence of such a conspiracy. I am disposed to take his answer as being as broad as though he had put it in these words. And now, I ask, even if he had done so, have not I a right to prove it on him, and to offer the evidence of more than two witnesses, by whom to prove it; and if the evidence proves the existence of the conspiracy, does his broader answer denying all knowledge, information, or belief, disturb the fact? It can only show that he was used by conspirators, and was not a leader of them.

Now, in regard to his reminding me of the moral rule that persons who tell

what they do not know to be true falsify as much as those who knowingly

tell falsehoods. I remember the rule, and it must be borne in mind that

in what I have read to you, I do not say that I know such a conspiracy

to exist. To that I reply, I believe it. If the Judge says that I do not

believe it, then he says what he does not know, and falls within his

own rule, that he who asserts a thing which he does not know to be true,

falsifies as much as he who knowingly tells a falsehood. I want to call

your attention to a little discussion on that branch of the case, and the

evidence which brought my mind to the conclusion which I expressed as

my belief. If, in arraying that evidence I had stated anything which was

false or erroneous, it needed but that Judge Douglas should point it out,

and I would have taken it back, with all the kindness in the world. I do not deal in that way. If I have brought forward anything not a fact, if he will point it out, it will not even ruffle me to take it back. But if he will not point out anything erroneous in the evidence, is it not rather for him to show, by a comparison of the evidence, that I have reasoned falsely, than to call the "kind, amiable, intelligent gentleman" a liar? If I have reasoned to a false conclusion, it is the vocation of an able debater to show by argument that I have wandered to an erroneous conclusion. I want to ask your attention to a portion of the Nebraska Bill, which Judge Douglas has quoted:

"It being the true intent and meaning of this Act, not to legislate slavery into any Territory or State, nor to exclude it therefrom, but to leave the people thereof perfectly free to form and regulate their domestic institutions in their own way, subject only to the Constitution of the United States."

Thereupon Judge Douglas and others began to argue in favor of "popular sovereignty," the right of the people to have slaves if they wanted them, and to exclude slavery if they did not want them. "But," said, in substance, a Senator from Ohio (Mr. Chase, I believe), "we more than suspect that you do not mean to allow the people to exclude slavery if they wish to; and if you do mean it, accept an amendment which I propose, expressly authorizing the people to exclude slavery."

I believe I have the amendment here before me, which was offered, and under which the people of the Territory, through their representatives, might, if they saw fit, prohibit the existence of slavery therein. And now I state it as a fact, to be taken back if there is any mistake about it, that Judge Douglas and those acting with him voted that amendment down. I now think that those men who voted it down had a real reason for doing so. They know what that reason was. It looks to us, since we have seen the Dred Scott decision pronounced, holding that "under the Constitution" the people cannot exclude slavery, I say it looks to outsiders, poor, simple, "amiable, intelligent gentlemen," as though the niche was left as a place to put that Dred Scott decision in,—a niche which would have been spoiled by adopting the amendment. And now, I say again, if this was not the reason, it will avail the Judge much more to calmly and good-humoredly point out to these people what that other reason was for voting the amendment down, than, swelling himself up, to vociferate that he may be provoked to call somebody a liar.

Again: There is in that same quotation from the Nebraska Bill this clause: "It being the true intent and meaning of this bill not to legislate slavery into any Territory or State." I have always been puzzled to know what business the word "State" had in that connection. Judge Douglas knows. He put it there. He knows what he put it there for. We outsiders cannot say what he put it there for. The law they were passing was not about States, and was not making provisions for States. What was it placed there for? After seeing the Dred Scott decision, which holds that the people cannot exclude slavery from a Territory, if another Dred Scott decision shall come, holding that they cannot exclude it from a State, we shall discover that when the word was originally put there, it was in view of something which was to come in due time, we shall see that it was the other half of something. I now say again, if there is any different reason for putting it there, Judge Douglas, in a good-humored way, without calling anybody a liar, can tell what the reason was.

When the Judge spoke at Clinton, he came very near making a charge of falsehood against me. He used, as I found it printed in a newspaper, which, I remember, was very nearly like the real speech, the following language:

"I did not answer the charge [of conspiracy] before, for the reason that I did not suppose there was a man in America with a heart so corrupt as to believe such a charge could be true. I have too much respect for Mr. Lincoln to suppose he is serious in making the charge."

I confess this is rather a curious view, that out of respect for me he should consider I was making what I deemed rather a grave charge in fun. I confess it strikes me rather strangely. But I let it pass. As the Judge did not for a moment believe that there was a man in America whose heart was so "corrupt" as to make such a charge, and as he places me among the "men in America" who have hearts base enough to make such a charge, I hope he will excuse me if I hunt out another charge very like this; and if it should turn out that in hunting I should find that other, and it should turn out to be Judge Douglas himself who made it, I hope he will reconsider this question of the deep corruption of heart he has thought fit to ascribe to me. In Judge Douglas's speech of March 22, 1858, which I hold in my hand, he says:

"In this connection there is another topic to which I desire to allude. I seldom refer to the course of newspapers, or notice the articles which they publish in regard to myself; but the course of the Washington Union has been so extraordinary for the last two or three months, that I think it well enough to make some allusion to it. It has read me out of the Democratic party every other day, at least for two or three months, and keeps reading me out, and, as if it had not succeeded, still continues to read me out, using such terms as 'traitor,' 'renegade,' 'deserter,' and other kind and polite epithets of that nature. Sir, I have no vindication to make of my Democracy against the Washington Union, or any other newspapers. I am willing to allow my history and action for the last twenty years to speak for themselves as to my political principles and my fidelity to political obligations. The Washington Union has a personal grievance. When its editor was nominated for public printer, I declined to vote for him, and stated that at some time I might give my reasons for doing so. Since I declined to give that vote, this scurrilous abuse, these vindictive and constant attacks have been repeated almost daily on me. Will any friend from Michigan read the article to which I allude?"

This is a part of the speech. You must excuse me from reading the entire article of the Washington Union, as Mr. Stuart read it for Mr. Douglas. The Judge goes on and sums up, as I think, correctly:

"Mr. President, you here find several distinct propositions advanced boldly by the Washington Union editorially, and apparently authoritatively; and any man who questions any of them is denounced as an Abolitionist, a Free-soiler, a fanatic. The propositions are, first, that the primary object of all government at its original institution is the protection of person and property; second, that the Constitution of the United States declares that the citizens of each State shall be entitled to all the privileges and immunities of citizens in the several States; and that, therefore, thirdly, all State laws, whether organic or otherwise, which prohibit the citizens of one State from settling in another with their slave property, and especially declaring it forfeited, are direct violations of the original intention of the government and Constitution of the United States; and, fourth, that the emancipation of the slaves of the Northern States was a gross outrage of the rights of property, inasmuch as it was involuntarily done on the part of the owner.

"Remember that this article was published in the Union on the 17th of November, and on the 18th appeared the first article giving the adhesion of the Union, to the Lecompton Constitution. It was in these words:

"KANSAS AND HER CONSTITUTION.—The vexed question is settled. The problem is saved. The dead point of danger is passed. All serious trouble to Kansas affairs is over and gone..."

And a column nearly of the same sort. Then, when you come to look into the Lecompton Constitution, you find the same doctrine incorporated in it which was put forth editorially in the Union. What is it?

"ARTICLE 7, Section I. The right of property is before and higher than any constitutional sanction; and the right of the owner of a slave to such slave and its increase is the same and as inviolable as the right of the owner of any property whatever."

Then in the schedule is a provision that the Constitution may be amended after 1864 by a two-thirds vote:

"But no alteration shall be made to affect the right of property in the ownership of slaves."

"It will be seen by these clauses in the Lecompton Constitution that they are identical in spirit with the authoritative article in the Washington Union of the day previous to its indorsement of this Constitution."

I pass over some portions of the speech, and I hope that any one who feels interested in this matter will read the entire section of the speech, and see whether I do the Judge injustice. He proceeds:

"When I saw that article in the Union of the 17th of November, followed by the glorification of the Lecompton Constitution on the 10th of November, and this clause in the Constitution asserting the doctrine that a State has no right to prohibit slavery within its limits, I saw that there was a fatal blow being struck at the sovereignty of the States of this Union."

I stop the quotation there, again requesting that it may all be read. I have read all of the portion I desire to comment upon. What is this charge that the Judge thinks I must have a very corrupt heart to make? It was a purpose on the part of certain high functionaries to make it impossible for the people of one State to prohibit the people of any other State from entering it with their "property," so called, and making it a slave State. In other words, it was a charge implying a design to make the institution of slavery national. And now I ask your attention to what Judge Douglas has himself done here. I know he made that part of the speech as a reason why he had refused to vote for a certain man for public printer; but when we get at it, the charge itself is the very one I made against him, that he thinks I am so corrupt for uttering. Now, whom does he make that charge against? Does he make it against that newspaper editor merely? No; he says it is identical in spirit with the Lecompton Constitution, and so the framers of that Constitution are brought in with the editor of the newspaper in that "fatal blow being struck." He did not call it a "conspiracy." In his language, it is a "fatal blow being struck." And if the words carry the meaning better when changed from a "conspiracy" into a "fatal blow being struck," I will change my expression, and call it "fatal blow being struck." We see the charge made not merely against the editor of the Union, but all the framers of the Lecompton Constitution; and not only so, but the article was an authoritative article. By whose authority? Is there any question but he means it was by the authority of the President and his Cabinet,—the Administration?

Is there any sort of question but he means to make that charge? Then there are the editors of the Union, the framers of the Lecompton Constitution, the President of the United States and his Cabinet, and all the supporters of the Lecompton Constitution, in Congress and out of Congress, who are all involved in this "fatal blow being struck." I commend to Judge Douglas's consideration the question of how corrupt a man's heart must be to make such a charge!

Now, my friends, I have but one branch of the subject, in the little time I have left, to which to call your attention; and as I shall come to a close at the end of that branch, it is probable that I shall not occupy quite all the time allotted to me. Although on these questions I would like to talk twice as long as I have, I could not enter upon another head and discuss it properly without running over my time. I ask the attention of the people here assembled and elsewhere to the course that Judge Douglas is pursuing every day as bearing upon this question of making slavery national. Not going back to the records, but taking the speeches he makes, the speeches he made yesterday and day before, and makes constantly all over the country, I ask your attention to them. In the first place, what is necessary to make the institution national? Not war. There is no danger that the people of Kentucky will shoulder their muskets, and, with a young nigger stuck on every bayonet, march into Illinois and force them upon us. There is no danger of our going over there and making war upon them. Then what is necessary for the nationalization of slavery? It is simply the next Dred Scott decision. It is merely for the Supreme Court to decide that no State under the Constitution can exclude it, just as they have already decided that under the Constitution neither Congress nor the Territorial Legislature can do it. When that is decided and acquiesced in, the whole thing is done. This being true, and this being the way, as I think, that slavery is to be made national, let us consider what Judge Douglas is doing every day to that end. In the first place, let us see what influence he is exerting on public sentiment. In this and like communities, public sentiment is everything. With public sentiment, nothing can fail; without it, nothing can succeed. Consequently, he who moulds public sentiment goes deeper than he who enacts statutes or pronounces decisions. He makes statutes and decisions possible or impossible to be executed. This must be borne in mind, as also the additional fact that Judge Douglas is a man of vast influence, so great that it is enough for many men to profess to believe anything when they once find out Judge Douglas professes to believe it. Consider also the attitude he occupies at the head of a large party,—a party which he claims has a majority of all the voters in the country. This man sticks to a decision which forbids the people of a Territory from excluding slavery, and he does so, not because he says it is right in itself,—he does not give any opinion on that,—but because it has been decided by the court; and being decided by the court, he is, and you are, bound to take it in your political action as law, not that he judges at all of its merits, but because a decision of the court is to him a "Thus saith the Lord." He places it on that ground alone; and you will bear in mind that thus committing himself unreservedly to this decision commits him to the next one just as firmly as to this. He did not commit himself on account of the merit or demerit of the decision, but it is a "Thus saith the Lord." The next decision, as much as this, will be a "Thus saith the Lord." There is nothing that can divert or turn him away from this decision. It is nothing that I point out to him that his great prototype, General Jackson, did not believe in the binding force of decisions. It is nothing to him that Jefferson did not so believe. I have said that I have often heard him approve of Jackson's course in disregarding the decision of the Supreme Court pronouncing a National Bank constitutional. He says I did not hear him say so. He denies the accuracy of my recollection. I say he ought to know better than I, but I will make no question about this thing, though it still seems to me that I heard him say it twenty times. I will tell him, though, that he now claims to stand on the Cincinnati platform, which affirms that Congress cannot charter a National Bank, in the teeth of that old standing decision that Congress can charter a bank. And I remind him of another piece of history on the question of respect for judicial decisions, and it is a piece of Illinois history belonging to a time when the large party to which Judge Douglas belonged were displeased with a decision of the Supreme Court of Illinois, because they had decided that a Governor could not remove a Secretary of State. You will find the whole story in Ford's History of Illinois, and I know that Judge Douglas will not deny that he was then in favor of over-slaughing that decision by the mode of adding five new judges, so as to vote down the four old ones. Not only so, but it ended in the Judge's sitting down on that very bench as one of the five new judges to break down the four old ones It was in this way precisely that he got his title of judge. Now, when the Judge tells me that men appointed conditionally to sit as members of a court will have to be catechized beforehand upon some subject, I say, "You know, Judge; you have tried it." When he says a court of this kind will lose the confidence of all men, will be prostituted and disgraced by such a proceeding, I say, "You know best, Judge; you have been through the mill." But I cannot shake Judge Douglas's teeth loose from the Dred Scott decision. Like some obstinate animal (I mean no disrespect) that will hang on when he has once got his teeth fixed, you may cut off a leg, or you may tear away an arm, still he will not relax his hold. And so I may point out to the Judge, and say that he is bespattered all over, from the beginning of his political life to the present time, with attacks upon judicial decisions; I may cut off limb after limb of his public record, and strive to wrench him from a single dictum of the court,—yet I cannot divert him from it. He hangs, to the last, to the Dred Scott decision. These things show there is a purpose strong as death and eternity for which he adheres to this decision, and for which he will adhere to all other decisions of the same court.

[A HIBERNIAN: "Give us something besides Dred Scott."]

Yes; no doubt you want to hear something that don't hurt. Now, having spoken of the Dred Scott decision, one more word, and I am done. Henry Clay, my beau-ideal of a statesman, the man for whom I fought all my humble life, Henry Clay once said of a class of men who would repress all tendencies to liberty and ultimate emancipation that they must, if they would do this, go back to the era of our Independence, and muzzle the cannon which thunders its annual joyous return; they must blow out the moral lights around us; they must penetrate the human soul, and eradicate there the love of liberty; and then, and not till then, could they perpetuate slavery in this country! To my thinking, Judge Douglas is, by his example and vast influence, doing that very thing in this community, when he says that the negro has nothing in the Declaration of Independence. Henry Clay plainly understood the contrary. Judge Douglas is going back to the era of our Revolution, and, to the extent of his ability, muzzling the cannon which thunders its annual joyous return. When he invites any people, willing to have slavery, to establish it, he is blowing out the moral lights around us. When he says he "cares not whether slavery is voted down or up,"—that it is a sacred right of self-government,—he is, in my judgment, penetrating the human soul and eradicating the light of reason and the love of liberty in this American people. And now I will only say that when, by all these means and appliances, Judge Douglas shall succeed in bringing public sentiment to an exact accordance with his own views; when these vast assemblages shall echo back all these sentiments; when they shall come to repeat his views and to avow his principles, and to say all that he says on these mighty questions,—then it needs only the formality of the second Dred Scott decision, which he indorses in advance, to make slavery alike lawful in all the States, old as well as new, North as well as South.

My friends, that ends the chapter. The Judge can take his half-hour.

SECOND JOINT DEBATE, AT FREEPORT,

AUGUST 27, 1858

LADIES AND GENTLEMEN:—On Saturday last, Judge Douglas and myself first met in public discussion. He spoke one hour, I an hour and a half, and he replied for half an hour. The order is now reversed. I am to speak an hour, he an hour and a half, and then I am to reply for half an hour. I propose to devote myself during the first hour to the scope of what was brought within the range of his half-hour speech at Ottawa. Of course there was brought within the scope in that half-hour's speech something of his own opening speech. In the course of that opening argument Judge Douglas proposed to me seven distinct interrogatories. In my speech of an hour and a half, I attended to some other parts of his speech, and incidentally, as I thought, intimated to him that I would answer the rest of his interrogatories on condition only that he should agree to answer as many for me. He made no intimation at the time of the proposition, nor did he in his reply allude at all to that suggestion of mine. I do him no injustice in saying that he occupied at least half of his reply in dealing with me as though I had refused to answer his interrogatories. I now propose that I will answer any of the interrogatories, upon condition that he will answer questions from me not exceeding the same number. I give him an opportunity to respond.

The Judge remains silent. I now say that I will answer his interrogatories, whether he answers mine or not; and that after I have done so, I shall propound mine to him.

I have supposed myself, since the organization of the Republican party at Bloomington, in May, 1856, bound as a party man by the platforms of the party, then and since. If in any interrogatories which I shall answer I go beyond the scope of what is within these platforms, it will be perceived that no one is responsible but myself.

Having said thus much, I will take up the Judge's interrogatories as I find them printed in the Chicago Times, and answer them seriatim. In order that there may be no mistake about it, I have copied the interrogatories in writing, and also my answers to them. The first one of these interrogatories is in these words:

Question 1.—"I desire to know whether Lincoln to-day stands, as he did in 1854, in favor of the unconditional repeal of the Fugitive Slave law?" Answer:—I do not now, nor ever did, stand in favor of the unconditional repeal of the Fugitive Slave law.

Q. 2.—"I desire him to answer whether he stands pledged to-day, as he did in 1854, against the admission of any more slave States into the Union, even if the people want them?" Answer:—I do not now, nor ever did, stand pledged against the admission of any more slave States into the Union.

Q. 3.—"I want to know whether he stands pledged against the admission of a new State into the Union with such a constitution as the people of that State may see fit to make?" Answer:—I do not stand pledged against the admission of a new State into the Union, with such a constitution as the people of that State may see fit to make.

Q. 4.—"I want to know whether he stands to-day pledged to the abolition of slavery in the District of Columbia?" Answer:—I do not stand to-day pledged to the abolition of slavery in the District of Columbia.

Q. 5.—"I desire him to answer whether he stands pledged to the prohibition of the slave-trade between the different States?" Answer:—I do not stand pledged to the prohibition of the slave-trade between the different States.

Q. 6.—"I desire to know whether he stands pledged to prohibit slavery in all the Territories of the United States, north as well as south of the Missouri Compromise line?" Answer:—I am impliedly, if not expressly, pledged to a belief in the right and duty of Congress to prohibit slavery in all the United States Territories.

Q. 7.—"I desire him to answer whether he is opposed to the acquisition of any new territory unless slavery is first prohibited therein?" Answer:—I am not generally opposed to honest acquisition of territory; and, in any given case, I would or would not oppose such acquisition, accordingly as I might think such acquisition would or would not aggravate the slavery question among ourselves.

Now, my friends, it will be perceived, upon an examination of these questions and answers, that so far I have only answered that I was not pledged to this, that, or the other. The Judge has not framed his interrogatories to ask me anything more than this, and I have answered in strict accordance with the interrogatories, and have answered truly, that I am not pledged at all upon any of the points to which I have answered. But I am not disposed to hang upon the exact form of his interrogatory. I am rather disposed to take up at least some of these questions, and state what I really think upon them.

As to the first one, in regard to the Fugitive Slave law, I have never hesitated to say, and I do not now hesitate to say, that I think, under the Constitution of the United States, the people of the Southern States are entitled to a Congressional Fugitive Slave law. Having said that, I have had nothing to say in regard to the existing Fugitive Slave law, further than that I think it should have been framed so as to be free from some of the objections that pertain to it, without lessening its efficiency. And inasmuch as we are not now in an agitation in regard to an alteration or modification of that law, I would not be the man to introduce it as a new subject of agitation upon the general question of slavery.

In regard to the other question, of whether I am pledged to the admission of any more slave States into the Union, I state to you very frankly that I would be exceedingly sorry ever to be put in a position of having to pass upon that question. I should be exceedingly glad to know that there would never be another slave State admitted into the Union; but I must add that if slavery shall be kept out of the Territories during the territorial existence of any one given Territory, and then the people shall, having a fair chance and a clear field, when they come to adopt the constitution, do such an extraordinary thing as to adopt a slave constitution, uninfluenced by the actual presence of the institution among them, I see no alternative, if we own the country, but to admit them into the Union.

The third interrogatory is answered by the answer to the second, it being, as I conceive, the same as the second.

The fourth one is in regard to the abolition of slavery in the District of Columbia. In relation to that, I have my mind very distinctly made up. I should be exceedingly glad to see slavery abolished in the District of Columbia. I believe that Congress possesses the constitutional power to abolish it. Yet as a member of Congress, I should not, with my present views, be in favor of endeavoring to abolish slavery in the District of Columbia, unless it would be upon these conditions: First, that the abolition should be gradual; second, that it should be on a vote of the majority of qualified voters in the District; and third, that compensation should be made to unwilling owners. With these three conditions, I confess I would be exceedingly glad to see Congress abolish slavery in the District of Columbia, and, in the language of Henry Clay, "sweep from our capital that foul blot upon our nation."

In regard to the fifth interrogatory, I must say here that, as to the question of the abolition of the slave-trade between the different States, I can truly answer, as I have, that I am pledged to nothing about it. It is a subject to which I have not given that mature consideration that would make me feel authorized to state a position so as to hold myself entirely bound by it. In other words, that question has never been prominently enough before me to induce me to investigate whether we really have the constitutional power to do it. I could investigate it if I had sufficient time to bring myself to a conclusion upon that subject; but I have not done so, and I say so frankly to you here, and to Judge Douglas. I must say, however, that if I should be of opinion that Congress does possess the constitutional power to abolish the slave-trade among the different States, I should still not be in favor of the exercise of that power, unless upon some conservative principle as I conceive it, akin to what I have said in relation to the abolition of slavery in the District of Columbia.

My answer as to whether I desire that slavery should be prohibited in all the Territories of the United States is full and explicit within itself, and cannot be made clearer by any comments of mine. So I suppose in regard to the question whether I am opposed to the acquisition of any more territory unless slavery is first prohibited therein, my answer is such that I could add nothing by way of illustration, or making myself better understood, than the answer which I have placed in writing.

Now in all this the Judge has me, and he has me on the record. I suppose he had flattered himself that I was really entertaining one set of opinions for one place, and another set for another place; that I was afraid to say at one place what I uttered at another. What I am saying here I suppose I say to a vast audience as strongly tending to Abolitionism as any audience in the State of Illinois, and I believe I am saying that which, if it would be offensive to any persons and render them enemies to myself, would be offensive to persons in this audience.

I now proceed to propound to the Judge the interrogatories, so far as I have framed them. I will bring forward a new installment when I get them ready. I will bring them forward now only reaching to number four. The first one is:

Question 1.—If the people of Kansas shall, by means entirely unobjectionable in all other respects, adopt a State constitution, and ask admission into the Union under it, before they have the requisite number of inhabitants according to the English bill,—some ninety-three thousand,—will you vote to admit them?

Q. 2.—Can the people of a United States Territory, in any lawful way, against the wish of any citizen of the United States, exclude slavery from its limits prior to the formation of a State constitution?

Q. 3. If the Supreme Court of the United States shall decide that States cannot exclude slavery from their limits, are you in favor of acquiescing in, adopting, and following such decision as a rule of political action?

Q. 4. Are you in favor of acquiring additional territory, in disregard of how such acquisition may affect the nation on the slavery question?

As introductory to these interrogatories which Judge Douglas propounded to me at Ottawa, he read a set of resolutions which he said Judge Trumbull and myself had participated in adopting, in the first Republican State Convention, held at Springfield in October, 1854. He insisted that I and Judge Trumbull, and perhaps the entire Republican party, were responsible for the doctrines contained in the set of resolutions which he read, and I understand that it was from that set of resolutions that he deduced the interrogatories which he propounded to me, using these resolutions as a sort of authority for propounding those questions to me. Now, I say here to-day that I do not answer his interrogatories because of their springing at all from that set of resolutions which he read. I answered them because Judge Douglas thought fit to ask them. I do not now, nor ever did, recognize any responsibility upon myself in that set of resolutions. When I replied to him on that occasion, I assured him that I never had anything to do with them. I repeat here to today that I never in any possible form had anything to do with that set of resolutions It turns out, I believe, that those resolutions were never passed in any convention held in Springfield.

It turns out that they were never passed at any convention or any public meeting that I had any part in. I believe it turns out, in addition to all this, that there was not, in the fall of 1854, any convention holding a session in Springfield, calling itself a Republican State Convention; yet it is true there was a convention, or assemblage of men calling themselves a convention, at Springfield, that did pass some resolutions. But so little did I really know of the proceedings of that convention, or what set of resolutions they had passed, though having a general knowledge that there had been such an assemblage of men there, that when Judge Douglas read the resolutions, I really did not know but they had been the resolutions passed then and there. I did not question that they were the resolutions adopted. For I could not bring myself to suppose that Judge Douglas could say what he did upon this subject without knowing that it was true. I contented myself, on that occasion, with denying, as I truly could, all connection with them, not denying or affirming whether they were passed at Springfield. Now, it turns out that he had got hold of some resolutions passed at some convention or public meeting in Kane County. I wish to say here, that I don't conceive that in any fair and just mind this discovery relieves me at all. I had just as much to do with the convention in Kane County as that at Springfield. I am as much responsible for the resolutions at Kane County as those at Springfield,—the amount of the responsibility being exactly nothing in either case; no more than there would be in regard to a set of resolutions passed in the moon.

I allude to this extraordinary matter in this canvass for some further purpose than anything yet advanced. Judge Douglas did not make his statement upon that occasion as matters that he believed to be true, but he stated them roundly as being true, in such form as to pledge his veracity for their truth. When the whole matter turns out as it does, and when we consider who Judge Douglas is, that he is a distinguished Senator of the United States; that he has served nearly twelve years as such; that his character is not at all limited as an ordinary Senator of the United States, but that his name has become of world-wide renown,—it is most extraordinary that he should so far forget all the suggestions of justice to an adversary, or of prudence to himself, as to venture upon the assertion of that which the slightest investigation would have shown him to be wholly false. I can only account for his having done so upon the supposition that that evil genius which has attended him through his life, giving to him an apparent astonishing prosperity, such as to lead very many good men to doubt there being any advantage in virtue over vice,—I say I can only account for it on the supposition that that evil genius has as last made up its mind to forsake him.

And I may add that another extraordinary feature of the Judge's conduct in this canvass—made more extraordinary by this incident—is, that he is in the habit, in almost all the speeches he makes, of charging falsehood upon his adversaries, myself and others. I now ask whether he is able to find in anything that Judge Trumbull, for instance, has said, or in anything that I have said, a justification at all compared with what we have, in this instance, for that sort of vulgarity.

I have been in the habit of charging as a matter of belief on my part that, in the introduction of the Nebraska Bill into Congress, there was a conspiracy to make slavery perpetual and national. I have arranged from time to time the evidence which establishes and proves the truth of this charge. I recurred to this charge at Ottawa. I shall not now have time to dwell upon it at very great length; but inasmuch as Judge Douglas, in his reply of half an hour, made some points upon me in relation to it, I propose noticing a few of them.

The Judge insists that, in the first speech I made, in which I very distinctly made that charge, he thought for a good while I was in fun! that I was playful; that I was not sincere about it; and that he only grew angry and somewhat excited when he found that I insisted upon it as a matter of earnestness. He says he characterized it as a falsehood so far as I implicated his moral character in that transaction. Well, I did not know, till he presented that view, that I had implicated his moral character. He is very much in the habit, when he argues me up into a position I never thought of occupying, of very cosily saying he has no doubt Lincoln is "conscientious" in saying so. He should remember that I did not know but what he was ALTOGETHER "CONSCIENTIOUS" in that matter. I can conceive it possible for men to conspire to do a good thing, and I really find nothing in Judge Douglas's course of arguments that is contrary to or inconsistent with his belief of a conspiracy to nationalize and spread slavery as being a good and blessed thing; and so I hope he will understand that I do not at all question but that in all this matter he is entirely "conscientious."

But to draw your attention to one of the points I made in this case, beginning at the beginning: When the Nebraska Bill was introduced, or a short time afterward, by an amendment, I believe, it was provided that it must be considered "the true intent and meaning of this Act not to legislate slavery into any State or Territory, or to exclude it therefrom, but to leave the people thereof perfectly free to form and regulate their own domestic institutions in their own way, subject only to the Constitution of the United States." I have called his attention to the fact that when he and some others began arguing that they were giving an increased degree of liberty to the people in the Territories over and above what they formerly had on the question of slavery, a question was raised whether the law was enacted to give such unconditional liberty to the people; and to test the sincerity of this mode of argument, Mr. Chase, of Ohio, introduced an amendment, in which he made the law—if the amendment were adopted—expressly declare that the people of the Territory should have the power to exclude slavery if they saw fit. I have asked attention also to the fact that Judge Douglas and those who acted with him voted that amendment down, notwithstanding it expressed exactly the thing they said was the true intent and meaning of the law. I have called attention to the fact that in subsequent times a decision of the Supreme Court has been made, in which it has been declared that a Territorial Legislature has no constitutional right to exclude slavery. And I have argued and said that for men who did, intend that the people of the Territory should have the right to exclude slavery absolutely and unconditionally, the voting down of Chase's amendment is wholly inexplicable. It is a puzzle, a riddle. But I have said, that with men who did look forward to such a decision, or who had it in contemplation that such a decision of the Supreme Court would or might be made, the voting down of that amendment would be perfectly rational and intelligible. It would keep Congress from coming in collision with the decision when it was made. Anybody can conceive that if there was an intention or expectation that such a decision was to follow, it would not be a very desirable party attitude to get into for the Supreme Court—all or nearly all its members belonging to the same party—to decide one way, when the party in Congress had decided the other way. Hence it would be very rational for men expecting such a decision to keep the niche in that law clear for it. After pointing this out, I tell Judge Douglas that it looks to me as though here was the reason why Chase's amendment was voted down. I tell him that, as he did it, and knows why he did it, if it was done for a reason different from this, he knows what that reason was and can tell us what it was. I tell him, also, it will be vastly more satisfactory to the country for him to give some other plausible, intelligible reason why it was voted down than to stand upon his dignity and call people liars. Well, on Saturday he did make his answer; and what do you think it was? He says if I had only taken upon myself to tell the whole truth about that amendment of Chase's, no explanation would have been necessary on his part or words to that effect. Now, I say here that I am quite unconscious of having suppressed anything material to the case, and I am very frank to admit if there is any sound reason other than that which appeared to me material, it is quite fair for him to present it. What reason does he propose? That when Chase came forward with his amendment expressly authorizing the people to exclude slavery from the limits of every Territory, General Cass proposed to Chase, if he (Chase) would add to his amendment that the people should have the power to introduce or exclude, they would let it go. This is substantially all of his reply. And because Chase would not do that, they voted his amendment down. Well, it turns out, I believe, upon examination, that General Cass took some part in the little running debate upon that amendment, and then ran away and did not vote on it at all. Is not that the fact? So confident, as I think, was General Cass that there was a snake somewhere about, he chose to run away from the whole thing. This is an inference I draw from the fact that, though he took part in the debate, his name does not appear in the ayes and noes. But does Judge Douglas's reply amount to a satisfactory answer?

[Cries of "Yes," "Yes," and "No," "No."]

There is some little difference of opinion here. But I ask attention to a few more views bearing on the question of whether it amounts to a satisfactory answer. The men who were determined that that amendment should not get into the bill, and spoil the place where the Dred Scott decision was to come in, sought an excuse to get rid of it somewhere. One of these ways—one of these excuses—was to ask Chase to add to his proposed amendment a provision that the people might introduce slavery if they wanted to. They very well knew Chase would do no such thing, that Mr. Chase was one of the men differing from them on the broad principle of his insisting that freedom was better than slavery,—a man who would not consent to enact a law, penned with his own hand, by which he was made to recognize slavery on the one hand, and liberty on the other, as precisely equal; and when they insisted on his doing this, they very well knew they insisted on that which he would not for a moment think of doing, and that they were only bluffing him. I believe (I have not, since he made his answer, had a chance to examine the journals or Congressional Globe and therefore speak from memory)—I believe the state of the bill at that time, according to parliamentary rules, was such that no member could propose an additional amendment to Chase's amendment. I rather think this is the truth,—the Judge shakes his head. Very well. I would like to know, then, if they wanted Chase's amendment fixed over, why somebody else could not have offered to do it? If they wanted it amended, why did they not offer the amendment? Why did they not put it in themselves? But to put it on the other ground: suppose that there was such an amendment offered, and Chase's was an amendment to an amendment; until one is disposed of by parliamentary law, you cannot pile another on. Then all these gentlemen had to do was to vote Chase's on, and then, in the amended form in which the whole stood, add their own amendment to it, if they wanted to put it in that shape. This was all they were obliged to do, and the ayes and noes show that there were thirty-six who voted it down, against ten who voted in favor of it. The thirty-six held entire sway and control. They could in some form or other have put that bill in the exact shape they wanted. If there was a rule preventing their amending it at the time, they could pass that, and then, Chase's amendment being merged, put it in the shape they wanted. They did not choose to do so, but they went into a quibble with Chase to get him to add what they knew he would not add, and because he would not, they stand upon the flimsy pretext for voting down what they argued was the meaning and intent of their own bill. They left room thereby for this Dred Scott decision, which goes very far to make slavery national throughout the United States.

I pass one or two points I have, because my time will very soon expire; but I must be allowed to say that Judge Douglas recurs again, as he did upon one or two other occasions, to the enormity of Lincoln, an insignificant individual like Lincoln,—upon his ipse dixit charging a conspiracy upon a large number of members of Congress, the Supreme Court, and two Presidents, to nationalize slavery. I want to say that, in the first place, I have made no charge of this sort upon my ipse dixit. I have only arrayed the evidence tending to prove it, and presented it to the understanding of others, saying what I think it proves, but giving you the means of judging whether it proves it or not. This is precisely what I have done. I have not placed it upon my ipse dixit at all. On this occasion, I wish to recall his attention to a piece of evidence which I brought forward at Ottawa on Saturday, showing that he had made substantially the same charge against substantially the same persons, excluding his dear self from the category. I ask him to give some attention to the evidence which I brought forward that he himself had discovered a "fatal blow being struck" against the right of the people to exclude slavery from their limits, which fatal blow he assumed as in evidence in an article in the Washington Union, published "by authority." I ask by whose authority? He discovers a similar or identical provision in

256

the Lecompton Constitution. Made by whom? The framers of that Constitution. Advocated by whom? By all the members of the party in the nation, who advocated the introduction of Kansas into the Union under the Lecompton Constitution. I have asked his attention to the evidence that he arrayed to prove that such a fatal blow was being struck, and to the facts which he brought forward in support of that charge,—being identical with the one which he thinks so villainous in me. He pointed it, not at a newspaper editor merely, but at the President and his Cabinet and the members of Congress advocating the Lecompton Constitution and those framing that instrument. I must again be permitted to remind him that although my ipse dixit may not be as great as his, yet it somewhat reduces the force of his calling my attention to the enormity of my making a like charge against him.

Go on, Judge Douglas.

Mr. LINCOLN'S REJOINDER.

MY FRIENDS:—It will readily occur to you that I cannot, in half an hour, notice all the things that so able a man as Judge Douglas can say in an hour and a half; and I hope, therefore, if there be anything that he has said upon which you would like to hear something from me, but which I omit to comment upon, you will bear in mind that it would be expecting an impossibility for me to go over his whole ground. I can but take up some of the points that he has dwelt upon, and employ my half-hour specially on them.

The first thing I have to say to you is a word in regard to Judge Douglas's declaration about the "vulgarity and blackguardism" in the audience, that no such thing, as he says, was shown by any Democrat while I was speaking. Now, I only wish, by way of reply on this subject, to say that while I was speaking, I used no "vulgarity or blackguardism" toward any Democrat.

Now, my friends, I come to all this long portion of the Judge's speech,—perhaps half of it,—which he has devoted to the various resolutions and platforms that have been adopted in the different counties in the different Congressional districts, and in the Illinois legislature, which he supposes are at variance with the positions I have assumed before you to-day. It is true that many of these resolutions are at variance with the positions I have here assumed. All I have to ask is that we talk reasonably and rationally about it. I happen to know, the Judge's opinion to the contrary notwithstanding, that I have never tried to conceal my opinions, nor tried to deceive any one in reference to them. He may go and examine all the members who voted for me for United States Senator in 1855, after the election of 1854. They were pledged to certain things here at home, and were determined to have pledges from me; and if he will find any of these persons who will tell him anything inconsistent with what I say now, I will resign, or rather retire from the race, and give him no more trouble. The plain truth is this: At the introduction of the Nebraska policy, we believed there was a new era being introduced in the history of the Republic, which tended to the spread and perpetuation of slavery. But in our opposition to that measure we did not agree with one another in everything. The people in the north end of the State were for stronger measures of opposition than we of the central and southern portions of the State, but we were all opposed to the Nebraska doctrine. We had that one feeling and that one sentiment in common. You at the north end met in your conventions and passed your resolutions. We in the middle of the State and farther south did not hold such conventions and pass the same resolutions, although we had in general a common view and a common sentiment. So that these meetings which the Judge has alluded to, and the resolutions he has read from, were local, and did not spread over the whole State. We at last met together in 1886, from all parts of the State, and we agreed upon a common platform. You, who held more extreme notions, either yielded those notions, or, if not wholly yielding them, agreed to yield them practically, for the sake of embodying the opposition to the measures which the opposite party were pushing forward at that time. We met you then, and if there was anything yielded, it was for practical purposes. We agreed then upon a platform for the party throughout the entire State of Illinois, and now we are all bound, as a party, to that platform.

And I say here to you, if any one expects of me—in case of my election—that I will do anything not signified by our Republican platform and my answers here to-day, I tell you very frankly that person will be deceived. I do not ask for the vote of any one who supposes that I have secret purposes or pledges that I dare not speak out. Cannot the Judge be satisfied? If he fears, in the unfortunate case of my election, that my going to Washington will enable me to advocate sentiments contrary to those which I expressed when you voted for and elected me, I assure him that his fears are wholly needless and groundless. Is the Judge really afraid of any such thing? I'll tell you what he is afraid of. He is afraid we'll all pull together. This is what alarms him more than anything else. For my part, I do hope that all of us, entertaining a common sentiment in opposition to what appears to us a design to nationalize and perpetuate slavery, will waive minor differences on questions which either belong to the dead past or the distant future, and all pull together in this struggle. What are your sentiments? If it be true that on the ground which I occupy—ground which I occupy as frankly and boldly as Judge Douglas does his,—my views, though partly coinciding with yours, are not as perfectly in accordance with your feelings as his are, I do say to you in all candor, go for him, and not for me. I hope to deal in all things fairly with Judge Douglas, and with the people of the State, in this contest. And if I should never be elected to any office, I trust I may go down with no stain of falsehood upon my reputation, notwithstanding the hard opinions Judge Douglas chooses to entertain of me.

The Judge has again addressed himself to the Abolition tendencies of a speech of mine made at Springfield in June last. I have so often tried to answer what he is always saying on that melancholy theme that I almost turn with disgust from the discussion,—from the repetition of an answer to it. I trust that nearly all of this intelligent audience have read that speech. If you have, I may venture to leave it to you to inspect it closely, and see whether it contains any of those "bugaboos" which frighten Judge Douglas.

The Judge complains that I did not fully answer his questions. If I have the sense to comprehend and answer those questions, I have done so fairly. If it can be pointed out to me how I can more fully and fairly answer him, I aver I have not the sense to see how it is to be done. He says I do not declare I would in any event vote for the admission of a slave State into the Union. If I have been fairly reported, he will see that I did give an explicit answer to his interrogatories; I did not merely say that I would dislike to be put to the test, but I said clearly, if I were put to the test, and a Territory from which slavery had been excluded should present herself with a State constitution sanctioning slavery,—a most extraordinary thing, and wholly unlikely to happen,—I did not see how I could avoid voting for her admission. But he refuses to understand that I said so, and he wants this audience to understand that I did not say so. Yet it will be so reported in the printed speech that he cannot help seeing it.

He says if I should vote for the admission of a slave State I would be voting for a dissolution of the Union, because I hold that the Union cannot permanently exist half slave and half free. I repeat that I do not believe this government can endure permanently half slave and half free; yet I do not admit, nor does it at all follow, that the admission of a single slave State will permanently fix the character and establish this as a universal slave nation. The Judge is very happy indeed at working up these quibbles. Before leaving the subject of answering questions, I aver as my confident belief, when you come to see our speeches in print, that you will find every question which he has asked me more fairly and boldly and fully answered than he has answered those which I put to him. Is not that so? The two speeches may be placed side by side, and I will venture to leave it to impartial judges whether his questions have not been more directly and circumstantially answered than mine.

Judge Douglas says he made a charge upon the editor of the Washington Union, alone, of entertaining a purpose to rob the States of their power to exclude slavery from their limits. I undertake to say, and I make the direct issue, that he did not make his charge against the editor of the Union alone. I will undertake to prove by the record here that he made that charge against more and higher dignitaries than the editor of the Washington Union. I am quite aware that he was shirking and dodging around the form in which he put it, but I can make it manifest that he leveled his "fatal blow" against more persons than this Washington editor. Will he dodge it now by alleging that I am trying to defend Mr. Buchanan against the charge? Not at all. Am I not making the same charge myself? I am trying to show that you, Judge Douglas, are a witness on my side. I am not defending Buchanan, and I will tell Judge Douglas that in my opinion, when he made that charge, he had an eye farther north than he has to-day. He was then fighting against people who called him a Black Republican and an Abolitionist. It is mixed all through his speech, and it is tolerably manifest that his eye was a great deal farther north than it is to-day. The Judge says that though he made this charge, Toombs got up and declared there was not a man in the United States, except the editor of the Union, who was in favor of the doctrines

258

put forth in that article. And thereupon I understand that the Judge withdrew the charge. Although he had taken extracts from the newspaper, and then from the Lecompton Constitution, to show the existence of a conspiracy to bring about a "fatal blow," by which the States were to be deprived of the right of excluding slavery, it all went to pot as soon as Toombs got up and told him it was not true. It reminds me of the story that John Phoenix, the California railroad surveyor, tells. He says they started out from the Plaza to the Mission of Dolores. They had two ways of determining distances. One was by a chain and pins taken over the ground. The other was by a "go-it-ometer,"—an invention of his own,—a three-legged instrument, with which he computed a series of triangles between the points. At night he turned to the chain-man to ascertain what distance they had come, and found that by some mistake he had merely dragged the chain over the ground, without keeping any record. By the "go-it-ometer," he found he had made ten miles. Being skeptical about this, he asked a drayman who was passing how far it was to the Plaza. The drayman replied it was just half a mile; and the surveyor put it down in his book,—just as Judge Douglas says, after he had made his calculations and computations, he took Toombs's statement. I have no doubt that after Judge Douglas had made his charge, he was as easily satisfied about its truth as the surveyor was of the drayman's statement of the distance to the Plaza. Yet it is a fact that the man who put forth all that matter which Douglas deemed a "fatal blow" at State sovereignty was elected by the Democrats as public printer.

Now, gentlemen, you may take Judge Douglas's speech of March 22, 1858, beginning about the middle of page 21, and reading to the bottom of page 24, and you will find the evidence on which I say that he did not make his charge against the editor of the Union alone. I cannot stop to read it, but I will give it to the reporters. Judge Douglas said:

"Mr. President, you here find several distinct propositions advanced boldly by the Washington Union editorially, and apparently authoritatively, and every man who questions any of them is denounced as an Abolitionist, a Free-soiler, a fanatic. The propositions are, first, that the primary object of all government at its original institution is the protection of persons and property; second, that the Constitution of the United States declares that the citizens of each State shall be entitled to all the privileges and immunities of citizens in the several States; and that, therefore, thirdly, all State laws, whether organic or otherwise, which prohibit the citizens of one State from settling in another with their slave property, and especially declaring it forfeited, are direct violations of the original intention of the Government and Constitution of the United States; and, fourth, that the emancipation of the slaves of the Northern States was a gross outrage on the rights of property, in as much as it was involuntarily done on the part of the owner.

"Remember that this article was published in the Union on the 17th of November, and on the 18th appeared the first article giving the adhesion of the Union to the Lecompton Constitution. It was in these words:

"'KANSAS AND HER CONSTITUTION.—The vexed question is settled. The problem is solved. The dead point of danger is passed. All serious trouble to Kansas affairs is over and gone....'"

"And a column, nearly, of the same sort. Then, when you come to look into the Lecompton Constitution, you find the same doctrine incorporated in it which was put forth editorially in the Union. What is it?

"'ARTICLE 7, Section i. The right of property is before and higher than any constitutional sanction; and the right of the owner of a slave to such slave and its increase is the same and as invariable as the right of the owner of any property whatever.'

"Then in the schedule is a provision that the Constitution may be amended after 1864 by a two-thirds vote.

"'But no alteration shall be made to affect the right of property in the ownership of slaves.'

"It will be seen by these clauses in the Lecompton Constitution that they are identical in spirit with this authoritative article in the Washington Union of the day previous to its indorsement of this Constitution.

"When I saw that article in the Union of the 17th of November, followed by the glorification of the Lecompton Constitution on the 18th of November, and this clause in the Constitution asserting the doctrine that a State has no right to prohibit slavery within its limits, I saw that there was a fatal blow being struck at the sovereignty of the States of this Union."

Here he says, "Mr. President, you here find several distinct propositions advanced boldly, and apparently authoritatively." By whose authority, Judge Douglas? Again, he says in another place, "It will be seen by these clauses in the Lecompton Constitution that they are identical in spirit with this authoritative article." By whose authority,—who do you mean to say authorized the publication of these articles? He knows that the Washington Union is considered the organ of the Administration. I demand of Judge Douglas by whose authority he meant to say those articles were published, if not by the authority of the President of the United States and his Cabinet? I defy him to show whom he referred to, if not to these high functionaries in the Federal Government. More than this, he says the articles in that paper and the provisions of the Lecompton Constitution are "identical," and, being identical, he argues that the authors are co-operating and conspiring together. He does not use the word "conspiring," but what other construction can you put upon it? He winds up:

"When I saw that article in the Union of the 17th of November, followed by the glorification of the Lecompton Constitution on the 18th of November, and this clause in the Constitution asserting the doctrine that a State has no right to prohibit slavery within its limits, I saw that there was a fatal blow being struck at the sovereignty of the States of this Union."

I ask him if all this fuss was made over the editor of this newspaper. It would be a terribly "fatal blow" indeed which a single man could strike, when no President, no Cabinet officer, no member of Congress, was giving strength and efficiency to the movement. Out of respect to Judge Douglas's good sense I must believe he did n't manufacture his idea of the "fatal" character of that blow out of such a miserable scapegrace as he represents that editor to be. But the Judge's eye is farther south now. Then, it was very peculiarly and decidedly north. His hope rested on the idea of visiting the great "Black Republican" party, and making it the tail of his new kite. He knows he was then expecting from day to day to turn Republican, and place himself at the head of our organization. He has found that these despised "Black Republicans" estimate him by a standard which he has taught them none too well. Hence he is crawling back into his old camp, and you will find him eventually installed in full fellowship among those whom he was then battling, and with whom he now pretends to be at such fearful variance.

THIRD JOINT DEBATE, AT JONESBORO,

SEPTEMBER 15, 1858

Mr. LINCOLN'S REPLY.

LADIES AND GENTLEMEN:—There is very much in the principles that Judge Douglas has here enunciated that I most cordially approve, and over which I shall have no controversy with him. In so far as he has insisted that all the States have the right to do exactly as they please about all their domestic relations, including that of slavery, I agree entirely with him. He places me wrong in spite of all I can tell him, though I repeat it again and again, insisting that I have no difference with him upon this subject. I have made a great many speeches, some of which have been printed, and it will be utterly impossible for him to find anything that I have ever put in print contrary to what I now say upon this subject. I hold myself under constitutional obligations to allow the people in all the States, without interference, direct or indirect, to do exactly as they please; and I deny that I have any inclination to interfere with them, even if there were no such constitutional obligation. I can only say again that I am placed improperly—altogether improperly, in spite of all I can say—when it is insisted that I entertain any other view or purposes in regard to that matter.

While I am upon this subject, I will make some answers briefly to certain propositions that Judge Douglas has put. He says, "Why can't this Union endure permanently half slave and half free?" I have said that I supposed it could not, and I will try, before this new audience, to give briefly some of the reasons for entertaining that opinion. Another form of his question is, "Why can't we let it stand as our fathers placed it?" That is the exact difficulty between us. I say that Judge Douglas and his friends have changed it from the position in which our fathers originally placed it. I say, in the way our father's originally left the slavery question, the institution was in the course of ultimate extinction, and the public mind rested in the belief that it was in the course of ultimate extinction. I say when this government was first established it was the policy of its founders to prohibit the spread of slavery into the new Territories of the United States, where it had not existed. But Judge Douglas and his friends have broken up that policy, and placed it upon a new basis, by which it is to become national and perpetual. All I have asked or desired anywhere is that it should be placed back again upon the basis that the fathers of our government originally placed it upon. I have no doubt that it would become extinct, for all time to come, if we but readopted the policy of the fathers, by restricting it to the limits it has already covered, restricting it from the new Territories.

I do not wish to dwell at great length on this branch of the subject at this time, but allow me to repeat one thing that I have stated before. Brooks—the man who assaulted Senator Sumner on the floor of the Senate, and who was complimented with dinners, and silver pitchers, and gold-headed canes, and a good many other things for that feat—in one of his speeches declared that when this government was originally established, nobody expected that the institution of slavery would last until this day. That was but the opinion of one man, but it was such an opinion as we can never get from Judge Douglas or anybody in favor of slavery, in the North, at all. You can sometimes get it from a Southern man. He said at the same time that the framers of our government did not have the knowledge that experience has taught us; that experience and the invention of the cotton-gin have taught us that the perpetuation of slavery is a necessity. He insisted, therefore, upon its being changed from the basis upon which the fathers of the government left it to the basis of its perpetuation and nationalization.

I insist that this is the difference between Judge Douglas and myself,—that Judge Douglas is helping that change along. I insist upon this government being placed where our fathers originally placed it.

I remember Judge Douglas once said that he saw the evidences on the statute books of Congress of a policy in the origin of government to divide slavery and freedom by a geographical line; that he saw an indisposition to maintain that policy, and therefore he set about studying up a way to settle the institution on the right basis,—the basis which he thought it ought to have been placed upon at first; and in that speech he confesses that he seeks to place it, not upon the basis that the fathers placed it upon, but upon one gotten up on "original principles." When he asks me why we cannot get along with it in the attitude where our fathers placed it, he had better clear up the evidences that he has himself changed it from that basis, that he has himself been chiefly instrumental in changing the policy of the fathers. Any one who will read his speech of the 22d of last March will see that he there makes an open confession, showing that he set about fixing the institution upon an altogether different set of principles. I think I have fully answered him when he asks me why we cannot let it alone upon the basis where our fathers left it, by showing that he has himself changed the whole policy of the government in that regard.

Now, fellow-citizens, in regard to this matter about a contract that was made between Judge Trumbull and myself, and all that long portion of Judge Douglas's speech on this subject,—I wish simply to say what I have said to him before, that he cannot know whether it is true or not, and I do know that there is not a word of truth in it. And I have told him so before. I don't want any harsh language indulged in, but I do not know how to deal with this persistent insisting on a story that I know to be utterly without truth. It used to be a fashion amongst men that when a charge was made, some sort of proof was brought forward to establish it, and if no proof was found to exist, the charge was dropped. I don't know how to meet this kind of an argument. I don't want to have a fight with Judge Douglas, and I have no way of making an argument up into the consistency of a corn-cob and stopping his mouth with it. All I can do is—good-humoredly—to say that, from the beginning to the end of all that story about a bargain between Judge Trumbull and myself, there is not a word of truth in it. I can only ask him to show some sort of evidence of the truth of his story. He brings forward here and reads from what he contends is a speech by James H. Matheny, charging such a bargain between Trumbull and myself. My own opinion is that Matheny did do some such immoral thing as to tell a story that he knew nothing about. I believe he did. I contradicted it instantly, and it has been contradicted by Judge Trumbull, while nobody has produced any proof, because there is none. Now, whether the speech which the Judge brings forward here is really the one Matheny made, I do not know, and I hope the Judge will pardon me for doubting the genuineness of this document, since his production of those Springfield resolutions at Ottawa. I do not wish to dwell at any great length upon this matter. I can say nothing when a long story like this is told, except it is not true, and demand that he who insists upon it shall produce some proof. That is all any man can do, and I leave it in that way, for I know of no other way of dealing with it.

[In an argument on the lines of: "Yes, you did.—No, I did not." It bears on the former to prove his point, not on the negative to "prove" that he did not—even if he easily can do so.]

The Judge has gone over a long account of the old Whig and Democratic parties, and it connects itself with this charge against Trumbull and myself. He says that they agreed upon a compromise in regard to the slavery question in 1850; that in a National Democratic Convention resolutions were passed to abide by that compromise as a finality upon the slavery question. He also says that the Whig party in National Convention agreed to abide by and regard as a finality the Compromise of 1850. I understand the Judge to be altogether right about that; I understand that part of the history of the country as stated by him to be correct I recollect that I, as a member of that party, acquiesced in that compromise. I recollect in the Presidential election which followed, when we had General Scott up for the presidency, Judge Douglas was around berating us Whigs as Abolitionists, precisely as he does to-day,—not a bit of difference. I have often heard him. We could do nothing when the old Whig party was alive that was not Abolitionism, but it has got an extremely good name since it has passed away.

[It almost a natural law that, when dead—no matter how bad we were—we are automatically beatified.]

When that Compromise was made it did not repeal the old Missouri Compromise. It left a region of United States territory half as large as the present territory of the United States, north of the line of 36 degrees 30 minutes, in which slavery was prohibited by Act of Congress. This Compromise did not repeal that one. It did not affect or propose to repeal it. But at last it became Judge Douglas's duty, as he thought (and I find no fault with him), as Chairman of the Committee on Territories, to bring in a bill for the organization of a territorial government,—first of one, then of two Territories north of that line. When he did so, it ended in his inserting a provision substantially repealing the Missouri Compromise. That was because the Compromise of 1850 had not repealed it. And now I ask why he could not have let that Compromise alone? We were quiet from the agitation of the slavery question. We were making no fuss about it. All had acquiesced in the Compromise measures of 1850. We never had been seriously disturbed by any Abolition agitation before that period. When he came to form governments for the Territories north of the line of 36 degrees 30 minutes, why could he not have let that matter stand as it was standing? Was it necessary to the organization of a Territory? Not at all. Iowa lay north of the line, and had been organized as a Territory and come into the Union as a State without disturbing that Compromise. There was no sort of necessity for destroying it to organize these Territories. But, gentlemen, it would take up all my time to meet all the little quibbling arguments of Judge Douglas to show that the Missouri Compromise was repealed by the Compromise of 1850. My own opinion is, that a careful investigation of all the arguments to sustain the position that that Compromise was virtually repealed by the Compromise of 1850 would show that they are the merest fallacies. I have the report that Judge Douglas first brought into Congress at the time of the introduction of the Nebraska Bill, which in its original form did not repeal the Missouri Compromise, and he there expressly stated that he had forborne to do so because it had not been done by the Compromise of 1850. I close this part of the discussion on my part by asking him the question again, "Why, when we had peace under the Missouri Compromise, could you not have let it alone?"

In complaining of what I said in my speech at Springfield, in which he says I accepted my nomination for the senatorship (where, by the way, he is at fault, for if he will examine it, he will find no acceptance in it), he again quotes that portion in which I said that "a house divided against itself cannot stand." Let me say a word in regard to that matter.

He tries to persuade us that there must be a variety in the different institutions of the States of the Union; that that variety necessarily proceeds from the variety of soil, climate, of the face of the country, and the difference in the natural features of the States. I agree to all that. Have these very matters ever produced any difficulty amongst us? Not at all. Have we ever had any quarrel over the fact that they have laws in Louisiana designed to regulate the commerce that springs from the production of sugar? Or because we have a different class relative to the production of flour in this State? Have they produced any differences? Not at all. They are the very cements of this Union. They don't make the house a house divided against itself. They are the props that hold up the house and sustain the Union.

But has it been so with this element of slavery? Have we not always had quarrels and difficulties over it? And when will we cease to have quarrels over it? Like causes produce like effects. It is worth while to observe that we have generally had comparative peace upon the slavery question, and that there has been no cause for alarm until it was excited by the effort to spread it into new territory. Whenever it has been limited to its present bounds, and there has been no effort to spread it, there has been peace. All the trouble and convulsion has proceeded from efforts to spread it over more territory. It was thus at the date of the Missouri Compromise. It was so again with the annexation of Texas; so with the territory acquired by the Mexican war; and it is so now. Whenever there has been an effort to spread it, there has been agitation and resistance. Now, I appeal to this audience (very few of whom are my political friends), as national men, whether we have reason to expect that the agitation in regard to this subject will cease while the causes that tend to reproduce agitation are actively at work? Will not the same cause that produced agitation in 1820, when the Missouri Compromise was formed, that which produced the agitation upon the annexation of Texas, and at other times, work out the same results always? Do you think that the nature of man will be changed, that the same causes that produced agitation at one time will not have the same effect at another?

This has been the result so far as my observation of the slavery question and my reading in history extends. What right have we then to hope that the trouble will cease,—that the agitation will come to an end,—until it shall either be placed back where it originally stood, and where the fathers originally placed it, or, on the other hand, until it shall entirely master all opposition? This is the view I entertain, and this is the reason why I entertained it, as Judge Douglas has read from my Springfield speech.

Now, my friends, there is one other thing that I feel myself under some sort of obligation to mention. Judge Douglas has here to-day—in a very rambling way, I was about saying—spoken of the platforms for which he seeks to hold me responsible. He says, "Why can't you come out and make an open avowal of principles in all places alike?" and he reads from an advertisement that he says was used to notify the people of a speech to be made by Judge Trumbull at Waterloo. In commenting on it he desires to know whether we cannot speak frankly and manfully, as he and his friends do. How, I ask, do his friends speak out their own sentiments? A Convention of his party in this State met on the 21st of April at Springfield, and passed a set of resolutions which they proclaim to the country as their platform. This does constitute their platform, and it is because Judge Douglas claims it is his platform—that these are his principles and purposes—that he has a right to declare he speaks his sentiments "frankly and manfully." On the 9th of June Colonel John Dougherty, Governor Reynolds, and others, calling themselves National Democrats, met in Springfield and adopted a set of resolutions which are as easily understood, as plain and as definite in stating to the country and to the world what they believed in and would stand upon, as Judge Douglas's platform Now, what is the reason that Judge Douglas is not willing that Colonel Dougherty and Governor Reynolds should stand upon their own written and printed platform as well as he upon his? Why must he look farther than their platform when he claims himself to stand by his platform?

Again, in reference to our platform: On the 16th of June the Republicans had their Convention and published their platform, which is as clear and distinct as Judge Douglas's. In it they spoke their principles as plainly and as definitely to the world. What is the reason that Judge Douglas is not willing I should stand upon that platform? Why must he go around hunting for some one who is supporting me or has supported me at some time in his life, and who has said something at some time contrary to that platform? Does the Judge regard that rule as a good one? If it turn out that the rule is a good one for me—that I am responsible for any and every opinion that any man has expressed who is my friend,—then it is a good rule for him. I ask, is it not as good a rule for him as it is for me? In my opinion, it is not a good rule for either of us. Do you think differently, Judge?

[Mr. DOUGLAS: I do not.]

Judge Douglas says he does not think differently. I am glad of it. Then can he tell me why he is looking up resolutions of five or six years ago, and insisting that they were my platform, notwithstanding my protest that they are not, and never were my platform, and my pointing out the platform of the State Convention which he delights to say nominated me for the Senate? I cannot see what he means by parading these resolutions, if it is not to hold me responsible for them in some way. If he says to me here that he does not hold the rule to be good, one way or the other, I do not comprehend how he could answer me more fully if he answered me at greater length. I will therefore put in as my answer to the resolutions that he has hunted up against me, what I, as a lawyer, would call a good plea to a bad declaration. I understand that it is an axiom of law that a poor plea may be a good plea to a bad declaration. I think that the opinions the Judge brings from those who support me, yet differ from me, is a bad declaration against me; but if I can bring the same things against him, I am putting in a good plea to that kind of declaration, and now I propose to try it.

At Freeport, Judge Douglas occupied a large part of his time in producing resolutions and documents of various sorts, as I understood, to make me somehow responsible for them; and I propose now doing a little of the same sort of thing for him. In 1850 a very clever gentleman by the name of Thompson Campbell, a personal friend of Judge Douglas and myself, a political friend of Judge Douglas and opponent of mine, was a candidate for Congress in the Galena District. He was interrogated as to his views on this same slavery question. I have here before me the interrogatories, and Campbell's answers to them—I will read them:

INTERROGATORIES:

"1st. Will you, if elected, vote for and cordially support a bill prohibiting slavery in the Territories of the United States?

"2d. Will you vote for and support a bill abolishing slavery in the District of Columbia?

"3d. Will you oppose the admission of any Slave States which may be formed out of Texas or the Territories?

"4th. Will you vote for and advocate the repeal of the Fugitive Slave law passed at the recent session of Congress?

"5th. Will you advocate and vote for the election of a Speaker of the House of Representatives who shall be willing to organize the committees of that House so as to give the Free States their just influence in the business of legislation?

"6th. What are your views, not only as to the constitutional right of Congress to prohibit the slave-trade between the States, but also as to the expediency of exercising that right immediately?"

CAMPBELL'S REPLY.

"To the first and second interrogatories, I answer unequivocally in the affirmative.

"To the third interrogatory I reply, that I am opposed to the admission of any more Slave States into the Union, that may be formed out of Texas or any other Territory.

"To the fourth and fifth interrogatories I unhesitatingly answer in the affirmative.

"To the sixth interrogatory I reply, that so long as the Slave States continue to treat slaves as articles of commerce, the Constitution confers power on Congress to pass laws regulating that peculiar COMMERCE, and that the protection of Human Rights imperatively demands the interposition of every constitutional means to prevent this most inhuman and iniquitous traffic.

"T. CAMPBELL."

I want to say here that Thompson Campbell was elected to Congress on that platform, as the Democratic candidate in the Galena District, against Martin P. Sweet.

[Judge DOUGLAS: Give me the date of the letter.]

The time Campbell ran was in 1850. I have not the exact date here. It was some time in 1850 that these interrogatories were put and the answer given. Campbell was elected to Congress, and served out his term. I think a second election came up before he served out his term, and he was not re-elected. Whether defeated or not nominated, I do not know. [Mr. Campbell was nominated for re-election by the Democratic party, by acclamation.] At the end of his term his very good friend Judge Douglas got him a high office from President Pierce, and sent him off to California. Is not that the fact? Just at the end of his term in Congress it appears that our mutual friend Judge Douglas got our mutual friend Campbell a good office, and sent him to California upon it. And not only so, but on the 27th of last month, when Judge Douglas and myself spoke at Freeport in joint discussion, there was his same friend Campbell, come all the way from California, to help the Judge beat me; and there was poor Martin P. Sweet standing on the platform, trying to help poor me to be elected. That is true of one of Judge Douglas's friends.

So again, in that same race of 1850, there was a Congressional Convention assembled at Joliet, and it nominated R. S. Molony for Congress, and unanimously adopted the following resolution:

"Resolved, That we are uncompromisingly opposed to the extension of slavery; and while we would not make such opposition a ground of interference with the interests of the States where it exists, yet we moderately but firmly insist that it is the duty of Congress to oppose its extension into Territory now free, by all means compatible with the obligations of the Constitution, and with good faith to our sister States; that these principles were recognized by the Ordinance of 1787, which received the sanction of Thomas Jefferson, who is acknowledged by all to be the great oracle and expounder of our faith."

Subsequently the same interrogatories were propounded to Dr. Molony which had been addressed to Campbell as above, with the exception of the 6th, respecting the interstate slave trade, to which Dr. Molony, the Democratic nominee for Congress, replied as follows:

"I received the written interrogatories this day, and, as you will see by the La Salle Democrat and Ottawa Free Trader, I took at Peru on the 5th, and at Ottawa on the 7th, the affirmative side of interrogatories 1st and 2d; and in relation to the admission of any more Slave States from Free Territory, my position taken at these meetings, as correctly reported in said papers, was emphatically and distinctly opposed to it. In relation to the admission of any more Slave States from Texas, whether I shall go against it or not will depend upon the opinion that I may hereafter form of the true meaning and nature of the resolutions of annexation. If, by said resolutions, the honor and good faith of the nation is pledged to admit more Slave States from Texas when she (Texas) may apply for the admission of such State, then I should, if in Congress, vote for their admission. But if not so PLEDGED and bound by sacred contract, then a bill for the admission of more Slave States from Texas would never receive my vote.

"To your fourth interrogatory I answer most decidedly in the affirmative, and for reasons set forth in my reported remarks at Ottawa last Monday.

"To your fifth interrogatory I also reply in the affirmative most cordially, and that I will use my utmost exertions to secure the nomination and election of a man who will accomplish the objects of said interrogatories. I most cordially approve of the resolutions adopted at the Union meeting held at Princeton on the 27th September ult.

"Yours, etc., R. S. MOLONY."

All I have to say in regard to Dr. Molony is that he was the regularly nominated Democratic candidate for Congress in his district; was elected at that time; at the end of his term was appointed to a land-office at Danville. (I never heard anything of Judge Douglas's instrumentality in this.) He held this office a considerable time, and when we were at Freeport the other day there were handbills scattered about notifying the public that after our debate was over R. S. Molony would make a Democratic speech in favor of Judge Douglas. That is all I know of my own personal knowledge. It is added here to this resolution, and truly I believe, that among those who participated in the Joliet Convention, and who supported its nominee, with his platform as laid down in the resolution of the Convention and in his reply as above given, we call at random the following names, all of which are recognized at this day as leading Democrats:

"Cook County,—E. B. Williams, Charles McDonell, Arno Voss, Thomas Hoyne, Isaac Cook."

I reckon we ought to except Cook.

"F. C. Sherman.

"Will,—Joel A. Matteson, S. W. Bowen.

"Kane,—B. F. Hall, G. W. Renwick, A. M. Herrington, Elijah Wilcox.

"McHenry,—W. M. Jackson, Enos W. Smith, Neil Donnelly.

La Salle,—John Hise, William Reddick."

William Reddick! another one of Judge Douglas's friends that stood on the stand with him at Ottawa, at the time the Judge says my knees trembled so that I had to be carried away. The names are all here:

"Du Page,—Nathan Allen.

"De Kalb,—Z. B. Mayo."

Here is another set of resolutions which I think are apposite to the matter in hand.

On the 28th of February of the same year a Democratic District Convention was held at Naperville to nominate a candidate for Circuit Judge. Among the delegates were Bowen and Kelly of Will; Captain Naper, H. H. Cody, Nathan Allen, of Du Page; W. M. Jackson, J. M. Strode, P. W. Platt, and Enos W. Smith of McHenry; J. Horssnan and others of Winnebago. Colonel Strode presided over the Convention. The following resolutions were unanimously adopted,— the first on motion of P. W. Platt, the second on motion of William M. Jackson:

"Resolved, That this Convention is in favor of the Wilmot Proviso, both in Principle and Practice, and that we know of no good reason why any person should oppose the largest latitude in Free Soil, Free Territory and Free speech.

"Resolved, That in the opinion of this Convention, the time has arrived when all men should be free, whites as well as others."

[Judge DOUGLAS: What is the date of those resolutions?]

I understand it was in 1850, but I do not know it. I do not state a thing and say I know it, when I do not. But I have the highest belief that this is so. I know of no way to arrive at the conclusion that there is an error in it. I mean to put a case no stronger than the truth will allow. But what I was going to comment upon is an extract from a newspaper in De Kalb County; and it strikes me as being rather singular, I confess, under the circumstances. There is a Judge Mayo in that county, who is a candidate for the Legislature, for the purpose, if he secures his election, of helping to re-elect Judge Douglas. He is the editor of a newspaper [De Kalb County Sentinel], and in that paper I find the extract I am going to read. It is part of an editorial article in which he was electioneering as fiercely as he could for Judge Douglas and against me. It was a curious thing, I think, to be in such a paper. I will agree to that, and the Judge may make the most of it:

"Our education has been such that we have been rather in favor of the equality of the blacks; that is, that they should enjoy all the privileges of the whites where they reside. We are aware that this is not a very popular doctrine. We have had many a confab with some who are now strong 'Republicans' we taking the broad ground of equality, and they the opposite ground.

"We were brought up in a State where blacks were voters, and we do not know of any inconvenience resulting from it, though perhaps it would not work as well where the blacks are more numerous. We have no doubt of the right of the whites to guard against such an evil, if it is one. Our opinion is that it would be best for all concerned to have the colored population in a State by themselves [in this I agree with him]; but if within the jurisdiction of the United States, we say by all means they should have the right to have their Senators and Representatives in Congress, and to vote for President. With us 'worth makes the man, and want of it the fellow.' We have seen many a 'nigger' that we thought more of than some white men."

That is one of Judge Douglas's friends. Now, I do not want to leave myself in an attitude where I can be misrepresented, so I will say I do not think the Judge is responsible for this article; but he is quite as responsible for it as I would be if one of my friends had said it. I think that is fair enough.

I have here also a set of resolutions passed by a Democratic State Convention in Judge Douglas's own good State of Vermont, that I think ought to be good for him too:

"Resolved, That liberty is a right inherent and inalienable in man, and that herein all men are equal.

"Resolved, That we claim no authority in the Federal Government to abolish slavery in the several States, but we do claim for it Constitutional power perpetually to prohibit the introduction of slavery into territory now free, and abolish it wherever, under the jurisdiction of Congress, it exists.

"Resolved, That this power ought immediately to be exercised in prohibiting the introduction and existence of slavery in New Mexico and California, in abolishing slavery and the slave-trade in the District of Columbia, on the high seas, and wherever else, under the Constitution, it can be reached.

"Resolved, That no more Slave States should be admitted into the Federal Union.

"Resolved, That the Government ought to return to its ancient policy, not to extend, nationalize, or encourage, but to limit, localize, and discourage slavery."

At Freeport I answered several interrogatories that had been propounded to me by Judge Douglas at the Ottawa meeting. The Judge has not yet seen fit to find any fault with the position that I took in regard to those seven interrogatories, which were certainly broad enough, in all conscience, to cover the entire ground. In my answers, which have been printed, and all have had the opportunity of seeing, I take the ground that those who elect me must expect that I will do nothing which will not be in accordance with those answers. I have some right to assert that Judge Douglas has no fault to find with them. But he chooses to still try to thrust me upon different ground, without paying any attention to my answers, the obtaining of which from me cost him so much trouble and concern. At the same time I propounded four interrogatories to him, claiming it as a right that he should answer as many interrogatories for me as I did for him, and I would reserve myself for a future instalment when I got them ready. The Judge, in answering me upon that occasion, put in what I suppose he intends as answers to all four of my interrogatories. The first one of these interrogatories I have before me, and it is in these words:

"Question 1.—If the people of Kansas shall, by means entirely unobjectionable in all other respects, adopt a State constitution, and ask admission into the Union under it, before they have the requisite number of inhabitants according to the English bill,"—some ninety-three thousand,—"will you vote to admit them?"

As I read the Judge's answer in the newspaper, and as I remember it as pronounced at the time, he does not give any answer which is equivalent to yes or no,—I will or I won't. He answers at very considerable length, rather quarreling with me for asking the question, and insisting that Judge Trumbull had done something that I ought to say something about, and finally getting out such statements as induce me to infer that he means to be understood he will, in that supposed case, vote for the admission of Kansas. I only bring this forward now for the purpose of saying that if he chooses to put a different construction upon his answer, he may do it. But if he does not, I shall from this time forward assume that he will vote for the admission of Kansas in disregard of the English bill. He has the right to remove any misunderstanding I may have. I only mention it now, that I may hereafter assume this to be the true construction of his answer, if he does not now choose to correct me.

The second interrogatory that I propounded to him was this:

"Question 2.—Can the people of a United States Territory, in any lawful way, against the wish of any citizen of the United States, exclude slavery from its limits prior to the formation of a State Constitution?"

To this Judge Douglas answered that they can lawfully exclude slavery from the Territory prior to the formation of a constitution. He goes on to tell us how it can be done. As I understand him, he holds that it can be done by the Territorial Legislature refusing to make any enactments for the protection of slavery in the Territory, and especially by adopting unfriendly legislation to it. For the sake of clearness, I state it again: that they can exclude slavery from the Territory, 1st, by withholding what he assumes to be an indispensable assistance to it in the way of legislation; and, 2d, by unfriendly legislation. If I rightly understand him, I wish to ask your attention for a while to his position.

In the first place, the Supreme Court of the United States has decided that any Congressional prohibition of slavery in the Territories is unconstitutional; that they have reached this proposition as a conclusion from their former proposition, that the Constitution of the United States expressly recognizes property in slaves, and from that other Constitutional provision, that no person shall be deprived of property without due process of law. Hence they reach the conclusion that as the Constitution of the United States expressly recognizes property in slaves, and prohibits any person from being deprived of property without due process of law, to pass an Act of Congress by which a man who owned a slave on one side of a line would be deprived of him if he took him on the other side, is depriving him of that property without due process of law. That I understand to be the decision of the Supreme Court. I understand also that Judge Douglas adheres most firmly to that decision; and the difficulty is, how is it possible for any power to exclude slavery from the Territory, unless in violation of that decision? That is the difficulty.

In the Senate of the United States, in 1850, Judge Trumbull, in a speech substantially, if not directly, put the same interrogatory to Judge Douglas, as to whether the people of a Territory had the lawful power to exclude slavery prior to the formation of a constitution. Judge Douglas then answered at considerable length, and his answer will be found in the Congressional Globe, under date of June 9th, 1856. The Judge said that whether the people could exclude slavery prior to the formation of a constitution or not was a question to be decided by the Supreme Court. He put that proposition, as will be seen by the Congressional Globe, in a variety of forms, all running to the same thing in substance,—that it was a question for the Supreme Court. I maintain that when he says, after the Supreme Court have decided the question, that the people may yet exclude slavery by any means whatever, he does virtually say that it is not a question for the Supreme Court. He shifts his ground. I appeal to you whether he did not say it was a question for the Supreme Court? Has not the Supreme Court decided that question? when he now says the people may exclude slavery, does he not make it a question for the people? Does he not virtually shift his ground and say that it is not a question for the Court, but for the people? This is a very simple proposition,—a very plain and naked one. It seems to me that there is no difficulty in deciding it. In a variety of ways he said that it was a question for the Supreme Court. He did not stop then to tell us that, whatever the Supreme Court decides, the people can by withholding necessary "police regulations" keep slavery out. He did not make any such answer I submit to you now whether the new state of the case has not induced the Judge to sheer away from his original ground. Would not this be the impression of every fair-minded man?

I hold that the proposition that slavery cannot enter a new country without police regulations is historically false. It is not true at all. I hold that the history of this country shows that the institution of slavery was originally planted upon this continent without these "police regulations," which the Judge now thinks necessary for the actual establishment of it. Not only so, but is there not another fact: how came this Dred Scott decision to be made? It was made upon the case of a negro being taken and actually held in slavery in Minnesota Territory, claiming his freedom because the Act of Congress prohibited his being so held there. Will the Judge pretend that Dred Scott was not held there without police regulations? There is at least one matter of record as to his having been held in slavery in the Territory, not only without police regulations, but in the teeth of Congressional legislation supposed to be valid at the time. This shows that there is vigor enough in slavery to plant itself in a new country even against unfriendly legislation. It takes not only law, but the enforcement of law to keep it out. That is the history of this country upon the subject.

I wish to ask one other question. It being understood that the Constitution of the United States guarantees property in slaves in the Territories, if there is any infringement of the right of that property, would not the United States courts, organized for the government of the Territory, apply such remedy as might be necessary in that case? It is a maxim held by the courts that there is no wrong without its remedy; and the courts have a remedy for whatever is acknowledged and treated as a wrong.

Again: I will ask you, my friends, if you were elected members of the Legislature, what would be the first thing you would have to do before entering upon your duties? Swear to support the Constitution of the United States. Suppose you believe, as Judge Douglas does, that the Constitution of the United States guarantees to your neighbor the right to hold slaves in that Territory; that they are his property: how can you clear your oaths unless you give him such legislation as is necessary to enable him to enjoy that property? What do you understand by supporting the Constitution of a State, or of the United States? Is it not to give such constitutional helps to the rights established by that Constitution as may be practically needed? Can you, if you swear to support the Constitution, and believe that the Constitution establishes a right, clear your oath, without giving it support? Do you support the Constitution if, knowing or believing there is a right established under it which needs specific legislation, you withhold that legislation? Do you not violate and disregard your oath? I can conceive of nothing plainer in the world. There can be nothing in the words "support the Constitution," if you may run counter to it by refusing support to any right established under the Constitution. And what I say here will hold with still more force against the Judge's doctrine of "unfriendly legislation." How could you, having sworn to support the Constitution, and believing it guaranteed the right to hold slaves in the Territories, assist in legislation intended to defeat that right? That would be violating your own view of the Constitution. Not only so, but if you were to do so, how long would it take the courts to hold your votes unconstitutional and void? Not a moment.

Lastly, I would ask: Is not Congress itself under obligation to give legislative support to any right that is established under the United States Constitution? I repeat the question: Is not Congress itself bound to give legislative support to any right that is established in the United States Constitution? A member of Congress swears to support the Constitution of the United States: and if he sees a right established by that Constitution which needs specific legislative protection, can he clear his oath without giving that protection? Let me ask you why many of us who are opposed to slavery upon principle give our acquiescence to a Fugitive Slave law? Why do we hold ourselves under obligations to pass such a law, and abide by it when it is passed? Because the Constitution makes provision that the owners of slaves shall have the right to reclaim them. It gives the right to reclaim slaves; and that right is, as Judge Douglas says, a barren right, unless there is legislation that will enforce it.

The mere declaration, "No person held to service or labor in one State under the laws thereof, escaping into another, shall in consequence of any law or regulation therein be discharged from such service or labor, but shall be delivered up on claim of the party to whom such service or labor may be due," is powerless without specific legislation to enforce it. Now, on what ground would a member of Congress, who is opposed to slavery in the abstract, vote for a Fugitive law, as I would deem it my duty to do? Because there is a constitutional right which needs legislation to enforce it. And although it is distasteful to me, I have sworn to support the Constitution; and having so sworn, I cannot conceive that I do support it if I withhold from that right any necessary legislation to make it practical. And if that is true in regard to a Fugitive Slave law, is the right to have fugitive slaves reclaimed any better fixed in the Constitution than the right to hold slaves in the Territories? For this decision is a just exposition of the Constitution, as Judge Douglas thinks. Is the one right any better than the other? Is there any man who, while a member of Congress, would give support to the one any more than the other? If I wished to refuse to give legislative support to slave property in the Territories, if a member of Congress, I could not do it, holding the view that the Constitution establishes that right. If I did it at all, it would be because I deny that this decision properly construes the Constitution. But if I acknowledge, with Judge Douglas, that this decision properly construes the Constitution, I cannot conceive that I would be less than a perjured man if I should refuse in Congress to give such protection to that property as in its nature it needed.

At the end of what I have said here I propose to give the Judge my fifth interrogatory, which he may take and answer at his leisure. My fifth interrogatory is this:

If the slaveholding citizens of a United States Territory should need and demand Congressional legislation for the protection of their slave property in such Territory, would you, as a member of Congress, vote for or against such legislation?

[Judge DOUGLAS: Will you repeat that? I want to answer that question.]

If the slaveholding citizens of a United States Territory should need and demand Congressional legislation for the protection of their slave property in such Territory, would you, as a member of Congress, vote for or against such legislation?

I am aware that in some of the speeches Judge Douglas has made, he has spoken as if he did not know or think that the Supreme Court had decided that a Territorial Legislature cannot exclude slavery. Precisely what the Judge would say upon the subject—whether he would say definitely that he does not understand they have so decided, or whether he would say he does understand that the court have so decided,—I do not know; but I know that in his speech at Springfield he spoke of it as a thing they had not decided yet; and in his answer to me at Freeport, he spoke of it, so far, again, as I can comprehend it, as a thing that had not yet been decided. Now, I hold that if the Judge does entertain that view, I think that he is not mistaken in so far as it can be said that the court has not decided anything save the mere question of jurisdiction. I know the legal arguments that can be made,—that after a court has decided that it cannot take jurisdiction in a case, it then has decided all that is before it, and that is the end of it. A plausible argument can be made in favor of that proposition; but I know that Judge Douglas has said in one of his speeches that the court went forward, like honest men as they were, and decided all the points in the case. If any points are really extra-judicially decided, because not necessarily before them, then this one as to the power of the Territorial Legislature, to exclude slavery is one of them, as also the one that the Missouri Compromise was null and void. They are both extra-judicial, or neither is, according as the court held that they had no jurisdiction in the case between the parties, because of want of capacity of one party to maintain a suit in that court. I want, if I have sufficient time, to show that the court did pass its opinion; but that is the only thing actually done in the case. If they did not decide, they showed what they were ready to decide whenever the matter was before them. What is that opinion? After having argued that Congress had no power to pass a law excluding slavery from a United States Territory, they then used language to this effect: That inasmuch as Congress itself could not exercise such a power, it followed as a matter of course that it could not authorize a Territorial government to exercise it; for the Territorial Legislature can do no more than Congress could do. Thus it expressed its opinion emphatically against the power of a Territorial Legislature to exclude slavery, leaving us in just as little doubt on that point as upon any other point they really decided.

Now, my fellow-citizens, I will detain you only a little while longer; my time is nearly out. I find a report of a speech made by Judge Douglas at Joliet, since we last met at Freeport,—published, I believe, in the Missouri Republican, on the 9th of this month, in which Judge Douglas says:

"You know at Ottawa I read this platform, and asked him if he concurred in each and all of the principles set forth in it. He would not answer these questions. At last I said frankly, I wish you to answer them, because when I get them up here where the color of your principles are a little darker than in Egypt, I intend to trot you down to Jonesboro. The very notice that I was going to take him down to Egypt made him tremble in his knees so that he had to be carried from the platform. He laid up seven days, and in the meantime held a consultation with his political physicians; they had Lovejoy and Farnsworth and all the leaders of the Abolition party, they consulted it all over, and at last Lincoln came to the conclusion that he would answer, so he came up to Freeport last Friday."

Now, that statement altogether furnishes a subject for philosophical contemplation. I have been treating it in that way, and I have really come to the conclusion that I can explain it in no other way than by believing the Judge is crazy. If he was in his right mind I cannot conceive how he would have risked disgusting the four or five thousand of his own friends who stood there and knew, as to my having been carried from the platform, that there was not a word of truth in it.

[Judge DOUGLAS: Did n't they carry you off?]

There that question illustrates the character of this man Douglas exactly. He smiles now, and says, "Did n't they carry you off?" but he said then "he had to be carried off"; and he said it to convince the country that he had so completely broken me down by his speech that I had to be carried away. Now he seeks to dodge it, and asks, "Did n't they carry you off?" Yes, they did. But, Judge Douglas, why didn't you tell the truth? I would like to know why you did n't tell the truth about it. And then again "He laid up seven days." He put this in print for the people of the country to read as a serious document. I think if he had been in his sober senses he would not have risked that barefacedness in the presence of thousands of his own friends who knew that I made speeches within six of the seven days at Henry, Marshall County, Augusta, Hancock County, and Macomb, McDonough County, including all the necessary travel to meet him again at Freeport at the end of the six days. Now I say there is no charitable way to look at that statement, except to conclude that he is actually crazy. There is another thing in that statement that alarmed me very greatly as he states it, that he was going to "trot me down to Egypt." Thereby he would have you infer that I would not come to Egypt unless he forced me—that I could not be got here unless he, giant-like, had hauled me down here. That statement he makes, too, in the teeth of the knowledge that I had made the stipulation to come down here and that he himself had been very reluctant to enter into the stipulation. More than all this: Judge Douglas, when he made that statement, must have been crazy and wholly out of his sober senses, or else he would have known that when he got me down here, that promise—that windy promise—of his powers to annihilate me, would n't amount to anything. Now, how little do I look like being carried away trembling? Let the Judge go on; and after he is done with his half-hour, I want you all, if I can't go home myself, to let me stay and rot here; and if anything happens to the Judge, if I cannot carry him to the hotel and put him to bed, let me stay here and rot. I say, then, here is something extraordinary in this statement. I ask you if you know any other living man who would make such a statement? I will ask my friend Casey, over there, if he would do such a thing? Would he send that out and have his men take it as the truth? Did the Judge talk of trotting me down to Egypt to scare me to death? Why, I know this people better than he does. I was raised just a little east of here. I am a part of this people. But the Judge was raised farther north, and perhaps he has some horrid idea of what this people might be induced to do. But really I have talked about this matter perhaps longer than I ought, for it is no great thing; and yet the smallest are often the most difficult things to deal with. The Judge has set about seriously trying to make the impression that when we meet at different places I am literally in his clutches—that I am a poor, helpless, decrepit mouse, and that I can do nothing at all. This is one of the ways he has taken to create that impression. I don't know any other way to meet it except this. I don't want to quarrel with him—to call him a liar; but when I come square up to him I don't know what else to call him if I must tell the truth out. I want to be at peace, and reserve all my fighting powers for necessary occasions. My time now is very nearly out, and I give up the trifle that is left to the Judge, to let him set my knees trembling again, if he can.

THE LINCOLN-DOUGLAS DEBATES II

LINCOLN AND DOUGLAS FOURTH DEBATE, AT CHARLESTON, SEPTEMBER 18, 1858.

LADIES AND GENTLEMEN:—It will be very difficult for an audience so large as this to hear distinctly what a speaker says, and consequently it is important that as profound silence be preserved as possible.

While I was at the hotel to-day, an elderly gentleman called upon me to know whether I was really in favor of producing a perfect equality between the negroes and white people. While I had not proposed to myself on this occasion to say much on that subject, yet as the question was asked me I thought I would occupy perhaps five minutes in saying something in regard to it. I will say, then, that I am not, nor ever have been, in favor of bringing about in any way the social and political equality of the white and black races; that I am not, nor ever have been, in favor of making voters or jurors of negroes, nor of qualifying them to hold office, nor to intermarry with white people; and I will say, in addition to this, that there is a physical difference between the white and black races which I believe will forever forbid the two races living together on terms of social and political equality. And in as much as they cannot so live, while they do remain together there must be the position of superior and inferior, and I as much as any other man am in favor of having the superior position assigned to the white race. I say upon this occasion I do not perceive that because the white man is to have the superior position the negro should be denied everything. I do not understand that because I do not want a negro woman for a slave I must necessarily want her for a wife. My understanding is that I can just let her alone. I am now in my fiftieth year, and I certainly never have had a black woman for either a slave or a wife. So it seems to me quite possible for us to get along without making either slaves or wives of negroes. I will add to this that I have never seen, to my knowledge, a man, woman, or child who was in favor of producing a perfect equality, social and political, between negroes and white men. I recollect of but one distinguished instance that I ever heard of so frequently as to be entirely satisfied of its correctness, and that is the case of Judge Douglas's old friend Colonel Richard M. Johnson. I will also add to the remarks I have made (for I am not going to enter at large upon this subject), that I have never had the least apprehension that I or my friends would marry negroes if there was no law to keep them from it; but as Judge Douglas and his friends seem to be in great apprehension that they might, if there were no law to keep them from it, I give him the most solemn pledge that I will to the very last stand by the law of this State which forbids the marrying of white people with negroes. I will add one further word, which is this: that I do not understand that there is any place where an alteration of the social and political relations of the negro and the white man can be made, except in the State Legislature,—not in the Congress of the United States; and as I do not really apprehend the approach of any such thing myself, and as Judge Douglas seems to be in constant horror that some such danger is rapidly approaching, I propose as the best means to prevent it that the Judge be kept at home, and placed in the State Legislature to fight the measure. I do not propose dwelling longer at this time on this subject.

When Judge Trumbull, our other Senator in Congress, returned to Illinois in the month of August, he made a speech at Chicago, in which he made what may be called a charge against Judge Douglas, which I understand proved to be very offensive to him. The Judge was at that time out upon one of his speaking tours through the country, and when the news of it reached him, as I am informed, he denounced Judge Trumbull in rather harsh terms for having said what he did in regard to that matter. I was traveling at that time, and speaking at the same places with Judge Douglas on subsequent days, and when I heard of what Judge Trumbull had said of Douglas, and what Douglas had said back again, I felt that I was in a position where I could not remain entirely silent in regard to the matter. Consequently, upon two or three occasions I alluded to it, and alluded to it in no other wise than to say that in regard to the charge brought by Trumbull against Douglas, I personally knew nothing, and sought to say nothing about it; that I did personally know Judge Trumbull; that I believed him to be a man of veracity; that I believed him to be a man of capacity sufficient to know very well whether an assertion he was making, as a conclusion drawn from a set of facts, was true or false; and as a conclusion of my own from that, I stated it as my belief if Trumbull should ever be called upon, he would prove everything he had said. I said this upon two or three occasions. Upon a subsequent occasion, Judge Trumbull spoke again before an audience at Alton, and upon that occasion not only repeated his charge against Douglas, but arrayed the evidence he relied upon to substantiate it. This speech was published at length; and subsequently at Jacksonville Judge Douglas alluded to the matter. In the course of his speech, and near the close of it, he stated in regard to myself what I will now read:

"Judge Douglas proceeded to remark that he should not hereafter occupy his time in refuting such charges made by Trumbull, but that, Lincoln having indorsed the character of Trumbull for veracity, he should hold him (Lincoln) responsible for the slanders."

I have done simply what I have told you, to subject me to this invitation to notice the charge. I now wish to say that it had not originally been my purpose to discuss that matter at all But in-as-much as it seems to be the wish of Judge Douglas to hold me responsible for it, then for once in my life I will play General Jackson, and to the just extent I take the responsibility.

I wish to say at the beginning that I will hand to the reporters that portion of Judge Trumbull's Alton speech which was devoted to this matter, and also that portion of Judge Douglas's speech made at Jacksonville in answer to it. I shall thereby furnish the readers of this debate with the complete discussion between Trumbull and Douglas. I cannot now read them, for the reason that it would take half of my first hour to do so. I can only make some comments upon them. Trumbull's charge is in the following words:

"Now, the charge is, that there was a plot entered into to have a constitution formed for Kansas, and put in force, without giving the people an opportunity to vote upon it, and that Mr. Douglas was in the plot."

I will state, without quoting further, for all will have an opportunity of reading it hereafter, that Judge Trumbull brings forward what he regards as sufficient evidence to substantiate this charge.

It will be perceived Judge Trumbull shows that Senator Bigler, upon the floor of the Senate, had declared there had been a conference among the senators, in which conference it was determined to have an enabling act passed for the people of Kansas to form a constitution under, and in this conference it was agreed among them that it was best not to have a provision for submitting the constitution to a vote of the people after it should be formed. He then brings forward to show, and showing, as he deemed, that Judge Douglas reported the bill back to the Senate with that clause stricken out. He then shows that there was a new clause inserted into the bill, which would in its nature prevent a reference of the constitution back for a vote of the people,—if, indeed, upon a mere silence in the law, it could be assumed that they had the right to vote upon it. These are the general statements that he has made.

I propose to examine the points in Judge Douglas's speech in which he attempts to answer that speech of Judge Trumbull's. When you come to examine Judge Douglas's speech, you will find that the first point he makes is:

"Suppose it were true that there was such a change in the bill, and that I struck it out,—is that a proof of a plot to force a constitution upon them against their will?"

His striking out such a provision, if there was such a one in the bill, he argues, does not establish the proof that it was stricken out for the purpose of robbing the people of that right. I would say, in the first place, that that would be a most manifest reason for it. It is true, as Judge Douglas states, that many Territorial bills have passed without having such a provision in them. I believe it is true, though I am not certain, that in some instances constitutions framed under such bills have been submitted to a vote of the people with the law silent upon the subject; but it does not appear that they once had their enabling acts framed with an express provision for submitting the constitution to be framed to a vote of the people, then that they were stricken out when Congress did not mean to alter the effect of the law. That there have been bills which never had the provision in, I do not question; but when was that provision taken out of one that it was in? More especially does the evidence tend to prove the proposition that Trumbull advanced, when we remember that the provision was stricken out of the bill almost simultaneously with the time that Bigler says there was a conference among certain senators, and in which it was agreed that a bill should be passed leaving that out. Judge Douglas, in answering Trumbull, omits to attend to the testimony of Bigler, that there was a meeting in which it was agreed they should so frame the bill that there should be no submission of the constitution to a vote of the people. The Judge does not notice this part of it. If you take this as one piece of evidence, and then ascertain that simultaneously Judge Douglas struck out a provision that did require it to be submitted, and put the two together, I think it will make a pretty fair show of proof that Judge Douglas did, as Trumbull says, enter into a plot to put in force a constitution for Kansas, without giving the people any opportunity of voting upon it.

But I must hurry on. The next proposition that Judge Douglas puts is this:

"But upon examination it turns out that the Toombs bill never did contain a clause requiring the constitution to be submitted."

This is a mere question of fact, and can be determined by evidence. I only want to ask this question: Why did not Judge Douglas say that these words were not stricken out of the Toomb's bill, or this bill from which it is alleged the provision was stricken out,—a bill which goes by the name of Toomb's, because he originally brought it forward? I ask why, if the Judge wanted to make a direct issue with Trumbull, did he not take the exact proposition Trumbull made in his speech, and say it was not stricken out? Trumbull has given the exact words that he says were in the Toomb's bill, and he alleges that when the bill came back, they were stricken out. Judge Douglas does not say that the words which Trumbull says were stricken out were not so stricken out, but he says there was no provision in the Toomb's bill to submit the constitution to a vote of the people. We see at once that he is merely making an issue upon the meaning of the words. He has not undertaken to say that Trumbull tells a lie about these words being stricken out, but he is really, when pushed up to it, only taking an issue upon the meaning of the words. Now, then, if there be any issue upon the meaning of the words, or if there be upon the question of fact as to whether these words were stricken out, I have before me what I suppose to be a genuine copy of the Toomb's bill, in which it can be shown that the words Trumbull says were in it were, in fact, originally there. If there be any dispute upon the fact, I have got the documents here to show they were there. If there be any controversy upon the sense of the words,—whether these words which were stricken out really constituted a provision for submitting the matter to a vote of the people,—as that is a matter of argument, I think I may as well use Trumbull's own argument. He says that the proposition is in these words:

"That the following propositions be and the same are hereby offered to the said Convention of the people of Kansas when formed, for their free acceptance or rejection; which, if accepted by the Convention and ratified by the people at the election for the adoption of the constitution, shall be obligatory upon the United States and the said State of Kansas."

Now, Trumbull alleges that these last words were stricken out of the bill when it came back, and he says this was a provision for submitting the constitution to a vote of the people; and his argument is this:

"Would it have been possible to ratify the land propositions at the election for the adoption of the constitution, unless such an election was to be held?"

This is Trumbull's argument. Now, Judge Douglas does not meet the charge at all, but he stands up and says there was no such proposition in that bill for submitting the constitution to be framed to a vote of the people. Trumbull admits that the language is not a direct provision for submitting it, but it is a provision necessarily implied from another provision. He asks you how it is possible to ratify the land proposition at the election for the adoption of the constitution, if there was no election to be held for the adoption of the constitution. And he goes on to show that it is not any less a law because the provision is put in that indirect shape than it would be if it were put directly. But I presume I have said enough to draw attention to this point, and I pass it by also.

Another one of the points that Judge Douglas makes upon Trumbull, and at very great length, is, that Trumbull, while the bill was pending, said in a speech in the Senate that he supposed the constitution to be made would have to be submitted to the people. He asks, if Trumbull thought so then, what ground is there for anybody thinking otherwise now? Fellow-citizens, this much may be said in reply: That bill had been in the hands of a party to which Trumbull did not belong. It had been in the hands of the committee at the head of which Judge Douglas stood. Trumbull perhaps had a printed copy of the original Toomb's bill. I have not the evidence on that point except a sort of inference I draw from the general course of business there. What alterations, or what provisions in the way of altering, were going on in committee, Trumbull had no means of knowing, until the altered bill was reported back. Soon afterwards, when it was reported back, there was a discussion over it, and perhaps Trumbull in reading it hastily in the altered form did not perceive all the bearings of the alterations. He was hastily borne into the debate, and it does not follow that because there was something in it Trumbull did not perceive, that something did not exist. More than this, is it true that what Trumbull did can have any effect on what Douglas did? Suppose Trumbull had been in the plot with these other men, would that let Douglas out of it? Would it exonerate Douglas that Trumbull did n't then perceive he was in the plot? He also asks the question: Why did n't Trumbull propose to amend the bill, if he thought it needed any amendment? Why, I believe that everything Judge Trumbull had proposed, particularly in connection with this question of Kansas and Nebraska, since he had been on the floor of the Senate, had been promptly voted down by Judge Douglas and his friends. He had no promise that an amendment offered by him to anything on this subject would receive the slightest consideration. Judge Trumbull did bring to the notice of the Senate at that time the fact that there was no provision for submitting the constitution about to be made for the people of Kansas to a vote of the people. I believe I may venture to say that Judge Douglas made some reply to this speech of Judge Trumbull's, but he never noticed that part of it at all. And so the thing passed by. I think, then, the fact that Judge Trumbull offered no amendment does not throw much blame upon him; and if it did, it does not reach the question of fact as to what Judge Douglas was doing. I repeat, that if Trumbull had himself been in the plot, it would not at all relieve the others who were in it from blame. If I should be indicted for murder, and upon the trial it should be discovered that I had been implicated in that murder, but that the prosecuting witness was guilty too, that would not at all touch the question of my crime. It would be no relief to my neck that they discovered this other man who charged the crime upon me to be guilty too.

Another one of the points Judge Douglas makes upon Judge Trumbull is, that when he spoke in Chicago he made his charge to rest upon the fact that the bill had the provision in it for submitting the constitution to a vote of the people when it went into his Judge Douglas's hands, that it was missing when he reported it to the Senate, and that in a public speech he had subsequently said the alterations in the bill were made while it was in committee, and that they were made in consultation between him (Judge Douglas) and Toomb's. And Judge Douglas goes on to comment upon the fact of Trumbull's adducing in his Alton speech the proposition that the bill not only came back with that proposition stricken out, but with another clause and another provision in it, saying that "until the complete execution of this Act there shall be no election in said Territory,"—which, Trumbull argued, was not only taking the provision for submitting to a vote of the people out of the bill, but was adding an affirmative one, in that it prevented the people from exercising the right under a bill that was merely silent on the question. Now, in regard to what he says, that Trumbull shifts the issue, that he shifts his ground,—and I believe he uses the term that, "it being proven false, he has changed ground," I call upon all of you, when you come to examine that portion of Trumbull's speech (for it will make a part of mine), to examine whether Trumbull has shifted his ground or not. I say he did not shift his ground, but that he brought forward his original charge and the evidence to sustain it yet more fully, but precisely as he originally made it. Then, in addition thereto, he brought in a new piece of evidence. He shifted no ground. He brought no new piece of evidence inconsistent with his former testimony; but he brought a new piece, tending, as he thought, and as I think, to prove his proposition. To illustrate: A man brings an accusation against another, and on trial the man making the charge introduces A and B to prove the accusation. At a second trial he introduces the same witnesses, who tell the same story as before, and a third witness, who tells the same thing, and in addition gives further testimony corroborative of the charge. So with Trumbull. There was no shifting of ground, nor inconsistency of testimony between the new piece of evidence and what he originally introduced.

But Judge Douglas says that he himself moved to strike out that last provision of the bill, and that on his motion it was stricken out and a substitute inserted. That I presume is the truth. I presume it is true that that last proposition was stricken out by Judge Douglas. Trumbull has not said it was not; Trumbull has himself said that it was so stricken out. He says: "I am now speaking of the bill as Judge Douglas reported it back. It was amended somewhat in the Senate before it passed, but I am speaking of it as he brought it back." Now, when Judge Douglas parades the fact that the provision was stricken out of the bill when it came back, he asserts nothing contrary to what Trumbull alleges. Trumbull has only said that he originally put it in, not that he did not strike it out. Trumbull says it was not in the bill when it went to the committee. When it came back it was in, and Judge Douglas said the alterations were made by him in consultation with Toomb's. Trumbull alleges, therefore, as his conclusion, that Judge Douglas put it in. Then, if Douglas wants to contradict Trumbull and call him a liar, let him say he did not put it in, and not that he did n't take it out again. It is said that a bear is sometimes hard enough pushed to drop a cub; and so I presume it was in this case. I presume the truth is that Douglas put it in, and afterward took it out. That, I take it, is the truth about it. Judge Trumbull says one thing, Douglas says another thing, and the two don't contradict one another at all. The question is, what did he put it in for? In the first place, what did he take the other provision out of the bill for,—the provision which Trumbull argued was necessary for submitting the constitution to a vote of the people? What did he take that out for; and, having taken it out, what did he put this in for? I say that in the run of things it is not unlikely forces conspire to render it vastly expedient for Judge Douglas to take that latter clause out again. The question that Trumbull has made is that Judge Douglas put it in; and he don't meet Trumbull at all unless he denies that.

In the clause of Judge Douglas's speech upon this subject he uses this language toward Judge Trumbull. He says:

"He forges his evidence from beginning to end; and by falsifying the record, he endeavors to bolster up his false charge."

Well, that is a pretty serious statement—Trumbull forges his evidence from beginning to end. Now, upon my own authority I say that it is not true. What is a forgery? Consider the evidence that Trumbull has brought forward. When you come to read the speech, as you will be able to, examine whether the evidence is a forgery from beginning to end. He had the bill or document in his hand like that [holding up a paper]. He says that is a copy of the Toomb's bill,—the amendment offered by Toomb's. He says that is a copy of the bill as it was introduced and went into Judge Douglas's hands. Now, does Judge Douglas say that is a forgery? That is one thing Trumbull brought forward. Judge Douglas says he forged it from beginning to end! That is the "beginning," we will say. Does Douglas say that is a forgery? Let him say it to-day, and we will have a subsequent examination upon this subject. Trumbull then holds up another document like this, and says that is an exact copy of the bill as it came back in the amended form out of Judge Douglas's hands. Does Judge Douglas say that is a forgery? Does he say it in his general sweeping charge? Does he say so now? If he does not, then take this Toomb's bill and the bill in the amended form, and it only needs to compare them to see that the provision is in the one and not in the other; it leaves the inference inevitable that it was taken out.

But, while I am dealing with this question, let us see what Trumbull's other evidence is. One other piece of evidence I will read. Trumbull says there are in this original Toomb's bill these words:

"That the following propositions be and the same are hereby offered to the said Convention of the people of Kansas, when formed, for their free acceptance or rejection; which, if accepted by the Convention and ratified by the people at the election for the adoption of the constitution, shall be obligatory upon the United States and the said State of Kansas."

Now, if it is said that this is a forgery, we will open the paper here and see whether it is or not. Again, Trumbull says, as he goes along, that Mr. Bigler made the following statement in his place in the Senate, December 9, 1857:

"I was present when that subject was discussed by senators before the bill was introduced, and the question was raised and discussed, whether the constitution, when formed, should be submitted to a vote of the people. It was held by those most intelligent on the subject that, in view of all the difficulties surrounding that Territory, the danger of any experiment at that time of a popular vote, it would be better there should be no such provision in the Toomb's bill; and it was my understanding, in all the intercourse I had, that the Convention would make a constitution, and send it here, without submitting it to the popular vote."

Then Trumbull follows on:

"In speaking of this meeting again on the 21st December, 1857 [Congressional Globe, same vol., page 113], Senator Bigler said:

"'Nothing was further from my mind than to allude to any social or confidential interview. The meeting was not of that character. Indeed, it was semi-official, and called to promote the public good. My recollection was clear that I left the conference under the impression that it had been deemed best to adopt measures to admit Kansas as a State through the agency of one popular election, and that for delegates to this Convention. This impression was stronger because I thought the spirit of the bill infringed upon the doctrine of non-intervention, to which I had great aversion; but with the hope of accomplishing a great good, and as no movement had been made in that direction in the Territory, I waived this objection, and concluded to support the measure. I have a few items of testimony as to the correctness of these impressions, and with their submission I shall be content. I have before me the bill reported by the senator from Illinois on the 7th of March, 1856, providing for the admission of Kansas as a State, the third section of which reads as follows:

"That the following propositions be, and the same are hereby offered to the said Convention of the people of Kansas, when formed, for their free acceptance or rejection; which, if accepted by the Convention and ratified by the people at the election for the adoption of the constitution, shall be obligatory upon the United States and the said State of Kansas."

The bill read in his place by the senator from Georgia on the 25th of June, and referred to the Committee on Territories, contained the same section word for word. Both these bills were under consideration at the conference referred to; but, sir, when the senator from Illinois reported the Toombs bill to the Senate with amendments, the next morning, it did not contain that portion of the third section which indicated to the Convention that the constitution should be approved by the people. The words "and ratified by the people at the election for the adoption of the constitution" had been stricken out.

Now, these things Trumbull says were stated by Bigler upon the floor of the Senate on certain days, and that they are recorded in the Congressional Globe on certain pages. Does Judge Douglas say this is a forgery? Does he say there is no such thing in the Congressional Globe? What does he mean when he says Judge Trumbull forges his evidence from beginning to end? So again he says in another place that Judge Douglas, in his speech, December 9, 1857 (Congressional Globe, part I., page 15), stated:

"That during the last session of Congress, I [Mr. Douglas] reported a bill from the Committee on Territories, to authorize the people of Kansas to assemble and form a constitution for themselves. Subsequently the senator from Georgia [Mr. Toombs] brought forward a substitute for my bill, which, after having been modified by him and myself in consultation, was passed by the Senate."

Now, Trumbull says this is a quotation from a speech of Douglas, and is recorded in the Congressional Globe. Is it a forgery? Is it there or not? It may not be there, but I want the Judge to take these pieces of evidence, and distinctly say they are forgeries if he dare do it.

[A voice: "He will."]

Well, sir, you had better not commit him. He gives other quotations,—another from Judge Douglas. He says:

"I will ask the senator to show me an intimation, from any one member of the Senate, in the whole debate on the Toombs bill, and in the Union, from any quarter, that the constitution was not to be submitted to the people. I will venture to say that on all sides of the chamber it was so understood at the time. If the opponents of the bill had understood it was not, they would have made the point on it; and if they had made it, we should certainly have yielded to it, and put in the clause. That is a discovery made since the President found out that it was not safe to take it for granted that that would be done, which ought in fairness to have been done."

Judge Trumbull says Douglas made that speech, and it is recorded. Does Judge Douglas say it is a forgery, and was not true? Trumbull says somewhere, and I propose to skip it, but it will be found by any one who will read this debate, that he did distinctly bring it to the notice of those who were engineering the bill, that it lacked that provision; and then he goes on to give another quotation from Judge Douglas, where Judge Trumbull uses this language:

"Judge Douglas, however, on the same day and in the same debate, probably recollecting or being reminded of the fact that I had objected to the Toombs bill when pending that it did not provide for a submission of the constitution to the people, made another statement, which is to be found in the same volume of the Globe, page 22, in which he says: 'That the bill was silent on this subject was true, and my attention was called to that about the time it was passed; and I took the fair construction to be, that powers not delegated were reserved, and that of course the constitution would be submitted to the people.'

"Whether this statement is consistent with the statement just before made, that had the point been made it would have been yielded to, or that it was a new discovery, you will determine."

So I say. I do not know whether Judge Douglas will dispute this, and yet maintain his position that Trumbull's evidence "was forged from beginning to end." I will remark that I have not got these Congressional Globes with me. They are large books, and difficult to carry about, and if Judge Douglas shall say that on these points where Trumbull has quoted from them there are no such passages there, I shall not be able to prove they are there upon this occasion, but I will have another chance. Whenever he points out the forgery and says, "I declare that this particular thing which Trumbull has uttered is not to be found where he says it is," then my attention will be drawn to that, and I will arm myself for the contest, stating now that I have not the slightest doubt on earth that I will find every quotation just where Trumbull says it is. Then the question is, How can Douglas call that a forgery? How can he make out that it is a forgery? What is a forgery? It is the bringing forward something in writing or in print purporting to be of certain effect when it is altogether untrue. If you come forward with my note for one hundred dollars when I have never given such a note, there is a forgery. If you come forward with a letter purporting to be written by me which I never wrote, there is another forgery. If you produce anything in writing or in print saying it is so and so, the document not being genuine, a forgery has been committed. How do you make this forgery when every piece of the evidence is genuine? If Judge Douglas does say these documents and quotations are false and forged, he has a full right to do so; but until he does it specifically, we don't know how to get at him. If he does say they are false and forged, I will then look further into it, and presume I can procure the certificates of the proper officers that they are genuine copies. I have no doubt each of these extracts will be found exactly where Trumbull says it is. Then I leave it to you if Judge Douglas, in making his sweeping charge that Judge Trumbull's evidence is forged from beginning to end, at all meets the case,—if that is the way to get at the facts. I repeat again, if he will point out which one is a forgery, I will carefully examine it, and if it proves that any one of them is really a forgery, it will not be me who will hold to it any longer. I have always wanted to deal with everyone I meet candidly and honestly. If I have made any assertion not warranted by facts, and it is pointed out to me, I will withdraw it cheerfully. But I do not choose to see Judge Trumbull calumniated, and the evidence he has brought forward branded in general terms "a forgery from beginning to end." This is not the legal way of meeting a charge, and I submit it to all intelligent persons, both friends of Judge Douglas and of myself, whether it is.

The point upon Judge Douglas is this: The bill that went into his hands had the provision in it for a submission of the constitution to the people; and I say its language amounts to an express provision for a submission, and that he took the provision out. He says it was known that the bill was silent in this particular; but I say, Judge Douglas, it was not silent when you got it. It was vocal with the declaration, when you got it, for a submission of the constitution to the people. And now, my direct question to Judge Douglas is, to answer why, if he deemed the bill silent on this point, he found it necessary to strike out those particular harmless words. If he had found the bill silent and without this provision, he might say what he does now. If he supposes it was implied that the constitution would be submitted to a vote of the people, how could these two lines so encumber the statute as to make it necessary to strike them out? How could he infer that a submission was still implied, after its express provision had been stricken from the bill? I find the bill vocal with the provision, while he silenced it. He took it out, and although he took out the other provision preventing a submission to a vote of the people, I ask, Why did you first put it in? I ask him whether he took the original provision out, which Trumbull alleges was in the bill. If he admits that he did take it, I ask him what he did it for. It looks to us as if he had altered the bill. If it looks differently to him,—if he has a different reason for his action from the one we assign him—he can tell it. I insist upon knowing why he made the bill silent upon that point when it was vocal before he put his hands upon it.

I was told, before my last paragraph, that my time was within three minutes of being out. I presume it is expired now; I therefore close.

Mr. LINCOLN'S REJOINDER.

FELLOW-CITIZENS: It follows as a matter of course that a half-hour answer to a speech of an hour and a half can be but a very hurried one. I shall only be able to touch upon a few of the points suggested by Judge Douglas, and give them a brief attention, while I shall have to totally omit others for the want of time.

Judge Douglas has said to you that he has not been able to get from me an answer to the question whether I am in favor of negro citizenship. So far as I know the Judge never asked me the question before. He shall have no occasion to ever ask it again, for I tell him very frankly that I am not in favor of negro citizenship. This furnishes me an occasion for saying a few words upon the subject. I mentioned in a certain speech of mine, which has been printed, that the Supreme Court had decided that a negro could not possibly be made a citizen; and without saying what was my ground of complaint in regard to that, or whether I had any ground of complaint, Judge Douglas has from that thing manufactured nearly everything that he ever says about my disposition to produce an equality between the negroes and the white people. If any one will read my speech, he will find I mentioned that as one of the points decided in the course of the Supreme Court opinions, but I did not state what objection I had to it. But Judge Douglas tells the people what my objection was when I did not tell them myself. Now, my opinion is that the different States have the power to make a negro a citizen under the Constitution of the United States if they choose. The Dred Scott decision decides that they have not that power. If the State of Illinois had that power, I should be opposed to the exercise of it. That is all I have to say about it.

Judge Douglas has told me that he heard my speeches north and my speeches south; that he had heard me at Ottawa and at Freeport in the north and recently at Jonesboro in the south, and there was a very different cast of sentiment in the speeches made at the different points. I will not charge upon Judge Douglas that he wilfully misrepresents me, but I call upon every fair-minded man to take these speeches and read them, and I dare him to point out any difference between my speeches north and south. While I am here perhaps I ought to say a word, if I have the time, in regard to the latter portion of the Judge's speech, which was a sort of declamation in reference to my having said I entertained the belief that this government would not endure half slave and half free. I have said so, and I did not say it without what seemed to me to be good reasons. It perhaps would require more time than I have now to set forth these reasons in detail; but let me ask you a few questions. Have we ever had any peace on this slavery question? When are we to have peace upon it, if it is kept in the position it now occupies? How are we ever to have peace upon it? That is an important question. To be sure, if we will all stop, and allow Judge Douglas and his friends to march on in their present career until they plant the institution all over the nation, here and wherever else our flag waves, and we acquiesce in it, there will be peace. But let me ask Judge Douglas how he is going to get the people to do that? They have been wrangling over this question for at least forty years. This was the cause of the agitation resulting in the Missouri Compromise; this produced the troubles at the annexation of Texas, in the acquisition of the territory acquired in the Mexican War. Again, this was the trouble which was quieted by the Compromise of 1850, when it was settled "forever" as both the great political parties declared in their National Conventions. That "forever" turned out to be just four years, when Judge Douglas himself reopened it. When is it likely to come to an end? He introduced the Nebraska Bill in 1854 to put another end to the slavery agitation. He promised that it would finish it all up immediately, and he has never made a speech since, until he got into a quarrel with the President about the Lecompton Constitution, in which he has not declared that we are just at the end of the slavery agitation. But in one speech, I think last winter, he did say that he did n't quite see when the end of the slavery agitation would come. Now he tells us again that it is all over and the people of Kansas have voted down the Lecompton Constitution. How is it over? That was only one of the attempts at putting an end to the slavery agitation—one of these "final settlements." Is Kansas in the Union? Has she formed a constitution that she is likely to come in under? Is not the slavery agitation still an open question in that Territory? Has the voting down of that constitution put an end to all the trouble? Is that more likely to settle it than every one of these previous attempts to settle the slavery agitation? Now, at this day in the history of the world we can no more foretell where the end of this slavery agitation will be than we can see the end of the world itself. The Nebraska-Kansas Bill was introduced four years and a half ago, and if the agitation is ever to come to an end we may say we are four years and a half nearer the end. So, too, we can say we are four years and a half nearer the end of the world, and we can just as clearly see the end of the world as we can see the end of this agitation. The Kansas settlement did not conclude it. If Kansas should sink to-day, and leave a great vacant space in the earth's surface, this vexed question would still be among us. I say, then, there is no way of putting an end to the slavery agitation amongst us but to put it back upon the basis where our fathers placed it; no way but to keep it out of our new Territories,—to restrict it forever to the old States where it now exists. Then the public mind will rest in the belief that it is in the course of ultimate extinction. That is one way of putting an end to the slavery agitation.

The other way is for us to surrender and let Judge Douglas and his friends have their way and plant slavery over all the States; cease speaking of it as in any way a wrong; regard slavery as one of the common matters of property, and speak of negroes as we do of our horses and cattle. But while it drives on in its state of progress as it is now driving, and as it has driven for the last five years, I have ventured the opinion, and I say to-day, that we will have no end to the slavery agitation until it takes one turn or the other. I do not mean that when it takes a turn toward ultimate extinction it will be in a day, nor in a year, nor in two years. I do not suppose that in the most peaceful way ultimate extinction would occur in less than a hundred years at least; but that it will occur in the best way for both races, in God's own good time, I have no doubt. But, my friends, I have used up more of my time than I intended on this point.

Now, in regard to this matter about Trumbull and myself having made a bargain to sell out the entire Whig and Democratic parties in 1854: Judge Douglas brings forward no evidence to sustain his charge, except the speech Matheny is said to have made in 1856, in which he told a cock-and-bull story of that sort, upon the same moral principles that Judge Douglas tells it here to-day. This is the simple truth. I do not care greatly for the story, but this is the truth of it: and I have twice told Judge Douglas to his face that from beginning to end there is not one word of truth in it. I have called upon him for the proof, and he does not at all meet me as Trumbull met him upon that of which we were just talking, by producing the record. He did n't bring the record because there was no record for him to bring. When he asks if I am ready to indorse Trumbull's veracity after he has broken a bargain with me, I reply that if Trumbull had broken a bargain with me I would not be likely to indorse his veracity; but I am ready to indorse his veracity because neither in that thing, nor in any other, in all the years that I have known Lyman Trumbull, have I known him to fail of his word or tell a falsehood large or small. It is for that reason that I indorse Lyman Trumbull.

[Mr. JAMES BROWN (Douglas postmaster): "What does Ford's History say about him?"]

Some gentleman asks me what Ford's History says about him. My own recollection is that Ford speaks of Trumbull in very disrespectful terms in several portions of his book, and that he talks a great deal worse of Judge Douglas. I refer you, sir, to the History for examination.

Judge Douglas complains at considerable length about a disposition on the part of Trumbull and myself to attack him personally. I want to attend to that suggestion a moment. I don't want to be unjustly accused of dealing illiberally or unfairly with an adversary, either in court or in a political canvass or anywhere else. I would despise myself if I supposed myself ready to deal less liberally with an adversary than I was willing to be treated myself. Judge Douglas in a general way, without putting it in a direct shape, revives the old charge against me in reference to the Mexican War. He does not take the responsibility of putting it in a very definite form, but makes a general reference to it. That charge is more than ten years old. He complains of Trumbull and myself because he says we bring charges against him one or two years old. He knows, too, that in regard to the Mexican War story the more respectable papers of his own party throughout the State have been compelled to take it back and acknowledge that it was a lie.

[Here Mr. LINCOLN turned to the crowd on the platform, and, selecting HON. ORLANDO B. FICKLIN, led him forward and said:]

I do not mean to do anything with Mr. FICKLIN except to present his face and tell you that he personally knows it to be a lie! He was a member of Congress at the only time I was in Congress, and [FICKLIN] knows that whenever there was an attempt to procure a vote of mine which would indorse the origin and justice of the war, I refused to give such indorsement and voted against it; but I never voted against the supplies for the army, and he knows, as well as Judge Douglas, that whenever a dollar was asked by way of compensation or otherwise for the benefit of the soldiers I gave all the votes that FICKLIN or Douglas did, and perhaps more.

[Mr. FICKLIN: My friends, I wish to say this in reference to the matter: Mr. Lincoln and myself are just as good personal friends as Judge Douglas and myself. In reference to this Mexican War, my recollection is that when Ashmun's resolution [amendment] was offered by Mr. Ashmun of Massachusetts, in which he declared that the Mexican War was unnecessary and unconstitutionally commenced by the President-my recollection is that Mr. Lincoln voted for that resolution.]

That is the truth. Now, you all remember that was a resolution censuring the President for the manner in which the war was begun. You know they have charged that I voted against the supplies, by which I starved the soldiers who were out fighting the battles of their country. I say that FICKLIN knows it is false. When that charge was brought forward by the Chicago Times, the Springfield Register [Douglas's organ] reminded the Times that the charge really applied to John Henry; and I do know that John Henry is now making speeches and fiercely battling for Judge Douglas. If the Judge now says that he offers this as a sort of setoff to what I said to-day in reference to Trumbull's charge, then I remind him that he made this charge before I said a word about Trumbull's. He brought this forward at Ottawa, the first time we met face to face; and in the opening speech that Judge Douglas made he attacked me in regard to a matter ten years old. Is n't he a pretty man to be whining about people making charges against him only two years old!

The Judge thinks it is altogether wrong that I should have dwelt upon this charge of Trumbull's at all. I gave the apology for doing so in my opening speech. Perhaps it did n't fix your attention. I said that when Judge Douglas was speaking at place—where I spoke on the succeeding day he used very harsh language about this charge. Two or three times afterward I said I had confidence in Judge Trumbull's veracity and intelligence; and my own opinion was, from what I knew of the character of Judge Trumbull, that he would vindicate his position and prove whatever he had stated to be true. This I repeated two or three times; and then I dropped it, without saying anything more on the subject for weeks—perhaps a month. I passed it by without noticing it at all till I found, at Jacksonville, Judge Douglas in the plenitude of his power is not willing to answer Trumbull and let me alone, but he comes out there and uses this language: "He should not hereafter occupy his time in refuting such charges made by Trumbull but that, Lincoln having indorsed the character of Trumbull for veracity, he should hold him [Lincoln] responsible for the slanders." What was Lincoln to do? Did he not do right, when he had the fit opportunity of meeting Judge Douglas here, to tell him he was ready for the responsibility? I ask a candid audience whether in doing thus Judge Douglas was not the assailant rather than I? Here I meet him face to face, and say I am ready to take the responsibility, so far as it rests on me.

Having done so I ask the attention of this audience to the question whether I have succeeded in sustaining the charge, and whether Judge Douglas has at all succeeded in rebutting it? You all heard me call upon him to say which of these pieces of evidence was a forgery. Does he say that what I present here as a copy of the original Toombs bill is a forgery? Does he say that what I present as a copy of the bill reported by himself is a forgery, or what is presented as a transcript from the Globe of the quotations from Bigler's speech is a forgery? Does he say the quotations from his own speech are forgeries? Does he say this transcript from Trumbull's speech is a forgery?

["He didn't deny one of them."]

I would then like to know how it comes about that when each piece of a story is true the whole story turns out false. I take it these people have some sense; they see plainly that Judge Douglas is playing cuttle-fish, a small species of fish that has no mode of defending itself when pursued except by throwing out a black fluid, which makes the water so dark the enemy cannot see it, and thus it escapes. Ain't the Judge playing the cuttle-fish?

Now, I would ask very special attention to the consideration of Judge Douglas's speech at Jacksonville; and when you shall read his speech of to-day, I ask you to watch closely and see which of these pieces of testimony, every one of which he says is a forgery, he has shown to be such. Not one of them has he shown to be a forgery. Then I ask the original question, if each of the pieces of testimony is true, how is it possible that the whole is a falsehood?

In regard to Trumbull's charge that he [Douglas] inserted a provision into the bill to prevent the constitution being submitted to the people, what was his answer? He comes here and reads from the Congressional Globe to show that on his motion that provision was struck out of the bill. Why, Trumbull has not said it was not stricken out, but Trumbull says he [Douglas] put it in; and it is no answer to the charge to say he afterwards took it out. Both are perhaps true. It was in regard to that thing precisely that I told him he had dropped the cub. Trumbull shows you that by his introducing the bill it was his cub. It is no answer to that assertion to call Trumbull a liar merely because he did not specially say that Douglas struck it out. Suppose that were the case, does it answer Trumbull? I assert that you [pointing to an individual] are here to-day, and you undertake to prove me a liar by showing that you were in Mattoon yesterday. I say that you took your hat off your head, and you prove me a liar by putting it on your head. That is the whole force of Douglas's argument.

Now, I want to come back to my original question. Trumbull says that Judge Douglas had a bill with a provision in it for submitting a constitution to be made to a vote of the people of Kansas. Does Judge Douglas deny that fact? Does he deny that the provision which Trumbull reads was put in that bill? Then Trumbull says he struck it out. Does he dare to deny that? He does not, and I have the right to repeat the question,—Why Judge Douglas took it out? Bigler has said there was a combination of certain senators, among whom he did not include Judge Douglas, by which it was agreed that the Kansas Bill should have a clause in it not to have the constitution formed under it submitted to a vote of the people. He did not say that Douglas was among them, but we prove by another source that about the same time Douglas comes into the Senate with that provision stricken out of the bill. Although Bigler cannot say they were all working in concert, yet it looks very much as if the thing was agreed upon and done with a mutual understanding after the conference; and while we do not know that it was absolutely so, yet it looks so probable that we have a right to call upon the man who knows the true reason why it was done to tell what the true reason was. When he will not tell what the true reason was, he stands in the attitude of an accused thief who has stolen goods in his possession, and when called to account refuses to tell where he got them. Not only is this the evidence, but when he comes in with the bill having the provision stricken out, he tells us in a speech, not then but since, that these alterations and modifications in the bill had been made by HIM, in consultation with Toombs, the originator of the bill. He tells us the same to-day. He says there were certain modifications made in the bill in committee that he did not vote for. I ask you to remember, while certain amendments were made which he disapproved of, but which a majority of the committee voted in, he has himself told us that in this particular the alterations and modifications were made by him, upon consultation with Toombs. We have his own word that these alterations were made by him, and not by the committee. Now, I ask, what is the reason Judge Douglas is so chary about coming to the exact question? What is the reason he will not tell you anything about How it was made, BY WHOM it was made, or that he remembers it being made at all? Why does he stand playing upon the meaning of words and quibbling around the edges of the evidence? If he can explain all this, but leaves it unexplained, I have the right to infer that Judge Douglas understood it was the purpose of his party, in engineering that bill through, to make a constitution, and have Kansas come into the Union with that constitution, without its being submitted to a vote of the people. If he will explain his action on this question, by giving a better reason for the facts that happened than he has done, it will be satisfactory. But until he does that—until he gives a better or more plausible reason than he has offered against the evidence in the case—I suggest to him it will not avail him at all that he swells himself up, takes on dignity, and calls people liars. Why, sir, there is not a word in Trumbull's speech that depends on Trumbull's veracity at all. He has only arrayed the evidence and told you what follows as a matter of reasoning. There is not a statement in the whole speech that depends on Trumbull's word. If you have ever studied geometry, you remember that by a course of reasoning Euclid proves that all the angles in a triangle are equal to two right angles. Euclid has shown you how to work it out. Now, if you undertake to disprove that proposition, and to show that it is erroneous, would you prove it to be false by calling Euclid a liar? They tell me that my time is out, and therefore I close.

FIFTH JOINT DEBATE, AT GALESBURGH, OCTOBER 7, 1858

Mr. LINCOLN'S REPLY.

MY FELLOW-CITIZENS: A very large portion of the speech which Judge Douglas has addressed to you has previously been delivered and put in print. I do not mean that for a hit upon the Judge at all.—If I had not been interrupted, I was going to say that such an answer as I was able to make to a very large portion of it had already been more than once made and published. There has been an opportunity afforded to the public to see our respective views upon the topics discussed in a large portion of the speech which he has just delivered. I make these remarks for the purpose of excusing myself for not passing over the entire ground that the Judge has traversed. I however desire to take up some of the points that he has attended to, and ask your attention to them, and I shall follow him backwards upon some notes which I have taken, reversing the order, by beginning where he concluded.

The Judge has alluded to the Declaration of Independence, and insisted that negroes are not included in that Declaration; and that it is a slander upon the framers of that instrument to suppose that negroes were meant therein; and he asks you: Is it possible to believe that Mr. Jefferson, who penned the immortal paper, could have supposed himself applying the language of that instrument to the negro race, and yet held a portion of that race in slavery? Would he not at once have freed them? I only have to remark upon this part of the Judge's speech (and that, too, very briefly, for I shall not detain myself, or you, upon that point for any great length of time), that I believe the entire records of the world, from the date of the Declaration of Independence up to within three years ago, may be searched in vain for one single affirmation, from one single man, that the negro was not included in the Declaration of Independence; I think I may defy Judge Douglas to show that he ever said so, that Washington ever said so, that any President ever said so, that any member of Congress ever said so, or that any living man upon the whole earth ever said so, until the necessities of the present policy of the Democratic party, in regard to slavery, had to invent that affirmation. And I will remind Judge Douglas and this audience that while Mr. Jefferson was the owner of slaves, as undoubtedly he was, in speaking upon this very subject he used the strong language that "he trembled for his country when he remembered that God was just"; and I will offer the highest premium in my power to Judge Douglas if he will show that he, in all his life, ever uttered a sentiment at all akin to that of Jefferson.

The next thing to which I will ask your attention is the Judge's comments upon the fact, as he assumes it to be, that we cannot call our public meetings as Republican meetings; and he instances Tazewell County as one of the places where the friends of Lincoln have called a public meeting and have not dared to name it a Republican meeting. He instances Monroe County as another, where Judge Trumbull and Jehu Baker addressed the persons whom the Judge assumes to be the friends of Lincoln calling them the "Free Democracy." I have the honor to inform Judge Douglas that he spoke in that very county of Tazewell last Saturday, and I was there on Tuesday last; and when he spoke there, he spoke under a call not venturing to use the word "Democrat." [Turning to Judge Douglas.] what think you of this?

So, again, there is another thing to which I would ask the Judge's attention upon this subject. In the contest of 1856 his party delighted to call themselves together as the "National Democracy"; but now, if there should be a notice put up anywhere for a meeting of the "National Democracy," Judge Douglas and his friends would not come. They would not suppose themselves invited. They would understand that it was a call for those hateful postmasters whom he talks about.

Now a few words in regard to these extracts from speeches of mine which Judge Douglas has read to you, and which he supposes are in very great contrast to each other. Those speeches have been before the public for a considerable time, and if they have any inconsistency in them, if there is any conflict in them, the public have been able to detect it. When the Judge says, in speaking on this subject, that I make speeches of one sort for the people of the northern end of the State, and of a different sort for the southern people, he assumes that I do not understand that my speeches will be put in print and read north and south. I knew all the while that the speech that I made at Chicago, and the one I made at Jonesboro and the one at Charleston, would all be put in print, and all the reading and intelligent men in the community would see them and know all about my opinions. And I have not supposed, and do not now suppose, that there is any conflict whatever between them. But the Judge will have it that if we do not confess that there is a sort of inequality between the white and black races which justifies us in making them slaves, we must then insist that there is a degree of equality that requires us to make them our wives. Now, I have all the while taken a broad distinction in regard to that matter; and that is all there is in these different speeches which he arrays here; and the entire reading of either of the speeches will show that that distinction was made. Perhaps by taking two parts of the same speech he could have got up as much of a conflict as the one he has found. I have all the while maintained that in so far as it should be insisted that there was an equality between the white and black races that should produce a perfect social and political equality, it was an impossibility. This you have seen in my printed speeches, and with it I have said that in their right to "life, liberty, and the pursuit of happiness," as proclaimed in that old Declaration, the inferior races are our equals. And these declarations I have constantly made in reference to the abstract moral question, to contemplate and consider when we are legislating about any new country which is not already cursed with the actual presence of the evil,—slavery. I have never manifested any impatience with the necessities that spring from the actual presence of black people amongst us, and the actual existence of slavery amongst us where it does already exist; but I have insisted that, in legislating for new countries where it does not exist there is no just rule other than that of moral and abstract right! With reference to those new countries, those maxims as to the right of a people to "life, liberty, and the pursuit of happiness" were the just rules to be constantly referred to. There is no misunderstanding this, except by men interested to misunderstand it. I take it that I have to address an intelligent and reading community, who will peruse what I say, weigh it, and then judge whether I advanced improper or unsound views, or whether I advanced hypocritical, and deceptive, and contrary views in different portions of the country. I believe myself to be guilty of no such thing as the latter, though, of course, I cannot claim that I am entirely free from all error in the opinions I advance.

The Judge has also detained us awhile in regard to the distinction between his party and our party. His he assumes to be a national party, ours a sectional one. He does this in asking the question whether this country has any interest in the maintenance of the Republican party. He assumes that our party is altogether sectional, that the party to which he adheres is national; and the argument is, that no party can be a rightful party—and be based upon rightful principles—unless it can announce its principles everywhere. I presume that Judge Douglas could not go into Russia and announce the doctrine of our national Democracy; he could not denounce the doctrine of kings and emperors and monarchies in Russia; and it may be true of this country that in some places we may not be able to proclaim a doctrine as clearly true as the truth of democracy, because there is a section so directly opposed to it that they will not tolerate us in doing so. Is it the true test of the soundness of a doctrine that in some places people won't let you proclaim it? Is that the way to test the truth of any doctrine? Why, I understood that at one time the people of Chicago would not let Judge Douglas preach a certain favorite doctrine of his. I commend to his consideration the question whether he takes that as a test of the unsoundness of what he wanted to preach.

There is another thing to which I wish to ask attention for a little while on this occasion. What has always been the evidence brought forward to prove that the Republican party is a sectional party? The main one was that in the Southern portion of the Union the people did not let the Republicans proclaim their doctrines amongst them. That has been the main evidence brought forward,—that they had no supporters, or substantially none, in the Slave States. The South have not taken hold of our principles as we announce them; nor does Judge Douglas now grapple with those principles. We have a Republican State Platform, laid down in Springfield in June last stating our position all the way through the questions before the country. We are now far advanced in this canvass. Judge Douglas and I have made perhaps forty speeches apiece, and we have now for the fifth time met face to face in debate, and up to this day I have not found either Judge Douglas or any friend of his taking hold of the Republican platform, or laying his finger upon anything in it that is wrong. I ask you all to recollect that. Judge Douglas turns away from the platform of principles to the fact that he can find people somewhere who will not allow us to announce those principles. If he had great confidence that our principles were wrong, he would take hold of them and demonstrate them to be wrong. But he does not do so. The only evidence he has of their being wrong is in the fact that there are people who won't allow us to preach them. I ask again, is that the way to test the soundness of a doctrine?

I ask his attention also to the fact that by the rule of nationality he is himself fast becoming sectional. I ask his attention to the fact that his speeches would not go as current now south of the Ohio River as they have formerly gone there I ask his attention to the fact that he felicitates himself to-day that all the Democrats of the free States are agreeing with him, while he omits to tell us that the Democrats of any slave State agree with him. If he has not thought of this, I commend to his consideration the evidence in his own declaration, on this day, of his becoming sectional too. I see it rapidly approaching. Whatever may be the result of this ephemeral contest between Judge Douglas and myself, I see the day rapidly approaching when his pill of sectionalism, which he has been thrusting down the throats of Republicans for years past, will be crowded down his own throat.

Now, in regard to what Judge Douglas said (in the beginning of his speech) about the Compromise of 1850 containing the principles of the Nebraska Bill, although I have often presented my views upon that subject, yet as I have not done so in this canvass, I will, if you please, detain you a little with them. I have always maintained, so far as I was able, that there was nothing of the principle of the Nebraska Bill in the Compromise of 1850 at all,—nothing whatever. Where can you find the principle of the Nebraska Bill in that Compromise? If anywhere, in the two pieces of the Compromise organizing the Territories of New Mexico and Utah. It was expressly provided in these two acts that when they came to be admitted into the Union they should be admitted with or without slavery, as they should choose, by their own constitutions. Nothing was said in either of those acts as to what was to be done in relation to slavery during the Territorial existence of those Territories, while Henry Clay constantly made the declaration (Judge Douglas recognizing him as a leader) that, in his opinion, the old Mexican laws would control that question during the Territorial existence, and that these old Mexican laws excluded slavery. How can that be used as a principle for declaring that during the Territorial existence as well as at the time of framing the constitution the people, if you please, might have slaves if they wanted them? I am not discussing the question whether it is right or wrong; but how are the New Mexican and Utah laws patterns for the Nebraska Bill? I maintain that the organization of Utah and New Mexico did not establish a general principle at all. It had no feature of establishing a general principle. The acts to which I have referred were a part of a general system of Compromises. They did not lay down what was proposed as a regular policy for the Territories, only an agreement in this particular case to do in that way, because other things were done that were to be a compensation for it. They were allowed to come in in that shape, because in another way it was paid for, considering that as a part of that system of measures called the Compromise of 1850, which finally included half-a-dozen acts. It included the admission of California as a free State, which was kept out of the Union for half a year because it had formed a free constitution. It included the settlement of the boundary of Texas, which had been undefined before, which was in itself a slavery question; for if you pushed the line farther west, you made Texas larger, and made more slave territory; while, if you drew the line toward the east, you narrowed the boundary and diminished the domain of slavery, and by so much increased free territory. It included the abolition of the slave trade in the District of Columbia. It included the passage of a new Fugitive Slave law. All these things were put together, and, though passed in separate acts, were nevertheless, in legislation (as the speeches at the time will show), made to depend upon each other. Each got votes with the understanding that the other measures were to pass, and by this system of compromise, in that series of measures, those two bills—the New Mexico and Utah bills—were passed: and I say for that reason they could not be taken as models, framed upon their own intrinsic principle, for all future Territories. And I have the evidence of this in the fact that Judge Douglas, a year afterward, or more than a year afterward, perhaps, when he first introduced bills for the purpose of framing new Territories, did not attempt to follow these bills of New Mexico and Utah; and even when he introduced this Nebraska Bill, I think you will discover that he did not exactly follow them. But I do not wish to dwell at great length upon this branch of the discussion. My own opinion is, that a thorough investigation will show most plainly that the New Mexico and Utah bills were part of a system of compromise, and not designed as patterns for future Territorial legislation; and that this Nebraska Bill did not follow them as a pattern at all.

The Judge tells, in proceeding, that he is opposed to making any odious distinctions between free and slave States. I am altogether unaware that the Republicans are in favor of making any odious distinctions between the free and slave States. But there is still a difference, I think, between Judge Douglas and the Republicans in this. I suppose that the real difference between Judge Douglas and his friends, and the Republicans on the contrary, is, that the Judge is not in favor of making any difference between slavery and liberty; that he is in favor of eradicating, of pressing out of view, the questions of preference in this country for free or slave institutions; and consequently every sentiment he utters discards the idea that there is any wrong in slavery. Everything that emanates from him or his coadjutors in their course of policy carefully excludes the thought that there is anything wrong in slavery. All their arguments, if you will consider them, will be seen to exclude the thought that there is anything whatever wrong in slavery. If you will take the Judge's speeches, and select the short and pointed sentences expressed by him,—as his declaration that he "don't care whether slavery is voted up or down,"—you will see at once that this is perfectly logical, if you do not admit that slavery is wrong. If you do admit that it is wrong, Judge Douglas cannot logically say he don't care whether a wrong is voted up or voted down. Judge Douglas declares that if any community wants slavery they have a right to have it. He can say that logically, if he says that there is no wrong in slavery; but if you admit that there is a wrong in it, he cannot logically say that anybody has a right to do wrong. He insists that upon the score of equality the owners of slaves and owners of property—of horses and every other sort of property—should be alike, and hold them alike in a new Territory. That is perfectly logical if the two species of property are alike and are equally founded in right. But if you admit that one of them is wrong, you cannot institute any equality between right and wrong. And from this difference of sentiment,—the belief on the part of one that the institution is wrong, and a policy springing from that belief which looks to the arrest of the enlargement of that wrong, and this other sentiment, that it is no wrong, and a policy sprung from that sentiment, which will tolerate no idea of preventing the wrong from growing larger, and looks to there never being an end to it through all the existence of things,—arises the real difference between Judge Douglas and his friends on the one hand and the Republicans on the other. Now, I confess myself as belonging to that class in the country who contemplate slavery as a moral, social, and political evil, having due regard for its actual existence amongst us and the difficulties of getting rid of it in any satisfactory way, and to all the constitutional obligations which have been thrown about it; but, nevertheless, desire a policy that looks to the prevention of it as a wrong, and looks hopefully to the time when as a wrong it may come to an end.

Judge Douglas has again, for, I believe, the fifth time, if not the seventh, in my presence, reiterated his charge of a conspiracy or combination between the National Democrats and Republicans. What evidence Judge Douglas has upon this subject I know not, inasmuch as he never favors us with any. I have said upon a former occasion, and I do not choose to suppress it now, that I have no objection to the division in the Judge's party. He got it up himself. It was all his and their work. He had, I think, a great deal more to do with the steps that led to the Lecompton Constitution than Mr. Buchanan had; though at last, when they reached it, they quarreled over it, and their friends divided upon it. I am very free to confess to Judge Douglas that I have no objection to the division; but I defy the Judge to show any evidence that I have in any way promoted that division, unless he insists on being a witness himself in merely saying so. I can give all fair friends of Judge Douglas here to understand exactly the view that Republicans take in regard to that division. Don't you remember how two years ago the opponents of the Democratic party were divided between Fremont and Fillmore? I guess you do. Any Democrat who remembers that division will remember also that he was at the time very glad of it, and then he will be able to see all there is between the National Democrats and the Republicans. What we now think of the two divisions of Democrats, you then thought of the Fremont and Fillmore divisions. That is all there is of it.

But if the Judge continues to put forward the declaration that there is an unholy and unnatural alliance between the Republicans and the National Democrats, I now want to enter my protest against receiving him as an entirely competent witness upon that subject. I want to call to the Judge's attention an attack he made upon me in the first one of these debates, at Ottawa, on the 21st of August. In order to fix extreme Abolitionism upon me, Judge Douglas read a set of resolutions which he declared had been passed by a Republican State Convention, in October, 1854, at Springfield, Illinois, and he declared I had taken part in that Convention. It turned out that although a few men calling themselves an anti-Nebraska State Convention had sat at Springfield about that time, yet neither did I take any part in it, nor did it pass the resolutions or any such resolutions as Judge Douglas read. So apparent had it become that the resolutions which he read had not been passed at Springfield at all, nor by a State Convention in which I had taken part, that seven days afterward, at Freeport, Judge Douglas declared that he had been misled by Charles H. Lanphier, editor of the State Register, and Thomas L. Harris, member of Congress in that district, and he promised in that speech that when he went to Springfield he would investigate the matter. Since then Judge Douglas has been to Springfield, and I presume has made the investigation; but a month has passed since he has been there, and so far as I know, he has made no report of the result of his investigation. I have waited as I think sufficient time for the report of that investigation, and I have some curiosity to see and hear it. A fraud, an absolute forgery was committed, and the perpetration of it was traced to the three,—Lanphier, Harris, and Douglas. Whether it can be narrowed in any way so as to exonerate any one of them, is what Judge Douglas's report would probably show.

It is true that the set of resolutions read by Judge Douglas were published in the Illinois State Register on the 16th of October, 1854, as being the resolutions of an anti-Nebraska Convention which had sat in that same month of October, at Springfield. But it is also true that the publication in the Register was a forgery then, and the question is still behind, which of the three, if not all of them, committed that forgery. The idea that it was done by mistake is absurd. The article in the Illinois State Register contains part of the real proceedings of that Springfield Convention, showing that the writer of the article had the real proceedings before him, and purposely threw out the genuine resolutions passed by the Convention and fraudulently substituted the others. Lanphier then, as now, was the editor of the Register, so that there seems to be but little room for his escape. But then it is to be borne in mind that Lanphier had less interest in the object of that forgery than either of the other two. The main object of that forgery at that time was to beat Yates and elect Harris to Congress, and that object was known to be exceedingly dear to Judge Douglas at that time. Harris and Douglas were both in Springfield when the Convention was in session, and although they both left before the fraud appeared in the Register, subsequent events show that they have both had their eyes fixed upon that Convention.

The fraud having been apparently successful upon the occasion, both Harris and Douglas have more than once since then been attempting to put it to new uses. As the fisherman's wife, whose drowned husband was brought home with his body full of eels, said when she was asked what was to be done with him, "Take the eels out and set him again," so Harris and Douglas have shown a disposition to take the eels out of that stale fraud by which they gained Harris's election, and set the fraud again more than once. On the 9th of July, 1856, Douglas attempted a repetition of it upon Trumbull on the floor of the Senate of the United States, as will appear from the appendix of the Congressional Globe of that date.

On the 9th of August, Harris attempted it again upon Norton in the House of Representatives, as will appear by the same documents,—the appendix to the Congressional Globe of that date. On the 21st of August last, all three—Lanphier, Douglas, and Harris—reattempted it upon me at Ottawa. It has been clung to and played out again and again as an exceedingly high trump by this blessed trio. And now that it has been discovered publicly to be a fraud we find that Judge Douglas manifests no surprise at it at all. He makes no complaint of Lanphier, who must have known it to be a fraud from the beginning. He, Lanphier, and Harris are just as cozy now and just as active in the concoction of new schemes as they were before the general discovery of this fraud. Now, all this is very natural if they are all alike guilty in that fraud, and it is very unnatural if any one of them is innocent. Lanphier perhaps insists that the rule of honor among thieves does not quite require him to take all upon himself, and consequently my friend Judge Douglas finds it difficult to make a satisfactory report upon his investigation. But meanwhile the three are agreed that each is "a most honorable man."

Judge Douglas requires an indorsement of his truth and honor by a re-election to the United States Senate, and he makes and reports against me and against Judge Trumbull, day after day, charges which we know to be utterly untrue, without for a moment seeming to think that this one unexplained fraud, which he promised to investigate, will be the least drawback to his claim to belief. Harris ditto. He asks a re-election to the lower House of Congress without seeming to remember at all that he is involved in this dishonorable fraud! The Illinois State Register, edited by Lanphier, then, as now, the central organ of both Harris and Douglas, continues to din the public ear with this assertion, without seeming to suspect that these assertions are at all lacking in title to belief.

After all, the question still recurs upon us, How did that fraud originally get into the State Register? Lanphier then, as now, was the editor of that paper. Lanphier knows. Lanphier cannot be ignorant of how and by whom it was originally concocted. Can he be induced to tell, or, if he has told, can Judge Douglas be induced to tell how it originally was concocted? It may be true that Lanphier insists that the two men for whose benefit it was originally devised shall at least bear their share of it! How that is, I do not know, and while it remains unexplained I hope to be pardoned if I insist that the mere fact of Judge Douglas making charges against Trumbull and myself is not quite sufficient evidence to establish them!

While we were at Freeport, in one of these joint discussions, I answered certain interrogatories which Judge Douglas had propounded to me, and then in turn propounded some to him, which he in a sort of way answered. The third one of these interrogatories I have with me, and wish now to make some comments upon it. It was in these words: "If the Supreme Court of States cannot exclude slavery from their limits, are you in favor of acquiescing in, adhering to, and following such decision as a rule of political action?"

To this interrogatory Judge Douglas made no answer in any just sense of the word. He contented himself with sneering at the thought that it was possible for the Supreme Court ever to make such a decision. He sneered at me for propounding the interrogatory. I had not propounded it without some reflection, and I wish now to address to this audience some remarks upon it.

In the second clause of the sixth article, I believe it is, of the Constitution of the United States, we find the following language:

"This Constitution and the laws of the United States which shall be made in pursuance thereof, and all treaties made, or which shall be made, under the authority of the United States, shall be the supreme law of the land; and the judges in every State shall be bound thereby, anything in the Constitution or laws of any State to the contrary notwithstanding."

The essence of the Dred Scott case is compressed into the sentence which I will now read:

"Now, as we have already said in an earlier part of this opinion, upon a different point, the right of property in a slave is distinctly and expressly affirmed in the Constitution."

I repeat it, "The right of property in a slave is distinctly and expressly affirmed in the Constitution"! What is it to be "affirmed" in the Constitution? Made firm in the Constitution, so made that it cannot be separated from the Constitution without breaking the Constitution; durable as the Constitution, and part of the Constitution. Now, remembering the provision of the Constitution which I have read—affirming that that instrument is the supreme law of the land; that the judges of every State shall be bound by it, any law or constitution of any State to the contrary notwithstanding; that the right of property in a slave is affirmed in that Constitution, is made, formed into, and cannot be separated from it without breaking it; durable as the instrument; part of the instrument;—what follows as a short and even syllogistic argument from it? I think it follows, and I submit to the consideration of men capable of arguing whether, as I state it, in syllogistic form, the argument has any fault in it:

Nothing in the Constitution or laws of any State can destroy a right distinctly and expressly affirmed in the Constitution of the United States.

The right of property in a slave is distinctly and expressly affirmed in the Constitution of the United States.

Therefore, nothing in the Constitution or laws of any State can destroy the right of property in a slave.

I believe that no fault can be pointed out in that argument; assuming the truth of the premises, the conclusion, so far as I have capacity at all to understand it, follows inevitably. There is a fault in it as I think, but the fault is not in the reasoning; but the falsehood in fact is a fault of the premises. I believe that the right of property in a slave is not distinctly and expressly affirmed in the Constitution, and Judge Douglas thinks it is. I believe that the Supreme Court and the advocates of that decision may search in vain for the place in the Constitution where the right of property in a slave is distinctly and expressly affirmed I say, therefore, that I think one of the premises is not true in fact. But it is true with Judge Douglas. It is true with the Supreme Court who pronounced it. They are estopped from denying it, and being estopped from denying it, the conclusion follows that, the Constitution of the United States being the supreme law, no constitution or law can interfere with it. It being affirmed in the decision that the right of property in a slave is distinctly and expressly affirmed in the Constitution, the conclusion inevitably follows that no State law or constitution can destroy that right. I then say to Judge Douglas and to all others that I think it will take a better answer than a sneer to show that those who have said that the right of property in a slave is distinctly and expressly affirmed in the Constitution, are not prepared to show that no constitution or law can destroy that right. I say I believe it will take a far better argument than a mere sneer to show to the minds of intelligent men that whoever has so said is not prepared, whenever public sentiment is so far advanced as to justify it, to say the other. This is but an opinion, and the opinion of one very humble man; but it is my opinion that the Dred Scott decision, as it is, never would have been made in its present form if the party that made it had not been sustained previously by the elections. My own opinion is, that the new Dred Scott decision, deciding against the right of the people of the States to exclude slavery, will never be made if that party is not sustained by the elections. I believe, further, that it is just as sure to be made as to-morrow is to come, if that party shall be sustained. I have said, upon a former occasion, and I repeat it now, that the course of arguement that Judge Douglas makes use of upon this subject (I charge not his motives in this), is preparing the public mind for that new Dred Scott decision. I have asked him again to point out to me the reasons for his first adherence to the Dred Scott decision as it is. I have turned his attention to the fact that General Jackson differed with him in regard to the political obligation of a Supreme Court decision. I have asked his attention to the fact that Jefferson differed with him in regard to the political obligation of a Supreme Court decision. Jefferson said that "Judges are as honest as other men, and not more so." And he said, substantially, that whenever a free people should give up in absolute submission to any department of government, retaining for themselves no appeal from it, their liberties were gone. I have asked his attention to the fact that the Cincinnati platform, upon which he says he stands, disregards a time-honored decision of the Supreme Court, in denying the power of Congress to establish a National Bank. I have asked his attention to the fact that he himself was one of the most active instruments at one time in breaking down the Supreme Court of the State of Illinois because it had made a decision distasteful to him,—a struggle ending in the remarkable circumstance of his sitting down as one of the new Judges who were to overslaugh that decision; getting his title of Judge in that very way.

So far in this controversy I can get no answer at all from Judge Douglas upon these subjects. Not one can I get from him, except that he swells himself up and says, "All of us who stand by the decision of the Supreme Court are the friends of the Constitution; all you fellows that dare question it in any way are the enemies of the Constitution." Now, in this very devoted adherence to this decision, in opposition to all the great political leaders whom he has recognized as leaders, in opposition to his former self and history, there is something very marked. And the manner in which he adheres to it,—not as being right upon the merits, as he conceives (because he did not discuss that at all), but as being absolutely obligatory upon every one simply because of the source from whence it comes, as that which no man can gainsay, whatever it may be,—this is another marked feature of his adherence to that decision. It marks it in this respect, that it commits him to the next decision, whenever it comes, as being as obligatory as this one, since he does not investigate it, and won't inquire whether this opinion is right or wrong. So he takes the next one without inquiring whether it is right or wrong. He teaches men this doctrine, and in so doing prepares the public mind to take the next decision when it comes, without any inquiry. In this I think I argue fairly (without questioning motives at all) that Judge Douglas is most ingeniously and powerfully preparing the public mind to take that decision when it comes; and not only so, but he is doing it in various other ways. In these general maxims about liberty, in his assertions that he "don't care whether slavery is voted up or voted down,"; that "whoever wants slavery has a right to have it"; that "upon principles of equality it should be allowed to go everywhere"; that "there is no inconsistency between free and slave institutions"—in this he is also preparing (whether purposely or not) the way for making the institution of slavery national! I repeat again, for I wish no misunderstanding, that I do not charge that he means it so; but I call upon your minds to inquire, if you were going to get the best instrument you could, and then set it to work in the most ingenious way, to prepare the public mind for this movement, operating in the free States, where there is now an abhorrence of the institution of slavery, could you find an instrument so capable of doing it as Judge Douglas, or one employed in so apt a way to do it?

I have said once before, and I will repeat it now, that Mr. Clay, when he was once answering an objection to the Colonization Society, that it had a tendency to the ultimate emancipation of the slaves, said that:

"Those who would repress all tendencies to liberty and ultimate emancipation must do more than put down the benevolent efforts of the Colonization Society: they must go back to the era of our liberty and independence, and muzzle the cannon that thunders its annual joyous return; they must blow out the moral lights around us; they must penetrate the human soul, and eradicate the light of reason and the love of liberty!"

And I do think—I repeat, though I said it on a former occasion—that Judge Douglas and whoever, like him, teaches that the negro has no share, humble though it may be, in the Declaration of Independence, is going back to the era of our liberty and independence, and, so far as in him lies, muzzling the cannon that thunders its annual joyous return; that he is blowing out the moral lights around us, when he contends that whoever wants slaves has a right to hold them; that he is penetrating, so far as lies in his power, the human soul, and eradicating the light of reason and the love of liberty, when he is in every possible way preparing the public mind, by his vast influence, for making the institution of slavery perpetual and national.

There is, my friends, only one other point to which I will call your attention for the remaining time that I have left me, and perhaps I shall not occupy the entire time that I have, as that one point may not take me clear through it.

Among the interrogatories that Judge Douglas propounded to me at Freeport, there was one in about this language:

"Are you opposed to the acquisition of any further territory to the United States, unless slavery shall first be prohibited therein?"

I answered, as I thought, in this way: that I am not generally opposed to the acquisition of additional territory, and that I would support a proposition for the acquisition of additional territory according as my supporting it was or was not calculated to aggravate this slavery question amongst us. I then proposed to Judge Douglas another interrogatory, which was correlative to that: "Are you in favor of acquiring additional territory, in disregard of how it may affect us upon the slavery question?" Judge Douglas answered,—that is, in his own way he answered it. I believe that, although he took a good many words to answer it, it was a little more fully answered than any other. The substance of his answer was that this country would continue to expand; that it would need additional territory; that it was as absurd to suppose that we could continue upon our present territory, enlarging in population as we are, as it would be to hoop a boy twelve years of age, and expect him to grow to man's size without bursting the hoops. I believe it was something like that. Consequently, he was in favor of the acquisition of further territory as fast as we might need it, in disregard of how it might affect the slavery question. I do not say this as giving his exact language, but he said so substantially; and he would leave the question of slavery, where the territory was acquired, to be settled by the people of the acquired territory. ["That's the doctrine."] May be it is; let us consider that for a while. This will probably, in the run of things, become one of the concrete manifestations of this slavery question. If Judge Douglas's policy upon this question succeeds, and gets fairly settled down, until all opposition is crushed out, the next thing will be a grab for the territory of poor Mexico, an invasion of the rich lands of South America, then the adjoining islands will follow, each one of which promises additional slave-fields. And this question is to be left to the people of those countries for settlement. When we get Mexico, I don't know whether the Judge will be in favor of the Mexican people that we get with it settling that question for themselves and all others; because we know the Judge has a great horror for mongrels, and I understand that the people of Mexico are most decidedly a race of mongrels. I understand that there is not more than one person there out of eight who is pure white, and I suppose from the Judge's previous declaration that when we get Mexico, or any considerable portion of it, that he will be in favor of these mongrels settling the question, which would bring him somewhat into collision with his horror of an inferior race.

It is to be remembered, though, that this power of acquiring additional territory is a power confided to the President and the Senate of the United States. It is a power not under the control of the representatives of the people any further than they, the President and the Senate, can be considered the representatives of the people. Let me illustrate that by a case we have in our history. When we acquired the territory from Mexico in the Mexican War, the House of Representatives, composed of the immediate representatives of the people, all the time insisted that the territory thus to be acquired should be brought in upon condition that slavery should be forever prohibited therein, upon the terms and in the language that slavery had been prohibited from coming into this country. That was insisted upon constantly and never failed to call forth an assurance that any territory thus acquired should have that prohibition in it, so far as the House of Representatives was concerned. But at last the President and Senate acquired the territory without asking the House of Representatives anything about it, and took it without that prohibition. They have the power of acquiring territory without the immediate representatives of the people being called upon to say anything about it, and thus furnishing a very apt and powerful means of bringing new territory into the Union, and, when it is once brought into the country, involving us anew in this slavery agitation. It is therefore, as I think, a very important question for due consideration of the American people, whether the policy of bringing in additional territory, without considering at all how it will operate upon the safety of the Union in reference to this one great disturbing element in our national politics, shall be adopted as the policy of the country. You will bear in mind that it is to be acquired, according to the Judge's view, as fast as it is needed, and the indefinite part of this proposition is that we have only Judge Douglas and his class of men to decide how fast it is needed. We have no clear and certain way of determining or demonstrating how fast territory is needed by the necessities of the country. Whoever wants to go out filibustering, then, thinks that more territory is needed. Whoever wants wider slave-fields feels sure that some additional territory is needed as slave territory. Then it is as easy to show the necessity of additional slave-territory as it is to assert anything that is incapable of absolute demonstration. Whatever motive a man or a set of men may have for making annexation of property or territory, it is very easy to assert, but much less easy to disprove, that it is necessary for the wants of the country.

And now it only remains for me to say that I think it is a very grave question for the people of this Union to consider, whether, in view of the fact that this slavery question has been the only one that has ever endangered our Republican institutions, the only one that has ever threatened or menaced a dissolution of the Union, that has ever disturbed us in such a way as to make us fear for the perpetuity of our liberty,—in view of these facts, I think it is an exceedingly interesting and important question for this people to consider whether we shall engage in the policy of acquiring additional territory, discarding altogether from our consideration, while obtaining new territory, the question how it may affect us in regard to this, the only endangering element to our liberties and national greatness. The Judge's view has been expressed. I, in my answer to his question, have expressed mine. I think it will become an important and practical question. Our views are before the public. I am willing and anxious that they should consider them fully; that they should turn it about and consider the importance of the question, and arrive at a just conclusion as to whether it is or is not wise in the people of this Union, in the acquisition of new territory, to consider whether it will add to the disturbance that is existing amongst us—whether it will add to the one only danger that has ever threatened the perpetuity of the Union or our own liberties. I think it is extremely important that they shall decide, and rightly decide, that question before entering upon that policy.

And now, my friends, having said the little I wish to say upon this head, whether I have occupied the whole of the remnant of my time or not, I believe I could not enter upon any new topic so as to treat it fully, without transcending my time, which I would not for a moment think of doing. I give way to Judge Douglas.

SIXTH JOINT DEBATE, AT QUINCY, OCTOBER 13, 1858.

LADIES AND GENTLEMEN: I have had no immediate conference with Judge Douglas, but I will venture to say that he and I will perfectly agree that your entire silence, both when I speak and when he speaks, will be most agreeable to us.

In the month of May, 1856, the elements in the State of Illinois which have since been consolidated into the Republican party assembled together in a State Convention at Bloomington. They adopted at that time what, in political language, is called a platform. In June of the same year the elements of the Republican party in the nation assembled together in a National Convention at Philadelphia. They adopted what is called the National Platform. In June, 1858,—the present year,—the Republicans of Illinois reassembled at Springfield, in State Convention, and adopted again their platform, as I suppose not differing in any essential particular from either of the former ones, but perhaps adding something in relation to the new developments of political progress in the country.

The Convention that assembled in June last did me the honor, if it be one, and I esteem it such, to nominate me as their candidate for the United States Senate. I have supposed that, in entering upon this canvass, I stood generally upon these platforms. We are now met together on the 13th of October of the same year, only four months from the adoption of the last platform, and I am unaware that in this canvass, from the beginning until to-day, any one of our adversaries has taken hold of our platforms, or laid his finger upon anything that he calls wrong in them.

In the very first one of these joint discussions between Senator Douglas and myself, Senator Douglas, without alluding at all to these platforms, or any one of them, of which I have spoken, attempted to hold me responsible for a set of resolutions passed long before the meeting of either one of these conventions of which I have spoken. And as a ground for holding me responsible for these resolutions, he assumed that they had been passed at a State Convention of the Republican party, and that I took part in that Convention. It was discovered afterward that this was erroneous, that the resolutions which he endeavored to hold me responsible for had not been passed by any State Convention anywhere, had not been passed at Springfield, where he supposed they had, or assumed that they had, and that they had been passed in no convention in which I had taken part. The Judge, nevertheless, was not willing to give up the point that he was endeavoring to make upon me, and he therefore thought to still hold me to the point that he was endeavoring to make, by showing that the resolutions that he read had been passed at a local convention in the northern part of the State, although it was not a local convention that embraced my residence at all, nor one that reached, as I suppose, nearer than one hundred and fifty or two hundred miles of where I was when it met, nor one in which I took any part at all. He also introduced other resolutions, passed at other meetings, and by combining the whole, although they were all antecedent to the two State Conventions and the one National Convention I have mentioned, still he insisted, and now insists, as I understand, that I am in some way responsible for them.

At Jonesboro, on our third meeting, I insisted to the Judge that I was in no way rightfully held responsible for the proceedings of this local meeting or convention, in which I had taken no part, and in which I was in no way embraced; but I insisted to him that if he thought I was responsible for every man or every set of men everywhere, who happen to be my friends, the rule ought to work both ways, and he ought to be responsible for the acts and resolutions of all men or sets of men who were or are now his supporters and friends, and gave him a pretty long string of resolutions, passed by men who are now his friends, and announcing doctrines for which he does not desire to be held responsible.

This still does not satisfy Judge Douglas. He still adheres to his proposition, that I am responsible for what some of my friends in different parts of the State have done, but that he is not responsible for what his have done. At least, so I understand him. But in addition to that, the Judge, at our meeting in Galesburgh, last week, undertakes to establish that I am guilty of a species of double dealing with the public; that I make speeches of a certain sort in the north, among the Abolitionists, which I would not make in the south, and that I make speeches of a certain sort in the south which I would not make in the north. I apprehend, in the course I have marked out for myself, that I shall not have to dwell at very great length upon this subject.

As this was done in the Judge's opening speech at Galesburgh, I had an opportunity, as I had the middle speech then, of saying something in answer to it. He brought forward a quotation or two from a speech of mine delivered at Chicago, and then, to contrast with it, he brought forward an extract from a speech of mine at Charleston, in which he insisted that I was greatly inconsistent, and insisted that his conclusion followed, that I was playing a double part, and speaking in one region one way, and in another region another way. I have not time now to dwell on this as long as I would like, and wish only now to requote that portion of my speech at Charleston which the Judge quoted, and then make some comments upon it. This he quotes from me as being delivered at Charleston, and I believe correctly:

"I will say, then, that I am not, nor ever have been, in favor of bringing about in any way the social and political equality of the white and black races; that I am not, nor ever have been, in favor of making voters or jurors of negroes, nor of qualifying them to hold office, nor to intermarry with white people; and I will say, in addition to this, that there is a physical difference between the white and black races which will forever forbid the two races living together on terms of social and political equality. And inasmuch as they cannot so live while they do remain together, there must be the position of superior and inferior. I am as much as any other man in favor of having the superior position assigned to the white race."

This, I believe, is the entire quotation from Charleston speech, as Judge Douglas made it his comments are as follows:

"Yes, here you find men who hurrah for Lincoln, and say he is right when he discards all distinction between races, or when he declares that he discards the doctrine that there is such a thing as a superior and inferior race; and Abolitionists are required and expected to vote for Mr. Lincoln because he goes for the equality of races, holding that in the Declaration of Independence the white man and negro were declared equal, and endowed by divine law with equality. And down South, with the old-line Whigs, with the Kentuckians, the Virginians and the Tennesseeans, he tells you that there is a physical difference between the races, making the one superior, the other inferior, and he is in favor of maintaining the superiority of the white race over the negro."

Those are the Judges comments. Now, I wish to show you that a month, or only lacking three days of a month, before I made the speech at Charleston, which the Judge quotes from, he had himself heard me say substantially the same thing It was in our first meeting, at Ottawa—and I will say a word about where it was, and the atmosphere it was in, after a while—but at our first meeting, at Ottawa, I read an extract from an old speech of mine, made nearly four years ago, not merely to show my sentiments, but to show that my sentiments were long entertained and openly expressed; in which extract I expressly declared that my own feelings would not admit a social and political equality between the white and black races, and that even if my own feelings would admit of it, I still knew that the public sentiment of the country would not, and that such a thing was an utter impossibility, or substantially that. That extract from my old speech the reporters by some sort of accident passed over, and it was not reported. I lay no blame upon anybody. I suppose they thought that I would hand it over to them, and dropped reporting while I was giving it, but afterward went away without getting it from me. At the end of that quotation from my old speech, which I read at Ottawa, I made the comments which were reported at that time, and which I will now read, and ask you to notice how very nearly they are the same as Judge Douglas says were delivered by me down in Egypt. After reading, I added these words:

"Now, gentlemen, I don't want to read at any great length; but this is the true complexion of all I have ever said in regard to the institution of slavery or the black race, and this is the whole of it: anything that argues me into his idea of perfect social and political equality with the negro, is but a specious and fantastical arrangement of words by which a man can prove a horse-chestnut to be a chestnut horse. I will say here, while upon this subject, that I have no purpose, directly or indirectly, to interfere with the institution in the States where it exists. I believe I have no right to do so. I have no inclination to do so. I have no purpose to introduce political and social equality between the white and black races. There is a physical difference between the two which, in my judgment, will probably forever forbid their living together on the footing of perfect equality; and inasmuch as it becomes a necessity that there must be a difference, I, as well as Judge Douglas, am in favor of the race to which I belong having the superior position. I have never said anything to the contrary, but I hold that, notwithstanding all this, there is no reason in the world why the negro is not entitled to all the rights enumerated in the Declaration of Independence,—the right of life, liberty, and the pursuit of happiness. I hold that he is as much entitled to these as the white man. I agree with Judge Douglas that he is not my equal in many respects, certainly not in color, perhaps not in intellectual and moral endowments; but in the right to eat the bread, without the leave of anybody else, which his own hand earns, he is my equal and the equal of Judge Douglas, and the equal of every other man."

I have chiefly introduced this for the purpose of meeting the Judge's charge that the quotation he took from my Charleston speech was what I would say down South among the Kentuckians, the Virginians, etc., but would not say in the regions in which was supposed to be more of the Abolition element. I now make this comment: That speech from which I have now read the quotation, and which is there given correctly—perhaps too much so for good taste—was made away up North in the Abolition District of this State par excellence, in the Lovejoy District, in the personal presence of Lovejoy, for he was on the stand with us when I made it. It had been made and put in print in that region only three days less than a month before the speech made at Charleston, the like of which Judge Douglas thinks I would not make where there was any Abolition element. I only refer to this matter to say that I am altogether unconscious of having attempted any double-dealing anywhere; that upon one occasion I may say one thing, and leave other things unsaid, and vice versa, but that I have said anything on one occasion that is inconsistent with what I have said elsewhere, I deny, at least I deny it so far as the intention is concerned. I find that I have devoted to this topic a larger portion of my time than I had intended. I wished to show, but I will pass it upon this occasion, that in the sentiment I have occasionally advanced upon the Declaration of Independence I am entirely borne out by the sentiments advanced by our old Whig leader, Henry Clay, and I have the book here to show it from but because I have already occupied more time than I intended to do on that topic, I pass over it.

At Galesburgh, I tried to show that by the Dred Scott decision, pushed to its legitimate consequences, slavery would be established in all the States as well as in the Territories. I did this because, upon a former occasion, I had asked Judge Douglas whether, if the Supreme Court should make a decision declaring that the States had not the power to exclude slavery from their limits, he would adopt and follow that decision as a rule of political action; and because he had not directly answered that question, but had merely contented himself with sneering at it, I again introduced it, and tried to show that the conclusion that I stated followed inevitably and logically from the proposition already decided by the court. Judge Douglas had the privilege of replying to me at Galesburgh, and again he gave me no direct answer as to whether he would or would not sustain such a decision if made. I give him his third chance to say yes or no. He is not obliged to do either, probably he will not do either; but I give him the third chance. I tried to show then that this result, this conclusion, inevitably followed from the point already decided by the court. The Judge, in his reply, again sneers at the thought of the court making any such decision, and in the course of his remarks upon this subject uses the language which I will now read. Speaking of me, the Judge says:

"He goes on and insists that the Dred Scott decision would carry slavery into the free States, notwithstanding the decision itself says the contrary." And he adds:

"Mr. Lincoln knows that there is no member of the Supreme Court that holds that doctrine. He knows that every one of them in their opinions held the reverse."

I especially introduce this subject again for the purpose of saying that I have the Dred Scott decision here, and I will thank Judge Douglas to lay his finger upon the place in the entire opinions of the court where any one of them "says the contrary." It is very hard to affirm a negative with entire confidence. I say, however, that I have examined that decision with a good deal of care, as a lawyer examines a decision and, so far as I have been able to do so, the court has nowhere in its opinions said that the States have the power to exclude slavery, nor have they used other language substantially that, I also say, so far as I can find, not one of the concurring judges has said that the States can exclude slavery, nor said anything that was substantially that. The nearest approach that any one of them has made to it, so far as I can find, was by Judge Nelson, and the approach he made to it was exactly, in substance, the Nebraska Bill,—that the States had the exclusive power over the question of slavery, so far as they are not limited by the Constitution of the United States. I asked the question, therefore, if the non-concurring judges, McLean or Curtis, had asked to get an express declaration that the States could absolutely exclude slavery from their limits, what reason have we to believe that it would not have been voted down by the majority of the judges, just as Chase's amendment was voted down by Judge Douglas and his compeers when it was offered to the Nebraska Bill.

Also, at Galesburgh, I said something in regard to those Springfield resolutions that Judge Douglas had attempted to use upon me at Ottawa, and commented at some length upon the fact that they were, as presented, not genuine. Judge Douglas in his reply to me seemed to be somewhat exasperated. He said he would never have believed that Abraham Lincoln, as he kindly called me, would have attempted such a thing as I had attempted upon that occasion; and among other expressions which he used toward me, was that I dared to say forgery, that I had dared to say forgery [turning to Judge Douglas]. Yes, Judge, I did dare to say forgery. But in this political canvass the Judge ought to remember that I was not the first who dared to say forgery. At Jacksonville, Judge Douglas made a speech in answer to something said by Judge Trumbull, and at the close of what he said upon that subject, he dared to say that Trumbull had forged his evidence. He said, too, that he should not concern himself with Trumbull any more, but thereafter he should hold Lincoln responsible for the slanders upon him. When I met him at Charleston after that, although I think that I should not have noticed the subject if he had not said he would hold me responsible for it, I spread out before him the statements of the evidence that Judge Trumbull had used, and I asked Judge Douglas, piece by piece, to put his finger upon one piece of all that evidence that he would say was a forgery! When I went through with each and every piece, Judge Douglas did not dare then to say that any piece of it was a forgery. So it seems that there are some things that Judge Douglas dares to do, and some that he dares not to do.

[A voice: It is the same thing with you.]

Yes, sir, it is the same thing with me. I do dare to say forgery when it is true, and don't dare to say forgery when it is false. Now I will say here to this audience and to Judge Douglas I have not dared to say he committed a forgery, and I never shall until I know it; but I did dare to say—just to suggest to the Judge—that a forgery had been committed, which by his own showing had been traced to him and two of his friends. I dared to suggest to him that he had expressly promised in one of his public speeches to investigate that matter, and I dared to suggest to him that there was an implied promise that when he investigated it he would make known the result. I dared to suggest to the Judge that he could not expect to be quite clear of suspicion of that fraud, for since the time that promise was made he had been with those friends, and had not kept his promise in regard to the investigation and the report upon it. I am not a very daring man, but I dared that much, Judge, and I am not much scared about it yet. When the Judge says he would n't have believed of Abraham Lincoln that he would have made such an attempt as that he reminds me of the fact that he entered upon this canvass with the purpose to treat me courteously; that touched me somewhat. It sets me to thinking. I was aware, when it was first agreed that Judge Douglas and I were to have these seven joint discussions, that they were the successive acts of a drama, perhaps I should say, to be enacted, not merely in the face of audiences like this, but in the face of the nation, and to some extent, by my relation to him, and not from anything in myself, in the face of the world; and I am anxious that they should be conducted with dignity and in the good temper which would be befitting the vast audiences before which it was conducted. But when Judge Douglas got home from Washington and made his first speech in Chicago, the evening afterward I made some sort of a reply to it. His second speech was made at Bloomington, in which he commented upon my speech at Chicago and said that I had used language ingeniously contrived to conceal my intentions, or words to that effect. Now, I understand that this is an imputation upon my veracity and my candor. I do not know what the Judge understood by it, but in our first discussion, at Ottawa, he led off by charging a bargain, somewhat corrupt in its character, upon Trumbull and myself,—that we had entered into a bargain, one of the terms of which was that Trumbull was to Abolitionize the old Democratic party, and I (Lincoln) was to Abolitionize the old Whig party; I pretending to be as good an old-line Whig as ever. Judge Douglas may not understand that he implicated my truthfulness and my honor when he said I was doing one thing and pretending another; and I misunderstood him if he thought he was treating me in a dignified way, as a man of honor and truth, as he now claims he was disposed to treat me. Even after that time, at Galesburgh, when he brings forward an extract from a speech made at Chicago and an extract from a speech made at Charleston, to prove that I was trying to play a double part, that I was trying to cheat the public, and get votes upon one set of principles at one place, and upon another set of principles at another place,—I do not understand but what he impeaches my honor, my veracity, and my candor; and because he does this, I do not understand that I am bound, if I see a truthful ground for it, to keep my hands off of him. As soon as I learned that Judge Douglas was disposed to treat me in this way, I signified in one of my speeches that I should be driven to draw upon whatever of humble resources I might have,—to adopt a new course with him. I was not entirely sure that I should be able to hold my own with him, but I at least had the purpose made to do as well as I could upon him; and now I say that I will not be the first to cry "Hold." I think it originated with the Judge, and when he quits, I probably will. But I shall not ask any favors at all. He asks me, or he asks the audience, if I wish to push this matter to the point of personal difficulty. I tell him, no. He did not make a mistake, in one of his early speeches, when he called me an "amiable" man, though perhaps he did when he called me an "intelligent" man. It really hurts me very much to suppose that I have wronged anybody on earth. I again tell him, no! I very much prefer, when this canvass shall be over, however it may result, that we at least part without any bitter recollections of personal difficulties.

The Judge, in his concluding speech at Galesburgh, says that I was pushing this matter to a personal difficulty, to avoid the responsibility for the enormity of my principles. I say to the Judge and this audience, now, that I will again state our principles, as well as I hastily can, in all their enormity, and if the Judge hereafter chooses to confine himself to a war upon these principles, he will probably not find me departing from the same course.

We have in this nation this element of domestic slavery. It is a matter of absolute certainty that it is a disturbing element. It is the opinion of all the great men who have expressed an opinion upon it, that it is a dangerous element. We keep up a controversy in regard to it. That controversy necessarily springs from difference of opinion; and if we can learn exactly—can reduce to the lowest elements—what that difference of opinion is, we perhaps shall be better prepared for discussing the different systems of policy that we would propose in regard to that disturbing element. I suggest that the difference of opinion, reduced to its lowest terms, is no other than the difference between the men who think slavery a wrong and those who do not think it wrong. The Republican party think it wrong; we think it is a moral, a social, and a political wrong. We think it as a wrong not confining itself merely to the persons or the States where it exists, but that it is a wrong in its tendency, to say the least, that extends itself to the existence of the whole nation. Because we think it wrong, we propose a course of policy that shall deal with it as a wrong. We deal with it as with any other wrong, in so far as we can prevent its growing any larger, and so deal with it that in the run of time there may be some promise of an end to it. We have a due regard to the actual presence of it amongst us, and the difficulties of getting rid of it in any satisfactory way, and all the constitutional obligations thrown about it. I suppose that in reference both to its actual existence in the nation, and to our constitutional obligations, we have no right at all to disturb it in the States where it exists, and we profess that we have no more inclination to disturb it than we have the right to do it. We go further than that: we don't propose to disturb it where, in one instance, we think the Constitution would permit us. We think the Constitution would permit us to disturb it in the District of Columbia. Still, we do not propose to do that, unless it should be in terms which I don't suppose the nation is very likely soon to agree to,—the terms of making the emancipation gradual, and compensating the unwilling owners. Where we suppose we have the constitutional right, we restrain ourselves in reference to the actual existence of the institution and the difficulties thrown about it. We also oppose it as an evil so far as it seeks to spread itself. We insist on the policy that shall restrict it to its present limits. We don't suppose that in doing this we violate anything due to the actual presence of the institution, or anything due to the constitutional guaranties thrown around it.

We oppose the Dred Scott decision in a certain way, upon which I ought perhaps to address you a few words. We do not propose that when Dred Scott has been decided to be a slave by the court, we, as a mob, will decide him to be free. We do not propose that, when any other one, or one thousand, shall be decided by that court to be slaves, we will in any violent way disturb the rights of property thus settled; but we nevertheless do oppose that decision as a political rule which shall be binding on the voter to vote for nobody who thinks it wrong, which shall be binding on the members of Congress or the President to favor no measure that does not actually concur with the principles of that decision. We do not propose to be bound by it as a political rule in that way, because we think it lays the foundation, not merely of enlarging and spreading out what we consider an evil, but it lays the foundation for spreading that evil into the States themselves. We propose so resisting it as to have it reversed if we can, and a new judicial rule established upon this subject.

I will add this: that if there be any man who does not believe that slavery is wrong in the three aspects which I have mentioned, or in any one of them, that man is misplaced, and ought to leave us; while on the other hand, if there be any man in the Republican party who is impatient over the necessity springing from its actual presence, and is impatient of the constitutional guaranties thrown around it, and would act in disregard of these, he too is misplaced, standing with us. He will find his place somewhere else; for we have a due regard, so far as we are capable of understanding them, for all these things. This, gentlemen, as well as I can give it, is a plain statement of our principles in all their enormity. I will say now that there is a sentiment in the country contrary to me,—a sentiment which holds that slavery is not wrong, and therefore it goes for the policy that does not propose dealing with it as a wrong. That policy is the Democratic policy, and that sentiment is the Democratic sentiment. If there be a doubt in the mind of any one of this vast audience that this is really the central idea of the Democratic party in relation to this subject, I ask him to bear with me while I state a few things tending, as I think, to prove that proposition. In the first place, the leading man—I think I may do my friend Judge Douglas the honor of calling him such advocating the present Democratic policy never himself says it is wrong. He has the high distinction, so far as I know, of never having said slavery is either right or wrong. Almost everybody else says one or the other, but the Judge never does. If there be a man in the Democratic party who thinks it is wrong, and yet clings to that party, I suggest to him, in the first place, that his leader don't talk as he does, for he never says that it is wrong. In the second place, I suggest to him that if he will examine the policy proposed to be carried forward, he will find that he carefully excludes the idea that there is anything wrong in it. If you will examine the arguments that are made on it, you will find that every one carefully excludes the idea that there is anything wrong in slavery. Perhaps that Democrat who says he is as much opposed to slavery as I am will tell me that I am wrong about this. I wish him to examine his own course in regard to this matter a moment, and then see if his opinion will not be changed a little. You say it is wrong; but don't you constantly object to anybody else saying so? Do you not constantly argue that this is not the right place to oppose it? You say it must not be opposed in the free States, because slavery is not here; it must not be opposed in the slave States, because it is there; it must not be opposed in politics, because that will make a fuss; it must not be opposed in the pulpit, because it is not religion. Then where is the place to oppose it? There is no suitable place to oppose it. There is no place in the country to oppose this evil overspreading the continent, which you say yourself is coming. Frank Blair and Gratz Brown tried to get up a system of gradual emancipation in Missouri, had an election in August, and got beat, and you, Mr. Democrat, threw up your hat, and hallooed "Hurrah for Democracy!" So I say, again, that in regard to the arguments that are made, when Judge Douglas Says he "don't care whether slavery is voted up or voted down," whether he means that as an individual expression of sentiment, or only as a sort of statement of his views on national policy, it is alike true to say that he can thus argue logically if he don't see anything wrong in it; but he cannot say so logically if he admits that slavery is wrong. He cannot say that he would as soon see a wrong voted up as voted down. When Judge Douglas says that whoever or whatever community wants slaves, they have a right to have them, he is perfectly logical, if there is nothing wrong in the institution; but if you admit that it is wrong, he cannot logically say that anybody has a right to do wrong. When he says that slave property and horse and hog property are alike to be allowed to go into the Territories, upon the principles of equality, he is reasoning truly, if there is no difference between them as property; but if the one is property held rightfully, and the other is wrong, then there is no equality between the right and wrong; so that, turn it in anyway you can, in all the arguments sustaining the Democratic policy, and in that policy itself, there is a careful, studied exclusion of the idea that there is anything wrong in slavery. Let us understand this. I am not, just here, trying to prove that we are right, and they are wrong. I have been stating where we and they stand, and trying to show what is the real difference between us; and I now say that whenever we can get the question distinctly stated, can get all these men who believe that slavery is in some of these respects wrong to stand and act with us in treating it as a wrong,—then, and not till then, I think we will in some way come to an end of this slavery agitation.

Mr. LINCOLN'S REJOINDER.

MY FRIENDS:—Since Judge Douglas has said to you in his conclusion that he had not time in an hour and a half to answer all I had said in an hour, it follows of course that I will not be able to answer in half an hour all that he said in an hour and a half.

I wish to return to Judge Douglas my profound thanks for his public annunciation here to-day, to be put on record, that his system of policy in regard to the institution of slavery contemplates that it shall last forever. We are getting a little nearer the true issue of this controversy, and I am profoundly grateful for this one sentence. Judge Douglas asks you, Why cannot the institution of slavery, or rather, why cannot the nation, part slave and part free, continue as our fathers made it, forever? In the first place, I insist that our fathers did not make this nation half slave and half free, or part slave and part free. I insist that they found the institution of slavery existing here. They did not make it so but they left it so because they knew of no way to get rid of it at that time. When Judge Douglas undertakes to say that, as a matter of choice, the fathers of the government made this nation part slave and part free, he assumes what is historically a falsehood. More than that: when the fathers of the government cut off the source of slavery by the abolition of the slave-trade, and adopted a system of restricting it from the new Territories where it had not existed, I maintain that they placed it where they understood, and all sensible men understood, it was in the course of ultimate extinction; and when Judge Douglas asks me why it cannot continue as our fathers made it, I ask him why he and his friends could not let it remain as our fathers made it?

It is precisely all I ask of him in relation to the institution of slavery, that it shall be placed upon the basis that our fathers placed it upon. Mr. Brooks, of South Carolina, once said, and truly said, that when this government was established, no one expected the institution of slavery to last until this day, and that the men who formed this government were wiser and better than the men of these days; but the men of these days had experience which the fathers had not, and that experience had taught them the invention of the cotton-gin, and this had made the perpetuation of the institution of slavery a necessity in this country. Judge Douglas could not let it stand upon the basis which our fathers placed it, but removed it, and put it upon the cotton-gin basis. It is a question, therefore, for him and his friends to answer, why they could not let it remain where the fathers of the government originally placed it. I hope nobody has understood me as trying to sustain the doctrine that we have a right to quarrel with Kentucky, or Virginia, or any of the slave States, about the institution of slavery,—thus giving the Judge an opportunity to be eloquent and valiant against us in fighting for their rights. I expressly declared in my opening speech that I had neither the inclination to exercise, nor the belief in the existence of, the right to interfere with the States of Kentucky or Virginia in doing as they pleased with slavery Or any other existing institution. Then what becomes of all his eloquence in behalf of the rights of States, which are assailed by no living man?

But I have to hurry on, for I have but a half hour. The Judge has informed me, or informed this audience, that the Washington Union is laboring for my election to the United States Senate. This is news to me,—not very ungrateful news either. [Turning to Mr. W. H. Carlin, who was on the stand]—I hope that Carlin will be elected to the State Senate, and will vote for me. [Mr. Carlin shook his head.] Carlin don't fall in, I perceive, and I suppose he will not do much for me; but I am glad of all the support I can get, anywhere, if I can get it without practicing any deception to obtain it. In respect to this large portion of Judge Douglas's speech in which he tries to show that in the controversy between himself and the Administration party he is in the right, I do not feel myself at all competent or inclined to answer him.

I say to him, "Give it to them,—give it to them just all you can!" and, on the other hand, I say to Carlin, and Jake Davis, and to this man Wogley up here in Hancock, "Give it to Douglas, just pour it into him!"

Now, in regard to this matter of the Dred Scott decision, I wish to say a word or two. After all, the Judge will not say whether, if a decision is made holding that the people of the States cannot exclude slavery, he will support it or not. He obstinately refuses to say what he will do in that case. The judges of the Supreme Court as obstinately refused to say what they would do on this subject. Before this I reminded him that at Galesburgh he said the judges had expressly declared the contrary, and you remember that in my Opening speech I told him I had the book containing that decision here, and I would thank him to lay his finger on the place where any such thing was said. He has occupied his hour and a half, and he has not ventured to try to sustain his assertion. He never will. But he is desirous of knowing how we are going to reverse that Dred Scott decision. Judge Douglas ought to know how. Did not he and his political friends find a way to reverse the decision of that same court in favor of the constitutionality of the National Bank? Didn't they find a way to do it so effectually that they have reversed it as completely as any decision ever was reversed, so far as its practical operation is concerned?

And let me ask you, did n't Judge Douglas find a way to reverse the decision of our Supreme Court when it decided that Carlin's father—old Governor Carlin had not the constitutional power to remove a Secretary of State? Did he not appeal to the "MOBS," as he calls them? Did he not make speeches in the lobby to show how villainous that decision was, and how it ought to be overthrown? Did he not succeed, too, in getting an act passed by the Legislature to have it overthrown? And did n't he himself sit down on that bench as one of the five added judges, who were to overslaugh the four old ones, getting his name of "judge" in that way, and no other? If there is a villainy in using disrespect or making opposition to Supreme Court decisions, I commend it to Judge Douglas's earnest consideration. I know of no man in the State of Illinois who ought to know so well about how much villainy it takes to oppose a decision of the Supreme Court as our honorable friend Stephen A. Douglas.

Judge Douglas also makes the declaration that I say the Democrats are bound by the Dred Scott decision, while the Republicans are not. In the sense in which he argues, I never said it; but I will tell you what I have said and what I do not hesitate to repeat to-day. I have said that as the Democrats believe that decision to be correct, and that the extension of slavery is affirmed in the National Constitution, they are bound to support it as such; and I will tell you here that General Jackson once said each man was bound to support the Constitution "as he understood it." Now, Judge Douglas understands the Constitution according to the Dred Scott decision, and he is bound to support it as he understands it. I understand it another way, and therefore I am bound to support it in the way in which I understand it. And as Judge Douglas believes that decision to be correct, I will remake that argument if I have time to do so. Let me talk to some gentleman down there among you who looks me in the face. We will say you are a member of the Territorial Legislature, and, like Judge Douglas, you believe that the right to take and hold slaves there is a constitutional right The first thing you do is to swear you will support the Constitution, and all rights guaranteed therein; that you will, whenever your neighbor needs your legislation to support his constitutional rights, not withhold that legislation. If you withhold that necessary legislation for the support of the Constitution and constitutional rights, do you not commit perjury? I ask every sensible man if that is not so? That is undoubtedly just so, say what you please. Now, that is precisely what Judge Douglas says, that this is a constitutional right. Does the Judge mean to say that the Territorial Legislature in legislating may, by withholding necessary laws, or by passing unfriendly laws, nullify that constitutional right? Does he mean to say that? Does he mean to ignore the proposition so long and well established in law, that what you cannot do directly, you cannot do indirectly? Does he mean that? The truth about the matter is this: Judge Douglas has sung paeans to his "Popular Sovereignty" doctrine until his Supreme Court, co-operating with him, has squatted his Squatter Sovereignty out. But he will keep up this species of humbuggery about Squatter Sovereignty. He has at last invented this sort of do-nothing sovereignty,—that the people may exclude slavery by a sort of "sovereignty" that is exercised by doing nothing at all. Is not that running his Popular Sovereignty down awfully? Has it not got down as thin as the homeopathic soup that was made by boiling the shadow of a pigeon that had starved to death? But at last, when it is brought to the test of close reasoning, there is not even that thin decoction of it left. It is a presumption impossible in the domain of thought. It is precisely no other than the putting of that most unphilosophical proposition, that two bodies can occupy the same space at the same time. The Dred Scott decision covers the whole ground, and while it occupies it, there is no room even for the shadow of a starved pigeon to occupy the same ground.

Judge Douglas, in reply to what I have said about having upon a previous occasion made the speech at Ottawa as the one he took and read an extract from at Charleston, says it only shows that I practiced the deception twice. Now, my friends, are any of you obtuse enough to swallow that? Judge Douglas had said I had made a speech at Charleston that I would not make up north, and I turned around and answered him by showing I had made that same speech up north,—had made it at Ottawa; made it in his hearing; made it in the Abolition District,—in Lovejoy's District,—in the personal presence of Lovejoy himself,—in the same atmosphere exactly in which I had made my Chicago speech, of which he complains so much.

Now, in relation to my not having said anything about the quotation from the Chicago speech: he thinks that is a terrible subject for me to handle. Why, gentlemen, I can show you that the substance of the Chicago speech I delivered two years ago in "Egypt," as he calls it. It was down at Springfield. That speech is here in this book, and I could turn to it and read it to you but for the lack of time. I have not now the time to read it. ["Read it, read it."] No, gentlemen, I am obliged to use discretion in disposing most advantageously of my brief time. The Judge has taken great exception to my adopting the heretical statement in the Declaration of Independence, that "all men are created equal," and he has a great deal to say about negro equality. I want to say that in sometimes alluding to the Declaration of Independence, I have only uttered the sentiments that Henry Clay used to hold. Allow me to occupy your time a moment with what he said. Mr. Clay was at one time called upon in Indiana, and in a way that I suppose was very insulting, to liberate his slaves; and he made a written reply to that application, and one portion of it is in these words:

"What is the foundation of this appeal to me in Indiana to liberate the slaves under my care in Kentucky? It is a general declaration in the act announcing to the world the independence of the thirteen American colonies, that men are created equal. Now, as an abstract principle, there is no doubt of the truth of that declaration, and it is desirable in the original construction of society, and in organized societies, to keep it in view as a great fundamental principle."

When I sometimes, in relation to the organization of new societies in new countries, where the soil is clean and clear, insisted that we should keep that principle in view, Judge Douglas will have it that I want a negro wife. He never can be brought to understand that there is any middle ground on this subject. I have lived until my fiftieth year, and have never had a negro woman either for a slave or a wife, and I think I can live fifty centuries, for that matter, without having had one for either. I maintain that you may take Judge Douglas's quotations from my Chicago speech, and from my Charleston speech, and the Galesburgh speech,—in his speech of to-day,—and compare them over, and I am willing to trust them with you upon his proposition that they show rascality or double-dealing. I deny that they do.

The Judge does not seem at all disposed to have peace, but I find he is disposed to have a personal warfare with me. He says that my oath would not be taken against the bare word of Charles H. Lanphier or Thomas L. Harris. Well, that is altogether a matter of opinion. It is certainly not for me to vaunt my word against oaths of these gentlemen, but I will tell Judge Douglas again the facts upon which I "dared" to say they proved a forgery. I pointed out at Galesburgh that the publication of these resolutions in the Illinois State Register could not have been the result of accident, as the proceedings of that meeting bore unmistakable evidence of being done by a man who knew it was a forgery; that it was a publication partly taken from the real proceedings of the Convention, and partly from the proceedings of a convention at another place, which showed that he had the real proceedings before him, and taking one part of the resolutions, he threw out another part, and substituted false and fraudulent ones in their stead. I pointed that out to him, and also that his friend Lanphier, who was editor of the Register at that time and now is, must have known how it was done. Now, whether he did it, or got some friend to do it for him, I could not tell, but he certainly knew all about it. I pointed out to Judge Douglas that in his Freeport speech he had promised to investigate that matter. Does he now say that he did not make that promise? I have a right to ask why he did not keep it. I call upon him to tell here to-day why he did not keep that promise? That fraud has been traced up so that it lies between him, Harris, and Lanphier. There is little room for escape for Lanphier. Lanphier is doing the Judge good service, and Douglas desires his word to be taken for the truth. He desires Lanphier to be taken as authority in what he states in his newspaper. He desires Harris to be taken as a man of vast credibility; and when this thing lies among them, they will not press it to show where the guilt really belongs. Now, as he has said that he would investigate it, and implied that he would tell us the result of his investigation, I demand of him to tell why he did not investigate it, if he did not; and if he did, why he won't tell the result. I call upon him for that.

This is the third time that Judge Douglas has assumed that he learned about these resolutions by Harris's attempting to use them against Norton on the floor of Congress. I tell Judge Douglas the public records of the country show that he himself attempted it upon Trumbull a month before Harris tried them on Norton; that Harris had the opportunity of learning it from him, rather than he from Harris. I now ask his attention to that part of the record on the case. My friends, I am not disposed to detain you longer in regard to that matter.

I am told that I still have five minutes left. There is another matter I wish to call attention to. He says, when he discovered there was a mistake in that case, he came forward magnanimously, without my calling his attention to it, and explained it. I will tell you how he became so magnanimous. When the newspapers of our side had discovered and published it, and put it beyond his power to deny it, then he came forward and made a virtue of necessity by acknowledging it. Now he argues that all the point there was in those resolutions, although never passed at Springfield, is retained by their being passed at other localities. Is that true? He said I had a hand in passing them, in his opening speech, that I was in the convention and helped to pass them. Do the resolutions touch me at all? It strikes me there is some difference between holding a man responsible for an act which he has not done and holding him responsible for an act that he has done. You will judge whether there is any difference in the "spots." And he has taken credit for great magnanimity in coming forward and acknowledging what is proved on him beyond even the capacity of Judge Douglas to deny; and he has more capacity in that way than any other living man.

Then he wants to know why I won't withdraw the charge in regard to a conspiracy to make slavery national, as he has withdrawn the one he made. May it please his worship, I will withdraw it when it is proven false on me as that was proven false on him. I will add a little more than that, I will withdraw it whenever a reasonable man shall be brought to believe that the charge is not true. I have asked Judge Douglas's attention to certain matters of fact tending to prove the charge of a conspiracy to nationalize slavery, and he says he convinces me that this is all untrue because Buchanan was not in the country at that time, and because the Dred Scott case had not then got into the Supreme Court; and he says that I say the Democratic owners of Dred Scott got up the case. I never did say that I defy Judge Douglas to show that I ever said so, for I never uttered it. [One of Mr. Douglas's reporters gesticulated affirmatively at Mr. Lincoln.] I don't care if your hireling does say I did, I tell you myself that I never said the "Democratic" owners of Dred Scott got up the case. I have never pretended to know whether Dred Scott's owners were Democrats, or Abolitionists, or Freesoilers or Border Ruffians. I have said that there is evidence about the case tending to show that it was a made-up case, for the purpose of getting that decision. I have said that that evidence was very strong in the fact that when Dred Scott was declared to be a slave, the owner of him made him free, showing that he had had the case tried and the question settled for such use as could be made of that decision; he cared nothing about the property thus declared to be his by that decision. But my time is out, and I can say no more.

LAST DEBATE, AT ALTON, OCTOBER 15, 1858

Mr. LINCOLN'S REPLY

LADIES AND GENTLEMEN:—I have been somewhat, in my own mind, complimented by a large portion of Judge Douglas's speech,—I mean that portion which he devotes to the controversy between himself and the present Administration. This is the seventh time Judge Douglas and myself have met in these joint discussions, and he has been gradually improving in regard to his war with the Administration. At Quincy, day before yesterday, he was a little more severe upon the Administration than I had heard him upon any occasion, and I took pains to compliment him for it. I then told him to give it to them with all the power he had; and as some of them were present, I told them I would be very much obliged if they would give it to him in about the same way. I take it he has now vastly improved upon the attack he made then upon the Administration. I flatter myself he has really taken my advice on this subject. All I can say now is to re-commend to him and to them what I then commended,—to prosecute the war against one another in the most vigorous manner. I say to them again: "Go it, husband!—Go it, bear!"

There is one other thing I will mention before I leave this branch of the discussion,—although I do not consider it much of my business, anyway. I refer to that part of the Judge's remarks where he undertakes to involve Mr. Buchanan in an inconsistency. He reads something from Mr. Buchanan, from which he undertakes to involve him in an inconsistency; and he gets something of a cheer for having done so. I would only remind the Judge that while he is very valiantly fighting for the Nebraska Bill and the repeal of the Missouri Compromise, it has been but a little while since he was the valiant advocate of the Missouri Compromise. I want to know if Buchanan has not as much right to be inconsistent as Douglas has? Has Douglas the exclusive right, in this country, of being on all sides of all questions? Is nobody allowed that high privilege but himself? Is he to have an entire monopoly on that subject?

So far as Judge Douglas addressed his speech to me, or so far as it was about me, it is my business to pay some attention to it. I have heard the Judge state two or three times what he has stated to-day, that in a speech which I made at Springfield, Illinois, I had in a very especial manner complained that the Supreme Court in the Dred Scott case had decided that a negro could never be a citizen of the United States. I have omitted by some accident heretofore to analyze this statement, and it is required of me to notice it now. In point of fact it is untrue. I never have complained especially of the Dred Scott decision because it held that a negro could not be a citizen, and the Judge is always wrong when he says I ever did so complain of it. I have the speech here, and I will thank him or any of his friends to show where I said that a negro should be a citizen, and complained especially of the Dred Scott decision because it declared he could not be one. I have done no such thing; and Judge Douglas, so persistently insisting that I have done so, has strongly impressed me with the belief of a predetermination on his part to misrepresent me. He could not get his foundation for insisting that I was in favor of this negro equality anywhere else as well as he could by assuming that untrue proposition. Let me tell this audience what is true in regard to that matter; and the means by which they may correct me if I do not tell them truly is by a recurrence to the speech itself. I spoke of the Dred Scott decision in my Springfield speech, and I was then endeavoring to prove that the Dred Scott decision was a portion of a system or scheme to make slavery national in this country. I pointed out what things had been decided by the court. I mentioned as a fact that they had decided that a negro could not be a citizen; that they had done so, as I supposed, to deprive the negro, under all circumstances, of the remotest possibility of ever becoming a citizen and claiming the rights of a citizen of the United States under a certain clause of the Constitution. I stated that, without making any complaint of it at all. I then went on and stated the other points decided in the case; namely, that the bringing of a negro into the State of Illinois and holding him in slavery for two years here was a matter in regard to which they would not decide whether it would make him free or not; that they decided the further point that taking him into a United States Territory where slavery was prohibited by Act of Congress did not make him free, because that Act of Congress, as they held, was unconstitutional. I mentioned these three things as making up the points decided in that case. I mentioned them in a lump, taken in connection with the introduction of the Nebraska Bill, and the amendment of Chase, offered at the time, declaratory of the right of the people of the Territories to exclude slavery, which was voted down by the friends of the bill. I mentioned all these things together, as evidence tending to prove a combination and conspiracy to make the institution of slavery national. In that connection and in that way I mentioned the decision on the point that a negro could not be a citizen, and in no other connection.

Out of this Judge Douglas builds up his beautiful fabrication of my purpose to introduce a perfect social and political equality between the white and black races. His assertion that I made an "especial objection" (that is his exact language) to the decision on this account is untrue in point of fact.

Now, while I am upon this subject, and as Henry Clay has been alluded to, I desire to place myself, in connection with Mr. Clay, as nearly right before this people as may be. I am quite aware what the Judge's object is here by all these allusions. He knows that we are before an audience having strong sympathies southward, by relationship, place of birth, and so on. He desires to place me in an extremely Abolition attitude. He read upon a former occasion, and alludes, without reading, to-day to a portion of a speech which I delivered in Chicago. In his quotations from that speech, as he has made them upon former occasions, the extracts were taken in such a way as, I suppose, brings them within the definition of what is called garbling,—taking portions of a speech which, when taken by themselves, do not present the entire sense of the speaker as expressed at the time. I propose, therefore, out of that same speech, to show how one portion of it which he skipped over (taking an extract before and an extract after) will give a different idea, and the true idea I intended to convey. It will take me some little time to read it, but I believe I will occupy the time that way.

You have heard him frequently allude to my controversy with him in regard to the Declaration of Independence. I confess that I have had a struggle with Judge Douglas on that matter, and I will try briefly to place myself right in regard to it on this occasion. I said—and it is between the extracts Judge Douglas has taken from this speech, and put in his published speeches:

"It may be argued that there are certain conditions that make necessities and impose them upon us, and to the extent that a necessity is imposed upon a man he must submit to it. I think that was the condition in which we found ourselves when we established this government. We had slaves among us, we could not get our Constitution unless we permitted them to remain in slavery, we could not secure the good we did secure if we grasped for more; and having by necessity submitted to that much, it does not destroy the principle that is the charter of our liberties. Let the charter remain as our standard."

Now, I have upon all occasions declared as strongly as Judge Douglas against the disposition to interfere with the existing institution of slavery. You hear me read it from the same speech from which he takes garbled extracts for the purpose of proving upon me a disposition to interfere with the institution of slavery, and establish a perfect social and political equality between negroes and white people.

Allow me while upon this subject briefly to present one other extract from a speech of mine, more than a year ago, at Springfield, in discussing this very same question, soon after Judge Douglas took his ground that negroes were, not included in the Declaration of Independence:

"I think the authors of that notable instrument intended to include all men, but they did not mean to declare all men equal in all respects. They did not mean to say all men were equal in color, size, intellect, moral development, or social capacity. They defined with tolerable distinctness in what they did consider all men created equal,—equal in certain inalienable rights, among which are life, liberty, and the pursuit of happiness. This they said, and this they meant. They did not mean to assert the obvious untruth that all were then actually enjoying that equality, or yet that they were about to confer it immediately upon them. In fact they had no power to confer such a boon. They meant simply to declare the right, so that the enforcement of it might follow as fast as circumstances should permit.

"They meant to set up a standard maxim for free society which should be familiar to all,—constantly looked to, constantly labored for, and even, though never perfectly attained, constantly approximated, and thereby constantly spreading and deepening its influence, and augmenting the happiness and value of life to all people, of all colors, everywhere."

There again are the sentiments I have expressed in regard to the Declaration of Independence upon a former occasion,—sentiments which have been put in print and read wherever anybody cared to know what so humble an individual as myself chose to say in regard to it.

At Galesburgh, the other day, I said, in answer to Judge Douglas, that three years ago there never had been a man, so far as I knew or believed, in the whole world, who had said that the Declaration of Independence did not include negroes in the term "all men." I reassert it to-day. I assert that Judge Douglas and all his friends may search the whole records of the country, and it will be a matter of great astonishment to me if they shall be able to find that one human being three years ago had ever uttered the astounding sentiment that the term "all men" in the Declaration did not include the negro. Do not let me be misunderstood. I know that more than three years ago there were men who, finding this assertion constantly in the way of their schemes to bring about the ascendency and perpetuation of slavery, denied the truth of it. I know that Mr. Calhoun and all the politicians of his school denied the truth of the Declaration. I know that it ran along in the mouth of some Southern men for a period of years, ending at last in that shameful, though rather forcible, declaration of Pettit of Indiana, upon the floor of the United States Senate, that the Declaration of Independence was in that respect "a self-evident lie," rather than a self-evident truth. But I say, with a perfect knowledge of all this hawking at the Declaration without directly attacking it, that three years ago there never had lived a man who had ventured to assail it in the sneaking way of pretending to believe it, and then asserting it did not include the negro. I believe the first man who ever said it was Chief Justice Taney in the Dred Scott case, and the next to him was our friend Stephen A. Douglas. And now it has become the catchword of the entire party. I would like to call upon his friends everywhere to consider how they have come in so short a time to view this matter in a way so entirely different from their former belief; to ask whether they are not being borne along by an irresistible current,—whither, they know not.

In answer to my proposition at Galesburgh last week, I see that some man in Chicago has got up a letter, addressed to the Chicago Times, to show, as he professes, that somebody had said so before; and he signs himself "An Old-Line Whig," if I remember correctly. In the first place, I would say he was not an old-line Whig. I am somewhat acquainted with old-line Whigs from the origin to the end of that party; I became pretty well acquainted with them, and I know they always had some sense, whatever else you could ascribe to them. I know there never was one who had not more sense than to try to show by the evidence he produces that some men had, prior to the time I named, said that negroes were not included in the term "all men" in the Declaration of Independence. What is the evidence he produces? I will bring forward his evidence, and let you see what he offers by way of showing that somebody more than three years ago had said negroes were not included in the Declaration. He brings forward part of a speech from Henry Clay,—the part of the speech of Henry Clay which I used to bring forward to prove precisely the contrary. I guess we are surrounded to some extent to-day by the old friends of Mr. Clay, and they will be glad to hear anything from that authority. While he was in Indiana a man presented a petition to liberate his negroes, and he (Mr. Clay) made a speech in answer to it, which I suppose he carefully wrote out himself and caused to be published. I have before me an extract from that speech which constitutes the evidence this pretended "Old-Line Whig" at Chicago brought forward to show that Mr. Clay did n't suppose the negro was included in the Declaration of Independence. Hear what Mr. Clay said:

"And what is the foundation of this appeal to me in Indiana to liberate the slaves under my care in Kentucky? It is a general declaration in the act announcing to the world the independence of the thirteen American colonies, that all men are created equal. Now, as an abstract principle, there is no doubt of the truth of that declaration; and it is desirable, in the original construction of society and in organized societies, to keep it in view as a great fundamental principle. But, then, I apprehend that in no society that ever did exist, or ever shall be formed, was or can the equality asserted among the members of the human race be practically enforced and carried out. There are portions, large portions, women, minors, insane, culprits, transient sojourners, that will always probably remain subject to the government of another portion of the community.

"That declaration, whatever may be the extent of its import, was made by the delegations of the thirteen States. In most of them slavery existed, and had long existed, and was established by law. It was introduced and forced upon the colonies by the paramount law of England. Do you believe that in making that declaration the States that concurred in it intended that it should be tortured into a virtual emancipation of all the slaves within their respective limits? Would Virginia and other Southern States have ever united in a declaration which was to be interpreted into an abolition of slavery among them? Did any one of the thirteen colonies entertain such a design or expectation? To impute such a secret and unavowed purpose, would be to charge a political fraud upon the noblest band of patriots that ever assembled in council,—a fraud upon the Confederacy of the Revolution; a fraud upon the union of those States whose Constitution not only recognized the lawfulness of slavery, but permitted the importation of slaves from Africa until the year 1808."

This is the entire quotation brought forward to prove that somebody previous to three years ago had said the negro was not included in the term "all men" in the Declaration. How does it do so? In what way has it a tendency to prove that? Mr. Clay says it is true as an abstract principle that all men are created equal, but that we cannot practically apply it in all cases. He illustrates this by bringing forward the cases of females, minors, and insane persons, with whom it cannot be enforced; but he says it is true as an abstract principle in the organization of society as well as in organized society and it should be kept in view as a fundamental principle. Let me read a few words more before I add some comments of my own. Mr. Clay says, a little further on:

"I desire no concealment of my opinions in regard to the institution of slavery. I look upon it as a great evil, and deeply lament that we have derived it from the parental government and from our ancestors. I wish every slave in the United States was in the country of his ancestors. But here they are, and the question is, How can they be best dealt with? If a state of nature existed, and we were about to lay the foundations of society, no man would be more strongly opposed than I should be to incorporate the institution of slavery amongst its elements."

Now, here in this same book, in this same speech, in this same extract, brought forward to prove that Mr. Clay held that the negro was not included in the Declaration of Independence, is no such statement on his part, but the declaration that it is a great fundamental truth which should be constantly kept in view in the organization of society and in societies already organized. But if I say a word about it; if I attempt, as Mr. Clay said all good men ought to do, to keep it in view; if, in this "organized society," I ask to have the public eye turned upon it; if I ask, in relation to the organization of new Territories, that the public eye should be turned upon it, forthwith I am vilified as you hear me to-day. What have I done that I have not the license of Henry Clay's illustrious example here in doing? Have I done aught that I have not his authority for, while maintaining that in organizing new Territories and societies this fundamental principle should be regarded, and in organized society holding it up to the public view and recognizing what he recognized as the great principle of free government?

And when this new principle—this new proposition that no human being ever thought of three years ago—is brought forward, I combat it as having an evil tendency, if not an evil design. I combat it as having a tendency to dehumanize the negro, to take away from him the right of ever striving to be a man. I combat it as being one of the thousand things constantly done in these days to prepare the public mind to make property, and nothing but property, of the negro in all the States of this Union.

But there is a point that I wish, before leaving this part of the discussion, to ask attention to. I have read and I repeat the words of Henry Clay:

"I desire no concealment of my opinions in regard to the institution of slavery. I look upon it as a great evil, and deeply lament that we have derived it from the parental government and from our ancestors. I wish every slave in the United States was in the country of his ancestors. But here they are, and the question is, How can they be best dealt with? If a state of nature existed, and we were about to lay the foundations of society, no man would be more strongly opposed than I should be to incorporate the institution of slavery amongst its elements."

The principle upon which I have insisted in this canvass is in relation to laying the foundations of new societies. I have never sought to apply these principles to the old States for the purpose of abolishing slavery in those States. It is nothing but a miserable perversion of what I have said, to assume that I have declared Missouri, or any other slave State, shall emancipate her slaves; I have proposed no such thing. But when Mr. Clay says that in laying the foundations of society in our Territories where it does not exist, he would be opposed to the introduction of slavery as an element, I insist that we have his warrant—his license—for insisting upon the exclusion of that element which he declared in such strong and emphatic language was most hurtful to him.

Judge Douglas has again referred to a Springfield speech in which I said "a house divided against itself cannot stand." The Judge has so often made the entire quotation from that speech that I can make it from memory. I used this language:

"We are now far into the fifth year since a policy was initiated with the avowed object and confident promise of putting an end to the slavery agitation. Under the operation of this policy, that agitation has not only not ceased, but has constantly augmented. In my opinion it will not cease until a crisis shall have been reached and passed. 'A house divided against itself cannot stand.' I believe this government cannot endure permanently, half slave and half free. I do not expect the house to fall, but I do expect it will cease to be divided. It will become all one thing, or all the other. Either the opponents of slavery will arrest the further spread of it, and place it where the public mind shall rest in the belief that it is in the course of ultimate extinction, or its advocates will push it forward till it shall become alike lawful in all the States, old as well as new, North as well as South."

That extract and the sentiments expressed in it have been extremely offensive to Judge Douglas. He has warred upon them as Satan wars upon the Bible. His perversions upon it are endless. Here now are my views upon it in brief:

I said we were now far into the fifth year since a policy was initiated with the avowed object and confident promise of putting an end to the slavery agitation. Is it not so? When that Nebraska Bill was brought forward four years ago last January, was it not for the "avowed object" of putting an end to the slavery agitation? We were to have no more agitation in Congress; it was all to be banished to the Territories. By the way, I will remark here that, as Judge Douglas is very fond of complimenting Mr. Crittenden in these days, Mr. Crittenden has said there was a falsehood in that whole business, for there was no slavery agitation at that time to allay. We were for a little while quiet on the troublesome thing, and that very allaying plaster of Judge Douglas's stirred it up again. But was it not understood or intimated with the "confident promise" of putting an end to the slavery agitation? Surely it was. In every speech you heard Judge Douglas make, until he got into this "imbroglio," as they call it, with the Administration about the Lecompton

Constitution, every speech on that Nebraska Bill was full of his felicitations that we were just at the end of the slavery agitation. The last tip of the last joint of the old serpent's tail was just drawing out of view. But has it proved so? I have asserted that under that policy that agitation "has not only not ceased, but has constantly augmented." When was there ever a greater agitation in Congress than last winter? When was it as great in the country as to-day?

There was a collateral object in the introduction of that Nebraska policy, which was to clothe the people of the Territories with a superior degree of self-government, beyond what they had ever had before. The first object and the main one of conferring upon the people a higher degree of "self-government" is a question of fact to be determined by you in answer to a single question. Have you ever heard or known of a people anywhere on earth who had as little to do as, in the first instance of its use, the people of Kansas had with this same right of "self-government"? In its main policy and in its collateral object, it has been nothing but a living, creeping lie from the time of its introduction till to-day.

I have intimated that I thought the agitation would not cease until a crisis should have been reached and passed. I have stated in what way I thought it would be reached and passed. I have said that it might go one way or the other. We might, by arresting the further spread of it, and placing it where the fathers originally placed it, put it where the public mind should rest in the belief that it was in the course of ultimate extinction. Thus the agitation may cease. It may be pushed forward until it shall become alike lawful in all the States, old as well as new, North as well as South. I have said, and I repeat, my wish is that the further spread of it may be arrested, and that it may be where the public mind shall rest in the belief that it is in the course of ultimate extinction—I have expressed that as my wish I entertain the opinion, upon evidence sufficient to my mind, that the fathers of this government placed that institution where the public mind did rest in the belief that it was in the course of ultimate extinction. Let me ask why they made provision that the source of slavery—the African slave-trade—should be cut off at the end of twenty years? Why did they make provision that in all the new territory we owned at that time slavery should be forever inhibited? Why stop its spread in one direction, and cut off its source in another, if they did not look to its being placed in the course of its ultimate extinction?

Again: the institution of slavery is only mentioned in the Constitution of the United States two or three times, and in neither of these cases does the word "slavery" or "negro race" occur; but covert language is used each time, and for a purpose full of significance. What is the language in regard to the prohibition of the African slave-trade? It runs in about this way:

"The migration or importation of such persons as any of the States now existing shall think proper to admit, shall not be prohibited by the Congress prior to the year one thousand eight hundred and eight."

The next allusion in the Constitution to the question of slavery and the black race is on the subject of the basis of representation, and there the language used is:

"Representatives and direct taxes shall be apportioned among the several States which may be included within this Union, according to their respective numbers, which shall be determined by adding to the whole number of free persons, including those bound to service for a term of years, and excluding Indians not taxed, three-fifths of all other persons."

It says "persons," not slaves, not negroes; but this "three-fifths" can be applied to no other class among us than the negroes.

Lastly, in the provision for the reclamation of fugitive slaves, it is said:

"No person held to service or labor in one State, under the laws thereof, escaping into another, shall in consequence of any law or regulation therein be discharged from such service or labor, but shall be delivered up, on claim of the party to whom such service or labor may be due."

There again there is no mention of the word "negro" or of slavery. In all three of these places, being the only allusions to slavery in the instrument, covert language is used. Language is used not suggesting that slavery existed or that the black race were among us. And I understand the contemporaneous history of those times to be that covert language was used with a purpose, and that purpose was that in our Constitution, which it was hoped and is still hoped will endure forever,—when it should be read by intelligent and patriotic men, after the institution of slavery had passed from among us,—there should be nothing on the face of the great charter of liberty suggesting that such a thing as negro slavery had ever existed among us. This is part of the evidence that the fathers of the government expected and intended the institution of slavery to come to an end. They expected and intended that it should be in the course of ultimate extinction. And when I say that I desire to see the further spread of it arrested, I only say I desire to see that done which the fathers have first done. When I say I desire to see it placed where the public mind will rest in the belief that it is in the course of ultimate extinction, I only say I desire to see it placed where they placed it. It is not true that our fathers, as Judge Douglas assumes, made this government part slave and part free. Understand the sense in which he puts it. He assumes that slavery is a rightful thing within itself,—was introduced by the framers of the Constitution. The exact truth is, that they found the institution existing among us, and they left it as they found it. But in making the government they left this institution with many clear marks of disapprobation upon it. They found slavery among them, and they left it among them because of the difficulty—the absolute impossibility—of its immediate removal. And when Judge Douglas asks me why we cannot let it remain part slave and part free, as the fathers of the government made it, he asks a question based upon an assumption which is itself a falsehood; and I turn upon him and ask him the question, when the policy that the fathers of the government had adopted in relation to this element among us was the best policy in the world, the only wise policy, the only policy that we can ever safely continue upon that will ever give us peace, unless this dangerous element masters us all and becomes a national institution,—I turn upon him and ask him why he could not leave it alone. I turn and ask him why he was driven to the necessity of introducing a new policy in regard to it. He has himself said he introduced a new policy. He said so in his speech on the 22d of March of the present year, 1858. I ask him why he could not let it remain where our fathers placed it. I ask, too, of Judge Douglas and his friends why we shall not again place this institution upon the basis on which the fathers left it. I ask you, when he infers that I am in favor of setting the free and slave States at war, when the institution was placed in that attitude by those who made the Constitution, did they make any war? If we had no war out of it when thus placed, wherein is the ground of belief that we shall have war out of it if we return to that policy? Have we had any peace upon this matter springing from any other basis? I maintain that we have not. I have proposed nothing more than a return to the policy of the fathers.

I confess, when I propose a certain measure of policy, it is not enough for me that I do not intend anything evil in the result, but it is incumbent on me to show that it has not a tendency to that result. I have met Judge Douglas in that point of view. I have not only made the declaration that I do not mean to produce a conflict between the States, but I have tried to show by fair reasoning, and I think I have shown to the minds of fair men, that I propose nothing but what has a most peaceful tendency. The quotation that I happened to make in that Springfield Speech, that "a house divided against itself cannot stand," and which has proved so offensive to the judge, was part and parcel of the same thing. He tries to show that variety in the democratic institutions of the different States is necessary and indispensable. I do not dispute it. I have no controversy with Judge Douglas about that. I shall very readily agree with him that it would be foolish for us to insist upon having a cranberry law here in Illinois, where we have no cranberries, because they have a cranberry law in Indiana, where they have cranberries. I should insist that it would be exceedingly wrong in us to deny to Virginia the right to enact oyster laws, where they have oysters, because we want no such laws here. I understand, I hope, quite as well as Judge Douglas or anybody else, that the variety in the soil and climate and face of the country, and consequent variety in the industrial pursuits and productions of a country, require systems of law conforming to this variety in the natural features of the country. I understand quite as well as Judge Douglas that if we here raise a barrel of flour more than we want, and the Louisianians raise a barrel of sugar more than they want, it is of mutual advantage to exchange. That produces commerce, brings us together, and makes us better friends. We like one another the more for it. And I understand as well as Judge Douglas, or anybody else, that these mutual accommodations are the cements which bind together the different parts of this Union; that instead of being a thing to "divide the house,"—figuratively expressing the Union,—they tend to sustain it; they are the props of the house, tending always to hold it up.

But when I have admitted all this, I ask if there is any parallel between these things and this institution of slavery? I do not see that there is any parallel at all between them. Consider it. When have we had any difficulty or quarrel amongst ourselves about the cranberry laws of Indiana, or the oyster laws of Virginia, or the pine-lumber laws of Maine, or the fact that Louisiana produces sugar, and Illinois flour? When have we had any quarrels over these things? When have we had perfect peace in regard to this thing which I say is an element of discord in this Union? We have sometimes had peace, but when was it? It was when the institution of slavery remained quiet where it was. We have had difficulty and turmoil whenever it has made a struggle to spread itself where it was not. I ask, then, if experience does not speak in thunder-tones telling us that the policy which has given peace to the country heretofore, being returned to, gives the greatest promise of peace again. You may say, and Judge Douglas has intimated the same thing, that all this difficulty in regard to the institution of slavery is the mere agitation of office-seekers and ambitious Northern politicians. He thinks we want to get "his place," I suppose. I agree that there are office-seekers amongst us. The Bible says somewhere that we are desperately selfish. I think we would have discovered that fact without the Bible. I do not claim that I am any less so than the average of men, but I do claim that I am not more selfish than Judge Douglas.

But is it true that all the difficulty and agitation we have in regard to this institution of slavery spring from office-seeking, from the mere ambition of politicians? Is that the truth? How many times have we had danger from this question? Go back to the day of the Missouri Compromise. Go back to the nullification question, at the bottom of which lay this same slavery question. Go back to the time of the annexation of Texas. Go back to the troubles that led to the Compromise of 1850. You will find that every time, with the single exception of the Nullification question, they sprung from an endeavor to spread this institution. There never was a party in the history of this country, and there probably never will be, of sufficient strength to disturb the general peace of the country. Parties themselves may be divided and quarrel on minor questions, yet it extends not beyond the parties themselves. But does not this question make a disturbance outside of political circles? Does it not enter into the churches and rend them asunder? What divided the great Methodist Church into two parts, North and South? What has raised this constant disturbance in every Presbyterian General Assembly that meets? What disturbed the Unitarian Church in this very city two years ago? What has jarred and shaken the great American Tract Society recently, not yet splitting it, but sure to divide it in the end? Is it not this same mighty, deep-seated power that somehow operates on the minds of men, exciting and stirring them up in every avenue of society,—in politics, in religion, in literature, in morals, in all the manifold relations of life? Is this the work of politicians? Is that irresistible power, which for fifty years has shaken the government and agitated the people, to be stifled and subdued by pretending that it is an exceedingly simple thing, and we ought not to talk about it? If you will get everybody else to stop talking about it, I assure you I will quit before they have half done so. But where is the philosophy or statesmanship which assumes that you can quiet that disturbing element in our society which has disturbed us for more than half a century, which has been the only serious danger that has threatened our institutions,—I say, where is the philosophy or the statesmanship based on the assumption that we are to quit talking about it, and that the public mind is all at once to cease being agitated by it? Yet this is the policy here in the North that Douglas is advocating, that we are to care nothing about it! I ask you if it is not a false philosophy. Is it not a false statesmanship that undertakes to build up a system of policy upon the basis of caring nothing about the very thing that everybody does care the most about—a thing which all experience has shown we care a very great deal about?

The Judge alludes very often in the course of his remarks to the exclusive right which the States have to decide the whole thing for themselves. I agree with him very readily that the different States have that right. He is but fighting a man of straw when he assumes that I am contending against the right of the States to do as they please about it. Our controversy with him is in regard to the new Territories. We agree that when the States come in as States they have the right and the power to do as they please. We have no power as citizens of the free-States, or in our Federal capacity as members of the Federal Union through the General Government, to disturb slavery in the States where it exists. We profess constantly that we have no more inclination than belief in the power of the government to disturb it; yet we are driven constantly to defend ourselves from the assumption that we are warring upon the rights of the Sates. What I insist upon is, that the new Territories shall be kept free from it while in the Territorial condition. Judge Douglas assumes that we have no interest in them,—that we have no right whatever to interfere. I think we have some interest. I think that as white men we have. Do we not wish for an outlet for our surplus population, if I may so express myself? Do we not feel an interest in getting to that outlet with such institutions as we would like to have prevail there? If you go to the Territory opposed to slavery, and another man comes upon the same ground with his slave, upon the assumption that the things are equal, it turns out that he has the equal right all his way, and you have no part of it your way. If he goes in and makes it a slave Territory, and by consequence a slave State, is it not time that those who desire to have it a free State were on equal ground? Let me suggest it in a different way. How many Democrats are there about here ["A thousand"] who have left slave States and come into the free State of Illinois to get rid of the institution of slavery? [Another voice: "A thousand and one."] I reckon there are a thousand and one. I will ask you, if the policy you are now advocating had prevailed when this country was in a Territorial condition, where would you have gone to get rid of it? Where would you have found your free State or Territory to go to? And when hereafter, for any cause, the people in this place shall desire to find new homes, if they wish to be rid of the institution, where will they find the place to go to?

Now, irrespective of the moral aspect of this question as to whether there is a right or wrong in enslaving a negro, I am still in favor of our new Territories being in such a condition that white men may find a home,—may find some spot where they can better their condition; where they can settle upon new soil and better their condition in life. I am in favor of this, not merely (I must say it here as I have elsewhere) for our own people who are born amongst us, but as an outlet for free white people everywhere the world over—in which Hans, and Baptiste, and Patrick, and all other men from all the world, may find new homes and better their conditions in life.

I have stated upon former occasions, and I may as well state again, what I understand to be the real issue in this controversy between Judge Douglas and myself. On the point of my wanting to make war between the free and the slave States, there has been no issue between us. So, too, when he assumes that I am in favor of producing a perfect social and political equality between the white and black races. These are false issues, upon which Judge Douglas has tried to force the controversy. There is no foundation in truth for the charge that I maintain either of these propositions. The real issue in this controversy—the one pressing upon every mind—is the sentiment on the part of one class that looks upon the institution of slavery as a wrong, and of another class that does not look upon it as a wrong. The sentiment that contemplates the institution of slavery in this country as a wrong is the sentiment of the Republican party. It is the sentiment around which all their actions, all their arguments, circle, from which all their propositions radiate. They look upon it as being a moral, social, and political wrong; and while they contemplate it as such, they nevertheless have due regard for its actual existence among us, and the difficulties of getting rid of it in any satisfactory way, and to all the constitutional obligations thrown about it. Yet, having a due regard for these, they desire a policy in regard to it that looks to its not creating any more danger. They insist that it should, as far as may be, be treated as a wrong; and one of the methods of treating it as a wrong is to make provision that it shall grow no larger. They also desire a policy that looks to a peaceful end of slavery at some time. These are the views they entertain in regard to it as I understand them; and all their sentiments, all their arguments and propositions, are brought within this range. I have said, and I repeat it here, that if there be a man amongst us who does not think that the institution of slavery is wrong in any one of the aspects of which I have spoken, he is misplaced, and ought not to be with us. And if there be a man amongst us who is so impatient of it as a wrong as to disregard its actual presence among us and the difficulty of getting rid of it suddenly in a satisfactory way, and to disregard the constitutional obligations thrown about it, that man is misplaced if he is on our platform. We disclaim sympathy with him in practical action. He is not placed properly with us.

On this subject of treating it as a wrong, and limiting its spread, let me say a word. Has anything ever threatened the existence of this Union save and except this very institution of slavery? What is it that we hold most dear amongst us? Our own liberty and prosperity. What has ever threatened our liberty and prosperity, save and except this institution of slavery? If this is true, how do you propose to improve the condition of things by enlarging slavery, by spreading it out and making it bigger? You may have a wen or cancer upon your person, and not be able to cut it out, lest you bleed to death; but surely it is no way to cure it, to engraft it and spread it over your whole body. That is no proper way of treating what you regard a wrong. You see this peaceful way of dealing with it as a wrong, restricting the spread of it, and not allowing it to go into new countries where it has not already existed. That is the peaceful way, the old-fashioned way, the way in which the fathers themselves set us the example.

On the other hand, I have said there is a sentiment which treats it as not being wrong. That is the Democratic sentiment of this day. I do not mean to say that every man who stands within that range positively asserts that it is right. That class will include all who positively assert that it is right, and all who, like Judge Douglas, treat it as indifferent and do not say it is either right or wrong. These two classes of men fall within the general class of those who do not look upon it as a wrong. And if there be among you anybody who supposes that he, as a Democrat, can consider himself "as much opposed to slavery as anybody," I would like to reason with him. You never treat it as a wrong. What other thing that you consider as a wrong do you deal with as you deal with that? Perhaps you say it is wrong—but your leader never does, and you quarrel with anybody who says it is wrong. Although you pretend to say so yourself, you can find no fit place to deal with it as a wrong. You must not say anything about it in the free States, because it is not here. You must not say anything about it in the slave States, because it is there. You must not say anything about it in the pulpit, because that is religion, and has nothing to do with it. You must not say anything about it in politics, because that will disturb the security of "my place." There is no place to talk about it as being a wrong, although you say yourself it is a wrong. But, finally, you will screw yourself up to the belief that if the people of the slave States should adopt a system of gradual emancipation on the slavery question, you would be in favor of it. You would be in favor of it. You say that is getting it in the right place, and you would be glad to see it succeed. But you are deceiving yourself. You all know that Frank Blair and Gratz Brown, down there in St. Louis, undertook to introduce that system in Missouri. They fought as valiantly as they could for the system of gradual emancipation which you pretend you would be glad to see succeed. Now, I will bring you to the test. After a hard fight they were beaten, and when the news came over here, you threw up your hats and hurrahed for Democracy. More than that, take all the argument made in favor of the system you have proposed, and it carefully excludes the idea that there is anything wrong in the institution of slavery. The arguments to sustain that policy carefully exclude it. Even here to-day you heard Judge Douglas quarrel with me because I uttered a wish that it might sometime come to an end. Although Henry Clay could say he wished every slave in the United States was in the country of his ancestors, I am denounced by those pretending to respect Henry Clay for uttering a wish that it might sometime, in some peaceful way, come to an end. The Democratic policy in regard to that institution will not tolerate the merest breath, the slightest hint, of the least degree of wrong about it. Try it by some of Judge Douglas's arguments. He says he "don't care whether it is voted up or voted down" in the Territories. I do not care myself, in dealing with that expression, whether it is intended to be expressive of his individual sentiments on the subject, or only of the national policy he desires to have established. It is alike valuable for my purpose. Any man can say that who does not see anything wrong in slavery; but no man can logically say it who does see a wrong in it, because no man can logically say he don't care whether a wrong is voted up or voted down. He may say he don't care whether an indifferent thing is voted up or down, but he must logically have a choice between a right thing and a wrong thing. He contends that whatever community wants slaves has a right to have them. So they have, if it is not a wrong. But if it is a wrong, he cannot say people have a right to do wrong. He says that upon the score of equality slaves should be allowed to go in a new Territory, like other property. This is strictly logical if there is no difference between it and other property. If it and other property are equal, this argument is entirely logical. But if you insist that one is wrong and the other right, there is no use to institute a comparison between right and wrong. You may turn over everything in the Democratic policy from beginning to end, whether in the shape it takes on the statute book, in the shape it takes in the Dred Scott decision, in the shape it takes in conversation, or the shape it takes in short maxim-like arguments,—it everywhere carefully excludes the idea that there is anything wrong in it.

That is the real issue. That is the issue that will continue in this country when these poor tongues of Judge Douglas and myself shall be silent. It is the eternal struggle between these two principles—right and wrong—throughout the world. They are the two principles that have stood face to face from the beginning of time, and will ever continue to struggle. The one is the common right of humanity, and the other the divine right of kings. It is the same principle in whatever shape it develops itself. It is the same spirit that says, "You work and toil and earn bread, and I'll eat it." No matter in what shape it comes, whether from the mouth of a king who seeks to bestride the people of his own nation and live by the fruit of their labor, or from one race of men as an apology for enslaving another race, it is the same tyrannical principle. I was glad to express my gratitude at Quincy, and I re-express it here, to Judge Douglas,—that he looks to no end of the institution of slavery. That will help the people to see where the struggle really is. It will hereafter place with us all men who really do wish the wrong may have an end. And whenever we can get rid of the fog which obscures the real question, when we can get Judge Douglas and his friends to avow a policy looking to its perpetuation,—we can get out from among that class of men and bring them to the side of those who treat it as a wrong. Then there will soon be an end of it, and that end will be its "ultimate extinction." Whenever the issue can be distinctly made, and all extraneous matter thrown out so that men can fairly see the real difference between the parties, this controversy will soon be settled, and it will be done peaceably too. There will be no war, no violence. It will be placed again where the wisest and best men of the world placed it. Brooks of South Carolina once declared that when this Constitution was framed its framers did not look to the institution existing until this day. When he said this, I think he stated a fact that is fully borne out by the history of the times. But he also said they were better and wiser men than the men of these days, yet the men of these days had experience which they had not, and by the invention of the cotton-gin it became a necessity in this country that slavery should be perpetual. I now say that, willingly or unwillingly—purposely or without purpose, Judge Douglas has been the most prominent instrument in changing the position of the institution of slavery,—which the fathers of the government expected to come to an end ere this, and putting it upon Brooks's cotton-gin basis; placing it where he openly confesses he has no desire there shall ever be an end of it.

I understand I have ten minutes yet. I will employ it in saying something about this argument Judge Douglas uses, while he sustains the Dred Scott decision, that the people of the Territories can still somehow exclude slavery. The first thing I ask attention to is the fact that Judge Douglas constantly said, before the decision, that whether they could or not, was a question for the Supreme Court. But after the court had made the decision he virtually says it is not a question for the Supreme Court, but for the people. And how is it he tells us they can exclude it? He says it needs "police regulations," and that admits of "unfriendly legislation." Although it is a right established by the Constitution of the United States to take a slave into a Territory of the United States and hold him as property, yet unless the Territorial Legislature will give friendly legislation, and more especially if they adopt unfriendly legislation, they can practically exclude him. Now, without meeting this proposition as a matter of fact, I pass to consider the real constitutional obligation. Let me take the gentleman who looks me in the face before me, and let us suppose that he is a member of the Territorial Legislature. The first thing he will do will be to swear that he will support the Constitution of the United States. His neighbor by his side in the Territory has slaves and needs Territorial legislation to enable him to enjoy that constitutional right. Can he withhold the legislation which his neighbor needs for the enjoyment of a right which is fixed in his favor in the Constitution of the United States which he has sworn to support? Can he withhold it without violating his oath? And, more especially, can he pass unfriendly legislation to violate his oath? Why, this is a monstrous sort of talk about the Constitution of the United States! There has never been as outlandish or lawless a doctrine from the mouth of any respectable man on earth. I do not believe it is a constitutional right to hold slaves in a Territory of the United States. I believe the decision was improperly made and I go for reversing it. Judge Douglas is furious against those who go for reversing a decision. But he is for legislating it out of all force while the law itself stands. I repeat that there has never been so monstrous a doctrine uttered from the mouth of a respectable man.

I suppose most of us (I know it of myself) believe that the people of the Southern States are entitled to a Congressional Fugitive Slave law,—that is a right fixed in the Constitution. But it cannot be made available to them without Congressional legislation. In the Judge's language, it is a "barren right," which needs legislation before it can become efficient and valuable to the persons to whom it is guaranteed. And as the right is constitutional, I agree that the legislation shall be granted to it, and that not that we like the institution of slavery. We profess to have no taste for running and catching niggers, at least, I profess no taste for that job at all. Why then do I yield support to a Fugitive Slave law? Because I do not understand that the Constitution, which guarantees that right, can be supported without it. And if I believed that the right to hold a slave in a Territory was equally fixed in the Constitution with the right to reclaim fugitives, I should be bound to give it the legislation necessary to support it. I say that no man can deny his obligation to give the necessary legislation to support slavery in a Territory, who believes it is a constitutional right to have it there. No man can, who does not give the Abolitionists an argument to deny the obligation enjoined by the Constitution to enact a Fugitive State law. Try it now. It is the strongest Abolition argument ever made. I say if that Dred Scott decision is correct, then the right to hold slaves in a Territory is equally a constitutional right with the right of a slaveholder to have his runaway returned. No one can show the distinction between them. The one is express, so that we cannot deny it. The other is construed to be in the Constitution, so that he who believes the decision to be correct believes in the right. And the man who argues that by unfriendly legislation, in spite of that constitutional right, slavery may be driven from the Territories, cannot avoid furnishing an argument by which Abolitionists may deny the obligation to return fugitives, and claim the power to pass laws unfriendly to the right of the slaveholder to reclaim his fugitive. I do not know how such an arguement may strike a popular assembly like this, but I defy anybody to go before a body of men whose minds are educated to estimating evidence and reasoning, and show that there is an iota of difference between the constitutional right to reclaim a fugitive and the constitutional right to hold a slave, in a Territory, provided this Dred Scott decision is correct, I defy any man to make an argument that will justify unfriendly legislation to deprive a slaveholder of his right to hold his slave in a Territory, that will not equally, in all its length, breadth, and thickness, furnish an argument for nullifying the Fugitive Slave law. Why, there is not such an Abolitionist in the nation as Douglas, after all!

THE WRITINGS OF ABRAHAM LINCOLN,
Volume Five, 1858-1862

1858

TO SYDNEY SPRING, GRAYVILLE, ILL.

SPRINGFIELD, June 19, 1858.

SYDNEY SPRING, Esq.
MY DEAR SIR:—Your letter introducing Mr. Faree was duly received. There was no opening to nominate him for Superintendent of Public Instruction, but through him Egypt made a most valuable contribution to the convention. I think it may be fairly said that he came off the lion of the day—or rather of the night. Can you not elect him to the Legislature? It seems to me he would be hard to beat. What objection could be made to him? What is your Senator Martin saying and doing? What is Webb about?
Please write me. Yours truly,
A. LINCOLN.

TO H. C. WHITNEY.

SPRINGFIELD, June 24, 1858

H. C. WHITNEY, ESQ.
DEAR SIR:—Your letter enclosing the attack of the Times upon me was received this morning. Give yourself no concern about my voting against the supplies. Unless you are without faith that a lie can be successfully contradicted, there is not a word of truth in the charge, and I am just considering a little as to the best shape to put a contradiction in. Show this to whomever you please, but do not publish it in the paper.
Your friend as ever,
A. LINCOLN.

TO J. W. SOMERS.

SPRINGFIELD, June 25, 1858.

JAMES W. SOMERS, Esq.
MY DEAR SIR:—Yours of the 22nd, inclosing a draft of two hundred dollars, was duly received. I have paid it on the judgment, and herewith you have the receipt. I do not wish to say anything as to who shall be the Republican candidate for the Legislature in your district, further than that I have full confidence in Dr. Hull. Have you ever got in the way of consulting with McKinley in political matters? He is true as steel, and his judgment is very good. The last I heard from him, he rather thought Weldon, of De Witt, was our best timber for representative, all things considered. But you there must settle it among yourselves. It may well puzzle older heads than yours to understand how, as the Dred Scott decision holds, Congress can authorize a Territorial Legislature to do everything else, and cannot authorize them to prohibit slavery. That is one of the things the court can decide, but can never give an intelligible reason for.
Yours very truly,
A. LINCOLN.

TO A. CAMPBELL.

SPRINGFIELD, June 28, 1858.

A. CAMPBELL, Esq.
MY DEAR SIR:—In 1856 you gave me authority to draw on you for any sum not exceeding five hundred dollars. I see clearly that such a privilege would be more available now than it was then. I am aware that times are tighter now than they were then. Please write me at all events, and whether you can now do anything or not I shall continue grateful for the past.
Yours very truly,
A. LINCOLN.

TO J. GILLESPIE.

SPRINGFIELD, July 16, 1858.

HON. JOSEPH GILLESPIE.
MY DEAR SIR:—I write this to say that from the specimens of Douglas Democracy we occasionally see here from Madison, we learn that they are making very confident calculation of beating you and your friends for the lower house, in that county. They offer to bet upon it. Billings and Job, respectively, have been up here, and were each as I learn, talking largely about it. If they do so, it can only be done by carrying the Fillmore men of 1856 very differently from what they seem to [be] going in the other party. Below is the vote of 1856, in your district:
Counties.

Counties.	Buchanan.	Fremont.	Fillmore.
Bond	607	153	659
Madison	1451	1111	1658
Montgomery	992	162	686
	3050	1426	3003

By this you will see, if you go through the calculation, that if they get one quarter of the Fillmore votes, and you three quarters, they will beat you 125 votes. If they get one fifth, and you four fifths, you beat them 179. In Madison, alone, if our friends get 1000 of the Fillmore votes, and their opponents the remainder, 658, we win by just two votes.
This shows the whole field, on the basis of the election of 1856.
Whether, since then, any Buchanan, or Fremonters, have shifted ground, and how the majority of new votes will go, you can judge better than I.
Of course you, on the ground, can better determine your line of tactics than any one off the ground; but it behooves you to be wide awake and actively working.
Don't neglect it; and write me at your first leisure. Yours as ever,
A. LINCOLN.

TO JOHN MATHERS, JACKSONVILLE, ILL.

SPRINGFIELD, JULY 20, 1858.

JNO. MATHERS, Esq.
MY DEAR SIR:—Your kind and interesting letter of the 19th was duly received. Your suggestions as to placing one's self on the offensive rather than the defensive are certainly correct. That is a point which I shall not disregard. I spoke here on Saturday night. The speech, not very well reported, appears in the State journal of this morning. You doubtless will see it; and I hope that you will perceive in it that I am already improving. I would mail you a copy now, but have not one [at] hand. I thank you for your letter and shall be pleased to hear from you again.
Yours very truly,

A. LINCOLN.

TO JOSEPH GILLESPIE.

SPRINGFIELD, JULY 25, 1858.

HON. J. GILLESPIE.
MY DEAR SIR:—Your doleful letter of the 8th was received on my return from Chicago last night. I do hope you are worse scared than hurt, though you ought to know best. We must not lose the district. We must make a job of it, and save it. Lay hold of the proper agencies, and secure all the Americans you can, at once. I do hope, on closer inspection, you will find they are not half gone. Make a little test. Run down one of the poll-books of the Edwardsville precinct, and take the first hundred known American names. Then quietly ascertain how many of them are actually going for Douglas. I think you will find less than fifty. But even if you find fifty, make sure of the other fifty, that is, make sure of all you can, at all events. We will set other agencies to work which shall compensate for the loss of a good many Americans. Don't fail to check the stampede at once. Trumbull, I think, will be with you before long.
There is much he cannot do, and some he can. I have reason to hope there will be other help of an appropriate kind. Write me again.
Yours as ever,
A. LINCOLN.

TO B. C. COOK.

SPRINGFIELD, Aug. 2, 1858.

Hon. B. C. COOK.
MY DEAR SIR:—I have a letter from a very true and intelligent man insisting that there is a plan on foot in La Salle and Bureau to run Douglas Republicans for Congress and for the Legislature in those counties, if they can only get the encouragement of our folks nominating pretty extreme abolitionists.
It is thought they will do nothing if our folks nominate men who are not very obnoxious to the charge of abolitionism. Please have your eye upon this. Signs are looking pretty fair.
Yours very truly,
A. LINCOLN.

TO HON. J. M. PALMER.

SPRINGFIELD, Aug. 5, 1858.

HON. J. M. PALMER.
DEAR SIR:—Since we parted last evening no new thought has occurred to [me] on the subject of which we talked most yesterday.
I have concluded, however, to speak at your town on Tuesday, August 31st, and have promised to have it so appear in the papers of to-morrow. Judge Trumbull has not yet reached here.
Yours as ever,
A. LINCOLN.

TO ALEXANDER SYMPSON.

SPRINGFIELD, Aug. 11, 1858.

ALEXANDER SYMPSON, Esq.
DEAR SIR:—Yours of the 6th received. If life and health continue I shall pretty likely be at Augusta on the 25th. Things look reasonably well. Will tell you more fully when I see you.
Yours truly,
A. LINCOLN.

TO J. O. CUNNINGHAM.

OTTAWA, August 22, 1858.

J. O. CUNNINGHAM, Esq.
MY DEAR SIR:—Yours of the 18th, signed as secretary of the Republican club, is received. In the matter of making speeches I am a good deal pressed by invitations from almost all quarters, and while I hope to be at Urbana some time during the canvass, I cannot yet say when. Can you not see me at Monticello on the 6th of September?
Douglas and I, for the first time this canvass, crossed swords here yesterday; the fire flew some, and I am glad to know I am yet alive. There was a vast concourse of people—more than could get near enough to hear.
Yours as ever,
A. LINCOLN.

ON SLAVERY IN A DEMOCRACY.

August??, 1858

As I would not be a slave, so I would not be a master. This expresses my idea of democracy. Whatever differs from this, to the extent of the difference, is no democracy.
A. LINCOLN.

TO B. C. COOK.

SPRINGFIELD, August 2, 1858

HON. B. C. COOK.
MY DEAR SIR:—I have a letter from a very true friend, and intelligent man, writing that there is a plan on foot in La Salle and Bureau, to run Douglas Republican for Congress and for the Legislature in those counties, if they can only get the encouragement of our folks nominating pretty extreme abolitionists. It is thought they will do nothing if our folks nominate men who are not very [undecipherable word looks like "obnoxious"] to the charge of abolitionism. Please have your eye upon this. Signs are looking pretty fair.
Yours very truly,
A. LINCOLN.

TO DR. WILLIAM FITHIAN, DANVILLE, ILL.

BLOOMINGTON, Sept. 3, 1858

DEAR DOCTOR:—Yours of the 1st was received this morning, as also one from Mr. Harmon, and one from Hiram Beckwith on the same subject. You will see by the Journal that I have been appointed to speak at Danville on the 22d of Sept.,—the day after Douglas speaks there. My recent experience shows that speaking at the same place the next day after D. is the very thing,—it is, in fact, a concluding speech on him. Please show this to Messrs. Harmon and Beckwith; and tell them they must excuse me from writing separate letters to them.
Yours as ever,
A. LINCOLN
P. S.—Give full notice to all surrounding country. A.L.

FRAGMENT OF SPEECH AT PARIS, ILL.,

SEPT. 8, 1858.

Let us inquire what Judge Douglas really invented when he introduced the Nebraska Bill? He called it Popular Sovereignty. What does that mean? It means the sovereignty of the people over their own affairs—in other words, the right of the people to govern themselves. Did Judge Douglas invent this? Not quite. The idea of popular sovereignty was floating about several ages before the author of the Nebraska Bill was born—indeed, before Columbus set foot on this continent. In the year 1776 it took form in the noble words which you are all familiar with: "We hold these truths to be self-evident, that all men are created equal," etc. Was not this the origin of popular sovereignty as applied to the American people? Here we are told that governments are instituted among men deriving their just powers from the consent of the governed. If that is not popular sovereignty, then I have no conception of the meaning of words. If Judge Douglas did not invent this kind of popular sovereignty, let us pursue the inquiry and find out what kind he did invent. Was it the right of emigrants to Kansas and Nebraska to govern themselves, and a lot of "niggers," too, if they wanted them? Clearly this was no invention of his because General Cass put forth the same doctrine in 1848 in his so called Nicholson letter, six years before Douglas thought of such a thing. Then what was it that the "Little Giant" invented? It never occurred to General Cass to call his discovery by the odd name of popular sovereignty. He had not the face to say that the right of the people to govern "niggers" was the right of the people to govern themselves. His notions of the fitness of things were not moulded to the brazenness of calling the right to put a hundred "niggers" through under the lash in Nebraska a "sacred" right of self-government. And here I submit to you was Judge Douglas's discovery, and the whole of it: He discovered that the right to breed and flog negroes in Nebraska was popular sovereignty.

SPEECH AT CLINTON, ILLINOIS,

SEPTEMBER 8, 1858.

The questions are sometimes asked "What is all this fuss that is being made about negroes? What does it amount to? And where will it end?" These questions imply that those who ask them consider the slavery question a very insignificant matter they think that it amounts to little or nothing and that those who agitate it are extremely foolish. Now it must be admitted that if the great question which has caused so much trouble is insignificant, we are very foolish to have anything to do with it—if it is of no importance we had better throw it aside and busy ourselves with something else. But let us inquire a little into this insignificant matter, as it is called by some, and see if it is not important enough to demand the close attention of every well-wisher of the Union. In one of Douglas's recent speeches, I find a reference to one which was made by me in Springfield some time ago. The judge makes one quotation from that speech that requires some little notice from me at this time. I regret that I have not my Springfield speech before me, but the judge has quoted one particular part of it so often that I think I can recollect it. It runs I think as follows:
"We are now far into the fifth year since a policy was initiated with the avowed object and confident promise of putting an end to slavery agitation. Under the operation of that policy that agitation has not only not ceased but has constantly augmented. In my opinion it will not cease until a crisis shall have been reached and passed.
"A house divided against itself cannot stand. I believe this government cannot endure permanently half slave and half free. I do not expect the Union to be dissolved. I do not expect the house to fall, but I do expect it will cease to be

divided. It will become all one thing or all the other. Either the opponents of slavery will arrest the further spread of it and place it where the public mind shall rest in the belief that it is in the course of ultimate extinction; or its advocates will push it forward till it shall become alike lawful in all the States, old as well as new, North as well as South."

Judge Douglas makes use of the above quotation, and finds a great deal of fault with it. He deals unfairly with me, and tries to make the people of this State believe that I advocated dangerous doctrines in my Springfield speech. Let us see if that portion of my Springfield speech of which Judge Douglas complains so bitterly, is as objectionable to others as it is to him. We are, certainly, far into the fifth year since a policy was initiated with the avowed object and confident promise of putting an end to slavery agitation. On the fourth day of January, 1854, Judge Douglas introduced the Kansas-Nebraska bill. He initiated a new policy, and that policy, so he says, was to put an end to the agitation of the slavery question. Whether that was his object or not I will not stop to discuss, but at all events some kind of a policy was initiated; and what has been the result? Instead of the quiet and good feeling which were promised us by the self-styled author of Popular Sovereignty, we have had nothing but ill-feeling and agitation. According to Judge Douglas, the passage of the Nebraska bill would tranquilize the whole country—there would be no more slavery agitation in or out of Congress, and the vexed question would be left entirely to the people of the Territories. Such was the opinion of Judge Douglas, and such were the opinions of the leading men of the Democratic Party. Even as late as the spring of 1856 Mr. Buchanan said, a short time subsequent to his nomination by the Cincinnati convention, that the territory of Kansas would be tranquil in less than six weeks. Perhaps he thought so, but Kansas has not been and is not tranquil, and it may be a long time before she may be so.

We all know how fierce the agitation was in Congress last winter, and what a narrow escape Kansas had from being admitted into the Union with a constitution that was detested by ninety-nine hundredths of her citizens. Did the angry debates which took place at Washington during the last season of Congress lead you to suppose that the slavery agitation was settled?

An election was held in Kansas in the month of August, and the constitution which was submitted to the people was voted down by a large majority. So Kansas is still out of the Union, and there is a probability that she will remain out for some time. But Judge Douglas says the slavery question is settled. He says the bill he introduced into the Senate of the United States on the 4th day of January, 1854, settled the slavery question forever! Perhaps he can tell us how that bill settled the slavery question, for if he is able to settle a question of such great magnitude he ought to be able to explain the manner in which he does it. He knows and you know that the question is not settled, and that his ill-timed experiment to settle it has made it worse than it ever was before.

And now let me say a few words in regard to Douglas's great hobby of negro equality. He thinks—he says at least—that the Republican party is in favor of allowing whites and blacks to intermarry, and that a man can't be a good Republican unless he is willing to elevate black men to office and to associate with them on terms of perfect equality. He knows that we advocate no such doctrines as these, but he cares not how much he misrepresents us if he can gain a few votes by so doing. To show you what my opinion of negro equality was in times past, and to prove to you that I stand on that question where I always stood, I will read you a few extracts from a speech that was made by me in Peoria in 1854. It was made in reply to one of Judge Douglas's speeches.

(Mr. Lincoln then read a number of extracts which had the ring of the true metal. We have rarely heard anything with which we have been more pleased. And the audience after hearing the extracts read, and comparing their conservative sentiments with those now advocated by Mr. Lincoln, testified their approval by loud applause. How any reasonable man can hear one of Mr. Lincoln's speeches without being converted to Republicanism is something that we can't account for. Ed.)

Slavery, continued Mr. Lincoln, is not a matter of little importance, it overshadows every other question in which we are interested. It has divided the Methodist and Presbyterian churches, and has sown discord in the American Tract Society. The churches have split and the society will follow their example before long. So it will be seen that slavery is agitated in the religious as well as in the political world. Judge Douglas is very much afraid in the triumph that the Republican party will lead to a general mixture of the white and black races. Perhaps I am wrong in saying that he is afraid, so I will correct myself by saying that he pretends to fear that the success of our party will result in the amalgamation of the blacks and whites. I think I can show plainly, from documents now before me, that Judge Douglas's fears are groundless. The census of 1800 tells us that in that year there were over four hundred thousand mulattoes in the United States. Now let us take what is called an Abolition State—the Republican, slavery-hating State of New Hampshire—and see how many mulattoes we can find within her borders. The number amounts to just one hundred and eighty-four. In the Old Dominion—in the Democratic and aristocratic State of Virginia—there were a few more mulattoes than the Census-takers found in New Hampshire. How many do you suppose there were? Seventy-nine thousand, seven hundred and seventy-five—twenty-three thousand more than there were in all the free States! In the slave States there were in 1800, three hundred and forty-eight thousand mulattoes all of home production; and in the free States there were less than sixty thousand mulattoes—and a large number of them were imported from the South.

FRAGMENT OF SPEECH AT EDWARDSVILLE, ILL.,

SEPT. 13, 1858.

I have been requested to give a concise statement of the difference, as I understand it, between the Democratic and Republican parties, on the leading issues of the campaign. This question has been put to me by a gentleman whom I do not know. I do not even know whether he is a friend of mine or a supporter of Judge Douglas in this contest, nor does that make any difference. His question is a proper one. Lest I should forget it, I will give you my answer before proceeding with the line of argument I have marked out for this discussion.
The difference between the Republican and the Democratic parties on the leading issues of this contest, as I understand it, is that the former consider slavery a moral, social and political wrong, while the latter do not consider it either a moral, a social or a political wrong; and the action of each, as respects the growth of the country and the expansion of our population, is squared to meet these views. I will not affirm that the Democratic party consider slavery morally, socially and politically right, though their tendency to that view has, in my opinion, been constant and unmistakable for the past five years. I prefer to take, as the accepted maxim of the party, the idea put forth by Judge Douglas, that he "don't care whether slavery is voted down or voted up." I am quite willing to believe that many Democrats would prefer that slavery should be always voted down, and I know that some prefer that it be always voted up; but I have a right to insist that their action, especially if it be their constant action, shall determine their ideas and preferences on this subject. Every measure of the Democratic party of late years, bearing directly or indirectly on the slavery question, has corresponded with this notion of utter indifference whether slavery or freedom shall outrun in the race of empire across to the Pacific—every measure, I say, up to the Dred Scott decision, where, it seems to me, the idea is boldly suggested that slavery is better than freedom. The Republican party, on the contrary, hold that this government was instituted to secure the blessings of freedom, and that slavery is an unqualified evil to the negro, to the white man, to the soil, and to the State. Regarding it as an evil, they will not molest it in the States where it exists, they will not overlook the constitutional guards which our fathers placed around it; they will do nothing that can give proper offence to those who hold slaves by legal sanction; but they will use every constitutional method to prevent the evil from becoming larger and involving more negroes, more white men, more soil, and more States in its deplorable consequences. They will, if possible, place it where the public mind shall rest in the belief that it is in course of ultimate peaceable extinction in God's own good time. And to this end they will, if possible, restore the government to the policy of the fathers, the policy of preserving the new Territories from the baneful influence of human bondage, as the Northwestern Territories were sought to be preserved by the Ordinance of 1787, and the Compromise Act of 1820. They will oppose, in all its length and breadth, the modern Democratic idea, that slavery is as good as freedom, and ought to have room for expansion all over the continent, if people can be found to carry it. All, or nearly all, of Judge Douglas's arguments are logical, if you admit that slavery is as good and as right as freedom, and not one of them is worth a rush if you deny it. This is the difference, as I understand it, between the Republican and Democratic parties.
My friends, I have endeavored to show you the logical consequences of the Dred Scott decision, which holds that the people of a Territory cannot prevent the establishment of slavery in their midst. I have stated what cannot be gainsaid, that the grounds upon which this decision is made are equally applicable to the free States as to the free Territories, and that the peculiar reasons put forth by Judge Douglas for indorsing this decision commit him, in advance, to the next decision and to all other decisions coming from the same source. And when, by all these means, you have succeeded in dehumanizing the negro; when you have put him down and made it impossible for him to be but as the beasts of the field; when you have extinguished his soul in this world and placed him where the ray of hope is blown out as in the darkness of the damned, are you quite sure that the demon you have roused will not turn and rend you? What constitutes the bulwark of our own liberty and independence? It is not our frowning battlements, our bristling sea coasts, our army and our navy. These are not our reliance against tyranny All of those may be turned against us without making us weaker for the struggle. Our reliance is in the love of liberty which God has planted in us. Our defense is in the spirit which prizes liberty as the heritage of all men, in all lands everywhere. Destroy this spirit and you have planted the seeds of despotism at your own doors. Familiarize yourselves with the chains of bondage and you prepare your own limbs to wear them. Accustomed to trample on the rights of others, you have lost the genius of your own independence and become the fit subjects of the first cunning tyrant who rises among you. And let me tell you, that all these things are prepared for you by the teachings of history, if the elections shall promise that the next Dred Scott decision and all future decisions will be quietly acquiesced in by the people.

VERSE TO "LINNIE"

September 30,? 1858.

TO "LINNIE":
    A sweet plaintive song did I hear
    And I fancied that she was the singer.
    May emotions as pure as that song set astir
    Be the wont that the future shall bring her.

NEGROES ARE MEN

TO J. U. BROWN.

SPRINGFIELD, OCT 18, 1858 HON. J. U. BROWN.
MY DEAR SIR:—I do not perceive how I can express myself more plainly than I have in the fore-going extracts. In four of them I have expressly disclaimed all intention to bring about social and political equality between the white and black races and in all the rest I have done the same thing by clear implication.
I have made it equally plain that I think the negro is included in the word "men" used in the Declaration of Independence.
I believe the declaration that "all men are created equal" is the great fundamental principle upon which our free institutions rest; that negro slavery is violative of that principle; but that, by our frame of government, that principle has not been made one of legal obligation; that by our frame of government, States which have slavery are to retain it, or surrender it at their own pleasure; and that all others—individuals, free States and national Government—are constitutionally bound to leave them alone about it.
I believe our Government was thus framed because of the necessity springing from the actual presence of slavery, when it was framed.
That such necessity does not exist in the Territories when slavery is not present.
In his Mendenhall speech Mr. Clay says: "Now as an abstract principle there is no doubt of the truth of that declaration (all men created equal), and it is desirable, in the original construction of society, to keep it in view as a great fundamental principle."
Again, in the same speech Mr. Clay says: "If a state of nature existed and we were about to lay the foundations of society, no man would be more strongly opposed than I should to incorporate the institution of slavery among its elements."
Exactly so. In our new free Territories, a state of nature does exist. In them Congress lays the foundations of society; and in laying those foundations, I say, with Mr. Clay, it is desirable that the declaration of the equality of all men shall be kept in view as a great fundamental principle, and that Congress, which lays the foundations of society, should, like Mr. Clay, be strongly opposed to the incorporation of slavery and its elements.
But it does not follow that social and political equality between whites and blacks must be incorporated because slavery must not. The declaration does not so require.
Yours as ever,
A. LINCOLN
[Newspaper cuttings of Lincoln's speeches at Peoria, in 1854, at Springfield, Ottawa, Chicago, and Charleston, in 1858. They were pasted in a little book in which the above letter was also written.]

TO A. SYMPSON.

BLANDINSVILLE, Oct 26, 1858

A. SYMPSON, Esq.

DEAR SIR:—Since parting with you this morning I heard some things which make me believe that Edmunds and Morrill will spend this week among the National Democrats, trying to induce them to content themselves by voting for Jake Davis, and then to vote for the Douglas candidates for senator and representative. Have this headed off, if you can. Call Wagley's attention to it and have him and the National Democrat for Rep. to counteract it as far as they can.
Yours as ever,
A. LINCOLN.

SENATORIAL ELECTION LOST AND OUT OF MONEY

TO N. B. JUDD.

SPRINGFIELD, NOVEMBER 16, 1858 HON. N. B. JUDD
DEAR SIR:—Yours of the 15th is just received. I wrote you the same day. As to the pecuniary matter, I am willing to pay according to my ability; but I am the poorest hand living to get others to pay. I have been on expenses so long without earning anything that I am absolutely without money now for even household purposes. Still, if you can put in two hundred and fifty dollars for me toward discharging the debt of the committee, I will allow it when you and I settle the private matter between us. This, with what I have already paid, and with an outstanding note of mine, will exceed my subscription of five hundred dollars. This, too, is exclusive of my ordinary expenses during the campaign, all of which, being added to my loss of time and business, bears pretty heavily upon one no better off in [this] world's goods than I; but as I had the post of honor, it is not for me to be over nice. You are feeling badly,—"And this too shall pass away," never fear.
Yours as ever,
A. LINCOLN.

THE FIGHT MUST GO ON

TO H. ASBURY.

SPRINGFIELD, November 19, 1858.
HENRY ASBURY, Esq.
DEAR SIR:—Yours of the 13th was received some days ago. The fight must go on. The cause of civil liberty must not be surrendered at the end of one or even one hundred defeats. Douglas had the ingenuity to be supported in the late contest both as the best means to break down and to uphold the slave interest. No ingenuity can keep these antagonistic elements in harmony long. Another explosion will soon come.
Yours truly,
A. LINCOLN.

REALIZATION THAT DEBATES MUST BE SAVED

TO C. H. RAY.

SPRINGFIELD, Nov.20, 1858
DR. C. H. RAY
MY DEAR SIR:—I wish to preserve a set of the late debates (if they may be called so), between Douglas and myself. To enable me to do so, please get two copies of each number of your paper containing the whole, and send them to me by express; and I will pay you for the papers and for your trouble. I wish the two sets in order to lay one away in the [undecipherable word] and to put the other in a scrapbook. Remember, if part of any debate is on both sides of the sheet it will take two sets to make one scrap-book.

I believe, according to a letter of yours to Hatch, you are "feeling like h-ll yet." Quit that—you will soon feel better. Another "blow up" is coming; and we shall have fun again. Douglas managed to be supported both as the best instrument to down and to uphold the slave power; but no ingenuity can long keep the antagonism in harmony.
Yours as ever,
A. LINCOLN

TO H. C. WHITNEY.

SPRINGFIELD, November 30, 1858

H. C. WHITNEY, ESQ.
MY DEAR SIR:—Being desirous of preserving in some permanent form the late joint discussion between Douglas and myself, ten days ago I wrote to Dr. Ray, requesting him to forward to me by express two sets of the numbers of the Tribune which contain the reports of those discussions. Up to date I have no word from him on the subject. Will you, if in your power, procure them and forward them to me by express? If you will, I will pay all charges, and be greatly obliged, to boot. Hoping to visit you before long, I remain
As ever your friend,
A. LINCOLN.

TO H. D. SHARPE.

SPRINGFIELD, Dec. 8, 1858.

H. D. SHARPE, Esq.
DEAR SIR:—Your very kind letter of Nov. 9th was duly received. I do not know that you expected or desired an answer; but glancing over the contents of yours again, I am prompted to say that, while I desired the result of the late canvass to have been different, I still regard it as an exceeding small matter. I think we have fairly entered upon a durable struggle as to whether this nation is to ultimately become all slave or all free, and though I fall early in the contest, it is nothing if I shall have contributed, in the least degree, to the final rightful result.
Respectfully yours,
A. LINCOLN.

TO A. SYMPSON.

SPRINGFIELD, Dec.12, 1858.

ALEXANDER SYMPSON, Esq.
MY DEAR SIR:—I expect the result of the election went hard with you. So it did with me, too, perhaps not quite so hard as you may have supposed. I have an abiding faith that we shall beat them in the long run. Step by step the objects of the leaders will become too plain for the people to stand them. I write merely to let you know that I am neither dead nor dying. Please give my respects to your good family, and all inquiring friends.
Yours as ever,
A. LINCOLN.

ON BANKRUPTCY

NOTES OF AN ARGUMENT.

December [?], 1858.

Legislation and adjudication must follow and conform to the progress of society.
The progress of society now begins to produce cases of the transfer for debts of the entire property of railroad corporations; and to enable transferees to use and enjoy the transferred property, legislation and adjudication begin to be necessary.
Shall this class of legislation just now beginning with us be general or special?

Section Ten of our Constitution requires that it should be general,

if possible. (Read the section.)

Special legislation always trenches upon the judicial department; and in so far violates Section Two of the Constitution. (Read it.)
Just reasoning—policy—is in favor of general legislation—else the Legislature will be loaded down with the investigation of smaller cases—a work which the courts ought to perform, and can perform much more perfectly. How can the Legislature rightly decide the facts between P. & B. and S.C.
It is said that under a general law, whenever a R. R. Co. gets tired of its debts, it may transfer fraudulently to get rid of them. So they may—so may individuals; and which—the Legislature or the courts—is best suited to try the question of fraud in either case?
It is said, if a purchaser have acquired legal rights, let him not be robbed of them, but if he needs legislation let him submit to just terms to obtain it.
Let him, say we, have general law in advance (guarded in every possible way against fraud), so that, when he acquires a legal right, he will have no occasion to wait for additional legislation; and if he has practiced fraud let the courts so decide.

A LEGAL OPINION BY ABRAHAM LINCOLN.

The 11th Section of the Act of Congress, approved Feb. 11, 1805, prescribing rules for the subdivision of sections of land within the United States system of surveys, standing unrepealed, in my opinion, is binding on the respective purchasers of different parts of the same section, and furnishes the true rule for surveyors in establishing lines between them. That law, being in force at the time each became a purchaser, becomes a condition of the purchase.
And, by that law, I think the true rule for dividing into quarters any interior section or sections, which is not fractional, is to run straight lines through the section from the opposite quarter section corners, fixing the point where such straight lines cross, or intersect each other, as the middle or centre of the section.
Nearly, perhaps quite, all the original surveys are to some extent erroneous, and in some of the sections, greatly so. In each of the latter, it is obvious that a more equitable mode of division than the above might be adopted; but as error is infinitely various perhaps no better single rules can be prescribed.
At all events I think the above has been prescribed by the competent authority.
SPRINGFIELD, Jany. 6, 1859.
A. LINCOLN.

TO M. W. DELAHAY.

SPRINGFIELD, March 4, 1859.

M. W. DELAHAY, Esq.
MY DEAR SIR: Your second letter in relation to my being with you at your Republican convention was duly received. It is not at hand just now, but I have the impression from it that the convention was to be at Leavenworth; but day before yesterday a friend handed me a letter from Judge M. F. Caraway, in which he also expresses a wish for me to come, and he fixes the place at Ossawatomie. This I believe is off of the river, and will require more time and labor to get to it. It will push me hard to get there without injury to my own business; but I shall try to do it, though I am not yet quite certain I shall succeed.
I should like to know before coming, that while some of you wish me to come, there may not be others who would quite as lief I would stay away. Write me again.
Yours as ever,
A. LINCOLN.

TO W. M. MORRIS.

SPRINGFIELD, March 28, 1859.

W. M. MORRIS, Esq.
DEAR SIR:—Your kind note inviting me to deliver a lecture at Galesburg is received. I regret to say I cannot do so now; I must stick to the courts awhile. I read a sort of lecture to three different audiences during the last month and this; but I did so under circumstances which made it a waste of no time whatever.
Yours very truly,

TO H. L. PIERCE AND OTHERS.

SPRINGFIELD, ILLINOIS, April 6, 1859.

GENTLEMEN:—Your kind note inviting me to attend a festival in Boston, on the 28th instant, in honor of the birthday of Thomas Jefferson, was duly received. My engagements are such that I cannot attend.
Bearing in mind that about seventy years ago two great political parties were first formed in this country, that Thomas Jefferson was the head of one of them and Boston the headquarters of the other, it is both curious and interesting that those supposed to descend politically from the party opposed to Jefferson should now be celebrating his birthday in their own original seat of empire, while those claiming political descent from him have nearly ceased to breathe his name everywhere.
Remembering, too, that the Jefferson party was formed upon its supposed superior devotion to the personal rights of men, holding the rights of property to be secondary only, and greatly inferior, and assuming that the so-called Democracy of to-day are the Jefferson, and their opponents the anti-Jefferson, party, it will be equally interesting to note how completely the two have changed hands as to the principle upon which they were originally supposed to be divided. The Democracy of to-day hold the liberty of one man to be absolutely nothing, when in conflict with another man's right of property; Republicans, on the contrary, are for both the man and the dollar, but in case of conflict the man before the dollar.
I remember being once much amused at seeing two partially intoxicated men engaged in a fight with their great-coats on, which fight, after a long and rather harmless contest, ended in each having fought himself out of his own coat and into that of the other. If the two leading parties of this day are really identical with the two in the days of Jefferson and Adams, they have performed the same feat as the two drunken men.
But soberly, it is now no child's play to save the principles of Jefferson from total overthrow in this nation. One would state with great confidence that he could convince any sane child that the simpler propositions of Euclid are true; but nevertheless he would fail, utterly, with one who should deny the definitions and axioms. The principles of Jefferson are the definitions and axioms of free society. And yet they are denied and evaded, with no small show of success. One dashingly calls them "glittering generalities." Another bluntly calls them "self-evident lies." And others insidiously argue

that they apply to "superior races." These expressions, differing in form, are identical in object and effect—the supplanting the principles of free government, and restoring those of classification, caste, and legitimacy. They would delight a convocation of crowned heads plotting against the people. They are the vanguard, the miners and sappers, of returning despotism. We must repulse them, or they will subjugate us. This is a world of compensation; and he who would be no slave must consent to have no slave. Those who deny freedom to others deserve it not for themselves, and, under a just God, cannot long retain it. All honor to Jefferson to the man who, in the concrete pressure of a struggle for national independence by a single people, had the coolness, forecast, and capacity to introduce into a mere revolutionary document an abstract truth, applicable to all men and all times, and so to embalm it there that to-day and in all coming days it shall be a rebuke and a stumbling-block to the very harbingers of reappearing tyranny and oppression.

Your obedient servant,
A. LINCOLN.

TO T. CANISIUS.

SPRINGFIELD, May 17, 1859.

DR. THEODORE CANISIUS.
DEAR SIR:—Your note asking, in behalf of yourself and other German citizens, whether I am for or against the constitutional provision in regard to naturalized citizens, lately adopted by Massachusetts, and whether I am for or against a fusion of the Republicans and other opposition elements for the canvass of 1860, is received.

Massachusetts is a sovereign and independent State; and it is no privilege of mine to scold her for what she does. Still, if from what she has done an inference is sought to be drawn as to what I would do, I may without impropriety speak out. I say, then, that, as I understand the Massachusetts provision, I am against its adoption in Illinois, or in any other place where I have a right to oppose it. Understanding the spirit of our institutions to aim at the elevation of men, I am opposed to whatever tends to degrade them. I have some little notoriety for commiserating the oppressed negro; and I should be strangely inconsistent if I could favor any project for curtailing the existing rights of white men, even though born in different lands, and speaking different languages from myself. As to the matter of fusion, I am for it if it can be had on Republican grounds; and I am not for it on any other terms. A fusion on any other terms would be as foolish as unprincipled. It would lose the whole North, while the common enemy would still carry the whole South. The question of men is a different one. There are good, patriotic men and able statesmen in the South whom I would cheerfully support, if they would now place themselves on Republican ground, but I am against letting down the Republican standard a hairsbreadth.

I have written this hastily, but I believe it answers your questions substantially.
Yours truly,
A. LINCOLN.

TO THE GOVERNOR, AUDITOR, AND TREASURER OF THE STATE OF ILLINOIS.

GENTLEMEN:

In reply to your inquiry; requesting our written opinion as to what your duty requires you to do in executing the latter clause of the Seventh Section of "An Act in relation to the payment of the principal and interest of the State debt," approved Feb'y 22, 1859, we reply that said last clause of said section is certainly indefinite, general, and ambiguous in its description of the bonds to be issued by you; giving no time at which the bonds are to be made payable, no place at which either principal or interest are to be paid, and no rate of interest which the bonds are to bear; nor any other description except that they are to be coupon bonds, which in commercial usage means interest-paying bonds with obligations or orders attached to them for the payment of annual or semiannual interest; there is we suppose no difficulty in ascertaining, if this act stood alone, what ought to be the construction of the terms "coupon bonds" and that it, would mean bonds bearing interest from the time of issuing the same. And under this act considered by itself the creditors would have a right to require such bonds. But your inquiry in regard to a class of bonds on which no interest is to be paid or shall begin to run until January 1, 1860, is whether the Act of February 18, 1857, would not authorize you to refuse to give bonds with any coupons attached payable before the first day of July, 1860. We have very maturely considered this question and have arrived at the conclusion that you have a right to use such measures as will secure the State against the loss of six months' interest on these bonds by the indefiniteness of the Act of 1859. While it cannot be denied that the letter of the laws favor the construction claimed by some of the creditors that interest-bearing bonds were required to be issued to them, inasmuch as the restriction that no interest is to run on said bonds until 1st January, 1860, relates solely to the bonds issued under the Act of 1857. And the Act of 1859 directing you to issue new bonds does not contain this restriction, but directs you to issue coupon bonds. Nevertheless the very indefiniteness and generality of the Act of 1859, giving no rate of interest, no time due, no place of payment, no postponement of the time when interest commences, necessarily implies that the Legislature intended to invest you with a discretion to impose such terms and restrictions as would protect the interest of the State; and we think you have a right and that it is your duty to see that the State Bonds are so issued that the State shall not lose six months' interest. Two plans present themselves either of which will secure the State. 1st. If in literal compliance with the law you issue bonds bearing interest from 1st July, 1859, you may deduct from the bonds presented three thousand from every $100,000 of bonds and issue $97,000 of coupon bonds; by this plan $3000 out of $100,000 of principal would be extinguished in consideration of paying $2910 interest on the first of January, 1860—and the interest on the $3000 would forever cease; this would be no doubt most advantageous to the State. But if the Auditor will not consent to this, then, 2nd. Cut off of each bond all the coupons payable before 1st July, 1860.

One of these plans would undoubtedly have been prescribed by the Legislature if its attention had been directed to this question.

May 28, 1859.

ON LINCOLN'S SCRAP BOOK

TO H. C. WHITNEY.

SPRINGFIELD, December 25, 1858.
H. C. WHITNEY, ESQ.
MY DEAR SIR:—I have just received yours of the 23rd inquiring whether I received the newspapers you sent me by express. I did receive them, and am very much obliged. There is some probability that my scrap-book will be reprinted, and if it shall, I will save you a copy.
Your friend as ever,
A. LINCOLN.

1859

FIRST SUGGESTION OF A PRESIDENTIAL OFFER.

TO S. GALLOWAY.

SPRINGFIELD, ILL., July 28, 1859.

HON. SAMUEL GALLOWAY.

MY DEAR SIR:—Your very complimentary, not to say flattering, letter of the 23d inst. is received. Dr. Reynolds had induced me to expect you here; and I was disappointed not a little by your failure to come. And yet I fear you have formed an estimate of me which can scarcely be sustained on a personal acquaintance.

Two things done by the Ohio Republican convention—the repudiation of Judge Swan, and the "plank" for a repeal of the Fugitive Slave Law—I very much regretted. These two things are of a piece; and they are viewed by many good men, sincerely opposed to slavery, as a struggle against, and in disregard of, the Constitution itself. And it is the very thing that will greatly endanger our cause, if it be not kept out of our national convention. There is another thing our friends are doing which gives me some uneasiness. It is their leaning toward "popular sovereignty." There are three substantial objections to this: First, no party can command respect which sustains this year what it opposed last. Secondly, Douglas (who is the most dangerous enemy of liberty, because the most insidious one) would have little support in the North, and by consequence, no capital to trade on in the South, if it were not for his friends thus magnifying him and his humbug. But lastly, and chiefly, Douglas's popular sovereignty, accepted by the public mind as a just principle, nationalizes slavery, and revives the African slave trade inevitably.

Taking slaves into new Territories, and buying slaves in Africa, are identical things, identical rights or identical wrongs, and the argument which establishes one will establish the other. Try a thousand years for a sound reason why Congress shall not hinder the people of Kansas from having slaves, and, when you have found it, it will be an equally good one why Congress should not hinder the people of Georgia from importing slaves from Africa.

As to Governor Chase, I have a kind side for him. He was one of the few distinguished men of the nation who gave us, in Illinois, their sympathy last year. I never saw him, but suppose him to be able and right-minded; but still he may not be the most suitable as a candidate for the Presidency.

I must say I do not think myself fit for the Presidency. As you propose a correspondence with me, I shall look for your letters anxiously.

I have not met Dr. Reynolds since receiving your letter; but when I shall, I will present your respects as requested.
Yours very truly,
A. LINCOLN.

IT IS BAD TO BE POOR.

TO HAWKINS TAYLOR

SPRINGFIELD, ILL. Sept. 6, 1859.
HAWKINS TAYLOR, Esq.
DEAR SIR:—Yours of the 3d is just received. There is some mistake about my expected attendance of the U.S. Court in your city on the 3d Tuesday of this month. I have had no thought of being there.

It is bad to be poor. I shall go to the wall for bread and meat if I neglect my business this year as well as last. It would please me much to see the city and good people of Keokuk, but for this year it is little less than an impossibility. I am constantly receiving invitations which I am compelled to decline. I was pressingly urged to go to Minnesota; and I now have two invitations to go to Ohio. These last are prompted by Douglas going there; and I am really tempted to make a flying trip to Columbus and Cincinnati.

I do hope you will have no serious trouble in Iowa. What thinks Grimes about it? I have not known him to be mistaken about an election in Iowa. Present my respects to Col. Carter, and any other friends, and believe me
Yours truly,
A. LINCOLN.

SPEECH AT COLUMBUS, OHIO.

SEPTEMBER 16, 1859.

FELLOW-CITIZENS OF THE STATE OF OHIO: I cannot fail to remember that I appear for the first time before an audience in this now great State,—an audience that is accustomed to hear such speakers as Corwin, and Chase, and Wade, and many other renowned men; and, remembering this, I feel that it will be well for you, as for me, that you should not raise your expectations to that standard to which you would have been justified in raising them had one of these distinguished men appeared before you. You would perhaps be only preparing a disappointment for yourselves, and, as a consequence of your disappointment, mortification to me. I hope, therefore, that you will commence with very moderate expectations; and perhaps, if you will give me your attention, I shall be able to interest you to a moderate degree.

Appearing here for the first time in my life, I have been somewhat embarrassed for a topic by way of introduction to my speech; but I have been relieved from that embarrassment by an introduction which the Ohio Statesman newspaper gave me this morning. In this paper I have read an article, in which, among other statements, I find the following:

"In debating with Senator Douglas during the memorable contest of last fall, Mr. Lincoln declared in favor of negro suffrage, and attempted to defend that vile conception against the Little Giant."

I mention this now, at the opening of my remarks, for the purpose of making three comments upon it. The first I have already announced,—it furnishes me an introductory topic; the second is to show that the gentleman is mistaken; thirdly, to give him an opportunity to correct it.

In the first place, in regard to this matter being a mistake. I have found that it is not entirely safe, when one is misrepresented under his very nose, to allow the misrepresentation to go uncontradicted. I therefore propose, here at the outset, not only to say that this is a misrepresentation, but to show conclusively that it is so; and you will bear with me while I read a couple of extracts from that very "memorable" debate with Judge Douglas last year, to which this newspaper refers. In the first pitched battle which Senator Douglas and myself had, at the town of Ottawa, I used the language which I will now read. Having been previously reading an extract, I continued as follows:

"Now, gentlemen, I don't want to read at any greater length, but this is the true complexion of all I have ever said in regard to the institution of slavery and the black race. This is the whole of it; and anything that argues me into his idea of perfect social and political equality with the negro, is but a specious and fantastic arrangement of words, by which a man can prove a horse-chestnut to be a chestnut horse. I will say here, while upon this subject, that I have no purpose directly or indirectly to interfere with the institution of slavery in the States where it exists. I believe I have no lawful right to do so, and I have no inclination to do so. I have no purpose to introduce political and social equality between the white and the black races. There is a physical difference between the two which, in my judgment, will probably forbid their ever living together upon the footing of perfect equality; and inasmuch as it becomes a necessity that there must be a difference, I, as well as Judge Douglas, am in favor of the race to which I belong having the superior position. I have never said anything to the contrary, but I hold that, notwithstanding all this, there is no reason in the world why the negro is not entitled to all the natural rights enumerated in the Declaration of Independence,—the right to life, liberty and the pursuit of happiness. I hold that he is as much entitled to these as the white man. I agree with judge Douglas, he is not my equal in many respects,—certainly not in color, perhaps not in moral or intellectual endowments. But in the right to eat the bread, without leave of anybody else, which his own hand earns, he is my equal, and the equal of Judge Douglas, and the equal of every living man."

Upon a subsequent occasion, when the reason for making a statement like this occurred, I said:

"While I was at the hotel to-day an elderly gentleman called upon me to know whether I was really in favor of producing perfect equality between the negroes and white people. While I had not proposed to myself on this occasion to say much on that subject, yet, as the question was asked me, I thought I would occupy perhaps five minutes in saying something in regard to it. I will say, then, that I am not, nor ever have been, in favor of bringing about in any way the social and political equality of the white and black races; that I am not, nor ever have been, in favor of making voters or jurors of negroes, nor of qualifying them to hold office, or intermarry with the white people; and I will say in addition to this that there is a physical difference between the white and black races which I believe will forever forbid the two races living together on terms of social and political equality. And inasmuch as they can not so live, while they do remain together there must be the position of superior and inferior, and I, as much as any other man, am in favor of having the superior position assigned to the white race. I say upon this occasion I do not perceive that because the white man is to have the superior position, the negro should be denied everything. I do not understand that because I do not want a negro woman for a slave, I must necessarily want her for a wife. My understanding is that I can just let her alone. I am now in my fiftieth year, and I certainly never have had a black woman for either a slave or a wife. So it seems to me quite possible for us to get along without making either slaves or wives of negroes. I will add to this that I have never seen, to my knowledge, a man, woman, or child, who was in favor of producing perfect equality, social and political, between negroes and white men. I recollect of but one distinguished instance that I ever heard of so frequently as to be satisfied of its correctness, and that is the case of Judge Douglas's old friend Colonel Richard M. Johnson. I will also add to the remarks I have made (for I am not going to enter at large upon this subject), that I have never had the least apprehension that I or my friends would marry negroes, if there was no law to keep them from it; but as judge Douglas and his friends seem to be in great apprehension that they might, if there were no law to keep them from it, I give him the most solemn pledge that I will to the very last stand by the law of the State which forbids the marrying of white people with negroes."

There, my friends, you have briefly what I have, upon former occasions, said upon this subject to which this newspaper, to the extent of its ability, has drawn the public attention. In it you not only perceive, as a probability, that in that contest I did not at any time say I was in favor of negro suffrage, but the absolute proof that twice—once substantially, and once expressly—I declared against it. Having shown you this, there remains but a word of comment upon that newspaper article. It is this, that I presume the editor of that paper is an honest and truth-loving man, and that he will be greatly obliged to me for furnishing him thus early an opportunity to correct the misrepresentation he has made, before it has run so long that malicious people can call him a liar.

The Giant himself has been here recently. I have seen a brief report of his speech. If it were otherwise unpleasant to me to introduce the subject of the negro as a topic for discussion, I might be somewhat relieved by the fact that he dealt exclusively in that subject while he was here. I shall, therefore, without much hesitation or diffidence, enter upon this subject.

The American people, on the first day of January, 1854, found the African slave trade prohibited by a law of Congress. In a majority of the States of this Union, they found African slavery, or any other sort of slavery, prohibited by State constitutions. They also found a law existing, supposed to be valid, by which slavery was excluded from almost all the territory the United States then owned. This was the condition of the country, with reference to the institution of slavery, on the first of January, 1854. A few days after that, a bill was introduced into Congress, which ran through its regular course in the two branches of the national legislature, and finally passed into a law in the month of May, by which the Act of Congress prohibiting slavery from going into the Territories of the United States was repealed. In connection with the law itself, and, in fact, in the terms of the law, the then existing prohibition was not only repealed, but there was a declaration of a purpose on the part of Congress never thereafter to exercise any power that they might have, real or supposed, to prohibit the extension or spread of slavery. This was a very great change; for the law thus repealed was of more than thirty years' standing. Following rapidly upon the heels of this action of Congress, a decision of the Supreme Court is made, by which it is declared that Congress, if it desires to prohibit the spread of slavery into the Territories, has no constitutional power to do so. Not only so, but that decision lays down principles which, if pushed to their logical conclusion,—I say pushed to their logical conclusion,—would decide that the constitutions of free States, forbidding slavery, are themselves unconstitutional. Mark me, I do not say the judges said this, and let no man say I affirm the judges used these words; but I only say it is my opinion that what they did say, if pressed to its logical conclusion, will inevitably result thus.

Looking at these things, the Republican party, as I understand its principles and policy, believes that there is great danger of the institution of slavery being spread out and extended until it is ultimately made alike lawful in all the States of this Union; so believing, to prevent that incidental and ultimate consummation is the original and chief purpose of the Republican organization. I say "chief purpose" of the Republican organization; for it is certainly true that if the National House shall fall into the hands of the Republicans, they will have to attend to all the other matters of national house-keeping, as well as this. The chief and real purpose of the Republican party is eminently conservative. It proposes nothing save and except to restore this government to its original tone in regard to this element of slavery, and there to maintain it, looking for no further change in reference to it than that which the original framers of the Government themselves expected and looked forward to.

The chief danger to this purpose of the Republican party is not just now the revival of the African slave trade, or the passage of a Congressional slave code, or the declaring of a second Dred Scott decision, making slavery lawful in all the States. These are not pressing us just now. They are not quite ready yet. The authors of these measures know that we are too strong for them; but they will be upon us in due time, and we will be grappling with them hand to hand, if they are not now headed off. They are not now the chief danger to the purpose of the Republican organization; but the most imminent danger that now threatens that purpose is that insidious Douglas popular sovereignty. This is the miner and sapper. While it does not propose to revive the African slave trade, nor to pass a slave code, nor to make a second Dred Scott decision, it is preparing us for the onslaught and charge of these ultimate enemies when they shall be ready to come on, and the word of command for them to advance shall be given. I say this "Douglas popular sovereignty"; for there is a broad distinction, as I now understand it, between that article and a genuine popular sovereignty.

I believe there is a genuine popular sovereignty. I think a definition of "genuine popular sovereignty," in the abstract, would be about this: That each man shall do precisely as he pleases with himself, and with all those things which exclusively concern him. Applied to government, this principle would be, that a general government shall do all those things which pertain to it, and all the local governments shall do precisely as they please in respect to those matters which exclusively concern them. I understand that this government of the United States, under which we live, is based upon this principle; and I am misunderstood if it is supposed that I have any war to make upon that principle.

Now, what is judge Douglas's popular sovereignty? It is, as a principle, no other than that if one man chooses to make a slave of another man neither that other man nor anybody else has a right to object. Applied in government, as he seeks to apply it, it is this: If, in a new Territory into which a few people are beginning to enter for the purpose of making their homes, they choose to either exclude slavery from their limits or to establish it there, however one or the other may affect the persons to be enslaved, or the infinitely greater number of persons who are afterwards to inhabit that Territory, or the other members of the families of communities, of which they are but an incipient member, or the general head of the family of States as parent of all, however their action may affect one or the other of these, there is no power or right to interfere. That is Douglas's popular sovereignty applied.

He has a good deal of trouble with popular sovereignty. His explanations explanatory of explanations explained are interminable. The most lengthy, and, as I suppose, the most maturely considered of this long series of explanations is his great essay in Harper's Magazine. I will not attempt to enter on any very thorough investigation of his argument as there made and presented. I will nevertheless occupy a good portion of your time here in drawing your attention to certain points in it. Such of you as may have read this document will have perceived that the judge early in the document quotes from two persons as belonging to the Republican party, without naming them, but who can readily be recognized as being Governor Seward of New York and myself. It is true that exactly fifteen months ago this day, I believe, I for the first time expressed a sentiment upon this subject, and in such a manner that it should get into print, that the public might see it beyond the circle of my hearers; and my expression of it at that time is the quotation that Judge Douglas makes. He has not made the quotation with accuracy, but justice to him requires me to say that it is sufficiently accurate not to change the sense.

The sense of that quotation condensed is this: that this slavery element is a durable element of discord among us, and that we shall probably not have perfect peace in this country with it until it either masters the free principle in our government, or is so far mastered by the free principle as for the public mind to rest in the belief that it is going to its end. This sentiment, which I now express in this way, was, at no great distance of time, perhaps in different language, and in connection with some collateral ideas, expressed by Governor Seward. Judge Douglas has been so much annoyed by the expression of that sentiment that he has constantly, I believe, in almost all his speeches since it was uttered, been referring to it. I find he alluded to it in his speech here, as well as in the copyright essay. I do not now enter upon this for the purpose of making an elaborate argument to show that we were right in the expression of that sentiment. In other words, I shall not stop to say all that might properly be said upon this point, but I only ask your attention to it for the purpose of making one or two points upon it.

If you will read the copyright essay, you will discover that judge Douglas himself says a controversy between the American Colonies and the Government of Great Britain began on the slavery question in 1699, and continued from that time until the Revolution; and, while he did not say so, we all know that it has continued with more or less violence ever since the Revolution.

Then we need not appeal to history, to the declarations of the framers of the government, but we know from judge Douglas himself that slavery began to be an element of discord among the white people of this country as far back as 1699, or one hundred and sixty years ago, or five generations of men,—counting thirty years to a generation. Now, it would seem to me that it might have occurred to Judge Douglas, or anybody who had turned his attention to these facts, that there was something in the nature of that thing, slavery, somewhat durable for mischief and discord.

There is another point I desire to make in regard to this matter, before I leave it. From the adoption of the Constitution down to 1820 is the precise period of our history when we had comparative peace upon this question,—the precise period of time when we came nearer to having peace about it than any other time of that entire one hundred and sixty years in which he says it began, or of the eighty years of our own Constitution. Then it would be worth our while to stop and examine into the probable reason of our coming nearer to having peace then than at any other time. This was the precise period of time in which our fathers adopted, and during which they followed, a policy restricting the spread of slavery, and the whole Union was acquiescing in it. The whole country looked forward to the ultimate extinction of the institution. It was when a policy had been adopted, and was prevailing, which led all just and right-minded men to suppose that slavery was gradually coming to an end, and that they might be quiet about it, watching it as it expired. I think Judge Douglas might have perceived that too; and whether he did or not, it is worth the attention of fair-minded men, here and elsewhere, to consider whether that is not the truth of the case. If he had looked at these two facts,— that this matter has been an element of discord for one hundred and sixty years among this people, and that the only comparative peace we have had about it was when that policy prevailed in this government which he now wars upon, he might then, perhaps, have been brought to a more just appreciation of what I said fifteen months ago,—that "a house divided against itself cannot stand. I believe that this government cannot endure permanently, half slave and half free. I do not expect the house to fall, I do not expect the Union to dissolve; but I do expect it will cease to be divided. It will become all one thing, or all the other. Either the opponents of slavery will arrest the further spread of it, and place it where the public mind will rest in the belief that it is in the course of ultimate extinction, or its advocates will push it forward until it shall become alike lawful in all the States, old as well as new, North as well as South." That was my sentiment at that time. In connection with it, I said: "We are now far into the fifth year since a policy was inaugurated with the avowed object and confident promise of putting an end to slavery agitation. Under the operation of the policy that agitation has not only not ceased, but has constantly augmented." I now say to you here that we are advanced still farther into the sixth year since that policy of Judge Douglas—that popular sovereignty of his—for quieting the slavery question was made the national policy. Fifteen months more have been added since I uttered that sentiment; and I call upon you and all other right-minded men to say whether that fifteen months have belied or corroborated my words.

While I am here upon this subject, I cannot but express gratitude that this true view of this element of discord among us—as I believe it is—is attracting more and more attention. I do not believe that Governor Seward uttered that sentiment because I had done so before, but because he reflected upon this subject and saw the truth of it. Nor do I believe because Governor Seward or I uttered it that Mr. Hickman of Pennsylvania, in different language, since that time, has declared his belief in the utter antagonism which exists between the principles of liberty and slavery. You see we are multiplying. Now, while I am speaking of Hickman, let me say, I know but little about him. I have never seen him, and know scarcely anything about the man; but I will say this much of him: Of all the anti-Lecompton Democracy that have been brought to my notice, he alone has the true, genuine ring of the metal. And now, without indorsing anything else he has said, I will ask this audience to give three cheers for Hickman. [The audience responded with three rousing cheers for Hickman.]

Another point in the copyright essay to which I would ask your attention is rather a feature to be extracted from the whole thing, than from any express declaration of it at any point. It is a general feature of that document, and, indeed, of all of Judge Douglas's discussions of this question, that the Territories of the United States and the States of this Union are exactly alike; that there is no difference between them at all; that the Constitution applies to the Territories precisely as it does to the States; and that the United States Government, under the Constitution, may not do in a State what it may not do in a Territory, and what it must do in a State it must do in a Territory. Gentlemen, is that a true view of the case? It is necessary for this squatter sovereignty, but is it true?

Let us consider. What does it depend upon? It depends altogether upon the proposition that the States must, without the interference of the General Government, do all those things that pertain exclusively to themselves,—that are local in their nature, that have no connection with the General Government. After Judge Douglas has established this proposition, which nobody disputes or ever has disputed, he proceeds to assume, without proving it, that slavery is one of those little, unimportant, trivial matters which are of just about as much consequence as the question would be to me whether my neighbor should raise horned cattle or plant tobacco; that there is no moral question about it, but that it is altogether a matter of dollars and cents; that when a new Territory is opened for settlement, the first man who goes into it may plant there a thing which, like the Canada thistle or some other of those pests of the soil, cannot be dug out by the millions of men who will come thereafter; that it is one of those little things that is so trivial in its nature that it has nor effect upon anybody save the few men who first plant upon the soil; that it is not a thing which in any way affects the family of communities composing these States, nor any way endangers the General Government. Judge Douglas ignores altogether the very well known fact that we have never had a serious menace to our political existence, except it sprang from this thing, which he chooses to regard as only upon a par with onions and potatoes.

Turn it, and contemplate it in another view. He says that, according to his popular sovereignty, the General Government may give to the Territories governors, judges, marshals, secretaries, and all the other chief men to govern them, but they, must not touch upon this other question. Why? The question of who shall be governor of a Territory for a year or two, and pass away, without his track being left upon the soil, or an act which he did for good or for evil being left behind, is a question of vast national magnitude; it is so much opposed in its nature to locality that the nation itself must decide it: while this other matter of planting slavery upon a soil,—a thing which, once planted, cannot be eradicated by the succeeding millions who have as much right there as the first comers, or, if eradicated, not without infinite difficulty and a long struggle, he considers the power to prohibit it as one of these little local, trivial things that the nation ought not to say a word about; that it affects nobody save the few men who are there.

Take these two things and consider them together, present the question of planting a State with the institution of slavery by the side of a question who shall be Governor of Kansas for a year or two, and is there a man here, is there a man on earth, who would not say the governor question is the little one, and the slavery question is the great one? I ask any honest Democrat if the small, the local, and the trivial and temporary question is not, Who shall be governor? while the durable, the important, and the mischievous one is, Shall this soil be planted with slavery?

This is an idea, I suppose, which has arisen in Judge Douglas's mind from his peculiar structure. I suppose the institution of slavery really looks small to him. He is so put up by nature that a lash upon his back would hurt him, but a lash upon anybody else's back does not hurt him. That is the build of the man, and consequently he looks upon the matter of slavery in this unimportant light.

Judge Douglas ought to remember, when he is endeavoring to force this policy upon the American people, that while he is put up in that way, a good many are not. He ought to remember that there was once in this country a man by the name of Thomas Jefferson, supposed to be a Democrat,—a man whose principles and policy are not very prevalent amongst Democrats to-day, it is true; but that man did not take exactly this view of the insignificance of the element of slavery which our friend judge Douglas does. In contemplation of this thing, we all know he was led to exclaim, "I tremble for my country when I remember that God is just!" We know how he looked upon it when he thus expressed himself. There was danger to this country,—danger of the avenging justice of God, in that little unimportant popular sovereignty question of judge Douglas. He supposed there was a question of God's eternal justice wrapped up in the enslaving of any race of men, or any man, and that those who did so braved the arm of Jehovah; that when a nation thus dared the Almighty, every friend of that nation had cause to dread his wrath. Choose ye between Jefferson and Douglas as to what is the true view of this element among us.

There is another little difficulty about this matter of treating the Territories and States alike in all things, to which I ask your attention, and I shall leave this branch of the case. If there is no difference between them, why not make the Territories States at once? What is the reason that Kansas was not fit to come into the Union when it was organized into a Territory, in Judge Douglas's view? Can any of you tell any reason why it should not have come into the Union at once? They are fit, as he thinks, to decide upon the slavery question,—the largest and most important with which they could possibly deal: what could they do by coming into the Union that they are not fit to do, according to his view, by staying out of it? Oh, they are not fit to sit in Congress and decide upon the rates of postage, or questions of ad valorem or specific duties on foreign goods, or live-oak timber contracts, they are not fit to decide these vastly important matters, which are national in their import, but they are fit, "from the jump," to decide this little negro question. But, gentlemen, the case is too plain; I occupy too much time on this head, and I pass on.

Near the close of the copyright essay, the judge, I think, comes very near kicking his own fat into the fire. I did not think, when I commenced these remarks, that I would read that article, but I now believe I will:

"This exposition of the history of these measures shows conclusively that the authors of the Compromise measures of 1850 and of the Kansas-Nebraska Act of 1854, as well as the members of the Continental Congress of 1774., and the founders of our system of government subsequent to the Revolution, regarded the people of the Territories and Colonies as political communities which were entitled to a free and exclusive power of legislation in their provisional legislatures, where their representation could alone be preserved, in all cases of taxation and internal polity."

When the judge saw that putting in the word "slavery" would contradict his own history, he put in what he knew would pass synonymous with it, "internal polity." Whenever we find that in one of his speeches, the substitute is used in this manner; and I can tell you the reason. It would be too bald a contradiction to say slavery; but "internal polity" is a general phrase, which would pass in some quarters, and which he hopes will pass with the reading community for the same thing.

"This right pertains to the people collectively, as a law-abiding and peaceful community, and not in the isolated individuals who may wander upon the public domain in violation of the law. It can only be exercised where there are inhabitants sufficient to constitute a government, and capable of performing its various functions and duties,—a fact to be ascertained and determined by" who do you think? Judge Douglas says "by Congress!" "Whether the number shall be fixed at ten, fifteen or twenty thousand inhabitants, does not affect the principle."

Now, I have only a few comments to make. Popular sovereignty, by his own words, does not pertain to the few persons who wander upon the public domain in violation of law. We have his words for that. When it does pertain to them, is when they are sufficient to be formed into an organized political community, and he fixes the minimum for that at ten thousand, and the maximum at twenty thousand. Now, I would like to know what is to be done with the nine thousand? Are they all to be treated, until they are large enough to be organized into a political community, as wanderers upon the public land, in violation of law? And if so treated and driven out, at what point of time would there ever be ten thousand? If they were not driven out, but remained there as trespassers upon the public land in violation of the law, can they establish slavery there? No; the judge says popular sovereignty don't pertain to them then. Can they exclude it then? No; popular sovereignty don't pertain to them then. I would like to know, in the case covered by the essay, what condition the people of the Territory are in before they reach the number of ten thousand?

But the main point I wish to ask attention to is, that the question as to when they shall have reached a sufficient number to be formed into a regular organized community is to be decided "by Congress." Judge Douglas says so. Well, gentlemen, that is about all we want. No, that is all the Southerners want. That is what all those who are for slavery want. They do not want Congress to prohibit slavery from coming into the new Territories, and they do not want popular sovereignty to hinder it; and as Congress is to say when they are ready to be organized, all that the South has to do is to get Congress to hold off. Let Congress hold off until they are ready to be admitted as a State, and the South has all it wants in taking slavery into and planting it in all the Territories that we now have or hereafter may have. In a word, the whole thing, at a dash of the pen, is at last put in the power of Congress; for if they do not have this popular sovereignty until Congress organizes them, I ask if it at last does not come from Congress? If, at last, it amounts to anything at all, Congress gives it to them. I submit this rather for your reflection than for comment. After all that is said, at last, by a dash of the pen, everything that has gone before is undone, and he puts the whole question under the control of Congress. After fighting through more than three hours, if you undertake to read it, he at last places the whole matter under the control of that power which he has been contending against, and arrives at a result directly contrary to what he had been laboring to do. He at last leaves the whole matter to the control of Congress.

There are two main objects, as I understand it, of this Harper's Magazine essay. One was to show, if possible, that the men of our Revolutionary times were in favor of his popular sovereignty, and the other was to show that the Dred Scott decision had not entirely squelched out this popular sovereignty. I do not propose, in regard to this argument drawn from the history of former times, to enter into a detailed examination of the historical statements he has made. I have the impression that they are inaccurate in a great many instances,—sometimes in positive statement, but very much more inaccurate by the suppression of statements that really belong to the history. But I do not propose to affirm that this is so to any very great extent, or to enter into a very minute examination of his historical statements. I avoid doing so upon this principle,—that if it were important for me to pass out of this lot in the least period of time possible, and I came to that fence, and saw by a calculation of my known strength and agility that I could clear it at a bound, it would be folly for me to stop and consider whether I could or not crawl through a crack. So I say of the whole history contained in his essay where he endeavored to link the men of the Revolution to popular sovereignty. It only requires an effort to leap out of it, a single bound to be entirely successful. If you read it over, you will find that he quotes here and there from documents of the Revolutionary times, tending to show that the people of the colonies were desirous of regulating their own concerns in their own way, that the British Government should not interfere; that at one time they struggled with the British Government to be permitted to exclude the African slave trade,—if not directly, to be permitted to exclude it indirectly, by taxation sufficient to discourage and destroy it. From these and many things of this sort, Judge Douglas argues that they were in favor of the people of our own Territories excluding slavery if they wanted to, or planting it there if they wanted to, doing just as they pleased from the time they settled upon the Territory. Now, however his history may apply and whatever of his argument there may be that is sound and accurate or unsound and inaccurate, if we can find out what these men did themselves do upon this very question of slavery in the Territories, does it not end the whole thing? If, after all this labor and effort to show that the men of the Revolution were in favor of his popular sovereignty and his mode of dealing with slavery in the Territories, we can show that these very men took hold of that subject, and dealt with it, we can see for ourselves how they dealt with it. It is not a matter of argument or inference, but we know what they thought about it.

It is precisely upon that part of the history of the country that one important omission is made by Judge Douglas. He selects parts of the history of the United States upon the subject of slavery, and treats it as the whole, omitting from his historical sketch the legislation of Congress in regard to the admission of Missouri, by which the Missouri Compromise was established and slavery excluded from a country half as large as the present United States. All this is left out of his history, and in nowise alluded to by him, so far as I can remember, save once, when he makes a remark, that upon his principle the Supreme Court were authorized to pronounce a decision that the act called the Missouri Compromise was unconstitutional. All that history has been left out. But this part of the history of the country was not made by the men of the Revolution.

There was another part of our political history, made by the very men who were the actors in the Revolution, which has taken the name of the Ordinance of '87. Let me bring that history to your attention. In 1784, I believe, this same Mr. Jefferson drew up an ordinance for the government of the country upon which we now stand, or rather, a frame or draft of an ordinance for the government of this country, here in Ohio, our neighbors in Indiana, us who live in Illinois, our neighbors in Wisconsin and Michigan. In that ordinance, drawn up not only for the government of that Territory, but for the Territories south of the Ohio River, Mr. Jefferson expressly provided for the prohibition of slavery. Judge Douglas says, and perhaps is right, that that provision was lost from that ordinance. I believe that is true. When the vote was taken upon it, a majority of all present in the Congress of the Confederation voted for it; but there were so many absentees that those voting for it did not make the clear majority necessary, and it was lost. But three years after that, the Congress of the Confederation were together again, and they adopted a new ordinance for the government of this Northwest Territory, not contemplating territory south of the river, for the States owning that territory had hitherto refrained from giving it to the General Government; hence they made the ordinance to apply only to what the Government owned. In fact, the provision excluding slavery was inserted aside, passed unanimously, or at any rate it passed and became a part of the law of the land. Under that ordinance we live. First here in Ohio you were a Territory; then an enabling act was passed, authorizing you to form a constitution and State Government, provided it was republican and not in conflict with the Ordinance of '87. When you framed your constitution and presented it for admission, I think you will find the legislation upon the subject will show that, whereas you had formed a constitution that was republican, and not in conflict with the Ordinance of '87, therefore you were admitted upon equal footing with the original States. The same process in a few years was gone through with in Indiana, and so with Illinois, and the same substantially with Michigan and Wisconsin.

Not only did that Ordinance prevail, but it was constantly looked to whenever a step was taken by a new Territory to become a State. Congress always turned their attention to it, and in all their movements upon this subject they traced their course by that Ordinance of '87. When they admitted new States, they advertised them of this Ordinance, as a part of the legislation of the country. They did so because they had traced the Ordinance of '87 throughout the history of this country. Begin with the men of the Revolution, and go down for sixty entire years, and until the last scrap of that Territory comes into the Union in the form of the State of Wisconsin, everything was made to conform with the Ordinance of '87, excluding slavery from that vast extent of country.

I omitted to mention in the right place that the Constitution of the United States was in process of being framed when that Ordinance was made by the Congress of the Confederation; and one of the first Acts of Congress itself, under the new Constitution itself, was to give force to that Ordinance by putting power to carry it out in the hands of the new officers under the Constitution, in the place of the old ones, who had been legislated out of existence by the change in the Government from the Confederation to the Constitution. Not only so, but I believe Indiana once or twice, if not Ohio, petitioned the General Government for the privilege of suspending that provision and allowing them to have slaves. A report made by Mr. Randolph, of Virginia, himself a slaveholder, was directly against it, and the action was to refuse them the privilege of violating the Ordinance of '87.

This period of history, which I have run over briefly, is, I presume, as familiar to most of this assembly as any other part of the history of our country. I suppose that few of my hearers are not as familiar with that part of history as I am, and I only mention it to recall your attention to it at this time. And hence I ask how extraordinary a thing it is that a man who has occupied a position upon the floor of the Senate of the United States, who is now in his third term, and who looks to see the government of this whole country fall into his own hands, pretending to give a truthful and accurate history o the slavery question in this country, should so entirely ignore the whole of that portion of our history—the most important of all. Is it not a most extraordinary spectacle that a man should stand up and ask for any confidence in his statements who sets out as he does with portions of history, calling upon the people to believe that it is a true and fair representation, when the leading part and controlling feature of the whole history is carefully suppressed?

But the mere leaving out is not the most remarkable feature of this most remarkable essay. His proposition is to establish that the leading men of the Revolution were for his great principle of nonintervention by the government in the question of slavery in the Territories, while history shows that they decided, in the cases actually brought before them, in exactly the contrary way, and he knows it. Not only did they so decide at that time, but they stuck to it during sixty years, through thick and thin, as long as there was one of the Revolutionary heroes upon the stage of political action. Through their whole course, from first to last, they clung to freedom. And now he asks the community to believe that the men of the Revolution were in favor of his great principle, when we have the naked history that they themselves dealt with this very subject matter of his principle, and utterly repudiated his principle, acting upon a precisely contrary ground. It is as impudent and absurd as if a prosecuting attorney should stand up before a jury and ask them to convict A as the murderer of B, while B was walking alive before them.

I say, again, if judge Douglas asserts that the men of the Revolution acted upon principles by which, to be consistent with themselves, they ought to have adopted his popular sovereignty, then, upon a consideration of his own argument, he had a right to make you believe that they understood the principles of government, but misapplied them, that he has arisen to enlighten the world as to the just application of this principle. He has a right to try to persuade you that he understands their principles better than they did, and, therefore, he will apply them now, not as they did, but as they ought to have done. He has a right to go before the community and try to convince them of this, but he has no right to attempt to impose upon any one the belief that these men themselves approved of his great principle. There are two ways of establishing a proposition. One is by trying to demonstrate it upon reason, and the other is, to show that great men in former times have thought so and so, and thus to pass it by the weight of pure authority. Now, if Judge Douglas will demonstrate somehow that this is popular sovereignty,—the right of one man to make a slave of another, without any right in that other or any one else to object,—demonstrate it as Euclid demonstrated propositions,—there is no objection. But when he comes forward, seeking to carry a principle by bringing to it the authority of men who themselves utterly repudiate that principle, I ask that he shall not be permitted to do it.

I see, in the judge's speech here, a short sentence in these words: "Our fathers, when they formed this government under which we live, understood this question just as well, and even better than, we do now." That is true; I stick to that. I will stand by Judge Douglas in that to the bitter end. And now, Judge Douglas, come and stand by me, and truthfully show how they acted, understanding it better than we do. All I ask of you, Judge Douglas, is to stick to the proposition that the men of the Revolution understood this subject better than we do now, and with that better understanding they acted better than you are trying to act now.

I wish to say something now in regard to the Dred Scott decision, as dealt with by Judge Douglas. In that "memorable debate" between Judge Douglas and myself, last year, the judge thought fit to commence a process of catechising me, and at Freeport I answered his questions, and propounded some to him. Among others propounded to him was one that I have here now. The substance, as I remember it, is, "Can the people of a United States Territory, under the Dred Scott decision, in any lawful way, against the wish of any citizen of the United States, exclude slavery from its limits, prior to the formation of a State constitution?" He answered that they could lawfully exclude slavery from the United States Territories, notwithstanding the Dred Scot decision. There was something about that answer that has probably been a trouble to the judge ever since.

The Dred Scott decision expressly gives every citizen of the United States a right to carry his slaves into the United States Territories. And now there was some inconsistency in saying that the decision was right, and saying, too, that the people of the Territory could lawfully drive slavery out again. When all the trash, the words, the collateral matter, was cleared away from it, all the chaff was fanned out of it, it was a bare absurdity,—no less than that a thing may be lawfully driven away from where it has a lawful right to be. Clear it of all the verbiage, and that is the naked truth of his proposition,—that a thing may be lawfully driven from the place where it has a lawful right to stay. Well, it was because the judge could n't help seeing this that he has had so much trouble with it; and what I want to ask your especial attention to, just now, is to remind you, if you have not noticed the fact, that the judge does not any longer say that the people can exclude slavery. He does not say so in the copyright essay; he did not say so in the speech that he made here; and, so far as I know, since his re-election to the Senate he has never said, as he did at Freeport, that the people of the Territories can exclude slavery. He desires that you, who wish the Territories to remain free, should believe that he stands by that position; but he does not say it himself. He escapes to some extent the absurd position I have stated, by changing his language entirely. What he says now is something different in language, and we will consider whether it is not different in sense too. It is now that the Dred Scott decision, or rather the Constitution under that decision, does not carry slavery into the Territories beyond the power of the people of the Territories to control it as other property. He does not say the people can drive it out, but they can control it as other property. The language is different; we should consider whether the sense is different. Driving a horse out of this lot is too plain a proposition to be mistaken about; it is putting him on the other side of the fence. Or it might be a sort of exclusion of him from the lot if you were to kill him and let the worms devour him; but neither of these things is the same as "controlling him as other property." That would be to feed him, to pamper him, to ride him, to use and abuse him, to make the most money out of him, "as other property"; but, please you, what do the men who are in favor of slavery want more than this? What do they really want, other than that slavery, being in the Territories, shall be controlled as other property? If they want anything else, I do not comprehend it. I ask your attention to this, first, for the purpose of pointing out the change of ground the judge has made; and, in the second place, the importance of the change,—that that change is not such as to give you gentlemen who want his popular sovereignty the power to exclude the institution or drive it out at all. I know the judge sometimes squints at the argument that in controlling it as other property by unfriendly legislation they may control it to death; as you might, in the case of a horse, perhaps, feed him so lightly and ride him so much that he would die. But when you come to legislative control, there is something more to be attended to. I have no doubt, myself, that if the Territories should undertake to control slave property as other property that is, control it in such a way that it would be the most valuable as property, and make it bear its just proportion in the way of burdens as property, really deal with it as property,—the Supreme Court of the United States will say, "God speed you, and amen." But I undertake to give the opinion, at least, that if the Territories attempt by any direct legislation to drive the man with his slave out of the Territory, or to decide that his slave is free because of his being taken in there, or to tax him to such an extent that he cannot keep him there, the Supreme Court will unhesitatingly decide all such legislation unconstitutional, as long as that Supreme Court is constructed as the Dred Scott Supreme Court is. The first two things they have already decided, except that there is a little quibble among lawyers between the words "dicta" and "decision." They have already decided a negro cannot be made free by Territorial legislation.

What is the Dred Scott decision? Judge Douglas labors to show that it is one thing, while I think it is altogether different. It is a long opinion, but it is all embodied in this short statement: "The Constitution of the United States forbids Congress to deprive a man of his property, without due process of law; the right of property in slaves is distinctly and expressly affirmed in that Constitution: therefore, if Congress shall undertake to say that a man's slave is no longer his slave when he crosses a certain line into a Territory, that is depriving him of his property without due process of law, and is unconstitutional." There is the whole Dred Scott decision. They add that if Congress cannot do so itself, Congress cannot confer any power to do so; and hence any effort by the Territorial Legislature to do either of these things is absolutely decided against. It is a foregone conclusion by that court.

Now, as to this indirect mode by "unfriendly legislation," all lawyers here will readily understand that such a proposition cannot be tolerated for a moment, because a legislature cannot indirectly do that which it cannot accomplish directly. Then I say any legislation to control this property, as property, for its benefit as property, would be hailed by this Dred Scott Supreme Court, and fully sustained; but any legislation driving slave property out, or destroying it as property, directly or indirectly, will most assuredly, by that court, be held unconstitutional.

Judge Douglas says if the Constitution carries slavery into the Territories, beyond the power of the people of the Territories to control it as other property; then it follows logically that every one who swears to support the Constitution of the United States must give that support to that property which it needs. And, if the Constitution carries slavery into the Territories, beyond the power of the people, to control it as other property, then it also carries it into the States, because the Constitution is the supreme law of the land. Now, gentlemen, if it were not for my excessive modesty, I would say that I told that very thing to Judge Douglas quite a year ago. This argument is here in print, and if it were not for my modesty, as I said, I might call your attention to it. If you read it, you will find that I not only made that argument, but made it better than he has made it since.

There is, however, this difference: I say now, and said then, there is no sort of question that the Supreme Court has decided that it is the right of the slave holder to take his slave and hold him in the Territory; and saying this, judge Douglas himself admits the conclusion. He says if that is so, this consequence will follow; and because this consequence would follow, his argument is, the decision cannot, therefore, be that way,—"that would spoil my popular sovereignty; and it cannot be possible that this great principle has been squelched out in this extraordinary way. It might be, if it were not for the extraordinary consequences of spoiling my humbug."

Another feature of the judge's argument about the Dred Scott case is, an effort to show that that decision deals altogether in declarations of negatives; that the Constitution does not affirm anything as expounded by the Dred Scott decision, but it only declares a want of power a total absence of power, in reference to the Territories. It seems to be his purpose to make the whole of that decision to result in a mere negative declaration of a want of power in Congress to do anything in relation to this matter in the Territories. I know the opinion of the Judges states that there is a total absence of power; but that is, unfortunately; not all it states: for the judges add that the right of property in a slave is distinctly and expressly affirmed in the Constitution. It does not stop at saying that the right of property in a slave is recognized in the Constitution, is declared to exist somewhere in the Constitution, but says it is affirmed in the Constitution. Its language is equivalent to saying that it is embodied and so woven in that instrument that it cannot be detached without breaking the Constitution itself. In a word, it is part of the Constitution.

Douglas is singularly unfortunate in his effort to make out that decision to be altogether negative, when the express language at the vital part is that this is distinctly affirmed in the Constitution. I think myself, and I repeat it here, that this decision does not merely carry slavery into the Territories, but by its logical conclusion it carries it into the States in which we live. One provision of that Constitution is, that it shall be the supreme law of the land,—I do not quote the language,—any constitution or law of any State to the contrary notwithstanding. This Dred Scott decision says that the right of property in a slave is affirmed in that Constitution which is the supreme law of the land, any State constitution or law notwithstanding. Then I say that to destroy a thing which is distinctly affirmed and supported by the supreme law of the land, even by a State constitution or law, is a violation of that supreme law, and there is no escape from it. In my judgment there is no avoiding that result, save that the American people shall see that constitutions are better construed than our Constitution is construed in that decision. They must take care that it is more faithfully and truly carried out than it is there expounded.

I must hasten to a conclusion. Near the beginning of my remarks I said that this insidious Douglas popular sovereignty is the measure that now threatens the purpose of the Republican party to prevent slavery from being nationalized in the United States. I propose to ask your attention for a little while to some propositions in affirmance of that statement. Take it just as it stands, and apply it as a principle; extend and apply that principle elsewhere; and consider where it will lead you. I now put this proposition, that Judge Douglas's popular sovereignty applied will reopen the African slave trade; and I will demonstrate it by any variety of ways in which you can turn the subject or look at it.

The Judge says that the people of the Territories have the right, by his principle, to have slaves, if they want them. Then I say that the people in Georgia have the right to buy slaves in Africa, if they want them; and I defy any man on earth to show any distinction between the two things,—to show that the one is either more wicked or more unlawful; to show, on original principles, that one is better or worse than the other; or to show, by the Constitution, that one differs a whit from the other. He will tell me, doubtless, that there is no constitutional provision against people taking slaves into the new Territories, and I tell him that there is equally no constitutional provision against buying slaves in Africa. He will tell you that a people, in the exercise of popular sovereignty, ought to do as they please about that thing, and have slaves if they want them; and I tell you that the people of Georgia are as much entitled to popular sovereignty and to buy slaves in Africa, if they want them, as the people of the Territory are to have slaves if they want them. I ask any man, dealing honestly with himself, to point out a distinction.

I have recently seen a letter of Judge Douglas's in which, without stating that to be the object, he doubtless endeavors to make a distinction between the two. He says he is unalterably opposed to the repeal of the laws against the African slave trade. And why? He then seeks to give a reason that would not apply to his popular sovereignty in the Territories. What is that reason? "The abolition of the African slave trade is a compromise of the Constitution!" I deny it. There is no truth in the proposition that the abolition of the African slave trade is a compromise of the Constitution. No man can put his finger on anything in the Constitution, or on the line of history, which shows it. It is a mere barren assertion, made simply for the purpose of getting up a distinction between the revival of the African slave trade and his "great principle."

At the time the Constitution of the United States was adopted, it was expected that the slave trade would be abolished. I should assert and insist upon that, if judge Douglas denied it. But I know that it was equally expected that slavery would be excluded from the Territories, and I can show by history that in regard to these two things public opinion was exactly alike, while in regard to positive action, there was more done in the Ordinance of '87 to resist the spread of slavery than was ever done to abolish the foreign slave trade. Lest I be misunderstood, I say again that at the time of the formation of the Constitution, public expectation was that the slave trade would be abolished, but no more so than the spread of slavery in the Territories should be restrained. They stand alike, except that in the Ordinance of '87 there was a mark left by public opinion, showing that it was more committed against the spread of slavery in the Territories than against the foreign slave trade.

Compromise! What word of compromise was there about it? Why, the public sense was then in favor of the abolition of the slave trade; but there was at the time a very great commercial interest involved in it, and extensive capital in that branch of trade. There were doubtless the incipient stages of improvement in the South in the way of farming, dependent on the slave trade, and they made a proposition to Congress to abolish the trade after allowing it twenty years,—a sufficient time for the capital and commerce engaged in it to be transferred to other channel. They made no provision that it should be abolished in twenty years; I do not doubt that they expected it would be, but they made no bargain about it. The public sentiment left no doubt in the minds of any that it would be done away. I repeat, there is nothing in the history of those times in favor of that matter being a compromise of the constitution. It was the public expectation at the time, manifested in a thousand ways, that the spread of slavery should also be restricted.

Then I say, if this principle is established, that there is no wrong in slavery, and whoever wants it has a right to have it, is a matter of dollars and cents, a sort of question as to how they shall deal with brutes, that between us and the negro here there is no sort of question, but that at the South the question is between the negro and the crocodile, that is all, it is a mere matter of policy, there is a perfect right, according to interest, to do just as you please,—when this is done, where this doctrine prevails, the miners and sappers will have formed public opinion for the slave trade. They will be ready for Jeff. Davis and Stephens and other leaders of that company to sound the bugle for the revival of the slave trade, for the second Dred Scott decision, for the flood of slavery to be poured over the free States, while we shall be here tied down and helpless and run over like sheep.

It is to be a part and parcel of this same idea to say to men who want to adhere to the Democratic party, who have always belonged to that party, and are only looking about for some excuse to stick to it, but nevertheless hate slavery, that Douglas's popular sovereignty is as good a way as any to oppose slavery. They allow themselves to be persuaded easily, in accordance with their previous dispositions, into this belief, that it is about as good a way of opposing slavery as any, and we can do that without straining our old party ties or breaking up old political associations. We can do so without being called negro-worshipers. We can do that without being subjected to the jibes and sneers that are so readily thrown out in place of argument where no argument can be found. So let us stick to this popular sovereignty,—this insidious popular sovereignty.

Now let me call your attention to one thing that has really happened, which shows this gradual and steady debauching of public opinion, this course of preparation for the revival of the slave trade, for the Territorial slave code, and the new Dred Scott decision that is to carry slavery into the Free States. Did you ever, five years ago, hear of anybody in the world saying that the negro had no share in the Declaration of National Independence; that it does not mean negroes at all; and when "all men" were spoken of, negroes were not included?

I am satisfied that five years ago that proposition was not put upon paper by any living being anywhere. I have been unable at any time to find a man in an audience who would declare that he had ever known of anybody saying so five years ago. But last year there was not a Douglas popular sovereign in Illinois who did not say it. Is there one in Ohio but declares his firm belief that the Declaration of Independence did not mean negroes at all? I do not know how this is; I have not been here much; but I presume you are very much alike everywhere. Then I suppose that all now express the belief that the Declaration of Independence never did mean negroes. I call upon one of them to say that he said it five years ago.

If you think that now, and did not think it then, the next thing that strikes me is to remark that there has been a change wrought in you,—and a very significant change it is, being no less than changing the negro, in your estimation, from the rank of a man to that of a brute. They are taking him down and placing him, when spoken of, among reptiles and crocodiles, as Judge Douglas himself expresses it.

Is not this change wrought in your minds a very important change? Public opinion in this country is everything. In a nation like ours, this popular sovereignty and squatter sovereignty have already wrought a change in the public mind to the extent I have stated. There is no man in this crowd who can contradict it.

Now, if you are opposed to slavery honestly, as much as anybody, I ask you to note that fact, and the like of which is to follow, to be plastered on, layer after layer, until very soon you are prepared to deal with the negro every where as with the brute. If public sentiment has not been debauched already to this point, a new turn of the screw in that direction is all that is wanting; and this is constantly being done by the teachers of this insidious popular sovereignty. You need but one or two turns further, until your minds, now ripening under these teachings, will be ready for all these things, and you will receive and support, or submit to, the slave trade, revived with all its horrors, a slave code enforced in our Territories, and a new Dred Scott decision to bring slavery up into the very heart of the free North. This, I must say, is but carrying out those words prophetically spoken by Mr. Clay,—many, many years ago,—I believe more than thirty years, when he told an audience that if they would repress all tendencies to liberty and ultimate emancipation they must go back to the era of our independence, and muzzle the cannon which thundered its annual joyous return on the Fourth of July; they must blow out the moral lights around us; they must penetrate the human soul, and eradicate the love of liberty: but until they did these things, and others eloquently enumerated by him, they could not repress all tendencies to ultimate emancipation.

I ask attention to the fact that in a pre-eminent degree these popular sovereigns are at this work: blowing out the moral lights around us; teaching that the negro is no longer a man, but a brute; that the Declaration has nothing to do with him; that he ranks with the crocodile and the reptile; that man, with body and soul, is a matter of dollars and cents. I suggest to this portion of the Ohio Republicans, or Democrats, if there be any present, the serious consideration of this fact that there is now going on among you a steady process of debauching public opinion on this subject. With this, my friends, I bid you adieu.

SPEECH AT CINCINNATI OHIO, SEPTEMBER 17, 1859

My Fellow-Citizens of the State of Ohio: This is the first time in my life that I have appeared before an audience in so great a city as this: I therefore—though I am no longer a young man—make this appearance under some degree of embarrassment. But I have found that when one is embarrassed, usually the shortest way to get through with it is to quit talking or thinking about it, and go at something else.

I understand that you have had recently with you my very distinguished friend Judge Douglas, of Illinois; and I understand, without having had an opportunity (not greatly sought, to be sure) of seeing a report of the speech that he made here, that he did me the honor to mention my humble name. I suppose that he did so for the purpose of making some objection to some sentiment at some time expressed by me. I should expect, it is true, that judge Douglas had reminded you, or informed you, if you had never before heard it, that I had once in my life declared it as my opinion that this government cannot endure permanently, half slave and half free; that a house divided against itself cannot stand, and, as I had expressed it, I did not expect the house to fall, that I did not expect the Union to be dissolved, but that I did expect that it would cease to be divided, that it would become all one thing, or all the other; that either the opponents of slavery would arrest the further spread of it, and place it where the public mind would rest in the belief that it was in the course of ultimate extinction, or the friends of slavery will push it forward until it becomes alike lawful in all the States, old or new, free as well as slave. I did, fifteen months ago, express that opinion, and upon many occasions Judge Douglas has denounced it, and has greatly, intentionally or unintentionally, misrepresented my purpose in the expression of that opinion.

I presume, without having seen a report of his speech, that he did so here. I presume that he alluded also to that opinion, in different language, having been expressed at a subsequent time by Governor Seward of New York, and that he took the two in a lump and denounced them; that he tried to point out that there was something couched in this opinion which led to the making of an entire uniformity of the local institutions of the various States of the Union, in utter disregard of the different States, which in their nature would seem to require a variety of institutions and a variety of laws, conforming to the differences in the nature of the different States.

Not only so: I presume he insisted that this was a declaration of war between the free and slave States, that it was the sounding to the onset of continual war between the different States, the slave and free States.

This charge, in this form, was made by Judge Douglas on, I believe, the 9th of July, 1858, in Chicago, in my hearing. On the next evening, I made some reply to it. I informed him that many of the inferences he drew from that expression of mine were altogether foreign to any purpose entertained by me, and in so far as he should ascribe these inferences to me, as my purpose, he was entirely mistaken; and in so far as he might argue that, whatever might be my purpose, actions conforming to my views would lead to these results, he might argue and establish if he could; but, so far as purposes were concerned, he was totally mistaken as to me.

When I made that reply to him, I told him, on the question of declaring war between the different States of the Union, that I had not said that I did not expect any peace upon this question until slavery was exterminated; that I had only said I expected peace when that institution was put where the public mind should rest in the belief that it was in course of ultimate extinction; that I believed, from the organization of our government until a very recent period of time, the institution had been placed and continued upon such a basis; that we had had comparative peace upon that question through a portion of that period of time, only because the public mind rested in that belief in regard to it, and that when we returned to that position in relation to that matter, I supposed we should again have peace as we previously had. I assured him, as I now, assure you, that I neither then had, nor have, or ever had, any purpose in any way of interfering with the institution of slavery, where it exists. I believe we have no power, under the Constitution of the United States, or rather under the form of government under which we live, to interfere with the institution of slavery, or any other of the institutions of our sister States, be they free or slave States. I declared then, and I now re-declare, that I have as little inclination to interfere with the institution of slavery where it now exists, through the instrumentality of the General Government, or any other instrumentality, as I believe we have no power to do so. I accidentally used this expression: I had no purpose of entering into the slave States to disturb the institution of slavery. So, upon the first occasion that Judge Douglas got an opportunity to reply to me, he passed by the whole body of what I had said upon that subject, and seized upon the particular expression of mine that I had no purpose of entering into the slave States to disturb the institution of slavery. "Oh, no," said he, "he [Lincoln] won't enter into the slave States to disturb the institution of slavery, he is too prudent a man to do such a thing as that; he only means that he will go on to the line between the free and slave States, and shoot over at them. This is all he means to do. He means to do them all the harm he can, to disturb them all he can, in such a way as to keep his own hide in perfect safety."

Well, now, I did not think, at that time, that that was either a very dignified or very logical argument but so it was, I had to get along with it as well as I could.

It has occurred to me here to-night that if I ever do shoot over the line at the people on the other side of the line into a slave State, and purpose to do so, keeping my skin safe, that I have now about the best chance I shall ever have. I should not wonder if there are some Kentuckians about this audience—we are close to Kentucky; and whether that be so or not, we are on elevated ground, and, by speaking distinctly, I should not wonder if some of the Kentuckians would hear me on the other side of the river. For that reason I propose to address a portion of what I have to say to the Kentuckians.

I say, then, in the first place, to the Kentuckians, that I am what they call, as I understand it, a "Black Republican." I think slavery is wrong, morally and politically. I desire that it should be no further spread in—these United States, and I should not object if it should gradually terminate in the whole Union. While I say this for myself, I say to you Kentuckians that I understand you differ radically with me upon this proposition; that you believe slavery is a good thing; that slavery is right; that it ought to be extended and perpetuated in this Union. Now, there being this broad difference between us, I do not pretend, in addressing myself to you Kentuckians, to attempt proselyting you; that would be a vain effort. I do not enter upon it. I only propose to try to show you that you ought to nominate for the next Presidency, at Charleston, my distinguished friend Judge Douglas. In all that there is a difference between you and him, I understand he is sincerely for you, and more wisely for you than you are for yourselves. I will try to demonstrate that proposition. Understand, now, I say that I believe he is as sincerely for you, and more wisely for you, than you are for yourselves.

What do you want more than anything else to make successful your views of slavery,—to advance the outspread of it, and to secure and perpetuate the nationality of it? What do you want more than anything else? What—is needed absolutely? What is indispensable to you? Why, if I may, be allowed to answer the question, it is to retain a hold upon the North, it is to retain support and strength from the free States. If you can get this support and strength from the free States, you can succeed. If you do not get this support and this strength from the free States, you are in the minority, and you are beaten at once.

If that proposition be admitted,—and it is undeniable,—then the next thing I say to you is, that Douglas, of all the men in this nation, is the only man that affords you any hold upon the free States; that no other man can give you any strength in the free States. This being so, if you doubt the other branch of the proposition, whether he is for you—whether he is really for you, as I have expressed it,—I propose asking your attention for a while to a few facts.

The issue between you and me, understand, is, that I think slavery is wrong, and ought not to be outspread; and you think it is right, and ought to be extended and perpetuated. [A voice, "Oh, Lord!"] That is my Kentuckian I am talking to now.

I now proceed to try to show you that Douglas is as sincerely for you and more wisely for you than you are for yourselves.

In the first place, we know that in a government like this, in a government of the people, where the voice of all the men of the country, substantially, enters into the execution—or administration, rather—of the government, in such a government, what lies at the bottom of all of it is public opinion. I lay down the proposition, that Judge Douglas is not only the man that promises you in advance a hold upon the North, and support in the North, but he constantly moulds public opinion to your ends; that in every possible way he can he constantly moulds the public opinion of the North to your ends; and if there are a few things in which he seems to be against you,—a few things which he says that appear to be against you, and a few that he forbears to say which you would like to have him say you ought to remember that the saying of the one, or the forbearing to say the other, would lose his hold upon the North, and, by consequence, would lose his capacity to serve you.

Upon this subject of moulding public opinion I call your attention to the fact—for a well established fact it is—that the Judge never says your institution of slavery is wrong. There is not a public man in the United States, I believe, with the exception of Senator Douglas, who has not, at some time in his life, declared his opinion whether the thing is right or wrong; but Senator Douglas never declares it is wrong. He leaves himself at perfect liberty to do all in your favor which he would be hindered from doing if he were to declare the thing to be wrong. On the contrary, he takes all the chances that he has for inveigling the sentiment of the North, opposed to slavery, into your support, by never saying it is right. This you ought to set down to his credit: You ought to give him full credit for this much; little though it be, in comparison to the whole which he does for you.

Some other, things I will ask your attention to. He said upon the floor of the United States Senate, and he has repeated it, as I understand, a great many times, that he does not care whether slavery is "voted up or voted down." This again shows you, or ought to show you, if you would reason upon it, that he does not believe it to be wrong; for a man may say when he sees nothing wrong in a thing; that he, does not care whether it be voted up or voted down but no man can logically say that he cares not whether a thing goes up or goes down which to him appears to be wrong. You therefore have a demonstration in this that to Judge Douglas's mind your favorite institution, which you would have spread out and made perpetual, is no wrong.

Another thing he tells you, in a speech made at Memphis in Tennessee, shortly after the canvass in Illinois, last year. He there distinctly told the people that there was a "line drawn by the Almighty across this continent, on the one side of which the soil must always be cultivated by slaves"; that he did not pretend to know exactly where that line was, but that there was such a line. I want to ask your attention to that proposition again; that there is one portion of this continent where the Almighty has signed the soil shall always be cultivated by slaves; that its being cultivated by slaves at that place is right; that it has the direct sympathy and authority of the Almighty. Whenever you can get these Northern audiences to adopt the opinion that slavery is right on the other side of the Ohio, whenever you can get them, in pursuance of Douglas's views, to adopt that sentiment, they will very readily make the other argument, which is perfectly logical, that that which is right on that side of the Ohio cannot be wrong on this, and that if you have that property on that side of the Ohio, under the seal and stamp of the Almighty, when by any means it escapes over here it is wrong to have constitutions and laws "to devil" you about it. So Douglas is moulding the public opinion of the North, first to say that the thing is right in your State over the Ohio River, and hence to say that that which is right there is not wrong here, and that all laws and constitutions here recognizing it as being wrong are themselves wrong, and ought to be repealed and abrogated. He will tell you, men of Ohio, that if you choose here to have laws against slavery, it is in conformity to the idea that your climate is not suited to it, that your climate is not suited to slave labor, and therefore you have constitutions and laws against it.

Let us attend to that argument for a little while and see if it be sound. You do not raise sugar-cane (except the new-fashioned sugar-cane, and you won't raise that long), but they do raise it in Louisiana. You don't raise it in Ohio, because you can't raise it profitably, because the climate don't suit it. They do raise it in Louisiana, because there it is profitable. Now, Douglas will tell you that is precisely the slavery question: that they do have slaves there because they are profitable, and you don't have them here because they are not profitable. If that is so, then it leads to dealing with the one precisely as with the other. Is there, then, anything in the constitution or laws of Ohio against raising sugar-cane? Have you found it necessary to put any such provision in your law? Surely not! No man desires to raise sugar-cane in Ohio, but if any man did desire to do so, you would say it was a tyrannical law that forbids his doing so; and whenever you shall agree with Douglas, whenever your minds are brought to adopt his argument, as surely you will have reached the conclusion that although it is not profitable in Ohio, if any man wants it, is wrong to him not to let him have it.

In this matter Judge Douglas is preparing the public mind for you of Kentucky to make perpetual that good thing in your estimation, about which you and I differ.

In this connection, let me ask your attention to another thing. I believe it is safe to assert that five years ago no living man had expressed the opinion that the negro had no share in the Declaration of Independence. Let me state that again: five years ago no living man had expressed the opinion that the negro had no share in the Declaration of Independence. If there is in this large audience any man who ever knew of that opinion being put upon paper as much as five years ago, I will be obliged to him now or at a subsequent time to show it.

If that be true I wish you then to note the next fact: that within the space of five years Senator Douglas, in the argument of this question, has got his entire party, so far as I know, without exception, in saying that the negro has no share in the Declaration of Independence. If there be now in all these United States one Douglas man that does not say this, I have been unable upon any occasion to scare him up. Now, if none of you said this five years ago, and all of you say it now, that is a matter that you Kentuckians ought to note. That is a vast change in the Northern public sentiment upon that question.

Of what tendency is that change? The tendency of that change is to bring the public mind to the conclusion that when men are spoken of, the negro is not meant; that when negroes are spoken of, brutes alone are contemplated. That change in public sentiment has already degraded the black man in the estimation of Douglas and his followers from the condition of a man of some sort, and assigned him to the condition of a brute. Now, you Kentuckians ought to give Douglas credit for this. That is the largest possible stride that can be made in regard to the perpetuation of your thing of slavery.

A voice: Speak to Ohio men, and not to Kentuckians!

Mr. LINCOLN: I beg permission to speak as I please.

In Kentucky perhaps, in many of the slave States certainly, you are trying to establish the rightfulness of slavery by reference to the Bible. You are trying to show that slavery existed in the Bible times by divine ordinance. Now, Douglas is wiser than you, for your own benefit, upon that subject. Douglas knows that whenever you establish that slavery was—right by the Bible, it will occur that that slavery was the slavery of the white man, of men without reference to color; and he knows very well that you may entertain that idea in Kentucky as much as you please, but you will never win any Northern support upon it. He makes a wiser argument for you: he makes the argument that the slavery of the black man; the slavery of the man who has a skin of a different color from your own, is right. He thereby brings to your support Northern voters who could not for a moment be brought by your own argument of the Bible right of

337

slavery. Will you give him credit for that? Will you not say that in this matter he is more wisely for you than you are for yourselves?

Now, having established with his entire party this doctrine, having been entirely successful in that branch of his efforts in your behalf, he is ready for another.

At this same meeting at Memphis he declared that in all contests between the negro and the white man he was for the white man, but that in all questions between the negro and the crocodile he was for the negro. He did not make that declaration accidentally at Memphis. He made it a great many times in the canvass in Illinois last year (though I don't know that it was reported in any of his speeches there, but he frequently made it). I believe he repeated it at Columbus, and I should not wonder if he repeated it here. It is, then, a deliberate way of expressing himself upon that subject. It is a matter of mature deliberation with him thus to express himself upon that point of his case. It therefore requires deliberate attention.

The first inference seems to be that if you do not enslave the negro, you are wronging the white man in some way or other, and that whoever is opposed to the negro being enslaved, is, in some way or other, against the white man. Is not that a falsehood? If there was a necessary conflict between the white man and the negro, I should be for the white man as much as Judge Douglas; but I say there is no such necessary conflict. I say that there is room enough for us all to be free, and that it not only does not wrong the white man that the negro should be free, but it positively wrongs the mass of the white men that the negro should be enslaved; that the mass of white men are really injured by the effects of slave labor in the vicinity of the fields of their own labor.

But I do not desire to dwell upon this branch of the question more than to say that this assumption of his is false, and I do hope that that fallacy will not long prevail in the minds of intelligent white men. At all events, you ought to thank Judge Douglas for it; it is for your benefit it is made.

The other branch of it is, that in the struggle between the negro and the crocodile; he is for the negro. Well, I don't know that there is any struggle between the negro and the crocodile, either. I suppose that if a crocodile (or, as we old Ohio River boatmen used to call them, alligators) should come across a white man, he would kill him if he could; and so he would a negro. But what, at last, is this proposition? I believe it is a sort of proposition in proportion, which may be stated thus: "As the negro is to the white man, so is the crocodile to the negro; and as the negro may rightfully treat the crocodile as a beast or reptile, so the white man may rightfully treat the negro as a beast or a reptile." That is really the "knip" of all that argument of his.

Now, my brother Kentuckians, who believe in this, you ought to thank Judge Douglas for having put that in a much more taking way than any of yourselves have done.

Again, Douglas's great principle, "popular sovereignty," as he calls it, gives you, by natural consequence, the revival of the slave trade whenever you want it. If you question this, listen awhile, consider awhile what I shall advance in support of that proposition.

He says that it is the sacred right of the man who goes into the Territories to have slavery if he wants it. Grant that for argument's sake. Is it not the sacred right of the man who don't go there equally to buy slaves in Africa, if he wants them? Can you point out the difference? The man who goes into the Territories of Kansas and Nebraska, or any other new Territory, with the sacred right of taking a slave there which belongs to him, would certainly have no more right to take one there than I would, who own no slave, but who would desire to buy one and take him there. You will not say you, the friends of Judge Douglas but that the man who does not own a slave has an equal right to buy one and take him to the Territory as the other does.

A voice: I want to ask a question. Don't foreign nations interfere with the slave trade?

Mr. LINCOLN: Well! I understand it to be a principle of Democracy to whip foreign nations whenever, they interfere with us.

Voice: I only asked for information. I am a Republican myself.

Mr. LINCOLN: You and I will be on the best terms in the world, but I do not wish to be diverted from the point I was trying to press.

I say that Douglas's popular sovereignty, establishing his sacred right in the people, if you please, if carried to its logical conclusion gives equally the sacred right to the people of the States or the Territories themselves to buy slaves wherever they can buy them cheapest; and if any man can show a distinction, I should like to hear him try it. If any man can show how the people of Kansas have a better right to slaves, because they want them, than the people of Georgia have to buy them in Africa, I want him to do it. I think it cannot be done. If it is "popular sovereignty" for the people to have slaves because they want them, it is popular sovereignty for them to buy them in Africa because they desire to do so.

I know that Douglas has recently made a little effort, not seeming to notice that he had a different theory, has made an effort to get rid of that. He has written a letter, addressed to somebody, I believe, who resides in Iowa, declaring his opposition to the repeal of the laws that prohibit the Africa slave trade. He bases his opposition to such repeal upon the ground that these laws are themselves one of the compromises of the Constitution of the United States. Now, it would be very interesting to see Judge Douglas or any of his friends turn, to the Constitution of the United States and point out that compromise, to show where there is any compromise in the Constitution, or provision in the Constitution; express or implied, by which the administrators of that Constitution are under any obligation to repeal the African slave trade. I know, or at least I think I know, that the framers of that Constitution did expect the African slave trade would be abolished at the end of twenty years, to which time their prohibition against its being abolished extended there is abundant contemporaneous history to show that the framers of the Constitution expected it to be abolished. But while they so expected, they gave nothing for that expectation, and they put no provision in the Constitution requiring it should be so abolished. The migration or importation of such persons as the States shall see fit to admit shall not be prohibited, but a certain tax might be levied upon such importation. But what was to be done after that time? The Constitution is as silent about that as it is silent, personally, about myself. There is absolutely nothing in it about that subject; there is only the expectation of the framers of the Constitution that the slave trade would be abolished at the end of that time; and they expected it would be abolished, owing to public sentiment, before that time; and the put that provision in, in order that it should not be abolished before that time, for reasons which I suppose they thought to be sound ones, but which I will not now try to enumerate before you.

But while, they expected the slave trade would be abolished at that time, they expected that the spread of slavery into the new Territories should also be restricted. It is as easy to prove that the framers of the Constitution of the United States expected that slavery should be prohibited from extending into the new Territories, as it is to prove that it was expected that the slave trade should be abolished. Both these things were expected. One was no more expected than the other, and one was no more a compromise of the Constitution than the other. There was nothing said in the Constitution in regard to the spread of slavery into the Territory. I grant that; but there was something very important said about it by the same generation of men in the adoption of the old Ordinance of '87, through the influence of which you here in Ohio, our neighbors in Indiana, we in Illinois, our neighbors in Michigan and Wisconsin, are happy, prosperous, teeming millions of free men. That generation of men, though not to the full extent members of the convention that framed the Constitution, were to some extent members of that convention, holding seats at the same time in one body and the other, so that if there was any compromise on either of these subjects, the strong evidence is that that compromise was in favor of the restriction of slavery from the new Territories.

But Douglas says that he is unalterably opposed to the repeal of those laws because, in his view, it is a compromise of the Constitution. You Kentuckians, no doubt, are somewhat offended with that. You ought not to be! You ought to be patient! You ought to know that if he said less than that, he would lose the power of "lugging" the Northern States to your support. Really, what you would push him to do would take from him his entire power to serve you. And you ought to remember how long, by precedent, Judge Douglas holds himself obliged to stick by compromises. You ought to remember that by the time you yourselves think you are ready to inaugurate measures for the revival of the African slave trade, that sufficient time will have arrived, by precedent, for Judge Douglas to break through, that compromise. He says now nothing more strong than he said in 1849 when he declared in favor of Missouri Compromise,—and precisely four years and a quarter after he declared that Compromise to be a sacred thing, which "no ruthless hand would ever daze to touch," he himself brought forward the measure ruthlessly to destroy it. By a mere calculation of time it will only be four years more until he is ready to take back his profession about the sacredness of the Compromise abolishing the slave trade. Precisely as soon as you are ready to have his services in that direction, by fair calculation, you may be sure of having them.

But you remember and set down to Judge Douglas's debt, or discredit, that he, last year, said the people of Territories can, in spite of the Dred Scott decision, exclude your slaves from those Territories; that he declared, by "unfriendly legislation" the extension of your property into the new Territories may be cut off, in the teeth of the decision of the Supreme Court of the United States.

He assumed that position at Freeport on the 27th of August, 1858. He said that the people of the Territories can exclude slavery, in so many words: You ought, however, to bear in mind that he has never said it since. You may hunt in every speech that he has since made, and he has never used that expression once. He has never seemed to notice that he is stating his views differently from what he did then; but by some sort of accident, he has always really stated it differently. He has always since then declared that "the Constitution does not carry slavery into the Territories of the United States beyond the power of the people legally to control it, as other property." Now, there is a difference in the language used upon that former occasion and in this latter day. There may or may not be a difference in the meaning, but it is worth while considering whether there is not also a difference in meaning.

What is it to exclude? Why, it is to drive it out. It is in some way to put it out of the Territory. It is to force it across the line, or change its character so that, as property, it is out of existence. But what is the controlling of it "as other property"? Is controlling it as other property the same thing as destroying it, or driving it away? I should think not. I should think the controlling of it as other property would be just about what you in Kentucky should want. I understand the controlling of property means the controlling of it for the benefit of the owner of it. While I have no doubt the Supreme Court of the United States would say "God speed" to any of the Territorial Legislatures that should thus control slave property, they would sing quite a different tune if, by the pretence of controlling it, they were to undertake to pass laws which virtually excluded it,—and that upon a very well known principle to all lawyers, that what a

Legislature cannot directly do, it cannot do by indirection; that as the Legislature has not the power to drive slaves out, they have no power, by indirection, by tax, or by imposing burdens in any way on that property, to effect the same end, and that any attempt to do so would be held by the Dred Scott court unconstitutional.

Douglas is not willing to stand by his first proposition that they can exclude it, because we have seen that that proposition amounts to nothing more nor less than the naked absurdity that you may lawfully drive out that which has a lawful right to remain. He admitted at first that the slave might be lawfully taken into the Territories under the Constitution of the United States, and yet asserted that he might be lawfully driven out. That being the proposition, it is the absurdity I have stated. He is not willing to stand in the face of that direct, naked, and impudent absurdity; he has, therefore, modified his language into that of being "controlled as other property."

The Kentuckians don't like this in Douglas! I will tell you where it will go. He now swears by the court. He was once a leading man in Illinois to break down a court, because it had made a decision he did not like. But he now not only swears by the court, the courts having got to working for you, but he denounces all men that do not swear by the courts, as unpatriotic, as bad citizens. When one of these acts of unfriendly legislation shall impose such heavy burdens as to, in effect, destroy property in slaves in a Territory, and show plainly enough that there can be no mistake in the purpose of the Legislature to make them so burdensome, this same Supreme Court will decide that law to be unconstitutional, and he will be ready to say for your benefit "I swear by the court; I give it up"; and while that is going on he has been getting all his men to swear by the courts, and to give it up with him. In this again he serves you faithfully, and, as I say, more wisely than you serve yourselves.

Again: I have alluded in the beginning of these remarks to the fact that Judge Douglas has made great complaint of my having expressed the opinion that this government "cannot endure permanently, half slave and half free." He has complained of Seward for using different language, and declaring that there is an "irrepressible conflict" between the principles of free and slave labor. [A voice: "He says it is not original with Seward. That it is original with Lincoln."] I will attend to that immediately, sir. Since that time, Hickman of Pennsylvania expressed the same sentiment. He has never denounced Mr. Hickman: why? There is a little chance, notwithstanding that opinion in the mouth of Hickman, that he may yet be a Douglas man. That is the difference! It is not unpatriotic to hold that opinion if a man is a Douglas man.

But neither I, nor Seward, nor Hickman is entitled to the enviable or unenviable distinction of having first expressed that idea. That same idea was expressed by the Richmond Enquirer, in Virginia, in 1856,—quite two years before it was expressed by the first of us. And while Douglas was pluming himself that in his conflict with my humble self, last year, he had "squelched out" that fatal heresy, as he delighted to call it, and had suggested that if he only had had a chance to be in New York and meet Seward he would have "squelched" it there also, it never occurred to him to breathe a word against Pryor. I don't think that you can discover that Douglas ever talked of going to Virginia to "squelch" out that idea there. No. More than that. That same Roger A. Pryor was brought to Washington City and made the editor of the par excellence Douglas paper, after making use of that expression, which, in us, is so unpatriotic and heretical. From all this, my Kentucky friends may see that this opinion is heretical in his view only when it is expressed by men suspected of a desire that the country shall all become free, and not when expressed by those fairly known to entertain the desire that the whole country shall become slave. When expressed by that class of men, it is in nowise offensive to him. In this again, my friends of Kentucky, you have Judge Douglas with you.

There is another reason why you Southern people ought to nominate Douglas at your convention at Charleston. That reason is the wonderful capacity of the man,—the power he has of doing what would seem to be impossible. Let me call your attention to one of these apparently impossible things:

Douglas had three or four very distinguished men of the most extreme anti-slavery views of any men in the Republican party expressing their desire for his re-election to the Senate last year. That would, of itself, have seemed to be a little wonderful; but that wonder is heightened when we see that Wise of Virginia, a man exactly opposed to them, a man who believes in the divine right of slavery, was also expressing his desire that Douglas should be reelected; that another man that may be said to be kindred to Wise, Mr. Breckinridge, the Vice-President, and of your own State, was also agreeing with the anti-slavery men in the North that Douglas ought to be re-elected. Still to heighten the wonder, a senator from Kentucky, whom I have always loved with an affection as tender and endearing as I have ever loved any man, who was opposed to the anti-slavery men for reasons which seemed sufficient to him, and equally opposed to Wise and Breckinridge, was writing letters into Illinois to secure the reelection of Douglas. Now, that all these conflicting elements should be brought, while at daggers' points with one another, to support him, is a feat that is worthy for you to note and consider. It is quite probable that each of these classes of men thought, by the re-election of Douglas, their peculiar views would gain something: it is probable that the anti-slavery men thought their views would gain something; that Wise and Breckinridge thought so too, as regards their opinions; that Mr. Crittenden thought that his views would gain something, although he was opposed to both these other men. It is probable that each and all of them thought that they were using Douglas; and it is yet an unsolved problem whether he was not using them all. If he was, then it is for you to consider whether that power to perform wonders is one for you lightly to throw away.

There is one other thing that I will say to you, in this relation. It is but my opinion, I give it to you without a fee. It is my opinion that it is for you to take him or be defeated; and that if you do take him you may be beaten. You will surely be beaten if you do not take him. We, the Republicans and others forming the opposition of the country, intend to "stand by our guns," to be patient and firm, and in the long run to beat you, whether you take him or not. We know that before we fairly beat you we have to beat you both together. We know that you are "all of a feather," and that we have to beat you all together, and we expect to do it. We don't intend to be very impatient about it. We mean to be as deliberate and calm about it as it is possible to be, but as firm and resolved as it is possible for men to be. When we do as we say,—beat you,—you perhaps want to know what we will do with you.

I will tell you, so far as I am authorized to speak for the opposition, what we mean to do with you. We mean to treat you, as near as we possibly can, as Washington, Jefferson, and Madison treated you. We mean to leave you alone, and in no way interfere with your institution; to abide by all and every compromise of the Constitution, and, in a word, coming back to the original proposition, to treat you, so far as degenerated men (if we have degenerated) may, according to the examples of those noble fathers, Washington, Jefferson, and Madison. We mean to remember that you are as good as we; that there is no difference between us other than the difference of circumstances. We mean to recognize and bear in mind always that you have as good hearts in your bosoms as other people, or as we claim to have, and treat you accordingly. We mean to marry your girls when we have a chance, the white ones I mean; and I have the honor to inform you that I once did have a chance in that way.

I have told you what we mean to do. I want to know, now, when that thing takes place, what do you mean to do? I often hear it intimated that you mean to divide the Union whenever a Republican, or anything like it, is elected President of the United States. [A voice: "That is so."] "That is so," one of them says; I wonder if he is a Kentuckian? [A voice: "He is a Douglas man."] Well, then, I want to know what you are going to do with your half of it? Are you going to split the Ohio down through, and push your half off a piece? Or are you going to keep it right alongside of us outrageous fellows? Or are you going to build up a wall some way between your country and ours, by which that movable property of yours can't come over here any more, to the danger of your losing it? Do you think you can better yourselves, on that subject, by leaving us here under no obligation whatever to return those specimens of your movable property that come hither? You have divided the Union because we would not do right with you, as you think, upon that subject; when we cease to be under obligations to do anything for you, how much better off do you think you will be? Will you make war upon us and kill us all? Why, gentlemen, I think you are as gallant and as brave men as live; that you can fight as bravely in a good cause, man for man, as any other people living; that you have shown yourselves capable of this upon various occasions: but, man for man, you are not better than we are, and there are not so many of you as there are of us. You will never make much of a hand at whipping us. If we were fewer in numbers than you, I think that you could whip us; if we were equal, it would likely be a drawn battle; but being inferior in numbers, you will make nothing by attempting to master us.

But perhaps I have addressed myself as long, or longer, to the Kentuckians than I ought to have done, inasmuch as I have said that whatever course you take we intend in the end to beat you. I propose to address a few remarks to our friends, by way of discussing with them the best means of keeping that promise that I have in good faith made.

It may appear a little episodical for me to mention the topic of which I will speak now. It is a favorite position of Douglas's that the interference of the General Government, through the Ordinance of '87, or through any other act of the General Government never has made or ever can make a free State; the Ordinance of '87 did not make free States of Ohio, Indiana, or Illinois; that these States are free upon his "great principle" of popular sovereignty, because the people of those several States have chosen to make them so. At Columbus, and probably here, he undertook to compliment the people that they themselves have made the State of Ohio free, and that the Ordinance of '87 was not entitled in any degree to divide the honor with them. I have no doubt that the people of the State of Ohio did make her free according to their own will and judgment, but let the facts be remembered.

In 1802, I believe, it was you who made your first constitution, with the clause prohibiting slavery, and you did it, I suppose, very nearly unanimously; but you should bear in mind that you—speaking of you as one people—that you did so unembarrassed by the actual presence of the institution amongst you; that you made it a free State not with the embarrassment upon you of already having among you many slaves, which if they had been here, and you had sought to make a free State, you would not know what to do with. If they had been among you, embarrassing difficulties, most probably, would have induced you to tolerate a slave constitution instead of a free one, as indeed these very difficulties have constrained every people on this continent who have adopted slavery.

Pray what was it that made you free? What kept you free? Did you not find your country free when you came to decide that Ohio should be a free State? It is important to inquire by what reason you found it so. Let us take an illustration between the States of Ohio and Kentucky. Kentucky is separated by this River Ohio, not a mile wide. A portion of Kentucky, by reason of the course of the Ohio, is farther north than this portion of Ohio, in which we now stand. Kentucky is entirely covered with slavery; Ohio is entirely free from it: What made that difference? Was it climate? No. A portion of Kentucky was farther north than this portion of Ohio. Was it soil? No. There is nothing in the soil of the one more favorable to slave than the other. It was not climate or soil that caused one side of the line to be entirely

341

covered with slavery, and the other side free of it. What was it? Study over it. Tell us, if you can, in all the range of conjecture, if there be anything you can conceive of that made that difference, other than that there was no law of any sort keeping it out of Kentucky, while the Ordinance of '87 kept it out of Ohio. If there is any other reason than this, I confess that it is wholly beyond my power to conceive of it. This, then, I offer to combat the idea that that Ordinance has never made any State free.

I don't stop at this illustration. I come to the State of Indiana; and what I have said as between Kentucky and Ohio, I repeat as between Indiana and Kentucky: it is equally applicable. One additional argument is applicable also to Indiana. In her Territorial condition she more than once petitioned Congress to abrogate the Ordinance entirely, or at least so far as to suspend its operation for a time, in order that they should exercise the "popular sovereignty" of having slaves if they wanted them. The men then controlling the General Government, imitating the men of the Revolution, refused Indiana that privilege. And so we have the evidence that Indiana supposed she could have slaves, if it were not for that Ordinance; that she besought Congress to put that barrier out of the way; that Congress refused to do so; and it all ended at last in Indiana being a free State. Tell me not then that the Ordinance of '87 had nothing to do with making Indiana a free State, when we find some men chafing against, and only restrained by, that barrier.

Come down again to our State of Illinois. The great Northwest Territory, including Ohio, Indiana, Illinois, Michigan, and Wisconsin, was acquired first, I believe, by the British Government, in part at least, from the French. Before the establishment of our independence it became a part of Virginia, enabling Virginia afterward to transfer it to the General Government. There were French settlements in what is now Illinois, and at the same time there were French settlements in what is now Missouri, in the tract of country that was not purchased till about 1803. In these French settlements negro slavery had existed for many years, perhaps more than a hundred; if not as much as two hundred years,—at Kaskaskia, in Illinois, and at St. Genevieve, or Cape Girardeau, perhaps, in Missouri. The number of slaves was not very great, but there was about the same number in each place. They were there when we acquired the Territory. There was no effort made to break up the relation of master and slave, and even the Ordinance of 1787 was not so enforced as to destroy that slavery in Illinois; nor did the Ordinance apply to Missouri at all.

What I want to ask your attention to; at this point, is that Illinois and Missouri came into the Union about the same time, Illinois in the latter part of 1818, and Missouri, after a struggle, I believe sometime in 1820. They had been filling up with American people about the same period of time; their progress enabling them to come into the Union about the same time. At the end of that ten years, in which they had been so preparing (for it was about that period of time), the number of slaves in Illinois had actually decreased; while in Missouri, beginning with very few, at the end of that ten years there were about ten thousand. This being so, and it being remembered that Missouri and Illinois are, to a certain extent, in the same parallel of latitude, that the northern half of Missouri and the southern half of Illinois are in the same parallel of latitude, so that climate would have the same effect upon one as upon the other, and that in the soil there is no material difference so far as bears upon the question of slavery being settled upon one or the other,—there being none of those natural causes to produce a difference in filling them, and yet there being a broad difference to their filling up, we are led again to inquire what was the cause of that difference.

It is most natural to say that in Missouri there was no law to keep that country from filling up with slaves, while in Illinois there was the Ordinance of The Ordinance being there, slavery decreased during that ten years; the Ordinance not being in the other, it increased from a few to ten thousand. Can anybody doubt the reason of the difference?

I think all these facts most abundantly prove that my friend Judge Douglas's proposition, that the Ordinance of '87, or the national restriction of slavery, never had a tendency to make a free State, is a fallacy,—a proposition without the shadow or substance of truth about it.

Douglas sometimes says that all the States (and it is part of this same proposition I have been discussing) that have become free have become so upon his "great principle"; that the State of Illinois itself came into the Union as a slave State, and that the people, upon the "great principle" of popular sovereignty, have since made it a free State. Allow me but a little while to state to you what facts there are to justify him in saying that Illinois came into the Union as a slave State.

I have mentioned to you that there were a few old French slaves there. They numbered, I think, one or two hundred. Besides that, there had been a Territorial law for indenturing black persons. Under that law, in violation of the Ordinance of '87, but without any enforcement of the Ordinance to overthrow the system, there had been a small number of slaves introduced as indentured persons. Owing to this, the clause for the prohibition of slavery was slightly modified. Instead of running like yours, that neither slavery nor involuntary servitude, except for crime, of which the party shall have been duly convicted, should exist in the State, they said that neither slavery nor involuntary servitude should thereafter be introduced; and that the children of indentured servants should be born free; and nothing was said about the few old French slaves. Out of this fact, that the clause for prohibiting slavery was modified because of the actual presence of it, Douglas asserts again and again that Illinois came into the Union as a slave State. How far the facts sustain the conclusion that he draws, it is for intelligent and impartial men to decide. I leave it with you, with these remarks, worthy of being remembered, that that little thing, those few indentured servants being there, was of itself sufficient to modify a constitution made by a people ardently desiring to have a free constitution; showing the power of the actual presence of the institution of slavery to prevent any people, however anxious to make a free State, from making it perfectly so.

I have been detaining you longer, perhaps, than I ought to do.

I am in some doubt whether to introduce another topic upon which I could talk a while. [Cries of "Go on," and "Give us it."] It is this, then: Douglas's Popular sovereignty, as a principle, is simply this: If one man chooses to make a slave of another man, neither that man nor anybody else has a right to object. Apply it to government, as he seeks to apply it, and it is this: If, in a new Territory into which a few people are beginning to enter for the purpose of making their homes, they choose to either exclude slavery from their limits, or to establish it there, however one or the other may affect the persons to be enslaved, or the infinitely greater number of persons who are afterward to inhabit that Territory, or the other members of the family of communities of which they are but an incipient member, or the general head of the family of States as parent of all, however their action may affect one or the other of these, there is no power or right to interfere. That is Douglas's popular sovereignty applied. Now, I think that there is a real popular sovereignty in the world. I think the definition of popular sovereignty, in the abstract, would be about this: that each man shall do precisely as he pleases with himself, and with all those things which exclusively concern him. Applied in government, this principle would be that a general government shall do all those things which pertain to it, and all the local governments shall do precisely as they please in respect to those matters which exclusively concern them.

Douglas looks upon slavery as so insignificant that the people must decide that question for themselves; and yet they are not fit to decide who shall be their governor, judge, or secretary, or who shall be any of their officers. These are vast national matters in his estimation; but the little matter in his estimation is that of planting slavery there. That is purely of local interest, which nobody should be allowed to say a word about.

Labor is the great source from which nearly all, if not all, human comforts and necessities are drawn. There is a difference in opinion about the elements of labor in society. Some men assume that there is necessary connection between capital and labor, and that connection draws within it the whole of the labor of the community. They assume that nobody works unless capital excites them to work. They begin next to consider what is the best way. They say there are but two ways: one is to hire men, and to allure them to labor by their consent; the other is to buy the men, and drive them, to it, and that is slavery. Having assumed that, they proceed to discuss the question of whether the laborers themselves are better off in the condition of slaves or of hired laborers, and they usually decide that they are better off in the condition of slaves.

In the first place, I say that the whole thing is a mistake. That there is a certain relation between capital and labor, I admit. That it does exist, and rightfully exists, I think is true. That men who are industrious, and sober, and honest in the pursuit of their own interests should after a while accumulate capital, and after that should be allowed to enjoy it in peace, and also, if they should choose, when they have accumulated it, to use it to save themselves from actual labor, and hire other people to labor for them, is right. In doing so they do not wrong the man they employ, for they find men who have not of their own land to work upon, or shops to work in, and who are benefited by working for others, hired laborers, receiving their capital for it. Thus a few men, that own capital, hire a few others, and these establish the relation of capital and labor rightfully, a relation of which I make no complaint. But I insist that that relation, after all, does not embrace more than one eighth of the labor of the country.

[The speaker proceeded to argue that the hired laborer, with his ability to become an employer, must have every precedence over him who labors under the inducement of force. He continued:]

I have taken upon myself in the name of some of you to say that we expect upon these principles to ultimately beat them. In order to do so, I think we want and must have a national policy in regard to the institution of slavery that acknowledges and deals with that institution as being wrong. Whoever desires the prevention of the spread of slavery and the nationalization of that institution yields all when he yields to any policy that either recognizes slavery as being right or as being an indifferent thing. Nothing will make you successful but setting up a policy which shall treat the thing as being wrong. When I say this, I do not mean to say that this General Government is charged with the duty of redressing or preventing all the wrongs in the world, but I do think that it is charged with preventing and redressing all wrongs which are wrongs to itself. This Government is expressly charged with the duty of providing for the general welfare. We believe that the spreading out and perpetuity of the institution of slavery impairs the general welfare. We believe—nay, we know—that that is the only thing that has ever threatened the perpetuity of the Union itself. The only thing which has ever menaced the destruction of the government under which we live is this very thing. To repress this thing, we think, is, Providing for the general welfare. Our friends in Kentucky differ from us. We need not make our argument for them, but we who think it is wrong in all its relations, or in some of them at least, must decide as to our own actions and our own course, upon our own judgment.

I say that we must not interfere with the institution of slavery in the States where it exists, because the Constitution forbids it, and the general welfare does not require us to do so. We must not withhold an efficient Fugitive Slave law, because the Constitution requires us, as I understand it, not to withhold such a law. But we must prevent the outspreading of the institution, because neither the Constitution nor general welfare requires us to extend it. We must prevent the revival of the African slave trade, and the enacting by Congress of a Territorial slave code. We must prevent each of these things being done by either Congresses or courts. The people of these United States are the rightful masters of both Congresses and courts, not to overthrow the Constitution, but to overthrow the men who pervert the Constitution.

To do these things we must employ instrumentalities. We must hold conventions; we must adopt platforms, if we conform to ordinary custom; we must nominate candidates; and we must carry elections. In all these things, I think that we ought to keep in view our real purpose, and in none do anything that stands adverse to our purpose. If we shall adopt a platform that fails to recognize or express our purpose, or elect a man that declares himself inimical to our purpose, we not only take nothing by our success, but we tacitly admit that we act upon no other principle than a desire to have "the loaves and fishes," by which, in the end, our apparent success is really an injury to us.

I know that this is very desirable with me, as with everybody else, that all the elements of the opposition shall unite in the next Presidential election and in all future time. I am anxious that that should be; but there are things seriously to be considered in relation to that matter. If the terms can be arranged, I am in favor of the union. But suppose we shall take up some man, and put him upon one end or the other of the ticket, who declares himself against us in regard to the prevention of the spread of slavery, who turns up his nose and says he is tired of hearing anything more about it, who is more against us than against the enemy, what will be the issue? Why, he will get no slave States, after all,—he has tried that already until being beat is the rule for him. If we nominate him upon that ground, he will not carry a slave State; and not only so, but that portion of our men who are high-strung upon the principle we really fight for will not go for him, and he won't get a single electoral vote anywhere, except, perhaps, in the State of Maryland. There is no use in saying to us that we are stubborn and obstinate because we won't do some such thing as this. We cannot do it. We cannot get our men to vote it. I speak by the card, that we cannot give the State of Illinois in such case by fifty thousand. We would be flatter down than the "Negro Democracy" themselves have the heart to wish to see us.

After saying this much let me say a little on the other side. There are plenty of men in the slave States that are altogether good enough for me to be either President or Vice-President, provided they will profess their sympathy with our purpose, and will place themselves on the ground that our men, upon principle, can vote for them. There are scores of them, good men in their character for intelligence and talent and integrity. If such a one will place himself upon the right ground, I am for his occupying one place upon the next Republican or opposition ticket. I will heartily go for him. But unless he does so place himself, I think it a matter of perfect nonsense to attempt to bring about a union upon any other basis; that if a union be made, the elements will scatter so that there can be no success for such a ticket, nor anything like success. The good old maxims of the Bible are applicable, and truly applicable, to human affairs, and in this, as in other things, we may say here that he who is not for us is against us; he who gathereth not with us, scattereth. I should be glad to have some of the many good and able and noble men of the South to place themselves where we can confer upon them the high honor of an election upon one or the other end of our ticket. It would do my soul good to do that thing. It would enable us to teach them that, inasmuch as we select one of their own number to carry out our principles, we are free from the charge that we mean more than we say.

But, my friends, I have detained you much longer than I expected to do. I believe I may do myself the compliment to say that you have stayed and heard me with great patience, for which I return you my most sincere thanks.

ON PROTECTIVE TARIFFS

TO EDWARD WALLACE.

CLINTON, October 11, 1859
Dr. EDWARD WALLACE.

MY DEAR SIR:—I am here just now attending court. Yesterday, before I left Springfield, your brother, Dr. William S. Wallace, showed me a letter of yours, in which you kindly mention my name, inquiring for my tariff views, and suggest the propriety of my writing a letter upon the subject. I was an old Henry-Clay-Tariff Whig. In old times I made more speeches on that subject than any other.

I have not since changed my views. I believe yet, if we could have a moderate, carefully adjusted protective tariff, so far acquiesced in as not to be a perpetual subject of political strife, squabbles changes, and uncertainties, it would be better for us. Still it is my opinion that just now the revival of that question will not advance the cause itself, or the man who revives it.

I have not thought much on the subject recently, but my general impression is that the necessity for a protective tariff will ere long force its old opponents to take it up; and then its old friends can join in and establish it on a more firm and durable basis. We, the Old Whigs, have been entirely beaten out on the tariff question, and we shall not be able to re-establish the policy until the absence of it shall have demonstrated the necessity for it in the minds of men heretofore

opposed to it. With this view, I should prefer to not now write a public letter on the subject. I therefore wish this to be considered confidential. I shall be very glad to receive a letter from you.
Yours truly,
A. LINCOLN.

ON MORTGAGES

TO W. DUNGY.

SPRINGFIELD, November, 2, 1859.
WM. DUNGY, Esq.
DEAR SIR:—Yours of October 27 is received. When a mortgage is given to secure two notes, and one of the notes is sold and assigned, if the mortgaged premises are only sufficient to pay one note, the one assigned will take it all. Also, an execution from a judgment on the assigned note may take it all; it being the same thing in substance. There is redemption on execution sales from the United States Court just as from any other court.
You did not mention the name of the plaintiff or defendant in the suit, and so I can tell nothing about it as to sales, bids, etc. Write again.
Yours truly,
A. LINCOLN.

FRAGMENT OF SPEECH AT LEAVENWORTH, KANSAS,

DECEMBER, 1859.

.... But you Democrats are for the Union; and you greatly fear the success of the Republicans would destroy the Union. Why? Do the Republicans declare against the Union? Nothing like it. Your own statement of it is that if the Black Republicans elect a President, you "won't stand it." You will break up the Union. If we shall constitutionally elect a President, it will be our duty to see that you submit. Old John Brown has been executed for treason against a State. We cannot object, even though he agreed with us in thinking slavery wrong. That cannot excuse violence, bloodshed and treason. It could avail him nothing that he might think himself right. So, if we constitutionally elect a President, and therefore you undertake to destroy the Union, it will be our duty to deal with you as old John Brown has been dealt with. We shall try to do our duty. We hope and believe that in no section will a majority so act as to render such extreme measures necessary.

TO G. W. DOLE, G. S. HUBBARD, AND W. H. BROWN.

SPRINGFIELD, Dec. 14, 1859

MESSRS. DOLE, HUBBARD & BROWN.
GENT.:—Your favor of the 12th is at hand, and it gives me pleasure to be able to answer it. It is not my intention to take part in any of the rivalries for the gubernatorial nomination; but the fear of being misunderstood upon that subject ought not to deter me from doing justice to Mr. Judd, and preventing a wrong being done to him by the use of nay name in connection with alleged wrongs to me.
In answer to your first question, as to whether Mr. Judd was guilty of any unfairness to me at the time of Senator Trumbull's election, I answer unhesitatingly in the negative; Mr. Judd owed no political allegiance to any party whose candidate I was. He was in the Senate, holding over, having been elected by a Democratic Constituency. He never was in any caucus of the friends who sought to make me U. S. Senator, never gave me any promises or pledges to support me, and subsequent events have greatly tended to prove the wisdom, politically, of Mr. Judd's course. The election of Judge Trumbull strongly tended to sustain and preserve the position of that lion of the Democrats who condemned

the repeal of the Missouri Compromise, and left them in a position of joining with us in forming the Republican party, as was done at the Bloomington convention in 1856.

During the canvass of 1858 for the senatorship my belief was, and still is, that I had no more sincere and faithful friend than Mr. Judd—certainly none whom I trusted more. His position as chairman of the State Central Committee led to my greater intercourse with him, and to my giving him a larger share of my confidence, than with or to almost any other friend; and I have never suspected that that confidence was, to any degree, misplaced.

My relations with Mr. Judo since the organization of the Republican party, in, our State, in 1856, and especially since the adjournment of the Legislature in Feb., 1857, have been so very intimate that I deem it an impossibility that he could have been dealing treacherously with me. He has also, at all times, appeared equally true and faithful to the party. In his position as chairman of the committee, I believe he did all that any man could have done. The best of us are liable to commit errors, which become apparent by subsequent developments; but I do not know of a single error, even, committed by Mr. Judd, since he and I have acted together politically.

I, had occasionally heard these insinuations against Mr. Judd, before the receipt of your letter; and in no instance have I hesitated to pronounce them wholly unjust, to the full extent of my knowledge and belief. I have been, and still am, very anxious to take no part between the many friends, all good and true, who are mentioned as candidates for a Republican gubernatorial nomination; but I can not feel that my own honor is quite clear if I remain silent when I hear any one of them assailed about matters of which I believe I know more than his assailants.

I take pleasure in adding that, of all the avowed friends I had in the canvass of last year, I do not suspect any of having acted treacherously to me, or to our cause; and that there is not one of them in whose honesty, honor, and integrity I, today, have greater confidence than I have in those of Mr. Judd.

I dislike to appear before the public in this matter; but you are at liberty to make such use of this letter as you may think justice requires.

Yours very truly,
A. LINCOLN.

TO G. M. PARSONS AND OTHERS.

SPRINGFIELD, ILLINOIS, December 19, 1859.

MESSRS. G. M. PARSONS AND OTHERS, CENTRAL EXECUTIVE COMMITTEE, ETC.

GENTLEMEN:—Your letter of the 7th instant, accompanied by a similar one from the governor-elect, the Republican State officers, and the Republican members of the State Board of Equalization of Ohio, both requesting of me, for publication in permanent form, copies of the political debates between Senator Douglas and myself last year, has been received. With my grateful acknowledgments to both you and them for the very flattering terms in which the request is communicated, I transmit you the copies. The copies I send you are as reported and printed by the respective friends of Senator Douglas and myself, at the time—that is, his by his friends, and mine by mine. It would be an unwarrantable liberty for us to change a word or a letter in his, and the changes I have made in mine, you perceive, are verbal only, and very few in number. I wish the reprint to be precisely as the copies I send, without any comment whatever.

Yours very truly,
A. LINCOLN.

AUTOBIOGRAPHICAL SKETCH

TO J. W. FELL,

SPRINGFIELD, December 20, 1859.
J. W. FELL, Esq.

MY DEAR SIR:—Herewith is a little sketch, as you requested. There is not much of it, for the reason, I suppose, that there is not much of me. If anything be made out of it, I wish it to be modest, and not to go beyond the material. If it were thought necessary to incorporate anything from any of my speeches I suppose there would be no objection. Of course it must not appear to have been written by myself.

Yours very truly, A. LINCOLN

I was born February 12, 1809, in Hardin County, Kentucky. My parents were both born in Virginia, of undistinguished families—second families, perhaps I should say. My mother, who died in my tenth year, was of a family of the name of Hanks, some of whom now reside in Adams, and others in Macon County, Illinois. My paternal grandfather, Abraham Lincoln, emigrated from Rockingham County, Virginia, to Kentucky about 1781 or 1782, where a year or two later he was killed by the Indians, not in battle, but by stealth, when he was laboring to open a farm in the forest. His ancestors, who were Quakers, went to Virginia from Berks County, Pennsylvania. An effort to identify them with the New England family of the same name ended in nothing more definite than a similarity of Christian names in both families, such as Enoch, Levi, Mordecai, Solomon, Abraham, and the like.

My father, at the death of his father, was but six years of age, and he grew up literally without education. He removed from Kentucky to what is now Spencer County, Indiana, in my eighth year. We reached our new home about the time that State came into the Union. It was a wild region, with many bears and other wild animals still in the woods. There I grew up. There were some schools, so called, but no qualification was ever required of a teacher beyond "readin', writin', and cipherin'" to the Rule of Three. If a straggler supposed to understand Latin happened to sojourn in the neighborhood he was looked upon as a wizard. There was absolutely nothing to excite ambition for education. Of course, when I came of age I did not know much. Still, somehow, I could read, write, and cipher to the Rule of Three, but that was all. I have not been to school since. The little advance I now have upon this store of education I have picked up from time to time under the pressure of necessity.

I was raised to farm work, which I continued till I was twenty-two. At twenty-one I came to Illinois, Macon County. Then I got to New Salem, at that time in Sangamon, now in Menard County, where I remained a year as a sort of clerk in a store. Then came the Black Hawk war; and I was elected a captain of volunteers, a success which gave me more pleasure than any I have had since. I went the campaign, was elected, ran for the Legislature the same year (1832), and was beaten—the only time I ever have been beaten by the people. The next and three succeeding biennial elections I was elected to the Legislature. I was not a candidate afterward. During this legislative period I had studied law, and removed to Springfield to practice it. In 1846 I was once elected to the lower House of Congress. Was not a candidate for re-election. From 1849 to 1854, both inclusive, practiced law more assiduously than ever before. Always a Whig in politics; and generally on the Whig electoral tickets, making active canvasses. I was losing interest in politics when the repeal of the Missouri Compromise aroused me again. What I have done since then is pretty well known.

If any personal description of me is thought desirable, it may be said I am, in height, six feet four inches, nearly; lean in flesh, weighing on an average one hundred and eighty pounds; dark complexion, with coarse black hair and gray eyes. No other marks or brands recollected.

Yours truly,
A. LINCOLN.

ON NOMINATION TO THE NATIONAL TICKET

To N. B. JUDD.

SPRINGFIELD, FEBRUARY 9, 1859 HON. N. B. JUDD.
DEAR Sir:—I am not in a position where it would hurt much for me to not be nominated on the national ticket; but I am where it would hurt some for me to not get the Illinois delegates. What I expected when I wrote the letter to Messrs. Dole and others is now happening. Your discomfited assailants are most bitter against me; and they will, for revenge upon me, lay to the Bates egg in the South, and to the Seward egg in the North, and go far toward squeezing me out in the middle with nothing. Can you help me a little in this matter in your end of the vineyard. I mean this to be private.
Yours as ever,
A. LINCOLN

1860

SPEECH AT THE COOPER INSTITUTE, NEW YORK FEBRUARY 27, 1860

MR. PRESIDENT AND FELLOW-CITIZENS OF NEW YORK:—The facts with which I shall deal this evening are mainly old and familiar; nor is there anything new in the general use I shall make of them. If there shall be any novelty, it will be in the mode of presenting the facts, and the inferences and observations following that presentation. In his speech last autumn at Columbus, Ohio, as reported in the New York Times, Senator Douglas said:

"Our fathers, when they framed the Government under which we live, understood this question just as well, and even better than we do now."

I fully indorse this, and I adopt it as a text for this discourse. I so adopt it because it furnishes a precise and an agreed starting-point for a discussion between Republicans and that wing of the Democracy headed by Senator Douglas. It simply leaves the inquiry: What was the understanding those fathers had of the question mentioned?

What is the frame of Government under which we live?

The answer must be—the Constitution of the United States. That Constitution consists of the original, framed in 1787 (and under which the present Government first went into operation), and twelve subsequently framed amendments, the first ten of which were framed in 1789.

Who were our fathers that framed the Constitution? I suppose the "thirty-nine" who signed the original instrument may be fairly called our fathers who framed that part of the present Government. It is almost exactly true to say they framed it, and it is altogether true to say they fairly represented the opinion and sentiment of the whole nation at that time.

Their names, being familiar to nearly all, and accessible to quite all, need not now be repeated.

I take these "thirty-nine," for the present, as being our "fathers who framed the Government under which we live."

What is the question which, according to the text, those fathers understood "just as well, and even better than we do now"?

It is this: Does the proper division of local from Federal authority, or anything in the Constitution, forbid our Federal Government to control as to slavery in our Federal Territories?

Upon this Senator Douglas holds the affirmative, and Republicans the negative. This affirmation and denial form an issue, and this issue—this question is precisely what the text declares our fathers understood "better than we."

Let us now inquire whether the "thirty-nine," or any of them, acted upon this question; and if they did, how they acted upon it—how they expressed that better understanding.

In 1784, three years before the Constitution—the United States then owning the Northwestern Territory, and no other—the Congress of the Confederation had before them the question of prohibiting slavery in that Territory; and four of the "thirty nine" who afterward framed the Constitution were in that Congress and voted on that question. Of these, Roger Sherman, Thomas Mifflin, and Hugh Williamson voted for the prohibition, thus showing that, in their understanding, no line dividing local from Federal authority, nor anything else, properly forbade the Federal Government to control as to slavery in Federal territory. The other of the four—James McHenry voted against the prohibition, showing that, for some cause, he thought it improper to vote for it.

In 1787, still before the Constitution, but while the convention was in session framing it, and while the Northwestern Territory still was the only Territory owned by the United States, the same question of prohibiting slavery in the Territory again came before the Congress of the Confederation; and two more of the "thirty-nine" who afterward signed the Constitution were in that Congress, and voted on the question. They were William Blount and William Few; and they both voted for the prohibition thus showing that, in their understanding, no line dividing local from Federal authority, nor anything else, properly forbade the Federal Government to control as to slavery in Federal territory. This time the prohibition became a law, being part of what is now well known as the Ordinance of '87.

The question of Federal control of slavery in the Territories seems not to have been directly before the convention which framed the original Constitution; and hence it is not recorded that the "thirty-nine," or any of them, while engaged on that instrument, expressed any opinion on that precise question.

In 1789, by the first Congress which sat under the Constitution, an act was passed to enforce the Ordinance of '87, including the prohibition of slavery in the Northwestern Territory. The bill for this act was reported by one of the "thirty-nine," Thomas Fitzsimmons, then a member of the House of Representatives from Pennsylvania. It went through all its stages without a word of opposition, and finally passed both branches without yeas and nays, which is equivalent to a unanimous passage. In this Congress there were sixteen of the thirty-nine fathers who framed the original Constitution. They were John Langdon, Nicholas Gilman, Wm. S. Johnnson, Roger Sherman, Robert Morris, Thos. Fitzsimmons, William Few, Abraham Baldwin, Rufus King, William Paterson, George Claimer, Richard Bassett, George Read, Pierce Butler, Daniel Carroll, James Madison.

This shows that, in their understanding, no line dividing local from Federal authority, nor anything in the Constitution, properly forbade Congress to prohibit slavery in the Federal territory; else both their fidelity to correct principles and their oath to support the Constitution would have constrained them to oppose the prohibition.

Again: George Washington, another of the "thirty nine," was then President of the United States, and, as such, approved and signed the bill; thus completing its validity as a law, and thus showing that, in his understanding, no line dividing local from Federal authority, nor anything in the Constitution, forbade the Federal Government to control as to slavery in Federal territory.

No great while after the adoption of the original Constitution, North Carolina ceded to the Federal Government the country now constituting the State of Tennessee; and, a few years later, Georgia ceded that which now constitutes the States of Mississippi and Alabama. In both deeds of cession it was made a condition by the ceding States that the Federal Government should not prohibit slavery in the ceded country. Besides this, slavery was then actually in the ceded country. Under these circumstances, Congress, on taking charge of these countries, did not absolutely prohibit slavery within them. But they did interfere with it—take control of it—even there, to a certain extent. In 1798, Congress organized the Territory of Mississippi: In the act of organization they prohibited the bringing of slaves into the Territory from any place without the United States, by fine and giving freedom to slaves so brought. This act passed both branches of Congress without yeas and nays. In that Congress were three of the "thirty-nine" who framed the original Constitution. They were John Langdon, George Read, and Abraham Baldwin. They all, probably, voted for it. Certainly they would have placed their opposition to it upon record, if, in their understanding, any line dividing local from Federal authority, or anything in the Constitution, properly forbade the Federal Government to control as to slavery in Federal territory.

In 1803, the Federal Government purchased the Louisiana country. Our former territorial acquisitions came from certain of our own States; but this Louisiana country was acquired from a foreign nation. In 1804, Congress gave a territorial organization to that part of it which now constitutes the State of Lousiana. New Orleans, lying within that part, was an old and comparatively large city. There were other considerable towns and settlements, and slavery was extensively and thoroughly intermingled with the people. Congress did not, in the Territorial Act, prohibit slavery; but they did interfere with it take control of it—in a more marked and extensive way than they did in the case of Mississippi. The substance of the provision therein made in relation to slaves was:

First. That no slave should be imported into the Territory from foreign parts.

Second. That no slave should be carried into it who had been imported into the United States since the first day of May, 1798.

Third. That no slave should be carried into it except by the owner, and for his own use as a settler; the penalty in all the cases being a fine upon the violator of the law, and freedom to the slave.

This act also was passed without yeas and nays. In the Congress which passed it there were two of the "thirty-nine." They were Abraham Baldwin and Jonathan Dayton. As stated in the case of Mississippi, it is probable they both voted for it. They would not have allowed it to pass without recording their opposition to it, if, in their understanding, it violated either the line properly dividing local from Federal authority, or any provision of the Constitution.

In 1819-20 came and passed the Missouri question. Many votes were taken, by yeas and nays, in both branches of Congress, upon the various phases of the general question. Two of the "thirty-nine"—Rufus King and Charles Pinckney were members of that Congress. Mr. King steadily voted for slavery prohibition and against all compromises, while Mr. Pinckney as steadily voted against slavery prohibition, and against all compromises. By this, Mr. King showed that, in his understanding, no line dividing local from Federal authority, nor anything in the Constitution, was violated by Congress prohibiting slavery in Federal territory; while Mr. Pinckney, by his vote, showed that in his understanding there was some sufficient reason for opposing such prohibition in that case.

The cases I have mentioned are the only acts of the "thirty-nine," or of any of them, upon the direct issue, which I have been able to discover.

To enumerate the persons who thus acted, as being four in 1784, two in 1787, seventeen in 1789, three in 1798, two in 1804, and two in 1819-20—there would be thirty of them. But this would be counting, John Langdon, Roger Sherman, William Few, Rufus King, and George Read, each twice, and Abraham Baldwin three times. The true number of those of the "thirty-nine" whom I have shown to have acted upon the question which, by the text, they understood better than we, is twenty-three, leaving sixteen not shown to have acted upon it in any way.

Here, then, we have twenty-three out of our thirty-nine fathers "who framed the Government under which we live," who have, upon their official responsibility and their corporal oaths, acted upon the very question which the text affirms they "understood just as well, and even better than we do now"; and twenty-one of them—a clear majority of the whole "thirty-nine"—so acting upon it as to make them guilty of gross political impropriety and wilful perjury, if, in their understanding, any proper division between local and Federal authority, or anything in the Constitution they had made themselves, and sworn to support, forbade the Federal Government to control as to slavery in the Federal Territories. Thus the twenty-one acted; and, as actions speak louder than words, so actions under such responsibilities speak still louder.

Two of the twenty-three voted against Congressional prohibition of slavery in the Federal Territories, in the instances in which they acted upon the question. But for what reasons they so voted is not known. They may have done so because they thought a proper division of local from Federal authority, or some provision or principle of the Constitution, stood in the way; or they may, without any such question, have voted against the prohibition on what appeared to them to be sufficient grounds of expediency. No one who has sworn to support the Constitution can conscientiously vote for what he understands to be an unconstitutional measure, however expedient he may think it; but one may and ought to vote against a measure which he deems constitutional, if, at the same time, he deems it inexpedient. It therefore would be unsafe to set down even the two who voted against the prohibition as having done so because, in their understanding, any proper division of local from Federal authority, or anything in the Constitution, forbade the Federal Government to control as to slavery in Federal territory.

The remaining sixteen of the "thirty-nine," so far as I have discovered, have left no record of their understanding upon the direct question of Federal control on slavery in the Federal Territories. But there is much reason to believe that their understanding upon that question would not have appeared different from that of their twenty-three compeers, had it been manifested at all.

For the purpose of adhering rigidly to the text, I have purposely omitted whatever understanding may have been manifested by any person, however distinguished, other than the thirty-nine fathers who framed the original Constitution; and, for the same reason, I have also omitted whatever understanding may have been manifested by any of the "thirty tine" even on any other phase of the general question of slavery. If we should look into their acts and declarations on those other phases, as the foreign slave trade, and the morality and policy of slavery generally, it would appear to us that on the direct question of Federal control of slavery in Federal Territories, the sixteen, if they had acted at all, would probably have acted just as the twenty-three did. Among that sixteen were several of the most noted anti-slavery men of those times—as Dr. Franklin, Alexander Hamilton, and Gouverneur Morris while there was not one now known to have been otherwise, unless it may be John Rutledge, of South Carolina.

The sum of the whole is, that of our thirty-nine fathers who framed the original Constitution, twenty-one—a clear majority of the whole—certainly understood that no proper division of local from Federal authority, nor any part of the Constitution, forbade the Federal Government to control slavery in the Federal Territories; whilst all the rest probably had the same understanding. Such, unquestionably, was the understanding of our fathers who framed the original Constitution; and the text affirms that they understood the question "better than we."

But, so far, I have been considering the understanding of the question manifested by the framers of the original Constitution. In and by the original instrument, a mode was provided for amending it; and, as I have already stated, the present frame of "the Government under which we live" consists of that original, and twelve amendatory articles framed and adopted since. Those who now insist that Federal control of slavery in Federal Territories violates the Constitution, point us to the provisions which they suppose it thus violates; and, as I understand, they all fix upon provisions in these amendatory articles, and not in the original instrument. The Supreme Court, in the Dred Scott case, plant themselves upon the fifth amendment, which provides that no person shall be deprived of "life, liberty, or property without due process of law"; while Senator Douglas and his peculiar adherents plant themselves upon the tenth amendment, providing that "the powers not delegated to the United States by the Constitution" "are reserved to the States respectively, or to the people."

Now, it so happens that these amendments were framed by the first Congress which sat under the Constitution—the identical Congress which passed the act already mentioned, enforcing the prohibition of slavery in the Northwestern Territory. Not only was it the same Congress, but they were the identical same individual men who, at the same session, and at the same time within the session, had under consideration, and in progress toward maturity, these Constitutional amendments, and this act prohibiting slavery in all the territory the nation then owned. The Constitutional amendments were introduced before and passed after the act enforcing the Ordinance of '87; so that, during the whole pendency of the act to enforce the Ordinance, the Constitutional amendments were also pending.

The seventy-six members of that Congress, including sixteen of the framers of the original Constitution, as before stated, were pre-eminently our fathers who framed that part of "the Government under which we live," which is now claimed as forbidding the Federal Government to control slavery in the Federal Territories.

Is it not a little presumptuous in any one at this day to affirm that the two things which that Congress deliberately framed, and carried to maturity at the same time, are absolutely inconsistent with each other? And does not such affirmation become impudently absurd when coupled with the other affirmation from the same mouth, that those who did the two things alleged to be inconsistent understood whether they really were inconsistent better than we—better than he who affirms that they are inconsistent?

It is surely safe to assume that the thirty-nine framers of the original Constitution, and the seventy-six members of the Congress which framed the amendments thereto, taken together, do certainly include those who may be fairly called "our fathers who framed the Government under which we live." And, so assuming, I defy any man to show that any one of them ever, in his whole life, declared that, in his understanding, any proper division of local from Federal authority, or any part of the Constitution, forbade the Federal Government to control as to slavery in the Federal Territories. I go a step further. I defy any one to show that any living man in the world ever did, prior to the beginning of the present century (and I might almost say prior to the beginning of the last half of the present century), declare that, in his understanding, any proper division of local from Federal authority, or any part of the Constitution, forbade the Federal Government to control as to slavery in the Federal Territories. To those who now so declare, I give not only "our fathers who framed the Government under which we live," but with them all other living men within the century in which it was framed, among whom to search, and they shall not be able to find the evidence of a single man agreeing with them.

Now and here let me guard a little against being misunderstood. I do not mean to say we are bound to follow implicitly in whatever our fathers did. To do so would be to discard all the lights of current experience to reject all progress, all improvement. What I do say is that, if we would supplant the opinions and policy of our fathers in any case, we should do so upon evidence so conclusive, and argument so clear, that even their great authority, fairly considered and weighed, cannot stand; and most surely not in a case whereof we ourselves declare they understood the question better than we. If any man at this day sincerely believes that proper division of local from Federal authority, or any part of the Constitution, forbids the Federal Government to control as to slavery in the Federal Territories, he is right to say so, and to enforce his position by all truthful evidence and fair argument which he can. But he has no right to mislead others who have less access to history, and less leisure to study it, into the false belief that "our fathers who framed the Government under which we live" were of the same opinion thus substituting falsehood and deception for truthful evidence and fair argument. If any man at this day sincerely believes "our fathers, who framed the Government under which we live," used and applied principles, in other cases, which ought to have led them to understand that a proper division of local from Federal authority, or some part of the Constitution, forbids the Federal Government to control as to slavery in the Federal Territories, he is right to say so. But he should, at the same time, brave the responsibility of declaring that, in his opinion, he understands their principles better than they did themselves; and especially should he not shirk that responsibility by asserting that they "understood the question just as well, and even better than we do now."

But enough! Let all who believe that "our fathers, who framed the Government under which we live, understood this question just as well, and even better than we do now," speak as they spoke, and act as they acted upon it. This is all Republicans ask—all Republicans desire—in relation to slavery. As those fathers marked it, so let it be again marked, as an evil not to be extended, but to be tolerated and protected only because of, and so far as, its actual presence among us makes that toleration and protection a necessity. Let all the guaranties those fathers gave it be not grudgingly, but fully and fairly maintained. For this Republicans contend, and with this, so far as I know or believe, they will be content.

And now, if they would listen—as I suppose they will not—I would address a few words to the Southern people.

I would say to them: You consider yourselves a reasonable and a just people; and I consider that in the general qualities of reason and justice you are not inferior to any other people. Still, when you speak of us Republicans, you do so only to denounce us as reptiles, or, at the best, as no better than outlaws. You will grant a hearing to pirates or murderers, but nothing like it to "Black Republicans." In all your contentions with one another, each of you deems an unconditional condemnation of "Black Republicanism" as the first thing to be attended to. Indeed, such condemnation of us seems to be an indispensable prerequisite license, so to speak among you, to be admitted or permitted to speak at all: Now; can you, or not, be prevailed upon to pause, and to consider whether this is quite just to us, or even to yourselves? Bring forward your charges and specifications, and then be patient long enough to hear us deny or justify.

You say we are sectional. We deny it. That makes an issue; and the burden of proof is upon you. You produce your proof; and what is it? Why, that our party has no existence in your section—gets no votes in your section. The fact is substantially true; but does it prove the issue? If it does, then in case we should, without change of principle, begin to get votes in your section, we should thereby cease to be sectional. You cannot escape this conclusion; and yet, are you willing to abide by it? If you are, you will probably soon find that we have ceased to be sectional, for we shall get votes in your section this very year. You will then begin to discover, as the truth plainly is, that your proof, does not touch the issue. The fact that we get no votes in your section is a fact of your making, and not of ours. And if there be fault in that fact, that fault is primarily yours, and remains so until you show that we repel you by, some wrong principle or practice. If we do repel you by any wrong principle or practice, the fault is ours; but this brings you to where you ought to have started to a discussion of the right or wrong of our principle. If our principle, put in practice, would wrong your section for the benefit of ours, or for any other object, then our principle, and we with it, are sectional, and are justly opposed and denounced as such. Meet us, then, on the question of whether our principle, put in practice, would wrong your section; and so meet us as if it were possible that something may be said on our side. Do you accept the challenge? No! Then you really believe that the principle which "our fathers who framed the Government under which we live" thought so clearly right as to adopt it, and indorse it again and again, upon their official oaths, is in fact so clearly wrong as to demand your condemnation without a moment's consideration.

Some of you delight to flaunt in our faces the warning against sectional parties given by Washington in his Farewell Address. Less than eight years before Washington gave that warning, he had, as President of the United States, approved and signed an act of Congress enforcing the prohibition of slavery in the Northwestern Territory, which act embodied the policy of the Government upon that subject up to, and at, the very moment he penned that warning; and about one year after he penned it, he wrote La Fayette that he considered that prohibition a wise measure, expressing in the same connection his hope that we should at some time have a confederacy of free States.

Bearing this in mind, and seeing that sectionalism has since arisen upon this same subject, is that warning a weapon in your hands against us, or in our hands against you? Could Washington himself speak, would he cast the blame of that sectionalism upon us, who sustain his policy, or upon you, who repudiate it? We respect that warning of Washington, and we commend it to you, together with his example pointing to the right application of it.

But you say you are conservative—eminently conservative—while we are revolutionary, destructive, or something, of the sort. What is conservatism? Is it not adherence to the old and tried, against a new and untried? We stick to, contend for, the identical old policy on the point in controversy which was adopted by "our fathers who framed the Government under which we live"; while you with one accord reject, and scout, and spit upon that old policy and insist upon substituting something new. True, you disagree among yourselves as to what that substitute shall be. You are divided on new propositions and plans, but you are unanimous in rejecting and denouncing the old policy of the fathers. Some of you are for reviving the foreign slave trade; some for a Congressional slave code for the Territories; some for Congress forbidding the Territories to prohibit slavery within their limits; some for maintaining slavery in the Territories through the judiciary; some for the "gur-reat pur-rinciple" that "if one man would enslave another, no third man should object," fantastically called "popular sovereignty"; but never a man among you in favor of Federal prohibition of slavery in Federal Territories, according to the practice of "our fathers who framed the Government under which we live." Not one of all your various plans can show a precedent or an advocate in the century within which our Government originated. Consider, then, whether your claim of conservatism for yourselves, and your charge of destructiveness against us, are based on the most clear and stable foundations.

Again: You say we have made the slavery question more prominent than it formerly was. We deny it. We admit that it is more prominent, but we deny that we made it so. It was not we, but you, who discarded the old policy of the fathers. We resisted and still resist your innovation; and thence comes the greater prominence of the question. Would you have that question reduced to its former proportions? Go back to that old policy. What has been will be again, under the same conditions. If you would have the peace of the old times, readopt the precepts and policy of the old times.

You charge that we stir up insurrections among your slaves. We deny it; and what is your proof? Harper's Ferry! John Brown!! John Brown was no Republican; and you have failed to implicate a single Republican in his Harper's Ferry enterprise. If any member of our party is guilty in that matter you know it or you do not know it. If you do know it, you are inexcusable for not designating the man and proving the fact. If you do not know it, you are inexcusable for asserting it, and especially for persisting in the assertion after you have tried and failed to make the proof. You need not be told that persisting in a charge which one does not know to be true is simply malicious slander.

Some of you admit that no Republican designedly aided or encouraged the Harper's Ferry affair, but still insist that our doctrines and declarations necessarily lead to such results. We do not believe it. We know we hold to no doctrine, and make no declaration, which were not held to and made by our fathers who framed the Government under which we live. You never dealt fairly by us in relation to this affair. When it occurred, some important State elections were near at hand, and you were in evident glee with the belief that, by charging the blame upon us, you could get an advantage of us in those elections. The elections came, and your expectations were not quite fulfilled. Every Republican man knew that, as to himself at least, your charge was a slander, and he was not much inclined by it to cast his vote in your favor. Republican doctrines and declarations are accompanied with a continued protest against any interference whatever with your slaves, or with you about your slaves. Surely, this does not encourage them to revolt. True, we do, in common with "our fathers, who framed the Government under which we live," declare our belief that slavery is wrong; but the slaves do not hear us declare even this. For any thing we say or do, the slaves would scarcely know there is a Republican party. I believe they would not, in fact, generally know it but for your misrepresentations of us in their hearing. In your political contests among yourselves, each faction charges the other with sympathy with Black Republicanism; and then, to give point to the charge, defines Black Republicanism to simply be insurrection, blood, and thunder among the slaves.

Slave insurrections are no more common now than they were before the Republican party was organized. What induced the Southampton insurrection, twenty-eight years ago, in which, at least, three times as many lives were lost as at Harper's Ferry? You can scarcely stretch your very elastic fancy to the conclusion that Southampton was "got up by Black Republicanism." In the present state of things in the United States, I do not think a general or even a very extensive slave insurrection is possible. The indispensable concert of action cannot be attained. The slaves have no means of rapid communication; nor can incendiary freemen, black or white, supply it. The explosive materials are everywhere in parcels; but there neither are, nor can be supplied the indispensable connecting trains.

Much is said by Southern people about the affection of slaves for their masters and mistresses; and a part of it, at least, is true. A plot for an uprising could scarcely be devised and communicated to twenty individuals before some one of them, to save the life of a favorite master or mistress, would divulge it. This is the rule; and the slave revolution in Hayti was not an exception to it, but a case occurring under peculiar circumstances. The gunpowder plot of British history, though not connected with slaves, was more in point. In that case, only about twenty were admitted to the secret; and yet one of them, in his anxiety to save a friend, betrayed the plot to that friend, and, by consequence, averted the calamity. Occasional poisonings from the kitchen, and open or stealthy assassinations in the field, and local revolts, extending to a score or so, will continue to occur as the natural results of slavery; but no general insurrection of slaves, as I think, can happen in this country for a long time. Whoever much fears or much hopes for such an event will be alike disappointed.

In the language of Mr. Jefferson, uttered many years ago, "It is still in our power to direct the process of emancipation and deportation peaceably, and in such slow degrees as that the evil will wear off insensibly, and their places be, pari passu, filled up by free white laborers. If, on the contrary, it is left to force itself on, human nature must shudder at the prospect held up."

Mr. Jefferson did not mean to say, nor do I, that the power of emancipation is in the Federal Government. He spoke of Virginia; and, as to the power of emancipation, I speak of the slave holding States only. The Federal Government, however, as we insist, has the power of restraining the extension of the institution—the power to insure that a slave insurrection shall never occur on any American soil which is now free from slavery.

John Brown's effort was peculiar. It was not a slave insurrection. It was an attempt by white men to get up a revolt among slaves, in which the slaves refused to participate. In fact, it was so absurd that the slaves, with all their ignorance, saw plainly enough it could not succeed. That affair, in its philosophy, corresponds with the many attempts related in history at the assassination of kings and emperors. An enthusiast broods over the oppression of a people till he fancies himself commissioned by Heaven to liberate them. He ventures the attempt, which ends in little else than his own execution. Orsini's attempt on Louis Napoleon and John Brown's attempt at Harper's Ferry were, in their philosophy, precisely the same. The eagerness to cast blame on old England in the one case, and on New England in the other, does not disprove the sameness of the two things.

And how much would it avail you, if you could, by the use of John Brown, Helper's Book, and the like, break up the Republican organization? Human action can be modified to some extent, but human nature cannot be changed. There is a judgment and a feeling against slavery in this nation, which cast at least a million and a half of votes. You cannot destroy that judgment and feeling—that sentiment—by breaking up the political organization which rallies around it. You can scarcely scatter and disperse an army which has been formed into order in the face of your heaviest fire; but if you could, how much would you gain by forcing the sentiment which created it out of the peaceful channel of the ballot-box, into some other channel? What would that other channel probably be? Would the number of John Browns be lessened or enlarged by the operation?

But you will break up the Union rather than submit to a denial of your constitutional rights.

That has a somewhat reckless sound; but it would be palliated, if not fully justified, were we proposing, by the mere force of numbers, to deprive you of some right plainly written down in the Constitution. But we are proposing no such thing.

When you make these declarations, you have a specific and well-understood allusion to an assumed constitutional right of yours to take slaves into the Federal Territories, and to hold them there as property. But no such right is specifically written in the Constitution. That instrument is literally silent about any such right. We, on the contrary, deny that such a right has any existence in the Constitution, even by implication.

Your purpose, then, plainly stated, is that you will destroy the Government unless you be allowed to construe and enforce the Constitution as you please on all points in dispute between you and us. You will rule or ruin, in all events.

This, plainly stated, is your language. Perhaps you will say the Supreme Court has decided the disputed constitutional question in your favor. Not quite so. But, waiving the lawyer's distinction between dictum and decision, the court have decided the question for you in a sort of way. The court have substantially said it is your constitutional right to take slaves into the Federal Territories, and to hold them there as property. When I say, the decision was made in a sort of way, I mean it was made in a divided court, by a bare majority of the judges, and they not quite agreeing with one another in the reasons for making it; that it is so made as that its avowed supporters disagree with one another about its meaning, and that it was mainly based upon a mistaken statement of fact—the statement in the opinion that "the right of property in a slave is distinctly and expressly affirmed in the Constitution."

An inspection of the Constitution will show that the right of property in a slave is not "distinctly and expressly affirmed" in it. Bear in mind, the judges do not pledge their judicial opinion that such right is impliedly affirmed in the Constitution; but they pledge their veracity that it is "distinctly and expressly" affirmed there—"distinctly," that is, not mingled with anything else; "expressly," that is, in words meaning just that, without the aid of any inference, and susceptible of no other meaning.

If they had only pledged their judicial opinion that such right is affirmed in the instrument by implication, it would be open to others to show that neither the word "slave" nor "slavery" is to be found in the Constitution, nor the word "property" even, in any connection with language alluding to the things slave or slavery; and that wherever in that instrument the slave is alluded to, he is called a "person"; and wherever his master's legal right in relation to him is alluded to, it is spoken of as "service or labor which may be due," as a debt payable in service or labor. Also, it would be open to show, by contemporaneous history, that this mode of alluding to slaves and slavery, instead of speaking of them, was employed on purpose to exclude from the Constitution the idea that there could be property in man.

To show all this, is easy and certain.

When this obvious mistake of the judges shall be brought to their notice, is it not reasonable to expect that they will withdraw the mistaken statement, and reconsider the conclusion based upon it?

And then it is to be remembered that "our fathers; who framed the Government under which we live",—the men who made the Constitution—decided this same constitutional question in our favor, long ago; decided it without division among themselves, when making the decision, without division among themselves about the meaning of it after it was made, and, so far as any evidence is left, without basing it upon any mistaken statement of facts.

Under all these circumstances, do you really feel yourselves justified to break up this Government unless such a court decision as yours is shall be at once submitted to as a conclusive and final rule of political action? But you will not abide the election of a Republican President! In that supposed event, you say, you will destroy the Union; and then, you say, the great crime of having destroyed it will be upon us! That is cool. A highwayman holds a pistol to my ear, and mutters through his teeth, "stand and deliver, or I shall kill you, and then you'll be a murderer!"

To be sure, what the robber demanded of me-my money was my own, and I had a clear right to keep it; but it was no more my own than my vote is my own; and the threat of death to me, to extort my money, and the threat of destruction to the Union, to extort my vote, can scarcely be distinguished in principle.

A few words now to Republicans: It is exceedingly desirable that all parts of this great confederacy shall be at peace and in harmony one with another. Let us Republicans do our part to have it so. Even though much provoked, let us do nothing through passion and ill temper. Even though the Southern people will not so much as listen to us, let us calmly consider their demands, and yield to them if, in our deliberate view of our duty, we possibly can. Judging by all they say and do, and by the subject and nature of their controversy with us, let us determine, if we can, what will satisfy them.

Will they be satisfied if the Territories be unconditionally surrendered to them? We know they will not. In all their present complaints against us, the Territories are scarcely mentioned. Invasions and insurrections are the rage now. Will it satisfy them if, in the future, we have nothing to do with invasions and, insurrections? We know it will not. We so know because we know we never had anything to do with invasions and insurrections; and yet this total abstaining does not exempt us from the charge and the denunciation.

The question recurs, what will satisfy them? Simply this: We must not only let them alone, but we must, somehow, convince them that we do let them alone. This, we know by experience, is no easy task. We have been so trying to convince them from the very beginning of our organization, but with no success. In all our platforms and speeches we have constantly protested our purpose to let them alone; but this has had no tendency to convince them. Alike unavailing to convince them is the fact that they have never detected a man of us in any attempt to disturb them.

These natural and apparently adequate means all failing, what will convince them? This, and this only: cease to call slavery wrong, and join them in calling it right. And this must be done thoroughly—done in acts as well as in words. Silence will not be tolerated—we must place ourselves avowedly with them. Senator Douglas's new sedition law must be enacted and enforced, suppressing all declarations that slavery is wrong, whether made in politics, in presses, in pulpits; or in private. We must arrest and return their fugitive slaves with greedy pleasure. We must pull down our free State constitutions. The whole atmosphere must be disinfected from all taint of opposition to slavery, before they will cease to believe that all their troubles proceed from us.

I am quite aware they do not state their case precisely in this way. Most of them would probably say to us, "Let us alone, do nothing to us, and say what you please about slavery." But we do let them alone have never disturbed them—so that after all it is what we say which dissatisfies them. They will continue to accuse us of doing, until we cease saying. I am also aware they have not as yet, in terms, demanded the overthrow of our free State constitutions. Yet those constitutions declare the wrong of slavery, with more solemn emphasis than do all other sayings against it; and when all these other sayings shall have been silenced, the overthrow of these constitutions will be demanded, and nothing be left to resist the demand. It is nothing to the contrary, that they do not demand the whole of this just now. Demanding what they do, and for the reason they do, they can voluntarily stop nowhere short of this consummation. Holding, as they do, that slavery is morally right, and socially elevating, they cannot cease to demand a full national recognition of it, as a legal right and a social blessing.

Nor can we justifiably withhold this on any ground save our conviction that slavery is wrong. If slavery is right, all words, acts, laws, and constitutions against it are themselves wrong, and should be silenced and swept away. If it is right, we cannot justly object to its nationality its universality; if it is wrong, they cannot justly insist upon its extension—its enlargement. All they ask we could readily grant if we thought slavery right; all we ask they could as readily grant, if they thought it wrong. Their thinking it right and our thinking it wrong is the precise fact upon which depends the whole controversy. Thinking it right, as they do, they are not to blame for desiring its full recognition, as being right; but thinking it wrong, as we do, can we yield to them? Can we cast our votes with their view, and against our own? In view of our moral, social, and political responsibilities, can we do this? Wrong as we think slavery is, we can yet afford to let it alone where it is, because that much is due to the necessity arising from its actual presence in the nation; but can we, while our votes will prevent it, allow it to spread into the national Territories, and to overrun us here in these free States? If our sense of duty forbids this, then let us stand by our duty, fearlessly and effectively. Let us be diverted by none of those sophistical contrivances wherewith we are so industriously plied and belabored-contrivances such as groping for some middle ground between the right and the wrong, vain as the search for a man who should be neither a living man nor a dead man-such as a policy of "don't care" on a question about which all true men do care—such as Union appeals beseeching true Union men to yield to Disunionists, reversing the divine rule, and calling, not the sinners, but the righteous to repentance—such as invocations to Washington, imploring men to unsay what Washington said, and undo what Washington did.

Neither let us be slandered from our duty by false accusations against us, nor frightened from it by menaces of destruction to the Government nor of dungeons to ourselves. LET US HAVE FAITH THAT RIGHT MAKES MIGHT, AND IN THAT FAITH LET US, TO THE END, DARE TO DO OUR DUTY AS WE UNDERSTAND IT.

SPEECH AT NEW HAVEN, CONNECTICUT, MARCH 6, 1860

MR. PRESIDENT, AND FELLOW-CITIZENS OF NEW HAVEN:—If the Republican party of this nation shall ever have the national House entrusted to its keeping, it will be the duty of that party to attend to all the affairs of national housekeeping. Whatever matters of importance may come up, whatever difficulties may arise in its way of administration of the Government, that party will then have to attend to. It will then be compelled to attend to other questions, besides this question which now assumes an overwhelming importance—the question of slavery. It is true that in the organization of the Republican party this question of slavery was more important than any other: indeed, so much more important has it become that no more national question can even get a hearing just at present. The old question of tariff—a matter that will remain one of the chief affairs of national house-keeping to all time; the question of the management of financial affairs; the question of the disposition of the public domain how shall it be managed for the purpose of getting it well settled, and of making there the homes of a free and happy people? these will remain open and require attention for a great while yet, and these questions will have to be attended to by whatever party has the control of the Government. Yet, just now, they cannot even obtain a hearing, and I do not propose to detain you upon these topics or what sort of hearing they should have when opportunity shall come.

For, whether we will or not, the question of slavery is the question, the all-absorbing topic of the day. It is true that all of us—and by that I mean, not the Republican party alone, but the whole American people, here and elsewhere—all of us wish this question settled, wish it out of the way. It stands in the way, and prevents the adjustment, and the giving of necessary attention to other questions of national house-keeping. The people of the whole nation agree that this question ought to be settled, and yet it is not settled. And the reason is that they are not yet agreed how it shall be settled. All wish it done, but some wish one way and some another, and some a third, or fourth, or fifth; different bodies are pulling in different directions, and none of them, having a decided majority, are able to accomplish the common object.

In the beginning of the year 1854, a new policy was inaugurated with the avowed object and confident promise that it would entirely and forever put an end to the slavery agitation. It was again and again declared that under this policy, when once successfully established, the country would be forever rid of this whole question. Yet under the operation of that policy this agitation has not only not ceased, but it has been constantly augmented. And this too, although, from the day of its introduction, its friends, who promised that it would wholly end all agitation, constantly insisted, down to the time that the Lecompton Bill was introduced, that it was working admirably, and that its inevitable tendency was to remove the question forever from the politics of the country. Can you call to mind any Democratic speech, made after the repeal of the Missouri Compromise, down to the time of the Lecompton Bill, in which it was not predicted that the slavery agitation was just at an end, that "the abolition excitement was played out," "the Kansas question was dead," "they have made the most they can out of this question and it is now forever settled"? But since the Lecompton Bill no Democrat, within my experience, has ever pretended that he could see the end. That cry has been dropped. They themselves do not pretend, now, that the agitation of this subject has come to an end yet.

The truth is that this question is one of national importance, and we cannot help dealing with it; we must do something about it, whether we will or not. We cannot avoid it; the subject is one we cannot avoid considering; we can no more avoid it than a man can live without eating. It is upon us; it attaches to the body politic as much and closely as the natural wants attach to our natural bodies. Now I think it important that this matter should be taken up in earnest, and really settled: And one way to bring about a true settlement of the question is to understand its true magnitude.

There have been many efforts made to settle it. Again and again it has been fondly hoped that it was settled; but every time it breaks out afresh, and more violently than ever. It was settled, our fathers hoped, by the Missouri Compromise, but it did not stay settled. Then the compromises of 1850 were declared to be a full and final settlement of the question. The two great parties, each in national convention, adopted resolutions declaring that the settlement made by the

Compromise of 1850 was a finality that it would last forever. Yet how long before it was unsettled again? It broke out again in 1854, and blazed higher and raged more furiously than ever before, and the agitation has not rested since.

These repeated settlements must have some faults about them. There must be some inadequacy in their very nature to the purpose to which they were designed. We can only speculate as to where that fault, that inadequacy, is, but we may perhaps profit by past experiences.

I think that one of the causes of these repeated failures is that our best and greatest men have greatly underestimated the size of this question. They have constantly brought forward small cures for great sores—plasters too small to cover the wound. That is one reason that all settlements have proved temporary—so evanescent.

Look at the magnitude of this subject: One sixth of our population, in round numbers—not quite one sixth, and yet more than a seventh,—about one sixth of the whole population of the United States are slaves. The owners of these slaves consider them property. The effect upon the minds of the owners is that of property, and nothing else it induces them to insist upon all that will favorably affect its value as property, to demand laws and institutions and a public policy that shall increase and secure its value, and make it durable, lasting, and universal. The effect on the minds of the owners is to persuade them that there is no wrong in it. The slaveholder does not like to be considered a mean fellow for holding that species of property, and hence, he has to struggle within himself and sets about arguing himself into the belief that slavery is right. The property influences his mind. The dissenting minister who argued some theological point with one of the established church was always met with the reply, "I can't see it so." He opened a Bible and pointed him a passage, but the orthodox minister replied, "I can't see it so." Then he showed him a single word—"Can you see that?" "Yes, I see it," was the reply. The dissenter laid a guinea over the word and asked, "Do you see it now?" So here. Whether the owners of this species of property do really see it as it is, it is not for me to say, but if they do, they see it as it is through two thousand millions of dollars, and that is a pretty thick coating. Certain it is that they do not see it as we see it. Certain it is that this two thousand millions of dollars, invested in this species of property, all so concentrated that the mind can grasp it at once—this immense pecuniary interest—has its influence upon their minds.

But here in Connecticut and at the North slavery does not exist, and we see it through no such medium.

To us it appears natural to think that slaves are human beings; men, not property; that some of the things, at least, stated about men in the Declaration of Independence apply to them as well as to us. I say we think, most of us, that this charter of freedom applies to the slaves as well as to ourselves; that the class of arguments put forward to batter down that idea are also calculated to break down the very idea of a free government, even for white men, and to undermine the very foundations of free society. We think slavery a great moral wrong, and, while we do not claim the right to touch it where it exists, we wish to treat it as a wrong in the Territories, where our votes will reach it. We think that a respect for ourselves, a regard for future generations and for the God that made us, require that we put down this wrong where our votes will properly reach it. We think that species of labor an injury to free white men—in short, we think slavery a great moral, social, and political evil, tolerable only because, and so far as, its actual existence makes it necessary to tolerate it, and that beyond that it ought to be treated as a wrong.

Now these two ideas, the property idea that slavery is right, and the idea that it is wrong, come into collision, and do actually produce that irrepressible conflict which Mr. Seward has been so roundly abused for mentioning. The two ideas conflict, and must conflict.

Again, in its political aspect, does anything in any way endanger the perpetuity of this Union but that single thing, slavery? Many of our adversaries are anxious to claim that they are specially devoted to the Union, and take pains to charge upon us hostility to the Union. Now we claim that we are the only true Union men, and we put to them this one proposition: Whatever endangers this Union, save and except slavery? Did any other thing ever cause a moment's fear? All men must agree that this thing alone has ever endangered the perpetuity of the Union. But if it was threatened by any other influence, would not all men say that the best thing that could be done, if we could not or ought not to destroy it, would be at least to keep it from growing any larger? Can any man believe, that the way to save the Union is to extend and increase the only thing that threatens the Union, and to suffer it to grow bigger and bigger?

Whenever this question shall be settled, it must be settled on some philosophical basis. No policy that does not rest upon some philosophical opinion can be permanently maintained. And hence there are but two policies in regard to slavery that can be at all maintained. The first, based on the property view that slavery is right, conforms to that idea throughout, and demands that we shall do everything for it that we ought to do if it were right. We must sweep away all opposition, for opposition to the right is wrong; we must agree that slavery is right, and we must adopt the idea that property has persuaded the owner to believe that slavery is morally right and socially elevating. This gives a philosophical basis for a permanent policy of encouragement.

The other policy is one that squares with the idea that slavery is wrong, and it consists in doing everything that we ought to do if it is wrong. Now, I don't wish to be misunderstood, nor to leave a gap down to be misrepresented, even. I don't mean that we ought to attack it where it exists. To me it seems that if we were to form a government anew, in view of the actual presence of slavery we should find it necessary to frame just such a government as our fathers did—giving to the slaveholder the entire control where the system was established, while we possessed the power to restrain it from going outside those limits. From the necessities of the case we should be compelled to form just such a government as our blessed fathers gave us; and, surely, if they have so made it, that adds another reason why we should let slavery alone where it exists.

If I saw a venomous snake crawling in the road, any man would say I might seize the nearest stick and kill it; but if I found that snake in bed with my children, that would be another question. I might hurt the children more than the snake, and it might bite them. Much more if I found it in bed with my neighbor's children, and I had bound myself by a solemn compact not to meddle with his children under any circumstances, it would become me to let that particular mode of getting rid of the gentleman alone. But if there was a bed newly made up, to which the children were to be taken, and it was proposed to take a batch of young snakes and put them there with them, I take it no man would say there was any question how I ought to decide!

That is just the case. The new Territories are the newly made bed to which our children are to go, and it lies with the nation to say whether they shall have snakes mixed up with them or not. It does not seem as if there could be much hesitation what our policy should be!

Now I have spoken of a policy based on the idea that slavery is wrong, and a policy based on the idea that it is right. But an effort has been made for a policy that shall treat it as neither right nor wrong. It is based upon utter indifference. Its leading advocate [Douglas] has said, "I don't care whether it be voted up or down." "It is merely a matter of dollars and cents." "The Almighty has drawn a line across this continent, on one side of which all soil must forever be cultivated by slave labor, and on the other by free." "When the struggle is between the white man and the negro, I am for the white man; when it is between the negro and the crocodile, I am for the negro." Its central idea is indifference. It holds that it makes no more difference to us whether the Territories become free or slave States than whether my neighbor stocks his farm with horned cattle or puts in tobacco. All recognize this policy, the plausible sugar-coated name of which is "popular sovereignty."

This policy chiefly stands in the way of a permanent settlement of the question. I believe there is no danger of its becoming the permanent policy of the country, for it is based on a public indifference. There is nobody that "don't care." All the people do care one way or the other! I do not charge that its author, when he says he "don't care," states his individual opinion; he only expresses his policy for the government. I understand that he has never said as an individual whether he thought slavery right or wrong—and he is the only man in the nation that has not! Now such a policy may have a temporary run; it may spring up as necessary to the political prospects of some gentleman; but it is utterly baseless: the people are not indifferent, and it can therefore have no durability or permanence.

But suppose it could: Then it could be maintained only by a public opinion that shall say, "We don't care." There must be a change in public opinion; the public mind must be so far debauched as to square with this policy of caring not at all. The people must come to consider this as "merely a question of dollars and cents," and to believe that in some places the Almighty has made slavery necessarily eternal. This policy can be brought to prevail if the people can be brought round to say honestly, "We don't care"; if not, it can never be maintained. It is for you to say whether that can be done.

You are ready to say it cannot, but be not too fast! Remember what a long stride has been taken since the repeal of the Missouri Compromise! Do you know of any Democrat, of either branch of the party—do you know one who declares that he believes that the Declaration of Independence has any application to the negro? Judge Taney declares that it has not, and Judge Douglas even vilifies me personally and scolds me roundly for saying that the Declaration applies to all men, and that negroes are men. Is there a Democrat here who does not deny that the Declaration applies to the negro? Do any of you know of one? Well, I have tried before perhaps fifty audiences, some larger and some smaller than this, to find one such Democrat, and never yet have I found one who said I did not place him right in that. I must assume that Democrats hold that, and now, not one of these Democrats can show that he said that five years ago! I venture to defy the whole party to produce one man that ever uttered the belief that the Declaration did not apply to negroes, before the repeal of the Missouri Compromise! Four or five years ago we all thought negroes were men, and that when "all men" were named, negroes were included. But the whole Democratic party has deliberately taken negroes from the class of men and put them in the class of brutes. Turn it as you will it is simply the truth! Don't be too hasty, then, in saying that the people cannot be brought to this new doctrine, but note that long stride. One more as long completes the journey from where negroes are estimated as men to where they are estimated as mere brutes—as rightful property!

That saying "In the struggle between white men and the negro," etc., which I know came from the same source as this policy—that saying marks another step. There is a falsehood wrapped up in that statement. "In the struggle between the white man and the negro" assumes that there is a struggle, in which either the white man must enslave the negro or the negro must enslave the white. There is no such struggle! It is merely the ingenious falsehood to degrade and brutalize the negro. Let each let the other alone, and there is no struggle about it. If it was like two wrecked seamen on a narrow plank, when each must push the other off or drown himself, I would push the negro off or a white man either, but it is not; the plank is large enough for both. This good earth is plenty broad enough for white man and negro both, and there is no need of either pushing the other off.

So that saying, "In the struggle between the negro and the crocodile," etc., is made up from the idea that down where the crocodile inhabits, a white man can't labor; it must be nothing else but crocodile or negro; if the negro does not the crocodile must possess the earth; in that case he declares for the negro. The meaning of the whole is just this: As a white man is to a negro, so is a negro to a crocodile; and as the negro may rightfully treat the crocodile, so may the white man rightfully treat the negro. This very dear phrase coined by its author, and so dear that he deliberately repeats it in many speeches, has a tendency to still further brutalize the negro, and to bring public opinion to the point of utter indifference whether men so brutalized are enslaved or not. When that time shall come, if ever, I think that policy to which I refer may prevail. But I hope the good freemen of this country will never allow it to come, and until then the policy can never be maintained.

Now consider the effect of this policy. We in the States are not to care whether freedom or slavery gets the better, but the people in the Territories may care. They are to decide, and they may think what they please; it is a matter of dollars and cents! But are not the people of the Territories detailed from the States? If this feeling of indifference this absence of moral sense about the question prevails in the States, will it not be carried into the Territories? Will not every man say, "I don't care, it is nothing to me"? If any one comes that wants slavery, must they not say, "I don't care whether freedom or slavery be voted up or voted down"? It results at last in nationalizing the institution of slavery. Even if fairly carried out, that policy is just as certain to nationalize slavery as the doctrine of Jeff Davis himself. These are only two roads to the same goal, and "popular sovereignty" is just as sure and almost as short as the other.

What we want, and all we want, is to have with us the men who think slavery wrong. But those who say they hate slavery, and are opposed to it, but yet act with the Democratic party—where are they? Let us apply a few tests. You say that you think slavery is wrong, but you denounce all attempts to restrain it. Is there anything else that you think wrong that you are not willing to deal with as wrong? Why are you so careful, so tender, of this one wrong and no other? You will not let us do a single thing as if it was wrong; there is no place where you will even allow it to be called wrong! We must not call it wrong in the free States, because it is not there, and we must not call it wrong in the slave States, because it is there; we must not call it wrong in politics because that is bringing morality into politics, and we must not call it wrong in the pulpit because that is bringing politics into religion; we must not bring it into the Tract Society or the other societies, because those are such unsuitable places—and there is no single place, according to you, where this wrong thing can properly be called wrong!

Perhaps you will plead that if the people of the slave States should themselves set on foot an effort for emancipation, you would wish them success, and bid them God-speed. Let us test that: In 1858 the emancipation party of Missouri, with Frank Blair at their head, tried to get up a movement for that purpose, and having started a party contested the State. Blair was beaten, apparently if not truly, and when the news came to Connecticut, you, who knew that Frank Blair was taking hold of this thing by the right end, and doing the only thing that you say can properly be done to remove this wrong—did you bow your heads in sorrow because of that defeat? Do you, any of you, know one single Democrat that showed sorrow over that result? Not one! On the contrary every man threw up his hat, and hallooed at the top of his lungs, "Hooray for Democracy!"

Now, gentlemen, the Republicans desire to place this great question of slavery on the very basis on which our fathers placed it, and no other. It is easy to demonstrate that "our fathers, who framed this Government under which we live," looked on slavery as wrong, and so framed it and everything about it as to square with the idea that it was wrong, so far as the necessities arising from its existence permitted. In forming the Constitution they found the slave trade existing, capital invested in it, fields depending upon it for labor, and the whole system resting upon the importation of slave labor. They therefore did not prohibit the slave trade at once, but they gave the power to prohibit it after twenty years. Why was this? What other foreign trade did they treat in that way? Would they have done this if they had not thought slavery wrong?

Another thing was done by some of the same men who framed the Constitution, and afterwards adopted as their own the act by the first Congress held under that Constitution, of which many of the framers were members, that prohibited the spread of slavery into Territories. Thus the same men, the framers of the Constitution, cut off the supply and prohibited the spread of slavery, and both acts show conclusively that they considered that the thing was wrong.

If additional proof is wanted it can be found in the phraseology of the Constitution. When men are framing a supreme law and chart of government, to secure blessings and prosperity to untold generations yet to come, they use language as short and direct and plain as can be found, to express their meaning In all matters but this of slavery the framers of the Constitution used the very clearest, shortest, and most direct language. But the Constitution alludes to slavery three times without mentioning it once The language used becomes ambiguous, roundabout, and mystical. They speak of the "immigration of persons," and mean the importation of slaves, but do not say so. In establishing a basis of representation they say "all other persons," when they mean to say slaves—why did they not use the shortest phrase? In providing for the return of fugitives they say "persons held to service or labor." If they had said slaves it would have been plainer, and less liable to misconstruction. Why did n't they do it? We cannot doubt that it was done on purpose. Only one reason is possible, and that is supplied us by one of the framers of the Constitution—and it is not possible for man to conceive of any other—they expected and desired that the system would come to an end, and meant that when it did, the Constitution should not show that there ever had been a slave in this good free country of ours.

I will dwell on that no longer. I see the signs of approaching triumph of the Republicans in the bearing of their political adversaries. A great deal of their war with us nowadays is mere bushwhacking. At the battle of Waterloo, when Napoleon's cavalry had charged again and again upon the unbroken squares of British infantry, at last they were giving up the attempt, and going off in disorder, when some of the officers in mere vexation and complete despair fired their pistols at those solid squares. The Democrats are in that sort of extreme desperation; it is nothing else. I will take up a few of these arguments.

There is "the irrepressible conflict." How they rail at Seward for that saying! They repeat it constantly; and, although the proof has been thrust under their noses again and again that almost every good man since the formation of our Government has uttered that same sentiment, from General Washington, who "trusted that we should yet have a confederacy of free States," with Jefferson, Jay, Monroe, down to the latest days, yet they refuse to notice that at all, and persist in railing at Seward for saying it. Even Roger A. Pryor, editor of the Richmond Enquirer, uttered the same sentiment in almost the same language, and yet so little offence did it give the Democrats that he was sent for to Washington to edit the States—the Douglas organ there—while Douglas goes into hydrophobia and spasms of rage because Seward dared to repeat it. This is what I call bushwhacking, a sort of argument that they must know any child can see through.

Another is John Brown: "You stir up insurrections, you invade the South; John Brown! Harper's Ferry!" Why, John Brown was not a Republican! You have never implicated a single Republican in that Harper's Ferry enterprise. We tell you that if any member of the Republican party is guilty in that matter, you know it or you do not know it. If you do know it, you are inexcusable not to designate the man and prove the fact. If you do not know it, you are inexcusable to assert it, and especially to persist in the assertion after you have tried and failed to make the proof. You need not be told that persisting in a charge which one does not know to be true is simply malicious slander. Some of you admit that no Republican designedly aided or encouraged the Harper's Ferry affair, but still insist that our doctrines and declarations necessarily lead to such results. We do not believe it. We know we hold to no doctrines, and make no declarations, which were not held to and made by our fathers who framed the Government 'under which we live, and we cannot see how declarations that were patriotic when they made them are villainous when we make them. You never dealt fairly by us in relation to that affair—and I will say frankly that I know of nothing in your character that should lead us to suppose that you would. You had just been soundly thrashed in elections in several States, and others were soon to come. You rejoiced at the occasion, and only were troubled that there were not three times as many killed in the affair. You were in evident glee; there was no sorrow for the killed nor for the peace of Virginia disturbed; you were rejoicing that by charging Republicans with this thing you might get an advantage of us in New York, and the other States. You pulled that string as tightly as you could, but your very generous and worthy expectations were not quite fulfilled. Each Republican knew that the charge was a slander as to himself at least, and was not inclined by it to cast his vote in your favor. It was mere bushwhacking, because you had nothing else to do. You are still on that track, and I say, go on! If you think you can slander a woman into loving you or a man into voting for you, try it till you are satisfied!

Another specimen of this bushwhacking, that "shoe strike." Now be it understood that I do not pretend to know all about the matter. I am merely going to speculate a little about some of its phases. And at the outset, I am glad to see that a system of labor prevails in New England under which laborers can strike when they want to, where they are not obliged to work under all circumstances, and are not tied down and obliged to labor whether you pay them or not! I like the system which lets a man quit when he wants to, and wish it might prevail everywhere. One of the reasons why I am opposed to slavery is just here. What is the true condition of the laborer? I take it that it is best for all to leave each man free to acquire property as fast as he can. Some will get wealthy. I don't believe in a law to prevent a man from getting rich; it would do more harm than good. So, while we do not propose any war upon capital, we do wish to allow the humblest man an equal chance to get rich with everybody else. When one starts poor, as most do in the race of life, free society is such that he knows he can better his condition; he knows that there is no fixed condition of labor for his whole life. I am not ashamed to confess that twenty-five years ago I was a hired laborer, mauling rails, at work on a flatboat—just what might happen to any poor man's son! I want every man to have a chance—and I believe a Black man is entitled to it—in which he can better his condition; when he may look forward and hope to be a hired laborer this year and the next, work for himself afterward, and finally to hire men to work for him! That is the system. Up here in New England, you have a soil that scarcely sprouts black-eyed beans, and yet where will you find wealthy men so wealthy, and poverty so rarely in extremity? There is not another such place on earth! I desire that if you get too thick here, and find it hard to better your condition on this soil, you may have a chance to strike and go somewhere else, where you may not be degraded, nor have your families corrupted, by forced rivalry with negro slaves. I want you to have a clean bed and no snakes in it! Then you can better your condition, and so it may go on and on in one endless round so long as man exists on the face of the earth!

Now, to come back to this shoe strike,—if, as the senator from Illinois asserts, this is caused by withdrawal of Southern votes, consider briefly how you will meet the difficulty. You have done nothing, and have protested that you have done nothing, to injure the South. And yet, to get back the shoe trade, you must leave off doing something which you are now doing. What is it? You must stop thinking slavery wrong! Let your institutions be wholly changed; let your State constitutions be subverted; glorify slavery, and so you will get back the shoe trade—for what? You have brought owned labor with it, to compete with your own labor, to underwork you, and to degrade you! Are you ready to get back the trade on those terms?

But the statement is not correct. You have not lost that trade; orders were never better than now! Senator Mason, a Democrat, comes into the Senate in homespun, a proof that the dissolution of the Union has actually begun! but orders are the same. Your factories have not struck work, neither those where they make anything for coats, nor for pants nor for shirts, nor for ladies' dresses. Mr. Mason has not reached the manufacturers who ought to have made him a coat and pants! To make his proof good for anything he should have come into the Senate barefoot!

Another bushwhacking contrivance; simply that, nothing else! I find a good many people who are very much concerned about the loss of Southern trade. Now either these people are sincere or they are not. I will speculate a little about that. If they are sincere, and are moved by any real danger of the loss of Southern trade, they will simply get their names on the white list, and then, instead of persuading Republicans to do likewise, they will be glad to keep you away! Don't you see that they cut off competition? They would not be whispering around to Republicans to come in and share the profits with them. But if they are not sincere, and are merely trying to fool Republicans out of their votes, they will grow very anxious about your pecuniary prospects; they are afraid you are going to get broken up and ruined; they do not care about Democratic votes, oh, no, no, no! You must judge which class those belong to whom you meet: I leave it to you to determine from the facts.

Let us notice some more of the stale charges against Republicans. You say we are sectional. We deny it. That makes an issue; and the burden of proof is upon you. You produce your proof; and what is it? Why, that our party has no existence in your section—gets no votes in your section. The fact is substantially true; but does it prove the issue? If it does, then in case we should, without change of principle, begin to get votes in your section, we should thereby cease to be sectional. You cannot escape this conclusion; and yet, are you willing to abide by it? If you are, you will probably soon find that we have ceased to be sectional, for we shall get votes in your section this very year. The fact that we get no votes in your section is a fact of your making and not of ours. And if there be fault in that fact, that fault is primarily yours, and remains so until you show that we repel you by some wrong principle or practice. If we ours; but this brings you to where you ought to have started—to a discussion of the right or wrong of our principle. If our principle, put in practice, would wrong your section for the benefit of ours, or for any other object, then our principle, and we with it, are sectional, and are justly opposed and denounced as such. Meet us, then, on the question of whether our principle put in practice would wrong your section; and so meet it as if it were possible that something may be said on our side. Do you accept the challenge? No? Then you really believe that the principle which our fathers who framed the Government under which we live thought so clearly right as to adopt it, and indorse it again and again, upon their official oaths, is in fact so clearly wrong as to demand our condemnation without a moment's consideration. Some of you delight to flaunt in our faces the warning against sectional parties given by Washington in his Farewell Address. Less than eight years before Washington gave that warning, he had, as President of the United States, approved and signed an act of Congress enforcing the prohibition of slavery in the Northwestern Territory, which act embodied the policy of government upon that subject, up to and at the very moment he penned that warning; and about one year after he penned it he wrote La Fayette that he considered that prohibition a wise measure, expressing in the same connection his hope that we should sometime have a confederacy of free States.

Bearing this in mind, and seeing that sectionalism has since arisen upon this same subject, is that warning a weapon in your hands against us, or in our hands against you? Could Washington himself speak, would he cast the blame of that sectionalism upon us, who sustain his policy, or upon you, who repudiate it? We respect that warning of Washington, and we commend it to you, together with his example pointing to the right application of it.

But you say you are conservative—eminently conservative—while we are revolutionary, destructive, or something of the sort. What is conservatism? Is it not adherence to the old and tried, against the new and untried? We stick to, contend for, the identical old policy on the point in controversy which was adopted by our fathers who framed the Government under which we live; while you with one accord reject and scout and spit upon that old policy, and insist upon substituting something new.

True, you disagree among yourselves as to what that substitute shall be. You have considerable variety of new propositions and plans, but you are unanimous in rejecting and denouncing the old policy of the fathers. Some of you are for reviving the foreign slave-trade; some for a congressional slave code for the Territories; some for Congress forbidding the Territories to prohibit slavery within their limits; some for maintaining slavery in the Territories through the judiciary; some for the "gur-reat pur-rinciple" that if one man would enslave another, no third man should object—fantastically called "popular sovereignty." But never a man among you in favor of prohibition of slavery in Federal Territories, according to the practice of our fathers who framed the Government under which we live. Not one of all your various plans can show a precedent or an advocate in the century within which our Government originated. And yet you draw yourselves up and say, "We are eminently conservative."

It is exceedingly desirable that all parts of this great confederacy shall be at peace, and in harmony one with another. Let us Republicans do our part to have it so. Even though much provoked, let us do nothing through passion and ill-temper. Even though the Southern people will not so much as listen to us, let us calmly consider their demands, and yield to them if, in our deliberate view of our duty, we possibly can. Judging by all they say and do, and by the subject and nature of their controversy with us, let us determine, if we can, what will satisfy them.

Will they be satisfied if the Territories be unconditionally surrendered to them? We know they will not. In all their present complaints against us, the Territories are scarcely mentioned. Invasions and insurrections are the rage now. Will it satisfy them, in the future, if we have nothing to do with invasions and insurrections? We know it will not. We so know because we know we never had anything to do with invasions and insurrections; and yet this total abstaining does not exempt us from the charge and the denunciation.

The question recurs, what will satisfy them? Simply this: we must not only let them alone, but we must, somehow, convince them that we do let them alone. This, we know by experience, is no easy task. We have been so trying to convince them, from the very beginning of our organization, but with no success. In all our platforms and speeches, we have constantly protested our purpose to let them alone; but this had no tendency to convince them. Alike unavailing to convince them is the fact that they have never detected a man of us in any attempt to disturb them.

These natural and apparently adequate means all failing, what will convince them? This, and this only: cease to call slavery wrong, and join them in calling it right. And this must be done thoroughly—done in acts as well as in words. Silence will not be tolerated—we must place ourselves avowedly with them. Douglas's new sedition law must be enacted and enforced, suppressing all declarations that slavery is wrong, whether made in politics, in presses, in pulpits, or in private. We must arrest and return their fugitive slaves with greedy pleasure. We must pull down our free State constitutions. The whole atmosphere must be disinfected of all taint of opposition to slavery, before they will cease to believe that all their troubles proceed from us. So long as we call slavery wrong, whenever a slave runs away they will overlook the obvious fact that he ran away because he was oppressed, and declare he was stolen off. Whenever a master cuts his slaves with a lash, and they cry out under it, he will overlook the obvious fact that the negroes cry out because they are hurt, and insist that they were put up to it by some rascally abolitionist.

I am quite aware that they do not state their case precisely in this way. Most of them would probably say to us, "Let us alone, do nothing to us, and say what you please about slavery." But we do let them alone—have never disturbed them—so that, after all, it is what we say which dissatisfies them. They will continue to accuse us of doing, until we cease saying.

I am also aware that they have not as yet in terms demanded the overthrow of our free-State constitutions. Yet those constitutions declare the wrong of slavery with more solemn emphasis than do all other sayings against it; and when all these other sayings shall have been silenced, the overthrow of these constitutions will be demanded. It is nothing to the contrary that they do not demand the whole of this just now. Demanding what they do, and for the reason they do, they can voluntarily stop nowhere short of this consummation. Holding as they do that slavery is morally right, and socially elevating, they cannot cease to demand a full national recognition of it, as a legal right, and a social blessing.

Nor can we justifiably withhold this on any ground save our conviction that slavery is wrong. If slavery is right, all words, acts, laws, and constitutions against it are themselves wrong and should be silenced and swept away. If it is right, we cannot justly object to its nationality—its universality: if it is wrong, they cannot justly insist upon its extension—its enlargement. All they ask, we could readily grant, if we thought slavery right; all we ask, they could as readily grant, if they thought it wrong. Their thinking it right and our thinking it wrong is the precise fact on which depends the whole controversy. Thinking it right as they do, they are not to blame for desiring its full recognition, as being right;

but, thinking it wrong, as we do, can we yield to them? Can we cast our votes with their view, and against our own? In view of our moral, social, and political responsibilities, can we do this?

Wrong as we think slavery is, we can yet afford to let it alone where it is because that much is due to the necessity arising from its actual presence in the nation; but can we, while our votes will prevent it, allow it to spread into the national Territories, and to overrun us here in these free States?

If our sense of duty forbids this, then let us stand by our duty, fearlessly and effectively. Let us be diverted by none of those sophistical contrivances wherewith we are so industriously plied and belabored—contrivances such as groping for some middle ground between the right and the wrong, vain as the search for a man who would be neither a living man nor a dead man—such as a policy of "don't care" on a question about which all free men do care—such as Union appeals beseeching true Union men to yield to Disunionists, reversing the divine rule, and caning, not the sinners, but the righteous to repentance—such as invocations of Washington, imploring men to unsay what Washington did.

Neither let us be slandered from our duty by false accusations against us, nor frightened from it by menaces of destruction to the Government, nor of dungeons to ourselves. Let us have faith that right makes might; and in that faith, let us, to the end, dare to do our duty as we understand it.

[As Mr. Lincoln concluded his address, there was witnessed the wildest scene of enthusiasm and excitement that has been in New Haven for years. The Palladium editorially says: "We give up most of our space to-day to a very full report of the eloquent speech of the HON. Abraham Lincoln, of Illinois, delivered last night at Union Hall."]

RESPONSE TO AN ELECTOR'S REQUEST FOR MONEY

TO —————— March 16, 1860

As to your kind wishes for myself, allow me to say I cannot enter the ring on the money basis—first, because in the main it is wrong; and secondly, I have not and cannot get the money.

I say, in the main, the use of money is wrong; but for certain objects in a political contest, the use of some is both right and indispensable. With me, as with yourself, the long struggle has been one of great pecuniary loss.

I now distinctly say this—if you shall be appointed a delegate to Chicago, I will furnish one hundred dollars to bear the expenses of the trip.

Your friend as ever,
A. LINCOLN.
[Extract from a letter to a Kansas delegate.]

TO J. W. SOMERS.

SPRINGFIELD, March 17, 1860

JAMES W. SOMERS, Esq.
DEAR SIR:—Reaching home three days ago, I found your letter of February 26th. Considering your difficulty of hearing, I think you had better settle in Chicago, if, as you say, a good man already in fair practice there will take you into partnership. If you had not that difficulty, I still should think it an even balance whether you would not better remain in Chicago, with such a chance for copartnership.

If I went west, I think I would go to Kansas, to Leavenworth or Atchison. Both of them are and will continue to be fine growing places.

I believe I have said all I can, and I have said it with the deepest interest for your welfare.
Yours truly,
A. LINCOLN.

ACCUSATION OF HAVING BEEN PAID FOR A POLITICAL SPEECH

TO C. F. McNEIL.

SPRINGFIELD, April 6, 1860
C. F. MCNEIL, Esq.
DEAR SIR:—Reaching home yesterday, I found yours of the 23d March, inclosing a slip from The Middleport Press. It is not true that I ever charged anything for a political speech in my life; but this much is true: Last October I was requested by letter to deliver some sort of speech in Mr. Beecher's church, in Brooklyn—two hundred dollars being offered in the first letter. I wrote that I could do it in February, provided they would take a political speech if I could find time to get up no other. They agreed; and subsequently I informed them the speech would have to be a political one. When I reached New York, I for the first time learned that the place was changed to "Cooper Institute." I made the speech, and left for New Hampshire, where I have a son at school, neither asking for pay nor having any offered me. Three days after a check for two hundred dollars was sent to me at New Hampshire; and I took it, and did not know it was wrong. My understanding now is—though I knew nothing of it at the time—that they did charge for admittance to the Cooper Institute, and that they took in more than twice two hundred dollars.

I have made this explanation to you as a friend; but I wish no explanation made to our enemies. What they want is a squabble and a fuss, and that they can have if we explain; and they cannot have it if we don't.

When I returned through New York from New England, I was told by the gentlemen who sent me the Check that a drunken vagabond in the club, having learned something about the two hundred dollars, made the exhibition out of which The Herald manufactured the article quoted by The Press of your town.

My judgment is, and therefore my request is, that you give no denial and no explanation.
Thanking you for your kind interest in the matter, I remain, Yours truly,
A. LINCOLN.

TO H. TAYLOR.

SPRINGFIELD, ILL., April 21, 1860.

HAWKINS TAYLOR, Esq.
DEAR SIR:—Yours of the 15th is just received. It surprises me that you have written twice, without receiving an answer. I have answered all I ever received from you; and certainly one since my return from the East.
Opinions here, as to the prospect of Douglas being nominated, are quite conflicting—some very confident he will, and others that he will not be. I think his nomination possible, but that the chances are against him.
I am glad there is a prospect of your party passing this way to Chicago. Wishing to make your visit here as pleasant as we can, we wish you to notify us as soon as possible whether you come this way, how many, and when you will arrive.
Yours very truly,
A. LINCOLN

TELEGRAM TO A MEMBER OF THE ILLINOIS DELEGATION

AT THE CHICAGO CONVENTION. SPRINGFIELD, May 17? 1860.

I authorize no bargains and will be bound by none.
A. LINCOLN.

REPLY TO THE COMMITTEE SENT BY THE CHICAGO CONVENTION TO INFORM

LINCOLN OF HIS NOMINATION,

MAY 19, 1860.

Mr. CHAIRMAN AND GENTLEMEN OF THE COMMITTEE:—I tender to you, and through you to the Republican National Convention, and all the people represented in it, my profoundest thanks for the high honor done me, which you now formally announce. Deeply and even painfully sensible of the great responsibility which is inseparable from this high honor—a responsibility which I could almost wish had fallen upon some one of the far more eminent men and experienced statesmen whose distinguished names were before the convention—I shall, by your leave, consider more fully the resolutions of the convention, denominated their platform, and without any unnecessary or unreasonable delay respond to you, Mr. Chairman, in writing—not doubting that the platform will be found satisfactory, and the nomination gratefully accepted.

And now I will not longer defer the pleasure of taking you, and each of you, by the hand.

ACCEPTANCE OF NOMINATION AS REPUBLICAN CANDIDATE FOR PRESIDENT

OF THE UNITED STATES

TO GEORGE ASHMUN AND OTHERS.
SPRINGFIELD ILLINOIS, May 23, 1860
HON. GEORGE ASHMUN, President of Republican National Convention.
SIR:—I accept the nomination tendered me by the convention over which you presided, and of which I am formally apprised in the letter of yourself and others, acting as a committee of the convention for that purpose.
The declaration of principles and sentiments which accompanies your letter meets my approval; and it shall be my care not to violate or disregard it in any part.
Imploring the assistance of Divine Providence, and with due regard to the views and feelings of all who were represented in the convention, to the rights of all the States and Territories and people of the nation, to the inviolability of the Constitution, and the perpetual union, harmony, and prosperity of all—I am most happy to co-operate for the practical success of the principles declared by the convention.
Your obliged friend and fellow-citizen,
A. LINCOLN.

To C. B. SMITH.

SPRINGFIELD, ILL., May 26, 1860.

HON. C. B. SMITH.
MY DEAR SIR:-Yours of the 21st was duly received, but have found no time until now to say a word in the way of answer. I am indeed much indebted to Indiana; and, as my home friends tell me, much to you personally. Your saying, you no longer consider it a doubtful State is very gratifying. The thing starts well everywhere—too well, I almost fear, to last. But we are in, and stick or go through must be the word.
Let me hear from Indiana occasionally.
Your friend, as ever,
A. LINCOLN.

FORM OF REPLY PREPARED BY MR. LINCOLN,

WITH WHICH HIS PRIVATE SECRETARY WAS INSTRUCTED TO ANSWER A NUMEROUS CLASS OF LETTERS IN THE CAMPAIGN OF 1860.
(Doctrine.)
SPRINGFIELD, ILLINOIS, ———, 1860
DEAR SIR:—Your letter to Mr. Lincoln of and by which you seek to obtain his opinions on certain political points, has been received by him. He has received others of a similar character, but he also has a greater number of the exactly

opposite character. The latter class beseech him to write nothing whatever upon any point of political doctrine. They say his positions were well known when he was nominated, and that he must not now embarrass the canvass by undertaking to shift or modify them. He regrets that he cannot oblige all, but you perceive it is impossible for him to do so.

Yours, etc.,
JNO. J. NICOLAY.

TO E. B. WASHBURNE.

SPRINGFIELD, ILLINOIS, MAY 26, 1860

HON. E. B. WASHBURNE.
MY DEAR SIR:—I have several letters from you written since the nomination, but till now have found no moment to say a word by way of answer. Of course I am glad that the nomination is well received by our friends, and I sincerely thank you for so informing me. So far as I can learn, the nominations start well everywhere; and, if they get no backset, it would seem as if they are going through. I hope you will write often; and as you write more rapidly than I do, don't make your letters so short as mine.

Yours very truly,
A. LINCOLN.

TO S. HAYCRAFT.

SPRINGFIELD, ILL., June 4, 1860.

HON. SAMUEL HAYCRAFT.
MY DEAR SIR:—Like yourself I belonged to the old Whig party from its origin to its close. I never belonged to the American party organization, nor ever to a party called a Union party; though I hope I neither am or ever have been less devoted to the Union than yourself or any other patriotic man.

Yours very truly,
A. LINCOLN.

ABRAHAM OR "ABRAM"

TO G. ASHMUN.

SPRINGFIELD, ILL. June 4, 1860
HON. GEORGE ASHMUN.
MY DEAR SIR:—It seems as if the question whether my first name is "Abraham" or "Abram" will never be settled. It is "Abraham," and if the letter of acceptance is not yet in print, you may, if you think fit, have my signature thereto printed "Abraham Lincoln." Exercise your judgment about this.

Yours as ever,
A. LINCOLN.

UNAUTHORIZED BIOGRAPHY

TO S. GALLOWAY.

SPRINGFIELD, ILL., June 19, 1860
HON. SAM'L GALLOWAY.

MY DEAR SIR:—Your very kind letter of the 15th is received. Messrs. Follett, Foster, & Co.'s Life of me is not by my authority; and I have scarcely been so much astounded by anything, as by their public announcement that it is authorized by me. They have fallen into some strange misunderstanding. I certainly knew they contemplated publishing a biography, and I certainly did not object to their doing so, upon their own responsibility. I even took pains to facilitate them. But, at the same time, I made myself tiresome, if not hoarse, with repeating to Mr. Howard, their only agent seen by me, my protest that I authorized nothing—would be responsible for nothing. How they could so misunderstand me, passes comprehension. As a matter wholly my own, I would authorize no biography, without time and opportunity [sic] to carefully examine and consider every word of it and, in this case, in the nature of things, I can have no such time and Opportunity [sic]. But, in my present position, when, by the lessons of the past, and the united voice of all discreet friends, I can neither write nor speak a word for the public, how dare I to send forth, by my authority, a volume of hundreds of pages, for adversaries to make points upon without end? Were I to do so, the convention would have a right to re-assemble and substitute another name for mine.

For these reasons, I would not look at the proof sheets—I am determined to maintain the position of [sic] truly saying I never saw the proof sheets, or any part of their work, before its publication.

Now, do not mistake me—I feel great kindness for Messrs. F., F., & Co.—do not think they have intentionally done wrong. There may be nothing wrong in their proposed book—I sincerely hope there will not. I barely suggest that you, or any of the friends there, on the party account, look it over, and exclude what you may think would embarrass the party bearing in mind, at all times, that I authorize nothing—will be responsible for nothing.

Your friend, as ever,
A. LINCOLN.

[The custom then, and it may have been a good one, was for the Presidential candidate to do no personal canvassing or speaking—or as we have it now "running for election." He stayed at home and kept his mouth shut. Ed.]

TO HANNIBAL HAMLIN.

SPRINGFIELD, ILLINOIS, July 18, 1860.

HON. HANNIBAL HAMLIN. MY DEAR SIR:—It appears to me that you and I ought to be acquainted, and accordingly I write this as a sort of introduction of myself to you. You first entered the Senate during the single term I was a member of the House of Representatives, but I have no recollection that we were introduced. I shall be pleased to receive a line from you.

The prospect of Republican success now appears very flattering, so far as I can perceive. Do you see anything to the contrary?

Yours truly,
A. LINCOLN.

TO A. JONAS.

(Confidential.) SPRINGFIELD, ILLINOIS, JULY 21, 1860.

HON. A. JONAS.

MY DEAR SIR:—Yours of the 20th is received. I suppose as good or even better men than I may have been in American or Know-Nothing lodges; but in point of fact, I never was in one at Quincy or elsewhere. I was never in Quincy but one day and two nights while Know-Nothing lodges were in existence, and you were with me that day and both those nights. I had never been there before in my life, and never afterward, till the joint debate with Douglas in 1858. It was in 1854 when I spoke in some hall there, and after the speaking, you, with others, took me to an oyster-saloon, passed an hour there, and you walked with me to, and parted with me at, the Quincy House, quite late at night. I left by stage for Naples before daylight in the morning, having come in by the same route after dark the evening, previous to the speaking, when I found you waiting at the Quincy House to meet me. A few days after I was there,

Richardson, as I understood, started this same story about my having been in a Know-Nothing lodge. When I heard of the charge, as I did soon after, I taxed my recollection for some incident which could have suggested it; and I remembered that on parting with you the last night I went to the office of the hotel to take my stage-passage for the morning, was told that no stage-office for that line was kept there, and that I must see the driver before retiring, to insure his calling for me in the morning; and a servant was sent with me to find the driver, who, after taking me a square or two, stopped me, and stepped perhaps a dozen steps farther, and in my hearing called to some one, who answered him, apparently from the upper part of a building, and promised to call with the stage for me at the Quincy House. I returned, and went to bed, and before day the stage called and took me. This is all.

That I never was in a Know-Nothing lodge in Quincy, I should expect could be easily proved by respectable men who were always in the lodges and never saw me there. An affidavit of one or two such would put the matter at rest.

And now a word of caution. Our adversaries think they can gain a point if they could force me to openly deny the charge, by which some degree of offence would be given to the Americans. For this reason it must not publicly appear that I am paying any attention to the charge.

Yours truly,
A. LINCOLN.

TO JOHN B. FRY.

SPRINGFIELD, ILLINOIS, August 15, 1860.

MY DEAR SIR:—Yours of the 9th, inclosing the letter of HON. John Minor Botts, was duly received. The latter is herewith returned according to your request. It contains one of the many assurances I receive from the South, that in no probable event will there be any very formidable effort to break up the Union. The people of the South have too much of good sense and good temper to attempt the ruin of the government rather than see it administered as it was administered by the men who made it. At least so I hope and believe. I thank you both for your own letter and a sight of that of Mr. Botts.

Yours very truly,
A. LINCOLN.

TO THURLOW WEED

SPRINGFIELD, ILL. August 17 1860.

MY DEAR SIR:—Yours of the 13th was received this morning. Douglas is managing the Bell element with great adroitness. He had his men in Kentucky to vote for the Bell candidate, producing a result which has badly alarmed and damaged Breckenridge, and at the same time has induced the Bell men to suppose that Bell will certainly be President, if they can keep a few of the Northern States away from us by throwing them to Douglas. But you, better than I, understand all this.

I think there will be the most extraordinary effort ever made to carry New York for Douglas. You and all others who write me from your State think the effort cannot succeed, and I hope you are right. Still, it will require close watching and great efforts on the other side.

Herewith I send you a copy of a letter written at New York, which sufficiently explains itself, and which may or may not give you a valuable hint. You have seen that Bell tickets have been put on the track both here and in Indiana. In both cases the object has been, I think, the same as the Hunt movement in New York—to throw States to Douglas. In our State, we know the thing is engineered by Douglas men, and we do not believe they can make a great deal out of it.

Yours very truly,
A. LINCOLN.

SLOW TO LISTEN TO CRIMINATIONS

TO HON. JOHN ―――――――

(Private.)
SPRINGFIELD, ILL., Aug. 31, 1860
MY DEAR SIR:—Yours of the 27th is duly received. It consists almost exclusively of a historical detail of some local troubles, among some of our friends in Pennsylvania; and I suppose its object is to guard me against forming a prejudice against Mr. McC―――――____, I have not heard near so much upon that subject as you probably suppose; and I am slow to listen to criminations among friends, and never expose their quarrels on either side. My sincere wish is that both sides will allow bygones to be bygones, and look to the present and future only.
Yours very truly,
A. LINCOLN.

TO HANNIBAL HAMLIN

SPRINGFIELD, ILLINOIS, September 4, 1860

HON. HANNIBAL HAMLIN.
MY DEAR SIR:—I am annoyed some by a letter from a friend in Chicago, in which the following passage occurs: "Hamlin has written Colfax that two members of Congress will, he fears, be lost in Maine, the first and sixth districts; and that Washburne's majority for governor will not exceed six thousand."
I had heard something like this six weeks ago, but had been assured since that it was not so. Your secretary of state,—Mr. Smith, I think,—whom you introduced to me by letter, gave this assurance; more recently, Mr. Fessenden, our candidate for Congress in one of those districts, wrote a relative here that his election was sure by at least five thousand, and that Washburne's majority would be from 14,000 to 17,000; and still later, Mr. Fogg, of New Hampshire, now at New York serving on a national committee, wrote me that we were having a desperate fight in Maine, which would end in a splendid victory for us.
Such a result as you seem to have predicted in Maine, in your letter to Colfax, would, I fear, put us on the down-hill track, lose us the State elections in Pennsylvania and Indiana, and probably ruin us on the main turn in November. You must not allow it.
Yours very truly,
A. LINCOLN.

TO E. B. WASHBURNE.

SPRINGFIELD, ILLINOIS, September 9, 1860

HON. E. B. WASHBURNE.
MY DEAR SIR: Yours of the 5th was received last evening. I was right glad to see it. It contains the freshest "posting" which I now have. It relieved me some from a little anxiety I had about Maine. Jo Medill, on August 30th, wrote me that Colfax had a letter from Mr. Hamlin saying we were in great danger of losing two members of Congress in Maine, and that your brother would not have exceeding six thousand majority for Governor. I addressed you at once, at Galena, asking for your latest information. As you are at Washington, that letter you will receive some time after the Maine election.
Yours very truly,
A. LINCOLN.

TO W. H. HERNDON.

SPRINGFIELD, ILL., OCTOBER 10, 1860

DEAR WILLIAM:—I cannot give you details, but it is entirely certain that Pennsylvania and Indiana have gone Republican very largely. Pennsylvania 25,000, and Indiana 5000 to 10,000. Ohio of course is safe.
Yours as ever,
A. LINCOLN.

TO L. M. BOND.

SPRINGFIELD, ILL., October 15, 1860

L. MONTGOMERY BOND, Esq.
MY DEAR SIR: I certainly am in no temper and have no purpose to embitter the feelings of the South, but whether I am inclined to such a course as would in fact embitter their feelings you can better judge by my published speeches than by anything I would say in a short letter if I were inclined now, as I am not, to define my position anew.
Yours truly,
A. LINCOLN.

LETTER SUGGESTING A BEARD

TO MISS GRACE BEDELL, RIPLEY N.Y.

SPRINGFIELD, ILL., October 19, 1860
MISS GRACE BEDELL.
MY DEAR LITTLE MISS:—Your very agreeable letter of the 15th is received. I regret the necessity of saying I have no daughter. I have three sons—one seventeen, one nine, and one seven. They with their mother constitute my whole family. As to the whiskers, as I have never worn any, do you not think that people would call it a piece of silly affectation were I to begin wearing them now?
I am your true friend and sincere well-wisher,
A. LINCOLN.

EARLY INFORMATION ON ARMY DEFECTION IN SOUTH

TO D. HUNTER.

(Private and Confidential.) SPRINGFIELD, ILLINOIS, October 26, 1860
MAJOR DAVID HUNTER
MY DEAR SIR:—Your very kind letter of the 20th was duly received, for which please accept my thanks. I have another letter, from a writer unknown to me, saying the officers of the army at Fort Kearny have determined in case of Republican success at the approaching Presidential election, to take themselves, and the arms at that point, south, for the purpose of resistance to the government. While I think there are many chances to one that this is a humbug, it occurs to me that any real movement of this sort in the Army would leak out and become known to you. In such case, if it would not be unprofessional or dishonorable (of which you are to be judge), I shall be much obliged if you will apprise me of it.
Yours very truly,
A. LINCOLN.

TO HANNIBAL HAMLIN

(Confidential.) SPRINGFIELD. ILLINOIS, November 8, 1860

HON. HANNIBAL HAMLIN.
MY DEAR SIR:—I am anxious for a personal interview with you at as early a day as possible. Can you, without much inconvenience, meet me at Chicago? If you can, please name as early a day as you conveniently can, and telegraph me, unless there be sufficient time before the day named to communicate by mail.
Yours very truly,
A. LINCOLN.

TO SAMUEL HAYCRAFT.

(Private and Confidential.)

SPRINGFIELD, ILL., Nov. 13, 1860
HON. SAMUEL HAYCRAFT.
MY DEAR SIR:—Yours of the 9th is just received. I can only answer briefly. Rest fully assured that the good people of the South who will put themselves in the same temper and mood towards me which you do will find no cause to complain of me.
Yours very truly,
A. LINCOLN. CELEBRATION OF LINCOLN'S ELECTION, REMARKS AT THE MEETING AT SPRINGFIELD, ILLINOIS NOVEMBER 20, 1860
FRIENDS AND FELLOW-CITIZENS:—Please excuse me on this occasion from making a speech. I thank you in common with all those who have thought fit by their votes to indorse the Republican cause. I rejoice with you in the success which has thus far attended that cause. Yet in all our rejoicings let us neither express nor cherish any hard feelings toward any citizen who by his vote has differed with us. Let us at all times remember that all American citizens are brothers of a common country, and should dwell together in the bonds of fraternal feeling. Let me again beg you to accept my thanks, and to excuse me from further speaking at this time.

TO ALEXANDER H. STEPHENS

SPRINGFIELD, ILL. NOV. 30, 1860

HON. A. H. STEPHENS.
MY DEAR SIR:—I have read in the newspapers your speech recently delivered (I think) before the Georgia Legislature, or its assembled members. If you have revised it, as is probable, I shall be much obliged if you will send me a copy.
Yours very truly,
A. LINCOLN.

TO HANNIBAL HAMLIN

(Private)

SPRINGFIELD, ILLINOIS, December 8, 1860
HON. HANNIBAL HAMLIN.

DEAR SIR:—Yours of the 4th was duly received. The inclosed to Governor Seward covers two notes to him, copies of which you find open for your inspection. Consult with Judge Trumbull; and if you and he see no reason to the contrary, deliver the letter to Governor Seward at once. If you see reason to the contrary write me at once.

I have an intimation that Governor Banks would yet accept a place in the Cabinet. Please ascertain and write me how this is,

Yours very truly,
A. LINCOLN.

BLOCKING "COMPROMISE" ON SLAVERY ISSUE

TO E. B. WASHBURNE

(Private and Confidential.)
SPRINGFIELD, ILL., December 13, 1860
HON. E. B. WASHBURNE.
MY DEAR SIR:—Your long letter received. Prevent, as far as possible, any of our friends from demoralizing themselves and our cause by entertaining propositions for compromise of any sort on "slavery extension." There is no possible compromise upon it but which puts us under again, and leaves all our work to do over again. Whether it be a Missouri line or Eli Thayer's popular sovereignty, it is all the same. Let either be done, and immediately filibustering and extending slavery recommences. On that point hold firm, as with a chain of steel.

Yours as ever,
A. LINCOLN.

OPINION ON SECESSION

TO THURLOW WEED

SPRINGFIELD, ILLINOIS, DECEMBER 17, 1860
MY DEAR SIR:—Yours of the 11th was received two days ago. Should the convocation of governors of which you speak seem desirous to know my views on the present aspect of things, tell them you judge from my speeches that I will be inflexible on the territorial question; but I probably think either the Missouri line extended, or Douglas's and Eli Thayer's popular sovereignty would lose us everything we gain by the election; that filibustering for all south of us and making slave States of it would follow in spite of us, in either case; also that I probably think all opposition, real and apparent, to the fugitive slave clause of the Constitution ought to be withdrawn.

I believe you can pretend to find but little, if anything, in my speeches, about secession. But my opinion is that no State can in any way lawfully get out of the Union without the consent of the others; and that it is the duty of the President and other government functionaries to run the machine as it is.

Truly yours,
A. LINCOLN.

SOME FORTS SURRENDERED TO THE SOUTH

TO E. B. WASHBURNE

(Confidential)
SPRINGFIELD, ILLINOIS, December 21, 1860
HON. E. B. WASHBURNE.

MY DEAR SIR:—Last night I received your letter giving an account of your interview with General Scott, and for which I thank you. Please present my respects to the General, and tell him, confidentially, I shall be obliged to him to be as well prepared as he can to either hold or retake the forts, as the case may require, at and after the inauguration.
Yours as ever,
A. LINCOLN.

TO A. H. STEPHENS.

(For your own eye only) SPRINGFIELD, ILLINOIS, DECEMBER 22, 1860

HON. ALEXANDER STEVENS
MY DEAR SIR:—Your obliging answer to my short note is just received, and for which please accept my thanks. I fully appreciate the present peril the country is in, and the weight of responsibility on me. Do the people of the South really entertain fear that a Republican administration would, directly or indirectly, interfere with the slaves, or with them about the slaves? If they do, I wish to assure you, as once a friend, and still, I hope, not an enemy, that there is no cause for such fears. The South would be in no more danger in this respect than it was in the days of Washington. I suppose, however, this does not meet the case. You think slavery is right and ought to be extended, while we think it is wrong and ought to be restricted. That, I suppose, is the rub. It certainly is the only substantial difference between us.
Yours very truly,
A. LINCOLN.

SUPPORT OF THE FUGITIVE SLAVE CLAUSE

MEMORANDUM

December [22?], 1860
Resolved: That the fugitive slave clause of the Constitution ought to be enforced by a law of Congress, with efficient provisions for that object, not obliging private persons to assist in its execution, but punishing all who resist it, and with the usual safeguards to liberty, securing free men against being surrendered as slaves.
That all State laws, if there be such, really or apparently in conflict with such law of Congress, ought to be repealed; and no opposition to the execution of such law of Congress ought to be made.
That the Federal Union must be preserved.
Prepared for the consideration of the Republican members of the Senate Committee of Thirteen.

TO D. HUNTER.

(Confidential.)

SPRINGFIELD, ILLINOIS December 22, 1860
MAJOR DAVID HUNTER.
MY DEAR SIR:—I am much obliged by the receipt of yours of the 18th. The most we can do now is to watch events, and be as well prepared as possible for any turn things may take. If the forts fall, my judgment is that they are to be retaken. When I shall determine definitely my time of starting to Washington, I will notify you.
Yours truly,
A. LINCOLN.

TO I. N. MORRIS

(Confidential.)

SPRINGFIELD, ILL., Dec 24, 1860
HON. I. N. MORRIS.
MY DEAR SIR:—Without supposing that you and I are any nearer together, politically, than heretofore, allow me to tender you my sincere thanks for your Union resolution, expressive of views upon which we never were, and, I trust, never will be at variance.
Yours very truly,
A. LINCOLN.

ATTEMPT TO FORM A COALITION CABINET

TO HANNIBAL HAMLIN

SPRINGFIELD, ILLINOIS, December 14, 1860.
HON. HANNIBAL HAMLIN.
MY DEAR SIR:—I need a man of Democratic antecedents from New England. I cannot get a fair share of that element in without. This stands in the way of Mr. Adams. I think of Governor Banks, Mr. Welles, and Mr. Tuck. Which of them do the New England delegation prefer? Or shall I decide for myself?
Yours as ever,
A. LINCOLN.

1861

TO WILLIAM H. SEWARD.
(Private.)
SPRINGFIELD. ILL., January 3, 1861.
HON. W. H. SEWARD.
DEAR SIR:—Yours without signature was received last night. I have been considering your suggestions as to my reaching Washington somewhat earlier than is usual. It seems to me the inauguration is not the most dangerous point for us. Our adversaries have us now clearly at disadvantage on the second Wednesday of February, when the votes should be officially counted. If the two houses refuse to meet at all, or meet without a quorum of each, where shall we be? I do not think that this counting is constitutionally essential to the election, but how are we to proceed in the absence of it? In view of this, I think it is best for me not to attempt appearing in Washington till the result of that ceremony is known.
It certainly would be of some advantage if you could know who are to be at the heads of the War and Navy departments, but until I can ascertain definitely whether I can get any suitable men from the South, and who, and how many, I can not well decide. As yet, I have no word from Mr. Gilmer in answer to my request for an interview with him. I look for something on the subject, through you, before long.
Yours very truly,
A. LINCOLN.

TO W. H. SEWARD.

(Private.)

SPRINGFIELD, ILL., January 12, 1861

HON. W. H. SEWARD.
MY DEAR SIR:—Yours of the 8th received. I still hope Mr. Gilmer will, on a fair understanding with us, consent to take a place in the Cabinet. The preference for him over Mr. Hunt or Mr. Gentry is that, up to date—he has a living position in the South, while they have not. He is only better than Winter Davis in that he is farther south. I fear, if we could get, we could not safely take more than one such man—that is, not more than one who opposed us in the election—the danger being to lose the confidence of our own friends. Your selection for the State Department having become public, I am happy to find scarcely any objection to it. I shall have trouble with every other Northern Cabinet appointment—so much so that I shall have to defer them as long as possible to avoid being teased into insanity, to make changes.
Your obedient servant,
A. LINCOLN

TO E. D. MORGAN

SPRINGFIELD, ILL. FEB. 4, 1861

SIR:—Your letter of the 30th ult. inviting me, on behalf of the Legislature of New York, to pass through that State on my way to Washington, and tendering me the hospitalities of her authorities and people, has been duly received. With the feelings of deep gratitude to you and them for this testimonial of regard and esteem I beg you to notify them that I accept the invitation so kindly tendered.
Your obedient servant,
A. LINCOLN
P.S.—Please let the ceremonies be only such as to take the least time possible. A. L.

PATRONAGE CLAIMS

TO THURLOW WEED

SPRINGFIELD, ILL., February 4, 1861
DEAR SIR:—I have both your letter to myself and that to Judge Davis, in relation to a certain gentleman in your State claiming to dispense patronage in my name, and also to be authorized to use my name to advance the chances of Mr. Greeley for an election to the United States Senate.
It is very strange that such things should be said by any one. The gentleman you mention did speak to me of Mr. Greeley in connection with the senatorial election, and I replied in terms of kindness toward Mr. Greeley, which I really feel, but always with an expressed protest that my name must not be used in the senatorial election in favor of or against any one. Any other representation of me is a misrepresentation.
As to the matter of dispensing patronage, it perhaps will surprise you to learn that I have information that you claim to have my authority to arrange that matter in New York. I do not believe you have so claimed; but still so some men say. On that subject you know all I have said to you is "justice to all," and I have said nothing more particular to any one. I say this to reassure you that I have not changed my position.
In the hope, however, that you will not use my name in the matter, I am,
Yours truly,
A. LINCOLN.

FAREWELL ADDRESS AT SPRINGFIELD, ILLINOIS,

FEBRUARY 11, 1861

MY FRIENDS:—One who has never been placed in a like position cannot understand my feelings at this hour, nor the oppressive sadness I feel at this parting. For more than twenty-five years I have lived among you, and during all that time I have received nothing but kindness at your hands. Here the most cherished ties of earth were assumed. Here my children were born, and here one of them lies buried. To you, my friends, I owe all that I have, all that I am. All the strange checkered past seems to crowd upon my mind. To-day I leave you. I go to assume a task more difficult than that which devolved upon General Washington. Unless the great God who assisted him shall be with and aid me I cannot prevail; but if the same almighty arm that directed and protected him shall guide and support me I shall not fail; I shall succeed. Let us pray that the God of our fathers may not forsake us now. To Him I commend you all. Permit me to ask that with equal sincerity and faith you will all invoke His wisdom and goodness for me.

With these words I must leave you; for how long I know not. Friends, one and all, I must now wish you an affectionate farewell.

REMARKS AT TOLONO, ILLINOIS, FEBRUARY 11, 1861

I am leaving you on an errand of national importance, attended, as you are aware, with considerable difficulties. Let us believe, as some poet has expressed it, "Behind the cloud the sun is still shining." I bid you an affectionate farewell.

REPLY TO ADDRESS OF WELCOME, INDIANAPOLIS,

INDIANA, FEBRUARY 11, 1861

GOVERNOR MORTON AND FELLOW CITIZENS OF THE STATE OF INDIANA:

Most heartily do I thank you for this magnificent reception, and while I cannot take to myself any share of the compliment thus paid, more than that which pertains to a mere instrument, an accidental instrument, perhaps I should say, of a great cause, I yet must look upon it as a most magnificent reception, and as such most heartily do thank you for it. You have been pleased to address yourself to me chiefly in behalf of this glorious Union in which we live, in all of which you have my hearty sympathy, and, as far as may be within my power, will have, one and inseparable, my hearty consideration. While I do not expect, upon this occasion, or until I get to Washington, to attempt any lengthy speech, I will only say to the salvation of the Union there needs but one single thing—the hearts of a people like yours. The people—when they rise in mass in behalf of the Union and the liberties of their country, truly may it be said, "The gates of hell cannot prevail against them." In all trying positions in which I shall be placed—and, doubtless, I shall be placed in many such—my reliance will be placed upon you and the people of the United States; and I wish you to remember, now and forever, that it is your business, and not mine; that if the union of these States and the liberties of this people shall be lost, it is but little to any one man of fifty-two years of age, but a great deal to the thirty millions of people who inhabit these United States, and to their posterity in all coming time. It is your business to rise up and preserve the Union and liberty for yourselves, and not for me.

I desire they should be constitutionally performed. I, as already intimated, am but an accidental instrument, temporary, and to serve but for a limited time; and I appeal to you again to constantly bear in mind that with you, and not with politicians, not with Presidents, not with office-seekers, but with you is the question, Shall the Union and shall the liberties of this country be preserved to the latest generations?

ADDRESS TO THE LEGISLATURE OF INDIANA, AT INDIANAPOLIS,

FEBRUARY 12, 1861

FELLOW-CITIZENS OF THE STATE OF INDIANA:—I am here to thank you much for this magnificent welcome, and still more for the generous support given by your State to that political cause which I think is the true and just cause of the whole country and the whole world.

Solomon says there is "a time to keep silence," and when men wrangle by the mouth with no certainty that they mean the same thing while using the same word, it perhaps were as well if they would keep silence.

The words "coercion" and "invasion" are much used in these days, and often with some temper and hot blood. Let us make sure, if we can, the meaning of those who use them. Let us get the exact definitions of these words, not from dictionaries, but from the men themselves, who certainly deprecate the things they would represent by the use of the words.

What, then, is coercion? What is invasion? Would the marching of an army into South Carolina, without the consent of her people, and with hostile intent toward them, be invasion? I certainly think it would, and it would be coercion also, if the South Carolinians were forced to submit. But if the United States should merely hold and retake its own forts and other property, and collect the duties on foreign importations, or even withhold the mails from places where they were habitually violated, would any or all of these things be invasion or coercion? Do our professed lovers of the Union, who spitefully resolve that they will resist coercion and invasion, understand that such things as these, on the part of the United States, would be coercion or invasion of a State? If so, their idea of means to preserve the object of their great affection would seem to be exceedingly thin and airy. If sick, the little pills of the homoeopathist would be much too large for it to swallow. In their view, the Union, as a family relation, would seem to be no regular marriage, but rather a sort of "free-love" arrangement, to be maintained on passional attraction.

By the way, in what consists the special sacredness of a State? I speak not of the position assigned to a State in the Union by the Constitution, for that is a bond we all recognize. That position, however, a State cannot carry out of the Union with it. I speak of that assumed primary right of a State to rule all which is less than itself, and to ruin all which is larger than itself. If a State and a county, in a given case, should be equal in number of inhabitants, in what, as a matter of principle, is the State better than the county? Would an exchange of name be an exchange of rights? Upon what principle, upon what rightful principle, may a State, being no more than one fiftieth part of the nation in soil and population, break up the nation, and coerce a proportionably large subdivision of itself in the most arbitrary way? What mysterious right to play tyrant is conferred on a district of country, with its people, by merely calling it a State? Fellow-citizens, I am not asserting anything. I am merely asking questions for you to consider. And now allow me to bid you farewell.

INTENTIONS TOWARD THE SOUTH

ADDRESS TO THE MAYOR AND CITIZENS OF

CINCINNATI, OHIO, FEBRUARY 12, 1861

Mr. MAYOR, AND GENTLEMEN:—Twenty-four hours ago, at the capital of Indiana, I said to myself, "I have never seen so many people assembled together in winter weather." I am no longer able to say that. But it is what might reasonably have been expected—that this great city of Cincinnati would thus acquit herself on such an occasion. My friends, I am entirely overwhelmed by the magnificence of the reception which has been given, I will not say to me, but to the President-elect of the United States of America. Most heartily do I thank you, one and all, for it.

I have spoken but once before this in Cincinnati. That was a year previous to the late Presidential election. On that occasion, in a playful manner, but with sincere words, I addressed much of what I said to the Kentuckians. I gave my opinion that we, as Republicans, would ultimately beat them as Democrats, but that they could postpone that result longer by nominating Senator Douglas for the Presidency than they could by any other way. They did not, in any true sense of the word, nominate Mr. Douglas, and the result has come certainly as soon as ever I expected. I also told them how I expected they would be treated after they should have been beaten, and I now wish to call their attention to what I then said upon that subject. I then said:

"When we do as we say, beat you, you perhaps want to know what we will do with you. I will tell you, as far as I am authorized to speak for the Opposition, what we mean to do with you. We mean to treat you, as near as we possibly can, as Washington, Jefferson, and Madison treated you. We mean to leave you alone, and in no way to interfere with your institutions; to abide by all and every compromise of the Constitution, and, in a word, coming back to the original proposition, to treat you so far as degenerate men, if we have degenerated, may, according to the example of those noble fathers, Washington, Jefferson, and Madison.

"We mean to remember that you are as good as we; that there is no difference between us other than the difference of circumstances. We mean to recognize and bear in mind always that you have as good hearts in your bosoms as other people, or as we claim to have, and treat you accordingly."

Fellow-citizens of Kentucky—friends and brethren, may I call you in my new position?—I see no occasion and feel no inclination to retract a word of this. If it shall not be made good, be assured the fault shall not be mine.

ADDRESS TO THE GERMAN CLUB OF CINCINNATI, OHIO,

FEBRUARY 12, 1861

Mr. CHAIRMAN:—I thank you and those whom you represent for the compliment you have paid me by tendering me this address. In so far as there is an allusion to our present national difficulties, which expresses, as you have said, the views of the gentlemen present, I shall have to beg pardon for not entering fully upon the questions which the address you have now read suggests.
I deem it my duty—a duty which I owe to my constituents—to you, gentlemen, that I should wait until the last moment for a development of the present national difficulties before I express myself decidedly as to what course I shall pursue. I hope, then, not to be false to anything that you have expected of me.
I agree with you, Mr. Chairman, that the working men are the basis of all governments, for the plain reason that they are all the more numerous, and as you added that those were the sentiments of the gentlemen present, representing not only the working class, but citizens of other callings than those of the mechanic, I am happy to concur with you in these sentiments, not only of the native-born citizens, but also of the Germans and foreigners from other countries.
Mr. Chairman, I hold that while man exists it is his duty to improve not only his own condition, but to assist in ameliorating the condition of mankind; and therefore, without entering upon the details of the question, I will simply say that I am for those means which will give the greatest good to the greatest number.
In regard to the Homestead law, I have to say that, in so far as the government lands can be disposed of, I am in favor of cutting up the wild lands into parcels, so that every poor man may have a home.
In regard to the Germans and foreigners, I esteem them no better than other people, nor any worse. It is not my nature, when I see a people borne down by the weight of their shackles—the oppression of tyranny—to make their life more bitter by heaping upon them greater burdens; but rather would I do all in my power to raise the yoke than to add anything that would tend to crush them.
Inasmuch as our own country is extensive and new, and the countries of Europe are densely populated, if there are any abroad who desire to make this the land of their adoption, it is not in my heart to throw aught in their way to prevent them from coming to the United States.
Mr. Chairman and gentlemen, I will bid you an affectionate farewell.

ADDRESS TO THE LEGISLATURE OF OHIO AT COLUMBUS

FEBRUARY 13, 1861

Mr. PRESIDENT AND Mr. SPEAKER, AND GENTLEMEN OF THE GENERAL ASSEMBLY OF OHIO:—It is true, as has been said by the president of the Senate, that very great responsibility rests upon me in the position to which the votes of the American people have called me. I am deeply sensible of that weighty responsibility. I cannot but know what you all know, that without a name, perhaps without a reason why I should have a name, there has fallen upon me a task such as did not rest even upon the Father of his Country; and so feeling, I can turn and look for that support without which it will be impossible for me to perform that great task. I turn, then, and look to the American people and to that God who has never forsaken them. Allusion has been made to the interest felt in relation to the policy of the new administration. In this I have received from some a degree of credit for having kept silence, and from others some deprecation. I still think that I was right.
In the varying and repeatedly shifting scenes of the present, and without a precedent which could enable me to judge by the past, it has seemed fitting that before speaking upon the difficulties of the country I should have gained a view of the whole field, being at liberty to modify and change the course of policy as future events may make a change necessary.
I have not maintained silence from any want of real anxiety. It is a good thing that there is no more than anxiety, for there is nothing going wrong. It is a consoling circumstance that when we look out there is nothing that really hurts anybody. We entertain different views upon political questions, but nobody is suffering anything. This is a most consoling circumstance, and from it we may conclude that all we want is time, patience, and a reliance on that God who has never forsaken this people.

Fellow-citizens, what I have said I have said altogether extemporaneously, and I will now come to a close.

ADDRESS AT STEUBENVILLE, OHIO,

FEBRUARY 14, 1861

I fear that the great confidence placed in my ability is unfounded. Indeed, I am sure it is. Encompassed by vast difficulties as I am, nothing shall be wanting on my part, if sustained by God and the American people. I believe the devotion to the Constitution is equally great on both sides of the river. It is only the different understanding of that instrument that causes difficulty. The only dispute on both sides is, "What are their rights?" If the majority should not rule, who would be the judge? Where is such a judge to be found? We should all be bound by the majority of the American people; if not, then the minority must control. Would that be right? Would it be just or generous? Assuredly not. I reiterate that the majority should rule. If I adopt a wrong policy, the opportunity for condemnation will occur in four years' time. Then I can be turned out, and a better man with better views put in my place.

ADDRESS AT PITTSBURGH, PENNSYLVANIA

FEBRUARY 15, 1861

I most cordially thank his Honor Mayor Wilson, and the citizens of Pittsburg generally, for their flattering reception. I am the more grateful because I know that it is not given to me alone, but to the cause I represent, which clearly proves to me their good-will, and that sincere feeling is at the bottom of it. And here I may remark that in every short address I have made to the people, in every crowd through which I have passed of late, some allusion has been made to the present distracted condition of the country. It is natural to expect that I should say something on this subject; but to touch upon it at all would involve an elaborate discussion of a great many questions and circumstances, requiring more time than I can at present command, and would, perhaps, unnecessarily commit me upon matters which have not yet fully developed themselves. The condition of the country is an extraordinary one, and fills the mind of every patriot with anxiety. It is my intention to give this subject all the consideration I possibly can before specially deciding in regard to it, so that when I do speak it may be as nearly right as possible. When I do speak I hope I may say nothing in opposition to the spirit of the Constitution, contrary to the integrity of the Union, or which will prove inimical to the liberties of the people, or to the peace of the whole country. And furthermore, when the time arrives for me to speak on this great subject, I hope I may say nothing to disappoint the people generally throughout the country, especially if the expectation has been based upon anything which I may have heretofore said. Notwithstanding the troubles across the river [the speaker pointing southwardly across the Monongahela, and smiling], there is no crisis but an artificial one. What is there now to warrant the condition of affairs presented by our friends over the river? Take even their own view of the questions involved, and there is nothing to justify the course they are pursuing. I repeat, then, there is no crisis, excepting such a one as may be gotten up at any time by turbulent men aided by designing politicians, My advice to them, under such circumstances, is to keep cool. If the great American people only keep their temper on both sides of the line, the troubles will come to an end, and the question which now distracts the country will be settled, just as surely as all other difficulties of a like character which have originated in this government have been adjusted. Let the people on both sides keep their self-possession, and just as other clouds have cleared away in due time, so will this great nation continue to prosper as heretofore. But, fellow-citizens, I have spoken longer on this subject than I intended at the outset.

It is often said that the tariff is the specialty of Pennsylvania. Assuming that direct taxation is not to be adopted, the tariff question must be as durable as the government itself. It is a question of national housekeeping. It is to the government what replenishing the meal-tub is to the family. Every varying circumstances will require frequent modifications as to the amount needed and the sources of supply. So far there is little difference of opinion among the people. It is as to whether, and how far, duties on imports shall be adjusted to favor home production in the home market, that controversy begins. One party insists that such adjustment oppresses one class for the advantage of another; while the other party argues that, with all its incidents, in the long run all classes are benefited. In the Chicago platform there is a plank upon this subject which should be a general law to the incoming administration. We should do neither more nor less than we gave the people reason to believe we would when they gave us their votes. Permit me, fellow-citizens, to read the tariff plank of the Chicago platform, or rather have it read in your hearing by one who has younger eyes.

[Mr. Lincoln's private secretary then read Section 12 of the Chicago platform, as follows:]

"That, while providing revenue for the support of the General Government by duties upon imports, sound policy requires such an adjustment of these imposts as will encourage the development of the industrial interest of the whole country; and we commend that policy of national exchanges which secures to working-men liberal wages, to agriculture remunerating prices, to mechanics and manufacturers adequate return for their skill, labor, and enterprise, and to the nation commercial prosperity and independence."

As with all general propositions, doubtless, there will be shades of difference in construing this. I have by no means a thoroughly matured judgment upon this subject, especially as to details; some general ideas are about all. I have long thought it would be to our advantage to produce any necessary article at home which can be made of as good quality and with as little labor at home as abroad, at least by the difference of the carrying from abroad. In such case the carrying is demonstrably a dead loss of labor. For instance, labor being the true standard of value, is it not plain that if equal labor get a bar of railroad iron out of a mine in England and another out of a mine in Pennsylvania, each can be laid down in a track at home cheaper than they could exchange countries, at least by the carriage? If there be a present cause why one can be both made and carried cheaper in money price than the other can be made without carrying, that cause is an unnatural and injurious one, and ought gradually, if not rapidly, to be removed. The condition of the treasury at this time would seem to render an early revision of the tariff indispensable. The Morrill [tariff] bill, now pending before Congress, may or may not become a law. I am not posted as to its particular provisions, but if they are generally satisfactory, and the bill shall now pass, there will be an end for the present. If, however, it shall not pass, I suppose the whole subject will be one of the most pressing and important for the next Congress. By the Constitution, the executive may recommend measures which he may think proper, and he may veto those he thinks improper, and it is supposed that he may add to these certain indirect influences to affect the action of Congress. My political education strongly inclines me against a very free use of any of these means by the executive to control the legislation of the country. As a rule, I think it better that Congress should originate as well as perfect its measures without external bias. I therefore would rather recommend to every gentleman who knows he is to be a member of the next Congress to take an enlarged view, and post himself thoroughly, so as to contribute his part to such an adjustment of the tariff as shall produce a sufficient revenue, and in its other bearings, so far as possible, be just and equal to all sections of the country and classes of the people.

ADDRESS AT CLEVELAND, OHIO,

FEBRUARY 15, 1861

Mr. CHAIRMAN AND FELLOW-CITIZENS OF CLEVELAND:—We have been marching about two miles through snow, rain, and deep mud. The large numbers that have turned out under these circumstances testify that you are in earnest about something or other. But do I think so meanly of you as to suppose that that earnestness is about me personally? I would be doing you an injustice to suppose you did. You have assembled to testify your respect for the Union, the Constitution, and the laws; and here let me say that it is with you, the people, to advance the great cause of the Union and the Constitution, and not with any one man. It rests with you alone. This fact is strongly impressed upon my mind at present. In a community like this, whose appearance testifies to their intelligence, I am convinced that the cause of liberty and the Union can never be in danger. Frequent allusion is made to the excitement at present existing in our national politics, and it is as well that I should also allude to it here. I think that there is no occasion for any excitement. The crisis, as it is called, is altogether an artificial crisis. In all parts of the nation there are differences of opinion on politics. There are differences of opinion even here. You did not all vote for the person who now addresses you. What is happening now will not hurt those who are farther away from here. Have they not all their rights now as they ever have had? Do they not have their fugitive slaves returned now as ever? Have they not the same Constitution that they have lived under for seventy-odd years? Have they not a position as citizens of this common country, and have we any power to change that position? What, then, is the matter with them? Why all this excitement? Why all these complaints?

As I said before, this crisis is all artificial! It has no foundation in facts. It is not argued up, as the saying is, and cannot, therefore, be argued down. Let it alone and it will go down of itself.

[Mr. Lincoln then said that they must be content with a few words from him, as he was tired, etc. Having been given to understand that the crowd was not all Republican, but consisted of men of all parties, he continued:]

This is as it should be. If Judge Douglas had been elected and had been here on his way to Washington, as I am tonight, the Republicans should have joined his supporters in welcoming him, just as his friends have joined with mine tonight. If all do not join now to save the good old ship of the Union this voyage, nobody will have a chance to pilot her on another voyage.

ADDRESS AT BUFFALO, NEW YORK,

FEBRUARY 16, 1861

Mr. MAYOR AND FELLOW-CITIZENS OF BUFFALO AND THE STATE OF NEW YORK:—I am here to thank you briefly for this grand reception given to me, not personally, but as the representative of our great and beloved country. Your worthy mayor has been pleased to mention, in his address to me, the fortunate and agreeable journey which I have had from home, on my rather circuitous route to the Federal capital. I am very happy that he was enabled in truth to congratulate myself and company on that fact. It is true we have had nothing thus far to mar the pleasure of the trip. We have not been met alone by those who assisted in giving the election to me—I say not alone by them, but by the whole population of the country through which we have passed. This is as it should be. Had the election fallen to any other of the distinguished candidates instead of myself, under the peculiar circumstances, to say the least, it would have been proper for all citizens to have greeted him as you now greet me. It is an evidence of the devotion of the whole people to the Constitution, the Union, and the perpetuity of the liberties of this country. I am unwilling on any occasion that I should be so meanly thought of as to have it supposed for a moment that these demonstrations are tendered to me personally. They are tendered to the country, to the institutions of the country, and to the perpetuity of the liberties of the country, for which these institutions were made and created.

Your worthy mayor has thought fit to express the hope that I may be able to relieve the country from the present, or, I should say, the threatened difficulties. I am sure I bring a heart true to the work. For the ability to perform it, I must trust in that Supreme Being who has never forsaken this favored land, through the instrumentality of this great and intelligent people. Without that assistance I shall surely fail; with it, I cannot fail. When we speak of threatened difficulties to the Country, it is natural that it should be expected that something should be said by myself with regard to particular measures. Upon more mature reflection, however, others will agree with me that, when it is considered that these difficulties are without precedent, and have never been acted upon by any individual situated as I am, it is most proper I should wait and see the developments, and get all the light possible, so that when I do speak authoritatively, I may be as near right as possible. When I shall speak authoritatively, I hope to say nothing inconsistent with the Constitution, the Union, the rights of all the States, of each State, and of each section of the country, and not to disappoint the reasonable expectations of those who have confided to me their votes. In this connection allow me to say that you, as a portion of the great American people, need only to maintain your composure, stand up to your sober convictions of right, to your obligations to the Constitution, and act in accordance with those sober convictions, and the clouds now on the horizon will be dispelled, and we shall have a bright and glorious future; and when this generation has passed away, tens of thousands will inhabit this country where only thousands inhabit it now. I do not propose to address you at length; I have no voice for it. Allow me again to thank you for this magnificent reception, and bid you farewell.

ADDRESS AT ROCHESTER, NEW YORK,

FEBRUARY 18, 1861

I confess myself, after having seen many large audiences since leaving home, overwhelmed with this vast number of faces at this hour of the morning. I am not vain enough to believe that you are here from any wish to see me as an individual, but because I am for the time being the representative of the American people. I could not, if I would, address you at any length. I have not the strength, even if I had the time, for a speech at each of these many interviews that are afforded me on my way to Washington. I appear merely to see you, and to let you see me, and to bid you farewell. I hope it will be understood that it is from no disinclination to oblige anybody that I do not address you at greater length.

ADDRESS AT SYRACUSE, NEW YORK,

FEBRUARY 18, 1861.

LADIES AND GENTLEMEN:—I See you have erected a very fine and handsome platform here for me, and I presume you expected me to speak from it. If I should go upon it, you would imagine that I was about to deliver you a much longer speech than I am. I wish you to understand that I mean no discourtesy to you by thus declining. I intend discourtesy to no one. But I wish you to understand that, though I am unwilling to go upon this platform, you are not at liberty to draw inferences concerning any other platform with which my name has been or is connected. I wish you long life and prosperity individually, and pray that with the perpetuity of those institutions under which we have all so long lived and prospered, our happiness may be secured, our future made brilliant, and the glorious destiny of our country established forever. I bid you a kind farewell.

ADDRESS AT UTICA, NEW YORK,

FEBRUARY 18, 1860

LADIES AND GENTLEMEN:—I have no speech to make to you; and no time to speak in. I appear before you that I may see you, and that you may see me; and I am willing to admit that so far as the ladies are concerned I have the best of the bargain, though I wish it to be understood that I do not make the same acknowledgment concerning the men.

REPLY TO THE MAYOR OF ALBANY, NEW YORK

FEBRUARY 18, 1861.

MR. MAYOR:—I can hardly appropriate to myself the flattering terms in which you communicate the tender of this reception, as personal to myself. I most gratefully accept the hospitalities tendered to me, and will not detain you or the audience with any extended remarks at this time. I presume that in the two or three courses through which I shall have to go, I shall have to repeat somewhat, and I will therefore only express to you my thanks for this kind reception.

REPLY TO GOVERNOR MORGAN OF NEW YORK, AT ALBANY,

FEBRUARY 18, 1861.

GOVERNOR MORGAN:—I was pleased to receive an invitation to visit the capital of the great Empire State of this nation while on my way to the Federal capital. I now thank you, Mr. Governor, and you, the people of the capital of the State of New York, for this most hearty and magnificent welcome. If I am not at fault, the great Empire State at this time contains a larger population than did the whole of the United States of America at the time they achieved their national independence, and I was proud—to be invited to visit its capital, to meet its citizens, as I now have the honor to do. I am notified by your governor that this reception is tendered by citizens without distinction of party. Because of this I accept it the more gladly. In this country, and in any country where freedom of thought is tolerated, citizens attach themselves to political parties. It is but an ordinary degree of charity to attribute this act to the supposition that, in thus attaching themselves to the various parties, each man in his own judgment supposes he thereby best advances the interests of the whole country. And when an election is past it is altogether befitting a free people, as I suppose, that, until the next election, they should be one people. The reception you have extended me to-day is not given to me personally,—it should not be so,—but as the representative, for the time being, of the majority of the nation. If the election had fallen to any of the more distinguished citizens who received the support of the people, this same honor should have greeted him that greets me this day, in testimony of the universal, unanimous devotion of the whole people to the Constitution, the Union, and to the perpetual liberties of succeeding generations in this country. I have neither the voice nor the strength to address you at any greater length. I beg you will therefore accept my most grateful thanks for this manifest devotion—not to me, but the institutions of this great and glorious country.

ADDRESS TO THE LEGISLATURE OF NEW YORK, AT ALBANY,

FEBRUARY 18, 1861.

MR. PRESIDENT AND GENTLEMEN OF THE GENERAL ASSEMBLY OF THE STATE OF NEW YORK:—
It is with feelings of great diffidence, and, I may say, with feelings of awe, perhaps greater than I have recently experienced, that I meet you here in this place. The history of this great State, the renown of those great men who have stood here, and have spoken here, and have been heard here, all crowd around my fancy, and incline me to shrink from any attempt to address you. Yet I have some confidence given me by the generous manner in which you have invited me, and by the still more generous manner in which you have received me, to speak further. You have invited and received me without distinction of party. I cannot for a moment suppose that this has been done in any considerable degree with reference to my personal services, but that it is done in so far as I am regarded, at this time, as the representative of the majesty of this great nation. I doubt not this is the truth, and the whole truth of the case, and this is as it should be. It is much more gratifying to me that this reception has been given to me as the elected representative of a free people, than it could possibly be if tendered merely as an evidence of devotion to me, or to any one man personally.

And now I think it were more fitting that I should close these hasty remarks. It is true that, while I hold myself, without mock modesty, the humblest of all individuals that have ever been elevated to the Presidency, I have a more difficult task to perform than any one of them.

You have generously tendered me the support—the united support—of the great Empire State. For this, in behalf of the nation—in behalf of the present and future of the nation—in behalf of civil and religious liberty for all time to come, most gratefully do I thank you. I do not propose to enter into an explanation of any particular line of policy, as to our present difficulties, to be adopted by the incoming administration. I deem it just to you, to myself, to all, that I should see everything, that I should hear everything, that I should have every light that can be brought within my reach, in order that, when I do so speak, I shall have enjoyed every opportunity to take correct and true ground; and for this reason I do not propose to speak at this time of the policy of the Government. But when the time comes, I shall speak, as well as I am able, for the good of the present and future of this country for the good both of the North and of the South—for the good of the one and the other, and of all sections of the country. In the meantime, if we have patience, if we restrain ourselves, if we allow ourselves not to run off in a passion, I still have confidence that the Almighty, the Maker of the universe, will, through the instrumentality of this great and intelligent people, bring us through this as He has through all the other difficulties of our country. Relying on this, I again thank you for this generous reception.

ADDRESS AT TROY, NEW YORK,

FEBRUARY 19, 1861

MR. MAYOR AND CITIZENS OF TROY:—I thank you very kindly for this great reception. Since I left my home it has not been my fortune to meet an assemblage more numerous and more orderly than this. I am the more gratified at this mark of your regard since you assure me it is tendered, not to the individual but to the high office you have called me to fill. I have neither strength nor time to make any extended remarks on this occasion, and I can only repeat to you my sincere thanks for the kind reception you have thought proper to extend to me.

ADDRESS AT POUGHKEEPSIE, NEW YORK,

FEBRUARY 19, 1861

FELLOW-CITIZENS:—It is altogether impossible I should make myself heard by any considerable portion of this vast assemblage; but, although I appear before you mainly for the purpose of seeing you, and to let you see rather than hear me, I cannot refrain from saying that I am highly gratified—as much here, indeed, under the circumstances, as I have been anywhere on my route—to witness this noble demonstration—made, not in honor of an individual, but of the man who at this time humbly, but earnestly, represents the majesty of the nation.

This reception, like all the others that have been tendered to me, doubtless emanates from all the political parties, and not from one alone. As such I accept it the more gratefully, since it indicates an earnest desire on the part of the whole people, with out regard to political differences, to save—not the country, because the country will save itself but to save the institutions of the country, those institutions under which, in the last three quarters of a century, we have grown to a great, and intelligent, and a happy people—the greatest, the most intelligent, and the happiest people in the world. These noble manifestations indicate, with unerring certainty, that the whole people are willing to make common cause for this object; that if, as it ever must be, some have been successful in the recent election and some have been beaten, if some are satisfied and some are dissatisfied, the defeated party are not in favor of sinking the ship, but are desirous of running it through the tempest in safety, and willing, if they think the people have committed an error in their verdict now, to wait in the hope of reversing it and setting it right next time. I do not say that in the recent election the people did the wisest thing, that could have been done—indeed, I do not think they did; but I do say that in accepting the great trust committed to me, which I do with a determination to endeavor to prove worthy of it, I must rely upon you, upon the people of the whole country, for support; and with their sustaining aid, even I, humble as I am, cannot fail to carry the ship of state safely through the storm.

I have now only to thank you warmly for your kind attendance, and bid you all an affectionate farewell.

ADDRESS AT HUDSON, NEW YORK.

FEBRUARY 19, 1860

FELLOW-CITIZENS:—I see that you are providing a platform for me. I shall have to decline standing upon it, because the president of the company tells me that I shall not have time to wait until it is brought to me. As I said yesterday, under similar circumstances at another gathering, you must not draw the inference that I have any intention of deserting any platform with which I have a legitimate connection because I do not stand on yours. Allow me to thank you for this splendid reception, and I now bid you farewell.

ADDRESS AT PEEKSKILL, NEW YORK,

FEBRUARY 19, 1861

LADIES AND GENTLEMEN:—I have but a moment to stand before you to listen to and return your kind greeting. I thank you for this reception, and for the pleasant manner in which it is tendered to me by our mutual friends. I will say in a single sentence, in regard to the difficulties that lie before me and our beloved country, that if I can only be as generously and unanimously sustained as the demonstrations I have witnessed indicate I shall be, I shall not fail; but without your sustaining hands I am sure that neither I nor any other man can hope to surmount these difficulties. I trust that in the course I shall pursue I shall be sustained not only by the party that elected me, but by the patriotic people of the whole country.

ADDRESS AT FISHKILL LANDING

FEBRUARY 19, 1861

LADIES AND GENTLEMEN:—I appear before you not to make a speech. I have not sufficient time, if I had the strength, to repeat speeches at every station where the people kindly gather to welcome me as we go along. If I had the strength, and should take the time, I should not get to Washington until after the inauguration, which you must be aware would not fit exactly. That such an untoward event might not transpire, I know you will readily forego any further remarks; and I close by bidding you farewell.

REMARKS AT THE ASTOR HOUSE, NEW YORK CITY, FEBRUARY 19, 1861

FELLOW-CITIZENS:—I have stepped before you merely in compliance with what appears to be your wish, and not with the purpose of making a speech. I do not propose making a speech this afternoon. I could not be heard by any but a small fraction of you, at best; but, what is still worse than that, I have nothing just now to say that is worthy of your hearing. I beg you to believe that I do not now refuse to address you from any disposition to disoblige you, but to the contrary. But, at the same time, I beg of you to excuse me for the present.

ADDRESS AT NEW YORK CITY,

FEBRUARY 19, 1861

Mr. CHAIRMAN AND GENTLEMEN:—I am rather an old man to avail myself of such an excuse as I am now about to do. Yet the truth is so distinct, and presses itself so distinctly upon me, that I cannot well avoid it—and that is, that I did not understand when I was brought into this room that I was to be brought here to make a speech. It was not intimated to me that I was brought into the room where Daniel Webster and Henry Clay had made speeches, and where one in my position might be expected to do something like those men or say something worthy of myself or my audience. I therefore beg you to make allowance for the circumstances in which I have been by surprise brought before you. Now I have been in the habit of thinking and sometimes speaking upon political questions that have for some years past agitated the country; and, if I were disposed to do so, and we could take up some one of the issues, as the lawyers call them, and I were called upon to make an argument about it to the best of my ability, I could do so without much preparation. But that is not what you desire to have done here to-night.

I have been occupying a position, since the Presidential election, of silence—of avoiding public speaking, of avoiding public writing. I have been doing so because I thought, upon full consideration, that was the proper course for me to take. I am brought before you now, and required to make a speech, when you all approve more than anything else of the fact that I have been keeping silence. And now it seems to me that the response you give to that remark ought to justify me in closing just here. I have not kept silence since the Presidential election from any party wantonness, or from any indifference to the anxiety that pervades the minds of men about the aspect of the political affairs of this country. I have kept silence for the reason that I supposed it was peculiarly proper that I should do so until the time came when, according to the custom of the country, I could speak officially.

I still suppose that, while the political drama being enacted in this country at this time is rapidly shifting its scenes—forbidding an anticipation with any degree of certainty to-day of what we shall see to-morrow—it is peculiarly fitting that I should see it all, up to the last minute, before I should take ground that I might be disposed, by the shifting of the scenes afterward, also to shift. I have said several times upon this journey, and I now repeat it to you, that when the time does come, I shall then take the ground that I think is right—right for the North, for the South, for the East, for the West, for the whole country. And in doing so I hope to feel no necessity pressing upon me to say anything in conflict with the Constitution, in conflict with the continued union of these States, in conflict with the perpetuation of the liberties of this people, or anything in conflict with anything whatever that I have ever given you reason to expect from me. And now, my friends, have I said enough? [Loud cries of "No, no!" and, "Three cheers for LINCOLN!"] Now, my friends, there appears to be a difference of opinion between you and me, and I really feel called upon to decide the question myself.

REPLY TO THE MAYOR OF NEW YORK CITY,

FEBRUARY 20, 1861

Mr. MAYOR:—It is with feelings of deep gratitude that I make my acknowledgments for the reception that has been given me in the great commercial city of New York. I cannot but remember that it is done by the people who do not, by a large majority, agree with me in political sentiment. It is the more grateful to me because in this I see that for the great principles of our Government the people are pretty nearly or quite unanimous. In regard to the difficulties that confront us at this time, and of which you have seen fit to speak so becomingly and so justly, I can only say I agree with the sentiments expressed. In my devotion to the Union I hope I am behind no man in the nation. As to my wisdom in conducting affairs so as to tend to the preservation of the Union, I fear too great confidence may have been placed in me. I am sure I bring a heart devoted to the work. There is nothing that could ever bring me to consent—willingly to consent—to the destruction of this Union (in which not only the great city of New York, but the whole country, has acquired its greatness), unless it would be that thing for which the Union itself was made. I understand that the ship is made for the carrying and preservation of the cargo; and so long as the ship is safe with the cargo, it shall not be abandoned. This Union shall never be abandoned, unless the possibility of its existence shall cease to exist without the necessity of throwing passengers and cargo overboard. So long, then, as it is possible that the prosperity and liberties of this people can be preserved within this Union, it shall be my purpose at all times to preserve it. And now, Mr. Mayor, renewing my thanks for this cordial reception, allow me to come to a close.

ADDRESS AT JERSEY CITY, NEW JERSEY

FEBRUARY 21, 1860

MR. DAYTON AND GENTLEMEN OF THE STATE OF NEW JERSEY:—I shall only thank you briefly for this very kind reception given me, not personally, but as the temporary representative of the majesty of the nation. To the kindness of your hearts, and of the hearts of your brethren in your State, I should be very proud to respond, but I shall not have strength to address you or other assemblages at length, even if I had the time to do so. I appear before you, therefore, for little else than to greet you, and to briefly say farewell. You have done me the very high honor to present your reception courtesies to me through your great man a man with whom it is an honor to be associated anywhere, and in owning whom no State can be poor. He has said enough, and by the saying of it suggested enough, to require a response of an hour, well considered. I could not in an hour make a worthy response to it. I therefore, ladies and gentlemen of New Jersey, content myself with saying, most heartily do I indorse all the sentiments he has expressed. Allow me, most gratefully, to bid you farewell.

REPLY TO THE MAYOR OF NEWARK, NEW JERSEY,

FEBRUARY 21, 1861.

MR. MAYOR:—I thank you for this reception at the city of Newark. With regard to the great work of which you speak, I will say that I bring to it a heart filled with love for my country, and an honest desire to do what is right. I am sure, however, that I have not the ability to do anything unaided of God, and that without His support and that of this free, happy, prosperous, and intelligent people, no man can succeed in doing that the importance of which we all comprehend. Again thanking you for the reception you have given me, I will now bid you farewell, and proceed upon my journey.

ADDRESS IN TRENTON AT THE TRENTON HOUSE,

FEBRUARY 21, 1861

I have been invited by your representatives to the Legislature to visit this the capital of your honored State, and in acknowledging their kind invitation, compelled to respond to the welcome of the presiding officers of each body, and I suppose they intended I should speak to you through them, as they are the representatives of all of you; and if I were to speak again here, I should only have to repeat in a great measure much that I have said, which would be disgusting to my friends around me who have met here. I have no speech to make, but merely appear to see you and let you look at me; and as to the latter I think I have greatly the best of the bargain. My friends, allow me to bid you farewell.

ADDRESS TO THE SENATE OF NEW JERSEY

FEBRUARY 21, 1861

MR. PRESIDENT AND GENTLEMEN OF THE SENATE OF THE STATE OF NEW JERSEY:—I am very grateful to you for the honorable reception of which I have been the object. I cannot but remember the place that New Jersey holds in our early history. In the Revolutionary struggle few of the States among the Old Thirteen had more of the battle-fields of the country within their limits than New Jersey. May I be pardoned if, upon this occasion, I mention that away back in my childhood, the earliest days of my being able to read, I got hold of a small book, such a one as few of the younger members have ever seen Weems's Life of Washington. I remember all the accounts there given of the battle-fields and struggles for the liberties of the country; and none fixed themselves upon my imagination so deeply as the struggle here at Trenton, New Jersey. The crossing of the river, the contest with the Hessians, the great hardships endured at that time, all fixed themselves on my memory more than any single Revolutionary event; and you all know, for you have all been boys, how these early impressions last longer than any others. I recollect thinking then, boy even though I was, that there must have been something more than common that these men struggled for. I am exceedingly anxious that that thing that something even more than national independence, that something that held out a great promise to all the people of the world to all time to come—I am exceedingly anxious that this Union, the Constitution, and the liberties of the people shall be perpetuated in accordance with the original idea for which that struggle was made; and I shall be most happy indeed if I shall be a humble instrument in the hands of the Almighty, and of this his almost chosen people, for perpetuating the object of that great struggle. You give me this reception, as I understand, without distinction of party. I learn that this body is composed of a majority of gentlemen who, in the exercise of their best judgment in the choice of a chief magistrate, did not think I was the man. I understand, nevertheless, that they come forward here to greet me as the constitutionally elected President of the United States—as citizens of the United States to meet the man who, for the time being, is the representative of the majesty of the nation—united by the single purpose to perpetuate the Constitution, the union, and the liberties of the people. As such, I accept this reception more gratefully than I could do did I believe it were tendered to me as an individual.

ADDRESS TO THE ASSEMBLY OF NEW JERSEY,

FEBRUARY 21, 1861

MR. SPEAKER AND GENTLEMEN: I have just enjoyed the honor of a reception by the other branch of this Legislature, and I return to you and them my thanks for the reception which the people of New Jersey have given through their chosen representatives to me as the representative, for the time being, of the majesty of the people of the United States. I appropriate to myself very little of the demonstrations of respect with which I have been greeted. I think little should be given to any man, but that it should be a manifestation of adherence to the Union and the Constitution. I understand myself to be received here by the representatives of the people of New Jersey, a majority of whom differ in opinion from those with whom I have acted. This manifestation is therefore to be regarded by me as expressing their devotion to the Union, the Constitution, and the liberties of the people.
You, Mr. Speaker, have well said that this is a time when the bravest and wisest look with doubt and awe upon the aspect presented by our national affairs. Under these circumstances you will readily see why I should not speak in detail of the course I shall deem it best to pursue. It is proper that I should avail myself of all the information and all the time at my command, in order that when the time arrives in which I must speak officially, I shall be able to take the ground

which I deem best and safest, and from which I may have no occasion to swerve. I shall endeavor to take the ground I deem most just to the North, the East, the West, the South, and the whole country. I shall take it, I hope, in good temper, certainly with no malice toward any section. I shall do all that may be in my power to promote a peaceful settlement of all our difficulties. The man does not live who is more devoted to peace than I am, none who would do more to preserve it, but it may be necessary to put the foot down firmly. And if I do my duty and do right, you will sustain me, will you not? [Loud cheers, and cries of "Yes, yes; we will."] Received as I am by the members of a Legislature the majority of whom do not agree with me in political sentiments, I trust that I may have their assistance in piloting the ship of state through this voyage, surrounded by perils as it is; for if it should suffer wreck now, there will be no pilot ever needed for another voyage.

Gentlemen, I have already spoken longer than I intended, and must beg leave to stop here.

REPLY TO THE MAYOR OF PHILADELPHIA, PENNSYLVANIA,

FEBRUARY 21, 1861

MR. MAYOR AND FELLOW-CITIZENS OF PHILADELPHIA:—I appear before you to make no lengthy speech, but to thank you for this reception. The reception you have given me to-night is not to me, the man, the individual, but to the man who temporarily represents, or should represent, the majesty of the nation. It is true, as your worthy mayor has said, that there is great anxiety amongst the citizens of the United States at this time. I deem it a happy circumstance that this dissatisfied portion of our fellow-citizens does not point us to anything in which they are being injured or about to be injured; for which reason I have felt all the while justified in concluding that the crisis, the panic, the anxiety of the country at this time is artificial. If there be those who differ with me upon this subject, they have not pointed out the substantial difficulty that exists. I do not mean to say that an artificial panic may not do considerable harm; that it has done such I do not deny. The hope that has been expressed by your mayor, that I may be able to restore peace, harmony, and prosperity to the country, is most worthy of him; and most happy, indeed, will I be if I shall be able to verify and fulfil that hope. I promise you that I bring to the work a sincere heart. Whether I will bring a head equal to that heart will be for future times to determine. It were useless for me to speak of details of plans now; I shall speak officially next Monday week, if ever. If I should not speak then, it were useless for me to do so now. If I do speak then, it is useless for me to do so now. When I do speak, I shall take such ground as I deem best calculated to restore peace, harmony, and prosperity to the country, and tend to the perpetuity of the nation and the liberty of these States and these people. Your worthy mayor has expressed the wish, in which I join with him, that it were convenient for me to remain in your city long enough to consult your merchants and manufacturers; or, as it were, to listen to those breathings rising within the consecrated walls wherein the Constitution of the United States and, I will add, the Declaration of Independence, were originally framed and adopted. I assure you and your mayor that I had hoped on this occasion, and upon all occasions during my life, that I shall do nothing inconsistent with the teachings of these holy and most sacred walls. I have never asked anything that does not breathe from those walls. All my political warfare has been in favor of the teachings that come forth from these sacred walls. May my right hand forget its cunning and my tongue cleave to the roof of my mouth if ever I prove false to those teachings. Fellow-citizens, I have addressed you longer than I expected to do, and now allow me to bid you goodnight.

ADDRESS IN THE HALL OF INDEPENDENCE, PHILADELPHIA,

FEBRUARY 22, 1861

MR. CUYLER:—I am filled with deep emotion at finding myself standing here, in this place, where were collected together the wisdom, the devotion to principle, from which sprang the institutions under which we live. You have kindly suggested to me that in my hands is the task of restoring peace to the present distracted condition of the country. I can say in return, sir, that all the political sentiments I entertain have been drawn, so far as I have been able to draw them, from the sentiments which originated and were given to the world from this hall. I have never had a feeling politically that did not spring from the sentiments embodied in the Declaration of Independence. I have often pondered over the dangers which were incurred by the men who assembled here and framed and adopted that Declaration of Independence. I have pondered over the toils that were endured by the officers and soldiers of the army who achieved that independence. I have often inquired of myself what great principle or idea it was that kept the confederacy so long together. It was not the mere matter of separation of the colonies from the motherland, but that sentiment in the Declaration of Independence which gave liberty, not alone to the people of this country, but, I hope, to the world for all future time. It was that which gave promise that in due time the weight would be lifted from the shoulders of all men. This is the sentiment embodied in the Declaration of Independence. Now, my friends, can the country be saved upon that basis? If it can, I will consider myself one of the happiest men in the world if I can help to save it. If it cannot be saved upon that principle, it will be truly awful. But if this country cannot be saved without giving up that principle, I was about to say I would rather be assassinated on this spot than surrender it. Now, in my view of the present aspect of affairs, there need be no bloodshed or war. There is no necessity for it. I am not in favor of such a course, and I may say, in advance, that there will be no bloodshed unless it is forced upon the Government, and then it will be compelled to act in self-defence.

My friends; this is wholly an unexpected speech, and I did not expect to be called upon to say a word when I came here. I supposed it was merely to do something toward raising the flag. I may, therefore, have said something indiscreet. I have said nothing but what I am willing to live by and, if it be the pleasure of Almighty God, die by.

REPLY TO THE WILMINGTON DELEGATION,

FEBRUARY 22, 1861

MR. CHAIRMAN:—I feel highly flattered by the encomiums you have seen fit to bestow upon me. Soon after the nomination of General Taylor, I attended a political meeting in the city of Wilmington, and have since carried with me a fond remembrance of the hospitalities of the city on that occasion. The programme established provides for my presence in Harrisburg in twenty-four hours from this time. I expect to be in Washington on Saturday. It is, therefore, an impossibility that I should accept your kind invitation. There are no people whom I would more gladly accommodate than those of Delaware; but circumstances forbid, gentlemen. With many regrets for the character of the reply I am compelled to give you, I bid you adieu.

ADDRESS AT LANCASTER, PENNSYLVANIA,

FEBRUARY 22, 1860

LADIES AND GENTLEMEN OF OLD LANCASTER:—I appear not to make a speech. I have not time to make a speech at length, and not strength to make them on every occasion; and, worse than all, I have none to make. There is plenty of matter to speak about in these times, but it is well known that the more a man speaks the less he is understood—the more he says one thing, the more his adversaries contend he meant something else. I shall soon have occasion to speak officially, and then I will endeavor to put my thoughts just as plain as I can express myself—true to the Constitution and Union of all the States, and to the perpetual liberty of all the people. Until I so speak, there is no need to enter upon details. In conclusion, I greet you most heartily, and bid you an affectionate farewell.

ADDRESS TO THE LEGISLATURE OF PENNSYLVANIA, AT HARRISBURG,

FEBRUARY 22, 1861

MR. SPEAKER OF THE SENATE, AND ALSO MR. SPEAKER OF THE HOUSE OF REPRESENTATIVES, AND GENTLEMEN OF THE GENERAL ASSEMBLY OF THE STATE OF PENNSYLVANIA:—I appear before you only for a very few brief remarks in response to what has been said to me. I thank you most sincerely for this reception, and the generous words in which support has been promised me upon this occasion. I thank your great commonwealth for the overwhelming support it recently gave, not me personally, but the cause which I think a just one, in the late election.

Allusion has been made to the fact—the interesting fact perhaps we should say—that I for the first time appear at the capital of the great commonwealth of Pennsylvania upon the birthday of the Father of his Country. In connection with that beloved anniversary connected with the history of this country, I have already gone through one exceedingly interesting scene this morning in the ceremonies at Philadelphia. Under the kind conduct of gentlemen there, I was for the first time allowed the privilege of standing in old Independence Hall to have a few words addressed to me there, and opening up to me an opportunity of manifesting my deep regret that I had not more time to express something of my own feelings excited by the occasion, that had been really the feelings of my whole life.

Besides this, our friends there had provided a magnificent flag of the country. They had arranged it so that I was given the honor of raising it to the head of its staff, and when it went up I was pleased that it went to its place by the strength of my own feeble arm. When, according to the arrangement, the cord was pulled, and it floated gloriously to the wind, without an accident, in the bright, glowing sunshine of the morning, I could not help hoping that there was in the entire success of that beautiful ceremony at least something of an omen of what is to come. Nor could I help feeling then, as I have often felt, that in the whole of that proceeding I was a very humbled instrument. I had not provided the flag; I had not made the arrangements for elevating it to its place; I had applied but a very small portion of even my feeble strength in raising it. In the whole transaction I was in the hands of the people who had arranged it, and if I can have the same generous co-operation of the people of this nation, I think the flag of our country may yet be kept flaunting gloriously.

I recur for a moment but to repeat some words uttered at the hotel in regard to what has been said about the military support which the General Government may expect from the commonwealth of Pennsylvania in a proper emergency. To guard against any possible mistake do I recur to this. It is not with any pleasure that I contemplate the possibility that a necessity may arise in this country for the use of the military arm. While I am exceedingly gratified to see the manifestation upon your streets of your military force here, and exceedingly gratified at your promise to use that force upon a proper emergency—while I make these acknowledgments I desire to repeat, in order to preclude any possible misconstruction, that I do most sincerely hope that we shall have no use for them; that it will never become their duty to shed blood, and most especially never to shed fraternal blood. I promise that so far as I may have wisdom to direct, if so painful a result shall in any wise be brought about, it shall be through no fault of mine.

Allusion has also been made by one of your honored speakers to some remarks recently made by myself at Pittsburg in regard to what is supposed to be the especial interest of this great commonwealth of Pennsylvania. I now wish only to say in regard to that matter, that the few remarks which I uttered on that occasion were rather carefully worded. I took pains that they should be so. I have seen no occasion since to add to them or subtract from them. I leave them precisely as they stand, adding only now that I am pleased to have an expression from you, gentlemen of Pennsylvania, signifying that they are satisfactory to you.

And now, gentlemen of the General Assembly of the Commonwealth of Pennsylvania, allow me again to return to you my most sincere thanks.

REPLY TO THE MAYOR OF WASHINGTON, D.C.,

FEBRUARY 27, 1861

Mr. MAYOR:—I thank you, and through you the municipal authorities of this city who accompany you, for this welcome. And as it is the first time in my life, since the present phase of politics has presented itself in this country, that I have said anything publicly within a region of country where the institution of slavery exists, I will take this occasion to say that I think very much of the ill feeling that has existed and still exists between the people in the section from which I came and the people here, is dependent upon a misunderstanding of one another. I therefore avail myself of this opportunity to assure you, Mr. Mayor, and all the gentlemen present, that I have not now, and never have had, any other than as kindly feelings toward you as to the people of my own section. I have not now, and never have had, any disposition to treat you in any respect otherwise than as my own neighbors. I have not now any purpose to withhold from you any of the benefits of the Constitution, under any circumstances, that I would not feel myself constrained to withhold from my own neighbors; and I hope, in a word, that when we shall become better acquainted—and I say it with great confidence—we shall like each other better. I thank you for the kindness of this reception.

REPLY TO A SERENADE AT WASHINGTON, D.C.,

FEBRUARY 28, 1861

MY FRIENDS:—I suppose that I may take this as a compliment paid to me, and as such please accept my thanks for it. I have reached this city of Washington under circumstances considerably differing from those under which any other man has ever reached it. I am here for the purpose of taking an official position amongst the people, almost all of whom were politically opposed to me, and are yet opposed to me, as I suppose.
I propose no lengthy address to you. I only propose to say, as I did on yesterday, when your worthy mayor and board of aldermen called upon me, that I thought much of the ill feeling that has existed between you and the people of your surroundings and that people from among whom I came, has depended, and now depends, upon a misunderstanding. I hope that, if things shall go along as prosperously as I believe we all desire they may, I may have it in my power to remove something of this misunderstanding; that I may be enabled to convince you, and the people of your section of the country, that we regard you as in all things our equals, and in all things entitled to the same respect and the same treatment that we claim for ourselves; that we are in no wise disposed, if it were in our power, to oppress you, to deprive you of any of your rights under the Constitution of the United States, or even narrowly to split hairs with you in regard to these rights, but are determined to give you, as far as lies in our hands, all your rights under the Constitution—not grudgingly, but fully and fairly. I hope that, by thus dealing with you, we will become better acquainted, and be better friends.
And now, my friends, with these few remarks, and again returning my thanks for this compliment, and expressing my desire to hear a little more of your good music, I bid you good-night.

WASHINGTON, SUNDAY, MARCH 3, 1861

[During the struggle over the appointments of LINCOLN's Cabinet, the President-elect spoke as follows:]
Gentlemen, it is evident that some one must take the responsibility of these appointments, and I will do it. My Cabinet is completed. The positions are not definitely assigned, and will not be until I announce them privately to the gentlemen whom I have selected as my Constitutional advisers.

FIRST INAUGURAL ADDRESS, MARCH 4, 1861

FELLOW-CITIZENS OF THE UNITED STATES:—In compliance with a custom as old as the Government itself, I appear before you to address you briefly, and to take in your presence the oath prescribed by the Constitution of the United States to be taken by the President "before he enters on the execution of his office."
I do not consider it necessary at present for me to discuss those matters of administration about which there is no special anxiety or excitement.
Apprehension seems to exist among the people of the Southern States that by the accession of a Republican administration their property and their peace and personal security are to be endangered. There has never been any reasonable cause for such apprehension. Indeed, the most ample evidence to the contrary has all the while existed and been open to their inspection. It is found in nearly all the published speeches of him who now addresses you. I do but quote from one of those speeches when I declare that
"I have no purpose, directly or indirectly, to interfere with the institution of slavery in the States where it exists. I believe I have no lawful right to do so, and I have no inclination to do so."
Those who nominated and elected me did so with full knowledge that I had made this and many similar declarations, and had never recanted them. And, more than this, they placed in the platform for my acceptance, and as a law to themselves and to me, the clear and emphatic resolution which I now read:
"Resolved, That the maintenance inviolate of the rights of the States, and especially the right of each State to order and control its own domestic institutions according to its own judgment exclusively, is essential to that balance of power on which the perfection and endurance of our political fabric depend, and we denounce the lawless invasion by armed force of the soil of any State or Territory, no matter under what pretext, as amongst the gravest of crimes."
I now reiterate these sentiments; and, in doing so, I only press upon the public attention the most conclusive evidence of which the case is susceptible, that the property, peace, and security of no section are to be in any wise endangered by the now incoming administration. I add, too, that all the protection which, consistently with the Constitution and

the laws, can be given, will be cheerfully given to all the States when lawfully demanded, for whatever cause—as cheerfully to one section as to another.

There is much controversy about the delivering up of fugitives from service or labor. The clause I now read is as plainly written in the Constitution as any other of its provisions:

"No person held to service or labor in one State, under the laws thereof, escaping into another, shall in consequence of any law or regulation therein be discharged from such service or labor, but shall be delivered up on claim of the party to whom such service or labor may be due."

It is scarcely questioned that this provision was intended by those who made it for the reclaiming of what we call fugitive slaves; and the intention of the lawgiver is the law. All members of Congress swear their support to the whole Constitution—to this provision as much as to any other. To the proposition, then, that slaves whose cases come within the terms of this clause "shall be delivered up," their oaths are unanimous. Now, if they would make the effort in good temper, could they not with nearly equal unanimity frame and pass a law by means of which to keep good that unanimous oath?

There is some difference of opinion whether this clause should be enforced by national or by State authority; but surely that difference is not a very material one. If the slave is to be surrendered, it can be of but little consequence to him or to others by which authority it is done. And should any one in any case be content that his oath shall go unkept on a merely unsubstantial controversy as to how it shall be kept?

Again, in any law upon this subject, ought not all the safeguards of liberty known in civilized and humane jurisprudence to be introduced, so that a free man be not, in any case, surrendered as a slave? And might it not be well at the same time to provide by law for the enforcement of that clause in the Constitution which guarantees that "the citizens of each State shall be entitled to all privileges and immunities of citizens in the several States"?

I take the official oath to-day with no mental reservations, and with no purpose to construe the Constitution or laws by any hypercritical rules. And, while I do not choose now to specify particular acts of Congress as proper to be enforced, I do suggest that it will be much safer for all, both in official and private stations, to conform to and abide by all those acts which stand unrepealed, than to violate any of them, trusting to find impunity in having them held to be unconstitutional.

It is seventy-two years since the first inauguration of a President under our national Constitution. During that period fifteen different and greatly distinguished citizens have, in succession, administered the executive branch of the Government. They have conducted it through many perils, and generally with great success. Yet, with all this scope of precedent, I now enter upon the same task for the brief constitutional term of four years under great and peculiar difficulty. A disruption of the Federal Union, heretofore only menaced, is now formidably attempted.

I hold that, in contemplation of universal law and of the Constitution, the Union of these States is perpetual. Perpetuity is implied, if not expressed, in the fundamental law of all national governments. It is safe to assert that no government proper ever had a provision in its organic law for its own termination. Continue to execute all the express provisions of our national Constitution, and the Union will endure forever—it being impossible to destroy it except by some action not provided for in the instrument itself.

Again, if the United States be not a government proper, but an association of States in the nature of contract merely, can it as a contract be peaceably unmade by less than all the parties who made it? One party to a contract may violate it—break it, so to speak; but does it not require all to lawfully rescind it?

Descending from these general principles, we find the proposition that in legal contemplation the Union is perpetual confirmed by the history of the Union itself. The Union is much older than the Constitution. It was formed, in fact, by the Articles of Association in 1774. It was matured and continued by the Declaration of Independence in 1776. It was further matured, and the faith of all the then thirteen States expressly plighted and engaged that it should be perpetual, by the Articles of Confederation in 1778. And, finally, in 1787 one of the declared objects for ordaining and establishing the Constitution was "to form a more perfect Union."

But if the destruction of the Union by one or by a part only of the States be lawfully possible, the Union is less perfect than before the Constitution, having lost the vital element of perpetuity.

It follows from these views that no State upon its own mere motion can lawfully get out of the Union; that resolves and ordinances to that effect are legally void; and that acts of violence, within any State or States, against the authority of the United States, are insurrectionary or revolutionary, according to circumstances.

I therefore consider that, in view of the Constitution and the laws, the Union is unbroken; and to the extent of my ability I shall take care, as the Constitution itself expressly enjoins upon me, that the laws of the Union be faithfully executed in all the States. Doing this I deem to be only a simple duty on my part; and I shall perform it so far as practicable, unless my rightful masters, the American people, shall withhold the requisite means, or in some authoritative manner direct the contrary. I trust this will not be regarded as a menace, but only as the declared purpose of the Union that it will constitutionally defend and maintain itself.

In doing this there needs to be no bloodshed or violence; and there shall be none, unless it be forced upon the national authority. The power confided to me will be used to hold, occupy, and possess the property and places belonging to the Government, and to collect the duties and imposts; but beyond what may be necessary for these objects, there will be no invasion, no using of force against or among the people anywhere. Where hostility to the United States, in any interior locality, shall be so great and universal as to prevent competent resident citizens from holding the Federal offices, there will be no attempt to force obnoxious strangers among the people for that object. While the strict legal right may exist in the government to enforce the exercise of these offices, the attempt to do so would be so irritating, and so nearly impracticable withal, that I deem it better to forego for the time the uses of such offices.

The mails, unless repelled, will continue to be furnished in all parts of the Union. So far as possible, the people everywhere shall have that sense of perfect security which is most favorable to calm thought and reflection. The course here indicated will be followed unless current events and experience shall show a modification or change to be proper, and in every case and exigency my best discretion will be exercised according to circumstances actually existing, and with a view and a hope of a peaceful solution of the national troubles and the restoration of fraternal sympathies and affections.

That there are persons in one section or another who seek to destroy the Union at all events, and are glad of any pretext to do it, I will neither affirm nor deny; but if there be such, I need address no word to them. To those, however, who really love the Union may I not speak?

Before entering upon so grave a matter as the destruction of our national fabric, with all its benefits, its memories, and its hopes, would it not be wise to ascertain precisely why we do it? Will you hazard so desperate a step while there is any possibility that any portion of the ills you fly from have no real existence? Will you, while the certain ills you fly to are greater than all the real ones you fly from—will you risk the commission of so fearful a mistake?

All profess to be content in the Union if all constitutional rights can be maintained. Is it true, then, that any right, plainly written in the Constitution, has been denied? I think not. Happily the human mind is so constituted that no party can reach to the audacity of doing this. Think, if you can, of a single instance in which a plainly written provision of the Constitution has ever been denied. If by the mere force of numbers a majority should deprive a minority of any clearly written constitutional right, it might, in a moral point of view, justify revolution—certainly would if such a right were a vital one. But such is not our case. All the vital rights of minorities and of individuals are so plainly assured to them by affirmations and negations, guaranties and prohibitions, in the Constitution, that controversies never arise concerning them. But no organic law can ever be framed with a provision specifically applicable to every question which may occur in practical administration. No foresight can anticipate, nor any document of reasonable length contain, express provisions for all possible questions. Shall fugitives from labor be surrendered by national or by State authority? The Constitution does not expressly say. May Congress prohibit slavery in the Territories? The Constitution does not expressly say. Must Congress protect slavery in the Territories? The Constitution does not expressly say.

From questions of this class spring all our constitutional controversies, and we divide upon them into majorities and minorities. If the minority will not acquiesce, the majority must, or the Government must cease. There is no other alternative; for continuing the Government is acquiescence on one side or the other.

If a minority in such case will secede rather than acquiesce, they make a precedent which in turn will divide and ruin them; for a minority of their own will secede from them whenever a majority refuses to be controlled by such minority. For instance, why may not any portion of a new confederacy a year or two hence arbitrarily secede again, precisely as portions of the present Union now claim to secede from it? All who cherish disunion sentiments are now being educated to the exact temper of doing this.

Is there such perfect identity of interests among the States to compose a new Union as to produce harmony only, and prevent renewed secession?

Plainly, the central idea of secession is the essence of anarchy. A majority held in restraint by constitutional checks and limitations, and always changing easily with deliberate changes of popular opinions and sentiments, is the only true sovereign of a free people. Whoever rejects it does, of necessity, fly to anarchy or to despotism. Unanimity is impossible; the rule of a minority, as a permanent arrangement, is wholly inadmissible; so that, rejecting the majority principle, anarchy or despotism in some form is all that is left.

I do not forget the position assumed by some, that constitutional questions are to be decided by the Supreme Court; nor do I deny that such decisions must be binding, in any case, upon the parties to a suit, as to the object of that suit, while they are also entitled to very high respect and consideration in all parallel cases by all other departments of the government. And, while it is obviously possible that such decision may be erroneous in any given case, still the evil effect following it, being limited to that particular case, with the chance that it may be overruled and never become a precedent for other cases, can better be borne than could the evils of a different practice. At the same time, the candid citizen must confess that if the policy of the government, upon vital questions affecting the whole people, is to be irrevocably fixed by decisions of the Supreme Court, the instant they are made, in ordinary litigation between parties in personal actions, the people will have ceased to be their own rulers, having to that extent practically resigned the government into the hands of that eminent tribunal. Nor is there in this view any assault upon the court or the judges. It is a duty from which they may not shrink to decide cases properly brought before them, and it is no fault of theirs if others seek to turn their decisions to political purposes.

One section of our country believes slavery is right, and ought to be extended, while the other believes it is wrong, and ought not to be extended. This is the only substantial dispute. The fugitive slave clause of the Constitution and the law for the suppression of the foreign slave trade are each as well enforced, perhaps, as any law can ever be in a community where the moral sense of the people imperfectly supports the law itself. The great body of the people abide by the dry legal obligation in both cases, and a few break over in each. This, I think, cannot be perfectly cured; and it would be worse in both cases after the separation of the sections than before. The foreign slave trade, now imperfectly suppressed, would be ultimately revived, without restriction, in one section, while fugitive slaves, now only partially surrendered, would not be surrendered at all by the other.

Physically speaking, we cannot separate. We cannot remove our respective sections from each other, nor build an impassable wall between them. A husband and wife may be divorced and go out of the presence and beyond the reach of each other; but the different parts of our country cannot do this. They cannot but remain face to face, and intercourse, either amicable or hostile, must continue between them. Is it possible, then, to make that intercourse more advantageous or more satisfactory after separation than before? Can aliens make treaties easier than friends can make laws? Can treaties be more faithfully enforced between aliens than laws can among friends? Suppose you go to war, you cannot fight always; and when, after much loss on both sides, and no gain on either, you cease fighting, the identical old questions as to terms of intercourse are again upon you.

This country, with its institutions, belongs to the people who inhabit it. Whenever they shall grow weary of the existing government, they can exercise their constitutional right of amending it, or their revolutionary right to dismember or overthrow it. I cannot be ignorant of the fact that many worthy and patriotic citizens are desirous of having the national Constitution amended. While I make no recommendation of amendments, I fully recognize the rightful authority of the people over the whole subject, to be exercised in either of the modes prescribed in the instrument itself, and I should, under existing circumstances, favor rather than oppose a fair opportunity being afforded the people to act upon it. I will venture to add that to me the convention mode seems preferable, in that it allows amendments to originate with the people themselves, instead of only permitting them to take or reject propositions originated by others not especially chosen for the purpose, and which might not be precisely such as they would wish to either accept or refuse. I understand a proposed amendment to the Constitution which amendment, however, I have not seen—has passed Congress, to the effect that the Federal Government shall never interfere with the domestic institutions of the States, including that of persons held to service. To avoid misconstruction of what I have said, I depart from my purpose not to speak of particular amendments so far as to say that, holding such a provision to now be implied constitutional law, I have no objection to its being made express and irrevocable.

The chief magistrate derives all his authority from the people, and they have conferred none upon him to fix terms for the separation of the States. The people themselves can do this also if they choose; but the executive, as such, has nothing to do with it. His duty is to administer the present government, as it came to his hands, and to transmit it, unimpaired by him, to his successors.

Why should there not be a patient confidence in the ultimate justice of the people? Is there any better or equal hope in the world? In our present differences is either party without faith of being in the right? If the Almighty Ruler of nations, with his eternal truth and justice, be on your side of the North, or on yours of the South, that truth and that justice will surely prevail by the judgment of this great tribunal of the American people.

By the frame of the government under which we live, this same people have wisely given their public servants but little power for mischief; and have, with equal wisdom, provided for the return of that little to their own hands at very short intervals. While the people retain their virtue and vigilance, no administration, by any extreme of wickedness or folly, can very seriously injure the government in the short space of four years.

My countrymen, one and all, think calmly and well upon this whole subject. Nothing valuable can be lost by taking time. If there be an object to hurry any of you in hot haste to a step which you would never take deliberately, that object will be frustrated by taking time; but no good object can be frustrated by it. Such of you as are now dissatisfied still have the old Constitution unimpaired, and, on the sensitive point, the laws of your own framing under it; while the new administration will have no immediate power, if it would, to change either. If it were admitted that you who are dissatisfied hold the right side in the dispute, there still is no single good reason for precipitate action. Intelligence, patriotism, Christianity, and a firm reliance on Him who has never yet forsaken this favored land, are still competent to adjust in the best way all our present difficulty.

In your hands, my dissatisfied fellow-countrymen, and not in mine, is the momentous issue of civil war. The government will not assail you. You can have no conflict without being yourselves the aggressors. You have no oath registered in heaven to destroy the government, while I shall have the most solemn one to "preserve, protect, and defend" it.

I am loath to close. We are not enemies, but friends. We must not be enemies. Though passion may have strained, it must not break, our bonds of affection. The mystic chords of memory, stretching from every battle-field and patriot grave to every living heart and hearthstone all over this broad land, will yet swell the chorus of the Union when again touched, as surely they will be, by the better angels of our nature.

REFUSAL OF SEWARD RESIGNATION

TO WM. H. SEWARD.

EXECUTIVE MANSION, March 4, 1861.
MY DEAR SIR:—Your note of the 2d instant, asking to withdraw your acceptance of my invitation to take charge of the State Department, was duly received. It is the subject of the most painful solicitude with me, and I feel constrained to beg that you will countermand the withdrawal. The public interest, I think, demands that you should; and my personal feelings are deeply enlisted in the same direction. Please consider and answer by 9 A.M. to-morrow.
Your obedient servant,
A. LINCOLN.

REPLY TO THE PENNSYLVANIA DELEGATION,

WASHINGTON, MARCH 5, 1861

Mr. CHAIRMAN AND GENTLEMEN OF THE PENNSYLVANIAN DELEGATION:—As I have so frequently said heretofore, when I have had occasion to address the people of the Keystone, in my visits to that State, I can now but repeat the assurance of my gratification at the support you gave me at the election, and at the promise of a continuation of that support which is now tendered to me.
Allusion has been made to the hope that you entertain that you have a President and a government. In respect to that I wish to say to you that in the position I have assumed I wish to do more than I have ever given reason to believe I would do. I do not wish you to believe that I assume to be any better than others who have gone before me. I prefer rather to have it understood that if we ever have a government on the principles we profess, we should remember, while we exercise our opinion, that others have also rights to the exercise of their opinions, and that we should endeavor to allow these rights, and act in such a manner as to create no bad feeling. I hope we have a government and a President. I hope, and wish it to be understood, that there may be no allusion to unpleasant differences.
We must remember that the people of all the States are entitled to all the privileges and immunities of the citizens of the several States. We should bear this in mind, and act in such a way as to say nothing insulting or irritating. I would inculcate this idea, so that we may not, like Pharisees, set ourselves up to be better than other people.
Now, my friends, my public duties are pressing to-day, and will prevent my giving more time to you. Indeed, I should not have left them now, but I could not well deny myself to so large and respectable a body.

REPLY TO THE MASSACHUSETTS DELEGATION,

WASHINGTON, MARCH 5, 1861

I am thankful for this renewed assurance of kind feeling and confidence, and the support of the old Bay State, in so far as you, Mr. Chairman, have expressed, in behalf of those whom you represent, your sanction of what I have enunciated in my inaugural address. This is very grateful to my feelings. The object was one of great delicacy, in presenting views at the opening of an administration under the peculiar circumstances attending my entrance upon the official duties connected with the Government. I studied all the points with great anxiety, and presented them with whatever of ability and sense of justice I could bring to bear. If it met the approbation of our good friends in Massachusetts, I shall be exceedingly gratified, while I hope it will meet the approbation of friends everywhere. I am thankful for the expressions of those who have voted with us; and like every other man of you, I like them as certainly as I do others. As the President in the administration of the Government, I hope to be man enough not to know one citizen of the United States from another, nor one section from another. I shall be gratified to have good friends of Massachusetts and others who have thus far supported me in these national views still to support me in carrying them out.

TO SECRETARY SEWARD

EXECUTIVE CHAMBER, MARCH 7, 1861

MY DEAR SIR:—Herewith is the diplomatic address and my reply. To whom the reply should be addressed—that is, by what title or style—I do not quite understand, and therefore I have left it blank.
Will you please bring with you to-day the message from the War Department, with General Scott's note upon it, which we had here yesterday? I wish to examine the General's opinion, which I have not yet done.
Yours very truly
A. LINCOLN.

REPLY TO THE DIPLOMATIC CORPS

WASHINGTON, THURSDAY, MARCH 7, 1861

Mr. FIGANIERE AND GENTLEMEN OF THE DIPLOMATIC BODY:—Please accept my sincere thanks for your kind congratulations. It affords me pleasure to confirm the confidence you so generously express in the friendly disposition of the United States, through me, towards the sovereigns and governments you respectively represent. With equal satisfaction I accept the assurance you are pleased to give, that the same disposition is reciprocated by your sovereigns, your governments, and yourselves.
Allow me to express the hope that these friendly relations may remain undisturbed, and also my fervent wishes for the health and happiness of yourselves personally.

TO SECRETARY SEWARD

EXECUTIVE MANSION, MARCH 11, 1861

HON. SECRETARY OF STATE. DEAR SIR:—What think you of sending ministers at once as follows: Dayton to England; Fremont to France; Clay to Spain; Corwin to Mexico?
We need to have these points guarded as strongly and quickly as possible. This is suggestion merely, and not dictation.
Your obedient servant,
A. LINCOLN.

TO J. COLLAMER

EXECUTIVE MANSION, MARCH 12, 1861

HON. JACOB COLLAMER. MY DEAR SIR:—God help me. It is said I have offended you. I hope you will tell me how.
Yours very truly,
A. LINCOLN.
March 14, 1861. DEAR SIR:—I am entirely unconscious that you have any way offended me. I cherish no sentiment towards you but that of kindness and confidence. Your humble servant, J. COLLAMER.
[Returned with indorsement:]
Very glad to know that I have n't.

A. LINCOLN.

TO THE POSTMASTER-GENERAL.

EXECUTIVE MANSION, MARCH 13, 1861

HON. P. M. G.
DEAR SIR:—The bearer of this, Mr. C. T. Hempstow, is a Virginian who wishes to get, for his son, a small place in your Dept. I think Virginia should be heard, in such cases.
LINCOLN.

NOTE ASKING CABINET OPINIONS ON FORT SUMTER.

EXECUTIVE MANSION, MARCH 15, 1861

THE HONORABLE SECRETARY OF WAR.
MY DEAR SIR:—Assuming it to be possible to now provision Fort Sumter, under all the circumstances is it wise to attempt it? Please give me your opinion in writing on this question.
Your obedient servant,
A. LINCOLN.
[Same to other members of the Cabinet.]

ON ROYAL ARBITRATION OF AMERICAN BOUNDARY LINE

TO THE SENATE OF THE UNITED STATES

The Senate has transmitted to me a copy of the message sent by my predecessor to that body on the 21st of February last, proposing to take its advice on the subject of a proposition made by the British Government through its minister here to refer the matter in controversy between that government and the Government of the United States to the arbitrament of the King of Sweden and Norway, the King of the Netherlands, or the Republic of the Swiss Confederation.
In that message my predecessor stated that he wished to present to the Senate the precise questions following, namely: "Will the Senate approve a treaty referring to either of the sovereign powers above named the dispute now existing between the governments of the United States and Great Britain concerning the boundary line between Vancouver's Island and the American continent? In case the referee shall find himself unable to decide where the line is by the description of it in the treaty of June 15, 1846, shall he be authorized to establish a line according to the treaty as nearly as possible? Which of the three powers named by Great Britain as an arbiter shall be chosen by the United States?"
I find no reason to disapprove of the course of my predecessor in this important matter; but, on the contrary, I not only shall receive the advice of the Senate thereon cheerfully, but I respectfully ask the Senate for their advice on the three questions before recited.
ABRAHAM LINCOLN.
WASHINGTON, March 16, 1861

AMBASSADORIAL APPOINTMENTS

TO SECRETARY SEWARD.

EXECUTIVE MANSION, MARCH 18, 1861 HON. SECRETARY OF STATE.
MY DEAR SIR:—I believe it is a necessity with us to make the appointments I mentioned last night—that is, Charles F. Adams to England, William L. Dayton to France, George P. Marsh to Sardinia, and Anson Burlingame to Austria. These gentlemen all have my highest esteem, but no one of them is originally suggested by me except Mr. Dayton. Mr. Adams I take because you suggested him, coupled with his eminent fitness for the place. Mr. Marsh and Mr. Burlingame I take because of the intense pressure of their respective States, and their fitness also.
The objection to this card is that locally they are so huddled up—three being in New England and two from a single State. I have considered this, and will not shrink from the responsibility. This, being done, leaves but five full missions undisposed of—Rome, China, Brazil, Peru, and Chili. And then what about Carl Schurz; or, in other words, what about our German friends?
Shall we put the card through, and arrange the rest afterward? What say you?
Your obedient servant,
A. LINCOLN.

TO G. E. PATTEN.

EXECUTIVE MANSION, March 19, 1861.

TO MASTER GEO. EVANS PATTEN.
WHOM IT MAY CONCERN:—I did see and talk with Master Geo. Evans Patten last May at Springfield, Ill.
Respectfully,
A. LINCOLN.
[Written because of a denial that any interview with young Patten, then a schoolboy, had ever taken place.]

RESPONSE TO SENATE INQUIRY RE. FORT SUMTER

MESSAGE TO THE SENATE.

TO THE SENATE OF THE UNITED STATES:—I have received a copy of the resolution of the Senate, passed on the 25th instant, requesting me, if in my opinion not incompatible with the public interest, to communicate to the Senate the despatches of Major Robert Anderson to the War Department during the time he has been in command of Fort Sumter. On examination of the correspondence thus called for, I have, with the highest respect for the Senate, come to the conclusion that at the present moment the publication of it would be inexpedient.
A. LINCOLN WASHINGTON, MARCH 16, 1861

PREPARATION OF FIRST NAVAL ACTION

TO THE SECRETARY OF WAR

EXECUTIVE MANSION, MARCH 29, 1861 HONORABLE SECRETARY OF WAR.
SIR:—I desire that an expedition to move by sea be got ready to sail as early as the 6th of April next, the whole according to memorandum attached, and that you cooperate with the Secretary of the Navy for that object.
Your obedient servant,
A. LINCOLN.
[Inclosure.]
Steamers Pocahontas at Norfolk, Paunee at Washington, Harriet Lane at New York, to be under sailing orders for sea, with stores, etc., for one month. Three hundred men to be kept ready for departure from on board the receiving-ships at New York. Two hundred men to be ready to leave Governor's Island in New York. Supplies for twelve months for

one hundred men to be put in portable shape, ready for instant shipping. A large steamer and three tugs conditionally engaged.

TO ——— STUART.

WASHINGTON, March 30, 1861

DEAR STUART:

Cousin Lizzie shows me your letter of the 27th. The question of giving her the Springfield post-office troubles me. You see I have already appointed William Jayne a Territorial governor and Judge Trumbull's brother to a land-office. Will it do for me to go on and justify the declaration that Trumbull and I have divided out all the offices among our relatives? Dr. Wallace, you know, is needy, and looks to me; and I personally owe him much.

I see by the papers, a vote is to be taken as to the post-office. Could you not set up Lizzie and beat them all? She, being here, need know nothing of it, so therefore there would be no indelicacy on her part.

Yours as ever,

TO THE COMMANDANT OF THE NEW YORK NAVY-YARD.

NAVY DEPT., WASHINGTON, April 1, 1861

TO THE COMMANDANT OF THE NAVY-YARD, Brooklyn, N. Y.

Fit out the Powhatan to go to sea at the earnest possible moment under sealed orders. Orders by a confidential messenger go forward to-morrow.

A. LINCOLN.

TO LIEUTENANT D. D. PORTER

EXECUTIVE MANSION, April 1, 1861

LIEUTENANT D. D. PORTER, United States Navy.

SIR:—You will proceed to New York, and with the least possible delay, assuming command of any naval steamer available, proceed to Pensacola Harbor, and at any cost or risk prevent any expedition from the mainland reaching Fort Pickens or Santa Rosa Island.

You will exhibit this order to any naval officer at Pensacola, if you deem it necessary, after you have established yourself within the harbor, and will request co-operation by the entrance of at least one other steamer.

This order, its object, and your destination will be communicated to no person whatever until you reach the harbor of Pensacola.

A. LINCOLN.

Recommended, WILLIAM H. SEWARD.

RELIEF EXPEDITION FOR FORT SUMTER

ORDER TO OFFICERS OF THE ARMY AND NAVY.

WASHINGTON, EXECUTIVE MANSION, April 1, 1861.

All officers of the army and navy to whom this order may be exhibited will aid by every means in their power the expedition under the command of Colonel Harvey Brown, supplying him with men and material, and co-operating with him as he may desire.

A. LINCOLN.

ORDER TO CAPTAIN SAMUEL MERCER.

(Confidential.)

WASHINGTON CITY, April 1, 1861

SIR:—Circumstances render it necessary to place in command of your ship (and for a special purpose) an officer who is fully informed and instructed in relation to the wishes of the Government, and you will therefore consider yourself detached. But in taking this step the Government does not in the least reflect upon your efficiency or patriotism; on the contrary, have the fullest confidence in your ability to perform any duty required of you. Hoping soon to be able to give you a better command than the one you now enjoy, and trusting that you will have full confidence in the disposition of the Government toward you, I remain, etc.,

A. LINCOLN.

SECRETARY SEWARD'S BID FOR POWER

MEMORANDUM FROM SECRETARY SEWARD, APRIL 1, 1861

Some thoughts for the President's Consideration,

First. We are at the end of a month's administration, and yet without a policy either domestic or foreign.

Second. This, however, is not culpable, and it has even been unavoidable. The presence of the Senate, with the need to meet applications for patronage, have prevented attention to other and more grave matters.

Third. But further delay to adopt and prosecute our policies for both domestic and foreign affairs would not only bring scandal on the administration, but danger upon the country.

Fourth. To do this we must dismiss the applicants for office. But how? I suggest that we make the local appointments forthwith, leaving foreign or general ones for ulterior and occasional action.

Fifth. The policy at home. I am aware that my views are singular, and perhaps not sufficiently explained. My system is built upon this idea as a ruling one, namely, that we must CHANGE THE QUESTION BEFORE THE PUBLIC FROM ONE UPON SLAVERY, OR ABOUT SLAVERY, for a question upon UNION OR DISUNION: In other words, from what would be regarded as a party question, to one of patriotism or union.

The occupation or evacuation of Fort Sumter, although not in fact a slavery or a party question, is so regarded. Witness the temper manifested by the Republicans in the free States, and even by the Union men in the South.

I would therefore terminate it as a safe means for changing the issue. I deem it fortunate that the last administration created the necessity.

For the rest, I would simultaneously defend and reinforce all the ports in the gulf, and have the navy recalled from foreign stations to be prepared for a blockade. Put the island of Key West under martial law.

This will raise distinctly the question of union or disunion. I would maintain every fort and possession in the South.

FOR FOREIGN NATIONS,

I would demand explanations from Spain and France, categorically, at once.

I would seek explanations from Great Britain and Russia, and send agents into Canada, Mexico, and Central America to rouse a vigorous continental spirit of independence on this continent against European intervention.

And, if satisfactory explanations are not received from Spain and France,

Would convene Congress and declare war against them.

But whatever policy we adopt, there must be an energetic prosecution of it.

For this purpose it must be somebody's business to pursue and direct it incessantly.

Either the President must do it himself, and be all the while active in it, or Devolve it on some member of his Cabinet. Once adopted, debates on it must end, and all agree and abide.

It is not in my especial province; But I neither seek to evade nor assume responsibility.

REPLY TO SECRETARY SEWARD'S MEMORANDUM

EXECUTIVE MANSION, APRIL 1, 1861

HON. W. H. SEWARD.
MY DEAR SIR:—Since parting with you I have been considering your paper dated this day, and entitled "Some Thoughts for the President's Consideration." The first proposition in it is, "First, We are at the end of a month's administration, and yet without a policy either domestic or foreign."
At the beginning of that month, in the inaugural, I said: "The power confided to me will be used to hold, occupy, and possess the property and places belonging to the Government, and to Collect the duties and imposts." This had your distinct approval at the time; and, taken in connection with the order I immediately gave General Scott, directing him to employ every means in his power to strengthen and hold the forts, comprises the exact domestic policy you now urge, with the single exception that it does not propose to abandon Fort Sumter.
Again, I do not perceive how the reinforcement of Fort Sumter would be done on a slavery or a party issue, while that of Fort Pickens would be on a more national and patriotic one.
The news received yesterday in regard to St. Domingo certainly brings a new item within the range of our foreign policy; but up to that time we have been preparing circulars and instructions to ministers and the like, all in perfect harmony, without even a suggestion that we had no foreign policy.
Upon your Closing propositions—that,
"Whatever policy we adopt, there must be an energetic prosecution of it.
"For this purpose it must be somebody's business to pursue and direct it incessantly.
"Either the President must do it himself, and be all the while active in it, or,
"Devolve it on some member of his Cabinet. Once adopted, debates on it must end, and all agree and abide"—
I remark that if this must be done, I must do it. When a general line of policy is adopted, I apprehend there is no danger of its being changed without good reason, or continuing to be a subject of unnecessary debate; still, upon points arising in its progress I wish, and suppose I am entitled to have, the advice of all the Cabinet.
Your obedient servant,
A. LINCOLN.

REPLY TO A COMMITTEE FROM THE VIRGINIA CONVENTION, APRIL 13, 1861

HON. WILLIAM BALLARD PRESTON, ALEXANDER H. H. STUART, GEORGE W. RANDOLPH, Esq.
GENTLEMEN:—As a committee of the Virginia Convention now in Session, you present me a preamble and resolution in these words:
"Whereas, in the opinion of this Convention, the uncertainty which prevails in the public mind as to the policy which the Federal Executive intends to pursue toward the seceded States is extremely injurious to the industrial and commercial interests of the country, tends to keep up an excitement which is unfavorable to the adjustment of pending difficulties, and threatens a disturbance of the public peace: therefore
"Resolved, that a committee of three delegates be appointed by this Convention to wait upon the President of the United States, present to him this preamble and resolution, and respectfully ask him to communicate to this Convention the policy which the Federal Executive intends to pursue in regard to the Confederate States."
"Adopted by the Convention of the State of Virginia, Richmond, April 8, 1861."
In answer I have to say that, having at the beginning of my official term expressed my intended policy as plainly as I was able, it is with deep regret and some mortification I now learn that there is great and injurious uncertainty in the public mind as to what that policy is, and what course I intend to pursue. Not having as yet seen occasion to change, it is now my purpose to pursue the course marked out in the inaugural address. I commend a careful consideration of the whole document as the best expression I can give of my purposes.
As I then and therein said, I now repeat: "The power confided to me will be used to hold, occupy, and possess the property and places belonging to the Government, and to collect the duties and imposts; but beyond what is necessary for these objects, there will be no invasion, no using of force against or among the people anywhere." By the words

"property and places belonging to the Government," I chiefly allude to the military posts and property which were in the possession of the Government when it came to my hands.

But if, as now appears to be true, in pursuit of a purpose to drive the United States authority from these places, an unprovoked assault has been made upon Fort Sumter, I shall hold myself at liberty to repossess, if I can, like places which had been seized before the Government was devolved upon me. And in every event I shall, to the extent of my ability, repel force by force. In case it proves true that Fort Sumter has been assaulted, as is reported, I shall perhaps cause the United States mails to be withdrawn from all the States which claim to have seceded, believing that the commencement of actual war against the Government justifies and possibly demands this.

I scarcely need to say that I consider the military posts and property situated within the States which claim to have seceded as yet belonging to the Government of the United States as much as they did before the supposed secession.

Whatever else I may do for the purpose, I shall not attempt to collect the duties and imposts by any armed invasion of any part of the country; not meaning by this, however, that I may not land a force deemed necessary to relieve a fort upon a border of the country.

From the fact that I have quoted a part of the inaugural address, it must not be inferred that I repudiate any other part, the whole of which I reaffirm, except so far as what I now say of the mails may be regarded as a modification.

PROCLAMATION CALLING FOR 75,000 MILITIA,

AND CONVENING CONGRESS IN EXTRA SESSION, APRIL 15, 1861.

BY THE PRESIDENT OF THE UNITED STATES OF AMERICA:
A Proclamation.

Whereas the laws of the United States have been for some time past and now are opposed, and the execution thereof obstructed, in the States of South Carolina, Georgia, Alabama, Florida, Mississippi, Louisiana, and Texas, by combinations too powerful to be suppressed by the ordinary course of judicial proceedings, or by the powers vested in the marshals bylaw:

Now, therefore, I, A. LINCOLN, President of the United States, in virtue of the power in me vested by the Constitution and the laws, have thought fit to call forth, and hereby do call forth, the militia of the several States of the Union, to the aggregate number of seventy-five thousand, in order to suppress said combinations, and to cause the laws to be duly executed.

The details for this object will be immediately communicated to the State authorities through the War Department.

I appeal to all loyal citizens to favor, facilitate, and aid this effort to maintain the honor, the integrity, and the existence of our National Union, and the perpetuity of popular government; and to redress wrongs already long enough endured.

I deem it proper to say that the first service assigned to the forces hereby called forth will probably be to repossess the forts, places, and property which have been seized from the Union; and in every event the utmost care will be observed, consistently with the objects aforesaid, to avoid any devastation, any destruction of or interference with property, or any disturbance of peaceful citizens in any part of the country.

And I hereby command the persons composing the combinations aforesaid to disperse and retire peacefully to their respective abodes within twenty days from date.

Deeming that the present condition of public affairs presents an extraordinary occasion, I do hereby, in virtue of the power in me vested by the Constitution, convene both Houses of Congress. Senators and Representatives are therefore summoned to assemble at their respective chambers, at twelve o'clock noon, on Thursday, the fourth day of July next, then and there to consider and determine such measures as, in their wisdom, the public safety and interest may seem to demand.

In witness whereof, I have hereunto set my hand, and caused the seal of the United States to be affixed.

Done at the city of Washington, this fifteenth day of April, in the year of our Lord one thousand eight hundred and sixty-one, and of the independence of the United States the eighty-fifth.

A. LINCOLN
By the President:
WILLIAM H. SEWARD, Secretary of State.

PROCLAMATION OF BLOCKADE, APRIL 19, 1861.

BY THE PRESIDENT OF THE UNITED STATES OF AMERICA:

A Proclamation.

Whereas an insurrection against the Government of the United States has broken out in the States of South Carolina, Georgia, Alabama, Florida, Mississippi, Louisiana, and Texas, and the laws of the United States for the collection of the revenue cannot be effectually executed therein conformably to that provision of the Constitution which requires duties to be uniform throughout the United States:

And Whereas a combination of persons engaged in such insurrection have threatened to grant pretended letters of marque to authorize the bearers thereof to commit assaults on the lives, vessels, and property of good citizens of the country lawfully engaged in commerce on the high seas, and in waters of the United States:

And Whereas an executive proclamation has been already issued requiring the persons engaged in these disorderly proceedings to desist therefrom, calling out a militia force for the purpose of repressing the same, and convening Congress in extraordinary session to deliberate and determine thereon:

Now, therefore, I, Abraham LINCOLN, President of the United States, with a view to the same purposes before mentioned, and to the protection of the public peace, and the lives and property of quiet and orderly citizens pursuing their lawful occupations, until Congress shall have assembled and deliberated on the said unlawful proceedings, or until the same shall have ceased, have further deemed it advisable to set on foot a blockade of the ports within the States aforesaid, in pursuance of the laws of the United States, and of the law of nations in such case provided. For this purpose a competent force will be posted so as to prevent entrance and exit of vessels from the ports aforesaid. If, therefore, with a view to violate such blockade, a vessel shall approach or shall attempt to leave either of the said ports, she will be duly warned by the commander of one of the blockading vessels, who will indorse on her register the fact and date of such warning, and if the same vessel shall again attempt to enter or leave the blockaded port, she will be captured and sent to the nearest convenient port, for such proceedings against her and her cargo, as prize, as may be deemed advisable.

And I hereby proclaim and declare that if any person, under the pretended authority of the said States, or under any other pretense, shall molest a vessel of the United States, or the persons or cargo on board of her, such person will be held amenable to the laws of the United States for the prevention and punishment of piracy.

In witness whereof, I have hereunto set my hand and caused the seal of the United States to be affixed.

Done at the city of Washington, this nineteenth day of April, in the year of our Lord one thousand eight hundred and sixty-one, and of the independence of the United States the eighty-fifth.

A. LINCOLN.

By the President: WILLIAM H. SEWARD, Secretary of State.

TO GOVERNOR HICKS AND MAYOR BROWN.

WASHINGTON, April 20, 1861

GOVERNOR HICKS AND MAYOR BROWN.

GENTLEMEN:—Your letter by Messrs. Bond, Dobbin, and Brune is received. I tender you both my sincere thanks for your efforts to keep the peace in the trying situation in which you are placed.

For the future troops must be brought here, but I make no point of bringing them through Baltimore. Without any military knowledge myself, of course I must leave details to General Scott. He hastily said this morning in the presence of these gentlemen, "March them around Baltimore, and not through it." I sincerely hope the General, on fuller reflection, will consider this practical and proper, and that you will not object to it. By this a collision of the people of Baltimore with the troops will be avoided, unless they go out of their way to seek it. I hope you will exert your influence to prevent this.

Now and ever I shall do all in my power for peace consistently with the maintenance of the Government.

Your obedient servant,

A. LINCOLN.

TO GOVERNOR HICKS.

WASHINGTON, April 20, 1861

GOVERNOR HICKS:
I desire to consult with you and the Mayor of Baltimore relative to preserving the peace of Maryland. Please come immediately by special train, which you can take at Baltimore; or, if necessary, one can be sent from here. Answer forthwith.
LINCOLN.

ORDER TO DEFEND FROM A MARYLAND INSURRECTION

ORDER TO GENERAL SCOTT. WASHINGTON, April 25, 1861

LIEUTENANT-GENERAL SCOTT.
MY DEAR SIR—The Maryland Legislature assembles to-morrow at Annapolis, and not improbably will take action to arm the people of that State against the United States. The question has been submitted to and considered by me whether it would not be justifiable, upon the ground of necessary defense, for you, as General in Chief of the United States Army, to arrest or disperse the members of that body. I think it would not be justifiable nor efficient for the desired object.
First. They have a clearly legal right to assemble, and we cannot know in advance that their action will not be lawful and peaceful, and if we wait until they shall have acted their arrest or dispersion will not lessen the effect of their action. Secondly. We cannot permanently prevent their action. If we arrest them, we cannot long hold them as prisoners, and when liberated they will immediately reassemble and take their action; and precisely the same if we simply disperse them—they will immediately reassemble in some other place.
I therefore conclude that it is only left to the Commanding General to watch and await their action, which, if it shall be to arm their people against the United States, he is to adopt the most prompt and efficient means to counteract, even, if necessary, to the bombardment of their cities and, in the extremist necessity, the suspension of the writ of habeas corpus.
Your obedient servant,
A. LINCOLN.

PROCLAMATION OF BLOCKADE, APRIL 27, 1861

BY THE PRESIDENT OF THE UNITED STATES OF AMERICA:

A Proclamation.
Whereas, for the reasons assigned in my proclamation of the nineteenth instant, a blockade of the ports of the States of South Carolina, Georgia, Florida, Alabama, Louisiana, Mississippi, and Texas was ordered to be established:
And whereas, since that date, public property of the United States has been seized, the collection of the revenue obstructed, and duly commissioned officers of the United States, while engaged in executing the orders of their superiors, have been arrested and held in custody as prisoners, or have been impeded in the discharge of their official duties, without due legal process, by persons claiming to act under authorities of the States of Virginia and North Carolina:
An efficient blockade of the ports of those States will also be established.
In witness whereof I have hereunto set my hand and caused the seal of the United States to be affixed.
Done at the city of Washington, this twenty seventh day of April, in the year of our Lord one thousand eight hundred and sixty-one, and of the independence of the United States the eighty-fifth.
A. LINCOLN.

REMARKS TO A MILITARY COMPANY, WASHINGTON, APRIL 27, 1861

I have desired as sincerely as any man, and I sometimes think more than any other man, that our present difficulties might be settled without the shedding of blood. I will not say that all hope has yet gone; but if the alternative is presented whether the Union is to be broken in fragments and the liberties of the people lost, or blood be shed, you will probably make the choice with which I shall not be dissatisfied.

LOCALIZED REPEAL OF WRIT OF HABEAS CORPUS

TO GENERAL SCOTT.

TO THE COMMANDING GENERAL, ARMY OF THE UNITED STATES.
You are engaged in suppressing an insurrection against the laws of the United States. If at any point on or in the vicinity of any military line which is now or which shall be used between the City of Philadelphia and the city of Washington you find resistance which renders it necessary to suspend the writ of habeas corpus for the public safety, you personally, or through the officer in command at the point at which resistance occurs, are authorized to suspend that writ.
A. LINCOLN.
WASHINGTON, April 17, 1861

MILITARY ENROLLMENT OF ST. LOUIS CITIZENS

FROM THE SECRETARY OF WAR WAR DEPARTMENT, April 30, 1861

TO CAPTAIN NATHANIEL LYON.
CAPT. NATHANIEL LYON, Commanding Department of the West.
SIR:—The President of the United States directs that you enroll in the military service of the United States the loyal citizens of Saint Louis and vicinity, not exceeding, with those heretofore enlisted, ten thousand in number, for the purpose of maintaining the authority of the United States; for the protection of the peaceful inhabitants of Missouri; and you will, if deemed necessary for that purpose by yourself, by Messrs. Oliver F. Ferny, John How, James O. Broadhead, Samuel T. Glover, J. Wilzie, Francis P. Blair, Jr., proclaim martial law in the city of Saint Louis.
The additional force hereby authorized shall be discharged in part or in whole, if enlisted. As soon as it appears to you and the gentlemen above mentioned that there is no danger of an attempt on the part of the enemies of the Government to take military possession of the city of Saint Louis, or put the city in control of the combination against the Government of the United States; and whilst such additional force remains in the service the same shall be governed by the Rules and Articles of War, and such special regulations as you may prescribe. I shall like the force hereafter directed to be enrolled to be under your command.
The arms and other military stores in the Saint Louis Arsenal not needed for the forces of the United States in Missouri must be removed to Springfield, or some other safe place of deposit in the State of Illinois, as speedily as practicable, by the ordnance officers in charge at Saint Louis.
(Indorsement.)
It is revolutionary times, and therefore I do not object to the irregularity of this. W. S.
Approved, April 30, 1861.
A. LINCOLN.
Colonel Thomas will make this order. SIMON CAMERON, Secretary of War.

CONDOLENCE OVER FAILURE OF FT. SUMTER RELIEF

TO GUSTAVUS V. FOX.

WASHINGTON, D.C., May 1, 1861
CAPTAIN G. V. Fox.

MY DEAR SIR:—I sincerely regret that the failure of the late attempt to provision Fort Sumter should be the source of any annoyance to you.

The practicability of your plan was not, in fact, brought to a test. By reason of a gale, well known in advance to be possible and not improbable, the tugs, an essential part of the plan, never reached the ground; while, by an accident for which you were in no wise responsible, and possibly I to some extent was, you were deprived of a war vessel, with her men, which you deemed of great importance to the enterprise.

I most cheerfully and truly declare that the failure of the undertaking has not lowered you a particle, while the qualities you developed in the effort have greatly heightened you in my estimation.

For a daring and dangerous enterprise of a similar character you would to-day be the man of all my acquaintances whom I would select. You and I both anticipated that the cause of the country would be advanced by making the attempt to provision Fort Sumter, even if it should fail; and it is no small consolation now to feel that our anticipation is justified by the result.

Very truly your friend,
A. LINCOLN.

PROCLAMATION CALLING FOR 42,034 VOLUNTEERS,

MAY 3, 1861

BY THE PRESIDENT OF THE UNITED STATES.
A Proclamation..

Whereas existing exigencies demand immediate and adequate measures for the protection of the National Constitution and the preservation of the National Union by the suppression of the insurrectionary combinations now existing in several States for opposing the laws of the Union and obstructing the execution thereof, to which end a military force in addition to that called forth by my proclamation of the 15th day of April in the present year appears to be indispensably necessary:

Now, therefore, I, Abraham Lincoln, President of the United States and Commander in Chief of the Army and Navy thereof and of the militia of the several States when called into actual service, do hereby call into the service of the United States 42,034 volunteers to serve for the period of three years, unless sooner discharged, and to be mustered into service as infantry and cavalry. The proportions of each arm and the details of enrollment and organization will be made known through the Department of War.

And I also direct that the Regular Army of the United States be increased by the addition of eight regiments of infantry, one regiment of cavalry, and one regiment of artillery, making altogether a maximum aggregate increase of 22,714 officers and enlisted men, the details of which increase will also be made known through the Department of War.

And I further direct the enlistment for not less than one or more than three years of 18,000 seamen, in addition to the present force, for the naval service of the United States. The details of the enlistment and organization will be made known through the Department of the Navy.

The call for volunteers hereby made and the direction for the increase of the Regular Army and for the enlistment of seamen hereby given, together with the plan of organization adopted for the volunteer and for the regular forces hereby authorized, will be submitted to Congress as soon as assembled.

In the meantime I earnestly invoke the co-operation of all good citizens in the measures hereby adopted for the effectual suppression of unlawful violence, for the impartial enforcement of constitutional laws, and for the speediest possible restoration of peace and order, and with these of happiness and prosperity, throughout our country.

In testimony whereof I have hereunto set my band and caused the seal of the United States to be affixed................
A. LINCOLN.
By the President: WILLIAM H. SEWARD, Secretary of State.

COMMUNICATION WITH VICE-PRESIDENT

TO VICE-PRESIDENT HAMLIN.

WASHINGTON, D.C., May 6, 1861
HON. H. HAMLIN, New York.
MY DEAR SIR:-Please advise me at the close of each day what troops left during the day, where going, and by what route; what remaining at New York, and what expected in the next day. Give the numbers, as near as convenient, and what corps they are. This information, reaching us daily, will be very useful as well as satisfactory.
Yours very truly,
A. LINCOLN.

ORDER TO COLONEL ANDERSON,

MAY 7, 1861

TO ALL WHO SHALL SEE THESE PRESENTS, GREETING:
Know ye that, reposing special trust and confidence in the patriotism, valor, fidelity, and ability of Colonel Robert Anderson, U. S. Army, I have empowered him, and do hereby empower him, to receive into the army of the United States as many regiments of volunteer troops from the State of Kentucky and from the western part of the State of Virginia as shall be willing to engage in the Service of the United States for the term of three years, upon the terms and according to the plan proposed by the proclamation of May 3, 1861, and General Orders No. 15, from the War Department, of May 4, 1861.
The troops whom he receives shall be on the same footing in every respect as those of the like kind called for in the proclamation above cited, except that the officers shall be commissioned by the United States. He is therefore carefully and diligently to discharge the duty hereby devolved upon him by doing and performing all manner of things thereunto belonging.
Given under my hand, at the city of Washington, this 7th day of May, A. D. 1861, and in the eighty-fifth year of the independence of the United States.
A. LINCOLN.
By the President: SIMON CAMERON, Secretary of War,

PROCLAMATION SUSPENDING THE WRIT OF HABEAS CORPUS IN FLORIDA,

MAY 10, 1861.

BY THE PRESIDENT OF THE UNITED STATES OP AMERICA:
A Proclamation.
Whereas an insurrection exists in the State of Florida, by which the lives, liberty, and property of loyal citizens of the United States are endangered:
And whereas it is deemed proper that all needful measures should be taken for the protection of such citizens and all officers of the United States in the discharge of their public duties in the State aforesaid:
Now, therefore, be it known that I, Abraham LINCOLN, President of the United States, do hereby direct the commander of the forces of the United States on the Florida coast to permit no person to exercise any office or authority upon the islands of Key West, the Tortugas, and Santa Rosa, which may be inconsistent with the laws and Constitution of the United States, authorizing him at the same time, if he shall find it necessary, to suspend there the writ of habeas corpus, and to remove from the vicinity of the United States fortresses all dangerous or suspected persons.
In witness whereof, I have hereunto set my hand and caused the seal of the United States to be affixed....................
A. LINCOLN.
By the President: WILLIAM H. SEWARD, Secretary of State.

TO SECRETARY WELLES.

EXECUTIVE MANSION, May 11, 1861

TO THE SECRETARY OF THE NAVY.
SIR:-Lieut. D. D. Porter was placed in command of the steamer Powhatan, and Captain Samuel Mercer was detached therefrom, by my special order, and neither of them is responsible for any apparent or real irregularity on their part or in connection with that vessel.

Hereafter Captain Porter is relieved from that special service and placed under the direction of the Navy Department, from which he will receive instructions and to which he will report.

Very respectfully,
A. LINCOLN.

PRESIDENT LINCOLN'S CORRECTIONS OF A DIPLOMATIC DESPATCH

WRITTEN BY THE SECRETARY OF STATE TO MINISTER ADAMS

NO. 10.
DEPARTMENT OF STATE. WASHINGTON, May 21, 1861
SIR:—Mr. Dallas, in a brief despatch of May 2d (No. 333), tells us that Lord John Russell recently requested an interview with him on account of the solicitude which his lordship felt concerning the effect of certain measures represented as likely to be adopted by the President. In that conversation the British secretary told Mr. Dallas that the three representatives of the Southern Confederacy were then in London, that Lord John Russell had not yet seen them, but that he was not unwilling to see them unofficially. He further informed Mr. Dallas that an understanding exists between the British and French governments which would lead both to take one and the same course as to recognition. His lordship then referred to the rumor of a meditated blockade by us of Southern ports, and a discontinuance of them as ports of entry. Mr. Dallas answered that he knew nothing on those topics, and therefore

(The President's corrections, both in notes and text, are in
caps. All matter between brackets was to be marked out.)

could say nothing. He added that you were expected to arrive in two weeks. Upon this statement Lord John Russell acquiesced in the expediency of waiting for the full knowledge you were expected to bring.

Mr. Dallas transmitted to us some newspaper reports of ministerial explanations made in Parliament.

You will base no proceedings on parliamentary debates further than to seek explanations when necessary and communicate them to this department. [We intend to have a clear and simple record of whatever issue may arise between us and Great Britain.]

The President [is surprised and grieved] regrets that Mr. Dallas did not protest against the proposed unofficial intercourse between the British Government and the missionaries of the insurgents [as well as against the demand for explanations made by the British Government]. It is due, however, to Mr. Dallas to say that our instructions had been given only to you and not to him, and that his loyalty and fidelity, too rare in these times [among our late representatives abroad, are confessed and] are appreciated.

Intercourse of any kind with the so-called commissioners is liable to be construed as a recognition of the authority which appointed them. Such intercourse would be none the less [wrongful] hurtful to us for being called unofficial, and it might be even more injurious, because we should have no means of knowing what points might be resolved by it. Moreover, unofficial intercourse is useless and meaningless if it is not expected to ripen into official intercourse and direct recognition. It is left doubtful here whether the proposed unofficial intercourse has yet actually begun. Your own [present] antecedent instructions are deemed explicit enough, and it is hoped that you have not misunderstood them. You will in any event desist from all intercourse whatever, unofficial as well as official, with the British Government, so long as it shall continue intercourse of either kind with the domestic enemies of this country [confining yourself to a delivery of a copy of this paper to the Secretary of State. After doing this.] When intercourse shall have been arrested for this cause, you will communicate with this department and receive further directions.

Lord John Russell has informed us of an understanding between the British and French governments that they will act together in regard to our affairs. This communication, however, loses something of its value from the circumstance that the communication was withheld until after knowledge of the fact had been acquired by us from other sources. We know also another fact that has not yet been officially communicated to us—namely, that other European States are apprised by France and England of their agreement, and are expected to concur with or follow them in whatever measures they adopt on the subject of recognition. The United States have been impartial and just in all their conduct toward the several nations of Europe. They will not complain, however, of the combination now announced by the two leading powers, although they think they had a right to expect a more independent, if not a more friendly, course from each of them. You will take no notice of that or any other alliance. Whenever the European governments shall see fit to communicate directly with us, we shall be, as heretofore, frank and explicit in our reply.

As to the blockade, you will say that by [the] our own laws [of nature] and the laws of nature and the laws of nations, this Government has a clear right to suppress insurrection. An exclusion of commerce from national ports which have been seized by the insurgents, in the equitable form of blockade, is the proper means to that end. You will [admit] not insist that our blockade is [not] to be respected if it be not maintained by a competent force; but passing by that question as not now a practical, or at least an urgent, one, you will add that [it] the blockade is now, and it will continue to be so maintained, and therefore we expect it to be respected by Great Britain. You will add that we have already revoked the exequatur of a Russian consul who had enlisted in the military service of the insurgents, and we shall dismiss or demand the recall of every foreign agent, consular or diplomatic, who shall either disobey the Federal laws or disown the Federal authority.

As to the recognition of the so-called Southern Confederacy, it is not to be made a subject of technical definition. It is, of course, [quasi] direct recognition to publish an acknowledgment of the sovereignty and independence of a new power. It is [quasi] direct recognition to receive its ambassadors, ministers, agents, or commissioners officially. A concession of belligerent rights is liable to be construed as a recognition of them. No one of these proceedings will [be borne] pass [unnoticed] unquestioned by the United States in this case.

Hitherto recognition has been moved only on the assumption that the so-called Confederate States are de facto a self-sustaining power. Now, after long forbearance, designed to soothe discontent and avert the need of civil war, the land and naval forces of the United States have been put in motion to repress the insurrection. The true character of the pretended new State is at once revealed. It is seen to be a power existing in pronunciamiento only, It has never won a field. It has obtained no forts that were not virtually betrayed into its hands or seized in breach of trust. It commands not a single port on the coast nor any highway out from its pretended capital by land. Under these circumstances Great Britain is called upon to intervene and give it body and independence by resisting our measures of suppression. British recognition would be British intervention to create within our own territory a hostile state by overthrowing this republic itself. [When this act of intervention is distinctly performed, we from that hour shall cease to be friends, and become once more, as we have twice before been forced to be, enemies of Great Britain.]

As to the treatment of privateers in the insurgent service, you will say that this is a question exclusively our own. We treat them as pirates. They are our own citizens, or persons employed by our citizens, preying on the commerce of our country. If Great Britain shall choose to recognize them as lawful belligerents, and give them shelter from our pursuit and punishment, the laws of nations afford an adequate and proper remedy [and we shall avail ourselves of it. And while you need not say this in advance, be sure that you say nothing inconsistent with it.]

Happily, however, her Britannic Majesty's government can avoid all these difficulties. It invited us in 1856 to accede to the declaration of the Congress of Paris, of which body Great Britain was herself a member, abolishing privateering everywhere in all cases and forever. You already have our authority to propose to her our accession to that declaration. If she refuse to receive it, it can only be because she is willing to become the patron of privateering when aimed at our devastation.

These positions are not elaborately defended now, because to vindicate them would imply a possibility of our waiving them.

1 We are not insensible of the grave importance of
1 (Drop all from this line to the end, and in lieu of it write, "This paper is for your own guidance only, and not [sic] to be read or shown to any one.")
(Secretary Seward, when the despatch was returned to him, added an introductory paragraph stating that the document was strictly confidential. For this reason these last two paragraphs remained as they are here printed.)

this occasion. We see how, upon the result of the debate in which we are engaged, a war may ensue between the United States and one, two, or even more European nations. War in any case is as exceptionable from the habits as it is revolting from the sentiments of the American people. But if it come, it will be fully seen that it results from the action of Great Britain, not our own; that Great Britain will have decided to fraternize with our domestic enemy, either without waiting to hear from you our remonstrances and our warnings, or after having heard them. War in defense of national life is not immoral, and war in defense of independence is an inevitable part of the discipline of nations.

The dispute will be between the European and the American branches of the British race. All who belong to that race will especially deprecate it, as they ought. It may well be believed that men of every race and kindred will deplore it. A war not unlike it between the same parties occurred at the close of the last century. Europe atoned by forty years of suffering for the error that Great Britain committed in provoking that contest. If that nation shall now repeat the same great error, the social convulsions which will follow may not be so long, but they will be more general. When they shall have ceased, it will, we think, be seen, whatever may have been the fortunes of other nations, that it is not the United

States that will have come out of them with its precious Constitution altered or its honestly obtained dominion in any degree abridged. Great Britain has but to wait a few months and all her present inconveniences will cease with all our own troubles. If she take a different course, she will calculate for herself the ultimate as well as the immediate consequences, and will consider what position she will hold when she shall have forever lost the sympathies and the affections of the only nation on whose sympathies and affections she has a natural claim. In making that calculation she will do well to remember that in the controversy she proposes to open we shall be actuated by neither pride, nor passion, nor cupidity, nor ambition; but we shall stand simply on the principle of self-preservation, and that our cause will involve the independence of nations and the rights of human nature.
I am, Sir, respectfully your obedient servant, W. H. S.
CHARLES FRANCIS ADAMS, Esq., etc,

TO THE SECRETARY OF WAR,

EXECUTIVE MANSION, May 21, 1861.

HON. SECRETARY OF WAR. MY DEAR SIR:—Why cannot Colonel Small's Philadelphia regiment be received? I sincerely wish it could. There is something strange about it. Give these gentlemen an interview, and take their regiment.
Yours truly,
A. LINCOLN.

TO GOVERNOR MORGAN.

WASHINGTON, May 12, 1861

GOVERNOR E. D. MORGAN, Albany, N.Y.
I wish to see you face to face to clear these difficulties about forwarding troops from New York.
A. LINCOLN.

TO CAPTAIN DAHLGREEN.

EXECUTIVE, MANSION, May 23, 1863.

CAPT. DAHLGREEN.
MY DEAR SIR:—Allow me to introduce Col. J. A. McLernand, M.C. of my own district in Illinois. If he should desire to visit Fortress Monroe, please introduce him to the captain of one of the vessels in our service, and pass him down and back.
Yours very truly,
A. LINCOLN.

LETTER OF CONDOLENCE TO ONE OF FIRST CASUALTIES

TO COLONEL ELLSWORTH'S PARENTS, WASHINGTON, D.C., May 25, 1861

TO THE FATHER AND MOTHER OF COL. ELMER E. ELLSWORTH.
MY DEAR SIR AND MADAME:—In the untimely loss of your noble son, our affliction here is scarcely less than your own. So much of promised usefulness to one's country, and of bright hopes for one's self and friends, have never

been so suddenly dashed as in his fall. In size, in years, and in youthful appearance a boy only, his power to command men was surpassingly great. This power, combined with a fine intellectual and indomitable energy, and a taste altogether military, constituted in him, as seemed to me, the best natural talent in that department I ever knew. And yet he was singularly modest and deferential in social intercourse. My acquaintance with him began less than two years ago; yet, through the latter half of the intervening period, it was as intense as the disparity of our ages and my engrossing engagements would permit. To me he appeared to have no indulgences or pastimes, and I never heard him utter a profane or an intemperate word. What was conclusive of his good heart, he never forgot his parents. The honors he labored for so laudably, and for which, in the sad end, he so gallantly gave his life, he meant for them no less than for himself.

In the hope that it may be no intrusion upon the sacredness of your sorrow, I have ventured to address you this tribute to the memory of my young friend and your brave and early fallen son.

May God give you the consolation which is beyond all early power.

Sincerely your friend in common affliction,

A. LINCOLN.

TO COLONEL BARTLETT.

WASHINGTON, May 27, 1861

COL. W. A. BARTLETT, New York.

The Naval Brigade was to go to Fort Monroe without trouble to the government, and must so go or not at all.

A. LINCOLN.

MEMORANDUM ABOUT INDIANA REGIMENTS.

WASHINGTON, JUNE 11, 1861

The government has already accepted ten regiments from the State of Indiana. I think at least six more ought to be received from that State, two to be those of Colonel James W. McMillan and Colonel William L. Brown, and the other four to be designated by the Governor of the State of Indiana, and to be received into the volunteer service of the United States according to the "Plan of Organization" in the General Orders of the War Department, No.15. When they report to Major-General McClellan in condition to pass muster according to that order, and with the approval of the Secretary of War to be indorsed hereon, and left in his department, I direct that the whole six, or any smaller number of such regiments, be received.

A. LINCOLN.

TO THE SECRETARY OF WAR.

EXECUTIVE MANSION, JUNE 13, 1861

HON. SECRETARY OF WAR.

MY DEAR SIR:—There is, it seems, a regiment in Massachusetts commanded by Fletcher Webster, and which HON. Daniel Webster's old friends very much wish to get into the service. If it can be received with the approval of your department and the consent of the Governor of Massachusetts I shall indeed be much gratified. Give Mr. Ashmun a chance to explain fully.

Yours truly,
A. LINCOLN.

TO THE SECRETARY OF WAR.

EXECUTIVE MANSION, JUNE 13, 1861 HON. SECRETARY OF WAR.

MY DEAR SIR—I think it is entirely safe to accept a fifth regiment from Michigan, and with your approbation I should say a regiment presented by Col. T. B. W. Stockton, ready for service within two weeks from now, will be received. Look at Colonel Stockton's testimonials.
Yours truly,
A. LINCOLN.

TO THE SECRETARY OF WAR.

EXECUTIVE MANSION, June 17, 1861

HON. SECRETARY Of WAR.
MY DEAR SIR:—With your concurrence, and that of the Governor of Indiana, I am in favor of accepting into what we call the three years' service any number not exceeding four additional regiments from that State. Probably they should come from the triangular region between the Ohio and Wabash Rivers, including my own old boyhood home. Please see HON. C. M. Allen, Speaker of the Indiana House of Representatives, and unless you perceive good reason to the contrary, draw up an order for him according to the above.
Yours truly,
A. LINCOLN.

TO THE SECRETARY OF WAR.

EXECUTIVE MANSION, JUNE 17, 1861

HON. SECRETARY OF WAR. MY DEAR SIR:—With your concurrence, and that of the Governor of Ohio, I am in favor of receiving into what we call the three years' service any number not exceeding six additional regiments from that State, unless you perceive good reasons to the contrary. Please see HON. John A. Gurley, who bears this, and make an order corresponding with the above.
Yours truly,
A. LINCOLN.

TO N. W. EDWARDS

WASHINGTON, D. C., June 19, 1861

Hon. N. W. EDWARDS MY DEAR SIR:
....When you wrote me some time ago in reference to looking up something in the departments here, I thought I would inquire into the thing and write you, but the extraordinary pressure upon me diverted me from it, and soon it passed out of my mind. The thing you proposed, it seemed to me, I ought to understand myself before it was set on foot by my direction or permission; and I really had no time to make myself acquainted with it. Nor have I yet. And yet I am

unwilling, of course, that you should be deprived of a chance to make something, if it can be done without injustice to the Government, or to any individual. If you choose to come here and point out to me how this can be done I shall not only not object, but shall be gratified to be able to oblige you.
Your friend as ever
A. LINCOLN.

TO SECRETARY CAMERON.

EXECUTIVE MANSION, June 20, 1861.

MY DEAR SIR:—Since you spoke to me yesterday about General J. H. Lane, of Kansas, I have been reflecting upon the subject, and have concluded that we need the service of such a man out there at once; that we had better appoint him a brigadier-general of volunteers to-day, and send him off with such authority to raise a force (I think two regiments better than three, but as to this I am not particular) as you think will get him into actual work quickest. Tell him, when he starts, to put it through not to be writing or telegraphing back here, but put it through.
Yours truly,
A. LINCOLN.

HON. SECRETARY OF WAR.

[Indorsement.]

General Lane has been authorized to raise two additional regiments of volunteers.
SIMON CAMERON, Secretary o f War.

TO THE KENTUCKY DELEGATION.

EXECUTIVE MANSION, June 29, 1861.

GENTLEMEN OF THE KENTUCKY DELEGATION WHO ARE FOR THE UNION:
I somewhat wish to authorize my friend Jesse Bayles to raise a Kentucky regiment, but I do not wish to do it without your consent. If you consent, please write so at the bottom of this.
Yours truly,
A. LINCOLN.
  We consent:
  R. MALLORY.
  H. GRIDER.
  G. W. DUNLAP.
  J. S. JACKSON.
  C. A. WICKLIFFE.

August 5, 1861.

I repeat, I would like for Col. Bayles to raise a regiment of cavalry whenever the Union men of Kentucky desire or consent to it.
A. LINCOLN.

ORDER AUTHORIZING GENERAL SCOTT TO SUSPEND THE WRIT OF HABEAS CORPUS, JULY 2, 1861 TO THE COMMANDING GENERAL, ARMY OF THE UNITED STATES:
You are engaged in suppressing an insurrection against the laws of the United States. If at any point on or in the vicinity of any military line which is now or which shall be used between the city of New York and the city of Washington you find resistance which renders it necessary to suspend the writ of habeas corpus for the public safety, you personally, or through the officer in command at the point where resistance occurs, are authorized to suspend that writ.
Given under my hand and the seal of the United States at the city of Washington, this second day of July, A.D. 1861, and of the independence of the United States the eighty-fifth.
A. LINCOLN.
By the President: WILLIAM H. SEWARD, Secretary of State.

TO SECRETARY SEWARD.

EXECUTIVE MANSION, JULY 3, 1861

HON. SECRETARY OF STATE.
MY DEAR SIR:—General Scott had sent me a copy of the despatch of which you kindly sent one. Thanks to both him and you. Please assemble the Cabinet at twelve to-day to look over the message and reports.
And now, suppose you step over at once and let us see General Scott (and) General Cameron about assigning a position to General Fremont.
Yours as ever,
A. LINCOLN.

MESSAGE TO CONGRESS IN SPECIAL SESSION,

JULY 4, 1861.

FELLOW-CITIZENS OF THE SENATE AND HOUSE OF REPRESENTATIVES:—Having been convened on an extraordinary occasion, as authorized by the Constitution, your attention is not called to any ordinary subject of legislation.
At the beginning of the present Presidential term, four months ago, the functions of the Federal Government were found to be generally suspended within the several States of South Carolina, Georgia, Alabama, Mississippi, Louisiana, and Florida, excepting only those of the Post-Office Department.
Within these States all the forts, arsenals, dockyards, custom-houses, and the like, including the movable and stationary property in and about them, had been seized, and were held in open hostility to this government, excepting only Forts Pickens, Taylor, and Jefferson, on and near the Florida coast, and Fort Sumter, in Charleston Harbor, South Carolina. The forts thus seized had been put in improved condition, new ones had been built, and armed forces had been organized and were organizing, all avowedly with the same hostile purpose.
The forts remaining in the possession of the Federal Government in and near these States were either besieged or menaced by warlike preparations, and especially Fort Sumter was nearly surrounded by well-protected hostile batteries, with guns equal in quality to the best of its own, and outnumbering the latter as perhaps ten to one. A disproportionate share of the Federal muskets and rifles had somehow found their way into these States, and had been seized to be used against the government. Accumulations of the public revenue lying within them had been seized for the same object. The navy was scattered in distant seas, leaving but a very small part of it within the immediate reach of the government. Officers of the Federal army and navy had resigned in great numbers; and of those resigning a large proportion had taken up arms against the government. Simultaneously, and in connection with all this, the purpose to sever the Federal Union was openly avowed. In accordance with this purpose, an ordinance had been adopted in each of these States,

declaring the States respectively to be separated from the national Union. A formula for instituting a combined government of these States had been promulgated; and this illegal organization, in the character of confederate States, was already invoking recognition, aid, and intervention from foreign powers.

Finding this condition of things, and believing it to be an imperative duty upon the incoming executive to prevent, if possible, the consummation of such attempt to destroy the Federal Union, a choice of means to that end became indispensable. This choice was made and was declared in the inaugural address. The policy chosen looked to the exhaustion of all peaceful measures before a resort to any stronger ones. It sought only to hold the public places and property not already wrested from the government, and to collect the revenue, relying for the rest on time, discussion, and the ballot-box. It promised a continuance of the mails, at government expense, to the very people who were resisting the government; and it gave repeated pledges against any disturbance to any of the people, or any of their rights. Of all that which a President might constitutionally and justifiably do in such a case, everything was forborne without which it was believed possible to keep the government on foot.

On the 5th of March (the present incumbent's first full day in office), a letter of Major Anderson, commanding at Fort Sumter, written on the 28th of February and received at the War Department on the 4th of March, was by that department placed in his hands. This letter expressed the professional opinion of the writer that reinforcements could not be thrown into that fort within the time for his relief, rendered necessary by the limited supply of provisions, and with a view of holding possession of the same, with a force of less than twenty thousand good and well-disciplined men. This opinion was concurred in by all the officers of his command, and their memoranda on the subject were made inclosures of Major Anderson's letter. The whole was immediately laid before Lieutenant-General Scott, who at once concurred with Major Anderson in opinion. On reflection, however, he took full time, consulting with other officers, both of the army and the navy, and at the end of four days came reluctantly but decidedly to the same conclusion as before. He also stated at the same time that no such sufficient force was then at the control of the government, or could be raised and brought to the ground within the time when the provisions in the fort would be exhausted. In a purely military point of view, this reduced the duty of the administration in the case to the mere matter of getting the garrison safely out of the fort.

It was believed, however, that to so abandon that position, under the circumstances, would be utterly ruinous; that the necessity under which it was to be done would not be fully understood; that by many it would be construed as a part of a voluntary policy; that at home it would discourage the friends of the Union, embolden its adversaries, and go far to insure to the latter a recognition abroad; that in fact, it would be our national destruction consummated. This could not be allowed. Starvation was not yet upon the garrison, and ere it would be reached Fort Pickens might be reinforced. This last would be a clear indication of policy, and would better enable the country to accept the evacuation of Fort Sumter as a military necessity. An order was at once directed to be sent for the landing of the troops from the steamship Brooklyn into Fort Pickens. This order could not go by land, but must take the longer and slower route by sea. The first return news from the order was received just one week before the fall of Fort Sumter. The news itself was that the officer commanding the Sabine, to which vessel the troops had been transferred from the Brooklyn, acting upon some quasi armistice of the late administration (and of the existence of which the present administration, up to the time the order was despatched, had only too vague and uncertain rumors to fix attention), had refused to land the troops. To now reinforce Fort Pickens before a crisis would be reached at Fort Sumter was impossible—rendered so by the near exhaustion of provisions in the latter-named fort. In precaution against such a conjuncture, the government had, a few days before, commenced preparing an expedition as well adapted as might be to relieve Fort Sumter, which expedition was intended to be ultimately used, or not, according to circumstances. The strongest anticipated case for using it was now presented, and it was resolved to send it forward. As had been intended in this contingency, it was also resolved to notify the governor of South Carolina that he might expect an attempt would be made to provision the fort; and that, if the attempt should not be resisted, there would be no effort to throw in men, arms, or ammunition, without further notice, or in case of an attack upon the fort. This notice was accordingly given; whereupon the fort was attacked and bombarded to its fall, without even awaiting the arrival of the provisioning expedition.

It is thus seen that the assault upon and reduction of Fort Sumter was in no sense a matter of self-defense on the part of the assailants. They well knew that the garrison in the fort could by no possibility commit aggression upon them. They knew—they were expressly notified—that the giving of bread to the few brave and hungry men of the garrison was all which would on that occasion be attempted, unless themselves, by resisting so much, should provoke more. They knew that this government desired to keep the garrison in the fort, not to assail them, but merely to maintain visible possession, and thus to preserve the Union from actual and immediate dissolution—trusting, as hereinbefore stated, to time, discussion, and the ballot-box for final adjustment; and they assailed and reduced the fort for precisely the reverse object—to drive out the visible authority of the Federal Union, and thus force it to immediate dissolution. That this was their object the executive well understood; and having said to them in the inaugural address, "You can have no conflict without being yourselves the aggressors," he took pains not only to keep this declaration good, but also to keep the case so free from the power of ingenious sophistry that the world should not be able to misunderstand it. By the affair at Fort Sumter, with its surrounding circumstances, that point was reached. Then and thereby the assailants of the government began the conflict of arms, without a gun in sight or in expectancy to return their fire, save only the few in the fort sent to that harbor years before for their own protection, and still ready to give that protection in whatever was lawful. In this act, discarding all else, they have forced upon the country the distinct issue, "immediate dissolution or blood."

And this issue embraces more than the fate of these United States. It presents to the whole family of man the question whether a constitutional republic or democracy—a government of the people by the same people—can or cannot maintain its territorial integrity against its own domestic foes. It presents the question whether discontented individuals, too few in numbers to control administration according to organic law in any case, can always, upon the pretenses made in this case, or on any other pretenses, or arbitrarily without any pretense, break up their government, and thus practically put an end to free government upon the earth. It forces us to ask: Is there in all republics this inherent and fatal weakness? Must a government, of necessity, be too strong for the liberties of its own people, or too weak to maintain its own existence?

So viewing the issue, no choice was left but to call out the war power of the government, and so to resist force employed for its destruction by force for its preservation.

The call was made, and the response of the country was most gratifying, surpassing in unanimity and spirit the most sanguine expectation. Yet none of the States commonly called slave States, except Delaware, gave a regiment through regular State organization. A few regiments have been organized within some others of those States by individual enterprise, and received into the government service. Of course the seceded States, so called (and to which Texas had been joined about the time of the inauguration), gave no troops to the cause of the Union.

The border States, so called, were not uniform in their action, some of them being almost for the Union, while in others—as Virginia, North Carolina, Tennessee, and Arkansas—the Union sentiment was nearly repressed and silenced. The course taken in Virginia was the most remarkable—perhaps the most important. A convention elected by the people of that State to consider this very question of disrupting the Federal Union was in session at the capital of Virginia when Fort Sumter fell. To this body the people had chosen a large majority of professed Union men. Almost immediately after the fall of Sumter, many members of that majority went over to the original disunion minority, and with them adopted an ordinance for withdrawing the State from the Union. Whether this change was wrought by their great approval of the assault upon Sumter, or their great resentment at the government's resistance to that assault, is not definitely known. Although they submitted the ordinance for ratification to a vote of the people, to be taken on a day then somewhat more than a month distant, the convention and the Legislature (which was also in session at the same time and place), with leading men of the State not members of either, immediately commenced acting as if the State were already out of the Union. They pushed military preparations vigorously forward all over the State. They seized the United States armory at Harper's Ferry, and the navy-yard at Gosport, near Norfolk. They received perhaps invited—into their State large bodies of troops, with their warlike appointments, from the so-called seceded States. They formally entered into a treaty of temporary alliance and co-operation with the so-called "Confederate States," and sent members to their congress at Montgomery. And finally, they permitted the insurrectionary government to be transferred to their capital at Richmond.

The people of Virginia have thus allowed this giant insurrection to make its nest within her borders; and this government has no choice left but to deal with it where it finds it. And it has the less regret as the loyal citizens have, in due form, claimed its protection. Those loyal citizens this government is bound to recognize and protect, as being Virginia.

In the border States, so called,—in fact, the middle States,—there are those who favor a policy which they call "armed neutrality"; that is, an arming of those States to prevent the Union forces passing one way, or the disunion the other, over their soil. This would be disunion completed. Figuratively speaking, it would be the building of an impassable wall along the line of separation—and yet not quite an impassable one, for under the guise of neutrality it would tie the hands of Union men and freely pass supplies from among them to the insurrectionists, which it could not do as an open enemy. At a stroke it would take all the trouble off the hands of secession, except only what proceeds from the external blockade. It would do for the disunionists that which, of all things, they most desire—feed them well and give them disunion without a struggle of their own. It recognizes no fidelity to the Constitution, no obligation to maintain the Union; and while very many who have favored it are doubtless loyal citizens, it is, nevertheless, very injurious in effect.

Recurring to the action of the government, it may be stated that at first a call was made for 75,000 militia; and, rapidly following this, a proclamation was issued for closing the ports of the insurrectionary districts by proceedings in the nature of blockade. So far all was believed to be strictly legal. At this point the insurrectionists announced their purpose to enter upon the practice of privateering.

Other calls were made for volunteers to serve for three years, unless sooner discharged, and also for large additions to the regular army and navy. These measures, whether strictly legal or not, were ventured upon, under what appeared to be a popular demand and a public necessity; trusting then, as now, that Congress would readily ratify them. It is believed that nothing has been done beyond the constitutional competency of Congress.

Soon after the first call for militia, it was considered a duty to authorize the commanding general in proper cases, according to his discretion, to suspend the privilege of the writ of habeas corpus, or, in other words, to arrest and detain, without resort to the ordinary processes and forms of law, such individuals as he might deem dangerous to the public safety. This authority has purposely been exercised but very sparingly. Nevertheless, the legality and propriety of what has been done under it are questioned, and the attention of the country has been called to the proposition that one who has sworn to "take care that the laws be faithfully executed" should not himself violate them. Of course some consideration was given to the questions of power and propriety before this matter was acted upon. The whole of the laws which were required to be faithfully executed were being resisted and failing of execution in nearly one third of the States. Must they be allowed to finally fail of execution, even had it been perfectly clear that by the use of the means necessary to their execution some single law, made in such extreme tenderness of the citizen's liberty that, practically, it relieves more of the guilty than of the innocent, should to a very limited extent be violated? To state the question more directly, are all the laws but one to go unexecuted, and the government itself go to pieces lest that one be violated? Even in such a case, would not the official oath be broken if the government should be overthrown when it was believed that disregarding the single law would tend to preserve it? But it was not believed that this question was presented. It was not believed that any law was violated. The provision of the Constitution that "the privilege of the writ of habeas corpus shall not be suspended, unless when, in cases of rebellion or invasion, the public safety may require it," is equivalent to a provision—is a provision—that such privilege may be suspended when, in case of rebellion or invasion, the public safety does require it. It was decided that we have a case of rebellion, and that the public safety does require the qualified suspension of the privilege of the writ which was authorized to be made. Now it is insisted that Congress, and not the executive, is vested with this power. But the Constitution itself is silent as to which or who is to exercise the power; and as the provision was plainly made for a dangerous emergency, it cannot be believed the framers of the instrument intended that in every case the danger should run its course until Congress could be called together, the very assembling of which might be prevented, as was intended in this case, by the rebellion.

No more extended argument is now offered, as an opinion at some length will probably be presented by the attorney-general. Whether there shall be any legislation upon the subject, and if any, what, is submitted entirely to the better judgment of Congress.

The forbearance of this government had been so extraordinary and so long continued as to lead some foreign nations to shape their action as if they supposed the early destruction of our national Union was probable. While this, on discovery, gave the executive some concern, he is now happy to say that the sovereignty and rights of the United States are now everywhere practically respected by foreign powers; and a general sympathy with the country is manifested throughout the world.

The reports of the Secretaries of the Treasury, War, and the Navy will give the information in detail deemed necessary and convenient for your deliberation and action; while the executive and all the departments will stand ready to supply omissions, or to communicate new facts considered important for you to know.

It is now recommended that you give the legal means for making this contest a short and decisive one: that you place at the control of the government for the work at least four hundred thousand men and $400,000,000. That number of men is about one-tenth of those of proper ages within the regions where, apparently, all are willing to engage; and the sum is less than a twenty-third part of the money value owned by the men who seem ready to devote the whole. A debt of $600,000,000 now is a less sum per head than was the debt of our Revolution when we came out of that struggle; and the money value in the country now bears even a greater proportion to what it was then than does the population. Surely each man has as strong a motive now to preserve our liberties as each had then to establish them.

A right result at this time will be worth more to the world than ten times the men and ten times the money. The evidence reaching us from the country leaves no doubt that the material for the work is abundant, and that it needs only the hand of legislation to give it legal sanction, and the hand of the executive to give it practical shape and efficiency. One of the greatest perplexities of the government is to avoid receiving troops faster than it can provide for them. In a word, the people will save their government if the government itself will do its part only indifferently well.

It might seem, at first thought, to be of little difference whether the present movement at the South be called "secession" or "rebellion." The movers, however, well understand the difference. At the beginning they knew they could never raise their treason to any respectable magnitude by any name which implies violation of law. They knew their people possessed as much of moral sense, as much of devotion to law and order, and as much pride in and reverence for the history and government of their common country as any other civilized and patriotic people. They knew they could make no advancement directly in the teeth of these strong and noble sentiments. Accordingly, they commenced by an insidious debauching of the public mind. They invented an ingenious sophism which, if conceded, was followed by perfectly logical steps, through all the incidents, to the complete destruction of the Union. The sophism itself is that any State of the Union may consistently with the national Constitution, and therefore lawfully and peacefully, withdraw from the Union without the consent of the Union or of any other State. The little disguise that the supposed right is to be exercised only for just cause, themselves to be the sole judges of its justice, is too thin to merit any notice.

With rebellion thus sugar-coated they have been drugging the public mind of their section for more than thirty years, and until at length they have brought many good men to a willingness to take up arms against the government the day after some assemblage of men have enacted the farcical pretense of taking their State out of the Union, who could have been brought to no such thing the day before.

This sophism derives much, perhaps the whole, of its currency from the assumption that there is some omnipotent and sacred supremacy pertaining to a State—to each State of our Federal Union. Our States have neither more nor less power than that reserved to them in the Union by the Constitution—no one of them ever having been a State out of the Union. The original ones passed into the Union even before they cast off their British colonial dependence; and the new ones each came into the Union directly from a condition of dependence, excepting Texas. And even Texas in its temporary independence was never designated a State. The new ones only took the designation of States on coming into the Union, while that name was first adopted for the old ones in and by the Declaration of Independence. Therein the "United Colonies" were declared to be "free and independent States"; but even then the object plainly was not to declare their independence of one another or of the Union, but directly the contrary, as their mutual pledge and their mutual action before, at the time, and afterward, abundantly show. The express plighting of faith by each and all of the original thirteen in the Articles of Confederation, two years later, that the Union shall be perpetual, is most conclusive. Having never been States either in substance or in name outside of the Union, whence this magical omnipotence of "State rights," asserting a claim of power to lawfully destroy the Union itself? Much is said about the "sovereignty" of the States; but the word even is not in the national Constitution, nor, as is believed, in any of the State constitutions. What is "sovereignty" in the political sense of the term? Would it be far wrong to define it as "a political community without a political superior"? Tested by this, no one of our States except Texas ever was a sovereignty. And even Texas gave up the character on coming into the Union; by which act she acknowledged the Constitution of the United States, and the laws and treaties of the United States made in pursuance of the Constitution, to be for her the supreme law of the land. The States have their status in the Union, and they have no other legal status. If they break from this, they can only do so against law and by revolution. The Union, and not themselves separately, procured their independence and their liberty. By conquest or purchase the Union gave each of them whatever of independence or liberty it has. The Union is older than any of the States, and, in fact, it created them as States. Originally some dependent colonies made the Union, and, in turn, the Union threw off their old dependence for them, and made them States, such as they are. Not one of them ever had a State constitution independent of the Union. Of course, it is not forgotten that all the new States framed their constitutions before they entered the Union nevertheless, dependent upon and preparatory to coming into the Union.

Unquestionably the States have the powers and rights reserved to them in and by the national Constitution; but among these surely are not included all conceivable powers, however mischievous or destructive, but, at most, such only as were known in the world at the time as governmental powers; and certainly a power to destroy the government itself had never been known as a governmental, as a merely administrative power. This relative matter of national power and State rights, as a principle, is no other than the principle of generality and locality. Whatever concerns the whole should be confided to the whole—to the General Government; while whatever concerns only the State should be left exclusively to the State. This is all there is of original principle about it. Whether the national Constitution in defining boundaries between the two has applied the principle with exact accuracy, is not to be questioned. We are all bound by that defining, without question.

What is now combated is the position that secession is consistent with the Constitution—is lawful and peaceful. It is not contended that there is any express law for it; and nothing should ever be implied as law which leads to unjust or absurd consequences. The nation purchased with money the countries out of which several of these States were formed. Is it just that they shall go off without leave and without refunding? The nation paid very large sums (in the aggregate, I believe, nearly a hundred millions) to relieve Florida of the aboriginal tribes. Is it just that she shall now be off without consent or without making any return? The nation is now in debt for money applied to the benefit of these so-called seceding States in common with the rest. Is it just either that creditors shall go unpaid or the remaining States pay the whole? A part of the present national debt was contracted to pay the old debts of Texas. Is it just that she shall leave and pay no part of this herself?

Again, if one State may secede, so may another; and when all shall have seceded, none is left to pay the debts. Is this quite just for creditors? Did we notify them of this sage view of ours when we borrowed their money? If we now recognize this doctrine by allowing the seceders to go in peace, it is difficult to see what we can do if others choose to go or to extort terms upon which they will promise to remain.

The seceders insist that our Constitution admits of secession. They have assumed to make a national constitution of their own, in which of necessity they have either discarded or retained the right of secession as they insist it exists in ours. If they have discarded it, they thereby admit that on principle it ought not to be in ours. If they have retained it, by their own construction of ours, they show that to be consistent they must secede from one another whenever they shall find it the easiest way of settling their debts, or effecting any other selfish or unjust object. The principle itself is one of disintegration and upon which no government can possibly endure.

If all the States save one should assert the power to drive that one out of the Union, it is presumed the whole class of seceder politicians would at once deny the power and denounce the act as the greatest outrage upon State rights. But suppose that precisely the same act, instead of being called "driving the one out," should be called "the seceding of the others from that one," it would be exactly what the seceders claim to do, unless, indeed, they make the point that the one, because it is a minority, may rightfully do what the others, because they are a majority, may not rightfully do. These politicians are subtle and profound on the rights of minorities. They are not partial to that power which made the Constitution and speaks from the preamble calling itself "We, the People."

It may well be questioned whether there is to-day a majority of the legally qualified voters of any State except perhaps South Carolina in favor of disunion. There is much reason to believe that the Union men are the majority in many, if not in every other one, of the so-called seceded States. The contrary has not been demonstrated in any one of them. It is ventured to affirm this even of Virginia and Tennessee; for the result of an election held in military camps, where the bayonets are all on one side of the question voted upon, can scarcely be considered as demonstrating popular sentiment. At such an election, all that large class who are at once for the Union and against coercion would be coerced to vote against the Union.

It may be affirmed without extravagance that the free institutions we enjoy have developed the powers and improved the condition of our whole people beyond any example in the world. Of this we now have a striking and an impressive illustration. So large an army as the government has now on foot was never before known without a soldier in it but who has taken his place there of his own free choice. But more than this, there are many single regiments whose members, one and another, possess full practical knowledge of all the arts, sciences, professions, and whatever else, whether useful or elegant, is known in the world; and there is scarcely one from which there could not be selected a President, a Cabinet, a Congress, and perhaps a court, abundantly competent to administer the government itself. Nor do I say this is not true also in the army of our late friends, now adversaries in this contest; but if it is, so much better the reason why the government which has conferred such benefits on both them and us should not be broken up. Whoever in any section proposes to abandon such a government would do well to consider in deference to what principle it is that he does it; what better he is likely to get in its stead; whether the substitute will give, or be intended to give, so much of good to the people. There are some foreshadowings on this subject. Our adversaries have adopted some declarations of independence in which, unlike the good old one, penned by Jefferson, they omit the words "all men are created equal." Why? They have adopted a temporary national constitution, in the preamble of which, unlike our good old one, signed by Washington, they omit "We, the People," and substitute, "We, the deputies of the sovereign and independent States." Why? Why this deliberate pressing out of view the rights of men and the authority of the people?

This is essentially a people's contest. On the side of the Union it is a struggle for maintaining in the world that form and substance of government whose leading object is to elevate the condition of men to lift artificial weights from all shoulders; to clear the paths of laudable pursuit for all; to afford all an unfettered start, and a fair chance in the race of life. Yielding to partial and temporary departures, from necessity; this is the leading object of the government for whose existence we contend.

I am most happy to believe that the plain people understand and appreciate this. It is worthy of note that, while in this the government's hour of trial large numbers of those in the army and navy who have been favored with the offices have resigned and proved false to the hand which had pampered them, not one common soldier or common sailor is known to have deserted his flag.

Great honor is due to those officers who remained true, despite the example of their treacherous associates; but the greatest honor, and most important fact of all, is the unanimous firmness of the common soldiers and common sailors. To the last man, so far as known, they have successfully resisted the traitorous efforts of those whose commands, but an hour before, they obeyed as absolute law. This is the patriotic instinct of the plain people. They understand, without an argument, that the destroying of the government which was made by Washington means no good to them.

Our popular government has often been called an experiment. Two points in it our people have already settled—the successful establishing and the successful administering of it. One still remains—its successful maintenance against a formidable internal attempt to overthrow it. It is now for them to demonstrate to the world that those who can fairly carry an election can also suppress a rebellion; that ballots are the rightful and peaceful successors of bullets; and that when ballots have fairly and constitutionally decided, there can be no successful appeal back to bullets; that there can be no successful appeal, except to ballots themselves, at succeeding elections. Such will be a great lesson of peace: teaching men that what they cannot take by an election, neither can they take it by a war; teaching all the folly of being the beginners of a war.

Lest there be some uneasiness in the minds of candid men as to what is to be the course of the government toward the Southern States after the rebellion shall have been suppressed, the executive deems it proper to say it will be his purpose then, as ever, to be guided by the Constitution and the laws; and that he probably will have no different understanding of the powers and duties of the Federal Government relatively to the rights of the States and the people, under the Constitution, than that expressed in the inaugural address.

He desires to preserve the government, that it may be administered for all as it was administered by the men who made it. Loyal citizens everywhere have the right to claim this of their government, and the government has no right to withhold or neglect it. It is not perceived that in giving it there is any coercion, any conquest, or any subjugation, in any just sense of those terms.

The Constitution provides, and all the States have accepted the provision, that "the United States shall guarantee to every State in this Union a republican form of government." But if a State may lawfully go out of the Union, having done so it may also discard the republican form of government, so that to prevent its going out is an indispensable means to the end of maintaining the guarantee mentioned; and when an end is lawful and obligatory, the indispensable means to it are also lawful and obligatory.

It was with the deepest regret that the executive found the duty of employing the war power in defense of the government forced upon him. He could but perform this duty or surrender the existence of the government. No compromise by public servants could, in this case, be a cure; not that compromises are not often proper, but that no popular government can long survive a marked precedent that those who carry an election can only save the government from immediate destruction by giving up the main point upon which the people gave the election. The people themselves, and not their servants, can safely reverse their own deliberate decisions.

As a private citizen the executive could not have consented that these institutions shall perish; much less could he in betrayal of so vast and so sacred a trust as these free people had confided to him. He felt that he had no moral right to shrink, nor even to count the chances of his own life, in what might follow. In full view of his great responsibility he has, so far, done what he has deemed his duty. You will now, according to your own judgment, perform yours. He sincerely hopes that your views and your action may so accord with his as to assure all faithful citizens who have been disturbed in their rights of a certain and speedy restoration to them, under the Constitution and the laws.

And having thus chosen our course, without guile and with pure purpose, let us renew our trust in God, and go forward without fear and with manly hearts.

A. LINCOLN,
July 4, 1861

TO THE SECRETARY OF THE INTERIOR.

EXECUTIVE MANSION, July 6, 1861.

HON. SEC. OF INTERIOR.

MY DEAR SIR:—Please ask the Comr. of Indian Affairs, and of the Gen'l Land Office to come with you, and see me at once. I want the assistance of all of you in overhauling the list of appointments a little before I send them to the Senate.

Yours truly,
A. LINCOLN.

MESSAGE TO THE HOUSE OF REPRESENTATIVES.

TO THE HOUSE OF REPRESENTATIVES:

In answer to the resolution of the House of Representatives of the 9th instant, requesting a copy of correspondence upon the subject of the incorporation of the Dominican republic with the Spanish monarchy, I transmit a report from the Secretary of State; to whom the resolution was referred.
WASHINGTON, July 11, 1861.

MESSAGE TO CONGRESS.

TO THE SENATE AND HOUSE OF REPRESENTATIVES:

I transmit to Congress a copy of correspondence between the Secretary of State and her Britannic Majesty's envoy extraordinary and minister plenipotentiary accredited to this government, relative to the exhibition of the products of industry of all nations, which is to take place at London in the course of next year. As citizens of the United States may justly pride themselves upon their proficiency in industrial arts, it is desirable that they should have proper facilities toward taking part in the exhibition. With this view I recommend such legislation by Congress at this session as may be necessary for that purpose.
A. LINCOLN.
WASHINGTON, July 16, 1861

MESSAGE TO CONGRESS.

TO THE SENATE AND HOUSE OF REPRESENTATIVES:

As the United States have, in common with Great Britain and France, a deep interest in the preservation and development of the fisheries adjacent to the northeastern coast and islands of this continent, it seems proper that we should concert with the governments of those countries such measures as may be conducive to those important objects. With this view I transmit to Congress a copy of a correspondence between the Secretary of State and the British minister here, in which the latter proposes, on behalf of his government, the appointment of a joint commission to inquire into the matter, in order that such ulterior measures may be adopted as may be advisable for the objects proposed. Such legislation recommended as may be necessary to enable the executive to provide for a commissioner on behalf of the United States:
WASHINGTON, JULY 19, 1861. A. LINCOLN.

TO THE ADJUTANT-GENERAL

WASHINGTON, JULY 19, 1861

ADJUTANT-GENERAL:
I have agreed, and do agree, that the two Indian regiments named within shall be accepted if the act of Congress shall admit it. Let there be no further question about it.
A. LINCOLN.

MEMORANDA OF MILITARY POLICY SUGGESTED BY THE BULL RUN DEFEAT. JULY 23, 1861

1. Let the plan for making the blockade effective be pushed forward with all possible despatch.
2. Let the volunteer forces at Fort Monroe and vicinity under General Butler be constantly drilled, disciplined, and instructed without more for the present.
3. Let Baltimore be held as now, with a gentle but firm and certain hand.
4. Let the force now under Patterson or Banks be strengthened and made secure in its position.
5. Let the forces in Western Virginia act till further orders according to instructions or orders from General McClellan.
6. [Let] General Fremont push forward his organization and operations in the West as rapidly as possible, giving rather special attention to Missouri.
7. Let the forces late before Manassas, except the three-months men, be reorganized as rapidly as possible in their camps here and about Arlington.
8. Let the three-months forces who decline to enter the longer service be discharged as rapidly as circumstances will permit.

9. Let the new volunteer forces be brought forward as fast as possible, and especially into the camps on the two sides of the river here.

When the foregoing shall be substantially attended to:

1. Let Manassas Junction (or some point on one or other of the railroads near it) and Strasburg be seized, and permanently held, with an open line from Washington to Manassas, and an open line from Harper's Ferry to Strasburg the military men to find the way of doing these.

2. This done, a joint movement from Cairo on Memphis; and from Cincinnati on East Tennessee.

TO THE GOVERNOR OF NEW JERSEY.

WASHINGTON, D.C., July 24, 1861

THE GOVERNOR OF NEW JERSEY.

SIR:—Together with the regiments of three years' volunteers which the government already has in service in your State, enough to make eight in all, if tendered in a reasonable time, will be accepted, the new regiments to be taken, as far as convenient, from the three months' men and officers just discharged, and to be organized, equipped, and sent forward as fast as single regiments are ready, On the same terms as were those already in the service from that State.

Your obedient servant,

A. LINCOLN.

[Indorsement.]

This order is entered in the War Department, and the Governor of New Jersey is authorized to furnish the regiments with wagons and horses.

S. CAMERON, Secretary of War.

MESSAGE TO THE HOUSE OF REPRESENTATIVES.

TO THE HOUSE OF REPRESENTATIVES:

In answer to the resolution of the House of Representatives of the 22d instant; requesting a copy of the correspondence between this, government and foreign powers with reference to maritime right, I transmit a report from the Secretary of State.

A. LINCOLN.

WASHINGTON, July 25, 1861

MESSAGE TO THE HOUSE OF REPRESENTATIVES.

TO THE HOUSE OF REPRESENTATIVES:

In answer to the resolution of the House of Representatives of the 15th instant, requesting a copy of the correspondence between this government and foreign powers on the subject of the existing insurrection in the United States, I transmit a report from the Secretary of State.

WASHINGTON, July 25, 1861.

A. LINCOLN.

TO SECRETARY CHASE.

EXECUTIVE MANSION, JULY 16, 1861

MR CHASE:—The bearer, Mr. ———, wants ——— in the custom house at Baltimore. If his recommendations are satisfactory, and I recollect them to have been so, the fact that he is urged by the Methodists should be in his favor, as they complain of us some.
LINCOLN.

MESSAGE TO THE HOUSE OF REPRESENTATIVES.

TO THE HOUSE OF REPRESENTATIVES:

In answer to the resolution of the House of Representatives of the 24th instant, asking the grounds, reasons, and evidence upon which the police Commissioners of Baltimore were arrested and are now detained as prisoners at Port McHenry, I have to state that it is judged to be incompatible with the public interest at this time to furnish the information called for by the resolution.
A. LINCOLN. WASHINGTON, JULY 27, 1861

MESSAGE TO THE SENATE.

TO THE SENATE OF THE UNITED STATES:

In answer to the resolution of the Senate of the 19th instant requesting information concerning the quasi armistice alluded to in my message of the 4th instant, I transmit a report from the Secretary of the Navy.
A. LINCOLN. JULY 30, 1861

MESSAGE TO THE SENATE.

TO THE SENATE OF THE UNITED STATES:

In answer to the resolution of the Senate of the 23d instant requesting information concerning the imprisonment of Lieutenant John J. Worden (John L. Worden) of the United States navy, I transmit a report from the Secretary of the Navy.
A. LINCOLN.
July 30, 1861

ORDER TO UNITED STATES MARSHALS.

EXECUTIVE MANSION, WASHINGTON, D.C., JULY 31, 1861

The Marshals of the United States in the vicinity of forts where political prisoners are held will supply decent lodging and sustenance for such prisoners unless they shall prefer to provide in those respects for themselves, in which case they will be allowed to do so by the commanding officer in charge.
Approved, and the Secretary of the State will transmit the order to the Marshals, to the Lieutenant-General, and the Secretary of the Interior.
A. LINCOLN.

MESSAGE TO THE HOUSE OF REPRESENTATIVES.

TO THE HOUSE OF REPRESENTATIVES:

In answer to the resolution of the House of Representatives of yesterday, requesting information regarding the imprisonment of loyal citizens of the United States by the forces now in rebellion against this government, I transmit a report from the Secretary of State, and the copy of a telegraphic despatch by which it was accompanied.
A. LINCOLN.
WASHINGTON, August 2, 1861.

MESSAGE TO THE SENATE.

TO THE SENATE OF THE UNITED STATES:

In answer to the resolution of your honorable body of date July 31, 1861, requesting the President to inform the Senate whether the Hon. James H. Lane, a member of that body from Kansas, has been appointed a brigadier-general in the army of the United States, and if so, whether he has accepted such appointment, I have the honor to transmit herewith certain papers, numbered 1, 2, 3, 4, 5, 6, and 7, which, taken together, explain themselves, and which contain all the information I possess upon the questions propounded.
It was my intention, as shown by my letter of June 20, 1861, to appoint Hon. James H. Lane, of Kansas, a brigadier-general of United States volunteers in anticipation of the act of Congress, since passed, for raising such volunteers; and I have no further knowledge upon the subject, except as derived from the papers herewith enclosed.
EXECUTIVE MANSION, August 5, 1861

TO SECRETARY CAMERON.

EXECUTIVE MANSION, AUGUST 7, 1861

HON. SECRETARY OF WAR
MY DEAR SIR:—The within paper, as you see, is by HON. John S. Phelps and HON. Frank P. Blair, Jr., both members of the present Congress from Missouri. The object is to get up an efficient force of Missourians in the southwestern part of the State. It ought to be done, and Mr. Phelps ought to have general superintendence of it. I see by a private report to me from the department that eighteen regiments are already accepted from Missouri. Can it not be arranged that part of them (not yet organized, as I understand) may be taken from the locality mentioned and put under the control of Mr. Phelps, and let him have discretion to accept them for a shorter term than three years—or the war—understanding, however, that he will get them for the full term if he can? I hope this can be done, because Mr. Phelps is too zealous and efficient and understands his ground too well for us to lose his service. Of course provision for arming, equipping, etc., must be made. Mr. Phelps is here, and wishes to carry home with him authority for this matter.
Yours truly,
A. LINCOLN

PROCLAMATION OF A NATIONAL FAST-DAY, AUGUST 12, 1861.

BY THE PRESIDENT OF THE UNITED STATES OF AMERICA

A Proclamation.

Whereas a joint committee of both houses of Congress has waited on the President of the United States and requested him to "recommend a day of public humiliation, prayer, and fasting to be observed by the people of the United States with religious solemnities and the offering of fervent supplications to Almighty God for the safety and welfare of these States, His blessings on their arms, and a speedy restoration of peace"; and

Whereas it is fit and becoming in all people at all times to acknowledge and revere the supreme government of God, to bow in humble submission to His chastisements, to confess and deplore their sins and transgressions in the full conviction that the fear of the Lord is the beginning of wisdom, and to pray with all fervency and contrition for the pardon of their past offences and for a blessing upon their present and prospective action; and

Whereas when our own beloved country, once, by the blessing of God, united, prosperous, and happy, is now afflicted with faction and civil war, it is peculiarly fit for us to recognize the hand of God in this terrible visitation, and in sorrowful remembrance of our own faults and crimes as a nation and as individuals to humble ourselves before Him and to pray for His mercy-to pray that we may be spared further punishment, though most justly deserved, that our arms may be blessed and made effectual for the re-establishment of order, law, and peace throughout the wide extent of our country, and that the inestimable boon of civil and religious liberty, earned under His guidance and blessing by the labors and sufferings of our fathers, may be restored in all its original excellence.

Therefore I, Abraham Lincoln, President of the United States, do appoint the last Thursday in September next as a day of humiliation, prayer, and fasting for all the people of the nation. And I do earnestly recommend to all the people, and especially to all ministers and teachers of religion of all denominations and to all heads of families, to observe and keep that day according to their several creeds and modes of worship in all humility and with all religious solemnity, to the end that the united prayer of the nation may ascend to the Throne of Grace and bring down plentiful blessings upon our country.

In testimony whereof I have hereunto set my hand
and caused the seal of the United States to
[SEAL.]
be affixed, this twelfth day of August, A. D.
1861, and of the independence of the United
States of America the eighty-sixth.
A. LINCOLN.
By the President: WILLIAM H. SEWARD,
Secretary of State.

TO JAMES POLLOCK.

WASHINGTON, AUGUST 15, 1861

HON. JAMES POLLOCK.
MY DEAR SIR:—You must make a job for the bearer of this—make a job of it with the collector and have it done. You can do it for me and you must.
Yours as ever,
A. LINCOLN.

TELEGRAM TO GOVERNOR O. P. MORTON.

WASHINGTON, D.C., AUGUST 15, 1861

GOVERNOR MORTON, Indiana: Start your four regiments to St. Louis at the earliest moment possible. Get such harness as may be necessary for your rifled guns. Do not delay a single regiment, but hasten everything forward as soon as any one regiment is ready. Have your three additional regiments organized at once. We shall endeavor to send you the arms this week.
A. LINCOLN

TELEGRAM TO GENERAL FREMONT,

WASHINGTON, August 15, 1861

TO MAJOR-GENERAL FREMONT:
Been answering your messages since day before yesterday. Do you receive the answers? The War Department has notified all the governors you designate to forward all available force. So telegraphed you. Have you received these messages? Answer immediately.
A. LINCOLN.

PROCLAMATION FORBIDDING INTERCOURSE WITH REBEL STATES, AUGUST 16, 1861.

BY THE PRESIDENT OF THE UNITED STATES OF AMERICA:

A Proclamation.
Whereas on the fifteenth day of April, eighteen hundred and sixty-one, the President of the United States, in view of an insurrection against the laws, Constitution, and government of the United States which had broken out within the States of South Carolina, Georgia, Alabama, Florida, Mississippi, Louisiana, and Texas, and in pursuance of the provisions of the act entitled "An act to provide for calling forth the militia to execute the laws of the Union, suppress insurrections, and repel invasions, and to repeal the act now in force for that purpose," approved February twenty-eighth, seventeen hundred and ninety-five, did call forth the militia to suppress said insurrection, and to cause the laws of the Union to be duly executed, and the insurgents have failed to disperse by the time directed by the President; and whereas such insurrection has since broken out and yet exists within the States of Virginia, North Carolina, Tennessee, and Arkansas; and whereas the insurgents in all the said States claim to act under the authority thereof, and such claim is not disclaimed or repudiated by the persons exercising the functions of government in such State or States, or in the part or parts thereof in which such combinations exist, nor has such insurrection been suppressed by said States:
Now, therefore, I, Abraham Lincoln, President of the United States, in pursuance of an act of Congress approved July thirteen, eighteen hundred and sixty-one, do hereby declare that the inhabitants of the said States of Georgia, South Carolina, Virginia, North Carolina, Tennessee, Alabama, Louisiana, Texas, Arkansas, Mississippi, and Florida (except the inhabitants of that part of the State of Virginia lying west of the Allegheny Mountains, and of such other parts of that State, and the other States hereinbefore named, as may maintain a loyal adhesion to the Union and the Constitution, or may be time to time occupied and controlled by forces of the United States engaged in the dispersion of said insurgents), are in a state of insurrection against the United States, and that all commercial intercourse between the same and the inhabitants thereof, with the exceptions aforesaid, and the citizens of other States and other parts of the United States, is unlawful, and will remain unlawful until such insurrection shall cease or has been suppressed; that all goods and chattels, wares and merchandise, coming from any of said States, with the exceptions aforesaid, into other parts of the United States, without the special license and permission of the President, through the Secretary of the Treasury, or proceeding to any of said States, with the exceptions aforesaid, by land or water, together with the vessel or vehicle conveying the same, or conveying persons to or from said States, with said exceptions, will be forfeited to the United States; and that from and after fifteen days from the issuing of this proclamation all ships and vessels belonging in whole or in part to any citizen or inhabitant of any of said States, with said exceptions, found at sea, or in any port of the United States, will be forfeited to the United States; and I hereby enjoin upon all district attorneys, marshals, and officers of the revenue and of the military and naval forces of the United States to be vigilant in the execution of said act, and in the enforcement of the penalties and forfeitures imposed or declared by it; leaving any party who may think himself aggrieved thereby to his application to the Secretary of the Treasury for the remission of any penalty or forfeiture, which the said Secretary is authorized by law to grant if, in his judgment, the special circumstances of any case shall require such remission.
In witness whereof, I have hereunto set my hand,....
A. LINCOLN.
By the President: WILLIAM H. SEWARD, Secretary of Sate.

TO SECRETARY CAMERON.

EXECUTIVE MANSION, August 17, 1861

HON. SECRETARY OF WAR.
MY DEAR SIR:—Unless there be reason to the contrary, not known to me, make out a commission for Simon B. Buckner, of Kentucky, as a brigadier-general of volunteers. It is to be put into the hands of General Anderson, and delivered to General Buckner or not, at the discretion of General Anderson. Of course it is to remain a secret unless and until the commission is delivered.
Yours truly, A. LINCOLN
Same day made.
[Indorsement.]

TO GOVERNOR MAGOFFIN,

WASHINGTON, D.C., AUGUST 24, 1861

To HIS EXCELLENCY B. MAGOFFIN, Governor of the State of Kentucky.
SIR:—Your letter of the 19th instant, in which you urge the "removal from the limits of Kentucky of the military force now organized and in camp within that State," is received.
I may not possess full and precisely accurate knowledge upon this subject; but I believe it is true that there is a military force in camp within Kentucky, acting by authority of the United States, which force is not very large, and is not now being augmented.
I also believe that some arms have been furnished to this force by the United States.
I also believe this force consists exclusively of Kentuckians, having their camp in the immediate vicinity of their own homes, and not assailing or menacing any of the good people of Kentucky.
In all I have done in the premises I have acted upon the urgent solicitation of many Kentuckians, and in accordance with what I believed, and still believe, to be the wish of a majority of all the Union-loving people of Kentucky.
While I have conversed on this subject with many eminent men of Kentucky, including a large majority of her members of Congress, I do not remember that any one of them, or any other person, except your Excellency and the bearers of your Excellency's letter, has urged me to remove the military force from Kentucky or to disband it. One other very worthy citizen of Kentucky did solicit me to have the augmenting of the force suspended for a time.
Taking all the means within my reach to form a judgment, I do not believe it is the popular wish of Kentucky that this force shall be removed beyond her limits; and, with this impression, I must respectfully decline to so remove it.
I most cordially sympathize with your Excellency in the wish to preserve the peace of my own native State, Kentucky. It is with regret I search, and cannot find, in your not very short letter, any declaration or intimation that you entertain any desire for the preservation of the Federal Union.
Your obedient servant,
A. LINCOLN.

TO GENERAL FREMONT.

WASHINGTON, D.C., SEPTEMBER 2, 1861

MAJOR-GENERAL FREMONT.
MY DEAR SIR:—Two points in your proclamation of August 30 give me some anxiety.
First. Should you shoot a man, according to the proclamation, the Confederates would very certainly shoot our best men in their hands in retaliation; and so, man for man, indefinitely. It is, therefore, my order that you allow no man to be shot under the proclamation without first having my approbation or consent.
Second. I think there is great danger that the closing paragraph, in relation to the confiscation of property and the liberating slaves of traitorous owners, will alarm our Southern Union friends and turn them against us; perhaps ruin

our rather fair prospect for Kentucky. Allow me, therefore, to ask that you will, as of your own motion, modify that paragraph so as to conform to the first and fourth sections of the act of Congress entitled "An act to confiscate property used for insurrectionary purposes," approved August 6, 1861, and a copy of which act I herewith send you.

This letter is written in a spirit of caution, and not of censure. I send it by special messenger, in order that it may certainly and speedily reach you.

Yours very truly,
A. LINCOLN.

TELEGRAM TO GOVERNORS

WASHBURN OF MAINE, FAIRBANKS OF VERMONT, BERRY OF NEW HAMPSHIRE, ANDREW OF MASSACHUSETTS, BUCKINGHAM OF CONNECTICUT, AND SPRAGUE OF RHODE ISLAND.
WAR DEPARTMENT, September 11, 1861.
General Butler proposes raising in New England six regiments, to be recruited and commanded by himself, and to go on special service.
I shall be glad if you, as governor of ————, will answer by telegraph if you consent.
A. LINCOLN.

TO GENERAL FREMONT.

WASHINGTON, D.C., SEPTEMBER 11, 1861

MAJOR-GENERAL JOHN C. FREMONT.
SIR:-Yours of the 8th, in answer to mine of the 2d instant, is just received. Assuming that you, upon the ground, could better judge of the necessities of your position than I could at this distance, on seeing your proclamation of August 30 I perceived no general objection to it. The particular clause, however, in relation to the confiscation of property and the liberation of slaves appeared to me to be objectionable in its nonconformity to the act of Congress passed the 6th of last August upon the same subjects; and hence I wrote you, expressing my wish that that clause should be modified accordingly. Your answer, just received, expresses the preference on your part that I should make an open order for the modification, which I very cheerfully do. It is therefore ordered that the said clause of said proclamation be so modified, held, and construed as to conform to, and not to transcend, the provisions on the same subject contained in the act of Congress entitled "An act to confiscate property used for insurrectionary purposes," approved August 6, 1861, and that said act be published at length with this order.
Your obedient servant,
A. LINCOLN.

TO MRS. FREMONT.

WASHINGTON, D.C., September 12, 1861

Mrs. GENERAL FREMONT.
MY DEAR MADAM:—Your two notes of to-day are before me. I answered the letter you bore me from General Fremont on yesterday, and not hearing from you during the day, I sent the answer to him by mail. It is not exactly correct, as you say you were told by the elder Mr. Blair, to say that I sent Postmaster-General Blair to St. Louis to examine into that department and report. Postmaster-General Blair did go, with my approbation, to see and converse with General Fremont as a friend. I do not feel authorized to furnish you with copies of letters in my possession without the consent of the writers. No impression has been made on my mind against the honor or integrity of General Fremont, and I now enter my protest against being understood as acting in any hostility toward him.
Your obedient servant,

A. LINCOLN.

TO JOSEPH HOLT,

EXECUTIVE MANSION, SEPTEMBER 12, 1861

HON. JOSEPH HOLT.
DEAR SIR:—Yours of this day in relation to the late proclamation of General Fremont is received yesterday I addressed a letter to him, by mail, on the same subject, and which is to be made public when he receives it. I herewith send you a copy of that letter, which perhaps shows my position as distinctly as any new one I could write. I will thank you not to make it public until General Fremont shall have had time to receive the original.
Your obedient servant,
A. LINCOLN.

TO GENERAL SCOTT

WASHINGTON, D.C., September 16, 1861.

DEAR SIR:—Since conversing with you I have concluded to request you to frame an order for recruiting North Carolinians at Fort Hatteras. I suggest it to be so framed as for us to accept a smaller force—even a company—if we cannot get a regiment or more. What is necessary to now say about officers you will judge. Governor Seward says he has a nephew (Clarence A. Seward, I believe) who would be willing to go and play colonel and assist in raising the force. Still it is to be considered whether the North Carolinians will not prefer officers of their own. I should expect they would.
Yours very truly,
A. LINCOLN.

TO SECRETARY CAMERON.

EXECUTIVE MANSION, September 18, 1861

HON. SECRETARY OF WAR. MY DEAR SIR:—To guard against misunderstanding, I think fit to say that the joint expedition of the army and navy agreed upon some time since, and in which General T. W. Sherman was and is to bear a conspicuous part, is in no wise to be abandoned, but must be ready to move by the 1st of, or very early in, October. Let all preparations go forward accordingly.
Yours truly,
A. LINCOLN.

TO GENERAL FREMONT,

WASHINGTON, SEPTEMBER 12, 1861

MAJOR-GENERAL FREMONT:
Governor Morton telegraphs as follows: "Colonel Lane, just arrived by special train, represents Owensborough, forty miles above Evansville, in possession of secessionists. Green River is navigable. Owensborough must be seized. We

want a gunboat sent up from Paducah for that purpose." Send up the gunboat if, in your discretion, you think it right. Perhaps you had better order those in charge of the Ohio River to guard it vigilantly at all points.
A. LINCOLN.

To O. H. BROWNING.

(Private and Confidential)

EXECUTIVE MANSION, WASHINGTON SEPTEMBER 22, 1861 HON. O. H. BROWNING.
MY DEAR SIR:—Yours of the 17th is just received; and coming from you, I confess it astonishes me. That you should object to my adhering to a law which you had assisted in making and presenting to me less than a month before is odd enough. But this is a very small part. General Fremont's proclamation as to confiscation of property and the liberation of slaves is purely political and not within the range of military law or necessity. If a commanding general finds a necessity to seize the farm of a private owner for a pasture, an encampment, or a fortification, he has the right to do so, and to so hold it as long as the necessity lasts; and this is within military law, because within military necessity. But to say the farm shall no longer belong to the owner, or his heirs forever, and this as well when the farm is not needed for military purposes as when it is, is purely political, without the savor of military law about it. And the same is true of slaves. If the general needs them, he can seize them and use them; but when the need is past, it is not for him to fix their permanent future condition. That must be settled according to laws made by law-makers, and not by military proclamations. The proclamation in the point in question is simply "dictatorship." It assumes that the general may do anything he pleases confiscate the lands and free the slaves of loyal people, as well as of disloyal ones. And going the whole figure, I have no doubt, would be more popular with some thoughtless people than that which has been done, But I cannot assume this reckless position, nor allow others to assume it on my responsibility.
You speak of it as being the only means of saving the government. On the contrary, it is itself the surrender of the government. Can it be pretended that it is any longer the Government of the United States—any government of constitution and laws wherein a general or a president may make permanent rules of property by proclamation? I do not say Congress might not with propriety pass a law on the point, just such as General Fremont proclaimed.
I do not say I might not, as a member of Congress, vote for it. What I object to is, that I, as President, shall expressly or impliedly seize and exercise the permanent legislative functions of the government.
So much as to principle. Now as to policy. No doubt the thing was popular in some quarters, and would have been more so if it had been a general declaration of emancipation. The Kentucky Legislature would not budge till that proclamation was modified; and General Anderson telegraphed me that on the news of General Fremont having actually issued deeds of manumission, a whole company of our volunteers threw down their arms and disbanded. I was so assured as to think it probable that the very arms we had furnished Kentucky would be turned against us. I think to lose Kentucky is nearly the same as to lose the whole game. Kentucky gone, we cannot hold Missouri, nor, as I think, Maryland. These all against us, and the job on our hands is too large for us. We would as well consent to separation at once, including the surrender of this Capital. On the contrary, if you will give up your restlessness for new positions, and back me manfully on the grounds upon which you and other kind friends gave me the election and have approved in my public documents, we shall go through triumphantly. You must not understand I took my course on the proclamation because of Kentucky. I took the same ground in a private letter to General Fremont before I heard from Kentucky.
You think I am inconsistent because I did not also forbid General Fremont to shoot men under the proclamation. I understand that part to be within military law, but I also think, and so privately wrote General Fremont, that it is impolitic in this, that our adversaries have the power, and will certainly exercise it, to shoot as many of our men as we shoot of theirs. I did not say this in the public letter, because it is a subject I prefer not to discuss in the hearing of our enemies.
There has been no thought of removing General Fremont on any ground connected with his proclamation, and if there has been any wish for his removal on any ground, our mutual friend Sam. Glover can probably tell you what it was. I hope no real necessity for it exists on any ground.
Your friend, as ever,
A. LINCOLN.

MEMORANDUM FOR A PLAN OF CAMPAIGN

[OCTOBER 1?] 1861

On or about the 5th of October (the exact date to be determined hereafter) I wish a movement made to seize and hold a point on the railroad connecting Virginia and Tennessee near the mountain-pass called Cumberland Gap. That point is now guarded against us by Zollicoffer, with 6000 or 8000 rebels at Barboursville Ky.,—say twenty-five miles from the Gap, toward Lexington. We have a force of 5000 or 6000 under General Thomas, at Camp Dick Robinson, about twenty-five miles from Lexington and seventy-five from Zollicoffer's camp, On the road between the two. There is not a railroad anywhere between Lexington and the point to be seized, and along the whole length of which the Union sentiment among the people largely predominates. We have military possession of the railroad from Cincinnati to Lexington, and from Louisville to Lexington, and some home guards, under General Crittenden, are on the latter line. We have possession of the railroad from Louisville to Nashville, Tenn., so far as Muldraugh's Hill, about forty miles, and the rebels have possession of that road all south of there. At the Hill we have a force of 8000, under General Sherman, and about an equal force of rebels is a very short distance south, under General Buckner.
We have a large force at Paducah, and a smaller at Port Holt, both on the Kentucky side, with some at Bird's Point, Cairo, Mound City, Evansville, and New Albany, all on the other side, and all which, with the gunboats on the river, are perhaps sufficient to guard the Ohio from Louisville to its mouth.
About supplies of troops, my general idea is that all from Wisconsin, Minnesota, Iowa, Illinois, Missouri, and Kansas, not now elsewhere, be left to Fremont. All from Indiana and Michigan, not now elsewhere, be sent to Anderson at Louisville. All from Ohio needed in western Virginia be sent there, and any remainder be sent to Mitchell at Cincinnati, for Anderson. All east of the mountains be appropriated to McClellan and to the coast.
As to movements, my idea is that the one for the coast and that on Cumberland Gap be simultaneous, and that in the meantime preparation, vigilant watching, and the defensive only be acted upon; this, however, not to apply to Fremont's operations in northern and middle Missouri. That before these movements Thomas and Sherman shall respectively watch but not attack Zollicoffer and Buckner. That when the coast and Gap movements shall be ready Sherman is merely to stand fast, while all at Cincinnati and all at Louisville, with all on the line, concentrate rapidly at Lexington, and thence to Thomas's camp, joining him, and the whole thence upon the Gap. It is for the military men to decide whether they can find a pass through the mountains at or near the Gap which cannot be defended by the enemy with a greatly inferior force, and what is to be done in regard to this.
The coast and Gap movements made, Generals McClellan and Fremont, in their respective departments, will avail themselves of any advantages the diversions may present.
[He was entirely unable to get this started, Sherman would have taken an active part if given him, the others were too busy getting lines of communication guarded—and discovering many "critical" supply items that had not been sent them. Also the commanding general did not like it. D.W.]

TO THE SECRETARY OF STATE.

EXECUTIVE MANSION, October 4, 1861

HONORABLE SECRETARY OF STATE.
DEAR SIR:—Please see Mr. Walker, well vouched as a Union man and son-in-law of Governor Morehead, and pleading for his release. I understand the Kentucky arrests were not made by special direction from here, and I am willing if you are that any of the parties may be released when James Guthrie and James Speed think they should be.
Yours truly,
A. LINCOLN.

TO THE VICEROY OF EGYPT.

WASHINGTON, October 11, 1861.

GREAT AND GOOD FRIEND:—I have received from Mr. Thayer, Consul-General of the United States at Alexandria, a full account of the liberal, enlightened, and energetic proceedings which, on his complaint, you have adopted in bringing to speedy and condign punishment the parties, subjects of your Highness in Upper Egypt, who were concerned in an act of criminal persecution against Faris, an agent of certain Christian missionaries in Upper Egypt. I pray your Highness to be assured that these proceedings, at once so prompt and so just, will be regarded as a new and unmistakable proof equally of your Highness's friendship for the United States and of the firmness, integrity and wisdom, with which the government of your Highness is conducted. Wishing you great prosperity and success, I am your friend,
A. LINCOLN.
HIS HIGHNESS MOHAMMED SAID PACHA, Viceroy of Egypt and its Dependencies, etc.
By the President: WILLIAM H. SEWARD, Secretary of State.

ORDER AUTHORIZING SUSPENSION OF THE WRIT OF HABEAS CORPUS.

October 14 1861

LIEUTENANT-GENERAL WINFIELD SCOTT:
The military line of the United States for the suppression of the insurrection may be extended so far as Bangor, in Maine. You and any officer acting under your authority are hereby authorized to suspend the writ of habeas corpus in any place between that place and the city of Washington.
A. LINCOLN.
By the President: WILLIAM H. SEWARD, Secretary of State.

TO SECRETARY OF INTERIOR.

EXECUTIVE MANSION, October 14, 1861

HON. SEC. OF INTERIOR.
DEAR SIR:—How is this? I supposed I was appointing for register of wills a citizen of this District. Now the commission comes to me "Moses Kelly, of New Hampshire." I do not like this.
Yours truly,
A. LINCOLN.

TWO SONS WHO WANT TO WORK

TO MAJOR RAMSEY.

EXECUTIVE MANSION, October 17, 1861
MAJOR RAMSEY.
MY DEAR SIR:—The lady bearer of this says she has two sons who want to work. Set them at it if possible. Wanting to work is so rare a want that it should be encouraged.
Yours truly,
A. LINCOLN.

TO GENERAL THOMAS W. SHERMAN.

WASHINGTON, October 18, 1861.

GENERAL THOMAS SHERMAN, Annapolis, Md.:
Your despatch of yesterday received and shown to General McClellan. I have promised him not to direct his army here without his consent. I do not think I shall come to Annapolis.
A. LINCOLN.

TO GENERAL CURTIS, WITH INCLOSURES.

WASHINGTON, October 24, 1861

BRIGADIER-GENERAL S. R. CURTIS.
MY DEAR SIR:—Herewith is a document—half letter, half order—which, wishing you to see, but not to make public, I send unsealed. Please read it and then inclose it to the officer who may be in command of the Department of the West at the time it reaches him. I cannot now know whether Fremont or Hunter will then be in command.
Yours truly,
A. LINCOLN.

WASHINGTON, October 24, 1861

BRIGADIER-GENERAL S. R. CURTIS.

DEAR SIR:—On receipt of this, with the accompanying inclosures, you will take safe, certain, and suitable measures to have the inclosure addressed to Major-General Fremont delivered to him with all reasonable despatch, subject to these conditions only: that if, when General Fremont shall be reached by the messenger—yourself or any one sent by you—he shall then have, in personal command, fought and won a battle, or shall then be actually in a battle, or shall then be in the immediate presence of the enemy in expectation of a battle, it is not to be delivered, but held for further orders. After, and not till after, the delivery to General Fremont, let the inclosure addressed to General Hunter be delivered to him.
Your obedient servant,
A. LINCOLN.
(General Orders No. 18.) HEADQUARTERS OF THE ARMY,
WASHINGTON, October 24, 1861
Major-General Fremont, of the United States Army, the present commander of the Western Department of the same, will, on the receipt of this order, call Major-General Hunter, of the United States Volunteers, to relieve him temporarily in that command, when he (Major-General Fremont) will report to general headquarters by letter for further orders.
WINFIELD SCOTT. By command: E. D. TOWNSEND, Assistant Adjutant-General.

WASHINGTON, October 24, 1861

TO THE COMMANDER OF THE DEPARTMENT OF THE WEST.

SIR:—The command of the Department of the West having devolved upon you, I propose to offer you a few suggestions. Knowing how hazardous it is to bind down a distant commander in the field to specific lines and operations, as so much always depends on a knowledge of localities and passing events, it is intended, therefore, to leave a considerable margin for the exercise of your judgment and discretion.
The main rebel army (Price's) west of the Mississippi is believed to have passed Dade County in full retreat upon northwestern Arkansas, leaving Missouri almost freed from the enemy, excepting in the southeast of the State. Assuming this basis of fact, it seems desirable, as you are not likely to overtake Price, and are in danger of making too

long a line from your own base of supplies and reinforcements, that you should give up the pursuit, halt your main army, divide it into two corps of observation, one occupying Sedalia and the other Rolla, the present termini of railroads; then recruit the condition of both corps by re-establishing and improving their discipline and instructions, perfecting their clothing and equipments, and providing less uncomfortable quarters. Of course, both railroads must be guarded and kept open, judiciously employing just so much force as is necessary for this. From these two points, Sedalia and Rolla, and especially in judicious cooperation with Lane on the Kansas border, it would be so easy to concentrate and repel any army of the enemy returning on Missouri from the southwest, that it is not probable any such attempt will be made before or during the approaching cold weather. Before spring the people of Missouri will probably be in no favorable mood to renew for next year the troubles which have so much afflicted and impoverished them during this. If you adopt this line of policy, and if, as I anticipate, you will see no enemy in great force approaching, you will have a surplus of force which you can withdraw from these points and direct to others as may be needed, the railroads furnishing ready means of reinforcing these main points if occasion requires. Doubtless local uprisings will for a time continue to occur, but these can be met by detachments and local forces of our own, and will ere long tire out of themselves.

While, as stated in the beginning of the letter, a large discretion must be and is left with yourself, I feel sure that an indefinite pursuit of Price or an attempt by this long and circuitous route to reach Memphis will be exhaustive beyond endurance, and will end in the loss of the whole force engaged in it.

Your obedient servant,

A. LINCOLN.

ORDER RETIRING GENERAL SCOTT AND APPOINTING

GENERAL McCLELLAN HIS SUCCESSOR. (General Orders, No.94.)

WAR DEPARTMENT, ADJUTANT-GENERAL'S OFFICE
WASHINGTON, November 1, 1861
The following order from the President of the United States, announcing the retirement from active command of the honored veteran Lieutenant general Winfield Scott, will be read by the army with profound regret:

EXECUTIVE MANSION, WASHINGTON.

November 1, 1861

On the 1st day of November, A.D. 1861, upon his own application to the President of the United States, Brevet Lieutenant-General Winfield Scott is ordered to be placed, and hereby is placed, upon the list of retired officers of the army of the United States, without reduction in his current pay, subsistence, or allowances.

The American people will hear with sadness and deep emotion that General Scott has withdrawn from the active control of the army, while the President and a unanimous Cabinet express their own and the nation's sympathy in his personal affliction and their profound sense of the important public services rendered by him to his country during his long and brilliant career, among which will ever be gratefully distinguished his faithful devotion to the Constitution, the Union, and the flag when assailed by parricidal rebellion.

A. LINCOLN

The President is pleased to direct that Major general George B. McClellan assume the command of the army of the United States. The headquarters of the army will be established in the city of Washington. All communications intended for the commanding general will hereafter be addressed direct to the adjutant-general. The duplicate returns, orders, and other papers heretofore sent to the assistant adjutant-general, headquarters of the army, will be discontinued.

By order of the Secretary of War: L. THOMAS, Adjutant General.

ORDER APPROVING THE PLAN OF GOVERNOR GAMBLE OF MISSOURI.

EXECUTIVE MANSION, WASHINGTON,

November 5, 1861.
The Governor of the State of Missouri, acting under the direction of the convention of that State, proposes to the Government of the United States that he will raise a military force to serve within the State as State militia during the war there, to cooperate with the troops in the service of the United States in repelling the invasion of the State and suppressing rebellion therein; the said State militia to be embodied and to be held in the camp and in the field, drilled, disciplined, and governed according to the Army Regulations and subject to the Articles of War; the said State militia not to be ordered out of the State except for the immediate defense of the State of Missouri, but to co-operate with the troops in the service of the United States in military operations within the State or necessary to its defense, and when officers of the State militia act with officers in the service of the United States of the same grade the officers of the United States service shall command the combined force; the State militia to be armed, equipped, clothed, subsisted, transported, and paid by the United States during such time as they shall be actually engaged as an embodied military force in service in accordance with regulations of the United States Army or general orders as issued from time to time. In order that the Treasury of the United States may not be burdened with the pay of unnecessary officers, the governor proposes that, although the State law requires him to appoint upon the general staff an adjutant-general, a commissary-general, an inspector-general, a quartermaster-general, a paymaster-general, and a surgeon-general, each with the rank of colonel of cavalry, yet he proposes that the Government of the United States pay only the adjutant-general, the quartermaster-general, and inspector-general, their services being necessary in the relations which would exist between the State militia and the United States. The governor further proposes that while he is allowed by the State law to appoint aides-de-camp to the governor at his discretion, with the rank of colonel, three only shall be reported to the United States for payment. He also proposes that the State militia shall be commanded by a single major-general and by such number of brigadier-generals as shall allow one for a brigade of not less than four regiments, and that no greater number of staff officers shall be appointed for regimental, brigade, and division duties than as provided for in the act of Congress of the 22d July, 1861; and that, whatever be the rank of such officers as fixed by the law of the State, the compensation that they shall receive from the United States shall only be that which belongs to the rank given by said act of Congress to officers in the United States service performing the same duties.

The field officers of a regiment in the State militia are one colonel, one lieutenant-colonel, and one major, and the company officers are a captain, a first lieutenant, and a second lieutenant. The governor proposes that, as the money to be disbursed is the money of the United States, such staff officers in the service of the United States as may be necessary to act as disbursing officers for the State militia shall be assigned by the War Department for that duty; or, if such cannot be spared from their present duty, he will appoint such persons disbursing officers for the State militia as the President of the United States may designate. Such regulations as may be required, in the judgment of the President, to insure regularity of returns and to protect the United States from any fraudulent practices shall be observed and obeyed by all in office in the State militia.

The above propositions are accepted on the part of the United States, and the Secretary of War is directed to make the necessary orders upon the Ordnance, Quartermaster's, Commissary, Pay, and Medical departments to carry this agreement into effect. He will cause the necessary staff officers in the United States service to be detailed for duty in connection with the Missouri State militia, and will order them to make the necessary provision in their respective offices for fulfilling this agreement. All requisitions upon the different officers of the United States under this agreement to be made in substance in the same mode for the Missouri State militia as similar requisitions are made for troops in the service of the United States; and the Secretary of War will cause any additional regulations that may be necessary to insure regularity and economy in carrying this agreement into effect to be adopted and communicated to the Governor of Missouri for the government of the Missouri State militia.

[Indorsement.]
November 6, 1861.
This plan approved, with the modification that the governor stipulates that when he commissions a major-general of militia it shall be the same person at the time in command of the United States Department of the West; and in case the United States shall change such commander of the department, he (the governor) will revoke the State commission given to the person relieved and give one to the person substituted to the United States command of said department.
A. LINCOLN.

REPLY TO THE MINISTER FROM SWEDEN.

November 8, 1861.

SIR:—I receive with great pleasure a Minister from Sweden. That pleasure is enhanced by the information which preceded your arrival here, that his Majesty, your sovereign, had selected you to fill the mission upon the grounds of your derivation from an ancestral stock identified with the most glorious era of your country's noble history, and your own eminent social and political standing in Sweden. This country, sir, maintains, and means to maintain, the rights of human nature, and the capacity of men for self-government. The history of Sweden proves that this is the faith of the people of Sweden, and we know that it is the faith and practice of their respected sovereign. Rest assured, therefore, that we shall be found always just and paternal in our transactions with your government, and that nothing will be omitted on my part to make your residence in this capital agreeable to yourself and satisfactory to your government.

INDORSEMENT AUTHORIZING MARTIAL LAW IN SAINT LOUIS.

St. Louis, November 20, 1861. (Received Nov. 20th.)

GENERAL McCLELLAN,
For the President of the United States.
No written authority is found here to declare and enforce martial law in this department. Please send me such written authority and telegraph me that it has been sent by mail.
H. W. HALLECK, Major-General.
[Indorsement.] November 21, 1861.
If General McClellan and General Halleck deem it necessary to declare and maintain martial law in Saint Louis, the same is hereby authorized.
A. LINCOLN.

OFFER TO COOPERATE AND GIVE SPECIAL LINE OF INFORMATION TO HORACE GREELEY

TO GOVERNOR WALKER.

WASHINGTON, November 21, 1861
DEAR GOVERNOR:—I have thought over the interview which Mr. Gilmore has had with Mr. Greeley, and the proposal that Greeley has made to Gilmore, namely, that he [Gilmore] shall communicate to him [Greeley] all that he learns from you of the inner workings of the administration, in return for his [Greeley's] giving such aid as he can to the new magazine, and allowing you [Walker] from time to time the use of his [Greeley's] columns when it is desirable to feel of, or forestall, public opinion on important subjects. The arrangement meets my unqualified approval, and I shall further it to the extent of my ability, by opening to you—as I do now—fully the policy of the Government,—its present views and future intentions when formed, giving you permission to communicate them to Gilmore for Greeley; and in case you go to Europe I will give these things direct to Gilmore. But all this must be on the express and explicit understanding that the fact of these communications coming from me shall be absolutely confidential,—not to be disclosed by Greeley to his nearest friend, or any of his subordinates. He will be, in effect, my mouthpiece, but I must not be known to be the speaker.
I need not tell you that I have the highest confidence in Mr. Greeley. He is a great power. Having him firmly behind me will be as helpful to me as an army of one hundred thousand men.
This was to be most severely regretted, when Greeley became a traitor to the cause, editorialized for compromise and separation—and promoted McClellan as Democratic candidate for the Presidency.
That he has ever kicked the traces has been owing to his not being fully informed. Tell Gilmore to say to him that, if he ever objects to my policy, I shall be glad to have him state to me his views frankly and fully. I shall adopt his if I can. If I cannot, I will at least tell him why. He and I should stand together, and let no minor differences come between us; for we both seek one end, which is the saving of our country. Now, Governor, this is a longer letter than I have written in a month,—longer than I would have written for any other man than Horace Greeley.
Your friend, truly,
A. LINCOLN.

P. S.—The sooner Gilmore sees Greeley the better, as you may before long think it wise to ventilate our policy on the Trent affair.

ORDER AUTHORIZING GENERAL HALLECK TO SUSPEND THE WRIT OF HABEAS CORPUS,

DECEMBER 2, 1861.

MAJOR-GENERAL H. W. HALLECK, Commanding in the Department of Missouri.
GENERAL:—As an insurrection exists in the United States, and is in arms in the State of Missouri, you are hereby authorized and empowered to suspend the writ of habeas corpus within the limits of the military division under your command, and to exercise martial law as you find it necessary in your discretion to secure the public safety and the authority of the United States.
In witness whereof I have hereunto set my hand and caused the seal of the United States to be affixed at Washington, this second day of December, A.D. 1861.
A. LINCOLN.
By the President: WILLIAM H. SEWARD, Secretary of State.

ANNUAL MESSAGE TO CONGRESS.

WASHINGTON, December 3, 1861

FELLOW-CITIZENS OF THE SENATE AND HOUSE OF REPRESENTATIVES:—In the midst of unprecedented political troubles we have cause of great gratitude to God for unusual good health and most abundant harvests.
You will not be surprised to learn that in the peculiar exigencies of the times our intercourse with foreign nations has been attended with profound solicitude, chiefly turning upon our own domestic affairs.
A disloyal portion of the American people have during the whole year been engaged in an attempt to divide and destroy the Union. A nation which endures factious domestic division is exposed to disrespect abroad, and one party, if not both, is sure sooner or later to invoke foreign intervention.
Nations thus tempted to interfere are not always able to resist the counsels of seeming expediency and ungenerous ambition, although measures adopted under such influences seldom fail to be unfortunate and injurious to those adopting them.
The disloyal citizens of the United States who have offered the ruin of our country in return for the aid and comfort which they have invoked abroad have received less patronage and encouragement than they probably expected. If it were just to suppose, as the insurgents have seemed to assume, that foreign nations in this case, discarding all moral, social, and treaty obligations, would act solely and selfishly for the most speedy restoration of commerce, including especially the acquisition of cotton, those nations appear as yet not to have seen their way to their object more directly or clearly through the destruction than through the preservation of the Union. If we could dare to believe that foreign nations are actuated by no higher principle than this, I am quite sure a sound argument could be made to show them that they can reach their aim more readily and easily by aiding to crush this rebellion than by giving encouragement to it.
The principal lever relied on by the insurgents for exciting foreign nations to hostility against us, as already intimated, is the embarrassment of commerce. Those nations, however, not improbably saw from the first that it was the Union which made as well our foreign as our domestic commerce. They can scarcely have failed to perceive that the effort for disunion produces the existing difficulty, and that one strong nation promises more durable peace and a more extensive, valuable, and reliable commerce than can the same nation broken into hostile fragments.
It is not my purpose to review our discussions with foreign states, because, whatever might be their wishes or dispositions, the integrity of our country and the stability of our government mainly depend not upon them, but on the loyalty, virtue, patriotism, and intelligence of the American people. The correspondence itself, with the usual reservations, is herewith submitted.
I venture to hope it will appear that we have practiced prudence and liberality toward foreign powers, averting causes of irritation and with firmness maintaining our own rights and honor.

Since, however, it is apparent that here, as in every other state, foreign dangers necessarily attend domestic difficulties, I recommend that adequate and ample measures be adopted for maintaining the public defenses on every side. While under this general recommendation provision for defending our seacoast line readily occurs to the mind, I also in the same connection ask the attention of Congress to our great lakes and rivers. It is believed that some fortifications and depots of arms and munitions, with harbor and navigation improvements, all at well-selected points upon these, would be of great importance to the national defense and preservation I ask attention to the views of the Secretary of War, expressed in his report, upon the same general subject.

I deem it of importance that the loyal regions of east Tennessee and western North Carolina should be connected with Kentucky and other faithful parts of the Union by rail-road. I therefore recommend, as a military measure, that Congress provide for the construction of such rail-road as speedily as possible. Kentucky will no doubt co-operate, and through her Legislature make the most judicious selection of a line. The northern terminus must connect with some existing railroad, and whether the route shall be from Lexington or Nicholasville to the Cumberland Gap, or from Lebanon to the Tennessee line, in the direction of Knoxville, or on some still different line, can easily be determined. Kentucky and the General Government co-operating, the work can be completed in a very short time, and when done it will be not only of vast present usefulness but also a valuable permanent improvement, worth its cost in all the future.

Some treaties, designed chiefly for the interests of commerce, and having no grave political importance, have been negotiated, and will be submitted to the Senate for their consideration.

Although we have failed to induce some of the commercial powers to adopt a desirable melioration of the rigor of maritime war, we have removed all obstructions from the way of this humane reform except such as are merely of temporary and accidental occurrence.

I invite your attention to the correspondence between her Britannic Majesty's minister accredited to this government and the Secretary of State relative to the detention of the British ship Perthshire in June last by the United States steamer Massachusetts for a supposed breach of the blockade. As this detention was occasioned by an obvious misapprehension of the facts, and as justice requires that we should commit no belligerent act not founded in strict right as sanctioned by public law, I recommend that an appropriation be made to satisfy the reasonable demand of the owners of the vessel for her detention.

I repeat the recommendation of my predecessor in his annual message to Congress in December last in regard to the disposition of the surplus which will probably remain after satisfying the claims of American citizens against China, pursuant to the awards of the commissioners under the act of the 3d of March, 1859. If, however, it should not be deemed advisable to carry that recommendation into effect, I would suggest that authority be given for investing the principal, or the proceeds of the surplus referred to, in good securities, with a view to the satisfaction of such other just claims of our citizens against China as are not unlikely to arise hereafter in the course of our extensive trade with that empire.

By the act of the 5th of August last Congress authorized the President to instruct the commanders of suitable vessels to defend themselves against and to capture pirates. His authority has been exercised in a single instance only. For the more effectual protection of our extensive and valuable commerce in the Eastern seas especially, it seems to me that it would also be advisable to authorize the commanders of sailing vessels to recapture any prizes which pirates may make of United States vessels and their cargoes, and the consular courts now established by law in Eastern countries to adjudicate the cases in the event that this should not be objected to by the local authorities.

If any good reason exists why we should persevere longer in withholding our recognition of the independence and sovereignty of Haiti and Liberia, I am unable to discern it. Unwilling, however, to inaugurate a novel policy in regard to them without the approbation of Congress, I submit for your consideration the expediency of an appropriation for maintaining a charge d'affaires near each of those new States. It does not admit of doubt that important commercial advantages might be secured by favorable treaties with them.

The operations of the treasury during the period which has elapsed since your adjournment have been conducted with signal success. The patriotism of the people has placed at the disposal of the government the large means demanded by the public exigencies. Much of the national loan has been taken by citizens of the industrial classes, whose confidence in their country's faith and zeal for their country's deliverance from present peril have induced them to contribute to the support of the government the whole of their limited acquisitions. This fact imposes peculiar obligations to economy in disbursement and energy in action.

The revenue from all sources, including loans, for the financial year ending on the 30th of June, 1861, was $86,835,900.27, and the expenditures for the same period, including payments on account of the public debt, were $84,578,834.47, leaving a balance in the treasury on the 1st of July of $2,257,065.80. For the first quarter of the financial year ending on the 30th of September, 1861, the receipts from all sources, including the balance of the 1st of July, were $102,532,509.27, and the expenses $98,239733.09, leaving a balance on the 1st of October, 1861, of $4,292,776.18.

Estimates for the remaining three quarters of the year and for the financial year 1863, together with his views of ways and means for meeting the demands contemplated by them, will be submitted to Congress by the Secretary of the Treasury. It is gratifying to know that the expenditures made necessary by the rebellion are not beyond the resources of the loyal people, and to believe that the same patriotism which has thus far sustained the government will continue to sustain it till peace and union shall again bless the land.

I respectfully refer to the report of the Secretary of War for information respecting the numerical strength of the army and for recommendations having in view an increase of its efficiency and the well-being of the various branches of the service intrusted to his care. It is gratifying to know that the patriotism of the people has proved equal to the occasion, and that the number of troops tendered greatly exceeds the force which Congress authorized me to call into the field. I refer with pleasure to those portions of his report which make allusion to the creditable degree of discipline already attained by our troops and to the excellent sanitary condition of the entire army.

The recommendation of the Secretary for an organization of the militia upon a uniform basis is a subject of vital importance to the future safety of the country, and is commended to the serious attention of Congress.

The large addition to the regular army, in connection with the defection that has so considerably diminished the number of its officers, gives peculiar importance to his recommendation for increasing the corps of cadets to the greatest capacity of the Military Academy.

By mere omission, I presume, Congress has failed to provide chaplains for hospitals occupied by volunteers. This subject was brought to my notice, and I was induced to draw up the form of a letter, one copy of which, properly addressed, has been delivered to each of the persons, and at the dates respectively named and stated in a schedule, containing also the form of the letter, marked A, and herewith transmitted.

These gentlemen, I understand, entered upon the duties designated at the times respectively stated in the schedule, and have labored faithfully therein ever since. I therefore recommend that they be compensated at the same rate as chaplains in the army. I further suggest that general provision be made for chaplains to serve at hospitals, as well as with regiments.

The report of the Secretary of the Navy presents in detail the operations of that branch of the service, the activity and energy which have characterized its administration, and the results of measures to increase its efficiency and power such have been the additions, by construction and purchase, that it may almost be said a navy has been created and brought into service since our difficulties commenced.

Besides blockading our extensive coast, squadrons larger than ever before assembled under our flag have been put afloat and performed deeds which have increased our naval renown.

I would invite special attention to the recommendation of the Secretary for a more perfect organization of the navy by introducing additional grades in the service.

The present organization is defective and unsatisfactory, and the suggestions submitted by the department will, it is believed, if adopted, obviate the difficulties alluded to, promote harmony, and increase the efficiency of the navy.

There are three vacancies on the bench of the Supreme Court—two by the decease of Justices Daniel and McLean and one by the resignation of Justice Campbell. I have so far forborne making nominations to fill these vacancies for reasons which I will now state. Two of the outgoing judges resided within the States now overrun by revolt, so that if successors were appointed in the same localities they could not now serve upon their circuits; and many of the most competent men there probably would not take the personal hazard of accepting to serve, even here, upon the Supreme bench. I have been unwilling to throw all the appointments north-ward, thus disabling myself from doing justice to the South on the return of peace; although I may remark that to transfer to the North one which has heretofore been in the South would not, with reference to territory and population, be unjust.

During the long and brilliant judicial career of Judge McLean his circuit grew into an empire-altogether too large for any one judge to give the courts therein more than a nominal attendance—rising in population from 1,470,018 in 1830 to 6,151,405 in 1860.

Besides this, the country generally has outgrown our present judicial system. If uniformity was at all intended, the system requires that all the States shall be accommodated with circuit courts, attended by Supreme judges, while, in fact, Wisconsin, Minnesota, Iowa, Kansas, Florida, Texas, California, and Oregon have never had any such courts. Nor can this well be remedied without a change in the system, because the adding of judges to the Supreme Court, enough for the accommodation of all parts of the country with circuit courts, would create a court altogether too numerous for a judicial body of any sort. And the evil, if it be one, will increase as new States come into the Union. Circuit courts are useful or they are not useful. If useful, no State should be denied them; if not useful, no State should have them. Let them be provided for all or abolished as to all.

Three modifications occur to me, either of which, I think, would be an improvement upon our present system. Let the Supreme Court be of convenient number in every event; then, first, let the whole country be divided into circuits of convenient size, the Supreme judges to serve in a number of them corresponding to their own number, and independent circuit judges be provided for all the rest; or, secondly, let the Supreme judges be relieved from circuit duties and circuit judges provided for all the circuits; or, thirdly, dispense with circuit courts altogether, leaving the judicial functions wholly to the district courts and an independent Supreme Court.

I respectfully recommend to the consideration of Congress the present condition of the statute laws, with the hope that Congress will be able to find an easy remedy for many of the inconveniences and evils which constantly embarrass those engaged in the practical administration of them. Since the Organization of the government, Congress has enacted some 5000 acts and joint resolutions, which fill more than 6000 closely printed pages and are scattered through many volumes. Many of these acts have been drawn in haste and without sufficient caution, so that their provisions are often obscure in themselves or in conflict with each other, or at least so doubtful as to render it very difficult for even the best-informed persons to ascertain precisely what the statute law really is.

It seems to me very important that the statute laws should be made as plain and intelligible as possible, and be reduced to as small a compass as may consist with the fullness and precision of the will of the Legislature and the perspicuity of its language. This well done would, I think, greatly facilitate the labors of those whose duty it is to assist in the administration of the laws, and would be a lasting benefit to the people, by placing before them in a more accessible and intelligible form the laws which so deeply concern their interests and their duties.

I am informed by some whose opinions I respect that all the acts of Congress now in force and of a permanent and general nature might be revised and rewritten so as to be embraced in one volume (or at most two volumes) of ordinary and convenient size; and I respectfully recommend to Congress to consider of the subject, and if my suggestion be approved to devise such plan as to their wisdom shall seem most proper for the attainment of the end proposed.

One of the unavoidable consequences of the present insurrection is the entire suppression in many places of all the ordinary means of administering civil justice by the officers and in the forms of existing law. This is the case, in whole or in part, in all the insurgent States; and as our armies advance upon and take possession of parts of those States the practical evil becomes more apparent. There are no courts or officers to whom the citizens of other States may apply for the enforcement of their lawful claims against citizens of the insurgent States, and there is a vast amount of debt constituting such claims. Some have estimated it as high as $200,000,000, due in large part from insurgents in open rebellion to loyal citizens who are even now making great sacrifices in the discharge of their patriotic duty to support the government.

Under these circumstances I have been urgently solicited to establish, by military power, courts to administer summary justice in such cases. I have thus far declined to do it, not because I had any doubt that the end proposed—the collection of the debts—was just and right in itself, but because I have been unwilling to go beyond the pressure of necessity in the unusual exercise of power. But the powers of Congress, I suppose, are equal to the anomalous occasion, and therefore I refer the whole matter to Congress, with the hope that a plan maybe devised for the administration of justice in all such parts of the insurgent States and Territories as may be under the control of this government, whether by a voluntary return to allegiance and order or by the power of our arms; this, however, not to be a permanent institution, but a temporary substitute, and to cease as soon as the ordinary courts can be reestablished in peace.

It is important that some more convenient means should be provided, if possible, for the adjustment of claims against the government, especially in view of their increased number by reason of the war. It is as much the duty of government to render prompt justice against itself in favor of citizens as it is to administer the same between private individuals. The investigation and adjudication of claims in their nature belong to the judicial department. Besides, it is apparent that the attention of Congress will be more than usually engaged for some time to come with great national questions. It was intended by the organization of the Court of Claims mainly to remove this branch of business from the halls of Congress; but, while the court has proved to be an effective and valuable means of investigation, it in great degree fails to effect the object of its creation for want of power to make its judgments final.

Fully aware of the delicacy, not to say the danger of the subject, I commend to your careful consideration whether this power of making judgments final may not properly be given to the court, reserving the right of appeal on questions of law to the Supreme Court, with such other provisions as experience may have shown to be necessary.

I ask attention to the report of the Postmaster general, the following being a summary statement of the condition of the department:

The revenue from all sources during the fiscal year ending June 30, 1861, including the annual permanent appropriation of $700,000 for the transportation of "free mail matter," was $9,049,296.40, being about 2 per cent. less than the revenue for 1860.

The expenditures were $13,606,759.11, showing a decrease of more than 8 per cent. as compared with those of the previous year and leaving an excess of expenditure over the revenue for the last fiscal year of $4,557,462.71.

The gross revenue for the year ending June 30, 1863, is estimated at an increase of 4 per cent. on that of 1861, making $8,683,000, to which should be added the earnings of the department in carrying free matter, viz., $700,000, making $9,383,000.

The total expenditures for 1863 are estimated at $12,528,000, leaving an estimated deficiency of $3,145,000 to be supplied from the treasury in addition to the permanent appropriation.

The present insurrection shows, I think, that the extension of this District across the Potomac River at the time of establishing the capital here was eminently wise, and consequently that the relinquishment of that portion of it which lies within the State of Virginia was unwise and dangerous. I submit for your consideration the expediency of regaining that part of the District and the restoration of the original boundaries thereof through negotiations with the State of Virginia.

The report of the Secretary of the Interior, with the accompanying documents, exhibits the condition of the several branches of the public business pertaining to that department. The depressing influences of the insurrection have been specially felt in the operations of the Patent and General Land Offices. The cash receipts from the sales of public lands during the past year have exceeded the expenses of our land system only about $200,000. The sales have been entirely suspended in the Southern States, while the interruptions to the business of the country and the diversion of large numbers of men from labor to military service have obstructed settlements in the new States and Territories of the Northwest.

The receipts of the Patent Office have declined in nine months about $100,000.00 rendering a large reduction of the force employed necessary to make it self-sustaining.

The demands upon the Pension Office will be largely increased by the insurrection. Numerous applications for pensions, based upon the casualties of the existing war, have already been made. There is reason to believe that many who are now upon the pension rolls and in receipt of the bounty of the government are in the ranks of the insurgent army or giving them aid and comfort. The Secretary of the Interior has directed a suspension of the payment of the pensions of such persons upon proof of their disloyalty. I recommend that Congress authorize that officer to cause the names of such persons to be stricken from the pension rolls.

The relations of the government with the Indian tribes have been greatly disturbed by the insurrection, especially in the southern superintendency and in that of New Mexico. The Indian country south of Kansas is in the possession of insurgents from Texas and Arkansas. The agents of the United States appointed since the 4th of March for this superintendency have been unable to reach their posts, while the most of those who were in office before that time have espoused the insurrectionary cause, and assume to exercise the powers of agents by virtue of commissions from the insurrectionists. It has been stated in the public press that a portion of those Indians have been organized as a military force and are attached to the army of the insurgents. Although the government has no official information upon this subject, letters have been written to the Commissioner of Indian Affairs by several prominent chiefs giving assurance of their loyalty to the United States and expressing a wish for the presence of Federal troops to protect them. It is believed that upon the repossession of the country by the Federal forces the Indians will readily cease all hostile demonstrations and resume their former relations to the government.

Agriculture, confessedly the largest interest of the nation, has not a department nor a bureau, but a clerkship only, assigned to it in the government. While it is fortunate that this great interest is so independent in its nature as not to have demanded and extorted more from the government, I respectfully ask Congress to consider whether something more cannot be given voluntarily with general advantage.

Annual reports exhibiting the condition of our agriculture, commerce, and manufactures would present a fund of information of great practical value to the country. While I make no suggestion as to details, I venture the opinion that an agricultural and statistical bureau might profitably be organized.

The execution of the laws for the suppression of the African slave trade has been confided to the Department of the Interior. It is a subject of gratulation that the efforts which have been made for the suppression of this inhuman traffic have been recently attended with unusual success. Five vessels being fitted out for the slave trade have been seized and condemned. Two mates of vessels engaged in the trade and one person in equipping a vessel as a slaver have been convicted and subjected to the penalty of fine and imprisonment, and one captain, taken with a cargo of Africans on board his vessel, has been convicted of the highest grade of offense under our laws, the punishment of which is death.

The Territories of Colorado, Dakota, and Nevada, created by the last Congress, have been organized, and civil administration has been inaugurated therein under auspices especially gratifying when it is considered that the leaven of treason was found existing in some of these new countries when the Federal officers arrived there.

The abundant natural resources of these Territories, with the security and protection afforded by organized government, will doubtless invite to them a large immigration when peace shall restore the business of the country to its accustomed channels. I submit the resolutions of the Legislature of Colorado, which evidence the patriotic spirit of the people of the Territory. So far the authority of the United States has been upheld in all the Territories, as it is hoped it will be in the future. I commend their interests and defense to the enlightened and generous care of Congress.

I recommend to the favorable consideration of Congress the interests of the District of Columbia. The insurrection has been the cause of much suffering and sacrifice to its inhabitants, and as they have no representative in Congress that body should not overlook their just claims upon the government.

At your late session a joint resolution was adopted authorizing the President to take measures for facilitating a proper representation of the industrial interests of the United States at the exhibition of the industry of all nations to be holden at London in the year 1862. I regret to say I have been unable to give personal attention to this subject—a subject at once so interesting in itself and so extensively and intimately connected with the material prosperity of the world. Through the Secretaries of State and of the Interior a plan or system has been devised and partly matured, and which will be laid before you.

Under and by virtue of the act of Congress entitled "An act to confiscate property used for insurrectionary purposes," approved August 6, 1861, the legal claims of certain persons to the labor and service of certain other persons have become forfeited, and numbers of the latter thus liberated are already dependent on the United States, and must be provided for in some way. Besides this, it is not impossible that some of the States will pass similar enactments for their own benefit respectively, and by operation of which persons of the same class will be thrown upon them for disposal. In such case I recommend that Congress provide for accepting such persons from such States, according to some mode of valuation, in lieu, pro tanto, of direct taxes, or upon some other plan to be agreed on with such States respectively; that such persons, on such acceptance by the General Government, be at once deemed free, and that in any event steps be taken for colonizing both classes (or the one first mentioned if the other shall not be brought into existence) at some place or places in a climate congenial to them. It might be well to consider, too, whether the free colored people already in the United States could not, so far as individuals may desire, be included in such colonization.

To carry out the plan of colonization may involve the acquiring of territory, and also the appropriation of money beyond that to be expended in the territorial acquisition. Having practised the acquisition of territory for nearly sixty years, the question of constitutional power to do so is no longer an open one with us. The power was questioned at first by Mr. Jefferson, who, however, in the purchase of Louisiana, yielded his scruples on the plea of great expediency. If it be said that the only legitimate object of acquiring territory is to furnish homes for white men, this measure effects that object, for emigration of colored men leaves additional room for white men remaining or coming here. Mr. Jefferson, however, placed the importance of procuring Louisiana more on political and commercial grounds than on providing room for population.

On this whole proposition, including the appropriation of money with the acquisition of territory, does not the expediency amount to absolute necessity—that without which the government itself cannot be perpetuated?

The war continues. In considering the policy to be adopted for suppressing the insurrection I have been anxious and careful that the inevitable conflict for this purpose shall not degenerate into a violent and remorseless revolutionary struggle. I have therefore in every case thought it proper to keep the integrity of the Union prominent as the primary object of the contest on our part, leaving all questions which are not of vital military importance to the more deliberate action of the Legislature.

In the exercise of my best discretion I have adhered to the blockade of the ports held by the insurgents, instead of putting in force by proclamation the law of Congress enacted at the late session for closing those ports.

So also, obeying the dictates of prudence, as well as the obligations of law, instead of transcending I have adhered to the act of Congress to confiscate property used for insurrectionary purposes. If a new law upon the same subject shall be proposed, its propriety will be duly considered. The Union must be preserved, and hence all indispensable means must be employed. We should not be in haste to determine that radical and extreme measures, which may reach the loyal as well as the disloyal, are indispensable.

The inaugural address at the beginning of the Administration and the message to Congress at the late special session were both mainly devoted to topics domestic controversy out of which the insurrection and consequent war have sprung. Nothing now occurs to add or subtract to or from the principles or general purposes stated and expressed in those documents.

The last ray of hope for preserving the Union peaceably expired at the assault upon Fort Sumter, and a general review of what has occurred since may not be unprofitable. What was painfully uncertain then is much better defined and more distinct now, and the progress of events is plainly in the right direction. The insurgents confidently claimed a strong support from north of Mason and Dixon's line, and the friends of the Union were not free from apprehension on the point. This, however, was soon settled definitely, and on the right side. South of the line noble little Delaware led off right from the first. Maryland was made to seem against the Union. Our soldiers were assaulted, bridges were burned, and railroads torn up within her limits, and we were many days at one time without the ability to bring a single regiment over her soil to the capital. Now her bridges and railroads are repaired and open to the government; she already gives seven regiments to the cause of the Union, and none to the enemy; and her people, at a regular election, have sustained the Union by a larger majority and a larger aggregate vote than they ever before gave to any candidate or any question. Kentucky, too, for some time in doubt, is now decidedly and, I think, unchangeably ranged on the side of the Union. Missouri is comparatively quiet, and, I believe, can, not again be overrun by the insurrectionists. These three States of Maryland, Kentucky, and Missouri, neither of which would promise a single soldier at first, have now an aggregate of not less than forty thousand in the field for the Union, while of their citizens certainly not more than a third of that number, and they of doubtful whereabouts and doubtful existence, are in arms against us. After a somewhat bloody struggle of months, winter closes on the Union people of western Virginia, leaving them masters of their own country.

An insurgent force of about fifteen hundred, for months dominating the narrow peninsular region constituting the counties of Accomac and Northampton, and known as Eastern Shore of Virginia, together with some contiguous parts of Maryland, have laid down their arms, and the people there have renewed their allegiance to and accepted the protection of the old flag. This leaves no armed insurrectionist north of the Potomac or east of the Chesapeake.

Also we have obtained a footing at each of the isolated points on the southern coast of Hatteras, Port Royal, Tybee Island (near Savannah), and Ship Island; and we likewise have some general accounts of popular movements in behalf of the Union in North Carolina and Tennessee.

These things demonstrate that the cause of the Union is advancing steadily and certainly southward.

Since your last adjournment Lieutenant-General Scott has retired from the head of the army. During his long life the nation has not been unmindful of his merit; yet on calling to mind how faithfully, ably, and brilliantly he has served the country, from a time far back in our history, when few of the now living had been born, and thenceforward continually, I cannot but think we are still his debtors. I submit, therefore, for your consideration what further mark of recognition is due to him, and to ourselves as a grateful people.

With the retirement of General Scott came the Executive duty of appointing in his stead a general-in-chief of the army. It is a fortunate circumstance that neither in council nor country was there, so far as I know, any difference of opinion as to the proper person to be selected. The retiring chief repeatedly expressed his judgment in favor of General McClellan for the position, and in this the nation seemed to give a unanimous concurrence. The designation of General McClellan is therefore in considerable degree the selection of the country as well as of the Executive, and hence there is better reason to hope there will be given him the confidence and cordial support thus by fair implication promised, and without which he cannot with so full efficiency serve the country.

It has been said that one bad general is better than two good ones, and the saying is true if taken to mean no more than that an army is better directed by a single mind, though inferior, than by two superior ones at variance and cross-purposes with each other.

And the same is true in all joint operations wherein those engaged can have none but a common end in view and can differ only as to the choice of means. In a storm at sea no one on board can wish the ship to sink, and yet not unfrequently all go down together because too many will direct and no single mind can be allowed to control.

It continues to develop that the insurrection is largely, if not exclusively, a war upon the first principle of popular government—the rights of the people. Conclusive evidence of this is found in the most grave and maturely considered public documents, as well as in the general tone of the insurgents. In those documents we find the abridgment of the existing right of suffrage and the denial to the people of all right to participate in the selection of public officers except the legislative boldly advocated, with labored arguments to prove that large control of the people in government is the source of all political evil. Monarchy itself is sometimes hinted at as a possible refuge from the power of the people.

In my present position I could scarcely be justified were I to omit raising a warning voice against this approach of returning despotism. It is not needed nor fitting here that a general argument should be made in favor of popular institutions, but there is one point, with its connections, not so hackneyed as most others, to which I ask a brief attention. It is the effort to place capital on an equal footing with, if not above, labor in the structure of government. It is assumed that labor is available only in connection with capital; that nobody labors unless somebody else, owning capital, somehow by the use of it induces him to labor. This assumed, it is next considered whether it is best that capital shall hire laborers, and thus induce them to work by their own consent, or buy them and drive them to it without their consent. Having proceeded so far, it is naturally concluded that all laborers are either hired laborers or what we call slaves. And further, it is assumed that whoever is once a hired laborer is fixed in that condition for life.

Now there is no such relation between capital and labor as assumed, nor is there any such thing as a free man being fixed for life in the condition of a hired laborer. Both these assumptions are false, and all inferences from them are groundless.

Labor is prior to and independent of capital. Capital is only the fruit of labor, and could never have existed if labor had not first existed. Labor is the superior of capital, and deserves much the higher consideration. Capital has its rights, which are as worthy of protection as any other rights. Nor is it denied that there is, and probably always will be, a relation between labor and capital producing mutual benefits. The error is in assuming that the whole labor of community exists within that relation. A few men own capital, and that few avoid labor themselves, and with their capital hire or buy another few to labor for them. A large majority belong to neither class—neither work for others nor have others working for them. In most of the Southern States a majority of the whole people of all colors are neither slaves nor masters, while in the Northern a large majority are neither hirers nor hired. Men, with their families—wives, sons, and daughters,—work for themselves on their farms, in their houses, and in their shops, taking the whole product to themselves, and asking no favors of capital on the one hand nor of hired laborers or slaves on the other. It is not forgotten that a considerable number of persons mingle their own labor with capital; that is, they labor with their own hands and also buy or hire others to labor for them; but this is only a mixed and not a distinct class. No principle stated is disturbed by the existence of this mixed class.

Again, as has already been said, there is not of necessity any such thing as the free hired laborer being fixed to that condition for life. Many independent men everywhere in these States a few years back in their lives were hired laborers. The prudent, penniless beginner in the world labors for wages awhile, saves a surplus with which to buy tools or land for himself, then labors on his own account another while, and at length hires another new beginner to help him. This is the just and generous and prosperous system which opens the way to all, gives hope to all, and consequent energy and progress and improvement of condition to all. No men living are more worthy to be trusted than those who toil up from poverty; none less inclined to take or touch aught which they have not honestly earned. Let them beware of surrendering a political power which they already possess, and which if surrendered will surely be used to close the door of advancement against such as they and to fix new disabilities and burdens upon them till all of liberty shall be lost.

From the first taking of our national census to the last are seventy years, and we find our population at the end of the period eight times as great as it was at the beginning. The increase of those other things which men deem desirable has been even greater. We thus have at one view what the popular principle, applied to government through the machinery of the States and the Union, has produced in a given time, and also what if firmly maintained it promises for the future. There are already among us those who if the Union be preserved will live to see it contain 200,000,000. The struggle of to-day is not altogether for to-day; it is for a vast future also. With a reliance on Providence all the more firm and earnest, let us proceed in the great task which events have devolved upon us.

A. LINCOLN.

MESSAGE TO CONGRESS.

WASHINGTON, December 20, 1861.

TO THE SENATE AND HOUSE OF REPRESENTATIVES:

I transmit to Congress a letter from the secretary of the executive committee of the commission appointed to represent the interests of those American citizens who may desire to become exhibitors at the industrial exhibition to be held in London in 1862, and a memorial of that commission, with a report of the executive committee thereof and copies of circulars announcing the decisions of Her Majesty's commissioners in London, giving directions to be observed in regard to articles intended for exhibition, and also of circular forms of application, demands for space, approvals, etc., according to the rules prescribed by the British commissioners.

As these papers fully set forth the requirements necessary to enable those citizens of the United States who may wish to become exhibitors to avail themselves of the privileges of the exhibition, I commend them to your early consideration, especially in view of the near approach of the time when the exhibition will begin.

A. LINCOLN.

LETTER OF REPRIMAND TO GENERAL HUNTER

TO GENERAL HUNTER.

EXECUTIVE MANSION, WASHINGTON,
Dec.31, 1861
MAJOR-GENERAL HUNTER.

DEAR SIR:—Yours of the 23d is received, and I am constrained to say it is difficult to answer so ugly a letter in good temper. I am, as you intimate, losing much of the great confidence I placed in you, not from any act or omission of yours touching the public service, up to the time you were sent to Leavenworth, but from the flood of grumbling despatches and letters I have seen from you since. I knew you were being ordered to Leavenworth at the time it was done; and I aver that with as tender a regard for your honor and your sensibilities as I had for my own, it never occurred to me that you were being "humiliated, insulted, and disgraced"; nor have I, up to this day, heard an intimation that you have been wronged, coming from any one but yourself. No one has blamed you for the retrograde movement from Springfield, nor for the information you gave General Cameron; and this you could readily understand, if it were not for your unwarranted assumption that the ordering you to Leavenworth must necessarily have been done as a punishment for some fault. I thought then, and think yet, the position assigned to you is as responsible, and as honorable, as that assigned to Buell—I know that General McClellan expected more important results from it. My impression is that at the time you were assigned to the new Western Department, it had not been determined to replace General Sherman in Kentucky; but of this I am not certain, because the idea that a command in Kentucky was very desirable, and one in the farther West undesirable, had never occurred to me. You constantly speak of being placed in command of only 3000. Now, tell me, is this not mere impatience? Have you not known all the while that you are to command four or five times that many.

I have been, and am sincerely your friend; and if, as such, I dare to make a suggestion, I would say you are adopting the best possible way to ruin yourself. "Act well your part, there all the honor lies." He who does something at the head of one regiment, will eclipse him who does nothing at the head of a hundred.

Your friend, as ever,
A. LINCOLN.

TELEGRAM TO GENERAL HALLECK.

WASHINGTON, D.C., December 31, 1861

GENERAL H. W. HALLECK, St. Louis, Missouri:
General McClellan is sick. Are General Buell and yourself in concert? When he moves on Bowling Green, what hinders it being reinforced from Columbus? A simultaneous movement by you on Columbus might prevent it.
A. LINCOLN.
[Similar despatch to Buell same date.]

1862

TELEGRAM TO GENERAL D. C. BUELL.

WASHINGTON CITY, January 1, 1862

BRIGADIER-GENERAL BUELL, Louisville:
General McClellan should not yet be disturbed with business. I think you better get in concert with General Halleck at once. I write you to-night. I also telegraph and write Halleck.
A. LINCOLN.

TO GENERAL H. W. HALLECK.

EXECUTIVE MANSION, January 1, 1862

DEAR GENERAL HALLECK:
General McClellan is not dangerously ill, as I hope, but would better not be disturbed with business. I am very anxious that, in case of General Buell's moving toward Nashville, the enemy shall not be greatly reinforced, and I think there is danger he will be from Columbus. It seems to me that a real or feigned attack upon Columbus from up the river at the same time would either prevent this or compensate for it by throwing Columbus into our hands. I wrote General Buell a letter similar to this, meaning that he and you shall communicate and act in concert, unless it be your judgment and his that there is no necessity for it. You and he will understand much better than I how to do it. Please do not lose time in this matter.
Yours very truly,
A. LINCOLN.

TO THE PEOPLE OF MARYLAND,

In view of the recent declaration of the people of Maryland of their adhesion to the Union, so distinctly made in their recent election, the President directs that all the prisoners who having heretofore been arrested in that State are now detained in military custody by the President's authority, be released from their imprisonment on the following conditions, namely: that if they were holding any civil or military offices when arrested, the terms of which have expired, they shall not resume or reclaim such office; and secondly, all persons availing themselves of this proclamation shall engage by oath or parole of honor to maintain the Union and the Constitution of the United States, and in no way to aid or abet by arms, counsel, conversation, or information of any kind the existing insurrection against the Government of the United States.

To guard against misapprehension it is proper to state that this proclamation does not apply to prisoners of war.

MESSAGE TO CONGRESS.

WASHINGTON, January 2, 1862

To THE SENATE AND HOUSE OF REPRESENTATIVES
I transmit to Congress a copy of a letter to the Secretary of State from James R. Partridge, secretary to the executive committee to the in exhibition to be held in London in the course present year, and a copy of the correspond which it refers, relative to a vessel for the of taking such articles as persons in this country may wish to exhibit on that occasion. As it appears no naval vessel can be spared for the purpose, I recommend that authority be given to charter a suitable merchant vessel, in order that facilities similar to those afforded by the government exhibition of 1851 may also be extended to citizens of the United States who may desire to contribute to the exhibition of this year.
A. LINCOLN

MESSAGES OF DISAPPOINTMENT WITH HIS GENERALS

TELEGRAM TO GENERAL D. C. BUELL.

WASHINGTON, January 4, 1862.
GENERAL BUELL:
Have arms gone forward for East Tennessee? Please tell me the progress and condition of the movement in that direction. Answer.
A. LINCOLN.

TO GENERAL D. C. BUELL.

EXECUTIVE MANSION, WASHINGTON,

January 6, 1862.
BRIGADIER-GENERAL BUELL.
MY DEAR SIR:—Your despatch of yesterday has been received, and it disappoints and distresses me. I have shown it to General McClellan, who says he will write you to-day. I am not competent to criticize your views, and therefore what I offer is in justification of myself. Of the two, I would rather have a point on the railroad south of Cumberland Gap than Nashville. First, because it cuts a great artery of the enemy's communication, which Nashville does not; and secondly, because it is in the midst of loyal people who would rally around it, while Nashville is not. Again, I cannot see why the movement on East Tennessee would not be a diversion in your favor rather than a disadvantage, assuming

that a movement toward Nashville is the main object. But my distress is that our friends in East Tennessee are being hanged and driven to despair, and even now, I fear, are thinking of taking rebel arms for the sake of personal protection. In this we lose the most valuable stake we have in the South. My despatch, to which yours is an answer, was sent with the knowledge of Senator Johnson and Representative Maynard of East Tennessee, and they will be upon me to know the answer, which I cannot safely show them. They would despair, possibly resign to go and save their families somehow, or die with them. I do not intend this to be an order in any sense, but merely, as intimated before, to show you the grounds of my anxiety.
Yours very truly,
A. LINCOLN.

TELEGRAM TO GENERAL BUELL.

WASHINGTON, January 7, 1862.

BRIGADIER-GENERAL D.C. BUELL, Louisville:
Please name as early a day as you safely can on or before which you can be ready to move southward in concert with Major-General Halleck. Delay is ruining us, and it is indispensable for me to have something definite. I send a like despatch to Major-General Halleck.
A. LINCOLN.

MESSAGE TO CONGRESS.

WASHINGTON, January 10, 1862

TO THE SENATE AND HOUSE OF REPRESENTATIVES:
I transmit to Congress a translation of an instruction to the minister of his Majesty the Emperor of Austria accredited to this government, and a copy of a note to that minister from the Secretary of State relative to the questions involved in the taking from the British steamer Trent of certain citizens of the United States by order of Captain Wilkes of the United States Navy. This correspondence may be considered as a sequel to that previously communicated to Congress relating to the same subject.
A. LINCOLN.

INDORSEMENT ON LETTER FROM GENERAL HALLECK,

JANUARY 10, 1862.

HEADQUARTERS DEPARTMENT OF THE MISSOURI ST. Louis, January 6, 1862.
To His EXCELLENCY THE PRESIDENT:
In reply to your Excellency's letter of the 1st instant, I have to state that on receiving your telegram I immediately communicated with General Buell and have since sent him all the information I could obtain of the enemy's movements about Columbus and Camp Beauregard. No considerable force has been sent from those places to Bowling Green. They have about 22,000 men at Columbus, and the place is strongly fortified. I have at Cairo, Port Holt, and Paducah only about 15,000, which, after leaving guards at these places, would give me but little over 10,000 men with which to assist General Buell. It would be madness to attempt anything serious with such a force, and I cannot at the present time withdraw any from Missouri without risking the loss of this State. The troops recently raised in other States of this department have, without my knowledge, been sent to Kentucky and Kansas.
I am satisfied that the authorities at Washington do not appreciate the difficulties with which we have to contend here. The operations of Lane, Jennison, and others have so enraged the people of Missouri that it is estimated that there is a

majority of 80,000 against the government. We are virtually in an enemy's country. Price and others have a considerable army in the southwest, against which I am operating with all my available force.

This city and most of the middle and northern counties are insurrectionary,—burning bridges, destroying telegraph lines, etc.,—and can be kept down only by the presence of troops. A large portion of the foreign troops organized by General Fremont are unreliable; indeed, many of them are already mutinous. They have been tampered with by politicians, and made to believe that if they get up a mutiny and demand Fremont's return the government will be forced to restore him to duty here. It is believed that some high officers are in the plot I have already been obliged to disarm several of these organizations, and I am daily expecting more serious outbreaks. Another grave difficulty is the want of proper general officers to command the troops and enforce order and discipline, and especially to protect public property from robbery and plunder. Some of the brigadier-generals assigned to this department are entirely ignorant of their duties and unfit for any command. I assure you, Mr. President, it is very difficult to accomplish much with such means. I am in the condition of a carpenter who is required to build a bridge with a dull axe, a broken saw, and rotten timber. It is true that I have some very good green timber, which will answer the purpose as soon as I can get it into shape and season it a little.

I know nothing of General Buell's intended operations, never having received any information in regard to the general plan of campaign. If it be intended that his column shall move on Bowling Green while another moves from Cairo or Paducah on Columbus or Camp Beauregard, it will be a repetition of the same strategic error which produced the disaster of Bull Run. To operate on exterior lines against an enemy occupying a central position will fail, as it always has failed, in ninety-nine cases out of a hundred. It is condemned by every military authority I have ever read.

General Buell's army and the forces at Paducah occupy precisely the same position in relation to each other and to the enemy as did the armies of McDowell and Patterson before the battle of Bull Run.

Very respectfully, your obedient servant,

H. W. HALLECK, Major-General

[Indorsement]

The within is a copy of a letter just received from General Halleck. It is exceedingly discouraging. As everywhere else, nothing can be done.

A. LINCOLN.

TELEGRAM TO GOVERNOR ANDREW.

WASHINGTON, D. C., January 11, 1862

GOVERNOR JOHN A. ANDREW, Boston:

I will be greatly obliged if you will arrange; somehow with General Butler to officer his two un-officered regiments.

A. LINCOLN

TO GENERAL D. C. BUELL.

EXECUTIVE MANSION, WASHINGTON, January 13, 1861

BRIGADIER-GENERAL BUELL.

MY DEAR SIR—Your despatch of yesterday is received, in which you say, "I received your letter and General McClellan's, and will at once devote my efforts to your views and his." In the midst of my many cares I have not seen, nor asked to see, General McClellan's letter to you. For my own views, I have not offered and do not now offer them as orders; and while I am glad to have them respectfully considered, I would blame you to follow them contrary to your own clear judgment, unless I should put them in the form of orders. As to General McClellan's views, you understand your duty in regard to them better than I do.

With this preliminary I state my general idea of this war to be, that we have the greater numbers and the enemy has the greater facility of concentrating forces upon points of collision; that we must fail unless we can find some way of making our advantage an overmatch for his; and that this can only be done by menacing him with superior forces at different points at the same time, so that we can safely attack one or both if he makes no change; and if he weakens one to strengthen the other, forbear to attack the strengthened one, but seize and hold the weakened one, gaining so much.

To illustrate: Suppose last summer, when Winchester ran away to reinforce Manassas, we had forborne to attack Manassas, but had seized and held Winchester. I mention this to illustrate and not to criticise. I did not lose confidence in McDowell, and I think less harshly of Patterson than some others seem to.... Applying the principle to your case, my idea is that Halleck shall menace Columbus and "down river" generally, while you menace Bowling Green and East Tennessee. If the enemy shall concentrate at Bowling Green, do not retire from his front, yet do not fight him there either, but seize Columbus and East Tennessee, one or both, left exposed by the concentration at Bowling Green. It is a matter of no small anxiety to me, and which I am sure you will not overlook, that the East Tennessee line is so long and over so bad a road.

Yours very truly,
A. LINCOLN.
(Indorsement.)
Having to-day written General Buell a letter, it occurs to me to send General Halleck a copy of it.
A. LINCOLN.

TO GENERAL H. W. HALLECK.

EXECUTIVE MANSION, WASHINGTON, January 1, 1862.

MAJOR-GENERAL HALLECK.

MY DEAR SIR:—The Germans are true and patriotic and so far as they have got cross in Missouri it is upon mistake and misunderstanding. Without a knowledge of its contents, Governor Koerner, of Illinois, will hand you this letter. He is an educated and talented German gentleman, as true a man as lives. With his assistance you can set everything right with the Germans.... My clear judgment is that, with reference to the German element in your command, you should have Governor Koerner with you; and if agreeable to you and him, I will make him a brigadier-general, so that he can afford to give his time. He does not wish to command in the field, though he has more military knowledge than some who do. If he goes into the place, he will simply be an efficient, zealous, and unselfish assistant to you. I say all this upon intimate personal acquaintance with Governor Koerner.

Yours very truly,
A. LINCOLN

MESSAGE TO CONGRESS.

WASHINGTON, January 17, 1862

TO THE SENATE AND HOUSE OF REPRESENTATIVES:
I transmit to Congress a translation of an instruction to the minister of his Majesty the King of Prussia accredited to this government, and a copy of a note to that minister from the Secretary of State relating to the capture and detention of certain citizens of the United States, passengers on board the British steamer Trent, by order of Captain Wilkes of the United States Navy.
A. LINCOLN

TO GENERAL McCLELLAN.

DEPARTMENT OF STATE, WASHINGTON.

January 20, 1862.
MAJOR-GENERAL GEORGE B. McCLELLAN,
Commanding Armies of the United States:

You or any officer you may designate will in your discretion suspend the writ of habeas corpus so far as may relate to Major Chase, lately of the Engineer Corps of the Army of the United States, now alleged to be guilty of treasonable practices against this government.

A. LINCOLN.

By the President: WILLIAM H. SEWARD.

PRESIDENT'S GENERAL WAR ORDER NO. 1

EXECUTIVE MANSION, WASHINGTON, January 27, 1862.

Ordered, That the 22d day of February, 1862, be the day for a general movement of the land and the naval forces of the United States against the insurgent forces.

That especially the army at and about Fortress Monroe, the Army of the Potomac, the Army of Western Virginia, the army near Munfordville, Kentucky, the army and flotilla at Cairo, and a naval force in the Gulf of Mexico, be ready for a movement on that day.

That all other forces, both land and naval, with their respective commanders, obey existing orders for the time, and be ready to obey additional orders when duly given.

That the heads of departments, and especially the Secretaries of War and of the Navy, with all their subordinates, and the General-in-chief, with all other commanders and subordinates of land and naval forces, will severally be held to their strict and full responsibilities for the prompt execution of this order.

A. LINCOLN.

TO SECRETARY STANTON,

EXECUTIVE MANSION WASHINGTON, January 31, 1862

HON. SECRETARY OF WAR.

MY DEAR SIR:—It is my wish that the expedition commonly called the "Lane Expedition" shall be, as much as has been promised at the adjutant-general's office, under the supervision of General McClellan, and not any more. I have not intended, and do not now intend, that it shall be a great, exhausting affair, but a snug, sober column of 10,000 or 15,000. General Lane has been told by me many times that he is under the command of General Hunter, and assented to it as often as told. It was the distinct agreement between him and me, when I appointed him, that he was to be under Hunter.

Yours truly,

A. LINCOLN.

PRESIDENT'S SPECIAL WAR ORDER NO. 1.

EXECUTIVE MANSION, WASHINGTON, January 31, 1862.

Ordered, That all the disposable force of the Army of the Potomac, after providing safely for the defence of Washington, be formed into an expedition for the immediate object of seizing and occupying a point upon the railroad southwestward of what is known as Manassas Junction, all details to be in the discretion of the commander-in-chief, and the expedition to move before or on the 22d day of February next.

A. LINCOLN.

OPPOSITION TO McCLELLAN'S PLANS

TO GENERAL G. B. McCLELLAN,

EXECUTIVE MANSION, WASHINGTON, February 3, 1862.
MAJOR-GENERAL MCCLELLAN.
DEAR SIR—You and I have distinct and different plans for a movement of the Army of the Potomac—yours to be down the Chesapeake, up the Rappahannock to Urbana, and across land to the terminus of the railroad on the York River; mine to move directly to a point on the railroad southwest of Manassas.
If you will give me satisfactory answers to the following questions, I shall gladly yield my plan to yours.
First. Does not your plan involve a greatly larger expenditure of time and money than mine?
Second. Wherein is a victory more certain by your plan than mine?
Third. Wherein is a victory more valuable by your plan than mine?
Fourth. In fact, would it not be less valuable in this, that it would break no great line of the enemy's communications, while mine would?
Fifth. In case of disaster, would not a retreat be more difficult by your plan than mine?
Yours truly,
A. LINCOLN.

Memorandum accompanying Letter of President Lincoln to General McClellan,

dated February 3, 1862.

First. Suppose the enemy should attack us in force before we reach the Occoquan, what?
Second. Suppose the enemy in force shall dispute the crossing of the Occoquan, what? In view of this, might it not be safest for us to cross the Occoquan at Coichester, rather than at the village of Occoquan? This would cost the enemy two miles of travel to meet us, but would, on the contrary, leave us two miles farther from our ultimate destination.
Third. Suppose we reach Maple Valley without an attack, will we not be attacked there in force by the enemy marching by the several roads from Manassas; and if so, what?

TO WM. H. HERNDON.

EXECUTIVE MANSION, WASHINGTON, February 3, 1862.

DEAR WILLIAM:—Yours of January 30th just received. Do just as you say about the money matter. As you well know, I have not time to write a letter of respectable length. God bless you, says
Your friend,
A. LINCOLN.

RESPITE FOR NATHANIEL GORDON

February 4, 1862

A. LINCOLN, PRESIDENT OF THE UNITED STATES OF AMERICA,
To all to whom these Presents shall come, Greeting:
Whereas it appears that at a term of the Circuit Court of the United States of America for the Southern District of New York held in the month of November, A.D. 1861, Nathaniel Gordon was indicted and convicted for being engaged in the slave trade, and was by the said court sentenced to be put to death by hanging by the neck, on Friday the 7th day of February, AD. 1862:

And whereas a large number of respectable citizens have earnestly besought me to commute the said sentence of the said Nathaniel Gordon to a term of imprisonment for life, which application I have felt it to be my duty to refuse:

And whereas it has seemed to me probable that the unsuccessful application made for the commutation of his sentence may have prevented the said Nathaniel Gordon from making the necessary preparation for the awful change which awaits him;

Now, therefore, be it known, that I, Abraham Lincoln, President of the United States of America, have granted and do hereby grant unto him, the said Nathaniel Gordon, a respite of the above recited sentence, until Friday the twenty-first day of February, A.D. 1862, between the hours of twelve o'clock at noon and three o'clock in the afternoon of the said day, when the said sentence shall be executed.

In granting this respite, it becomes my painful duty to admonish the prisoner that, relinquishing all expectation of pardon by human authority, he refer himself alone to the mercy of the common God and Father of all men.

In testimony whereof I have hereunto signed my name and caused the seal of the United States to be affixed.

Done at the City of Washington, this fourth day of February, A.D. 1862, and of the independence of the United States the eighty-sixth.

A. LINCOLN.

By the President: WILLIAM H. SEWARD, Secretary of State.

MESSAGE TO THE SENATE.

WASHINGTON CITY, February 4. 1862

To THE SENATE OF THE UNITED STATES:

The third section of the "Act further to promote the efficiency of the Navy," approved December 21, 1862, provides: "That the President of the United States, by and with the advice and consent of the Senate, shall have the authority to detail from the retired list of the navy for the command of squadrons and single ships such officers as he may believe that the good of the service requires to be thus placed in command; and such officers may, if upon the recommendation of the President of the United States they shall receive a vote of thanks of Congress for their services and gallantry in action against an enemy, be restored to the active list, and not otherwise."

In conformity with this law, Captain Samuel F. Du Pont, of the navy, was nominated to the Senate for continuance as the flag-officer in command of the squadron which recently rendered such important service to the Union in the expedition to the coast of South Carolina.

Believing that no occasion could arise which would more fully correspond with the intention of the law, or be more pregnant with happy influence as an example, I cordially recommend that Captain Samuel F. Du Pont receive a vote of thanks of Congress for his services and gallantry displayed in the capture of Forts Walker and Beauregard, commanding the entrance of Port Royal Harbor, on the 7th of November, 1861.

A. LINCOLN.

TO GENERALS D. HUNTER AND J. H. LANE.

EXECUTIVE MANSION WASHINGTON, FEBRUARY 4, 1862.

MAJOR-GENERAL HUNTER AND BRIGADIER-GENERAL LANE, Leavenworth, Kansas:

My wish has been and is to avail the government of the services of both General Hunter and General Lane, and, so far as possible, to personally oblige both. General Hunter is the senior officer, and must command when they serve together; though in so far as he can consistently with the public service and his own honor oblige General Lane, he will also oblige me. If they cannot come to an amicable understanding, General Lane must report to General Hunter for duty, according to the rules, or decline the service.

A. LINCOLN.

EXECUTIVE ORDER NO. 1, RELATING TO POLITICAL PRISONERS.

WAR DEPARTMENT, WASHINGTON, February 14, 1862.

The breaking out of a formidable insurrection based on a conflict of political ideas, being an event without precedent in the United States, was necessarily attended by great confusion and perplexity of the public mind. Disloyalty before unsuspected suddenly became bold, and treason astonished the world by bringing at once into the field military forces superior in number to the standing army of the United States.

Every department of the government was paralyzed by treason. Defection appeared in the Senate, in the House of Representatives, in the Cabinet, in the Federal courts; ministers and consuls returned from foreign countries to enter the insurrectionary councils of land or naval forces; commanding and other officers of the army and in the navy betrayed our councils or deserted their posts for commands in the insurgent forces. Treason was flagrant in the revenue and in the post-office service, as well as in the Territorial governments and in the Indian reserves.

Not only governors, judges, legislators, and ministerial officers in the States, but even whole States rushed one after another with apparent unanimity into rebellion. The capital was besieged and its connection with all the States cut off. Even in the portions of the country which were most loyal, political combinations and secret societies were formed furthering the work of disunion, while, from motives of disloyalty or cupidity or from excited passions or perverted sympathies, individuals were found furnishing men, money, and materials of war and supplies to the insurgents' military and naval forces. Armies, ships, fortifications, navy yards, arsenals, military posts, and garrisons one after another were betrayed or abandoned to the insurgents.

Congress had not anticipated, and so had not provided for, the emergency. The municipal authorities were powerless and inactive. The judicial machinery seemed as if it had been designed, not to sustain the government, but to embarrass and betray it.

Foreign intervention, openly invited and industriously instigated by the abettors of the insurrection, became imminent, and has only been prevented by the practice of strict and impartial justice, with the most perfect moderation, in our intercourse with nations.

The public mind was alarmed and apprehensive, though fortunately not distracted or disheartened. It seemed to be doubtful whether the Federal Government, which one year before had been thought a model worthy of universal acceptance, had indeed the ability to defend and maintain itself.

Some reverses, which, perhaps, were unavoidable, suffered by newly levied and inefficient forces, discouraged the loyal and gave new hopes to the insurgents. Voluntary enlistments seemed about to cease and desertions commenced. Parties speculated upon the question whether conscription had not become necessary to fill up the armies of the United States. In this emergency the President felt it his duty to employ with energy the extraordinary powers which the Constitution confides to him in cases of insurrection. He called into the field such military and naval forces, unauthorized by the existing laws, as seemed necessary. He directed measures to prevent the use of the post-office for treasonable correspondence. He subjected passengers to and from foreign countries to new passport regulations, and he instituted a blockade, suspended the writ of habeas corpus in various places, and caused persons who were represented to him as being or about to engage in disloyal and treasonable practices to be arrested by special civil as well as military agencies and detained in military custody when necessary to prevent them and deter others from such practices. Examinations of such cases were instituted, and some of the persons so arrested have been discharged from time to time under circumstances or upon conditions compatible, as was thought, with the public safety.

Meantime a favorable change of public opinion has occurred. The line between loyalty and disloyalty is plainly defined. The whole structure of the government is firm and stable. Apprehension of public danger and facilities for treasonable practices have diminished with the passions which prompted heedless persons to adopt them. The insurrection is believed to have culminated and to be declining.

The President, in view of these facts, and anxious to favor a return to the normal course of the administration as far as regard for the public welfare will allow, directs that all political prisoners or state prisoners now held in military custody be released on their subscribing to a parole engaging them to render no aid or comfort to the enemies in hostility to the United States.

The Secretary of War will, however, in his discretion, except from the effect of this order any persons detained as spies in the service of the insurgents, or others whose release at the present moment may be deemed incompatible with the public safety.

To all persons who shall be so released, and who shall keep their parole, the President grants an amnesty for any past offences of treason or disloyalty which they may have comminuted.

Extraordinary arrests will hereafter be made under the direction of the military authorities alone.

By order of the President EDWIN M. STANTON, Secretary of War.

MESSAGE TO CONGRESS. WASHINGTON CITY, February 15, 1862

TO THE SENATE AND HOUSE OF REPRESENTATIVES OF THE UNITED STATES:

The third section of the "Act further to promote the efficiency of the Navy," approved December 21, 1861, provides "That the President of the United States, by and with the advice and consent of the Senate, shall have the authority to detail from the retired list of the navy for the command of squadrons and single ships such officers as he may believe that the good of the service requires to be thus placed in command; and such officers may, if upon the recommendation of the President of the United States they shall receive a vote of thanks of Congress for their services and gallantry in action against an enemy, be restored to the active list, and not otherwise."
In conformity with this law, Captain Louis M. Goldsborough, of the navy, was nominated to the Senate for continuance as the flag-officer in command of the North Atlantic Blockading Squadron, which recently rendered such important service to the Union in the expedition to the coast of North Carolina.
Believing that no occasion could arise which would more fully correspond with the intention of the law or be more pregnant with happy influence as an example, I cordially recommend that Captain Louis M. Goldsborough receive a vote of thanks of Congress for his services and gallantry displayed in the combined attack of the forces commanded by him and Brigadier-General Burnside in the capture of Roanoke Island and the destruction of rebel gunboats On the 7th, 8th, and 10th of February, 1862.
A. LINCOLN.

FIRST WRITTEN NOTICE OF GRANT

TO GENERAL H. W. HALLECK.

EXECUTIVE MANSION, WASHINGTON,
February 16, 1862.
MAJOR-GENERAL HALLECK, St. Louis, Missouri:
You have Fort Donelson safe, unless Grant shall be overwhelmed from outside; to prevent which latter will, I think, require all the vigilance, energy, and skill of yourself and Buell, acting in full co-operation. Columbus will not get at Grant, but the force from Bowling Green will. They hold the railroad from Bowling Green to within a few miles of Fort Donelson, with the bridge at Clarksville undisturbed. It is unsafe to rely that they will not dare to expose Nashville to Buell. A small part of their force can retire slowly toward Nashville, breaking up the railroad as they go, and keep Buell out of that city twenty days. Meanwhile Nashville will be abundantly defended by forces from all South and perhaps from hers at Manassas. Could not a cavalry force from General Thomas on the upper Cumberland dash across, almost unresisted, and cut the railroad at or near Knoxville, Tennessee? In the midst of a bombardment at Fort Donelson, why could not a gunboat run up and destroy the bridge at Clarksville? Our success or failure at Fort Donelson is vastly important, and I beg you to put your soul in the effort. I send a copy of this to Buell.
A. LINCOLN.

EXECUTIVE ORDER NO. 2.—IN RELATION TO STATE PRISONERS.

WAR DEPARTMENT, WASHINGTON CITY, FEBRUARY 27, 1862

It is ordered:
First. That a special commission of two persons, one of military rank and the other in civil life, be appointed to examine the cases of the state prisoners remaining in the military custody of the United States, and to determine whether in view of the public Safety and the existing rebellion they should be discharged, or remain in military custody, or be remitted to the civil tribunals for trial.
Second. That Major-General John A. Dix, commanding in Baltimore, and the HON. Edwards Pierrepont, of New York, be, and they are hereby, appointed commissioners for the purpose above mentioned; and they are authorized to

examine, hear, and determine the cases aforesaid ex parte and in a summary manner, at such times and places as in their discretion they may appoint, and make full report to the War Department.
By order of the President EDWIN M. STANTON, Secretary of War.

ORDER RELATING TO COMMERCIAL INTERCOURSE.

Considering that the existing circumstances of the country allow a partial restoration of commercial intercourse between the inhabitants of those parts of the United States heretofore declared to be in insurrection and the citizens of the loyal States of the Union, and exercising the authority and discretion confided to me by the act of Congress, approved July 13, 1861, entitled "An act further to provide for the collection of duties on imports, and for other purposes," I hereby license and permit such commercial intercourse in all cases within the rules and regulations which have been or may be prescribed by the Secretary of the Treasury for conducting and carrying on the same on the inland waters and ways of the United States.
WASHINGTON, February 28, 1862.
A. LINCOLN.

SPEECH TO THE PERUVIAN MINISTER,

WASHINGTON, D. C., MARCH 4, 1862

The United States have no enmities, animosities, or rivalries, and no interests which conflict with the welfare, safety, and rights or interests of any other nation. Their own prosperity, happiness, and aggrandizement are sought most safely and advantageously through the preservation not only of peace on their own part, but peace among all other nations. But while the United States are thus a friend to all other nations, they do not seek to conceal the fact that they cherish especial sentiments of friendship for, and sympathies with, those who, like themselves, have founded their institutions on the principle of the equal rights of men; and such nations being more prominently neighbors of the United States, the latter are co-operating with them in establishing civilization and culture on the American continent. Such being the general principles which govern the United States in their foreign relations, you may be assured, sir, that in all things this government will deal justly, frankly, and, if it be possible, even liberally with Peru, whose liberal sentiments toward us you have so kindly expressed.

MESSAGE TO CONGRESS RECOMMENDING COMPENSATED EMANCIPATION.

March 6, 1862

FELLOW-CITIZENS OF THE SENATE AND HOUSE OF REPRESENTATIVES:—I recommend the adoption of a joint resolution by your honorable bodies which shall be substantially as follows:
"Resolved, That the United States ought to co-operate with any State which may adopt gradual abolishment of slavery, giving to such State pecuniary aid, to be used by such State, in its discretion, to compensate for the inconveniences, public and private, produced by such change of system."
If the proposition contained in the resolution does not meet the approval of Congress and the country, there is the end; but if it does command such approval, I deem it of importance that the States and people immediately interested should be at once distinctly notified of the fact, so that they may begin to consider whether to accept or reject it. The Federal Government would find its highest interest in such a measure, as one of the most efficient means of self-preservation. The leaders of the existing insurrection entertain the hope that this government will ultimately be forced to acknowledge the independence of some part of the disaffected region, and that all the slave States north of such part will then say, "The Union for which we have struggled being already gone, we now choose to go with the Southern section." To deprive them of this hope substantially ends the rebellion, and the initiation of emancipation completely deprives them of it as to all the States initiating it. The point is not that all the States tolerating slavery would very soon,

if at all, initiate emancipation; but that, while the offer is equally made to all, the more northern shall by such initiation make it certain to the more southern that in no event will the former ever join the latter in their proposed confederacy. I say "initiation" because, in my judgment, gradual and not sudden emancipation is better for all. In the mere financial or pecuniary view, any member of Congress with the census tables and treasury reports before him can readily see for himself how very soon the current expenditures of this war would purchase, at fair valuation, all the slaves in any named State. Such a proposition on the part of the General Government sets up no claim of a right by Federal authority to interfere with slavery within State limits, referring, as it does, the absolute control of the subject in each case to the State and its people immediately interested. It is proposed as a matter of perfectly free choice with them.

In the annual message last December, I thought fit to say, "The Union must be preserved, and hence all indispensable means must be employed." I said this not hastily, but deliberately. War has been made and continues to be an indispensable means to this end. A practical reacknowledgment of the national authority would render the war unnecessary, and it would at once cease. If, however, resistance continues, the war must also continue; and it is impossible to foresee all the incidents which may attend and all the ruin which may follow it. Such as may seem indispensable or may obviously promise great efficiency toward ending the struggle must and will come.

The proposition now made (though an offer only), I hope it may be esteemed no offense to ask whether the pecuniary consideration tendered would not be of more value to the States and private persons concerned than are the institution and property in it in the present aspect of affairs.

While it is true that the adoption of the proposed resolution would be merely initiatory, and not within itself a practical measure, it is recommended in the hope that it would soon lead to important practical results. In full view of my great responsibility to my God and to my country, I earnestly beg the attention of Congress and the people to the subject.
A. LINCOLN.

INDORSEMENT ON LETTER FROM GOVERNOR YATES.

STATE OF ILLINOIS, EXECUTIVE DEPARTMENT, SPRINGFIELD, ILL., March 1, 1862

HON. EDWIN M. STANTON, SECRETARY OF WAR, Washington, D. C.

SIR:—The government at my special request a few months since contracted for fourteen batteries of the James rifled gun, 6-pounder calibre, and a limited quantity of the James projectiles, weighing about fourteen pounds each. The reports showing the superiority of this gun and projectile, both as regards range, accuracy, and execution, for field service over that of all others at the battle of Fort Donelson, leads me to request that there be furnished to the State of Illinois in the shortest time practicable seven batteries of 12-pounder calibre James rifled guns, with carriages, harness, implements, etc., complete and ready for field service, together with the following fixed ammunition to each gun, viz., 225 shells, 225 canister, and 50 solid projectiles, weighing about 24 pounds each, and also 200 shells, 100 canister, and 100 solid projectiles for each of the guns of the fourteen batteries named above, weighing about 14 pounds each, all to be of the James model.
Very respectfully,
RICHARD YATES, Governor of Illinois.
[Indorsement.]
March 8, 1862.
The within is from the Governor of Illinois. I understand the seven additional batteries now sought are to be 6-gun batteries, and the object is to mix them with the fourteen batteries they already have so as to make each battery consist of four 6-pounders and two 12-pounders. I shall be very glad to have the requisition filled if it can be without detriment to the service.
A. LINCOLN.

PRESIDENT'S GENERAL WAR ORDER NO.2.

EXECUTIVE MANSION, WASHINGTON

March 8, 1862.

Ordered: 1. That the major-general commanding the Army of the Potomac proceed forthwith to organize that part of the said army destined to enter upon active operations (including the reserve, but excluding the troops to be left in the fortifications about Washington) into four army corps, to be commanded according to seniority of rank, as follows: First Corps to consist of four divisions, and to be commanded by Major-General I. McDowell. Second Corps to consist of three divisions, and to be commanded by Brigadier-General E. V. Sumner. Third Corps to consist of three divisions, and to be commanded by Brigadier-General S. P. Heintzelman. Fourth Corps to consist of three divisions, and to be commanded by Brigadier-General E. D. Keyes.
2. That the divisions now commanded by the officers above assigned to the commands of army corps shall be embraced in and form part of their respective corps.
3. The forces left for the defense of Washington will be placed in command of Brigadier-General James S. Wadsworth, who shall also be military governor of the District of Columbia.
4. That this order be executed with such promptness and dispatch as not to delay the commencement of the operations already directed to be underwritten by the Army of the Potomac.
5. A fifth army corps, to be commanded by Major general N. P. Banks, will be formed from his own and General Shields's (late General Lander's) divisions.
A. LINCOLN.

PRESIDENT'S GENERAL WAR ORDER NO.3.

EXECUTIVE MANSION, WASHINGTON, MARCH 8, 1862

Ordered: That no change of the base of operations of the Army of the Potomac shall be made without leaving in and about Washington such a force as in the opinion of the general-in-chief and the commanders of all the army corps shall leave said city entirely secure.
That no more than two army corps (about 50,000 troops) of said Army of the Potomac shall be moved en route for a new base of operations until the navigation of the Potomac from Washington to the Chesapeake Bay shall be freed from enemy's batteries and other obstructions, or until the President shall hereafter give express permission.
That any movements as aforesaid en route for a new base of operations which may be ordered by the general-in-chief, and which may be intended to move upon the Chesapeake Bay, shall begin to move upon the bay as early as the 18th day of March instant, and the general-in-chief shall be responsible that it so move as early as that day.
Ordered, That the army and navy co-operate in an immediate effort to capture the enemy's batteries upon the Potomac between Washington and the Chesapeake Bay.
A. LINCOLN

INTERVIEW BETWEEN THE PRESIDENT AND SOME BORDER SLAVE STATE

REPRESENTATIVES, BY HON. J. W. CRISFIELD.

MEMORANDUM
"DEAR SIR:—I called, at the request of the President, to ask you to come to the White House tomorrow morning, at nine o'clock, and bring such of your colleagues as are in town."
WASHINGTON, March 10, 1862.
Yesterday, on my return from church, I found Mr. Postmaster-General Blair in my room, writing the above note, which he immediately suspended, and verbally communicated the President's invitation, and stated that the President's purpose was to have some conversation with the delegations of Kentucky, Missouri, Maryland, Virginia, and Delaware, in explanation of his message of the 6th instant.
This morning these delegations, or such of them as were in town, assembled at the White House at the appointed time, and after some little delay were admitted to an audience. Mr. Leary and myself were the only members from Maryland present, and, I think, were the only members of the delegation at that time in the city. I know that Mr. Pearce, of the Senate, and Messrs. Webster and Calvert, of the House, were absent.
After the usual salutations, and we were seated, the President said, in substance, that he had invited us to meet him to have some conversation with us in explanation of his message of the 6th; that since he had sent it in several of the

gentlemen then present had visited him, but had avoided any allusion to the message, and he therefore inferred that the import of the message had been misunderstood, and was regarded as inimical to the interests we represented; and he had resolved he would talk with us, and disabuse our minds of that erroneous opinion.

The President then disclaimed any intent to injure the interests or wound the sensibilities of the slave States. On the contrary, his purpose was to protect the one and respect the other; that we were engaged in a terrible, wasting, and tedious war; immense armies were in the field, and must continue in the field as long as the war lasts; that these armies must, of necessity, be brought into contact with slaves in the States we represented and in other States as they advanced; that slaves would come to the camps, and continual irritation was kept up; that he was constantly annoyed by conflicting and antagonistic complaints: on the one side a certain class complained if the slave was not protected by the army; persons were frequently found who, participating in these views, acted in a way unfriendly to the slaveholder; on the other hand, slaveholders complained that their rights were interfered with, their slaves induced to abscond and protected within the lines; these complaints were numerous, loud and deep; were a serious annoyance to him and embarrassing to the progress of the war; that it kept alive a spirit hostile to the government in the States we represented; strengthened the hopes of the Confederates that at some day the border States would unite with them, and thus tend to prolong the war; and he was of opinion, if this resolution should be adopted by Congress and accepted by our States, these causes of irritation and these hopes would be removed, and more would be accomplished toward shortening the war than could be hoped from the greatest victory achieved by Union armies; that he made this proposition in good faith, and desired it to be accepted, if at all, voluntarily, and in the same patriotic spirit in which it was made; that emancipation was a subject exclusively under the control of the States, and must be adopted or rejected by each for itself; that he did not claim nor had this government any right to coerce them for that purpose; that such was no part of his purpose in making this proposition, and he wished it to be clearly understood; that he did not expect us there to be prepared to give him an answer, but he hoped we would take the subject into serious consideration, confer with one another, and then take such course as we felt our duty and the interests of our constituents required of us.

Mr. Noell, of Missouri, said that in his State slavery was not considered a permanent institution; that natural causes were there in operation which would at no distant day extinguish it, and he did not think that this proposition was necessary for that; and, besides that, he and his friends felt solicitous as to the message on account of the different constructions which the resolution and message had received. The New York Tribune was for it, and understood it to mean that we must accept gradual emancipation according to the plan suggested, or get something worse.

The President replied that he must not be expected to quarrel with the New York Tribune before the right time; he hoped never to have to do it; he would not anticipate events. In respect to emancipation in Missouri, he said that what had been observed by Mr. Noell was probably true, but the operation of these natural causes had not prevented the irritating conduct to which he had referred, or destroyed the hopes of the Confederates that Missouri would at some time merge herself alongside of them, which, in his judgment, the passage of this resolution by Congress and its acceptance by Missouri would accomplish.

Mr. Crisfield, of Maryland, asked what would be the effect of the refusal of the State to accept this proposal, and he desired to know if the President looked to any policy beyond the acceptance or rejection of this scheme.

The President replied that he had no designs beyond the actions of the States on this particular subject. He should lament their refusal to accept it, but he had no designs beyond their refusal of it.

Mr. Menzies, of Kentucky, inquired if the President thought there was any power except in the States themselves to carry out his scheme of emancipation.

The President replied that he thought there could not be. He then went off into a course of remarks not qualifying the foregoing declaration nor material to be repeated to a just understanding of his meaning.

Mr. Crisfield said he did not think the people of Maryland looked upon slavery as a permanent institution; and he did not know that they would be very reluctant to give it up if provision was made to meet the loss and they could be rid of the race; but they did not like to be coerced into emancipation, either by the direct action of the government or by indirection, as through the emancipation of slaves in this District, or the confiscation of Southern property as now threatened; and he thought before they would consent to consider this proposition they would require to be informed on these points. The President replied that, unless he was expelled by the act of God or the Confederate armies he should occupy that house for three years; and as long as he remained there Maryland had nothing to fear either for her institutions or her interests on the points referred to.

Mr. Crisfield immediately added: "Mr. President, if what you now say could be heard by the people of Maryland, they would consider your proposition with a much better feeling than I fear without it they will be inclined to do."

The President: "That [meaning a publication of what he said] will not do; it would force me into a quarrel before the proper time "; and, again intimating, as he had before done, that a quarrel with the "Greeley faction" was impending, he said he did not wish to encounter it before the proper time, nor at all if it could be avoided.

[The Greely faction wanted an immediate Emancipation Proclamation. D.W.]

Governor Wickliffe, of Kentucky, then asked him respecting the constitutionality of his scheme.

The President replied: "As you may suppose, I have considered that; and the proposition now submitted does not encounter any constitutional difficulty. It proposes simply to co-operate with any State by giving such State pecuniary aid"; and he thought that the resolution, as proposed by him, would be considered rather as the expression of a sentiment than as involving any constitutional question.

Mr. Hall, of Missouri, thought that if this proposition was adopted at all it should be by the votes of the free States, and come as a proposition from them to the slave States, affording them an inducement to put aside this subject of discord; that it ought not to be expected that members representing slaveholding constituencies should declare at once, and in advance of any proposition to them, for the emancipation of slavery.

The President said he saw and felt the force of the objection; it was a fearful responsibility, and every gentleman must do as he thought best; that he did not know how this scheme was received by the members from the free States; some of them had spoken to him and received it kindly; but for the most part they were as reserved and chary as we had been, and he could not tell how they would vote. And in reply to some expression of Mr. Hall as to his own opinion regarding slavery, he said he did not pretend to disguise his anti-slavery feeling; that he thought it was wrong, and should continue to think so; but that was not the question we had to deal with now. Slavery existed, and that, too, as well by the act of the North as of the South; and in any scheme to get rid of it the North as well as the South was morally bound to do its full and equal share. He thought the institution wrong and ought never to have existed; but yet he recognized the rights of property which had grown out of it, and would respect those rights as fully as similar rights in any other property; that property can exist and does legally exist. He thought such a law wrong, but the rights of property resulting must be respected; he would get rid of the odious law, not by violating the rights, but by encouraging the proposition and offering inducements to give it up.

Here the interview, so far as this subject is concerned, terminated by Mr. Crittenden's assuring the President that, whatever might be our final action, we all thought him solely moved by a high patriotism and sincere devotion to the happiness and glory of his country; and with that conviction we should consider respectfully the important suggestions he had made.

After some conversation on the current war news, we retired, and I immediately proceeded to my room and wrote out this paper. J. W. CRISFIELD.

We were present at the interview described in the foregoing paper of Mr. Crisfield, and we certify that the substance of what passed on the occasion is in this paper faithfully and fully given.

J. W. MENZIES, J. J. CRITTENDEN, R. MALLORY.

March 10, 1862.

PRESIDENT'S SPECIAL WAR ORDER NO.3.

EXECUTIVE MANSION, WASHINGTON, March 11, 1862.

Major-General McClellan having personally taken the field at the head of the Army of the Potomac, until otherwise ordered he is relieved from the command of the other military departments, he retaining command of the Department of the Potomac.

Ordered further, That the departments now under the respective commands of Generals Halleck and Hunter, together with so much of that under General Buell as lies west of a north and south line indefinitely drawn through Knoxville, Tenn., be consolidated and designated the Department of the Mississippi, and that until otherwise ordered Major General Halleck have command of said department.

Ordered also, That the country west of the Department of the Potomac and east of the Department of the Mississippi be a military department, to be called the Mountain Department, and that the same be commanded by Major-General Fremont.

That all the commanders of departments, after the receipt of this order by them, respectively report severally and directly to the Secretary of War, and that prompt, full, and frequent reports will be expected of all and each of them.

A. LINCOLN.

FROM SECRETARY STANTON TO GENERAL MCCLELLAN.

WAR DEPARTMENT, March 13, 1862.

MAJOR-GENERAL GEORGE B. MCCLELLAN:
The President, having considered the plan of operations agreed upon by yourself and the commanders of army corps, makes no objection to the same but gives the following directions as to its execution:
1. Leave such force at Manassas Junction as shall make it entirely certain that the enemy shall no repossess himself of that position and line of communication.
2. Leave Washington entirely secure.
3. Move the remainder of the force down the Potomac, choosing a new base at Fortress Monroe or anywhere between here and there, or, at all events, move such remainder of the army at once in pursuit of the enemy by some route.
EDWARD M. STANTON, Secretary of War.

SPEECH TO A PARTY OF MASSACHUSETTS GENTLEMAN

WASHINGTON, MARCH 13, 1862

I thank you, Mr. Train, for your kindness in presenting me with this truly elegant and highly creditable specimen of the handiwork of the mechanics of your State of Massachusetts, and I beg of you to express my hearty thanks to the donors. It displays a perfection of workmanship which I really wish I had time to acknowledge in more fitting words, and I might then follow your idea that it is suggestive, for it is evidently expected that a good deal of whipping is to be done. But as we meet here socially let us not think only of whipping rebels, or of those who seem to think only of whipping negroes, but of those pleasant days, which it is to be hoped are in store for us, when seated behind a good pair of horses we can crack our whips and drive through a peaceful, happy, and prosperous land. With this idea, gentlemen, I must leave you for my business duties. [It was likely a Buggy-Whip D.W.]

MESSAGE TO CONGRESS.

WASHINGTON CITY, March 20, 1862.

TO THE SENATE AND HOUSE OF REPRESENTATIVES:
The third section of the "Act further to promote the efficiency of the Navy," approved December 21, 1861, provides: "That the President of the United States, by and with the advice and consent of the Senate, shall have the authority to detail from the retired list of the navy for the command of squadrons and single ships such officers as he may believe the good of the service requires to be thus placed in command; and such officers may, if upon the recommendation of the President of the United States they shall receive a vote of thanks cf Congress for their services and gallantry in action against an enemy, be restored to the active list, and not otherwise."
In conformity with this law, Captain Samuel F. Du Pont, of the navy, was nominated to the Senate for continuance as the flag-officer in command of the squadron which recently rendered such important service to the Union in the expedition to the coasts of South Carolina, Georgia, and Florida.
Believing that no occasion could arise which would more fully correspond with the intention of the law or be more pregnant with happy influence as an example, I cordially recommend that Captain Samuel F. Du Pont receive a vote of thanks of Congress for his service and gallantry displayed in the capture since the 21st December, 1861, of various ports on the coasts of Georgia and Florida, particularly Brunswick, Cumberland Island and Sound, Amelia Island, the towns of St. Mary's, St. Augustine, and Jacksonville and Fernandina.
A. LINCOLN.

TO GENERAL G. B. McCLELLAN.

EXECUTIVE MANSION, WASHINGTON, MARCH 31, 1862

MAJOR-GENERAL McCLELLAN.
MY DEAR SIR:-This morning I felt constrained to order Blenker's division to Fremont, and I write this to assure you I did so with great pain, understanding that you would wish it otherwise. If you could know the full pressure of the case, I am confident that you would justify it, even beyond a mere acknowledgment that the commander-in-chief may order what he pleases.
Yours very truly,
A. LINCOLN.

GIFT OF SOME RABBITS

TO MICHAEL CROCK. 360 N. Fourth St., Philadelphia.

EXECUTIVE MANSION, WASHINGTON, April 2, 1862.
MY DEAR SIR:-Allow me to thank you in behalf of my little son for your present of white rabbits. He is very much pleased with them.
Yours truly,
A. LINCOLN.

INSTRUCTION TO SECRETARY STANTON.

EXECUTIVE MANSION, April 3, 1862.

The Secretary of War will order that one or the other of the corps of General McDowell and General Sumner remain in front of Washington until further orders from the department, to operate at or in the direction of Manassas Junction, or otherwise, as occasion may require; that the other Corps not so ordered to remain go forward to General McClellan as speedily as possible; that General McClellan commence his forward movements from his new base at once, and that such incidental modifications as the foregoing may render proper be also made. A. LINCOLN.

TELEGRAM TO GENERAL McCLELLAN.

WASHINGTON, April 6, 1862.

GENERAL G. B. McCLELLAN:
Yours of 11 A. M. today received. Secretary of War informs me that the forwarding of transportation, ammunition, and Woodbury's brigade, under your orders, is not, and will not be, interfered with. You now have over one hundred thousand troops with you, independent of General Wool's command. I think you better break the enemy's line from Yorktown to Warwick River at once. This will probably use time as advantageously as you can.
A. LINCOLN, President

TO GENERAL G. B. McCLELLAN.

WASHINGTON, April 9, 1862

MAJOR-GENERAL McCLELLAN.
MY DEAR SIR+—Your despatches, complaining that you are not properly sustained, while they do not offend me, do pain me very much.

Blenker's division was withdrawn from you before you left here, and you knew the pressure under which I did it, and, as I thought, acquiesced in it certainly not without reluctance.

After you left I ascertained that less than 20,000 unorganized men, without a single field battery, were all you designed to be left for the defense of Washington and Manassas Junction, and part of this even to go to General Hooker's old position; General Banks's corps, once designed for Manassas Junction, was divided and tied up on the line of Winchester and Strasburg, and could not leave it without again exposing the upper Potomac and the Baltimore and Ohio Railroad. This presented (or would present when McDowell and Sumner should be gone) a great temptation to the enemy to turn back from the Rappahannock and sack Washington. My explicit order that Washington should, by the judgment of all the Commanders of corps, be left entirely secure, had been neglected. It was precisely this that drove me to detain McDowell.

I do not forget that I was satisfied with your arrangement to leave Banks at Manassas Junction; but when that arrangement was broken up and nothing substituted for it, of course I was not satisfied. I was constrained to substitute something for it myself.

And now allow me to ask, do you really think I should permit the line from Richmond via Manaasas Junction to this city to be entirely open, except what resistance could be presented by less than 20,000 unorganized troops? This is a question which the country will not allow me to evade.

There is a curious mystery about the number of the troops now with you. When I telegraphed you on the 6th, saying you had over 100,000 with you, I had just obtained from the Secretary of War a statement, taken as he said from your own returns, making 108,000 then with you and en route to you. You now say you will have but 85,000 when all enroute to you shall have reached you. How can this discrepancy of 23,000 be accounted for?

As to General Wool's command, I understand it is doing for you precisely what a like number of your own would have to do if that command was away. I suppose the whole force which has gone forward to you is with you by this time; and if so, I think it is the precise time for you to strike a blow. By delay the enemy will relatively gain upon you—that is, he will gain faster by fortifications and reinforcements than you can by reinforcements alone.

And once more let me tell you it is indispensable to you that you strike a blow. I am powerless to help this. You will do me the justice to remember I always insisted that going down the bay in search of a field, instead of fighting at or near Manassas, was only shifting and not surmounting a difficulty; that we would find the same enemy and the same or equal entrenchments at either place. The country will not fail to note—is noting now—that the present hesitation to move upon an entrenched enemy is but the story of Manassas repeated.

I beg to assure you that I have never written you or spoken to you in greater kindness of feeling than now, nor with a fuller purpose to sustain you, so far as in my most anxious judgment I consistently can; but you must act.

Yours very truly,
A. LINCOLN.

TO GENERAL H. W. HALLECK.

EXECUTIVE MANSION, WASHINGTON, April 9, 1862.

MAJOR-GENERAL HALLECK, Saint Louis, Mo.: If the rigor of the confinement of Magoffin (Governor of Kentucky) at Alton is endangering his life, or materially impairing his health, I wish it mitigated as far as it can be consistently with his safe detention.
A. LINCOLN.
Please send above, by order of the President. JOHN HAY.

PROCLAMATION RECOMMENDING THANKSGIVING FOR VICTORIES,

APRIL 10, 1862.

BY THE PRESIDENT OF THE UNITED STATES OF AMERICA:
A Proclamation
It has pleased Almighty God to vouchsafe signal victories to the land and naval forces engaged in suppressing, an internal rebellion, and at the same time to avert from our country the dangers of foreign intervention and invasion.

It is therefore recommended to the people of the United States that at their next weekly assemblages in their accustomed places of public worship which shall occur after notice of this proclamation shall have been received, they especially acknowledge and render thanks to our Heavenly Father for these inestimable blessings, that they then and there implore spiritual consolation in behalf of all who have been brought into affliction by the casualties and calamities of sedition and civil war, and that they reverently invoke the divine guidance for our national counsels, to the end that they may speedily result in the restoration of peace, harmony, and unity throughout our borders and hasten the establishment of fraternal relations among all the countries of the earth.

In witness whereof I have hereunto set my hand and caused the seal of the United States to be affixed.

Done at the city of Washington, this tenth day of April, A.D. 1862, and of the independence of the United States the eighty-sixth.

A. LINCOLN.

By the President: WILLIAM H. SEWARD, Secretary of State.

ABOLISHING SLAVERY IN WASHINGTON, D.C.

MESSAGE TO CONGRESS. April 16, 1862.

FELLOW-CITIZENS OF THE SENATE AND HOUSE OF REPRESENTATIVES: The act entitled "An act for the relief of certain persons held to service or labor in the District of Columbia" has this day been approved and signed. I have never doubted the constitutional authority of Congress to abolish slavery in this District, and I have ever desired to see the national capital freed from the institution in some satisfactory way. Hence there has never been in my mind any question on the subject except the one of expediency, arising in view of all the circumstances. If there be matters within and about this act which might have taken a course or shape more satisfactory to my judgment, I do not attempt to specify them. I am gratified that the two principles of compensation and colonization are both recognized and practically applied in the act.

In the matter of compensation, it is provided that claims may be presented within ninety days from the passage of the act, "but not thereafter"; and there is no saving for minors, femmes covert, insane or absent persons. I presume this is an omission by mere oversight, and I recommend that it be supplied by an amendatory or supplemental act.

A. LINCOLN.

TELEGRAM TO GENERAL G. B. McCLELLAN.

WASHINGTON, April 21, 1862.

MAJOR-GENERAL McCLELLAN:

Your despatch of the 19th was received that day. Fredericksburg is evacuated and the bridges destroyed by the enemy, and a small part of McDowell's command occupies this side of the Rappahannock, opposite the town. He purposes moving his whole force to that point.

A. LINCOLN.

TO POSTMASTER-GENERAL

A. LINCOLN. EXECUTIVE MANSION, WASHINGTON, April 24, 1862.

Hon. POSTMASTER-GENERAL.

MY DEAR SIR:—The member of Congress from the district including Tiffin, O., calls on me about the postmaster at that place. I believe I turned over a despatch to you from some persons there, asking a suspension, so as for them to be heard, or something of the sort. If nothing, or nothing amounting to anything, has been done, I think the suspension might now be suspended, and the commission go forward.

Yours truly,

A. LINCOLN.

TELEGRAM TO GENERAL G. B. McCLELLAN.

WASHINGTON, April 29, 1862.

MAJOR-GENERAL McCLELLAN:
Would it derange or embarrass your operations if I were to appoint Captain Charles Griffin a brigadier-general of volunteers? Please answer.
A. LINCOLN.

MESSAGE TO THE SENATE, MAY 1, 1862.

TO THE SENATE OF THE UNITED STATES:

In answer to the resolution of the Senate [of April 22] in relation to Brigadier-General Stone, I have the honor to state that he was arrested and imprisoned under my general authority, and upon evidence which whether he be guilty or innocent, required, as appears to me, such proceedings to be had against him for the public safety. I deem it incompatible with the public interest, as also, perhaps, unjust to General Stone, to make a more particular statement of the evidence.
He has not been tried because, in the state of military operations at the time of his arrest and since, the officers to constitute a court martial and for witnesses could not be withdrawn from duty without serious injury to the service. He will be allowed a trial without any unnecessary delay; the charges and specifications will be furnished him in due season, and every facility for his defense will be afforded him by the War Department.
A. LINCOLN, WASHINGTON, MAY 1, 1862

TELEGRAM TO GENERAL McCLELLAN

EXECUTIVE MANSION, WASHINGTON, MAY 1, 1862

MAJOR-GENERAL McCLELLAN:
Your call for Parrott guns from Washington alarms me, chiefly because it argues indefinite procrastination. Is anything to be done?
A. LINCOLN.

TELEGRAM TO GENERAL H. W. HALLECK.

WAR DEPARTMENT, MAY 1, 1862

MAJOR-GENERAL HALLECK, Pittsburgh Landing, Tennessee:
I am pressed by the Missouri members of Congress to give General Schofield independent command in Missouri. They insist that for want of this their local troubles gradually grow worse. I have forborne, so far, for fear of interfering with and embarrassing your operations. Please answer telling me whether anything, and what, I can do for them without injuriously interfering with you.
A. LINCOLN.

RESPONSE TO EVANGELICAL LUTHERANS, MAY 6, 1862

GENTLEMEN:—I welcome here the representatives of the Evangelical Lutherans of the United States. I accept with gratitude their assurances of the sympathy and support of that enlightened, influential, and loyal class of my fellow citizens in an important crisis which involves, in my judgment, not only the civil and religious liberties of our own dear land, but in a large degree the civil and religious liberties of mankind in many countries and through many ages. You well know, gentlemen, and the world knows, how reluctantly I accepted this issue of battle forced upon me on my advent to this place by the internal enemies of our country. You all know, the world knows, the forces and the resources the public agents have brought into employment to sustain a government against which there has been brought not one complaint of real injury committed against society at home or abroad. You all may recollect that in taking up the sword thus forced into our hands this government appealed to the prayers of the pious and the good, and declared that it placed its whole dependence on the favor of God. I now humbly and reverently, in your presence, reiterate the acknowledgment of that dependence, not doubting that, if it shall please the Divine Being who determines the destinies of nations, this shall remain a united people, and that they will, humbly seeking the divine guidance, make their prolonged national existence a source of new benefits to themselves and their successors, and to all classes and conditions of mankind.

TELEGRAM TO FLAG-OFFICER L. M. GOLDSBOROUGH.

FORT MONROE, VIRGINIA, MAY 7, 1862

FLAG-OFFICER GOLDSBOROUGH.
SIR:—Major-General McClellan telegraphs that he has ascertained by a reconnaissance that the battery at Jamestown has been abandoned, and he again requests that gunboats may be sent up the James River.
If you have tolerable confidence that you can successfully contend with the Merrimac without the help of the Galena and two accompanying gunboats, send the Galena and two gunboats up the James River at once. Please report your action on this to me at once. I shall be found either at General Wool's headquarters or on board the Miami.
Your obedient servant,
A. LINCOLN.

FURTHER REPRIMAND OF McCLELLAN

TO GENERAL G. B. McCLELLAN.

FORT MONROE, VIRGINIA, May 9, 1862
MAJOR-GENERAL McCLELLAN:
MY DEAR SIR:—I have just assisted the Secretary of War in framing part of a despatch to you relating to army corps, which despatch, of course, will have reached you long before this will. I wish to say a few words to you privately on this subject. I ordered the army corps organization not only on the unanimous opinion of the twelve generals whom you had selected and assigned as generals of divisions, but also on the unanimous opinion of every military man I could get an opinion from, and every modern military book, yourself only excepted. Of course, I did not on my own judgment pretend to understand the subject. I now think it indispensable for you to know how your struggle against it is received in quarters which we cannot entirely disregard. It is looked upon as merely an effort to pamper one or two pets, and to persecute and degrade their supposed rivals. I have had no word from Sumner, Heintzleman, or Keyes the commanders of these corps are, of course, the three highest officers with you; but I am constantly told that you have no consultation or communication with them; that you consult and communicate with nobody but General Fitz John Porter, and perhaps General Franklin. I do not say these complaints are true or just; but at all events, it is proper you should know of their existence. Do the commanders of corps disobey your orders in anything?

When you relieved General Hamilton of his command the other day, you thereby lost the confidence of at least one of your best friends in the Senate. And here let me say, not as applicable to you personally, that Senators and Representatives speak of me in their places without question, and that officers of the army must cease addressing insulting letters to them for taking no greater liberty with them.

But to return. Are you strong enough—are you strong enough even with my help—to set your foot upon the necks of Sumner, Heintzelman, and Keyes all at once? This is a practical and very serious question to you?

The success of your army and the cause of the country are the same, and, of course, I only desire the good of the cause.

Yours truly,

A. LINCOLN.

TO FLAG-OFFICER L. M. GOLDSBOROUGH,

FORT MONROE, VIRGINIA, May 10, 1862

FLAG-OFFICER GOLDSBOROUGH.

MY DEAR SIR:—I send you this copy of your report of yesterday for the purpose of saying to you in writing that you are quite right in supposing the movement made by you and therein reported was made in accordance with my wishes verbally expressed to you in advance. I avail myself of the occasion to thank you for your courtesy and all your conduct, so far as known to me, during my brief visit here.

Yours very truly,

A. LINCOLN.

PROCLAMATION RAISING THE BLOCKADE OF CERTAIN PORTS.

May 12, 1862.

BY THE PRESIDENT OF THE UNITED STATES OF AMERICA:

A Proclamation.

Whereas, by my proclamation of the 19th of April, one thousand eight hundred and sixty-one, it was declared that the ports of certain States, including those of Beaufort, in the State of North Carolina, Port Royal, in the State of South Carolina, and New Orleans, in the State of Louisiana, were, for reasons therein set forth, intended to be placed under blockade; and whereas the said ports of Beaufort, Port Royal, and New Orleans have since been blockaded; but as the blockade of the same ports may now be safely relaxed with advantage to the interests of commerce:

Now, therefore, be it known that I, Abraham Lincoln, President of the United States, pursuant to the authority in me vested by the fifth section of the act of Congress approved on the 13th of July last, entitled "An act further to provide for the collection of duties on imports, and for other purposes," do hereby declare that the blockade of the said ports of Beaufort, Port Royal, and New Orleans shall so far cease and determine, from and after the first day of June next, that commercial intercourse with those ports, except as to persons, things, and information contraband of war, may from that time be carried on, subject to the laws of the United States, and to the limitations and in pursuance of the regulations which are prescribed by the Secretary of the Treasury in his order of this date, which is appended to this proclamation.

In witness whereof, I have hereunto set my hand and caused the seal of the United States to be affixed.

Done at the city of Washington, this twelfth day of May, in the year of our Lord one thousand eight hundred and sixty-two, and of the independence of the United States the eighty-sixth.

A. LINCOLN.

By the President: WILLIAM H. SEWARD, Secretary of State.

THE WRITINGS OF A. LINCOLN,
Volume Six, 1862-1863

1862

RECOMMENDATION OF NAVAL OFFICERS

MESSAGE TO CONGRESS.

WASHINGTON, D.C., May 14, 1862.
TO SENATE AND HOUSE OF REPRESENTATIVES:
The third section of the "Act further to promote the efficiency of the Navy," approved 21st of December, 1861, provides:
"That the President of the United States by and with the advice and consent of the Senate, shall have the authority to detail from the retired list of the navy for the command of squadrons and single ships such officers as he may believe that the good of the service requires to be thus placed in command; and such officers may, if upon the recommendation of the President of the United States they shall receive a vote of thanks of Congress for their services and gallantry in action against an enemy, be restored to the active list, and not otherwise."
In conformity with this law, Captain David G. Farragut was nominated to the Senate for continuance as the flag-officer in command of the squadron which recently rendered such important service to the Union by his successful operations on the lower Mississippi and capture of New Orleans.
Believing that no occasion could arise which would more fully correspond with the intention of the law or be more pregnant with happy influence as an example, I cordially recommend that Captain D. G. Farragut receive a vote of thanks of Congress for his services and gallantry displayed in the capture since 21st December, 1861, of Forts Jackson and St. Philip, city of New Orleans, and the destruction of various rebel gunboats, rams, etc.....

TO THE SENATE AND HOUSE OF REPRESENTATIVES:

I submit herewith a list of naval officers who commanded vessels engaged in the recent brilliant operations of the squadron commanded by Flag-officer Farragut which led to the capture of Forts Jackson and St. Philip, city of New Orleans, and the destruction of rebel gunboats, rams, etc., in April 1862. For their services and gallantry on those occasions I cordially recommend that they should, by name, receive a vote of thanks of Congress:
LIST:
    Captain Theodorus Bailey.
    Captain Henry W. Morris.
    Captain Thomas T. Craven.
    Commander Henry H. Bell.
    Commander Samuel Phillips Lee.
    Commander Samuel Swartwout.
    Commander Melancton Smith.
    Commander Charles Stewart Boggs
    Commander John De Camp
    Commander James Alden.
    Commander David D. Porter.
    Commander Richard Wainwright.
    Commander William B. Renshaw.
    Lieutenant Commanding Abram D. Harrell.

Lieutenant Commanding Edward Donaldson.
Lieutenant Commanding George H. Preble.
Lieutenant Commanding Edward T. Nichols.
Lieutenant Commanding Jonathan M. Wainwright.
Lieutenant Commanding John Guest.
Lieutenant Commanding Charles H. B. Caldwell.
Lieutenant Commanding Napoleon B. Harrison.
Lieutenant Commanding Albert N. Smith.
Lieutenant Commanding Pierce Crosby.
Lieutenant Commanding George M. Ransom.
Lieutenant Commanding Watson Smith.
Lieutenant Commanding John H. Russell.
Lieutenant Commanding Walter W. Queen.
Lieutenant Commanding K. Randolph Breese.
Acting Lieutenant Commanding Sellin E. Woolworth.
Acting Lieutenant Commanding Charles H. Baldwin.
A. LINCOLN.
WASHINGTON, D.C., May 14, 1862

TELEGRAM TO GENERAL G. B. McCLELLAN.

WASHINGTON CITY, May 15, 1862.

MAJOR-GENERAL McCLELLAN, Cumberland, Virginia:
Your long despatch of yesterday is just received. I will answer more fully soon. Will say now that all your despatches to the Secretary of War have been promptly shown to me. Have done and shall do all I could and can to sustain you. Hoped that the opening of James River and putting Wool and Burnside in communication, with an open road to Richmond, or to you, had effected something in that direction. I am still unwilling to take all our force off the direct line between Richmond and here.
A. LINCOLN.

SPEECH TO THE 12TH INDIANA REGIMENT, MAY [15?] 1862

SOLDIERS, OF THE TWELFTH INDIANA REGIMENT:

It has not been customary heretofore, nor will it be hereafter, for me to say something to every regiment passing in review. It occurs too frequently for me to have speeches ready on all occasions. As you have paid such a mark of respect to the chief magistrate, it appears that I should say a word or two in reply. Your colonel has thought fit, on his own account and in your name, to say that you are satisfied with the manner in which I have performed my part in the difficulties which have surrounded the nation. For your kind expressions I am extremely grateful, but on the other hand I assure you that the nation is more indebted to you, and such as you, than to me. It is upon the brave hearts and strong arms of the people of the country that our reliance has been placed in support of free government and free institutions. For the part which you and the brave army of which you are a part have, under Providence, performed in this great struggle, I tender more thanks especially to this regiment, which has been the subject of good report. The thanks of the nation will follow you, and may God's blessing rest upon you now and forever. I hope that upon your return to your homes you will find your friends and loved ones well and happy. I bid you farewell.

TELEGRAM TO GENERAL I. McDOWELL.

WASHINGTON, May 16, 1862.

MAJOR-GENERAL McDOWELL:
What is the strength of your force now actually with you?
A. LINCOLN.

MEMORANDUM OF PROPOSED ADDITIONS TO INSTRUCTIONS OF ABOVE DATE

TO GENERAL McDOWELL, AND GENERAL MEIGS'S INDORSEMENT THEREON.

May 17, 1862. You will retain the separate command of the forces taken with you; but while co-operating with General McClellan you will obey his orders, except that you are to judge, and are not to allow your force to be disposed otherwise than so as to give the greatest protection to this capital which may be possible from that distance.
[Indorsement.]
TO THE SECRETARY OF WAR:
The President having shown this to me, I suggested that it is dangerous to direct a subordinate not to obey the orders of his superior in any case, and that to give instructions to General McClellan to this same end and furnish General McDowell with a copy thereof would effect the object desired by the President. He desired me to say that the sketch of instructions to General McClellan herewith he thought made this addition unnecessary.
Respectfully, M. C. M.

MILITARY EMANCIPATION

INDORSEMENT RELATING TO GENERAL DAVID HUNTER'S ORDER OF MILITARY EMANCIPATION,
MAY 17, 1862
No commanding general shall do such a thing upon my responsibility without consulting me.
A. LINCOLN.

FROM SECRETARY STANTON TO GENERAL McCLELLAN.

WASHINGTON, May 18, 1862.

GENERAL: Your despatch to the President, asking reinforcements, has been received and carefully considered.
The President is not willing to uncover the capital entirely; and it is believed that, even if this were prudent, it would require more time to effect a junction between your army and that of the Rappahannock by the way of the Potomac and York rivers than by a land march. In order, therefore, to increase the strength of the attack upon Richmond at the earliest moment, General McDowell has been ordered to march upon that city by the shortest route. He is ordered, keeping himself always in position to save the capital from all possible attack, so to operate as to put his left wing in communication with your right wing, and you are instructed to co-operate so as to establish this communication as soon as possible by extending your right-wing to the north of Richmond.
It is believed that this communication can be safely established either north or south of the Pamunkey River.
In any event, you will be able to prevent the main body of the enemy's forces from leaving Richmond and falling in overwhelming force upon General McDowell. He will move with between thirty-five and forty thousand men.
A copy of the instructions to General McDowell are with this. The specific task assigned to his command has been to provide against any danger to the capital of the nation.
At your earnest call for reinforcements, he is sent forward to co-operate in the reduction of Richmond, but charged, in attempting this, not to uncover the city of Washington; and you will give no order, either before or after your junction, which can put him out of position to cover this city. You and he will communicate with each other by telegraph or

otherwise as frequently as may be necessary for efficient cooperation. When General McDowell is in position on your right, his supplies must be drawn from West Point, and you will instruct your staff-officers to be prepared to supply him by that route.

The President desires that General McDowell retain the command of the Department of the Rappahannock and of the forces with which he moves forward.

By order of the President: EDWIN M. STANTON, Secretary of War.

MAJOR-GENERAL GEORGE B. McCLELLAN, Commanding Army of the Potomac, before Richmond.

PROCLAMATION REVOKING GENERAL HUNTER'S ORDER OF MILITARY EMANCIPATION,

MAY 19, 1862.

BY THE PRESIDENT OF THE UNITED STATES OF AMERICA:
A Proclamation
Whereas there appears in the public prints what purports to be a proclamation of Major general Hunter, in the words and figures following, to wit:
(General Orders No. 11) HEADQUARTERS DEPARTMENT OF THE SOUTH, HILTON HEAD, PORT ROYAL, S. C., May 9, 1862.
"The three States of Georgia, Florida, and South Carolina, comprising the military department of the South, having deliberately declared themselves no longer under the protection of the United States of America, and having taken up arms against the said United States, it became a military necessity to declare martial law. This was accordingly done on the 25th day of April, 1862. Slavery and martial law in a free country are altogether incompatible. The persons in these three States: Georgia Florida, and South Carolina—heretofore held as slaves are therefore declared forever free.
"By command of Major-General D. Hunter: "(Official.)ED. W. SMITH, "Acting Assistant Adjutant-General."
And whereas the same is producing some excitement and misunderstanding: therefore,
I, Abraham Lincoln, President of the United States, proclaim and declare that the Government of the United States, had no knowledge, information, or belief of an intention on the part of General Hunter to issue such a proclamation; nor has it yet any authentic information that the document is genuine. And further, that neither General Hunter nor any other commander or person has been authorized by the Government of the United States to make a proclamation declaring the slaves of any State free; and that the supposed proclamation now in question, whether genuine or false, is altogether void so far as respects such a declaration.
I further make known that whether it be competent for me, as commander-in-chief of the army and navy, to declare the slaves of any State or States free, and whether, at any time, in any case, it shall have become a necessity indispensable to the maintenance of the government to exercise such supposed power, are questions which under my responsibility I reserve to myself, and which I cannot feel justified in leaving to the decision of commanders in the field.
These are totally different questions from those of police regulations in armies and camps.
On the sixth day of March last, by special message, I recommended to Congress the adoption of a joint resolution, to be substantially as follows:
Resolved, That the United States ought to co-operate with any State which may adopt gradual abolishment of slavery, giving to such State pecuniary aid, to be used by such State, in its discretion, to compensate for the inconvenience, public and private, produced by such change of system.
The resolution in the language above quoted was adopted by large majorities in both branches of Congress, and now stands an authentic, definite, and solemn proposal of the nation to the States and people most immediately interested in the subject-matter. To the people of those States I now earnestly appeal. I do not argue—I beseech you to make arguments for yourselves. You cannot, if you would, be blind to the signs of the times. I beg of you a calm and enlarged consideration of them, ranging, if it may be, far above personal and partisan politics. This proposal makes common cause for a common object, casting no reproaches upon any. It acts not the Pharisee. The change it contemplates would come gently as the dews of heaven, not rending or wrecking anything. Will you not embrace it? So much good has not been done, by one effort, in all past time, as in the providence of God it is now your high privilege to do. May the vast future not have to lament that you have neglected it.
In witness whereof, I have hereunto set my hand and caused the seal of the United States to be affixed.
Done at the city of Washington, this nineteenth day of May, in the year of our Lord one thousand eight hundred and sixty-two, and of the independence of the United States the eighty-sixth.
A. LINCOLN.
By the President: WILLIAM H. SEWARD, Secretary of State.

TELEGRAM TO GENERAL G. E. McCLELLAN.

WASHINGTON, May 21, 1862.

MAJOR-GENERAL McCLELLAN:
I have just been waited on by a large committee who present a petition signed by twenty-three senators and eighty-four representatives asking me to restore General Hamilton to his division. I wish to do this, and yet I do not wish to be understood as rebuking you. Please answer at once.
A. LINCOLN.

TELEGRAM TO GENERAL G. B. McCLELLAN.

WASHINGTON CITY, May 22, 1862.

MAJOR-GENERAL McCLELLAN:
Your long despatch of yesterday just received. You will have just such control of General McDowell and his forces as you therein indicate. McDowell can reach you by land sooner than he could get aboard of boats, if the boats were ready at Fredericksburg, unless his march shall be resisted, in which case the force resisting him will certainly not be confronting you at Richmond. By land he can reach you in five days after starting, whereas by water he would not reach you in two weeks, judging by past experience. Franklin's single division did not reach you in ten days after I ordered it.
A. LINCOLN,
President United States.

TELEGRAM TO GENERAL McCLELLAN.

WASHINGTON, May 24, 1862. 4 PM.

MAJOR-GENERAL G. B. McCLELLAN:
In consequence of General Banks's critical position, I have been compelled to suspend General McDowell's movements to join you. The enemy are making a desperate push upon Harper's Ferry, and we are trying to throw General Fremont's force and part of General McDowell's in their rear.
A. LINCOLN, President.

TELEGRAM TO GENERAL McCLELLAN

WASHINGTON May 24, 1862.

MAJOR-GENERAL GEORGE B. McCLELLAN:
I left General McDowell's camp at dark last evening. Shields's command is there, but it is so worn that he cannot move before Monday morning, the 26th. We have so thinned our line to get troops for other places that it was broken yesterday at Front Royal, with a probable loss to us of one regiment infantry, two Companies cavalry, putting General Banks in some peril.
The enemy's forces under General Anderson now opposing General McDowell's advance have as their line of supply and retreat the road to Richmond.

If, in conjunction with McDowell's movement against Anderson, you could send a force from your right to cut off the enemy's supplies from Richmond, preserve the railroad bridges across the two forks of the Pamunkey, and intercept the enemy's retreat, you will prevent the army now opposed to you from receiving an accession of numbers of nearly 15,000 men; and if you succeed in saving the bridges you will secure a line of railroad for supplies in addition to the one you now have. Can you not do this almost as well as not while you are building the Chickahominy bridges? McDowell and Shields both say they can, and positively will, move Monday morning. I wish you to move cautiously and safely.

You will have command of McDowell, after he joins you, precisely as you indicated in your long despatch to us of the 21st.

A. LINCOLN.

TELEGRAM TO GENERAL RUFUS SAXTON.

WAR DEPARTMENT, May, 24 1862. 2 P.M.

GENERAL SAXTON:

Geary reports Jackson with 20,000 moving from Ashby's Gap by the Little River turnpike, through Aldie, toward Centreville. This he says is reliable. He is also informed of large forces south of him. We know a force of some 15,000 broke up Saturday night from in front of Fredericksburg and went we know not where. Please inform us, if possible, what has become of the force which pursued Banks yesterday; also any other information you have.

A. LINCOLN

TELEGRAM TO COLONEL D. S. MILES.

WAR DEPARTMENT, May 24, 1862. 1.30 P.M.

COLONEL MILES, Harper's Ferry, Virginia

Could you not send scouts from Winchester who would tell whether enemy are north of Banks, moving on Winchester? What is the latest you have?

A. LINCOLN.

TELEGRAM TO GENERAL J. C. FREMONT.

WAR DEPARTMENT, May 24, 1862. 4 P.M.

MAJOR-GENERAL FREMONT, Franklin:

You are authorized to purchase the 400 horses, or take them wherever or however you can get them. The exposed condition of General Banks makes his immediate relief a point of paramount importance. You are therefore directed by the President to move against Jackson at Harrisonburg and operate against the enemy in such way as to relieve Banks. This movement must be made immediately. You will acknowledge the receipt of this order, and specify the hour it is received by you.

A. LINCOLN.

TELEGRAM TO GENERAL J. C. FREMONT.

WAR DEPARTMENT, May 24, 1862. 7.15 P.M.

MAJOR-GENERAL FREMONT, Franklin, Virginia:
Many thanks for the promptness with which you have answered that you will execute the order. Much—perhaps all—depends upon the celerity with which you can execute it. Put the utmost speed into it. Do not lose a minute.
A. LINCOLN.

TELEGRAM TO GENERAL H. W. HALLECK.

WAR DEPARTMENT, May 24, 1862.

MAJOR-GENERAL HALLECK, near Corinth, Mississippi:
Several despatches from Assistant Secretary Scott and one from Governor Morton asking reinforcements for you have been received. I beg you to be assured we do the best we can. I mean to cast no blame where I tell you each of our commanders along our line from Richmond to Corinth supposes himself to be confronted by numbers superior to his own. Under this pressure We thinned the line on the upper Potomac, until yesterday it was broken with heavy loss to us, and General Banks put in great peril, out of which he is not yet extricated, and may be actually captured. We need men to repair this breach, and have them not at hand. My dear General, I feel justified to rely very much on you. I believe you and the brave officers and men with you can and will get the victory at Corinth.
A. LINCOLN.

TELEGRAM TO GENERAL I. McDOWELL
WAR DEPARTMENT, May 24, 1862.
MAJOR-GENERAL McDOWELL, Fredricksburg:
General Fremont has been ordered by telegraph to move from Franklin on Harrisonburg to relieve General Banks, and capture or destroy Jackson's and Ewell's forces. You are instructed, laying aside for the present the movement on Richmond, to put 20,000 men in motion at once for the Shenandoah, moving on the line or in advance of the line of the Manassas Gap railroad. Your object will be to capture the forces of Jackson and Ewell, either in co-operation with General Fremont, or, in case want of supplies or of transportation, interferes with his movements, it is believed that the force which you move will be sufficient to accomplish this object alone. The information thus far received here makes it probable that if the enemy operate actively against General Banks, you will not be able to count upon much assistance from him, but may even have to release him. Reports received this moment are that Banks is fighting with Ewell eight miles from Winchester.
A. LINCOLN.

TELEGRAM TO GENERAL McDOWELL.

WAR DEPARTMENT, WASHINGTON CITY, D.C., May 24, 1862

MAJOR-GENERAL I. McDOWELL:
I am highly gratified by your alacrity in obeying my order. The change was as painful to me as it can possibly be to you or to any one. Everything now depends upon the celerity and vigor of your movement.
A. LINCOLN

TELEGRAM TO GENERAL J. W. GEARY.

WAR DEPARTMENT, May 25, 1862 1.45 P.M.

GENERAL GEARY, White Plains:
Please give us your best present impression as to the number of the enemy's forces north of Strasburg and Front Royal. Are the forces still moving north through the gap at Front Royal and between you and there?

A. LINCOLN.

TELEGRAM TO GENERAL G. B. McCLELLAN.

WASHINGTON, May 25, 1862. 2 P.M.

MAJOR-GENERAL McCLELLAN:
The enemy is moving north in sufficient force to drive General Banks before him—precisely in what force we cannot tell. He is also threatening Leesburg and Geary, on the Manassas Gap railroad, from both north and south—in precisely what force we cannot tell. I think the movement is a general and concerted one, such as would not be if he was acting upon the purpose of a very desperate defense of Richmond. I think the time is near when you must either attack Richmond or give up the job and come to the defense of Washington. Let me hear from you instantly.
A. LINCOLN, President.

ORDER TAKING MILITARY POSSESSION OF RAILROADS.

WAR DEPARTMENT, May 25, 1862.

Ordered: By virtue of the authority vested by act of Congress, the President takes military possession of all the railroads in the United States from and after this date until further order, and directs that the respective railroad companies, their officers and servants, shall hold themselves in readiness for the transportation of such troops and munitions of war as may be ordered by the military authorities, to the exclusion of all other business.
By order of the Secretary of War.
M. C. MEIGS

TELEGRAM TO SECRETARY CHASE.

WAR DEPARTMENT, May 25, 1862.

SECRETARY CHASE, Fredericksburg, Virginia:
It now appears that Banks got safely into Winchester last night, and is this morning retreating on Harper's Ferry. This justifies the inference that he is pressed by numbers superior to his own. I think it not improbable that Ewell, Jackson, and Johnson are pouring through the gap they made day before yesterday at Front Royal, making a dash northward. It will be a very valuable and very honorable service for General McDowell to cut them off. I hope he will put all possible energy and speed into the effort.
A. LINCOLN.

TELEGRAM TO GENERAL R. SAXTON.

WAR DEPARTMENT, May 25, 1862.

GENERAL SAXTON, Harper's Ferry:
If Banks reaches Martinsburg, is he any the better for it? Will not the enemy cut him from thence to Harper's Ferry? Have you sent anything to meet him and assist him at Martinsburg? This is an inquiry, not an order.
A. LINCOLN.

TELEGRAM TO GENERAL R. SAXTON.

WAR DEPARTMENT, May 25, 1862. 6.30 P.M.

GENERAL SAXTON, Harper's Ferry:
One good six-gun battery, complete in its men and appointments, is now on its way to you from Baltimore. Eleven other guns, of different sorts, are on their way to you from here. Hope they will all reach you before morning. As you have but 2500 men at Harper's Ferry, where are the rest which were in that vicinity and which we have sent forward? Have any of them been cut off?
A. LINCOLN.

TELEGRAM TO GENERAL R. SAXTON.

WAR DEPARTMENT, May 25, 1862.

GENERAL SAXTON, Harper's Ferry:
I fear you have mistaken me. I did not mean to question the correctness of your conduct; on the contrary! I approve what you have done. As the 2500 reported by you seemed small to me, I feared some had got to Banks and been cut off with him. Please tell me the exact number you now have in hand.
A. LINCOLN.

TELEGRAM TO GENERAL G. B. McCLELLAN.

[Sent in cipher.]

WAR DEPARTMENT, WASHINGTON CITY, D. C., May 25,1862. 8.30 P.M.
MAJOR-GENERAL McCLELLAN:
Your despatch received. General Banks was at Strasburg, with about 6,000 men, Shields having been taken from him to swell a column for McDowell to aid you at Richmond, and the rest of his force scattered at various places. On the 23d a rebel force of 7000 to 10,000 fell upon one regiment and two companies guarding the bridge at Front Royal, destroying it entirely; crossed the Shenandoah, and on the 24th (yesterday) pushed to get north of Banks, on the road to Winchester. Banks ran a race with them, beating them into Winchester yesterday evening. This morning a battle ensued between the two forces, in which Banks was beaten back into full retreat toward Martinsburg, and probably is broken up into a total rout. Geary, on the Manassas Gap railroad, just now reports that Jackson is now near Front Royal, With 10,000, following up and supporting, as I understand, the forces now pursuing Banks, also that another force of 10,000 is near Orleans, following on in the same direction. Stripped here, as we are here, it will be all we can do to prevent them crossing the Potomac at Harper's Ferry or above. We have about 20,000 of McDowell's force moving back to the vicinity of Front Royal, and General Fremont, who was at Franklin, is moving to Harrisonburg; both these movements intended to get in the enemy's rear.
One more of McDowell's brigades is ordered through here to Harper's Ferry; the rest of his force remains for the present at Fredericksburg. We are sending such regiments and dribs from here and Baltimore as we can spare to Harper's Ferry, supplying their places in some sort by calling in militia from the adjacent States. We also have eighteen cannon on the road to Harper's Ferry, of which arm there is not a single one yet at that point. This is now our situation. If McDowell's force was now beyond our reach, we should be utterly helpless. Apprehension of something like this, and no unwillingness to sustain you, has always been my reason for withholding McDowell's force from you. Please understand this, and do the best you can with the force you have.
A. LINCOLN.

HISTORY OF CONSPIRACY OF REBELLION

MESSAGE TO CONGRESS.

MAY 16, 1862 TO THE SENATE AND HOUSE OF REPRESENTATIVES:
The insurrection which is yet existing in the United States and aims at the overthrow of the Federal Constitution and the Union, was clandestinely prepared during the Winter of 1860 and 1861, and assumed an open organization in the form of a treasonable provisional government at Montgomery, in Alabama on the 18th day of February, 1861. On the 12th day of April, 1861, the insurgents committed the flagrant act of civil war by the bombardment and the capture of Fort Sumter, Which cut off the hope of immediate conciliation. Immediately afterward all the roads and avenues to this city were obstructed, and the capital was put into the condition of a siege. The mails in every direction were stopped and the lines of telegraph cut off by the insurgents, and military and naval forces which had been called out by the government for the defense of Washington were prevented from reaching the city by organized and combined treasonable resistance in the State of Maryland. There was no adequate and effective organization for the public defense. Congress had indefinitely adjourned. There was no time to convene them. It became necessary for me to choose whether, using only the existing means, agencies, and processes which Congress had provided, I should let the government fall at once into ruin or whether, availing myself of the broader powers conferred by the Constitution in cases of insurrection, I would make an effort to save it, with all its blessings, for the present age and for posterity.

I thereupon summoned my constitutional advisers, the heads of all the departments, to meet on Sunday, the 20th day of April, 1861, at the office of the Navy Department, and then and there, with their unanimous concurrence, I directed that an armed revenue cutter should proceed to sea to afford protection to the commercial marine, and especially the California treasure ships then on their way to this coast. I also directed the commandant of the navy-yard at Boston to purchase or charter and arm as quickly as possible five steamships for purposes of public defense. I directed the commandant of the navy-yard at Philadelphia to purchase or charter and arm an equal number for the same purpose. I directed the commandant at New York to purchase or charter and arm an equal number. I directed Commander Gillis to purchase or charter and arm and put to sea two other vessels. Similar directions were given to Commodore Dupont, with a view to the opening of passages by water to and from the capital. I directed the several officers to take the advice and obtain the aid and efficient services, in the matter, of his Excellency Edwin D. Morgan, the Governor of New York, or in his absence George D. Morgan, William M. Evarts, R. M. Blatchford, and Moses H. Grinnell, who were by my directions especially empowered by the Secretary of the Navy to act for his department in that crisis in matters pertaining to the forwarding of troops and supplies for the public defense.

The several departments of the government at that time contained so large a number of disloyal persons that it would have been impossible to provide safely through official agents only for the performance of the duties thus confided to citizens favorably known for their ability, loyalty, and patriotism.

The several orders issued upon these occurrences were transmitted by private messengers, who pursued a circuitous way to the seaboard cities, inland across the States of Pennsylvania and Ohio and the northern lakes. I believe by these and other similar measures taken in that crisis, some of which were without any authority of law, the government was saved from overthrow. I am not aware that a dollar of the public funds thus confided without authority of law to unofficial persons was either lost or wasted, although apprehensions of such misdirection occurred to me as objections to those extraordinary proceedings, and were necessarily overruled.

I recall these transactions now because my attention has been directed to a resolution which was passed by the House of Representatives on the 30th day of last month, which is in these words:

"Resolved, That Simon Cameron, late Secretary of War by investing Alexander Cummings with the control of large sums of the public money and authority to purchase military supplies without restriction, without requiring from him any guaranty for the faithful performance of his duties, when the services of competent public officers were available, and by involving the government in a vast number of contracts with persons not legitimately engaged in the business pertaining to the subject-matter of such contracts, especially in the purchase of arms for future delivery, has adopted a policy highly injurious to the public service, and deserves the censure of the House."

Congress will see that I should be wanting equally in candor and in justice if I should leave the censure expressed in this resolution to rest exclusively or chiefly upon Mr. Cameron. The same sentiment is unanimously entertained by the heads of department who participated in the proceedings which the House of Representatives have censured. It is due to Mr. Cameron to say that although he fully approved the proceedings they were not moved nor suggested by himself, and that not only the President, but all the other heads of departments, were at least equally responsible with him for whatever error, wrong, or fault was committed in the premises.
A. LINCOLN.

TELEGRAM TO GENERAL G. B. McCLELLAN.

WASHINGTON, May 26, 1862. 12.40

MAJOR-GENERAL McCLELLAN:
We have General Banks's official report. He has saved his army and baggage, and has made a safe retreat to the river, and is probably safe at Williamsport. He reports the attacking force at 15,000.
A. LINCOLN, President.

TELEGRAM TO GENERAL I. McDOWELL.

WAR DEPARTMENT, May 26, 1862. 1 P.M.

MAJOR-GENERAL McDOWELL, Falmouth, Virginia:
Despatches from Geary just received have been sent you. Should not the remainder of your forces, except sufficient to hold the point at Fredericksburg, move this way—to Manassas Junction or Alexandria? As commander of this department, should you not be here? I ask these questions.
A. LINCOLN.

TELEGRAM TO GENERAL McCLELLAN.

WASHINGTON, May 26, 1862.

MAJOR-GENERAL GEORGE B. McCLELLAN:
Can you not cut the Alula Creek railroad? Also, what impression have you as to intrenched works for you to contend with in front of Richmond? Can you get near enough to throw shells into the city?
A. LINCOLN, President.

TELEGRAM TO GENERAL J. C. FREMONT.

May 27. 1862. 9.58 P.M.

MAJOR-GENERAL FREMONT:
I see that you are at Moorefield. You were expressly ordered to march to Harrisonburg. What does this mean?
A. LINCOLN.

TELEGRAM FROM SECRETARY STANTON TO GOVERNOR ANDREW.

WASHINGTON, May 27, 1862.

GOVERNOR ANDREW, Boston:

The President directs that the militia be relieved, and the enlistments made for three years, or during the war. This, I think, will practically not be longer than for a year. The latest intelligence from General Banks states that he has saved nearly his whole command with small loss.
Concentrations of our force have been made, which it is hoped will capture the enemy.
EDWIN M. STANTON, Secretary of War.

TELEGRAM FROM SECRETARY STANTON TO GENERAL J. C. FREMONT,

WASHINGTON, May 28, 1862

MAJOR-GENERAL FREMONT, Moorefield
The President directs you to halt at Moorefield and await orders, unless you hear of the enemy being in the general direction of Rodney, in which case you will move upon him. Acknowledge the receipt of this order, and the hour it is received.
EDWIN M. STANTON, Secretary of War.

TELEGRAM TO GENERAL I. McDOWELL.

WASHINGTON, May 28, 1862.

GENERAL McDOWELL, Manassas Junction:
General McClellan at 6.30 P.M. yesterday telegraphed that Fitz-John Porter's division had fought and driven 13,000 of the enemy, under General Branch, from Hanover Court-House, and was driving them from a stand they had made on the railroad at the time the messenger left. Two hours later he telegraphed that Stoneman had captured an engine and six cars on the Virginia Central, which he at once sent to communicate with Porter. Nothing further from McClellan. If Porter effects a lodgment on both railroads near Hanover Court-House, consider whether your forces in front of Fredericksburg should not push through and join him.
A. LINCOLN.

TELEGRAM TO GENERAL G. B. McCLELLAN.

WASHINGTON, May 28, 1862.

MAJOR-GENERAL McCLELLAN:
What of F.J. Porter's expedition? Please answer.
A. LINCOLN.

TELEGRAM TO GENERAL I. McDOWELL.

WASHINGTON. May 28, 1862. 4 P.M.

GENERAL McDOWELL, Manassas Junction:
You say General Geary's scouts report that they find no enemy this side of the Blue Ridge. Neither do I. Have they been to the Blue Ridge looking for them.
A. LINCOLN.

TELEGRAM TO GENERAL I. McDOWELL.

WASHINGTON, May 28, 1862. 5.40 P.M.

GENERAL McDOWELL, Manassas Junction:
I think the evidence now preponderates that Ewell and Jackson are still about Winchester. Assuming this, it is for you a question of legs. Put in all the speed you can. I have told Fremont as much, and directed him to drive at them as fast as possible. By the way, I suppose you know Fremont has got up to Moorefield, instead of going into Harrisonburg.
A. LINCOLN.

TELEGRAM TO GENERAL G. B. McCLELLAN

WASHINGTON May 28, 1862. 8.40 P.M.

MAJOR-GENERAL McCLELLAN:
I am very glad of General F. J. Porter's victory. Still, if it was a total rout of the enemy, I am puzzled to know why the Richmond and Fredericksburg railroad was not seized again, as you say you have all the railroads but the Richmond and Fredericksburg. I am puzzled to see how, lacking that, you can have any, except the scrap from Richmond to West Point. The scrap of the Virginia Central from Richmond to Hanover Junction, without more, is simply nothing. That the whole of the enemy is concentrating on Richmond, I think cannot be certainly known to you or me. Saxton, at Harper's Ferry informs us that large forces, supposed to be Jackson's and Ewells, forced his advance from Charlestown today. General King telegraphs us from Fredericksburg that contrabands give certain information that 15,000 left Hanover Junction Monday morning to reinforce Jackson. I am painfully impressed with the importance of the struggle before you, and shall aid you all I can consistently with my view of due regard to all points.
A. LINCOLN.

TELEGRAM FROM SECRETARY STANTON TO GENERAL FREMONT.

WASHINGTON, May 28, 1862.

MAJOR-GENERAL JOHN C. FREMONT, Moorefield:
The order to remain at Moorefield was based on the supposition that it would find you there.
Upon subsequent information that the enemy were still operating in the vicinity of Winchester and Martinsburg, you were directed to move against the enemy.
The President now again directs you to move against the enemy without delay. Please acknowledge the receipt of this, and the time received.
EDWIN M. STANTON, Secretary of War.

TELEGRAM TO GENERAL MARCY.

WASHINGTON, May 29, 1862. 10 A.M.

GENERAL R. B. MARCY, McClellan's Headquarters:
Yours just received. I think it cannot be certainly known whether the force which fought General Porter is the same which recently confronted McDowell. Another item of evidence bearing on it is that General Branch commanded

against Porter, while it was General Anderson who was in front of McDowell. He and McDowell were in correspondence about prisoners.
A. LINCOLN.

TELEGRAM TO GENERAL G. B. McCLELLAN.

WAR DEPARTMENT, WASHINGTON CITY, D. C., May 29, 1862. 10.30 A.M.

MAJOR-GENERAL McCLELLAN:
I think we shall be able within three days to tell you certainly whether any considerable force of the enemy—Jackson or any one else—is moving on to Harper's Ferry or vicinity. Take this expected development into your calculations.
A. LINCOLN.

TELEGRAM TO GENERAL N. P. BANKS.

WASHINGTON, May 29, 1862.

MAJOR-GENERAL BANKS, Williamsport, Maryland:
General McDowell's advance should, and probably will, be at or near Front Royal at twelve (noon) tomorrow. General Fremont will be at or near Strasburg as soon. Please watch the enemy closely, and follow and harass and detain him if he attempts to retire. I mean this for General Saxton's force as well as that immediately with you.
A. LINCOLN.

TELEGRAM TO GENERAL FREMONT

WASHINGTON, May 29, 1862. 12 M.

MAJOR-GENERAL FREMONT, Moorefield, Virginia:
General McDowell's advance, if not checked by the enemy, should, and probably will, be at Front Royal by twelve (noon) to-morrow. His force, when up, will be about 20,000. Please have your force at Strasburg, or, if the route you are moving on does not lead to that point, as near Strasburg as the enemy may be by the same time. Your despatch No.30 received and satisfactory.
A. LINCOLN.

TELEGRAM TO GENERAL I. McDOWELL.

WASHINGTON, May 29, 1862.

MAJOR-GENERAL McDOWELL, Manassas Junction:
General Fremont's force should, and probably will, be at or near Strasburg by twelve (noon) tomorrow. Try to have your force, or the advance of it, at Front Royal as soon.
A. LINCOLN.

TELEGRAM TO GENERAL MARCY.

WASHINGTON, May 29, 1862. 1.20 P.M.

GENERAL R. B. MARCY:
Your despatch as to the South Anna and Ashland being seized by our forces this morning is received. Understanding these points to be on the Richmond and Fredericksburg railroad, I heartily congratulate the country, and thank General McClellan and his army for their seizure.
A. LINCOLN.

TELEGRAM TO GENERAL I. McDOWELL.

WASHINGTON, May 30, 1862. 10 A.M.

MAJOR-GENERAL McDOWELL, Manassas Junction:
I somewhat apprehend that Fremont's force, in its present condition, may not be quite strong enough in case it comes in collision with the enemy. For this additional reason I wish you to push forward your column as rapidly as possible. Tell me what number your force reaching Front Royal will amount to.
A. LINCOLN.

TELEGRAM TO GENERAL N. P. BANKS.

WASHINGTON, May 30, 1862. 10.15 A.M.

MAJOR-GENERAL BANKS,
Williamsport, Maryland, via Harper's Ferry:
If the enemy in force is in or about Martinsburg, Charlestown, and Winchester, Or any or all of them, he may come in collision with Fremont, in which case I am anxious that your force, with you and at Harper's Ferry, should so operate as to assist Fremont if possible; the same if the enemy should engage McDowell. This was the meaning of my despatch yesterday.
A. LINCOLN.

TELEGRAM TO GENERAL I. McDOWELL.

WASHINGTON, May 30, 1862. 12.40.

MAJOR-GENERAL McDOWELL, Rectortown:
Your despatch of to-day received and is satisfactory. Fremont has nominally 22,000, really about 17,000. Blenker's division is part of it. I have a despatch from Fremont this morning, not telling me where he is; but he says: "Scouts and men from Winchester represent Jackson's force variously at 30,000 to 60,000. With him Generals Ewell and Longstreet."
The high figures erroneous, of course. Do you know where Longstreet is? Corinth is evacuated and occupied by us.
A. LINCOLN.

TELEGRAM TO GENERAL FREMONT.

WASHINGTON, May 30, 1862. 2.30 P.M.

MAJOR-GENERAL FREMONT, Moorefield, Virginia:
Yours, saying you will reach Strasburg or vicinity at 5 P.M. Saturday, has been received and sent to General McDowell, and he directed to act in view of it. You must be up to the time you promised, if possible.
Corinth was evacuated last night, and is occupied by our troops to-day; the enemy gone south to Okolotia, on the railroad to Mobile.
A. LINCOLN.

TELEGRAM TO GENERAL I. McDOWELL.

WAR DEPARTMENT WASHINGTON CITY, May 30, 1862. 9.30 P.M.

MAJOR-GENERAL McDOWELL, Rectortown, Va.:
I send you a despatch just received from Saxton at Harper's Ferry: "The rebels are in line of battle in front of our lines. They have nine pieces of artillery, and in position, and cavalry. I shelled the woods in which they were, and they in return threw a large number of shells into the lines and tents from which I moved last night to take up a stronger position. I expect a great deal from the battery on the mountain, having three 9 inch Dahlgren bearing directly on the enemy's approaches. The enemy appeared this morning and then retired, with the intention of drawing us on. I shall act on the defensive, as my position is a strong one. In a skirmish which took place this afternoon I lost one horse, The enemy lost two men killed and seven wounded.
"R. SAXTON, Brigadier General."
It seems the game is before you. Have sent a copy to General Fremont.
A. LINCOLN.

TELEGRAM TO GENERAL G. B. McCLELLAN.

WASHINGTON, May 31, 1862. 10.20 PM.

MAJOR-GENERAL McCLELLAN:
A circle whose circumference shall pass through Harper's Ferry, Front Royal, and Strasburg, and whose center shall be a little northeast of Winchester, almost certainly has within it this morning the forces of Jackson, Ewell, and Edward Johnson. Quite certainly they were within it two days ago. Some part of their forces attacked Harper's Ferry at dark last evening, and are still in sight this morning. Shields, with McDowell's advance, retook Front Royal at 11 A.M. yesterday, with a dozen of our own prisoners taken there a week ago, 150 of the enemy, two locomotives, and eleven cars, some other property and stores, and saved the bridge.
General Fremont, from the direction of Moorefield, promises to be at or near Strasburg at 5 P.M. to-day. General Banks at Williamsport, with his old force and his new force at Harper's Ferry, is directed to co-operate. Shields at Front Royal reports a rumor of still an additional force of the enemy, supposed to be Anderson's, having entered the valley of Virginia. This last may or may not be true. Corinth is certainly in the hands of General Halleck.
A. LINCOLN.

TELEGRAM FROM SECRETARY STANTON

TO GENERAL G. A. McCALL, WASHINGTON, May 31, 1562.

GENERAL McCALL:
The President directs me to say to you that there can be nothing to justify a panic at Fredericksburg. He expects you to maintain your position there as becomes a soldier and a general.

EDWIN M. STANTON, Secretary of War.

TELEGRAM TO GENERAL G. B. McCLELLAN.

WASHINGTON CITY, D.C., June 1, 1862. 9.30.

MAJOR-GENERAL McCLELLAN:
You are probably engaged with the enemy. I suppose he made the attack. Stand well on your guard, hold all your ground, or yield any only inch by inch and in good order. This morning we merge General Wool's department into yours, giving you command of the whole, and sending General Dix to Port Monroe and General Wool to Fort McHenry. We also send General Sigel to report to you for duty.
A. LINCOLN.

TELEGRAM TO GENERAL G. B. McCLELLAN.

WASHINGTON, June 3, 1862.

MAJOR-GENERAL McCLELLAN:
With these continuous rains I am very anxious about the Chickahominy so close in your rear and crossing your line of communication. Please look to it.
A. LINCOLN, President.

TELEGRAM TO GENERAL I. McDOWELL.

WASHINGTON, June 3, 1862. 6.15 P.M.

MAJOR-GENERAL McDOWELL, Front Royal, Virginia:
Anxious to know whether Shields can head or flank Jackson. Please tell about where Shields and Jackson, respectively, are at the time this reaches you.
A. LINCOLN.

TELEGRAM TO GENERAL H. W. HALLECK.

WASHINGTON, June 4, 1862.

MAJOR-GENERAL HALLECK, Corinth:
Your despatch of to-day to Secretary of War received. Thanks for the good news it brings. Have you anything from Memphis or other parts of the Mississippi River? Please answer.
A. LINCOLN.

TELEGRAM TO GOVERNOR JOHNSON.

[cipher.]

WASHINGTON, June 4, 1862.
HON. ANDREW JOHNSON, Nashville, Tennessee:
Do you really wish to have control of the question of releasing rebel prisoners so far as they may be Tennesseeans? If you do, please tell us so. Your answer not to be made public.
A. LINCOLN.

TO GENERAL G. B. McCLELLAN.

[Cipher.]

WAR DEPARTMENT, WASHINGTON, D.C., June 7, 1862.
MAJOR-GENERAL McCLELLAN:
Your despatch about Chattanooga and Dalton was duly received and sent to General Halleck. I have just received the following answer from him:
We have Fort Pillow, Randolph, and Memphis.
A. LINCOLN.

TELEGRAM TO GENERAL H. W. HALLECK.

WASHINGTON, June 8, 1862.

MAJOR-GENERAL HALLECK, Corinth, Mississippi:
We are changing one of the departmental lines, so as to give you all of Kentucky and Tennessee. In your movement upon Chattanooga I think it probable that you include some combination of the force near Cumberland Gap under General Morgan.
Do you?
A. LINCOLN.

TELEGRAM TO GENERAL N. P. BANKS.

WASHINGTON, June 9, 1862.

MAJOR-GENERAL BANKS, Winchester:
We are arranging a general plan for the valley of the Shenandoah, and in accordance with this you will move your main force to the Shenandoah at or opposite Front Royal as soon as possible.
A. LINCOLN.

TELEGRAM TO GENERAL J. C. FREMONT.

WASHINGTON, June 9, 1862.

MAJOR-GENERAL FREMONT:
Halt at Harrisonburg, pursuing Jackson no farther. Get your force well in hand and stand on the defensive, guarding against a movement of the enemy either back toward Strasburg or toward Franklin, and await further orders, which will soon be sent you.

A. LINCOLN.

TELEGRAM TO GOVERNOR JOHNSON.

[Cipher.]

WASHINGTON, June 9, 1862.
HON. ANDREW JOHNSON, Nashville, Tennessee:
Your despatch about seizing seventy rebels to exchange for a like number of Union men was duly received. I certainly do not disapprove the proposition.
A. LINCOLN.

TO GENERAL J. C. FREMONT. WASHINGTON, June 12, 1862.

MAJOR-GENERAL FREMONT:

Accounts, which we do not credit, represent that Jackson is largely reinforced and turning upon you. Get your forces well in hand and keep us well and frequently advised; and if you find yourself really pressed by a superior force of the enemy, fall back cautiously toward or to Winchester, and we will have in due time Banks in position to sustain you. Do not fall back upon Harrisonburg unless upon tolerably clear necessity. We understand Jackson is on the other side of the Shenandoah from you, and hence cannot in any event press you into any necessity of a precipitate withdrawal.
A. LINCOLN.
P.S.—Yours, preferring Mount Jackson to Harrisonburg, is just received. On this point use your discretion, remembering that our object is to give such protection as you can to western Virginia. Many thanks to yourself, officers, and men for the gallant battle of last Sunday. A. L.

MESSAGE TO CONGRESS.

EXECUTIVE MANSION, WASHINGTON,

June 13, 1862.
FELLOW-CITIZENS OF THE SENATE AND HOUSE OF REPRESENTATIVES: I herewith transmit a memorial addressed and presented to me in behalf of the State of New York in favor of enlarging the locks of the Erie and Oswego Canal. While I have not given nor have leisure to give the subject a careful examination, its great importance is obvious and unquestionable. The large amount of valuable statistical information which is collated and presented in the memorial will greatly facilitate the mature consideration of the subject, which I respectfully ask for it at your hands.
A. LINCOLN.

TO GENERAL J. C. FREMONT.

WASHINGTON; June 13. 1862

MAJOR-GENERAL FREMONT:
We cannot afford to keep your force and Banks's and McDowell's engaged in keeping Jackson south of Strasburg and Front Royal. You fought Jackson alone and worsted him. He can have no substantial reinforcements so long as a battle

is pending at Richmond. Surely you and Banks in supporting distance are capable of keeping him from returning to Winchester. But if Sigel be sent forward to you, and McDowell (as he must) be put to other work, Jackson will break through at Front Royal again. He is already on the right side of the Shenandoah to do it, and on the wrong side of it to attack you. The orders already sent you and Banks place you and him in the proper positions for the work assigned you. Jackson cannot move his whole force on either of you before the other can learn of it and go to his assistance. He cannot divide his force, sending part against each of you, because he will be too weak for either. Please do as I directed in the order of the 8th and my despatch of yesterday, the 12th, and neither you nor Banks will be overwhelmed by Jackson. By proper scout lookouts, and beacons of smoke by day and fires by night you can always have timely notice of the enemy's approach. I know not as to you, but by some this has been too much neglected.

A. LINCOLN. TO GENERAL J. C. FREMONT

WAR DEPARTMENT, WASHINGTON CITY, D. C., June 15, 1862.

MAJOR-GENERAL FREMONT:

MY DEAR SIR:—Your letter of the 12th by Colonel Zagonyi is just received. In answer to the principal part of it, I repeat the substance of an order of the 8th and one or two telegraphic despatches sent you since.

We have no definite power of sending reinforcements; so that we are compelled rather to consider the proper disposal of the forces we have than of those we could wish to have. We may be able to send you some dribs by degrees, but I do not believe we can do more. As you alone beat Jackson last Sunday, I argue that you are stronger than he is to-day, unless he has been reinforced; and that he cannot have been materially reinforced, because such reinforcement could only have come from Richmond, and he is much more likely to go to Richmond than Richmond is to come to him. Neither is very likely. I think Jackson's game—his assigned work—now is to magnify the accounts of his numbers and reports of his movements, and thus by constant alarms keep three or four times as many of our troops away from Richmond as his own force amounts to. Thus he helps his friends at Richmond three or four times as much as if he were there. Our game is not to allow this. Accordingly, by the order of the 8th, I directed you to halt at Harrisonburg, rest your force, and get it well in hand, the objects being to guard against Jackson's returning by the same route to the upper Potomac over which you have just driven him out, and at the same time give some protection against a raid into West Virginia.

Already I have given you discretion to occupy Mount Jackson instead, if, on full consideration, you think best. I do not believe Jackson will attack you, but certainly he cannot attack you by surprise; and if he comes upon you in superior force, you have but to notify us, fall back cautiously, and Banks will join you in due time. But while we know not whether Jackson will move at all, or by what route, we cannot safely put you and Banks both on the Strasburg line, and leave no force on the Front Royal line—the very line upon which he prosecuted his late raid. The true policy is to place one of you on one line and the other on the other in such positions that you can unite once you actually find Jackson moving upon it. And this is precisely what we are doing. This protects that part of our frontier, so to speak, and liberates McDowell to go to the assistance of McClellan. I have arranged this, and am very unwilling to have it deranged. While you have only asked for Sigel, I have spoken only of Banks, and this because Sigel's force is now the principal part of Bank's force.

About transferring General Schenck's commands, the purchase of supplies, and the promotion and appointment of officers, mentioned in your letter, I will consult with the Secretary of War to-morrow.

Yours truly,

A. LINCOLN.

TO GENERAL J. C. FREMONT.

WASHINGTON, June 16, 1862

MAJOR-GENERAL FREMONT, Mount Jackson, Virginia:

Your despatch of yesterday, reminding me of a supposed understanding that I would furnish you a corps of 35,000 men, and asking of me the "fulfilment of this understanding," is received. I am ready to come to a fair settlement of accounts with you on the fulfilment of understandings.

Early in March last, when I assigned you to the command of the Mountain Department, I did tell you I would give you all the force I could, and that I hoped to make it reach 35,000. You at the same time told me that within a reasonable time you would seize the railroad at or east of Knoxville, Tenn., if you could. There was then in the department a force supposed to be 25,000, the exact number as well known to you as to me. After looking about two or three days, you called and distinctly told me that if I would add the Blenker division to the force already in the department, you would undertake the job. The Blenker division contained 10,000, and at the expense of great dissatisfaction to General

485

McClellan I took it from his army and gave it to you. My promise was literally fulfilled. I have given you all I could, and I have given you very nearly, if not quite, 35,000.

Now for yours. On the 23d of May, largely over two months afterward, you were at Franklin, Va., not within 300 miles of Knoxville, nor within 80 miles of any part of the railroad east of it, and not moving forward, but telegraphing here that you could not move for lack of everything. Now, do not misunderstand me. I do not say you have not done all you could. I presume you met unexpected difficulties; and I beg you to believe that as surely as you have done your best, so have I. I have not the power now to fill up your Corps to 35,000. I am not demanding of you to do the work of 35,000. I am only asking of you to stand cautiously on the defensive, get your force in order, and give such protection as you can to the valley of the Shenandoah and to western Virginia.

Have you received the orders, and will you act upon them?

A. LINCOLN.

TO GENERAL C. SCHURZ.

WASHINGTON, June 16, 1862

BRIGADIER-GENERAL SCHURZ, Mount Jackson, Virginia:

Your long letter is received. The information you give is valuable. You say it is fortunate that Fremont did not intercept Jackson; that Jackson had the superior force, and would have overwhelmed him. If this is so, how happened it that Fremont fairly fought and routed him on the 8th? Or is the account that he did fight and rout him false and fabricated? Both General Fremont and you speak of Jackson having beaten Shields. By our accounts he did not beat Shields. He had no engagement with Shields. He did meet and drive back with disaster about 2000 of Shields's advance till they were met by an additional brigade of Shields's, when Jackson himself turned and retreated. Shields himself and more than half his force were not nearer than twenty miles to any of it.

A. LINCOLN.

TELEGRAM TO GENERAL H. W. HALLECK.

WASHINGTON, June 18, 1862.

MAJOR-GENERAL HALLECK, Corinth, Mississippi:

It would be of both interest and value to us here to know how the expedition toward East Tennessee is progressing, if in your judgment you can give us the information with safety.

A. LINCOLN.

TELEGRAM TO GENERAL G. B. McCLELLAN.

WAR DEPARTMENT, WASHINGTON, D. C., June 18, 1862.

MAJOR-GENERAL McCLELLAN:

Yours of to-day, making it probable that Jackson has been reinforced by about 10,000 from Richmond, is corroborated by a despatch from General King at Fredericksburg, saying a Frenchman, just arrived from Richmond by way of Gordonsville, met 10,000 to 15,000 passing through the latter place to join Jackson.

If this is true, it is as good as a reinforcement to you of an equal force. I could better dispose of things if I could know about what day you can attack Richmond, and would be glad to be informed, if you think you can inform me with safety.

A. LINCOLN.

TELEGRAM TO GENERAL G. B. McCLELLAN.

WASHINGTON, JUNE 19, 1862

MAJOR-GENERAL McCLELLAN:
Yours of last night just received, and for which I thank you.
If large reinforcements are going from Richmond to Jackson, it proves one of two things: either they are very strong at Richmond, or do not mean to defend the place desperately.
On reflection, I do not see how reinforcements from Richmond to Jackson could be in Gordonsville, as reported by the Frenchman and your deserters. Have not all been sent to deceive?
A. LINCOLN.

TELEGRAM TO GENERAL G. B. McCLELLAN.

WAR DEPARTMENT, WASHINGTON, June 20, 1862.

MAJOR-GENERAL McCLELLAN:
In regard to the contemplated execution of Captains Spriggs and Triplett the government has no information whatever, but will inquire and advise you.
A. LINCOLN.

TELEGRAM TO GENERAL G. B. McCLELLAN.

WASHINGTON CITY, June 20, 1862.

MAJOR-GENERAL McCLELLAN:
We have this morning sent you a despatch of General Sigel corroborative of the proposition that Jackson is being reinforced from Richmond. This may be reality, and yet may only be contrivance for deception, and to determine which is perplexing. If we knew it was not true, we could send you some more force; but as the case stands we do not think we safely can. Still, we will watch the signs and do so if possible.
In regard to a contemplated execution of Captains Spriggs and Triplett the government has no information whatever, but will inquire and advise you.
A. LINCOLN.

TELEGRAM TO GENERAL G. B. McCLELLAN.

WASHINGTON, June 21 1862 6 PM.

MAJOR-GENERAL GEORGE B. McCLELLAN:
Your despatch of yesterday (2 P. M.) was received this morning. If it would not divert too much of your time and attention from the army under your immediate command, I would be glad to have your views as to the present state of military affairs throughout the whole country, as you say you would be glad to give them. I would rather it should be by letter than by telegraph, because of the better chance of secrecy. As to the numbers and positions of the troops not under your command in Virginia and elsewhere, even if I could do it with accuracy, which I cannot, I would rather not transmit either by telegraph or by letter, because of the chances of its reaching the enemy. I would be very glad to talk with you, but you cannot leave your camp, and I cannot well leave here.
A. LINCOLN, President

TELEGRAM TO GENERAL N. P. BANKS.

WAR DEPARTMENT, June 22, 1862

MAJOR-GENERAL BANKS, Middletown:
I am very glad you are looking well to the west for a movement of the enemy in that direction. You know my anxiety on that point.
All was quiet at General McClellan's headquarters at two o'clock to-day.
A. LINCOLN.

TREATY WITH MEXICO

MESSAGE TO THE SENATE.

WASHINGTON, June 23, 1862.
TO THE SENATE OF THE UNITED STATES:
On the 7th day of December, 1861, I submitted to the Senate the project of a treaty between the United States and Mexico which had been proposed to me by Mr. Corwin, our minister to Mexico, and respectfully requested the advice of the Senate thereupon.
On the 25th day of February last a resolution was adopted by the Senate to the effect:
"That it is not advisable to negotiate a treaty that will require the United States to assume any portion of the principal or interest of the debt of Mexico, or that will require the concurrence of European powers."
This resolution having been duly communicated to me, notice thereof was immediately given by the Secretary of State to Mr. Corwin, and he was informed that he was to consider his instructions upon the subject referred to modified by this resolution and would govern his course accordingly. That despatch failed to reach Mr. Corwin, by reason of the disturbed condition of Mexico, until a very recent date, Mr. Corwin being without instructions, or thus practically left without instructions, to negotiate further with Mexico.
In view of the very important events Occurring there, he has thought that the interests of the United States would be promoted by the conclusion of two treaties which should provide for a loan to that republic. He has therefore signed such treaties, and they having been duly ratified by the Government of Mexico, he has transmitted them to me for my consideration. The action of the Senate is of course conclusive against an acceptance of the treaties On my part. I have, nevertheless, thought it just to our excellent minister in Mexico and respectful to the Government of that republic to lay the treaties before the Senate, together with the correspondence which has occurred in relation to them. In performing this duty I have only to add that the importance of the subject thus submitted to the Senate, can not be over estimated, and I shall cheerfully receive and consider with the highest respect any further advice the Senate may think proper to give upon the subject.
A. LINCOLN.

VETO OF A CURRENCY BILL

MESSAGE TO THE SENATE, JUNE 23, 1862.

TO THE SENATE OF THE UNITED STATES:
The bill which has passed the House of Representatives and the Senate, entitled "An act to repeal that part of an act of Congress which prohibits the circulation of bank-notes of a less denomination than five dollars in the District of Columbia," has received my attentive consideration, and I now return it to the Senate, in which it originated, with the following objections:

1. The bill proposes to repeal the existing legislation prohibiting the circulation of bank-notes of a less denomination than five dollars within the District of Columbia, without permitting the issuing of such bills by banks not now legally authorized to issue them. In my judgment, it will be found impracticable, in the present condition of the currency, to make such a discrimination. The banks have generally suspended specie payments, and a legal sanction given to the circulation of the irredeemable notes of one class of them will almost certainly be so extended, in practical operation, as to include those of all classes, whether authorized or unauthorized. If this view be correct, the currency of the District, should this act become a law, will certainly and greatly deteriorate, to the serious injury of honest trade and honest labor.

2. This bill seems to contemplate no end which cannot be otherwise more certainly and beneficially attained. During the existing war it is peculiarly the duty of the National Government to secure to the people a sound circulating medium. This duty has been, under existing circumstances, satisfactorily performed, in part at least, by authorizing the issue of United States notes, receivable for all government dues except customs, and made a legal tender for all debts, public and private, except interest on public debt. The object of the bill submitted to me—namely, that of providing a small note currency during the present suspension—can be fully accomplished by authorizing the issue, as part of any new emission of United States notes made necessary by the circumstances of the country, of notes of a similar character, but of less denomination than five dollars. Such an issue would answer all the beneficial purposes of the bill, would save a considerable amount to the treasury in interest, would greatly facilitate payments to soldiers and other creditors of small sums, and would furnish; to the people a currency as safe as their own government.

Entertaining these objections to the bill, I feel myself constrained to withhold from it my approval and return it for the further consideration and action of Congress.

A. LINCOLN

SPEECH AT JERSEY CITY, JUNE 24, 1862.

When birds and animals are looked at through a fog, they are seen to disadvantage, and so it might be with you if I were to attempt to tell you why I went to see General Scott. I can only say that my visit to West Point did not have the importance which has been attached to it; but it concerned matters that you understand quite as well as if I were to tell you all about them. Now, I can only remark that it had nothing whatever to do with making or unmaking any general in the country. The Secretary of War, you know, holds a pretty tight rein on the press, so that they shall not tell more than they ought to; and I'm afraid that if I blab too much, he might draw a tight rein on me.

TO GENERAL G. B. McCLELLAN.

WASHINGTON, June 26, 1862.

MAJOR-GENERAL McCLELLAN:

Your three despatches of yesterday in relation to the affair, ending with the statement that you completely succeeded in making your point, are very gratifying.

The later one of 6.15 P.M., suggesting the probability of your being overwhelmed by two hundred thousand, and talking of where the responsibility will belong, pains me very much. I give you all I can, and act on the presumption that you will do the best you can with what you have, while you continue, ungenerously I think, to assume that I could give you more if I would. I have omitted, and shall omit, no opportunity to send you reinforcements whenever I possibly can.

A. LINCOLN.

P. S. General Pope thinks if you fall back it would be much better towards York River than towards the James. As Pope now has charge of the capital, please confer with him through the telegraph.

ORDER CONSTITUTING THE ARMY OF VIRGINIA.

EXECUTIVE MANSION, WASHINGTON, D. C., June 26, 1862.

Ordered: 1st. The forces under Major-Generals Fremont, Banks, and McDowell, including the troops now under Brigadier-General Sturgis at Washington, shall be consolidated and form one army, to be called the Army of Virginia.
2d. The command of the Army of Virginia is specially assigned to Major-General John Pope, as commanding general. The troops of the Mountain Department, heretofore under command of General Fremont, shall constitute the First Army Corps, under the command of General Fremont; the troops of the Shenandoah Department, now under General Banks, shall constitute the Second Army Corps, and be commanded by him; the troops under the command of General McDowell, except those within the fortifications and city of Washington, shall form the Third Army Corps, and be under his command.
3d. The Army of Virginia shall operate in such manner as, while protecting western Virginia and the national capital from danger or insult, it shall in the speediest manner attack and overcome the rebel forces under Jackson and Ewell, threaten the enemy in the direction of Charlottesville, and render the most effective aid to relieve General McClellan and capture Richmond.
4th. When the Army of the Potomac and the Army of Virginia shall be in position to communicate and directly cooperate at or before Richmond, the chief command, while so operating together, shall be governed, as in like cases, by the Rules and Articles of War.
A. LINCOLN.

TELEGRAM FROM SECRETARY STANTON TO GENERAL H. W. HALLECK.

WAR DEPARTMENT, June 28, 1862.

MAJOR-GENERAL HALLECK:
The enemy have concentrated in such force at Richmond as to render it absolutely necessary, in the opinion of the President, for you immediately to detach 25,000 of your force and forward it by the nearest and quickest route by way of Baltimore and Washington to Richmond. It is believed that the quickest route would be by way of Columbus, Ky., and up the Ohio River. But in detaching your force the President directs that it be done in such a way as to enable you to hold your ground and not interfere with the movement against Chattanooga and East Tennessee. This condition being observed, the forces to be detached and the routes they are to be sent are left to your own judgment.
The direction to send these forces immediately is rendered imperative by a serious reverse suffered by General McClellan before Richmond yesterday, the full extent of which is not yet known.
You will acknowledge the receipt of this despatch, stating the day and hour it is received, and inform me what your action will be, so that we may take measures to aid in river and railroad transportation.
EDWIN M. STANTON, Secretary of War.

TELEGRAMS TO GENERAL A. E. BURNSIDE.

WASHINGTON, June 28, 1862.

GENERAL BURNSIDE:
I think you had better go, with any reinforcements you can spare, to General McClellan.
A. LINCOLN.

WAR DEPARTMENT, June, 28, 1862

MAJOR-GENERAL BURNSIDE, Newbern:

We have intelligence that General McClellan has been attacked in large force and compelled to fall back toward the James River. We are not advised of his exact condition, but the President directs that you shall send him all the

reinforcements from your command to the James River that you can safely do without abandoning your own position. Let it be infantry entirely, as he said yesterday that he had cavalry enough.
EDWIN M. STANTON,
Secretary of War.

TELEGRAM TO GENERAL G. B. McCLELLAN.

WAR DEPARTMENT, WASHINGTON CITY, June 28, 1862.

MAJOR-GENERAL McCLELLAN:
Save your army, at all events. Will send reinforcements as fast as we can. Of course they cannot reach you to-day, to-morrow, or next day. I have not said you were ungenerous for saying you needed reinforcements. I thought you were ungenerous in assuming that I did not send them as fast as I could. I feel any misfortune to you and your army quite as keenly as you feel it yourself. If you have had a drawn battle, or a repulse, it is the price we pay for the enemy not being in Washington. We protected Washington, and the enemy concentrated on you. Had we stripped Washington, he would have been upon us before the troops could have gotten to you. Less than a week ago you notified us that reinforcements were leaving Richmond to come in front of us. It is the nature of the case, and neither you nor the government is to blame. Please tell at once the present condition and aspect of things.
A. LINCOLN

TO SECRETARY SEWARD.

EXECUTIVE MANSION, June 28, 1862

HON. W. H. SEWARD.
MY DEAR SIR:—My view of the present condition of the war is about as follows:
The evacuation of Corinth and our delay by the flood in the Chickahominy have enabled the enemy to concentrate too much force in Richmond for McClellan to successfully attack. In fact there soon will be no substantial rebel force anywhere else. But if we send all the force from here to McClellan, the enemy will, before we can know of it, send a force from Richmond and take Washington. Or if a large part of the western army be brought here to McClellan, they will let us have Richmond, and retake Tennessee, Kentucky, Missouri, etc. What should be done is to hold what we have in the West, open the Mississippi, and take Chattanooga and East Tennessee without more. A reasonable force should in every event be kept about Washington for its protection. Then let the country give us a hundred thousand new troops in the shortest possible time, which, added to McClellan directly or indirectly, will take Richmond without endangering any other place which we now hold, and will substantially end the war. I expect to maintain this contest until successful, or till I die, or am conquered, or my term expires, or Congress or the country forsake me; and I would publicly appeal to the country for this new force were it not that I fear a general panic and stampede would follow, so hard it is to have a thing understood as it really is. I think the new force should be all, or nearly all, infantry, principally because such can be raised most cheaply and quickly.
Yours very truly,
A. LINCOLN.

TELEGRAM TO GENERAL J. A. DIX.

WAR DEPARTMENT, WASHINGTON, D.C., June 28, 1862.

GENERAL DIX:
Communication with McClellan by White House is cut off. Strain every nerve to open communication with him by James River, or any other way you can. Report to me.

A. LINCOLN.

TELEGRAM TO FLAG-OFFICER L. M. GOLDSBOROUGH.

WASHINGTON, D.C., June 28, 1862.

FLAG-OFFICER GOLDSBOROUGH, Fort Monroe:
Enemy has cut McClellan's communication with White House, and is driving Stoneman back on that point. Do what you can for him with gunboats at or near that place. McClellan's main force is between the Chickahominy and the James. Also do what you can to communicate with him and support him there.
A. LINCOLN

To GOVERNOR MORTON.

WAR DEPARTMENT, WASHINGTON, D.C. June 28, 1862.

GOVERNOR O. P. MORTON, Indianapolis, Ind:
Your despatch of to-day is just received. I have no recollection of either John R. Cravens or Cyrus M. Allen having been named to me for appointment under the tax law. The latter particularly has been my friend, and I am sorry to learn that he is not yours. No appointment has been or will be made by me for the purpose of stabbing you.
A. LINCOLN.

TELEGRAM TO SECRETARY SEWARD.

WAR DEPARTMENT, June 29, 1862.6 P.M.

HON. WILLIAM H. SEWARD, Astor House, New York:
Not much more than when you left. Fulton of Baltimore American is now with us. He left White House at 11 A.M. yesterday. He conversed fully with a paymaster who was with Porter's force during the fight of Friday and fell back to nearer McClellan's quarters just a little sooner than Porter did, seeing the whole of it; stayed on the Richmond side of the Chickahominy over night, and left for White House at 5 A.M. Saturday. He says Porter retired in perfect order under protection of the guns arranged for the purpose, under orders and not from necessity; and with all other of our forces, except what was left on purpose to go to White House, was safely in pontoons over the Chickahominy before morning, and that there was heavy firing on the Richmond side, begun at 5 and ceased at 7 A.M. Saturday. On the whole, I think we have had the better of it up to that point of time. What has happened since we still know not, as we have no communication with General McClellan. A despatch from Colonel Ingalls shows that he thinks McClellan is fighting with the enemy at Richmond to-day, and will be to-morrow. We have no means of knowing upon what Colonel Ingalls founds his opinion. Confirmed about saving all property. Not a single unwounded straggler came back to White House from the field, and the number of wounded reaching there up to 11 A.M. Saturday was not large.
A. LINCOLN.
To what the President has above stated I will only add one or two points that may be satisfactory for you to know.
First. All the sick and wounded were safely removed
Second. A despatch from Burnside shows that he is from White House; not a man left behind in condition to afford efficient support, and is probably doing so.
Third. The despatch from Colonel Ingalls impresses me with the conviction that the movement was made by General McClellan to concentrate on Richmond, and was successful to the latest point of which we have any information.
Fourth. Mr. Fulton says that on Friday night, between twelve and one o'clock, General McClellan telegraphed Commodore Goldsborough that the result of the movement was satisfactory to him.

Fifth. From these and the facts stated by the President, my inference is that General McClellan will probably be in Richmond within two days.

EDWIN M. STANTON, Secretary of War.

[Unfortunately McClellan did not do any of the things he was ordered, and that it was very likely possible to do. It is still some mystery what he was doing all these days other than hiding in the woods and staying out of communication so he would not receive any more uncomfortable orders. This was another place where the North was close to wining the war and did not. D.W.]

TELEGRAM TO SECRETARY SEWARD. WAR DEPARTMENT, June 30, 1862.

HON. WM. H. SEWARD, New York:

We are yet without communication with General McClellan, and this absence of news is our point of anxiety. Up to the latest point to which we are posted he effected everything in such exact accordance with his plan, contingently announced to us before the battle began, that we feel justified to hope that he has not failed since. He had a severe engagement in getting the part of his army on this side of the Chickahominy over to the other side, in which the enemy lost certainly as much as we did. We are not dissatisfied with this, only that the loss of enemies does not compensate for the loss of friends. The enemy cannot come below White House; certainly is not there now, and probably has abandoned the whole line. Dix's pickets are at New Kent Court-House.

A. LINCOLN.

CALL FOR TROOPS. NEW YORK, June 30, 1862.

TO THE GOVERNORS OF THE SEVERAL STATES:

The capture of New Orleans, Norfolk, and Corinth by the national forces has enabled the insurgents to concentrate a large force at and about Richmond, which place we must take with the least possible delay; in fact, there will soon be no formidable insurgent force except at Richmond. With so large an army there, the enemy can threaten us on the Potomac and elsewhere. Until we have re-established the national authority, all these places must be held, and we must keep a respectable force in front of WASHINGTON. But this, from the diminished strength of our army by sickness and casualties, renders an addition to it necessary in order to close the struggle which has been prosecuted for the last three months with energy and success. Rather than hazard the misapprehension of our military condition and of groundless alarm by a call for troops by proclamation, I have deemed it best to address you in this form. To accomplish the object stated we require without delay 150,000 men, including those recently called for by the Secretary of War. Thus reinforced our gallant army will be enabled to realize the hopes and expectations of the government and the people.

A. LINCOLN.

TELEGRAM TO GENERAL J. A. DIX.

WAR DEPARTMENT, WASHINGTON CITY, June 30, 1862.

MAJOR-GENERAL Dix, Fort Monroe:

Is it not probable that the enemy has abandoned the line between White House and McClellan's rear? He could have but little object to maintain it, and nothing to subsist upon. Would not Stoneman better move up and see about it? I think a telegraphic communication can at once be opened to White House from Williamsburg. The wires must be up still.

A. LINCOLN.

TELEGRAMS TO GENERAL H. W. HALLECK.

WAR DEPARTMENT, JUNE 30, 1862. 3 P. M.

MAJOR-GENERAL HALLECK, Corinth:
Your telegram of this date just received. The Chattanooga expedition must not on any account be given up. The President regards that and the movement against East Tennessee as one of the most important movements of the war, and its occupation nearly as important as the capture of Richmond. He is not pleased with the tardiness of the movement toward Chattanooga, and directs that no force be sent here if you cannot do it without breaking up the operations against that point and East Tennessee. Infantry only are needed; our cavalry and artillery are strong enough. The first reports from Richmond were more discouraging than the truth warranted. If the advantage is not on our side, it is balanced. General McClellan has moved his whole force on the line of the James River, and is supported there by our gunboats; but he must be largely strengthened before advancing, and hence the call on you, which I am glad you answered so promptly. Let me know to what point on the river you will send your forces, so as to provide immediately for transportation.
EDWIN M. STANTON,
Secretary of War.

WASHINGTON, D.C., June 30, 1862.

MAJOR-GENERAL HALLECK, Corinth, Mississippi:

Would be very glad of 25,000 infantry; no artillery or cavalry; but please do not send a man if it endangers any place you deem important to hold, or if it forces you to give up or weaken or delay the expedition against Chattanooga. To take and hold the railroad at or east of Cleveland, in East Tennessee, I think fully as important as the taking and holding of Richmond.
A. LINCOLN.

CALL FOR 300,000 VOLUNTEERS, JULY 1, 1862.

June 28, 1861.

The undersigned, governors of States of the Union, impressed with the belief that the citizens of the States which they respectively represent are of one accord in the hearty desire that the recent successes of the Federal arms may be followed up by measures which must insure the speedy restoration of the Union, and believing that, in view of the present state of the important military movements now in progress, and the reduced condition of our effective forces in the field, resulting from the usual and unavoidable casualties in the service, the time has arrived for prompt and vigorous measures to be adopted by the people in support of the great interests committed to your charge, respectfully request, if it meets with your entire approval, that you at once call upon the several States for such number of men as may be required to fill up all military organizations now in the field, and add to the armies heretofore organized such additional number of men as may, in your judgment, be necessary to garrison and hold all the numerous cities and military positions that have been captured by our armies, and to speedily crush the rebellion that still exists in several of the Southern States, thus practically restoring to the civilized world our great and good government. All believe that the decisive moment is near at hand, and to that end the people of the United States are desirous to aid promptly in furnishing all reinforcements that you may deem needful to sustain our government.
    ISRAEL WASHBURN, JR., Governor of Maine.
    H. S. BERRY, Governor of New Hampshire.
    FREDERICK HOLBROOK, Governor of Vermont.
    WILLIAM A. BUCKINGHAM, Governor of Connecticut.

E. D. MORGAN, Governor of New York.
CHARLES S. OLDEN, Governor of New Jersey.
A. G. CURTIN, Governor of Pennsylvania.
A. W. BRADFORD, Governor of Maryland.
F. H. PIERPOINT, Governor of Virginia.
AUSTIN BLAIR, Governor of Michigan.
J. B. TEMPLE, President Military Board of Kentucky.
ANDREW JOHNSON, Governor of Tennessee.
H. R. GAMBLE, Governor of Missouri.
O. P. MORTON, Governor of Indiana.
DAVID TODD, Governor of Ohio.
ALEXANDER RAMSEY, Governor of Minnesota.
RICHARD YATES, Governor of Illinois.
EDWARD SALOMON, Governor of Wisconsin.
THE PRESIDENT

EXECUTIVE MANSION, WASHINGTON, July 1, 1862

GENTLEMEN:—Fully concurring in the wisdom of the views expressed to me in so patriotic a manner by you, in the communication of the twenty-eighth day of June, I have decided to call into the service an additional force of 300,000 men. I suggest and recommend that the troops should be chiefly of infantry. The quota of your State would be —— ——. I trust that they may be enrolled without delay, so as to bring this unnecessary and injurious civil war to a speedy and satisfactory conclusion. An order fixing the quotas of the respective States will be issued by the War Department to-morrow.
A. LINCOLN.

PROCLAMATION CONCERNING TAXES IN REBELLIOUS STATES, JULY 1, 1862.

BY THE PRESIDENT OF THE UNITED STATES OF AMERICA:

A Proclamation.
Whereas in and by the second section of an act of Congress passed on the 7th day of June, A. D. 1862, entitled "An act for the collection of direct taxes in insurrectionary districts within the United States, and for other purposes," it is made the duty of the President to declare, on or before the first day of July then next following, by his proclamation, in what States and parts of States insurrection exists:
Now, therefore, be it known that I, Abraham Lincoln, President of the United States of America, do hereby declare and proclaim that the States of South Carolina, Florida, Georgia, Alabama, Louisiana, Texas, Mississippi, Arkansas, Tennessee, North Carolina, and the State of Virginia except the following counties-Hancock, Brooke, Ohio, Marshall, Wetzel, Marion, Monongalia, Preston, Taylor, Pleasants, Tyler, Ritchie, Doddridge, Harrison, Wood, Jackson, Wirt, Roane, Calhoun, Gilmer, Barbour, Tucker, Lewis, Braxton, Upshur, Randolph, Mason, Putnam, Kanawha, Clay, Nicholas, Cabell, Wayne, Boone, Logan, Wyoming, Webster, Fayette, and Raleigh-are now in insurrection and rebellion, and by reason thereof the civil authority of the United States is obstructed so that the provisions of the "Act to provide increased revenue from imports, to pay the interest on the public debt, and for other purposes," approved August 5, 1861, can not be peaceably executed; and that the taxes legally chargeable upon real estate under the act last aforesaid lying within the States and parts of States as aforesaid, together with a penalty of 50 per centum of said taxes, shall be a lien upon the tracts or lots of the same, severally charged, till paid.
In witness whereof I have hereunto set my hand and caused the seal of the United States to be affixed............
A. LINCOLN.
By the President: F. W. SEWARD, Acting Secretary of State.

MESSAGE TO CONGRESS, JULY 1, 1862.

TO THE SENATE AND HOUSE OF REPRESENTATIVES

I most cordially recommend that Captain Andrew H. Foote, of the United States Navy, receive a vote of thanks of Congress for his eminent services in Organizing the flotilla on the western Waters, and for his gallantry at Fort Henry, Fort Donelson, Island Number Ten, and at various other places, whilst in command of the naval forces, embracing a period of nearly ten months.
A. LINCOLN.
WASHINGTON, D. C. July 1, 1862

TELEGRAM TO GENERAL McCLELLAN.

WASHINGTON, JULY 1,1862. 3.30 P.M.

MAJOR-GENERAL GEORGE B. McCLELLAN:
It is impossible to reinforce you for your present emergency. If we had a million of men, We could not get them to you in time. We have not the men to send. If you are not strong enough to face the enemy, you must find a place of security, and wait, rest, and repair. Maintain your ground if you can, but save the army at all events, even if you fall back to Fort Monroe. We still have strength enough in the country, and will bring it out.
A. LINCOLN.

TO GENERAL G. B. McCLELLAN.

WAR DEPARTMENT, WASHINGTON, D.C., July 2, 1862.

MAJOR-GENERAL McCLELLAN:
Your despatch of Tuesday morning induces me to hope your army is having some rest. In this hope allow me to reason with you a moment. When you ask for 50,000 men to be promptly sent you, you surely labor under some gross mistake of fact. Recently you sent papers showing your disposal of forces made last spring for the defense of WASHINGTON, and advising a return to that plan. I find it included in and about WASHINGTON 75,000 men. Now, please be assured I have not men enough to fill that very plan by 15,000. All of Fremont's in the valley, all of Banks's, all of McDowell's not with you, and all in WASHINGTON, taken together, do not exceed, if they reach, 60,000. With Wool and Dix added to those mentioned, I have not, outside of your army, 75,000 men east of the mountains. Thus the idea of sending you 50,000, or any other considerable force, promptly, is simply absurd. If, in your frequent mention of responsibility, you have the impression that I blame you for not doing more than you can, please be relieved of such impression. I only beg that in like manner you will not ask impossibilities of me. If you think you are not strong enough to take Richmond just now, I do not ask you to try just now. Save the army, material and personal, and I will strengthen it for the offensive again as fast as I can. The governors of eighteen States offer me a new levy of 300,000, which I accept.
A. LINCOLN.

TELEGRAM TO GENERAL H. W. HALLECK.

WASHINGTON, D.C. July 2, 1862.

MAJOR-GENERAL HALLECK, Corinth, Mississippi:

Your several despatches of yesterday to Secretary of War and myself received. I did say, and now repeat, I would be exceedingly glad for some reinforcements from you. Still do not send a man if in your judgment it will endanger any point you deem important to hold, or will force you to give up or weaken or delay the Chattanooga expedition.
Please tell me could you not make me a flying visit for consultation without endangering the Service in your department.
A. LINCOLN.

MESSAGE TO THE SENATE.

EXECUTIVE MANSION, July 2, 1862.

TO THE SENATE OF THE UNITED STATES:
I herewith return to your honorable body, in which it originated, an act entitled "An act to provide for additional medical officers of the volunteer service," without my approval.
My reason for so doing is that I have approved an act of the same title passed by Congress after the passage of the one first mentioned for the express purpose of correcting errors in and superseding the same, as I am informed.
A. LINCOLN.

CIRCULAR LETTER TO THE GOVERNORS.

(Private and Confidential.)

WAR DEPARTMENT, July 3, 1862.10.30 A.M.
GOVERNOR WASHBURN, Maine [and other governors] I should not want the half of 300,000 new troops if I could have them now. If I had 50,000 additional troops here now, I believe I could substantially close the war in two weeks. But time is everything, and if I get 50,000 new men in a month, I shall have lost 20,000 old ones during the same month, having gained only 30,000, with the difference between old and new troops still against me. The quicker you send, the fewer you will have to send. Time is everything. Please act in view of this. The enemy having given up Corinth, it is not wonderful that he is thereby enabled to check us for a time at Richmond.
Yours truly,
A. LINCOLN.

TO GENERAL G. B. McCLELLAN.

WAR DEPARTMENT WASHINGTON, D.C., JULY 3, 1862

MAJOR-GENERAL GEORGE B. McCLELLAN:
Yours of 5.30 yesterday is just received. I am satisfied that yourself, officers, and men have done the best you could. All accounts say better fighting was never done. Ten thousand thanks for it.
On the 28th we sent General Burnside an order to send all the force he could spare to you. We then learned that you had requested him to go to Goldsborough; upon which we said to him our order was intended for your benefit, and we did not wish to be in conflict with your views.
We hope you will have help from him soon. Today we have ordered General Hunter to send you all he can spare. At last advices General Halleck thinks he cannot send reinforcements without endangering all he has gained.
A. LINCOLN, President

TO GENERAL G. B. McCLELLAN.

WAR DEPARTMENT, WASHINGTON CITY, D.C., July 4, 1862.

MAJOR-GENERAL McCLELLAN:
I understand your position as stated in your letter and by General Marcy. To reinforce you so as to enable you to resume the offensive within a month, or even six weeks, is impossible. In addition to that arrived and now arriving from the Potomac (about 10,000 men, I suppose), and about 10,000 I hope you will have from Burnside very soon, and about 5000 from Hunter a little later, I do not see how I can send you another man within a month. Under these circumstances the defensive for the present must be your only care. Save the army first, where you are, if you can; secondly, by removal, if you must. You, on the ground, must be the judge as to which you will attempt, and of the means for effecting it. I but give it as my opinion that with the aid of the gunboats and the reinforcements mentioned above you can hold your present position—provided, and so long as, you can keep the James River open below you. If you are not tolerably confident you can keep the James River open, you had better remove as soon as possible. I do not remember that you have expressed any apprehension as to the danger of having your communication cut on the river below you, yet I do not suppose it can have escaped your attention.
Yours very truly,
A. LINCOLN.
P.S.—If at any time you feel able to take the offensive, you are not restrained from doing so. A.L.

TELEGRAM TO GENERAL H. W. HALLECK.

WAR DEPARTMENT, July 4, 1862.

MAJOR-GENERAL HALLECK, Corinth, Mississippi:
You do not know how much you would oblige us if, without abandoning any of your positions or plans, you could promptly send us even 10,000 infantry. Can you not? Some part of the Corinth army is certainly fighting McClellan in front of Richmond. Prisoners are in our hands from the late Corinth army.
A. LINCOLN.

TELEGRAM TO GENERAL J. A. DIX.

WASHINGTON CITY, July 4, 1862.

MAJOR-GENERAL Dix, Fort Monroe:
Send forward the despatch to Colonel Hawkins and this also. Our order and General McClellan's to General Burnside being the same, of course we wish it executed as promptly as possible.
A. LINCOLN.

TELEGRAM TO GENERAL G. B. McCLELLAN.

WASHINGTON, July 5, 1862. 9 A.M.

MAJOR-GENERAL GEORGE B. McCLELLAN:
A thousand thanks for the relief your two despatches of 12 and 1 P.M. yesterday gave me. Be assured the heroism and skill of yourself and officers and men is, and forever will be, appreciated.
If you can hold your present position, we shall have the enemy yet.
A. LINCOLN

TO GENERAL H. W. HALLECK.

WAR DEPARTMENT, WASHINGTON CITY, D.C., July 6, 1862.

MAJOR-GENERAL HALLECK, Corinth, Mississippi.
MY DEAR SIR:—This introduces Governor William Sprague, of Rhode Island. He is now Governor for the third time, and senator-elect of the United States.
I know the object of his visit to you. He has my cheerful consent to go, but not my direction. He wishes to get you and part of your force, one or both, to come here. You already know I should be exceedingly glad of this if, in your judgment, it could be without endangering positions and operations in the southwest; and I now repeat what I have more than once said by telegraph: "Do not come or send a man if, in your judgment, it will endanger any point you deem important to hold, or endangers or delays the Chattanooga expedition."
Still, please give my friend, Governor Sprague, a full and fair hearing.
Yours very truly,
A. LINCOLN.

MEMORANDUM OF AN INTERVIEW BETWEEN THE PRESIDENT AND GENERAL McCLELLAN

AND OTHER OFFICERS DURING A VISIT TO THE ARMY OF THE POTOMAC AT HARRISON'S LANDING, VIRGINIA.
July 9, 1862.
THE PRESIDENT: What amount of force have you now?
GENERAL McCLELLAN: About 80,000, can't vary much, certainly 75,000.
THE PRESIDENT:[to the corps commanders] What is the whole amount of your corps with you now.
    GENERAL SUMNER: About 15,000.
    GENERAL HEINTZELMAN: 15,000 for duty.
    GENERAL KEYES: About 12,500.
    GENERAL PORTER: About 23,000—fully 20,000 fit for duty.
    GENERAL FRANKLIN: About 15,000.
THE PRESIDENT: What is likely to be your condition as to health in this camp?
GENERAL McCLELLAN: Better than in any encampment since landing at Fortress Monroe.
PRESIDENT LINCOLN:[to the corps commanders] In your present encampment what is the present and prospective condition as to health?
GENERAL SUMNER: As good as any part of Western Virginia.
GENERAL HEINTZELMAN: Excellent for health, and present health improving.
GENERAL KEYES: A little improved, but think camp is getting worse.
GENERAL PORTER: Very good.
GENERAL FRANKLIN: Not good.
THE PRESIDENT: Where is the enemy now?
GENERAL McCLELLAN: From four to five miles from us on all the roads—I think nearly the whole army—both Hills, Longstreet, Jackson, Magruder, Huger.
THE PRESIDENT: [to the corps commanders] Where and in what condition do you believe the enemy to be now?
GENERAL SUMNER: I think they have retired from our front; were very much damaged, especially in their best troops, in the late actions, from superiority of arms.
GENERAL HEINTZELMAN: Don't think they are in force in our vicinity.
GENERAL KEYES: Think he has withdrawn, and think preparing to go to WASHINGTON.
GENERAL PORTER: Believe he is mainly near Richmond. He feels he dare not attack us here.
GENERAL FRANKLIN: I learn he has withdrawn from our front and think that is probable.
THE PRESIDENT: [to the corps commanders] What is the aggregate of your killed, wounded, and missing from the attack on the 26th ultimo till now?
    GENERAL SUMNER: 1175.
    GENERAL HEINTZELMAN: Not large 745.
    GENERAL KEYES: Less than 500.

GENERAL PORTER: Over 5000.
GENERAL FRANKLIN: Not over 3000.
THE PRESIDENT: If you desired could you remove the army safely?
GENERAL McCLELLAN: It would be a delicate and very difficult matter.
THE PRESIDENT: [to the corps commanders] If it were desired to get the army away, could it be safely effected?
GENERAL SUMNER: I think we could, but I think we give up the cause if we do.
GENERAL HEINTZELMAN: Perhaps we could, but I think it would be ruinous to the country.
GENERAL KEYES: I think it could if done quickly.
GENERAL PORTER: Impossible—move the army and ruin the country.
GENERAL FRANKLIN: I think we could, and that we had better—think Rappahannock the true line.
THE PRESIDENT: [to the corps commanders] Is the army secure in its present position?
    GENERAL SUMNER: Perfectly so, in my judgment.
    GENERAL HEINTZELMAN: I think it is safe.
    GENERAL KEYES: With help of General B. [Burnside] can hold position.
    GENERAL PORTER: Perfectly so. Not only, but we are ready to begin moving forward.
    GENERAL FRANKLIN: Unless river can be closed it is.

ORDER MAKING HALLECK GENERAL-IN-CHIEF.

EXECUTIVE MANSION, WASHINGTON, July 11, 1862.

Ordered, That Major-General Henry W. Halleck be assigned to command the whole land forces of the United States, as general-in-chief, and that he repair to this capital so soon as he can with safety to the positions and operations within the department now under his charge.
A. LINCOLN

ORDER CONCERNING THE SOUTHWEST BRANCH OF THE PACIFIC RAILROAD.

Whereas, in the judgment of the President, the public safety does require that the railroad line called and known as the Southwest Branch of the Pacific Railroad in the State of Missouri be repaired, extended, and completed from Rolla to Lebanon, in the direction to Springfield, in the said State, the same being necessary to the successful and economical conduct of the war and to the maintenance of the authority of the government in the Southwest:
Therefore, under and in virtue of the act of Congress entitled "An act to authorize the President of the United States in certain cases to take possession of railroad and telegraph lines, and for other purposes," approved January 31, 1862, it is ordered, That the portion of the said railroad line which reaches from Rolla to Lebanon be repaired, extended, and completed, so as to be made available for the military uses of the government, as speedily as may be. And, inasmuch as upon the part of the said line from Rolla to the stream called Little Piney a considerable portion of the necessary work has already been done by the railroad company, and the road to this extent may be completed at comparatively small cost, it is ordered that the said line from Rolla to and across Little Piney be first completed, and as soon as possible.
The Secretary of War is charged with the execution of this order. And to facilitate the speedy execution of the work, he is directed, at his discretion, to take possession and control of the whole or such part of the said railroad line, and the whole or such part of the rolling stock, offices, shops, buildings, and all their appendages and appurtenances, as he may judge necessary or convenient for the early completion of the road from Rolla to Lebanon.
Done at the city of WASHINGTON, July 11, 1862.
A. LINCOLN.

MESSAGE TO CONGRESS.

WASHINGTON, D C., July 11, 1862

TO THE SENATE AND HOUSE OF REPRESENTATIVES:
I recommend that the thanks of Congress be given to the following officers of the United States Navy:
Captain James L. Lardner, for meritorious conduct at the battle of Port Royal and distinguished services on the coast of the United States against the enemy.
Captain Charles Henry Davis, for distinguished services in conflict with the enemy at Fort Pillow, at Memphis, and for successful operations at other points in the waters of the Mississippi River.
Commander John A. Dahlgren, for distinguished services in the line of his profession, improvements in ordnance, and zealous and efficient labors in the ordnance branch of the service.
Commander Stephen C. Rowan, for distinguished services in the waters of North Carolina, and particularly in the capture of Newbern, being in chief command of the naval forces.
Commander David D. Porter, for distinguished services in the conception and preparation of the means used for the capture of the forts below New Orleans, and for highly meritorious conduct in the management of the mortar flotilla during the bombardment of Forts Jackson and St. Philip.
Captain Silas H. Stringham, now on the retired list, for distinguished services in the capture of Forts Hatteras and Clark.
A. LINCOLN.

TELEGRAM TO GOVERNOR JOHNSON. WAR DEPARTMENT, July 11, 1862.

HON. ANDREW JOHNSON.

MY DEAR SIR:—Yours of yesterday is received. Do you not, my good friend, perceive that what you ask is simply to put you in command in the West? I do not suppose you desire this. You only wish to control in your own localities; but this you must know may derange all other posts. Can you not, and will you not, have a full conference with General Halleck? Telegraph him, and meet him at such place as he and you can agree upon. I telegraph him to meet you and confer fully with you.
A. LINCOLN.

TELEGRAM TO GENERAL H. W. HALLECK. WAR DEPARTMENT, July 11, 1862.

MAJOR-GENERAL HALLECK, Corinth:

Governor Johnson, at Nashville, is in great trouble and anxiety about a raid into Kentucky. The governor is a true and valuable man—indispensable to us in Tennessee. Will you please get in communication with him, and have a full conference with him before you leave for here? I have telegraphed him on the subject.
A. LINCOLN.

APPEAL TO BORDER-STATES IN FAVOR OF COMPENSATED EMANCIPATION.

July 12, 1862.

GENTLEMEN:—After the adjournment of Congress now very near, I shall have no opportunity of seeing you for several months. Believing that you of the border States hold more power for good than any other equal number of members, I feel it a duty which I cannot justifiably waive to make this appeal to you. I intend no reproach or complaint when I assure you that, in my opinion, if you all had voted for the resolution in the gradual-emancipation message of last March, the war would now be substantially ended. And the plan therein proposed is yet one of the most potent and swift means of ending it. Let the States which are in rebellion see definitely and certainly that in no event will the States you represent ever join their proposed confederacy, and they cannot much longer maintain the contest. But you cannot divest them of their hope to ultimately have you with them so long as you show a determination to perpetuate the institution within your own States. Beat them at elections, as you have overwhelmingly done, and, nothing daunted, they still claim you as their own. You and I know what the lever of their power is. Break that lever before their faces, and they can shake you no more forever. Most of you have treated me with kindness and consideration and I trust you will not now think I improperly touch what is exclusively your own, when, for the sake of the whole country, I ask, Can you, for your States, do better than to take the course I urge? Discarding punctilio and maxims adapted to more manageable times, and looking only to the unprecedentedly stern facts of our case, can you do better in any possible event? You prefer that the constitutional relation of the States to the nation shall be practically restored without disturbance of the institution; and if this were done, my whole duty in this respect, under the Constitution and my oath of office, would be performed. But it is not done, and we are trying to accomplish it by war. The incidents of the war cannot be avoided. If the war continues long, as it must if the object be not sooner attained, the institution in your States will be extinguished by mere friction and abrasion—by the mere incidents of the war. It will be gone, and you will have nothing valuable in lieu of it. Much of its value is gone already. How much better for you and for your people to take the step which at once shortens the war and secures substantial compensation for that which is sure to be wholly lost in any other event! How much better to thus save the money which else we sink forever in war! How much better to do it while we can, lest the war ere long render us pecuniarily unable to do it! How much better for you as seller, and the nation as buyer, to sell out and buy out that without which the war could never have been, than to sink both the thing to be sold and the price of it in cutting one another's throats! I do not speak of emancipation at once, but of a decision at once to emancipate gradually. Room in South America for colonization can be obtained cheaply and in abundance, and when numbers shall be large enough to be company and encouragement for one another, the freed people will not be so reluctant to go.

I am pressed with a difficulty not yet mentioned—one which threatens division among those who, united, are none too strong. An instance of it is known to you. General Hunter is an honest man. He was, and I hope still is, my friend. I valued him none the less for his agreeing with me in the general wish that all men everywhere could be free. He proclaimed all men free within certain States, and I repudiated the proclamation. He expected more good and less harm from the measure than I could believe would follow. Yet, in repudiating it, I gave dissatisfaction, if not offence, to many whose support the country cannot afford to lose. And this is not the end of it. The pressure in this direction is still upon me, and is increasing. By conceding what I now ask you can relieve me, and, much more, can relieve the country in this important point.

Upon these considerations, I have again begged your attention to the message of March last. Before leaving the Capital, consider and discuss it among yourselves. You are patriots and statesmen, and as such I pray you consider this proposition; and, at the least, commend it to the consideration of your States and people. As you would perpetuate popular government for the best people in the world, I beseech you that you do in nowise omit this. Our common country is in great peril, demanding the loftiest views and boldest action to bring a speedy relief. Once relieved, its form of government is saved to the world; its beloved history and cherished memories are vindicated, and its happy future fully assured and rendered inconceivably grand. To you, more than to any others, the privilege is given to assure that happiness and swell that grandeur, and to link your own names therewith forever.

TO GENERAL G. B. McCLELLAN.

EXECUTIVE MANSION, WASHINGTON, July 13, 1862.

MAJOR-GENERAL McCLELLAN:
MY DEAR SIR:—I am told that over 160,000 men have gone into your army on the Peninsula. When I was with you the other day we made out 86,500 remaining, leaving 73,500 to be accounted for. I believe 23,500 will cover all the killed, wounded, and missing in all your battles and skirmishes, leaving 50,000 who have left otherwise. No more than 5000 of these have died, leaving 45,000 of your army still alive and not with it. I believe half or two-thirds of them are fit for duty to-day. Have you any more perfect knowledge of this than I have? If I am right, and you had these men with you, you could go into Richmond in the next three days. How can they be got to you, and how can they be prevented from getting away in such numbers for the future?
A. LINCOLN.

TELEGRAM TO GENERAL H. W. HALLECK.

WAR DEPARTMENT, July 13, 1862.

MAJOR-GENERAL HALLECK, Corinth, Mississippi:
They are having a stampede in Kentucky. Please look to it.
A. LINCOLN.

TELEGRAM TO GENERAL J. T. BOYLE.

WASHINGTON, July 13, 1862.

GENERAL J. T. BOYLE, Louisville, Kentucky:
Your several despatches received. You should call on General Halleck. Telegraph him at once. I have telegraphed him that you are in trouble.
A. LINCOLN.

TELEGRAM TO GENERAL J. T. BOYLE.

WAR DEPARTMENT, July 13, 1862.

GENERAL J. T. BOYLE, Louisville, Kentucky:
We cannot venture to order troops from General Buell. We know not what condition he is in. He maybe attacked himself. You must call on General Halleck, who commands, and whose business it is to understand and care for the whole field If you cannot telegraph to him, send a messenger to him. A dispatch has this moment come from Halleck at Tuscombia, Alabama.
A. LINCOLN.

ACT OF COMPENSATED EMANCIPATION

MESSAGE TO CONGRESS.

July 4, 1862.
FELLOW-CITIZENS OF THE SENATE AND HOUSE OF REPRESENTATIVES:
Herewith is the draft of the bill to compensate any State which may abolish slavery within its limits, the passage of which, substantially as presented, I respectfully and earnestly recommend.
A. LINCOLN.
Be it enacted by the Senate and House of Representatives of the United States of America in Congress assembled:—
That whenever the President of the United States shall be satisfied that any State shall have lawfully abolished slavery within and through-out such State, either immediately or gradually, it shall be the duty of the President, assisted by the Secretary of the Treasury, to prepare and deliver to each State an amount of six per cent. interest-bearing bonds of the United States equal to the aggregate value at ——— dollars per head of all the slaves within such State, as reported by the census of 1860; the whole amount for any one State to be delivered at once if the abolishment be immediate, or in equal annual instalments if it be gradual, interest to begin running on each bond at the time of delivery, and not before. And be it further enacted, That if any State, having so received any such bonds, shall at any time afterwards by law reintroduce or tolerate slavery within its limits, contrary to the act of abolishment upon which such bonds shall have been received, said bonds so received by said State shall at once be null and void, in whosesoever hands they may be, and such State shall refund to the United States all interest which may have been paid on such bonds.

TELEGRAM TO GENERAL H. W. HALLECK.

WAR DEPARTMENT, July 14, 1862.

MAJOR-GENERAL HALLECK, Corinth, Mississippi:
I am very anxious—almost impatient—to have you here. Have due regard to what you leave behind. When can you reach here?
A. LINCOLN.

TELEGRAM TO GENERAL G. B. McCLELLAN.

WAR DEPARTMENT, WASHINGTON CITY, July 14, 1862.

MAJOR-GENERAL McCLELLAN:
General Burnside's force is at Newport News, ready to move, on short notice, one way or the other, when ordered.
A. LINCOLN.

TO SOLOMON FOOT.

EXECUTIVE MANSION, WASHINGTON, July 15, 1862.

HON. SOLOMON FOOT, President pro tempore of the Senate.
SIR:—Please inform the Senate that I shall be obliged if they will postpone the adjournment at least one day beyond the time which I understand to be now fixed for it.
Your obedient servant,
A. LINCOLN.
[The same message was addressed to Hon. Galusha A. Grow Speaker of the House of Representatives.]

MESSAGE TO CONGRESS. July 17, 1862.

FELLOW-CITIZENS OF THE SENATE AND HOUSE OF REPRESENTATIVES:

I have inadvertently omitted so long to inform you that in March last Mr. Cornelius Vanderbilt, of New York, gratuitously presented to the United States the ocean steamer Vanderbilt, by many esteemed the finest merchant ship in the world. She has ever since been and still is doing valuable service to the government. For the patriotic act of making this magnificent and valuable present to the country I recommend that some suitable acknowledgment be made.
A. LINCOLN.

MESSAGE TO CONGRESS. July 17, 1862.

FELLOW-CITIZENS OF THE SENATE AND HOUSE OF REPRESENTATIVES:

Considering the bill for "An act to suppress insurrection, to punish treason and rebellion, to seize and confiscate the property of rebels, and for other purposes," and the joint resolution explanatory of said act as being substantially one, I have approved and signed both.

Before I was informed of the passage of the resolution I had prepared the draft of a message stating objections to the bill becoming a law, a copy of which draft is herewith transmitted.

A. LINCOLN.

FELLOW-CITIZENS OF THE HOUSE OF REPRESENTATIVES:

I herewith return to your honorable body, in which it originated, the bill for an act entitled "An act to suppress treason and rebellion, to seize and confiscate the property of rebels, and for other purposes," together with my objections to its becoming a law.

There is much in the bill to which I perceive no objection. It is wholly prospective, and touches neither person nor property of any loyal citizen, in which particulars it is just and proper. The first and second sections provide for the conviction and punishment of persons who shall be guilty of treason and persons who shall "incite, set on foot, assist, or engage in any rebellion or insurrection against the authority of the United States or the laws thereof, or shall give aid and comfort thereto, or shall engage in or give aid and comfort to any such existing rebellion or insurrection." By fair construction persons within these sections are not to be punished without regular trials in duly constituted courts, under the forms and all the substantial provisions of law and of the Constitution applicable to their several cases. To this I perceive no objection, especially as such persons would be within the general pardoning power and also the special provision for pardon and amnesty contained in this act.

It is also provided that the slaves of persons convicted under these sections shall be free. I think there is an unfortunate form of expression rather than a substantial objection in this. It is startling to say that Congress can free a slave within a State, and yet if it were said the ownership of the slave had first been transferred to the nation and that Congress had then liberated him the difficulty would at once vanish. And this is the real case. The traitor against the General Government forfeits his slave at least as justly as he does any other property, and he forfeits both to the government against which he offends. The government, so far as there can be ownership, thus owns the forfeited slaves, and the question for Congress in regard to them is, "Shall they be made free or be sold to new masters?" I perceive no objection to Congress deciding in advance that they shall be free. To the high honor of Kentucky, as I am informed, she is the owner of some slaves by escheat, and has sold none, but liberated all. I hope the same is true of some other States. Indeed, I do not believe it will be physically possible for the General Government to return persons so circumstanced to actual slavery. I believe there would be physical resistance to it which could neither be turned aside by argument nor driven away by force. In this view I have no objection to this feature of the bill. Another matter involved in these two sections, and running through other parts of the act, will be noticed hereafter.

I perceive no objection to the third or fourth sections.

So far as I wish to notice the fifth and sixth sections, they may be considered together. That the enforcement of these sections would do no injustice to the persons embraced within them, is clear. That those who make a causeless war should be compelled to pay the cost of it, is too obviously just to be called in question. To give governmental protection to the property of persons who have abandoned it, and gone on a crusade to overthrow the same government, is absurd, if considered in the mere light of justice. The severest justice may not always be the best policy. The principle of seizing and appropriating the property of the persons embraced within these sections is certainly not very objectionable, but a justly discriminating application of it would be very difficult and, to a great extent, impossible. And would it not be wise to place a power of remission somewhere, so that these persons may know they have something to lose by persisting and something to gain by desisting?

[A man without hope is a most dangerous man—he has nothing to lose!]

I am not sure whether such power of remission is or is not in section thirteen. Without any special act of Congress, I think our military commanders, when—in military phrase, "they are within the enemy's country," should, in an orderly manner, seize and use whatever of real or personal property may be necessary or convenient for their commands; at the same time preserving, in some way, the evidence of what they do.

What I have said in regard to slaves, while commenting on the first and second sections, is applicable to the ninth, with the difference that no provision is made in the whole act for determining whether a particular individual slave does or does not fall within the classes defined in that section. He is to be free upon certain conditions but whether those conditions do or do not pertain to him no mode of ascertaining is provided. This could be easily supplied.

To the tenth section I make no objection. The oath therein required seems to be proper, and the remainder of the section is substantially identical with a law already existing.

The eleventh section simply assumes to confer discretionary power upon the executive. Without the law, I have no hesitation to go as far in the direction indicated as I may at any time deem expedient. And I am ready to say now—I think it is proper for our military commanders to employ, as laborers, as many persons of African descent as can be used to advantage.

The twelfth and thirteenth sections are something better than unobjectionable; and the fourteenth is entirely proper, if all other parts of the act shall stand.

That to which I chiefly object pervades most parts of the act, but more distinctly appears in the first, second, seventh, and eighth sections. It is the sum of those provisions which results in the divesting of title forever.

For the causes of treason and ingredients of treason, not amounting to the full crime, it declares forfeiture extending beyond the lives of the guilty parties; whereas the Constitution of the United States declares that "no attainder of treason shall work corruption of blood or forfeiture except during the life of the person attainted." True, there is to be no formal attainder in this case; still, I think the greater punishment cannot be constitutionally inflicted, in a different form, for the same offence.

With great respect I am constrained to say I think this feature of the act is unconstitutional. It would not be difficult to modify it.

I may remark that the provision of the Constitution, put in language borrowed from Great Britain, applies only in this country, as I understand, to real or landed estate.

Again, this act in rem forfeits property for the ingredients of treason without a conviction of the supposed criminal, or a personal hearing given him in any proceeding. That we may not touch property lying within our reach, because we cannot give personal notice to an owner who is absent endeavoring to destroy the government, is certainly not satisfactory. Still, the owner may not be thus engaged; and I think a reasonable time should be provided for such parties to appear and have personal hearings. Similar provisions are not uncommon in connection with proceedings in rem.

For the reasons stated, I return the bill to the House in which it originated.

TELEGRAM TO GENERAL G. B. McCLELLAN.

WAR DEPARTMENT, WASHINGTON CITY, D.C., July 21, 1862.

MAJOR-GENERAL McCLELLAN:
This is Monday. I hope to be able to tell you on Thursday what is to be done with Burnside.
A. LINCOLN.

ORDER IN REGARD TO BEHAVIOR OF ALIENS

WAR DEPARTMENT, ADJUTANT-GENERAL'S OFFICE,

WASHINGTON, July 21, 1862.
The following order has been received from the President of the United States:
Representations have been made to the President by the ministers of various foreign powers in amity with the United States that subjects of such powers have during the present insurrection been obliged or required by military authorities to take an oath of general or qualified allegiance to this government. It is the duty of all aliens residing in the United States to submit to and obey the laws and respect the authority of the government. For any proceeding or conduct inconsistent with this obligation and subversive of that authority they may rightfully be subjected to military restraints when this may be necessary. But they cannot be required to take an oath of allegiance to this government, because it conflicts with the duty they owe to their own sovereigns. All such obligations heretofore taken are therefore remitted and annulled. Military commanders will abstain from imposing similar obligations in future, and will in lieu thereof adopt such other restraints of the character indicated as they shall find necessary, convenient, and effectual for the public safety. It is further directed that whenever any order shall be made affecting the personal liberty of an alien reports of the same and of the causes thereof shall be made to the War Department for the consideration of the Department of State.
By order of the Secretary of War:
L. THOMAS, Adjutant-General.

ORDER AUTHORIZING EMPLOYMENT OF "CONTRABANDS."

WAR DEPARTMENT, July 22, 1862.

Ordered:
1. That military commanders within the States of Virginia, South Carolina, Georgia, Florida, Alabama, Mississippi, Louisiana, Texas, and Arkansas in an orderly manner seize and use any property, real or personal, which may be necessary or convenient for their several commands as supplies or for other military purposes; and that while property may be destroyed for proper military objects, none shall be destroyed in wantonness or malice.
2. That military and naval commanders shall employ as laborers within and from said States so many persons of African descent as can be advantageously used for military or naval purposes, giving them reasonable wages for their labor.
3. That as to both property and persons of African descent accounts shall be kept sufficiently accurate and in detail to show quantities and amounts and from whom both property and such persons shall have come, as a basis upon which compensation can be made in proper cases; and the several departments of this government shall attend to and perform their appropriate parts toward the execution of these orders.
By order of the President: EDWIN M. STANTON, Secretary of War.

WARNING TO REBEL SYMPATHIZERS

PROCLAMATION, JULY 25, 1862.

THE PRESIDENT OF THE UNITED STATES OF AMERICA:
A Proclamation.
In pursuance of the sixth section of the act of Congress entitled "An act to suppress insurrection and to punish treason and rebellion, to seize and confiscate property of rebels, and for other purposes," approved July 17, 1862, and which act and the joint resolution explanatory thereof are herewith published, I, Abraham Lincoln, President of the United States, do hereby proclaim to and warn all persons within the contemplation of said sixth section to cease participating in, aiding, countenancing, or abetting the existing rebellion or any rebellion against the Government of the United States and to return to their proper allegiance to the United States, on pain of the forfeitures and seizures as within and by said sixth section provided.
In testimony whereof I have hereunto set my hand and caused the seal of the United States to be affixed.
Done at the city of Washington, this twenty-fifth day of July, A.D. 1862, and of the independence of the United States the eighty-seventh.
A. LINCOLN.
By the President: WILLIAM H. SEWARD, Secretary of State.

HOLD MY HAND WHILST THE ENEMY STABS ME

TO REVERDY JOHNSON.

(Private.)
EXECUTIVE MANSION, WASHINGTON, July 26, 1862.
HON. REVERDY JOHNSON.
MY DEAR SIR:—Yours of the 16th is received...........
You are ready to say I apply to friends what is due only to enemies. I distrust the wisdom if not the sincerity of friends who would hold my hands while my enemies stab me. This appeal of professed friends has paralyzed me more in this struggle than any other one thing. You remember telling me, the day after the Baltimore mob in April, 1861, that it would crush all Union feeling in Maryland for me to attempt bringing troops over Maryland soil to Washington. I

brought the troops notwithstanding, and yet there was Union feeling enough left to elect a Legislature the next autumn, which in turn elected a very excellent Union United States senator! I am a patient man—always willing to forgive on the Christian terms of repentance, and also to give ample time for repentance. Still, I must save this government, if possible. What I cannot do, of course, I will not do; but it may as well be understood, once for all, that I shall not surrender this game leaving any available card unplayed.

Yours truly,
A. LINCOLN.

TO CUTHBERT BULLITT.

(Private.)

WASHINGTON, D. C., July 28, 1862.
CUTHBERT BULLITT, Esq., New Orleans, Louisiana.
SIR:—The copy of a letter addressed to yourself by Mr. Thomas J. Durant has been shown to me. The writer appears to be an able, a dispassionate, and an entirely sincere man. The first part of the letter is devoted to an effort to show that the secession ordinance of Louisiana was adopted against the will of a majority of the people. This is probably true, and in that fact may be found some instruction. Why did they allow the ordinance to go into effect? Why did they not assert themselves? Why stand passive and allow themselves to be trodden down by minority? Why did they not hold popular meetings and have a convention of their own to express and enforce the true sentiment of the State? If preorganization was against them then, why not do this now that the United States army is present to protect them? The paralysis—the dead palsy—of the government in this whole struggle is that this class of men will do nothing for the government, nothing for themselves, except demanding that the government shall not strike its open enemies, lest they be struck by accident!

Mr. Durant complains that in various ways the relation of master and slave is disturbed by the presence of our army, and he considers it particularly vexatious that this, in part, is done under cover of an act of Congress, while constitutional guaranties are suspended on the plea of military necessity. The truth is, that what is done and omitted about slaves is done and omitted on the same military necessity. It is a military necessity to have men and money; and we can get neither in sufficient numbers or amounts if we keep from or drive from our lines slaves coming to them. Mr. Durant cannot be ignorant of the pressure in this direction, nor of my efforts to hold it within bounds till he and such as he shall have time to help themselves.

I am not posted to speak understandingly on all the police regulations of which Mr. Durant complains. If experience shows any one of them to be wrong, let them be set right. I think I can perceive in the freedom of trade which Mr. Durant urges that he would relieve both friends and enemies from the pressure of the blockade. By this he would serve the enemy more effectively than the enemy is able to serve himself. I do not say or believe that to serve the enemy is the purpose, of Mr. Durant, or that he is conscious of any purpose other than national and patriotic ones. Still, if there were a class of men who, having no choice of sides in the contest, were anxious only to have quiet and comfort for themselves while it rages, and to fall in with the victorious side at the end of it without loss to themselves, their advice as to the mode of conducting the contest would be precisely such as his is. He speaks of no duty—apparently thinks of none—resting upon Union men. He even thinks it injurious to the Union cause that they should be restrained in trade and passage without taking sides. They are to touch neither a sail nor a pump, but to be merely passengers—deadheads at that—to be carried snug and dry throughout the storm, and safely landed right side up. Nay, more: even a mutineer is to go untouched, lest these sacred passengers receive an accidental wound. Of course the rebellion will never be suppressed in Louisiana if the professed Union men there will neither help to do it nor permit the government to do it without their help. Now, I think the true remedy is very different from what is suggested by Mr. Durant. It does not lie in rounding the rough angles of the war, but in removing the necessity for the war. The people of Louisiana who wish protection to person and property have but to reach forth their hands and take it. Let them in good faith reinaugurate the national authority, and set up a State government conforming thereto under the Constitution. They know how to do it and can have the protection of the army while doing it. The army will be withdrawn so soon as such State government can dispense with its presence; and the people of the State can then, upon the old constitutional terms, govern themselves to their own liking. This is very simple and easy.

If they will not do this—if they prefer to hazard all for the sake of destroying the government—it is for them to consider whether it is probable I will surrender the government to save them from losing all. If they decline what I suggest, you scarcely need to ask what I will do. What would you do in my position? Would you drop the war where it is? Or would you prosecute it in future with elder-stalk squirts charged with rose water? Would you deal lighter blows rather than

heavier ones? Would you give up the contest, leaving any available means unapplied? I am in no boastful mood. I shall not do more than I can, and I shall do all I can, to save the government, which is my sworn duty as well as my personal inclination. I shall do nothing in malice. What I deal with is too vast for malicious dealing.
Yours truly,
A. LINCOLN.

TO LOYAL GOVERNORS.

WAR DEPARTMENT, WASHINGTON, D.C.,

July 28, 1862.
GOVERNORS OF ALL LOYAL STATES:
It would be of great service here for us to know, as fully as you can tell, what progress is made and making in recruiting for old regiments in your State. Also about what day the first regiments can move with you, what the second, what the third, and so on. This information is important to us in making calculations. Please give it as promptly and accurately as you call.
A. LINCOLN.

BROKEN EGGS CANNOT BE MENDED

EXTRACT FROM LETTER TO AUGUST BELMONT.

July 31, 1862.
Broken eggs cannot be mended; but Louisiana has nothing to do now but to take her place in the Union as it was, barring the already broken eggs. The sooner she does so, the smaller will be the amount of that which will be past mending. This government cannot much longer play a game in which it stakes all, and its enemies stake nothing. Those enemies must understand that they cannot experiment for ten years trying to destroy the government, and if they fail, still come back into the Union unhurt. If they expect in any contingency to ever have the Union as it was, I join with the writer in saying, "Now is the time."
How much better it would have been for the writer to have gone at this, under the protection of the army at New Orleans, than to have sat down in a closet writing complaining letters northward!
Yours truly,
A. LINCOLN.

TO COUNT GASPARIN.

EXECUTIVE MANSION, WASHINGTON,

August 4, 1863.
TO COUNT A. DE GASPARIN.
DEAR SIR—Your very acceptable letter, dated Orbe, Canton de Vaud, Switzerland, 18th of July, 1862, is received. The moral effect was the worst of the affair before Richmond, and that has run its course downward. We are now at a stand, and shall soon be rising again, as we hope. I believe it is true that, in men and material, the enemy suffered more than we in that series of conflicts, while it is certain that he is less able to bear it.
With us every soldier is a man of character, and must be treated with more consideration than is customary in Europe. Hence our great army, for slighter causes than could have prevailed there, has dwindled rapidly, bringing the necessity for a new call earlier than was anticipated. We shall easily obtain the new levy, however. Be not alarmed if you shall learn that we shall have resorted to a draft for part of this. It seems strange even to me, but it is true, that the government is now pressed to this course by a popular demand. Thousands who wish not to personally enter the service are

nevertheless anxious to pay and send substitutes, provided they can have assurance that unwilling persons, similarly situated, will be compelled to do likewise. Besides this, volunteers mostly choose to enter newly forming regiments, while drafted men can be sent to fill up the old ones, wherein man for man they are quite doubly as valuable.

You ask, "Why is it that the North with her great armies so often is found with inferiority of numbers face to face with the armies of the South?" While I painfully know the fact, a military man, which I am not, would better answer the question. The fact I know has not been overlooked, and I suppose the cause of its continuance lies mainly in the other facts that the enemy holds the interior and we the exterior lines, and that we operate where the people convey information to the enemy, while he operates where they convey none to us.

I have received the volume and letter which you did me the honor of addressing to me, and for which please accept my sincere thanks. You are much admired in America for the ability of your writings, and much loved for your generosity to us and your devotion to liberal principles generally.

You are quite right as to the importance to us, for its bearing upon Europe, that we should achieve military successes, and the same is true for us at home as well as abroad. Yet it seems unreasonable that a series of successes, extending through half a year, and clearing more than 100,000 square miles of country, should help us so little, while a single half-defeat should hurt us so much. But let us be patient.

I am very happy to know that my course has not conflicted with your judgment of propriety and policy I can only say that I have acted upon my best convictions, without selfishness or malice, and that by the help of God I shall continue to do so.

Please be assured of my highest respect and esteem.

A. LINCOLN.

SPEECH AT A WAR MEETING, WASHINGTON, AUGUST 6, 1862

FELLOW CITIZENS: I believe there is no precedent for my appearing before you on this occasion, but it is also true that there is no precedent for your being here yourselves, and I offer in justification of myself and of you that, upon examination, I have found nothing in the Constitution against it. I, however, have an impression that; there are younger gentlemen who will entertain you better and better address your understanding than I will or could, and therefore I propose but to detain you a moment longer. I am very little inclined on any occasion to say anything unless I hope to produce some good by it. The only thing I think of just now not likely to be better said by some one else is a matter in which we have heard some other persons blamed for what I did myself There has been a very widespread attempt to have a quarrel between General McClellan and the Secretary of War Now, I occupy a position that enables me to believe that these two gentlemen are not nearly so deep in the quarrel as some presuming to be their friends. General McClellan's attitude is such that in the very selfishness of his nature he cannot but wish to be successful—and I hope he will—and the Secretary of War is precisely in the same situation. If the military commanders in the field cannot be successful, not only the Secretary of War, but myself, for the time being the master of both, cannot but be failures. I know General McClellan wishes to be successful, and I know he does not wish it any more than the Secretary of War for him, and both of them together no more than I wish it. Sometimes we have a dispute about how many men General McClellan has had, and those who would disparage him say he has had a very large number, and those who would disparage the Secretary of War insist that General McClellan has had a very small number. The basis for this is, there is always a wide difference, and on this occasion perhaps a wider one, between the grand total on McClellan's rolls and the men actually fit for duty; and those who would disparage him talk of the grand total on paper, and those who would disparage the Secretary of War talk of those at present fit for duty. General McClellan has sometimes asked for things that the Secretary of War did not give him. General McClellan is not to blame for asking for what he wanted and needed, and the Secretary of War is not to blame for not giving when he had none to give. And I say here, so far as I know, the Secretary of War has withheld no one thing at any time in my power to give him. I have no accusation against him. I believe he is a brave and able man, and I stand here, as justice requires me to do, to take upon myself what has been charged on the Secretary of War as withholding from him. I have talked longer than I expected to do, and now I avail myself of my privilege of saying no more.

TELEGRAM TO GOVERNOR ANDREW. August 12, 1862.

WAR DEPARTMENT, WASHINGTON CITY, D.C.

GOVERNOR ANDREW, Boston, Mass.:

Your despatch saying "I can't get those regiments off because I can't get quick work out of the V. S. disbursing officer and the paymaster" is received. Please say to these gentlemen that if they do not work quickly I will make quick work with them. In the name of all that is reasonable, how long does it take to pay a couple of regiments? We were never more in need of the arrival of regiments than now—even to-day.

A. LINCOLN.

TELEGRAM TO GOVERNOR CURTIN. August 12, 1862.

WAR DEPARTMENT, WASHINGTON, D.C.

GOVERNOR CURTIN, Harrisburg, Penn.:

It is very important for some regiments to arrive here at once. What lack you from us? What can we do to expedite matters? Answer.

A. LINCOLN.

TELEGRAM TO GENERAL S. R. CURTIS. August 12, 1862.

WASHINGTON, D. C.

MAJOR-GENERAL CURTIS, St. Louis, Missouri:

Would the completion of the railroad some distance farther in the direction of Springfield, Mo., be of any military advantage to you? Please answer.

A. LINCOLN.

ADDRESS ON COLONIZATION TO A DEPUTATION OF COLORED MEN.

WASHINGTON, Thursday, August 14, 1862.

This afternoon the President of the United States gave an audience to a committee of colored men at the White House. They were introduced by Rev. J. Mitchell, Commissioner of Emigration, E. M. Thomas, the chairman, remarked that they were there by invitation to hear what the Executive had to say to them.

Having all been seated, the President, after a few preliminary observations, informed them that a sum of money had been appropriated by Congress, and placed at his disposition, for the purpose of aiding the colonization, in some country, of the people, or a portion of them, of African descent, thereby making it his duty, as it had for a long time been his inclination, to favor that cause. And why, he asked, should the people of your race be colonized, and where? Why should they leave this country? This is, perhaps, the first question for proper consideration. You and we are different races. We have between us a broader difference than exists between almost any other two races. Whether it is right or wrong I need not discuss; but this physical difference is a great disadvantage to us both, as I think. Your race suffer very greatly, many of them, by living among us, while ours suffer from your presence. In a word, we suffer on each side. If this is admitted, it affords a reason, at least, why we should be separated. You here are free men, I suppose. [A voice—"Yes, sir!"]

Perhaps you have long been free, or all your lives. Your race are suffering, in my judgment, the greatest wrong inflicted on any people. But even when you cease to be slaves, you are yet far removed from being placed on an equality with the white race. You are cut off from many of the advantages which the other race enjoys. The aspiration of men is to enjoy equality with the best when free, but on this broad continent not a single man of your race is made the equal of a single man of ours. Go where you are treated the best, and the ban is still upon you. I do not propose to discuss this, but to present it as a fact, with which we have to deal. I cannot alter it if I would. It is a fact about which we all think and feel alike, I and you. We look to our condition. Owing to the existence of the two races on this continent, I need not recount to you the effects upon white men, growing out of the institution of slavery.

I believe in its general evil effects on the white race. See our present condition—the country engaged in war—white men cutting one another's throats—none knowing how far it will extend—and then consider what we know to be the truth: But for your race among us there could not be war, although many men engaged on either side do not care for you one way or the other. Nevertheless I repeat, without the institution of slavery and the colored race as a basis, the war could not have an existence. It is better for us both, therefore, to be separated. I know that there are free men among you, who, even if they could better their condition, are not as much inclined to go out of the country as those who, being slaves, could obtain their freedom on this condition. I suppose one of the principal difficulties in the way of colonization is that the free colored man cannot see that his comfort would be advanced by it. You may believe that you can live in WASHINGTON, or elsewhere in the United States, the remainder of your life, as easily, perhaps more so, than you can in any foreign Country; and hence you may come to the conclusion that you have nothing to do with the idea of going to a foreign country.

This is (I speak in no unkind sense) an extremely selfish view of the case. You ought to do something to help those who are not so fortunate as yourselves. There is an unwillingness on the part of our people, harsh as it may be, for you free colored people to remain with us. Now, if you could give a start to the white people, you would open a wide door for many to be made free. If we deal with those who are not free at the beginning, and whose intellects are clouded by slavery, we have very poor material to start with. If intelligent colored men, such as are before me, would move in this matter, much might be accomplished.

It is exceedingly important that we have men at the beginning capable of thinking as white men, and not those who have been systematically oppressed. There is much to encourage you. For the sake of your race you should sacrifice something of your present comfort for the purpose of being as grand in that respect as the white people. It is a cheering thought throughout life that something can be done to ameliorate the condition of those who have been subject to the hard usages of the world. It is difficult to make a man miserable while he feels he is worthy of himself and claims kindred to the great God who made him. In the American Revolutionary war sacrifices were made by men engaged in it, but they were cheered by the future. General WASHINGTON himself endured greater physical hardships than if he had remained a British subject, yet he was a happy man because he had engaged in benefiting his race, in doing something for the children of his neighbors, having none of his own.

The colony of Liberia has been in existence a long time. In a certain sense it is a success. The old President of Liberia, Roberts, has just been with me—the first time I ever saw him. He says they have within the bounds of that colony between three and four hundred thousand people, or more than in some of our old States, such as Rhode Island or Delaware, or in some of our newer States, and less than in some of our larger ones. They are not all American colonists or their descendants. Something less than 12,000 have been sent thither from this country. Many of the original settlers have died; yet, like people else-where, their offspring outnumber those deceased. The question is, if the colored people are persuaded to go anywhere, why not there?

One reason for unwillingness to do so is that some of you would rather remain within reach of the country of your nativity. I do not know how much attachment you may have toward our race. It does not strike me that you have the greatest reason to love them. But still you are attached to them, at all events.

The place I am thinking about for a colony is in Central America. It is nearer to us than Liberia not much more than one fourth as far as Liberia, and within seven days' run by steamers. Unlike Liberia, it is a great line of travel—it is a highway. The country is a very excellent one for any people, and with great natural resources and advantages, and especially because of the similarity of climate with your native soil, thus being suited to your physical condition. The particular place I have in view is to be a great highway from the Atlantic or Caribbean Sea to the Pacific Ocean, and this particular place has all the advantages for a colony. On both sides there are harbors—among the finest in the world. Again, there is evidence of very rich coal-mines. A certain amount of coal is valuable in any country. Why I attach so much importance to coal is, it will afford an opportunity to the inhabitants for immediate employment till they get ready to settle permanently in their homes. If you take colonists where there is no good landing, there is a bad show; and so where there is nothing to cultivate and of which to make a farm. But if something is started so that you can get your daily bread as soon as reach you there, it is a great advantage. Coal land is the best thing I know of with which to commence an enterprise. To return—you have been talked to upon this subject, and told that a speculation is intended by gentlemen who have an interest in the country, including the coal-mines. We have been mistaken all our lives if we do not know whites, as well as blacks, look to their self-interest. Unless among those deficient of intellect, everybody you trade with makes something. You meet with these things here and everywhere. If such persons have what will be an advantage to them, the question is whether it cannot be made of advantage to you. You are intelligent, and know that success does not so much depend on external help as on self-reliance. Much, therefore, depends upon yourselves. As to the coal-mines, I think I see the means available for your self-reliance. I shall, if I get a sufficient number of you engaged, have provision made that you shall not be wronged. If you will engage in the enterprise, I will spend some of the money intrusted to me. I am not sure you will succeed. The government may lose the money; but we cannot succeed unless we try, and we think with care we can succeed. The political affairs in Central America are not in quite as satisfactory a condition as I wish. There are contending factions in that quarter, but it is true all the factions are agreed alike on the subject of colonization, and want it, and are more generous than we are here.

To your colored race they have no objection I would endeavor to have you made the equals, and have the best assurance that you should be the equals, of the best.

The practical thing I want to ascertain is whether I can get a number of able-bodied men, with their wives and children, who are willing to go when I present evidence of encouragement and protection. Could I get a hundred tolerably intelligent men, with their wives and children, and able to "cut their own fodder," so to speak? Can I have fifty? If I could find twenty-five able-bodied men, with a mixture of women and children—good things in the family relation, I think,—I could make a successful commencement. I want you to let me know whether this can be done or not. This is the practical part of my wish to see you. These are subjects of very great importance, worthy of a month's study, instead of a speech delivered in an hour. I ask you, then, to consider seriously, not pertaining to yourselves merely, nor for your race and ours for the present time, but as one of the things, if successfully managed, the good of mankind—not confined to the present generation, but as

"From age to age descends the lay
To millions yet to be,
Till far its echoes roll away
Into eternity."

The above is merely given as the substance of the President's remarks.

The chairman of the delegation briefly replied that they would hold a consultation, and in a short time give an answer. The President said: Take your full time-no hurry at all.

The delegation then withdrew.

TELEGRAM TO OFFICER AT CAMP CHASE, OHIO.

WAR DEPARTMENT, WASHINGTON, D. C., August 14, 1862.

OFFICER in charge of Confederate prisoners at Camp Chase, Ohio:
It is believed that a Dr. J. J. Williams is a prisoner in your charge, and if so tell him his wife is here and allow him to telegraph to her.
A. LINCOLN.

TO HIRAM BARNEY.

EXECUTIVE MANSION, WASHINGTON, August 16, 1862.

HON. HIRAM BARNEY, New York:
Mrs. L. has $1000 for the benefit of the hospitals and she will be obliged, and send the pay, if you will be so good as to select and send her $200 worth of good lemons and $100 worth of good oranges.
A. LINCOLN.

NOTE OF INTRODUCTION.

The Secretary of the Treasury and the Commissioner of Internal Revenue will please see Mr. Talcott, one of the best men there is, and, if any difference, one they would like better than they do me.
August 18, 1862
A. LINCOLN TELEGRAM TO S. B. MOODY
EXECUTIVE MANSION, WASHINGTON August 18, 1862
S. B. MOODY, Springfield, Ill.:

Which do you prefer—commissary or quartermaster? If appointed it must be without conditions.
A. LINCOLN.
Operator please send above for President. JOHN HAY

TO Mrs. PRESTON.

WAR DEPARTMENT, WASHINGTON, D. C., August 21, 1862.

Mrs. MARGARET PRESTON, Lexington, Ky.:
Your despatch to Mrs. L. received yesterday. She is not well. Owing to her early and strong friendship for you, I would gladly oblige you, but I cannot absolutely do it. If General Boyle and Hon. James Guthrie, one or both, in their discretion see fit to give you the passes, this is my authority to them for doing so.
A. LINCOLN.

TELEGRAM TO GENERAL BURNSIDE OR GENERAL PARKE.

WASHINGTON, August 21.

TO GENERAL BURNSIDE OR GENERAL PARKE:
What news about arrival of troops?
A. LINCOLN.

TO G. P. WATSON.

EXECUTIVE MANSION, WASHINGTON, D. C., August 21, 1862.

GILLET F. WATSON, Williamsburg, Va.:
Your telegram in regard to the lunatic asylum has been received. It is certainly a case of difficulty, but if you cannot remain, I cannot conceive who under my authority can. Remain as long as you safely can and provide as well as you can for the poor inmates of the institution.
A. LINCOLN.

TO HORACE GREELEY.

EXECUTIVE MANSION, WASHINGTON, August 22, 1862.

HON. HORACE GREELEY.
DEAR SIR:—I have just read yours of the 19th, addressed to myself through the New York Tribune. If there be in it any statements or assumptions of fact which I may know to be erroneous, I do not now and here controvert them. If there be in it any inferences which I may believe to be falsely drawn, I do not now and here argue against them. If there be perceptible in it an impatient and dictatorial tone, I waive it in deference to an old friend, whose heart I have always supposed to be right.
As to the policy I "seem to be pursuing," as you say, I have not meant to leave any one in doubt.
I would save the Union. I would save it the shortest way under the Constitution. The sooner the national authority can be restored, the nearer the Union will be, "the Union as it was." If there be those who would not save the Union unless they could at the same time save slavery, I do not agree with them. If there be those who would not save the Union

unless they could at the same time destroy slavery, I do not agree with them. My paramount object in this struggle is to save the Union, and is not either to save or destroy slavery. If I could save the Union without freeing any slave, I would do it; and if I could save it by freeing all the slaves, I would do it; and if I could do it by freeing some and leaving others alone, I would also do that. What I do about slavery and the colored race, I do because I believe it helps to save this Union; and what I forbear, I forbear because I do not believe it would help to save the Union. I shall do less whenever I shall believe what I am doing hurts the cause, and I shall do more whenever I shall believe doing more will help the cause. I shall try to correct errors when shown to be errors; and I shall adopt new views so fast as they shall appear to be true views. I have here stated my purpose according to my view of official duty, and I intend no modification of my oft expressed personal wish that all men, everywhere, could be free.
Yours,
A. LINCOLN.

TELEGRAM TO GOVERNOR YATES.

WAR DEPARTMENT, WASHINGTON, D.C., August 13.1862. 8 A.M.

HON. R. YATES, Springfield, Ill.:
I am pained to hear that you reject the service of an officer we sent to assist in organizing and getting off troops. Pennsylvania and Indiana accepted such officers kindly, and they now have more than twice as many new troops in the field as all the other States together. If Illinois had got forward as many troops as Indiana, Cumberland Gap would soon be relieved from its present peril. Please do not ruin us on punctilio.
A. LINCOLN.

TELEGRAM TO GOVERNOR RAMSEY.

EXECUTIVE MANSION, August 27, 1862

GOVERNOR RAMSEY, St. Paul, Minnesota:
Yours received. Attend to the Indians. If the draft cannot proceed, of course it will not proceed. Necessity knows no law. The government cannot extend the time.
A. LINCOLN.

TELEGRAM TO GENERAL G. B. McCLELLAN.

WASHINGTON CITY, August 27, 1862 4 P.M.

MAJOR-GENERAL McCLELLAN, Alexandria, Virginia:
What news from the front?
A. LINCOLN.

TELEGRAM TO GENERAL A. E. BURNSIDE.

August 27, 1862 4.30 p.m.

MAJOR-GENERAL BURNSIDE, Falmouth, Virginia:
Do you hear anything from Pope?

A. LINCOLN.

TELEGRAM TO GENERAL A. E. BURNSIDE.

August 28, 1862. 2.40 P. M.

MAJOR-GENERAL BURNSIDE, Falmouth, Virginia:
Any news from General Pope?
A. LINCOLN

TELEGRAM TO COLONEL HAUPT.

August 28, 1862. 2.40 p. m.

COLONEL HAUPT, Alexandria, Virginia:
Yours received. How do you learn that the rebel forces at Manassas are large and commanded by several of their best generals?
A. LINCOLN,

TELEGRAM TO GENERAL A. E. BURNSIDE.

WASHINGTON, D. C., August 29, 1862. 2.30 P.M.

MAJOR-GENERAL BURNSIDE, Falmouth, Virginia:
Any further news? Does Colonel Devon mean that sound of firing was heard in direction of Warrenton, as stated, or in direction of Warrenton Junction?
A. LINCOLN

TELEGRAM TO GENERAL G. B. McCLELLAN.

WASHINGTON, August 29, 1862. 2.30 p.m.

MAJOR-GENERAL McCLELLAN
What news from direction of Manassas Junction? What generally?
A. LINCOLN.

TELEGRAM TO GENERAL G. B. McCLELLAN.

WASHINGTON, August 29, 1862. 4.10 P.M.

MAJOR-GENERAL McCLELLAN: Yours of to-day just received. I think your first alternative—to wit, "to concentrate all our available forces to open communication with Pope"—is the right one, but I wish not to control. That I now leave to General Halleck, aided by your counsels.

A. LINCOLN.

TELEGRAM TO COLONEL HAUPT.

WAR DEPARTMENT, WASHINGTON, D. C., August 30, 1862. 10.20 A.M.

COLONEL HAUPT Alexandria, Virginia:
What news?
A. LINCOLN.

TELEGRAM TO COLONEL HAUPT.

WAR DEPARTMENT, August 30, 1862. 3.50 P.M. COLONEL HAUPT, Alexandria, Virginia
Please send me the latest news.
A. LINCOLN.

TELEGRAM TO GENERAL BANKS.

August 30, 1862. 8.35 P.M.

MAJOR-GENERAL BANKS, Manassas Junction, Virginia:
Please tell me what news.
A. LINCOLN.

TELEGRAM TO GENERAL J. T. BOYLE.

WAR DEPARTMENT, August 31, 1862.

GENERAL BOYLE, Louisville, Kentucky:
What force, and what the numbers of it, which General Nelson had in the engagement near Richmond yesterday?
A. LINCOLN.

ORDER TO GENERAL H. W. HALLECK.

WASHINGTON, D. C., September 3, 1862.

Ordered, That the general-in-chief, Major-General Halleck, immediately commence, and proceed with all possible despatch; to organize an army, for active operations, from all the material within and coming within his control, independent of the forces he may deem necessary for the defense of Washington when such active army shall take the field.
By order of the President:
EDWIN M. STANTON, Secretary of War.
[Indorsement.]

Copy delivered to Major-General Halleck, September 3, 1862, at 10 p.m.
E. D. TOWNSEND, Assistant-Adjutant General.

TELEGRAM TO GENERAL H. G. WRIGHT.

WAR DEPARTMENT, WASHINGTON, D. C., September 7, 1862.

GENERAL WRIGHT, Cincinnati, Ohio:
Do you know to any certainty where General Bragg is? May he not be in Virginia?
A. LINCOLN.

TELEGRAM TO GENERAL J. T. BOYLE.

WAR DEPARTMENT, WASHINGTON, D. C., September 7, 1862.

GENERAL BOYLE, Louisville, Kentucky:
Where is General Bragg? What do you know on the subject?
A. LINCOLN.

TELEGRAM TO GENERAL J. E. WOOL.

WAR DEPARTMENT, WASHINGTON, D.C.

September 7, 1862.
MAJOR-GENERAL Wool, Baltimore:
What about Harper's Ferry? Do you know anything about it? How certain is your information about Bragg being in the valley of the Shenandoah?
A. LINCOLN.

TELEGRAM TO GENERAL G. B, McCLELLAN.

WASHINGTON, September 8, 1862. 5 P.M.

MAJOR-GENERAL McCLELLAN, Rockville, Maryland:
How does it look now?
A. LINCOLN.

TELEGRAM TO GENERAL D. C. BUELL.

WAR DEPARTMENT, WASHINGTON, September 8, 1862. 7.20 P.M.

GENERAL BUELL:
What degree of certainty have you that Bragg, with his command, is not now in the valley of the Shenandoah, Virginia?

A. LINCOLN.

TELEGRAM TO T. WEBSTER.

WASHINGTON, September 9, 1862.

THOMAS WEBSTER, Philadelphia:
Your despatch received, and referred to General Halleck, who must control the questions presented. While I am not surprised at your anxiety, I do not think you are in any danger. If half our troops were in Philadelphia, the enemy could take it, because he would not fear to leave the other half in his rear; but with the whole of them here, he dares not leave them in his rear.
A. LINCOLN.

TELEGRAM TO GENERAL G. B. McCLELLAN.

WAR DEPARTMENT, WASHINGTON CITY, September 10, 1862. 10.15 AM.

MAJOR-GENERAL McCLELLAN, Rockville, Maryland:
How does it look now?
A. LINCOLN.

TO GOVERNOR CURTIN. September 11, 1862.

WAR DEPARTMENT, WASHINGTON, D.C.,

HIS EXCELLENCY ANDREW G. CURTIN, Governor of Pennsylvania, Harrisburg, Pennsylvania.
SIR:—The application made to me by your adjutant general for authority to call out the militia of the State of Pennsylvania has received careful consideration. It is my anxious desire to afford, as far as possible, the means and power of the Federal Government to protect the State of Pennsylvania from invasion by the rebel forces; and since, in your judgment, the militia of the State are required, and have been called upon by you, to organize for home defense and protection, I sanction the call that you have made, and will receive them into the service and pay of the United States to the extent they can be armed, equipped, and usefully employed. The arms and equipments now belonging to the General Government will be needed for the troops called out for the national armies, so that arms can only be furnished for the quota of militia furnished by the draft of nine months' men, heretofore ordered. But as arms may be supplied by the militia under your call, these, with the 30,000 in your arsenal, will probably be sufficient for the purpose contemplated by your call. You will be authorized to provide such equipments as may be required, according to the regulations of the United States service, which, upon being turned over to the United States Quartermaster's Department, will be paid for at regulation prices, or the rates allowed by the department for such articles. Railroad transportation will also be paid for, as in other cases. Such general officers will be supplied as the exigencies of the service will permit.
Yours truly,
A. LINCOLN.

TELEGRAM TO GOVERNOR CURTIN.

WASHINGTON, September 11, 1862 12M

HON. ANDREW G. CURTIN:
Please tell me at once what is your latest news from or toward Hagerstown, or of the enemy's movement in any direction.
A. LINCOLN.

TELEGRAM TO GENERAL C. B. McCLELLAN.

EXECUTIVE MANSION, SEPTEMBER 11, 1862. 6 PM

MAJOR-GENERAL McCLELLAN:
This is explanatory. If Porter, Heintzelman, and Sigel were sent you, it would sweep everything from the other side of the river, because the new troops have been distributed among them, as I understand. Porter reports himself 21,000 strong, which can only be by the addition of new troops. He is ordered tonight to join you as quickly as possible. I am for sending you all that can be spared, and I hope others can follow Porter very soon,
A. LINCOLN.

TELEGRAM TO GENERAL G. B. McCLELLAN.

WASHINGTON CITY, D.C., SEPTEMBER 12, 1862

MAJOR-GENERAL McCLELLAN, Clarksburg, Maryland:
How does it look now?
A. LINCOLN.

TELEGRAM TO GOVERNOR CURTIN.

WAR DEPARTMENT, WASHINGTON D.C., SEPTEMBER 12, 1862 10.35 AM

HON. ANDREW G. CURTIN, Harrisburg, Pennsylvania:
Your despatch asking for 80,000 disciplined troops to be sent to Pennsylvania is received. Please consider we have not to exceed 80,000 disciplined troops, properly so called, this side of the mountains; and most of them, with many of the new regiments, are now close in the rear of the enemy supposed to be invading Pennsylvania. Start half of them to Harrisburg, and the enemy will turn upon and beat the remaining half, and then reach Harrisburg before the part going there, and beat it too when it comes. The best possible security for Pennsylvania is putting the strongest force possible in rear of the enemy.
A. LINCOLN.

TELEGRAM TO GENERAL H. G. WRIGHT.

MILITARY TELEGRAPH, WASHINGTON, September 12, 1862.

MAJOR-GENERAL WRIGHT, Cincinnati, Ohio:
I am being appealed to from Louisville against your withdrawing troops from that place. While I cannot pretend to judge of the propriety of what you are doing, you would much oblige me by furnishing me a rational answer to make to the governor and others at Louisville.

A. LINCOLN.

TELEGRAM TO GENERAL J. T. BOYLE.

WASHINGTON, September 12, 1862.

MAJOR-GENERAL BOYLE, Louisville, Kentucky:
Your despatch of last evening received. Where is the enemy which you dread in Louisville? How near to you? What is General Gilbert's opinion? With all possible respect for you, I must think General Wright's military opinion is the better. He is as much responsible for Louisville as for Cincinnati. General Halleck telegraphed him on this very subject yesterday, and I telegraph him now; but for us here to control him there on the ground would be a babel of confusion which would be utterly ruinous. Where do you understand Buell to be, and what is he doing?
A. LINCOLN.

TELEGRAM TO A. HENRY.

WAR DEPARTMENT, WASHINGTON, D. C, September 12, 1862.

HON. ALEXANDER HENRY, Philadelphia:
Yours of to-day received. General Halleck has made the best provision he can for generals in Pennsylvania. Please do not be offended when I assure you that in my confident belief Philadelphia is in no danger. Governor Curtin has just telegraphed me: "I have advices that Jackson is crossing the Potomac at Williamsport, and probably the whole rebel army will be drawn from Maryland." At all events, Philadelphia is more than 150 miles from Hagerstown, and could not be reached by the rebel army in ten days, if no hindrance was interposed.
A. LINCOLN.

TELEGRAM TO GENERAL G. B. McCLELLAN.

WASHINGTON CITY, D.C., September 12, 1862. 5.45 PM

MAJOR-GENERAL McCLELLAN:
Governor Curtin telegraphs me:
"I have advices that Jackson is crossing the Potomac at Williamsport, and probably the whole rebel army will be down from Maryland."
Receiving nothing from Harper's Ferry or Martinsburg to-day, and positive information from Wheeling that the line is cut, corroborates the idea that the enemy is crossing the Potomac. Please do not let him get off without being hurt.
A. LINCOLN.
[But he did! D.W.]

REPLY TO REQUEST THE PRESIDENT ISSUE A PROCLAMATION OF EMANCIPATION.

A COMMITTEE FROM THE RELIGIOUS DENOMINATIONS OF CHICAGO,

September 13,1862.
The subject presented in the memorial is one upon which I have thought much for weeks past, and I may even say for months. I am approached with the most opposite opinions and advice, and that by religious men, who are equally

certain that they represent the Divine will. I am sure that either the one or the other class is mistaken in that belief, and perhaps in some respects both. I hope it will not be irreverent for me to say that if it is probable that God would reveal his will to others, on a point so connected with my duty, it might be supposed he would reveal it directly to me; for, unless I am more deceived in myself than I often am, it is my earnest desire to know the will of Providence in this matter. And if I can learn what it is I will do it! These are not, however, the days of miracles, and I suppose it will be granted that I am not to expect a direct revelation. I must study the plain physical facts of the case, ascertain what is possible, and learn what appears to be wise and right.

The subject is difficult, and good men do not agree. For instance, the other day, four gentlemen of standing and intelligence from New York called as a delegation on business connected with the war; but before leaving two of them earnestly besought me to proclaim general emancipation, upon which the other two at once attacked them. You know also that the last session of Congress had a decided majority of antislavery men, yet they could not unite on this policy. And the same is true of the religious people. Why, the rebel soldiers are praying with a great deal more earnestness, I fear, than our own troops, and expecting God to favor their side: for one of our soldiers who had been taken prisoner told Senator Wilson a few days since that he met nothing so discouraging as the evident sincerity of those he was among in their prayers. But we will talk over the merits of the case.

What good would a proclamation of emancipation from me do, especially as we are now situated? I do not want to issue a document that the whole world will see must necessarily be inoperative, like the Pope's bull against the comet! Would my word free the slaves, when I cannot even enforce the Constitution in the rebel States? Is there a single court, or magistrate or individual that would be influenced by it there? And what reason is there to think it would have any greater effect upon the slaves than the late law of Congress, which I approved, and which offers protection and freedom to the slaves of rebel masters who come within our lines? Yet I cannot learn that that law has caused a single slave to come over to us. And suppose they could be induced by a proclamation of freedom from me to throw themselves upon us, what should we do with them? How can we feed and care for such a multitude? General Butler wrote me a few days since that he was issuing more rations to the slaves who have rushed to him than to all the white troops under his command. They eat, and that is all; though it is true General Butler is feeding the whites also by the thousand; for it nearly amounts to a famine there. If, now, the pressure of the war should call off our forces from New Orleans to defend some other point, what is to prevent the masters from reducing the blacks to slavery again? for I am told that whenever the rebels take any black prisoners, free or slave, they immediately auction them off. They did so with those they took from a boat that was aground in the Tennessee River a few days ago. And then I am very ungenerously attacked for it! For instance, when, after the late battles at and near Bull Run, an expedition went out from Washington under a flag of truce to bury the dead and bring in the wounded, and the rebels seized the blacks who went along to help, and sent them into slavery, Horace Greeley said in his paper that the government would probably do nothing about it. What could I do?

Now, then, tell me, if you please, what possible result of good would follow the issuing of such a proclamation as you desire? Understand, I raise no objections against it on legal or constitutional grounds; for, as commander-in-chief of the army and navy, in time of war I suppose I have a right to take any measure which may best subdue the enemy; nor do I urge objections of a moral nature, in view of possible consequences of insurrection and massacre at the South. I view this matter as a practical war measure, to be decided on according to the advantages or disadvantages it may offer to the suppression of the rebellion.

I admit that slavery is the root of the rebellion, or at least its sine qua non. The ambition of politicians may have instigated them to act, but they would have been impotent without slavery as their instrument. I will also concede that emancipation would help us in Europe, and convince them that we are incited by something more than ambition. I grant, further, that it would help somewhat at the North, though not so much, I fear, as you and those you represent imagine. Still, some additional strength would be added in that way to the war, and then, unquestionably, it would weaken the rebels by drawing off their laborers, which is of great importance; but I am not so sure we could do much with the blacks. If we were to arm them, I fear that in a few weeks the arms would be in the hands of the rebels; and, indeed, thus far we have not had arms enough to equip our white troops. I will mention another thing, though it meet only your scorn and contempt. There are fifty thousand bayonets in the Union armies from the border slave States. It would be a serious matter if, in consequence of a proclamation such as you desire, they should go over to the rebels. I do not think they all would—not so many, indeed, as a year ago, or as six months ago—not so many to-day as yesterday. Every day increases their Union feeling. They are also getting their pride enlisted, and want to beat the rebels. Let me say one thing more: I think you should admit that we already have an important principle to rally and unite the people, in the fact that constitutional government is at stake. This is a fundamental idea going down about as deep as anything. Do not misunderstand me because I have mentioned these objections. They indicate the difficulties that have thus far prevented my action in some such way as you desire. I have not decided against a proclamation of liberty to the slaves, but hold the matter under advisement; and I can assure you that the subject is on my mind, by day and night, more than any other. Whatever shall appear to be God's will, I will do. I trust that in the freedom with which I have canvassed your views I have not in any respect injured your feelings.

TELEGRAM TO GENERAL H. G. WRIGHT.

WAR DEPARTMENT, WASHINGTON, D. C., September 14, 1862.

GENERAL WRIGHT, Cincinnati, Ohio:
Thanks for your despatch. Can you not pursue the retreating enemy, and relieve Cumberland Gap?
A. LINCOLN.

TELEGRAM TO GENERAL G. B. McCLELLAN.

WAR DEPARTMENT, WASHINGTON,

September 15, 1862. 2.45 P.M.
MAJOR-GENERAL McCLELLAN:
Your despatch of to-day received. God bless you, and all with you. Destroy the rebel army if possible.
A. LINCOLN.

TELEGRAM TO J. K. DUBOIS. WASHINGTON, D.C.,

September 15, 1862. 3 P.M.

HON. K. DUBOIS, Springfield, Illinois:
I now consider it safe to say that General McClellan has gained a great victory over the great rebel army in Maryland, between Fredericktown and Hagerstown. He is now pursuing the flying foe.
A. LINCOLN.
[But not very fast—and he did not catch them! D.W.]

TELEGRAM TO GOVERNOR CURTIN,

WASHINGTON, D. C., September 16, 1862. Noon.

GOVERNOR CURTIN, Harrisburg:
What do you hear from General McClellan's army? We have nothing from him to-day.
A. LINCOLN.

TELEGRAM TO GOVERNOR MORTON.

WASHINGTON, D.C., September 17, 1862.

GOVERNOR O. P. MORTON, Indianapolis, Indiana:
I have received your despatch in regard to recommendations of General Wright. I have received no such despatch from him, at least not that I can remember. I refer yours for General Halleck's consideration.

A. LINCOLN.

TELEGRAM TO GENERAL KETCHUM.

EXECUTIVE MANSION, WASHINGTON, September 20, 1862.

GENERAL KETCHUM, Springfield, Illinois:
How many regiments are there in Illinois, ready for service but for want of arms? How many arms have you there ready for distribution?
A. LINCOLN.

PRELIMINARY EMANCIPATION PROCLAMATION, SEPTEMBER 22, 1862.

THE PRESIDENT OF THE UNITED STATES OF AMERICA:

A Proclamation.
I, Abraham Lincoln, President of the United States of America and Commander-in-Chief of the Army and Navy thereof, do hereby proclaim and declare that hereafter, as heretofore, the war will be prosecuted for the object of practically restoring the constitutional relation between the United States and each of the States and the people thereof in which States that relation is or may be suspended or disturbed.
That it is my purpose, upon the next meeting of Congress, to again recommend the adoption of a practical measure tendering pecuniary aid to the free acceptance or rejection of all slave States, so called, the people whereof may not then be in rebellion against the United States, and which States may then have voluntarily adopted, or thereafter may voluntarily adopt, immediate or gradual abolishment of slavery within their respective limits; and that the effort to colonize persons of African descent with their consent upon this continent or elsewhere, with the previously obtained consent of the governments existing there, will be continued.
That on the 1st day of January, A.D. 1863, all persons held as slaves within any State or designated part of a State the people whereof shall then be in rebellion against the United States shall be then, thenceforward, and forever free; and the executive government of the United States, including the military and naval authority thereof, will recognize and maintain the freedom of such persons and will do no act or acts to repress such persons, or any of them, in any efforts they may make for their actual freedom.
That the Executive will on the 1st day of January aforesaid, by proclamation, designate the States and parts of States, if any, in which the people thereof, respectively, shall then be in rebellion against the United States; and the fact that any State or the people thereof shall on that day be in good faith represented in the Congress of the United States by members chosen thereto at elections wherein a majority of the qualified voters of such State shall have participated shall, in the absence of strong countervailing testimony, be deemed conclusive evidence that such State and the people thereof are not then in rebellion against the United States.
That attention is hereby called to an act of Congress entitled "An act to make an additional article of war," approved March 13, 1862, and which act is in the words and figure following:
"Be it enacted by the Senate and House of Representatives of the United States of America in Congress assembled, That hereafter the following shall be promulgated as an additional article of war for the government of the Army of the United States and shall be obeyed and observed as such.
"ART. All officers or persons in the military or naval service of the United States are prohibited from employing any of the forces under their respective commands for the purpose of returning fugitives from service or labor who may have escaped from any person, to whom such service or labor is claimed to be due, and any officer who shall be found guilty by a court-martial of violating this article shall be dismissed from the service.
"SEC. 2. And be it further enacted, That this act shall take effect from and after its passage."
Also to the ninth and tenth sections of an act entitled "An act to suppress insurrection, to punish treason and rebellion, to seize and confiscate the property of rebels, and for other purposes," approved July 17, 1862, and which sections are in the words and figures following:
"SEC. 9. And be it further enacted, That all slaves of persons who shall hereafter be engaged in rebellion against the Government of the United States, or who shall in any way give aid or comfort thereto, escaping from such persons and

taking refuge within the lines of the army, and all slaves captured from such persons or deserted by them and coming under the control of the Government of the United States, and all slaves of such persons found on (or) being within any place occupied by rebel forces and afterwards occupied by the forces of the United States, shall be deemed captives of war and shall be forever free of their servitude and not again held as slaves.

"SEC. 9. And be it further enacted, That no slave escaping into any State, Territory, or the District of Columbia from any other State shall be delivered up or in any way impeded or hindered of his liberty, except for crime, or some offence against the laws, unless the person claiming said fugitive shall first make oath that the person to whom the labor or service of such fugitive is alleged to be due is his lawful owner, and has not borne arms against the United States in the present rebellion, nor in any way given aid and comfort thereto; and no person engaged in the military or naval service of the United States shall, under any pretense whatever, assume to decide on the validity of the claim of any person to the service or labor of any other person, or surrender up any such person to the claimant, on pain of being dismissed from the service."

And I do hereby enjoin upon and order all persons engaged in the military and naval service of the United States to observe, obey, and enforce, within their respective spheres of service, the act and sections above recited.

And the Executive will in due time recommend that all citizens of the United States who shall have remained loyal thereto throughout the rebellion shall (upon the restoration of the constitutional relation between the United States and their respective States and people, if that relation shall have been suspended or disturbed) be compensated for all losses by acts of the United States, including the loss of slaves.

In witness whereof, I have hereunto set my hand and caused the seal of the United States to be affixed.

Done at the City of Washington, this twenty-second day of September, in the year of our Lord one thousand eight hundred and sixty-two, and of the independence of the United States the eighty-seventh.

A. LINCOLN.

By the President: WILLIAM H. SEWARD, Secretary of State.

PROCLAMATION SUSPENDING THE WRIT OF HABEAS CORPUS,

SEPTEMBER 24, 1862.

THE PRESIDENT OF THE UNITED STATES OF AMERICA

A Proclamation

Whereas it has become necessary to call into service not only volunteers, but also portions of the militia of the States by draft, in order to suppress the insurrection existing in the United States, and disloyal persons are not adequately restrained by the ordinary processes of law from hindering this measure, and from giving aid and comfort in various ways to the insurrection:

Now, therefore, be it ordered

First. That during the existing insurrection, and as a necessary measure for suppressing the same, all rebels and insurgents, their aiders and abettors within the United States, and all persons discouraging volunteer enlistments, resisting militia drafts, or guilty of any disloyal practice affording aid and comfort to rebels against the authority of the United States, shall be subject to martial law, and liable to trial and punishment by courts-martial or military commissions.

Second. That the writ of habeas corpus is suspended in respect to all persons arrested, or who are now, or hereafter during the rebellion shall be, imprisoned in any fort camp, arsenal, military prison or other place of confinement by any military authority or by the sentence of any court-martial or military commission.

In witness whereof I have hereunto set my hand and caused the seal of the United States to be affixed.

Done at the city of WASHINGTON, this twenty-fourth day of September. A.D. eighteen hundred and sixty-two, and of the independence of the United States the eighty-seventh.

A. LINCOLN.

By the President: WILLIAM H. SEWARD, Secretary of State.

REPLY TO SERENADE, SEPTEMBER 24, 1862.

I appear before you to do little more than acknowledge the courtesy you pay me, and to thank you for it. I have not been distinctly informed why it is that on this occasion you appear to do me this honor, though I suppose it is because of the proclamation. What I did, I did after a very full deliberation, and under a very heavy and solemn sense of responsibility. I can only trust in God I have made no mistake. I shall make no attempt on this occasion to sustain what I have done or said by any comment. It is now for the country and the world to pass judgment and, maybe, take action upon it.

I will say no more upon this subject. In my position I am environed with difficulties. Yet they are scarcely so great as the difficulties of those who upon the battle-field are endeavoring to purchase with their blood and their lives the future happiness and prosperity of this country. Let us never forget them. On the fourteenth and seventeenth days of this present month there have been battles bravely, skillfully, and successfully fought. We do not yet know the particulars. Let us be sure that, in giving praise to certain individuals, we do no injustice to others. I only ask you, at the conclusion of these few remarks, to give three hearty cheers for all good and brave officers and men who fought those successful battles.

RECORD EXPLAINING THE DISMISSAL OF MAJOR JOHN J. KEY

FROM THE MILITARY SERVICE OF THE UNITED STATES.

EXECUTIVE MANSION, WASHINGTON,
September 26, 1862.
MAJOR JOHN J. KEY:
I am informed that, in answer to the question, "Why was not the rebel army bagged immediately after the battle near Sharpsburg?" propounded to you by Major Levi C. Turner, Judge Advocate, etc., you said: "That is not the game. The object is, that neither army shall get much advantage of the other; that both shall be kept in the field till they are exhausted, when we will make a compromise and save slavery."
I shall be very happy if you will, within twenty-four hours from the receipt of this, prove to me by Major Turner that you did not, either literally or in substance, make the answer stated.
[Above delivered to Major Key at 10.25 a.m. September 27th.]
At about 11 o'clock A.M., September 27, 1862, Major Key and Major Turner appeared before me. Major Turner says: "As I remember it, the conversation was: 'Why did we not bag them after the battle of Sharpsburg?' Major Key's reply was: 'That was not the game; that we should tire the rebels out and ourselves; that that was the only way the Union could be preserved, we come together fraternally, and slavery be saved.'"
On cross-examination, Major Turner says he has frequently heard Major Key converse in regard to the present troubles, and never heard him utter a sentiment unfavorable to the maintenance of the Union. He has never uttered anything which he, Major T., would call disloyalty. The particular conversation detailed was a private one.
[Indorsement on the above.]
In my view, it is wholly inadmissible for any gentleman holding a military commission from the United States to utter such sentiments as Major Key is within proved to have done. Therefore, let Major John J. Key be forthwith dismissed from the military service of the United States.
A. LINCOLN.

TO HANNIBAL HAMLIN.

(Strictly private.)

EXECUTIVE MANSION, WASHINGTON,
September 28, 1862.
HON. HANNIBAL HAMLIN.
MY DEAR SIR: Your kind letter of the 25th is just received. It is known to some that, while I hope something from the proclamation, my expectations are not as sanguine as are those of some friends. The time for its effect southward has not come; but northward the effect should be instantaneous. It is six days old, and, while commendation in newspapers and by distinguished individuals is all that a vain man could wish, the stocks have declined, and troops

come forward more slowly than ever. This, looked soberly in the face, is not very satisfactory. We have fewer troops in the field at the end of the six days than we had at the beginning—the attrition among the old outnumbering the addition by the new. The North responds to the proclamation sufficiently in breath; but breath alone kills no rebels.
I wish I could write more cheerfully; nor do I thank you the less for the kindness of your letter.
Yours very truly,
A. LINCOLN.

TO GENERAL HALLECK.

McCLELLAN'S HEADQUARTERS, October 3, 1862.

MAJOR-GENERAL HALLECK:
General Stuart, of the rebel army, has sent in a few of our prisoners under a flag of truce, paroled with terms to prevent their fighting the Indians, and evidently seeking to commit us to their right to parole prisoners in that way. My inclination is to send the prisoners back with a definite notice that we will recognize no paroles given to our prisoners by the rebels as extending beyond a prohibition against fighting them, though I wish your opinion upon it, based both upon the general law and our cartel. I wish to avoid violations of the law and bad faith. Answer as quickly as possible, as the thing, if done at all, should be done at once.
A. LINCOLN, President

REMARKS TO THE ARMY OF THE POTOMAC AT FREDERICK, MARYLAND,

OCTOBER, 4, 1862.

I am surrounded by soldiers and a little farther off by the citizens of this good City of Frederick. Nevertheless I can only say, as I did five minutes ago, it is not proper for me to make speeches in my present position. I return thanks to our soldiers for the good services they have rendered, the energy they have shown, the hardships they have endured, and the blood they have shed for this Union of ours; and I also return thanks, not only to the soldiers, but to the good citizens of Frederick, and to the good men, women, and children in this land of ours, for their devotion to this glorious cause; and I say this with no malice in my heart towards those who have done otherwise. May our children and children's children, for a thousand generations, continue to enjoy the benefits conferred upon us by a united country, and have cause yet to rejoice under these glorious institutions, bequeathed to us by WASHINGTON and his compeers. Now, my friends, soldiers and citizens, I can only say once more-farewell.

TELEGRAM FROM GENERAL HALLECK

TO GENERAL G. B. McCLELLAN., WASHINGTON, D. C., October 6, 1862.

MAJOR-GENERAL McCLELLAN:
I am instructed to telegraph you as follows: The President directs that you cross the Potomac and give battle to the enemy, or drive him south. Your army must move now, while the roads are good. If you cross the river between the enemy and Washington, and cover the latter by your operation, you can be reinforced by thirty thousand men. If you move up the valley of the Shenandoah, not more than twelve or fifteen thousand can be sent you. The President advises the interior line between Washington and the enemy, but does not order it. He is very desirous that your army move as soon as possible. You will immediately report what line you adopt, and when you intend to cross the river; also to what point the reinforcements are to be sent. It is necessary that the plan of your operations be positively determined on, before orders are given for building bridges and repairing railroads. I am directed to add that the Secretary of War and the General-in-chief fully concur with the President in these directions.
H. W. HALLECK, General-in-Chief.

TELEGRAM TO GENERAL McCLELLAN.

EXECUTIVE MANSION, WASHINGTON, October 7, 1862.

MAJOR-GENERAL McCLELLAN, Hdqs. Army of the Potomac:
You wish to see your family and I wish to oblige you. It might be left to your own discretion; certainly so, if Mrs. M. could meet you here at Washington.
A. LINCOLN.

TO T. H. CLAY.

WAR DEPARTMENT, October 8, 1862.

THOMAS H. CLAY, Cincinnati, Ohio:
You cannot have reflected seriously when you ask that I shall order General Morgan's command to Kentucky as a favor because they have marched from Cumberland Gap. The precedent established by it would evidently break up the whole army. Buell's old troops, now in pursuit of Bragg, have done more hard marching recently; and, in fact, if you include marching and fighting, there are scarcely any old troops east or west of the mountains that have not done as hard service. I sincerely wish war was an easier and pleasanter business than it is; but it does not admit of holidays. On Morgan's command, where it is now sent, as I understand, depends the question whether the enemy will get to the Ohio River in another place.
A. LINCOLN.

TELEGRAM TO GENERAL U. S. GRANT.

WASHINGTON, D.C., October 8, 1862

MAJOR-GENERAL GRANT:
I congratulate you and all concerned in your recent battles and victories. How does it all sum up? I especially regret the death of General Hackleman, and am very anxious to know the condition of General Oglesby, who is an intimate personal friend.
A. LINCOLN.

TELEGRAM TO GENERAL J. T. BOYLE.

WAR DEPARTMENT, October 11, 1862. 4 P.M.

GENERAL BOYLE, Louisville, Kentucky:
Please send any news you have from General Buell to-day.
A. LINCOLN.

TELEGRAM TO GENERAL J. T. BOYLE.

WAR DEPARTMENT, October 12, 1862. 4.10 P.M.

GENERAL BOYLE, Louisville, Kentucky:
We are anxious to hear from General Buell's army. We have heard nothing since day before yesterday. Have you anything?
A. LINCOLN.

TELEGRAM TO GENERAL CURTIS.

WASHINGTON, D. C., October 12, 1862.

MAJOR-GENERAL CURTIS, Saint Louis, Missouri:
Would the completion of the railroad some distance further in the direction of Springfield, Mo., be of any military advantage to you? Please answer.
A. LINCOLN.

TO GENERAL G. B. McCLELLAN.

EXECUTIVE MANSION, WASHINGTON, October 13, 1862.

MY DEAR SIR—You remember my speaking to you of what I called your over-cautiousness. Are you not over-cautious when you assume that you cannot do what the enemy is constantly doing? Should you not claim to be at least his equal in prowess, and act upon the claim?
As I understand, you telegraphed General Halleck that you cannot subsist your army at Winchester unless the railroad from Harper's Ferry to that point be put in working order. But the enemy does now subsist his army at Winchester, at a distance nearly twice as great from railroad transportation as you would have to do, without the railroad last named. He now wagons from Culpepper Court-House, which is just about twice as far as you would have to do from Harper's Ferry. He is certainly not more than half as well provided with wagons as you are. I certainly should be pleased for you to have the advantage of the railroad from Harper's Ferry to Winchester; but it wastes all the remainder of autumn to give it to you, and, in fact, ignores the question of time, which cannot and must not be ignored.
Again, one of the standard maxims of war, as you know, is "to operate upon the enemy's communications as much as possible, without exposing your own." You seem to act as if this applies against you, but cannot apply in your favor. Change positions with the enemy, and think you not he would break your communication with Richmond within the next twenty-four hours? You dread his going into Pennsylvania. But if he does so in full force, he gives up his communications to you absolutely, and you have nothing to do but to follow and ruin him; if he does so with less than full force, fall upon and beat what is left behind all the easier.
Exclusive of the water line, you are now nearer to Richmond than the enemy is, by the route that you can and he must take. Why can you not reach there before him, unless you admit that he is more than your equal on a march? His route is the arc of a circle, while yours is the chord. The roads are as good on yours as on his.
You know I desired, but did not order, you to cross the Potomac below instead of above the Shenandoah and Blue Ridge. My idea was, that this would at once menace the enemy's communications, which I would seize if he would permit. If he should move northward, I would follow him closely, holding his communications. If he should prevent our seizing his communications, and move toward Richmond, I would press closely to him, fight him if a favorable opportunity should present, and at least try to beat him to Richmond on the inside track. I say "try;" if we never try, we shall never succeed. If he makes a stand at Winchester, moving neither north or south, I would fight him there, on the idea that if we cannot beat him when he bears the wastage of coming to us, we never can when we bear the wastage of going to him. This proposition is a simple truth, and is too important to be lost sight of for a moment. In coming to us he tenders us an advantage which we should not waive. We should not so operate as to merely drive him away. As we must beat him somewhere or fail finally, we can do it, if at all, easier near to us than far away. If we cannot beat the enemy where he now is, we never can, he again being within the entrenchments of Richmond.

[And, indeed, the enemy was let back into Richmond and it took another two years and thousands of dead for McClelland cowardice—if that was all that it was. I still suspect, and I think the evidence is overwhelming that he was, either secretly a supporter of the South, or, what is more likely, a politician readying for a different campaign: that of the Presidency of the United States.]

Recurring to the idea of going to Richmond on the inside track, the facility of supplying from the side away from the enemy is remarkable, as it were, by the different spokes of a wheel extending from the hub toward the rim, and this whether you move directly by the chord or on the inside arc, hugging the Blue Ridge more closely. The chord line, as you see, carries you by Aldie, Hay Market, and Fredericksburg; and you see how turnpikes, railroads, and finally the Potomac, by Aquia Creek, meet you at all points from WASHINGTON; the same, only the lines lengthened a little, if you press closer to the Blue Ridge part of the way.

The gaps through the Blue Ridge I understand to be about the following distances from Harper's Ferry, to wit: Vestal's, 5 miles; Gregory's, 13; Snicker's, 18; Ashby's, 28; Manassas, 38; Chester, 45; and Thornton's, 53. I should think it preferable to take the route nearest the enemy, disabling him to make an important move without your knowledge, and compelling him to keep his forces together for dread of you. The gaps would enable you to attack if you should wish. For a great part of the way you would be practically between the enemy and both WASHINGTON and Richmond, enabling us to spare you the greatest number of troops from here. When at length running for Richmond ahead of him enables him to move this way, if he does so, turn and attack him in rear. But I think he should be engaged long before such a point is reached. It is all easy if our troops march as well as the enemy, and it is unmanly to say they cannot do it. This letter is in no sense an order.

Yours truly,
A. LINCOLN.

TELEGRAM TO GOVERNOR PIERPOINT.

WAR DEPARTMENT, WASHINGTON CITY, D. C., October 16, 1862.

GOVERNOR PIERPOINT, Wheeling, Virginia:

Your despatch of to-day received. I am very sorry to have offended you. I appointed the collector, as I thought, on your written recommendation, and the assessor also with your testimony of worthiness, although I know you preferred a different man. I will examine to-morrow whether I am mistaken in this.
A. LINCOLN.

EXECUTIVE ORDER ESTABLISHING A PROVISIONAL COURT IN LOUISIANA.

EXECUTIVE MANSION, WASHINGTON CITY,

October 20, 1862.

The insurrection which has for some time prevailed in several of the States of this Union, including Louisiana, having temporarily subverted and swept away the civil institutions of that State, including the judiciary and the judicial authorities of the Union, so that it has become necessary to hold the State in military Occupation, and it being indispensably necessary that there shall be some judicial tribunal existing there capable of administering justice, I have therefore thought it proper to appoint, and I do hereby constitute, a provisional court, which shall be a court of record, for the State of Louisiana; and I do hereby appoint Charles A Peabody, of New York, to be a provisional judge to hold said court, with authority to hear, try, and determine all causes, civil and criminal, including causes in law, equity, revenue, and admiralty, and particularly all such powers and jurisdiction as belong to the district and circuit courts of the United States, conforming his proceedings so far as possible to the course of proceedings and practice which has been customary in the courts of the United States and Louisiana, his judgment to be final and conclusive. And I do hereby authorize and empower the said judge to make and establish such rules and regulations as may be necessary for the exercise of his jurisdiction, and empower the said judge to appoint a prosecuting attorney, marshal, and clerk of the said court, who shall perform the functions of attorney, marshal, and clerk according to such proceedings and practice as before mentioned and such rules and regulations as may be made and established by said judge. These appointments are to continue during the pleasure of the President, not extending beyond the military occupation of the city of New

Orleans or the restoration of the civil authority in that city and in the State of Louisiana. These officers shall be paid, out of the contingent fund of the War Department, compensation as follows:

The judge at the rate of $3500 per annum; the prosecuting attorney, including the fees, at the rate of $3000 per annum; the marshal, including the fees, at the rate of $3000 per annum; and the clerk, including the fees, at the rate of $2500 per annum; such compensations to be certified by the Secretary of War. A copy of this order, certified by the Secretary of War and delivered to such judge, shall be deemed and held to be a sufficient commission.

A. LINCOLN,
President of the United States.

TO GENERAL U.S. GRANT.

EXECUTIVE MANSION, WASHINGTON,

October 21, 1862.
MAJOR-GENERAL U. S. GRANT:
The bearer of this, Thomas R. Smith, a citizen of Tennessee, goes to that State seeking to have such of the people thereof as desire to avoid the unsatisfactory prospect before them, and to have peace again upon the old terms, under the Constitution of the United States, to manifest such desire by elections of members to the Congress of the United States particularly, and perhaps a Legislature, State officers, and a United States senator friendly to their object.

I shall be glad for you and each of you to aid him, and all others acting for this object, as much as possible. In all available ways give the people a show to express their wishes at these elections.

Follow law, and forms of law, as far as convenient, but at all events get the expression of the largest number of the people possible. All see how such action will connect with and affect the proclamation of September 22. Of course the men elected should be gentlemen of character, willing to swear support to the Constitution as of old, and known to be above reasonable suspicion of duplicity.

Yours very respectfully,
A. LINCOLN.

TELEGRAM TO GENERAL JAMESON.

EXECUTIVE MANSION, WASHINGTON, October 21, 1862.

GENERAL JAMESON, Upper Stillwater, Me.:
How is your health now? Do you or not wish Lieut. R. P. Crawford to be restored to his office?
A. LINCOLN.

GENERAL McCLELLAN'S TIRED HORSES

TELEGRAM TO GENERAL G. B. McCLELLAN.

WAR DEPARTMENT, WASHINGTON CITY, October 24 [25?], 1862.
MAJOR-GENERAL McCLELLAN:
I have just read your despatch about sore-tongued and fatigued horses. Will you pardon me for asking what the horses of your army have done since the battle of Antietam that fatigues anything?
A. LINCOLN.

TELEGRAM TO GENERAL G. B. McCLELLAN.

EXECUTIVE MANSION WASHINGTON, October 26, 1862. 11.30am

MAJOR-GENERAL McCLELLAN:
Yours, in reply to mine about horses, received. Of course you know the facts better than I; still two considerations remain: Stuart's cavalry outmarched ours, having certainly done more marked service on the Peninsula and everywhere since. Secondly, will not a movement of our army be a relief to the cavalry, compelling the enemy to concentrate instead of foraging in squads everywhere? But I am so rejoiced to learn from your despatch to General Halleck that you begin crossing the river this morning.
A. LINCOLN.

TO GENERAL DIX.

(Private and confidential.)

EXECUTIVE MANSION, WASHINGTON October 26, 1862.
MAJOR-GENERAL Dix, Fort Monroe, Virginia:
Your despatch to Mr. Stanton, of which the enclosed is a copy, has been handed me by him. It would be dangerous for me now to begin construing and making specific applications of the proclamation.
It is obvious to all that I therein intended to give time and opportunity. Also, it is seen I left myself at liberty to exempt parts of States. Without saying more, I shall be very glad if any Congressional district will, in good faith, do as your despatch contemplates.
Could you give me the facts which prompted you to telegraph?
Yours very truly,
A. LINCOLN.

TELEGRAM TO GENERAL G. B. McCLELLAN.

EXECUTIVE MANSION, WASHINGTON, October 27, 1862, 12.10

MAJOR-GENERAL McCLELLAN:
Yours of yesterday received. Most certainly I intend no injustice to any, and if I have done any I deeply regret it. To be told, after more than five weeks' total inaction of the army, and during which period we have sent to the army every fresh horse we possibly could, amounting in the whole to 7918, that the cavalry horses were too much fatigued to move, presents a very cheerless, almost hopeless, prospect for the future, and it may have forced something of impatience in my despatch. If not recruited and rested then, when could they ever be? I suppose the river is rising, and I am glad to believe you are crossing.
A. LINCOLN.

TELEGRAM TO GENERAL G. B. McCLELLAN.

EXECUTIVE MANSION, WASHINGTON, October 27, 1862. 3.25pm

MAJOR-GENERAL McCLELLAN:
Your despatch of 3 P.M. to-day, in regard to filling up old regiments with drafted men, is received, and the request therein shall be complied with as far as practicable.
And now I ask a distinct answer to the question, Is it your purpose not to go into action again until the men now being drafted in the States are incorporated into the old regiments?

A. LINCOLN

TELEGRAM TO GENERAL G. B. McCLELLAN.

EXECUTIVE MANSION, WASHINGTON, October 29, 1863.

MAJOR-GENERAL McCLELLAN:
Your despatches of night before last, yesterday, and last night all received. I am much pleased with the movement of the army. When you get entirely across the river let me know. What do you know of the enemy?
A. LINCOLN.

TELEGRAM TO GOVERNOR CURTIN.

EXECUTIVE MANSION, WASHINGTON, October 30, 1862.

GOVERNOR CURTIN, Harrisburg:
By some means I have not seen your despatch of the 27th about order No.154 until this moment. I now learn, what I knew nothing of before, that the history of the order is as follows:
When General McClellan telegraphed asking General Halleck to have the order made, General Halleck went to the Secretary of War with it, stating his approval of the plan. The Secretary assented and General Halleck wrote the order. It was a military question, which the Secretary supposed the General understood better than he.
I wish I could see Governor Curtin.
A. LINCOLN.

TELEGRAM TO GOVERNOR JOHNSON.

WAR DEPARTMENT, October 31, 1862.

GOV. ANDREW JOHNSON, Nashville, Tenn., via Louisville, Ky.:
Yours of the 29th received. I shall take it to General Halleck, but I already know it will be inconvenient to take General Morgan's command from where it now is. I am glad to hear you speak hopefully of Tennessee. I sincerely hope Rosecrans may find it possible to do something for her. David Nelson, son of the M. C. of your State, regrets his father's final defection, and asks me for a situation. Do you know him? Could he be of service to you or to Tennessee in any capacity in which I could send him?
A. LINCOLN.

MEMORANDUM.

EXECUTIVE MANSION, WASHINGTON,

November 1, 1862.
TO WHOM IT MAY CONCERN: Captain Derrickson, with his company, has been for some time keeping guard at my residence, now at the Soldiers' Retreat. He and his company are very agreeable to me, and while it is deemed proper for any guard to remain, none would be more satisfactory than Captain Derrickson and his company.
A. LINCOLN.

ORDER RELIEVING GENERAL G. B. McCLELLAN

AND MAKING OTHER CHANGES.

EXECUTIVE MANSION WASHINGTON, November 5, 1862.
By direction of the President, it is ordered that Major-General McClellan be relieved from the command of the Army of the Potomac, and that Major-General Burnside take the command of that army. Also that Major-General Hunter take command of the corps in said army which is now commanded by General Burnside. That Major-General Fitz. John Porter be relieved from command of the corps he now commands in said army, and that Major-General Hooker take command of said corps.
The general-in-chief is authorized, in [his] discretion, to issue an order substantially as the above forthwith, or so soon as he may deem proper.
A. LINCOLN.

TELEGRAM TO M. F. ODELL.

EXECUTIVE MANSION WASHINGTON, November 5, 1862.

HON. M. F. ODELL, Brooklyn, New York:
You are re-elected. I wish to see you at once will you come? Please answer.
A. LINCOLN.

TELEGRAM TO COLONEL LOWE.

EXECUTIVE MANSION, WASHINGTON, November 7, 1862.

COL. W. W. LOWE, Fort Henry, Tennessee:
Yours of yesterday received. Governor Johnson, Mr. Ethridge, and others are looking after the very thing you telegraphed about.
A. LINCOLN.

TELEGRAM TO GENERAL J. POPE.

EXECUTIVE MANSION, WASHINGTON, November 10, 1862.

MAJOR-GENERAL POPE, St. Paul, Minnesota:
Your despatch giving the names of 300 Indians condemned to death is received. Please forward as soon as possible the full and complete record of their convictions; and if the record does not fully indicate the more guilty and influential of the culprits, please have a careful statement made on these points and forwarded to me. Send all by mail.
A. LINCOLN.

TO COMMODORE FARRAGUT.

EXECUTIVE MANSION, WASHINGTON, November 11, 1862.

COMMODORE FARRAGUT:
DEAR SIR:—This will introduce Major-General Banks. He is in command of a considerable land force for operating in the South, and I shall be glad for you to co-Operate with him and give him such assistance as you can consistently with your orders from the Navy Department.
Your obedient servant,
A. LINCOLN.

ORDER CONCERNING BLOCKADE.

EXECUTIVE MANSION, WASHINGTON, November 12, 1862.

Ordered, First: that clearances issued by the Treasury Department for vessels or merchandise bound for the port of Norfolk, for the military necessities of the department, certified by the military commandant at Fort Monroe, shall be allowed to enter said port.
Second: that vessels and domestic produce from Norfolk, permitted by the military commandant at Fort Monroe for the military purposes of his command, shall on his permit be allowed to pass from said port to their destination in any port not blockaded by the United States.
A. LINCOLN

ORDER CONCERNING THE CONFISCATION ACT.

EXECUTIVE MANSION, November 13, 1862.

Ordered, by the President of the United States, That the Attorney-General be charged with the superintendence and direction of all proceedings to be had under the act of Congress of the 17th of July, 1862, entitled "An act to suppress insurrection, to punish treason and rebellion, to seize and confiscate the property of rebels, and for other purposes," in so far as may concern the seizure, prosecution, and condemnation of the estate, property, and effects of rebels and traitors, as mentioned and provided for in the fifth, sixth, and seventh sections of the said act of Congress. And the Attorney-General is authorized and required to give to the attorneys and marshals of the United States such instructions and directions as he may find needful and convenient touching all such seizures, prosecutions, and condemnations, and, moreover, to authorize all such attorneys and marshals, whenever there may be reasonable ground to fear any forcible resistance to them in the discharge of their respective duties in this behalf, to call upon any military officer in command of the forces of the United States to give to them such aid, protection, and support as may be necessary to enable them safely and efficiently to discharge their respective duties; and all such commanding officers are required promptly to obey such call, and to render the necessary service as far as may be in their power consistently with their other duties.
A. LINCOLN.
By the President: EDWARD BATES, Attorney-General

TELEGRAM TO GOVERNOR JOHNSON.

WAR DEPARTMENT, November 14, 1862.

GOV. ANDREW JOHNSON, Nashville, Tennessee:
Your despatch of the 4th, about returning troops from western Virginia to Tennessee, is just received, and I have been to General Halleck with it. He says an order has already been made by which those troops have already moved, or soon will move, to Tennessee.

A. LINCOLN.

GENERAL ORDER RESPECTING THE OBSERVANCE OF THE SABBATH DAY

IN THE ARMY AND NAVY.

EXECUTIVE MANSION, WASHINGTON, November 15, 1862.
The President, Commander-in-Chief of the Army and Navy, desires and enjoins the orderly observance of the Sabbath by the officers and men in the military and naval service. The importance for man and beast of the prescribed weekly rest, the sacred rights of Christian soldiers and sailors, a becoming deference to the best sentiment of a Christian people, and a due regard for the divine will demand that Sunday labor in the army and navy be reduced to the measure of strict necessity.
The discipline and character of the national forces should not suffer nor the cause they defend be imperilled by the profanation of the day or name of the Most High. "At this time of public distress," adopting the words of Washington in 1776, "men may find enough to do in the service of God and their country without abandoning themselves to vice and immorality." The first general order issued by the Father of his Country after the Declaration of Independence indicates the spirit in which our institutions were founded and should ever be defended:
"The General hopes and trusts that every officer and man will endeavor to live and act as becomes a Christian soldier defending the dearest rights and liberties of his country."
A. LINCOLN.

TELEGRAM TO GENERAL BLAIR

EXECUTIVE MANSION, WASHINGTON, November 17,1862.

HON. F. P. BLAIR:
Your brother says you are solicitous to be ordered to join General McLernand. I suppose you are ordered to Helena; this means that you are to form part of McLernand's expedition as it moves down the river; and General McLernand is so informed. I will see General Halleck as to whether the additional force you mention can go with you.
A. LINCOLN.

TELEGRAM TO GENERAL J. A. DIX.

WASHINGTON, D. C., November 18, 1861.

MAJOR-GENERAL Dix, Fort Monroe:
Please give me your best opinion as to the number of the enemy now at Richmond and also at Petersburg.
A. LINCOLN.

TO GOVERNOR SHEPLEY.

EXECUTIVE MANSION, WASHINGTON, November 21, 1862.

HON. G. F. SHEPLEY.
DEAR SIR:—Dr. Kennedy, bearer of this, has some apprehension that Federal officers not citizens of Louisiana may be set up as candidates for Congress in that State. In my view there could be no possible object in such an election. We

do not particularly need members of Congress from there to enable us to get along with legislation here. What we do want is the conclusive evidence that respectable citizens of Louisiana are willing to be members of Congress and to swear support to the Constitution, and that other respectable citizens there are willing to vote for them and send them. To send a parcel of Northern men here as representatives, elected, as would be understood (and perhaps really so), at the point of the bayonet, would be disgusting and outrageous; and were I a member of Congress here, I would vote against admitting any such man to a seat.
Yours very truly,
A. LINCOLN,

ORDER PROHIBITING THE EXPORT OF ARMS AND MUNITIONS OF WAR.

EXECUTIVE MANSION, WASHINGTON,

November 21, 1862.
Ordered, That no arms, ammunition, or munitions of war be cleared or allowed to be exported from the United States until further orders. That any clearance for arms, ammunition, or munitions of war issued heretofore by the Treasury Department be vacated, if the articles have not passed without the United States, and the articles stopped. That the Secretary of War hold possession of the arms, etc., recently seized by his order at Rouse's Point, bound for Canada.
A. LINCOLN.

DELAYING TACTICS OF GENERALS

TO GENERAL N. P. BANKS.

EXECUTIVE MANSION, WASHINGTON, November 22, 1862.
MY DEAR GENERAL BANKS:—Early last week you left me in high hope with your assurance that you would be off with your expedition at the end of that week, or early in this. It is now the end of this, and I have just been overwhelmed and confounded with the sight of a requisition made by you which, I am assured, cannot be filled and got off within an hour short of two months. I enclose you a copy of the requisition, in some hope that it is not genuine—that you have never seen it. My dear General, this expanding and piling up of impedimenta has been, so far, almost our ruin, and will be our final ruin if it is not abandoned. If you had the articles of this requisition upon the wharf, with the necessary animals to make them of any use, and forage for the animals, you could not get vessels together in two weeks to carry the whole, to say nothing of your twenty thousand men; and, having the vessels, you could not put the cargoes aboard in two weeks more. And, after all, where you are going you have no use for them. When you parted with me you had no such ideas in your mind. I know you had not, or you could not have expected to be off so soon as you said. You must get back to something like the plan you had then, or your expedition is a failure before you start. You must be off before Congress meets. You would be better off anywhere, and especially where you are going, for not having a thousand wagons doing nothing but hauling forage to feed the animals that draw them, and taking at least two thousand men to care for the wagons and animals, who otherwise might be two thousand good soldiers. Now, dear General, do not think this is an ill-natured letter; it is the very reverse. The simple publication of this requisition would ruin you.
Very truly your friend,
A. LINCOLN.

TO CARL SCHURZ.

EXECUTIVE MANSION, WASHINGTON, November 24, 1862.

GENERAL CARL SCHURZ.

MY DEAR SIR—I have just received and read your letter of the 20th. The purport of it is that we lost the late elections and the administration is failing because the war is unsuccessful, and that I must not flatter myself that I am not justly to blame for it. I certainly know that if the war fails the administration fails, and that I will be blamed for it, whether I deserve it or not. And I ought to be blamed if I could do better. You think I could do better; therefore you blame me already. I think I could not do better; therefore I blame you for blaming me. I understand you now to be willing to accept the help of men who are not Republicans, provided they have "heart in it." Agreed. I want no others. But who is to be the judge of hearts, or of "heart in it"? If I must discard my own judgment and take yours, I must also take that of others and by the time I should reject all I should be advised to reject, I should have none left, Republicans or others not even yourself. For be assured, my dear sir, there are men who have "heart in it" that think you are performing your part as poorly as you think I am performing mine. I certainly have been dissatisfied with the slowness of Buell and McClellan; but before I relieved them I had great fears I should not find successors to them who would do better; and I am sorry to add that I have seen little since to relieve those fears.

I do not see clearly the prospect of any more rapid movements. I fear we shall at last find out that the difficulty is in our case rather than in particular generals. I wish to disparage no one certainly not those who sympathize with me; but I must say I need success more than I need sympathy, and that I have not seen the so much greater evidence of getting success from my sympathizers than from those who are denounced as the contrary. It does seem to me that in the field the two classes have been very much alike in what they have done and what they have failed to do. In sealing their faith with their blood, Baker and Lyon and Bohien and Richardson, Republicans, did all that men could do; but did they any more than Kearny and Stevens and Reno and Mansfield, none of whom were Republicans, and some at least of whom have been bitterly and repeatedly denounced to me as secession sympathizers? I will not perform the ungrateful task of comparing cases of failure.

In answer to your question, "Has it not been publicly stated in the newspapers, and apparently proved as a fact, that from the commencement of the war the enemy was continually supplied with information by some of the confidential subordinates of as important an officer as Adjutant-General Thomas?" I must say "No," as far as my knowledge extends. And I add that if you can give any tangible evidence upon the subject, I will thank you to come to this city and do so.

Very truly your friend,
A. LINCOLN.

TELEGRAM TO GENERAL A. E. BURNSIDE.

EXECUTIVE MANSION, WASHINGTON, November 25, 1862.

MAJOR-GENERAL BURNSIDE, Falmouth, Virginia:
If I should be in boat off Aquia Creek at dark tomorrow (Wednesday) evening, could you, without inconvenience, meet me and pass an hour or two with me?
A. LINCOLN.

TO ATTORNEY-GENERAL BATES.

EXECUTIVE MANSION, WASHINGTON,

November 29, 1862.
HON. ATTORNEY-GENERAL.
MY DEAR SIR:—Few things perplex me more than this question between Governor Gamble and the War Department, as to whether the peculiar force organized by the former in Missouri are State troops or United States troops. Now, this is either an immaterial or a mischievous question. First, if no more is desired than to have it settled what name the force is to be called by, it is immaterial. Secondly, if it is desired for more than the fixing a name, it can only be to get a position from which to draw practical inferences; then it is mischievous. Instead of settling one dispute by deciding the question, I should merely furnish a nest-full of eggs for hatching new disputes. I believe the force is not strictly either "State troops" or "United States troops." It is of mixed character. I therefore think it is safer, when a practical question arises, to decide that question directly, and not indirectly by deciding a general abstraction supposed

to include it, and also including a great deal more. Without dispute Governor Gamble appoints the officers of this force, and fills vacancies when they occur. The question now practically in dispute is: Can Governor Gamble make a vacancy by removing an officer or accepting a resignation? Now, while it is proper that this question shall be settled, I do not perceive why either Governor Gamble or the government here should care which way it is settled. I am perplexed with it only because there seems to be pertinacity about it. It seems to me that it might be either way without injury to the service; or that the offer of the Secretary of War to let Governor Gamble make vacancies, and he (the Secretary) to ratify the making of them, ought to be satisfactory.
Yours truly,
A. LINCOLN

TELEGRAM TO GENERAL CURTIS.

[Cipher.]

WASHINGTON, November 30, 1862.
MAJOR-GENERAL CURTIS, Saint Louis, Missouri:
Frank Blair wants Manter's Thirty-second, Curly's Twenty seventh, Boyd's Twenty-fourth and the Ninth and Tenth Cavalry to go with him down the river. I understand it is with you to decide whether he shall have them and if so, and if also it is consistent with the public service, you will oblige me a good deal by letting him have them.
A. LINCOLN.

ON EXECUTING 300 INDIANS

LETTER TO JUDGE-ADVOCATE-GENERAL.

EXECUTIVE MANSION, WASHINGTON, December 1, 1862.
JUDGE-ADVOCATE-GENERAL.
SIR:—Three hundred Indians have been sentenced to death in Minnesota by a military commission, and execution only awaits my action. I wish your legal opinion whether if I should conclude to execute only a part of them, I must myself designate which, or could I leave the designation to some officer on the ground?
Yours very truly,
A. LINCOLN.

ANNUAL MESSAGE TO CONGRESS, DECEMBER 1, 1862.

FELLOW-CITIZENS OF THE SENATE AND HOUSE OF REPRESENTATIVES—Since your last annual assembling another year of health and bountiful harvests has passed; and while it has not pleased the Almighty to bless us with a return of peace, we can but press on, guided by the best light he gives us, trusting that in his own good time and wise way all will yet be well.
The correspondence touching foreign affairs which has taken place during the last year is herewith submitted, in virtual compliance with a request to that effect, made by the House of Representatives near the close of the last session of Congress.
If the condition of our relations with other nations is less gratifying than it has usually been at former periods, it is certainly more satisfactory than a nation so unhappily distracted as we are might reasonably have apprehended. In the month of June last there were some grounds to expect that the maritime powers which, at the beginning of our domestic difficulties, so unwisely and unnecessarily, as we think, recognized the insurgents as a belligerent, would soon recede from that position, which has proved only less injurious to themselves than to our own country. But the temporary reverses which afterward befell the national arms, and which were exaggerated by our own disloyal citizens abroad, have hitherto delayed that act of simple justice.

The civil war, which has so radically changed, for the moment, the occupations and habits of the American people, has necessarily disturbed the social condition, and affected very deeply the prosperity, of the nations with which we have carried on a commerce that has been steadily increasing throughout a period of half a century. It has, at the same time, excited political ambitions and apprehensions which have produced a profound agitation throughout the civilized world. In this unusual agitation we have forborne from taking part in any controversy between foreign states, and between parties or factions in such states. We have attempted no propagandism and acknowledged no revolution, but we have left to every nation the exclusive conduct and management of its own affairs. Our struggle has been, of course, contemplated by foreign nations with reference less to its own merits than to its supposed and often exaggerated effects and consequences resulting to those nations themselves, nevertheless, complaint on the part of this government, even if it were just, would certainly be unwise.

The treaty with Great Britain for the suppression of the slave trade has been put into operation with a good prospect of complete success. It is an occasion of special pleasure to acknowledge that the execution of it on the part of her Majesty's government has been marked with a jealous respect for the authority of the United States and the rights of their moral and loyal citizens.

The convention with Hanover for the abolition of the state dues has been carried into full effect under the act of Congress for that purpose.

A blockade of 3000 miles of seacoast could not be established and vigorously enforced in a season of great commercial activity like the present without committing occasional mistakes and inflicting unintentional injuries upon foreign nations and their subjects.

A civil war occurring in a country where foreigners reside and carry on trade under treaty stipulations is necessarily fruitful of complaints of the violation of neutral rights. All such collisions tend to excite misapprehensions, and possibly to produce mutual reclamations between nations which have a common interest in preserving peace and friendship. In clear cases of these kinds I have so far as possible heard and redressed complaints which have been presented by friendly powers. There is still, however, a large and an augmenting number of doubtful cases upon which the government is unable to agree with the governments whose protection is demanded by the claimants. There are, moreover, many cases in which the United States or their citizens suffer wrongs from the naval or military authorities of foreign nations which the governments of those states are not at once prepared to redress. I have proposed to some of the foreign states thus interested mutual conventions to examine and adjust such complaints. This proposition has been made especially to Great Britain, to France, to Spain, and to Prussia. In each case it has been kindly received, but has not yet been formally adopted.

I deem it my duty to recommend an appropriation in behalf of the owners of the Norwegian bark Admiral P. Tordenskiold, which vessel was in May, 1861, prevented by the commander of the blockading force off Charleston from leaving that port with cargo, notwithstanding a similar privilege had shortly before been granted to an English vessel. I have directed the Secretary of State to cause the papers in the case to be communicated to the proper committees.

Applications have been made to me by many free Americans of African descent to favor their emigration, with a view to such colonization as was contemplated in recent acts of Congress, Other parties, at home and abroad—some from interested motives, others upon patriotic considerations, and still others influenced by philanthropic sentiments—have suggested similar measures, while, on the other hand, several of the Spanish American republics have protested against the sending of such colonies to their respective territories. Under these circumstances I have declined to move any such colony to any state without first obtaining the consent of its government, with an agreement on its part to receive and protect such emigrants in all the rights of freemen; and I have at the same time offered to the several states situated within the Tropics, or having colonies there, to negotiate with them, subject to the advice and consent of the Senate, to favor the voluntary emigration of persons of that class to their respective territories, upon conditions which shall be equal, just, and humane. Liberia and Haiti are as yet the only countries to which colonists of African descent from here could go with certainty of being received and adopted as citizens; and I regret to say such persons contemplating colonization do not seem so willing to migrate to those countries as to some others, nor so willing as I think their interest demands. I believe, however, opinion among them in this respect is improving, and that ere long there will be an augmented and considerable migration to both these countries from the United States.

The new commercial treaty between the United States and the Sultan of Turkey has been carried into execution.

A commercial and consular treaty has been negotiated, subject to the Senate's consent, with Liberia, and a similar negotiation is now pending with the Republic of Haiti. A considerable improvement of the national commerce is expected to result from these measures.

Our relations with Great Britain, France, Spain, Portugal, Russia, Prussia, Denmark, Sweden, Austria, the Netherlands, Italy, Rome, and the other European states remain undisturbed. Very favorable relations also continue to be maintained with Turkey, Morocco, China, and Japan.

During the last year there has not only been no change of our previous relations with the independent states of our own continent, but more friendly sentiments than have heretofore existed are believed to be entertained by these neighbors, whose safety and progress are so intimately connected with our own. This statement especially applies to Mexico, Nicaragua, Costa Rica, Honduras, Peru, and Chile.

The commission under the convention with the Republic of New Granada closed its session without having audited and passed upon all the claims which were submitted to it. A proposition is pending to revive the convention, that it may be able to do more complete justice. The joint commission between the United States and the Republic of Costa Rica has completed its labors and submitted its report.

I have favored the project for connecting the United States with Europe by an Atlantic telegraph, and a similar project to extend the telegraph from San Francisco to connect by a Pacific telegraph with the line which is being extended across the Russian Empire.

The Territories of the United States, with unimportant exceptions, have remained undisturbed by the civil war; and they are exhibiting such evidence of prosperity as justifies an expectation that some of them will soon be in a condition to be organized as States and be constitutionally admitted into the Federal Union.

The immense mineral resources of some of those Territories ought to be developed as rapidly as possible. Every step in that direction would have a tendency to improve the revenues of the government and diminish the burdens of the people. It is worthy of your serious consideration whether some extraordinary measures to promote that end cannot be adopted. The means which suggests itself as most likely to be effective is a scientific exploration of the mineral regions in those Territories with a view to the publication of its results at home and in foreign countries—results which cannot fail to be auspicious.

The condition of the finances win claim your most diligent consideration. The vast expenditures incident to the military and naval operations required for the suppression of the rebellion have hitherto been met with a promptitude and certainty unusual in similar circumstances, and the public credit has been fully maintained. The continuance of the war, however, and the increased disbursements made necessary by the augmented forces now in the field demand your best reflections as to the best modes of providing the necessary revenue without injury to business and with the least possible burdens upon labor.

The suspension of specie payments by the banks soon after the commencement of your last session made large issues of United States notes unavoidable. In no other way could the payment of troops and the satisfaction of other just demands be so economically or so well provided for. The judicious legislation of Congress, securing the receivability of these notes for loans and internal duties and making them a legal tender for other debts, has made them an universal currency, and has satisfied, partially at least, and for the time, the long-felt want of an uniform circulating medium, saving thereby to the people immense sums in discounts and exchanges.

A return to specie payments, however, at the earliest period compatible with due regard to all interests concerned should ever be kept in view. Fluctuations in the value of currency are always injurious, and to reduce these fluctuations to the lowest possible point will always be a leading purpose in wise legislation. Convertibility, prompt and certain convertibility, into coin is generally acknowledged to be the best and surest safeguard against them; and it is extremely doubtful whether a circulation of United States notes payable in coin and sufficiently large for the wants of the people can be permanently, usefully, and safely maintained.

Is there, then, any other mode in which the necessary provision for the public wants can be made and the great advantages of a safe and uniform currency secured?

I know of none which promises so certain results and is at the same time so unobjectionable as the organization of banking associations, under a general act of Congress, well guarded in its provisions. To such associations the government might furnish circulating notes, on the security of United States bonds deposited in the treasury. These notes, prepared under the supervision of proper officers, being uniform in appearance and security and convertible always into coin, would at once protect labor against the evils of a vicious currency and facilitate commerce by cheap and safe exchanges.

A moderate reservation from the interest on the bonds would compensate the United States for the preparation and distribution of the notes and a general supervision of the system, and would lighten the burden of that part of the public debt employed as securities. The public credit, moreover, would be greatly improved and the negotiation of new loans greatly facilitated by the steady market demand for government bonds which the adoption of the proposed system would create.

It is an additional recommendation of the measure, of considerable weight, in my judgment, that it would reconcile as far as possible all existing interests by the opportunity offered to existing institutions to reorganize under the act, substituting only the secured uniform national circulation for the local and various circulation, secured and unsecured, now issued by them.

The receipts into the treasury from all sources, including loans and balance from the preceding year, for the fiscal year ending on the 30th June, 1862, were $583,885,247.06, of which sum $49,056,397.62 were derived from customs; $1,795,331.73 from the direct tax; from public lands, $152,203.77; from miscellaneous sources, $931,787.64; from loans in all forms, $529,692,460.50. The remainder, $2,257,065.80, was the balance from last year.

The disbursements during the same period were: For congressional, executive, and judicial purposes, $5,939,009.29; for foreign intercourse, $1,339,710.35; for miscellaneous expenses, including the mints, loans, post-office deficiencies, collection of revenue, and other like charges, $14,129,771.50; for expenses under the Interior Department, $3,102,985.52; under the War Department, $394,368,407.36; under the Navy Department, $42,674,569.69; for interest on public debt, $13,190,324.45; and for payment of public debt, including reimbursement of temporary loan and redemptions, $96,096,922.09; making an aggregate of $570,841,700.25, and leaving a balance in the treasury on the 1st day of July, 1862, of $13,043,546.81.

It should be observed that the sum of $96,096,922.09, expended for reimbursements and redemption of public debt, being included also in the loans made, may be properly deducted both from receipts and expenditures, leaving the actual receipts for the year $487,788,324.97, and the expenditures $474,744,778.16.

Other information on the subject of the finances will be found in the report of the Secretary of the Treasury, to whose statements and views I invite your most candid and considerate attention.

The reports of the Secretaries of War and of the Navy are herewith transmitted. These reports, though lengthy, are scarcely more than brief abstracts of the very numerous and extensive transactions and operations conducted through those departments. Nor could I give a summary of them here upon any principle which would admit of its being much shorter than the reports themselves. I therefore content myself with laying the reports before you and asking your attention to them.

It gives me pleasure to report a decided improvement in the financial condition of the Post-Office Department as compared with several preceding years. The receipts for the fiscal year 1861 amounted to $8,349,296.40, which embraced the revenue from all the States of the Union for three quarters of that year. Notwithstanding the cessation of revenue from the so-called seceded States during the last fiscal year, the increase of the correspondence of the loyal States has been sufficient to produce a revenue during the same year of $8,299,820.90, being only $50,000 less than was derived from all the States of the Union during the previous year. The expenditures show a still more favorable result. The amount expended in 1861 was $13,606,759.11. For the last year the amount has been reduced to $11,125,364.13, showing a decrease of about $2,481,000 in the expenditures as compared with the preceding year, and about $3,750,000 as compared with the fiscal year 1860. The deficiency in the department for the previous year was $4,551,966.98. For the last fiscal year it was reduced to $2,112,814.57. These favorable results are in part owing to the cessation of mail service in the insurrectionary States and in part to a careful review of all expenditures in that department in the interest of economy. The efficiency of the postal service, it is believed, has also been much improved. The Postmaster-General has also opened a correspondence through the Department of State with foreign governments proposing a convention of postal representatives for the purpose of simplifying the rates of foreign postage and to expedite the foreign mails. This proposition, equally important to our adopted citizens and to the commercial interests of this country, has been favorably entertained and agreed to by all the governments from whom replies have been received.

I ask the attention of Congress to the suggestions of the Postmaster-General in his report respecting the further legislation required, in his opinion, for the benefit of the postal service.

The Secretary of the Interior reports as follows in regard to the public lands:

"The public lands have ceased to be a source of revenue. From the 1st July, 1861, to the 30th September, 1862, the entire cash receipts from the sale of lands were $137,476.2—a sum much less than the expenses of our land system during the same period. The homestead law, which will take effect on the 1st of January next, offers such inducements to settlers that sales for cash cannot be expected to an extent sufficient to meet the expenses of the General Land Office and the cost of surveying and bringing the land into market."

The discrepancy between the sum here stated as arising from the sales of the public lands and the sum derived from the same source as reported from the Treasury Department arises, as I understand, from the fact that the periods of time, though apparently were not really coincident at the beginning point, the Treasury report including a considerable sum now which had previously been reported from the Interior, sufficiently large to greatly overreach the sum derived from the three months now reported upon by the Interior and not by the Treasury.

The Indian tribes upon our frontiers have during the past year manifested a spirit of insubordination, and at several points have engaged in open hostilities against the white settlements in their vicinity. The tribes occupying the Indian country south of Kansas renounced their allegiance to the United States and entered into treaties with the insurgents. Those who remained loyal to the United States were driven from the country. The chief of the Cherokees has visited this city for the purpose of restoring the former relations of the tribe with the United States. He alleges that they were constrained by superior force to enter into treaties with the insurgents, and that the United States neglected to furnish the protection which their treaty stipulations required.

In the month of August last the Sioux Indians in Minnesota attacked the settlements in their vicinity with extreme ferocity, killing indiscriminately men, women, and children. This attack was wholly unexpected, and therefore no means of defense had been provided. It is estimated that not less than 800 persons were killed by the Indians, and a large amount of property was destroyed. How this outbreak was induced is not definitely known, and suspicions, which may be unjust, need not to be stated. Information was received by the Indian Bureau from different sources about the time hostilities were commenced that a simultaneous attack was to be made upon white settlements by all the tribes between the Mississippi River and the Rocky Mountains. The State of Minnesota has suffered great injury from this Indian war. A large portion of her territory has been depopulated, and a severe loss has been sustained by the destruction of property. The people of that State manifest much anxiety for the removal of the tribes beyond the limits of the State as a guaranty against future hostilities. The Commissioner of Indian Affairs will furnish full details. I submit for your especial consideration whether our Indian system shall not be remodeled. Many wise and good men have impressed me with the belief that this can be profitably done.

I submit a statement of the proceedings of commissioners, which shows the progress that has been made in the enterprise of constructing the Pacific Railroad. And this suggests the earliest completion of this road, and also the favorable action of Congress upon the projects now pending before them for enlarging the capacities of the great canals in New York and Illinois, as being of vital and rapidly increasing importance to the whole nation, and especially to the vast interior region hereinafter to be noticed at some greater length. I purpose having prepared and laid before you at an early day some interesting and valuable statistical information upon this subject. The military and commercial importance of enlarging the Illinois and Michigan Canal and improving the Illinois River is presented in the report of Colonel Webster to the Secretary of War, and now transmitted to Congress. I respectfully ask attention to it.

To carry out the provisions of the act of Congress of the 15th of May last, I have caused the Department of Agriculture of the United States to be organized.

The Commissioner informs me that within the period of a few months this department has established an extensive system of correspondence and exchanges, both at home and abroad, which promises to effect highly beneficial results in the development of a correct knowledge of recent improvements in agriculture, in the introduction of new products, and in the collection of the agricultural statistics of the different States.

Also, that it will soon be prepared to distribute largely seeds, cereals, plants, and cuttings, and has already published and liberally diffused much valuable information in anticipation of a more elaborate report, which will in due time be furnished, embracing some valuable tests in chemical science now in progress in the laboratory.

The creation of this department was for the more immediate benefit of a large class of our most valuable citizens, and I trust that the liberal basis upon which it has been organized will not only meet your approbation, but that it will realize at no distant day all the fondest anticipations of its most sanguine friends and become the fruitful source of advantage to all our people.

On the 22d day of September last a proclamation was issued by the Executive, a copy of which is herewith submitted. In accordance with the purpose expressed in the second paragraph of that paper, I now respectfully recall your attention to what may be called "compensated emancipation."

A nation may be said to consist of its territory, its people, and its laws. The territory is the only part which is of certain durability. "One generation passeth away and another generation cometh, but the earth abideth forever." It is of the first importance to duly consider and estimate this ever enduring part. That portion of the earth's surface which is owned and inhabited by the people of the United States is well adapted to be the home of one national family, and it is not well adapted for two or more. Its vast extent and its variety of climate and productions are of advantage in this age for one people, whatever they might have been in former ages. Steam, telegraphs, and intelligence have brought these to be an advantageous combination for one united people.

In the inaugural address I briefly pointed out the total inadequacy of disunion as a remedy for the differences between the people of the two sections. I did so in language which I cannot improve, and which, therefore, I beg to repeat:

"One section of our country believes slavery is right and ought to be extended, while the other believes it is wrong and ought not to be extended. This is the only substantial dispute. The fugitive-slave clause of the Constitution and the laws for the suppression of the foreign slave trade are each as well enforced, perhaps, as any law can ever be in a community where the moral Sense of the people imperfectly supports the law itself. The great body of the people abide by the dry legal obligation in both cases, and a few break over in each. This, I think, cannot be perfectly cured, and it would be worse in both cases after the separation of the sections than before. The foreign slave trade, now imperfectly suppressed, would be ultimately revived without restriction in one section, while fugitive slaves, now only partially surrendered, would not be surrendered at all by the other.

"Physically speaking, we can not separate. We can not remove our respective sections from each other nor build an impassable wall between them. A husband and wife may be divorced and go out of the presence and beyond the reach of each other, but the different parts of our country cannot do this. They cannot but remain face to face, and intercourse, either amicable or hostile, must continue between them. Is it possible, then, to make that intercourse more advantageous or more satisfactory after separation than before? Can aliens make treaties easier than friends can make laws? Can treaties be more faithfully enforced between aliens than laws can among friends? Suppose you go to war, you cannot fight always; and when, after much loss on both sides and no gain on either, you cease fighting, the identical old questions, as to terms of intercourse, are again upon you."

There is no line, straight or crooked, suitable for a national boundary upon which to divide. Trace through, from east to west, upon the line between the free and slave country, and we shall find a little more than one third of its length are rivers, easy to be crossed, and populated, or soon to be populated, thickly upon both sides; while nearly all its remaining length are merely surveyors' lines, over which people may walk back and forth without any consciousness of their presence. No part of this line can be made any more difficult to pass by writing it down on paper or parchment as a national boundary. The fact of separation, if it comes, gives up on the part of the seceding section the fugitive-slave clause along with all other constitutional obligations upon the section seceded from, while I should expect no treaty stipulation would ever be made to take its place.

But there is another difficulty. The great interior region bounded east by the Alleghenies, north by the British dominions, west by the Rocky Mountains, and south by the line along which the culture of corn and cotton meets, and which includes part of Virginia, part of Tennessee, all of Kentucky, Ohio, Indiana, Michigan, Wisconsin, Illinois, Missouri, Kansas, Iowa, Minnesota, and the Territories of Dakota, Nebraska, and part of Colorado, already has above 10,000,000 people, and will have 50,000,000 within fifty years if not prevented by any political folly or mistake. It contains more than one third of the country owned by the United States—certainly more than 1,000,000 square miles. Once half as populous as Massachusetts already is, it would have more than 75,000,000 people. A glance at the map shows that, territorially speaking, it is the great body of the Republic. The other parts are but marginal borders to it, the magnificent region sloping west from the Rocky Mountains to the Pacific being the deepest and also the richest in undeveloped resources. In the production of provisions, grains, grasses, and all which proceed from them this great interior region is naturally one of the most important in the world. Ascertain from statistics the small proportion of the region which has yet been brought into cultivation, and also the large and rapidly increasing amount of products, and we shall be overwhelmed with the magnitude of the prospect presented. And yet this region has no seacoast—touches no ocean anywhere. As part of one nation, its people now find, and may forever find, their way to Europe by New York, to South America and Africa by New Orleans, and to Asia by San Francisco; but separate our common country into two nations, as designed by the present rebellion, and every man of this great interior region is thereby cut off from some one or more of these outlets, not perhaps by a physical barrier, but by embarrassing and onerous trade regulations.

And this is true, wherever a dividing or boundary line may be fixed. Place it between the now free and slave country, or place it south of Kentucky or north of Ohio, and still the truth remains that none south of it can trade to any port or place north of it, and none north of it can trade to any port or place south of it, except upon terms dictated by a government foreign to them. These outlets, east, west, and south, are indispensable to the well-being of the people inhabiting and to inhabit this vast interior region. Which of the three may be the best is no proper question. All are better than either, and all of right belong to that people and to their successors forever. True to themselves, they will not ask where a line of separation shall be, but will vow rather that there shall be no such line.

Nor are the marginal regions less interested in these communications to and through them to the great outside world. They, too, and each of them, must have access to this Egypt of the West without paying toll at the crossing of any national boundary.

Our national strife springs not from our permanent part; not from the land we inhabit; not from our national homestead. There is no possible severing of this but would multiply and not mitigate evils among us. In all its adaptations and aptitudes it demands union and abhors separation. In fact, it would ere long force reunion, however much of blood and treasure the separation might have cost.

Our strife pertains to ourselves—to the passing generations of men—and it can without convulsion be hushed forever with the passing of one generation.

In this view I recommend the adoption of the following resolution and articles amendatory to the Constitution of the United States:

Resolved by the Senate and House of Representatives of the United States of America, in Congress assembled, (two thirds of both Houses concurring), That the following articles be proposed to the Legislatures (or conventions) of the several States as amendments to the Constitution of the United States, all or any of which articles, when ratified by three fourths of the said Legislatures (or conventions), to be valid as part or parts of the said Constitution, viz.

ART.—Every State wherein slavery now exists which shall abolish the same therein at any time or times before the 1st day of January, A.D. 1900, shall receive compensation from the United States as follows, to wit:

The President of the United States shall deliver to every such State bonds of the United States bearing interest at the rate of — per cent. per annum to an amount equal to the aggregate sum of ——— for each slave shown to have been therein by the Eighth Census of the United States, said bonds to be delivered to such State by instalments or in one parcel at the completion of the abolishment, accordingly as the same shall have been gradual or at one time within such State; and interest shall begin to run upon any such bond only from the proper time of its delivery as aforesaid. Any State having received bonds as aforesaid and afterwards reintroducing or tolerating slavery therein shall refund to the United States the bonds so received, or the value thereof, and all interest paid thereon.

ART.—All slaves who shall have enjoyed actual freedom by the chances of the war at any time before the end of the rebellion shall be forever free; but all owners of such who shall not have been disloyal shall be compensated for them at the same rates as is provided for States adopting abolishment of slavery, but in such way that no slave shall be twice accounted for.

ART.—Congress may appropriate money and otherwise provide for colonizing free colored persons with their own consent at any place or places without the United States.

I beg indulgence to discuss these proposed articles at some length. Without slavery the rebellion could never have existed; without slavery it could not continue.

Among the friends of the Union there is great diversity of sentiment and of policy in regard to slavery and the African race amongst us. Some would perpetuate slavery; some would abolish it suddenly and without compensation; some would abolish it gradually and with compensation; some would remove the freed people from us, and some would retain them with us; and there are yet other minor diversities. Because of these diversities we waste much strength in struggles among ourselves. By mutual concession we should harmonize and act together. This would be compromise, but it would be compromise among the friends and not with the enemies of the Union. These articles are intended to embody a plan of such mutual concessions. If the plan shall be adopted, it is assumed that emancipation will follow, at least in several of the States.

As to the first article, the main points are, first, the emancipation; secondly, the length of time for consummating it (thirty-seven years); and, thirdly, the compensation.

The emancipation will be unsatisfactory to the advocates of perpetual slavery, but the length of time should greatly mitigate their dissatisfaction. The time spares both races from the evils of sudden derangement—in fact, from the necessity of any derangement—while most of those whose habitual course of thought will be disturbed by the measure will have passed away before its consummation. They will never see it. Another class will hail the prospect of emancipation, but will deprecate the length of time. They will feel that it gives too little to the now living slaves. But it really gives them much. It saves them from the vagrant destitution which must largely attend immediate emancipation in localities where their numbers are very great, and it gives the inspiring assurance that their posterity shall be free forever. The plan leaves to each State choosing to act under it to abolish slavery now or at the end of the century, or at any intermediate time, or by degrees extending over the whole or any part of the period, and it obliges no two States to proceed alike. It also provides for compensation, and generally the mode of making it. This, it would seem, must further mitigate the dissatisfaction of those who favor perpetual slavery, and especially of those who are to receive the compensation. Doubtless some of those who are to pay and not to receive will object. Yet the measure is both just and economical. In a certain sense the liberation of slaves is the destruction of property—property acquired by descent or by purchase, the same as any other property. It is no less true for having been often said that the people of the South are not more responsible for the original introduction of this property than are the people of the North; and when it is remembered how unhesitatingly we all use cotton and sugar and share the profits of dealing in them, it may not be quite safe to say that the South has been more responsible than the North for its continuance. If, then, for a common object this property is to be sacrificed, is it not just that it be done at a common charge?

And if with less money, or money more easily paid, we can preserve the benefits of the Union by this means than we can by the war alone, is it not also economical to do it? Let us consider it, then. Let us ascertain the sum we have expended in the war Since compensated emancipation was proposed last March, and consider whether if that measure had been promptly accepted by even some of the slave States the same sum would not have done more to close the war than has been otherwise done. If so, the measure would save money, and in that view would be a prudent and economical measure. Certainly it is not so easy to pay something as it is to pay nothing, but it is easier to pay a large sum than it is to pay a larger one. And it is easier to pay any sum when we are able than it is to pay it before we are able. The war requires large sums, and requires them at once. The aggregate sum necessary for compensated emancipation of course would be large. But it would require no ready cash, nor the bonds even any faster than the emancipation progresses. This might not, and probably would not, close before the end of the thirty-seven years. At that time we shall probably have a hundred millions of people to share the burden, instead of thirty-one millions as now. And not only so, but the increase of our population may be expected to continue for a long time after that period as rapidly as before, because our territory will not have become full. I do not state this inconsiderately. At the same ratio of increase which we have maintained, on an average, from our first national census, in 1790, until that of 1860, we should in 1900 have a population of 103,208,415. And why may we not continue that ratio far beyond that period? Our abundant room, our broad national homestead, is our ample resource. Were our territory as limited as are the British Isles, very certainly our population could not expand as stated. Instead of receiving the foreign born as now, we should be compelled to send part of the native born away. But such is not our condition. We have 2,963,000 square miles. Europe has 3,800,000, with a population averaging 73 persons to the square mile. Why may not our country at some time average as many? Is it less fertile? Has it more waste surface by mountains, rivers, lakes, deserts, or other causes? Is it inferior to Europe in any natural advantage? If, then, we are at some time to be as populous as Europe, how soon? As to when this may be, we can judge by the past and the present; as to when it will be, if ever, depends much on whether we maintain the Union...............

[a page of tables of projected statistics]

These figures show that our country may be as populous as Europe now is at some point between 1920 and 1930, say about 1925—our territory, at 73 persons to the square mile, being of capacity to contain 217,186,000.

And we will reach this, too, if we do not ourselves relinquish the chance by the folly and evils of disunion or by long and exhausting war springing from the only great element of national discord among us. While it cannot be foreseen exactly how much one huge example of secession, breeding lesser ones indefinitely, would retard population, civilization, and prosperity, no one can doubt that the extent of it would be very great and injurious.

The proposed emancipation would shorten the war, perpetuate peace, insure this increase of population, and proportionately the wealth of the country. With these we should pay all the emancipation would cost, together with our other debt, easier than we should pay our other debt without it. If we had allowed our old national debt to run at six per cent. per annum, simple interest, from the end of our revolutionary struggle until to-day, without paying anything on either principal or interest, each man of us would owe less upon that debt now than each man owed upon it then; and this because our increase of men through the whole period has been greater than six per cent.—has run faster than the interest upon the debt. Thus time alone relieves a debtor nation, so long as its population increases faster than unpaid interest accumulates on its debt.

This fact would be no excuse for delaying payment of what is justly due, but it shows the great importance of time in this connection—the great advantage of a policy by which we shall not have to pay until we number 100,000,000 what by a different policy we would have to pay now, when we number but 31,000,000. In a word, it shows that a dollar will be much harder to pay for the war than will be a dollar for emancipation on the proposed plan. And then the latter will cost no blood, no precious life. It will be a saving of both.

As to the second article, I think it would be impracticable to return to bondage the class of persons therein contemplated. Some of them, doubtless, in the property sense belong to loyal owners, and hence Provision is made in this article for compensating such.

The third article relates to the future of the freed people. It does not oblige, but merely authorizes Congress to aid in colonizing such as may consent. This ought not to be regarded as objectionable on the one hand or on the other, insomuch as it comes to nothing unless by the mutual consent of the people to be deported and the American voters through their representatives in Congress.

I cannot make it better known than it already is that I strongly favor colonization; and yet I wish to say there is an objection urged against free colored persons remaining in the country which is largely imaginary, if not sometimes malicious.

It is insisted that their presence would injure and displace white labor and white laborers. If there ever could be a proper time for mere catch arguments that time surely is not now. In times like the present men should utter nothing for which they would not willingly be responsible through time and in eternity. Is it true, then, that colored people can displace any more white labor by being free than by remaining slaves? If they stay in their old places, they jostle no white laborers; if they leave their old places, they leave them open to white laborers. Logically, there is neither more nor less of it. Emancipation, even without deportation, would probably enhance the wages of white labor, and very surely would not reduce them. Thus the customary amount of labor would still have to be performed. The freed people would surely not do more than their old proportion of it, and very probably for a time would do less, leaving an increased part to white laborers, bringing their labor into greater demand, and consequently enhancing the wages of it. With deportation, even to a limited extent, enhanced wages to white labor is mathematically certain. Labor is like any other commodity in the market-increase the demand for it and you increase the price of it. Reduce the supply of black labor by colonizing the black laborer out of the country, and by precisely so much you increase the demand for and wages of white labor.

But it is dreaded that the freed people will swarm forth and cover the whole land. Are they not already in the land? Will liberation make them any more numerous? Equally distributed among the whites of the whole country, and there would be but one colored to seven whites. Could the one in any way greatly disturb the seven? There are many communities now having more than one free colored person to seven whites, and this without any apparent consciousness of evil from it. The District of Columbia and the States of Maryland and Delaware are all in this condition. The District has more than one free colored to six whites, and yet in its frequent petitions to Congress I believe it has never presented the presence of free colored persons as one of its grievances. But why should emancipation South send the free people North? People of any color seldom run unless there be something to run from. Heretofore colored people to some extent have fled North from bondage, and now, perhaps, from both bondage and destitution. But if gradual emancipation and deportation be adopted, they will have neither to flee from. Their old masters will give them wages at least until new laborers can be procured, and the freedmen in turn will gladly give their labor for the wages till new homes can be found for them in congenial climes and with people of their own blood and race. This proposition can be trusted on the mutual interests involved. And in any event, cannot the North decide for itself whether to receive them?

Again, as practice proves more than theory in any case, has there been any irruption of colored people northward because of the abolishment of slavery in this District last spring?

What I have said of the proportion of free colored persons to the whites in the District is from the census of 1860, having no reference to persons called contrabands nor to those made free by the act of Congress abolishing slavery here.

The plan consisting of these articles is recommended, not but that a restoration of the national authority would be accepted without its adoption.

Nor will the war nor proceedings under the proclamation of September 22, 1862, be stayed because of the recommendation of this plan. Its timely adoption, I doubt not, would bring restoration, and thereby stay both.

And notwithstanding this plan, the recommendation that Congress provide by law for compensating any State which may adopt emancipation before this plan shall have been acted upon is hereby earnestly renewed. Such would be only an advance part of the plan, and the same arguments apply to both.

This plan is recommended as a means, not in exclusion of, but additional to, all others for restoring and preserving the national authority throughout the Union. The subject is presented exclusively in its economical aspect. The plan would, I am confident, secure peace more speedily and maintain it more permanently than can be done by force alone, while all it would cost, considering amounts and manner of payment and times of payment, would be easier paid than will be the additional cost of the war if we rely solely upon force. It is much, very much, that it would cost no blood at all.

The plan is proposed as permanent constitutional law. It cannot become such without the concurrence of, first, two thirds of Congress, and afterwards three fourths of the States. The requisite three fourths of the States will necessarily include seven of the slave States. Their concurrence, if obtained, will give assurance of their severally adopting emancipation at no very distant day upon the new constitutional terms. This assurance would end the struggle now and save the Union forever.

I do not forget the gravity which should characterize a paper addressed to the Congress of the nation by the chief magistrate of the nation, nor do I forget that some of you are my seniors, nor that many of you have more experience than I in the conduct of public affairs. Yet I trust that in view of the great responsibility resting upon me you will perceive no want of respect to yourselves in any undue earnestness I may seem to display.

Is it doubted, then, that the plan I propose, if adopted, would shorten the war, and thus lessen its expenditure of money and of blood? Is it doubted that it would restore the national authority and national prosperity and perpetuate both indefinitely? Is it doubted that we here—Congress and executive—can secure its adoption? Will not the good people respond to a united and earnest appeal from us? Can we, can they, by any other means so certainly or so speedily assure these vital objects? We can succeed only by concert. It is not "Can any of us imagine better?" but "Can we all do better?" Object whatsoever is possible, still the question recurs, "Can we do better?" The dogmas of the quiet past are inadequate to the stormy present. The occasion is piled high with difficulty, and we must rise with the occasion. As our case is new, so we must think anew and act anew. We must disenthrall ourselves, and then we shall save our country.

Fellow-citizens, we can not escape history. We of this Congress and this administration will be remembered in spite of ourselves. No personal significance or insignificance can spare one or another of us. The fiery trial through which we pass will light us down in honor or dishonor to the latest generation. We say we are for the Union. The world will not forget that we say this. We know how to save the Union. The world knows we do know how to save it. We, even we here, hold the power and bear the responsibility. In giving freedom to the slave we assure freedom to the free—honorable alike in what we give and what we preserve. We shall nobly save or meanly lose the last, best hope of earth. Other means may succeed; this could not fail. The way is plain, peaceful, generous, just—a way which if followed the world will forever applaud and God must forever bless.

A. LINCOLN.

MESSAGE TO CONGRESS.

WASHINGTON, December 3, 1862.

TO THE SENATE AND HOUSE OF REPRESENTATIVES:

On the 3d of November, 1861, a collision took place off the coast of Cuba between the United States war steamer San Jacinto and the French brig Jules et Marie, resulting in serious damage to the latter. The obligation of this Government to make amends therefor could not be questioned if the injury resulted from any fault On the part of the San Jacinto. With a view to ascertain this, the subject was referred to a commission of the United States and French naval officers at New York, with a naval officer of Italy as an arbiter. The conclusion arrived at was that the collision was occasioned by the failure of the San Jacinto seasonably to reverse her engine. It then became necessary to ascertain the amount of indemnification due to the injured party. The United States consul-general at Havana was consequently instructed to confer with the consul of France on this point, and they have determined that the sum of $9,500 is an equitable allowance under the circumstances.

I recommend an appropriation of this sum for the benefit of the owners of the Jules et Marie.

A copy of the letter of Mr. Shufeldt, the consul-general of the United States at Havana, to the Secretary of State on the subject is herewith transmitted.

A. LINCOLN.

TELEGRAM TO H. J. RAYMOND.

EXECUTIVE MANSION, WASHINGTON,

December 7, 1862.
Hon. H. J. RAYMOND, Times Office, New York:
Yours of November 25 reached me only yesterday. Thank you for it. I shall consider and remember your suggestions.
A. LINCOLN.

TELEGRAM TO B. G. BROWN.

EXECUTIVE MANSION, WASHINGTON December 7, 1862.

HON. B. GRATZ BROWN, Saint Louis, Missouri:
Yours of the 3d received yesterday. Have already done what I can in the premises.
A. LINCOLN.

TELEGRAM TO GOVERNOR JOHNSON.

EXECUTIVE MANSION, WASHINGTON, December 8, 1862. GOVERNOR ANDREW JOHNSON, Nashville, Tenn.:
Jesse H. Strickland is here asking authority to raise a regiment of Tennesseeans. Would you advise that the authority be given him?
A. LINCOLN.

MESSAGE TO CONGRESS. December 8, 1862.

WASHINGTON, D. C.

TO THE SENATE AND HOUSE OF REPRESENTATIVES:
In conformity to the law of July 16, 1862, I most cordially recommend, that Commander John L. Worden, United States Navy, receive a vote of thanks of Congress for the eminent skill and gallantry exhibited by him in the late remarkable battle between the United States ironclad steamer Monitor, under his command, and the rebel ironclad steamer Merrimac, in March last.

The thanks of Congress for his services on the occasion referred to were tendered by a resolution approved July 11, 1862, but the recommendation is now specially made in order to comply with the requirements of the ninth section of the act of July 16, 1862, which is in the following words, viz.:

"That any line officer of the navy or marine corps may be advanced one grade if upon recommendation of the President by name he receives the thanks of Congress for highly distinguished conduct in conflict with the enemy or for extraordinary heroism in the line of his profession."
A. LINCOLN.

TO GENERAL S. R. CURTIS.

EXECUTIVE MANSION, WASHINGTON,

December 10, 1862.
MAJOR-GENERAL CURTIS, St. Louis, Missouri:
Please suspend, until further order, all proceeding on the order made by General Schofield, on the twenty-eighth day of August last, for assessing and collecting from secessionists and Southern sympathizers the sum of five hundred thousand dollars, etc., and in the meantime make out and send me a statement of facts pertinent to the question, together with your opinion upon it.
A. LINCOLN.

TO J. K. DUBOIS.

EXECUTIVE MANSION, WASHINGTON,

December 10, 1862.
Hon. J. K. DuBois.
MY DEAR SIR:—In the summer of 1859, when Mr. Freeman visited Springfield, Illinois, in relation to the McCallister and Stebbins bonds I promised him that, upon certain conditions, I would ask members of the Legislature to give him a full and fair hearing of his case. I do not now remember, nor have I time to recall, exactly what the conditions were, nor whether they were completely performed; but there can be in no case any harm [in] his having a full and fair hearing, and I sincerely wish it may be given him.
Yours truly,
A. LINCOLN.

MESSAGE TO THE SENATE.

December 11, 1862.

TO THE SENATE OF THE UNITED STATES:
In compliance with your resolution of December 5, 1862, requesting the President "to furnish the Senate with all information in his possession touching the late Indian barbarities in the State of Minnesota, and also the evidence in his possession upon which some of the principal actors and head men were tried and condemned to death," I have the honor to state that on receipt of said resolution, I transmitted the same to the Secretary of the Interior, accompanied by a note, a copy of which is herewith inclosed, marked A, and in response to which I received, through that department, a letter of the Commissioner of Indian Affairs, a copy of which is herewith inclosed, marked B.
I further state that on the eighth day of November last I received a long telegraphic despatch from Major-General Pope, at St. Paul, Minnesota, simply announcing the names of the persons sentenced to be hanged. I immediately telegraphed to have transcripts of the records in all cases forwarded to me, which transcripts, however, did not reach me until two or three days before the present meeting of Congress. Meantime I received, through telegraphic despatches and otherwise, appeals in behalf of the condemned, appeals for their execution, and expressions of opinion as to the proper policy in regard to them and to the Indians generally in that vicinity, none of which, as I understand, falls within the scope of your inquiry. After the arrival of the transcripts of records, but before I had sufficient opportunity to

examine them, I received a joint letter from one of the senators and two of the representatives from Minnesota, which contains some statements of fact not found in the records of the trials, and for which reason I herewith transmit a copy, marked C. I also, for the same reason, inclose a printed memorial of the citizens of St. Paul, addressed to me, and forwarded with the letter aforesaid.

Anxious to not act with so much clemency as to encourage another outbreak on the one hand, nor with so much severity as to be real cruelty on the other, I caused a careful examination of the records of trials to be made, in view of first ordering the execution of such as had been proved guilty of violating females. Contrary to my expectation, only two of this class were found. I then directed a further examination and a classification of all who were proven to have participated in massacres, as distinguished from participation in battles. This class numbered forty, and included the two convicted of female violation. One of the number is strongly recommended, by the commission which tried them, for commutation to ten years imprisonment I have ordered the other thirty-nine to be executed on Friday the 19th instant. The order was despatched from here on Monday, the 8th instant, by a messenger to General Sibley, and a copy of which order is herewith transmitted, marked D.

An abstract of the evidence as to the forty is herewith inclosed, marked E.

To avoid the immense amount of copying, I lay before the Senate the original transcripts of the records of trials, as received by me.

This is as full and complete a response to the resolution as it is in my power to make.

A. LINCOLN.

MESSAGE TO CONGRESS.

December 12, 1862.

FELLOW-CITIZENS OF THE SENATE AND HOUSE OF REPRESENTATIVES:
I have in my possession three valuable swords, formerly the property of General David E. Twiggs, which I now place at the disposal of Congress. They are forwarded to me from New Orleans by Major-General Benjamin F. Butler. If they or any of them shall be by Congress disposed of in reward or compliment of military service, I think General Butler is entitled to the first consideration. A copy of the General's letter to me accompanying the swords is herewith transmitted.
A. LINCOLN.

TO FERNANDO WOOD.

EXECUTIVE MANSION, WASHINGTON DECEMBER 12, 1862.

HON. FERNANDO WOOD.
MY DEAR SIR:—Your letter of the 8th, with the accompanying note of same date, was received yesterday. The most important paragraph in the letter, as I consider, is in these words:

"On the 25th of November last I was advised by an authority which I deemed likely to be well informed, as well as reliable and truthful, that the Southern States would send representatives to the next Congress, provided that a full and general amnesty should permit them to do so. No guarantee or terms were asked for other than the amnesty referred to."

I strongly suspect your information will prove to be groundless; nevertheless, I thank you for communicating it to me. Understanding the phrase in the paragraph just quoted—"the Southern States would send representatives to the next Congress"—to be substantially the same as that "the people of the Southern States would cease resistance, and would reinaugurate, submit to, and maintain the national authority within the limits of such States, under the Constitution of the United States," I say that in such case the war would cease on the part of the United States; and that if within a reasonable time "a full and general amnesty" were necessary to such end, it would not be withheld.

I do not think it would be proper now to communicate this, formally or informally, to the people of the Southern States. My belief is that they already know it; and when they choose, if ever, they can communicate with me unequivocally. Nor do I think it proper now to suspend military operations to try any experiment of negotiation.

I should nevertheless receive with great pleasure the exact information you now have, and also such other as you may in any way obtain. Such information might be more valuable before the 1st of January than afterwards.

While there is nothing in this letter which I shall dread to see in history, it is, perhaps, better for the present that its existence should not become public. I therefore have to request that you will regard it as confidential.

Your obedient servant,
A. LINCOLN.

TELEGRAM TO GENERAL CURTIS.

EXECUTIVE MANSION, WASHINGTON, December 14, 1862

MAJOR-GENERAL CURTIS, St. Louis, Missouri:
If my friend Dr. William Fithian, of Danville, Ill., should call on YOU, please give him such facilities as you consistently can about recovering the remains of a step-son, and matters connected therewith.
A. LINCOLN.

TELEGRAM TO GENERAL H. H. SIBLEY.

EXECUTIVE MANSION, WASHINGTON, December 16, 1862.

BRIG. GEN. H. H. SIBLEY, Saint Paul, Minn.:
As you suggest, let the executions fixed for Friday the 19th instant be postponed to, and be done on, Friday the 26th instant.
A. LINCOLN. (Private.) Operator please send this very carefully and accurately. A. L.

TELEGRAM TO GENERAL CURTIS.

EXECUTIVE MANSION, WASHINGTON, December 16, 1862.

MAJOR-GENERAL CURTIS, Saint Louis, Missouri:
N. W. Watkins, of Jackson, Mo., (who is half brother to Henry Clay), writes me that a colonel of ours has driven him from his home at Jackson. Will you please look into the case and restore the old man to his home if the public interest will admit?
A. LINCOLN.

TELEGRAM TO GENERAL BURNSIDE.

WAR DEPARTMENT, WASHINGTON CITY, D. C., December 16, 1862.

MAJOR-GENERAL BURNSIDE, Falmouth:
Your despatch about General Stahel is received. Please ascertain from General Sigel and his old corps whether Stahel or Schurz is preferable and telegraph the result, and I will act immediately. After all I shall be governed by your preference.
A. LINCOLN.

TELEGRAM TO GENERAL CURTIS.

EXECUTIVE MANSION, WASHINGTON, December 17, 1862.

MAJOR-GENERAL CURTIS:
Could the civil authority be reintroduced into Missouri in lieu of the military to any extent, with advantage and safety?
A. LINCOLN.

TELEGRAM TO GENERAL BURNSIDE.

EXECUTIVE MANSION, WASHINGTON, December 17, 1862.

MAJOR-GENERAL BURNSIDE
George Patten says he was a classmate of yours and was in the same regiment of artillery. Have you a place you would like to put him in? And if so what is it?
A. LINCOLN.

TELEGRAM TO GOVERNOR GAMBLE.

EXECUTIVE MANSION, WASHINGTON, December 18, 1862.

GOVERNOR GAMBLE, Saint Louis, MO.:
It is represented to me that the enrolled militia alone would now maintain law and order in all the counties of your State north of the Missouri River. If so all other forces there might be removed south of the river, or out of the State. Please post yourself and give me your opinion upon the subject.
A. LINCOLN.

TELEGRAM TO GENERAL CURTIS.

EXECUTIVE MANSION, WASHINGTON,

December 19, 1862.
MAJOR-GENERAL CURTIS, Saint Louis, Mo.:
Hon. W. A. Hall, member of Congress here, tells me, and Governor Gamble telegraphs me; that quiet can be maintained in all the counties north of the Missouri River by the enrolled militia. Confer with Governor Gamble and telegraph me.
A. LINCOLN.

TELEGRAM TO GENERAL A. E. BURNSIDE.

WASHINGTON, December 19, 1862.

MAJOR-GENERAL BURNSIDE:
Come, of course, if in your own judgment it is safe to do so.
A. LINCOLN.

TO SECRETARIES SEWARD AND CHASE.

EXECUTIVE MANSION, WASHINGTON,

December 20, 1862.
HON. WILLIAM H. SEWARD AND HON. SALMON P. CHASE.
GENTLEMEN:—You have respectively tendered me your resignations as Secretary of State and Secretary of the Treasury of the United States. I am apprised of the circumstances which may render this course personally desirable to each of you; but after most anxious consideration my deliberate judgment is that the public interest does not admit of it. I therefore have to request that you will resume the duties of your departments respectively.
Your obedient servant,
A. LINCOLN.

TELEGRAM TO GOVERNOR ANDREW.

WASHINGTON, D. C., December 20, 1862.

GOVERNOR ANDREW, Boston, Mass.:
Neither the Secretary of War nor I know anything except what you tell us about the "published official document" you mention.
A. LINCOLN.

TO T. J. HENDERSON.

EXECUTIVE MANSION, WASHINGTON, December 20, 1862.

HON. T. J. HENDERSON.
DEAR SIR:-Your letter of the 8th to Hon. William Kellogg has just been shown me. You can scarcely overestimate the pleasure it would give me to oblige you, but nothing is operating so ruinously upon us everywhere as "absenteeism." It positively will not do for me to grant leaves of absence in cases not sufficient to procure them under the regular rules.
It would astonish you to know the extent of the evil of "absenteeism." We scarcely have more than half the men we are paying on the spot for service anywhere.
Yours very truly,
A. LINCOLN.

CONGRATULATIONS TO THE ARMY OF THE POTOMAC

EXECUTIVE MANSION, WASHINGTON,

December 22, 1862.
TO THE ARMY OF THE POTOMAC:
I have just read your general's report of the battle of Fredericksburg. Although you were not successful, the attempt was not an error, nor the failure other than accident. The courage with which you, in an open field, maintained the contest against an intrenched foe, and the consummate skill and success with which you crossed and recrossed the river

in the face of the enemy, show that you possess all the qualities of a great army, which will yet give victory to the cause of the country and of popular government.

Condoling with the mourners for the dead, and sympathizing with the severely wounded, I congratulate you that the number of both is comparatively so small.

I tender to you, officers and soldiers, the thanks of the nation.

A. LINCOLN.

LETTER OF CONDOLENCE

TO MISS FANNY McCULLOUGH.

EXECUTIVE MANSION, WASHINGTON, December, 23, 1862.

DEAR FANNY:—It is with deep regret that I learn of the death of your kind and brave father, and especially that it is affecting your young heart beyond what is common in such cases. In this sad world of ours sorrow comes to all, and to the young it comes with bittered agony because it takes them unawares.

The older have learned ever to expect it. I am anxious to afford some alleviation of your present distress, perfect relief is not possible, except with time. You cannot now realize that you will ever feel better. Is not this so? And yet it is a mistake. You are sure to be happy again. To know this, which is certainly true, will make you some less miserable now. I have had experience enough to know what I say, and you need only to believe it to feel better at once. The memory of your dear father, instead of an agony, will yet be a sad, sweet feeling in your heart, of a purer and holier sort than you have known before.

Please present my kind regards to your afflicted mother.

Your sincere friend,

A. LINCOLN.

TO SECRETARY OF WAR.

EXECUTIVE MANSION, WASHINGTON, December 26, 1862

HONORABLE SECRETARY OF WAR.

Sir:—Two Ohio regiments and one Illinois regiment which were captured at Hartsville have been paroled and are now at Columbus, Ohio. This brings the Ohio regiments substantially to their homes. I am strongly impressed with the belief that the Illinois regiment better be sent to Illinois, where it will be recruited and put in good condition by the time they are exchanged so as to re-enter the service. They did not misbehave, as I am satisfied, so that they should receive no treatment nor have anything withheld from them by way of punishment.

Yours truly,

A. LINCOLN.

TELEGRAM TO GENERAL CURTIS.

EXECUTIVE MANSION, WASHINGTON, December 27, 1862.

MAJOR-GENERAL CURTIS, Saint Louis, Mo.:

Let the order in regard to Dr. McPheeters and family be suspended until you hear from me.

A. LINCOLN.

TELEGRAM TO GOVERNOR GAMBLE.

WAR DEPARTMENT, December 27, 1862.

HIS EXCELLENCY GOVERNOR GAMBLE:
I do not wish to leave the country north of the Missouri to the care of the enrolled militia except upon the concurrent judgment of yourself and General Curtis. His I have not yet obtained. Confer with him, and I shall be glad to act when you and he agree.
A. LINCOLN

TELEGRAM TO GENERAL A. E. BURNSIDE.

WAR DEPARTMENT, WASHINGTON CITY, D.C., December 30, 1862. 3.30 PM.

MAJOR-GENERAL BURNSIDE:
I have good reason for saying you must not make a general movement of the army without letting me know.
A. LINCOLN.

TELEGRAM TO GENERAL DIX.

EXECUTIVE MANSION, WASHINGTON, December 31, 1862.

MAJOR-GENERAL Dix, Fort Monroe, Va.:
I hear not a word about the Congressional election of which you and I corresponded. Time clearly up.
A. LINCOLN.

TELEGRAM TO H. J. RAYMOND.

(Private.)

EXECUTIVE MANSION, WASHINGTON, December 31, 1862.
HON. H. J. RAYMOND:
The proclamation cannot be telegraphed to you until during the day to-morrow.
JNO. G. NICOLAY.
[Same to Horace Greeley]

1863

EMANCIPATION PROCLAMATION, JANUARY 1, 1863.

THE PRESIDENT OF THE UNITED STATES OF AMERICA:

A Proclamation.

Whereas on the 22d day of September, A.D. 1862, a proclamation was issued by the President of the United States, containing, among other things, the following, to wit:

"That on the 1st day of January, A.D., 1863, all persons held as slaves within any State or designated part of a State the people whereof shall then be in rebellion against the United States shall be then, thenceforward, and forever free; and the executive government of the United States, including the military and naval authority thereof, will recognize and maintain the freedom of such persons, and will do no act or acts to repress such persons, or any of them, in any efforts they may make for their actual freedom.

"That the executive will on the 1st day of January aforesaid, by proclamation, designate the States and parts of States, if any, in which the people thereof, respectively, shall then be in rebellion against the United States; and the fact that any State or the people thereof shall on that day be in good faith represented in the Congress of the United States by members chosen thereto at elections wherein a majority of the qualified voters of such States shall have participated shall, in the absence of strong countervailing testimony, be deemed conclusive evidence that such State and the people thereof are not then in rebellion against the United States."

Now, therefore, I, Abraham Lincoln, President of the United States, by virtue of the power in me vested as Commander-in-Chief of the Army and Navy of the United States in time of actual armed rebellion against the authority and government of the United States, and as a fit and necessary war measure for suppressing said rebellion, do, on this 1st day of January, A. D. 1863, and in accordance with my purpose so to do, publicly proclaimed for the full period of one hundred days from the first day above mentioned, order and designate as the States and parts of States wherein the people thereof, respectively, are this day in rebellion against the United States the following, to wit:

Arkansas, Texas, Louisiana (except the parishes of St. Bernard, Plaquemines, Jefferson, St. John, St. Charles, St. James, Ascension, Assumption, Terre Bonne, Lafourche, St. Mary, St. Martin, and Orleans, including the city of New Orleans), Mississippi, Alabama, Florida, Georgia, South Carolina, North Carolina, and Virginia (except the forty-eight counties designated as West Virginia, and also the counties of Berkeley, Accomac, Northampton, Elizabeth City, York, Princess Anne, and Norfolk, including the cities of Norfolk and Portsmouth), and which excepted parts are for the present left precisely as if this proclamation were not issued.

And by virtue of the power and for the purpose aforesaid, I do order and declare that all persons held as slaves within said designated States and parts of States are, and henceforward shall be, free; and that the Executive Government of the United States, including the military and naval authorities thereof, will recognize and maintain the freedom of said persons.

And I hereby enjoin upon the people so declared to be free to abstain from all violence, unless in necessary self-defense; and I recommend to them that, in all cases when allowed, they labor faithfully for reasonable wages.

And I further declare and make known that such persons of suitable condition will be received into the armed service of the United States to garrison forts, positions, stations, and other places, and to man vessels of all sorts in said service.

And upon this act, sincerely believed to be an act of justice, warranted by the Constitution upon military necessity, I invoke the considerate judgment of mankind and the gracious favor of Almighty God.

In witness whereof I have hereunto set my hand and caused the seal of the United States to be affixed.

Done at the city of Washington, this first day of January, A.D. 1863, and of the independence of the United States of America the eighty-seventh.

A. LINCOLN.

By the President: WILLIAM H. SEWARD, Secretary of State.

TO GENERAL H. W. HALLECK.

EXECUTIVE MANSION, WASHINGTON January 1, 1863

MAJOR-GENERAL HALLECK.

DEAR SIR:—General Burnside wishes to cross the Rappahannock with his army, but his grand division commanders all oppose the movement. If in such a difficulty as this you do not help, you fail me precisely in the point for which I sought your assistance You know what General Burnside's plan is, and it is my wish that you go with him to the ground, examine it as far as practicable, confer with the officers, getting their judgment, and ascertaining their temper—in a word, gather all the elements for forming a judgment of your own, and then tell General Burnside that you do approve or that you do not approve his plan. Your military skill is useless to me if you will not do this.

Yours very truly,
A. LINCOLN

[Indorsement]
January 1, 1863 Withdrawn, because considered harsh by General Halleck.
A. LINCOLN.

MESSAGE TO CONGRESS

WASHINGTON, January 2, 1863

TO THE SENATE AND HOUSE OF REPRESENTATIVES:
I submit to Congress the expediency of extending to other departments of the government the authority conferred on the President by the eighth section of the act of the 8th of May, 1792, to appoint a person to temporarily discharge the duties of Secretary of State, Secretary of the Treasury, and Secretary of War, in case of the death, absence from the seat of government, or sickness of either of those officers.
A. LINCOLN.

TO GENERAL S. R. CURTIS.

EXECUTIVE MANSION, WASHINGTON JANUARY 2, 1863

MAJOR-GENERAL CURTIS.
MY DEAR SIR:—Yours of December 29 by the hand of Mr. Strong is just received. The day I telegraphed you suspending the order in relation to Dr. McPheeters, he, with Mr. Bates, the Attorney-General, appeared before me and left with me a copy of the order mentioned. The doctor also showed me the Copy of an oath which he said he had taken, which is indeed very strong and specific. He also verbally assured me that he had constantly prayed in church for the President and government, as he had always done before the present war. In looking over the recitals in your order, I do not see that this matter of the prayer, as he states it, is negatived, nor that any violation of his oath is charged nor, in fact, that anything specific is alleged against him. The charges are all general: that he has a rebel wife and rebel relations, that he sympathies with rebels, and that he exercises rebel influence. Now, after talking with him, I tell you frankly I believe he does sympathize with the rebels, but the question remains whether such a man, of unquestioned good moral character, who has taken such an oath as he has, and cannot even be charged with violating it, and who can be charged with no other specific act or omission, can, with safety to the government, be exiled upon the suspicion of his secret sympathies. But I agree that this must be left to you, who are on the spot; and if, after all, you think the public good requires his removal, my suspension of the order is withdrawn, only with this qualification, that the time during the suspension is not to be counted against him. I have promised him this. But I must add that the United States Government must not, as by this order, undertake to run the churches. When an individual in a church or out of it becomes dangerous to the public interest, he must be checked; but let the churches, as such, take care of themselves. It will not do for the United States to appoint trustees, supervisors, or other agents for the churches.
Yours very truly,
A. LINCOLN.
P. S.—The committee composed of Messrs. Yeatman and Filley (Mr. Broadhead not attending) has presented your letter and the memorial of sundry citizens. On the whole subject embraced exercise your best judgment, with a sole view to the public interest, and I will not interfere without hearing you.
A. LINCOLN., January 3, 1863.

TO SECRETARY WELLES.

EXECUTIVE MANSION, WASHINGTON, January 4, 1863.

HON. GIDEON WELLES, Secretary of the Navy.

DEAR SIR:—As many persons who come well recommended for loyalty and service to the Union cause, and who are refugees from rebel oppression in the State of Virginia, make application to me for authority and permission to remove their families and property to protection within the Union lines, by means of our armed gunboats on the Potomac River and Chesapeake Bay, you are hereby requested to hear and consider all such applications, and to grant such assistance to this class of persons as in your judgment their merits may render proper, and as may in each case be consistent with the perfect and complete efficiency of the naval service and with military expediency.
A. LINCOLN.

TO GENERAL S. L CURTIS.

EXECUTIVE MANSION, WASHINGTON, January 5, 1863

MAJOR-GENERAL CURTIS.
MY DEAR SIR:—I am having a good deal of trouble with Missouri matters, and I now sit down to write you particularly about it. One class of friends believe in greater severity and another in greater leniency in regard to arrests, banishments, and assessments. As usual in such cases, each questions the other's motives. On the one hand, it is insisted that Governor Gamble's unionism, at most, is not better than a secondary spring of action; that hunkerism and a wish for political influence stand before Unionism with him. On the other hand, it is urged that arrests, banishments, and assessments are made more for private malice, revenge, and pecuniary interest than for the public good. This morning I was told, by a gentleman who I have no doubt believes what he says, that in one case of assessments for $10,000 the different persons who paid compared receipts, and found they had paid $30,000. If this be true, the inference is that the collecting agents pocketed the odd $20,000. And true or not in the instance, nothing but the sternest necessity can justify the making and maintaining of a system so liable to such abuses. Doubtless the necessity for the making of the system in Missouri did exist, and whether it continues for the maintenance of it is now a practical and very important question. Some days ago Governor Gamble telegraphed me, asking that the assessments outside of St. Louis County might be suspended, as they already have been within it, and this morning all the members of Congress here from Missouri but one laid a paper before me asking the same thing. Now, my belief is that Governor Gamble is an honest and true man, not less so than yourself; that you and he could confer together on this and other Missouri questions with great advantage to the public; that each knows something which the other does not; and that acting together you could about double your stock of pertinent information. May I not hope that you and he will attempt this? I could at once safely do (or you could safely do without me) whatever you and he agree upon. There is absolutely no reason why you should not agree.
Yours as ever,
A. LINCOLN.
P. S.—I forgot to say that Hon. James S. Rollins, member of Congress from one of the Missouri districts, wishes that, upon his personal responsibility, Rev. John M. Robinson, of Columbia, Missouri; James L. Matthews, of Boone County, Missouri; and James L. Stephens, also of Boone County, Missouri, may be allowed to return to their respective homes. Major Rollins leaves with me very strong papers from the neighbors of these men, whom he says he knows to be true men. He also says he has many constituents who he thinks are rightly exiled, but that he thinks these three should be allowed to return. Please look into the case, and oblige Major Rollins if you consistently can.
Yours truly,
A. LINCOLN.
[Copy sent to Governor Gamble.]

TO CALEB RUSSELL AND SALLIE A. FENTON.

EXECUTIVE MANSION, WASHINGTON, January 5, 1863.

MY GOOD FRIENDS: The Honorable Senator Harlan has just placed in my hands your letter of the 27th of December, which I have read with pleasure and gratitude.
It is most cheering and encouraging for me to know that in the efforts which I have made and am making for the restoration of a righteous peace to our country, I am upheld and sustained by the good wishes and prayers of God's

people. No one is more deeply than myself aware that without His favor our highest wisdom is but as foolishness and that our most strenuous efforts would avail nothing in the shadow of His displeasure.

I am conscious of no desire for my country's welfare that is not in consonance with His will, and of no plan upon which we may not ask His blessing. It seems to me that if there be one subject upon which all good men may unitedly agree, it is imploring the gracious favor of the God of Nations upon the struggles our people are making for the preservation of their precious birthright of civil and religious liberty.

Very truly your friend;
A. LINCOLN.

TELEGRAM TO GENERAL ROSECRANS.

EXECUTIVE MANSION, WASHINGTON, January 5. 1863.

MAJOR-GENERAL W. S. ROSECRANS, Murfreesborough, Tenn.: Your despatch announcing retreat of enemy has just reached here. God bless you and all with you! Please tender to all, and accept for yourself, the nation's gratitude for your and their skill, endurance, and dauntless courage.
A. LINCOLN.

TELEGRAM TO GENERAL DIX.

WAR DEPARTMENT, WASHINGTON, D.C., January 7, 1863.

MAJOR-GENERAL DIX, Fort Monroe, Va.:
Do Richmond papers of 6th say nothing about Vicksburg, or if anything, what?
A. LINCOLN.

TO GENERAL H. W. HALLECK.

EXECUTIVE MANSION, WASHINGTON January 7, 1863.

MAJOR-GENERAL HALLECK.
MY DEAR SIR:—What think you of forming a reserve cavalry corps of, say, 6000 for the Army of the Potomac? Might not such a corps be constituted from the cavalry of Sigel's and Slocum's corps, with scraps we could pick up here and there?
Yours truly,
A. LINCOLN.

TELEGRAM TO B. G. BROWN.

WASHINGTON, D. C., January 7, 1863. 5.30 P.M.

HON. B. GRATZ BROWN, Jefferson City, Mo.:
Yours of to-day just received. The administration takes no part between its friends in Missouri, of whom I, at least, consider you one; and I have never before had an intimation that appointees there were interfering, or were inclined to interfere.
A. LINCOLN.

CORRESPONDENCE WITH GENERAL A. E. BURNSIDE, JANUARY 8, 1863.

HEADQUARTERS ARMY OF THE POTOMAC January 5, 1863.
HIS EXCELLENCY THE PRESIDENT OF THE UNITED STATES:
Since my return to the army I have become more than ever convinced that the general officers of this command are almost unanimously opposed to another crossing of the river; but I am still of the opinion that the crossing should be attempted, and I have accordingly issued orders to the engineers and artillery to prepare for it. There is much hazard in it, as there always is in the majority of military movements, and I cannot begin the movement without giving you notice of it, particularly as I know so little of the effect that it may have upon other movements of distant armies.
The influence of your telegram the other day is still upon me, and has impressed me with the idea that there are many parts of the problem which influence you that are not known to me.
In order to relieve you from all embarrassment in my case, I inclose with this my resignation of my commission as major-general of volunteers, which you can have accepted if my movement is not in accordance with the views of yourself and your military advisers.
I have taken the liberty to write to you personally upon this subject, because it was necessary, as I learned from General Halleck, for you to approve of my general plan, written at Warrenton, before I could commence the movement; and I think it quite as necessary that you should know of the important movement I am about to make, particularly as it will have to be made in opposition to the views of nearly all my general officers, and after the receipt of a despatch from you informing me of the opinion of some of them who had visited you.
In conversation with you on New Year's morning I was led to express some opinions which I afterward felt it my duty to place on paper, and to express them verbally to the gentleman of whom we were speaking, which I did in your presence, after handing you the letter. You were not disposed then, as I saw, to retain the letter, and I took it back, but I now return it to you for record if you wish it.
I beg leave to say that my resignation is not sent in in any spirit of insubordination, but, as I before said, simply to relieve you from any embarrassment in changing commanders where lack of confidence may have rendered it necessary.
The bearer of this will bring me any answer, or I should be glad to hear from you by telegraph in cipher.
I have the honor to be, very respectfully, your obedient servant,
A. E. BURNSIDE,
Major-General, Commanding Army of the Potomac.

HEADQUARTERS OF THE ARMY, WASHINGTON, January 7, 1863.

MAJOR-GENERAL BURNSIDE, Commanding, etc., Falmouth:

GENERAL:—Your communication of the 5th was delivered to me by your aide-de-camp at 12 M. to-day.
In all my communications and interviews with you since you took command of the Army of the Potomac I have advised a forward movement across the Rappahannock. At our interview at Warrenton I urged that you should cross by the fords above Fredericksburg rather than to fall down to that place; and when I left you at Warrenton it was understood that at least a considerable part of your army would cross by the fords, and I so represented to the President. It was this modification of the plan proposed by you that I telegraphed you had received his approval. When the attempt at Fredericksburg was abandoned, I advised you to renew the attempt at some other point, either in whole or in part, to turn the enemy's works, or to threaten their wings or communications; in other words, to keep the enemy occupied till a favorable opportunity offered to strike a decisive blow. I particularly advised you to use your cavalry and light artillery upon his communications, and attempt to cut off his supplies and engage him at an advantage.
In all our interviews I have urged that our first object was, not Richmond, but the defeat or scattering of Lee's army, which threatened Washington and the line of the upper Potomac. I now recur to these things simply to remind you of the general views which I have expressed, and which I still hold.
The circumstances of the case, however, have somewhat changed since the early part of November. The chances of an extended line of operations are now, on account of the advanced season, much less than then. But the chances are still in our favor to meet and defeat the enemy on the Rappahannock, if we can effect a crossing in a position where we can meet the enemy on favorable or even equal terms. I therefore still advise a movement against him. The character of

that movement, however, must depend upon circumstances which may change any day and almost any hour. If the enemy should concentrate his forces at the place you have selected for a crossing, make it a feint and try another place. Again, the circumstances at the time may be such as to render an attempt to cross the entire army not advisable. In that case, theory suggests that, while the enemy concentrates at that point, advantages can be gained by crossing smaller forces at other points to cut off his lines, destroy his communication, and capture his rear-guards, outposts, etc. The great object is to occupy the enemy to prevent his making large detachments or distant raids, and to injure him all you can with the least injury to yourself. If this can be best accomplished by feints of a general crossing and detached real crossings, take that course; if by an actual general crossing, with feints on other points, adopt that course. There seem to me to be many reasons why a crossing at some point should be attempted. It will not do to keep your large army inactive. As you yourself admit, it devolves on you to decide upon the time, place, and character of the crossing which you may attempt. I can only advise that an attempt be made, and as early as possible.
Very respectfully, your obedient servant,
H. W. HALLECK, General-in-Chief.
[Indorsement.]
January 8, 1863.
GENERAL BURNSIDE:
I understand General Halleck has sent you a letter of which this is a copy. I approve this letter. I deplore the want of concurrence with you in opinion by your general officers, but I do not see the remedy. Be cautious, and do not understand that the government or country is driving you. I do not yet see how I could profit by changing the command of the Army of the Potomac; and if I did, I should not wish to do it by accepting the resignation of your commission.
A. LINCOLN.

TELEGRAM TO GOVERNOR JOHNSON.

EXECUTIVE MANSION, WASHINGTON, January 8, 1863.

GOVERNOR JOHNSON, Nashville Tenn.:
A dispatch of yesterday from Nashville says the body of Captain Todd, of the Sixth Kentucky, was brought in to-day. Please tell me what was his Christian name, and whether he was in our service or that of the enemy. I shall also be glad to have your impression as to the effect the late operations about Murfreesborough will have on the prospects of Tennessee.
A. LINCOLN.

TELEGRAM TO GENERAL S. R. CURTIS.

EXECUTIVE MANSION, WASHINGTON, January 10, 1863.

MAJOR-GENERAL CURTIS, St. Louis, MO.:
I understand there is considerable trouble with the slaves in Missouri. Please do your best to keep peace on the question for two or three weeks, by which time we hope to do something here toward settling the question in Missouri.
A. LINCOLN.

TELEGRAM TO GOVERNOR JOHNSON.

EXECUTIVE MANSION, WASHINGTON, January 10, 1863

GOVERNOR JOHNSON, Nashville, Tenn.:

Yours received. I presume the remains of Captain Todd are in the hands of his family and friends, and I wish to give no order on the subject; but I do wish your opinion of the effects of the late battles about Murfreesborough upon the prospects of Tennessee.
A. LINCOLN.

INSTRUCTION TO THE JUDGE-ADVOCATE-GENERAL.

WAR DEPARTMENT, WASHINGTON CITY, January 12, 1863.

The Judge-Advocate-General is instructed to revise the proceedings of the court-martial in the case of Major-General Fitz-John Porter, and to report fully upon any legal questions that may have arisen in them, and upon the bearing of the testimony in reference to the charges and specifications exhibited against the accused, and upon which he was tried.
A. LINCOLN.

MESSAGE TO THE HOUSE OF REPRESENTATIVES. JANUARY 14, 1863.

TO THE HOUSE OF REPRESENTATIVES: The Secretary of State has submitted to me a resolution of the House of Representatives of the 5th instant, which has been delivered to him, and which is in the following words:
"Resolved, That the Secretary of State be requested to communicate to this House, if not, in his judgment, incompatible with the public interest, why our Minister in New Granada has not presented his credentials to the actual government of that country; also the reasons for which Senor Murillo is not recognized by the United States as the diplomatic representative of the Mosquera government of that country; also, what negotiations have been had, if any, with General Herran as the representative of Ospina's government in New Granada since it went into existence."
On the 12th day of December, 1846, a treaty of amity, peace, and concord was concluded between the United States of America and the Republic of New Granada, which is still in force. On the 7th day of December, 1847, General Pedro Alcantara Herran, who had been duly accredited, was received here as the envoy extraordinary and minister plenipotentiary of that, republic. On the 30th day of August, 1849, Senor Don Rafael Rivas was received by this government as charge d'affaires of the same republic. On the 5th day of December, 1851, a consular convention was concluded between that republic and the United States, which treaty was signed on behalf of the Republic of Granada by the same Senor Rivas. This treaty is still in force. On the 27th of April, 1852, Senor Don Victoriano de Diego Paredes was received as charge d'affaires of the Republic of New Granada. On the 20th of June, 1855, General Pedro Alcantara Herran was again received as envoy extraordinary and minister plenipotentiary, duly accredited by the Republic of New Granada, and he has ever since remained, under the same credentials, as the representative of that republic near the Government of the United States. On the 10th day of September, 1857, a claims convention was concluded between the United States and the Republic of Granada. This convention is still in force, and has in part been executed. In May, 1858, the constitution of the republic was remodelled; and the nation assumed the political title of "The Granadian Confederacy." This fact was formally announced to this Government, but without any change in their representative here. Previously to the 4th day of March, 1861, a revolutionary war against the Republic of New Granada, which had thus been recognized and treated with by the United States, broke out in New Granada, assuming to set up a new government under the name of "United States of Colombia." This war has had various vicissitudes, sometimes favorable, sometimes adverse, to the revolutionary movements. The revolutionary organization has hitherto been simply a military provisionary power, and no definitive constitution of government has yet been established in New Granada in place of that organized by the constitution of 1858. The minister of the United States to the Granadian Confederacy, who was appointed on the 29th day of May, 1861, was directed, in view of the occupation of the capital by the revolutionary party and of the uncertainty of the civil war, not to present his credentials to either the government of the Granadian Confederacy or to the provisional military government, but to conduct his affairs informally, as is customary in such cases, and to report the progress of events and await the instructions of this Government. The advices which have been received from him have not hitherto, been sufficiently conclusive to determine me to recognize the revolutionary government. General Herran being here, with full authority from the Government of New Canada, which has been so long recognized by the United States, I have not received any representative from the revolutionary government, which has not yet been recognized, because such a proceeding would be in itself an act of recognition.

Official communications have been had on various incidental and occasional questions with General Herran as the minister plenipotentiary and envoy extraordinary of the Granadian Confederacy, but in no other character. No definitive measure or proceeding has resulted from these communications, and a communication of them at present would not, in my judgment, be compatible with the public interest.

A. LINCOLN.

TO SECRETARY OF WAR.

WASHINGTON, January 15, 1863.

SECRETARY OF WAR:
Please see Mr. Stafford, who wants to assist in raising colored troops in Missouri.

A. LINCOLN.

PRINTING MONEY

MESSAGE TO CONGRESS.

January 17, 1863.
TO THE SENATE AND HOUSE OF REPRESENTATIVES:
I have signed the joint resolution to provide for the immediate payment of the army and navy of the United States, passed by the House of Representatives on the 14th and by the Senate on the 15th instant.

The joint resolution is a simple authority, amounting, however, under existing circumstances, to a direction, to the Secretary of the Treasury to make an additional issue of $100,000,000 in United States notes, if so much money is needed, for the payment of the army and navy.

My approval is given in order that every possible facility may be afforded for the prompt discharge of all arrears of pay due to our soldiers and our sailors.

While giving this approval, however, I think it my duty to express my sincere regret that it has been found necessary to authorize so large an additional issue of United States notes, when this circulation and that of the suspended banks together have become already so redundant as to increase prices beyond real values, thereby augmenting the cost of living to the injury of labor, and the cost of supplies to the injury of the whole country.

It seems very plain that continued issues of United States notes without any check to the issues of suspended banks, and without adequate provision for the raising of money by loans and for funding the issues so as to keep them within due limits, must soon produce disastrous consequences; and this matter appears to me so important that I feel bound to avail myself of this occasion to ask the special attention of Congress to it.

That Congress has power to regulate the currency of the country can hardly admit of doubt, and that a judicious measure to prevent the deterioration of this currency, by a seasonable taxation of bank circulation or otherwise, is needed seems equally clear. Independently of this general consideration, it would be unjust to the people at large to exempt banks enjoying the special privilege of circulation from their just proportion of the public burdens.

In order to raise money by way of loans most easily and cheaply, it is clearly necessary to give every possible support to the public credit. To that end a uniform currency, in which taxes, subscriptions to loans, and all other ordinary public dues as well as all private dues may be paid, is almost if not quite indispensable. Such a currency can be furnished by banking associations organized under a general act of Congress, as suggested in my message at the beginning of the present session. The securing of this circulation by the pledge of United States bonds, as therein suggested, would still further facilitate loans, by increasing the present and causing a future demand for such bonds.

In view of the actual financial embarrassments of the government, and of the greater embarrassment sure to come if the necessary means of relief be not afforded, I feel that I should not perform my duty by a simple announcement of my approval of the joint resolution, which proposes relief only by increased circulation, without expressing my earnest desire that measures such in substance as those I have just referred to may receive the early sanction of Congress. By such measures, in my opinion, will payment be most certainly secured, not only to the army and navy, but to all honest creditors of the government, and satisfactory provision made for future demands on the treasury.

A. LINCOLN.

TO THE WORKING-MEN OF MANCHESTER, ENGLAND.

EXECUTIVE MANSION, WASHINGTON, January, 1863.

TO THE WORKING-MEN OF MANCHESTER:
I have the honor to acknowledge the receipt of the address and resolutions which you sent me on the eve of the new year. When I came, on the 4th of March, 1861, through a free and constitutional election to fireside in the Government of the United States, the country was found at the verge of civil war. Whatever might have been the cause, or whosesoever the fault, one duty, paramount to all others, was before me, namely, to maintain and preserve at once the Constitution and the integrity of the Federal Republic. A conscientious purpose to perform this duty is the key to all the measures of administration which have been and to all which will hereafter be pursued. Under our frame of government and my official oath, I could not depart from this purpose if I would. It is not always in the power of governments to enlarge or restrict the scope of moral results which follow the policies that they may deem it necessary for the public safety from time to time to adopt.

I have understood well that the duty of self-preservation rests solely with the American people; but I have at the same time been aware that favor or disfavor of foreign nations might have a material influence in enlarging or prolonging the struggle with disloyal men in which the country is engaged. A fair examination of history has served to authorize a belief that the past actions and influences of the United States were generally regarded as having been beneficial toward mankind. I have, therefore, reckoned upon the forbearance of nations. Circumstances—to some of which you kindly allude—induce me especially to expect that if justice and good faith should be practised by the United States, they would encounter no hostile influence on the part of Great Britain. It is now a pleasant duty to acknowledge the demonstration you have given of your desire that a spirit of amity and peace toward this country may prevail in the councils of your Queen, who is respected and esteemed in your own country only more than she is by the kindred nation which has its home on this side of the Atlantic.

I know and deeply deplore the sufferings which the workingmen at Manchester, and in all Europe, are called to endure in this crisis. It has been often and studiously represented that the attempt to overthrow this government, which was built upon the foundation of human rights, and to substitute for it one which should rest exclusively on the basis of human slavery, was likely to obtain the favor of Europe. Through the action of our disloyal citizens, the working-men of Europe have been subjected to severe trials, for the purpose of forcing their sanction to that attempt. Under the circumstance, I cannot but regard your decisive utterances upon the question as an instance of sublime Christian heroism which has not been surpassed in any age or in any country. It is indeed an energetic and inspiring assurance of the inherent power of truth and of the ultimate and universal triumph of justice, humanity, and freedom. I do not doubt that the sentiments, you have expressed will be sustained by your great nation; and, on the other hand, I have no hesitation in assuring you that they will excite admiration, esteem, and the most reciprocal feelings of friendship among the American people.

I hail this interchange of sentiment, therefore, as an augury that whatever else may happen, whatever misfortune may befall your country or my own, the peace and friendship which now exist between the two nations will be, as it shall be my desire to make them, perpetual.
A. LINCOLN.

MESSAGE TO CONGRESS.

WASHINGTON, January 21, 1863.

GENTLEMEN OF THE SENATE AND HOUSE OF REPRESENTATIVES:
I submit herewith for your consideration the joint resolutions of the corporate authorities of the city of Washington, adopted September a 7, 1862, and a memorial of the same under date of October 28, 1862, both relating to and urging the construction of certain railroads concentrating upon the city of Washington.
In presenting this memorial and the joint resolutions to you, I am not prepared to say more than that the subject is one of great practical importance, and that I hope it will receive the attention of Congress.
A. LINCOLN.

FITZ-JOHN PORTER COURT-MARTIAL.

INDORSEMENT ON THE PROCEEDINGS AND SENTENCE

HEADQUARTERS OF THE ARMY, WASHINGTON,
January 13, 1863.
In compliance with the Sixty-fifth Article of War, these whole proceedings are transmitted to the Secretary of War, to be laid before the President of the United States.
H. W. HALLECK,
General-in-Chief.
January 21, 1863.
The foregoing proceedings, findings, and sentence in the foregoing case of Major-General Fitz-John Porter are approved and confirmed, and it is ordered that the said Fitz-John Porter be, and he hereby is, cashiered and dismissed from the service of the United States as a major-general of volunteers, and as colonel and brevet brigadier-general in the regular service of the United States, and forever disqualified from holding any office of trust or profit under the Government of the United States.
A. LINCOLN.

FROM GENERAL HALLECK TO GENERAL U. S. GRANT.

HEADQUARTERS OF THE ARMY, WASHINGTON

January 21, 1863.
MAJOR-GENERAL GRANT, Memphis.
GENERAL:—The President has directed that so much of Arkansas as you may desire to control be temporarily attached to your department. This will give you control of both banks of the river.
In your operations down the Mississippi you must not rely too confidently upon any direct co-operation of General Banks and the lower flotilla, as it is possible that they may not be able to pass or reduce Port Hudson. They, however, will do everything in their power to form a junction with you at Vicksburg. If they should not be able to effect this, they will at least occupy a portion of the enemy's forces, and prevent them from reinforcing Vicksburg. I hope, however, that they will do still better and be able to join you.
It may be proper to give you some explanation of the revocation of your order expelling all Jews from your department. The President has no objection to your expelling traitors and Jew peddlers, which, I suppose, was the object of your order; but as it in terms proscribed an entire religious class, some of whom are fighting in our ranks, the President deemed it necessary to revoke it.
Very respectfully, your obedient servant,
H. W. HALLECK, General-in-Chief.

TELEGRAM TO GENERAL BURNSIDE.

EXECUTIVE MANSION, WASHINGTON, January 23, 1863

GENERAL BURNSIDE:
Will see you any moment when you come.
A. LINCOLN.

ORDER RELIEVING GENERAL A. E. BURNSIDE AND MAKING OTHER CHANGES.

(General Orders No.20.)

WAR DEPARTMENT, ADJUTANT-GENERAL'S OFFICE, WASHINGTON, D.C. JANUARY 25, 1863.
I. The President of the United States has directed:
1st. That Major-General A. E. Burnside, at his own request, be relieved from the command of the Army of the Potomac.
2d. That Major-General E. V. Sumner, at his own request, be relieved from duty in the Army of the Potomac.
3d. That Major-General W. B. Franklin be relieved from duty in the Army of the Potomac.
4th. That Major-General J. Hooker be assigned to the command of the Army of the Potomac.
II. The officers relieved as above will report in person to the adjutant-general of the army.
By order of the Secretary of War: D. TOWNSEND, Assistant Adjutant-General

TO GENERAL J. HOOKER.

EXECUTIVE MANSION, WASHINGTON, D. C., January 26, 1863.

MAJOR-GENERAL HOOKER.
GENERAL:—I have placed you at the head of the Army of the Potomac. Of course I have done this upon what appear to me to be sufficient reasons, and yet I think it best for you to know that there are some things in regard to which I am not quite satisfied with you. I believe you to be a brave and skillful soldier, which of course I like. I also believe you do not mix politics with your profession, in which you are right. You have confidence in yourself, which is a valuable if not an indispensable quality. You are ambitious, which within reasonable bounds does good rather than harm; but I think that during General Burnside's command of the army you have taken counsel of your ambition and thwarted him as much as you could, in which you did a great wrong to the country and to a most meritorious and honorable brother officer. I have heard, in such a way as to believe it, of your recently saying that both the army and the government needed a dictator. Of course it was not for this, but in spite of it, that I have given you the command. Only those generals who gain successes can set up dictators. What I now ask of you is military success, and I will risk the dictatorship. The government will support you to the utmost of its ability, which is neither more nor less than it has done and will do for all commanders. I much fear that the spirit that you have aided to infuse into the army, of criticizing their commander and withholding confidence from him, will now turn upon you. I shall assist you as far as I can to put it down. Neither you nor Napoleon, if he were alive again, could get any good out of an army while such a spirit prevails in it. And now beware of rashness. Beware of rashness, but with energy and sleepless vigilance go forward and give us victories.
Yours very truly,
A. LINCOLN.

MESSAGE TO CONGRESS.

WASHINGTON CITY, January 28,1863,

TO THE SENATE AND HOUSE OF REPRESENTATIVES:
In conformity to the law of July 16, 1862, I most cordially recommend that Commander David D. Porter, United States Navy, acting rear-admiral, commanding the Mississippi Squadron, receive a vote of thanks of Congress for the bravery and skill displayed in the attack on the post of Arkansas, which surrendered to the combined military and naval forces on the 10th instant.
A. LINCOLN.

TELEGRAM TO GENERAL BUTLER

EXECUTIVE MANSION, WASHINGTON, January 28, 1863.

MAJOR-GENERAL BUTLER, Lowell, Mass.:
Please come here immediately. Telegraph me about what time you will arrive.
A. LINCOLN.

TELEGRAM TO GENERAL DIX.

EXECUTIVE MANSION, WASHINGTON, January 29, 1863

MAJOR-GENERAL DIx, Fort Monroe, Va.:
Do Richmond papers have anything from Vicksburg?
A. LINCOLN.

TO THURLOW WEED.

WASHINGTON, January 29, 1863.

HON. THURLOW WEED.
DEAR SIR:—Your valedictory to the patrons of the Albany Evening journal brings me a good deal of uneasiness. What does it mean?
Truly Yours,
A. LINCOLN.

TELEGRAM TO GENERAL DIX.

WAR DEPARTMENT, WASHINGTON CITY,

January 30, 1863. 5.45 P.M.
MAJOR-GENERAL Dix, Fort Monroe, Va.:
What iron-clads, if any, have gone out of Hampton Roads within the last two days?
A. LINCOLN.

TELEGRAM TO GENERAL DIX.

WAR DEPARTMENT, WASHINGTON CITY, D. C., January 31, 1863.

MAJOR-GENERAL Dix, Fort Monroe, Va.: Corcoran's and Pryor's battle terminated. Have you any news through Richmond papers or otherwise?
A. LINCOLN.

TELEGRAM TO GENERAL SCHENCK.

WAR DEPARTMENT, WASHINGTON CITY, D. C., January 31, 1863.

MAJOR-GENERAL SCHENCK, Baltimore, Md.:
I do not take jurisdiction of the pass question. Exercise your own discretion as to whether Judge Pettis shall have a pass.
A. LINCOLN.

TO THE WORKING-MEN OF LONDON, ENGLAND.

EXECUTIVE MANSION, February 1, 1863.

TO THE WORKING-MEN OF LONDON:
I have received the New Year's address which you have sent me, with a sincere appreciation of the exalted and humane sentiments by which it was inspired.

As these sentiments are manifestly the enduring support of the free institutions of England, so I am sure also that they constitute the only reliable basis for free institutions throughout the world.

The resources, advantages, and powers of the American people are very great, and they have consequently succeeded to equally great responsibilities. It seems to have devolved upon them to test whether a government established on the principles of human freedom can be maintained against an effort to build one upon the exclusive foundation of human bondage. They will rejoice with me in the new evidences which your proceedings furnish that the magnanimity they are exhibiting is justly estimated by the true friends of freedom and humanity in foreign countries.

Accept my best wishes for your individual welfare, and for the welfare and happiness of the whole British people.
A. LINCOLN.

TELEGRAM TO GENERAL SCHENCK. [Cipher.] WAR DEPARTMENT, WASHINGTON, D. C.,

February 4, 1863.

MAJOR-GENERAL SCHENCK, Baltimore, Md.:
I hear of some difficulty in the streets of Baltimore yesterday. What is the amount of it?
A. LINCOLN.

MESSAGE TO THE SENATE.

WASHINGTON, D. C., February 12, 1863.

TO THE SENATE OF THE UNITED STATES:
On the 4th of September, 1862, Commander George Henry Preble, United States Navy, then senior officer in command of the naval force off the harbor of Mobile, was guilty of inexcusable neglect in permitting the armed steamer Oreto in open daylight to run the blockade. For his omission to perform his whole duty on that occasion, and the injury thereby inflicted on the service and the country, his name was stricken from the list of naval officers and he was dismissed [from] the service.

Since his dismissal earnest application has been made for his restoration to his former position by senators and naval officers, on the ground that his fault was an error of judgment, and that the example in his case has already had its effect in preventing a repetition of similar neglect.

I therefore on this application and representation, and in consideration of his previous fair record, do hereby nominate George Henry Preble to be a commander in the navy from the 16th July, 1862, to take rank on the active list next after Commander Edward Donaldson, and to fill a vacancy occasioned by the death of Commander J. M. Wainwright.
A. LINCOLN.

MESSAGE TO THE SENATE.

WASHINGTON, D. C., February 12, 1863.

TO THE SENATE OF THE UNITED STATES:
On the 24th August, 1861, Commander Roger Perry, United. States Navy, was dismissed from the service under a misapprehension in regard to his loyalty to the Government, from the circumstance that several oaths were transmitted to him and the Navy Department failed to receive any recognition of them. After his dismissal, and upon his assurance that the oath failed to reach him and his readiness to execute it, he was recommissioned to his original position on the 4th September following. On the same day, 4th September, he was ordered to command the sloop of war Vandalia; on the 22d this order was revoked and he was ordered to duty in the Mississippi Squadron, and on the 23d January, 1862, was detached sick, and has since remained unemployed. The advisory board under the act of 16th July, 1862, did not recommend him for further promotion.

This last commission, having been issued during the recess of the Senate, expired at the end of the succeeding session, 17th July, 1862, from which date, not having been nominated to the Senate, he ceased to be a commander in the navy. To correct the omission to nominate this officer to the Senate at its last session, I now nominate Commander Roger Perry to be a commander in the navy from the 14th September, 1855, to take his relative position on the list of commanders not recommended for further promotion.
A. LINCOLN.

TELEGRAM TO GENERAL W. S. ROSECRANS.

EXECUTIVE MANSION, WASHINGTON, February 12,1863.

MAJOR-GENERAL ROSECRANS, Murfreesborough, Tenn.:
Your despatch about "river patrolling" received. I have called the Secretary of the Navy, Secretary of War, and General-in-Chief together, and submitted it to them, who promise to do their very best in the case. I cannot take it into my own hands without producing inextricable confusion.
A. LINCOLN.

TELEGRAM TO SIMON CAMERON.

EXECUTIVE MANSION, WASHINGTON, February 13, 1863.

HON. SIMON CAMERON, Harrisburg, Pa.: General Clay is here and I suppose the matter we spoke of will have to be definitely settled now. Please answer.
A. LINCOLN.

TO ALEXANDER REED.

EXECUTIVE MANSION, WASHINGTON, February 22, 1863.

REV. ALEXANDER REED. MY DEAR SIR:—Your note, by which you, as General Superintendent of the United States Christian Commission, invite me to preside at a meeting to be held this day at the hall of the House of Representatives in this city, is received.

While, for reasons which I deem sufficient, I must decline to preside, I cannot withhold my approval of the meeting and its worthy objects.

Whatever shall be, sincerely and in God's name, devised for the good of the soldiers and seamen in their hard spheres of duty, can scarcely fail to be blessed; and whatever shall tend to turn our thoughts from the unreasoning and uncharitable passions, prejudices, and jealousies incident to a great national trouble such as ours, and to fix them on the vast and long enduring consequences, for weal or for woe, which are to result from the struggle, and especially to strengthen our reliance on the Supreme Being for the final triumph of the right, cannot but be well for us all.

The birthday of Washington and the Christian Sabbath coinciding this year, and suggesting together the highest interests of this life and of that to come, is most propitious for the meeting proposed.

Your obedient servant,
A. LINCOLN

TELEGRAM TO J. K. DUBOIS.

[Cipher]

WAR DEPARTMENT, WASHINGTON, D. C. February 26,1863.
HON. J. K. DuBois, Springfield, Ill.: General Rosecrans respectfully urges the appointment of William P. Caslin as a brigadier-general, What say you?
A. LINCOLN.

TELEGRAM TO GENERAL HOOKER

EXECUTIVE MANSION, WASHINGTON, February 27,1863

MAJOR-GENERAL HOOKER:
If it will be no detriment to the service I will be obliged for Capt. Henry A. Marchant, of Company I, Twenty-third Pennsylvania Volunteers, to come here and remain four or five days.
A. LINCOLN.

PROCLAMATION CONVENING THE SENATE, FEBRUARY 28, 1863

BY THE PRESIDENT OF THE UNITED STATES OF AMERICA

A Proclamation.
Whereas objects of interest to the United States require that the Senate should be convened at 12 o'clock on the 4th of March next to receive and act upon such communications as may be made to it on the part of the Executive:
Now, therefore, I, Abraham Lincoln, President of the United States, have considered it to be my duty to issue this my proclamation, declaring that an extraordinary occasion requires the Senate of the United States to convene for the transaction of business at the Capitol, in the city of Washington, on the 4th day of March next, at 12 o'clock at noon on that day, of which all who shall at that time be entitled to act as members of that body are hereby required to take notice.
Given under my hand and the seal of the United States, at Washington, the twenty eighth day of February A.D. 1863, and of the independence of the United States of America, the eighty-seventh.
A. LINCOLN.

By the President WILLIAM H. SEWARD,
Secretary of State.

TO SECRETARY SEWARD.

WASHINGTON, March, 7, 1863.

Mr. M. is now with me on the question of the Honolulu Commissioner. It pains me some that this tilt for the place of Colonel Baker's friend grows so fierce, now that the Colonel is no longer alive to defend him. I presume, however, we shall have no rest from it. In self-defense I am disposed to say, "Make a selection and send it to me."
A. LINCOLN

TELEGRAM TO GOVERNOR TOD,

EXECUTIVE MANSION, WASHINGTON, March 9, 1863.

GOVERNOR DAVID TOD, Columbus, Ohio:
I think your advice with that of others would be valuable in the selection of provost-marshals for Ohio.
A. LINCOLN.

PROCLAMATION RECALLING SOLDIERS TO THEIR REGIMENTS, MARCH 10, 1863

BY THE PRESIDENT OF THE UNITED STATES:

A Proclamation
In pursuance of the twenty-sixth section of the act of Congress entitled "An act for enrolling and calling out the national forces, and for other purposes," approved on the 3d day of March, 1863, I, Abraham Lincoln, President and Commander-in-Chief of the Army and Navy of the United States, do hereby order and command that all soldiers enlisted or drafted in the service of the United States now absent from their regiments without leave shall forthwith return to their respective regiments.
And I do hereby declare and proclaim that all soldiers now absent from their respective regiments without leave who shall, on or before the first day of April, 1863, report themselves at any rendezvous designated by the general orders of the War Department No. 58, hereto annexed, may be restored to their respective regiments without punishment, except the forfeiture of pay and allowances during their absence; and all who do not return within the time above specified shall be arrested as deserters and punished as the law provides; and
Whereas evil-disposed and disloyal persons at sundry places have enticed and procured soldiers to desert and absent themselves from their regiments, thereby weakening the strength of the armies and prolonging the war, giving aid and comfort to the enemy, and cruelly exposing the gallant and faithful soldiers remaining in the ranks to increased hardships and danger:
I do therefore call upon all patriotic and faithful citizens to oppose and resist the aforementioned dangerous and treasonable crimes, and to aid in restoring to their regiments all soldiers absent without leave, and to assist in the execution of the act of Congress "for enrolling and calling out the national forces, and for other purposes," and to support the proper authorities in the prosecution and punishment of offenders against said act and in suppressing the insurrection and rebellion.
In testimony whereof I have hereunto set my hand. Done at the city of Washington, this tenth day of March, A.D. 1863, and of the independence of the United States the eighty-seventh.
A. LINCOLN.
By the President: EDWIN M. STANTON, Secretary of War.

TELEGRAM TO GENERAL HOOKER.

EXECUTIVE MANSION, WASHINGTON, March 13, 1863.

MAJOR-GENERAL HOOKER:
General Stahel wishes to be assigned to General Heintzelman and General Heintzelman also desires it. I would like to oblige both if it would not injure the service in your army, or incommode you. What say you?
A. LINCOLN.

TO SECRETARY SEWARD.

WASHINGTON, Match 15, 1863.

I am very glad of your note saying "recent despatches from him are able, judicious, and loyal," and that if I agree; we will leave him there. I am glad to agree, so long as the public interest does not seem to require his removal.

TELEGRAM TO J. O. MORTON.

EXECUTIVE MANSION, WASHINGTON, March 16, 1863.

HON. J. O. MORTON, Joliet, Ill.: William Chumasero is proposed for provost-marshal of your district. What think you of it? I understand he is a good man.
A. LINCOLN.

GRANT'S EXCLUSION OF A NEWSPAPER REPORTER

REVOCATION OF SENTENCE OF T. W. KNOX.

EXECUTIVE MANSION, WASHINGTON, March 20, 1863.
WHOM IT MAY CONCERN:—Whereas, it appears to my satisfaction that Thomas W. Knox, a correspondent of the New York Herald, has been by the sentence of a court-martial excluded from the military department under command of Major-General Grant, and also that General Thayer, president of the court-martial which rendered the sentence, and Major-General McClernand, in command of a corps of that department, and many other respectable persons, are of opinion that Mr. Knox's offense was technical rather than wilfully wrong, and that the sentence should be revoked: now, therefore, said sentence is hereby so far revoked as to allow Mr. Knox to return to General Grant's headquarters, and to remain if General Grant shall give his express assent, and to again leave the department if General Grant shall refuse such assent.
A. LINCOLN.

TO BENJAMIN GRATZ.

EXECUTIVE MANSION, WASHINGTON, March 25,1863.

Mr. BENJAMIN GRATZ, Lexington, Ky.:

Show this to whom it may concern as your authority for allowing Mrs. Selby to remain at your house, so long as you choose to be responsible for what she may do.

A. LINCOLN.

TELEGRAM TO GENERAL ROSECRANS.

EXECUTIVE MANSION, WASHINGTON, March 25, 1863.

MAJOR-GENERAL ROSECRANS, Murfreesborough, Tenn.:

Your dispatches about General Davis and General Mitchell are received. General Davis' case is not particular, being simply one of a great many recommended and not nominated because they would transcend the number allowed by law. General Mitchell (was) nominated and rejected by the Senate and I do not think it proper for me to renominate him without a change of circumstances such as the performance of additional service, or an expressed change of purpose on the part of at least some senators who opposed him.

A. LINCOLN.

TELEGRAM TO GENERAL S. A. HURLBUT.

WASHINGTON, March 25, 1863.

MAJOR-GENERAL HURLBUT, Memphis:

What news have you? What from Vicksburg? What from Yazoo Pass? What from Lake Providence? What generally?

A. LINCOLN.

QUESTION OF RAISING NEGRO TROOPS

TO GOVERNOR JOHNSON.

(Private.)
EXECUTIVE MANSION, WASHINGTON March 26, 1863.
HON. ANDREW JOHNSON.

MY DEAR SIR:—I am told you have at least thought of raising a negro military force. In my opinion the country now needs no specific thing so much as some man of your ability and position to go to this work. When I speak of your position, I mean that of an eminent citizen of a slave State and himself a slaveholder. The colored population is the great available and yet unavailed of force for restoring the Union. The bare sight of fifty thousand armed and drilled black soldiers upon the banks of the Mississippi would end the rebellion at once; and who doubts that we can present that sight if we but take hold in earnest? If you have been thinking of it, please do not dismiss the thought.

Yours very truly,
A. LINCOLN.

PROCLAMATION APPOINTING A NATIONAL FAST-DAY.

BY THE PRESIDENT OF THE UNITED STATES OF AMERICA:

A Proclamation.

March 30, 1863.

Whereas the Senate of the United States, devoutly recognizing the supreme authority and just government of Almighty God in all the affairs of men and of nations, has by a resolution requested the President to designate and set apart a day for national prayer and humiliation:

And whereas it is the duty of nations as well as men to own their dependence upon the overruling power of God; to confess their sins and transgressions in humble sorrow, yet with assured hope that genuine repentance will lead to mercy and pardon; and to recognize the sublime truth, announced in the Holy Scriptures and proven by all history, that those nations only are blessed whose God is the Lord:

And insomuch as we know that by His divine law nations, like individuals, are subjected to punishments and chastisements in this world, may we not justly fear that the awful calamity of civil war which now desolates the land may be but a punishment inflicted upon us for our presumptuous sins, to the needful end of our national reformation as a whole people? We have been the recipients of the choicest bounties of Heaven. We have been preserved, these many years, in peace and prosperity. We have grown in numbers, wealth, and power as no other nation has ever grown; but we have forgotten God. We have forgotten the gracious hand which preserved us in peace, and multiplied and enriched and strengthened us; and we have vainly imagined, in the deceitfulness of our hearts, that all these blessings were produced by some superior wisdom and virtue of our own. Intoxicated with unbroken success, we have become too self-sufficient to feel the necessity of redeeming and preserving grace, too proud to pray to the God that made us: It behooves us, then, to humble ourselves before the offended Power, to confess our national sins, and to pray for clemency and forgiveness:

Now, therefore, in compliance with the request, and fully concurring in the views, of the Senate, I do by this my proclamation designate and set apart Thursday, the 30th day of April, 1863, as a day of national humiliation, fasting, and prayer. And I do hereby request all the people to abstain on that day from their ordinary secular pursuits, and to unite at their several places of public worship and their respective homes in keeping the day holy to the Lord, and devoted to the humble discharge of the religious duties proper to that solemn occasion. All this being done in sincerity and truth, let us then rest humbly in the hope, authorized by the divine teachings, that the united cry of the nation will be heard on high, and answered with blessings no less than the pardon of our national sins, and the restoration of our now divided and suffering country to its former happy condition of unity and peace.

In witness whereof, I have hereunto set my hand, and caused the seal of the United States to be affixed.

Done at the city of Washington, this thirtieth day of March, in the year of our Lord one thousand eight hundred and sixty-three, and of the independence of the United States the eighty-seventh.

A. LINCOLN.

By the President: WILLIAM H. SEWARD,
  Secretary of State.

LICENSE OF COMMERCIAL INTERCOURSE.

EXECUTIVE MANSION, WASHINGTON, March 31, 1863.

Whereas by the act of Congress approved July 13, 1861, entitled "An act to provide for the collection of duties on imports, and for other purposes," all commercial intercourse between the inhabitants of such States as should by proclamation be declared in insurrection against the United States and the citizens of the rest of the United States was prohibited so long as such condition of hostility should continue, except as the same shall be licensed and permitted by the President to be conducted and carried on only in pursuance of rules and regulations prescribed by the Secretary of the Treasury; and:

Whereas it appears that a partial restoration of such intercourse between the inhabitants of sundry places and sections heretofore declared in insurrection in pursuance of said act and the citizens of the rest of the United States will favorably affect the public interests:

Now, therefore, I, Abraham Lincoln, President of the United States, exercising the authority and discretion confided to me by the said act of Congress, do hereby license and permit such commercial intercourse between the citizens of loyal States and the inhabitants of such insurrectionary States in the cases and under the restrictions described and expressed in the regulations prescribed by the Secretary of the Treasury bearing even date with these presents, or in such other regulations as he may hereafter, with my approval, prescribe.

A. LINCOLN.

TO GENERAL D. HUNTER.

(Private.) EXECUTIVE MANSION, WASHINGTON, D. C April 1, 1863.

MAJOR-GENERAL HUNTER.
MY DEAR SIR:—I am glad to see the accounts of your colored force at Jacksonville, Florida. I see the enemy are driving at them fiercely, as is to be expected. It is important to the enemy that such a force shall not take shape and grow and thrive in the South, and in precisely the same proportion it is important to us that it shall. Hence the utmost caution and vigilance is necessary on our part. The enemy will make extra efforts to destroy them, and we should do the same to preserve and increase them.
Yours truly,
A. LINCOLN.

PROCLAMATION ABOUT COMMERCIAL INTERCOURSE, APRIL 2, 1863

BY THE PRESIDENT OF THE UNITED STATES OF AMERICA:

A Proclamation.
Whereas, in pursuance of the act of Congress approved July 13, 1861, I did, by proclamation dated August 16, 1861, declare that the inhabitants of the States of Georgia, South Carolina, Virginia, North Carolina, Tennessee, Alabama, Louisiana, Texas, Arkansas, Mississippi, and Florida (except the inhabitants of that part of Virginia lying west of the Alleghany Mountains, and of such other parts of that State and the other States hereinbefore named as might maintain a legal adhesion to the Union and the Constitution or might be from time to time occupied and controlled by forces of the United States engaged in the dispersion of said insurgents) were in a state of insurrection against the United States, and that all commercial intercourse between the same and the inhabitants thereof, with the exceptions aforesaid, and the citizens of other States and other parts of the United States was unlawful and would remain unlawful until such insurrection should cease or be suppressed, and that all goods and chattels, wares and merchandise, coming from any of said States, with the exceptions aforesaid, into other parts of the United States without the license and permission of the President, through the Secretary of the Treasury, or proceeding to any of said States, with the exceptions aforesaid, by land or water, together with the vessel or vehicle conveying the same to or from said States, with the exceptions aforesaid, would be forfeited to the United States, and:
Whereas experience has shown that the exceptions made in and by said proclamation embarrass the due enforcement of said act of July 13, 1861, and the proper regulation of the commercial intercourse authorized by said act with the loyal citizens of said States:
Now, therefore, I, Abraham Lincoln, President of the United States, do hereby revoke the said exceptions, and declare that the inhabitants of the States of Georgia, South Carolina, North Carolina, Tennessee, Alabama, Louisiana, Texas, Arkansas, Mississippi, Florida, and Virginia (except the forty-eight counties of Virginia designated as West Virginia, and except also the ports of New Orleans, Key West; Port Royal, and Beaufort in North Carolina) are in a state of insurrection against the United States, and that all commercial intercourse not licensed and conducted as provided in said act between the said States and the inhabitants thereof, with the exceptions aforesaid, and the citizens of other States and other parts of the United States is unlawful and will remain unlawful until such insurrection shall cease or has been suppressed and notice thereof has been duly given by proclamation; and all cotton, tobacco, and other products, and all other goods and chattels, wares and merchandise, coming from any of said States, with the exceptions aforesaid, into other parts of the United States, or proceeding to any of said States, with the exceptions aforesaid, without the license and permission of the President, through the Secretary of the Treasury, will together with the vessel or vehicle conveying the same, be forfeited to the United States.
In witness whereof I have hereunto set my hand and caused the seal of the United States to be affixed.
Done at the city of Washington, this second day of April, A.D. 1863, and of the independence of the United States of America the eighty-seventh.
A. LINCOLN.
By the President: WILLIAM H. SEWARD,
  Secretary of State.

TELEGRAM TO GENERAL HOOKER.

EXECUTIVE MANSION, WASHINGTON, April 3, 1863.

MAJOR-GENERAL HOOKER:
Our plan is to pass Saturday night on the boat, go over from Aquia Creek to your camp Sunday morning, remain with you till Tuesday morning, and then return. Our party will probably not exceed six persons of all sorts.
A. LINCOLN.

OPINION ON HARBOR DEFENSE.

April 4, 1863.

On this general subject I respectfully refer Mr.————__ to the Secretaries of War and Navy for conference and consultation. I have a single idea of my own about harbor defense. It is a steam ram, built so as to sacrifice nearly all capacity for carrying to those of speed and strength, so as to be able to split any vessel having hollow enough in her to carry supplies for a voyage of any distance. Such ram, of course, could not herself carry supplies for a voyage of considerable distance, and her business would be to guard a particular harbor as a bulldog guards his master's door.
A. LINCOLN.

TELEGRAM TO THE SECRETARY OF THE NAVY.

HEADQUARTERS ARMY POTOMAC, April 9, 1863.

HON. SECRETARY OF THE NAVY:
Richmond Whig of the 8th has no telegraphic despatches from Charleston, but has the following as editorial:
"All thoughts are now centred upon Charleston. Official intelligence was made public early yesterday morning that the enemy's iron-clad fleet had attempted to cross the bar and failed, but later in the day it was announced that the gunboats and transports had succeeded in crossing and were at anchor. Our iron-clads lay between the forts quietly awaiting the attack. Further intelligence is looked for with eager anxiety. The Yankees have made no secret of this vast preparation for an attack on Charleston, and we may well anticipate a desperate conflict. At last the hour of trial has come for Charleston, the hour of deliverance or destruction, for no one believes the other alternative, surrender, possible. The heart of the whole country yearns toward the beleaguered city with intense solicitude, yet with hopes amounting to confidence. Charleston knows what is expected of her, and which is due to her fame, and to the relation she sustains to the cause. The devoted, the heroic, the great-hearted Beauregard is there, and he, too, knows what is expected of him and will not disappoint that expectation. We predict a Saragossa defense, and that if Charleston is taken it will be only a heap of ruins."
The rebel pickets are reported as calling over to our pickets today that we had taken some rebel fort. This is not very intelligible, and I think is entirely unreliable.
A. LINCOLN.

TELEGRAM TO OFFICER IN COMMAND AT NASHVILLE.

EXECUTIVE MANSION, WASHINGTON, April 11,1863.

OFFICER IN COMMAND at Nashville, Tenn: Is there a soldier by the name of John R. Minnick of Wynkoop's cavalry under sentence of death, by a court-martial or military commission, in Nashville? And if so what was his offense, and when is he to be executed?
A. LINCOLN.
If necessary let the execution be staid till I can be heard from again.
A. LINCOLN.

> [President Lincoln sent many telegrams similar in form to this one in order to avoid tiresome repetition the editor has omitted all those without especial interest. Hardly a day went by that there were not people in the White House begging mercy for a sentenced soldier. A mother one day, pleaded with Lincoln to remit the sentence of execution on her son. "Well, I don't think it will do him a bit of good" said Mr. Lincoln—"Pardoned." D.W.]

TELEGRAM TO GENERAL HOOKER.

WASHINGTON D.C., April 12, 1863

MAJOR-GENERAL HOOKER:
Your letter by the hand of General Butterfield is received, and will be conformed to. The thing you dispense with would have been ready by mid-day to-morrow.
A. LINCOLN

TELEGRAM TO ADMIRAL S. P. DUPONT.

EXECUTIVE MANSION, WASHINGTON, April 13, 1863

ADMIRAL DUPONT:
Hold your position inside the bar near Charleston; or, if you shall have left it, return to it, and hold it until further orders. Do not allow the enemy to erect new batteries or defenses on Morris Island. If he has begun it, drive him out. I do not herein order you to renew the general attack. That is to depend on your own discretion or a further order.
A. LINCOLN.

TO GENERAL D. HUNTER AND ADMIRAL S. F. DUPONT.

EXECUTIVE MANSION, WASHINGTON, April 54, 1863.

GENERAL HUNTER AND ADMIRAL DUPONT:
This is intended to clear up an apparent inconsistency between the recent order to continue operations before Charleston and the former one to remove to another point in a certain contingency. No censure upon you, or either of you, is intended. We still hope that by cordial and judicious co-operation you can take the batteries on Morris Island and Sullivan's Island and Fort Sumter. But whether you can or not, we wish the demonstration kept up for a time, for a collateral and very important object. We wish the attempt to be a real one, though not a desperate one, if it affords any considerable chance of success. But if prosecuted as a demonstration only, this must not become public, or the whole effect will be lost. Once again before Charleston, do not leave until further orders from here. Of course this is not intended to force you to leave unduly exposed Hilton Head or other near points in your charge.
Yours truly,
A. LINCOLN.

P. S.—Whoever receives this first, please send a copy to the other immediately. A.L.

TELEGRAM TO GENERAL S. HOOKER.

WASHINGTON, D. C., April 15, 1863. 10.15 P.M.

MAJOR-GENERAL HOOKER:
It is now 10.15 P.M. An hour ago I received your letter of this morning, and a few moments later your despatch of this evening. The latter gives me considerable uneasiness. The rain and mud of course were to be calculated upon. General S. is not moving rapidly enough to make the expedition come to anything. He has now been out three days, two of which were unusually fair weather, and all three without hindrance from the enemy, and yet he is not twenty-five miles from where he started. To reach his point he still has sixty to go, another river (the Rapidan) to cross, and will be hindered by the enemy. By arithmetic, how many days will it take him to do it? I do not know that any better can be done, but I greatly fear it is another failure already. Write me often. I am very anxious.
Yours truly,
A. LINCOLN.

ON COLONIZATION ARRANGEMENTS

REPUDIATION OF AN AGREEMENT WITH BERNARD KOCK

APRIL 16, 1863. A. LINCOLN, PRESIDENT OF THE UNITED STATES OF AMERICA, TO ALL TO WHOM THESE PRESENTS SHALL COME, GREETING:
Know ye that, whereas a paper bearing date the 3rd day of December last, purporting to be an agreement between the United States and one Bernard Kock for immigration of persons of African extraction to a dependency of the Republic of Haiti, was signed by me on behalf of the party of the first part; but whereas the said instrument was and has since remained incomplete in consequence of the seal of the United States not having been thereunto affixed; and whereas I have been moved by considerations by me deemed sufficient to withhold my authority for affixing the said seal:
Now, therefore, be it known that I, Abraham Lincoln, President of the United States, do hereby authorize the Secretary of State to cancel my signature to the instrument aforesaid.
Done at Washington, this sixteenth day of April, A.D. 1863.
A. LINCOLN.
By the President: WILLIAM H. SEWARD, Secretary of State.

STATEHOOD FOR WEST VIRGINIA, APRIL 20, 1863.

PROCLAMATION ADMITTING WEST VIRGINIA INTO THE UNION,

BY THE PRESIDENT OF THE UNITED STATES OF AMERICA:
A Proclamation.
Whereas by the act of Congress approved the 31st day of December last the State of West Virginia was declared to be one of the United States of America, and was admitted into the Union on an equal footing with the original States in all respects whatever, upon the condition that certain changes should be duly made in the proposed constitution for that State; and
Whereas proof of a compliance with that condition, as required by the second section of the act aforesaid, has been submitted to me:
Now, therefore, be it known that I, Abraham Lincoln, President of the United States, do hereby, in pursuance of the act of Congress aforesaid, declare and proclaim that the said act shall take effect and be in force from and after sixty days from the date hereof.

In witness whereof I have hereunto set my hand and caused the seal of the United States to be affixed.
Done at the city of Washington, this twentieth day of April, A.D. 1863, and of the independence of the United States the eighty-seventh.
A. LINCOLN.

TELEGRAM TO GENERAL W. S. ROSECRANS.

EXECUTIVE MANSION, WASHINGTON, APRIL 23, 1863 10.10am

MAJOR-GENERAL ROSECRANS, Murfreesborough, Tenn.:
Your despatch of the 21st received. I really cannot say that I have heard any complaint of you. I have heard complaint of a police corps at Nashville, but your name was not mentioned in connection with it, so far as I remember. It may be that by inference you are connected with it, but my attention has never been drawn to it in that light.
A. LINCOLN.

TELEGRAM TO GENERAL J. HOOKER.

WASHINGTON, D.C., April 27, 1863. 3.30 P.M.

MAJOR-GENERAL HOOKER:
How does it look now?
A. LINCOLN.

TELEGRAM TO GOVERNOR CURTIN.

WAR DEPARTMENT, WASHINGTON, April 28, 1863.

HON. A. O. CURTIN, Harrisburg, Penn.:
I do not think the people of Pennsylvania should be uneasy about an invasion. Doubtless a small force of the enemy is flourishing about in the northern part of Virginia, on the "skewhorn" principle, on purpose to divert us in another quarter. I believe it is nothing more. We think we have adequate force close after them.
A. LINCOLN.

TELEGRAM TO W. A. NEWELL.

EXECUTIVE MANSION, WASHINGTON, April 29, 1863.

HON. W. A. NEWELL, Allentown, N.J.:
I have some trouble about provost-marshal in your first district. Please procure HON. Mr. Starr to come with you and see me, or come to an agreement with him and telegraph me the result.
A. LINCOLN.

TELEGRAM TO GOVERNOR CURTIN,

EXECUTIVE MANSION, MAY 1, 1863

GOVERNOR CURTIN, Harrisburg, Penn.:
The whole disposable force at Baltimore and else where in reach have already been sent after the enemy which alarms you. The worst thing the enemy could do for himself would be to weaken himself before Hooker, and therefore it is safe to believe he is not doing it; and the best thing he could do for himself would be to get us so scared as to bring part of Hooker's force away, and that is just what he is trying to do. I will telegraph you in the morning about calling out the militia.
A. LINCOLN,

TELEGRAM TO GOVERNOR CURTIN

EXECUTIVE MANSION, MAY 2, 1863

GOVERNOR CURTIN, Harrisburg, Penn.:
General Halleck tells me he has a despatch from General Schenck this morning, informing him that our forces have joined, and that the enemy menacing Pennsylvania will have to fight or run today. I hope I am not less anxious to do my duty to Pennsylvania than yourself, but I really do not yet see the justification for incurring the trouble and expense of calling out the militia. I shall keep watch, and try to do my duty.
A. LINCOLN P. S.—Our forces are exactly between the enemy and Pennsylvania.

TELEGRAM TO GENERAL D. BUTTERFIELD.

WASHINGTON, D. C., May 3, 1863.

MAJOR-GENERAL BUTTERFIELD, Chief of Staff:
The President thanks you for your telegrams, and hopes you will keep him advised as rapidly as any information reaches you.
EDWIN M. STANTON, Secretary of War.

GENERALS LOST

TELEGRAM TO GENERAL D. BUTTERFIELD.

WASHINGTON, D. C., May 3, 1863. 4.35 P.M.
MAJOR-GENERAL BUTTERFIELD:
Where is General Hooker? Where is Sedgwick Where is Stoneman?
A. LINCOLN.

TELEGRAM TO GENERAL J. HOOKER.

WASHINGTON, D.C., May 4, 1863. 3.10 P M.

MAJOR-GENERAL HOOKER:
We have news here that the enemy has reoccupied heights above Fredericksburg. Is that so?

A. LINCOLN.

TELEGRAM TO GENERAL BURNSIDE.

EXECUTIVE MANSION, WASHINGTON, May 4, 1863.

MAJOR-GENERAL BURNSIDE, Cincinnati, O.:
Our friend General Sigel claims that you owe him a letter. If you so remember please write him at once. He is here.
A. LINCOLN.

TELEGRAM TO GENERAL HOOKER.

WASHINGTON, D.C., May 6, 1863. 2.25. P.M.

MAJOR-GENERAL HOOKER:
We have through General Dix the contents of Richmond papers of the 5th. General Dix's despatch in full is going to you by Captain Fox of the navy. The substance is General Lee's despatch of the 3d (Sunday), claiming that he had beaten you and that you were then retreating across the Rappahannock, distinctly stating that two of Longstreet's divisions fought you on Saturday, and that General [E. F.] Paxton was killed, Stonewall Jackson severely wounded, and Generals Heth and A. P. Hill slightly wounded. The Richmond papers also stated, upon what authority not mentioned, that our cavalry have been at Ashland, Hanover Court-House, and other points, destroying several locomotives and a good deal of other property, and all the railroad bridges to within five miles of Richmond.
A. LINCOLN.

TELEGRAM TO GENERAL HOOKER

WASHINGTON, D.C., May 6, 1863. 12.30 P.M.

Just as I telegraphed you contents of Richmond papers showing that our cavalry has not failed, I received General Butterfield's of 11 A.M. yesterday. This, with the great rain of yesterday and last night securing your right flank, I think puts a new face upon your case; but you must be the judge.
A. LINCOLN.

TELEGRAM TO COLONEL R. INGALLS.

WASHINGTON, D. C., May 6, 1863 1.45 PM

COLONEL INGALLS:
News has gone to General Hooker which may change his plans. Act in view of such contingency.
A. LINCOLN.

TO GENERAL J. HOOKER.

HEADQUARTERS ARMY OF THE POTOMAC, May 7, 1863.

MAJOR-GENERAL HOOKER.
MY DEAR SIR:—The recent movement of your army is ended without effecting its object, except, perhaps, some important breakings of the enemy's communications. What next? If possible, I would be very glad of another movement early enough to give us some benefit from the fact of the enemy's communication being broken; but neither for this reason nor any other do I wish anything done in desperation or rashness. An early movement would also help to supersede the bad moral effect of there certain, which is said to be considerably injurious. Have you already in your mind a plan wholly or partially formed? If you have, prosecute it without interference from me. If you have not, please inform me, so that I, incompetent as I may be, can try and assist in the formation of some plan for the army.
Yours as ever,
A. LINCOLN.

DRAFTING OF ALIENS

PROCLAMATION CONCERNING ALIENS,

MAY 8, 1863. BY THE PRESIDENT OF THE UNITED STATES OF AMERICA:
A Proclamation
Whereas the Congress of the United States, at its last session, enacted a law entitled "An act for enrolling and calling out the national forces and for other purposes," which was approved on the 3d day of March last; and
Whereas it is recited in the said act that there now exists in the United States an insurrection and rebellion against the authority thereof, and it is, under the Constitution of the United States, the duty of the government to suppress insurrection and rebellion, to guarantee to each State a republican form of government, and to preserve the public tranquillity; and
Whereas for these high purposes a military force is indispensable, to raise and support which all persons Ought willingly to contribute; and
Whereas no service can be more praiseworthy and honorable than that which is rendered for the maintenance of the Constitution and the Union, and the consequent preservation of free government; and
Whereas, for the reasons thus recited, it was enacted by the said statute that all able-bodied male citizens of the United States, and persons of foreign birth who shall have declared on oath their intention to become citizens under and in pursuance of the laws thereof, between the ages of twenty and forty-five years (with certain exceptions not necessary to be here mentioned), are declared to constitute the national forces, and shall be liable to perform military duty in the service of the United States when called out by the President for that purpose; and
Whereas it is claimed by and in behalf of persons of foreign birth within the ages specified in said act, who have heretofore declared on oath their intentions to become citizens under and in pursuance of the laws of the United States, and who have not exercised the right of suffrage or any other political franchise under the laws of the United States, or of any of the States thereof, that they are not absolutely concluded by their aforesaid declaration of intention from renouncing their purpose to become citizens, and that, on the contrary, such persons under treaties or the law of nations retain a right to renounce that purpose and to forego the privileges of citizenship and residence within the United States under the obligations imposed by the aforesaid act of Congress:
Now, therefore, to avoid all misapprehensions concerning the liability of persons concerned to perform the service required by such enactment, and to give it full effect, I do hereby order and proclaim that no plea of alienage will be received or allowed to exempt from the obligations imposed by the aforesaid act of Congress any person of foreign birth who shall have declared on oath his intention to become a citizen of the United States under the laws thereof, and who shall be found within the United States at any time during the continuance of the present insurrection and rebellion, at or after the expiration of the period of sixty-five days from the date of this proclamation; nor shall any such plea of alienage be allowed in favor of any such person who has so, as aforesaid, declared his intention to become a citizen of the United States, and shall have exercised at any time the right of suffrage, or any other political franchise, within the United States, under the laws thereof, or under the laws of any of the several States.
In witness whereof, I have hereunto set my hand, and caused the seal of the United States to be affixed. Done at the city of Washington, this eighth day of May, in the year of our Lord one thousand eight hundred and sixty-three, and of the independence of the United States the eighty-seventh.
A. LINCOLN.
By the President: WILLIAM H. SEWARD

TELEGRAM TO GENERAL J. HOOKER.

WASHINGTON, D. C. May 8, 1863. 4 P.M.

MAJOR-GENERAL HOOKER:
The news is here of the capture by our forces of Grand Gulf—a large and very important thing. General Willich, an exchanged prisoner just from Richmond, has talked with me this morning. He was there when our cavalry cut the roads in that vicinity. He says there was not a sound pair of legs in Richmond, and that our men, had they known it, could have safely gone in and burned everything and brought in Jeff Davis. We captured and paroled 300 or 400 men. He says as he came to City Point there was an army three miles long (Longstreet's, he thought) moving toward Richmond. Muroy has captured a despatch of General Lee, in which he says his loss was fearful in his last battle with you.
A. LINCOLN.

TELEGRAM TO GENERAL J. A. DIX.

WAR DEPARTMENT, May 9, 1863.

MAJOR-GENERAL DIX:
It is very important for Hooker to know exactly what damage is done to the railroads at all points between Fredericksburg and Richmond. As yet we have no word as to whether the crossings of the North and South Anna, or any of them, have been touched. There are four of these Crossings; that is, one on each road on each stream. You readily perceive why this information is desired. I suppose Kilpatrick or Davis can tell. Please ascertain fully what was done, and what is the present condition, as near as you can, and advise me at once.
A. LINCOLN.

TO SECRETARY SEWARD.

WASHINGTON, May 9, 1863

I believe Mr. L. is a good man, but two things need to be remembered.
1st. Mr. R.'s rival was a relative of Mr. L.
2d. I hear of nobody calling Mr. R. a "Copperhead," but Mr. L. However, let us watch.
A. L.

TO SECRETARY STANTON.

EXECUTIVE MANSION, WASHINGTON, MAY 11, 1863

HON. SECRETARY OF WAR.
DEAR SIR:—I have again concluded to relieve General Curtis. I see no other way to avoid the worst consequences there. I think of General Schofield as his successor, but I do not wish to take the matter of a successor out of the hands of yourself and General Halleck.
Yours truly,
A. LINCOLN.

TELEGRAM TO GENERAL DIX.

WAR DEPARTMENT, WASHINGTON CITY, May 11, 1863.

MAJOR-GENERAL DIX:
Do the Richmond papers have anything about Grand Gulf or Vicksburg?
A. LINCOLN.

TELEGRAM TO GENERAL BUTTERFIELD.

[Cipher.]

WAR DEPARTMENT, WASHINGTON CITY, May 11, 1863.
MAJOR-GENERAL BUTTERFIELD:
About what distance is it from the observatory we stopped at last Thursday to the line of enemies' works you ranged the glass upon for me?
A. LINCOLN.

TELEGRAM TO GOVERNOR SEYMOUR

EXECUTIVE MANSION, WASHINGTON, May 12, 1863.

GOVERNOR SEYMOUR, Albany, N.Y.:
Dr. Swinburne and Mr. Gillett are here, having been refused, as they say, by the War Department, permission to go to the Army of the Potomac. They now appeal to me, saying you wish them to go. I suppose they have been excluded by a rule which experience has induced the department to deem proper; still they shall have leave to go, if you say you desire it. Please answer.
A. LINCOLN

TELEGRAM TO A. G. HENRY.

EXECUTIVE MANSION, WASHINGTON May 13, 1863.

Dr. A. G. HENRY, Metropolitan Hotel, New York:
Governor Chase's feelings were hurt by my action in his absence. Smith is removed, but Governor Chase wishes to name his successor, and asks a day or two to make the designation.
A. LINCOLN.

TO GENERAL J. HOOKER.

EXECUTIVE MANSION, WASHINGTON, D.C. May 14, 1863.

MAJOR-GENERAL HOOKER, Commanding.

MY DEAR SIR:—When I wrote on the 7th, I had an impression that possibly by an early movement you could get some advantage from the supposed facts that the enemy's communications were disturbed and that he was somewhat deranged in position. That idea has now passed away, the enemy having re-established his communications, regained his positions, and actually received reinforcements. It does not now appear probable to me that you can gain anything by an early renewal of the attempt to cross the Rappahannock. I therefore shall not complain if you do no more for a time than to keep the enemy at bay and out of other mischief by menaces and occasional cavalry raids, if practicable, and to put your own army in good condition again. Still, if in your own clear judgment you can renew the attack successfully, I do not mean to restrain you. Bearing upon this last point, I must tell you that I have some painful intimations that some of your corps and division commanders are not giving you their entire confidence. This would be ruinous, if true, and you should therefore, first of all, ascertain the real facts beyond all possibility of doubt.
Yours truly,
A. LINCOLN.

FACTIONAL QUARRELS

TELEGRAM TO H. T. BLOW AND OTHERS.

EXECUTIVE MANSION, WASHINGTON, May 15, 1863.
HON. H. T. BLOW, C. D. DRAKE, AND OTHERS, St. Louis, Mo.:
Your despatch of to-day is just received. It is very painful to me that you in Missouri cannot or will not settle your factional quarrel among yourselves. I have been tormented with it beyond endurance for months by both sides. Neither side pays the least respect to my appeals to your reason. I am now compelled to take hold of the case.
A. LINCOLN.

TELEGRAM TO JAMES GUTHRIE.

WAR DEPARTMENT, WASHINGTON CITY, May 16, 1863.

HON. JAMES GUTHRIE, Louisville, Ky.:
Your despatch of to-day is received. I personally know nothing of Colonel Churchill, but months ago and more than once he has been represented to me as exerting a mischievous influence at Saint Louis, for which reason I am unwilling to force his continuance there against the judgment of our friends on the ground; but if it will oblige you, he may come to and remain at Louisville upon taking the oath of allegiance, and your pledge for his good behavior.
A. LINCOLN.

TO SECRETARY OF WAR.

WAR DEPARTMENT, WASHINGTON CITY, May 16, 1863.

HON. SECRETARY OF WAR.
MY DEAR SIR:—The commander of the Department at St. Louis has ordered several persons south of our military lines, which order is not disapproved by me. Yet at the special request of the HON. James Guthrie I have consented to one of the number, Samuel Churchill, remaining at Louisville, Ky., upon condition of his taking the oath of allegiance and Mr. Guthrie's word of honor for his good behavior.
Yours truly,
A. LINCOLN.

ORDERS SENDING C. L. VALLANDIGHAM BEYOND MILITARY LINES.

[Cipher.]

UNITED STATES MILITARY TELEGRAPH, May 10, 1863. By telegraph from Washington, 9.40 PM, 1863
TO MAJOR-GENERAL BURNSIDE, Commanding Department of Ohio.
SIR:—The President directs that without delay you send C. L. Vallandigham under secure guard to the Headquarters of General Rosecrans, to be put by him beyond our military lines; and in case of his return within our lines, he be arrested and kept in close custody for the term specified in his sentence.
By order of the President: E. R. S. CANBY, Assistant Adjutant-General.

WAR DEPARTMENT, May 20, 1863.

MAJOR-GENERAL A. B. BURNSIDE, Commanding Department of Ohio, Cincinnati, O.
Your despatch of three o'clock this afternoon to the Secretary of War has been received and shown to the President. He thinks the best disposition to be made of Vallandigham is to put him beyond the lines, as directed in the order transmitted to you last evening, and directs that you execute that order by sending him forward under secure guard without delay to General Rosecrans.
By order of the President: ED. R. S. CANBY, Brigadier-General

TELEGRAM TO GENERAL W. S. ROSECRANS.

WASHINGTON, May 20, 1863.

MAJOR-GENERAL ROSECRANS:
Yours of yesterday in regard to Colonel Haggard is received. I am anxious that you shall not misunderstand me. In no case have I intended to censure you or to question your ability. In Colonel Haggard's case I meant no more than to suggest that possibly you might have been mistaken in a point that could [be] corrected. I frequently make mistakes myself in the many things I am compelled to do hastily.
A. LINCOLN.

TELEGRAM TO GENERAL W. S. ROSECRANS.

WASHINGTON, May 21, 1863. 4.40 PM.

MAJOR-GENERAL ROSECRANS:
For certain reasons it is thought best for Rev. Dr. Jaquess not to come here.
Present my respects to him, and ask him to write me fully on the subject he has in contemplation.
A. LINCOLN.

TELEGRAM TO GENERAL S. A. HURLBUT.

WASHINGTON, May 22, 1863.

MAJOR-GENERAL HURLBUT, Memphis, Tenn.:

We have news here in the Richmond newspapers of 20th and 21st, including a despatch from General Joe Johnston himself, that on the 15th or 16th—a little confusion as to the day—Grant beat Pemberton and [W. W.] Loring near Edwards Station, at the end of a nine hours' fight, driving Pemberton over the Big Black and cutting Loring off and driving him south to Crystal Springs, twenty-five miles below Jackson. Joe Johnston telegraphed all this, except about Loring, from his camp between Brownsville and Lexington, on the 18th. Another despatch indicates that Grant was moving against Johnston on the 18th.
A. LINCOLN.

TELEGRAM TO ANSON STAGER.

WAR DEPARTMENT, WASHINGTON, D. C., May 24, 1863.10.40

ANSON STAGER, Cleveland, O.:
Late last night Fuller telegraphed you, as you say, that "the Stars and Stripes float over Vicksburg and the victory is complete." Did he know what he said, or did he say it without knowing it? Your despatch of this afternoon throws doubt upon it.
A. LINCOLN.

TELEGRAM TO COLONEL HAGGARD.

EXECUTIVE MANSION, WASHINGTON. May 25, 1863.

COLONEL HAGGARD, Nashville, Tenn.:
Your despatch to Green Adams has just been shown me. General Rosecrans knows better than we can know here who should be in charge of the Fifth Cavalry.
A. LINCOLN

TELEGRAM TO GENERAL BURNSIDE.

WAR DEPARTMENT, WASHINGTON, D. C., May 26, 1863.

MAJOR-GENERAL BURNSIDE, Cincinnati, O.:
Your despatch about Campbell, Lyle, and others received and postponement ordered by you approved. I will consider and telegraph you again in a few days.
A. LINCOLN.

TELEGRAM TO GENERAL SCHENCK.

EXECUTIVE MANSION, WASHINGTON, May 27, 1863.

MAJOR-GENERAL SCHENCK, Baltimore, Md.:
Let the execution of William B. Compton be respited or suspended till further order from me, holding him in safe custody meanwhile. On receiving this notify me.
A. LINCOLN.

TELEGRAM TO GOVERNOR BUCKINGHAM.

EXECUTIVE MANSION, WASHINGTON, May 27,1863.

GOVERNOR BUCKINGHAM, Hartford, Conn.:
The execution of Warren Whitemarch is hereby respited or suspended until further order from me, he to be held in safe custody meanwhile. On receiving this notify me.
A. LINCOLN.

TELEGRAM TO GENERAL W. S. ROSECRANS.

WAR DEPARTMENT, May 27,1863.

MAJOR-GENERAL ROSECRANS, Murfreesborough, Tenn.:
Have you anything from Grant? Where is Forrest's headquarters?
A. LINCOLN.

TO GENERAL SCHOFIELD.

EXECUTIVE MANSION, WASHINGTON May 27, 1863.

GENERAL JOHN M. SCHOFIELD.
MY DEAR SIR:—Having relieved General Curtis and assigned you to the command of the Department of the Missouri, I think it may be of some advantage for me to state why I did it. I did not relieve General Curtis because of any full conviction that he had done wrong by commission or omission. I did it because of a conviction in my mind that the Union men of Missouri, constituting, when united, a vast majority of the whole people, have entered into a pestilent factional quarrel among themselves—General Curtis, perhaps not of choice, being the head of one faction and Governor Gamble that of the other. After months of labor to reconcile the difficulty, it seemed to grow worse and worse, until I felt it my duty to break it up somehow; and as I could not remove Governor Gamble, I had to remove General Curtis. Now that you are in the position, I wish you to undo nothing merely because General Curtis or Governor Gamble did it, but to exercise your own judgment, and do right for the public interest. Let your military measures be strong enough to repel the invader and keep the peace, and not so strong as to unnecessarily harass and persecute the people. It is a difficult role, and so much greater will be the honor if you perform it well. If both factions, or neither, shall abuse you, you will probably be about right. Beware of being assailed by one and praised by the other.
Yours truly,
A. LINCOLN.

TELEGRAM TO GENERAL HOOKER.

WASHINGTON, May 27, 1863.11 P.M.

MAJOR-GENERAL HOOKER:
Have you Richmond papers of this morning? If so, what news?
A. LINCOLN.

TO ERASTUS CORNING.

EXECUTIVE MANSION, WASHINGTON, May 28, 1863.

HON. ERASTUS CORNING, Albany, N.Y.:
The letter of yourself and others dated the 19th and inclosing the resolutions of a public meeting held at Albany on the 16th, was received night before last. I shall give the resolutions the consideration you ask, and shall try to find time and make a respectful response.
Your obedient servant,
A. LINCOLN.

TELEGRAM TO GENERAL W. S. ROSECRANS.

WASHINGTON, May 28, 1863.

MAJOR-GENERAL ROSECRANS, Murfreesborough, Tenn..
I would not push you to any rashness, but I am very anxious that you do your utmost, short of rashness, to keep Bragg from getting off to help Johnston against Grant.
A. LINCOLN

TELEGRAM TO GOVERNOR JOHNSON.

WASHINGTON, May 29, 1863.

GOVERNOR ANDREW JOHNSON, Louisville, Ky.:
General Burnside has been frequently informed lately that the division under General Getty cannot be spared. I am sorry to have to tell you this, but it is true, and cannot be helped.
A. LINCOLN.

TO J. K. DUBOIS AND OTHERS.

EXECUTIVE MANSION, WASHINGTON, May 29, 1863.

MESSRS. JESSE K. DUBOIS, O. M. HATCH, JOHN WILLIAMS, JACOB BUNN, JOHN BUNN, GEORGE R. WEBER, WILLIAM YATES, S. M. CULLOM, CHARLES W. MATHENY, WILLIAM F. ELKIN, FRANCIS SPRINGER, B. A. WATSON, ELIPHALET HAWLEY, AND JAMES CAMPBELL.
GENTLEMEN:—Agree among yourselves upon any two of your own number—one of whom to be quartermaster and the other to be commissary to serve at Springfield, Illinois, and send me their names, and I will appoint them.
Yours truly,
A. LINCOLN.

TELEGRAM TO GENERAL A. E. BURNSIDE.

WASHINGTON, May 29, 1863

MAJOR-GENERAL BURNSIDE, Cincinnati, O.:
Your despatch of to-day received. When I shall wish to supersede you I will let you know. All the Cabinet regretted the necessity of arresting, for instance, Vallandigham, some perhaps doubting there was a real necessity for it; but, being done, all were for seeing you through with it.
A. LINCOLN.

TELEGRAM TO COLONEL LUDLOW.

[Cipher.]

EXECUTIVE MANSION, WASHINGTON, June 1, 1863.
COLONEL LUDLOW, Fort Monroe:
Richardson and Brown, correspondents of the Tribune captured at Vicksburg, are detained at Richmond. Please ascertain why they are detained, and get them off if you can.
A. LINCOLN.

TELEGRAM TO GENERAL HOOKER.

EXECUTIVE MANSION, WASHINGTON, June 2, 1863.

MAJOR-GENERAL HOOKER:
It is said that Philip Margraf, in your army, is under sentence to be shot on Friday the 5th instant as a deserter. If so please send me up the record of his case at once.
A. LINCOLN.

TELEGRAM TO GENERAL U.S. GRANT.

WAR DEPARTMENT, June 2, 1863.

MAJOR-GENERAL GRANT, Vicksburg, via Memphis:
Are you in communication with General Banks? Is he coming toward you or going farther off? Is there or has there been anything to hinder his coming directly to you by water from Alexandria?
A. LINCOLN.

TELEGRAM TO MAJOR-GENERAL HOOKER. [Cipher.] EXECUTIVE MANSION, WASHINGTON,

June 4,1863.
MAJOR-GENERAL HOOKER:

Let execution of sentences in the cases of Daily, Margraf, and Harrington be respited till further orders from me, they remaining in close custody meanwhile.
A. LINCOLN.

TELEGRAM TO GENERAL BUTTERFIELD.

WAR DEPARTMENT, WASHINGTON, D.C., June 4, 1863.

MAJOR-GENERAL BUTTERFIELD:
The news you send me from the Richmond Sentinel of the 3d must be greatly if not wholly incorrect. The Thursday mentioned was the 28th, and we have despatches here directly from Vicksburg of the 28th, 29th, 30th, and 31st; and, while they speak of the siege progressing, they speak of no assault or general fighting whatever, and in fact they so speak as to almost exclude the idea that there can have been any since Monday the 25th, which was not very heavy. Neither do they mention any demand made by Grant upon Pemberton for a surrender. They speak of our troops as being in good health, condition, and spirits. Some of them do say that Banks has Port Hudson invested.
A. LINCOLN.

TO SECRETARY STANTON.

EXECUTIVE MANSION, WASHINGTON, June 4, 1863.

HON. SECRETARY OF WAR.
MY DEAR SIR:—I have received additional despatches, which, with former ones, induce me to believe we should revoke or suspend the order suspending the Chicago Times; and if you concur in opinion, please have it done.
Yours truly,
A. LINCOLN.

TELEGRAM TO GENERAL HOOKER.

WASHINGTON, D.C. JUNE 5, 1863

MAJOR-GENERAL HOOKER:
Yours of to-day was received an hour ago. So much of professional military skill is requisite to answer it that I have turned the task over to General Halleck. He promises to perform it with his utmost care. I have but one idea which I think worth suggesting to you, and that is, in case you find Lee coming to the north of the Rappahannock, I would by no means cross to the south of it. If he should leave a rear force at Fredericksburg, tempting you to fall upon it, it would fight in entrenchments and have you at advantage, and so, man for man, worst you at that point, While his main force would in some way be getting an advantage of you northward. In one word, I would not take any risk of being entangled up on the river like an ox jumped half over a fence and liable to be torn by dogs front and rear without a fair chance to gore one way or to kick the other.
If Lee would come to my side of the river I would keep on the same side and fight him, or act on the defensive, according as might be my estimate of his strength relatively to my own. But these are mere suggestions, which I desire to be controlled by the judgment of yourself and General Halleck.
A. LINCOLN.

TELEGRAM TO MRS. GRIMSLEY.

WASHINGTON, D. C., June 6, 1863.

Mrs. ELIZABETH J. GRIMSLEY, Springfield, Ill.:
Is your John ready to enter the naval school? If he is, telegraph me his full name.
A. LINCOLN.

TELEGRAM TO GENERAL DIX,

WAR DEPARTMENT, WASHINGTON, D.C., June 6, 1863.

MAJOR-GENERAL Dix, Fort Monroe, Va.:
By noticing the news you send from the Richmond Dispatch of this morning you will see one of the very latest despatches says they have nothing reliable from Vicksburg since Sunday. Now we here have a despatch from there Sunday and others of almost every day preceding since the investment, and while they show the siege progressing they do not show any general fighting since the 21st and 22d. We have nothing from Port Hudson later than the 29th when things looked reasonably well for us. I have thought this might be of some interest to you.
A. LINCOLN.

TELEGRAM TO GENERAL DIX.

EXECUTIVE MANSION, WASHINGTON, June 8, 1863.

MAJOR-GENERAL Dix, Fort Monroe:
We have despatches from Vicksburg of the 3d. Siege progressing. No general fighting recently. All well. Nothing new from Port Hudson.
A. LINCOLN.

TELEGRAM TO GENERAL DIX.

WAR DEPARTMENT, WASHINGTON, D.C. JUNE 8, 1863.

MAJOR-GENERAL Dix, Fort Monroe:
The substance of news sent of the fighting at Port Hudson on the 27th we have had here three or four days, and I supposed you had it also, when I said this morning, "No news from Port Hudson." We knew that General Sherman was wounded, but we hoped not so dangerously as your despatch represents. We still have nothing of that Richmond newspaper story of Kirby Smith crossing and of Banks losing an arm.
A. LINCOLN

TELEGRAM TO J. P. HALE.

EXECUTIVE MANSION, WASHINGTON, June 9, 1863.

HON. JOHN P. HALE, Dover, N. H.:
I believe that it was upon your recommendation that B. B. Bunker was appointed attorney for Nevada Territory. I am pressed to remove him on the ground that he does not attend to the office, nor in fact pass much time in the Territory. Do you wish to say anything on the subject?
A. LINCOLN

TELEGRAM TO MRS. LINCOLN.

EXECUTIVE MANSION, WASHINGTON, June 9, 1863.

MRS. LINCOLN, Philadelphia, Pa.:
Think you had better put "Tad's" pistol away. I had an ugly dream about him.
A. LINCOLN.

TELEGRAM TO GENERAL HOOKER.

WASHINGTON, D.C. June 9, 1863

MAJOR-GENERAL HOOKER:
I am told there are 50 incendiary shells here at the arsenal made to fit the 100 pounder Parrott gun now with you. If this be true would you like to have the shells sent to you?
A. LINCOLN

TELEGRAM TO GENERAL HOOKER.

WASHINGTON, D. C., June 10, 1863

MAJOR-GENERAL HOOKER:
Your long despatch of to-day is just received. If left to me, I would not go south of the Rappahannock upon Lee's moving north of it. If you had Richmond invested to-day you would not be able to take it in twenty days; meanwhile your communications, and with them your army, would be ruined. I think Lee's army, and not Richmond, is your true objective point. If he comes towards the upper Potomac, follow on his flank, and on the inside track, shortening your lines while he lengthens his. Fight him, too, when opportunity offers. If he stay where he is, fret him and fret him.
A. LINCOLN.

TELEGRAM TO MRS. LINCOLN.

EXECUTIVE MANSION, WASHINGTON, June 11,1863.

MRS. LINCOLN, Philadelphia:
Your three despatches received. I am very well and am glad to know that you and "Tad" are so.
A. LINCOLN.

TELEGRAM TO GENERAL HOOKER.

[Cipher.]

EXECUTIVE MANSION, WASHINGTON, JUNE 12, 1863. MAJOR-GENERAL HOOKER:
If you can show me a trial of the incendiary shells on Saturday night, I will try to join you at 5 P.M. that day Answer.
A. LINCOLN.

TO ERASTUS CORNING AND OTHERS.

EXECUTIVE MANSION, WASHINGTON, June 12, 1863.

HON. ERASTUS CORNING AND OTHERS.
GENTLEMEN:—Your letter of May 19, inclosing the resolutions of a public meeting held at Albany, New York, on the 16th of the same month, was received several days ago.
The resolutions, as I understand them, are resolvable into two propositions—first, the expression of a purpose to sustain the cause of the Union, to secure peace through victory, and to support the administration in every constitutional and lawful measure to suppress the rebellion; and, secondly, a declaration of censure upon the administration for supposed unconstitutional action, such as the making of military arrests. And from the two propositions a third is deduced, which is that the gentlemen composing the meeting are resolved on doing their part to maintain our common government and country, despite the folly or wickedness, as they may conceive, of any administration. This position is eminently patriotic, and as such I thank the meeting, and congratulate the nation for it. My own purpose is the same; so that the meeting and myself have a common object, and can have no difference, except in the choice of means or measures for effecting that object.
And here I ought to close this paper, and would close it, if there were no apprehension that more injurious consequences than any merely personal to myself might follow the censures systematically cast upon me for doing what, in my view of duty, I could not forbear. The resolutions promise to support me in every constitutional and lawful measure to suppress the rebellion; and I have not knowingly employed, nor shall knowingly employ, any other. But the meeting, by their resolutions, assert and argue that certain military arrests, and proceedings following them, for which I am ultimately responsible, are unconstitutional. I think they are not. The resolutions quote from the Constitution the definition of treason, and also the limiting safeguards and guarantees therein provided for the citizen on trial for treason, and on his being held to answer for capital or otherwise infamous crimes, and in criminal prosecutions his right to a speedy and public trial by an impartial jury. They proceed to resolve "that these safeguards of the rights of the citizen against the pretensions of arbitrary power were intended more especially for his protection in times of civil commotion." And, apparently to demonstrate the proposition, the resolutions proceed: "They were secured substantially to the English people after years of protracted civil war, and were adopted into our Constitution at the close of the Revolution." Would not the demonstration have been better if it could have been truly said that these safeguards had been adopted and applied during the civil wars and during our Revolution, instead of after the one and at the close of the other? I too am devotedly for them after civil war, and before civil war, and at all times, "except when, in cases of rebellion or invasion, the public safety may require" their suspension. The resolutions proceed to tell us that these safeguards "have stood the test of seventy-six years of trial under our republican system, under circumstances which show that, while they constitute the foundation of all free government, they are the elements of the enduring stability of the republic." No one denies that they have so stood the test up to the beginning of the present rebellion, if we except a certain occurrence at New Orleans hereafter to be mentioned; nor does any one question that they will stand the same test much longer after the rebellion closes. But these provisions of the Constitution have no application to the case we have in hand, because the arrests complained of were not made for treason—that is, not for the treason defined in the Constitution, and upon the conviction of which the punishment is death—nor yet were they made to hold persons to answer for any capital or otherwise infamous crimes; nor were the proceedings following, in any constitutional or legal sense, "criminal prosecutions." The arrests were made on totally different grounds, and the proceedings following accorded with the grounds of the arrests. Let us consider the real case with which we are dealing, and apply to it the parts of the Constitution plainly made for such cases.
Prior to my installation here it had been inculcated that any State had a lawful right to secede from the national Union, and that it would be expedient to exercise the right whenever the devotees of the doctrine should fail to elect a president to their own liking. I was elected contrary to their liking; and accordingly, so far as it was legally possible, they had taken seven States out of the Union, had seized many of the United States forts, and had fired upon the United States flag, all before I was inaugurated, and, of course, before I had done any official act whatever. The rebellion thus begun soon ran into the present civil war; and, in certain respects, it began on very unequal terms between the parties. The insurgents had been preparing for it more than thirty years, while the government had taken no steps to resist them. The former had carefully considered all the means which could be turned to their account. It undoubtedly was a well-pondered reliance with them that in their own unrestricted effort to destroy Union, Constitution and law, all together, the government would, in great degree, be restrained by the same Constitution and law from arresting their progress. Their sympathizers invaded all departments of the government and nearly all communities of the people. From this material, under cover of "liberty of speech," "liberty of the press," and "habeas corpus," they hoped to keep on foot amongst us a most efficient corps of spies, informers, suppliers, and aiders and abettors of their cause in a thousand ways. They knew that in times such as they were inaugurating, by the Constitution itself the "habeas corpus" might be suspended;

but they also knew they had friends who would make a question as to who was to suspend it; meanwhile their spies and others might remain at large to help on their cause. Or if, as has happened, the Executive should suspend the writ without ruinous waste of time, instances of arresting innocent persons might occur, as are always likely to occur in such cases; and then a clamor could be raised in regard to this, which might be at least of some service to the insurgent cause. It needed no very keen perception to discover this part of the enemies program, so soon as by open hostilities their machinery was fairly put in motion. Yet, thoroughly imbued with a reverence for the guaranteed rights of individuals, I was slow to adopt the strong measures which by degrees I have been forced to regard as being within the exceptions of the Constitution, and as indispensable to the public safety. Nothing is better known to history than that courts of justice are utterly incompetent to such cases. Civil courts are organized chiefly for trials of individuals—or, at most, a few individuals acting in concert, and this in quiet times, and on charges of crimes well defined in the law. Even in times of peace bands of horse-thieves and robbers frequently grow too numerous and powerful for the ordinary courts of justice. But what comparison, in numbers have such bands ever borne to the insurgent sympathizers even in many of the loyal States? Again, a jury too frequently has at least one member more ready to hang the panel than to hang the traitor. And yet again, he who dissuades one man from volunteering, or induces one soldier to desert, weakens the Union cause as much as he who kills a Union soldier in battle. Yet this dissuasion or inducement may be so conducted as to be no defined crime of which any civil court would take cognizance.

Ours is a case of rebellion—so called by the resolutions before me—in fact, a clear, flagrant, and gigantic case of rebellion; and the provision of the Constitution that "the privilege of the writ of habeas corpus shall not be suspended unless when, in cases of rebellion or invasion, the public safety may require it," is the provision which specially applies to our present case. This provision plainly attests the understanding of those who made the Constitution that ordinary courts of justice are inadequate to "cases of rebellion"—attests their purpose that, in such cases, men may be held in custody whom the courts, acting on ordinary rules, would discharge. Habeas corpus does not discharge men who are proved to be guilty of defined crime, and its suspension is allowed by the Constitution on purpose that men may be arrested and held who can not be proved to be guilty of defined crime, "when, in cases of rebellion or invasion, the public safety may require it."

This is precisely our present case—a case of rebellion wherein the public safety does require the suspension—Indeed, arrests by process of courts and arrests in cases of rebellion do not proceed altogether upon the same basis. The former is directed at the small percentage of ordinary and continuous perpetration of crime, while the latter is directed at sudden and extensive uprisings against the government, which, at most, will succeed or fail in no great length of time. In the latter case arrests are made not so much for what has been done as for what probably would be done. The latter is more for the preventive and less for the vindictive than the former. In such cases the purposes of men are much more easily understood than in cases of ordinary crime. The man who stands by and says nothing when the peril of his government is discussed, cannot be misunderstood. If not hindered, he is sure to help the enemy; much more if he talks ambiguously—talks for his country with "buts," and "ifs," and "ands." Of how little value the constitutional provision I have quoted will be rendered if arrests shall never be made until defined crimes shall have been committed, may be illustrated by a few notable examples: General John C. Breckinridge, General Robert E. Lee, General Joseph E. Johnston, General John B. Magruder, General William B. Preston, General Simon B. Buckner, and Commodore Franklin Buchanan, now occupying the very highest places in the rebel war service, were all within the power of the government since the rebellion began, and were nearly as well known to be traitors then as now. Unquestionably if we had seized and had them the insurgent cause would be much weaker. But no one of them had then committed any crime defined in the law. Every one of them, if arrested, would have been discharged on habeas corpus were the writ allowed to operate. In view of these and similar cases, I think the time not unlikely to come when I shall be blamed for having made too few arrests rather than too many.

By the third resolution the meeting indicate their opinion that military arrests may be constitutional in localities where rebellion actually exists, but that such arrests are unconstitutional in localities where rebellion or insurrection does not actually exist. They insist that such arrests shall not be made "outside of the lines of necessary military occupation and the scenes of insurrection." Inasmuch, however, as the Constitution itself makes no such distinction, I am unable to believe that there is any such constitutional distinction. I concede that the class of arrests complained of can be constitutional only when, in cases of rebellion or invasion, the public safety may require them; and I insist that in such cases—they are constitutional wherever the public safety does require them, as well in places to which they may prevent the rebellion extending, as in those where it may be already prevailing; as well where they may restrain mischievous interference with the raising and supplying of armies to suppress the rebellion as where the rebellion may actually be; as well where they may restrain the enticing men out of the army as where they would prevent mutiny in the army; equally constitutional at all places where they will conduce to the public safety as against the dangers of rebellion or invasion. Take the particular case mentioned by the meeting. It is asserted in substance that Mr. Vallandigham was, by a military commander, seized and tried "for no other reason than words addressed to a public meeting in criticism of the course of the administration, and in condemnation of the military orders of the general." Now, if there be no mistake about this, if this assertion is the truth, and the whole truth, if there were no other reason for the arrest, then I concede that the arrest was wrong. But the arrest, as I understand, was made for a very different reason. Mr. Vallandigham avows his hostility to the war on the part of the Union; and his arrest was made because he was laboring, with some effect, to prevent the raising of troops, to encourage desertions from the army, and to leave the rebellion without an adequate military force to suppress it. He was not arrested because he was damaging the political prospects of the administration or the personal interests of the commanding general, but because he was damaging the army, upon the existence and vigor of which the life of the nation depends. He was warring upon the military, and thus gave the military constitutional jurisdiction to lay hands upon him. If Mr. Vallandigham was not damaging the military power of the country, then his arrest was made on mistake of fact, which I would be glad to correct on reasonably satisfactory evidence.

I understand the meeting whose resolutions I am considering to be in favor of suppressing the rebellion by military force—by armies. Long experience has shown that armies cannot be maintained unless desertion shall be punished by the severe penalty of death. The case requires, and the law and the Constitution sanction, this punishment. Must I shoot a simple-minded boy and not touch a hair of a wily agitator who induced him to desert. This is none the less injurious when effected by getting a father, or brother, or friend into a public meeting, and there working upon his feelings till he is persuaded to write the soldier boy that he is fighting in a bad cause, for a wicked administration of a contemptible government, too weak to arrest and punish him if he shall desert. I think that, in such a case, to silence the agitator and save the boy is not only constitutional, but withal a great mercy.

If I be wrong on this question of constitutional power, my error lies in believing that certain proceedings are constitutional when, in cases of rebellion or invasion, the public safety requires them, which would not be constitutional when, in absence of rebellion or invasion, the public safety does not require them: in other words, that the Constitution is not in its application in all respects the same in cases of rebellion or invasion involving the public safety as it is in times of profound peace and public security. The Constitution itself makes the distinction, and I can no more be persuaded that the government can constitutionally take no strong measures in time of rebellion, because it can be shown that the same could not be lawfully taken in times of peace, than I can be persuaded that a particular drug is not good medicine for a sick man because it can be shown to not be good food for a well one. Nor am I able to appreciate the danger apprehended by the meeting, that the American people will by means of military arrests during the rebellion lose the right of public discussion, the liberty of speech and the press, the law of evidence, trial by jury, and habeas corpus throughout the indefinite peaceful future which I trust lies before them, any more than I am able to believe that a man could contract so strong an appetite for emetics during temporary illness as to persist in feeding upon them during the remainder of his healthful life.

In giving the resolutions that earnest consideration which you request of me, I cannot overlook the fact that the meeting speak as "Democrats." Nor can I, with full respect for their known intelligence, and the fairly presumed deliberation with which they prepared their resolutions, be permitted to suppose that this occurred by accident, or in any way other than that they preferred to designate themselves "Democrats" rather than "American citizens." In this time of national peril I would have preferred to meet you upon a level one step higher than any party platform, because I am sure that from such more elevated position we could do better battle for the country we all love than we possibly can from those lower ones where, from the force of habit, the prejudices of the past, and selfish hopes of the future, we are sure to expend much of our ingenuity and strength in finding fault with and aiming blows at each other. But since you have denied me this I will yet be thankful for the country's sake that not all Democrats have done so. He on whose discretionary judgment Mr. Vallandigham was arrested and tried is a Democrat, having no old party affinity with me, and the judge who rejected the constitutional view expressed in these resolutions, by refusing to discharge Mr. Vallandigham on habeas corpus is a Democrat of better days than these, having received his judicial mantle at the hands of President Jackson. And still more: of all those Democrats who are nobly exposing their lives and shedding their blood on the battle-field, I have learned that many approve the course taken with Mr. Vallandigham, while I have not heard of a single one condemning it. I cannot assert that there are none such. And the name of President Jackson recalls an instance of pertinent history. After the battle of New Orleans, and while the fact that the treaty of peace had been concluded was well known in the city, but before official knowledge of it had arrived, General Jackson still maintained martial or military law. Now that it could be said that the war was over, the clamor against martial law, which had existed from the first, grew more furious. Among other things, a Mr. Louaillier published a denunciatory newspaper article. General Jackson arrested him. A lawyer by the name of Morel procured the United States Judge Hall to order a writ of habeas corpus to release Mr. Louaillier. General Jackson arrested both the lawyer and the judge. A Mr. Hollander ventured to say of some part of the matter that "it was a dirty trick." General Jackson arrested him. When the officer undertook to serve the writ of habeas corpus, General Jackson took it from him, and sent him away with a copy. Holding the judge in custody a few days, the general sent him beyond the limits of his encampment, and set him at liberty with an order to remain till the ratification of peace should be regularly announced, or until the British should have left the southern coast. A day or two more elapsed, the ratification of the treaty of peace was regularly announced, and the judge and others were fully liberated. A few days more, and the judge called General Jackson into court and fined him $1000 for having arrested him and the others named. The General paid the fine, and then the matter rested for nearly thirty years, when Congress refunded principal and interest. The late Senator Douglas, then in the House of Representatives, took a leading part in the debates, in which the constitutional question was much discussed. I am not prepared to say whom the journals would show to have voted for the measure.

It may be remarked—first, that we had the same Constitution then as now; secondly, that we then had a case of invasion, and now we have a case of rebellion; and, thirdly, that the permanent right of the people to public discussion, the liberty of speech and of the press, the trial by jury, the law of evidence, and the habeas corpus suffered no detriment whatever by that conduct of General Jackson, or its subsequent approval by the American Congress.

And yet, let me say that, in my own discretion, I do not know whether I would have ordered the arrest of Mr. Vallandigham. While I cannot shift the responsibility from myself, I hold that, as a general rule, the commander in the field is the better judge of the necessity in any particular case. Of course I must practice a general directory and revisory power in the matter.

One of the resolutions expresses the opinion of the meeting that arbitrary arrests will have the effect to divide and distract those who should be united in suppressing the rebellion, and I am specifically called on to discharge Mr. Vallandigham. I regard this as, at least, a fair appeal to me on the expediency of exercising a constitutional power which I think exists. In response to such appeal I have to say, it gave me pain when I learned that Mr. Vallandigham had been arrested (that is, I was pained that there should have seemed to be a necessity for arresting him), and that it will afford me great pleasure to discharge him so soon as I can by any means believe the public safety will not suffer by it.

I further say that, as the war progresses, it appears to me, opinion and action, which were in great confusion at first, take shape and fall into more regular channels, so that the necessity for strong dealing with them gradually decreases. I have every reason to desire that it should cease altogether, and far from the least is my regard for the opinions and wishes of those who, like the meeting at Albany, declare their purpose to sustain the government in every constitutional and lawful measure to suppress the rebellion. Still, I must continue to do so much as may seem to be required by the public safety.

A. LINCOLN.

TO THE SECRETARY OF THE TREASURY.

EXECUTIVE MANSION, June 14, 1863.

HON. SECRETARY OF THE TREASURY.
SIR:—Your note of this morning is received. You will co-operate by the revenue cutters under your direction with the navy in arresting rebel depredations on American commerce and transportation and in capturing rebels engaged therein.
A. LINCOLN.

TELEGRAM TO GENERAL TYLER.

WAR DEPARTMENT, June 14, 1863.

GENERAL TYLER, Martinsburg: Is Milroy invested so that he cannot fall back to Harper's Ferry?
A. LINCOLN.

RESPONSE TO A "BESIEGED" GENERAL

TELEGRAM TO GENERAL TYLER.

WAR DEPARTMENT, June 14, 1863.
GENERAL TYLER, Martinsburg:
If you are besieged, how do you despatch me? Why did you not leave before being besieged?
A. LINCOLN.

TELEGRAM TO GENERAL KELLEY.

WASHINGTON, June 14, 1863. 1.27 P.M.

MAJOR-GENERAL KELLEY, Harper's Ferry:
Are the forces at Winchester and Martinsburg making any effort to get to you?
A. LINCOLN.

TELEGRAM TO GENERAL HOOKER.

WASHINGTON, D. C., June 14, 1863. 3.50 P.M.,

MAJOR-GENERAL HOOKER:
So far as we can make out here, the enemy have Muroy surrounded at Winchester, and Tyler at Martinsburg. If they could hold out a few days, could you help them? If the head of Lee's army is at Martinsburg and the tail of it on the plank-road between Fredericksburg and Chancellorsville, the animal must be very slim somewhere; could you not break him?
A. LINCOLN.

TELEGRAM TO GENERAL R. C. SCHENCK.

WAR DEPARTMENT, June 14, 1863.

MAJOR-GENERAL SCHENCK:
Get General Milroy from Winchester to Harper's Ferry, if possible. He will be "gobbled up" if he remains, if he is not already past salvation.
A. LINCOLN, President, United States.

NEEDS NEW TIRES ON HIS CARRIAGE

TELEGRAM TO MRS. LINCOLN.

WAR DEPARTMENT, June 15, 1863.
MRS. LINCOLN, Philadelphia, Pa.:
Tolerably well. Have not rode out much yet, but have at last got new tires on the carriage wheels and perhaps shall ride out soon.
A. LINCOLN.

CALL FOR 100,000 MILITIA TO SERVE FOR SIX MONTHS, JUNE 15, 1863.

BY THE PRESIDENT OF THE UNITED STATES OF AMERICA:

A Proclamation

Whereas the armed insurrectionary combinations now existing in several of the States are threatening to make inroads into the States of Maryland, West Virginia, Pennsylvania, and Ohio, requiring immediately an additional military force for the service of the United States:

Now, therefore, I, Abraham Lincoln, President of the United States and Commander-in-Chief of the Army and Navy thereof and of the militia of the several States when called into actual service, do hereby call into the service of the United States 100,000 militia from the States following, namely:

From the State of Maryland, 10,000; from the State of Pennsylvania, 50,000; from the State of Ohio, 30,000; from the State of West Virginia, 10,000—to be mustered into the service of the United States forthwith and to serve for a period of six months from the date of such muster into said service, unless sooner discharged; to be mustered in as infantry, artillery, and cavalry, in proportions which will be made known through the War Department, which Department will also designate the several places of rendezvous. These militia to be organized according to the rules and regulations of the volunteer service and such orders as may hereafter be issued. The States aforesaid will be respectively credited under the enrollment act for the militia services entered under this proclamation. In testimony whereof...............

A. LINCOLN

TELEGRAM TO P. KAPP AND OTHERS.

WAR DEPARTMENT, WASHINGTON, D. C., June 10, 1863

FREDERICK KAPP AND OTHERS, New York:

The Governor of New York promises to send us troops, and if he wishes the assistance of General Fremont and General Sigel, one or both, he can have it. If he does not wish them it would but breed confusion for us to set them to work independently of him.

A. LINCOLN.

TELEGRAM TO GENERAL MEAGHER.

WAR DEPARTMENT, WASHINGTON, D. C., June 16, 1863.

GENERAL T. FRANCIS MEAGHER, New York:

Your despatch received. Shall be very glad for you to raise 3000 Irish troops if done by the consent of and in concert with Governor Seymour.

A. LINCOLN.

TELEGRAM TO MRS. LINCOLN.

WAR DEPARTMENT, WASHINGTON, D. C., June 16, 1863.

MRS. LINCOLN, Philadelphia:

It is a matter of choice with yourself whether you come home. There is no reason why you should not, that did not exist when you went away. As bearing on the question of your coming home, I do not think the raid into Pennsylvania amounts to anything at all.

A. LINCOLN.

TELEGRAM TO COLONEL BLISS.

EXECUTIVE MANSION, WASHINGTON, June 16, 1863.

COL. WILLIAM S. BLISS, New York Hotel:
Your despatch asking whether I will accept "the Loyal Brigade of the North" is received. I never heard of that brigade by name and do not know where it is; yet, presuming it is in New York, I say I will gladly accept it, if tendered by and with the consent and approbation of the Governor of that State. Otherwise not.
A. LINCOLN.

TELEGRAM TO GENERAL HOOKER.

WASHINGTON, June 16, 1863. 10 P.M.

MAJOR-GENERAL HOOKER:
To remove all misunderstanding, I now place you in the strict military relation to General Halleck of a commander of one of the armies to the general-in-chief of all the armies. I have not intended differently, but as it seems to be differently understood I shall direct him to give you orders and you to obey them.
A. LINCOLN.

TELEGRAM TO GENERAL HOOKER.

WAR DEPARTMENT WASHINGTON D. C., June 17, 1863.

MAJOR-GENERAL HOOKER:
Mr. Eckert, superintendent in the telegraph office, assures me that he has sent and will send you everything that comes to the office.
A. LINCOLN.

TELEGRAM TO JOSHUA TEVIS.

EXECUTIVE MANSION, WASHINGTON, June 17, 1863.

JOSHUA TEVIS, Esq., U. S. Attorney, Frankfort, Ky.:
A Mr. Burkner is here shoving a record and asking to be discharged from a suit in San Francisco, as bail for one Thompson. Unless the record shown me is defectively made out I think it can be successfully defended against. Please examine the case carefully and, if you shall be of opinion it cannot be sustained, dismiss it and relieve me from all trouble about it. Please answer.
A. LINCOLN.

TELEGRAM TO GOVERNOR TOD.

[Cipher.]

EXECUTIVE MANSION, WASHINGTON,
June 18, 1863.
GOVERNOR D. TOD, Columbus, O.:

Yours received. I deeply regret that you were not renominated, not that I have aught against Mr. Brough. On the contrary, like yourself, I say hurrah for him.
A. LINCOLN.

TELEGRAM TO GENERAL DINGMAN.

WAR DEPARTMENT, WASHINGTON, D. C., June 18, 1863.

GENERAL A. DINGMAN, Belleville, C. W.:
Thanks for your offer of the Fifteenth Battalion. I do not think Washington is in danger.
A. LINCOLN

TO B. B. MALHIOT AND OTHERS.

EXECUTIVE MANSION, WASHINGTON, June 19, 1863.

MESSRS. B. B. MALHIOT, BRADISH JOHNSON, AND THOMAS COTTMAN.
GENTLEMEN:—Your letter, which follows, has been received and Considered.
"The undersigned, a committee appointed by the planters of the State of Louisiana, respectfully represent that they have been delegated to seek of the General Government a full recognition of all the rights of the State as they existed previous to the passage of an act of secession, upon the principle of the existence of the State constitution unimpaired, and no legal act having transpired that could in any way deprive them of the advantages conferred by that constitution. Under this constitution the State wishes to return to its full allegiance, in the enjoyment of all rights and privileges exercised by the other States under the Federal Constitution. With the view of accomplishing the desired object, we further request that your Excellency will, as commander-in-chief of the army of the United States, direct the Military Governor of Louisiana to order an election, in conformity with the constitution and laws of the State, on the first Monday of November next, for all State and Federal officers.
"With high consideration and resect, we have the honor to subscribe ourselves,
"Your obedient servants,
 "E. E. MALHIOT.
 "BRADISH JOHNSON.
 "THOMAS COTTMAN."
Since receiving the letter, reliable information has reached me that a respectable portion of the Louisiana people desire to amend their State constitution, and contemplate holding a State convention for that object. This fact alone, as it seems to me, is a sufficient reason why the General Government should not give the committal you seek to the existing State constitution. I may add that, while I do not perceive how such committal could facilitate our military operations in Louisiana, I really apprehend it might be so used as to embarrass them.
As to an election to be held next November, there is abundant time without any order or proclamation from me just now. The people of Louisiana shall not lack an opportunity for a fair election for both Federal and State officers by want of anything within my power to give them.
Your obedient servant,
A. LINCOLN.

TO GENERAL J. M. SCHOFIELD.

EXECUTIVE MANSION, WASHINGTON

June 22, 1863.

GENERAL JOHN M. SCHOFIELD. MY DEAR SIR:—Your despatch, asking in substance whether, in case Missouri shall adopt gradual emancipation, the General Government will protect slave owners in that species of property during the short time it shall be permitted by the State to exist within it, has been received. Desirous as I am that emancipation shall be adopted by Missouri, and believing as I do that gradual can be made better than immediate for both black and white, except when military necessity changes the case, my impulse is to say that such protection would be given. I cannot know exactly what shape an act of emancipation may take. If the period from the initiation to the final end should be comparatively short, and the act should prevent persons being sold during that period into more lasting slavery, the whole would be easier. I do not wish to pledge the General Government to the affirmative support of even temporary slavery beyond what can be fairly claimed under the Constitution. I suppose, however, this is not desired, but that it is desired for the military force of the United States, while in Missouri, to not be used in subverting the temporarily reserved legal rights in slaves during the progress of emancipation. This I would desire also. I have very earnestly urged the slave States to adopt emancipation; and it ought to be, and is, an object with me not to overthrow or thwart what any of them may in good faith do to that end. You are therefore authorized to act in the spirit of this letter in conjunction with what may appear to be the military necessities of your department. Although this letter will become public at some time, it is not intended to be made so now.
Yours truly,
A. LINCOLN.

TELEGRAM TO GENERAL J. HOOKER.

WASHINGTON, June 22, 1863

MAJOR-GENERAL HOOKER:
Operator at Leesburg just now says: "I heard very little firing this A.M. about daylight, but it seems to have stopped now. It was in about the same direction as yesterday, but farther off."
A. LINCOLN.

TO SECRETARY OF WAR.

EXECUTIVE MANSION, WASHINGTON, June 23, 1863.

HON. SECRETARY OF WAR:
You remember that Hon. W. D. Kelly and others are engaged in raising or trying to raise some colored regiments in Philadelphia. The bearer of this, Wilton M. Huput, is a friend of Judge Kelly, as appears by the letter of the latter. He is a private in the 112th Penn. and has been disappointed in a reasonable expectation of one of the smaller offices. He now wants to be a lieutenant in one of the colored regiments. If Judge Kelly will say in writing he wishes to so have him, I am willing for him to be discharged from his present position, and be so appointed. If you approve, so indorse and let him carry the letter to Kelly.
Yours truly,
A. LINCOLN.

TELEGRAM TO MAJOR VAN VLIET.

[Cipher.]

WAR DEPARTMENT, WASHINGTON, D. C., June 23, 1863.
MAJOR VAN VLIET, New York:
Have you any idea what the news is in the despatch of General Banks to General Halleck?
A. LINCOLN.

TELEGRAM TO GENERAL COUCH.

WAR DEPARTMENT, June 24, 1863.

MAJOR-GENERAL COUCH, Harrisburg, Pa.:
Have you any reports of the enemy moving into Pennsylvania? And if any, what?
A. LINCOLN.

TELEGRAM TO GENERAL DIX.

WASHINGTON, June 24, 1863

MAJOR-GENERAL Dix, Yorktown, Va.:
We have a despatch from General Grant of the 19th. Don't think Kirby Smith took Milliken's Bend since, allowing time to get the news to Joe Johnston and from him to Richmond. But it is not absolutely impossible. Also have news from Banks to the 16th, I think. He had not run away then, nor thought of it.
A. LINCOLN.

TELEGRAM TO GENERAL PECK.

WAR DEPARTMENT, WASHINGTON, D. C., June 25, 1863.

GENERAL PECK, Suffolk, Va.:
Colonel Derrom, of the Twenty-fifth New Jersey Volunteers, now mustered out, says there is a man in your hands under conviction for desertion, who formerly belonged to the above named regiment, and whose name is Templeton— Isaac F. Templeton, I believe. The Colonel and others appeal to me for him. Please telegraph to me what is the condition of the case, and if he has not been executed send me the record of the trial and conviction.
A. LINCOLN.

TELEGRAM TO GENERAL SLOCUM.

WAR DEPARTMENT, WASHINGTON, D. C., June 25,1863.

MAJOR-GENERAL SLOCUM, Leesburg, Va.:
Was William Gruvier, Company A, Forty-sixth, Pennsylvania, one of the men executed as a deserter last Friday?
A. LINCOLN.

TELEGRAM TO GENERAL HOOKER.

WAR DEPARTMENT, WASHINGTON, D. C., June 27, 1863. 8A.M.

MAJOR-GENERAL HOOKER:

It did not come from the newspapers, nor did I believe it, but I wished to be entirely sure it was a falsehood.
A. LINCOLN.

TELEGRAM TO GENERAL BURNSIDE.

EXECUTIVE MANSION, WASHINGTON, June 28, 1863.

MAJOR-GENERAL BURNSIDE, Cincinnati, O.:
There is nothing going on in Kentucky on the subject of which you telegraph, except an enrolment. Before anything is done beyond this, I will take care to understand the case better than I now do.
A. LINCOLN.

TELEGRAM TO GOVERNOR BOYLE.

EXECUTIVE MANSION, WASHINGTON, D. C., June 28, 1863.

GOVERNOR J. T. BOYLE, Cincinnati, O.:
There is nothing going on in Kentucky on the subject of which you telegraph, except an enrolment. Before anything is done beyond this, I will take care to understand the case better than I now do.
A. LINCOLN.

TELEGRAM TO GENERAL SCHENCK.

WAR DEPARTMENT, WASHINGTON, D. C., June 28, 1863.

MAJOR GENERAL SCHENCK, Baltimore, Md.:
Every place in the Naval school subject to my appointment is full, and I have one unredeemed promise of more than half a year's standing.
A. LINCOLN.

FURTHER DEMOCRATIC PARTY CRITICISM

TO M. BIRCHARD AND OTHERS.

WASHINGTON, D. C., June 29, 1863.
MESSRS. M. BIRCHARD, DAVID A. HOUK, et al:
GENTLEMEN:—The resolutions of the Ohio Democratic State convention, which you present me, together with your introductory and closing remarks, being in position and argument mainly the same as the resolutions of the Democratic meeting at Albany, New York, I refer you to my response to the latter as meeting most of the points in the former.
This response you evidently used in preparing your remarks, and I desire no more than that it be used with accuracy. In a single reading of your remarks, I only discovered one inaccuracy in matter, which I suppose you took from that paper. It is where you say: "The undersigned are unable to agree with you in the opinion you have expressed that the Constitution is different in time of insurrection or invasion from what it is in time of peace and public security."
A recurrence to the paper will show you that I have not expressed the opinion you suppose. I expressed the opinion that the Constitution is different in its application in cases of rebellion or invasion, involving the public safety, from

what it is in times of profound peace and public security; and this opinion I adhere to, simply because, by the Constitution itself, things may be done in the one case which may not be done in the other.

I dislike to waste a word on a merely personal point, but I must respectfully assure you that you will find yourselves at fault should you ever seek for evidence to prove your assumption that I "opposed in discussions before the people the policy of the Mexican war."

You say: "Expunge from the Constitution this limitation upon the power of Congress to suspend the writ of habeas corpus, and yet the other guarantees of personal liberty would remain unchanged." Doubtless, if this clause of the Constitution, improperly called, as I think, a limitation upon the power of Congress, were expunged, the other guarantees would remain the same; but the question is not how those guarantees would stand with that clause out of the Constitution, but how they stand with that clause remaining in it, in case of rebellion or invasion involving the public safety. If the liberty could be indulged of expunging that clause, letter and spirit, I really think the constitutional argument would be with you.

My general view on this question was stated in the Albany response, and hence I do not state it now. I only add that, as seems to me, the benefit of the writ of habeas corpus is the great means through which the guarantees of personal liberty are conserved and made available in the last resort; and corroborative of this view is the fact that Mr. Vallandigham, in the very case in question, under the advice of able lawyers, saw not where else to go but to the habeas corpus. But by the Constitution the benefit of the writ of habeas corpus itself may be suspended when, in case of rebellion or invasion, the public safety may require it.

You ask, in substance, whether I really claim that I may override all the guaranteed rights of individuals, on the plea of conserving the public safety when I may choose to say the public safety requires it. This question, divested of the phraseology calculated to represent me as struggling for an arbitrary personal prerogative, is either simply a question who shall decide, or an affirmation that nobody shall decide, what the public safety does require in cases of rebellion or invasion.

The Constitution contemplates the question as likely to occur for decision, but it does not expressly declare who is to decide it. By necessary implication, when rebellion or invasion comes, the decision is to be made from time to time; and I think the man whom, for the time, the people have, under the Constitution, made the commander-in-chief of their army and navy, is the man who holds the power and bears the responsibility of making it. If he uses the power justly, the same people will probably justify him; if he abuses it, he is in their hands to be dealt with by all the modes they have reserved to themselves in the Constitution.

The earnestness with which you insist that persons can only, in times of rebellion, be lawfully dealt with in accordance with the rules for criminal trials and punishments in times of peace, induces me to add a word to what I said on that point in the Albany response.

You claim that men may, if they choose, embarrass those whose duty it is to combat a giant rebellion, and then be dealt with in turn only as if there were no rebellion. The Constitution itself rejects this view. The military arrests and detentions which have been made, including those of Mr. Vallandigham, which are not different in principle from the others, have been for prevention, and not for punishment—as injunctions to stay injury, as proceedings to keep the peace; and hence, like proceedings in such cases and for like reasons, they have not been accompanied with indictments, or trials by juries, nor in a single case by any punishment whatever, beyond what is purely incidental to the prevention. The original sentence of imprisonment in Mr. Vallandigham's case was to prevent injury to the military service only, and the modification of it was made as a less disagreeable mode to him of securing the same prevention.

I am unable to perceive an insult to Ohio in the case of Mr. Vallandigham. Quite surely nothing of the sort was or is intended. I was wholly unaware that Mr. Vallandigham was, at the time of his arrest, a candidate for the Democratic nomination for governor until so informed by your reading to me the resolutions of the convention. I am grateful to the State of Ohio for many things, especially for the brave soldiers and officers she has given in the present national trial to the armies of the Union.

You claim, as I understand, that according to my own position in the Albany response, Mr. Vallandigham should be released; and this because, as you claim, he has not damaged the military service by discouraging enlistments, encouraging desertions, or otherwise; and that if he had, he should have been turned over to the civil authorities under the recent acts of Congress. I certainly do not know that Mr. Vallandigham has specifically and by direct language advised against enlistments and in favor of desertion and resistance to drafting.

We all know that combinations, armed in some instances, to resist the arrest of deserters began several months ago; that more recently the like has appeared in resistance to the enrolment preparatory to a draft; and that quite a number of assassinations have occurred from the same animus. These had to be met by military force, and this again has led to bloodshed and death. And now, under a sense of responsibility more weighty and enduring than any which is merely official, I solemnly declare my belief that this hindrance of the military, including maiming and murder, is due to the course in which Mr. Vallandigham has been engaged in a greater degree than to any other cause; and it is due to him personally in a greater degree than to any other one man.

These things have been notorious, known to all, and of course known to Mr. Vallandigham. Perhaps I would not be wrong to say they originated with his special friends and adherents. With perfect knowledge of them, he has frequently if not constantly made speeches in Congress and before popular assemblies; and if it can be shown that, with these things staring him in the face he has ever uttered a word of rebuke or counsel against them, it will be a fact greatly in his favor with me, and one of which as yet I am totally ignorant. When it is known that the whole burden of his speeches has been to stir up men against the prosecution of the war, and that in the midst of resistance to it he has not been known in any instance to counsel against such resistance, it is next to impossible to repel the inference that he has counseled directly in favor of it.

With all this before their eyes, the convention you represent have nominated Mr. Vallandigham for governor of Ohio, and both they and you have declared the purpose to sustain the national Union by all constitutional means. But of course they and you in common reserve to yourselves to decide what are constitutional means; and, unlike the Albany meeting, you omit to state or intimate that in your opinion an army is a constitutional means of saving the Union against a rebellion, or even to intimate that you are conscious of an existing rebellion being in progress with the avowed object of destroying that very Union. At the same time your nominee for governor, in whose behalf you appeal, is known to you and to the world to declare against the use of an army to suppress the rebellion. Your own attitude, therefore, encourages desertion, resistance to the draft, and the like, because it teaches those who incline to desert and to escape the draft to believe it is your purpose to protect them, and to hope that you will become strong enough to do so.

After a short personal intercourse with you, gentlemen of the committee, I cannot say I think you desire this effect to follow your attitude; but I assure your that both friends and enemies of the Union look upon it in this light. It is a substantial hope, and by consequence a real strength to the enemy. If it is a false hope, and one which you would willingly dispel, I will make the way exceedingly easy.

I send you duplicates of this letter in order that you, or a majority of you, may, if you choose, indorse your names upon one of them and return it thus indorsed to me with the understanding that those signing are thereby committed to the following propositions and to nothing else:

1. That there is now a rebellion in the United States, the object and tendency of which is to destroy the National Union; and that, in your opinion, an army and navy are constitutional means for suppressing that rebellion;

2. That no one of you will do anything which, in his own judgment, will tend to hinder the increase, or favor the decrease, or lessen the efficiency of the army or navy while engaged in the effort to suppress that rebellion; and

3. That each of you will, in his sphere, do all he can to have the officers, soldiers, and seamen of the army and navy, while engaged in the effort to suppress the rebellion, paid, fed, clad, and otherwise well provided for and supported.

And with the further understanding that upon receiving the letter and names thus indorsed, I will cause them to be published, which publication shall be, within itself, a revocation of the order in relation to Mr. Vallandigham. It will not escape observation that I consent to the release of Mr. Vallandigham upon terms not embracing any pledge from him or from others as to what he will or will not do. I do this because he is not present to speak for himself, or to authorize others to speak for him; and because I should expect that on his returning he would not put himself practically in antagonism with the position of his friends. But I do it chiefly because I thereby prevail on other influential gentlemen of Ohio to so define their position as to be of immense value to the army—thus more than compensating for the consequences of any mistake in allowing Mr. Vallandigham to return; so that, on the whole, the public safety will not have suffered by it. Still, in regard to Mr. Vallandigham and all others, I must hereafter, as heretofore, do so much as the public safety may seem to require.

I have the honor to be respectfully yours, etc.,
A. LINCOLN.

TELEGRAM TO GOVERNOR PARKER.

EXECUTIVE MANSION, WASHINGTON, June 30, 1863. 10.55

GOVERNOR PARKER, Trenton, N.J.:

Your despatch of yesterday received. I really think the attitude of the enemy's army in Pennsylvania presents us the best opportunity we have had since the war began. I think you will not see the foe in New Jersey. I beg you to be assured that no one out of my position can know so well as if he were in it the difficulties and involvements of replacing General McClellan in command, and this aside from any imputations upon him.

Please accept my sincere thanks for what you have done and are doing to get troops forward.
A. LINCOLN.

TELEGRAM TO A. K. McCLURE.

WAR DEPARTMENT, WASHINGTON CITY, June 30, 1863.

A. K. McCLURE, Philadelphia:
Do we gain anything by opening one leak to stop another? Do we gain anything by quieting one merely to open another, and probably a larger one?
A. LINCOLN.

TELEGRAM TO GENERAL COUCH. [Cipher] WASHINGTON CITY, June 30, 1863. 3.23

P.M.
MAJOR-GENERAL COUCH, Harrisburg, Pa.:
I judge by absence of news that the enemy is not crossing or pressing up to the Susquehanna. Please tell me what you know of his movements.
A. LINCOLN

TO GENERAL D. HUNTER.

EXECUTIVE MANSION, WASHINGTON, June 30, 1863.

MAJOR-GENERAL HUNTER.
MY DEAR GENERAL:—I have just received your letter of the 25th of June.
I assure you, and you may feel authorized in stating, that the recent change of commanders in the Department of the South was made for no reasons which convey any imputation upon your known energy, efficiency, and patriotism; but for causes which seemed sufficient, while they were in no degree incompatible with the respect and esteem in which I have always held you as a man and an officer.
I cannot, by giving my consent to a publication of whose details I know nothing, assume the responsibility of whatever you may write. In this matter your own sense of military propriety must be your guide, and the regulations of the service your rule of conduct.
I am very truly your friend,
A. LINCOLN.

TELEGRAM TO GENERAL BURNSIDE.

WAR DEPARTMENT, WASHINGTON, D. C., July 3, 1863

MAJOR-GENERAL BURNSIDE, Cincinnati, Ohio:
Private Downey, of the Twentieth or Twenty-sixth Kentucky Infantry, is said to have been sentenced to be shot for desertion to-day. If so, respite the execution until I can see the record.
A. LINCOLN.

REASSURING SON IN COLLEGE

TELEGRAM TO ROBERT T. LINCOLN.

EXECUTIVE MANSION, WASHINGTON, July 3,1863.
ROBERT T. LINCOLN, Esq., Cambridge, Mass.:
Don't be uneasy. Your mother very slightly hurt by her fall.
A.L.
Please send at once.

ANNOUNCEMENT OF NEWS FROM GETTYSBURG.

WASHINGTON,

July 4, 10.30 A.M.
The President announces to the country that news from the Army of the Potomac, up to 10 P.M. of the 3d, is such as to cover that army with the highest honor, to promise a great success to the cause of the Union, and to claim the condolence of all for the many gallant fallen; and that for this he especially desires that on this day He whose will, not ours, should ever be done be everywhere remembered and reverenced with profoundest gratitude.
A. LINCOLN.

TELEGRAM TO GENERAL FRENCH. [Cipher] WAR DEPARTMENT, WASHINGTON, D. C.,

July 5, 1863.
MAJOR-GENERAL FRENCH, Fredericktown, Md.:

I see your despatch about destruction of pontoons. Cannot the enemy ford the river?
A. LINCOLN.

CONTINUED FAILURE TO PURSUE ENEMY

TELEGRAM TO GENERAL H. W. HALLECK.

SOLDIERS' HOME, WASHINGTON, JULY 6 1863.7 P.M., MAJOR-GENERAL HALLECK:
I left the telegraph office a good deal dissatisfied. You know I did not like the phrase—in Orders, No. 68, I believe— "Drive the invaders from our soil." Since that, I see a despatch from General French, saying the enemy is crossing his wounded over the river in flats, without saying why he does not stop it, or even intimating a thought that it ought to be stopped. Still later, another despatch from General Pleasonton, by direction of General Meade, to General French, stating that the main army is halted because it is believed the rebels are concentrating "on the road towards Hagerstown, beyond Fairfield," and is not to move until it is ascertained that the rebels intend to evacuate Cumberland Valley.
These things appear to me to be connected with a purpose to cover Baltimore and Washington and to get the enemy across the river again without a further collision, and they do not appear connected with a purpose to prevent his crossing and to destroy him. I do fear the former purpose is acted upon and the latter rejected.
If you are satisfied the latter purpose is entertained, and is judiciously pursued, I am content. If you are not so satisfied, please look to it.
Yours truly,
A. LINCOLN.

RESPONSE TO A SERENADE,

JULY 7, 1863.

FELLOW-CITIZENS:—I am very glad indeed to see you to-night, and yet I will not say I thank you for this call; but I do most sincerely thank Almighty God for the occasion on which you have called. How long ago is it Eighty-odd years since, on the Fourth of July, for the first time in the history of the world, a nation, by its representatives, assembled and declared as a self-evident truth "that all men are created equal." That was the birthday of the United States of America. Since then the Fourth of July has had several very peculiar recognitions. The two men most distinguished in the framing and support of the Declaration were Thomas Jefferson and John Adams, the one having penned it, and the other sustained it the most forcibly in debate—the only two of the fifty-five who signed it and were elected Presidents of the United States. Precisely fifty years after they put their hands to the paper, it pleased Almighty God to take both from this stage of action. This was indeed an extraordinary and remarkable event in our history. Another President, five years after, was called from this stage of existence on the same day and month of the year; and now on this last Fourth of July just passed, when we have a gigantic rebellion, at the bottom of which is an effort to overthrow the principle that all men were created equal, we have the surrender of a most powerful position and army on that very day. And not only so, but in the succession of battles in Pennsylvania, near to us, through three days, so rapidly fought that they might be called one great battle, on the first, second, and third of the month of July; and on the fourth the cohorts of those who opposed the Declaration that all men are created equal, "turned tail" and run.

Gentlemen, this is a glorious theme, and the occasion for a speech, but I am not prepared to make one worthy of the occasion. I would like to speak in terms of praise due to the many brave officers and soldiers who have fought in the cause of the Union and liberties of their country from the beginning of the war. These are trying occasions, not only in success, but for the want of success. I dislike to mention the name of one single officer, lest I might do wrong to those I might forget. Recent events bring up glorious names, and particularly prominent ones; but these I will not mention. Having said this much, I will now take the music.

SURRENDER OF VICKSBURG TO GENERAL GRANT

TELEGRAM FROM GENERAL HALLECK TO GENERAL G. C. MEADE.

WASHINGTON, D.C., July 7, 1863.
MAJOR-GENERAL MEADE, Army of the Potomac:
I have received from the President the following note, which I respectfully communicate:
"We have certain information that Vicksburg surrendered to General Grant on the Fourth of July. Now if General Meade can complete his work, so gloriously prosecuted this far, by the literal or substantial destruction of Lee's army, the rebellion will be over.
"Yours truly,
"A. LINCOLN."
H. W. HALLECK. General-in-Chief.

TELEGRAM FROM GENERAL HALLECK TO GENERAL G. C. MEADE.

WASHINGTON, D. C., July 8, 1863.

MAJOR-GENERAL MEADE, Frederick, Md.:
There is reliable information that the enemy is crossing at Williamsport. The opportunity to attack his divided forces should not be lost. The President is urgent and anxious that your army should move against him by forced marches.
H. W. HALLECK, General-in-Chief

TELEGRAM TO GENERAL THOMAS.

WAR DEPARTMENT, WASHINGTON, July 8, 1863.12.30 P.M.

GENERAL LORENZO THOMAS, Harrisburg, Pa.:
Your despatch of this morning to the Secretary of War is before me. The forces you speak of will be of no imaginable service if they cannot go forward with a little more expedition. Lee is now passing the Potomac faster than the forces you mention are passing Carlisle. Forces now beyond Carlisle to be joined by regiments still at Harrisburg, and the united force again to join Pierce somewhere, and the whole to move down the Cumberland Valley, will in my unprofessional opinion be quite as likely to capture the "man in the moon" as any part of Lee's army.
A. LINCOLN.

NEWS OF GRANT'S CAPTURE OF VICKSBURG

TELEGRAM TO E. D. SMITH.

WAR DEPARTMENT, WASHINGTON, D.C., July 8, 1863.
E. DELAFIELD SMITH, New York:
Your kind despatch in behalf of self and friends is gratefully received. Capture of Vicksburg confirmed by despatch from General Grant himself.
A. LINCOLN.

TELEGRAM TO F. F. LOWE.

WAR DEPARTMENT, WASHINGTON, D.C., July 8, 1863.

HON. F. F. LOWE, San Francisco, Cal.:
There is no doubt that General Meade, now commanding the Army of the Potomac, beat Lee at Gettysburg, Pa., at the end of a three days' battle, and that the latter is now crossing the Potomac at Williamsport over the swollen stream and with poor means of crossing, and closely pressed by Meade. We also have despatches rendering it entirely certain that Vicksburg surrendered to General Grant on the glorious old 4th.
A. LINCOLN.

TELEGRAM TO L. SWETT AND P. F. LOWE.

[Cipher.]

WAR DEPARTMENT, WASHINGTON CITY, D.C., July 9, 1863.
HON. LEONARD SWETT, HON. F. F. LOWE, San Francisco, Cal.:
Consult together and do not have a riot, or great difficulty about delivering possession.
A. LINCOLN.

TELEGRAM TO J. K. DUBOIS.

WASHINGTON, D.C., July 11, 1863. 9 A.M.

HON. J. K. DUBOIS, Springfield, Ill.:
It is certain that, after three days' fighting at Gettysburg, Lee withdrew and made for the Potomac, that he found the river so swollen as to prevent his crossing; that he is still this side, near Hagerstown and Williamsport, preparing to defend himself; and that Meade is close upon him, and preparing to attack him, heavy skirmishing having occurred nearly all day yesterday.
I am more than satisfied with what has happened north of the Potomac so far, and am anxious and hopeful for what is to come.
A. LINCOLN.
> [Nothing came! Lee was allowed to escape again and the war went on for another two years. D.W.]

TELEGRAM TO GENERAL SCHENCK.

[Cipher.]

WAR DEPARTMENT, WASHINGTON CITY, July 11, 1863.
MAJOR-GENERAL SCHENCK, Baltimore, Md.:
How many rebel prisoners captured within Maryland and Pennsylvania have reached Baltimore within this month of July?
A. LINCOLN.

TO GENERAL GRANT.

EXECUTIVE MANSION, WASHINGTON, July 13, 1863.

MAJOR-GENERAL GRANT:
MY DEAR GENERAL:—I do not remember that you and I ever met personally. I write this now as a grateful acknowledgment of the almost inestimable service you have done the Country. I write to say a word further. When you first reached the vicinity of Vicksburg, I thought you should do what you finally did—march the troops across the neck, run the batteries with the transports, and thus go below; and I never had any faith except a general hope that you knew better than I, that the Yazoo Pass expedition and the like could succeed. When you dropped below, and took Port Gibson, Grand Gulf, and vicinity, I thought you should go down the river and join General Banks; and when you turned northward, east of the Big Black, I feared it was a mistake. I now wish to make the personal acknowledgment that you were right and I was wrong.
Yours very truly,
A. LINCOLN.

TELEGRAM TO GENERAL J. M. SCHOFIELD.

WAR DEPARTMENT, WASHINGTON, July 13, 1863.

GENERAL SCHOFIELD. St. Louis, Mo.:
I regret to learn of the arrest of the Democrat editor. I fear this loses you the middle position I desired you to occupy. I have not learned which of the two letters I wrote you it was that the Democrat published, but I care very little for the publication of any letter I have written. Please spare me the trouble this is likely to bring.
A. LINCOLN.

SON IN COLLEGE DOES NOT WRITE HIS PARENTS

TELEGRAM TO R. T. LINCOLN.

WAR DEPARTMENT, WASHINGTON D.C., July 14, 1863.
ROBERT T. LINCOLN: New York, Fifth Avenue Hotel:
Why do I hear no more of you?
A. LINCOLN.

INTIMATION OF ARMISTICE PROPOSALS

FROM JAMES R. GILMORE TO GOVERNOR VANCE OF NORTH CAROLINA,

WITH THE PRESIDENT'S INDORSEMENT. PRESIDENT'S ROOM, WHITE HOUSE, WASHINGTON,
July [15?] 1864.
HIS EXCELLENCY ZEBULON B. VANCE.
MY DEAR SIR:—My former business partner, Mr. Frederic Kidder, of Boston, has forwarded to me a letter he has recently received from his brother, Edward Kidder, of Wilmington, in which (Edward Kidder) says that he has had an interview with you in which you expressed an anxiety for any peace compatible with honor; that you regard slavery as already dead, and the establishment of the Confederacy as hopeless; and that you should exert all your influence to bring about any reunion that would admit the South on terms of perfect equality with the North.
On receipt of this letter I lost no time in laying it before the President of the United States, who expressed great gratification at hearing such sentiments from you, one of the most influential and honored of the Southern governors, and he desires me to say that he fully shares your anxiety for the restoration of peace between the States and for a reunion of all the States on the basis of the abolition of slavery—the bone we are fighting over—and the full reinstatement of every Confederate citizen in all the rights of citizenship in our common country. These points conceded, the President authorizes me to say that he will be glad to receive overtures from any man, or body of men, who have authority to control the armies of the Confederacy; and that he and the United States Congress will be found very liberal on all collateral points that may come up in the settlement.
His views on the collateral points that may naturally arise, the President desires me to say he will communicate to you through me if you should suggest the personal interview that Mr. Edward Kidder recommends in his letter to his brother. In that case you will please forward to me, through Mr. Kidder, your official permit, as Governor of North Carolina, to enter and leave the State, and to remain in it in safety during the pendency of these negotiations, which, I suppose, should be conducted in entire secrecy until they assume an official character. With high consideration, I am, Sincerely yours,
JAMES R. GILMORE.
[Indorsement.]
This letter has been written in my presence, has been read by me, and has my entire approval. A.L.

PROCLAMATION FOR THANKSGIVING, JULY 15, 1863

BY THE PRESIDENT OF THE UNITED STATES OF AMERICA:

A Proclamation.
It has pleased Almighty God to hearken to the supplications and prayers of an afflicted people, and to vouchsafe to the army and navy of the United States victories on land and on the sea so signal and so effective as to furnish reasonable grounds for augmented confidence that the Union of these States will be maintained, their Constitution preserved, and their peace and prosperity permanently restored. But these victories have been accorded not without sacrifices of life, limb, health, and liberty, incurred by brave, loyal, and patriotic citizens. Domestic affliction in every part of the country

follows in the train of these fearful bereavements. It is meet and right to recognize and confess the presence of the Almighty Father, and the power of His hand equally in these triumphs and in these sorrows.

Now, therefore, be it known that I do set apart Thursday, the 6th day of August next, to be observed as a day for national thanksgiving, praise, and prayer, and I invite the people of the United States to assemble on that occasion in their customary places of worship, and, in the forms approved by their own consciences, render the homage due to the Divine Majesty for the wonderful things He has done in the nation's behalf, and invoke the influence of His Holy Spirit to subdue the anger which has produced and so long sustained a needless and cruel rebellion, to change the hearts of the insurgents, to guide the counsels of the Government with wisdom adequate to so great a national emergency, and to visit with tender care and consolation throughout the length and breadth of our land all those who, through the vicissitudes of marches, voyages, battles, and sieges have been, brought to suffer in mind, body, or estate, and finally to lead the whole nation through the paths of repentance and submission to the Divine Will back to the perfect enjoyment of union and fraternal peace.

In witness whereof, I have hereunto set my hand and caused the seal of the United States to be affixed.

Done at the city of Washington, this fifteenth day of July, in the year of our Lord one thousand eight hundred and sixty-three, and of the independence of the United States of America the eighty-eighth.

A. LINCOLN.

By, the President WILLIAM H. SEWARD,
 Secretary of State.

TELEGRAM TO L. SWETT.

[Cipher.]

WAR DEPARTMENT, WASHINGTON CITY, July 15, 1863.
HON. L SWETT, San Francisco, Cal.:

Many persons are telegraphing me from California, begging me for the peace of the State to suspend the military enforcement of the writ of possession in the Almaden case, while you are the single one who urges the contrary. You know I would like to oblige you, but it seems to me my duty in this case is the other way.

A. LINCOLN.

TELEGRAM TO SIMON CAMERON.

[Cipher.]

WAR DEPARTMENT, WASHINGTON CITY, JULY 15, 1863.
HON. SIMON CAMERON, Harrisburg, Pa.:

Your despatch of yesterday received. Lee was already across the river when you sent it. I would give much to be relieved of the impression that Meade, Couch, Smith, and all since the battle at Gettysburg, have striven only to get Lee over the river without another fight. Please tell me, if you know, who was the one corps commander who was for fighting in the council of war on Sunday night.

A. LINCOLN.

TELEGRAM TO J. O. BROADHEAD.

WASHINGTON, D.C., JULY 15, 1863.

J. O. BROADHEAD, St. Louis, Mo.:

The effect on political position of McKee's arrest will not be relieved any by its not having been made with that purpose.

A. LINCOLN.

TO GENERAL LANE.

EXECUTIVE MANSION, WASHINGTON, July 17 1863.

HON. S. H. LANE.
MY DEAR SIR:—Governor Carney has not asked to [have] General Blunt removed, or interfered with, in his military operations. He has asked that he, the Governor, be allowed to commission officers for troops raised in Kansas, as other governors of loyal States do; and I think he is right in this.
He has asked that General Blunt shall not take persons charged with civil crimes out of the hands of the courts and turn them over to mobs to be hung; and I think he is right in this also. He has asked that General Ewing's department be extended to include all Kansas; and I have not determined whether this is right or not.
Yours truly,
A. LINCOLN.

TELEGRAM TO GOVERNOR MORTON.

WASHINGTON, D. C., July 18, 1863.

GOVERNOR O. P. MORTON, Indianapolis:
What do you remember about the case of John O. Brown, convicted of mutinous conduct and sentenced to death? What do you desire about it?
A. LINCOLN.

TO GOVERNOR PARKER

EXECUTIVE MANSION, WASHINGTON

July 20, 1863.
HIS EXCELLENCY JOEL PARKER, Governor of New Jersey.
DEAR SIR:—Yours of the 15th has been received, and considered by the Secretary of War and myself. I was pained to be informed this morning by the Provost-Marshal-General that New Jersey is now behind twelve thousand, irrespective of the draft. I did not have time to ascertain by what rules this was made out; and I shall be very glad if it shall, by any means, prove to be incorrect. He also tells me that eight thousand will be about the quota of New Jersey on the first draft; and the Secretary of War says the first draft in that State would not be made for some time in any event. As every man obtained otherwise lessens the draft so much, and this may supersede it altogether, I hope you will push forward your volunteer regiments as fast as possible.
It is a very delicate matter to postpone the draft in one State, because of the argument it furnishes others to have postponement also. If we could have a reason in one case which would be good if presented in all cases, we could act upon it.
I will thank you, therefore, to inform me, if you can, by what day, at the earliest, you can promise to have ready to be mustered into the United States service the eight thousand men.
If you can make a reliable promise (I mean one which you can rely on yourself) of this sort, it will be of great value, if the day is not too remote.
I beg you to be assured I wish to avoid the difficulties you dread as much as yourself.
Your obedient servant,
A. LINCOLN

TO GENERAL SCHOFIELD.

EXECUTIVE MANSION, WASHINGTON D.C. JULY 20, 1863

MAJOR GENERAL JOHN M. SCHOFIELD.
MY DEAR GENERAL:—I have received and read your letter of the 14th of July.
I think the suggestion you make, of discontinuing proceedings against Mr. McKee, a very proper one. While I admit that there is an apparent impropriety in the publication of the letter mentioned, without my consent or yours, it is still a case where no evil could result, and which I am entirely willing to overlook.
Yours truly,
A. LINCOLN.

TELEGRAM TO GENERAL J. M. SCHOFIELD

WASHINGTON, D.C. JULY 22, 1863

MAJOR GENERAL SCHOFIELD, St. Louis, Mo.:
The following despatch has been placed in my hands. Please look to the subject of it.
LEXINGTON, Mo., JULY 21, 1863 HON. S C. POMEROY: Under Orders No.63 the sheriff is arresting slaves of rebels inside our lines, and returning them in great numbers. Can he do it? Answer. GOULD.
A. LINCOLN

TO POSTMASTER-GENERAL BLAIR

EXECUTIVE MANSION, WASHINGTON,

JULY 24, 1863. HON. POSTMASTER-GENERAL
SIR:-Yesterday little indorsements of mine went to you in two cases of postmasterships sought for widows whose husbands have fallen in the battles of this war. These cases occurring on the same day brought me to reflect more attentively than I had before done, as to what is fairly due from us herein the dispensing of patronage toward the men who, by fighting our battles, bear the chief burden of serving our country. My conclusion is that, other claims and qualifications being equal, they have the better right and this is especially applicable to the disabled and the soldier, deceased soldier's family.
Your obedient servant,
A. LINCOLN

TO SECRETARY OF THE NAVY.

EXECUTIVE MANSION, WASHINGTON, July 25, 1863.

HON. SECRETARY OF THE NAVY.
SIR:—Certain matters have come to my notice, and considered by me, which induce me to believe that it will conduce to the public interest for you to add to the general instructions given to our naval commanders in relation to contraband trade propositions substantially as follows, to wit:
First. You will avoid the reality, and as far as possible the appearance, of using any neutral port to watch neutral vessels and then to dart out and seize them on their departure.

615

NOTE.—Complaint is made that this has been practiced at the port of St Thomas, which practice, if it exists, is disapproved and must cease.

Second. You will not in any case detain the crew of a captured neutral vessel or any other subject of a neutral power on board such vessel, as prisoners of war or otherwise, except the small number necessary as witnesses in the prize court.

NOTE.-The practice here forbidden is also charged to exist, which, if true, is disapproved and must cease.

My dear sir, it is not intended to be insinuated that you have been remiss in the performance of the arduous and responsible duties of your department, which, I take pleasure in affirming, has in your hands been conducted with admirable success. Yet, while your subordinates are almost of necessity brought into angry collision with the subjects of foreign states, the representatives of those states and yourself do not come into immediate contact for the purpose of keeping the peace, in spite of such collisions. At that point there is an ultimate and heavy responsibility upon me.

What I propose is in strict accordance with international law, and is therefore unobjectionable; whilst, if it does no other good, it will contribute to sustain a considerable portion of the present British ministry in their places, who, if displaced, are sure to be replaced by others more unfavorable to us.

Your obedient servant,

A. LINCOLN

LETTER TO GOVERNOR PARKER.

EXECUTIVE MANSION, WASHINGTON,

July 25, 1863.

HIS EXCELLENCY GOVERNOR JOEL PARKER.

SIR:—Yours of the 21st is received, and I have taken time and considered and discussed the subject with the Secretary of War and Provost-Marshal General, in order, if possible, to make you a more favorable answer than I finally find myself able to do.

It is a vital point with us to not have a special stipulation with the governor of any one State, because it would breed trouble in many, if not all, other States; and my idea was when I wrote you, as it still is, to get a point of time to which we could wait, on the reason that we were not ready ourselves to proceed, and which might enable you to raise the quota of your State, in whole, or in large part, without the draft. The points of time you fix are much farther off than I had hoped. We might have got along in the way I have indicated for twenty, or possibly thirty, days. As it stands, the best I can say is that every volunteer you will present us within thirty days from this date, fit and ready to be mustered into the United States service, on the usual terms, shall be pro tanto an abatement of your quota of the draft. That quota I can now state at eight thousand seven hundred and eighty-three (8783). No draft from New Jersey, other than for the above quota, will be made before an additional draft, common to [all] the States, shall be required; and I may add that if we get well through with this draft, I entertain a strong hope that any further one may never be needed. This expression of hope, however, must not be construed into a promise.

As to conducting the draft by townships, I find it would require such a waste of labor already done, and such an additional amount of it, and such a loss of time, as to make it, I fear, inadmissible.

Your obedient servant,

A. LINCOLN.

P. S.—Since writing the above, getting additional information, I am enabled to say that the draft may be made in subdistricts, as the enrolment has been made, or is in process of making. This will amount practically to drafting by townships, as the enrollment subdistricts are generally about the extent of townships. A.L.

To GENERAL G. G. MEADE. (Private.)

EXECUTIVE MANSION, WASHINGTON, July 27, 1863.

MAJOR-GENERAL MEADE:

I have not thrown General Hooker away; and therefore I would like to know whether it would be agreeable to you, all things considered, for him to take a corps under you, if he himself is willing to do so. Write me in perfect freedom,

with the assurance that I will not subject you to any embarrassment by making your letter or its contents known to any one. I wish to know your wishes before I decide whether to break the subject to him. Do not lean a hair's breadth against your own feelings, or your judgment of the public service, on the idea of gratifying me.
Yours truly,
A. LINCOLN.

TELEGRAM TO GENERAL A. B. BURNSIDE.

WAR DEPARTMENT, WASHINGTON, July 27, 1863.

MAJOR-GENERAL BURNSIDE, Cincinnati, O.:
Let me explain. In General Grant's first despatch after the fall of Vicksburg, he said, among other things, he would send the Ninth Corps to you. Thinking it would be pleasant to you, I asked the Secretary of War to telegraph you the news. For some reasons never mentioned to us by General Grant, they have not been sent, though we have seen outside intimations that they took part in the expedition against Jackson. General Grant is a copious worker and fighter, but a very meager writer or telegrapher. No doubt he changed his purpose in regard to the Ninth Corps for some sufficient reason, but has forgotten to notify us of it.
A. LINCOLN.

TO GENERAL H. W. HALLECK.

EXECUTIVE MANSION, July 29, 1863

MAJOR-GENERAL HALLECK:
Seeing General Meade's despatch of yesterday to yourself causes me to fear that he supposes the Government here is demanding of him to bring on a general engagement with Lee as soon as possible. I am claiming no such thing of him. In fact, my judgment is against it; which judgment, of course, I will yield if yours and his are the contrary. If he could not safely engage Lee at Williamsport, it seems absurd to suppose he can safely engage him now, when he has scarcely more than two thirds of the force he had at Williamsport, while it must be that Lee has been reinforced. True, I desired General Meade to pursue Lee across the Potomac, hoping, as has proved true, that he would thereby clear the Baltimore and Ohio Railroad, and get some advantages by harassing him on his retreat. These being past, I am unwilling he should now get into a general engagement on the impression that we here are pressing him, and I shall be glad for you to so inform him, unless your own judgment is against it.
Yours truly,
A. LINCOLN.
H. W. HALLECK, General-in-Chief.

TO SECRETARY STANTON.

EXECUTIVE MANSION, WASHINGTON, July 29, 1863

HON. SECRETARY OF WAR.
SIR:—Can we not renew the effort to organize a force to go to western Texas?
Please consult with the general-in-chief on the subject.
If the Governor of New Jersey shall furnish any new regiments, might not they be put into such an expedition? Please think of it.
I believe no local object is now more desirable.
Yours truly,
A. LINCOLN.

ORDER OF RETALIATION.

EXECUTIVE MANSION, WASHINGTON, July 30, 1863.

It is the duty of every government to give protection to its citizens, of whatever class, color, or condition, and especially to those who are duly organized as soldiers in the public service. The law of nations and the usages and customs of war, as carried on by civilized powers, permit no distinction as to color in the treatment of prisoners of war as public enemies. To sell or enslave any captured person, on account of his color and for no offense against the laws of war, is a relapse into barbarism, and a crime against the civilization of the age.
The Government of the United States will give the same protection to all its soldiers; and if the enemy shall sell or enslave any one because of his color, the offense shall be punished by retaliation upon the enemy's prisoners in our possession.
It is therefore ordered that for every soldier of the United States killed in violation of the laws of war, a rebel soldier shall be executed; and for every one enslaved by the enemy or sold into slavery, a rebel soldier shall be placed at hard labor on the public works, and continued at such labor until the other shall be released and receive the treatment due to a prisoner of war.
A. LINCOLN.

TO GENERAL S. A. HURLBUT.

EXECUTIVE MANSION, WASHINGTON, July 31, 1863.

MY DEAR GENERAL HURLBUT:
Your letter by Mr. Dana was duly received. I now learn that your resignation has reached the War Department. I also learn that an active command has been assigned you by General Grant. The Secretary of War and General Halleck are very partial to you, as you know I also am. We all wish you to reconsider the question of resigning; not that we would wish to retain you greatly against your wish and interest, but that your decision may be at least a very well-considered one.
I understand that Senator [William K.] Sebastian, of Arkansas, thinks of offering to resume his place in the Senate. Of course the Senate, and not I, would decide whether to admit or reject him. Still I should feel great interest in the question. It may be so presented as to be one of the very greatest national importance; and it may be otherwise so presented as to be of no more than temporary personal consequence to him.
The Emancipation Proclamation applies to Arkansas. I think it is valid in law, and will be so held by the courts. I think I shall not retract or repudiate it. Those who shall have tasted actual freedom I believe can never be slaves or quasi-slaves again. For the rest, I believe some plan substantially being gradual emancipation would be better for both white and black. The Missouri plan recently adopted, I do not object to on account of the time for ending the institution; but I am sorry the beginning should have been postponed for seven years, leaving all that time to agitate for the repeal of the whole thing. It should begin at once, giving at least the new-born a vested interest in freedom which could not be taken away. If Senator Sebastian could come with something of this sort from Arkansas, I, at least, should take great interest in his case; and I believe a single individual will have scarcely done the world so great a service. See him if you can, and read this to him; but charge him not to make it public for the present. Write me again.
Yours very truly,
A. LINCOLN.

TELEGRAM FROM GOVERNOR SEYMOUR.

ALBANY, August 1, 1863. Recvd 2 P.M.

TO THE PRESIDENT OF THE UNITED STATES:
I ask that the draft be suspended in this State until I can send you a communication I am preparing.
HORATIO SEYMOUR.

TELEGRAM TO GOVERNOR SEYMOUR

WASHINGTON, D.C., August 1, 1863. 4 P.M.

HIS EXCELLENCY GOVERNOR SEYMOUR, Albany, N.Y.:
By what day may I expect your communication to reach me? Are you anxious about any part except the city and vicinity?
A. LINCOLN.

TELEGRAM TO GENERAL FOSTER.

EXECUTIVE MANSION, WASHINGTON, August 3, 1863.

MAJOR-GENERAL FOSTER (or whoever may be in command of the military department with headquarters at Fort Monroe, Va.):
If Dr. Wright, on trial at Norfolk, has been or shall be convicted, send me a transcript of his trial and conviction, and do not let execution be done upon him until my further order.
A. LINCOLN.

TO GENERAL N. P. BANKS.

EXECUTIVE MANSION, WASHINGTON, August 5, 1863.

MY DEAR GENERAL BANKS:
While I very well know what I would be glad for Louisiana to do, it is quite a different thing for me to assume direction of the matter. I would be glad for her to make a new constitution, recognizing the emancipation proclamation, and adopting emancipation in those parts of the State to which the proclamation does not apply. And while she is at it, I think it would not be objectionable for her to adopt some practical system by which the two races could gradually live themselves out of their old relation to each other, and both come out better prepared for the new. Education for young blacks should be included in the plan. After all, the power or element of "contract" may be sufficient for this probationary period, and by its simplicity and flexibility may be the better.
As an antislavery man, I have a motive to desire emancipation which proslavery men do not have but even they have strong enough reason to thus place themselves again under the shield of the Union, and to thus perpetually hedge against the recurrence of the scenes through which we are now passing.
Governor Shepley has informed me that Mr. Durant is now taking a registry, with a view to the election of a constitutional convention in Louisiana. This, to me, appears proper. If such convention were to ask my views, I could present little else than what I now say to you. I think the thing should be pushed forward, so that, if possible, its mature work may reach here by the meeting of Congress.
For my own part, I think I shall not, in any event, retract the emancipation proclamation: nor, as executive, ever return to slavery any person who is free by the terms of that proclamation, or by any of the acts of Congress.
If Louisiana shall send members to Congress, their admission to seats will depend, as you know, upon the respective Houses, and not upon the President.
Yours very truly,
A. LINCOLN.

TO GOVERNOR SEYMOUR.

EXECUTIVE MANSION, WASHINGTON, August 7, 1863.

HIS EXCELLENCY HORATIO SEYMOUR, Governor of New York:
Your communication of the 3rd instant has been received and attentively considered.
I cannot consent to suspend the draft in New York, as you request, because, among other reasons, time is too important. By the figures you send, which I presume are correct, the twelve districts represented fall into two classes of eight and four respectively. The disparity of the quotas for the draft in these two classes is certainly very striking, being the difference between an average of 2200 in one class and 4864 in the other. Assuming that the districts are equal one to another in entire population, as required by the plan on which they were made, this disparity is such as to require attention. Much of it, however, I suppose will be accounted for by the fact that so many more persons fit for soldiers are in the city than are in the country who have too recently arrived from other parts of the United States and from Europe to be either included in the census of 1860, or to have voted in 1862. Still, making due allowance for this, I am yet unwilling to stand upon it as an entirely sufficient explanation of the great disparity.
I shall direct the draft to proceed in all the districts, drawing, however, at first from each of the four districts—to wit, the Second, Fourth, Sixth, and Eighth—only, 2200 being the average quota of the other class. After this drawing, these four districts, and also the Seventeenth and Twenty-ninth, shall be carefully re-enrolled; and, if you please, agents of yours may witness every step of the process. Any deficiency which may appear by the new enrolment will be supplied by a special draft for that object, allowing due credit for volunteers who may be obtained from these districts respectively during the interval; and at all points, so far as consistent with practical convenience, due credits shall be given for volunteers, and your Excellency shall be notified of the time fixed for commencing the draft in each district. I do not object to abide a decision of the United States Supreme Court, or of the judges thereof, on the constitutionality of the draft law. In fact, I should be willing to facilitate the obtaining of it. But I cannot consent to lose the time while it is being obtained. We are contending with an enemy who, as I understand, drives every able-bodied man he can reach into his ranks, very much as a butcher drives bullocks into the slaughter-pen. No time is wasted, no argument is used. This produces an army which will soon turn upon our now victorious soldiers already in the field, if they shall not be sustained by recruits as they should be. It produces an army with a rapidity not to be matched on our side if we first waste time to re-experiment with the volunteer system, already deemed by Congress, and palpably, in fact, so far exhausted as to be inadequate; and then more time to obtain a court decision as to whether a law is constitutional, which requires a part of those not now in the service to go to the aid of those who are already in it; and still more time to determine with absolute certainty that we get those who are to go in the precisely legal proportion to those who are not to go. My purpose is to be in my action just and constitutional, and yet practical, in performing the important duty with which I am charged, of maintaining the unity and the free principles of our common country.
Your obedient servant,
A. LINCOLN.

TO GENERAL U.S. GRANT.

EXECUTIVE MANSION WASHINGTON, August 9, 1863.

MY DEAR GENERAL GRANT:
I see by a despatch of yours that you incline quite strongly toward an expedition against Mobile. This would appear tempting to me also, were it not that in view of recent events in Mexico I am greatly impressed with the importance of re-establishing the national authority in western Texas as soon as possible. I am not making an order, however, that I leave, for the present at least, to the general-in-chief.
A word upon another subject: General Thomas has gone again to the Mississippi Valley, with the view of raising colored troops. I have no reason to doubt that you are doing what you reasonably can upon the same subject. I believe it is a resource which if vigorously applied now will soon close the contest. It works doubly, weakening the enemy and strengthening us. We were not fully ripe for it until the river was opened. Now, I think at least one hundred thousand can and ought to be rapidly organized along its shores, relieving all white troops to serve elsewhere. Mr. Dana understands you as believing that the Emancipation Proclamation has helped some in your military operations. I am very glad if this is so.

Did you receive a short letter from me dated the 13th of July?
Yours very truly,
A. LINCOLN.

TO GENERAL W. S. ROSECRANS.

EXECUTIVE MANSION, WASHINGTON, August 10, 1863.

MY DEAR GENERAL ROSECRANS:
Yours of the 1st was received two days ago. I think you must have inferred more than General Halleck has intended, as to any dissatisfaction of mine with you. I am sure you, as a reasonable man, would not have been wounded could you have heard all my words and seen all my thoughts in regard to you. I have not abated in my kind feeling for and confidence in you. I have seen most of your despatches to General Halleck—probably all of them. After Grant invested Vicksburg I was very anxious lest Johnston should overwhelm him from the outside, and when it appeared certain that part of Bragg's force had gone and was going to Johnston, it did seem to me it was exactly the proper time for you to attack Bragg with what force he had left. In all kindness let me say it so seems to me yet. Finding from your despatches to General Halleck that your judgment was different, and being very anxious for Grant, I, on one occasion, told General Halleck I thought he should direct you to decide at once to immediately attack Bragg or to stand on the defensive and send part of your force to Grant. He replied he had already so directed in substance. Soon after, despatches from Grant abated my anxiety for him, and in proportion abated my anxiety about any movement of yours. When afterward, however, I saw a despatch of yours arguing that the right time for you to attack Bragg was not before, but would be after, the fall of Vicksburg, it impressed me very strangely, and I think I so stated to the Secretary of War and General Halleck. It seemed no other than the proposition that you could better fight Bragg when Johnston should be at liberty to return and assist him than you could before he could so return to his assistance.
Since Grant has been entirely relieved by the fall of Vicksburg, by which Johnston is also relieved, it has seemed to me that your chance for a stroke has been considerably diminished, and I have not been pressing you directly or indirectly. True, I am very anxious for East Tennessee to be occupied by us; but I see and appreciate the difficulties you mention. The question occurs, Can the thing be done at all? Does preparation advance at all? Do you not consume supplies as fast as you get them forward? Have you more animals to-day than you had at the battle of Stone's River? And yet have not more been furnished you since then than your entire present stock? I ask the same questions as to your mounted force.
Do not misunderstand: I am not casting blame upon you; I rather think by great exertion you can get to East Tennessee; but a very important question is, Can you stay there? I make no order in the case—that I leave to General Halleck and yourself.
And now be assured once more that I think of you in all kindness and confidence, and that I am not watching you with an evil eye.
Yours very truly,
A. LINCOLN.

TO GOVERNOR SEYMOUR.

EXECUTIVE MANSION WASHINGTON, August 11.1863.

HIS EXCELLENCY HORATIO SEYMOUR, Governor of New York:
Yours of the 8th, with Judge-Advocate-General Waterbury's report, was received to-day.
Asking you to remember that I consider time as being very important, both to the general cause of the country and to the soldiers in the field, I beg to remind you that I waited, at your request, from the 1st until the 6th inst., to receive your communication dated the 3d. In view of its great length, and the known time and apparent care taken in its preparation, I did not doubt that it contained your full case as you desired to present it. It contained the figures for twelve districts, omitting the other nineteen, as I suppose, because you found nothing to complain of as to them. I answered accordingly. In doing so I laid down the principle to which I purpose adhering, which is to proceed with the draft, at the same time employing infallible means to avoid any great wrong. With the communication received to-day

you send figures for twenty-eight districts, including the twelve sent before, and still omitting three, for which I suppose the enrolments are not yet received. In looking over the fuller list of twenty-eight districts, I find that the quotas for sixteen of them are above 2000 and below 2700, while, of the rest, six are above 2700 and six are below 2000. Applying the principle to these new facts, the Fifth and Seventh districts must be added to the four in which the quotas have already been reduced to 2200 for the first draft; and with these four others just be added to those to be re-enrolled. The correct case will then stand: the quotas of the Second, Fourth, Fifth, Sixth, Seventh, and Eighth districts fixed at 2200 for the first draft. The Provost-Marshal-General informs me that the drawing is already completed in the Sixteenth, Seventeenth, Eighteenth, Twenty-second, Twenty-fourth, Twenty-sixth, Twenty-seventh, Twenty-eighth, Twenty-ninth, and Thirtieth districts. In the others, except the three outstanding, the drawing will be made upon the quotas as now fixed. After the first draft, the Second, Fourth, Fifth, Sixth, Seventh, Eighth, Sixteenth, Seventeenth, Twenty-first, Twenty-fifth, Twenty-ninth, and Thirty-first will be enrolled for the purpose and in the manner stated in my letter of the 7th inst. The same principle will be applied to the now outstanding districts when they shall come in. No part of my former letter is repudiated by reason of not being restated in this, or for any other cause.
Your obedient servant,
A. LINCOLN.

TO GENERAL J. A. McCLERNAND.

EXECUTIVE MANSION, WASHINGTON, August 12, 1863.

MAJOR-GENERAL McCLERNAND.
MY DEAR SIR:—Our friend William G. Greene has just presented a kind letter in regard to yourself, addressed to me by our other friends Yates, Hatch, and Dubois.
I doubt whether your present position is more painful to you than to myself. Grateful for the patriotic stand so early taken by you in this life-and-death struggle of the nation, I have done whatever has appeared practicable to advance you and the public interest together. No charges, with a view to a trial, have been preferred against you by any one; nor do I suppose any will be. All there is, so far as I have heard, is General Grant's statement of his reasons for relieving you. And even this I have not seen or sought to see; because it is a case, as appears to me, in which I could do nothing without doing harm. General Grant and yourself have been conspicuous in our most important successes; and for me to interfere and thus magnify a breach between you could not but be of evil effect. Better leave it where the law of the case has placed it. For me to force you back upon General Grant would be forcing him to resign. I cannot give you a new command, because we have no forces except such as already have commanders.
I am constantly pressed by those who scold before they think, or without thinking at all, to give commands respectively to Fremont, McClellan, Butler, Sigel, Curtis, Hunter, Hooker, and perhaps others, when, all else out of the way, I have no commands to give them. This is now your case; which, as I have said, pains me not less than it does you. My belief is that the permanent estimate of what a general does in the field is fixed by the "cloud of witnesses" who have been with him in the field, and that, relying on these, he who has the right needs not to fear.
Your friend as ever,
A. LINCOLN.

TELEGRAM TO GOVERNOR SEYMOUR.

EXECUTIVE MANSION, WASHINGTON, AUGUST 16, 1863.

GOVERNOR SEYMOUR, New York:
Your despatch of this morning is just received, and I fear I do not perfectly understand it.
My view of the principle is that every soldier obtained voluntarily leaves one less to be obtained by draft. The only difficulty is in applying the principle properly. Looking to time, as heretofore, I am unwilling to give up a drafted man now, even for the certainty, much less for the mere chance, of getting a volunteer hereafter. Again, after the draft in any district, would it not make trouble to take any drafted man out and put a volunteer in—for how shall it be determined which drafted man is to have the privilege of thus going out, to the exclusion of all the others? And even before the draft in any district the quota must be fixed; and the draft must be postponed indefinitely if every time a

volunteer is offered the officers must stop and reconstruct the quota. At least I fear there might be this difficulty; but, at all events, let credits for volunteers be given up to the last moment which will not produce confusion or delay. That the principle of giving credits for volunteers shall be applied by districts seems fair and proper, though I do not know how far by present statistics it is practicable. When for any cause a fair credit is not given at one time, it should be given as soon thereafter as practicable. My purpose is to be just and fair, and yet to not lose time.
A. LINCOLN

To J. H. HACKETT.

EXECUTIVE MANSION, WASHINGTON August 17, 1863.

JAMES H. HACKETT, Esq.
MY DEAR SIR:—Months ago I should have acknowledged the receipt of your book and accompanying kind note; and I now have to beg your pardon for not having done so.
For one of my age I have seen very little of the drama. The first presentation of Falstaff I ever saw was yours here, last winter or spring. Perhaps the best compliment I can pay is to say, as I truly can, I am very anxious to see it again. Some of Shakespeare's plays I have never read, while others I have gone over perhaps as frequently as any un-professional reader. Among the latter are Lear, Richard III., Henry VIII., Hamlet, and especially Macbeth. I think nothing equals Macbeth. It is wonderful.
Unlike you gentlemen of the profession, I think the soliloquy in Hamlet commencing "Oh, my offense is rank," surpasses that commencing "To be or not to be." But pardon this small attempt at criticism. I should like to hear you pronounce the opening speech of Richard III. Will you not soon visit Washington again? If you do, please call and let me make your personal acquaintance.
Yours truly,
A. LINCOLN

TO F. F. LOWE.

WASHINGTON, D. C., August 17, 1863.

HON. P. F. LOWE, San Francisco, Cal.:
There seems to be considerable misunderstanding about the recent movement to take possession of the "New Almaden" mine. It has no reference to any other mine or mines.
In regard to mines and miners generally, no change of policy by the Government has been decided on, or even thought of, so far as I know.
The "New Almaden" mine was peculiar in this: that its occupants claimed to be the legal owners of it on a Mexican grant, and went into court on that claim. The case found its way into the Supreme Court of the United States, and last term, in and by that court, the claim of the occupants was decided to be utterly fraudulent. Thereupon it was considered the duty of the Government by the Secretary of the Interior, the Attorney-General, and myself to take possession of the premises; and the Attorney-General carefully made out the writ and I signed it. It was not obtained surreptitiously, although I suppose General Halleck thought it had been, when he telegraphed, simply because he thought possession was about being taken by a military order, while he knew no such order had passed through his hands as general-in-chief.
The writ was suspended, upon urgent representations from California, simply to keep the peace. It never had any direct or indirect reference to any mine, place, or person, except the "New Almaden" mine and the persons connected with it.
A. LINCOLN.

TELEGRAM TO GENERAL MEADE.

EXECUTIVE MANSION, WASHINGTON, August 21, 1863.

MAJOR-GENERAL MEADE, Warrenton, Va.:
At this late moment I am appealed to in behalf of William Thompson of Company K, Third Maryland Volunteers, in Twelfth Army Corps, said to be at Kelly's Ford, under sentence to be shot to-day as a deserter. He is represented to me to be very young, with symptoms of insanity. Please postpone the execution till further order.
A. LINCOLN.

TELEGRAM TO GENERAL SCHOFIELD.

WASHINGTON, D. C., August 22, 1863.

GENERAL SCHOFIELD, Saint Louis, Mo.:
Please send me if you can a transcript of the record in the case of McQuin and Bell, convicted of murder by a military commission. I telegraphed General Strong for it, but he does not answer.
A. LINCOLN.

TELEGRAM TO MRS. GRIMSLEY.

WAR DEPARTMENT, WASHINGTON, D. C., August 24, 1863.

MRS. ELIZABETH J. GRIMSLEY, Springfield, Ill.:
I mail the papers to you to-day appointing Johnny to the Naval school.
A. LINCOLN

TO CRITICS OF EMANCIPATION

To J. C. CONKLING.

EXECUTIVE MANSION, WASHINGTON, August 26, 1863.
HON. JAMES C. CONKLING.
MY DEAR SIR:—Your letter inviting me to attend a mass meeting of unconditional Union men, to be held at the capital of Illinois, on the 3d day of September, has been received. It would be very agreeable for me thus to meet my old friends at my own home, but I cannot just now be absent from here so long as a visit there would require.
The meeting is to be of all those who maintain unconditional devotion to the Union, and I am sure that my old political friends will thank me for tendering, as I do, the nation's gratitude to those other noble men whom no partisan malice or partisan hope can make false to the nation's life.
There are those who are dissatisfied with me. To such I would say: You desire peace, and you blame me that we do not have it. But how can we obtain it? There are but three conceivable ways:
First—to suppress the rebellion by force of arms. This I am trying to do. Are you for it? If you are, so far we are agreed. If you are not for it, a second way is to give up the Union. I am against this. Are you for it? If you are you should say so plainly. If you are not for force nor yet for dissolution, there only remains some imaginable compromise.
I do not believe that any compromise embracing the maintenance of the Union is now possible. All that I learn leads to a directly opposite belief. The strength of the rebellion is its military, its army. That army dominates all the country and all the people within its range. Any offer of terms made by any man or men within that range, in opposition to that army, is simply nothing for the present; because such man or men have no power whatever to enforce their side of a compromise, if one were made with them.

To illustrate: Suppose refugees from the South and peace men of the North get together in convention, and frame and proclaim a compromise embracing a restoration of the Union. In what way can that compromise be used to keep Lee's army out of Pennsylvania? Meade's army can keep Lee's army out of Pennsylvania, and, I think, can ultimately drive it out of existence. But no paper compromise to which the controllers of Lee's army are not agreed can at all affect that army. In an effort at such compromise we would waste time, which the enemy would improve to our disadvantage; and that would be all.

A compromise, to be effective, must be made either with those who control the rebel army, or with the people, first liberated from the domination of that army by the success of our own army. Now allow me to assure you that no word or intimation from that rebel army, or from any of the men controlling it, in relation to any peace compromise, has ever come to my knowledge or belief. All charges and insinuations to the contrary are deceptive and groundless. And I promise you that if any such proposition shall hereafter come, it shall not be rejected and kept a secret from you. I freely acknowledge myself to be the servant of the people, according to the bond of service, the United States Constitution, and that, as such, I am responsible to them.

But, to be plain: You are dissatisfied with me about the negro. Quite likely there is a difference of opinion between you and myself upon that subject. I certainly wish that all men could be free, while you, I suppose, do not. Yet, I have neither adopted nor proposed any measure which is not consistent with even your view, provided you are for the Union. I suggested compensated emancipation; to which you replied you wished not to be taxed to buy negroes. But I had not asked you to be taxed to buy negroes, except in such way as to save you from greater taxation to save the Union exclusively by other means.

You dislike the Emancipation Proclamation, and perhaps would have it retracted. You say it is unconstitutional. I think differently. I think the Constitution invests its commander-in-chief with the law of war in time of war. The most that can be said, if so much, is, that slaves are property. Is there, has there ever been, any question that by the law of war, property, both of enemies and friends, may be taken when needed? And is it not needed whenever it helps us and hurts the enemy? Armies, the world over, destroy enemies' property when they cannot use it, and even destroy their own to keep it from the enemy. Civilized belligerents do all in their power to help themselves or hurt the enemy, except a few things regarded as barbarous or cruel. Among the exceptions are the massacre of vanquished foes and non-combatants, male and female.

But the proclamation, as law, either is valid or is not valid. If it is not valid it needs no retraction. If it is valid it cannot be retracted, any more than the dead can be brought to life. Some of you profess to think its retraction would operate favorably for the Union, why better after the retraction than before the issue? There was more than a year and a half of trial to suppress the rebellion before the proclamation was issued, the last one hundred days of which passed under an explicit notice that it was coming, unless averted by those in revolt returning to their allegiance. The war has certainly progressed as favorably for us since the issue of the proclamation as before.

I know, as fully as one can know the opinions of others, that some of the commanders of our armies in the field, who have given us our most important victories, believe the emancipation policy and the use of colored troops constitute the heaviest blows yet dealt to the rebellion, and that at least one of those important successes could not have been achieved when it was but for the aid of black soldiers.

Among the commanders who hold these views are some who have never had any affinity with what is called "Abolitionism," or with "Republican Party politics," but who hold them purely as military opinions. I submit their opinions are entitled to some weight against the objections often urged that emancipation and arming the blacks are unwise as military measures, and were not adopted as such in good faith.

You say that you will not fight to free negroes. Some of them seem willing to fight for you; but no matter. Fight you, then, exclusively, to save the Union. I issued the proclamation on purpose to aid you in saving the Union. Whenever you shall have conquered all resistance to the Union, if I shall urge you to continue fighting, it will be an apt time then for you to declare you will not fight to free negroes. I thought that in your struggle for the Union, to whatever extent the negroes should cease helping the enemy, to that extent it weakened the enemy in his resistance to you. Do you think differently? I thought that whatever negroes can be got to do as soldiers, leaves just so much less for white soldiers to do in saving the Union. Does it appear otherwise to you? But negroes, like other people, act upon motives. Why should they do anything for us if we will do nothing for them? If they stake their lives for us they must be prompted by the strongest motive, even the promise of freedom. And the promise, being made, must be kept.

The signs look better. The Father of Waters again goes unvexed to the sea. Thanks to the great Northwest for it; nor yet wholly to them. Three hundred miles up they met New England, Empire, Keystone, and Jersey, hewing their way right and left. The sunny South, too, in more colors than one, also lent a helping hand. On the spot, their part of the history was jotted down in black and white. The job was a great national one, and let none be slighted who bore an honorable part in it And while those who have cleared the great river may well be proud, even that is not all. It is hard to say that anything has been more bravely and well done than at Antietam, Murfreesboro, Gettysburg, and on many fields of less note. Nor must Uncle Sam's web-feet be forgotten. At all the watery margins they have been present; not only on the deep sea, the broad bay, and the rapid river, but also up the narrow, muddy bayou, and wherever the ground was a little damp, they have been and made their tracks. Thanks to all. For the great Republic—for the principle it lives by and keeps alive—for man's vast future—thanks to all.

Peace does not appear so distant as it did. I hope it will come soon, and come to stay, and so come as to be worth the keeping in all future time. It will then have been proved that among freemen there can be no successful appeal from the ballot to the bullet, and that they who take such appeal are sure to lose their case and pay the cost. And there will be some black men who can remember that with silent tongue, and clinched teeth, and steady eye, and well-poised bayonet, they have helped mankind on to this great consummation; while I fear there will be some white ones unable to forget that with malignant heart and deceitful speech they have striven to hinder it.

Still, let us not be over-sanguine of a speedy, final triumph. Let us be quite sober. Let us diligently apply the means, never doubting that a just God, in His own good time, will give us the rightful result.

Yours very truly,
A. LINCOLN.

TO JAMES CONKLING.

(Private.)

WAR DEPARTMENT, WASHINGTON CITY, D. C., August 27.1863.
HON. JAMES CONKLING.
MY DEAR CONKLING:—I cannot leave here now. Herewith is a letter instead. You are one of the best public readers. I have but one suggestion—read it very slowly. And now God bless you, and all good Union men.
Yours as ever,
A. LINCOLN.

TO SECRETARY STANTON.

EXECUTIVE MANSION, WASHINGTON, D. C., August 26, 1863.

HON. SECRETARY OF WAR SIR:-In my correspondence with Governor Seymour in relation to the draft, I have said to him, substantially, that credits shall be given for volunteers up to the latest moment, before drawing in any district, that can be done without producing confusion or delay. In order to do this, let our mustering officers in New York and elsewhere be at, once instructed that whenever they muster into our service any number of volunteers, to at once make return to the War Department, both by telegraph and mail, the date of the muster, the number mustered, and the Congressional or enrolment district or districts, of their residences, giving the numbers separately for each district. Keep these returns diligently posted, and by them give full credit on the quotas, if possible, on the last day before the draft begins in any district.

Again, I have informed Governor Seymour that he shall be notified of the time when the draft is to commence in each district in his State. This is equally proper for all the States. In order to carry it out, I propose that so soon as the day for commencing the draft in any district is definitely determined, the governor of the State, including the district, be notified thereof, both by telegraph and mail, in form about as follows:

——————————————————
—————————————— 1863.
Governor of ————————————————
——————————————————
You are notified that the draft will commence in the
—————————————— ———— district, at ———— on the
———— day ——————
1863, at ———— A.M. of said day.
Please acknowledge receipt of this by telegraph and mail.
——————————————
——————————————

This notice may be given by the Provost-Marshal-General here, the sub-provost-marshal-generals in the States, or perhaps by the district provost-marshals.

Whenever we shall have so far proceeded in New York as to make the re-enrolment specially promised there practicable, I wish that also to go forward, and I wish Governor Seymour notified of it; so that if he choose, he can place agents of his with ours to see the work fairly done.

Yours truly,
A. LINCOLN.

TO GOVERNOR SEYMOUR.

EXECUTIVE MANSION, WASHINGTON, D. C., August 27. 1863.

HIS EXCELLENCY HORATIO SEYMOUR,
Governor of New York:

Yours of the 21st, with exhibits, was received on the 24th.

In the midst of pressing duties I have been unable to answer it sooner. In the meantime the Provost Marshal-General has had access to yours, and has addressed a communication in relation to it to the Secretary of War, a copy of which communication I herewith enclose to you.

Independently of this, I addressed a letter on the same subject to the Secretary of War, a copy of which I also enclose to you. The Secretary has sent my letter to the Provost-Marshal General, with direction that he adopt and follow the course therein pointed out. It will, of course, overrule any conflicting view of the Provost-Marshal-General, if there be such.

Yours very truly,
A. LINCOLN.

P. S.-I do not mean to say that if the Provost-Marshal-General can find it practicable to give credits by subdistricts, I overrule him in that. On the contrary, I shall be glad of it; but I will not take the risk of over-burdening him by ordering him to do it. A. L.

Abraham Lincoln

TELEGRAM TO GENERAL J. M. SCHOFIELD.

WASHINGTON, D. C., August 27, 1863 8.30 P. M.

GENERAL SCHOFIELD, St. LOUIS:

I have just received the despatch which follows, from two very influential citizens of Kansas, whose names I omit. The severe blow they have received naturally enough makes them intemperate even without there being any just cause for blame. Please do your utmost to give them future security and to punish their invaders.

A. LINCOLN.

TELEGRAM TO GENERAL G. G. MEADE.

WAR DEPARTMENT, WASHINGTON, D. C., August 27, 1863 9 A.M.

MAJOR-GENERAL MEADE, Warrenton, Va.:

Walter, Rionese, Folancy, Lai, and Kuhn appealed to me for mercy, without giving any ground for it whatever. I understand these are very flagrant cases, and that you deem their punishment as being indispensable to the service. If I am not mistaken in this, please let them know at once that their appeal is denied.

A. LINCOLN.

TELEGRAM TO F. C. SHERMAN AND J. S. HAYES.

WASHINGTON, August 27, 1863.

F. C. SHERMAN, Mayor, J. S. HAYES, Comptroller, Chicago, Ill.:
Yours of the 24th, in relation to the draft, is received. It seems to me the Government here will be overwhelmed if it undertakes to conduct these matters with the authorities of cities and counties. They must be conducted with the governors of States, who will, of course, represent their cities and counties. Meanwhile you need not be uneasy until you again hear from here.
A. LINCOLN.

TELEGRAM TO GENERAL FOSTER.

WAR DEPARTMENT, WASHINGTON, August 28, 1863.

MAJOR-GENERAL FOSTER, Fort Monroe, Va.:
Please notify, if you can, Senator Bowden, Mr. Segar, and Mr. Chandler, all or any of them, that I now have the record in Dr. Wright's case, and am ready to hear them. When you shall have got the notice to them, please let me know.
A. LINCOLN.

TELEGRAM TO GENERAL CRAWFORD.

EXECUTIVE MANSION, WASHINGTON, D. C., August 28, 1863.

GENERAL CRAWFORD, Rappahannock Station, Va.:
I regret that I cannot be present to witness the presentation of a sword by the gallant Pennsylvania Reserve Corps to one so worthy to receive it as General Meade.
A. LINCOLN.

TELEGRAM TO L. SWETT.

WASHINGTON, D. C., August 29, 1863.

HON. L. SWETT, San Francisco, Cal.: If the Government's rights are reserved, the Government will be satisfied, and at all events it will consider.
A. LINCOLN.

TELEGRAM TO MRS. LINCOLN.

EXECUTIVE MANSION, WASHINGTON, D. C. August 29, 1863.

MRS. A. LINCOLN, Manchester, N. H.:

All quite well. Fort Sumter is certainly battered down and utterly useless to the enemy, and it is believed here, but not entirely certain, that both Sumter and Fort Wagner are occupied by our forces. It is also certain that General Gilmore has thrown some shot into the city of Charleston.
A. LINCOLN.

TELEGRAM TO J. C. CONKLING.

EXECUTIVE MANSION, WASHINGTON,

August 31, 1863.
HON. JAMES C. CONKLING, Springfield, Ill.:
In my letter of the 26th insert between the sentence ending "since the issue of the Emancipation Proclamation as before" and the next, commencing "You say you will not fight, etc.," what follows below my signature hereto.
A. LINCOLN.
"I know as fully as one can know the opinions of others that some of the commanders of our armies in the field, who have given us our most important successes, believe the emancipation policy and the use of colored troops constitute the heaviest blow yet dealt to the rebellion, and that at least one of those important successes could not have been achieved when it was, but for the aid of black soldiers. Among the commanders holding these views are some who have never had any affinity with what is called abolitionism, or with Republican party politics, but who hold them purely as military opinions. I submit these opinions as being entitled to some weight against the objections, often urged, that emancipation and arming the blacks are unwise as military measures and were not adopted as such in good faith."

TO GENERAL W. S. ROSECRANS.

EXECUTIVE MANSION, WASHINGTON, August 31, 1863.

MY DEAR GENERAL ROSECRANS:
Yours of the 22d was received yesterday. When I wrote you before, I did not intend, nor do I now, to engage in an argument with you on military questions. You had informed me you were impressed through General Halleck that I was dissatisfied with you, and I could not bluntly deny that I was without unjustly implicating him. I therefore concluded to tell you the plain truth, being satisfied the matter would thus appear much smaller than it would if seen by mere glimpses. I repeat that my appreciation of you has not abated. I can never forget whilst I remember anything, that about the end of last year and the beginning of this, you gave us a hard-earned victory, which, had there been a defeat instead, the nation could hardly have lived over. Neither can I forget the check you so opportunely gave to a dangerous sentiment which was spreading in the North.
Yours, as ever,
A. LINCOLN

TO GENERAL H. W. HALLECK.

August 31, 1863

It is not improbable that retaliation for the recent great outrage at Lawrence, in Kansas, may extend to indiscriminate slaughter on the Missouri border, unless averted by very judicious action. I shall be obliged if the general-in-chief can make any suggestions to General Schofield upon the subject.
A. LINCOLN.

POLITICAL MOTIVATED MISQUOTATION IN NEWSPAPER

TELEGRAM TO J. C. CONKLING.

EXECUTIVE MANSION, WASHINGTON, September 3, 1863.
HON. JAMES C. CONKLING, Springfield, Ill.:
I am mortified this morning to find the letter to you botched up in the Eastern papers, telegraphed from Chicago. How did this happen?
A. LINCOLN.

ORDER CONCERNING COMMERCIAL REGULATIONS.

EXECUTIVE MANSION, WASHINGTON, September 4, 1863.

Ordered, That the executive order dated November 21, 1862, prohibiting the exportation from the United States of arms, ammunition, or munitions of war, under which the commandants of departments were, by order of the Secretary of War dated May 13, 1863, directed to prohibit the purchase and sale, for exportation from the United States, of all horses and mules within their respective commands, and to take and appropriate for the use of the United States any horses, mules, and live stock designed for exportation, be so far modified that any arms heretofore imported into the United States may be re-exported to the place of original shipment, and that any live stock raised in any State or Territory bounded by the Pacific Ocean may be exported from, any port of such State or Territory.
A. LINCOLN.

TELEGRAM TO J. SEGAR.

WAR DEPARTMENT, WASHINGTON, D. C.. September 5, 1863.

HON. JOSEPH SEGAR, Fort Monroe, Va.:
I have just seen your despatch to the Secretary of War, who is absent. I also send a despatch from Major Hayner of the 3d showing that he had notice of my order, and stating that the people were jubilant over it, as a victory over the Government extorted by fear, and that he had already collected about $4000 of the money. If he has proceeded since, I shall hold him accountable for his contumacy. On the contrary, no dollar shall be refunded by my order until it shall appear that my act in the case has been accepted in the right spirit.
A. LINCOLN

TELEGRAM TO MRS. LINCOLN.

WAR DEPARTMENT, WASHINGTON. D. C. September 6, 1863.

MRS. A. LINCOLN, Manchester, Vt.:
All well and no news except that General Burnside has Knoxville, Ten.
A. LINCOLN.

TELEGRAM TO SECRETARY STANTON.

WAR DEPARTMENT, WASHINGTON, September 6, 1863. 6 P.M.

HON. SECRETARY OF WAR, Bedford, Pa.:
Burnside has Kingston and Knoxville, and drove the enemy across the river at Loudon, the enemy destroying the bridge there; captured some stores and one or two trains; very little fighting; few wounded and none killed. No other news of consequence.
A. LINCOLN.

TELEGRAM TO F. C. SHERMAN AND J. S. HAYES.

WASHINGTON, September 7, 1863.

Yours of August 29 just received. I suppose it was intended by Congress that this government should execute the act in question without dependence upon any other government, State, city, or county. It is, however, within the range of practical convenience to confer with the governments of States, while it is quite beyond that range to have correspondence on the subject with counties and cities. They are too numerous. As instances, I have corresponded with Governor Seymour, but Not with Mayor Opdyke; with Governor Curtin, but not with Mayor Henry.
A. LINCOLN.

TELEGRAM TO GOVERNOR JOHNSON.

EXECUTIVE MANSION, WASHINGTON, September 8, 1863. 9.30

HON. ANDREW JOHNSON, Nashville, Tenn.:
Despatch of yesterday just received. I shall try to find the paper you mention and carefully consider it. In the meantime let me urge that you do your utmost to get every man you can, black and white, under arms at the very earliest moment, to guard roads, bridges, and trains, allowing all the better trained soldiers to go forward to Rosecrans. Of course I mean for you to act in co-operation with and not independently of, the military authorities.
A. LINCOLN.

TELEGRAM TO GENERAL MEADE.

EXECUTIVE MANSION, WASHINGTON, September 9, 1863.

MAJOR-GENERAL MEADE, Warrenton, Va.:
It would be a generous thing to give General Wheaton a leave of absence for ten or fifteen days, and if you can do so without injury to the service, please do it.
A. LINCOLN.

TELEGRAM TO GENERAL WHEATON.

WASHINGTON, D.C., September 10, 1863.

GENERAL WHEATON, Army of Potomac:

Yesterday at the instance of Mr. Blair, senator, I telegraphed General Meade asking him to grant you a leave of absence, to which he replied that you had not applied for such leave, and that you can have it when you do apply. I suppose it is proper for you to know this.
A. LINCOLN.

TO GOVERNOR JOHNSON.

EXECUTIVE MANSION, WASHINGTON, SEPTEMBER, 11, 1863

HON. ANDREW JOHNSON.
MY DEAR SIR:—All Tennessee is now clear of armed insurrectionists. You need not to be reminded that it is the nick of time for reinaugurating a loyal State government. Not a moment should be lost. You and the co-operating friends there can better judge of the ways and means than can be judged by any here. I only offer a few suggestions. The reinauguration must not be such as to give control of the State and its representation in Congress to the enemies of the Union, driving its friends there into political exile. The whole struggle for Tennessee will have been profitless to both State and nation if it so ends that Governor Johnson is put down and Governor Harris put up. It must not be so. You must have it otherwise. Let the reconstruction be the work of such men only as can be trusted for the Union. Exclude all others, and trust that your government so organized will be recognized here as being the one of republican form to be guaranteed to the State, and to be protected against invasion and domestic violence. It is something on the question of time to remember that it cannot be known who is next to occupy the position I now hold, nor what he will do. I see that you have declared in favor of emancipation in Tennessee, for which may God bless you. Get emancipation into your new State government constitution and there will be no such word as fail for your cause. The raising of colored troops, I think, will greatly help every way.
Yours very truly,
A. LINCOLN.

TELEGRAM TO GENERAL A. E. BURNSIDE.

WASHINGTON, September 11, 1863.

MAJOR-GENERAL BURNSIDE, Cumberland Gap:
Yours received. A thousand thanks for the late successes you have given us. We cannot allow you to resign until things shall be a little more settled in East Tennessee. If then, purely on your own account, you wish to resign, we will not further refuse you.
A. LINCOLN

TELEGRAM TO GENERAL MEADE.

EXECUTIVE MANSION, WASHINGTON, September 11, 1863.

MAJOR-GENERAL MEADE, Warrenton, Va.:
It is represented to me that Thomas Edds, in your army, is under sentence of death for desertion, to be executed next Monday. It is also said his supposed desertion is comprised in an absence commencing with his falling behind last winter, being captured and paroled by the enemy, and then going home. If this be near the truth, please suspend the execution till further order and send in the record of the trial.
A. LINCOLN

TELEGRAM TO GENERAL MEADE.

WASHINGTON, D.C., September 12, 1863.

MAJOR-GENERAL MEAD, Warrenton, Va.:
The name is "Thomas Edds" not "Eddies" as in your despatch. The papers left with me do not designate the regiment to which he belongs. The man who gave me the papers, I do not know how to find again. He only told me that Edds is in the Army of the Potomac, and that he fell out of the ranks during Burnside's mud march last winter. If I get further information I will telegraph again.
A. LINCOLN

TELEGRAM TO H. H. SCOTT.

EXECUTIVE MANSION, WASHINGTON, September 13, 1863.

Dr. WILLIAM H. H. SCOTT, Danville, Ill.:
Your niece, Mrs. Kate Sharp, can now have no difficulty in going to Knoxville, Tenn., as that place is within our military lines.
A. LINCOLN.

TELEGRAM TO J. G. BLAINE.

WAR DEPARTMENT, WASHINGTON, D. C., September 25, 1863.

J. G. BLAINE, Augusta, Me.: Thanks both for the good news you send and for the sending of it.
A. LINCOLN.

PROCLAMATION SUSPENDING WRIT OF HABEAS CORPUS, SEPTEMBER 15, 1863.

BY THE PRESIDENT OF THE UNITED STATES OF AMERICA:

A Proclamation.
Whereas the Constitution of the United States has ordained that the privilege of the writ of habeas corpus shall not be suspended unless when, in cases of rebellion or invasion, the public safety may require it; and:
Whereas a rebellion was existing on the third day of March, 1863, which rebellion is still existing; and:
Whereas by a statute which was approved on that day it was enacted by the Senate and House of Representatives of the United States in Congress assembled that during the present insurrection the President of the United States, whenever in his judgment the public safety may require, is authorized to suspend the privilege of the writ of habeas corpus in any case throughout the United States or any part thereof; and:
Whereas, in the judgment of the President, the public safety does require that the privilege of the said writ shall new be suspended throughout the United States in the cases where, by the authority of the President of the United States, military, naval, and civil officers of the United States, or any of them, hold persons under their command or in their custody, either as prisoners of war, spies, or aiders or abettors of the enemy, or officers, soldiers, or seamen enrolled or drafted or mustered or enlisted in or belonging to the land or naval forces of the United States, or as deserters therefrom, or otherwise amenable to military law or the rules and articles of war or the rules or regulations prescribed for the military or naval services by authority of the President of the United States, or for resisting a draft, or for any other offense against the military or naval service.

Now, therefore, I, Abraham Lincoln, President of the United States, do hereby proclaim and make known to all whom it may concern that the privilege of the writ of habeas corpus is suspended throughout the United States in the several cases before mentioned, and that this suspension will continue throughout the duration of the said rebellion or until this proclamation shall, by a subsequent one to be issued by the President of the United States, be modified or revoked. And I do hereby require all magistrates, attorneys, and other civil officers within the United States and all officers and others in the military and naval services of the United States to take distinct notice of this suspension and to give it full effect, and all citizens of the United States to conduct and govern themselves accordingly and in conformity with the Constitution of the United States and the laws of Congress in such case made and provided.

In testimony whereof I have hereunto set my hand and caused the seal of the United States to be affixed, this fifteenth day of September, A.D. 1863, and of the independence of the United States of America the eighty-eighth.

A. LINCOLN.

By the President: WILLIAM H. SEWARD,
 Secretary of State.

TO GENERAL H. W. HALLECK.

EXECUTIVE MANSION, WASHINGTON, September 13, 1863.

MAJOR-GENERAL HALLECK:
If I did not misunderstand General Meade's last despatch, he posts you on facts as well as he can, and desires your views and those of the Government as to what he shall do. My opinion is that he should move upon Lee at once in manner of general attack, leaving to developments whether he will make it a real attack. I think this would develop Lee's real condition and purposes better than the cavalry alone can do. Of course my opinion is not to control you and General Meade.

Yours truly,
A. LINCOLN.

TELEGRAM TO MRS. SPEED.

WASHINGTON, D.C., September 16, 1862.

MRS. J. F. SPEED, Louisville, Ky.:
Mr. Holman will not be jostled from his place with my knowledge and consent.
A. LINCOLN.

TELEGRAM TO GENERAL MEADE.

EXECUTIVE MANSION, WASHINGTON, September 16, 1863.

MAJOR-GENERAL MEADE, Warrenton, Va.:
Is Albert Jones of Company K, Third Maryland Volunteers, to be shot on Friday next? If so please state to me the general features of the case.
A. LINCOLN.

TELEGRAM TO GENERAL SCHENCK.

EXECUTIVE MANSION, WASHINGTON, September 17, 1863.

MAJOR-GENERAL SCHENCK, Baltimore, Md.:
Major Haynor left here several days ago under a promise to put down in writing, in detail, the facts in relation to the misconduct of the people on the eastern shore of Virginia. He has not returned. Please send him over.
A. LINCOLN.

TELEGRAM TO GENERAL MEADE.

EXECUTIVE MANSION, WASHINGTON, September 17, 1863.

MAJOR-GENERAL MEADE, Headquarters Army of Potomac:
Yours in relation to Albert Jones is received. I am appealed to in behalf of Richard M. Abrams of Company A, Sixth New Jersey Volunteers, by Governor Parker, Attorney-General Frelinghuysen, Governor Newell, Hon. Mr. Middleton, M. C., of the district, and the marshal who arrested him. I am also appealed to in behalf of Joseph S. Smith, of Company A, Eleventh New Jersey Volunteers, by Governor Parker, Attorney-General Frelinghuysen, and Hon. Marcus C. Ward. Please state the circumstances of their cases to me.
A. LINCOLN.

REQUEST TO SUGGEST NAME FOR A BABY

TELEGRAM TO C. M. SMITH.

WASHINGTON, D. C., September 18, 1863.
C.M. SMITH, Esq., Springfield, Ill.:
Why not name him for the general you fancy most? This is my suggestion.
A. LINCOLN

TELEGRAM TO MRS. ARMSTRONG.

WASHINGTON, September 18, 1863.

MRS. HANNAH ARMSTRONG, Petersburg, Ill.:
I have just ordered the discharge of your boy William, as you say, now at Louisville, Ky.
A. LINCOLN.

TO GOVERNOR JOHNSON.

(Private.)

EXECUTIVE MANSION, WASHINGTON, D. C., September 19.1863.
HON. ANDREW JOHNSON.
MY DEAR SIR:—Herewith I send you a paper, substantially the same as the one drawn up by yourself and mentioned in your despatch, but slightly changed in two particulars: First, yours was so drawn as that I authorized you to carry into effect the fourth section, etc., whereas I so modify it as to authorize you to so act as to require the United States to carry into effect that section.

Secondly, you had a clause committing me in some sort to the State constitution of Tennessee, which I feared might embarrass you in making a new constitution, if you desire; so I dropped that clause.

Yours very truly,
A. LINCOLN.
[Inclosure.]
EXECUTIVE MANSION, WASHINGTON, D. C.,
September 19, 1863.
HON. ANDREW JOHNSON, Military Governor of Tennessee:
In addition to the matters contained in the orders and instructions given you by the Secretary of War, you are hereby authorized to exercise such powers as may be necessary and proper to enable the loyal people of Tennessee to present such a republican form of State government as will entitle the State to the guaranty of the United States therefor, and to be protected under such State government by the United States against invasion and domestic violence, all according to the fourth Section of the fourth article of the Constitution of the United States.
A. LINCOLN

MILITARY STRATEGY

TO GENERAL H. W. HALLECK

EXECUTIVE MANSION, WASHINGTON D.C. September 19, 1863.
MAJOR-GENERAL HALLECK:
By General Meade's despatch to you of yesterday it appears that he desires your views and those of the government as to whether he shall advance upon the enemy. I am not prepared to order, or even advise, an advance in this case, wherein I know so little of particulars, and wherein he, in the field, thinks the risk is so great and the promise of advantage so small.

And yet the case presents matter for very serious consideration in another aspect. These two armies confront each other across a small river, substantially midway between the two capitals, each defending its own capital, and menacing the other. General Meade estimates the enemy's infantry in front of him at not less than 40,000. Suppose we add fifty per cent. to this for cavalry, artillery, and extra-duty men stretching as far as Richmond, making the whole force of the enemy 60,000.

General Meade, as shown by the returns, has with him, and between him and Washington, of the same classes, of well men, over 90,000. Neither can bring the whole of his men into a battle; but each can bring as large a percentage in as the other. For a battle, then, General Meade has three men to General Lee's two. Yet, it having been determined that choosing ground and standing on the defensive gives so great advantage that the three cannot safely attack the two, the three are left simply standing on the defensive also.

If the enemy's 60,000 are sufficient to keep our 90,000 away from Richmond, why, by the same rule, may not 40,000 of ours keep their 60,000 away from Washington, leaving us 50,000 to put to some other use? Having practically come to the mere defensive, it seems to be no economy at all to employ twice as many men for that object as are needed. With no object, certainly, to mislead myself, I can perceive no fault in this statement, unless we admit we are not the equal of the enemy, man for man. I hope you will consider it.

To avoid misunderstanding, let me say that to attempt to fight the enemy slowly back into his entrenchments at Richmond, and then to capture him, is an idea I have been trying to repudiate for quite a year.

My judgment is so clear against it that I would scarcely allow the attempt to be made if the general in command should desire to make it. My last attempt upon Richmond was to get McClellan, when he was nearer there than the enemy was, to run in ahead of him. Since then I have constantly desired the Army of the Potomac to make Lee's army, and not Richmond, its objective point. If our army cannot fall upon the enemy and hurt him where he is, it is plain to me it can gain nothing by attempting to follow him over a succession of intrenched lines into a fortified city.

Yours truly,
A. LINCOLN.

TELEGRAM TO MRS. LINCOLN.

WAR DEPARTMENT, WASHINGTON, D. C., September 20, 1863.

MRS. A. LINCOLN, New York:
I neither see nor hear anything of sickness here now, though there may be much without my knowing it. I wish you to stay or come just as is most agreeable to yourself.
A. LINCOLN.

TELEGRAM TO MRS. LINCOLN.

WAR DEPARTMENT, WASHINGTON, D. C, September 21, 1863.

MRS. A. LINCOLN. Fifth Avenue Hotel. New York:
The air is so clear and cool and apparently healthy that I would be glad for you to come. Nothing very particular, but I would be glad to see you and Tad.
A. LINCOLN.

TO GENERAL H. W. HALLECK.

EXECUTIVE MANSION WASHINGTON, D. C., September 21, 1863.

MAJOR-GENERAL HALLECK:
I think it very important for General Rosecrans to hold his position at or about Chattanooga, because if held from that place to Cleveland, both inclusive, it keeps all Tennessee clear of the enemy, and also breaks one of his most important railroad lines. To prevent these consequences is so vital to his cause that he cannot give up the effort to dislodge us from the position, thus bringing him to us and saving us the labor, expense, and hazard of going farther to find him, and also giving us the advantage of choosing our own ground and preparing it to fight him upon. The details must, of course, be left to General Rosecrans, while we must furnish him the means to the utmost of our ability. If you concur, I think he would better be informed that we are not pushing him beyond this position; and that, in fact, our judgment is rather against his going beyond it. If he can only maintain this position, without more, this rebellion can only eke out a short and feeble existence, as an animal sometimes may with a thorn in its vitals.
Yours truly,
A. LINCOLN.

TELEGRAM TO GENERAL A. E. BURNSIDE

EXECUTIVE MANSION, WASHINGTON, D.C., September 21, 1863.

GENERAL BURNSIDE, Greenville, Tenn.:
If you are to do any good to Rosecrans it will not do to waste time with Jonesboro. It is already too late to do the most good that might have been done, but I hope it will still do some good. Please do not lose a moment.
A. LINCOLN.

TELEGRAM TO GENERAL A. E. BURNSIDE

WAR DEPARTMENT, September 21, 1863. 11 A.M.

GENERAL BURNSIDE, Knoxville, Tenn.:
Go to Rosecrans with your force without a moment's delay.
A. LINCOLN,

TELEGRAM TO GENERAL W. S. ROSECRANS

WASHINGTON, September 21, 1863. 12.55 PM.

MAJOR-GENERAL ROSECRANS, Chattanooga:
Be of good cheer. We have unabated confidence in you, and in your soldiers and officers. In the main you must be the judge as to what is to be done. If I were to suggest, I would say, save your army by taking strong positions until Burnside joins you, when, I hope, you can turn the tide. I think you had better send a courier to Burnside to hurry him up. We cannot reach him by telegraph. We suppose some force is going to you from Corinth, but for want of communication we do not know how they are getting along. We shall do our utmost to assist you. Send us your present positions.
A. LINCOLN.

TELEGRAM TO GENERAL W. S. ROSECRANS.

[Cipher.]

WAR DEPARTMENT, September 22, 1863.8.30 A.M.
MAJOR-GENERAL ROSECRANS, Chattanooga, Tenn.:
We have not a word here as to the whereabouts or condition of your army up to a later hour than sunset, Sunday, the 20th. Your despatches to me of 9 A.M., and to General Halleck of 2 P. M., yesterday, tell us nothing later on those points. Please relieve my anxiety as to the position and condition of your army up to the latest moment.
A. LINCOLN.

TELEGRAM TO O. M. HATCH AND J. K. DUBOIS.

EXECUTIVE MANSION, WASHINGTON. September 22, 1863.

HON. O. M. HATCH, HON. J. K. DUBOIS, Springfield, Ill.:
Your letter is just received. The particular form of my despatch was jocular, which I supposed you gentlemen knew me well enough to understand. General Allen is considered here as a very faithful and capable officer, and one who would be at least thought of for quartermaster-general if that office were vacant.
A. LINCOLN.

TELEGRAM TO MRS. LINCOLN.

EXECUTIVE MANSION, WASHINGTON, September 22, 1863.

MRS. A. LINCOLN, Fifth Avenue House, New York:—Did you receive my despatch of yesterday? Mrs. Cuthbert did not correctly understand me. I directed her to tell you to use your own pleasure whether to stay or come, and I did not say it is sickly and that you should on no account come. So far as I see or know, it was never healthier, and I really wish to see you. Answer this on receipt.
A. LINCOLN.

TELEGRAM TO GENERAL W. S. ROSECRANS.

WASHINGTON, September 23, 1863. 9.13 A.M.

MAJOR-GENERAL ROSECRANS, Chattanooga, Tenn:
Below is Bragg's despatch as found in the Richmond papers. You see he does not claim so many prisoners or captured guns as you were inclined to concede. He also confesses to heavy loss. An exchanged general of ours leaving Richmond yesterday says two of Longstreet's divisions and his entire artillery and two of Pickett's brigades and Wise's legion have gone to Tennessee. He mentions no other.
"CHICAMAUGA RIVER, SEPTEMBER 20.
"GENERAL COOPER, Adjutant-General:
"After two days' hard fighting we have driven the enemy, after a desperate resistance, from several positions, and now hold the field; but he still confronts us. The loses are heavy on both sides, especially in our officers....
"BRAXTON BRAGG" A. LINCOLN

PROCLAMATION OPENING THE PORT OF ALEXANDRIA, VIRGINIA,

SEPTEMBER 24, 1863.

BY THE PRESIDENT OF THE UNITED STATES OF AMERICA:
A Proclamation.
Whereas, in my proclamation of the twenty-seventh of April, 1861, the ports of the States of Virginia and North Carolina were, for reasons therein set forth, placed under blockade; and whereas the port of Alexandria, Virginia, has since been blockaded, but as the blockade of said port may now be safely relaxed with advantage to the interests of commerce:
Now, therefore, be it known that I, Abraham Lincoln, President of the United Sates, pursuant to the authority in me vested by the fifth section of the act of Congress, approved on the 13th of July, 1861, entitled "An act further to provide for the collection of duties on imports, and for other purposes," do hereby declare that the blockade of the said port of Alexandria shall so far cease and determine, from and after this date, that commercial intercourse with said port, except as to persons, things, and information contraband of war, may from this date be carried on, subject to the laws of the United States, and to the limitations and in pursuance of the regulations which are prescribed by the Secretary of the Treasury in his order which is appended to my proclamation of the 12th of May, 1862.
In witness whereof, I have hereunto set my hand, and caused the seal of the United States to be affixed.
Done at the city of Washington, this twenty-fourth day of September in the year of our Lord one thousand eight hundred and sixty-three, and of the independence of the United States the eighty-eighth.
A. LINCOLN.
By the President WILLIAM H. SEWARD,
    Secretary of State.

TELEGRAM TO GENERAL W. S. ROSECRANS.

WAR DEPARTMENT, September 24, 1863. 10 A.M.

MAJOR-GENERAL ROSECRANS, Chattanooga, Term.:
Last night we received the rebel accounts, through Richmond papers, of your late battle. They give Major-General Hood as mortally wounded, and Brigadiers Preston Smith, Wofford, Walthall, Helm of Kentucky, and DesMer killed, and Major-Generals Preston, Cleburne, and Gregg, and Brigadier-Generals Benning, Adams, Burm, Brown, and John

[B. H.] Helm wounded. By confusion the two Helms may be the same man, and Bunn and Brown may be the same man. With Burnside, Sherman, and from elsewhere we shall get to you from forty to sixty thousand additional men.
A. LINCOLN

MRS. LINCOLN'S REBEL BROTHER-IN-LAW KILLED

TELEGRAM TO MRS. LINCOLN.

WAR DEPARTMENT, SEPTEMBER 24, 1863
MRS. A. LINCOLN, Fifth Avenue Hotel, New York:
We now have a tolerably accurate summing up of the late battle between Rosecrans and Braag. The result is that we are worsted, if at all, only in the fact that we, after the main fighting was over, yielded the ground, thus leaving considerable of our artillery and wounded to fall into the enemy's hands., for which we got nothing in turn. We lost in general officers one killed and three or four wounded, all brigadiers, while, according to the rebel accounts which we have, they lost six killed and eight wounded: of the killed one major-general and five brigadiers including your brother-in-law, Helm; and of the wounded three major-generals and five brigadiers. This list may be reduced two in number by corrections of confusion in names. At 11.40 A.M. yesterday General Rosecrans telegraphed from Chattanooga: "We hold this point, and I cannot be dislodged except by very superior numbers and after a great battle." A despatch leaving there after night yesterday says, "No fight to-day."
A. LINCOLN.

TELEGRAM TO GENERAL McCALLUM.

WAR DEPARTMENT, WASHINGTON, D. C., September 25, 1863.

GENERAL McCALLUM, Alexandria, Va.:
I have sent to General Meade, by telegraph, to suspend the execution of Daniel Sullivan of Company F, Thirteenth Massachusetts, which was to be to-day, but understanding there is an interruption on the line, may I beg you to send this to him by the quickest mode in your power?
A. LINCOLN.

TELEGRAM TO GENERAL MEADE.

WAR DEPARTMENT, WASHINGTON, D. C., September 25, 1863.

MAJOR-GENERAL MEADE, Army of Potomac:
Owing to the press in behalf of Daniel Sullivan, Company E, Thirteenth Massachusetts, and the doubt; though small, which you express of his guilty intention, I have concluded to say let his execution be suspended till further order, and copy of record sent me.
A. LINCOLN.

TO GENERAL W. S. ROSECRANS.

EXECUTIVE MANSION, WASHINGTON, September 25, 1863.

MY DEAR GENERAL ROSECRANS:

We are sending you two small corps, one under General Howard and one under General Slocum, and the whole under General Hooker.

Unfortunately the relations between Generals Hooker and Slocum are not such as to promise good, if their present relative positions remain. Therefore, let me beg—almost enjoin upon you—that on their reaching you, you will make a transposition by which General Slocum with his Corps, may pass from under the command of General Hooker, and General Hooker, in turn receive some other equal force. It is important for this to be done, though we could not well arrange it here. Please do it.

Yours very truly,
A. LINCOLN.

TELEGRAM TO GENERAL W. S. ROSECRANS.

WAR DEPARTMENT, September 28, 1863. 8 A.M.

MAJOR-GENERAL ROSECRANS, Chattanooga., Tenn.:
You can perhaps communicate with General Burnside more rapidly by sending telegrams directly to him at Knoxville. Think of it. I send a like despatch to him.
A. LINCOLN.

TELEGRAM TO GENERAL SCHOFIELD.

EXECUTIVE MANSION, WASHINGTON, D. C, September 30, 1863.

GENERAL SCHOFIELD, Saint Louis, Mo.:
Following despatch just received:
"Union Men Driven out of Missouri."
"Leavenworth, September 29, 1863.
"Governor Gamble having authorized Colonel Moss, of Liberty, Missouri, to arm the men in Platte and Clinton Counties, he has armed mostly the returned rebel soldiers and men under bonds. Moss's men are now driving the Union men out of Missouri. Over one hundred families crossed the river to-day. Many of the wives of our Union soldiers have been compelled to leave. Four or five Union men have been murdered by Colonel Moss's men."
Please look to this and, if true, in main or part, put a stop to it.
A. LINCOLN

TELEGRAM TO F. S. CORKRAN.

EXECUTIVE MANSION, WASHINGTON, September 30, 1863.

HON. FRANCIS S. CORKRAN, Baltimore, Md.: MRS. L. is now at home and would be pleased to see you any time. If the grape time has not passed away, she would be pleased to join in the enterprise you mention.
Yours truly,
A. LINCOLN.

TELEGRAM TO GENERAL TYLER

WAR DEPARTMENT, WASHINGTON, D.C., October 1, 1863.

GENERAL TYLER, Baltimore:

Take care of colored troops in your charge, but do nothing further about that branch of affairs until further orders. Particularly do nothing about General Vickers of Kent County.

A. LINCOLN.

Send a copy to Colonel Birney. A. L.

TO GENERAL SCHOFIELD.

EXECUTIVE MANSION, WASHINGTON,

OCTOBER 1, 1863 GENERAL JOHN M. SCHOFIELD:

There is no organized military force in avowed opposition to the General Government now in Missouri, and if any shall reappear, your duty in regard to it will be too plain to require any special instruction. Still, the condition of things, both there and elsewhere, is such as to render it indispensable to maintain, for a time, the United States military establishment in that State, as well as to rely upon it for a fair contribution of support to that establishment generally. Your immediate duty in regard to Missouri now is to advance the efficiency of that establishment, and to so use it, as far as practicable, to compel the excited people there to let one another alone.

Under your recent order, which I have approved, you will only arrest individuals, and suppress assemblies or newspapers, when they may be working palpable injury to the military in your charge; and in no other case will you interfere with the expression of opinion in any form, or allow it to be interfered with violently by others. In this you have a discretion to exercise with great caution, calmness, and forbearance.

With the matter of removing the inhabitants of certain counties en masse, and of removing certain individuals from time to time, who are supposed to be mischievous, I am not now interfering, but am leaving to your own discretion.

Nor am I interfering with what may still seem to you to be necessary restrictions upon trade and intercourse. I think proper, however, to enjoin upon you the following: Allow no part of the military under your command to be engaged in either returning fugitive slaves or in forcing or enticing slaves from their homes; and, so far as practicable, enforce the same forbearance upon the people.

Report to me your opinion upon the availability for good of the enrolled militia of the State. Allow no one to enlist colored troops, except upon orders from you, or from here through you.

Allow no one to assume the functions of confiscating property, under the law of Congress, or otherwise, except upon orders from here.

At elections see that those, and only those, are allowed to vote who are entitled to do so by the laws of Missouri, including as of those laws the restrictions laid by the Missouri convention upon those who may have participated in the rebellion.

So far as practicable, you will, by means of your military force, expel guerrillas, marauders, and murderers, and all who are known to harbor, aid, or abet them. But in like manner you will repress assumptions of unauthorized individuals to perform the same service, because under pretense of doing this they become marauders and murderers themselves.

To now restore peace, let the military obey orders, and those not of the military leave each other alone, thus not breaking the peace themselves.

In giving the above directions, it is not intended to restrain you in other expedient and necessary matters not falling within their range.

Your obedient servant,

A. LINCOLN.

TELEGRAM TO GENERAL S. M. SCHOFIELD.

WASHINGTON, D.C. OCTOBER 2, 1863

MAJOR-GENERAL SCHOFIELD:

I have just seen your despatch to Halleck about Major-General Blunt. If possible, you better allow me to get through with a certain matter here, before adding to the difficulties of it. Meantime supply me the particulars of Major-General Blunt's case.

A. LINCOLN.

TELEGRAM TO COLONEL BIRNEY. [Cipher.] WAR DEPARTMENT, WASHINGTON, D.C., October 3, 1863.
COLONEL BIRNEY, Baltimore, Md.:

Please give me, as near as you can, the number of slaves you have recruited in Maryland. Of course the number is not to include the free colored.

A. LINCOLN.

PROCLAMATION FOR THANKSGIVING, OCTOBER 3, 1863.

BY THE PRESIDENT OF THE UNITED STATES AMERICA:

A Proclamation.

The year that is drawing towards its close has been filled with the blessings of fruitful fields and healthful skies. To these bounties, which are so constantly enjoyed that we are prone to forget the source from which they come, others have been added which are of so extraordinary a nature that they cannot fail to penetrate and soften even the heart which is habitually insensible to the ever-watchful providence of Almighty God. In the midst of a civil war of unequalled magnitude and severity which has sometimes seemed to invite and provoke the aggressions of foreign states; peace has been preserved with all nations, order has been maintained, the laws have been respected and obeyed, and harmony has prevailed everywhere except in the theatre of military conflict; while that theatre has been greatly contracted by the advancing armies and navies of the Union. The needful diversion of wealth and strength from the fields of peaceful industry, to the national defense has not arrested the plough, the shuttle, or the ship: The axe has enlarged the borders of our settlements, and the mines, as well of, iron and coal as of the precious metals, have yielded even more abundantly than heretofore. Population has steadily increased, notwithstanding the waste that has been made in the camp, the siege, and the battle-field; and the country, rejoicing in the consciousness of augmented strength and vigor, is permitted to expect a continuance of years, with large increase of freedom.

No human counsel hath devised, nor hath any mortal hand worked out these great things. They are the gracious gifts of the Most High God, who, while dealing with us in anger for our sins, hath nevertheless remembered mercy.

It has seemed to me fit and proper that they should be reverently, solemnly, and gratefully acknowledged, as with one heart and voice, by the whole American people. I do, therefore, invite my fellow-citizens in every part of the United States, and also those who are at sea, and those who are sojourning in foreign lands, to set apart and observe the last Thursday of November next as a day of thanksgiving and prayer to our beneficent Father who dwelleth in the heavens. And I recommend to them that, while offering up the ascriptions justly due to Him for such singular deliverances and blessings, they do also, with humble penitence for our national perverseness and disobedience, commend to His tender care all those who have become widows, orphans, mourners, or sufferers in the lamentable civil strife in which we are unavoidably engaged, and fervently implore the interposition of the Almighty hand to heal the wounds of the nation, and to restore it, as soon as may be consistent with divine purposes, to the full enjoyment of peace, harmony, tranquillity, and union.

In testimony whereof, I have hereunto set my hand, and caused the seal of the United States to be affixed.

Done at the city of Washington, this third day of October, in the year of our Lord one thousand eight hundred and sixty-three, and of the independence of the United States the eighty-eighth.

A. LINCOLN.

By the President: WILLIAM H. SEWARD,
 Secretary of State

TELEGRAM TO GENERAL J. M. SCHOFIELD.

WASHINGTON D.C., OCTOBER 4, 1863

MAJOR-GENERAL SCHOFIELD, St. Louis, Mo.:

I think you will not have just cause to complain of my action.
A. LINCOLN.

TELEGRAM TO GENERAL W. S. ROSECRANS.

WAR DEPARTMENT, October 4, 1863. 11.30 A.M.

MAJOR-GENERAL ROSECRANS, Chattanooga, Tenn.:
Yours of yesterday received. If we can hold Chattanooga and East Tennessee, I think the rebellion must dwindle and die. I think you and Burnside can do this, and hence doing so is your main object. Of course to greatly damage or destroy the enemy in your front would be a greater object, because it would include the former and more, but it is not so certainly within your power. I understand the main body of the enemy is very near you, so near that you could "board at home," so to speak, and menace or attack him any day. Would not the doing of this be your best mode of counteracting his raid on your communications? But this is not an order. I intend doing something like what you suggest whenever the case shall appear ripe enough to have it accepted in the true understanding rather than as a confession of weakness and fear.
A. LINCOLN.

TO C. D. DRAKE AND OTHERS.

EXECUTIVE MANSION, WASHINGTON, October 5, 1863.

HON. CHARLES D. DRAKE AND OTHERS, Committee.
GENTLEMEN:-Your original address, presented on the 30th ult., and the four supplementary ones presented on the 3d inst., have been carefully considered. I hope you will regard the other duties claiming my attention, together with the great length and importance of these documents, as constituting a sufficient apology for not having responded sooner.
These papers, framed for a common object, consist of the things demanded and the reasons for demanding them.
The things demanded are
First. That General Schofield shall be relieved, and General Butler be appointed as Commander of the Military Department of Missouri.
Second. That the system of enrolled militia in Missouri may be broken up, and national forces be substituted for it; and
Third. That at elections persons may not be allowed to vote who are not entitled by law to do so.
Among the reasons given, enough of suffering and wrong to Union men is certainly, and I suppose truly, stated. Yet the whole case, as presented, fails to convince me that General Schofield, or the enrolled militia, is responsible for that suffering and wrong. The whole can be explained on a more charitable, and, as I think, a more rational hypothesis.
We are in a civil war. In such cases there always is a main question, but in this case that question is a perplexing compound—Union and slavery. It thus becomes a question not of two sides merely, but of at least four sides, even among those who are for the Union, saying nothing of those who are against it. Thus, those who are for the Union with, but not without slavery; those for it without, but not with; those for it with or without, but prefer it with; and those for it with or without, but prefer it without.
Among these, again, is a subdivision of those who are for gradual, but not for immediate, and those who are for immediate, but not for gradual extinction of slavery.
It is easy to conceive that all these shades of opinion, and even more, may be sincerely entertained by honest and truthful men. Yet, all being for the Union, by reason of these differences each will prefer a different way of sustaining the Union. At once, sincerity is questioned, and motives are assailed. Actual war comming, blood grows hot and blood is spilled. Thought is forced from old channels into confusion. Deception breeds and thrives. Confidence dies, and universal suspicion reigns. Each man feels an impulse to kill his neighbor, lest he be killed by him. Revenge and retaliation follow. And all this, as before said, may be among honest men only. But this is not all. Every foul bird comes abroad, and every dirty reptile rises up. These add crime to confusion. Strong measures deemed indispensable, but harsh at best, such men make worse by maladministration. Murders for old grudges, and murders for self, proceed under any cloak that will best serve for the occasion.

These causes amply account for what has occurred in Missouri, without ascribing it to the weakness or wickedness of any general. The newspaper files, those chroniclers of current events, will show that the evils now complained of were quite as prevalent under Fremont, Hunter, Halleck, and Curtis, as under Schofield. If the former had greater force opposed to them, they also had greater force with which to meet it. When the organized rebel army left the State, the main Federal force had to go also, leaving the department commander at home relatively no stronger than before. Without disparaging any, I affirm with confidence that no commander of that department has, in proportion to his means, done better than General Schofield.

The first specific charge against General Schofield is, that the enrolled militia was placed under his command, whereas it had not been placed under the command of General Curtis. The fact is, I believe, true; but you do not point out, nor can I conceive, how that did, or could, injure loyal men or the Union cause.

You charge that, General Curtis being superseded by General Schofield, Franklin A. Dick was superseded by James O. Broadhead as Provost-Marshal General. No very specific showing is made as to how this did or could injure the Union cause. It recalls, however, the condition of things, as presented to me, which led to a change of commander of that department.

To restrain contraband intelligence and trade, a system of searches, seizures, permits, and passes, had been introduced, I think, by General Fremont. When General Halleck came, he found and continued the system, and added an order, applicable to some parts of the State, to levy and collect contributions from noted rebels, to compensate losses and relieve destitution caused by the rebellion. The action of General Fremont and General Halleck, as stated, constituted a sort of system which General Curtis found in full operation when he took command of the department. That there was a necessity for something of the sort was clear; but that it could only be justified by stern necessity, and that it was liable to great abuse in administration, was equally clear. Agents to execute it, contrary to the great prayer, were led into temptation. Some might, while others would not, resist that temptation. It was not possible to hold any to a very strict accountability; and those yielding to the temptation would sell permits and passes to those who would pay most and most readily for them, and would seize property and collect levies in the aptest way to fill their own pockets. Money being the object, the man having money, whether loyal or disloyal, would be a victim. This practice doubtless existed to some extent, and it was, a real additional evil that it could be, and was, plausibly charged to exist in greater extent than it did.

When General Curtis took command of the department, Mr. Dick, against whom I never knew anything to allege, had general charge of this system. A controversy in regard to it rapidly grew into almost unmanageable proportions. One side ignored the necessity and magnified the evils of the system, while the other ignored the evils and magnified the necessity; and each bitterly assailed the other. I could not fail to see that the controversy enlarged in the same proportion as the professed Union men there distinctly took sides in two opposing political parties. I exhausted my wits, and very nearly my patience also, in efforts to convince both that the evils they charged on each other were inherent in the case, and could not be cured by giving either party a victory over the other.

Plainly, the irritating system was not to be perpetual; and it was plausibly urged that it could be modified at once with advantage. The case could scarcely be worse, and whether it could be made better could only be determined by a trial. In this view, and not to ban or brand General Curtis, or to give a victory to any party, I made the change of commander for the department. I now learn that soon after this change Mr. Dick was removed, and that Mr. Broadhead, a gentleman of no less good character, was put in the place. The mere fact of this change is more distinctly complained of than is any conduct of the new officer, or other consequence of the change.

I gave the new commander no instructions as to the administration of the system mentioned, beyond what is contained in the private letter afterwards surreptitiously published, in which I directed him to act solely for the public good, and independently of both parties. Neither any thing you have presented me, nor anything I have otherwise learned, has convinced me that he has been unfaithful to this charge.

Imbecility is urged as one cause for removing General Schofield; and the late massacre at Lawrence, Kansas, is pressed as evidence of that imbecility. To my mind that fact scarcely tends to prove the proposition. That massacre is only an example of what Grierson, John Morgan, and many others might have repeatedly done on their respective raids, had they chosen to incur the personal hazard, and possessed the fiendish hearts to do it.

The charge is made that General Schofield, on purpose to protect the Lawrence murderers, would not allow them to be pursued into Missouri. While no punishment could be too sudden or too severe for those murderers, I am well satisfied that the preventing of the threatened remedial raid into Missouri was the only way to avoid an indiscriminate massacre there, including probably more innocent than guilty. Instead of condemning, I therefore approve what I understand General Schofield did in that respect.

The charges that General Schofield has purposely withheld protection from loyal people and purposely facilitated the objects of the disloyal are altogether beyond my power of belief. I do not arraign the veracity of gentlemen as to the facts complained of, but I do more than question the judgment which would infer that those facts occurred in accordance with the purposes of General Schofield.

With my present views, I must decline to remove General Schofield. In this I decide nothing against General Butler. I sincerely wish it were convenient to assign him a suitable command. In order to meet some existing evils I have addressed a letter of instructions to General Schofield, a copy of which I enclose to you.

As to the enrolled militia, I shall endeavor to ascertain better than I now know what is its exact value. Let me say now, however, that your proposal to substitute national forces for the enrolled militia implies that in your judgment the latter is doing something which needs to be done; and if so, the proposition to throw that force away and to supply its place by bringing other forces from the field where they are urgently needed seems to me very extraordinary. Whence shall they come? Shall they be withdrawn from Banks, or Grant, or Steele, or Rosecrans? Few things have been so grateful to my anxious feelings as when, in June last, the local force in Missouri aided General Schofield to so promptly send a large general force to the relief of General Grant, then investing Vicksburg and menaced from without by General Johnston. Was this all wrong? Should the enrolled militia then have been broken up and General Herron kept from Grant to police Missouri? So far from finding cause to object, I confess to a sympathy for whatever relieves our general force in Missouri and allows it to serve elsewhere. I therefore, as at present advised, cannot attempt the destruction of the enrolled militia of Missouri. I may add that, the force being under the national military control, it is also within the proclamation in regard to the habeas corpus.

I concur in the propriety of your request in regard to elections, and have, as you see, directed General Schofield accordingly. I do not feel justified to enter upon the broad field you present in regard to the political differences between Radicals and Conservatives. From time to time I have done and said what appeared to me proper to do and say. The public knows it all. It obliges nobody to follow me, and I trust it obliges me to follow nobody. The Radicals and Conservatives each agree with me in some things and disagree in others. I could wish both to agree with me in all things, for then they would agree with each other, and would be too strong for any foe from any quarter. They, however, choose to do otherwise; and I do not question their right. I too shall do what seems to be my duty. I hold whoever commands in Missouri or elsewhere responsible to me and not to either Radicals or Conservatives. It is my duty to hear all, but at last I must, within my sphere, judge what to do and what to forbear.

Your obedient servant,
A. LINCOLN.

THE CASE OF DR. DAVID M. WRIGHT

APPROVAL OF THE DECISION OF THE COURT

WAR DEPARTMENT, ADJUTANT-GENERALS OFFICE,
WASHINGTON, October 8, 1863.
MAJOR-GENERAL J. G. FOSTER, Commanding Department of Virginia and North Carolina, Fort Monroe, Va.
SIR:—The proceedings of the military commission instituted for the trial of David Wright, of Norfolk, in Special Orders Nos. 195, 196, and 197, of 1863, from headquarters Department of Virginia, have been submitted to the President of the United States. The following are his remarks on the case:

Upon the presentation of the record in this case and the examination thereof, aided by the report thereon of the Judge-Advocate-General, and on full hearing of counsel for the accused, being specified that no proper question remained open except as to the sanity of the accused, I caused a very full examination to be made on that question, upon a great amount of evidence, including all effort by the counsel for accused, by an expert of high reputation in that professional department, who thereon reports to me, as his opinion, that the accused, Dr. David M. Wright, was not insane prior to or on the 11th day of July, 1863, the date of the homicide of Lieutenant Sanborn; that he has not been insane since, and is not insane now (Oct. 7, 1863). I therefore approve the finding and sentence of the military commission, and direct that the major-general in command of the department including the place of trial, and wherein the convict is now in custody, appoint a time and place and carry such sentence into execution.
A. LINCOLN.

TELEGRAM TO GENERAL MEADE.

WAR DEPARTMENT, WASHINGTON, D. C., October 8, 1863.

MAJOR-GENERAL MEADE, Army of Potomac:
I am appealed to in behalf of August Blittersdorf, at Mitchell's Station, Va., to be shot to-morrow as a deserter. I am unwilling for any boy under eighteen to be shot, and his father affirms that he is yet under sixteen. Please answer. His regiment or company not given me.
A. LINCOLN.

TELEGRAM TO GENERAL MEADE.

EXECUTIVE MANSION, WASHINGTON, October 8, 1863.

MAJOR-GENERAL MEADE, Army of Potomac:
The boy telegraphs from Mitchell's Station, Va. The father thinks he is in the One hundred and nineteenth Pennsylvania Volunteers. The father signs the name "Blittersdorf." I can tell no more.
A. LINCOLN.

TELEGRAM TO GENERAL MEADE.

EXECUTIVE MANSION, WASHINGTON, October 12, 1863.

MAJOR-GENERAL MEADE, Army of Potomac:
The father and mother of John Murphy, of the One hundred and nineteenth Pennsylvania Volunteers, have filed their own affidavits that he was born June 22, 1846, and also the affidavits of three other persons who all swear that they remembered the circumstances of his birth and that it was in the year 1846, though they do not remember the particular day. I therefore, on account of his tender age, have concluded to pardon him, and to leave it to yourself whether to discharge him or continue him in the service.
A. LINCOLN.

TELEGRAM TO W. S. ROSECRANS.

[Cipher.]

WAR DEPARTMENT, October 12, 1863.8.35 A.M.
MAJOR-GENERAL ROSECRANS, Chattanooga, Tenn.:
As I understand, Burnside is menaced from the west, and so cannot go to you without surrendering East Tennessee. I now think the enemy will not attack Chattanooga, and I think you will have to look out for his making a concentrated drive at Burnside. You and Burnside now have him by the throat, and he must break your hold or perish I therefore think you better try to hold the road up to Kingston, leaving Burnside to what is above there. Sherman is coming to you, though gaps in the telegraph prevent our knowing how far he is advanced. He and Hooker will so support you on the west and northwest as to enable you to look east and northeast. This is not an order. General Halleck will give his views.
A. LINCOLN.

TELEGRAM TO GENERAL G. G. MEADE.

WASHINGTON, October 12, 1863. 9 A.M.

MAJOR-GENERAL MEADE: What news this morning? A despatch from Rosecrans, leaving him at 7.30 P.M. yesterday, says:
"Rebel rumors that head of Ewell's column reached Dalton yesterday."
I send this for what it is worth.
A. LINCOLN.

TELEGRAM TO WAYNE McVEIGH.

EXECUTIVE MANSION, WASHINGTON, October 13, 1863.

McVEIGH, Philadelphia:
The enemy some days ago made a movement, apparently to turn General Meade's right. This led to a maneuvering of the two armies and to pretty heavy skirmishing on Saturday, Sunday, and Monday. We have frequent despatches from General Meade and up to 10 o'clock last night nothing had happened giving either side any marked advantage. Our army reported to be in excellent condition. The telegraph is open to General Meade's camp this morning, but we have not troubled him for a despatch.
A. LINCOLN.

TO THURLOW WEED.

EXECUTIVE MANSION, WASHINGTON, October 14, 1863.

HON. THURLOW WEED.
DEAR SIR:—I have been brought to fear recently that somehow, by commission or omission, I have caused you some degree of pain. I have never entertained an unkind feeling or a disparaging thought toward you; and if I have said or done anything which has been construed into such unkindness or disparagement, it has been misconstrued. I am sure if we could meet we would not part with any unpleasant impression on either side.
Yours as ever,
A. LINCOLN.

TO L. B. TODD.

WAR DEPARTMENT, WASHINGTON, D. C., October 15, 1863.

L. B. TODD, Lexington, Ky.:
I send the following pass to your care.
A. LINCOLN.

AID TO MRS. HELM, MRS. LINCOLN'S SISTER

WASHINGTON, D. C., October 15, 1863.

To WHOM IT MAY CONCERN:
Allow MRS. Robert S. Todd, widow, to go south and bring her daughter, MRS. General B. Hardin Helm, with her children, north to Kentucky.
A. LINCOLN.

TELEGRAM TO GENERAL FOSTER.

WAR DEPARTMENT, WASHINGTON, D. C., October 15, 1863.

MAJOR-GENERAL FOSTER, Fort Monroe, Va.:
Postpone the execution of Dr. Wright to Friday the 23d instant (October). This is intended for his preparation and is final.
A. LINCOLN.

TELEGRAM TO GENERAL MEADE.

EXECUTIVE MANSION, WASHINGTON, October 15, 1863.

MAJOR-GENERAL MEADE, Army of Potomac:
On the 4th instant you telegraphed me that Private Daniel Hanson, of Ninety-seventh New York Volunteers, had not yet been tried. When he shall be, please notify me of the result, with a brief statement of his case, if he be convicted. Gustave Blittersdorf, who you say is enlisted in the One hundred and nineteenth Pennsylvania Volunteers as William Fox, is proven to me to be only fifteen years old last January. I pardon him, and you will discharge him or put him in the ranks at your discretion. Mathias Brown, of Nineteenth Pennsylvania Volunteers, is proven to me to be eighteen last May, and his friends say he is convicted on an enlistment and for a desertion both before that time. If this last be true he is pardoned, to be kept or discharged as you please. If not true suspend his execution and report the facts of his case. Did you receive my despatch of 12th pardoning John Murphy?
A. LINCOLN.
[The Lincoln papers during this time have a suspended execution on almost every other page, I have omitted most of these D.W.]

TELEGRAM TO T. W. SWEENEY.

WAR DEPARTMENT, WASHINGTON, D. C., October 16, 1863.

THOMAS W. SWEENEY, Continental, Philadelphia:
Tad is teasing me to have you forward his pistol to him.
A. LINCOLN.

TELEGRAM TO T. C. DURANT.

WASHINGTON, D. C., October 16, 1863.

T. C. DURANT, New York:
I remember receiving nothing from you of the 10th, and I do not comprehend your despatch of to-day. In fact I do not remember, if I ever knew, who you are, and I have very little conception as to what you are telegraphing about.
A. LINCOLN.

COMMENT ON A NOTE.

NEW YORK, October 15, 1863.

DEAR SIR: On the point of leaving I am told, by a gentleman to whose statements I attach credit, that the opposition policy for the Presidential campaign will be to "abstain from voting." J.
[Comment.]
More likely to abstain from stopping, once they get at it, until they shall have voted several times each.
October 16. A. L.

TO GENERAL H. W. HALLECK.

EXECUTIVE MANSION, WASHINGTON, October 16, 1863.

MAJOR GENERAL HALLECK:
I do not believe Lee can have over 60,000 effective men.
Longstreet's corps would not be sent away to bring an equal force back upon the same road; and there is no other direction for them to have come from.
Doubtless, in making the present movement, Lee gathered in all available scraps, and added them to Hill's and Ewell's corps; but that is all, and he made the movement in the belief that four corps had left General Meade; and General Meade's apparently avoiding a collision with him has confirmed him in that belief. If General Meade can now attack him on a field no worse than equal for us, and will do so now with all the skill and courage which he, his officers, and men possess, the honor will be his if he succeeds, and the blame may be mine if he fails.
Yours truly,
A. LINCOLN.

CALL FOR 300,000 VOLUNTEERS, OCTOBER 17, 1863.

BY THE PRESIDENT OF THE UNITED STATES OF AMERICA:

A Proclamation.
Whereas the term of service of a part of the Volunteer forces of the United States will expire during the coming year; and whereas, in addition to the men raised by the present draft, it is deemed expedient to call out three hundred thousand volunteers to serve for three years or during the war, not, however, exceeding three years:
Now, therefore, I, Abraham Lincoln, President of the United States, and Commander-in-Chief of the Army and Navy thereof, and of the militia of the several States when called into actual service, do issue this my proclamation, calling upon the governors of the different States to raise, and have enlisted into the United States service, for the various companies and regiments in the field from their respective States, the quotas of three hundred thousand men.
I further proclaim that all the volunteers thus called out and duly enlisted shall receive advance pay, premium, and bounty, as heretofore communicated to the governors of States by the War Department through the Provost-Marshal-General's office, by special letters.
I further proclaim that all volunteers received under this call, as well as all others not heretofore credited, shall be duly credited and deducted from the quotas established for the next draft.
I further proclaim that if any State shall fail to raise the quota assigned to it by the War Department under this call, then a draft for the deficiency in said quota shall be made in said State, or in the districts of said State, for their due proportion of said quota, and the said draft shall commence on the 5th day of January, 1864.
And I further proclaim that nothing in this proclamation shall interfere with existing orders, or with those which may be issued for the present draft in the States where it is now in progress, or where it has not yet been commenced.
The quotas of the States and districts will be assigned by the War Department through the Provost-Marshal-General's office, due regard being had for the men heretofore furnished, whether by volunteering or drafting; and the recruiting will be conducted in accordance with such instructions as have been or may be issued by that department.

In issuing this proclamation, I address myself not only to the governors of the several States, but also to the good and loyal people thereof, invoking them to lend their cheerful, willing, and effective aid to the measures thus adopted, with a view to reinforce our victorious army now in the field, and bring our needful military operations to a prosperous end, thus closing forever the fountains of sedition and civil war.
In witness whereof, I have hereunto set my hand and caused the seal of the United States to be affixed....................
A. LINCOLN.
By the President: WILLIAM H. SEWARD, Secretary of State.

TELEGRAM TO GENERAL FOSTER.

WAR DEPARTMENT, WASHINGTON, D.C., October 17, 1863.

MAJOR-GENERAL FOSTER, Port Monroe, Va.:
It would be useless for Mrs. Dr. Wright to come here. The subject is a very painful one, but the case is settled.
A. LINCOLN.

TELEGRAM TO W. B. THOMAS

EXECUTIVE MANSION, WASHINGTON, D.C., OCTOBER 17, 1863

HON. WILLIAM B. THOMAS, Philadelphia, Pa.
I am grateful for your offer of 100,000 men, but as at present advised I do not consider that Washington is in danger, or that there is any emergency requiring 60 or 90 days men.
A. LINCOLN.

TELEGRAM TO J. WILLIAMS AND N. G. TAYLOR.

WAR DEPARTMENT, October 17, 1863.

JOHN WILLIAMS AND N G. TAYLOR, Knoxville, Tenn.:
You do not estimate the holding of East Tennessee more highly than I do. There is no absolute purpose of withdrawing our forces from it, and only a contingent one to withdraw them temporarily for the purpose of not losing the position permanently. I am in great hope of not finding it necessary to withdraw them at all, particularly if you raise new troops rapidly for us there.
A. LINCOLN.

TELEGRAM TO T. C. DURANT.

EXECUTIVE MANSION, WASHINGTON CITY, October 18, 1863.

T. C. DURANT, New York:
As I do with others, so I will try to see you when you come.
A. LINCOLN.

TELEGRAM TO GENERAL W. S. ROSECRANS.

WAR DEPARTMENT, October 19, 1863. 9. A.M.

MAJOR-GENERAL ROSECRANS, Chattanooga, Tenn:
There has been no battle recently at Bull Run. I suppose what you have heard a rumor of was not a general battle, but an "affair" at Bristow Station on the railroad, a few miles beyond Manassas Junction toward the Rappahannock, on Wednesday, the 14th. It began by an attack of the enemy upon General Warren, and ended in the enemy being repulsed with a loss of four cannon and from four to seven hundred prisoners.
A. LINCOLN.

TELEGRAM TO GENERAL R. C. SCHENCK.

EXECUTIVE MANSION, WASHINGTON, October 21, 1863. 2.45

MAJOR-GENERAL SCHENCK, Baltimore, Md.:
A delegation is here saying that our armed colored troops are at many, if not all, the landings on the Patuxent River, and by their presence with arms in their hands are frightening quiet people and producing great confusion. Have they been sent there by any order, and if so, for what reason?
A. LINCOLN.

TELEGRAM TO GENERAL R. C. SCHENCK.

EXECUTIVE MANSION, WASHINGTON, October 22, 1863. 1.30 P.M.

MAJOR-GENERAL SCHENCK, Baltimore, Md.:
Please come over here. The fact of one of our officers being killed on the Patuxent is a specimen of what I would avoid. It seems to me we could send white men to recruit better than to send negroes and thus inaugurate homicides on punctilio.
Please come over.
A. LINCOLN.

TO GENERAL H. W. HALLECK.

EXECUTIVE MANSION, WASHINGTON, October 24, 1863.

MAJOR-GENERAL HALLECK:
Taking all our information together, I think it probable that Ewell's corps has started for East Tennessee by way of Abingdon, marching last Monday, say from Meade's front directly to the railroad at Charlottesville.
First, the object of Lee's recent movement against Meade; his destruction of the Alexandria and Orange Railroad, and subsequent withdrawal without more motive, not otherwise apparent, would be explained by this hypothesis.
Secondly, the direct statement of Sharpe's men that Ewell has gone to Tennessee.
Thirdly, the Irishman's [Northern Spy in Richmond] statement that he has not gone through Richmond, and his further statement of an appeal made to the people at Richmond to go and protect their salt, which could only refer to the works near Abingdon.
Fourthly, Graham's statement from Martinsburg that Imboden is in retreat for Harrisonburg. This last matches with the idea that Lee has retained his cavalry, sending Imboden and perhaps other scraps to join Ewell. Upon this probability what is to be done?

If you have a plan matured, I have nothing to say. If you have not, then I suggest that, with all possible expedition, the Army of the Potomac get ready to attack Lee, and that in the meantime a raid shall, at all hazards, break the railroad at or near Lynchburg.

Yours truly,
A. LINCOLN.

TO E. B. WASHBURNE.

(Private and Confidential.)

EXECUTIVE MANSION, WASHINGTON, October 26, 1863.
HON. E. B. WASHBURNE.
MY DEAR SIR:—Yours of the 12th has been in my hands several days. Inclosed I send the leave of absence for your brother, in as good form as I think I can safely put it. Without knowing whether he would accept it. I have tendered the collectorship at Portland, Maine, to your other brother, the governor.

Thanks to both you and our friend Campbell for your kind words and intentions. A second term would be a great honor and a great labor, which, together, perhaps I would not decline if tendered.

Yours truly,
A. LINCOLN.

TO SECRETARY CHASE.

EXECUTIVE MANSION, WASHINGTON, October 26, 1863.

HON. SECRETARY OF THE TREASURY.
MY DEAR SIR:—The writer of the accompanying letter is one of Mrs. Lincoln's numerous cousins. He is a grandson of "Milliken's Bend," near Vicksburg—that is, a grandson of the man who gave name to Milliken's Bend. His father was a brother to MRS. Lincoln's mother. I know not a thing about his loyalty beyond what he says. Supposing he is loyal, can any of his requests be granted, and if any, which of them?

Yours truly,
A. LINCOLN.

THE WRITINGS OF A. LINCOLN,
Volume Seven, 1863-1865

1863

OPINION ON THE LOSS OF GENERAL R. H. MILROY'S DIVISION.
October 27, 1863.
In June last a division was substantially lost at or near Winchester, Va. At the time, it was under General Milroy as immediate commander in the field, General Schenck as department commander at Baltimore, and General Halleck as general-in-chief at Washington.
General Milroy, as immediate commander, was put in arrest, and subsequently a court of inquiry examined chiefly with reference to disobedience of orders, and reported the evidence.
The foregoing is a synoptical statement of the evidence, together with the judge-advocate-general's conclusions. The disaster, when it came, was a surprise to all. It was very well known to Generals Shenck and Milroy for some time before, that General Halleck thought the division was in great danger of a surprise at Winchester; that it was of no service commensurate with the risk it incurred, and that it ought to be withdrawn; but, although he more than once advised its withdrawal, he never positively ordered it. General Schenck, on the contrary, believed the service of the force at Winchester was worth the hazard, and so did not positively order its withdrawal until it was so late that the enemy cut the wire and prevented the order reaching General Milroy.
General Milroy seems to have concurred with General Schenck in the opinion that the force should be kept at Winchester at least until the approach of danger, but he disobeyed no order upon the subject.
Some question can be made whether some of General Halleck's dispatches to General Schenk should not have been construed to be orders to withdraw the force, and obeyed accordingly; but no such question can be made against General Milroy. In fact, the last order he received was to be prepared to withdraw, but not to actually withdraw until further order, which further order never reached him.
Serious blame is not necessarily due to any serious disaster, and I cannot say that in this case any of the officers are deserving of serious blame. No court-martial is deemed necessary or proper in the case.
A. LINCOLN.

TO GENERAL SCHOFIELD.

Private and confidential

EXECUTIVE MANSION, WASHINGTON, October 28, 1863.
GENERAL JOHN M. SCHOFIELD:
There have recently reached the War Department, and thence been laid before me, from Missouri, three communications, all similar in import and identical in object. One of them, addressed to nobody, and without place or date, but having the signature of (apparently) the writer, is a letter of eight closely written foolscap pages. The other two are written by a different person, at St. Joseph, Mo., and of the dates, respectively, October 12 and 13, 1863, and each inclosing a large number of affidavits. The general statements of the whole are that the Federal and State authorities are arming the disloyal and disarming the loyal, and that the latter will all be killed or driven out of the State unless there shall be a change. In particular, no loyal man who has been disarmed is named, but the affidavits show by name forty-two persons as disloyal who have been armed. They are as follows: [The names are omitted.]
A majority of these are shown to have been in the rebel service. I believe it could be shown that the government here has deliberately armed more than ten times as many captured at Gettysburg, to say nothing of similar operations in East Tennessee. These papers contain altogether thirty—one manuscript pages, and one newspaper in extenso, and yet I do not find it anywhere charged in them that any loyal man has been harmed by reason of being disarmed, or that any disloyal one has harmed anybody by reason of being armed by the Federal or State Government. Of course, I have not had time to carefully examine all; but I have had most of them examined and briefed by others, and the result is as stated. The remarkable fact that the actual evil is yet only anticipated—inferred—induces me to suppose I understand the case; but I do not state my impression, because I might be mistaken, and because your duty and mine is plain in

any event. The locality of nearly all this seems to be St. Joseph and Buchanan County. I wish you to give special attention to this region, particularly on election day. Prevent violence from whatever quarter, and see that the soldiers themselves do no wrong.
Yours truly,
A. LINCOLN.

TELEGRAM TO GOVERNOR JOHNSON.

[Cipher.]

EXECUTIVE MANSION, WASHINGTON, D. C., October 28, 1863.
HON. ANDREW JOHNSON, Nashville, Tenn.: If not too inconvenient, please come at once and have a personal conversation with me.
A. LINCOLN.

TO VICE-PRESIDENT HAMLIN.

AN ACT TO REGULATE THE DUTIES OF THE CLERK OF THE HOUSE OF REPRESENTATIVES IN PREPARING FOR THE ORGANIZATION OF THE HOUSE.
Be it enacted by the Senate and House of Representatives of the United States of America in Congress assembled, that, before the first meeting of the next Congress, and of every subsequent Congress, the clerk of the next preceding House of Representatives shall make a roll of the Representatives elect, and place thereon the names of all persons, and of such persons only, whose credentials show that they were regularly elected in accordance with the laws of their States respectively, or the laws of the United States.
Approved March 3, 1863.

TO J. W. GRIMES.

EXECUTIVE MANSION,

WASHINGTON, D.C., October 29, 1863.
HON. JAMES W. GRIMES.
MY DEAR SIR:—The above act of Congress was passed, as I suppose, for the purpose of shutting out improper applicants for seats in the House of Representatives; and I fear there is some danger that it will be used to shut out proper ones. Iowa, having an entire Union delegation, will be one of the States the attempt will be made, if upon any. The Governor doubtless has made out the certificates, and they are already in the hands of the members. I suggest that they come on with them; but that, for greater caution, you, and perhaps Mr. Harlan with you, consult with the Governor, and have an additional set made out according to the form on the other half of this sheet; and still another set, if you can, by studying the law, think of a form that in your judgment, promises additional security, and quietly bring the whole on with you, to be used in case of necessity. Let what you do be kept still.
Yours truly,
A. LINCOLN.

TELEGRAM TO P. F. LOWE.

[Cipher.]

EXECUTIVE MANSION, WASHINGTON, D. C., October 30, 1863.
HON. F. F. LOWE, San Francisco, Cal.:
Below is an act of Congress, passed last session, intended to exclude applicants not entitled to seats, but which, there is reason to fear, will be used to exclude some who are entitled. Please get with the Governor and one or two other discreet friends, study the act carefully, and make certificates in two or three forms, according to your best judgement, and have them sent to me, so as to multiply the chances of the delegation getting their seats. Let it be done without publicity. Below is a form which may answer for one. If you could procure the same to be done for the Oregon member it might be well.
A. LINCOLN.

TELEGRAM TO GENERAL MEADE.

EXECUTIVE MANSION, WASHINGTON, D. C., October 30, 1863.

MAJOR-GENERAL MEADE, Army of Potomac:
Much obliged for the information about deserters contained in your dispatch of yesterday, while I have to beg your pardon for troubling you in regard to some of them, when, as it appears by yours, I had the means of answering my own questions.
A. LINCOLN.

MEMORANDUM.

EXECUTIVE MANSION, WASHINGTON, October 31, 1863.

The Provost-Marshal-General has issued no proclamation at all. He has in no form announced anything recently in regard to troops in New York, except in his letter to Governor Seymour of October 21, which has been published in the newspapers of that State. It has not been announced or decided in any form by the Provost-Marshal-General, or any one else in authority of the Government, that every citizen who has paid his three hundred dollars commutation is liable to be immediately drafted again, or that towns that have just raised the money to pay their quotas will have again to be subject to similar taxation or suffer the operations of the new conscription, nor it is probable that the like of them ever will be announced or decided.

TELEGRAM TO W. H. SEWARD.

WAR DEPARTMENT, WASHINGTON, D. C., November 1, 1863.

HON. W. H. SEWARD, Auburn, N.Y.:
No important news. Details of Hooker's night fight do great credit to his command, and particularly to the Eleventh Corps and Geary's part of the Twelfth. No discredit on any.
A. LINCOLN.

TO POSTMASTER-GENERAL BLAIR.

EXECUTIVE MANSION,

WASHINGTON, November 2, 1863.
HON. MONTGOMERY BLAIR.
MY DEAR SIR:—Some days ago I understood you to say that your brother, General Frank Blair, desires to be guided by my wishes as to whether he will occupy his seat in Congress or remain in the field. My wish, then, is compounded of what I believe will be best for the country; and it is that he will come here, put his military commission in my hands, take his seat, go into caucus with our friends, abide the nominations, help elect the nominees, and thus aid to organize a House of Representatives which will really support the Government in the war. If the result shall be the election of himself as Speaker, let him serve in that position. If not, let him retake his commission and return to the army for the benefit of the country.

This will heal a dangerous schism for him. It will relieve him from a dangerous position or a misunderstanding, as I think he is in danger of being permanently separated from those with whom only he can ever have a real sympathy—the sincere opponents of slavery.

It will be a mistake if he shall allow the provocations offered him by insincere time-servers to drive him from the house of his own building. He is young yet. He has abundant talents—quite enough to occupy all his time without devoting any to temper.

He is rising in military skill and usefulness. His recent appointment to the command of a corps, by one so competent to judge as General Sherman, proves this. In that line he can serve both the country and himself more profitably than he could as a member of Congress upon the floor.

The foregoing is what I would say if Frank Blair was my brother instead of yours.
Yours truly,
A. LINCOLN.

TO GOVERNOR BRADFORD.

EXECUTIVE MANSION, WASHINGTON, November 2, 1863.

His EXCELLENCY A. W. BRADFORD, Governor of Maryland.
SIR:—Yours of the 31st ult. was received yesterday about noon, and since then I have been giving most earnest attention to the subject-matter of it. At my call General Schenck has attended, and he assures me it is almost certain that violence will be used at some of the voting places on election day unless prevented by his provost-guards. He says that at some of those places Union voters will not attend at all, or run a ticket, unless they have some assurance of protection. This makes the Missouri case, of my action in regard to which you express your approval.

The remaining point of your letter is a protest against any person offering to vote being put to any test not found in the laws of Maryland. This brings us to a difference between Missouri and Maryland. With the same reason in both States, Missouri has, by law, provided a test for the voter with reference to the present rebellion, while Maryland has not. For example, General Trimble, captured fighting us at Gettysburg, is, without recanting his treason, a legal voter by the laws of Maryland. Even General Schenck's order admits him to vote, if he recants upon oath. I think that is cheap enough. My order in Missouri, which you approve, and General Scherick's order here, reach precisely the same end. Each assures the right of voting to all loyal men, and whether a man is loyal, each allows that man to fix by his own oath. Your suggestion that nearly all the candidates are loyal, I do not think quite meets the case. In this struggle for the nation's life, I cannot so confidently rely on those whose elections may have depended upon disloyal votes. Such men, when elected, may prove true; but such votes are given them in the expectation that they will prove false.

Nor do I think that to keep the peace at the polls, and to prevent the persistently disloyal from voting, constitutes just cause of offense to Maryland. I think she has her own example for it. If I mistake not, it is precisely what General Dix did when your Excellency was elected Governor.

I revoke the first of the three propositions in General Schenck's General Order No. 53; not that it is wrong in principle, but because the military, being of necessity exclusive judges as to who shall be arrested, the provision is too liable to abuse. For the revoked part I substitute the following:

That, all provost-marshals and other military officers do prevent all disturbance and violence at or about the polls, whether offered by such persons as above described, or by any other person or persons whomsoever.

The other two propositions of the order I allow to stand. General Schenck is fully determined, and has my strict orders besides, that all loyal men may vote, and vote for whom they please.
Your obedient servant,
A. LINCOLN.

TO J. H. HACKETT

[Private.]

EXECUTIVE MANSION, WASHINGTON, November 2, 1863.
JAMES H. HACKETT.
MY DEAR SIR:—Yours of October 22d is received, as also was, in due course, that of October 3d. I look forward with pleasure to the fulfillment of the promise made in the former to visit Washington the following winter and to "call."
Give yourself no uneasiness on the subject mentioned in that of the 22d. My note to you I certainly did not expect to see in print, yet I have not been much shocked by the newspaper comments upon it.
Those comments constitute a fair specimen of what has occurred to me through life. I have endured a great deal of ridicule, without much malice; and have received a great deal of kindness not quite free from ridicule. I am used to it.

TELEGRAM TO W. H. SEWARD.

WAR DEPARTMENT, WASHINGTON CITY, November 3, 1863.

HON. W. H. SEWARD, Auburn, N. Y.:
Nothing new. Dispatches up to 12 last night from Chattanooga show all quiet and doing well. How is your son?
A. LINCOLN.

TELEGRAM TO GENERAL MEADE EXECUTIVE MANSION, WASHINGTON, November 3, 1863.

MAJOR-GENERAL MEADE, Army of Potomac:

Samuel Wellers, private in Company B, Forty-ninth Pennsylvania Volunteers, writes that he is to be shot for desertion on the 6th instant. His own story is rather a bad one, and yet he tells it so frankly, that I am somewhat interested in him. Has he been a good soldier except the desertion? About how old is he?
A. LINCOLN.

TELEGRAM TO GENERAL MEADE.

EXECUTIVE, MANSION WASHINGTON, D. C., November 5, 1863.

MAJOR-GENERAL MEADE, Army of Potomac:
Please suspend the execution of Samuel Wellers, Forty-ninth Pennsylvania Volunteers, until further orders.
A. LINCOLN.

TELEGRAM TO GENERAL A. E. BURNSIDE. WAR DEPARTMENT, WASHINGTON, November

9, 1863.4 P.M.
MAJOR-GENERAL BURNSIDE, Knoxville, Tenn.:

Have seen dispatch from General Grant about your loss at Rogersville. Per contra, about the same time, Averell and Duffle got considerable advantage of the enemy at and about Lewisburg, Virginia: and on Saturday, the seventh, Meade drove the enemy from Rappahannock Station and Kelly's Ford, capturing eight battle-flags, four guns, and over 1800 prisoners, with very little loss to himself. Let me hear from you.
A. LINCOLN.

TELEGRAM TO GENERAL G. G. MEADE.

WASHINGTON, November 9, 1863 7.30 P.M.

MAJOR-GENERAL MEADE:
I have seen your dispatches about operations on the Rappahannock on Saturday, and I wish to say, "Well done!" Do the 1500 prisoners reported by General Sedgwick include the 400 taken by General French, or do the Whole amount to 1900?
A. LINCOLN.

ORDER CONCERNING THE EXPORT OF TOBACCO PURCHASED BY FOREIGN NATIONS.

EXECUTIVE MANSION,

WASHINGTON, November 10, 1863.
In consideration of the peculiar circumstances and pursuant to the comity deemed to be due to friendly powers, any tobacco in the United States belonging to the government either of France, Austria, or any other state with which this country is at peace, and which tobacco was purchased and paid for by such government prior to the 4th day of March, 1861, may be exported from any port of the United States under the supervision and upon the responsibility of naval officers of such governments and in conformity to such regulations as may be presented by the Secretary of State of the United States, and not otherwise.
A. LINCOLN.

TELEGRAM TO GENERAL SCHOFIELD.

WAR DEPARTMENT, WASHINGTON, D. C., November 10, 1863.

GENERAL SCHOFIELD, Saint Louis, Mo.:
I see a dispatch here from Saint Louis, which is a little difficult for me to understand. It says "General Schofield has refused leave of absence to members in military service to attend the legislature. All such are radical and administration men. The election of two Senators from this place on Thursday will probably turn upon this thing." what does this mean? Of course members of the legislation must be allowed to attend its sessions. But how is there a session before the recent election returns are in? And how is it to be at "this place"—and that is Saint Louis? Please inform me.
A. LINCOLN.

TELEGRAM TO GENERAL SCHOFIELD.

WAR DEPARTMENT, WASHINGTON, D. C., November 11, 1863.

GENERAL SCHOFIELD, Saint Louis, Mo.:
I believe the Secretary of War has telegraphed you about members of the legislation. At all events, allow those in the service to attend the session, and we can afterward decide whether they can stay through the entire session.
A. LINCOLN.

TELEGRAM TO HIRAM BARNEY.

[Cipher.]
EXECUTIVE MANSION, WASHINGTON, D. C., November 11, 1863.
HON. HIRAM BARNEY, New York; I would like an interview with you. Can you not come?
A. LINCOLN.

TELEGRAM TO J. MILDERBORGER.

EXECUTIVE MANSION,

WASHINGTON, D. C., November 11, 1863.
JOHN MILDERBORGER, Peru, Ind.:
I cannot comprehend the object of your dispatch. I do not often decline seeing people who call upon me, and probably will see you if you call.
A. LINCOLN.

TELEGRAM to E. H. AND E. JAMESON.

WAR DEPARTMENT,

WASHINGTON, D. C., November 13, 1863.
E. H. and E. JAMESON, Jefferson City, Mo.:
Yours saying Brown and Henderson are elected Senators is received. I understand this is one and one. If so it is knocking heads together to some.
A. LINCOLN.

TELEGRAM TO GENERAL W. S. ROSECRANS.

WAR DEPARTMENT, WASHINGTON, November 14, 1863. 12.15 P.M.

MAJOR-GENERAL ROSECRANS, Cincinnati, Ohio:
I have received and considered your dispatch of yesterday. Of the reports you mention, I have not the means of seeing any except your own. Besides this, the publication might be improper in view of the court of inquiry which has been ordered. With every disposition, not merely to do justice, but to oblige you, I feel constrained to say I think the publications better not be made now.
A. LINCOLN.

TELEGRAM TO GENERAL BURNSIDE.

WAR DEPARTMENT, WASHINGTON CITY, November 16, 1863.

MAJOR-GENERAL BURNSIDE, Knoxville, Tenn.:
What is the news?
A. LINCOLN.

TO SECRETARY CHASE

EXECUTIVE MANSION, WASHINGTON, November 17, 1863.

HON. SECRETARY OF THE TREASURY.
MY DEAR SIR:—I expected to see you here at Cabinet meeting, and to say something about going to Gettysburg. There will be a train to take and return us. The time for starting is not yet fixed, but when it shall be I will notify you.
Yours truly,
A. LINCOLN.

ADDRESS AT GETTYSBURG

NOVEMBER 19, 1863.

Four score and seven years ago our fathers brought forth on this continent, a new nation, conceived in Liberty, and dedicated to the proposition that all men are created equal.
Now we are engaged in a great civil war, testing whether that nation or any nation so conceived and so dedicated, can long endure. We are met on a great battle-field of that war. We have come to dedicate a portion of that field, as a final resting place for those who here gave their lives that that nation might live. It is altogether fitting and proper that we should do this.
But, in a larger sense, we can not dedicate—we can not consecrate—we can not hallow—this ground. The brave men, living and dead, who struggled here, have consecrated it, far above our poor power to add or detract. The world will little note, nor long remember what we say here, but it can never forget what they did here. It is for us the living, rather, to be dedicated here to the unfinished work which they who fought here have thus far so nobly advanced. It is rather for us to be here dedicated to the great task remaining before us—that from these honored dead we take increased devotion to that cause for which they gave the last full measure of devotion that we here highly resolve that these dead shall not have died in vain—that this nation, under God, shall have a new birth of freedom—and that government of the people, by the people, for the people, shall not perish from the earth.

TELEGRAM TO GENERAL MEADE.

EXECUTIVE MANSION, WASHINGTON, D. C., November 20, 1863.

MAJOR-GENERAL MEADE, Army of Potomac:
If there is a man by the name of King under sentence to be shot, please suspend execution till further order, and send record.
A. LINCOLN.

TELEGRAM TO GENERAL MEADE.

EXECUTIVE MANSION, WASHINGTON. November 20, 1863.

MAJOR-GENERAL MEADE, Army of Potomac:
An intelligent woman in deep distress, called this morning, saying her husband, a lieutenant in the Army of Potomac, was to be shot next Monday for desertion, and putting a letter in my hand, upon which I relied for particulars, she left without mentioning a name or other particular by which to identify the case. On opening the letter I found it equally vague, having nothing to identify by, except her own signature, which seems to be "Mrs. Anna S. King." I could not again find her. If you have a case which you shall think is probably the one intended, please apply my dispatch of this morning to it.
A. LINCOLN.

TELEGRAM TO E. P. EVANS.

EXECUTIVE MANSION, WASHINGTON, D. C., November 23, 1863.

E. P. EVANS, West Union, Adams County, Ohio:
Yours to Governor Chase in behalf of John A Welch is before me. Can there be a worse case than to desert and with letters persuading others to desert? I cannot interpose without a better showing than you make. When did he desert? when did he write the letters?
A. LINCOLN.

TO SECRETARY SEWARD.

EXECUTIVE MANSION, WASHINGTON, D. C., November 23, 1863.

MY DEAR SIR:—Two despatches since I saw you; one not quite so late on firing as we had before, but giving the points that Burnside thinks he can hold the place, that he is not closely invested, and that he forages across the river. The other brings the firing up to 11 A.M. yesterday, being twenty-three hours later than we had before.
Yours truly,
A. LINCOLN.

TELEGRAM TO GENERAL GRANT.

WASHINGTON, November 25, 1863. 8.40 A.M.

MAJOR-GENERAL U.S. GRANT:
Your despatches as to fighting on Monday and Tuesday are here. Well done! Many thanks to all. Remember Burnside.
A. LINCOLN.

TO C. P. KIRKLAND.

EXECUTIVE MANSION, WASHINGTON, December 7, 1863.

CHARLES P. KIRKLAND, ESQ., New York:
I have just received and have read your published letter to the HON. Benjamin R. Curtis. Under the circumstances I may not be the most competent judge, but it appears to me to be a paper of great ability, and for the country's sake more than for my own I thank you for it.
Yours very truly,
A. LINCOLN.

ANNOUNCEMENT OF UNION SUCCESS IN EAST TENNESSEE.

EXECUTIVE MANSION, WASHINGTON, D. C., December 7, 1863.

Reliable information being received that the insurgent force is retreating from East Tennessee, under circumstances rendering it probable that the Union forces cannot hereafter be dislodged from that important position; and esteeming this to be of high national consequence, I recommend that all loyal people do, on receipt of this information, assemble at their places of worship, and render special homage and gratitude to Almighty God for this great advancement of the national cause.
A. LINCOLN.

PROCLAMATION OF AMNESTY AND RECONSTRUCTION. DECEMBER 8, 1863.

BY THE PRESIDENT OF THE UNITED STATES OF AMERICA:

A Proclamation.
Whereas in and by the Constitution of the United States it is provided that the President "shall have power to grant reprieves and pardons for offenses against the United States, except in cases of impeachment;" and,
Whereas a rebellion now exists whereby the loyal State governments of several States have for a long time been subverted, and many persons have committed and are now guilty of treason against the United States; and
Whereas, with reference to said rebellion and treason, laws have been enacted by Congress declaring forfeitures and confiscation of property and liberation of slaves, all upon terms and conditions therein stated, and also declaring that the President was thereby authorized at any time thereafter, by proclamation, to extend to persons who may have participated in the existing rebellion in any State or part thereof pardon and amnesty, with such exceptions and at such times and on such conditions as he may deem expedient for the public welfare; and
Whereas the Congressional declaration for limited and conditional pardon accords with well-established judicial exposition of the pardoning power; and
Whereas, with reference to said rebellion, the President of the United States has issued several proclamations with provisions in regard to the liberation of slaves; and
Whereas it is now desired by some persons heretofore engaged in said rebellion to resume their allegiance to the United States and to reinaugurate loyal State governments within and for their respective States:
Therefore, I, Abraham Lincoln, President of the United States, do proclaim, declare, and make known to all persons who have, directly or by implication, participated in the existing rebellion, except as hereinafter excepted, that a full pardon is hereby granted to them and each of them, with restoration of all rights of property, except as to slaves and in property cases where rights of third parties shall have intervened, and upon the condition that every such person shall take and subscribe an oath and thenceforward keep and maintain said oath inviolate, and which oath shall be registered for permanent preservation and shall be of the tenor and effect following, to wit:
"I, ———, do solemnly swear, in presence of Almighty God, that I will henceforth faithfully support, protect, and defend the Constitution of the United States and the Union of the States thereunder; and that I will in like manner abide by and faithfully support all acts of Congress passed during the existing rebellion with reference to slaves, so long and so far as not repealed, modified, or held void by Congress or by decision of the Supreme Court; and that I will in like manner abide by and faithfully support all proclamations of the President made during the existing rebellion having

reference to slaves, so long and so far as not modified or declared void by decision of the Supreme Court. So help me God."

The persons excepted from the benefits of the foregoing provisions are all who are or shall have been civil or diplomatic officers or agents of the so-called Confederate Government; all who have left judicial stations under the United States to aid the rebellion; all who are or shall have been military or naval officers of said so-called Confederate Government above the rank of colonel in the army or of lieutenant in the navy; all who left seats in the United States Congress to aid the rebellion; all who resigned commissions in the Army or Navy of the United States and afterwards aided the rebellion; and all who have engaged in any way in treating colored persons, or white persons in charge of such, otherwise than lawfully as prisoners of war, and which persons may have been found in the United States service as soldiers, seamen, or in any other capacity.

And I do further proclaim, declare, and make known that whenever, in any of the States of Arkansas, Texas, Louisiana, Mississippi, Tennessee, Alabama, Georgia, Florida, South Carolina, and North Carolina, a number of persons, not less than one-tenth in number of the votes cast in such State at the Presidential election of the year A.D. 1860, each having taken oath aforesaid, and not having since violated it, and being a qualified voter by the election law of the State existing immediately before the so-called act of secession, and excluding all others, shall reestablish a State government which shall be republican and in nowise contravening said oath, such shall be recognized as the true government of the State, and the State shall receive thereunder the benefits of the constitutional provision which declares that "the United States shall guarantee to every State in this Union a republican form of government and shall protect each of them against invasion, and, on application of the legislature, or the EXECUTIVE (when the legislature can not be convened), against domestic violence."

And I do further proclaim, declare, and make known that any provision which may be adopted by such State government in relation to the freed people of such State which shall recognize and declare their permanent freedom, provide for their education, and which may yet be consistent as a temporary arrangement with their present condition as a laboring, landless, and homeless class, will not be objected to by the National EXECUTIVE.

And it is suggested as not improper that in constructing a loyal State government in any State the name of the State, the boundary, the subdivisions, the constitution, and the general code of laws as before the rebellion be maintained, subject only to the modifications made necessary by the conditions hereinbefore stated, and such others, if any, not contravening said co and which may be deemed expedient by those framing the new State government.

To avoid misunderstanding, it may be proper to say that this proclamation, so far as it relates to State governments, has no reference to States wherein loyal State governments have all the while been maintained. And for the same reason it may be proper to further say that whether members sent to Congress from any State shall be admitted to seats constitutionally rests exclusively with the respective Houses, and not to any extent with the EXECUTIVE. And, still further, that this proclamation is intended to present the people of the States wherein the national authority has been suspended and loyal State governments have been subverted a mode in and by which the national authority and loyal State governments may be re-established within said States or in any of them; and while the mode presented is the best the EXECUTIVE can suggest, with his present impressions, it must not be understood that no other possible mode would be acceptable.

Given under my hand at the city of WASHINGTON, the 8th day of December, A. D. 1863, and of the Independence of the United States of America the eighty-eighth.
A. LINCOLN.
By the President: WILLIAM H. SEWARD, Secretary of State.

ANNUAL MESSAGE TO CONGRESS, DECEMBER 8, 1863.

FELLOW-CITIZENS OF THE SENATE AND HOUSE OF REPRESENTATIVES:—
Another year of health, and of sufficiently abundant harvests, has passed. For these, and especially for the improved condition of our national affairs, our renewed and profoundest gratitude to God is due.
We remain in peace and friendship with foreign powers.
The efforts of disloyal citizens of the United States to involve us in foreign wars, to aid an inexcusable insurrection, have been unavailing. Her Britannic Majesty's government, as was justly expected, have exercised their authority to prevent the departure of new hostile expeditions from British ports. The Emperor of France has, by a like proceeding, promptly vindicated the neutrality which he proclaimed at the beginning of the contest. Questions of great intricacy and importance have arisen out of the blockade, and other belligerent operations, between the Government and several of the maritime powers, but they have been discussed, and, as far as was possible, accommodated, in a spirit of

frankness, justice, and mutual good-will. It is especially gratifying that our prize courts, by the impartiality of their adjudications, have commanded the respect and confidence of maritime powers.

The supplemental treaty between the United States and Great Britain for the suppression of the African slave-trade, made on the 17th day of February last, has been duly ratified and carried into execution. It is believed that, so far as American ports and American citizens are concerned, that inhuman and odious traffic has been brought to an end.

I shall submit, for the consideration of the Senate, a convention for the adjustment of possessory claims in Washington Territory, arising out of the treaty of the 15th of June, 1846, between the United States and Great Britain, and which have been the source of some disquiet among the citizens of that now rapidly improving part of the country.

A novel and important question, involving the extent of the maritime jurisdiction of Spain in the waters which surround the island of Cuba, has been debated without reaching an agreement, and it is proposed, in an amicable spirit, to refer it to the arbitrament of a friendly power. A convention for that purpose will be submitted to the Senate.

I have thought it proper, subject to the approval of the Senate, to concur with the interested commercial powers in an arrangement for the liquidation of the Scheldt dues upon the principles which have been heretofore adopted in regard to the imposts upon navigation in the waters of Denmark.

The long-pending controversy between this government and that of Chile touching the seizure at Sitana, in Peru, by Chilean officers, of a large amount in treasure belonging to citizens of the United States has been brought to a close by the award of His Majesty the King of the Belgians, to whose arbitration the question was referred by the parties. The subject was thoroughly and patiently examined by that justly respected magistrate, and although the sum awarded to the claimants may not have been as large as they expected there is no reason to distrust the wisdom of His Majesty's decision. That decision was promptly complied with by Chile when intelligence in regard to it reached that country.

The joint commission under the act of the last session of carrying into effect the convention with Peru on the subject of claims has been organized at Lima, and is engaged in the business intrusted to it.

Difficulties concerning interoceanic transit through Nicaragua are in course of amicable adjustment.

In conformity with principles set forth in my last annual message, I have received a representative from the United States of Colombia, and have accredited a minister to that Republic.

Incidents occurring in the progress of our civil war have forced upon my attention the uncertain state of international questions touching the rights of foreigners in this country and of United States citizens abroad. In regard to some governments these rights are at least partially defined by treaties. In no instance, however, is it expressly stipulated that in the event of civil war a foreigner residing in this country within the lines of the insurgents is to be exempted from the rule which classes him as a belligerent, in whose behalf the government of his country can not expect any privileges or immunities distinct from that character. I regret to say, however, that such claims have been put forward, and in some instances in behalf of foreigners who have lived in the United States the greater part of their lives.

There is reason to believe that many persons born in foreign countries who have declared their intention to become citizens, or who have been fully naturalized have evaded the military duty required of them by denying the fact and thereby throwing upon the Government the burden of proof. It has been found difficult or impracticable to obtain this proof from the want of guides to the proper sources of information. These might be supplied by requiring clerks of courts where declarations of intention may be made or naturalizations effected to send periodically lists of the names of the persons naturalized or declaring their intention to become citizens to the Secretary of the Interior, in whose Department those names might be arranged and printed for general information.

There is also reason to believe that foreigners frequently become citizens of the United States for the sole purpose of evading duties imposed by the laws of their native countries, to which on becoming naturalized here they at once repair, and though never returning to the United States they still claim the interposition of this government as citizens. Many altercations and great prejudices have heretofore arisen out of this abuse. It is therefore submitted to your serious consideration. It might be advisable to fix a limit beyond which no citizen of the United States residing abroad may claim the interposition of his government.

The right of suffrage has often been assumed and exercised by aliens under pretenses of naturalization, which they have disavowed when drafted into the military service. I submit the expediency of such an amendment of the law as will make the fact of voting an estoppe against any plea of exemption from military service or other civil obligation on the ground of alienage.

In common with other Western powers, our relations with Japan have been brought into serious jeopardy through the perverse opposition of the hereditary aristocracy of the Empire to the enlightened and liberal policy of the Tycoon, designed to bring the country into the society of nations. It is hoped, although not with entire confidence, that these difficulties may be peacefully overcome. I ask your attention to the claim of the minister residing there for the damages he sustained in the destruction by fire of the residence of the legation at Yedo.

Satisfactory arrangements have been made with the Emperor of Russia, which, it is believed, will result in effecting a continuous line of telegraph through that Empire from our Pacific coast.

I recommend to your favorable consideration the subject of an international telegraph across the Atlantic Ocean, and also of a telegraph between this capital and the national forts along the Atlantic seaboard and the Gulf of Mexico. Such communications, established with any reasonable outlay, would be economical as well as effective aids to the diplomatic, military, and naval service.

The consular system of the United States, under the enactments of the last Congress, begins to be self-sustaining, and there is reason to hope that it may become entirely so with the increase of trade which will ensue whenever peace is restored. Our ministers abroad have been faithful in defending American rights. In protecting commercial interests our consuls have necessarily had to encounter increased labors and responsibilities growing out of the war. These they have for the most part met and discharged with zeal and efficiency. This acknowledgment justly includes those consuls who, residing in Morocco, Egypt, Turkey, Japan, China, and other Oriental countries, are charged with complex functions and extraordinary powers.

The condition of the several organized Territories is generally satisfactory, although Indian disturbances in New Mexico have not been entirely suppressed. The mineral resources of Colorado, Nevada, Idaho, New Mexico, and Arizona are proving far richer than has been heretofore understood. I lay before you a communication on this subject from the Governor of New Mexico. I again submit to your consideration the expediency of establishing a system for the encouragement of immigration. Although this source of national wealth and strength is again flowing with greater freedom than for several years before the insurrection occurred, there is still a great deficiency of laborers in every field of industry, especially in agriculture and in our mines, as well of iron and coal as of the precious metals. While the demand for labor is much increased here, tens of thousands of persons, destitute of remunerative occupation, are thronging our foreign consulates and offering to emigrate to the United States if essential, but very cheap, assistance can be afforded them. It is easy to see that under the sharp discipline of civil war the nation is beginning a new life. This noble effort demands the aid and ought to receive the attention and support of the Government.

Injuries unforeseen by the Government and unintended may in some cases have been inflicted on the subjects or citizens of foreign countries, both at sea and on land, by persons in the service of the United States. As this government expects redress from other powers when similar injuries are inflicted by persons in their service upon citizens of the United States, we must be prepared to do justice to foreigners. If the existing judicial tribunals are inadequate to this purpose, a special court may be authorized, with power to hear and decide such claims of the character referred to as may have arisen under treaties and the public law. Conventions for adjusting the claims by joint commission have been proposed to some governments, but no definitive answer to the proposition has yet been received from any.

In the course of the session I shall probably have occasion to request you to provide indemnification to claimants where decrees of restitution have been rendered and damages awarded by admiralty courts, and in other cases where this government may be acknowledged to be liable in principle and where the amount of that liability has been ascertained by an informal arbitration.

The proper officers of the Treasury have deemed themselves required by the law of the United States upon the subject to demand a tax upon the incomes of foreign consuls in this country. While such a demand may not in strictness be in derogation of public law, or perhaps of any existing treaty between the United States and a foreign country, the expediency of so far modifying the act as to exempt from tax the income of such consuls as are not citizens of the United States, derived from the emoluments of their office or from property not situated in the United States, is submitted to your serious consideration. I make this suggestion upon the ground that a comity which ought to be reciprocated exempts our consuls in all other countries from taxation to the extent thus indicated. The United States, I think, ought not to be exceptionally illiberal to international trade and commerce.

The operations of the Treasury during the last year have been successfully conducted. The enactment by Congress of a national banking law has proved a valuable support of the public credit, and the general legislation in relation to loans has fully answered the expectations of its favorers. Some amendments may be required to perfect existing laws, but no change in their principles or general scope is believed to be needed.

Since these measures have been in operation all demands on the Treasury, including the pay of the Army and Navy, have been promptly met and fully satisfied. No considerable body of troops, it is believed, were ever more amply provided and more liberally and punctually paid, and it may be added that by no people were the burdens incident to a great war ever more cheerfully borne.

The receipts during the year from all sources, including loans and balance in the Treasury at its commencement, were $901,125,674.86, and the aggregate disbursements $895,796,630.65, leaving a balance on the 1st of July, 1863, of $5,329,044.21. Of the receipts there were derived from customs $69,059,642.40, from internal revenue $37,640,787.95, from direct tax $1,485,103.61, from lands $167,617.17, from miscellaneous sources $3,046,615.35, and from loans $776,682,361.57, making the aggregate $901,125,674.86. Of the disbursements there were for the civil service $23,253,922.08, for pensions and Indians $4,216,520.79, for interest on public debt $24,729,846.51, for the War Department $599,298,600.83, for the Navy Department $63,211,105.27, for payment of funded and temporary debt $181,086,635.07, making the aggregate $895,796,630.65 and leaving the balance of $5,329,044.21. But the payment of funded and temporary debt, having been made from moneys borrowed during the year, must be regarded as merely nominal payments and the moneys borrowed to make them as merely nominal receipts, and their amount,

$181,086,635.07, should therefore be deducted both from receipts and disbursements. This being done there remains as actual receipts $720,039,039.79 and the actual disbursements $714,709,995.58, leaving the balance as already stated. The actual receipts and disbursements for the first quarter and the estimated receipts and disbursements for the remaining three-quarters of the current fiscal year (1864) will be shown in detail by the report of the Secretary of the Treasury, to which I invite your attention. It is sufficient to say here that it is not believed that actual results will exhibit a state of the finances less favorable to the country than the estimates of that officer heretofore submitted while it is confidently expected that at the close of the year both disbursements and debt will be found very considerably less than has been anticipated.

The report of the Secretary of War is a document of great interest. It consists of:

1. The military operations of the year, detailed in the report of the General in Chief.
2. The organization of colored persons into the war service.
3. The exchange of prisoners, fully set forth in the letter of General Hitchcock.
4. The operations under the act for enrolling and calling out the national forces, detailed in the report of the Provost Marshal General.
5. The organization of the invalid corps, and
6. The operation of the several departments of the Quartermaster-General, Commissary-General, Paymaster-General, Chief of Engineers, Chief of Ordnance, and Surgeon-General.

It has appeared impossible to make a valuable summary of this report, except such as would be too extended for this place, and hence I content myself by asking your careful attention to the report itself.

The duties devolving on the naval branch of the service during the year and throughout the whole of this unhappy contest have been discharged with fidelity and eminent success. The extensive blockade has been constantly increasing in efficiency as the Navy has expanded, yet on so long a line it has so far been impossible to entirely suppress illicit trade. From returns received at the Navy Department it appears that more than 1,000 vessels have been captured since the blockade was instituted? and that the value of prizes already sent in for adjudication amounts to over $13,000,000. The naval force of the United States consists at this time of five hundred and eighty-eight vessels completed and in the course of completion, and of these seventy-five are ironclad or armored steamers. The events of the war give an increased interest and importance to the Navy which will probably extend beyond the war itself.

The armored vessels in our Navy completed and in service, or which are under contract and approaching completion, are believed to exceed in number those of any other power; but while these may be relied upon for harbor defense and coast service, others of greater strength and capacity will be necessary for cruising purposes and to maintain our rightful position on the ocean.

The change that has taken place in naval vessels and naval warfare since the introduction of steam as a motive power for ships of war demands either a corresponding change in some of our existing navy yards or the establishment of new ones for the construction and necessary repair of modern naval vessels. No inconsiderable embarrassment, delay, and public injury have been experienced from the want of such governmental establishments. The necessity of such a navy-yard, so furnished, at some suitable place upon the Atlantic seaboard has on repeated occasions been brought to the attention of Congress by the Navy Department, and is again presented in the report of the Secretary which accompanies this communication. I think it my duty to invite your special attention to this subject, and also to that of establishing a yard and depot for naval purposes upon one of the Western rivers. A naval force has been created on those interior waters, and under many disadvantages, within little more than two years, exceeding in numbers the whole naval force of the country at the commencement of the present Administration. Satisfactory and important as have been the performances of the heroic men of the Navy at this interesting period, they are scarcely more wonderful than the success of our mechanics and artisans in the production of war vessels, which has created a new form of naval power.

Our country has advantages superior to any other nation in our resources of iron and timber, with inexhaustible quantities of fuel in the immediate vicinity of both, and all available and in close proximity to navigable waters. Without the advantage of public works, the resources of the nation have been developed and its power displayed in the construction of a Navy of such magnitude, which has at the very period of its creation rendered signal service to the Union.

The increase of the number of seamen in the public service from 7,500 men in the spring of 1861 to about 34,000 at the present time has been accomplished without special legislation or extraordinary bounties to promote that increase. It has been found, however, that the operation of the draft, with the high bounties paid for army recruits, is beginning to affect injuriously the naval service, and will, if not corrected, be likely to impair its efficiency by detaching seamen from their proper vocation and inducing them to enter the Army. I therefore respectfully suggest that Congress might aid both the army and naval services by a definite provision on this subject which would at the same time be equitable to the communities more especially interested.

I commend to your consideration the suggestions of the Secretary of the Navy in regard to the policy of fostering and training seamen and also the education of officers and engineers for the naval service. The Naval Academy is rendering signal service in preparing midshipmen for the highly responsible duties which in after life they will be required to perform. In order that the country should not be deprived of the proper quota of educated officers, for which legal provision has been made at the naval school, the vacancies caused by the neglect or omission to make nominations from the States in insurrection have been filled by the Secretary of the Navy. The school is now more full and complete than at any former period, and in every respect entitled to the favorable consideration of Congress.

During the past fiscal year the financial condition of the Post-Office Department has been one of increasing prosperity, and I am gratified in being able to state that the actual postal revenue has nearly equaled the entire expenditures, the latter amounting to $11,314,206.84 and the former to $11,163,789.59, leaving a deficiency of but $150,417.25. In 1860, the year immediately preceding the rebellion, the deficiency amounted to $5,656,705.49, the postal receipts of that year being $2,645,722.19 less that those of 1863. The decrease since 1860 in the annual amount of transportation has been only about twenty-five per cent, but the annual expenditure on account of the same has been reduced thirty-five per cent. It is manifest, therefore, that the Post-Office Department may become self-sustaining in a few years, even with the restoration of the whole service.

The international conference of postal delegates from the principal countries of Europe and America, which was called at the suggestion of the Postmaster-General, met at Paris on the 11th of May last and concluded its deliberations on the 8th of June. The principles established by the conference as best adapted to facilitate postal intercourse between nations and as the basis of future postal conventions inaugurate a general system of uniform international charges at reduced rates of postage, and can not fail to produce beneficial results.

I refer you to the report of the Secretary of the Interior, which is herewith laid before you, for useful and varied information in relation to the public lands, Indian affairs, patents, pensions, and other matters of public concern pertaining to his Department.

The quantity of land disposed of during the last and the first quarter of the present fiscal years was 3,841,549 acres, of which 161,911 acres were sold for cash, 1,456,514 acres were taken up under the homestead law, and the residue disposed of under laws granting lands for military bounties, for railroad and other purposes. It also appears that the sale of the public lands is largely on the increase.

It has long been a cherished opinion of some of our wisest statesmen that the people of the United States had a higher and more enduring interest in the early settlement and substantial cultivation of the public lands than in the amount of direct revenue to be derived from the sale of them. This opinion has had a controlling influence in shaping legislation upon the subject of our national domain. I may cite as evidence of this the liberal measures adopted in reference to actual settlers; the grant to the States of the overflowed lands within their limits, in order to their being reclaimed and rendered fit for cultivation; the grants to railway companies of alternate sections of land upon the contemplated lines of their roads, which when completed will so largely multiply the facilities for reaching our distant possessions. This policy has received its most signal and beneficent illustration in the recent enactment granting homesteads to actual settlers. Since the 1st day of January last the before-mentioned quantity of 1,456,514 acres of land have been taken up under its provisions. This fact and the amount of sales furnish gratifying evidence of increasing settlement upon the public lands, notwithstanding the great struggle in which the energies of the nation have been engaged, and which has required so large a withdrawal of our citizens from their accustomed pursuits. I cordially concur in the recommendation of the Secretary of the Interior suggesting a modification of the act in favor of those engaged in the military and naval service of the United States. I doubt not that Congress will cheerfully adopt such measures as will, without essentially changing the general features of the system, secure to the greatest practicable extent its benefits to those who have left their homes in the defense of the country in this arduous crisis.

I invite your attention to the views of the Secretary as to the propriety of raising by appropriate legislation a revenue from the mineral lands of the United States.

The measures provided at your last session for the removal of certain Indian tribes have been carried into effect. Sundry treaties have been negotiated, which will in due time be submitted for the constitutional action of the Senate. They contain stipulations for extinguishing the possessory rights of the Indians to large and valuable tracts of lands. It is hoped that the effect of these treaties will result in the establishment of permanent friendly relations with such of these tribes as have been brought into frequent and bloody collision with our outlying settlements and emigrants. Sound policy and our imperative duty to these wards of the Government demand our anxious and constant attention to their material well-being, to their progress in the arts of civilization, and, above all, to that moral training which under the blessing of Divine Providence will confer upon them the elevated and sanctifying influences, the hopes and consolations, of the Christian faith.

I suggested in my last annual message the propriety of remodeling our Indian system. Subsequent events have satisfied me of its necessity. The details set forth in the report of the Secretary evince the urgent need for immediate legislative action.

I commend the benevolent institutions established or patronized by the Government in this District to your generous and fostering care.

The attention of Congress during the last session was engaged to some extent with a proposition for enlarging the water communication between the Mississippi River and the northeastern seaboard, which proposition, however, failed for the time. Since then, upon a call of the greatest respectability, a convention has been held at Chicago upon the same subject, a summary of whose views is contained in a memorial addressed to the President and Congress, and which I now have the honor to lay before you. That this interest is one which ere long will force its own way I do not entertain a doubt, while it is submitted entirely to your wisdom as to what can be done now. Augmented interest is given to this subject by the actual commencement of work upon the Pacific Railroad, under auspices so favorable to rapid progress and completion. The enlarged navigation becomes a palpable need to the great road.

I transmit the second annual report of the Commissioner of the Department of Agriculture, asking your attention to the developments in that vital interest of the nation.

When Congress assembled a year ago, the war had already lasted nearly twenty months, and there had been many conflicts on both land and sea, with varying results; the rebellion had been pressed back into reduced limits; yet the tone of public feeling and opinion, at home and abroad, was not satisfactory. With other signs, the popular elections then just past indicated uneasiness among ourselves, while, amid much that was cold and menacing, the kindest words coming from Europe were uttered in accents of pity that we are too blind to surrender a hopeless cause. Our commerce was suffering greatly by a few armed vessels built upon and furnished from foreign shores, and we were threatened with such additions from the same quarter as would sweep our trade from the sea and raise our blockade. We had failed to elicit from European governments anything hopeful upon this subject. The preliminary emancipation proclamation, issued in September, was running its assigned period to the beginning of the new year. A month later the final proclamation came, including the announcement that colored men of suitable condition would be received into the war service. The policy of emancipation and of employing black soldiers gave to the future a new aspect, about which hope and fear and doubt contended in uncertain conflict. According to our political system, as a matter of civil administration, the General Government had no lawful power to effect emancipation in any State, and for a long time it had been hoped that the rebellion could be suppressed without resorting to it as a military measure. It was all the while deemed possible that the necessity for it might come, and that if it should the crisis of the contest would then be presented. It came, and, as was anticipated, it was followed by dark and doubtful days. Eleven months having now passed, we are permitted to take another review. The rebel borders are pressed still farther back, and by the complete opening of the Mississippi the country dominated by the rebellion is divided into distinct parts, with no practical communication between them. Tennessee and Arkansas have been substantially cleared of insurgent control, and influential citizens in each, owners of slaves and advocates of slavery at the beginning of the rebellion, now declare openly for emancipation in their respective States. Of those States not included in the emancipation proclamation, Maryland and Missouri, neither of which three years ago would tolerate any restraint upon the extension of slavery into new Territories, dispute now only as to the best mode of removing it within their own limits.

Of those who were slaves at the beginning of the rebellion full 100,000 are now in the United States military service, about one-half of which number actually bear arms in the ranks, thus giving the double advantage of taking so much labor from the insurgent cause and supplying the places which otherwise must be filled with so many white men. So far as tested, it is difficult to say they are not as good soldiers as any. No servile insurrection or tendency to violence or cruelty has marked the measures of emancipation and arming the blacks. These measures have been much discussed in foreign countries, and, contemporary with such discussion, the tone of public sentiment there is much improved. At home the same measures have been fully discussed, supported, criticized, and denounced, and the annual elections following are highly encouraging to those whose official duty it is to bear the country through this great trial. Thus we have the new reckoning. The crisis which threatened to divide the friends of the Union is past.

Looking now to the present and future, and with reference to a resumption of the national authority within the States wherein that authority has been suspended, I have thought fit to issue a proclamation, a copy of which is herewith transmitted. On examination of this proclamation it will appear, as is believed, that nothing will be attempted beyond what is amply justified by the Constitution. True, the form of an oath is given, but no man is coerced to take it. The man is promised a pardon only in case he voluntarily takes the oath. The Constitution authorizes the Executive to grant or withhold the pardon at his own absolute discretion, and this includes the power to grant on terms, as is fully established by judicial and other authorities.

It is also proffered that if in any of the States named a State government shall be in the mode prescribed set up, such government shall be recognized and guaranteed by the United States, and that under it the State shall, on the constitutional conditions, be protected against invasion and domestic violence. The constitutional obligation of the United States to guarantee to every State in the Union a republican form of government and to protect the State in the cases stated is explicit and full. But why tender the benefits of this provision only to a State government set up in this particular way? This section of the Constitution contemplates a case wherein the element within a State favorable to republican government in the Union may be too feeble for an opposite and hostile element external to or even within the State, and such are precisely the cases with which we are now dealing.

An attempt to guarantee and protect a revived State government, constructed in whole or in preponderating part from the very element against whose hostility and violence it is to be protected, is simply absurd. There must be a test by which to separate the opposing elements, so as to build only from the sound; and that test is a sufficiently liberal one which accepts as sound whoever will make a sworn recantation of his former unsoundness.

But if it be proper to require as a test of admission to the political body an oath of allegiance to the Constitution of the United States and to the Union under it, why also to the laws and proclamations in regard to slavery? Those laws and proclamations were enacted and put forth for the purpose of aiding in the suppression of the rebellion. To give them their fullest effect there had to be a pledge for their maintenance. In my judgment, they have aided and will further aid the cause for which they were intended. To now abandon them would be not only to relinquish a lever of power, but would also be a cruel and an astounding breach of faith. I may add at this point that while I remain in my present position I shall not attempt to retract or modify the emancipation proclamation, nor shall I return to slavery any person who is free by the terms of that proclamation or by any of the acts of Congress. For these and other reasons it is thought best that support of these measures shall be included in the oath, and it is believed the Executive may lawfully claim it in return for pardon and restoration of forfeited rights, which he has clear constitutional power to withhold altogether or grant upon the terms which he shall deem wisest for the public interest. It should be observed also that this part of the oath is subject to the modifying and abrogating power of legislation and supreme judicial decision.

The proposed acquiescence of the National Executive in any reasonable temporary State arrangement for the freed people is made with the view of possibly modifying the confusion and destitution which must at best attend all classes by a total revolution of labor throughout whole States. It is hoped that the already deeply afflicted people in those States may be somewhat more ready to give up the cause of their affliction if to this extent this vital matter be left to themselves, while no power of the National Executive to prevent an abuse is abridged by the proposition.

The suggestion in the proclamation as to maintaining the political framework of the States on what is called reconstruction is made in the hope that it may do good without danger of harm. It will save labor and avoid great confusion.

But why any proclamation now upon this subject? This question is beset with the conflicting views that the step might be delayed too long or be taken too soon. In some States the elements for resumption seem ready for action, but remain inactive apparently for want of a rallying point—a plan of action. Why shall A adopt the plan of B rather than B that of A? And if A and B should agree, how can they know but that the General Government here will reject their plan? By the proclamation a plan is presented which may be accepted by them as a rallying point, and which they are assured in advance will not be rejected here. This may bring them to act sooner than they otherwise would.

The objections to a premature presentation of a plan by the National Executive consist in the danger of committals on points which could be more safely left to further developments. Care has been taken to so shape the document as to avoid embarrassments from this source. Saying that on certain terms certain classes will be pardoned with rights restored, it is not said that other classes or other terms will never be included. Saying that reconstruction will be accepted if presented in a specified way, it is not said it will never be accepted in any other way.

The movements by State action for emancipation in several of the States not included in the emancipation proclamation are matters of profound gratulation. And while I do not repeat in detail what I have heretofore so earnestly urged upon this subject my general views and feelings remain unchanged and I trust that Congress will omit no fair opportunity of aiding these important steps to a great consummation.

In the midst of other cares, however important we must not lose sight of the fact that the war power is still our main reliance. To that power alone we look yet for a time to give confidence to the people in the contested regions that the insurgent power will not again overrun them. Until that confidence shall be established little can be done anywhere what is called reconstruction. Hence our chiefest care must still be directed to the Army and Navy who have thus far borne their harder part so nobly and well; and it may be esteemed fortunate that giving the greatest efficiency to these indispensable arms we do also honorably recognize the gallant men, from commander to sentinel, who compose them, and to whom more than to others the world must stand indebted for the home of freedom disenthralled, regenerated, enlarged, and perpetuated.

A. LINCOLN.

MESSAGE TO CONGRESS. WASHINGTON D. C., December 8, 1863.

TO THE SENATE AND HOUSE OF REPRESENTATIVES:

In conformity to the law of July 16, 1862, I most cordially recommend that Captain John Rogers United States Navy, receive a vote of thanks from Congress for the eminent skill and gallantry exhibited by him in the engagement with the rebel armed ironclad steamer Fingal, alias Atlanta, whilst in command of the United States ironclad steamer Weehawken, which led to her capture on the 17th June, 1863, and also for the zeal, bravery, and general good conduct shown by this officer on many occasions.

This recommendation is specially made in order to comply with the requirements of the ninth section of the aforesaid act, which is in the following words, viz:

That any line officer of the Navy or Marine Corps may be advanced one grade if upon recommendation of the President by name he receives the thanks of Congress for highly distinguished conduct in conflict with the enemy or for extraordinary heroism in the line of his profession.

A. LINCOLN.

MESSAGE TO THE SENATE. WASHINGTON, D. C., December 8, 1863.

TO THE SENATE OF THE UNITED STATES:

Congress, on my recommendation, passed a resolution, approved 7th February, 1863, tendering its thanks to Commander D. D. Porter "for the bravery and skill displayed in the attack on the post of Arkansas on the 10th January, 1863," and in consideration of those services, together with his efficient labors and vigilance subsequently displayed in thwarting the efforts of the rebels to obstruct the Mississippi and its tributaries and the important part rendered by the squadron under his command, which led to the surrender of Vicksburg.

I do therefore, in conformity to the seventh section of the act approved 16th July, 1862, nominate Commander D. D. Porter to be a rear-admiral in the Navy on the active list from the 4th July, 1863, to fill an existing vacancy.

A. LINCOLN.

TELEGRAM TO GENERAL U. S. GRANT.

WASHINGTON, December 8, 1863.

MAJOR-GENERAL GRANT:

Understanding that your lodgment at Chattanooga and Knoxville is now secure, I wish to tender you, and all under your command, my more than thanks, my profoundest gratitude, for the skill, courage, and perseverance with which you and they, over so great difficulties, have effected that important object. God bless you all!

A. LINCOLN.

TO GOVERNOR CURTIN.

EXECUTIVE MANSION, WASHINGTON, December 9, 1863

HIS EXCELLENCY A. G. CURTIN,
Governor of Pennsylvania.

DEAR SIR:—I have to urge my illness, and the preparation of the message, in excuse for not having sooner transmitted you the inclosed from the Secretary of War and Provost Marshal General in response to yours in relation to recruiting in Pennsylvania. Though not quite as you desire, I hope the grounds taken will be reasonably satisfactory to you. Allow me to exchange congratulations with you on the organization of the House of Representatives, and especially on recent military events in Georgia and Tennessee.

Yours very truly,
A. LINCOLN.

TELEGRAM TO GENERAL BUTLER.

EXECUTIVE MANSION, WASHINGTON, D. C., December 10, 1863.

MAJOR-GENERAL BUTLER, Fort Monroe, Va.:
Please suspend execution in any and all sentences of death in your department until further order.
A. LINCOLN.

TELEGRAM TO GENERAL MEADE.

EXECUTIVE MANSION, WASHINGTON, December 11, 1863.

MAJOR-GENERAL MEADE, Army of the Potomac:
Lieut. Col. James B. Knox, Tenth Regiment Pennsylvania Reserves, offers his resignation under circumstances inducing me to wish to accept it. But I prefer to know your pleasure upon the subject. Please answer.
A. LINCOLN.

TO JUDGE HOFFMAN.

EXECUTIVE MANSION, December 15, 1863.

HON. OGDEN HOFFMAN, U. S. District Judge, San Francisco, Cal.:
The oath in the proclamation of December 8 is intended for those who may voluntarily take it, and not for those who may be constrained to take it in order to escape actual imprisonment or punishment. It is intended that the latter class shall abide the granting or withholding of the pardoning power in the ordinary way.
A. LINCOLN.

TELEGRAM TO MARY GONYEAG.

EXECUTIVE MANSION, WASHINGTON, December 15, 1863.

MOTHER MARY GONYEAG, Superior, Academy of Visitation, Keokuk, Iowa:
The President has no authority as to whether you may raffle for the benevolent object you mention. If there is no objection in the Iowa laws, there is none here.
A. LINCOLN.

PROCLAMATION CONCERNING DISCRIMINATING DUTIES, DECEMBER 16, 1863.

BY THE PRESIDENT OF THE UNITED STATES OF AMERICA:

A Proclamation.
Whereas by an act of the Congress of the United States of the 24th of May, 1828, entitled "An act in addition to an act entitled 'An act concerning discriminating duties of tonnage and impost' and to equalize the duties on Prussian vessels and their cargoes," it is provided that upon satisfactory evidence being given to the President of the United States by the government of any foreign nation that no discriminating duties of tonnage or impost are imposed or levied in the

ports of the said nation upon vessels wholly belonging to citizens of the United States or upon the produce, manufactures, or merchandise imported in the same from the United States or from any foreign country, the President is thereby authorized to issue his proclamation declaring that the foreign discriminating duties of tonnage and impost within the United States are and shall be suspended and discontinued so far as respects the vessels of the said foreign nation and the produce, manufactures, or merchandise imported into the United States in the same from the said foreign nation or from any other foreign country, the said suspension to take effect from the time of such notification being given to the President of the United States and to continue so long as the reciprocal exemption of vessels belonging to citizens of the United States and their cargoes, as aforesaid, shall be continued, and no longer; and

Whereas satisfactory evidence has lately been received by me through an official communication of Senor Don Luis Molina, Envoy Extraordinary and Minister Plenipotentiary of the Republic of Nicaragua, under date of the 28th of November, 1863, that no other or higher duties of tonnage and impost have been imposed or levied since the second day of August, 1838, in the ports of Nicaragua, upon vessels wholly belonging to citizens of the United States, and upon the produce, manufactures, or merchandise imported in the same from the United States, and from any foreign country whatever, than are levied on Nicaraguan ships and their cargoes in the same ports under like circumstances:

Now, therefore, I, Abraham Lincoln, President of the United States of America, do hereby declare and proclaim that so much of the several acts imposing discriminating duties of tonnage and impost within the United States are, and shall be, suspended and discontinued so far as respects the vessels of Nicaragua, and the produce, manufactures, and the merchandise imported into the United States in the same from the dominions of Nicaragua, and from any other foreign country whatever; the said suspension to take effect from the day above mentioned, and to continue thenceforward so long as the reciprocal exemption of the vessels of the United States, and the produce, manufactures, and merchandise imported into the dominions of Nicaragua in the same, as aforesaid, shall be continued on the part of the government of Nicaragua.

Given under my hand at the city of Washington, the sixteenth day of December, in the year of our Lord one thousand eight hundred and sixty-three, and the eighty-eighth of the Independence of the United States.

A. LINCOLN.

By the President: WILLIAM H. SEWARD, Secretary of State.

MESSAGE TO CONGRESS,

DECEMBER 17, 1863.

TO THE SENATE AND HOUSE OF REPRESENTATIVES OF THE UNITED STATES:

Herewith I lay before you a letter addressed to myself by a committee of gentlemen representing the freedmen's aid societies in Boston, New York, Philadelphia, and Cincinnati. The subject of the letter, as indicated above, is one of great magnitude and importance, and one which these gentlemen, of known ability and high character, seem to have considered with great attention and care. Not having the time to form a mature judgment of my own as to whether the plan they suggest is the best, I submit the whole subject to Congress, deeming that their attention thereto is almost imperatively demanded.

A. LINCOLN.

TELEGRAM TO GENERAL HURLBUT.

[Cipher.]

EXECUTIVE MANSION, WASHINGTON, D. C., December 17, 1863.
MAJOR-GENERAL HURLBUT, Memphis, Tenn.:

I understand you have under sentence of death, a tall old man, by the name of Henry F. Luckett. I personally knew him, and did not think him a bad man. Please do not let him be executed unless upon further order from me, and in the meantime send me a transcript of the record.

A. LINCOLN.

TELEGRAM TO GENERAL U.S. GRANT.

WAR DEPARTMENT, WASHINGTON, December 19, 1863.

GENERAL GRANT, Chattanooga, Tennessee:
The Indiana delegation in Congress, or at least a large part of them, are very anxious that General Milroy shall enter active service again, and I share in this feeling. He is not a difficult man to satisfy, sincerity and courage being his strong traits. Believing in our cause, and wanting to fight for it, is the whole matter with him. Could you, without embarrassment, assign him a place, if directed to report to you?
A. LINCOLN.

TO SECRETARY STANTON.

(Private.)

EXECUTIVE MANSION, WASHINGTON, D. C., December 21, 1863.
HON. SECRETARY OF WAR.
MY DEAR SIR:—Sending a note to the Secretary of the Navy, as I promised, he called over and said that the strikes in the ship-yards had thrown the completion of vessels back so much that he thought General Gilimore's proposition entirely proper. He only wishes (and in which I concur) that General Gillmore will courteously confer with, and explain to, Admiral Dahlgren.
In regard to the Western matter, I believe the program will have to stand substantially as I first put it. Henderson, and especially Brown, believe that the social influence of St. Louis would inevitably tell injuriously upon General Pope in the particular difficulty existing there, and I think there is some force in that view.
As to retaining General Schofield temporarily, if this should be done, I believe I should scarcely be able to get his nomination through the Senate. Send me over his nomination, which, however, I am not quite ready to send to the Senate.
Yours as ever,
A. LINCOLN.

TO O. D. FILLEY.

EXECUTIVE MANSION, WASHINGTON, December 22, 1863.

O. D. FILLEY, ST. Louis, Missouri:
I have just looked over a petition signed by some three dozen citizens of St. Louis, and three accompanying letters, one by yourself, one by a Mr. Nathan Ranney, and one by a Mr. John D. Coalter, the whole relating to the Rev. Dr. McPheeters. The petition prays, in the name of justice and mercy, that I will restore Dr. McPheeters to all his ecclesiastical rights. This gives no intimation as to what ecclesiastical rights are withheld.
Your letter states that Provost-Marshal Dick, about a year ago, ordered the arrest of Dr. McPheeters, pastor of the Vine Street Church, prohibited him from officiating, and placed the management of the affairs of the church out of the control of its chosen trustees; and near the close you state that a certain course "would insure his release." Mr. Ranney's letter says: "Dr. Samuel S. McPheeters is enjoying all the rights of a civilian, but cannot preach the Gospel!!!!" Mr. Coalter, in his letter, asks: "Is it not a strange illustration of the condition of things, that the question of who shall be allowed to preach in a church in St. Louis shall be decided by the President of the United States?"
Now, all this sounds very strangely; and, withal, a little as if you gentlemen making the application do not understand the case alike; one affirming that the doctor is enjoying all the rights of a civilian, and another pointing out to me what will secure his release! On the second day of January last, I wrote to General Curtis in relation to Mr. Dick's order upon Dr. McPheeters; and, as I suppose the doctor is enjoying all the rights of a civilian, I only quote that part of my letter which relates to the church. It is as follows: "But I must add that the United States Government must not, as by this

order, undertake to run the churches. When an individual, in a church or out of it, becomes dangerous to the public interest, he must be checked; but the churches, as such, must take care of themselves. It will not do for the United States to appoint trustees, supervisors, or other agents for the churches."

This letter going to General Curtis, then in command there, I supposed, of course, it was obeyed, especially as I heard no further complaint from Dr. McPheeters or his friends for nearly an entire year. I have never interfered, nor thought of interfering, as to who shall or shall not preach in any church; nor have I knowingly or believingly tolerated any one else to so interfere by my authority. If any one is so interfering by color of my authority, I would like to have it specifically made known to me. If, after all, what is now sought is to have me put Dr. McPheeters back over the heads of a majority of his own congregation, that, too, will be declined. I will not have control of any church on any side.

Yours respectfully,
A. LINCOLN.

TELEGRAM TO MILITARY COMMANDER AT POINT LOOKOUT.

EXECUTIVE MANSION, WASHINGTON, December 22, 1863.

MILITARY COMMANDER, Point Lookout, Md.:

If you have a prisoner by the name Linder—Daniel Linder, I think, and certainly the son of U. F. Linder, of Illinois, please send him to me by an officer.

A. LINCOLN.

TELEGRAM TO MILITARY COMMANDER AT POINT LOOKOUT.

EXECUTIVE MANSION, WASHINGTON, D. C., December 24, 1863.

MILITARY COMMANDER, Point Lookout, Md.:

If you send Linder to me as directed a day or two ago, also send Edwin C. Claybrook, of Ninth Virginia rebel cavalry.

A. LINCOLN.

TELEGRAM TO U. F. LINDER.

EXECUTIVE MANSION, WASHINGTON D. C., December 26, 1863.

HON. U. F. LINDER, Chicago, Ill.: Your son Dan has just left me with my order to the Secretary of War, to administer to him the oath of allegiance, discharge him and send him to you.

A. LINCOLN.

TO GENERAL N. P. BANKS.

EXECUTIVE MANSION, WASHINGTON, December 29, 1863.

MAJOR-GENERAL BANKS:

Yours of the sixteenth is received, and I send you, as covering the ground of it, a copy of my answer to yours of the sixth, it being possible the original may not reach you. I intend you to be master in every controversy made with you.

Yours truly,
A. LINCOLN.

TELEGRAM TO GENERAL BUTLER.

EXECUTIVE MANSION, WASHINGTON, D. C., December 30, 1863.

MAJOR-GENERAL BUTLER, Fort Monroe, Va.:
Jacob Bowers is fully pardoned for past offence, upon condition that he returns to duty and re-enlists for three years or during the war.
A. LINCOLN.

TO SECRETARY STANTON.

EXECUTIVE MANSION WASHINGTON, December 31, 1863.

HON. SECRETARY OF WAR.
SIR:—Please fix up the department to which Curtis is to go, without waiting to wind up the Missouri matter. Lane is very anxious to have Fort Smith in it, and I am willing, unless there be decided military reasons to the contrary, in which case of course, I am not for it. It will oblige me to have the Curtis department fixed at once.
Yours truly,
A. LINCOLN.

1864

TELEGRAM TO GENERAL SULLIVAN.
WAR DEPARTMENT, WASHINGTON, D.C., January 1, 1864. 3.30 p.m.
GENERAL SULLIVAN, Harper's Ferry:
Have you anything new from Winchester, Martinsburg or thereabouts?
A. LINCOLN.

TELEGRAM TO GOVERNOR PIERPOINT.

EXECUTIVE MANSION, WASHINGTON, D. C., January 2, 1864.

GOVERNOR PIERPOINT, Alexandria, Va.:
Please call and see me to-day if not too inconvenient.
A. LINCOLN.

TELEGRAM TO GENERAL BUTLER.

EXECUTIVE MANSION, WASHINGTON, January 2, 1864

MAJOR-GENERAL BUTLER.

SIR:—The Secretary of War and myself have concluded to discharge of the prisoners at Point Lookout the following classes: First, those who will take the oath prescribed in the proclamation of December 8, and issued by the consent of General Marston, will enlist in our service. Second, those who will take the oath and be discharged and whose homes lie safely within our military lines.

I send by Mr. Hay this letter and a blank-book and some other blanks, the way of using which I propose for him to explain verbally better than I can in writing.

Yours, very truly,
A. LINCOLN.

TELEGRAM TO GENERAL MEADE.

EXECUTIVE MANSION, WASHINGTON, January 5, 1864.

MAJOR-GENERAL MEADE:
If not inconsistent with the service, please allow General William Harrow as long a leave of absence as the rules permit with the understanding that I may lengthen it if I see fit. He is an acquaintance and friend of mine, and his family matters very urgently require his presence.
A. LINCOLN.

MESSAGE TO CONGRESS,

JANUARY 5, 1864.

GENTLEMEN OF THE SENATE AND HOUSE OF REPRESENTATIVES:
By a joint resolution of your honorable bodies approved December 23, 1863, the paying of bounties to veteran volunteers, as now practiced by the War Department, is, to the extent of three hundred dollars in each case, prohibited after this 5th day of the present month. I transmit for your consideration a communication from the Secretary of War, accompanied by one from the Provost-Marshal General to him, both relating to the subject above mentioned. I earnestly recommend that the law be so modified as to allow bounties to be paid as they now are, at least until the ensuing 1st day of February.

I am not without anxiety lest I appear to be importunate in thus recalling your attention to a subject upon which you have so recently acted, and nothing but a deep conviction that the public interest demands it could induce me to incur the hazard of being misunderstood on this point. The Executive approval was given by me to the resolution mentioned, and it is now by a closer attention and a fuller knowledge of facts that I feel constrained to recommend a reconsideration of the subject.
A. LINCOLN.

TELEGRAM TO GOVERNOR BRAMLETTE.

EXECUTIVE MANSION, WASHINGTON, January 6, 1864. 2 P.M.

GOVERNOR BRAMLETTE, Frankfort, Kentucky:
Yours of yesterday received. Nothing is known here about General Foster's order, of which you complain, beyond the fair presumption that it comes from General Grant, and that it has an object which, if you understood, you would be loath to frustrate. True, these troops are, in strict law, only to be removed by my order; but General Grant's judgment would be the highest incentive to me to make such order. Nor can I understand how doing so is bad faith and dishonor, nor yet how it so exposes Kentucky to ruin. Military men here do not perceive how it exposes Kentucky, and I am sure Grant would not permit it if it so appeared to him.
A. LINCOLN.

TO GENERAL Q. A. GILLMORE.

EXECUTIVE MANSION, WASHINGTON, January 13, 1864.

MAJOR-GENERAL GILLMORE:
I understand an effort is being made by some worthy gentlemen to reconstruct a legal State government in Florida. Florida is in your Department, and it is not unlikely you may be there in person. I have given Mr. Hay a commission of major, and sent him to you, with some blank-books and other blanks, to aid in the reconstruction. He will explain as to the manner of using the blanks, and also my general views on the subject. It is desirable for all to co-operate, but if irreconcilable differences of opinion shall arise, you are master. I wish the thing done in the most speedy way, so that when done it be within the range of the late proclamation on the subject. The detail labor will, of course, have to be done by others; but I will be greatly obliged if you will give it such general supervision as you can find consistent with your more strictly military duties.
A. LINCOLN.

TELEGRAM TO GOVERNOR BROUGH. EXECUTIVE MANSION, WASHINGTON, January 15, 1864.

GOVERNOR BROUGH, Columbus, Ohio:
If Private William G. Toles, of Fifty-ninth Ohio Volunteers, returns to his regiment and faithfully serves out his term, he is fully pardoned for all military offenses prior to this.
A. LINCOLN.

TO CROSBY AND NICHOLS.

EXECUTIVE MANSION, WASHINGTON, January 16, 1864.

MESSRS. CROSBY AND NICHOLS.
GENTLEMEN: The number for this month and year of the North American Review was duly received, and for which please accept my thanks. Of course I am not the most impartial judge; yet, with due allowance for this, I venture to hope that the article entitled "The President's Policy" will be of value to the country. I fear I am not worthy of all which is therein kindly said of me personally.
The sentence of twelve lines, commencing at the top of page 252, I could wish to be not exactly what it is. In what is there expressed, the writer has not correctly understood me. I have never had a theory that secession could absolve States or people from their obligations. Precisely the contrary is asserted in the inaugural address; and it was because of my belief in the continuation of those obligations that I was puzzled, for a time, as to denying the legal rights of those citizens who remained individually innocent of treason or rebellion. But I mean no more now than to merely call attention to this point.
Yours respectfully,
A. LINCOLN.

TO GENERAL F. STEELE.

EXECUTIVE MANSION, WASHINGTON, January 20, 1864.

MAJOR-GENERAL STEELE:

Sundry citizens of the State of Arkansas petition me that an election may be held in that State, at which to elect a Governor; that it be assumed at that election, and thenceforward, that the constitution and laws of the State, as before the rebellion, are in full force, except that the constitution is so modified as to declare that there shall be neither slavery nor involuntary servitude, except in the punishment of crimes whereof the party shall have been duly convicted; that the General Assembly may make such provisions for the freed people as shall recognize and declare their permanent freedom, and provide for their education, and which may yet be construed as a temporary arrangement suitable to their condition as a laboring, landless, and homeless class; that said election shall be held on the 28th of March, 1864, at all the usual places of the State, or all such as voters may attend for that purpose, that the voters attending at eight o'clock in the morning of said day may choose judges and clerks of election for such purpose; that all persons qualified by said constitution and laws, and taking the oath presented in the President's proclamation of December 8, 1863, either before or at the election, and none others, may be voters; that each set of judges and clerks may make returns directly to you on or before the —th day of —— next; that in all other respects said election may be conducted according to said constitution and laws: that on receipt of said returns, when five thousand four hundred and six votes shall have been cast, you can receive said votes, and ascertain all who shall thereby appear to have been elected; that on the —th day of ——— next, all persons so appearing to have been elected, who shall appear before you at Little Rock, and take the oath, to be by you severally administered, to support the Constitution of the United States and said modified Constitution of the State of Arkansas, may be declared by you qualified and empowered to enter immediately upon the duties of the offices to which they shall have been respectively elected.

You will please order an election to take place on the 28th of March, 1864, and returns to be made in fifteen days thereafter.

A. LINCOLN.

MESSAGE TO CONGRESS, JANUARY 20, 1864

GENTLEMEN OF THE SENATE AND HOUSE OF REPRESENTATIVES:

In accordance with a letter addressed by the Secretary of State, with my approval, to the Hon. Joseph A. Wright, of Indiana, that patriotic and distinguished gentleman repaired to Europe and attended the International Agricultural Exhibition, held at Hamburg last year, and has since his return made a report to me, which, it is believed, can not fail to be of general interest, and especially so to the agricultural community. I transmit for your consideration copies of the letters and report. While it appears by the letter that no reimbursement of expenses or compensation was promised him, I submit whether reasonable allowance should not be made him for them.

A. LINCOLN.

ORDER APPROVING TRADE REGULATIONS.

EXECUTIVE MANSION, WASHINGTON, January 26, 1864.

I, Abraham Lincoln, President of the United States having seen and considered the additional regulations of trade prescribed by the Secretary of the Treasury, and numbered LI, LII, LIII, LIV, LV, and LVI, do hereby approve the same; and I further declare and order that all property brought in for sale, in good faith, and actually sold in pursuance of said Regulations LII, LIII, LIV, LV, and LVI, after the same shall have taken effect and come in force as provided in Regulation LVI, shall be exempt from confiscation or forfeiture to the United States.

A. LINCOLN.

TELEGRAM TO GENERAL FOSTER.

WAR DEPARTMENT, WASHINGTON, D. C., January 27, 1864.

MAJOR-GENERAL FOSTER, Knoxville, Tenn.:
Is a supposed correspondence between General Longstreet and yourself about the amnesty proclamation, which is now in the newspapers, genuine?
A. LINCOLN.

TELEGRAM TO E. STANLEY.

EXECUTIVE MANSION, WASHINGTON, January 28, 1864

HON. EDWARD STANLEY, San Francisco, Cal.:
Yours of yesterday received. We have rumors similar to the dispatch received by you, but nothing very definite from North Carolina. Knowing Mr. Stanley to be an able man, and not doubting that he is a patriot, I should be glad for him to be with his old acquaintances south of Virginia, but I am unable to suggest anything definite upon the subject.
A. LINCOLN.

TO GENERAL H. W. HALLECK.

EXECUTIVE MANSION

WASHINGTON, January 28, 1864.
MAJOR-GENERAL HALLECK:
Some citizens of Missouri, vicinity of Kansas City, are apprehensive that there is special danger of renewed troubles in that neighborhood, and thence on the route toward New Mexico. I am not impressed that the danger is very great or imminent, but I will thank you to give Generals Rosecrans and Curtis, respectively, such orders as may turn their attention thereto and prevent as far as possible the apprehended disturbance.
Yours truly,
A. LINCOLN.

TELEGRAM TO GENERAL SICKLES.

EXECUTIVE MANSION, WASHINGTON, January 29, 1864.

MAJOR-GENERAL SICKLES, New York:
Could you, without it being inconvenient or disagreeable to yourself, immediately take a trip to Arkansas for me?
A. LINCOLN.

TELEGRAM TO GOVERNOR BRAMLETTE.

EXECUTIVE MANSION, WASHINGTON, D. C., January 31, 1864.

GOVERNOR BRAMLETTE, Frankfort, Ky.:
General Boyle's resignation is accepted, so that your Excellency can give him the appointment proposed.
A. LINCOLN.

COLONIZATION EXPERIMENT

ORDER TO SECRETARY STANTON.

EXECUTIVE MANSION, February 1, 1864
HON. EDWIN M. STANTON, Secretary of War.

SIR:-You are directed to have a transport (either a steam or sailing vessel, as may be deemed proper by the Quartermaster-General) sent to the colored colony established by the United States at the island of Vache, on the coast of San Domingo, to bring back to this country such of the colonists there as desire to return. You will have the transport furnished with suitable supplies for that purpose, and detail an officer of the Quartermaster's Department, who, under special instructions to be given, shall have charge of the business. The colonists will be brought to Washington, unless otherwise hereafter directed, and be employed and provided for at the camps for colored persons around that city. Those only will be brought from the island who desire to return, and their effects will be brought with them.
A. LINCOLN.

ORDER FOR A DRAFT OF FIVE HUNDRED THOUSAND MEN.

EXECUTIVE MANSION, February 1, 1864.

Ordered, That a draft of five hundred thousand (500,000) men, to serve for three years or during the war, be made on the tenth (10th) day of March next, for the military service of the United States, crediting and deducting therefrom so many as may have been enlisted or drafted into the service prior to the first (1st) day of March, and not before credited.
A. LINCOLN.

TELEGRAM TO GOVERNOR YATES.

EXECUTIVE MANSION, WASHINGTON, February 3, 1864.

GOVERNOR YATES, Springfield, Ill.:
The United States Government lot in Springfield can be used for a soldiers' home, with the understanding that the Government does not incur any expense in the case.
A. LINCOLN.

TELEGRAM TO GOVERNOR MURPHY.

WASHINGTON, February 6, 1864.

GOVERNOR J. MURPHY:
My order to General Steele about an election was made in ignorance of the action your convention had taken or would take. A subsequent letter directs General Steele to aid you on your own plan, and not to thwart or hinder you. Show this to him.
A. LINCOLN.

THE STORY OF THE EMANCIPATION PROCLAMATION

TOLD BY THE PRESIDENT, TO THE ARTIST F. B. CARPENTER,

FEBRUARY 6, 1864.
"It had got to be," said Mr. Lincoln, "midsummer, 1862. Things had gone on from bad to worse, until I felt that we had reached the end of our rope on the plan of operations we had been pursuing; that we had about played our last card, and must change our tactics, or lose the game. I now determined upon the adoption of the emancipation policy; and without consultation with, or the knowledge of, the Cabinet, I prepared the original draft of the proclamation, and, after much anxious thought, called a Cabinet meeting upon the subject. This was the last of July or the first part of the month of August, 1862. [The exact date was July 22, 1862.]... All were present excepting Mr. Blair, the Postmaster-General, who was absent at the opening of the discussion, but came in subsequently. I said to the Cabinet that I had resolved upon this step, and had not called them together to ask their advice, but to lay the subject-matter of a proclamation before them, suggestions as to which would be in order after they had heard it read. Mr. Lovejoy was in error when he informed you that it excited no comment excepting on the part of Secretary Seward. Various suggestions were offered. Secretary Chase wished the language stronger in reference to the arming of the blacks.

"Mr. Blair, after he came in, deprecated the policy on the ground that it would cost the administration the fall elections. Nothing, however, was offered that I had not already fully anticipated and settled in my mind, until Secretary Seward spoke. He said in substance, 'Mr. President, I approve of the proclamation, but I question the expediency of its issue at this juncture. The depression of the public mind, consequent upon our repeated reverses, is so great that I fear the effect of so important a step. It may be viewed as the last measure of an exhausted government, a cry for help; the government stretching forth its hands to Ethiopia, instead of Ethiopia stretching forth her hands to the government.' His idea," said the President, "was that it would be considered our last shriek on the retreat." [This was his precise expression.] 'Now,' continued Mr. Seward, 'while I approve the measure, I suggest, sir, that you postpone its issue until you can give it to the country supported by military success, instead of issuing it, as would be the case now, upon the greatest disasters of the war.' Mr. Lincoln continued "The wisdom of the view of the Secretary of State struck me with very great force. It was an aspect of the case that, in all my thought upon the subject, I had entirely overlooked. The result was that I put the draft of the proclamation aside, as you do your sketch for a picture, waiting for a victory.

"From time to time I added or changed a line, touching it up here and there, anxiously watching the process of events. Well, the next news we had was of Pope's disaster at Bull Run. Things looked darker than ever. Finally came the week of the battle of Antietam. I determined to wait no longer. The news came, I think, on Wednesday, that the advantage was on our side. I was then staying at the Soldiers' Home [three miles out of Washington]. Here I finished writing the second draft of the preliminary proclamation; came up on Saturday; called the Cabinet together to hear it, and it was published on the following Monday."

TELEGRAM TO GENERAL SEDGWICK.

EXECUTIVE MANSION, WASHINGTON, February 11, 1864.

MAJOR-GENERAL SEDGWICK, Army of Potomac:
Unless there be some strong reason to the contrary, please send General Kilpatrick to us here, for two or three days.
A. LINCOLN.

TELEGRAM TO HORACE MAYNARD.

EXECUTIVE MANSION, WASHINGTON, February 13, 1864.

HON. HORACE MAYNARD, Nashville, Tenn.:
Your letter of [the] second received. Of course Governor Johnson will proceed with reorganization as the exigencies of the case appear to him to require. I do not apprehend he will think it necessary to deviate from my views to any ruinous extent. On one hasty reading I see no such deviation in his program, which you send.
A. LINCOLN.

TO W. M. FISHBACK.

WAR DEPARTMENT, WASHINGTON, February 17, 1864.

WILLIAM M. FISHBACK, Little Rock, Arkansas:
When I fixed a plan for an election in Arkansas I did it in ignorance that your convention was doing the same work. Since I learned the latter fact I have been constantly trying to yield my plan to them. I have sent two letters to General Steele, and three or four despatches to you and others, saying that he, General Steele, must be master, but that it will probably be best for him to merely help the convention on its own plan. Some single mind must be master, else there will be no agreement in anything, and General Steele, commanding the military and being on the ground, is the best man to be that master. Even now citizens are telegraphing me to postpone the election to a later day than either that fixed by the convention or by me. This discord must be silenced.
A. LINCOLN.

TELEGRAM TO GENERAL STEELE.

EXECUTIVE MANSION, WASHINGTON, February 17, 1864.

MAJOR-GENERAL STEELE, Little Rock, Arkansas:
The day fixed by the convention for the election is probably the best, but you on the ground, and in consultation with gentlemen there, are to decide. I should have fixed no day for an election, presented no plan for reconstruction, had I known the convention was doing the same things. It is probably best that you merely assist the convention on their own plan, as to election day and all other matters I have already written and telegraphed this half a dozen times.
A. LINCOLN.

TELEGRAM TO A. ROBINSON.

EXECUTIVE MANSION, WASHINGTON, February 18, 1864.

A. ROBINSON, Leroy, N. Y.:
The law only obliges us to keep accounts with States, or at most Congressional Districts, and it would overwhelm us to attempt in counties, cities and towns. Nevertheless we do what we can to oblige in particular cases. In this view I send your dispatch to the Provost-Marshal General, asking him to do the best he can for you.
A. LINCOLN.

PROCLAMATION CONCERNING BLOCKADE, FEBRUARY 18, 1864.

BY THE PRESIDENT OF THE UNITED STATES

A Proclamation.
Whereas, by my proclamation of the nineteenth of April, one thousand eight hundred and sixty-one, the ports of the States of South Carolina, Georgia, Alabama, Florida, Mississippi, Louisiana, and Texas were, for reasons therein set forth, placed under blockade; and whereas, the port of Brownsville, in the district of Brazos Santiago, in the State of Texas, has since been blockaded, but as the blockade of said port may now be safely relaxed with advantage to the interests of commerce:

Now, therefore, be it known that I, Abraham Lincoln, President of the United States, pursuant to the authority in me vested by the fifth section of the act of Congress approved on the 13th of July, 1861, entitled "An act further to provide for the collection of duties on imports, and for other purposes," do hereby declare that the blockade of the said port of Brownsville shall so far cease and determine from and after this date, that commercial intercourse with said port, except as to persons, things, and information hereinafter specified, may, from this date, be carried on, subject to the laws of the United States, to the regulations prescribed by the Secretary of the Treasury, and, until the rebellion shall have been suppressed, to such orders as may be promulgated by the general commanding the department, or by an officer duly authorized by him and commanding at said port. This proclamation does not authorize or allow the shipment or conveyance of persons in, or intending to enter, the service of the insurgents, or of things or information intended for their use, or for their aid or comfort, nor, except upon the permission of the Secretary of War, or of some officer duly authorized by him, of the following prohibited articles, namely: cannon, mortars, firearms, pistols, bombs, grenades, powder, saltpeter, sulphur, balls, bullets, pikes, swords, boarding-caps (always excepting the quantity of the said articles which may be necessary for the defense of the ship and those who compose the crew), saddles, bridles, cartridge-bag material, percussion and other caps, clothing adapted for uniforms; sail-cloth of all kinds, hemp and cordage, intoxicating drinks other than beer and light native wines.

To vessels clearing from foreign ports and destined to the port of Brownsville, opened by this proclamation, licenses will be granted by consuls of the United States upon satisfactory evidence that the vessel so licensed will convey no persons, property, or information excepted or prohibited above, either to or from the said port; which licenses shall be exhibited to the collector of said port immediately on arrival, and, if required, to any officer in charge of the blockade, and on leaving said port every vessel will be required to have a clearance from the collector of the customs, according to law, showing no violation of the conditions of the license. Any violations of said conditions will involve the forfeiture and condemnation of the vessel and cargo, and the exclusion of all parties concerned from any further privilege of entering the United States during the war for any purpose whatever.

In all respects, except as herein specified, the existing blockade remains in full force and effect as hitherto established and maintained, nor is it relaxed by this proclamation except in regard to the port to which relaxation is or has been expressly applied.

In witness whereof, I have hereunto set my hand, and caused the seal of the United States to be affixed. Done at the city of Washington, this eighteenth day of February, in the year of our Lord one thousand eight hundred and sixty-four, and of the independence of the United States the eighty-eighth.

A. LINCOLN.
By the President WILLIAM H. SEWARD, Secretary of State.

TELEGRAM TO COMMANDER BLAKE.

EXECUTIVE, MANSION, February 19, 1864.

COMMANDER GEORGE S. BLAKE, Commandant Naval Academy, Newport, R. I.:
I desire the case of Midshipman C. Lyon re-examined and if not clearly inconsistent I shall be much obliged to have the recommendation changed.
A. LINCOLN.

TELEGRAM FROM WARREN JORDAN.

NASHVILLE, February 20, 1864.

HON. W. H. SEWARD, Secretary of State, Washington, D.C.:
In county and State elections, must citizens of Tennessee take the oath prescribed by Governor Johnson, or will the President's oath of amnesty entitle them to vote? I have been appointed to hold the March election in Cheatham County, and wish to act understandingly.
WARREN JORDAN.
WASHINGTON, February 20, 1864.
WARREN JORDAN, NASHVILLE:

In county elections you had better stand by Governor Johnson's plan; otherwise you will have conflict and confusion. I have seen his plan.
A. LINCOLN.

TELEGRAM TO GENERAL ROSECRANS.

WAR DEPARTMENT, WASHINGTON, D. C., February 22, 1864.

MAJOR-GENERAL ROSECRANS, Saint LOUIS, MO.:
Colonel Sanderson will be ordered to you to-day, a mere omission that it was not done before. The other questions in your despatch I am not yet prepared to answer.
A. LINCOLN.

TELEGRAM TO GENERAL STEELE.

WAR DEPARTMENT, WASHINGTON, D. C., February 22, 1864.

MAJOR-GENERAL STEELE, Little Rock, Ark.:
Yours of yesterday received. Your conference with citizens approved. Let the election be on the 14th of March as they agreed.
A. LINCOLN.

TO GENERAL F. STEELE.

WAR DEPARTMENT, WASHINGTON, February 25, 1864.

MAJOR-GENERAL STEELE, Little Rock, Arkansas:
General Sickles is not going to Arkansas. He probably will make a tour down the Mississippi and home by the gulf and ocean, but he will not meddle in your affairs.
At one time I did intend to have him call on you and explain more fully than I could do by letter or telegraph, so as to avoid a difficulty coming of my having made a plan here, while the convention made one there, for reorganizing Arkansas; but even his doing that has been given up for more than two weeks. Please show this to Governor Murphy to save me telegraphing him.
A. LINCOLN.

DESERTERS DEATH SENTENCES REMITTED

GENERAL ORDERS, NO.76.

WAR DEPARTMENT, ADJUTANT-GENERALS OFFICE,
WASHINGTON, February 26, 1864.
Sentence of Deserters.
The President directs that the sentences of all deserters who have been condemned by court-martial to death, and that have not been otherwise acted upon by him, be mitigated to imprisonment during the war at the Dry Tortugas, Florida, where they will be sent under suitable guards by orders from army commanders.

The commanding generals, who have power to act on proceedings of courts-martial in such cases, are authorized in special cases to restore to duty deserters under sentence, when in their judgment the service will be thereby benefited. Copies of all orders issued under the foregoing instructions will be immediately forwarded to the Adjutant-General and to the Judge-Advocate General.
By order of the Secretary of War: B. D. TOWNSEND, Assistant Adjutant-General

FEMALE SPY

TELEGRAM TO GENERAL BUTLER.

EXECUTIVE MANSION, WASHINGTON, February 26, 1864
MAJOR-GENERAL BUTLER, Fort. Monroe, Va.:
I cannot remember at whose request it was that I gave the pass to Mrs. Bulky. Of course detain her, if the evidence of her being a spy is strong against her.
A. LINCOLN.

TO W. JAYNE.

EXECUTIVE MANSION, WASHINGTON, February 26, 1864.

HON. W. JAYNE.
DEAR SIR—I dislike to make changes in office so long as they can be avoided. It multiplies my embarrassments immensely. I dislike two appointments when one will do. Send me the name of some man not the present marshal, and I will nominate him to be Provost-Marshal for Dakota.
Yours truly,
A. LINCOLN.

TO E. H. EAST.

WASHINGTON, February 27, 1864.

HON. E. H: EAST, Secretary of State, Nashville, Tennessee
Your telegram of the twenty-sixth instant asking for a copy of my despatch to Warren Jordan, Esq., at Nashville Press office, has just been referred to me by Governor Johnson. In my reply to Mr. Jordan, which was brief and hurried, I intended to say that in the county and State elections of Tennessee, the oath prescribed in the proclamation of Governor Johnson on the twenty-sixth of January, 1864, ordering an election in Tennessee on the first Saturday in March next, is entirely satisfactory to me as a test of loyalty of all persons proposing or offering to vote in said elections; and coming from him would better be observed and followed. There is no conflict between the oath of amnesty in my proclamation of eighth December, 1863, and that prescribed by Governor Johnson in his proclamation of the twenty-sixth ultimo. No person who has taken the oath of amnesty of eighth December, 1863, and obtained a pardon thereby, and who intends to observe the same in good faith, should have any objection to taking that prescribed by Governor Johnson as a test of loyalty.
I have seen and examined Governor Johnson's proclamation, and am entirely satisfied with his plan, which is to restore the State government and place it under the control of citizens truly loyal to the Government of the United States.
A. LINCOLN.
Please send above to Governor Johnson. A. L.

TO SECRETARY STANTON.

EXECUTIVE MANSION, WASHINGTON, February 27, 1864

HON. SECRETARY OF WAR.
SIR:—You ask some instructions from me in relation to the Report of Special Commission constituted by an order of the War Department, dated December 5, 1863, "to revise the enrolment and quotas of the City and State of New York, and report whether there be any, and what, errors or irregularities therein, and what corrections, if any, should be made."
In the correspondence between the Governor of New York and myself last summer, I understood him to complain that the enrolments in several of the districts of that State had been neither accurately nor honestly made; and in view of this, I, for the draft then immediately ensuing, ordered an arbitrary reduction of the quotas in several of the districts wherein they seemed too large, and said: "After this drawing, these four districts, and also the seventeenth and twenty-ninth, shall be carefully re-enrolled, and, if you please, agents of yours may witness every step of the process." In a subsequent letter I believe some additional districts were put into the list of those to be re-enrolled. My idea was to do the work over according to the law, in presence of the complaining party, and thereby to correct anything which might be found amiss. The commission, whose work I am considering, seem to have proceeded upon a totally different idea. Not going forth to find men at all, they have proceeded altogether upon paper examinations and mental processes. One of their conclusions, as I understand, is that, as the law stands, and attempting to follow it, the enrolling officers could not have made the enrolments much more accurately than they did. The report on this point might be useful to Congress. The commission conclude that the quotas for the draft should be based upon entire population, and they proceed upon this basis to give a table for the State of New York, in which some districts are reduced and some increased. For the now ensuing draft, let the quotas stand as made by the enrolling officers, in the districts wherein this table requires them to be increased; and let them be reduced according to the table in the others: this to be no precedent for subsequent action. But, as I think this report may, on full consideration, be shown to have much that is valuable in it, I suggest that such consideration be given it, and that it be especially considered whether its suggestions can be conformed to without an alteration of the law.
Yours truly,
A. LINCOLN. TELEGRAM TO GENERAL THOMAS.
WAR DEPARTMENT, WASHINGTON, February 28, 1864.
GENERAL L. THOMAS, Louisville, Kentucky:
I see your despatch of yesterday to the Secretary of War.
I wish you would go to the Mississippi River at once, and take hold of and be master in the contraband and leasing business. You understand it better than any other man does. Mr. Miller's system doubtless is well intended, but from what I hear I fear that, if persisted in, it would fall dead within its own entangling details. Go there and be the judge. A Mr. Lewis will probably follow you with something from me on this subject, but do not wait for him. Nor is this to induce you to violate or neglect any military order from the General-in-Chief or Secretary of War.
A. LINCOLN.

TO SECRETARY CHASE.

EXECUTIVE MANSION, WASHINGTON, February 29, 1864.

HON. SECRETARY OF THE TREASURY.
MY DEAR SIR:—I would have taken time to answer yours of the 22d inst. sooner, only that I did not suppose any evil could result from the delay, especially as, by a note, I promptly acknowledged the receipt of yours, and promised a fuller answer. Now, on consideration I find there is really very little to say. My knowledge of Mr. Pomeroy's letter having been made public came to me only the day you wrote; but I had, in spite of myself, known of its existence several days before. I have not yet read it, and I think I shall not. I was not shocked or surprised by the appearance of the letter, because I had had knowledge of Mr. Pomeroy's committee, and of secret issues which, I supposed, came from it, and of secret agents who, I supposed, were sent out by it for several weeks. I have known just as little a these things as my friends have allowed me to know. They bring the documents to me, but I do not read them; they tell me what they think fit to tell me, but I do not inquire for more.

I fully concur with you that neither of us can justly be held responsible for what our respective friends may do without our instigation or countenance and I assure you, as you have assured me, that no assault has been made upon you by my instigation, or with my countenance.

Whether you shall remain at the head of the Treasury Department is a question which I will not allow myself to consider from any standpoint other than my judgment of the public service, and, in that view, I do not perceive occasion for a change.

Yours truly,
A. LINCOLN.

TO GENERAL THOMAS.

EXECUTIVE MANSION WASHINGTON, March 1,1864.

GENERAL L. THOMAS:
This introduces Mr. Lewis, mentioned in my despatch sent you at Louisville some days ago. I have but little personal acquaintance with him; but he has the confidence of several members of Congress here who seem to know him well. He hopes to be useful, without charge to the government, in facilitating the introduction of the free-labor system on the Mississippi plantations. He is acquainted with, and has access to, many of the planters who wish to adopt the system. He will show you two letters of mine on this subject, one somewhat General, and the other relating to named persons; they are not different in principle. He will also show you some suggestions coming from some of the planters themselves. I desire that all I promise in these letters, so far as practicable, may be in good faith carried out, and that suggestions from the planters may be heard and adopted, so far as they may not contravene the principles stated, nor justice, nor fairness, to laborers. I do not herein intend to overrule your own mature judgment on any point.
Yours truly,
A. LINCOLN.

TELEGRAM TO GENERAL STEELE.

WAR DEPARTMENT, WASHINGTON, D. C., March 3, 1864.

MAJOR-GENERAL STEELE, Little Rock, Ark.:
Yours including address to people of Arkansas is received. I approve the address and thank you for it. Yours in relation to William M. Randolph also received. Let him take the oath of December 8, and go to work for the new constitution, and on your notifying me of it, I will immediately issue the special pardon for him.
A. LINCOLN.

TELEGRAM TO GENERAL BUTLER.

EXECUTIVE MANSION, WASHINGTON, March 4,1864. MAJOR-GENERAL BUTLER, Fort Monroe, Va.:
Admiral Dahlgren is here, and of course is very anxious about his son. Please send me at once all you know or can learn of his fate.
A. LINCOLN.

ORDER IN REGARD TO THE EXPORTATION OF TOBACCO BELONGING TO THE FRENCH

GOVERNMENT. EXECUTIVE MANSION,

WASHINGTON, March 7, 1864.
Whereas, by an Executive order of the 10th of November last permission was given to export certain tobacco belonging to the French government from insurgent territory, which tobacco was supposed to have been purchased and paid for prior to the 4th day of March, 1861; but whereas it was subsequently ascertained that a part at least of the said tobacco had been purchased subsequently to that date, which fact made it necessary to suspend the carrying into effect of the said order; but whereas, pursuant to mutual explanations, a satisfactory understanding upon the subject has now been reached, it is directed that the order aforesaid may be carried into effect, it being understood that the quantity of French tobacco so to be exported shall not exceed seven thousand hogsheads, and that it is the same tobacco respecting the exportation of which application was originally made by the French government.
A. LINCOLN.

TELEGRAM TO UNITED STATES MARSHAL, LOUISVILLE.

EXECUTIVE MANSION, WASHINGTON, March 7, 1864.

U.S. MARSHAL, Louisville, Ky.:
Until further order suspend sale of property and further proceedings in cases of the United States against Dr. John B. English, and S. S. English, qt al., sureties for John L. Hill. Also same against same sureties for Thomas A. Ireland.
A. LINCOLN.
MAJOR ECKERT: Please send the above dispatch. JNO. G. NICOLAY, Private Secretary

TELEGRAM TO GENERAL MEADE.

EXECUTIVE MANSION, WASHINGTON, March 9, 1864.

MAJOR-GENERAL MEADE, Army of Potomac:
New York City votes ninety-five hundred majority for allowing soldiers to vote, and the rest of the State nearly all on the same side. Tell the soldiers.
A. LINCOLN.

MESSAGE TO SENATE.

EXECUTIVE MANSION, March 9, 1864.

TO THE SENATE OF THE UNITED STATES
In compliance with a resolution of the Senate of the 1st instant, respecting the points of commencement of the Union Pacific Railroad, on the one hundredth degree of west longitude, and of the branch road, from the western boundary of Iowa to the said one hundredth degree of longitude, I transmit the accompanying report from the Secretary of the Interior, containing the information called for.
I deem it proper to add that on the 17th day of November last an Executive order was made upon this subject and delivered to the vice-president of the Union Pacific Railroad Company, which fixed the point on the western boundary of the State of Iowa from which the company should construct their branch road to the one hundredth degree of west longitude, and declared it to be within the limits of the township in Iowa opposite the town of Omaha, in Nebraska. Since then the company has represented to me that upon actual surveys made it has determined upon the precise point of departure of their said branch road from the Missouri River, and located the same as described in the accompanying report of the Secretary of the Interior, which point is within the limits designated in the order of November last; and inasmuch as that order is not of record in any of the Executive Departments, and the company having desired a more definite one, I have made the order of which a copy is herewith, and caused the same to be filed in the Department of the Interior.

A. LINCOLN.

ADDRESS TO GENERAL GRANT,

MARCH 9, 1864.

GENERAL GRANT:—The expression of the nation's approbation of what you have already done, and its reliance on you for what remains to do in the existing great struggle, is now presented with this commission constituting you Lieutenant-General of the Army of the United States.

With this high honor, devolves on you an additional responsibility. As the country herein trusts you, so, under God, it will sustain you. I scarcely need add, that with what I here speak for the country, goes my own hearty personal concurrence.

GENERAL GRANT'S REPLY.

Mr. PRESIDENT:—I accept this commission, with gratitude for the high honor conferred.

With the aid of the noble armies that have fought on so many fields for our common country, it will be my earnest endeavor not to disappoint your expectations.

I feel the full weight of the responsibilities now devolving on me, and I know that if they are met, it will be due to those armies; and above all, to the favor of that Providence which leads both nations and men.

ORDER ASSIGNING U. S. GRANT COMMAND OF THE ARMIES OF THE UNITED STATES.

EXECUTIVE MANSION, WASHINGTON, D. C., March 10, 1864.

Under the authority of an act of Congress to revive the grade of lieutenant-General in the United States Army, approved February 29, 1864, Lieutenant-General Ulysses S. Grant, United States Army, is assigned to the command of the Armies of the United States.
A. LINCOLN.

TELEGRAM TO GOVERNOR MURPHY.

WASHINGTON, D. C., March 12, 1864.

GOVERNOR MURPHY, Little Rock, Arkansas:

I am not appointing officers for Arkansas now, and I will try to remember your request. Do your best to get out the largest vote possible, and of course as much of it as possible on the right side.
A. LINCOLN.

TO GENERAL HAHN. (Private.)

EXECUTIVE MANSION, WASHINGTON, March 13, 1864

HON. MICHAEL HAHN.

MY DEAR SIR:—I congratulate you on having fixed your name in history as the first free-state governor of Louisiana. Now, you are about to have a convention, which among other things will probably define the elective franchise. I barely suggest for your private consideration, whether some of the colored people may not be let in,—as, for instance, the very intelligent, and especially those who have fought gallantly in our ranks. They would probably help, in some trying time to come, to keep the jewel of liberty within the family of freedom. But this is only a suggestion,—not to the public, but to you alone.

Yours truly,
A. LINCOLN.

CALL FOR TWO HUNDRED THOUSAND MEN.

EXECUTIVE MANSION WASHINGTON, MARCH 14, 1864.

In order to supply the force required to be drafted for the Navy and to provide an adequate reserve force for all contingencies, in addition to the five hundred thousand men called for February 1, 1864, a call is hereby made and a draft ordered for two hundred thousand men for the military service (Army, Navy, and Marine Corps) of the United States.

The proportional quotas for the different wards, towns, townships, precincts, or election districts, or counties, will be made known through the Provost Marshal-General's Bureau, and account will be taken of the credits and deficiencies on former quotas.

The 15th day of April, 1864, is designated as the time up to which the numbers required from each ward of a city, town, etc., may be raised by voluntary enlistment, and drafts will be made in each ward of a city, town, etc., which shall not have filled the quota assigned to it within the time designated for the number required to fill said quotas. The drafts will be commenced as soon after the 15th of April as practicable.

The Government bounties as now paid continue until April I, 1864, at which time the additional bounties cease. On and after that date one hundred dollars bounty only will be paid, as provided by the act approved July 22, 1861.
A. LINCOLN.

TELEGRAM TO GENERAL U. S. GRANT.

(Private.)

EXECUTIVE MANSION, WASHINGTON, March 15, 1864
LIEUTENANT-GENERAL GRANT, Nashville, Tenn.:

General McPherson having been assigned to the command of a department, could not General Frank Blair, without difficulty or detriment to the service, be assigned to command the Corps he commanded a while last autumn?
A. LINCOLN.

PASS FOR GENERAL D. E. SICKLES.

EXECUTIVE MANSION, WASHINGTON, March 15, 1864.

WHOM IT MAY CONCERN

Major-General Sickles is making a tour for me from here by way of Cairo, New Orleans, and returning by the gulf, and ocean, and all land and naval officers and, employees are directed to furnish reasonable transportation and other reasonable facilities to himself and personal staff not inconsistent with the public service.
A. LINCOLN.

ORDER TO GOVERNOR HAHN.

EXECUTIVE MANSION, WASHINGTON, March 15, 1864.

HIS EXCELLENCY MICHAEL HAHN, Governor of Louisiana
Until further order, you are hereby invested with the powers exercised hitherto by the military governor of Louisiana.
Yours truly,
A. LINCOLN.

REMARKS AT A FAIR IN THE PATENT OFFICE,

WASHINGTON, MARCH 16, 1864.

LADIES AND GENTLEMEN:
I appear to say but a word. This extraordinary war in which we are engaged falls heavily upon all classes of people but the most heavily upon the soldier. For it has been said, "All that a man hath will he give for his life;" and while all contribute of their substance, the soldier puts his life at stake, and often yields it up in his country's cause. The highest merit, then, is due to the soldier.
In this extraordinary war, extraordinary developments have manifested themselves, such as have not been seen in former wars; and among these manifestations nothing has been more remarkable than these fairs for the relief of suffering soldiers and their families. And the chief agents of these fairs are the women of America.
I am not accustomed to the use of language of eulogy: I have never studied the art of paying compliments to women; but I must say, that if all that has been said by orators and poets since the creation of the world in praise of women were applied to the women of America, it would not do them justice for their conduct during this war. I will close by saying, God bless the women of America.

REPLY TO A COMMITTEE FROM THE WORKINGMEN'S ASSOCIATION OF NEW YORK,

MARCH 21, 1864.

GENTLEMEN OF THE COMMITTEE:
The honorary membership in your association, as generously tendered, is gratefully accepted.
You comprehend, as your address shows, that the existing rebellion means more and tends to do more than the perpetuation of African slavery—that it is, in fact, a war upon the rights of all working people. Partly to show that this view has not escaped my attention, and partly that I cannot better express myself, I read a passage from the message to Congress in December, 1861:
"It continues to develop that the insurrection is largely, if not exclusively, a war upon the first principle of popular government, the rights of the people. Conclusive evidence of this is found in the most grave and maturely considered public documents, as well as in the General tone of the insurgents. In those documents we find the abridgment of the existing right of suffrage, and the denial to the people of all right to participate in the selection of public officers, except the legislature, boldly advocated, with labored argument to prove that large control of the people in government is the source of all political evil. Monarchy itself is sometimes hinted at as a possible refuge from the power of the people. In my present position I could scarcely be justified were I to omit raising a warning voice against this approach of returning despotism.
"It is not needed, nor fitting here, that a General argument should be made in favor of popular institutions; but there is one point, with its connections, not so hackneyed as most others, to which I ask a brief attention. It is the effort to place capital on an equal footing, if not above labor, in the structure of government. It is assumed that labor is available only in connection with capital; that nobody labors unless somebody else, owning capital, somehow by the use of it induces him to labor. This assumed, it is next considered whether it is best that capital shall hire laborers, and thus induce them to work by their own consent or buy them, and drive them to it without their consent. Having proceeded so it is naturally concluded that all laborers are either hired laborers, or what we call slaves. And, further, it is assumed that whoever is once a hired laborer, is fixed in that condition for life. Now there is no such relation between capital and labor as assumed, nor is there any such thing as a free man being fixed for life in the condition of a hired laborer. Both these assumptions are false, and all inferences from them are groundless.

"Labor is prior to, and independent of, capital. Capital is only the fruit of labor, and could never have existed if labor had not first existed. Labor is the superior of capital, and deserves much the higher consideration. Capital has its rights, which are as worthy of protection as any other rights. Nor is it denied that there is, and probably always will be, a relation between capital and labor, producing mutual benefits. The error is in assuming that the whole labor of a community exists within that relation. A few men own capital, and that few avoid labor themselves, and, with their capital, hire or buy another few to labor for them. A large majority belong to neither class—neither work for others, nor have others working for them. In most of the Southern States, a majority of the whole people, of all colors, are neither slaves nor masters; while in the Northern, a large majority are neither hirers nor hired. Men with their families, wives, sons, and daughters—work for themselves, on their farms, in their houses, and in their shops, taking the whole product to themselves, and asking no favors of capital on the one hand, nor of hired laborers or slaves on the other. It is not forgotten that a considerable number of persons mingle their own labor with capital; that is, they labor with their own hands, and also buy or hire others to labor for them, but this is only a mixed and not a distinct class. No principle stated is disturbed by the existence of this mixed class.

"Again, as has already been said, there is not, of necessity, any such thing as the free hired laborer being fixed to that condition for life. Many independent men everywhere in these States, a few years back in their lives, were hired laborers. The prudent penniless beginner in the world labors for wages a while, saves a surplus with which to buy tools or land for himself, then labors on his own account another while, and at length hires another new beginner to help him. This is the just and generous and prosperous system which opens the way to all—gives hope to all, and consequent energy and progress, and improvement of condition to all. No men living are more worthy to be trusted than those who toil up from poverty—none less inclined to touch or take aught which they have not honestly earned. Let them beware of surrendering a political power they already possess, and which, if surrendered, will surely be used to close the door of advancement against such as they, and to fix new disabilities and burdens upon them, till all of liberty shall be lost."

The views then expressed remain unchanged, nor have I much to add. None are so deeply interested to resist the present rebellion as the working people. Let them beware of prejudices, working division and hostility among themselves. The most notable feature of a disturbance in your city last summer was the hanging of some working people by other working people. It should never be so. The strongest bond of human sympathy, outside of the family relation, should be one uniting all working people, of all nations, and tongues, and kindreds. Nor should this lead to a war upon property, or the owners of property. Property is the fruit of labor; property is desirable; is a positive good in the world. That some should be rich shows that others may become rich, and, hence, is just encouragement to industry and enterprise. Let not him who is houseless pull down the house of another, but let him labor diligently and build one for himself, thus by example assuring that his own shall be safe from violence when built.

TELEGRAM TO GENERAL BUTLER.

EXECUTIVE MANSION, WASHINGTON, March 22, 1864.

MAJOR-GENERAL BUTLER, Fort Monroe, Va.:
Hon. W. R. Morrison says he has requested you by letter to effect a special exchange of Lieut. Col. A. F. Rogers, of Eightieth Illinois Volunteers, now in Libby Prison, and I shall be glad if you can effect it.
A. LINCOLN.

CORRESPONDENCE WITH GENERAL C. SCHURZ.

(Private.)

WASHINGTON, March 13, 1864.
MAJOR-GENERAL SCHURZ..
MY DEAR SIR:—Yours of February 29 reached me only four days ago; but the delay was of little consequence, because I found, on feeling around, I could not invite you here without a difficulty which at least would be unpleasant, and perhaps would be detrimental to the public service. Allow me to suggest that if you wish to remain in the military service, it is very dangerous for you to get temporarily out of it; because, with a major-general once out, it is next to impossible for even the President to get him in again. With my appreciation of your ability and correct principle, of

course I would be very glad to have your service for the country in the approaching political canvass; but I fear we cannot properly have it without separating you from the military.
Yours truly,
A. LINCOLN.

PROCLAMATION ABOUT AMNESTY,

MARCH 26, 1864.

BY THE PRESIDENT OF THE UNITED STATES OF AMERICA:
A Proclamation.
Whereas, it has become necessary to define the cases in which insurgent enemies are entitled to the benefits of the Proclamation of the President of the United States, which was made on the 8th day of December, 1863, and the manner in which they shall proceed to avail themselves of these benefits; and whereas the objects of that Proclamation were to suppress the insurrection and to restore the authority of the United States; and whereas the amnesty therein proposed by the President was offered with reference to these objects alone:
Now, therefore, I, Abraham Lincoln, President of the United States, do hereby proclaim and declare that the said Proclamation does not apply to the cases of persons who, at the time when they seek to obtain the benefits thereof by taking the oath thereby prescribed, are in military, naval, or civil confinement or custody, or under bonds, or on parole of the civil, military, or naval authorities, or agents of the United States, as prisoners of war, or persons detained for offences of any kind, either before or after conviction; and that on the contrary it does apply only to those persons who, being yet at large, and free from any arrest, confinement, or duress, shall voluntarily come forward and take the said oath, with the purpose of restoring peace, and establishing the national authority.
Persons excluded from the amnesty offered in the said Proclamation may apply to the President for clemency, like all other offenders, and their application will receive due consideration.
I do further declare and proclaim that the oath presented in the aforesaid proclamation of the 8th of December, 1863, may be taken and subscribed before any commissioned officer, civil, military, or naval, in the service of the United States, or any civil or military officer of a State or Territory not in insurrection, who, by the laws thereof, may be qualified for administering oaths.
All officers who receive such oaths are hereby authorized to give certificates thereof to the persons respectively by whom they are made, and such officers are hereby required to transmit the original records of such oaths, at as early a day as may be convenient, to the Department of State, where they will be deposited, and remain in the archives of the Government.
The Secretary of State will keep a registry thereof, and will, on application, in proper cases, issue certificates of such records in the customary form of official certificates.
In testimony whereof I have hereunto set my hand and caused the seal of the United States to be affixed............
A. LINCOLN.
By the President: WILLIAM H. SEWARD, Secretary of State.

TO SECRETARY STANTON.

EXECUTIVE MANSION, WASHINGTON, March 28, 1864.

HON. SECRETARY OF WAR.
MY DEAR SIR:—The Governor of Kentucky is here, and desires to have the following points definitely fixed:
First. That the quotas of troops furnished, and to be furnished, by Kentucky may be adjusted upon the basis as actually reduced by able-bodied men of hers having gone into the rebel service; and that she be required to furnish no more than her just quotas upon fair adjustment upon such basis.
Second. To whatever extent the enlistment and drafting, one or both, of colored troops may be found necessary within the State, it may be conducted within the law of Congress; and, so far as practicable, free from collateral embarrassments, disorders, and provocations.

I think these requests of the Governor are reasonable; and I shall be obliged if you will give him a full hearing, and do the best you can to effect these objects.
Yours very truly,
A. LINCOLN.

TO GENERAL G. G. MEADE.

EXECUTIVE MANSION, WASHINGTON, March 29, 1864.

MAJOR-GENERAL MEADE.
MY DEAR SIR:—Your letter to Colonel Townsend, inclosing a slip from the "Herald," and asking a court of inquiry, has been laid before me by the Secretary of War, with the request that I would consider it. It is quite natural that you should feel some sensibility on the subject; yet I am not impressed, nor do I think the country is impressed, with the belief that your honor demands, or the public interest demands, such an inquiry. The country knows that at all events you have done good service; and I believe it agrees with me that it is much better for you to be engaged in trying to do more, than to be diverted, as you necessarily would be, by a court of inquiry.
Yours truly,
A. LINCOLN.

TELEGRAM TO GENERAL U. S. GRANT.

EXECUTIVE MANSION, WASHINGTON, March 29,1864.

LIEUTENANT-GENERAL GRANT, Army of the Potomac:
Captain Kinney, of whom I spoke to you as desiring to go on your staff, is now in your camp, in company with Mrs. Senator Dixon. Mrs. Grant and I, and some others, agreed last night that I should, by this despatch, kindly call your attention to Captain Kinney.
A. LINCOLN.

TO A. G. HODGES.

EXECUTIVE MANSION, WASHINGTON, April 4, 1864.

A. G. HODGES, ESQ., Frankfort, Kentucky:
MY DEAR SIR:—You ask me to put in writing the substance of what I verbally said the other day, in your presence, to Governor Bramlette and Senator Dixon. It was about as follows:
"I am naturally anti-slavery. If slavery is not wrong, nothing is wrong. I cannot remember when I did not so think and feel, and yet I have never understood that the Presidency conferred upon me an unrestricted right to act officially upon this judgment and feeling. It was in the oath I took that I would, to the best of my ability preserve, protect, and defend the Constitution of the United States. I could not take the office without taking the oath. Nor was it my view that I might take an oath to get power, and break the oath in using the power. I understood, too, that in ordinary civil administration this oath even forbade me to practically indulge my primary abstract judgment on the moral question of slavery. I had publicly declared this many times, and in many ways. And I aver that, to this day, I have done no official act in mere deference to my abstract judgment and feeling on slavery. I did understand, however, that my oath to preserve the Constitution to the best of my ability, imposed upon me the duty of preserving, by every indispensable means, that government, that nation, of which that Constitution was the organic law. Was it possible to lose the nation and yet preserve the Constitution? By General law, life and limb must be protected; yet often a limb must be amputated to save a life; but a life is never wisely given to save a limb. I felt that measures, otherwise unconstitutional, might become lawful, by becoming indispensable to the preservation of the Constitution, through the preservation of the

nation. Right or wrong, I assumed this ground, and now avow it. I could not feel that to the best of my ability I had even tried to preserve the Constitution, if, to save slavery, or any minor matter, I should permit the wreck of government, country, and Constitution, altogether. When, early in the war, General Fremont attempted military emancipation, I forbade it, because I did not then think it an indispensable necessity. When, a little later, General Cameron, then Secretary of War, suggested the arming of the blacks, I objected, because I did not yet think it an indispensable necessity. When, still later, General Hunter attempted military emancipation, I again forbade it, because I did not yet think the indispensable necessity had come. When, in March, and May, and July, 1862, I made earnest and successive appeals to the Border States to favor compensated emancipation, I believed the indispensable necessity for military emancipation and arming the blacks would come, unless averted by that measure. They declined the proposition, and I was, in my best judgment, driven to the alternative of either surrendering the Union, and with it the Constitution, or of laying strong hand upon the colored element. I chose the latter. In choosing it, I hoped for greater gain than loss, but of this I was not entirely confident. More than a year of trial now shows no loss by it in our foreign relations, none in our home popular sentiment, none in our white military force, no loss by it any how, or anywhere. On the contrary, it shows a gain of quite one hundred and thirty thousand soldiers, seamen, and laborers. These are palpable facts, about which, as facts, there can be no caviling. We have the men; and we could not have had them without the measure.

"And now let any Union man who complains of the measure test himself by writing down in one line that he is for subduing the rebellion by force of arms; and in the next, that he is for taking these hundred and thirty thousand men from the Union side, and placing them where they would be but for the measure he condemns. If he cannot face his case so stated, it is only because he cannot face the truth."

I add a word which was not in the verbal conversation. In telling this tale I attempt no compliment to my own sagacity. I claim not to have controlled events, but confess plainly that events have controlled me. Now, at the end of three years' struggle, the nation's condition is not what either party, or any man, devised or expected. God alone can claim it. Whither it is tending seems plain. If God now wills the removal of a great wrong, and wills also that we of the North, as well as you of the South, shall pay fairly for our complicity in that wrong, impartial history will find therein new cause to attest and revere the justice and goodness of God.

Yours truly,
A. LINCOLN.

TO MRS. HORACE MANN.

EXECUTIVE MANSION, WASHINGTON, April 5, 1864.

MRS HORACE MANN:
MADAM:—The petition of persons under eighteen, praying that I would free all slave children, and the heading of which petition it appears you wrote, was handed me a few days since by Senator Sumner. Please tell these little people I am very glad their young hearts are so full of just and generous sympathy, and that, while I have not the power to grant all they ask, I trust they will remember that God has, and that, as it seems, he wills to do it.
Yours truly,
A. LINCOLN.

TELEGRAM TO GENERAL BUTLER.

EXECUTIVE MANSION, WASHINGTON, April 12, 1864.

MAJOR-GENERAL BUTLER, Fort Monroe, Va.:
I am pressed to get from Libby, by special exchange, Jacob C. Hagenbuek, first lieutenant, Company H, Sixty-seventh Pennsylvania Volunteers. Please do it if you can without detriment or embarrassment.
A. LINCOLN.

TELEGRAM TO GENERAL MEADE.

EXECUTIVE MANSION, WASHINGTON, April 17, 1864.

MAJOR-GENERAL MEADE, Army of the Potomac:
Private William Collins of Company B, of the Sixty-ninth New York Volunteers, has been convicted of desertion, and execution suspended as in numerous other cases. Now Captain O'Neill, commanding the regiment, and nearly all its other regimental and company officers, petition for his full pardon and restoration to his company. Is there any good objection?
A. LINCOLN.

LECTURE ON LIBERTY

ADDRESS AT SANITARY FAIR IN BALTIMORE,

APRIL 18, 1864.
LADIES AND GENTLEMEN:—Calling to mind that we are in Baltimore, we cannot fail to note that the world moves. Looking upon these many people assembled here to serve, as they best may, the soldiers of the Union, it occurs at once that three years ago the same soldiers could not so much as pass through Baltimore. The change from then till now is both great and gratifying. Blessings on the brave men who have wrought the change, and the fair women who strive to reward them for it!
But Baltimore suggests more than could happen within Baltimore. The change within Baltimore is part only of a far wider change. When the war began, three years ago, neither party, nor any man, expected it would last till now. Each looked for the end, in some way, long ere to-day. Neither did any anticipate that domestic slavery would be much affected by the war. But here we are; the war has not ended, and slavery has been much affected how much needs not now to be recounted. So true is it that man proposes and God disposes.
But we can see the past, though we may not claim to have directed it; and seeing it, in this case, we feel more hopeful and confident for the future.
The world has never had a good definition of the word liberty, and the American people, just now, are much in want of one. We all declare for liberty; but in using the same word we do not all mean the same thing. With some the word liberty may mean for each man to do as he pleases with himself, and the product of his labor; while with others the same word may mean for some men to do as they please with other men, and the product of other men's labor. Here are two, not only different, but incompatible things, called by the same name, liberty. And it follows that each of the things is, by the respective parties, called by two different and incompatible names—liberty and tyranny.
The shepherd drives the wolf from the sheep's throat, for which the sheep thanks the shepherd as his liberator, while the wolf denounces him for the same act, as the destroyer of liberty, especially as the sheep was a black one. Plainly, the sheep and the wolf are not agreed upon a definition of the word liberty; and precisely the same difference prevails to-day among us human creatures, even in the North, and all professing to love liberty. Hence we behold the process by which thousands are daily passing from under the yoke of bondage hailed by some as the advance of liberty, and bewailed by others as the destruction of all liberty. Recently, as it seems, the people of Maryland have been doing something to define liberty, and thanks to them that, in what they have done, the wolf's dictionary has been repudiated.
It is not very becoming for one in my position to make speeches at length; but there is another subject upon which I feel that I ought to say a word. A painful rumor, true, I fear, has reached us, of the massacre, by the rebel forces at Fort Pillow, in the west end of Tennessee, on the Mississippi River, of some three hundred colored soldiers and white officers [I believe it latter turned out to be 500], who had just been overpowered by their assailants [numbering 5000]. There seems to be some anxiety in the public mind whether the Government is doing its duty to the colored soldier, and to the service, at this point. At the beginning of the war, and for some time, the use of colored troops was not contemplated; and how the change of purpose was wrought I will not now take time to explain. Upon a clear conviction of duty I resolved to turn that element of strength to account; and I am responsible for it to the American people, to the Christian world, to history, and in my final account to God. Having determined to use the negro as a soldier, there is no way but to give him all the protection given to any other soldier. The difficulty is not in stating the principle, but in practically applying it. It is a mistake to suppose the Government is indifferent to this matter, or is not doing the best it can in regard to it. We do not to-day know that a colored soldier, or white officer commanding colored soldiers, has been massacred by the rebels when made a prisoner. We fear it, we believe it, I may say,—but we do not know it.

697

To take the life of one of their prisoners on the assumption that they murder ours, when it is short of certainty that they do murder ours, might be too serious, too cruel, a mistake. We are having the Fort Pillow affair thoroughly investigated; and such investigation will probably show conclusively how the truth is. If after all that has been said it shall turn out that there has been no massacre at Fort Pillow, it will be almost safe to say there has been none, and will be none, elsewhere. If there has been the massacre of three hundred there, or even the tenth part of three hundred, it will be conclusively proved; and being so proved, the retribution shall as surely come. It will be matter of grave consideration in what exact course to apply the retribution; but in the supposed case it must come.

[There was a massacre of a black company and their officers at Fort Pillow—they were prisoners who later on, the day of their capture, were ordered executed. The black soldiers were tied alive to individual planks—then man and plank were cobbled up like cord wood and burned. The white officers were shot. D.W.]

TO CALVIN TRUESDALE.

EXECUTIVE MANSION, WASHINGTON, April 20, 1864.

CALVIN TRUESDALE, ESQ., Postmaster, Rock Island, Ill.:
Thomas J. Pickett, late agent of the Quartermaster's Department for the island of Rock Island, has been removed or suspended from that position on a charge of having sold timber and stone from the island for his private benefit. Mr. Pickett is an old acquaintance and friend of mine, and I will thank you, if you will, to set a day or days and place on and at which to take testimony on the point. Notify Mr. Pickett and one J. B. Danforth (who, as I understand, makes the charge) to be present with their witnesses. Take the testimony in writing offered by both sides, and report it in full to me. Please do this for me.
Yours truly,
A. LINCOLN.

TELEGRAM TO OFFICER COMMANDING AT FORT WARREN.

EXECUTIVE MANSION, WASHINGTON, April 20, 1864.

OFFICER IN MILITARY COMMAND, Fort Warren, Boston Harbor, Mass.:
If there is a man by the name of Charles Carpenter, under sentence of death for desertion, at Fort Warren, suspend execution until further order and send the record of his trial. If sentenced for any other offence, telegraph what it is and when he is to be executed. Answer at all events.
A. LINCOLN.

TELEGRAM TO OFFICER COMMANDING AT FORT WARREN.

EXECUTIVE MANSION, WASHINGTON, April 21,1864.

OFFICER IN COMMAND AT FORT WARREN, Boston Harbor, Mass.:
The order I sent yesterday in regard to Charles Carpenter is hereby withdrawn and you are to act as if it never existed.
A. LINCOLN.

TELEGRAM TO GENERAL DIX.

EXECUTIVE MANSION, WASHINGTON, D. C., April 21, 1864.

MAJOR-GENERAL Dix, New York:

Yesterday I was induced to telegraph the officer in military command at Fort Warren, Boston Harbor, Massachusetts, suspending the execution of Charles Carpenter, to be executed tomorrow for desertion. Just now, on reaching your order in the case, I telegraphed the same officer withdrawing the suspension, and leave the case entirely with you. The man's friends are pressing me, but I refer them to you, intending to take no further action myself.
A. LINCOLN.

TELEGRAM TO GENERAL BUTLER.

EXECUTIVE MANSION, WASHINGTON, April 23, 1864.

MAJOR-GENERAL BUTLER, Fort Monroe, Va.:

Senator Ten Eyck is very anxious to have a special exchange of Capt. Frank J. McLean, of Ninth Tennessee Cavalry now, or lately, at Johnson's Island, for Capt. T. Ten Eyck, Eighteenth U. S. Infantry, and now at Richmond. I would like to have it done. Can it be?
A. LINCOLN.

INDORSEMENT ON OFFER OF TROOPS, APRIL 23, 1864.

TO THE PRESIDENT OF THE UNITED STATES:

1. The Governors of Ohio, Indiana, Illinois, Iowa, and Wisconsin offer to the President infantry troops for the approaching campaign as follows: Ohio, thirty thousand; Indiana, twenty thousand; Illinois, twenty thousand; Iowa, ten thousand; Wisconsin, five thousand.
2. The term of service to be one hundred days, reckoned from the date of muster into the service of the United States, unless sooner discharged.
3. The troops to be mustered into the service of the United States by regiments, when the regiments are filled up, according to regulations, to the minimum strength—the regiments to be organized according to the regulations of the War Department. The whole number to be furnished within twenty days from date of notice of the acceptance of this proposition.
4. The troops to be clothed, armed, equipped, subsisted; transported, and paid as other United States infantry volunteers, and to serve in fortifications,—or wherever their services may be required, within or without their respective States.
5. No bounty to be paid the troops, nor the service charged or credited on any draft.
6. The draft for three years' service to go on in any State or district where the quota is not filled up; but if any officer or soldier in this special service should be drafted, he shall be credited for the service rendered.
JOHN BROUGH, Governor of Ohio. O. P. MORTON, Governor of Indiana. RICHARD PATES, Governor of Illinois. WILLIAM M. STONE, Governor of Iowa. JAMES T. LEWIS, Governor of Wisconsin
(Indorsement.)
April 23, 1864.
The foregoing proposition of the governors is accepted, and the Secretary of War is directed to carry it into execution.
A. LINCOLN.

TO SECRETARY STANTON.

EXECUTIVE MANSION, WASHINGTON, April 23, 1864.

HON. SECRETARY OF WAR:

MY DEAR SIR:—According to our understanding with Major-General Frank P. Blair at the time he took his seat in Congress last winter, he now asks to withdraw his resignation as Major-General, then tendered, and be sent to the field. Let this be done. Let the order sending him be such as shown me to-day by the Adjutant-General, only dropping from it the names of Maguire and Tompkins.
Yours truly,
A. LINCOLN.

TELEGRAM TO JOHN WILLIAMS.

WAR DEPARTMENT, WASHINGTON CITY, April 25, 1864.

JOHN WILLIAMS, Springfield, Ill.:
Yours of the 15th is just received. Thanks for your kind remembrance. I would accept your offer at once, were it not that I fear there might be some impropriety in it, though I do not see that there would. I will think of it a while.
A. LINCOLN.

TELEGRAM TO GENERAL MEADE.

WAR DEPARTMENT, WASHINGTON CITY, April 25, 1864.

MAJOR-GENERAL MEADE, Army of Potomac:
A Mr. Corby brought you a note from me at the foot of a petition I believe, in the case of Dawson, to be executed to-day. The record has been examined here, and it shows too strong a case for a pardon or commutation, unless there is something in the poor man's favor outside of the record, which you on the ground may know, but I do not. My note to you only means that if you know of any such thing rendering a suspension of the execution proper, on your own judgment, you are at liberty to suspend it. Otherwise I do not interfere.
A. LINCOLN.

TELEGRAM TO GENERAL THOMAS.

EXECUTIVE MANSION, WASHINGTON, D. C., April 26, 1864.

MAJOR-GENERAL THOMAS, Chattanooga, Term.:
Suspend execution of death sentence of young Perry, of Wisconsin, condemned for sleeping on his post, till further orders, and forward record for examination.
A. LINCOLN.

TO GOVERNOR MURPHY.

WASHINGTON, D. C., April 27, 1864.

GOVERNOR MURPHY, Little Rock, Arkansas:
I am much gratified to learn that you got out so large a vote, so nearly all the right way, at the late election; and not less so that your State government including the legislature, is organized and in good working order. Whatever I can I will do to protect you; meanwhile you must do your utmost to protect yourselves. Present my greeting to all.
A. LINCOLN.

MESSAGE TO CONGRESS, APRIL 28, 1864.

TO THE HONORABLE THE SENATE AND HOUSE OF REPRESENTATIVES:

I have the honor to transmit herewith an address to the President of the United States, and through him to both Houses of Congress, on the condition and wants of the people of east Tennessee, and asking their attention to the necessity of some action on the part of the Government for their relief, and which address is presented by a committee of an organization called "The East Tennessee Relief Association."
Deeply commiserating the condition of these most loyal and suffering people, I am unprepared to make any specific recommendation for their relief. The military is doing and will continue to do the best for them within its power. Their address represents that the construction of direct railroad communication between Knoxville and Cincinnati by way of central Kentucky would be of great consequence in the present emergency. It may be remembered that in the annual message of December, 1861, such railroad construction was recommended. I now add that, with the hearty concurrence of Congress, I would yet be pleased to construct a road, both for the relief of these people and for its continuing military importance.
A. LINCOLN.

MESSAGE TO THE HOUSE OF REPRESENTATIVES,

APRIL 28, 1864.

TO THE HOUSE OF REPRESENTATIVES:
In obedience to the resolution of your honorable body, a copy of which is herewith returned, I have the honor to make the following brief statement, which is believed to contain the information sought:
Prior to and at the meeting of the present Congress, Robert C. Schenck, of Ohio, and Frank P. Blair, Jr., of Missouri, members elect thereto, by and with the consent of the Senate held commissions from the Executive as major-generals in the volunteer army. General Schenck tendered the resignation of his said commission, and took his seat in the House of Representatives, at the assembling thereof, upon the distinct verbal understanding with the Secretary of War and the Executive that he might, at any time during the session, at his own pleasure, withdraw said resignation and return to the field.
General Blair was, by temporary assignment of General Sherman, in command of a corps through the battles in front of Chattanooga, and in the march to the relief of Knoxville, which occurred in the latter days of November and early days of December last, and of course was not present at the assembling of Congress. When he subsequently arrived here, he sought, and was allowed by the Secretary of War and the Executive, the same conditions and promise as allowed and made to General Schenck.
General Schenck has not applied to withdraw his resignation; but when General Grant was made Lieutenant-General, producing some change of commanders, General Blair sought to be assigned to the command of a corps. This was made known to Generals Grant and Sherman, and assented to by them, and the particular corps for him designated.
This was all arranged and understood, as now remembered, so much as a month ago; but the formal withdrawal of General Blair's resignation, and making the order assigning him to the command of the corps, were not consummated at the War Department until last week, perhaps on the 23d of April instant. As a summary of the whole, it may be stated that General Blair holds no military commission or appointment other than as herein stated, and that it is believed he is now acting as major-General upon the assumed validity of the commission herein stated, in connection with the facts herein stated, and not otherwise. There are some letters, notes, telegrams, orders, entries, and perhaps other documents in connection with this subject, which it is believed would throw no additional light upon it, but which will be cheerfully furnished if desired.
A. LINCOLN.

TO GENERAL U. S. GRANT.

EXECUTIVE MANSION, WASHINGTON, April 30, 1864.

LIEUTENANT-GENERAL GRANT:
Not expecting to see you before the spring campaign opens, I wish to express in this way my entire satisfaction with what you have done up to this time, so far as I understand it.
The particulars of your plans I neither know nor seek to know. You are vigilant and self-reliant; and, pleased with this, I wish not to obtrude any restraints or constraints upon you. While I am very anxious that any great disaster or capture of our men in great number shall be avoided, I know that these points are less likely to escape your attention than they would be mine. If there be anything wanting which is within my power to give, do not fail to let me know it.
And now, with a brave army and a just cause, may God sustain you.
Yours very truly,
A. LINCOLN.

MESSAGE TO THE HOUSE OF REPRESENTATIVES

MAY 2, 1864.

TO THE HONORABLE THE HOUSE OF REPRESENTATIVES:
In compliance with the request contained in your resolution of the 29th ultimo, a copy of which resolution is herewith returned, I have the honor to transmit the following:
[Correspondence and orders relating to the resignation and reinstatement of Major-General Frank P. Blair, Jr., of Missouri.]
The foregoing constitutes all sought by the resolution so far as is remembered or has been found upon diligent search.
A. LINCOLN.

TELEGRAM TO GENERAL W. T. SHERMAN.

WASHINGTON, D. C., May 4, 1864.

MAJOR-GENERAL SHERMAN, Chattanooga, Tenn.:
I have an imploring appeal in behalf of the citizens who say your Order No.8 will compel them to go north of Nashville. This is in no sense an order, nor is it even a request that you will do anything which in the least shall be a drawback upon your military operations, but anything you can do consistently with those operations for those suffering people I shall be glad of.
A. LINCOLN.

TELEGRAM TO GENERAL ROSECRANS.

EXECUTIVE MANSION, WASHINGTON, May 5, 1864.

MAJOR-GENERAL ROSECRANS, Commanding, Saint Louis, Mo.:
The President directs me to inquire whether a day has yet been fixed for the execution of citizen Robert Louden, and if so what day?
JOHN HAY, Major and Assistant Adjutant-General.

TO MRS. S. B. McCONKEY.

EXECUTIVE MANSION, WASHINGTON, May 9, 1864.

MRS. SARAH B. McCONKEY, West Chester, Pa.:
MADAM:—Our mutual friend, Judge Lewis, tells me you do me the honor to inquire for my personal welfare. I have been very anxious for some days in regard to our armies in the field, but am considerably cheered, just now, by favorable news from them.

I am sure you will join me in the hope for their further success; while yourself, and other good mothers, wives, sisters, and daughters, do all you and they can, to relieve and comfort the gallant soldiers who compose them.
Yours truly,
A. LINCOLN.

RECOMMENDATION OF THANKSGIVING.

EXECUTIVE MANSION, WASHINGTON, May 9, 1864

TO THE FRIENDS OF UNION AND LIBERTY:
Enough is known of army operations, within the last five days, to claim our special gratitude to God. While what remains undone demands our most sincere prayers to and reliance upon Him (without whom all effort is vain), I recommend that all patriots at their homes, in their places of public worship, and wherever they may be, unite in common thanksgiving and prayer to Almighty God.
A. LINCOLN.

RESPONSE TO A SERENADE,

MAY 9, 1864.

FELLOW-CITIZENS:—I am very much obliged to you for the compliment of this call, though I apprehend it is owing more to the good news received to-day from the Army, than to a desire to see me. I am indeed very grateful to the brave men who have been struggling with the enemy in the field, to their noble commanders who have directed them, and especially to our Maker. Our commanders are following up their victories resolutely and successfully. I think, without knowing the particulars of the plans of General Grant, that what has been accomplished is of more importance than at first appears. I believe, I know (and am especially grateful to know) that General Grant has not been jostled in his purposes, that he has made all his points, and to-day he is on his line as he purposed before he moved his armies. I will volunteer to say that I am very glad at what has happened, but there is a great deal still to be done. While we are grateful to all the brave men and officers for the events of the past few days, we should, above all, be very grateful to Almighty God, who gives us victory.

There is enough yet before us requiring all loyal men and patriots to perform their share of the labor and follow the example of the modest General at the head of our armies, and sink all personal consideration for the sake of the country. I commend you to keep yourselves in the same tranquil mood that is characteristic of that brave and loyal man. I have said more than I expected when I came before you. Repeating my thanks for this call, I bid you good-bye.

TELEGRAM TO GENERAL LEW WALLACE.

WAR DEPARTMENT, WASHINGTON, D. C., May 10, 1864.

MAJOR-GENERAL WALLACE, Baltimore:

Please tell me what is the trouble with Dr. Hawks. Also please ask Bishop Whittington to give me his view of the case.
A. LINCOLN.

TELEGRAM TO GENERAL W. S. ROSECRANS,

EXECUTIVE MANSION, WASHINGTON, May 11, 1864.

MAJOR-GENERAL ROSECRANS, St. Louis, Missouri:
Complaints are coming to me of disturbances in Canoll, Platte, and Buchanan counties. Please ascertain the truth, correct what is found wrong, and telegraph me.
A. LINCOLN.

TO P. B. LOOMIS.

EXECUTIVE MANSION, WASHINGTON, May 12, 1864

F. B. LOOMIS, ESQ.
MY DEAR SIR:—I have the honor to acknowledge the receipt of your communication of the 28th April, in which you offer to replace the present garrison at Port Trumbull with volunteers, which you propose to raise at your own expense. While it seems inexpedient at this time to accept this proposition on account of the special duties now devolving upon the garrison mentioned, I cannot pass unnoticed such a meritorious instance of individual patriotism. Permit me, for the Government, to express my cordial thanks to you for this generous and public-spirited offer, which is worthy of note among the many called forth in these times of national trial.
I am very truly, your obedient servant,
A. LINCOLN.

RESPONSE TO A METHODIST DELEGATION, MAY 14, 1864.

GENTLEMEN:-In response to your address, allow me to attest the accuracy of its historical statements, indorse the sentiments it expresses, and thank you in the nation's name for the sure promise it gives. Nobly sustained, as the Government has been, by all the churches, I would utter nothing which might in the least appear invidious against any. Yet without this, it may fairly be said, that the Methodist Episcopal Church, not less devoted than the best, is by its greatest numbers the most important of all. It is no fault in others that the Methodist Church sends more soldiers to the field, more nurses to the hospitals, and more prayers to Heaven than—any other. God bless the Methodist Church Bless all the churches; and blessed be God, who in this our great trial giveth us the churches.

TELEGRAM TO GOVERNOR YATES. EXECUTIVE MANSION, WASHINGTON, May 18, 1864.

His EXCELLENCY RICHARD YATES, Springfield, Ill.:

If any such proclamation has appeared, it is a forgery.
A. LINCOLN.

ARREST AND IMPRISONMENT OF IRRESPONSIBLE NEWSPAPER REPORTERS AND EDITORS

ORDER TO GENERAL J. A. DIX.

EXECUTIVE MANSION, WASHINGTON, May 18, 1864.
MAJOR-GENERAL JOHN A. DIX, Commanding at New York:
Whereas there has been wickedly and traitorously printed and published this morning in the New York World and New York Journal of Commerce, newspapers printed and published in the city of New York, a false and spurious proclamation purporting to be signed by the President and to be countersigned by the Secretary of State, which publication is of a treasonable nature, designed to give aid and comfort to the enemies of the United States and to the rebels now at war against the Government and their aiders and abettors, you are therefore hereby commanded forthwith to arrest and imprison in any fort or military prison in your command, the editors, proprietors, and publishers of the aforesaid newspapers, and all such persons as, after public notice has been given of the falsehood of said publication, print and publish the same with intent to give aid and comfort to the enemy; and you will hold the persons so arrested in close custody until they can be brought to trial before a military commission for their offense. You will also take possession by military force of the printing establishments of the New York World and Journal of Commerce, and hold the same until further orders, and prohibit any further publication therefrom.
A. LINCOLN.
[On the morning of May 18, 3864, a forged proclamation was published in the World, and Journal of Commerce, of New York. The proclamation named a day for fasting and prayer, called for 400,000 fresh troops, and purposed to raise by an "immediate and peremptory draft," whatever quotas were not furnished on the day specified. Ed.]

TELEGRAM TO GENERAL B. P. BUTLER.

(Cipher.)

WASHINGTON, D. C., May 18, 1864.
MAJOR-GENERAL BUTLER, Bermuda Hundred, Va.:
Until receiving your dispatch of yesterday, the idea of commissions in the volunteers expiring at the end of three years had not occurred to me. I think no trouble will come of it; and, at all events, I shall take care of it so far as in me lies. As to the major-generalships in the regular army, I think I shall not dispose of another, at least until the combined operations now in progress, under direction of General Grant, and within which yourself and command are included, shall be terminated.
Meanwhile, on behalf of yourself, officers, and men, please accept my hearty thanks for what you and they have so far done.
A. LINCOLN.

ORDER CONCERNING THE EXEMPTION OF AMERICAN CONSULS FROM MILITARY SERVICE

MAY 19, 1864.

It is officially announced by the State Department that citizens of the United States holding commissions and recognized as Consuls of foreign powers, are not by law exempt from military service if drafted:
Therefore the mere enrolment of a citizen holding a foreign consulate will not be held to vacate his commission, but if he shall be drafted his exequatur will be revoked unless he shall have previously resigned in order that another Consul may be received.
An exequatur bearing date the 3d day of May, 1858, having been issued to Charles Hunt, a citizen of the United States, recognizing him as a Consul of Belgium for St. Louis, Missouri, and declaring him free to exercise and enjoy such functions, powers, and privileges as are allowed to the Consuls of the most favored nations in the United States, and the said Hunt having sought to screen himself from his military duty to his country, in consequence of thus being invested with the consular functions of a foreign power in the United States, it is deemed advisable that the said Charles Hunt should no longer be permitted to continue in the exercise of said functions, powers, and privileges.

These are therefore to declare that I no longer recognize the said Hunt as Consul of Belgium, for St. Louis, Missouri, and will not permit him to exercise or enjoy any of the functions, powers or privileges allowed to consuls of that nation, and that I do hereby wholly revoke and annul the said exequatur heretofore given, and do declare the same to be absolutely null and void from this day forward.

In testimony whereof, I have caused these letters to be made patent, and the seal of the United States of America to be hereunto affixed................

A. LINCOLN.

By the President: WILLIAM H. SEWARD, Secretary of State.

TELEGRAM TO GOVERNOR MORTON AND OTHERS. EXECUTIVE MANSION, May 21, 1864

GOVERNOR O. P. MORTON:

The getting forward of hundred-day troops to sustain General Sherman's lengthening lines promises much good. Please put your best efforts into the work.

A. LINCOLN.

Same to Governor Yates, Springfield, Illinois; Governor Stone, Davenport, Iowa; Governor Lewis, Madison, Wisconsin.

TELEGRAM TO CHRISTIANA A. SACK. WAR DEPARTMENT WASHINGTON, D. C., May 21, 1864

CHRISTIANA A. SACK, Baltimore, Md.:

I cannot postpone the execution of a convicted spy on a mere telegraphic despatch signed with a name I never heard before. General Wallace may give you a pass to see him if he chooses.

A. LINCOLN.

TELEGRAM TO GOVERNOR BROUGH. WASHINGTON CITY, May 24, 1864.

GOVERNOR BROUGH, Columbus, Ohio:

Yours to Secretary of War [received] asking for something cheering. We have nothing bad from anywhere. I have just seen a despatch of Grant, of 11 P.M., May 23, on the North Anna and partly across it, which ends as follows: "Everything looks exceedingly favorable for us." We have nothing later from him.

A. LINCOLN.

TELEGRAM TO GENERAL MEADE. EXECUTIVE MANSION, WASHINGTON, May 25,1864.

MAJOR-GENERAL MEADE, Army of Potomac:

Mr. J. C. Swift wishes a pass from me to follow your army to pick up rags and cast-off clothing. I will give it to him if you say so, otherwise not.

A. LINCOLN.

["No job to big or too small" for this president—not even a request from a Rag Picker. D.W.]

MEMORANDUM CONCERNING THE TRANSPORTATION OF THE NEW YORK NAVAL BRIGADE.

EXECUTIVE MANSION, WASHINGTON, May 26, 1864.

WHOM IT MAY CONCERN:
I am again pressed with the claim of Mr. Marshall O. Roberts, for transportation of what was called the Naval Brigade from New York to Fortress Monroe. This force was a special organization got up by one Bartlett, in pretended pursuance of written authority from me, but in fact, pursuing the authority in scarcely anything whatever. The credit given him by Mr. Roberts, was given in the teeth of the express declaration that the Government would not be responsible for the class of expenses to which it belonged. After all some part of the transportation became useful to the Government, and equitably should be paid for; but I have neither time nor means to ascertain this equitable amount, or any appropriation to pay it with if ascertained. If the Quartermaster at New York can ascertain what would compensate for so much of the transportation as did result usefully to the Government, it might be a step towards reaching justice. I write this from memory, but I believe it is substantially correct.
A. LINCOLN.

TO P. A. CONKLING AND OTHERS.

EXECUTIVE MANSION,

WASHINGTON, June 3, 1864.
HON. F. A. CONKLING AND OTHERS.
GENTLEMEN:—Your letter, inviting me to be present at a mass meeting of loyal citizens, to be held at New York on the 4th instant, for the purpose of expressing gratitude to Lieutenant-General Grant for his signal services, was received yesterday. It is impossible for me to attend. I approve, nevertheless, of whatever may tend to strengthen and sustain General Grant and the noble armies now under his direction. My previous high estimate of General Grant has been maintained and heightened by what has occurred in the remarkable campaign he is now conducting, while the magnitude and difficulty of the task before him does not prove less than I expected. He and his brave soldiers are now in the midst of their great trial, and I trust that at your meeting you will so shape your good words that they may turn to men and guns, moving to his and their support.
Yours truly,
A. LINCOLN.

INDORSEMENT ON A LETTER TOUCHING THE REPUBLICAN NATIONAL CONVENTION.

JUNE 5, 1864.

(Indorsement.)
Swett is unquestionably all right. Mr. Holt is a good man, but I had not heard or thought of him for Vice-President. Wish not to interfere about Vice-President. Cannot interfere about platform. Convention must judge for itself.
A. LINCOLN.

TELEGRAM TO GENERAL MEADE. EXECUTIVE MANSION, WASHINGTON, June 6, 1864.

MAJOR-GENERAL MEADE, Army of the Potomac:

Private James McCarthy, of the One-hundred and fortieth New York Volunteers, is here under sentence to the Dry Tortugas for an attempt to desert. His friends appeal to me and if his colonel and you consent, I will send him to his regiment. Please answer.
A. LINCOLN.

TELEGRAM TO GENERAL W. S. ROSECRANS. WASHINGTON, June 8, 1864.

MAJOR-GENERAL ROSECRANS, St. Louis, Missouri:

Yours of to-day received. I am unable to conceive how a message can be less safe by the express than by a staff-officer. If you send a verbal message, the messenger is one additional person let into the secret.
A. LINCOLN

REPLY TO THE COMMITTEE NOTIFYING PRESIDENT LINCOLN OF HIS RENOMINATION,

JUNE 9, 1864.

Mr. CHAIRMAN AND GENTLEMEN OF THE COMMITTEE:
I will neither conceal my gratification nor restrain the expression of my gratitude that the Union people, through their convention, in their continued effort to save and advance the nation, have deemed me not unworthy to remain in my present position. I know no reason to doubt that I shall accept the nomination tendered; and yet perhaps I should not declare definitely before reading and considering what is called the platform. I will say now, however, I approve the declaration in favor of so amending the Constitution as to prohibit slavery throughout the nation. When the people in revolt, with a hundred days of explicit notice that they could within those days resume their allegiance without the overthrow of their institution, and that they could not so resume it afterward, elected to stand out, such amendment of the Constitution as now proposed became a fitting and necessary conclusion to the final success of the Union cause. Such alone can meet and cover all cavils. Now the unconditional Union men, North and South, perceive its importance and embrace it. In the joint names of Liberty and Union, let us labor to give it legal form and practical effect.

PLATFORM OF THE UNION NATIONAL CONVENTION HELD IN BALTIMORE, MD., JUNE 7 AND 8, 1864.
1. Resolved, That it is the highest duty of every American citizen to maintain against all their enemies the integrity of the Union and the paramount authority of the Constitution and laws of the United States; and that, laying aside all differences of political opinion, we pledge ourselves, as Union men, animated by a common sentiment and aiming at a common object, to do everything in our power to aid the Government in quelling by force of arms the rebellion now raging against its authority, and in bringing to the punishment due to their crimes the rebels and traitors arrayed against it.
2. Resolved, That we approve the determination of the Government of the United States not to compromise with rebels, or to offer them any terms of peace, except such as may be based upon an unconditional surrender of their hostility and a return to their just allegiance to the Constitution and laws of the United States, and that we call upon the Government to maintain this position, and to prosecute the war with the utmost possible vigor to the complete suppression of the rebellion, in full reliance upon the self-sacrificing patriotism, the heroic valor, and the undying devotion of the American people to their Country and its free institutions.
3. Resolved, That as slavery was the cause, and now constitutes the strength, of this rebellion, and as it must be, always and everywhere, hostile to the principles of republican government, justice and the national safety demand its utter and complete extirpation from the soil of the republic; and that while we uphold and maintain the acts and proclamations by which the Government, in its own defense, has aimed a death-blow at this gigantic evil, we are in favor, furthermore,

of such an amendment to the Constitution, to be made by the people in conformity with its provisions, as shall terminate and forever prohibit the existence of slavery within the limits or the jurisdiction of the United States.

4. Resolved, That the thanks of the American people are due to the soldiers and sailors of the Army and Navy, who have periled their lives in defense of their country and in vindication of the honor of its flag; that the nation owes to them some permanent recognition of their patriotism and their valor, and ample and permanent provision for those of their survivors who have received disabling and honorable wounds in the service of the country; and that the memories of those who have fallen in its defense shall be held in grateful and everlasting remembrance.

5. Resolved, That we approve and applaud the practical wisdom, the unselfish patriotism, and the unswerving fidelity to the Constitution and the principles of American liberty, with which Abraham Lincoln has discharged under circumstances of unparalleled difficulty the great duties and responsibilities of the Presidential office; that we approve and indorse as demanded by the emergency and essential to the preservation of the nation, and as within the provisions of the Constitution, the measures and acts which he has adopted to defend the nation against its open and secret foes; that we approve, especially, the Proclamation of Emancipation, and the employment as Union soldiers of men heretofore held in slavery; and that we have full confidence in his determination to carry these and all other constitutional measures essential to the salvation of the country into full and complete effect.

6. Resolved, That we deem it essential to the General welfare that harmony should prevail in the national councils, and we regard as worthy of public confidence and official trust those only who cordially indorse the principles proclaimed in these resolutions, and which should characterize the administration of the Government.

7. Resolved, That the Government owes to all men employed in its armies, without regard to distinction of color, the full protection of the laws of war, and that any violation of these laws, or of the usages of civilized nations in time of war, by the rebels now in arms, should be made the subject of prompt and full redress.

8. Resolved, That foreign immigration, which in the past has added so much to the wealth, development of resources, and increase of power to this nation, the asylum of the oppressed of all nations, should be fostered and encouraged by a liberal and just policy.

9. Resolved, That we are in favor of the speedy construction of the railroad to the Pacific coast.

10. Resolved, That the national faith, pledged for the redemption of the public debt, must be kept inviolate, and that for this purpose we recommend economy and rigid responsibility in the public expenditures, and a vigorous and just system of taxation: and that it is the duty of every loyal State to sustain the credit and promote the use of the national currency.

11. Resolved, That we approve the position taken by the Government that the people of the United States can never regard with indifference the attempt of any European power to overthrow by force or to supplant by fraud the institutions of any republican government on the Western Continent, and that they will view with extreme jealousy, as menacing to the peace and independence of their own country, the efforts of any such power to obtain new footholds for monarchical governments, sustained by foreign military force, in near proximity to the United States.

REPLY TO A DELEGATION FROM THE NATIONAL UNION LEAGUE,

JUNE 9, 1864.

GENTLEMEN—I can only say in response to the remarks of your chairman, that I am very grateful for the renewed confidence which has been accorded to me, both by the convention and by the National League. I am not insensible at all to the personal compliment there is in this, yet I do not allow myself to believe that any but a small portion of it is to be appropriated as a personal compliment to me. The convention and the nation, I am assured, are alike animated by a higher view of the interests of the country, for the present and the great future, and the part I am entitled to appropriate as a compliment is only that part which I may lay hold of as being the opinion of the convention and of the League, that I am not entirely unworthy to be intrusted with the place I have occupied for the last three years. I have not permitted myself, gentlemen, to conclude that I am the best man in the country; but I am reminded in this connection of a story of an old Dutch farmer, who remarked to a companion once that "it was not best to swap horses when crossing a stream."

REPLY TO A DELEGATION FROM OHIO,

JUNE 9, 1864.

GENTLEMEN:—I am very much obliged to you for this compliment. I have just been saying, and will repeat it, that the hardest of all speeches I have to answer is a serenade. I never know what to say on these occasions. I suppose that you have done me this kindness in connection with the action of the Baltimore convention, which has recently taken place, and with which, of course, I am very well satisfied. What we want still more than Baltimore conventions, or Presidential elections, is success under General Grant. I propose that you constantly bear in mind that the support you owe to the brave officers and soldiers in the field is of the very first importance, and we should therefore bend all our energies to that point. Now without detaining you any longer, I propose that you help me to close up what I am now saying with three rousing cheers for General Grant and the officers and soldiers under his command.

ADDRESS TO THE ENVOY FROM THE HAWAIIAN ISLANDS,

JUNE 11, 1864.

SIR:—In every light in which the State of the Hawaiian Islands can be contemplated, it is an object of profound interest for the United States. Virtually it was once a colony. It is now a near and intimate neighbor. It is a haven of shelter and refreshment for our merchants, fishermen, seamen, and other citizens, when on their lawful occasions they are navigating the eastern seas and oceans. Its people are free, and its laws, language, and religion are largely the fruit of our own teaching and example. The distinguished part which you, Mr. Minister, have acted in the history of that interesting country, is well known here. It gives me pleasure to assure you of my sincere desire to do what I can to render now your sojourn in the United States agreeable to yourself, satisfactory to your sovereign, and beneficial to the Hawaiian people.

REMARKS TO AN OHIO REGIMENT,

JUNE 11, 1864.

Soldiers! I understand you have just come from Ohio; come to help us in this the nation's day of trial, and also of its hopes. I thank you for your promptness in responding to the call for troops. Your services were never needed more than now. I know not where you are going. You may stay here and take the places of those who will be sent to the front, or you may go there yourselves. Wherever you go I know you will do your best. Again I thank you. Good-by.

TELEGRAM TO GENERAL L. THOMAS. EXECUTIVE MANSION, WASHINGTON, June 13,

1864.
MAJOR-GENERAL THOMAS, Louisville, Kentucky:
Complaint is made to me that in the vicinity of Henderson, our militia is seizing negroes and carrying them off without their own consent, and according to no rules whatever, except those of absolute violence. I wish you would look into this and inform me, and see that the making soldiers of negroes is done according to the rules you are acting upon, so that unnecessary provocation and irritation be avoided.
A. LINCOLN.

TELEGRAM TO THOMAS WEBSTER. WASHINGTON, D. C., June 13, 1864.

THOMAS WEBSTER, Philadelphia:

Will try to leave here Wednesday afternoon, say at 4 P.M., remain till Thursday afternoon and then return. This subject to events.
A. LINCOLN.

TELEGRAM TO GENERAL U. S. GRANT. WASHINGTON, June 15, 1864. 7 A.M.

LIEUTENANT-GENERAL GRANT, Headquarters Army of the Potomac:

I have just received your dispatch of 1 P.M. yesterday. I begin to see it: you will succeed. God bless you all.
A. LINCOLN.

ADDRESS AT A SANITARY FAIR IN PHILADELPHIA,

JUNE 16, 1864.

I suppose that this toast is intended to open the way for me to say something. War at the best is terrible, and this of ours in its magnitude and duration is one of the most terrible the world has ever known. It has deranged business totally in many places, and perhaps in all. It has destroyed property, destroyed life, and ruined homes. It has produced a national debt and a degree of taxation unprecedented in the history of this country. It has caused mourning among us until the heavens may almost be said to be hung in black. And yet it continues. It has had accompaniments not before known in the history of the world. I mean the Sanitary and Christian Commissions, with their labors for the relief of the soldiers, and the Volunteer Refreshment Saloons, understood better by those who hear me than by myself, and these fairs, first begun at Chicago and next held in Boston, Cincinnati, and other cities. The motive and object that lie at the bottom of them are worthy of the most that we can do for the soldier who goes to fight the battles of his country. From the fair and tender hand of women is much, very much, done for the soldier, continually reminding him of the care and thought for him at home. The knowledge that he is not forgotten is grateful to his heart. Another view of these institutions is worthy of thought. They are voluntary contributions, giving proof that the national resources are not at all exhausted, and that the national patriotism will sustain us through all. It is a pertinent question, When is this war to end? I do not wish to name the day when it will end, lest the end should not come at the given time. We accepted this war, and did not begin it. We accepted it for an object, and when that object is accomplished the war will end, and I hope to God that it will never end until that object is accomplished. We are going through with our task, so far as I am concerned, if it takes us three years longer. I have not been in the habit of making predictions, but I am almost tempted now to hazard one. I will. It is, that Grant is this evening in a position, with Meade and Hancock, of Pennsylvania, whence he can never be dislodged by the enemy until Richmond is taken. If I shall discover that General Grant may be greatly facilitated in the capture of Richmond by rapidly pouring to him a large number of armed men at the briefest notice, will you go? Will you march on with him? [Cries of "Yes, yes."] Then I shall call upon you when it is necessary.

TO ATTORNEY-GENERAL BATES.

EXECUTIVE MANSION, WASHINGTON, Jun. 24, 1864

HONORABLE ATTORNEY-GENERAL.

SIR:—By authority of the Constitution, and moved thereto by the fourth section of the act of Congress, entitled "An act making appropriations for the support of the army for the year ending the thirtieth of June, eighteen hundred and sixty-five, and for other purposes, approved June is, 1864," I require your opinion in writing as to what pay, bounty, and clothing are allowed by law to persons of color who were free on the nineteenth day of April, 1861, and who have

been enlisted and mustered into the military service of the United States between the month of December, 1862, and the sixteenth of June, 1864.
Please answer as you would do, on my requirement, if the act of June 15, 1864, had not been passed, and I will so use your opinion as to satisfy that act.
Your obedient servant,
A. LINCOLN.

TELEGRAM TO MRS. LINCOLN.

EXECUTIVE MANSION, WASHINGTON, June 24, 1864.

MRS. A. LINCOLN, Boston, Massachusetts:
All well and very warm. Tad and I have been to General Grant's army. Returned yesterday safe and sound.
A. LINCOLN.

TELEGRAM TO GENERAL W. S. ROSECRANS. WASHINGTON, June 24, 1864.

MAJOR-GENERAL ROSECRANS, St. Louis, Missouri:

Complaint is made to me that General Brown does not do his best to suppress bushwhackers. Please ascertain and report to me.
A. LINCOLN.

LETTER ACCEPTING THE NOMINATION FOR PRESIDENT.

EXECUTIVE MANSION, WASHINGTON, June 27, 1864.

HON. WILLIAM DENNISON AND OTHERS, a Committee of the Union National Convention.
GENTLEMEN:—Your letter of the 14th inst.., formally notifying me that I have been nominated by the convention you represent for the Presidency of the United States for four years from the 4th of March next, has been received. The nomination is gratefully accepted, as the resolutions of the convention, called the platform, are heartily approved. While the resolution in regard to the supplanting of republican government upon the Western Continent is fully concurred in, there might be misunderstanding were I not to say that the position of the Government in relation to the action of France in Mexico, as assumed through the State Department and indorsed by the convention among the measures and acts of the Executive, will be faithfully maintained so long as the state of facts shall leave that position pertinent and applicable.
I am especially gratified that the soldier and seaman were not forgotten by the convention, as they forever must and will be remembered by the grateful country for whose salvation they devote their lives.
Thanking you for the kind and complimentary terms in which you have communicated the nomination and other proceedings of the convention, I subscribe myself,
Your obedient servant,
A. LINCOLN.

TO GENERAL P. STEELE.

EXECUTIVE MANSION, WASHINGTON, June 29, 1864

MAJOR-GENERAL STEELE:
I understand that Congress declines to admit to seats the persons sent as Senators and Representatives from Arkansas. These persons apprehend that, in consequence, you may not support the new State government there as you otherwise would. My wish is that you give that government and the people there the same support and protection that you would if the members had been admitted, because in no event, nor in any view of the case, can this do any harm, while it will be the best you can do toward suppressing the rebellion.
Yours truly,
A. LINCOLN.

TELEGRAM TO GENERAL GRANT. EXECUTIVE MANSION, WASHINGTON, June 29, 1864.

LIEUTENANT-GENERAL GRANT, City Point:

Dr. Worster wishes to visit you with a view of getting your permission to introduce into the army "Harmon's Sandal Sock." Shall I give him a pass for that object?
A. LINCOLN.

TELEGRAM TO DAVID TOD.

EXECUTIVE MANSION, WASHINGTON, D. C., June 30, 1864.

HON. DAVID TOD, Youngstown, Ohio: I have nominated you to be Secretary of the Treasury, in place of Governor Chase, who has resigned. Please come without a moment's delay.
A. LINCOLN.

TO J. L. SCRIPPS.

EXECUTIVE MANSION, WASHINGTON, July 4, 1864.

To JOHN L. SCRIPPS, ESQ.
DEAR SIR:—Complaint is made to me that you are using your official power to defeat Mr. Arnold's nomination to Congress. I am well satisfied with Mr. Arnold as a member of Congress, and I do not know that the man who might supplant him would be as satisfactory; but the correct principle, I think, is that all our friends should have absolute freedom of choice among our friends. My wish, therefore, is that you will do just as you think fit with your own suffrage in the case, and not constrain any of your subordinates to [do] other than [as] he thinks fit with his. This is precisely the rule I inculcated and adhered to on my part, when a certain other nomination, now recently made, was being canvassed for.
Yours very truly,
A. LINCOLN.
TELEGRAM TO J. W. GARRETT. WASHINGTON, July 5, 1864.
J. W. GARRETT, President [B. & O. R. R.], Camden Station:
You say telegraphic communication is re-established with Sandy Hook. Well, what does Sandy Hook say about operations of enemy and of Sigel during to-day?
A. LINCOLN.

FROM SECRETARY STANTON TO GOVERNOR SEYMOUR.

WAR DEPARTMENT, WASHINGTON, July 5, 1864.

HIS EXCELLENCY HORATIO SEYMOUR, Governor of New York, Albany:
The President directs me to inform you that a rebel force, variously estimated at from fifteen to twenty thousand men, have invaded the State of Maryland, and have taken Martinsburg and Harper's Ferry, and are threatening other points; that the public safety requires him to call upon the State executives for a militia force to repel this invasion. He therefore directs me to call on you for a militia force of twelve thousand men from your State to serve not more than one hundred days, and to request that you will with the utmost despatch forward the troops to Washington by rail or steamboat as may be most expeditious.
Please favor me with an answer at your earliest convenience.
EDWIN M. STANTON,
Secretary of War.

PROCLAMATION SUSPENDING THE WRIT OF HABEAS CORPUS,

JULY 5, 1864.

BY THE PRESIDENT OF THE UNITED STATES:
A Proclamation.
Whereas, by a proclamation which was issued on the 15th day of April, 1861, the President of the United States announced and declared that the laws of the United States had been for some time past, and then were, opposed and the execution thereof obstructed in certain States therein mentioned, by combinations too powerful to be suppressed by the ordinary course of judicial proceedings or by the power vested in the marshals by law; and
Whereas, immediately after the issuing of the said proclamation the land and naval forces of the United States were put into activity to suppress the said insurrections and rebellion; and
Whereas, the Congress of the United States, by an act approved on the third day of March, 1863, did enact that during the said rebellion the President of the United States, whenever in his judgment the public safety may require it, is authorized to suspend the privilege of the writ of habeas corpus in any case throughout the United States, or any part thereof; and
Whereas, the said insurrection and rebellion still continue, endangering the existence of the Constitution and Government of the United States; and
Whereas, the military forces of the United States are now actively engaged in suppressing the said insurrection and rebellion in various parts of the States where the said rebellion has been successful in obstructing the laws and public authorities, especially in the States of Virginia and Georgia; and
Whereas, on the fifteenth day of September last, the President of the United States duly issued his proclamation, wherein he declared that the privilege of the writ of habeas corpus should be suspended throughout the United States, in Cases whereby the authority of the President of the United States, the military, naval, and civil officers of the United States, or any of them, hold persons under their command or in their custody, either as prisoners of war, spies, or aiders or abettors of the enemy, or officers, soldiers, or seamen enrolled or drafted, or mustered, or enlisted in, or belonging to the land or naval forces of the United States, or as deserters therefrom, or otherwise amenable to military law, or the rules and articles of war, or the rules and regulations prescribed for the military and naval service by authority of the President of the United States, or for resisting a draft, or for any other offence against the military or naval service; and
Whereas, many citizens of the State of Kentucky have joined the forces of the insurgents, who have on several occasions entered the said State of Kentucky in large force and not without aid and comfort furnished by disaffected and disloyal citizens of the United States residing therein, have not only greatly disturbed the public peace but have overborne the civil authorities and made flagrant civil war, destroying property and life in various parts of the State; and
Whereas, it has been made known to the President of the United States, by the officers commanding the National armies, that combinations have been formed in the said State of Kentucky, with a purpose of inciting the rebel forces to renew the said operations of civil war within the said State, and thereby to embarrass the United States armies now operating in the said States of Virginia and Georgia, and even to endanger their safety.
Now, therefore, I, Abraham Lincoln, President of the United States, by virtue of the authority vested in me by the Constitution and laws, do hereby declare that in my judgment the public safety especially requires that the suspension of the privilege of the writ of habeas corpus so proclaimed in the said proclamation of the 15th of September, 1863,

be made effectual and be duly enforced in and throughout the said State of Kentucky, and that martial law be for the present declared therein. I do therefore hereby require of the military officers of the said State that the privilege of the habeas corpus be effectually suspended within the said State, according to the aforesaid proclamation, and that martial law be established therein to take effect from the date of this proclamation, the said suspension and establishment of martial law to continue until this proclamation shall be revoked or modified, but not beyond the period when the said rebellion shall have been suppressed or come to an end. And I do hereby require and command, as well as military officers, all civil officers and authorities existing or found within the said State of Kentucky, to take notice of this proclamation and to give full effect to the same. The martial laws herein proclaimed and the things in that respect herein ordered will not be deemed or taken to interfere with the holding of lawful elections, or with the proceedings of the constitutional Legislature of Kentucky, or with the administration of justice in the courts of law existing therein between citizens of the United States in suits or proceedings which do not affect the military operations or the constituted authorities of the government of the United States.

In testimony whereof I have hereunto set my hand and caused the seal of the United States to be affixed.

Done at the City of Washington this 5th day of July, in the year of our Lord 1864, and of the independence of the United States the eighty-eighth.

A. LINCOLN. By the President: WILLIAM H. SEWARD, Secretary of State.

PROCLAMATION FOR A DAY OF PRAYER, JULY 7, 1864.

BY THE PRESIDENT OF THE UNITED STATES OF AMERICA:

A Proclamation.

Whereas, the Senate and House of Representatives at their last session adopted a concurrent resolution, which was approved on the second day of July instant, and which `was in the words following, namely:

That the President of the United States be requested to appoint a day of humiliation and prayer by the people of the United States, that he request his constitutional advisers at the head of the Executive Departments to unite with him, as Chief Magistrate of the nation, at the City of Washington, and the members of Congress, and all magistrates, all civil, military, and naval officers, all soldiers, sailors, and marines, with all loyal and law-abiding people, to convene at their usual places of worship, or wherever they may be, to confess and to repent of their manifold sins, to implore the compassion and forgiveness of the Almighty, that, if consistent with His will, the existing rebellion may be speedily suppressed, and the supremacy of the Constitution and laws of the United States may be established throughout all the States; to implore Him, as the Supreme Ruler of the world, not to destroy us as a people, nor suffer us to be destroyed by the hostility or connivance of other nations, or by obstinate adhesion to our own counsels which may be in conflict with His eternal, purposes, and to implore Him to enlighten the mind of the nation to know and do His will, humbly believing that it is in accordance with His will that our place should be maintained as a united people among the family of nations; to implore Him to grant to our armed defenders, and the masses of the people, that courage, power of resistance, and endurance necessary to secure that result; to implore Him in His infinite goodness to soften the hearts, enlighten the minds, and quicken the conscience of those in rebellion, that they may lay down their arms, and speedily return to their allegiance to the United States, that they may not be utterly destroyed, that the effusion of blood may be stayed, and that unity and fraternity may be restored, and peace established throughout all our borders.

Now, therefore, I, Abraham Lincoln, President of the `United States, cordially concurring with the Congress of the United States, in the penitential and pious sentiments expressed in the aforesaid resolutions, and heartily approving of the devotional design and purpose thereof, do hereby appoint the first Thursday of August next to be observed by the people of the United States as a day of national humiliation and prayer.

I do hereby further invite and request the heads of the Executive Departments of this Government, together with all legislators, all judges and magistrates, and all other persons exercising authority in the land, whether civil, military, or naval, and all soldiers, seamen, and marines in the national service, and all other loyal and law-abiding people of the United States, to assemble in their preferred places of public worship on that day, and there to render to the Almighty and merciful Ruler of the Universe, such homage and such confessions, and to offer to Him such supplications as the Congress of the United States have, in their aforesaid resolution, so solemnly, so earnestly, and so reverently recommended.

In testimony whereof, I have hereunto set my hand and caused the seal of the United States to be affixed. Done at the city of Washington this seventh day of July, in the year of our Lord one thousand eight hundred and sixty-four, and of the independence of the United States the eighty-ninth.

A. LINCOLN.

By the President WILLIAM H. SEWARD, Secretary of State.

PROCLAMATION CONCERNING A BILL "TO GUARANTEE TO CERTAIN STATES,

WHOSE GOVERNMENTS HAVE BEEN USURPED OR OVERTHROWN, A REPUBLICAN FORM OF GOVERNMENT," AND CONCERNING RECONSTRUCTION,
JULY 8, 1864. BY THE PRESIDENT OF THE UNITED STATES:
A Proclamation.
Whereas at the late session Congress passed a bill "to guarantee to certain states whose governments have been usurped or overthrown a republican form of government," a copy of which is hereunto annexed; and
Whereas, the said bill was presented to the President of the United States for his approval less than one hour before the sine die adjournment of said session, and was not signed by him; and
Whereas the said bill contains, among other things, a plan for restoring the States in rebellion to their proper practical relation in the Union, which plan expresses the sense of Congress upon that subject, and which plan it is now thought fit to lay before the people for their consideration:
Now, therefore, I, Abraham Lincoln, President of the United States, do proclaim, declare, and make known that while I am (as I was in December last, when, by proclamation, I propounded a plan for restoration) unprepared by a formal approval of this bill to be inflexibly committed to any single plan of restoration, and while I am also unprepared to declare that the free State constitutions and governments already adopted and installed in Arkansas and Louisiana shall be set aside and held for naught, thereby repelling and discouraging the loyal citizens who have set up the same as to further effort, or to declare a constitutional competency in Congress to abolish slavery in States, but am at the same time sincerely hoping and expecting that a constitutional amendment abolishing slavery throughout the nation may be adopted, nevertheless I am fully satisfied with the system for restoration contained in the bill as one very proper plan for the loyal people of any State choosing to adopt it, and that I am and at all times shall be prepared to give the Executive aid and assistance to any such people so soon as the military resistance to the United States shall have been suppressed in any such States and the people thereof shall have sufficiently returned to their obedience to the Constitution and the laws of the United States, in which cases militia-governors will be appointed with directions to proceed according to the bill.
In testimony whereof I have hereunto set my hand and caused the seal of the United States to be affixed..............
A. LINCOLN.
By the President: WILLIAM H. SEWARD, Secretary of State.

TO HORACE GREELEY.

WASHINGTON, D. C., July 9, 1864

HON. HORACE GREELEY.
DEAR SIR:—Your letter of the 7th, with inclosures, received.
If you can find any person, anywhere, professing to have any proposition of Jefferson Davis in writing, for peace, embracing the restoration of the Union and abandonment of slavery, whatever else it embraces, say to him he may come to me with you; and that if he really brings such proposition, he shall at the least have safe conduct with the paper (and without publicity, if he chooses) to the point where you shall have to meet him. The same if there be two or more persons.
Yours truly,
A. LINCOLN.

TELEGRAM TO J. W. GARRETT. WASHINGTON, D. C., July 9, 1864

J. W. GARRETT, Camden Station:

What have you heard about a battle at Monocacy to-day? We have nothing about it here except what you say.
A. LINCOLN.

TELEGRAM FROM GENERAL HALLECK TO GENERAL WALLACE.

WASHINGTON, July 9, 1864. 11.57 P.M.

MAJOR-GENERAL L. WALLACE, Commanding Middle Department:
I am directed by the President to say that you will rally your forces and make every possible effort to retard the enemy's march on Baltimore.
H. W. HALLECK, Major-General and Chief of Staff.

TELEGRAM TO T. SWAN AND OTHERS. WASHINGTON, D. C., July 10, 1864. 9.20

A.M.
THOMAS SWAN AND OTHERS, Baltimore, Maryland:
Yours of last night received. I have not a single soldier but whom is being disposed by the military for the best protection of all. By latest accounts the enemy is moving on Washington. They cannot fly to either place. Let us be vigilant, but keep cool. I hope neither Baltimore nor Washington will be sacked.
A. LINCOLN.

TELEGRAM TO GENERAL U.S. GRANT. WASHINGTON CITY, July TO, 1864. 2 P.M.

LIEUTENANT-GENERAL GRANT, City Point, Va.:

Your dispatch to General Halleck, referring to what I may think in the present emergency, is shown me. General Halleck says we have absolutely no force here fit to go to the field. He thinks that with the hundred-day men and invalids we have here we can defend Washington, and, scarcely, Baltimore. Besides these there are about eight thousand, not very reliable, under Howe, at Harper's Ferry with Hunter approaching that point very slowly, with what number I suppose you know better than I. Wallace, with some odds and ends, and part of what came up with Ricketts, was so badly beaten yesterday at Monocacy, that what is left can attempt no more than to defend Baltimore. What we shall get in from Pennsylvania and New York will scarcely be worth counting, I fear. Now, what I think is, that you should provide to retain your hold where you are, certainly, and bring the rest with you personally, and make a vigorous effort to destroy the enemy's forces in this vicinity. I think there is really a fair chance to do this, if the movement is prompt. This is what I think upon your suggestion, and is not an order.
A. LINCOLN.

TELEGRAM TO GENERAL U.S. GRANT. WASHINGTON, July 11, 1864. 8 A.M.

LIEUTENANT-GENERAL GRANT, City Point, Va.:

Yours of 10.30 P.M. yesterday received, and very satisfactory. The enemy will learn of Wright's arrival, and then the difficulty will be to unite Wright and Hunter south of the enemy before he will recross the Potomac. Some firing between Rockville and here now.
A. LINCOLN.

TELEGRAM TO GENERAL U.S. GRANT. WASHINGTON, D. C., July 12, 1864. 11.30 AM.

LIEUTENANT-GENERAL GRANT, City Point, Va.:
Vague rumors have been reaching us for two or three days that Longstreet's corps is also on its way [to] this vicinity. Look out for its absence from your front.
A. LINCOLN.

TELEGRAM AND LETTER TO HORACE GREELEY. EXECUTIVE MANSION, WASHINGTON, July 12, 1864.
HON. HORACE GREELEY, New York:
I suppose you received my letter of the 9th. I have just received yours of the 13th, and am disappointed by it. I was not expecting you to send me a letter, but to bring me a man, or men. Mr. Hay goes to you with my answer to yours of the 13th.
A. LINCOLN.
[Carried by Major John Hay.]

EXECUTIVE MANSION, WASHINGTON, JULY 15, 1864.

HON. HORACE GREELEY.

MY DEAR SIR:-Yours of the 13th is just received, and I am disappointed that you have not already reached here with those commissioners, if they would consent to come on being shown my letter to you of the 9th instant. Show that and this to them, and if they will come on the terms stated in the former, bring them. I not only intend a sincere effort for peace, but I intend that you shall be a personal witness that it is made.
Yours truly,
A. LINCOLN.

SAFE CONDUCT FOR CLEMENT C. CLAY AND OTHERS,

JULY 16, 1864.

The President of the United States directs that the four persons whose names follow, to wit, HON. Clement C. Clay, HON. Jacob Thompson, Professor James P. Holcombe, George N. Sanders, shall have safe conduct to the city of Washington in company with the HON. HORACE GREELEY, and shall be exempt from arrest or annoyance of any kind from any officer of the United States during their journey to the said city of Washington.
By order of the President: JOHN HAY, Major and Assistant Adjutant-General

TELEGRAM TO GENERAL U. S. GRANT. [WASHINGTON] July 17. 1864. 11.25 A.M.

LIEUTENANT-GENERAL GRANT, City Point, Va.:

In your dispatch of yesterday to General Sherman, I find the following, to wit:
"I shall make a desperate effort to get a position here, which will hold the enemy without the necessity of so many men."
Pressed as we are by lapse of time I am glad to hear you say this; and yet I do hope you may find a way that the effort shall not be desperate in the sense of great loss of life.
A. LINCOLN, President.

TELEGRAM TO GENERAL D. HUNTER WASHINGTON JULY 17, 1864.

MAJOR-GENERAL HUNTER, Harper's Ferry, West Va.

Yours of this morning received. You misconceive. The order you complain of was only nominally mine, and was framed by those who really made it with no thought of making you a scapegoat. It seemed to be General Grant's wish that the forces under General Wright and those under you should join and drive at the enemy under General Wright. Wright had the larger part of the force, but you had the rank. It was thought that you would prefer Crook's commanding your part to your serving in person under Wright. That is all of it. General Grant wishes you to remain in command of the department, and I do not wish to order otherwise.
A. LINCOLN.

TELEGRAM TO GENERAL W. T. SHERMAN.

EXECUTIVE MANSION, WASHINGTON, July 18, 1864. 11.25 A.M.

MAJOR-GENERAL SHERMAN, Chattahoochee River, Georgia:
I have seen your despatches objecting to agents of Northern States opening recruiting stations near your camps. An act of Congress authorizes this, giving the appointment of agents to the States, and not to the Executive Government. It is not for the War Department, or myself, to restrain or modify the law, in its execution, further than actual necessity may require. To be candid, I was for the passage of the law, not apprehending at the time that it would produce such inconvenience to the armies in the field as you now cause me to fear. Many of the States were very anxious for it, and I hoped that, with their State bounties, and active exertions, they would get out substantial additions to our colored forces, which, unlike white recruits, help us where they come from, as well as where they go to. I still hope advantage from the law; and being a law, it must be treated as such by all of us. We here will do what we consistently can to save you from difficulties arising out of it. May I ask, therefore, that you will give your hearty co-operation.
A. LINCOLN.

ANNOUNCEMENT CONCERNING TERMS OF PEACE.

EXECUTIVE MANSION,

WASHINGTON, July 18, 1864.
TO WHOM IT MAY CONCERN:
Any proposition which embraces the restoration of peace, the integrity of the whole Union, and the abandonment of slavery, and which comes by and with an authority that can control the armies now at war against the United States, will be received and considered by the Executive Government of the United States, and will be met by liberal terms on other substantial and collateral points; and the bearer or bearers thereof shall have safe conduct both ways.
A. LINCOLN.

PROCLAMATION CALLING FOR FIVE HUNDRED THOUSAND VOLUNTEERS,

JULY 18, 1864,

BY THE PRESIDENT OF THE UNITED STATES OF AMERICA:
A Proclamation.

Whereas by the act approved July 4, 1864, entitled "An act further to regulate and provide for the enrolling and calling out the national forces and for other purposes," it is provided that the President of the United States may, "at his discretion, at any time hereafter, call for any number of men, as volunteers for the respective terms of one, two, and three years for military service," and "that in case the quota or any part thereof of any town, township, ward of a city, precinct, or election district, or of a county not so subdivided, shall not be filled within the space of fifty days after such call, then the President shall immediately order a draft for one year to fill such quota or any part thereof which may be unfilled;" and

Whereas the new enrolment heretofore ordered is so far completed as that the aforementioned act of Congress may now be put in operation for recruiting and keeping up the strength of the armies in the field, for garrisons, and such military operations as may be required for the purpose of suppressing the rebellion and restoring the authority of the United States Government in the insurgent States:

Now, therefore, I, Abraham Lincoln, President of the United States, do issue this my last call for five hundred thousand volunteers for the military service: Provided, nevertheless, That this call shall be reduced by all credits which may be established under section eight of the aforesaid act on account of persons who have entered the naval service during the present rebellion and by credits for men furnished to the military service in excess of calls heretofore made. Volunteers will be accepted under this call for one, two, or three years, as they may elect, and will be entitled to the bounty provided by the law for the period of services for which they enlist.

And I hereby proclaim, order, and direct that immediately after the 5th day of September, 1864, being fifty days from the date of this call, a draft for troops to serve for one year shall be had in every town, township, ward of a city, precinct, or election district, or county not so subdivided, to fill the quota which shall be assigned to it under this call or any part thereof which may be unfilled by volunteers on the said 5th day of September, 1864.

In testimony whereof I have hereunto set my hand and caused the seal of the United States to be affixed.

Done at the City of Washington, this 18th day of July, A.D. 1864, and of the independence of the United States the eighty-ninth.
A. LINCOLN.
By the President: WILLIAM H. SEWARD, Secretary of State.

TELEGRAM TO GENERAL U.S. GRANT.

EXECUTIVE MANSION, WASHINGTON, July 20, 1864. 4.30 p.m.

LIEUTENANT-GENERAL GRANT, City Point, Va.:
Yours of yesterday, about a call for three hundred thousand, is received. I suppose you had not seen the call for five hundred thousand, made the day before, and which, I suppose, covers the case. Always glad to have your suggestions.
A. LINCOLN.

TELEGRAM TO J. L. WRIGHT.

WAR DEPARTMENT, JULY. 20, 1864.

J. L. WRIGHT, Indianapolis, Ind.:
All a mistake. Mr. Stanton has not resigned.
A. LINCOLN.

TELEGRAM TO GENERAL D. HUNTER. (Cipher.)

WAR DEPARTMENT, JULY 23, 1864.

MAJOR-GENERAL HUNTER, Harper's Ferry, West Va.
Are you able to take care of the enemy, when he turns back upon you, as he probably will on finding that Wright has left?
A. LINCOLN.

TO GOVERNOR CURTIN, ENCLOSING A LETTER TO WILLIAM O. SNIDER.

EXECUTIVE MANSION, WASHINGTON, July 25, 1864.

GOVERNOR CURTIN:
Herewith is the manuscript letter for the gentleman who sent me a cane through your hands. For my life I cannot make out his name; and therefore I cut it from his letter and pasted it on, as you see. I suppose [sic] will remember who he is, and I will thank you to forward him the letter. He dates his letter at Philadelphia.
Yours truly,
A. LINCOLN.

PRESENTATION OF A CANE

EXECUTIVE MANSION, WASHINGTON, July 25, 1864.

WILLIAM O. SNIDER:
The cane you did me the honor to present through Governor Curtin was duly placed in my hand by him. Please accept my thanks; and, at the same time, pardon me for not having sooner found time to tender them. Your obedient servant,
A. LINCOLN.

FROM JOHN HAY TO J. C. WELLING.

EXECUTIVE MANSION, WASHINGTON. July 25, 1864.

J. C. WELLING, ESQ.
SIR:—According to the request contained in your note, I have placed Mr. Gibson's letter of resignation in the hands of the President. He has read the letter, and says he accepts the resignation, as he will be glad to do with any other, which may be tendered, as this is, for the purpose of taking an attitude of hostility against him.
He says he was not aware that he was so much indebted to Mr. Gibson for having accepted the office at first, not remembering that he ever pressed him to do so, or that he gave it otherwise than as was usual, upon request made on behalf of Mr. Gibson.
He thanks Mr. Gibson for his acknowledgment that he has been treated with personal kindness and consideration, and says he knows of but two small drawbacks upon Mr. Gibson's right to still receive such treatment, one of which is that he never could learn of his giving much attention to the duties of his office, and the other is this studied attempt of Mr. Gibson's to stab him.
I am very truly,
Your obedient servant,

JOHN HAY.

TO COLONEL, FIRST N. Y. VETERAN CAVALRY.

EXECUTIVE MANSION, WASHINGTON, JULY 25, 1864.

Thomas Connor, a private in the First Veteran New York Cavalry, is now imprisoned at hard labor for desertion. If the Colonel of said Regiment will say in writing on this sheets that he is willing to receive him back to the Regiment, I will pardon, and send him.
A. LINCOLN.

TELEGRAM TO GENERAL W. T. SHERMAN.

WASHINGTON, July 26, 1864. 2.30 P.M.

MAJOR-GENERAL SHERMAN, near Atlanta:
I have just seen yours complaining of the appointment of Hovey and Osterhaus. The point you make is unquestionably a good one, and yet please hear a word from us. My recollection is that both General Grant and yourself recommended both H [ovey] and O [sterhaus] for promotion, and these, with other strong recommendations, drew committals from us which we could neither honorably or safely disregard. We blamed H [ovey] for coming away in the manner in which he did, but he knew he had apparent reason to feel disappointed and mortified, and we felt it was not best to crush one who certainly had been a good soldier. As to [Osterhaus], we did not know of his leaving at the time we made the appointment, and do not now know the terms on which he left. Not to have appointed him, as the case appeared to us at the time, would have been almost, if not quite, a violation of our word. The word was given on what we thought was high merit and somewhat on his nationality. I beg you to believe we do not act in a spirit of disregarding merit. We expect to await your programme for further changes and promotions in your army. My profoundest thanks to you and your whole army for the present campaign so far.
A. LINCOLN.

FROM SECRETARY STANTON TO GENERAL HALLECK.

WASHINGTON CITY, July 27, 1864

MAJOR-GENERAL HALLECK, Chief of Staff of the Army:
GENERAL:—Lieutenant-General Grant having signified that, owing to the difficulties and delay of communication between his headquarters and Washington, it is necessary that in the present emergency military orders must be issued directly from Washington, the President directs me to instruct you that all the military operations for the defense of the Middle Department, the Department of the Susquehanna, the Department of Washington, and the Department of West Virginia, and all the forces in those departments, are placed under your general command, and that you will be expected to take all military measures necessary for defense against any attack of the enemy and for his capture and destruction. You will issue from time to time such orders to the commanders of the respective departments and to the military authorities therein as may be proper.
Your obedient servant,
EDWIN M. STANTON, Secretary of War.

TELEGRAM TO GOVERNOR JOHNSON. WASHINGTON, July 27, 1864.

GOVERNOR JOHNSON, Nashville, Tennessee:

Yours in relation to General A. C. Gillam just received. Will look after the matter to-day.
I also received yours about General Carl Schurz. I appreciate him certainly, as highly as you do; but you can never know until you have the trial, how difficult it is to find a place for an officer of so high rank when there is no place seeking him.
A. LINCOLN.

TO Mrs. ANNE WILLIAMSON,

EXECUTIVE MANSION, WASHINGTON, July 29, 1864.

Mrs. ANNE WILLIAMSON.
MADAM:—The plaid you send me is just now placed in my hands. I thank you for that pretty and useful present, but still more for those good wishes for myself and our country, which prompted you to present it.
Your obedient servant,
A. LINCOLN. INDORSEMENT, AUGUST 3, 1864.
WAR DEPARTMENT, WASHINGTON CITY, August 2, 1864.
MR. PRESIDENT:—This note will introduce to you Mr. Schley of Baltimore, who desires to appeal to you for the revocation of an order of General Hunter, removing some persons, citizens of Frederick, beyond his lines, and imprisoning others. This Department has no information of the reasons or proofs on which General Hunter acts, and I do not therefore feel at liberty to suspend or interfere with his action except under your direction.
Yours truly,
EDWIN M. STANTON, Secretary of War.
[Indorsement.]
August 3, 1864.
The Secretary of War will suspend the order of General Hunter mentioned within, until further order and direct him to send to the Department a brief report of what is known against each one proposed to be dealt with.
A. LINCOLN.

TELEGRAM TO GENERAL U, S. GRANT.

(Cipher.)

WASHINGTON, D. C.. August 3, 1864
LIEUTENANT-GENERAL GRANT, City Point, Va.:
I have seen your despatch in which you say, "I want Sheridan put in command of all the troops in the field, with instructions to put himself south of the enemy, and follow him to the death. Wherever the enemy goes, let our troops go also."
This, I think, is exactly right as to how our forces should move; but please look over the despatches you may have received from here, ever since you made that order, and discover, if you can, that there is any idea in the head of any one here of "putting our army south of the enemy," or of following him to the "death," in any direction. I repeat to you, it will neither be done nor attempted, unless you watch it every day and hour, and force it.
A. LINCOLN.
 [Here the President was mistaken in thinking that Sherman,
 Sheridan, and Grant had the same inability of most of his
 previous general officers. No one needed to watch Grant or
 Sherman or Sheridan, they only needed to get out of their
 way. D.W.]

TELEGRAM TO HORACE GREELEY.

EXECUTIVE MANSION, WASHINGTON, August 6, 1864

HON. HORACE GREELEY, New York:
Yours to Major Hay about publication of our correspondence received. With the suppression of a few passages in your letters in regard to which I think you and I would not disagree, I should be glad of the publication. Please come over and see me.
A. LINCOLN.

TELEGRAM TO HORACE GREELEY.

EXECUTIVE MANSION, WASHINGTON, August 8, 1864

HON. HORACE GREELEY, New York:
I telegraphed you Saturday. Did you receive the despatch? Please answer.
A. LINCOLN.

ON DISLOYAL FAMILY MEMBER

TO GENERAL S. O. BURBRIDGE.

WASHINGTON, D. C., August 8, 1864
MAJOR-GENERAL BURBRIDGE, Lexington, Ky.:
Last December Mrs. Emily T. Helm, half-sister of Mrs. Lincoln, and widow of the rebel general, Ben Hardin Helm, stopped here on her way from Georgia to Kentucky, and I gave her a paper, as I remember, to protect her against the mere fact of her being General Helm's widow. I hear a rumor to-day that you recently sought to arrest her, but were prevented by her presenting the paper from me. I do not intend to protect her against the consequences of disloyal words or acts, spoken or done by her since her return to Kentucky, and if the paper given her by me can be construed to give her protection for such words and acts, it is hereby revoked pro tanto. Deal with her for current conduct just as you would with any other.
A. LINCOLN.

TELEGRAM TO GENERAL U. S. GRANT.

WASHINGTON, D. C., August 14, 1864. 1.30 P.M.

LIEUTENANT-GENERAL GRANT, City Point, Va.:
The Secretary of War and I concur that you had better confer with General Lee, and stipulate for a mutual discontinuance of house-burning and other destruction of private property. The time and manner of conference and particulars of stipulation we leave, on our part, to your convenience and judgment.
A. LINCOLN.

TELEGRAM TO GENERAL W. T. SHERMAN.

EXECUTIVE MANSION, WASHINGTON, D. C., August 15, 1864.

MAJOR-GENERAL SHERMAN, near Atlanta, Ga.:
If the Government should purchase, on its own account, cotton northward of you, and on the line of your communications, would it be an inconvenience to you, or detriment to the military service, for it to come to the north on the railroad?
A. LINCOLN.

INTERVIEW WITH JOHN T. MILLS,

AUGUST [15?], 1864.

"Mr. President," said Governor Randall, "why can't you seek seclusion, and play hermit for a fortnight? It would reinvigorate you."

"Ah," said the President, "two or three weeks would do me no good. I cannot fly from my thoughts—my solicitude for this great country follows me wherever I go. I do not think it is personal vanity or ambition, though I am not free from these infirmities, but I cannot but feel that the weal or woe of this great nation will be decided in November. There is no program offered by any wing of the Democratic party but that must result in the permanent destruction of the Union."

"But, Mr. President, General McClellan is in favor of crushing out this rebellion by force. He will be the Chicago candidate."

"Sir, the slightest knowledge of arithmetic will prove to any man that the rebel armies cannot be destroyed by Democratic strategy. It would sacrifice all the white men of the North to do it. There are now in the service of the United States nearly one hundred and fifty thousand able-bodied colored men, most of them under arms, defending and acquiring Union territory. The Democratic strategy demands that these forces be disbanded, and that the masters be conciliated by restoring them to slavery. The black men who now assist Union prisoners to escape are to be converted into our enemies, in the vain hope of gaining the good-will of their masters. We shall have to fight two nations instead of one.

"You cannot conciliate the South if you guarantee to them ultimate success; and the experience of the present war proves their success is inevitable if you fling the compulsory labor of millions of black men into their side of the scale. Will you give our enemies such military advantages as insure success, and then depend on coaxing, flattery, and concession to get them back into the Union? Abandon all the posts now garrisoned by black men, take one hundred and fifty thousand men from our side and put them in the battle-field or corn-field against us, and we would be compelled to abandon the war in three weeks.

"We have to hold territory in inclement and sickly places; where are the Democrats to do this? It was a free fight, and the field was open to the war Democrats to put down this rebellion by fighting against both master and slave, long before the present policy was inaugurated.

"There have been men base enough to propose to me to return to slavery the black warriors of Port Hudson and Olustee, and thus win the respect of the masters they fought. Should I do so, I should deserve to be damned in time and eternity. Come what will, I will keep my faith with friend and foe. My enemies pretend I am now carrying on this war for the sole purpose of abolition. So long as I am President, it shall be carried on for the sole purpose of restoring the Union. But no human power can subdue this rebellion without the use of the emancipation policy, and every other policy calculated to weaken the moral and physical forces of the rebellion.

"Freedom has given us one hundred and fifty thousand men, raised on Southern soil. It will give us more yet. Just so much it has subtracted from the enemy, and, instead of alienating the South, there are now evidences of a fraternal feeling growing up between our men and the rank and file of the rebel soldiers. Let my enemies prove to the country that the destruction of slavery is not necessary to a restoration of the Union. I will abide the issue."

ENDORSEMENT OF APPLICATION FOR EMPLOYMENT, AUGUST 15, 1864.

I am always for the man who wishes to work; and I shall be glad for this man to get suitable employment at Cavalry Depot, or elsewhere.
A. LINCOLN.

TO H. J. RAYMOND.

EXECUTIVE MANSION WASHINGTON, August 15, 1864

HON. HENRY J. RAYMOND.
MY DEAR SIR:—I have proposed to Mr. Greeley that the Niagara correspondence be published, suppressing only the parts of his letters over which the red pencil is drawn in the copy which I herewith send. He declines giving his consent to the publication of his letters unless these parts be published with the rest. I have concluded that it is better for me to submit, for the time, to the consequences of the false position in which I consider he has placed me, than to subject the country to the consequences of publishing these discouraging and injurious parts. I send you this, and the accompanying copy, not for publication, but merely to explain to you, and that you may preserve them until their proper time shall come.
Yours truly,
A. LINCOLN.

TELEGRAM TO GENERAL U. S. GRANT.

EXECUTIVE MANSION, WASHINGTON, August 17, 1864.

LIEUTENANT-GENERAL GRANT, City Point, Va.:
I have seen your despatch expressing your unwillingness to break your hold where you are. Neither am I willing. Hold on with a bulldog grip, and chew and choke as much as possible.
A. LINCOLN.

PROCLAMATION CONCERNING COMMERCIAL REGULATIONS, AUGUST 18, 1864.

BY THE PRESIDENT OF THE UNITED STATES OF AMERICA:

A Proclamation.
Whereas the act of Congress of the 28th of September, 1850, entitled "An act to create additional collection districts in the State of California, and to change the existing districts therein, and to modify the existing collection districts in the United States," extends to merchandise warehoused under bond the privilege of being exported to the British North American provinces adjoining the United States, in the manner prescribed in the act of Congress of the 3d of March, 1845, which designates certain frontier ports through which merchandise may be exported, and further provides "that such other ports, situated on the frontiers of the United States adjoining the British North American provinces, as may hereafter be found expedient, may have extended to them the like privileges, on the recommendation of the Secretary of the Treasury, and proclamation duly made by the President of the United States, specially designating the ports to which the aforesaid privileges are to be extended."
Now, therefore, I, Abraham Lincoln, President of the United States of America, in accordance with the recommendation of the Secretary of the Treasury, do hereby declare and proclaim that the port of Newport, in the State of Vermont, is and shall be entitled to all the privileges in regard to the exportation of merchandise in bond to the British North American provinces adjoining the United States, which are extended to the ports enumerated in the seventh section of the act of Congress of the 3d of March, 1845, aforesaid, from and after the date of this proclamation.

In witness whereof, I have hereunto set my hand and caused the seal of the United States to be affixed. Done at the city of Washington, this eighteenth day of August, in the year of our Lord one thousand eight hundred and sixty-four, and of the independence of the United States of America, the eighty-ninth.
A. LINCOLN.
By the President: WILLIAM H. SEWARD, Secretary of State.

INDORSEMENT CONCERNING AN EXCHANGE OF PRISONERS, AUGUST 18, 1864.

If General Hitchcock can effect a special exchange of Thomas D. Armesy, now under conviction as a spy, or something of the sort, and in prison at for Major Nathan Goff, made a prisoner of war, and now in prison at Richmond, let it be done.
A. LINCOLN.

ADDRESS TO THE 164TH OHIO REGIMENT,

AUGUST 18, 1864.

SOLDIERS:—You are about to return to your homes and your friends, after having, as I learn, performed in camp a comparatively short term of duty in this great contest. I am greatly obliged to you, and to all who have come forward at the call of their country. I wish it might be more generally and universally understood what the country is now engaged in. We have, as all will agree, a free government, where every man has a right to be equal with every other man. In this great struggle, this form of government and every form of human right is endangered if our enemies succeed. There is more involved in this contest than is realized by every one. There is involved in this struggle, the question whether your children and my children shall enjoy the privileges we have enjoyed. I say this, in order to impress upon you, if you are not already so impressed, that no small matter should divert us from our great purpose.
There may be some inequalities in the practical application of our system. It is fair that each man shall pay taxes in exact proportion to the value of his property; but if we should wait, before collecting a tax, to adjust the taxes upon each man in exact proportion with every other man, we should never collect any tax at all. There may be mistakes made sometimes; and things may be done wrong, while the officers of the Government do all they can to prevent mistakes. But I beg of you, as citizens of this great Republic, not to let your minds be carried off from the great work we have before us. This struggle is too large for you to be diverted from it by any small matter. When you return to your homes, rise up to the height of a generation of men worthy of a free government, and we will carry out the great work we have commenced. I return to you my sincere thanks, soldiers, for the honor you have done me this afternoon.

TELEGRAM TO GENERAL BUTLER. EXECUTIVE MANSION, WASHINGTON, D. C., August

20, 1864.
MAJOR-GENERAL BUTLER, Bermuda Hundred, Va.:
Please allow Judge Snead to go to his family on Eastern Shore, or give me some good reason why not.
A. LINCOLN.

ADDRESS TO THE 166TH OHIO REGIMENT,

AUGUST 22, 1864.

SOLDIERS—I suppose you are going home to see your families and friends. For the services you have done in this great struggle in which we are engaged, I present you sincere thanks for myself and the country.

I almost always feel inclined, when I say anything to soldiers, to impress upon them, in a few brief remarks, the importance of success in this contest. It is not merely for the day, but for all time to come, that we should perpetuate for our children's children that great and free government which we have enjoyed all our lives. I beg you to remember this, not merely for my sake, but for yours. I happen, temporarily, to occupy this big White House. I am a living witness that any one of your children may look to come here as my father's child has. It is in order that each one of you may have, through this free government which we have enjoyed, an open field, and a fair chance for your industry, enterprise, and intelligence; that you may all have equal privileges in the race of life with all its desirable human aspirations—it is for this that the struggle should be maintained, that we may not lose our birthrights—not only for one, but for two or three years, if necessary. The nation is worth fighting for, to secure such an inestimable jewel.

MEMORANDUM.

EXECUTIVE MANSION, WASHINGTON, August 23, 1864.

This morning, as for some days past, it seems exceedingly probable that this administration will not be re-elected. Then it will be my duty to so co-operate with the President-elect as to save the Union between the election and the inauguration; as he will have secured his election on such ground that he cannot possibly save it afterward.
A. LINCOLN.

TELEGRAM TO GOVERNOR JOHNSON. EXECUTIVE MANSION, WASHINGTON, August 26, 1864.
GOVERNOR JOHNSON, Nashville, Tenn.:
Thanks to General Gillam for making the news and also to you for sending it. Does Joe Heiskell's "walking to meet us" mean any more than that "Joe" was scared and wanted to save his skin?
A. LINCOLN.

TELEGRAM TO B. H. BREWSTER. EXECUTIVE MANSION, WASHINGTON, D. C., August 30,1864.
HON. B. H. BREWSTER, Astor House, New York:
Your letter of yesterday received. Thank you for it. Please have no fears.
A. LINCOLN.

ORDER CONCERNING COTTON.

EXECUTIVE MANSION, WASHINGTON, August 31, 1864.

Any person or persons engaged in bringing out cotton, in strict conformity with authority given by W. P. Fessenden, Secretary of the United States Treasury, must not be hindered by the War, Navy, or any other Department of the Government, or any person engaged under any of said Departments.
A. LINCOLN.

TO COLONEL HUIDEKOPER.

EXECUTIVE MANSION, SEPTEMBER 1, 1864

COLONEL H. C. HUIDEKOPER, Meadville, Penn.

SIR: It is represented to me that there are at Rock Island, Illinois, as rebel prisoners of war, many persons of Northern and foreign birth who are unwilling to be exchanged and sent South, but who wish to take the oath of allegiance and enter the military service of the Union. Colonel Huidekoper, on behalf of the people of some parts of Pennsylvania, wishes to pay the bounties the Government would have to pay to proper persons of this class, have them enter the service of the United States, and be credited to the localities furnishing the bounty money. He will therefore proceed to Rock Island, ascertain the names of such persons (not including any who have attractions Southward), and telegraph them to the Provost-Marshal-General here, whereupon direction will be given to discharge the persons named upon their taking the oath of allegiance; and then upon the official evidence being furnished that they shall have been duly received and mustered into the service of the United States, their number will be credited as may be directed by Colonel Huidekoper.

A. LINCOLN.

PROCLAMATION OF THANKSGIVING,

EXECUTIVE MANSION, WASHINGTON CITY, September 3, 1864.

The signal success that Divine Providence has recently vouchsafed to the operations of the United States fleet and army in the harbor of Mobile, and the reduction of Fort Powell, Fort Gaines, and Fort Morgan, and the glorious achievements of the army under Major-General Sherman, in the State of Georgia, resulting in the capture of the city of Atlanta, call for devout acknowledgment to the Supreme Being in whose hands are the destinies of nations. It is therefore requested that on next Sunday, in all places of worship in the United States, thanksgivings be offered to Him for His mercy in preserve our national existence against the insurgent rebels who have been waging a cruel war against the Government of the United States for its overthrow, and also that prayer be made for Divine protection to our brave soldiers and their leaders in the field who have so often and so gallantly periled their lives in battling with the enemy, and for blessings and comfort from the Father of mercies to the sick, wounded, and prisoners, and to the orphans and widows of those who have fallen in the service of their country, and that He will continue to uphold the Government of the United States against all the efforts of public enemies and secret foes.

A. LINCOLN.

ORDERS OF GRATITUDE AND REJOICING.

EXECUTIVE MANSION, September 3, 1864.

The national thanks are tendered by the President to Admiral Farragut and Major-General Canby, for the skill and harmony with which the recent operations in Mobile Harbor and against Fort Powell, Fort Gaines, and Fort Morgan were planned and carried into execution. Also to Admiral Farragut and Major-General Granger, under whose immediate command they were conducted, and to the gallant commanders on sea and land, and to the sailors and soldiers engaged in the operations, for their energy and courage, which, under the blessing of Providence, have been crowned with brilliant success, and have won for them the applause and thanks of the nation.

A. LINCOLN.

EXECUTIVE MANSION, September 3, 1864.

The national thanks are tendered by the President to Major-General William T. Sherman and the gallant officers and soldiers of his command before Atlanta, for the distinguished ability, courage, and perseverance displayed in the campaign in Georgia, which under Divine power resulted in the capture of the city of Atlanta. The marches, battles, sieges, and other military operations that have signalized this campaign must render it famous in the annals of war, and have entitled those who have participated therein to the applause and thanks of the nation.
A. LINCOLN.

EXECUTIVE MANSION, September 3, 1864.

Ordered: First, That on Monday, the fifth day of September, commencing at the hour of twelve o'clock noon, there shall be given a salute of one hundred guns at the arsenal and navy-yard, at Washington, and on Tuesday, the 6th of September, or on the day after the receipt of this order, at each arsenal and navy-yard in the United States, for the recent brilliant achievements of the fleet and land forces of the United States in the harbor of Mobile, and in the reduction of Fort Powell, Fort Gaines, and Fort Morgan. The Secretary of War and the Secretary of the Navy will issue the necessary directions in their respective departments for the execution of this order.
Second, That on Wednesday, the 7th of September, commencing at the hour of twelve o'clock noon, there shall be fired a salute of one hundred guns at the arsenal at Washington, and at New York, Boston, Philadelphia, Baltimore, Pittsburg, Newport (Ky.), and St. Louis, and New Orleans, Mobile, and Pensacola, Hilton Head, and Newbern, the day after the receipt of this order, for the brilliant achievements of the army under command of Major-General Sherman, in the State of Georgia, and for the capture of Atlanta. The Secretary of War will issue directions for the execution of this order.
A. LINCOLN, President Of the United States.

TO MRS. GURNEY.

EXECUTIVE MANSION, WASHINGTON, SEPTEMBER 4, 1864.

ELIZA P. GURNEY.
MY ESTEEMED FRIEND:—I have not forgotten probably never shall forget the very impressive occasion when yourself and friends visited me on a Sabbath forenoon two years ago—nor has your kind letter, written nearly a year later, even been for gotten. In all, it has been your purpose to strengthen my reliance on God. I am much indebted to the good Christian people of the country for their constant prayer and consolations; and to no one of them, more than to yourself. The purposes of the Almighty are perfect, and must prevail, though we erring mortals may fail to accurately perceive them in advance. We hoped for a happy termination of this terrible war long before this; but God knows best, and has ruled otherwise. We shall yet acknowledge His wisdom, and our own error therein. Mean while we must work earnestly in the best light He gives us, trusting that so working still conduces to the great ends He ordains. Surely He intends some great good to follow this mighty convulsion, which no mortal could make, and no mortal could stay.
Your people—the Friends—have had, and are having, a very great trial. On principle, and faith, opposed to both war and oppression, they can only practically oppose oppression by war. For those appealing to me on conscientious grounds, I have done, and shall do, the best I could and can, in my own conscience, under my oath to the law. That you believe this I doubt not, and believing it, I shall still receive, for our country and myself your earnest prayers to our Father in Heaven.
Your sincere friend,
A. LINCOLN.

REPLY TO A COMMITTEE OF COLORED PEOPLE FROM BALTIMORE

WHO PRESENTED HIM WITH A BIBLE,

SEPTEMBER 7, 1864.
I can only say now, as I have often said before, it has always been a sentiment with me, that all mankind should be free. So far as I have been able, so far as came within my sphere, I have always acted as I believed was just and right, and done all I could for the good of mankind. I have, in letters sent forth from this office, expressed myself better than I can now.

In regard to the great Book, I have only to say it is the best gift which God has ever given to man. All the good from the Saviour of the world is communicated to us through this book. But for that Book, we could not know right from wrong. All those things desirable to man are contained in it. I return you sincere thanks for this very elegant copy of this great Book of God which you present.

TELEGRAM TO GOVERNOR PICKERING.

WAR DEPARTMENT, WASHINGTON, D. C., September 8, 1864:

GOVERNOR PICKERING, Olympia, W. T.:
Your patriotic despatch of yesterday received and will be published.
A. LINCOLN.

ORDER OF THANKS TO HUNDRED-DAY TROOPS FROM OHIO.

EXECUTIVE MANSION, WASHINGTON CITY, September 10, 1864.

The term of one hundred days for which the National Guard of Ohio volunteered having expired, the President directs an official acknowledgment to be made of their patriotic and valuable services during the recent campaigns. The term of service of their enlistment was short, but distinguished by memorable events. In the Valley of the Shenandoah, on the Peninsula, in the operations on the James River, around Petersburg and Richmond, in the battle of Monocacy, and in the intrenchments of Washington, and in other important service, the National Guard of Ohio performed with alacrity the duty of patriotic volunteers, for which they are entitled to and are hereby tendered, through the Governor of their State, the national thanks.
A. LINCOLN.

TO GENERAL U.S. GRANT.

EXECUTIVE MANSION, WASHINGTON, September 12, 1864.

LIEUTENANT-GENERAL GRANT:
Sheridan and Early are facing each other at a dead-lock. Could we not pick up a regiment here and there, to the number of say ten thousand men, and quietly but suddenly concentrate them at Sheridan's camp and enable him to make a strike?
This is but a suggestion.
Yours truly,
A. LINCOLN.

TELEGRAM TO JAMES G. BLAINE. WAR DEPARTMENT, WASHINGTON, D. C., September

13, 1864.
HON. J. G. BLAINE, Augusta, Me.: On behalf of the Union, thanks to Maine. Thanks to you personally for sending the news.
A. LINCOLN.
P. S.—Send same to L. B. Smith and M. A. Blanchard, Portland, Me. A. L.
TELEGRAM TO GENERAL ROSECRANS. EXECUTIVE MANSION, WASHINGTON, September 13, 1864
MAJOR-GENERAL ROSECRANS, Saint Louis:
Postpone the execution of S. H. Anderson for two weeks. Hear what his friends can say in mitigation and report to me.
A. LINCOLN.
MAJOR ECKERT: Please send the above telegram.
JNO. G. NICOLAY, Private Secretary.

TELEGRAM TO GENERAL SLOUGH.

WAR DEPARTMENT, WASHINGTON, D. C., September 16, 1864.

GENERAL SLOUGH, Alexandria, Va.:
On the 14th I commuted the sentence of Conley, but fearing you may not have received notice I send this. Do not execute him.
A. LINCOLN.

TELEGRAM TO GENERAL W. T. SHERMAN. WASHINGTON, D. C., September 17, 1864.

MAJOR-GENERAL SHERMAN, Atlanta, Georgia:

I feel great interest in the subjects of your despatch mentioning corn and sorghum, and the contemplated visit to you.
A. LINCOLN, President of the United States.

TO GENERAL W. T. SHERMAN.

EXECUTIVE MANSION, WASHINGTON, September 19, 1864.

MAJOR-GENERAL SHERMAN:
The State election of Indiana occurs on the 11th of October, and the loss of it to the friends of the Government would go far towards losing the whole Union cause. The bad effect upon the November election, and especially the giving the State government to those who will oppose the war in every possible way, are too much to risk if it can be avoided. The draft proceeds, notwithstanding its strong tendency to lose us the State. Indiana is the only important State voting in October whose soldiers cannot vote in the field. Anything you can safely do to let her soldiers or any part of them go home and vote at the State election will be greatly in point. They need not remain for the Presidential election, but may return to you at once. This is in no sense an order, but is merely intended to impress you with the importance to the Army itself of your doing all you safely can, yourself being the judge of what you can safely do.
Yours truly,
A. LINCOLN.

INDORSEMENT CONCERNING AN EXCHANGE OF PRISONERS, SEPTEMBER 1864.

The writer of this, who appeals for his brother, is our minister to Ecuador, and whom, if at all compatible, I would like to have obliged by a special exchange of his brother.
A. LINCOLN.

TELEGRAM TO GENERAL P. SHERIDAN. EXECUTIVE MANSION, WASHINGTON, September

20, 1864
MAJOR-GENERAL SHERIDAN, Winchester, Va.:
Have just heard of your great victory. God bless you all, officers and men. Strongly inclined to come up and See you.
A. LINCOLN.

TO GENERAL HITCHCOCK,

EXECUTIVE MANSION, WASHINGTON, September 21, 1864.

GENERAL HITCHCOCK:
Please see the bearer, Mr. Broadwell, on a question about a mutual supplying of clothes to prisoners.
Yours truly,
A. LINCOLN.

TO GENERAL U.S. GRANT.

EXECUTIVE MANSION, WASHINGTON, September 22, 1864.

LIEUTENANT-GENERAL GRANT:
I send this as an explanation to you, and to do justice to the Secretary of War. I was induced, upon pressing application, to authorize the agents of one of the districts of Pennsylvania to recruit in one of the prison depots in Illinois; and the thing went so far before it came to the knowledge of the Secretary that, in my judgment, it could not be abandoned without greater evil than would follow its going through. I did not know at the time that you had protested against that class of thing being done; and I now say that while this particular job must be completed, no other of the sort will be authorized, without an understanding with you, if at all. The Secretary of War is wholly free of any part in this blunder.
Yours truly,
A. LINCOLN.

TO POSTMASTER-GENERAL BLAIR.

EXECUTIVE MANSION, WASHINGTON, September 23, 1864.

HON. MONTGOMERY BLAIR.
MY DEAR SIR:—You have generously said to me, more than once, that whenever your resignation could be a relief to me, it was at my disposal. The time has come. You very well know that this proceeds from no dissatisfaction of mine with you personally or officially. Your uniform kindness has been unsurpassed by that of any other friend, and while it is true that the war does not so greatly add to the difficulties of your department as to those of some others, it is yet much to say, as I most truly can, that in the three years and a half during which you have administered the General Post-Office, I remember no single complaint against you in connection therewith.
Yours, as ever,

A. LINCOLN.

ORDER CONCERNING THE PURCHASE OF PRODUCTS IN INSURRECTIONARY STATES.

EXECUTIVE MANSION, September 24, 1864.

I. Congress having authorized the purchase for the United States of the products of States declared in insurrection, and the Secretary of the Treasury having designated New Orleans, Memphis, Nashville, Pensacola, Port Royal, Beaufort (North Carolina), and Norfolk, as places of purchase, and, with my approval, appointed agents and made regulations under which said products may be purchased, therefore:
II. All persons except such as may be in the civil, military, or naval service of the government, having in their possession any products of States or parts of States declared in insurrection, which said agents are authorized to purchase; and all persons owning or controlling such products therein are authorized to convey such products to either of the places which have been hereby or may hereafter be designated as places of purchase, and such products so destined shall not be liable to detention, seizure, or forfeiture while in transitu, or in store waiting transportation.
III. Any person having the certificate of a purchasing agent, as prescribed by Treasury Regulation VIII, is authorized to pass with the necessary means of transportation to the points named in said certificate, and to return therefrom with the products required for the fulfilment of the stipulations set forth in said certificate.
IV. Any person having sold and delivered to a purchasing agent any products of an insurrectionary State in accordance with the regulations in relation thereto, and having in his possession a certificate setting forth the fact of such purchase and sale; the character and quantity of products, and the aggregate amount paid therefor, as prescribed by Regulation I, shall be permitted by the military authority commanding at the place of sale to purchase from any authorized dealer at such place merchandise and other articles not contraband of war nor prohibited by order of the War Department, nor coin, bullion, or foreign exchange, to an amount not exceeding in value one-third of the aggregate value of the products sold by him as certified by the agents purchasing, and the merchandise and other articles so purchased may be transported by the same route, and to the same place, from and by which the products sold and delivered reached the purchasing agent, as set forth in the certificate, and such merchandise and other articles shall have safe conduct, and shall not be subject to detention, seizure, or forfeiture while being transported to the places and by the routes set forth in the said certificate.
V. Generals commanding military districts, and commandants of military posts and detachments, and officers commanding fleets, flotillas, and gunboats, will give safe conduct to persons and products, merchandise, and other articles duly authorized as aforesaid, and not contraband of war, or prohibited by order of the War Department, or of the order of such generals commanding, or other duly authorized military or naval officer, made in pursuance hereof, and all persons hindering or preventing such safe conduct of persons or property will, be deemed guilty of a military offense and punished accordingly.
VI. Any person transporting or attempting to transport any merchandise or other articles except in pursuance of regulations of the Secretary of the Treasury, dated July 29, 1864, or in pursuance of this order, or transporting or attempting to transport any merchandise or other articles contraband of war or forbidden by any order of the War Department, will be deemed guilty of a military offense and punished accordingly; and all products of insurrectionary States found in transitu to any other person or than a purchasing agent and a designated of purchase shall be seized and forfeited to the States, except such as may be moving to a loyal state under duly authorized permits of a proper officer of the Treasury Department, as prescribed by Regulation XXXVIII, concerning commercial intercourse, dated July 29, 1864, or such as may have been found abandoned, or have been captured and are moving in pursuance of the act of March 12, 1864.
VII. No military or naval officer of the United States, or person in the military or naval service, nor any civil officer, except such as are appointed for that purpose, shall engage in trade or traffic in the products of the insurrectionary States, or furnish transportation therefor under pain of being deemed guilty of unlawful trading with the enemy and punished accordingly.
VIII. The Secretary of War will make such general orders or regulations as will insure the proper observance and execution of,, this order, and the Secretary of the Navy will give instructions to officers commanding fleets,, flotillas, and gunboats in conformity therewith.
A. LINCOLN.

TELEGRAM TO GENERAL W. T. SHERMAN. WASHINGTON, D. C., September 27, 1864.

MAJOR-GENERAL SHERMAN, Atlanta, Georgia:

You say Jefferson Davis is on a visit to Hood. I judge that Brown and Stephens are the objects of his visit.
A. LINCOLN.

TELEGRAM TO GENERAL U. S. GRANT. WASHINGTON, D.C., September 29,1864.

LIEUTENANT-GENERAL GRANT, City Point, Va.:

I hope it will have no constraint on you, nor do harm any way, for me to say I am a little afraid lest Lee sends reinforcements to Early, and thus enables him to turn upon Sheridan.
A. LINCOLN.

INDORSEMENT.

September 29, 1864.

I think the bearer of this, Second Lieutenant Albee, deserves a hearing. Will the Secretary of War please accord it to him?
A. LINCOLN.

ORDER RETURNING THANKS TO THE VOLUNTEERS FOR ONE HUNDRED DAYS

FROM THE STATES OF INDIANA, ILLINOIS, IOWA, AND WISCONSIN.

EXECUTIVE MANSION,
WASHINGTON, October 1, 1864.
The term of one hundred days for which volunteers from the States of Indiana, Illinois, Iowa, and Wisconsin volunteered, under the call of their respective governors, in the months of May and June, to aid in the campaign of General Sherman, having expired; the President directs an official acknowledgment to be made of their patriotic service. It was their good fortune to render efficient service in the brilliant operations in the Southwest and to contribute to the victories of the national arms over the rebel forces in Georgia under command of Johnston and Hood. On all occasions and in every service to which they were assigned their duty as patriotic volunteers was performed with alacrity and courage, for which they are entitled to and are hereby tendered the national thanks through the governors of their respective States.
The Secretary of War is directed to transmit a copy of this order to the governors of Indiana, Illinois, Iowa, and Wisconsin and to cause a certificate of their honorable service to be delivered to the officers and soldiers of the States above named who recently served in the military force of the United States as volunteers for one hundred days.
A. LINCOLN.

TO GENERAL U.S. GRANT.

EXECUTIVE MANSION, WASHINGTON, October 5, 1864

LIEUTENANT-GENERAL GRANT:
I inclose you a copy of a correspondence in regard to a contemplated exchange of naval prisoners through your lines, and not very distant from your headquarters. It only came to the knowledge of the War Department and of myself yesterday, and it gives us some uneasiness. I therefore send it to you with the statement that, as the numbers to be exchanged under it are small, and so much has already been done to effect the exchange, I hope you may find it consistent to let it go forward under the general supervision of General Butler, and particularly in reference to the points he holds vital in exchanges. Still, you are at liberty to arrest the whole operation if in your judgment the public good requires it.
Yours truly,
A. LINCOLN.

INDORSEMENT ON A MEMORANDUM BY GENERAL McDOWELL, OCTOBER 7, 1864

I well remember the meetings herein narrated. See nothing for me to object to in the narrative as being made by General McDowell, except the phrase attributed to me "of the Jacobinism of Congress",
   [This memorandum describes the private discussions that
   preceded the transfer of McClellan's army from the Potomac,
   where it had confronted the Confederates at Manassas. See H.
   J. Raymond: Life of Lincoln, p. 772]
which phrase I do not remember using literally or in substance, and which I wish not to be published in any event.
A. LINCOLN.

TO H. W. HOFFMAN.

EXECUTIVE MANSION WASHINGTON, October 10, 1864.

HON. HENRY W. HOFFMAN.
MY DEAR SIR:—A convention of Maryland has framed a new constitution for the State; a public meeting is called for this evening at Baltimore to aid in securing its ratification by the people, and you ask a word from me for the occasion. I presume the only feature of the instrument about which there is serious controversy is that which provides for the extinction of slavery. It needs not to be a secret and I presume it is no secret, that I wish success to this provision. I desire it on every consideration. I wish all men to be free. I wish the material prosperity of the already free, which I feel sure the extinction of slavery would bring. I wish to see in process of disappearing that only thing which ever could bring this nation to civil war. I attempt no argument. Argument upon the question is already exhausted by the abler, better informed, and more immediately interested sons of Maryland herself. I only add that I shall be gratified exceedingly if the good people of the State shall, by their votes, ratify the new constitution.
Yours truly,
A. LINCOLN.

TELEGRAM TO GOVERNOR CURTIN.

WAR DEPARTMENT, WASHINGTON, D. C., October 10, 1864, 5 P.M.

GOVERNOR CURTIN, Harrisburg, Pa.:
Yours of to-day just this moment received, and the Secretary having left it is impossible for me to answer to-day. I have not received your letter from Erie.
A. LINCOLN.

TELEGRAM TO ROBERT T. LINCOLN, Cambridge, Mass.:

Your letter makes us a little uneasy about your health. Telegraph us how you are. If you think it would help you, make us a visit.
A. LINCOLN.

TELEGRAM TO GENERAL U. S. GRANT. WASHINGTON, D. C., October 12, 1864.

LIEUTENANT-GENERAL GRANT, City Point, Va.:

Secretary of War not being in, I answer yours about election. Pennsylvania very close, and still in doubt on home vote. Ohio largely for us, with all the members of Congress but two or three. Indiana largely for us,—Governor, it is said, by fifteen thousand, and eight of the eleven members of Congress. Send us what you may know of your army vote.
A. LINCOLN.

RESPONSE TO A SERENADE,

OCTOBER 19, 1864.

FRIENDS AND FELLOW-CITIZENS:—I am notified that this is a compliment paid me by the loyal Marylanders resident in this District. I infer that the adoption of the new constitution for the State furnishes the occasion, and that in your view the extirpation of slavery constitutes the chief merit of the new constitution. Most heartily do I congratulate you, and Maryland, and the nation, and the world, upon this event. I regret that it did not occur two years sooner, which, I am sure, would have saved the nation more money than would have met all the private loss incident to the measure; but it has come at last, and I sincerely hope its friends may fully realize all their anticipations of good from it, and that its opponents may by its effects be agreeably and profitably disappointed.
A word upon another subject. Something said by the Secretary of State in his recent speech at Auburn, has been construed by some into a threat, that if I shall be beaten at the election, I will, between then and the end of my constitutional term, do what I may be able to ruin the Government.
Others regard the fact that the Chicago Convention adjourned, not sine die, but to meet again, if called to do so by a particular individual, as the intimation of a purpose that if their nominee shall be elected he will at once seize control of the Government. I hope the good people will permit themselves to suffer no uneasiness on either point. I am struggling to maintain the Government, not to overthrow it. I am struggling especially to prevent others from overthrowing it. I therefore say, that if I live, I shall remain President until the 4th of next March, and that whoever shall be constitutionally elected, in November, shall be duly installed as President on the 4th of March, and in the interval I shall do my utmost that whoever is to hold the helm for the next voyage shall start with the best possible chance of saving the ship. This is due to the people, both on principle and under the Constitution. Their will, constitutionally expressed, is the ultimate law for all. If they should deliberately resolve to have immediate peace, even at the loss of their country and their liberties, I know not the power or the right to resist them. It is their own business, and they must do as they please with their own. I believe, however, they are still resolved to preserve their country and their liberties; and in this, in office or out of it, I am resolved to stand by them. I may add, that in this purpose to save the country and its liberties, no classes of people seem so nearly unanimous as the soldiers in the field and the sailors afloat. Do they not have the hardest of it? Who should quail while they do not? God bless the soldiers and seamen, with all their brave commanders.

PROCLAMATION OF THANKSGIVING, OCTOBER 20, 1864.

BY THE PRESIDENT OF THE UNITED STATES OF AMERICA:

A Proclamation.
It has pleased Almighty God to prolong our national life another year, defending us with his guardian care against unfriendly designs from abroad, and vouchsafing to us in His mercy many and signal victories over the enemy, who is of our own household. It has also pleased our Heavenly Father to favor as well our citizens in their homes as our soldiers in their camps, and our sailors on the rivers and seas, with unusual health. He has largely augmented our free population by emancipation and by immigration, while he has opened to us new: sources of wealth, and has crowned the labor of our working-men in every department of industry with abundant rewards. Moreover, he has been pleased to animate and inspire our minds and hearts with fortitude, courage, and resolution sufficient for the great trial of civil war into which we have been brought by our adherence as a nation to the cause of freedom and humanity, and to afford to us reasonable hopes of an ultimate and happy deliverance from all our dangers and afflictions.
Now, therefore, I, Abraham Lincoln, President of the United States, do hereby appoint and set apart the last Thursday in November next as a day which I desire to be observed by all my fellow-citizens, wherever they may be then, as a day of thanksgiving and praise to Almighty God, the beneficent Creator and Ruler of the Universe. And I do further recommend to my fellow-citizens aforesaid, that on that occasion they do reverently humble themselves in the dust, and from thence offer up penitent and fervent prayers and supplications to the great Disposer of events for a return of the inestimable blessings of peace, union, and harmony throughout the, land which it has pleased him to assign as a dwelling-place for ourselves and for our posterity throughout all generations.
In testimony whereof, I have hereunto set my hand and caused the seal of the United States to be affixed.
Done at the city of Washington, this twentieth day of October, in the year of our Lord one thousand eight hundred and sixty-four, and of the independence of the United States the eighty-ninth.
A. LINCOLN.
By the President WILLIAM H. SEWARD, Secretary of State.

TELEGRAM To J. G. NICOLAY. WASHINGTON, D. C., October 21, 1864. 9.45 P.M.

J. G. NICOLAY, Saint Louis, Missouri:

While Curtis is fighting Price, have you any idea where the force under Rosecrans is, or what it is doing?
A. LINCOLN.

TO WILLIAM B. CAMPBELL AND OTHERS.

EXECUTIVE MANSION, WASHINGTON, D. C., October 22, 1864.

MESSRS WILLIAM B. CAMPBELL, THOMAS A. R. NELSON, JAMES T. P. CARTER, JOHN WILLIAMS, A. BLIZZARD, HENRY COOPER, BAILLIE PEYTON, JOHN LELLYET, EMERSON ETHERIDGE, and JOHN D. PERRYMAN.
GENTLEMEN:—On the 15th day of this month, as I remember, a printed paper manuscript, with a few manuscript interlineations, called a protest, with your names appended thereto, and accompanied by another printed paper, purporting to be a proclamation by Andrew Johnson, Military Governor of Tennessee, and also a manuscript paper, purporting to be extracts from the Code of Tennessee, were laid before me.
The protest, proclamation, and extracts are respectively as follows:
[The protest is here recited, and also the proclamation of Governor Johnson, dated September 30, to which it refers, together with a list of the counties in East, Middle, and West Tennessee; also extracts from the Code of Tennessee in relation to electors of President and Vice-President, qualifications of voters for members of the General Assembly, places of holding elections, and officers of popular elections.]
At the time these papers were presented, as before stated, I had never seen either of them, nor heard of the subject to which they related, except in a general way one day previously.

Up to the present moment, nothing whatever upon the subject has passed between Governor Johnson, or any one else, connected with the proclamation, and myself.

Since receiving the papers, as stated, I have given the subject such brief consideration as I have been able to do, in the midst of so many pressing public duties.

My conclusion is, that I can have nothing to do with the matter, either to sustain the plan as the convention and Governor Johnson have initiated it, or to revoke or modify it as you demand.

By the Constitution and laws, the President is charged with no duty in the presidential election in any State, nor do I in this case perceive any military reason for his interference in the matter.

The movement set on foot by the convention and Governor Johnson does not, as seems to be assumed by you, emanate from the National Executive.

In no proper sense can it be considered other than an independent movement of, at least, a portion of the loyal people of Tennessee.

I do not perceive in the plan any menace, or violence, or coercion towards any one.

Governor Johnson, like any other loyal citizen of Tennessee, has the right to favor any political plan he chooses, and, as military governor, it is his duty to keep peace among and for the loyal people of the State.

I cannot discern that by this plan he purposes any more. But you object to the plan.

Leaving it alone will be your perfect security against it. It is not proposed to force you into it. Do as you please, on your own account, peaceably and loyally, and Governor Johnson will not molest you, but will protect you against violence as far as in his power.

I presume that the conducting of a presidential election in Tennessee in strict accordance with the old Code of the State, is not now a possibility.

It is scarcely necessary to add, that if any election shall be held and any votes shall be cast in the State of Tennessee for President and Vice-President of the United States, it will belong, not to the military agents, nor yet to the Executive Department, but exclusively to another department of the Government, to determine whether they are entitled to be counted in conformity with the Constitution and laws of the United States.

Except it be to give protection against violence, I decline to interfere in any way with any presidential election.
A. LINCOLN.

TELEGRAM TO GENERAL P. H. SHERIDAN. EXECUTIVE MANSION, WASHINGTON, October 22, 1864
MAJOR-GENERAL SHERIDAN:

With great pleasure I tender to you and your brave army the thanks of the nation, and my own personal admiration and gratitude, for the month's operations in the Shenandoah Valley; and especially for the splendid work of October 19, 1864.

Your obedient servant,
A. LINCOLN.

TELEGRAM TO GENERAL G. H. THOMAS. WASHINGTON, D. C., October 23, 1864 5

P.M.
MAJOR-GENERAL THOMAS, Nashville, Tennessee:

I have received information to-day, having great appearance of authenticity, that there is to be a rebel raid into Western Kentucky; that it is to consist of four thousand infantry and three thousand cavalry, and is to start from Corinth, Mississippi, On the fourth day of November.
A. LINCOLN, President.
Send copy to General Washburn at Memphis. A. L.

TELEGRAM TO T. T. DAVIS. EXECUTIVE MANSION, WASHINGTON, D.C., October 31,

1864.
HON. THOMAS T. DAVIS, Syracuse, N.Y.:

I have ordered that Milton D. Norton be discharged on taking the oath. Please notify his mother.
A. LINCOLN.

PROCLAMATION ADMITTING NEVADA INTO THE UNION

OCTOBER 31, 1864.

BY THE PRESIDENT OF THE UNITED STATES OF AMERICA:
A Proclamation
Whereas the Congress of the United States passed an act, which was approved on the 21st day of March last, entitled "An act to enable the people of Nevada to form a constitution and State government, and for the admission of such State into the Union on an equal footing with the original States;" and,
Whereas the said constitution and State government have been formed, pursuant to the conditions prescribed by the fifth section of the act of Congress aforesaid, and the certificate required by the said act and also a copy of the constitution and ordinances have been submitted to the President of the United States:
Now, therefore, be it known that I, Abraham Lincoln, President of the United States, in accordance with the duty imposed upon me by the act of Congress aforesaid, do hereby declare and proclaim that the said State of Nevada is admitted into the Union on an equal footing with the original States.
In witness whereof I have hereunto set my hand and caused the seal of the United States to be affixed..........
A. LINCOLN.
By the President: WILLIAM H. SEWARD, Secretary of State.

TELEGRAM TO GENERAL BURBRIDGE.

EXECUTIVE MANSION, WASHINGTON, November 4, 1864

MAJOR-GENERAL BURBRIDGE, Lexington, Ky.
Suspend execution of all the deserters ordered to be executed on Sunday at Louisville, until further order, and send me the records in the cases. Acknowledge receipt.
A. LINCOLN.

TELEGRAM TO NAVAL OFFICER AT MOBILE BAY.

EXECUTIVE MANSION, WASHINGTON, November 6, 1864. 9 P.M.

MAJOR-GENERAL CANBY, New Orleans, La.:
Please forward with all possible despatch to the naval officer commanding at Mobile Bay the following order.
A. LINCOLN.
(Inclosure.)
EXECUTIVE MANSION, WASHINGTON, November 6, 1864.
NAVAL OFFICER IN COMMAND AT MOBILE BAY
Do not on any account, or on any showing of authority whatever, from whomsoever purporting to come, allow the blockade to be violated.
A. LINCOLN.

TELEGRAM TO SAILORS' FAIR, BOSTON, MASSACHUSETTS.

WASHINGTON, D. C., November 8, 1864.

TO THE MANAGING COMMITTEE OF THE SAILORS' FAIR, Boston, Massachusetts

Allow me to wish you a great success. With the old fame of the Navy made brighter in the present war you cannot fail. I name none lest I wrong others by omission. To all, from rear-admiral to honest Jack, I tender the nation's admiration and gratitude.

A. LINCOLN.

TELEGRAM TO A. H. RICE.

EXECUTIVE MANSION, WASHINGTON, November 8, 1864.

HON. A. H. RICE, Boston, Massachusetts:

Yours received. I have no other notice that the ox is mine. If it be really so, I present it to the Sailors' Fair as a contribution.

A. LINCOLN.

TELEGRAM TO SECRETARY SEWARD. WASHINGTON, November 8, 1864.

HON. WILLIAM H. SEWARD, Auburn, New York:

News from Grant, Sherman, Thomas and Rosecrans satisfactory, but not important. Pirate Florida captured by the Wachusett October 7, on the coast of Brazil. The information is certain.

A. LINCOLN.

RESPONSE TO A SERENADE, NOVEMBER 9, 1864.

FRIENDS AND FELLOW-CITIZENS:—Even before I had been informed by you that this compliment was paid me by loyal citizens of Pennsylvania, friendly to me, I had inferred that you were of that portion of my countrymen who think that the best interests of the nation are to be subserved by the support of the present administration. I do not pretend to say that you, who think so, embrace all the patriotism and loyalty of the country, but I do believe, and I trust without personal interest, that the welfare of the country does require that such support and indorsement should be given.

I earnestly believe that the consequences of this day's work, if it be as you assume, and as now seems probable, will be to the lasting advantage, if not to the very salvation, of the country. I cannot at this hour say what has been the result of the election. But, whatever it may be, I have no desire to modify this opinion: that all who have labored to-day in behalf of the Union have wrought for the best interests of the country and the world; not only for the present, but for all future ages.

I am thankful to God for this approval of the people; but, while deeply grateful for this mark of their confidence in me, if I know my heart, my gratitude is free from any taint of personal triumph. I do not impugn the motives of any one opposed to me. It is no pleasure to me to triumph over any one, but I give thanks to the Almighty for this evidence of the people's resolution to stand by free government and the rights of humanity.

TELEGRAM TO H. W. HOFFMAN. WAR DEPARTMENT, WASHINGTON, D. C. November 10, 1864.

H. HOFFMAN, Baltimore, Md.:

The Maryland soldiers in the Army of the Potomac cast a total vote of fourteen hundred and twenty-eight, out of which we get eleven hundred and sixty majority. This is directly from General Meade and General Grant.
A. LINCOLN.

ON DEMOCRATIC GOVERNMENT

RESPONSE TO A SERENADE, NOVEMBER 10, 1864.

It has long been a grave question whether any government, not too strong for the liberties of its people, can be strong enough to maintain its existence in great emergencies. On this point the present rebellion brought our government to a severe test, and a presidential election occurring in regular course during the rebellion, added not a little to the strain. If the loyal people united were put to the utmost of their strength by the rebellion, must they not fail when divided and partially paralyzed by a political war among themselves? But the election was a necessity. We cannot have free government without elections; and if the election could force us to forego or postpone a national election, it might fairly claim to have already conquered and ruined us. The strife of the election is but human nature practically applied to the facts of the case. What has occurred in this case must ever recur in similar cases. Human nature will not change. In any future great national trial, compared with the men of this, we will have as weak and as strong, as silly and as wise, as bad and as good. Let us, therefore, study the incidents of this as philosophy to learn wisdom from, and none of them as wrongs to be revenged.

But the election, along with its incidental and undesirable strife, has done good, too. It has demonstrated that a people's government can sustain a national election in the midst of a great civil war. Until now, it has not been known to the world that this was a possibility. It shows, also, how sound and strong we still are. It shows that even among the candidates of the same party, he who is most devoted to the Union and most opposed to treason can receive most of the people's votes. It shows, also, to the extent yet known, that we have more men now than we had when the war began. Gold is good in its place; but living, brave, and patriotic men are better than gold.

But the rebellion continues, and, now that the election is over, may not all have a common interest to reunite in a common effort to save our common country? For my own part, I have striven and shall strive to avoid placing any obstacle in the way. So long as I have been here, I have not willingly planted a thorn in any man's bosom. While I am duly sensible to the high compliment of a re-election, and duly grateful, as I trust, to Almighty God, for having directed my countrymen to a right conclusion, as I think, for their good, it adds nothing to my satisfaction that any other man may be disappointed by the result.

May I ask those who have not differed with me to join with me in this same spirit towards those who have? And now, let me close by asking three hearty cheers for our brave soldiers and seamen, and their gallant and skillful commanders.

TELEGRAM TO GENERAL S. O. BURBRIDGE. WASHINGTON, D.C., November 10, 1864.

MAJOR-GENERAL BURBRIDGE, Lexington, Ky.:

I have just received a telegram from Governor Bramlette saying: "General John B. Houston, a loyal man and prominent citizen, was arrested, and yesterday, started off by General Burbridge, to be sent beyond our lines by way of Catlettsburg, for no other offense than opposition to your re-election," and I have answered him as follows below, of which please take notice and report to me.
A. LINCOLN.

WASHINGTON, D.C., November 10, 1864. GOVERNOR BRAMLETTE, Frankfort, Ky.:

Yours of yesterday received. I can scarcely believe that General John B. Houston has been arrested "for no other offense than opposition to my re-election;" for, if that had been deemed sufficient cause of arrest, I should have heard of more than one arrest in Kentucky on election day. If, however, General Houston has been arrested for no other cause than opposition to my re-election, General Burbridge will discharge him at once, I sending him a copy of this as an order to that effect.

A. LINCOLN.

TO GENERAL S. A. HURLBUT.

(Private.)

EXECUTIVE MANSION, WASHINGTON, November 14, 1864.
MAJOR-GENERAL HURLBUT:
Few things since I have been here have impressed me more painfully than what, for four or five months past, has appeared a bitter military opposition to the new State government of Louisiana. I still indulged some hope that I was mistaken in the fact; but copies of a correspondence on the subject between General Canby and yourself, and shown me to-day, dispel that hope. A very fair proportion of the people of Louisiana have inaugurated a new State government, making an excellent new constitution—better for the poor black man than we have in Illinois. This was done under military protection, directed by me, in the belief, still sincerely entertained, that with such a nucleus around which to build we could get the State into position again sooner than otherwise. In this belief a general promise of protection and support, applicable alike to Louisiana and other States, was given in the last annual message. During the formation of the new government and constitution they were supported by nearly every loyal person, and opposed by every secessionist. And this support and this opposition, from the respective standpoints of the parties, was perfectly consistent and logical. Every Unionist ought to wish the new government to succeed; and every disunionist must desire it to fail. Its failure would gladden the heart of Slidell in Europe, and of every enemy of the old flag in the world. Every advocate of slavery naturally desires to see blasted and crushed the liberty promised the black man by the new constitution. But why General Canby and General Hurlbut should join on the same side is to me incomprehensible.

Of course, in the condition of things at New Orleans, the military must not be thwarted by the civil authority; but when the Constitutional Convention, for what it deems a breach of privilege, arrests an editor in no way connected with the military, the military necessity for insulting the convention and forcibly discharging the editor is difficult to perceive. Neither is the military necessity for protecting the people against paying large salaries fixed by a legislature of their own choosing very apparent. Equally difficult to perceive is the military necessity for forcibly interposing to prevent a bank from loaning its own money to the State. These things, if they have occurred, are, at the best, no better than gratuitous hostility. I wish I could hope that they may be shown not to have occurred. To make assurance against misunderstanding, I repeat that in the existing condition of things in Louisiana, the military must not be thwarted by the civil authority; and I add that on points of difference the commanding general must be judge and master. But I also add that in the exercise of this judgment and control, a purpose, obvious, and scarcely unavowed, to transcend all military necessity, in order to crush out the civil government, will not be overlooked.

Yours truly,
A. LINCOLN.

REPLY TO MARYLAND UNION COMMITTEE, NOVEMBER 17, 1864.

The President, in reply, said that he had to confess he had been duly notified of the intention to make this friendly call some days ago, and in this he had had a fair opportunity afforded to be ready with a set speech; but he had not prepared one, being too busy for that purpose. He would say, however, that he was gratified with the result of the presidential election. He had kept as near as he could to the exercise of his best judgment for the interest of the whole country, and to have the seal of approbation stamped on the course he had pursued was exceedingly grateful to his feelings. He thought he could say, in as large a sense as any other man, that his pleasure consisted in belief that the policy he had pursued was the best, if not the only one, for the safety of the country.

He had said before, and now repeated, that he indulged in no feeling of triumph over any man who thought or acted differently from himself. He had no such feeling toward any living man. When he thought of Maryland, in particular, he was of the opinion that she had more than double her share in what had occurred in the recent elections. The adoption of a free-State constitution was a greater thing than the part taken by the people of the State in the presidential election. He would any day have stipulated to lose Maryland in the presidential election to save it by the adoption of a free-State constitution, because the presidential election comes every four years, while that is a thing which, being done, cannot be undone. He therefore thought that in that they had a victory for the right worth a great deal more than their part in the presidential election, though of the latter he thought highly. He had once before said, but would say again, that those who have differed with us and opposed us will see that the result of the presidential election is better for their own good than if they had been successful.

Thanking the committee for their compliment, he brought his brief speech to a close.

PROCLAMATION CONCERNING BLOCKADE, NOVEMBER 19, 1864

BY THE PRESIDENT OF THE UNITED STATES OF AMERICA:

A Proclamation.

Whereas by my proclamation of the 19th of April, 1861, it was declared that the ports of certain States, including those of Norfolk, in the State of Virginia, Fernandina and Pensacola, in the State of Florida, were, for reasons therein set forth, intended to be placed under blockade; and:

Whereas the said ports were subsequently blockaded accordingly, but having for some time past been in the military possession of the United States, it is deeemd advisable that they should be opened to domestic and foreign commerce: Now, therefore, be it known that I, Abraham Lincoln, President of the United States, pursuant to the authority in me vested by the fifth section of the act of Congress approved on the 13th of July, 1861, entitled "An act further to provide for the collection of duties on imports, and for other purposes," do hereby declare that the blockade of the said ports of Norfolk, Fernandina, and Pensacola shall so far cease and determine, from and after the first day of December next, that commercial intercourse with those ports, except as to persons, things, and information contraband of war, may, from that time, be carried on, subject to the laws of the United States, to the limitations and in pursuance of the regulations which may be prescribed by the Secretary of the Treasury, and to such military and naval regulations as are now in force, or may hereafter be found necessary.

In witness whereof, I have hereunto set my hand and caused the seal of the United States to be affixed. Done at the city of Washington, this nineteenth day of November, in the year of our Lord one thousand eight hundred and sixty-four, and of the independence of the United States the eighty-ninth.

A. LINCOLN.

By the President: WILLIAM H. SEWARD, Secretary of State.

FIVE-STAR MOTHER

TO MRS. BIXBY.

EXECUTIVE MANSION, WASHINGTON, November 21, 1864.

MRS. BIXBY, Boston, Massachusetts.

DEAR MADAM:—I have been shown in the files of the War Department a statement of the Adjutant-General of Massachusetts that you are the mother of five sons who have died gloriously on the field of battle. I feel how weak and fruitless must be any words of mine which should attempt to beguile you from the grief of a loss so overwhelming. But I cannot refrain from tendering to you the consolation that may be found in the thanks of the Republic they died to save. I pray that our Heavenly Father may assuage the anguish of your bereavement, and leave you only the cherished memory of the loved and lost, and the solemn pride that must be yours to have laid so costly a sacrifice upon the altar of freedom.

Yours very sincerely and respectfully,

A. LINCOLN.

TO J. PHILLIPS.

EXECUTIVE MANSION, WASHINGTON, November 21, 1864.

DEACON JOHN PHILLIPS.
MY DEAR SIR:—I have heard of the incident at the polls in your town, in which you acted so honorable a part, and I take the liberty of writing to you to express my personal gratitude for the compliment paid me by the suffrage of a citizen so venerable.
The example of such devotion to civic duties in one whose days have already been extended an average lifetime beyond the Psalmist's limit, cannot but be valuable and fruitful. It is not for myself only, but for the country which you have in your sphere served so long and so well, that I thank you.
Your friend and servant,
A. LINCOLN.

TELEGRAM TO GOVERNOR BRAMLETTE. WASHINGTON, D. C. NOVEMBER 22, 1864.

GOVERNOR BRAMLETTE, Frankfort, Ky.:

Yours of to-day received. It seems that Lieutenant-Governor Jacobs and Colonel Wolford are stationary now. General Sudarth and Mr. Hodges are here, and the Secretary of War and myself are trying to devise means of pacification and harmony for Kentucky, which we hope to effect soon, now that the passion-exciting subject of the election is past.
A. LINCOLN.

TELEGRAM TO GOVERNOR CURTIN, WASHINGTON, D.C., NOVEMBER 25, 1864

GOVERNOR CURTIN, Harrisburg, Pennsylvania;

I have no knowledge, information, or belief, that three States—or any States, offer to resume allegiance.
A. LINCOLN.

TELEGRAM TO GENERAL ROSECRANS. EXECUTIVE MANSION, WASHINGTON D.C., NOV.

26, 1864 MAJOR-GENERAL ROSECRANS:
Please telegraph me briefly on what charge and evidence Mrs. Anna B. Martin has been sent to the penitentiary at Alton.
A. LINCOLN.

MEMORANDUM,

DECEMBER 3, 1864.

On Thursday of last week, two ladies from Tennessee came before the President, asking the release of their husbands held as prisoners of war at Johnson's Island. They were put off until Friday, when they came again, and were again put off until Saturday. At each of the interviews one of the ladies urged that her husband was a religious man, and on Saturday the President ordered the release of the prisoners, when he said to this lady: "You say your husband is a religious man; tell him when you meet him, that I say I am not much of a judge of religion, but that, in my opinion, the religion that sets men to rebel and fight against their own government, because, as they think, that government does

not sufficiently help some men to eat their bread in the sweat of other men's faces, is not the sort of religion upon which people can get to heaven."
A. LINCOLN.

ORDER CONCERNING THE STEAMER "FUNAYMA SOLACE."

EXECUTIVE MANSION, WASHINGTON, December 3, 1864.

A war steamer, called the Funayma Solace, having been built in this country, for the Japanese government and at the instance of that government, it is deemed to comport with the public interest, in view of the unsettled condition of the relations of the United States with that Empire, that the steamer should not be allowed to proceed to Japan. If, however, the Secretary of the Navy should ascertain that the steamer is adapted to our service, he is authorized to purchase her, but the purchase money will be held in trust toward satisfying any valid claims which may be presented by the Japanese on account of the construction of the steamer and the failure to deliver the same, as above set forth.
A. LINCOLN. MESSAGE TO CONGRESS.
WASHINGTON CITY, December 5, 1864
TO THE SENATE AND HOUSE OF REPRESENTATIVES:
In conformity to the law of July 16, 1862, I most cordially recommend that Captain John A. Winslow, United States Navy, receive a vote of thanks from Congress for the skill and gallantry exhibited by him in the brilliant action whilst in command of the United States steamer Keaysarge, which led to the total destruction of the piratical craft Alabama, on the 19th of June, 1864., a vessel superior in tonnage, superior in number of guns, and superior in number of crew.
This recommendation is specially made in order to comply with the requirements of the ninth section of the aforesaid act, which is in the following words, viz:
That any line officer of the navy or marine corps may be advanced one grade, if, upon recommendation by the President by name he receives the thanks of Congress for highly distinguished conduct in conflict with the enemy, or far extraordinary heroism in the line of his profession.
A. LINCOLN,

MESSAGE TO CONGRESS.

WASHINGTON CITY, December 5, 1864.

TO THE SENATE AND HOUSE OF REPRESENTATIVES:
In conformity to the law of July 16, 1862, I most cordially recommend that Lieutenant William B. Gushing, United States Navy, receive a vote of thanks from Congress for his important, gallant, and perilous achievement in destroying the rebel ironclad steamer Albemarle on the night of the 27th of October, 1864., at Plymouth, N. C.
The destruction of so formidable a vessel, which had resisted the continued attacks of a number of our vessels on former occasions, is an important event touching our future naval and military operations, and would reflect honor on any officer, and redounds to the credit of this young officer and the few brave comrades who assisted in this successful and daring undertaking.
This recommendation is specially made in order to comply with the requirements of the ninth section of the Aforesaid act, which is in the following words, namely:
That any line officer of the navy or marine corps may be advanced one grade if upon recommendation of the President by name he receives the thanks of Congress for highly distinguished conduct in conflict with the enemy, or for extraordinary heroism in the line of his profession.
A. LINCOLN.

ANNUAL MESSAGE TO CONGRESS,

DECEMBER 6, 1864.

FELLOW-CITIZENS OF THE SENATE AND HOUSE OF REPRESENTATIVES:
Again the blessings of health and abundant harvests claim our profoundest gratitude to Almighty God.
The condition of our foreign affairs is reasonably satisfactory.
Mexico continues to be a theater of civil war. While our political relations with that country have undergone no change, we have at the same time strictly maintained neutrality between the belligerents.
At the request of the States of Costa Rica and Nicaragua, a competent engineer has been authorized to make a survey of the river San Juan and the port of San Juan. It is a source of much satisfaction that the difficulties which for a moment excited some political apprehensions and caused a closing of the interoceanic transit route have been amicably adjusted, and that there is a good prospect that the route will soon be reopened with an increase of capacity and adaptation. We could not exaggerate either the commercial or the political importance of that great improvement.
It would be doing injustice to an important South American State not to acknowledge the directness, frankness, and cordiality with which the United States of Colombia have entered into intimate relations with this government. A claims convention has been constituted to complete the unfinished work of the one which closed its session in 1861.
The new liberal constitution of Venezuela having gone into effect with the universal acquiescence of the people, the government under it has been recognized and diplomatic intercourse with it has opened in a cordial and friendly spirit. The long-deferred Aves Island claim has been satisfactorily paid and discharged.
Mutual payments have been made of the claims awarded by the late joint commission for the settlement of claims between the United States and Peru. An earnest and cordial friendship continues to exist between the two countries, and such efforts as were in my power have been used to remove misunderstanding, and avert a threatened war between Peru and Spain.
Our relations are of the most friendly nature with Chile, the Argentine Republic, Bolivia, Costa Rica, Paraguay, San Salvador, and Haiti.
During the past year no differences of any kind have arisen with any of these republics, and on the other hand, their sympathies with the United States are constantly expressed with cordiality and earnestness.
The claim arising from the seizure of the cargo of the brig Macedonian in 1821 has been paid in full by the Government of Chile.
Civil war continues in the Spanish part of San Domingo, apparently without prospect of an early close.
Official correspondence has been freely opened with Liberia, and it gives us a pleasing view of social and political progress in that republic. It may be expected to derive new vigor from American influence improved by the rapid disappearance of slavery in the United States.
I solicit your authority to furnish to the republic a gunboat, at moderate cost, to be reimbursed to the United States by instalments. Such a vessel is needed for the safety of that state against the native African races, and in Liberian hands it would be more effective in arresting the African slave-trade than a squadron in our own hands. The possession of the least organized naval force would stimulate a generous ambition in the republic, and the confidence which we should manifest by furnishing it would win forbearance and favor toward the colony from all civilized nations.
The proposed overland telegraph between America and Europe, by the way of Bering Straits and Asiatic Russia, which was sanctioned by Congress at the last session, has been undertaken, under very favorable circumstances, by an association of American citizens, with the cordial good-will and support as well of this Government as of those of Great Britain and Russia. Assurances have been received from most of the South American States of their high appreciation of the enterprise and their readiness to co-operate in constructing lines tributary to that world-encircling communication. I learn with much satisfaction that the noble design of a telegraphic communication between the eastern coast of America and Great Britain has been renewed, with full expectation of its early accomplishment.
Thus it is hoped that with the return of domestic peace the country will be able to resume with energy and advantage its former high career of commerce and civilization.
Our very popular and estimable representative in Egypt died in April last. An unpleasant altercation which arose between the temporary incumbent of the office and the Government of the Pasha resulted in a suspension of intercourse. The evil was promptly corrected on the arrival of the successor in the consulate, and our relations with Egypt, as well as our relations with the Barbary Powers, are entirely satisfactory.
The rebellion which has so long been flagrant in China has at last been suppressed, with the co-operating good offices of this Government and of the other Western commercial States. The judicial consular establishment there has become very difficult and onerous, and it will need legislative revision to adapt it to the extension of our commerce and to the more intimate intercourse which has been instituted with the Government and people of that vast Empire. China seems to be accepting with hearty good-will the conventional laws which regulate commercial and social intercourse among the Western nations.
Owing to the peculiar situation of Japan and the anomalous form of its Government, the action of that empire in performing treaty stipulations is inconstant and capricious. Nevertheless, good progress has been effected by the

Western powers, moving with enlightened concert. Our own pecuniary claims have been allowed or put in course of settlement, and the inland sea has been reopened to commerce. There is reason also to believe that these proceedings have increased rather than diminished the friendship of Japan toward the United States.

The ports of Norfolk, Fernandina, and Pensacola have been opened by proclamation. It is hoped that foreign merchants will now consider whether it is not safer and more profitable to themselves, as well as just to the United States, to resort to these and other open ports than it is to pursue, through many hazards and at vast cost, a contraband trade with other ports which are closed, if not by actual military occupation, at least by a lawful and effective blockade.

For myself, I have no doubt of the power and duty of the Executive, under the law of nations, to exclude enemies of the human race from an asylum in the United States. If Congress should think that proceedings in such cases lack the authority of law, or ought to be further regulated by it, I recommend that provision be made for effectually preventing foreign slave traders from acquiring domicile and facilities for their criminal occupation in our country.

It is possible that if it were a new and open question the maritime powers, with the lights they now enjoy, would not concede the privileges of a naval belligerent to the insurgents of the United States, destitute, as they are, and always have been, equally of ships of war and of ports and harbors. Disloyal emissaries have been neither assiduous nor more successful during the last year than they were before that time in their efforts, under favor of that privilege, to embroil our country in foreign wars. The desire and determination of the governments of the maritime states to defeat that design are believed to be as sincere as and can not be more earnest than our own. Nevertheless, unforeseen political difficulties have arisen, especially in Brazilian and British ports and on the northern boundary of the United States, which have required, and are likely to continue to require, the practice of constant vigilance and a just and conciliatory spirit on the part of the United States, as well as of the nations concerned and their governments.

Commissioners have been appointed under the treaty with Great Britain on the adjustment of the claims of the Hudson Bay and Puget Sound Agricultural Companies, in Oregon, and are now proceeding to the execution of the trust assigned to them.

In view of the insecurity of life and property in the region adjacent to the Canadian border, by reason of recent assaults and depredations committed by inimical and desperate persons who are harbored there, it has been thought proper to give notice that after the expiration of six months, the period conditionally stipulated in the existing arrangement with Great Britain, the United States must hold themselves at liberty to increase their naval armament upon the Lakes if they shall find that proceeding necessary. The condition of the border will necessarily come into consideration in connection with the question of continuing or modifying the rights of transit from Canada through the United States, as well as the regulation of imposts, which were temporarily established by the reciprocity treaty of the 5th June, 1854.

I desire, however, to be understood while making this statement that the colonial authorities of Canada are not deemed to be intentionally unjust or unfriendly toward the United States, but, on the contrary, there is every reason to expect that, with the approval of the Imperial Government, they will take the necessary measures to prevent new incursions across the border.

The act passed at the last session for the encouragement of immigration has so far as was possible been put into operation. It seems to need amendment which will enable the officers of the Government to prevent the practice of frauds against the immigrants while on their way and on their arrival in the ports, so as to secure them here a free choice of avocations and places of settlement. A liberal disposition toward this great national policy is manifested by most of the European States, and ought to be reciprocated on our part by giving the immigrants effective national protection. I regard our immigrants as one of the principal replenishing streams which are appointed by Providence to repair the ravages of internal war and its wastes of national strength and health. All that is necessary is to secure the flow of that stream in its present fullness, and to that end the Government must in every way make it manifest that it neither needs nor designs to impose involuntary military service upon those who come from other lands to cast their lot in our country. The financial affairs of the Government have been successfully administered during the last year. The legislation of the last session of Congress has beneficially affected the revenues, although sufficient time has not yet elapsed to experience the full effect of several of the provisions of the acts of Congress imposing increased taxation.

The receipts during the year from all sources, upon the basis of warrants signed by the Secretary of the Treasury, including loans and the balance in the Treasury on the 1st day of July, 1863, were $1,394,196,007.62, and the aggregate disbursements, upon the same basis, were $1,298,056,101.89, leaving a balance in the Treasury, as shown by warrants, of $96,739,905.73.

Deduct from these amounts the amount of the principal of the public debt redeemed and the amount of issues in substitution therefor, and the actual cash operations of the Treasury were: receipts, $884,076,646.57; disbursements, $865,234,087.86; which leaves a cash balance in the Treasury of $18,842,558.71.

Of the receipts there were derived from customs $102,316,152.99, from lands $588,333.29, from direct taxes $475,648.96, from internal revenue $109,741,134.10, from miscellaneous sources $47,511,448.10, and from loans applied to actual expenditures, including former balance, $623,443,929.13.

There were disbursed for the civil service $27,505,599.46, for pensions and Indians $7,517,930.97, for the War Department $690,791,842.97, for the Navy Department $85,733,292.77, for interest on the public debt $53,685,421.69, making an aggregate of $865,234,087.86, and leaving a balance in the Treasury of $18,842,558.71, as before stated.

For the actual receipts and disbursements for the first quarter and the estimated receipts and disbursements for the three remaining quarters of the current fiscal year, and the general operations of the Treasury in detail, I refer you to the report of the Secretary of the Treasury. I concur with him in the opinion that the proportion of moneys required to meet the expenses consequent upon the war derived from taxation should be still further increased; and I earnestly invite your attention to this subject to the end that there be such additional legislation as shall be required to meet the just expectations of the Secretary.

The public debt on the first day of July last, as appears by the books of the Treasury, amounted to $1,740,690,489.49. Probably, should the war continue for another year, that amount may be increased by not far from $500,000,000. Held, as it is, for the most part by our own people, it has become a substantial branch of national, though private, property. For obvious reasons the more nearly this property can be distributed among all the people the better. To favor such general distribution, greater inducements to become owners might, perhaps, with good effect and without injury be presented to persons of limited means. With this view I suggest whether it might not be both competent and expedient for Congress to provide that a limited amount of some future issue of public securities might be held by any bona fide purchaser exempt from taxation and from seizure for debt, under such restrictions and limitations as might be necessary to guard against abuse of so important a privilege. This would enable every prudent person to set aside a small annuity against a possible day of want.

Privileges like these would render the possession of such securities to the amount limited most desirable to every person of small means who might be able to save enough for the purpose. The great advantage of citizens being creditors as well as debtors with relation to the public debt is obvious. Men readily perceive that they can not be much oppressed by a debt which they owe to themselves.

The public debt on the first day of July last, although somewhat exceeding the estimate of the Secretary of the Treasury made to Congress at the commencement of the last session, falls short of the estimate of that officer made in the preceding December as to its probable amount at the beginning of this year by the sum of $3,995,097.31. This fact exhibits a satisfactory condition and conduct of the operations of the Treasury.

The national banking system is proving to be acceptable to capitalists and to the people. On the twenty-fifth day of November five hundred and eighty-four national banks had been organized, a considerable number of which were conversions from State banks. Changes from State systems to the national system are rapidly taking place, and it is hoped that very soon there will be in the United States no banks of issue not authorized by Congress and no bank-note circulation not secured by the Government. That the Government and the people will derive great benefit from this change in the banking systems of the country can hardly be questioned. The national system will create a reliable and permanent influence in support of the national credit and protect the people against losses in the use of paper money. Whether or not any further legislation is advisable for the suppression of State-bank issues, it will be for Congress to determine. It seems quite clear that the Treasury can not be satisfactorily conducted unless the Government can exercise a restraining power over the bank-note circulation of the country.

The report of the Secretary of War and the accompanying documents will detail the campaigns of the armies in the field since the date of the last annual message, and also the operations of the several administrative bureaus of the War Department during the last year. It will also specify the measures deemed essential for the national defense and to keep up and supply the requisite military force.

The report of the Secretary of the Navy presents a comprehensive and satisfactory exhibit of the affairs of that Department and of the naval service. It is a subject of congratulation and laudable pride to our countrymen that a Navy of such vast proportions has been organized in so brief a period and conducted with so much efficiency and success.

The general exhibit of the Navy, including vessels under construction on the first of December, 1864, shows a total of 671 vessels, carrying 4610 guns, and of 510,396 tons, being an actual increase during the year, over and above all losses by shipwreck or in battle, of 83 vessels, 167 guns, and 42,427 tons.

The total number of men at this time in the naval service, including officers, is about 51,000.

There have been captured by the Navy during the year 324 vessels, and the whole number of naval captures since hostilities commenced is 1379, of which 267 are steamers.

The gross proceeds arising from the sale of condemned prize property thus far reported amount to $14,369,250.51. A large amount of such proceeds is still under adjudication and yet to be reported.

The total expenditure of the Navy Department of every description, including the cost of the immense squadrons that have been called into existence from the fourth of March, 1861, to the first of November, 1864, is $238,647,262.35.

Your favorable consideration is invited to the various recommendations of the Secretary of the Navy, especially in regard to a navy-yard and suitable establishment for the construction and repair of iron vessels and the machinery and armature for our ships, to which reference was made in my last annual message.

Your attention is also invited to the views expressed in the report in relation to the legislation of Congress at its last session in respect to prize on our inland waters.

I cordially concur in the recommendation of the Secretary as to the propriety of creating the new rank of vice-admiral in our naval service.

Your attention is invited to the report of the Postmaster-General for a detailed account of the operations and financial condition of the Post-Office Department.

The postal revenues for the year ending June 30, 1864, amounted to $12,438,253.78, and the expenditures to $12,644,786.20, the excess of expenditures over receipts being $206,532.42.

The views presented by the Postmaster-General on the subject of special grants by the Government in aid of the establishment of new lines of ocean mail steamships and the policy he recommends for the development of increased commercial intercourse with adjacent and neighboring countries should receive the careful consideration of Congress.

It is of noteworthy interest that the steady expansion of population, improvement, and governmental institutions over the new and unoccupied portions of our country have scarcely been checked, much less impeded or destroyed, by our great civil war, which at first glance would seem to have absorbed almost the entire energies of the nation.

The organization and admission of the State of Nevada has been completed in conformity with law, and thus our excellent system is firmly established in the mountains, which once seemed a barren and uninhabitable waste between the Atlantic States and those which have grown up on the coast of the Pacific Ocean.

The Territories of the Union are generally in a condition of prosperity and rapid growth. Idaho and Montana, by reason of their great distance and the interruption of communication with them by Indian hostilities, have been only partially organized; but it is understood that these difficulties are about to disappear, which will permit their governments, like those of the others, to go into speedy and full operation.

As intimately connected with and promotive of this material growth of the nation, I ask the attention of Congress to the valuable information and important recommendations relating to the public lands, Indian affairs, the Pacific Railroad, and mineral discoveries contained in the report of the Secretary of the Interior which is herewith transmitted, and which report also embraces the subjects of patents, pensions, and other topics of public interest pertaining to his Department.

The quantity of public land disposed of during the five quarters ending on the thirtieth of September last was 4,221,342 acres, of which 1,538,614 acres were entered under the homestead law. The remainder was located with military land warrants, agricultural scrip certified to States for railroads, and sold for cash. The cash received from sales and location fees was $1,019,446.

The income from sales during the fiscal year ending June 30, 1864, was $678,007.21, against $136,077.95 received during the preceding year. The aggregate number of acres surveyed during the year has been equal to the quantity disposed of, and there is open to settlement about 133,000,000 acres of surveyed land.

The great enterprise of connecting the Atlantic with the Pacific States by railways and telegraph lines has been entered upon with a vigor that gives assurance of success, notwithstanding the embarrassments arising from the prevailing high prices of materials and labor. The route of the main line of the road has been definitely located for one hundred miles westward from the initial point at Omaha City, Nebraska, and a preliminary location of the Pacific Railroad of California has been made from Sacramento eastward to the great bend of the Truckee River in Nevada.

Numerous discoveries of gold, silver, and cinnabar mines have been added to the many heretofore known, and the country occupied by the Sierra Nevada and Rocky mountains and the subordinate ranges now teems with enterprising labor, which is richly remunerative. It is believed that the produce of the mines of precious metals in that region has during the year reached, if not exceeded, $100,000,000 in value.

It was recommended in my last annual message that our Indian system be remodeled. Congress at its last session, acting upon the recommendation, did provide for reorganizing the system in California, and it is believed that under the present organization the management of the Indians there will be attended with reasonable success. Much yet remains to be done to provide for the proper government of the Indians in other parts of the country, to render it secure for the advancing settler, and to provide for the welfare of the Indian. The Secretary reiterates his recommendations, and to them the attention of Congress is invited.

The liberal provisions made by Congress for paying pensions to invalid soldiers and sailors of the Republic and to the widows, orphans, and dependent mothers of those who have fallen in battle or died of disease contracted or of wounds received in the service of their country have been diligently administered. There have been added to the pension rolls during the year ending the 30th day of June last the names of 16,770 invalid soldiers and of 271 disabled seamen, making the present number of army invalid pensioners 22,767 and of navy invalid pensioners 712.

Of widows, orphans, and mothers 22,198 have been placed on the army pension rolls and 248 on the navy rolls. The present number of army pensioners of this class is 25,433 and of navy pensioners 793. At the beginning of the year the number of Revolutionary pensioners was 1430. Only twelve of them were soldiers, of whom seven have since died. The remainder are those who under the law receive pensions because of relationship to Revolutionary soldiers. During the year ending the thirtieth of June, 1864, $4,504,616.92 have been paid to pensioners of all classes.

I cheerfully commend to your continued patronage the benevolent institutions of the District of Columbia which have hitherto been established or fostered by Congress, and respectfully refer for information concerning them and in relation to the Washington Aqueduct, the Capitol, and other matters of local interest to the report of the Secretary.

The Agricultural Department, under the supervision of its present energetic and faithful head, is rapidly commending itself to the great and vital interest it was created to advance. It is peculiarly the people's department, in which they feel more directly concerned than in any other. I commend it to the continued attention and fostering care of Congress.

The war continues. Since the last annual message all the important lines and positions then occupied by our forces have been maintained and our arms have steadily advanced, thus liberating the regions left in rear, so that Missouri, Kentucky, Tennessee, and parts of other States have again produced reasonably fair crops.

The most remarkable feature in the military operations of the year is General Sherman's attempted march of three hundred miles directly through the insurgent region. It tends to show a great increase of our relative strength that our General-in-Chief should feel able to confront and hold in check every active force of the enemy, and yet to detach a well-appointed large army to move on such an expedition. The result not yet being known, conjecture in regard to it is not here indulged.

Important movements have also occurred during the year to the effect of molding society for durability in the Union. Although short of complete success, it is much in the right direction that twelve thousand citizens in each of the States of Arkansas and Louisiana have organized loyal State governments, with free constitutions, and are earnestly struggling to maintain and administer them. The movements in the same direction more extensive though less definite in Missouri, Kentucky, and Tennessee, should not be overlooked. But Maryland presents the example of complete success. Maryland is secure to liberty and union for all the future. The genius of rebellion will no more claim Maryland. Like another foul spirit being driven out, it may seek to tear her, but it will woo her no more.

At the last session of Congress a proposed amendment of the Constitution abolishing slavery throughout the United States passed the Senate, but failed for lack of the requisite two-thirds vote in the House of Representatives. Although the present is the same Congress and nearly the same members, and without questioning the wisdom or patriotism of those who stood in opposition, I venture to recommend the reconsideration and passage of the measure at the present session. Of course the abstract question is not changed; but an intervening election shows almost certainly that the next Congress will pass the measure if this does not. Hence there is only a question of time as to when the proposed amendment will go to the States for their action. And as it is to so go at all events, may we not agree that the sooner the better? It is not claimed that the election has imposed a duty on members to change their views or their votes any further than, as an additional element to be considered, their judgment may be affected by it. It is the voice of the people now for the first time heard upon the question. In a great national crisis like ours, unanimity of action among those seeking a common end is very desirable, almost indispensable. And yet no approach to such unanimity is attainable unless some deference shall be paid to the will of the majority simply because it is the will of the majority. In this case the common end is the maintenance of the Union, and among the means to secure that end such will, through the election, is most clearly declared in favor of such Constitutional amendment.

The most reliable indication of public purpose in this country is derived through our popular elections. Judging by the recent canvass and its result, the purpose of the people within the loyal States to maintain the integrity of the Union was never more firm nor more nearly unanimous than now. The extraordinary calmness and good order with which the millions of voters met and mingled at the polls give strong assurance of this. Not only all those who supported the Union ticket, so called, but a great majority of the opposing party also may be fairly claimed to entertain and to be actuated by the same purpose. It is an unanswerable argument to this effect that no candidate for any office whatever, high or low, has ventured to seek votes on the avowal that he was for giving up the Union. There have been much impugning of motives and much heated controversy as to the proper means and best mode of advancing the Union cause, but on the distinct issue of Union or no Union the politicians have shown their instinctive knowledge that there is no diversity among the people. In affording the people the fair opportunity of showing one to another and to the world this firmness and unanimity of purpose, the election has been of vast value to the national cause.

The election has exhibited another fact not less valuable to be known—the fact that we do not approach exhaustion in the most important branch of national resources, that of living men. While it is melancholy to reflect that the war has filled so many graves and carried mourning to so many hearts, it is some relief to know that, compared with the surviving, the fallen have been so few. While corps and divisions and brigades and regiments have formed and fought and dwindled and gone out of existence, a great majority of the men who composed them are still living. The same is true of the naval service. The election returns prove this. So many voters could not else be found. The States regularly holding elections, both now and four years ago, to wit, California, Connecticut, Delaware, Illinois, Indiana, Iowa, Kentucky, Maine, Maryland, Massachusetts, Michigan, Minnesota, Missouri, New Hampshire, New Jersey, New York, Ohio, Oregon, Pennsylvania, Rhode Island, Vermont, West Virginia, and Wisconsin, cast 3,982,011 votes now, against 3,870,222 cast then, showing an aggregate now of 3,982,011. To this is to be added 33,762 cast now in the new States of Kansas and Nevada, which States did not vote in 1860, thus swelling the aggregate to 4,015,773 and the net increase during the three years and a half of war to 145,551. A table is appended showing particulars. To this again should be added the number of all soldiers in the field from Massachusetts, Rhode Island, New Jersey, Delaware, Indiana, Illinois, and California, who by the laws of those States could not vote away from their homes, and which number can not be less than 90,000. Nor yet is this all. The number in organized Territories is triple now what it was four years ago—while thousands, white and black, join us as the national arms press back the insurgent lines. So much is shown, affirmatively and negatively, by the election. It is not material to inquire how the increase has been produced or to show that it would have been greater but for the war, which is probably true. The important fact remains demonstrated that we have more men now than we had when the war began; that we are not exhausted nor in process of exhaustion; that we are gaining strength and may if need be maintain the contest indefinitely. [This sentence recognizes the concern of a guerilla war after the main war finished.]This as to men. Material resources are now more complete and abundant than ever.

The national resources, then, are unexhausted, and, as we believe, inexhaustible. The public purpose to re-establish and maintain the national authority is unchanged, and, as we believe, unchangeable. The manner of continuing the effort remains to choose. On careful consideration of all the evidence accessible it seems to me that no attempt at negotiation with the insurgent leader could result in any good. He would accept nothing short of severance of the Union, precisely what we will not and can not give. His declarations to this effect are explicit and oft repeated. He does not attempt to deceive us. He affords us no excuse to deceive ourselves. He can not voluntarily reaccept the Union; we can not voluntarily yield it. Between him and us the issue is distinct, simple, and inflexible. It is an issue which can only be tried by war and decided by victory. If we yield, we are beaten; if the Southern people fail him, he is beaten. Either way it would be the victory and defeat following war. What is true, however, of him who heads the insurgent cause is not necessarily true of those who follow. Although he can not reaccept the Union, they can. Some of them, we know, already desire peace and reunion. The number of such may increase. They can at any moment have peace simply by laying down their arms and submitting to the national authority under the Constitution. After so much the Government could not, if it would, maintain war against them. The loyal people would not sustain or allow it. If questions should remain, we would adjust them by the peaceful means of legislation, conference, courts, and votes, operating only in Constitutional and lawful channels. Some certain, and other possible, questions are and would be beyond the Executive power to adjust; as, for instance, the admission of members into Congress and whatever might require the appropriation of money. The Executive power itself would be greatly diminished by the cessation of actual war. Pardons and remissions of forfeitures, however, would still be within Executive control. In what spirit and temper this control would be exercised can be fairly judged of by the past.

A year ago general pardon and amnesty, upon specified terms, were offered to all except certain designated classes, and it was at the same time made known that the excepted classes were still within contemplation of special clemency. During the year many availed themselves of the general provision, and many more would, only that the signs of bad faith in some led to such precautionary measures as rendered the practical process less easy and certain. During the same time also special pardons have been granted to individuals of the excepted classes, and no voluntary application has been denied. Thus practically the door has been for a full year open to all except such as were not in condition to make free choice; that is, such as were in custody or under constraint. It is still so open to all. But the time may come, probably will come, when public duty shall demand that it be closed and that in lieu more rigorous measures than heretofore shall be adopted.

In presenting the abandonment of armed resistance to the national authority on the part of the insurgents as the only indispensable condition to ending the war on the part of the Government, I retract nothing heretofore said as to slavery. I repeat the declaration made a year ago, that "while I remain in my present position I shall not attempt to retract or modify the emancipation proclamation, nor shall I return to slavery any person who is free by the terms of that proclamation or by any of the acts of Congress." If the people should, by whatever mode or means, make it an Executive duty to re-enslave such persons, another, and not I, must be their instrument to perform it.

In stating a single condition of peace I mean simply to say that the war will cease on the part of the Government whenever it shall have ceased on the part of those who began it.

A. LINCOLN.

RESPONSE TO A SERENADE, DECEMBER 6, 1864.

FRIENDS AND FELLOW-CITIZENS:—I believe I shall never be old enough to speak without embarrassment when I have nothing to talk about. I have no good news to tell you, and yet I have no bad news to tell. We have talked of elections until there is nothing more to say about them. The most interesting news now we have is from Sherman. We all know where he went in at, but I can't tell where he will come out at. I will now close by proposing three cheers for General Sherman and his army.

TELEGRAM TO GOVERNOR HALL.

EXECUTIVE MANSION, WASHINGTON, December 7, 1864.

GOVERNOR HALL, Jefferson City, Mo.:
Complaint is made to me of the doings of a man at Hannibal, Mo., by the name of Haywood, who, as I am told, has charge of some militia force, and is not in the United States service. Please inquire into the matter and correct anything you may find amiss if in your power.
A. LINCOLN.

TELEGRAM TO COLONEL FASLEIGH.

EXECUTIVE MANSION, WASHINGTON, D. C., December 8, 1864.

COLONEL FASLEIGH, Louisville, Ky.:
I am appealed to in behalf of a man by the name of Frank Fairbairns, said to have been for a long time and still in prison, without any definite ground stated. How is it?
A. LINCOLN.

ORDER APPOINTING COMMISSIONERS

TO INVESTIGATE THE MILITARY DIVISION WEST OF THE MISSISSIPPI.

EXECUTIVE MANSION, December 10, 1864.
ORDERED, First, that Major-General William P. Smith and the Hon. Henry Stanbery be, and they are hereby, appointed special commissioners to investigate and report, for the information of the President; upon the civil and military administration in the military division bordering upon and west of the Mississippi, under such instructions as shall be issued by authority of the President and the War Department.
Second, said commissioners shall have power to examine witnesses upon oath, and to take such proofs orally or in writing, upon the subject-matters of investigation as they may deem expedient, and return the same together with their report.
Third, all officers and persons in the military, naval and revenue services, or in any branch of the public service under the authority of the United States Government, are required, upon subpoena issued by direction of the said commissioners, to appear before them at such time and place as may be designated in said subpoena and to give testimony on oath touching such matters as may be inquired of by the commissioners, and to produce such books, papers, writings, and documents as they may be notified or required to produce by the commissioners, and as may be in their possession.
Fourth, said special commissioners shall also investigate and report upon any other matters that may hereafter be directed by the Secretary of War, and shall with all convenient dispatch make report to him in writing of their investigation, and shall also from time to time make special reports to the Secretary of War upon such matters as they may deem of importance to the public interests.
Fifth, the Secretary of War shall assign to the said commissioners such aid and assistance as may be required for the performance of their duties, and make such just and reasonable allowances and compensation for the said commissioners and for the persons employed by them as he may deem proper.
A. LINCOLN.

TELEGRAM TO GENERAL G, H. THOMAS. WASHINGTON, D.C., December 16, 1864.

MAJOR-GENERAL THOMAS, Nashville, Tennessee:

Please accept for yourself, officers, and men, the nation's thanks for your good work of yesterday. You made a magnificent beginning; a grand consummation is within your easy reach. Do not let it slip.
A. LINCOLN,

ORIGIN OF THE "GREENBACK" CURRENCY

TO COLONEL B. D. TAYLOR

EXECUTIVE MANSION, WASHINGTON, December [16?], 1864.
DEAR COLONEL DICK:—I have long determined to make public the origin of the greenback and tell the world that it is Dick Taylor's creation. You had always been friendly to me, and when troublous times fell on us, and my shoulders, though broad and willing, were weak, and myself surrounded by such circumstances and such people that I knew not whom to trust, then I said in my extremity: "I will send for Colonel Taylor; he will know what to do." I think it was in January, 1862, on or about the 16th, that I did so. You came, and I said to you:
"What can we do?" Said you, "Why, issue Treasury notes bearing no interest, printed on the best banking paper. Issue enough to pay off the Army expenses and declare it legal tender."
Chase thought it a hazardous thing, but we finally accomplished it, and gave the people of this Republic the greatest blessing they ever had—their own paper to pay their own debts.
It is due to you, the father of the present greenback, that the people should know it, and I take great pleasure in making it known. How many times have I laughed at you telling me plainly that I was too lazy to be anything but a lawyer.
Yours truly,
A. LINCOLN.

TELEGRAM TO OFFICER IN COMMAND AT CHATTANOOGA. EXECUTIVE MANSION,

WASHINGTON, December 16, 1864
OFFICER IN COMMAND at Chattanooga, Tenn.:

It is said that Harry Walters, a private in the Anderson cavalry, is now and for a long time has been in prison at Chattanooga. Please report to me what is his condition, and for what he is imprisoned.
A. LINCOLN.

CALL FOR 300,000 VOLUNTEERS, DECEMBER 19, 1864.

BY THE PRESIDENT OF THE UNITED STATES:

A Proclamation
Whereas, by the act approved July 4, 1864, entitled "An act further to regulate and provide for the enrolling and calling out the national forces, and for other purposes," it is provided that the President of the United States may, "at his discretion, at any time hereafter, call for any number of men, as volunteers for the respective terms of one, two, and three years for military service," and "that in case the quota or any part thereof of any town, township, ward of a city, precinct, or election district, or of any country not so subdivided, shall not be filled within the space of fifty days after such call, then the President shall immediately order a draft for one year to fill such quota or any part thereof which may be unfilled;" and

Whereas, by the credits allowed in accordance with the act of Congress on the call for 500,000 men, made July 18, 1864, the number of men to be obtained under that call was reduced to 280,000; and

Whereas, the operations of the enemy in certain States have rendered it impracticable to procure from them their full quotas of troops under said call; and

Whereas, from the foregoing causes but 240,000 men have been put into the Army, Navy, and Marine Corps under the said call of July 18, 1864, leaving a deficiency on that call of two hundred and sixty thousand (260,000):

Now, therefore, I, Abraham Lincoln, President of the United States of America, in order to supply the aforesaid deficiency and to provide for casualties in the military and naval service of the United States, do issue this my call for three hundred thousand (300,000) volunteers to serve for one, two, or three years. The quotas of the States, districts, and subdistricts under this call will be assigned by the War Department through the bureau of the Provost-Marshal General of the United States, and "in case the quota or any part thereof of any town, township, ward of a city, precinct, or election district, or of any county not so subdivided, shall not be filled" before the fifteenth of February, 1865, then a draft shall be made to fill such quota or any part thereof under this call which may be unfilled on said fifteenth day of February, 1865.

In testimony whereof I have hereunto set my hand and caused the seal of the United States to be affixed..........
A. LINCOLN.
By the President: WILLIAM H. SEWARD, Secretary of State.

SHERMAN'S MARCH TO THE SEA

TO GENERAL W. T. SHERMAN.

EXECUTIVE MANSION, WASHINGTON, December 26, 1864
MY DEAR GENERAL SHERMAN:—Many, many thanks for your Christmas gift, the capture of Savannah.

When you were about leaving Atlanta for the Atlantic coast, I was anxious, if not fearful; but feeling that you were the better judge, and remembering that "nothing risked, nothing gained," I did not interfere. Now, the undertaking being a success, the honor is all yours; for I believe none of us went further than to acquiesce.

And taking the work of General Thomas into the count, as it should be taken, it is indeed a great success. Not only does it afford the obvious and immediate military advantages; but in showing to the world that your army could be divided, putting the stronger part to an important new service, and yet leaving enough to vanquish the old opposing force of the whole,—Hood's army,—it brings those who sat in darkness to see a great light. But what next?

I suppose it will be safe if I leave General Grant and yourself to decide.

Please make my grateful acknowledgments to your whole army of officers and men.

Yours very truly,
A. LINCOLN.

TELEGRAM TO OFFICER IN COMMAND AT LEXINGTON.

EXECUTIVE MANSION, WASHINGTON, December 27, 1864.

OFFICER IN COMMAND at Lexington, Ky.:
If within your power send me the particulars of the causes for which Lieutenant-Governor Jacob was arrested and sent away.
A. LINCOLN.

TO J. MACLEAN.

EXECUTIVE MANSION, WASHINGTON, December 27, 1864.

Dr. JOHN MACLEAN:

MY DEAR SIR:—I have the honor to acknowledge the reception of your note of the twentieth of December, conveying the announcement that the Trustees of the College of New Jersey had conferred upon me the degree of Doctor of Laws.

The assurance conveyed by this high compliment, that the course of the Government which I represent, has received the approval of a body of gentlemen of such character and intelligence, in this time of public trial, is most grateful to me.

Thoughtful men must feel that the fate of civilization upon this continent is involved in the issue of our contest. Among the most gratifying proofs of this conviction is the hearty devotion everywhere exhibited by our schools and colleges to the national cause.

I am most thankful if my labors have seemed to conduct to the preservation of those institutions, under which alone we can expect good government and in its train sound learning, and the progress of the liberal arts.

I am, sir, very truly, your obedient servant,

A. LINCOLN.

TELEGRAM TO OFFICER IN COMMAND AT NASHVILLE.

EXECUTIVE MANSION, WASHINGTON, December 28, 1864.

OFFICER IN COMMAND at Nashville, Tenn.:

Suspend execution of James R. Mallory, for six weeks from Friday the thirtieth of this month, which time I have given his friends to make proof, if they can, upon certain points.

A. LINCOLN,

TELEGRAM TO GENERAL U. S. GRANT.

WASHINGTON, D. C., December 28, 1864. 5.30 p.m.

LIEUTENANT-GENERAL GRANT, City Point, Va.:

If there be no objection, please tell me what you now understand of the Wilmington expedition, present and prospective.

A. LINCOLN.

TELEGRAM TO GENERAL BUTLER.

EXECUTIVE MANSION, WASHINGTON, December 29, 1864.

MAJOR-GENERAL BUTLER:

There is a man in Company I, Eleventh Connecticut Volunteers, First Brigade, Third Division, Twenty-fourth Army Corps, at Chapin's Farm, Va.; under the assumed name of William Stanley, but whose real name is Frank R. Judd, and who is under arrest, and probably about to be tried for desertion. He is the son of our present minister to Prussia, who is a close personal friend of Senator Trumbull and myself. We are not willing for the boy to be shot, but we think it as well that his trial go regularly on, suspending execution until further order from me and reporting to me.

A. LINCOLN.

TELEGRAM TO COLONEL WARNER.

EXECUTIVE MANSION, WASHINGTON, December 30, 1864.

COLONEL WARNER, Indianapolis, Ind.:
It is said that you were on the court-martial that tried John Lennon, and that you are disposed to advise his being pardoned and sent to his regiment. If this be true, telegraph me to that effect at once.
A. LINCOLN.

1865

TELEGRAM TO J. WILLIAMS.

EXECUTIVE MANSION, WASHINGTON, January 4, 1865.

JOHN WILLIAMS, Springfield, Ill.:
Let Trumbo's substitute be regularly mustered in, send me the evidence that it is done and I will then discharge Trumbo.
A. LINCOLN.

MESSAGE TO THE HOUSE OF REPRESENTATIVES.

WASHINGTON, January 5, 1865.

TO THE HOUSE OF REPRESENTATIVES OF THE UNITED STATES:
I herewith return to your honorable body, in which it originated, a "joint resolution to correct certain clerical errors in the internal revenue act," without my approval.
My reason for so doing is that I am informed that this joint resolution was prepared during the last moments of the last session of Congress for the purpose of correcting certain errors of reference in the internal revenue act, which were discovered on an examination of an official copy procured from the State Department a few hours only before the adjournment. It passed the House and went to the Senate, where a vote was taken upon it, but by some accident it was not presented to the President of the Senate for his signature.
Since the adjournment of the last session of Congress, other errors of a kind similar to those which this resolution was designed to correct, have been discovered in the law, and it is now thought most expedient to include all the necessary corrections in one act or resolution.
The attention of the proper committee of the House has, I am informed, been already directed to the preparation of a bill for this purpose.
A. LINCOLN.

TO GENERAL U. S. GRANT.

EXECUTIVE MANSION, WASHINGTON, January 5, 1865.

LIEUTENANT-GENERAL GRANT, City Point, Va.:
Richard T. Jacob, Lieutenant-Governor of Kentucky, is at the Spotswood House, in Richmond, under an order of General Burbridge not to return to Kentucky. Please communicate leave to him to pass our lines, and come to me here at Washington.
A. LINCOLN.

TELEGRAM TO GENERAL GRANT.

EXECUTIVE MANSION,

WASHINGTON, January 6, 1865, LIEUTENANT-GENERAL GRANT, City Point:
If there is a man at City Point by the name of Waterman Thornton who is in trouble about desertion, please have his case briefly stated to me and do not let him be executed meantime.
A. LINCOLN.

MESSAGE TO CONGRESS,

WASHINGTON, January 9, 1865.

TO THE SENATE AND HOUSE OF REPRESENTATIVES: I transmit to Congress a copy of two treaties between the United States and Belgium, for the extinguishment of the Scheldt dues, etc., concluded on the twentieth of May, 1863, and twentieth of July, 1863, respectively, the ratifications of which were exchanged at Brussels on the twenty-fourth of June last; and I recommend an appropriation to carry into effect the provisions thereof relative to the payment of the proportion of the United States toward the capitalization of the said dues.
A. LINCOLN.

TO SCHUYLER COLFAX.

EXECUTIVE MANSION, WASHINGTON, January 9, 1865.

HON. SCHUYLER COLFAX, Speaker of the House of Representatives.
SIR:—I transmit herewith the letter of the Secretary of War, with accompanying report of the Adjutant-General, in reply to the resolution of the House of Representatives, dated December 7, 1864, requesting me "to communicate to the House the report made by Col. Thomas M. Key of an interview between himself and General Howell Cobb on the fourteenth [15th] day of June, 1862, on the banks of the Chickahominy, on the subject of the exchange of prisoners of war."
I am, sir, very respectfully, your obedient servant,
A. LINCOLN.

PROCLAMATION CONCERNING COMMERCE, JANUARY 10, 1865.

BY THE PRESIDENT OF THE UNITED STATES OF AMERICA:

A Proclamation.
Whereas the act of Congress of the twenty-eighth of September, 1850, entitled "An act to create additional collection districts in the State of California, and to change the existing districts therein, and to modify the existing collection districts in the United States," extends to merchandise warehoused under bond the privilege of being exported to the British North American provinces adjoining the United States, in the manner prescribed in the act of Congress of the third of March, 1845, which designates certain frontier ports through which merchandise may be exported, and further provides "that such other ports situated on the frontiers of the United States, adjoining the British North American provinces, as may hereafter be found expedient, may have extended to them the like privileges on the recommendation

of the Secretary of the Treasury, and proclamation duly made by the President of the United States, specially designating the ports to which the aforesaid privileges are to be extended;"

Now, therefore, I, Abraham Lincoln, President of the United States of America, in accordance with the recommendation of the Secretary of the Treasury, do hereby declare and proclaim that the port of St. Albans, in the State of Vermont, is, and shall be, entitled to all the privileges in regard to the exportation of merchandise in bond to the British North American provinces adjoining the United States, which are extended to the ports enumerated in the seventh section of the act of Congress of the third of March, 1845, aforesaid, from and after the date of this proclamation.

In witness whereof, I have hereunto set my hand, and caused the seal of the United States to be affixed.

Done at the city of Washington, this tenth day of January, in the year of our Lord one thousand eight hundred-and sixty-five, and of the independence of the United States of America the eighty-ninth.

A. LINCOLN.

By the President: WILLIAM H. SEWARD, Secretary of State.

TELEGRAM TO GENERAL B. F. BUTLER.

EXECUTIVE MANSION, WASHINGTON, January 10, 1865.

MAJOR-GENERAL BUTLER, Fort Monroe, Va.:

No principal report of yours on the Wilmington expedition has ever reached the War Department, as I am informed there. A preliminary report did reach here, but was returned to General Grant at his request. Of course, leave to publish cannot be given without inspection of the paper, and not then if it should be deemed to be detrimental to the public service.

A. LINCOLN.

TELEGRAM TO GENERAL B. F. BUTLER.

EXECUTIVE MANSION, WASHINGTON, January 13, 1865.

MAJOR-GENERAL BUTLER, Fort Monroe, Va.:

Yours asking leave to come to Washington is received. You have been summoned by the Committee on the Conduct of the War to attend here, which, of course, you will do.

A. LINCOLN.

TELEGRAM TO GOVERNOR JOHNSON.

WASHINGTON, D. C., January 15, 1865.

GOVERNOR JOHNSON, Nashville, Tennessee:

Yours announcing ordinance of emancipation received. Thanks to the convention and to you. When do you expect to be here? Would be glad to have your suggestion as to supplying your place of military governor.

A. LINCOLN.

TELEGRAM TO GENERAL G. M. DODGE. EXECUTIVE MANSION, WASHINGTON, January 15, 1865.

MAJOR-GENERAL DODGE, St. Louis, Missouri:
It is represented to me that there is so much irregular violence in northern Missouri as to be driving away the people and almost depopulating it. Please gather information, and consider whether an appeal to the people there to go to their homes and let one another alone recognizing as a full right of protection for each that he lets others alone, and banning only him who refuses to let others alone may not enable you to withdraw the troops, their presence itself [being] a cause of irritation and constant apprehension, and thus restore peace and quiet, and returning prosperity. Please consider this and telegraph or write me.
A. LINCOLN.

FIRST OVERTURES FOR SURRENDER FROM DAVIS

TO P. P. BLAIR, SR.

WASHINGTON, January 18, 1865.
F. P. BLAIR, ESQ.
SIR:-You having shown me Mr. Davis's letter to you of the twelfth instant, you may say to him that I have constantly been, am now, and shall continue, ready to receive any agent whom he or any other influential person now resisting the national authority may informally send to me with the view of securing peace to the people of our one common country.
Yours, etc.,
A. LINCOLN.

EXECUTIVE MANSION,

WASHINGTON, January 19, 1865.

LIEUTENANT-GENERAL GRANT:
Please read and answer this letter as though I was not President, but only a friend. My son, now in his twenty-second year, having graduated at Harvard, wishes to see something of the war before it ends. I do not wish to put him in the ranks, nor yet to give him a commission, to which those who have already served long are better entitled and better qualified to hold. Could he, without embarrassment to you, or detriment to the service, go into your military family with some nominal rank, I, and not the public, furnishing his necessary means? If no, say so without the least hesitation, because I am as anxious and as deeply interested that you shall not be encumbered as you can be yourself.
Yours truly,
A. LINCOLN.

TELEGRAM TO GENERAL DODGE.

EXECUTIVE MANSION, WASHINGTON, January 19, 1865.

MAJOR-GENERAL DODGE, Saint Louis, Mo.:
If Mrs. Beattie, alias Mrs. Wolff, shall be sentenced to death, notify me, and postpone the execution till further order.
A. LINCOLN.

TELEGRAM TO GENERAL ORD.

EXECUTIVE MANSION, WASHINGTON, January 19, 1864

MAJOR-GENERAL ORD:
You have a man in arrest for desertion passing by the name of Stanley. William Stanley, I think, but whose real name is different. He is the son of so close a friend of mine that I must not let him be executed. Please let me know what is his present and prospective condition.
A. LINCOLN.

TELEGRAM TO GENERAL G. M. DODGE.

EXECUTIVE MANSION, WASHINGTON, January 24, 1865.

MAJOR-GENERAL DODGE, St. Louis, Mo.:
It is said an old lady in Clay County, Missouri, by name Mrs. Winifred B. Price, is about being sent South. If she is not misbehaving let her remain.
A. LINCOLN.

TELEGRAM TO GOVERNOR JOHNSON.

EXECUTIVE MANSION, WASHINGTON, January 24, 1865.

HON. ANDREW JOHNSON, Nashville, Tennessee:
Several members of the Cabinet, with myself, considered the question, to-day, as to the time of your coming on here. While we fully appreciate your wish to remain in Tennessee until her State government shall be completely reinaugurated, it is our unanimous conclusion that it is unsafe for you to not be here on the 4th of March. Be sure to reach here by that time.
A. LINCOLN.

REPLY TO A COMMITTEE, JANUARY 24, 1865.

REVEREND SIR, AND LADIES AND GENTLEMEN:

I accept with emotions of profoundest gratitude, the beautiful gift you have been pleased to present to me. You will, of course, expect that I acknowledge it. So much has been said about Gettysburg and so well, that for me to attempt to say more may perhaps only serve to weaken the force of that which has already been said. A most graceful and eloquent tribute was paid to the patriotism and self-denying labors of the American ladies, on the occasion of the consecration of the National Cemetery at Gettysburg, by our illustrious friend, Edward Everett, now, alas! departed from earth. His life was a truly great one, and I think the greatest part of it was that which crowned its closing years, I wish you to read, if you have not already done so, the eloquent and truthful words which he then spoke of the women of America. Truly, the services they have rendered to the defenders of our country in this perilous time, and are yet rendering, can never be estimated as they ought to be. For your kind wishes to me personally, I beg leave to render you likewise my sincerest thanks. I assure you they are reciprocated. And now, gentlemen and ladies, may God bless you all.

TELEGRAM TO GENERAL GRANT.

EXECUTIVE MANSION, WASHINGTON, January 25, 1865.

LIEUTENANT-GENERAL GRANT, City Point
If Newell W. Root, of First Connecticut Heavy Artillery, is under sentence of death, please telegraph me briefly the circumstances.
A. LINCOLN.

TELEGRAM TO GENERAL GRANT.

WAR DEPARTMENT, WASHINGTON, D. C., January 25, 1865.

LIEUTENANT-GENERAL GRANT, City Point, Va.:
Having received the report in the case of Newell W. Root, I do not interfere further in the case.
A. LINCOLN.

EARLY CONSULTATIONS WITH REBELS

INSTRUCTIONS TO MAJOR ECKERT.

EXECUTIVE MANSION, WASHINGTON, January 30, 1865.
MAJOR T. T. ECKERT.
SIR:-You will proceed with the documents placed in your hands, and on reaching General Ord will deliver him the letter addressed to him by the Secretary of War. Then, by General Ord's assistance procure an interview with Messrs. Stephens, Hunter, and Campbell, or any of them, deliver to him or them the paper on which your own letter is written. Note on the copy which you retain the time of delivery and to whom delivered. Receive their answer in writing, waiting a reasonable time for it, and which, if it contain their decision to come through without further condition, will be your warrant to ask General Ord to pass them through as directed in the letter of the Secretary of War to him. If by their answer they decline to come, or propose other terms, do not have them pass through. And this being your whole duty, return and report to me.
Yours truly,
A. LINCOLN.

TELEGRAM FROM SECRETARY OF WAR TO GENERAL ORD.

(Cipher.)

WAR DEPARTMENT, WASHINGTON, D. C., January 30, 1865.
MAJOR-GENERAL ORD, Headquarters Army of the James:
By direction of the President you are instructed to inform the three gentlemen, Messrs. Stephens, Hunter, and Campbell, that a messenger will be dispatched to them at or near where they now are, without unnecessary delay.
EDWIN M. STANTON, Secretary of War.

INDORSEMENT ON A LETTER FROM J. M. ASHLEY.

HOUSE OF REPRESENTATIVES, January 31, 1865.

DEAR SIR:—The report is in circulation in the House that Peace Commissioners are on their way or in the city, and is being used against us. If it is true, I fear we shall lose the bill. Please authorize me to contradict it, if it is not true.
Respectfully, J. M. ASHLEY.
To the President.
(Indorsement.)
So far as I know there are no Peace Commissioners in the city or likely to be in it.
A. LINCOLN. January 31, 1865

TELEGRAM TO GENERAL U.S. GRANT.

EXECUTIVE MANSION, WASHINGTON, January 31, 1865

LIEUTENANT-GENERAL GRANT, City Point, Va.:
A messenger is coming to you on the business contained in your despatch. Detain the gentlemen in comfortable quarters until he arrives, and then act upon the message he brings, as far as applicable, it having been made up to pass through General Ord's hands, and when the gentlemen were supposed to be beyond our lines.
A. LINCOLN.

INSTRUCTIONS TO SECRETARY SEWARD.

EXECUTIVE MANSION, WASHINGTON, January 31, 1865.

HON. WILLIAM H. SEWARD, Secretary of State
You will proceed to Fortress Monroe, Virginia, there to meet and informally confer with Messrs. Stephens, Hunter, and Campbell, on the basis of my letter to F. P. Blair, Esq., of January 18, 1865, a copy of which you have. You will make known to them that three things are indispensable to wit:
1. The restoration of the national authority throughout all the States.
2. No receding by the Executive of the United States on the slavery question from the position assumed thereon in the late annual message to Congress, and in preceding documents.
3. No cessation of hostilities short of an end of the war and the disbanding of all forces hostile to the Government.
You will inform them that all propositions of theirs, not inconsistent with the above, will be considered and passed upon in a spirit of sincere liberality. You will hear all they may choose to say and report it to me. You will not assume to definitely consummate anything.
Yours, etc.,
A. LINCOLN.

CONSTITUTIONAL AMENDMENT FOR THE ABOLISHING OF SLAVERY

PASSAGE THROUGH CONGRESS OF THE CONSTITUTIONAL AMENDMENT FOR THE ABOLISHING OF SLAVERY
RESPONSE TO A SERENADE, JANUARY 31, 1865.
He supposed the passage through Congress of the Constitutional amendment for the abolishing of slavery throughout the United States was the occasion to which he was indebted for the honor of this call.
The occasion was one of congratulation to the country, and to the whole world. But there is a task yet before us—to go forward and consummate by the votes of the States that which Congress so nobly began yesterday. He had the honor to inform those present that Illinois had already done the work. Maryland was about half through, but he felt proud that Illinois was a little ahead.
He thought this measure was a very fitting if not an indispensable adjunct to the winding up of the great difficulty. He wished the reunion of all the States perfected, and so effected as to remove all causes of disturbance in the future; and,

to attain this end, it was necessary that the original disturbing cause should, if possible, be rooted out. He thought all would bear him witness that he had never shirked from doing all that he could to eradicate slavery, by issuing an Emancipation Proclamation. But that proclamation falls short of what the amendment will be when fully consummated. A question might be raised whether the proclamation was legally valid. It might be added, that it only aided those who came into our lines, and that it was inoperative as to those who did not give themselves up; or that it would have no effect upon the children of the slaves born hereafter; in fact, it would be urged that it did not meet the evil. But this amendment is a king's cure for all evils. It winds the whole thing up. He would repeat, that it was the fitting if not the indispensable adjunct to the consummation of the great game we are playing. He could not but congratulate all present—himself, the country, and the whole world upon this great moral victory.

TELEGRAM TO GENERAL U. S. GRANT. WASHINGTON, February 1, 1865

LIEUTENANT-GENERAL GRANT, City Point:

Let nothing which is transpiring change, hinder, or delay your military movements or plans.
A. LINCOLN.

TELEGRAM TO MAJOR ECKERT. WASHINGTON, D. C., February 1, 1865.

MAJOR T. T. ECKERT, Care of General Grant, City Point, Va.:

Call at Fortress Monroe, and put yourself under direction of Mr. Seward, whom you will find there.
A. LINCOLN.

TELEGRAM TO GENERAL U. S. GRANT. WASHINGTON, D. C., February 2, 1865

LIEUTENANT-GENERAL GRANT, City Point, Va.:

Say to the gentlemen I will meet them personally at Fortress Monroe as soon as I can get there.
A. LINCOLN.

TELEGRAM TO SECRETARY SEWARD, WASHINGTON, D. C., February 2, 1865.

HON. WILLIAM H. SEWARD, Fortress Monroe, Va.

Induced by a despatch of General Grant, I join you at Fort Monroe, as soon as I can come.
A. LINCOLN.

ORDER TO MAKE CORRECTIONS IN THE DRAFT.

EXECUTIVE MANSION, WASHINGTON CITY, February 6, 1865

Whereas complaints are made in some localities respecting the assignments of quotas and credits allowed for the pending call of troops to fill up the armies: Now, in order to determine all controversies in respect thereto, and to avoid any delay in filling up the armies, it is ordered,

1. That the Attorney-General, Brigadier-General Richard Delafield, and Colonel C. W. Foster, be, and they are hereby constituted, a board to examine into the proper quotas and credits of the respective States and districts under the call of December 19, 1864, with directions, if any errors be found therein, to make such corrections as the law and facts may require, and report their determination to the Provost-Marshal-General. The determination of said board to be final and conclusive, and the draft to be made in conformity therewith.

2. The Provost-Marshal-General is ordered to make the draft in the respective districts as speedily as the same can be done after the fifteenth of this month.

A. LINCOLN.

TO PROVOST-MARSHAL-GENERAL.

EXECUTIVE MANSION, WASHINGTON, February 6, 1865.

PROVOST-MARSHAL-GENERAL:
These gentlemen distinctly say to me this morning that what they want is the means from your office of showing their people that the quota assigned to them is right. They think it will take but little time—two hours, they say. Please give there double the time and every facility you can.
Yours truly,
A. LINCOLN.
February 6, 1865.
The Provost-Marshal brings this letter back to me and says he cannot give the facility required without detriment to the service, and thereupon he is excused from doing it.
A. LINCOLN.

TELEGRAM TO LIEUTENANT-COLONEL GLENN.

EXECUTIVE MANSION, WASHINGTON, February 7, 1865.

LIEUTENANT-COLONEL GLENN, Commanding Post at Henderson, Ky.:
Complaint is made to me that you are forcing negroes into the military service, and even torturing them—riding them on rails and the like to extort their consent. I hope this may be a mistake. The like must not be done by you, or any one under you. You must not force negroes any more than white men. Answer me on this.
A. LINCOLN.

TO GOVERNOR SMITH.

EXECUTIVE MANSION, WASHINGTON, February 8, 1865.

HIS EXCELLENCY GOVERNOR SMITH, of Vermont:
Complaint is made to me, by Vermont, that the assignment of her quota for the draft on the pending call is intrinsically unjust, and also in bad faith of the Government's promise to fairly allow credits for men previously furnished. To illustrate, a supposed case is stated as follows:
Vermont and New Hampshire must between them furnish six thousand men on the pending call; and being equal, each must furnish as many as the other in the long run. But the Government finds that on former calls Vermont furnished a surplus of five hundred, and New Hampshire a surplus, of fifteen hundred. These two surpluses making two thousand and added to the six thousand, making eight thousand to be furnished by the two States, or four thousand each less,

by fair credits. Then subtract Vermont's surplus of five hundred from her four thousand, leaves three thousand five hundred as her quota on the pending call; and likewise subtract New Hampshire's surplus of fifteen hundred from her four thousand, leaves two thousand five hundred as her quota on the pending call. These three thousand five hundred and two thousand five hundred make precisely six thousand, which the supposed case requires from the two States, and it is just equal for Vermont to furnish one thousand more now than New Hampshire, because New Hampshire has heretofore furnished one thousand more than Vermont, which equalizes the burdens of the two in the long run. And this result, so far from being bad faith to Vermont, is indispensable to keeping good faith with New Hampshire. By no other result can the six thousand men be obtained from the two States, and, at the same time deal justly and keep faith with both, and we do but confuse ourselves in questioning the process by which the right result is reached. The supposed case is perfect as an illustration.

The pending call is not for three hundred thousand men subject to fair credits, but is for three hundred thousand remaining after all fair credits have been deducted, and it is impossible to concede what Vermont asks without coming out short of three hundred thousand men, or making other localities pay for the partiality shown her.

This upon the case stated. If there be different reasons for making an allowance to Vermont, let them be presented and considered.

Yours truly,
A. LINCOLN.

MESSAGE TO CONGRESS.

EXECUTIVE MANSION, February 8, 1865.

TO THE HONORABLE THE SENATE AND HOUSE OF REPRESENTATIVES:
The joint resolution entitled "Joint resolution declaring certain States not entitled to representation in the electoral college" has been signed by the Executive in deference to the view of Congress implied in its passage and presentation to him. In his own view, however, the two Houses of Congress, convened under the twelfth article of the Constitution, have complete power to exclude from counting all electoral votes deemed by them to be illegal, and it is not competent for the Executive to defeat or obstruct that power by a veto, as would be the case if his action were at all essential in the matter. He disclaims all right of the Executive to interfere in any way in the matter of canvassing or counting electoral votes, and he also disclaims that by signing said resolution he has expressed any opinion on the recitals of the preamble or any judgment of his own upon the subject of the resolution.
A. LINCOLN.

TELEGRAM TO GENERAL U. S. GRANT. EXECUTIVE MANSION, WASHINGTON, February 8, 1865

LIEUTENANT-GENERAL GRANT, City Point. Va.:
I am called on by the House of Representatives to give an account of my interview with Messrs. Stephens, Hunter, and Campbell, and it is very desirable to me to put your despatch of February 1, to the Secretary of War, in which, among other things, you say: "I fear now their going back without any expression from any one in authority will have a bad influence." I think the despatch does you credit, while I do not see that it can embarrass you. May I use it?
A. LINCOLN.

RESULT OF THE ELECTORAL COUNT

REPLY TO A COMMITTEE OF CONGRESS, REPORTING THE RESULT OF THE ELECTORAL COUNT, FEBRUARY 9, 1865.
With deep gratitude to my countrymen for this mark of their confidence; with a distrust of my own ability to perform the duty required under the most favorable circumstances, and now rendered doubly difficult by existing national perils;

yet with a firm reliance on the strength of our free government, and the eventual loyalty of the people to the just principles upon which it is founded, and above all with an unshaken faith in the Supreme Ruler of nations, I accept this trust. Be pleased to signify this to the respective Houses of Congress.

CHRONOLOGIC REVIEW OF PEACE PROPOSALS

MESSAGE TO THE HOUSE OF REPRESENTATIVES.

EXECUTIVE MANSION, February 10, 1865
TO THE HONORABLE THE HOUSE OF REPRESENTATIVES:
In response to your resolution of the eighth instant, requesting information in relation to a conference recently held in Hampton Roads, I have the honor to state that on the day of the date I gave Francis P. Blair, Sr., a card, written on as follows, to wit:
December 28, 1864.
Allow the bearer, F. P. Blair, Sr., to pass our lines, go South, and return.
A. LINCOLN.
That at the time I was informed that Mr. Blair sought the card as a means of getting to Richmond, Va., but he was given no authority to speak or act for the Government, nor was I informed of anything he would say or do on his own account or otherwise. Afterwards Mr. Blair told me that he had been to Richmond and had seen Mr. Jefferson Davis; and he (Mr. B.) at the same time left with me a manuscript letter, as follows, to wit:
RICHMOND, VA., January 12, 1865. F. P. BLAIR, ESQ.
SIR: I have deemed it proper, and probably desirable to you, to give you in this for in the substance of remarks made by me, to be repeated by you to President Lincoln, etc., etc.
I have no disposition to find obstacles in forms, and am willing, now as heretofore, to enter into negotiations for the restoration of peace, and am ready to send a commission whenever I have reason to suppose it will be received, or to receive a commission if the United States Government shall choose to send one. That notwithstanding the rejection of our former offers, I would, if you could promise that a commissioner, minister, or other agent would be received, appoint one immediately, and renew the effort to enter into conference with a view to secure peace to the two countries.
Yours, etc., JEFFERSON DAVIS.
Afterwards, and with the view that it should be shown to Mr. Davis, I wrote and delivered to Mr. Blair a letter, as follows, to wit:
WASHINGTON, January 18, 1865.
P. P. BLAIR, ESQ.
SIR:—Your having shown me Mr. Davis's letter to you of the twelfth instant, you may say to him that I have constantly been, am now, and shall continue ready to receive any agent whom he or any other influential person now resisting the national authority may informally send to me with the view of securing peace to the people of our one common country.
Yours, etc.,
A. LINCOLN.

Afterwards Mr. Blair dictated for and authorized me to make an entry on

the back of my retained copy of the letter last above recited, which entry is as follows:
January 28, 1865

To-day Mr. Blair tells me that on the twenty-first instant he delivered to Mr. Davis the original of which the within is a copy, and left it with him; that at the time of delivering it Mr. Davis read it over twice in Mr. Blair's presence, at the close of which he (Mr. Blair) remarked that the part about "our one common country" related to the part of Mr. Davis' letter about "the two countries," to which Mr. Davis replied that he so understood it.
A. LINCOLN.

Afterwards the Secretary of War placed in my hands the following telegram,
indorsed by him, as appears:
OFFICE UNITED STATES MILITARY TELEGRAPH WAR DEPARTMENT. The following telegram received at Washington January 29, 1865, from headquarters Army of James,
6.30 P.M., January 29, 1865:
"HON. EDWIN M. STANTON," Secretary of War:
"The following despatch just received from Major-General Parke, who refers it to me for my action. I refer it to you in Lieutenant-General Grant's absence:
"E. O. C. ORD, Major-General, Commanding.
HEADQUARTERS ARMY OF POTOMAC,
January 29, 1863. 4 P.M."

'MAJOR-GENERAL E. O. C. ORD,
'Headquarters Army of James:
'The following despatch is forwarded to you for your action. Since I have no knowledge of General Grant's having had any understanding of this kind, I refer the matter to you as the ranking officer present in the two armies.
'JNO. G. PARKE, Major-General, Commanding.'
"'FROM HEADQUARTERS NINTH ARMY Cos, 29th.
'MAJOR-GENERAL JNO. G. PARKE, 'Headquarters Army of Potomac:
'Alexander H. Stephens, R. M. T. Hunter, and J. A. Campbell desire to cross my lines, in accordance with an understanding claimed to exist with Lieutenant-General Grant, on their way to Washington as peace commissioners. Shall they be admitted? They desire an early answer, to come through immediately. Would like to reach City Point tonight if they can. If they can not do this, they would like to come through at 10 A.M. to-morrow morning.
'O. B. WILCOX,
'Major-General, Commanding Ninth Corps.'
"January 29, 8.30 P.M.
"Respectfully referred to the President for such instructions as he may be pleased to give.
"EDWIN M. STANTON, "Secretary of War."
It appears that about the time of placing the foregoing telegram in my hands the Secretary of War dispatched General Ord as follows, to wit:
WAR DEPARTMENT, WASHINGTON CITY, January 29, 1865. 10 P.M. (Sent at 2 A.M., 30th.) MAJOR-GENERAL ORD.
SIR:—This Department has no knowledge of any understanding by General Grant to allow any person to come within his lines as commissioner of any sort. You will therefore allow no one to come into your lines under such character or profession until you receive the President's instructions, to whom your telegraph will be submitted for his directions.
EDWIN M. STANTON, Secretary of War.
Afterwards, by my direction, the Secretary of War telegraphed General Ord as follows, to wit:
WAR DEPARTMENT, WASHINGTON, D.C., January 30. 10.30 A.M.
MAJOR-GENERAL E. O. C. ORD, Headquarters Army of the James.
SIR:—By direction of the President, you are instructed to inform the three gentlemen, Messrs. Stephens, Hunter and Campbell, that a messenger will be dispatched to them at or near where they now are without unnecessary delay.
EDWIN M. STANTON, Secretary of War.
Afterwards I prepared and put into the hands of Major Thomas T. Eckert the following instructions and message:
EXECUTIVE MANSION,
MAJOR T. T. ECKERT. WASHINGTON, January 30, 1865
SIR:—You will proceed with the documents placed in your hands, and on reaching General Ord will deliver him the letter addressed to him by the Secretary of War; then, by General Ord's assistance, procure an interview with Messrs. Stephens, Hunter, and Campbell, or any of them. Deliver to him or them the paper on which your own letter is written. Note on the copy which you retain the time of delivery and to whom delivered. Receive their answer in writing, waiting a reasonable time for it, and which, if it contain their decision to come through without further condition, will be your

warrant to ask General Ord to pass them through, as directed in the letter of the Secretary of War to him. If by their answer they decline to come, or propose other terms, do not have them pass through. And this being your whole duty, return and report to me.
A. LINCOLN.
CITY POINT, VA.. February 1, 1865.
MESSRS. ALEXANDER H. STEPHENS, J. A. CAMPBELL AND R. M. T. HUNTER.
GENTLEMEN:—I am instructed by the President of the United States to place this paper in your hands, with the information that if you pass through the United States military lines it will be understood that you do so for the purpose of an informal conference on the basis of the letter a copy of which is on the reverse side of this sheet, and that if you choose to pass on such understanding, and so notify me in writing, I will procure the commanding general to pass you through the lines and to Fortress Monroe under such military precautions as he may deem prudent, and at which place you will be met in due time by some person or persons for the purpose of such informal conference; and, further, that you shall have protection, safe conduct, and safe return in all events.
THOMAS T. ECKERT, Major and Aide-de-Camp.
WASHINGTON, January 18, 1865. F. P. BLAIR, ESQ.
SIR:—Your having shown me Mr. Davis's letter to you of the twelfth instant, you may say to him that I have constantly been, am now, and shall continue ready to receive any agent whom he or any other influential person now resisting the national authority may informally send to me with the view of securing peace to the people of our one common country.
Yours, etc.,
A. LINCOLN.
Afterwards, but before Major Eckert had departed, the following dispatch was received from General Grant:
OFFICE UNITED STATES MILITARY TELEGRAPH, WAR DEPARTMENT.
The following telegram received at Washington January 30, 1865, from City Point, Va., 10.30 A.M., January 30, 1865:
"His EXCELLENCY
A. LINCOLN,
President of the United States:

"The following communication was received here last evening:

"'PETERSBURG, VA., January 30, 1865.
'LIEUTENANT-GENERAL U.S. GRANT,
Commanding Armies United States.
'SIR: We desire to pass your lines under safe conduct, and to proceed to Washington to hold a conference with President Lincoln upon the subject of the existing war, and with a view of ascertaining upon what terms it may be terminated, in pursuance of the course indicated by him in his letter to Mr. Blair of January 18, 1865, of which we presume you have a copy; and if not, we wish to see you in person, if convenient, and to confer with you upon the subject.
'Very respectfully, yours,
'ALEXANDER H. STEPHENS.
'J. A. CAMPBELL.
'R. M. T. HUNTER.'"
"I have sent directions to receive these gentlemen, and expect to have them at my quarters this evening, awaiting your instructions. U.S. GRANT, Lieutenant-General, Commanding Armies United States."
This, it will be perceived, transferred General Ord's agency in the matter to General Grant. I resolved, however, to send Major Eckert forward with his message, and accordingly telegraphed General Grant as follows, to wit:
EXECUTIVE MANSION WASHINGTON, January 13, 1865 (Sent at 1.30 P.M.)
LIEUTENANT-GENERAL GRANT, City Point, Va.:
A messenger is coming to you on the business contained in your despatch. Detain the gentlemen in comfortable quarters until he arrives, and then act upon the message he brings as far as applicable, it having been made up to pass through General Ord's hands, and when the gentlemen were supposed to be beyond our lines.
A. LINCOLN.
When Major Eckert departed, he bore with him a letter of the Secretary of War to General Grant, as follows, to wit:
WAR DEPARTMENT, WASHINGTON, D. C., January 30, 1865.
LIEUTENANT-GENERAL GRANT, Commanding, etc.
GENERAL:—The President desires that you will please procure for the bearer, Major Thomas T. Eckert, an interview with Messrs. Stephens, Hunter, and Campbell, and if on his return to you he requests it pass them through our lines to

Fortress Monroe by such route and under such military precautions as you may deem prudent, giving them protection and comfortable quarters while there, and that you let none of this have any effect upon your movements or plans.
By order of the President: EDWIN M. STANTON, Secretary of War.

Supposing the proper point to be then reached, I dispatched the Secretary of State with the following instructions, Major Eckert, however, going ahead of him:

EXECUTIVE MANSION, WASHINGTON, January 31, 1865.
HON. WILLIAM H. SEWARD, Secretary of State:

You will proceed to Fortress Monroe, Va., there to meet and informally confer with Messrs. Stephens, Hunter, and Campbell on the basis of my letter to F. P. Blair, Esq., of January 18, 1865, a copy of which you have.

You will make known to them that three things are indispensable, to Wit:

1. The restoration of the national authority throughout all the States.
2. No receding by the Executive of the United States on the slavery question from the position assumed thereon in the late annual message to Congress and in preceding documents.
3. No cessation of hostilities short of an end of the war and the disbanding of all forces hostile to the Government.

You will inform them that all propositions of theirs not inconsistent with the above will be considered and passed upon in a spirit of sincere liberality. You will hear all they may choose to say and report it to me.

You will not assume to definitely consummate anything.

Yours, etc.,
A. LINCOLN.

On the day of its date the following telegram was sent to General Grant:
WAR DEPARTMENT, WASHINGTON, D. C., February 1, 1865 (Sent at 9.30 A.M.)
LIEUTENANT-GENERAL GRANT, City Point, Va.:
Let nothing which is transpiring change, hinder, or delay your military movements or plans.
A. LINCOLN.

Afterwards the following despatch was received from General Grant:
OFFICE UNITED STATES MILITARY TELEGRAPH WAR DEPARTMENT. The following telegram received at Washington, 2.30 P.M., February 1, 1865, from City Point, Va., February 1, 12.30 P.M., 1865:
"His EXCELLENCY A. LINCOLN, President United States:
"Your despatch received. There will be no armistice in consequence of the presence of Mr. Stephens and others within our lines. The troops are kept in readiness to move at the shortest notice if occasion should justify it.
"U.S. GRANT, Lieutenant-General."

To notify Major Eckert that the Secretary of State would be at Fortress Monroe, and to put them in communication, the following despatch was sent:
WAR DEPARTMENT, WASHINGTON, D. C., February 1, 1865.
MAJOR T. T. ECKERT, Care of General Grant, City Point, Va.:
Call at Fortress Monroe and put yourself under direction of Mr. S., whom you will find there.
A. LINCOLN.

On the morning of the 2d instant the following telegrams were received by me respectively from the Secretary of State and Major Eckert:
FORT MONROE, VA., February 1, 1865. 11.30 P.M.
THE PRESIDENT OF THE UNITED STATES:
Arrived at 10 this evening. Richmond party not here. I remain here.
WILLIAM H. SEWARD.

CITY POINT, VA., February 1, 1865. 10 P.M.
HIS EXCELLENCY A. LINCOLN, President of the United States: I have the honor to report the delivery of your communication and my letter at 4.15 this afternoon, to which I received a reply at 6 P.M., but not satisfactory.

At 8 P.M. the following note, addressed to General Grant, was received:
CITY POINT, VA., February 1, 1865
"LIEUTENANT-GENERAL GRANT.
"SIR:—We desire to go to Washington City to confer informally with the President personally in reference to the matters mentioned in his letter to Mr. Blair of the 18th January ultimo, without any personal compromise on any question in the letter. We have the permission to do so from the authorities in Richmond.
Very respectfully yours,
ALEX. H. STEPHENS R. M. T. HUNTER. J. A. CAMPBELL."

At 9.30 P.M. I notified them that they could not proceed further unless they complied with the terms expressed in my letter. The point of meeting designated in the above note would not, in my opinion, be insisted upon. Think Fort Monroe would be acceptable. Having complied with my instructions, I will return to Washington to-morrow unless otherwise ordered.

THOS. T. ECKERT, Major, etc.

On reading this despatch of Major Eckert I was about to recall him and the Secretary of State, when the following telegram of General Grant to the Secretary of War was shown me:

OFFICE UNITED STATES MILITARY TELEGRAPH, WAR DEPARTMENT.

The following telegram received at Washington 4.35 A.M., February 2, 1865, from City Point, Va., February 1, 10.30 P.M., 1865:

"HON. EDWIN M. STANTON, "Secretary of War:

"Now that the interview between Major Eckert, under his written instructions, and Mr. Stephens and party has ended, I will state confidentially, but not officially to become a matter of record, that I am convinced upon conversation with Messrs. Stephens and Hunter that their intentions are good and their desire sincere to restore peace and union. I have not felt myself at liberty to express even views of my own or to account for my reticency. This has placed me in an awkward position, which I could have avoided by not seeing them in the first instance. I fear now their going back without any expression from anyone in authority will have a bad influence. At the same time, I recognize the difficulties in the way of receiving these informal commissioners at this time, and do not know what to recommend. I am sorry, however, that Mr. Lincoln can not have an interview with the two named in this despatch, if not all three now within our lines. Their letter to me was all that the President's instructions contemplated to secure their safe conduct if they had used the same language to Major Eckert.

"U.S. GRANT "Lieutenant-General."

This despatch of General Grant changed my purpose, and accordingly I telegraphed him and the Secretary of State, respectively, as follows:

WAR DEPARTMENT, WASHINGTON, D. C., February 2, 1865. (Sent at 9 A.M.)
LIEUTENANT-GENERAL GRANT, City Point, Va.:
Say to the gentlemen I will meet them personally at Fortress Monroe as soon as I can get there.
A. LINCOLN.

WAR DEPARTMENT, WASHINGTON, D. C., February 2, 1865. (Sent at 9 A.M.)
HON. WILLIAM H. SEWARD, Fortress Monroe, Va.:
Induced by a despatch from General Grant, I join you at Fort Monroe as soon as I can come.
A. LINCOLN.

Before starting, the following despatch was shown me. I proceeded, nevertheless:

OFFICE UNITED STATES MILITARY TELEGRAPH, WAR DEPARTMENT.

The following telegram received at Washington, February 2, 1865, from City Point, Va., 9 A.M., February 2, 1865:

"HON. WILLIAM H. SEWARD, Secretary of State, Fort Monroe:

"The gentlemen here have accepted the proposed terms, and will leave for Fort Monroe at 9.30 A.M.

"U. S. GRANT, Lieutenant-General."

(Copy to HON. Edwin M. Stanton, Secretary of War, Washington.)

On the night of the 2nd I reached Hampton Roads, found the Secretary of State and Major Eckert on a steamer anchored offshore, and learned of them that the Richmond gentlemen were on another steamer also anchored offshore, in the Roads, and that the Secretary of State had not yet seen or communicated with them. I ascertained that Major Eckert had literally complied with his instructions, and I saw for the first time the answer of the Richmond gentlemen to him, which in his despatch to me of the 1st he characterizes as "not satisfactory." That answer is as follows, to wit:

CITY POINT, VA., February 1, 1865. THOMAS T. ECKERT, Major and Aid-de-Camp. MAJOR:-Your note, delivered by yourself this day, has been considered. In reply we have to say that we were furnished with a copy of the letter of President Lincoln to Francis P. Blair, Esq., of the 18th of January ultimo, another copy of which is appended to your note. Our instructions are contained in a letter of which the following is a copy:

"RICHMOND, January 28, 1865. "In conformity with the letter of Mr. Lincoln, of which the foregoing is a copy, you are to proceed to Washington City for informal conference with him upon the issues involved in the existing war, and for the purpose of securing peace to the two countries. "With great respect, your obedient servant, "JEFFERSON DAVIS."

The substantial object to be obtained by the informal conference is to ascertain upon what terms the existing war can be terminated honorably.

Our instructions contemplate a personal interview between President Lincoln and ourselves at Washington City, but with this explanation we are ready to meet any person or persons that President Lincoln may appoint at such place as he may designate.

Our earnest desire is that a just and honorable peace may be agreed upon, and we are prepared to receive or to submit propositions which may possibly lead to the attainment of that end.

Very respectfully, yours,
ALEXANDER H. STEPHENS.
R. M. T. HUNTER.

JOHN A. CAMPBELL.

A note of these gentlemen, subsequently addressed to General Grant, has already been given in Major Eckert's despatch of the 1st instant.

I also here saw, for the first time, the following note, addressed by the Richmond gentlemen to Major Eckert:

CITY POINT, VA., February 2, 1865. THOMAS T. ECKERT, Major and Aid-de-Camp. MAJOR:—In reply to your verbal statement that your instructions did not allow you to alter the conditions upon which a passport could be given to us, we say that we are willing to proceed to Fortress Monroe and there to have an informal conference with any person or persons that President Lincoln may appoint on the basis of his letter to Francis P. Blair of the 18th of January ultimo, or upon any other terms or conditions that he may hereafter propose not inconsistent with the essential principles of self-government and popular rights, upon which our institutions are founded.

It is our earnest wish to ascertain, after a free interchange of ideas and information, upon what principles and terms, if any, a just and honorable peace can be established without the further effusion of blood, and to contribute our utmost efforts to accomplish such a result.

We think it better to add that in accepting your passport we are not to be understood as committing ourselves to anything but to carry to this informal conference the views and feelings above expressed.

Very respectfully, yours, etc.,

ALEXANDER H. STEPHENS, J. A. CAMPBELL, R. M. T. HUNTER.

Note.-The above communication was delivered to me at Fort Monroe at 4.30 P.M. February 2 by Lieutenant-Colonel Babcock, of General Grant's staff.

THOMAS T. ECKERT Major and Aid-de-Camp.

On the morning of the third the three gentlemen, Messrs. Stephens, Hunter, and Campbell, came aboard of our steamer and had an interview with the Secretary of State and myself of several hours' duration. No question of preliminaries to the meeting was then and there made or mentioned; no other person was present; no papers were exchanged or produced; and it was in advance agreed that the conversation was to be informal and verbal merely. On our part the whole substance of the instructions to the Secretary of State hereinbefore recited was stated and insisted upon, and nothing was said inconsistent therewith; while by the other party it was not said that in any event or on any condition they ever would consent to reunion, and yet they equally omitted to declare that they never would consent. They seemed to desire a postponement of that question and the adoption of some other course first, which, as some of them seemed to argue, might or might not lead to reunion, but which course we thought would amount to an indefinite postponement. The conference ended without result.

The foregoing, containing, as is believed, all the information sought is respectfully submitted.

A. LINCOLN.

MESSAGE TO THE SENATE. WASHINGTON, February 10, 1865

To THE SENATE OF THE UNITED STATES:

In answer to the resolution of the Senate of the eighth instant, requesting information concerning recent conversations or communications with insurgents, under executive sanction, I transmit a report from the Secretary of State, to whom the resolution was referred.

A. LINCOLN. TO THE PRESIDENT:

The Secretary of State, to whom was referred a resolution of the Senate of the 8th instant, requesting "the President of the United States, if, in his opinion, not incompatible with the public interests, to furnish to the Senate any information in his possession concerning recent conversations or communications with certain rebels, said to have taken place under executive sanction, including communications with the rebel Jefferson Davis, and any correspondence relating thereto," has the honor to report that the Senate may properly be referred to a special message of the President bearing upon the subject of the resolution, and transmitted to the House this day. Appended to this report is a copy of an instruction which has been addressed to Charles Francis Adams, Esq., envoy extraordinary and minister plenipotentiary of the United States at London, and which is the only correspondence found in this department touching the subject referred to in the resolution.

Respectfully submitted,

WILLIAM H. SEWARD.

DEPARTMENT OF STATE, WASHINGTON, February 10, 1865.

MR. SEWARD TO MR. ADAMS.

(Extract.) No. 1258.

DEPARTMENT OF STATE, WASHINGTON, February 7, 1865

On the morning of the 3d, the President, attended by the Secretary, received Messrs. Stephens, Hunter, and Campbell on board the United States steam transport River Queen in Hampton Roads. The conference was altogether informal. There was no attendance of secretaries, clerks, or other witnesses. Nothing was written or read. The conversation, although earnest and free, was calm, and courteous, and kind on both sides. The Richmond party approached the discussion rather indirectly, and at no time did they either make categorical demands, or tender formal stipulations or absolute refusals. Nevertheless, during the conference, which lasted four hours, the several points at issue between the Government and the insurgents were distinctly raised, and discussed fully, intelligently, and in an amicable spirit. What the insurgent party seemed chiefly to favor was a postponement of the question of separation, upon which the war is waged, and a mutual direction of efforts of the Government, as well as those of the insurgents, to some extrinsic policy or scheme for a season during which passions might be expected to subside, and the armies be reduced, and trade and intercourse between the people of both sections resumed. It was suggested by them that through such postponement we might now have immediate peace, with some not very certain prospect of an ultimate satisfactory adjustment of political relations between this Government and the States, section, or people now engaged in conflict with it.

This suggestion, though deliberately considered, was nevertheless regarded by the President as one of armistice or truce, and he announced that we can agree to no cessation or suspension of hostilities, except on the basis of the disbandment of the insurgent forces, and the restoration of the national authority throughout all the States in the Union. Collaterally, and in subordination to the proposition which was thus announced, the antislavery policy of the United States was reviewed in all its bearings, and the President announced that he must not be expected to depart from the positions he had heretofore assumed in his proclamation of emancipation and other documents, as these positions were reiterated in his last annual message. It was further declared by the President that the complete restoration of the national authority was an indispensable condition of any assent on our part to whatever form of peace might be proposed. The President assured the other party that, while he must adhere to these positions, he would be prepared, so far as power is lodged with the Executive, to exercise liberality. His power, however, is limited by the Constitution; and when peace should be made, Congress must necessarily act in regard to appropriations of money and to the admission of representatives from the insurrectionary States. The Richmond party were then informed that Congress had, on the 31st ultimo, adopted by a constitutional majority a joint resolution submitting to the several States the proposition to abolish slavery throughout the Union, and that there is every reason to expect that it will be soon accepted by three fourths of the States, so as to become a part of the national organic law.

The conference came to an end by mutual acquiescence, without producing an agreement of views upon the several matters discussed, or any of them. Nevertheless, it is perhaps of some importance that we have been able to submit our opinions and views directly to prominent insurgents, and to hear them in answer in a courteous and not unfriendly manner.

I am, sir, your obedient servant,
WILLIAM H. SEWARD.

TO ADMIRAL DAVID D. PORTER.

EXECUTIVE MANSION, February 10, 1865

REAR-ADMIRAL DAVID D. PORTER, Commanding North Atlantic Squadron, Hampton Roads, Va.
SIR:—It is made my agreeable duty to enclose herewith the joint resolution approved 24th January, 1865, tendering the thanks of Congress to yourself, the officers and men under your command for their gallantry and good conduct in the capture of Fort Fisher, and through you to all who participated in that brilliant and decisive victory under your command.
Very respectfully,
A. LINCOLN.

TELEGRAM TO GENERAL S. POPE.

EXECUTIVE MANSION, WASHINGTON, February 12, 1865

MAJOR-GENERAL POPE, St. Louis, Missouri:
I understand that provost-marshals in different parts of Missouri are assuming to decide that the conditions of bonds are forfeited, and therefore are seizing and selling property to pay damages. This, if true, is both outrageous and ridiculous. Do not allow it. The courts, and not provost-marshals, are to decide such questions unless when military necessity makes an exception. Also excuse John Eaton, of Clay County, and Wesley Martin, of Platte, from being sent South, and let them go East if anywhere.
A. LINCOLN

TO THE COMMANDING OFFICERS IN WEST TENNESSEE

WASHINGTON, February 13, 1865.

TO THE MILITARY OFFICERS COMMANDING IN WEST TENNESSEE:
While I cannot order as within requested, allow me to say that it is my wish for you to relieve the people from all burdens, harassments, and oppressions, so far as is possible consistently with your military necessities; that the object of the war being to restore and maintain the blessings of peace and good government, I desire you to help, and not hinder, every advance in that direction.
Of your military necessities you must judge and execute, but please do so in the spirit and with the purpose above indicated.
A. LINCOLN.

TELEGRAM TO GENERAL J. POPE.

EXECUTIVE MANSION, WASHINGTON, February 14, 1865.

MAJOR-GENERAL POPE, St. Louis, Missouri:
Yours of yesterday about provost-marshal system received. As part of the same subject, let me say I am now pressed in regard to a pending assessment in St. Louis County. Please examine and satisfy yourself whether this assessment should proceed or be abandoned; and if you decide that it is to proceed, please examine as to the propriety of its application to a gentleman by the name of Charles McLaran.
A. LINCOLN.

TELEGRAM TO GENERAL POPE.

EXECUTIVE MANSION, WASHINGTON February 15, 1865.

MAJOR-GENERAL POPE, St. Louis, Missouri:
Please ascertain whether General Fisk's administration is as good as it might be, and answer me.
A. LINCOLN.

PROCLAMATION CONVENING THE SENATE IN EXTRA SESSION,

FEBRUARY 17, 1865.

BY THE PRESIDENT OF THE UNITED STATES OF AMERICA:
A Proclamation
Whereas objects of interest to the United States require that the Senate should be convened at twelve o'clock on the fourth of March next to receive and act upon such communications as may be made to it on the part of the Executive; Now, therefore, I, Abraham Lincoln, President of the United States, have considered it to be my duty to issue this, my proclamation, declaring that an extraordinary occasion requires the Senate of the United States to convene for the transaction of business at the Capitol, in the city of Washington, on the fourth day of March next, at twelve o'clock at noon on that day, of which all who shall at that time be entitled to act as members of that body are hereby required to take notice.
Given under my hand and the seal of the United States, at Washington..............
A. LINCOLN. By the President: WILLIAM H. SEWARD, Secretary of State.

TELEGRAM TO OFFICER IN COMMAND AT HARPER'S FERRY.

EXECUTIVE MANSION, WASHINGTON, February 17, 1865

OFFICER IN COMMAND AT HARPER'S FERRY:
Chaplain Fitzgibbon yesterday sent me a despatch invoking Clemency for Jackson, Stewart, and Randall, who are to be shot to-day. The despatch is so vague that there is no means here of ascertaining whether or not the execution of sentence of one or more of them may not already have been ordered. If not suspend execution of sentence m their cases until further orders and forward records of trials for examination.
A. LINCOLN
MAJOR ECKERT: Please send above telegram JNO. G. NICOLAY.

TELEGRAM TO GENERAL U.S. GRANT.

WASHINGTON, D. C., February 24, 1865

LIEUTENANT-GENERAL GRANT, City Point, Virginia:
I am in a little perplexity. I was induced to authorize a gentleman to bring Roger A. Pryor here with a view of effecting an exchange of him; but since then I have seen a despatch of yours showing that you specially object to his exchange. Meantime he has reached here and reported to me. It is an ungracious thing for me to send him back to prison, and yet inadmissible for him to remain here long. Cannot you help me out with it? I can conceive that there may be difference to you in days, and I can keep him a few days to accommodate on that point. I have not heard of my son's reaching you.
A. LINCOLN.

TELEGRAM TO GENERAL POPE.

EXECUTIVE MANSION, WASHINGTON, February 24, 1865

MAJOR-GENERAL POPE, Saint Louis, Mo.:
Please inquire and report to me whether there is any propriety of longer keeping in Gratiott Street Prison a man said to be there by the name of Riley Whiting.
A. LINCOLN.

TELEGRAM TO GENERAL U. S. GRANT. WASHINGTON, February 25, 1865

LIEUTENANT-GENERAL GRANT, City Point, Virginia:

General Sheridan's despatch to you, of to-day, in which he says he "will be off on Monday," and that he "will leave behind about two thousand men," causes the Secretary of War and myself considerable anxiety. Have you well considered whether you do not again leave open the Shenandoah Valley entrance to Maryland and Pennsylvania, or, at least, to the Baltimore and Ohio Railroad?
A. LINCOLN.

TELEGRAM TO GENERAL U. S. GRANT. WASHINGTON, D. C., February 27, 1865.

LIEUTENANT-GENERAL GRANT, City Point, Virginia:

Subsequent reflection, conference with General Halleck, your despatch, and one from General Sheridan, have relieved my anxiety; and so I beg that you will dismiss any concern you may have on my account, in the matter of my last despatch.
A. LINCOLN.

TO T. W. CONWAY.

EXECUTIVE MANSION, WASHINGTON, D. C., March 1, 1865.

MR. THOMAS W. CONWAY, General Superintendent Freedmen, Department of the Gulf.
SIR:—Your statement to Major-General Hurlbut of the condition of the freedmen of your department, and of your success in the work of their moral and physical elevation, has reached me and given me much pleasure.
That we shall be entirely successful in our efforts I firmly believe.
The blessing of God and the efforts of good and faithful men will bring us an earlier and happier consummation than the most sanguine friends of the freedmen could reasonably expect.
Yours,
A. LINCOLN,

TELEGRAM TO GENERAL U.S. GRANT. WASHINGTON, D. C., March 2, 1865.

LIEUTENANT-GENERAL GRANT, City Point, Va.:

You have not sent contents of Richmond papers for Tuesday or Wednesday. Did you not receive them? If not, does it indicate anything?
A. LINCOLN.

TELEGRAM FROM SECRETARY STANTON TO GENERAL GRANT.

WASHINGTON, March 3, 1865. 12 PM.

LIEUTENANT-GENERAL GRANT:
The President directs me to say to you that he wishes you to have no conference with General Lee unless it be for the capitulation of General Lee's army, or on some minor and purely military matter. He instructs me to say that you are not to decide, discuss, or confer upon any political question. Such questions the President holds in his own hands, and will submit them to no military conferences or conventions. Meantime you are to press to the utmost your military advantages.
EDWIN M. STANTON, Secretary of War.

SECOND INAUGURAL ADDRESS, MARCH 4, 1865.

FELLOW-COUNTRYMEN:—At this second appearing to take the oath of the presidential office there is less occasion for an extended address than there was at the first. Then a statement somewhat in detail of a course to be pursued seemed fitting and proper. Now, at the expiration of four years, during which public declarations have been constantly called forth on every point and phase of the great contest which still absorbs the attention and engrosses the energies of the nation, little that is new could be presented. The progress of our arms, upon which all else chiefly depends, is as well known to the public as to myself, and it is, I trust, reasonably satisfactory and encouraging to all. With high hope for the future, no prediction in regard to it is ventured.

On the occasion corresponding to this four years ago all thoughts were anxiously directed to an impending civil war. All dreaded it, all sought to avert it. While the inaugural address was being delivered from this place, devoted altogether to saving the Union without war, insurgent agents were in the city seeking to destroy it without war seeking to dissolve the Union and divide effects by negotiation. Both parties deprecated war, but one of them would make war rather than let the nation survive, and the other would accept war rather than let it perish, and the war came.

One eighth of the whole population was colored slaves, not distributed generally over the Union, but localized in the southern part of it. These slaves constituted a peculiar and powerful interest. All knew that this interest was somehow the cause of the war. To strengthen, perpetuate, and extend this interest was the object for which the insurgents would rend the Union even by war, while the Government claimed no right to do more than to restrict the territorial enlargement of it. Neither party expected for the war the magnitude or the duration which it has already attained. Neither anticipated that the cause of the conflict might cease with or even before the conflict itself should cease. Each looked for an easier triumph, and a result less fundamental and astounding. Both read the same Bible and pray to the same God, and each invokes His aid against the other. It may seem strange that any men should dare to ask a just God's assistance in wringing their bread from the sweat of other men's faces, but let us judge not, that we be not judged. The prayers of both could not be answered. That of neither has been answered fully. The Almighty has His own purposes. "Woe unto the world because of offenses; for it must needs be that offenses come, but woe to that man by whom the offense cometh." If we shall suppose that American slavery is one of those offenses which, in the providence of God, must needs come, but which, having continued through His appointed time, He now wills to remove, and that He gives to both North and South this terrible war as the woe due to those by whom the offense came, shall we discern therein any departure from those divine attributes which the believers in a living God always ascribe to Him? Fondly do we hope, fervently do we pray, that this mighty scourge of war may speedily pass away. Yet, if God wills that it continue until all the wealth piled by the bondsman's two hundred and fifty years of unrequited toil shall be sunk, and until every drop of blood drawn with the lash shall be paid by another drawn with the sword, as was said three thousand years ago, so still it must be said, "The judgments of the Lord are true and righteous altogether."

With malice toward none, with charity for all, with firmness in the right as God gives us to see the right, let us strive on to finish the work we are in, to bind up the nation's wounds, to care for him who shall have borne the battle and for his widow and his orphan, to do all which may achieve and cherish a just and lasting peace among ourselves and with all nations.

TELEGRAM TO GENERAL JOHN POPE.

EXECUTIVE MANSION, WASHINGTON, March 7, 1865

MAJOR-GENERAL POPE, St. Louis, Missouri:

Please state briefly, by telegraph, what you concluded about the assessments in St. Louis County. Early in the war one Samuel B. Churchill was sent from St. Louis to Louisville, where I have quite satisfactory evidence that he has not misbehaved. Still I am told his property at St. Louis is subjected to the assessment, which I think it ought not to be. Still I wish to know what you think.

A. LINCOLN.

TO GENERAL U.S. GRANT. WASHINGTON, D. C., March 8, 1865.

LIEUTENANT-GENERAL GRANT, City Point, Va:

Your two despatches to the Secretary of War, one relating to supplies for the enemy going by the Blackwater, and the other to General Singleton and Judge Hughes, have been laid before me by him. As to Singleton and Hughes, I think they are not in Richmond by any authority, unless it be from you. I remember nothing from me which could aid them in getting there, except a letter to you, as follows, to wit:

EXECUTIVE MANSION, WASHINGTON CITY, February 7, 1865. LIEUTENANT-GENERAL GRANT, City Point, Va.: General Singleton, who bears you this, claims that he already has arrangements made, if you consent, to bring a large amount of Southern produce through your lines. For its bearing on our finances, I would be glad for this to be done, if it can be, without injuriously disturbing your military operations, or supplying the enemy. I wish you to be judge and master on these points. Please see and hear him fully, and decide whether anything, and, if anything, what, can be done in the premises. Yours truly,

A. LINCOLN.

I believe I gave Hughes a card putting him with Singleton on the same letter. However this may be, I now authorize you to get Singleton and Hughes away from Richmond, if you choose, and can. I also authorize you, by an order, or in what form you choose, to suspend all operations on the Treasury trade permits, in all places southeastward of the Alleghenies. If you make such order, notify me of it, giving a copy, so that I can give corresponding direction to the Navy.

A. LINCOLN.

PROCLAMATION OFFERING PARDON TO DESERTERS,

MARCH 11, 1865

BY THE PRESIDENT OF THE UNITED STATES OF AMERICA
A Proclamation

Whereas, the twenty-first section of the act of Congress, approved on the 3d instant, entitled "An Act to amend the several acts heretofore passed to provide for the enrolling and calling out the national forces and for other purposes," requires that in addition to the other lawful penalties of the crime of desertion from the military or naval service, all persons who have deserted the military or naval service of the United States who shall not return to said service or report themselves to a provost-marshal within sixty days after the proclamation hereinafter mentioned, shall be deemed and taken to have voluntarily relinquished and forfeited their citizenship and their right to become citizens, and such deserters shall be forever incapable of holding any office of trust or profit under the United States, or of exercising any rights of citizens thereof; and all persons who shall hereafter desert the military or naval service, and all persons who, being duly enrolled, shall depart the jurisdiction of the district in which they are enrolled, or go beyond the limits of the United States with intent to avoid any draft into the military or naval service duly ordered, shall be liable to the penalties of this section; and the President is hereby authorized and required forthwith, on the passage of this act, to issue his proclamation setting forth the provisions of this section, in which proclamation the President is requested to notify all deserters returning within sixty days as aforesaid that they shall be pardoned on condition of returning to their regiments and companies, or to such other organizations as they may be assigned to, until they shall have served for a period of time equal to their original term of enlistment:

Now, therefore, be it known that I, Abraham Lincoln, President of the United States, do issue this my proclamation as required by said act, ordering and requiring all deserters to return to their proper posts; and I do hereby notify them

that all deserters who shall within sixty days from the date of this proclamation, viz., on or before the 10th day of May, 1865, return to service or report themselves to a provost-marshal, shall be pardoned on condition that they return to their regiments or companies or to such other organization as they may be assigned to, and serve the remainder of their original terms of enlistment, and in addition thereto a period equal to the time lost by desertion.
In testimony whereof, I have hereunto set my hand and caused the seal of the United States to be affixed...............
A. LINCOLN.
By the President: WILLIAM H. SEWARD, Secretary of State

TELEGRAM TO H. T. BLOW.

WASHINGTON, March 13, 1865.

HON. HENRY T. BLOW, Saint Louis, Mo.:
A Miss E. Snodgrass, who was banished from Saint Louis in May,1863, wishes to take the oath and return home. What say you?
A. LINCOLN.

LETTER TO THURLOW WEED,

MARCH 15, 1865.

EXECUTIVE MANSION, WASHINGTON, D. C.
DEAR Mr. WEED:
Every one likes a compliment. Thank you for yours on my little notification speech and on the recent inaugural address. I expect the latter to wear as well as perhaps better than—anything I have produced; but I believe it is not immediately popular. Men are not flattered by being shown that there has been a difference of purpose between the Almighty and them. To deny it, however, in this case, is to deny that there is a God governing the world. It is a truth which I thought needed to be told, and, as whatever of humiliation there is in it falls most directly on myself, I thought others might afford for me to tell it.
Truly yours,
A. LINCOLN.

TELEGRAM TO COLONEL ROUGH AND OTHERS.

WAR DEPARTMENT, WASHINGTON, D. C., March 17, 1865.

COL. R. M. ROUGH AND OTHERS, Chicago, Ill.:
Yours received. The best I can do with it is, to refer it to the War Department. The Rock Island case referred to, was my individual enterprise; and it caused so much difficulty in so many ways that I promised to never undertake another.
A. LINCOLN.

ADDRESS TO AN INDIANA REGIMENT,

MARCH 17, 1865.

FELLOW-CITIZENS:—It will be but a very few words that I shall undertake to say. I was born in Kentucky, raised in Indiana, and lived in Illinois; and now I am here, where it is my business to care equally for the good people of all the States. I am glad to see an Indiana regiment on this day able to present the captured flag to the Governor of Indiana. I am not disposed, in saying this, to make a distinction between the States, for all have done equally well.

There are but few views or aspects of this great war upon which I have not said or written something whereby my own opinions might be known. But there is one—the recent attempt of our erring brethren, as they are sometimes called, to employ the negro to fight for them. I have neither written nor made a speech on that subject, because that was their business, not mine, and if I had a wish on the subject, I had not the power to introduce it, or make it effective. The great question with them was whether the negro, being put into the army, will fight for them. I do not know, and therefore cannot decide. They ought to know better than me. I have in my lifetime heard many arguments why the negroes ought to be slaves; but if they fight for those who would keep them in slavery, it will be a better argument than any I have yet heard. He who will fight for that, ought to be a slave. They have concluded, at last, to take one out of four of the slaves and put them in the army, and that one out of the four who will fight to keep the others in slavery, ought to be a slave himself, unless he is killed in a fight. While I have often said that all men ought to be free, yet would I allow those colored persons to be slaves who want to be, and next to them those white people who argue in favor of making other people slaves. I am in favor of giving an appointment to such white men to try it on for these slaves. I will say one thing in regard to the negroes being employed to fight for them. I do know he cannot fight and stay at home and make bread too. And as one is about as important as the other to them, I don't care which they do. I am rather in favor of having them try them as soldiers. They lack one vote of doing that, and I wish I could send my vote over the river so that I might cast it in favor of allowing the negro to fight. But they cannot fight and work both. We must now see the bottom of the enemy's resources. They will stand out as long as they can, and if the negro will fight for them they must allow him to fight. They have drawn upon their last branch of resources, and we can now see the bottom. I am glad to see the end so near at hand. I have said now more than I intended, and will therefore bid you good-by.

PROCLAMATION CONCERNING INDIANS,

MARCH 17, 1865.

BY THE PRESIDENT OF THE UNITED STATES OF AMERICA:
A Proclamation.
Whereas reliable information has been received that hostile Indians, within the limits of the United States, have been furnished with arms and munitions of war by persons dwelling in conterminous foreign territory, and are thereby enabled to prosecute their savage warfare upon the exposed and sparse settlements of the frontier;
Now, therefore, be it known that I, Abraham Lincoln, President of the United States of America, do hereby proclaim and direct that all persons detected in that nefarious traffic shall be arrested and tried by court-martial at the nearest military post, and if convicted, shall receive the punishment due to their deserts.
In witness whereof, I have hereunto set my hand, and caused the seal of the United States to be affixed..................
A. LINCOLN.
By the President: WILLIAM H. SEWARD, Secretary of State.

ORDER ANNULLING THE SENTENCE

AGAINST BENJAMIN G. SMITH AND FRANKLIN W. SMITH,

MARCH 18, 1865.
I am unwilling for the sentence to stand, and be executed, to any extent in this case. In the absence of a more adequate motive than the evidence discloses, I am wholly unable to believe in the existence of criminal or fraudulent intent on the part of men of such well established good character. If the evidence went as far to establish a guilty profit of one or two hundred thousand dollars, as it does of one or two hundred dollars, the case would, on the question of guilt, bear a far different aspect. That on this contract, involving some twelve hundred thousand dollars, the contractors would plan, and attempt to execute a fraud which, at the most, could profit them only one or two hundred, or even

one thousand dollars, is to my mind beyond the power of rational belief. That they did not, in such a case, make far greater gains, proves that they did not, with guilty or fraudulent intent, make at all. The judgment and sentence are disapproved, and declared null, and the defendants are fully discharged.
A. LINCOLN March 18, 1865.

TELEGRAM TO GENERAL J. POPE.

EXECUTIVE MANSION, WASHINGTON, March 19, 1865.

MAJOR-GENERAL POPE, St. Louis, Missouri:
Understanding that the plan of action for Missouri contained in your letter to the Governor of that State, and your other letter to me, is concurred in by the Governor, it is approved by me, and you will be sustained in proceeding upon it.
A. LINCOLN.

TELEGRAM TO GENERAL ORD.

EXECUTIVE MANSION, WASHINGTON, May [March] 20, 1865.

MAJOR-GENERAL ORD, Army of the James
Is it true that George W. Lane is detained at Norfolk without any charge against him? And if so why is it done?
A. LINCOLN.

TELEGRAM TO JUDGE SCATES.

EXECUTIVE MANSION,

WASHINGTON, March 21, 1865.
HON. WALTER B. SCATES, Centralia, Illinois:
If you choose to go to New Mexico and reside, I will appoint you chief justice there. What say you? Please answer.
A. LINCOLN.

TELEGRAM TO GENERAL W. S. HANCOCK.

WASHINGTON, D. C., March 22, 1865. MAJOR-GENERAL HANCOCK, Winchester, Va.:

Seeing your despatch about General Crook, and fearing that through misapprehension something unpleasant may occur, I send you below two despatches of General Grant, which I suppose will fully explain General Crook's movements.
A. LINCOLN.

ANOTHER FEMALE SPY

TELEGRAM TO GENERAL DODGE. EXECUTIVE MANSION, WASHINGTON, March 23, 1865.

GENERAL DODGE, Commanding, &c, Saint Louis, Mo.:
Allow Mrs. R. S. Ewell the benefit of my amnesty proclamation on her taking the oath.
A. LINCOLN.

TELEGRAM TO SECRETARY STANTON.

CITY POINT, VIRGINIA, March 25, 1865. 8.30 A.M.

HON. SECRETARY OF WAR, Washington, D. C.:
Arrived here all safe about 9 P.M. yesterday. No war news. General Grant does not seem to know very much about Yeatman, but thinks very well of him so far as he does know.
I like Mr. Whiting very much, and hence would wish him to remain or resign as best suits himself. Hearing this much from me, do as you think best in the matter. General Lee has sent the Russell letter back, concluding, as I understand from Grant, that their dignity does not admit of their receiving the document from us. Robert just now tells me there was a little rumpus up the line this morning, ending about where it began.
A. LINCOLN.

TELEGRAM TO SECRETARY STANTON.

(Cipher.)

HEADQUARTERS ARMY OF THE POTOMAC, March 25, 1865. (Received 5 P.M.)
HON. EDWIN M. STANTON, Secretary of War:
I am here within five miles of the scene of this morning's action. I have nothing to add to what General Meade reports except that I have seen the prisoners myself and they look like there might be the number he states—1600.
A. LINCOLN

TELEGRAM TO SECRETARY STANTON.

CITY POINT, VA., March 26, 1865. (Received 11.30 A.M.)

HON. SECRETARY OF WAR:
I approve your Fort Sumter programme. Grant don't seem to know Yeatman very well, but thinks very well of him so far as he knows. Thinks it probable that Y. is here now, for the place. I told you this yesterday as well as that you should do as you think best about Mr. Whiting's resignation, but I suppose you did not receive the dispatch. I am on the boat and have no later war news than went to you last night.
A. LINCOLN.

TELEGRAM TO SECRETARY STANTON.

CITY POINT, VIRGINIA, March 27, 1865.3.35 P.M.

HON. SECRETARY OF WAR, Washington, D.C.:

Yours inclosing Fort Sumter order received. I think of but one suggestion. I feel quite confident that Sumter fell on the 13th, and not on the 14th of April, as you have it. It fell on Saturday, the 13th; the first call for troops on our part was got up on Sunday, the 14th, and given date and issued on Monday, the 15th. Look up the old almanac and other data, and see if I am not right.
A. LINCOLN.

TELEGRAM TO SECRETARY STANTON.

CITY POINT, VIRGINIA, March 28, 1865. 12 M.

HON. SECRETARY OF WAR, Washington, D.C.: After your explanation, I think it is little or no difference whether the Fort Sumter ceremony takes place on the 13th or 14th.
General Sherman tells me he is well acquainted with James Yeatman, and that he thinks him almost the best man in the country for anything he will undertake.
A. LINCOLN.

TELEGRAM TO SECRETARY STANTON.

CITY POINT, VA., March 30, 1865. 7.30 P.M. (Received 8.30 P.M.)

HON. SECRETARY OF WAR:
I begin to feel that I ought to be at home and yet I dislike to leave without seeing nearer to the end of General Grant's present movement. He has now been out since yesterday morning and although he has not been diverted from his programme no considerable effort has yet been produced so far as we know here. Last night at 10.15 P. M. when it was dark as a rainy night without a moon could be, a furious cannonade soon joined in by a heavy musketry fire opened near Petersburg and lasted about two hours. The sound was very distinct here as also were the flashes of the guns up the clouds. It seemed to me a great battle, but the older hands here scarcely noticed it and sure enough this morning it was found that very little had been done.
A. LINCOLN.

TELEGRAM TO SECRETARY STANTON.

CITY POINT, VIRGINIA, March 31, 1865. 3 P.M.

SECRETARY STANTON:
At 12.30 P.M. to-day General Grant telegraphed me as follows: "There has been much hard fighting this morning. The enemy drove our left from near Dabney's house back well toward the Boydton plank road. We are now about to take the offensive at that point, and I hope will more than recover the lost ground."
Later he telegraphed again as follows:
"Our troops, after being driven back to the Boydton plank road, turned and drove the enemy in turn, and took the White Oak road, which we now have. This gives us the ground occupied by the enemy this morning. I will send you a rebel flag captured by our troops in driving the enemy back. There have been four flags captured to-day."
Judging by the two points from which General Grant telegraphs, I infer that he moved his headquarters about one mile since he sent the first of the two despatches.
A. LINCOLN.

TELEGRAM TO GENERAL U. S. GRANT.

CITY POINT, April 1, 1865.

LIEUTENANT-GENERAL GRANT:
Yours to Colonel Bowers about the Secretary of War is shown to me. He is not here, nor have I any notice that he is coming. I presume the mistake comes of the fact that the Secretary of State was here. He started back to Washington this morning. I have your two despatches of this morning, and am anxious to hear from Sheridan.
A. LINCOLN.

TELEGRAM TO SECRETARY STANTON.

CITY POINT, April 1, 1865. 12.50 P.M.

HON. SECRETARY OF WAR, Washington, D.C.:
I have had two despatches from General Grant since my last to you, but they contain little additional, except that Sheridan also had pretty hot work yesterday, that infantry was sent to his support during the night, and that he (Grant) has not since heard from Sheridan.
Mrs. Lincoln has started home, and I will thank you to see that our coachman is at the Arsenal wharf at eight o'clock to-morrow morning, there to wait until she arrives.
A. LINCOLN. TELEGRAM TO SECRETARY SEWARD.
CITY POINT, V.A., April, 1865. 5.30?.M.
HON. W. H. SEWARD, Secretary of State, Fort Monroe:
Despatch just received, showing that Sheridan, aided by Warren, had, at 2 P.M., pushed the enemy back, so as to retake the Five Forks and bring his own headquarters up to J. Boisseau's. The Five Forks were barricaded by the enemy and carried by Devin's division of cavalry. This part of the enemy seem to now be trying to work along the White Oak road, to join the main force in front of Grant, while Sheridan and Warren are pressing them as closely as possible.
A. LINCOLN.

TELEGRAM TO GENERAL U.S. GRANT. CITY POINT, April 1, 1865.

LIEUTENANT-GENERAL GRANT:

Yours showing Sheridan's success of to-day is just received and highly appreciated. Having no great deal to do here, I am still sending the substance of your despatches to the Secretary of War.
A. LINCOLN.

TELEGRAM TO MRS. LINCOLN.

CITY POINT, V.A., April 2, 1865. 8.30 A.M. (Received 9 A.M.)

MRS. A. LINCOLN, Executive Mansion:
Last night General Grant telegraphed that General Sheridan with his cavalry and the Fifth Corps had captured three brigades of infantry, a train of wagons, and several batteries, prisoners amounting to several thousand. This morning General Grant having ordered an attack along the whole line telegraphs as follows.
Robert yesterday wrote a little cheerful note to Captain Penrose, which is all he has heard of him since you left.
A. LINCOLN.

TELEGRAMS TO SECRETARY STANTON. CITY POINT, VIRGINIA, April 2, 1865. 8.30 A.M.

HON. E. M. STANTON, Secretary of War:

Last night General Grant telegraphed that General Sheridan, with his cavalry and the Fifth Corps, had captured three brigades of infantry, a train of wagons, and several batteries; the prisoners amounting to several thousand.

This morning General Grant, having ordered an attack along the whole line, telegraphs as follows:

"Both Wright and Parke got through the enemy's lines. The battle now rages furiously. General Sheridan, with his cavalry, the Fifth corps, and Miles's Division of the Second Corps, which was sent to him this morning, is now sweeping down from the west.

"All now looks highly favorable. General Ord is engaged, but I have not yet heard the result in his front."

A. LINCOLN.

CITY POINT, April 1. 11.00 A.M.

Despatches are frequently coming in. All is going on finely. Generals Parke, Wright, and Ord's lines are extending from the Appomattox to Hatcher's Run. They have all broken through the enemy's intrenched lines, taking some forts, guns, and prisoners. Sheridan, with his own cavalry, the Fifth Corps, and part of the Second, is coming in from the west on the enemy's flank. Wright is already tearing up the Southside Railroad.

A. LINCOLN

CITY POINT, VIRGINIA, April 2. 2 P.M.

At 10.45 A.M. General Grant telegraphs as follows:

"Everything has been carried from the left of the Ninth Corps. The Sixth Corps alone captured more than three thousand prisoners. The Second and Twenty-fourth Corps captured forts, guns, and prisoners from the enemy, but I cannot tell the numbers. We are now closing around the works of the line immediately enveloping Petersburg. All looks remarkably well. I have not yet heard from Sheridan. His headquarters have been moved up to Banks's house, near the Boydton road, about three miles southwest of Petersburg."

A. LINCOLN.

CITY POINT, VIRGINIA, April 2. 8.30 P.M.

At 4.30 P.M. to-day General Grant telegraphs as follows:

"We are now up and have a continuous line of troops, and in a few hours will be intrenched from the Appomattox below Petersburg to the river above. The whole captures since the army started out will not amount to less than twelve thousand men, and probably fifty pieces of artillery. I do not know the number of men and guns accurately, however. A portion of Foster's Division, Twenty Fourth Corps, made a most gallant charge this afternoon, and captured a very important fort from the enemy, with its entire garrison. All seems well with us, and everything is quiet just now."

A. LINCOLN.

TELEGRAM TO MRS. LINCOLN. CITY POINT, VA., April 1, 1865.

MRS. LINCOLN:

At 4.30 P.M. to-day General Grant telegraphs that he has Petersburg completely enveloped from river below to river above, and has captured, since he started last Wednesday, about twelve thousand prisoners and fifty guns. He suggests that I shall go out and see him in the morning, which I think I will do. Tad and I are both well, and will be glad to see you and your party here at the time you name.

A. LINCOLN.

TELEGRAM TO GENERAL U. S. GRANT.

CITY POINT, April 2, 1865

LIEUTENANT-GENERAL GRANT:

Allow me to tender to you and all with you the nation's grateful thanks for this additional and magnificent success. At your kind suggestion I think I will meet you to-morrow.
A. LINCOLN.

TELEGRAM TO SECRETARY STANTON.

CITY POINT, VIRGINIA, April 3, 1865. 8.30 A.M.

HON. E. M. STANTON, Secretary of War:
This morning Lieutenant-General Grant reports Petersburg evacuated, and he is confident that Richmond also is. He is pushing forward to cut off, if possible, the retreating rebel army.
A. LINCOLN.

TELEGRAM TO SECRETARY STANTON.

CITY POINT, VA., April 3, 1865. 5 P.M.

HON. EDWIN M. STANTON, Secretary of War:
Yours received. Thanks for your caution, but I have already been to Petersburg. Staid with General Grant an hour and a half and returned here. It is certain now that Richmond is in our hands, and I think I will go there to-morrow. I will take care of myself.
A. LINCOLN.

TELEGRAM TO SECRETARY STANTON.

CITY POINT, VA., April 4, 1865 (Received 8.45 A.M.)

HON. EDWIN M. STANTON, Secretary of War:
General Weitzel telegraphs from Richmond that of railroad stock he found there twenty-eight locomotives, forty-four passenger and baggage cars, and one hundred and six freight cars. At 3.30 this evening General Grant, from Sutherland's Station, ten miles from Petersburg toward Burkevllle, telegraphs as follows:
"General Sheridan picked up twelve hundred prisoners to-day, and from three hundred to five hundred more have been gathered by other troops. The majority of the arms that were left in the hands of the remnant of Lee's army are now scattered between Richmond and where his troops are. The country is also full of stragglers; the line of retreat marked with artillery, ammunition, burned or charred wagons, caissons, ambulances, etc."
A. LINCOLN.

TELEGRAM TO SECRETARY SEWARD.

CITY POINT, APRIL 5, 1865. (Received 11.55 PM.)

HON. SECRETARY OF STATE:
Yours of to-day received. I think there is no probability of my remaining here more than two days longer. If that is too long come down. I passed last night at Richmond and have just returned.
A. LINCOLN.

TELEGRAM TO GENERAL U. S. GRANT.

HEADQUARTERS ARMIES OF THE UNITED STATES, CITY POINT, April 6, 1865.

LIEUTENANT-GENERAL GRANT, in the Field:
Secretary Seward was thrown from his carriage yesterday and seriously injured. This, with other matters, will take me to Washington soon. I was at Richmond yesterday and the day before, when and where Judge Campbell, who was with Messrs. Hunter and Stephens in February, called on me, and made such representations as induced me to put in his hands an informal paper, repeating the propositions in my letter of instructions to Mr. Seward, which you remember, and adding that if the war be now further persisted in by the rebels, confiscated property shall at the least bear the additional cost, and that confiscation shall be remitted to the people of any State which will now promptly and in good faith withdraw its troops and other support from resistance to the Government.
Judge Campbell thought it not impossible that the rebel legislature of Virginia would do the latter if permitted; and accordingly I addressed a private letter to General Weitzel, with permission to Judge Campbell to see it, telling him (General Weitzel) that if they attempt this, to permit and protect them, unless they attempt something hostile to the United States, in which case to give them notice and time to leave, and to arrest any remaining after such time.
I do not think it very probable that anything win come of this, but I have thought best to notify you so that if you should see signs you may understand them.
From your recent despatches it seems that you are pretty effectually withdrawing the Virginia troops from opposition to the Government. Nothing that I have done, or probably shall do, is to delay, hinder, or interfere with your work.
Yours truly,
A. LINCOLN.

TELEGRAM TO GENERAL G. WEITZEL.

HEADQUARTERS ARMIES OF THE UNITED STATES CITY POINT, April 6, 1865.

MAJOR-GENERAL WEITZEL, Richmond, Va.:
It has been intimated to me that the gentlemen who have acted as the legislature of Virginia in support of the rebellion may now desire to assemble at Richmond and take measures to withdraw the Virginia troops and other support from resistance to the General Government. If they attempt it, give them permission and protection, until, if at all, they attempt some action hostile to the United States, in which case you will notify them, give them reasonable time to leave, and at the end of which time arrest any who remain. Allow Judge Campbell to see this, but do not make it public.
A. LINCOLN.

TELEGRAM TO SECRETARY STANTON.

CITY POINT, VA., April 7, 1865 (Received 10.30 AM.)

HON. SECRETARY OF WAR:
At 11.15 P.M. yesterday at Burkesville Station, General Grant sends me the following from General Sheridan:
"April 6, 11.15 P.M.
"LIEUTENANT-GENERAL GRANT:
I have the honor to report that the enemy made a stand at the intersection of the Burks Station road with the road upon which they were retreating. I attacked them with two divisions of the Sixth Army Corps and routed them handsomely, making a connection with the cavalry. I am still pressing on with both cavalry and infantry. Up to the present time we have captured Generals Ewell, Kershaw, Button, Corse, DeBare, and Custis Lee, several thousand prisoners, fourteen pieces of artillery with caissons and a large number of wagons. If the thing is pressed I think Lee will surrender.

"P. H. SHERIDAN,
"Major-General, Commanding."
A. LINCOLN.

LET THE THING BE PRESSED.

TELEGRAM TO GENERAL U. S. GRANT.

HEADQUARTERS ARMIES OF THE UNITED STATES,
CITY POINT, April 7, 11 A.M., 1865.
LIEUTENANT-GENERAL GRANT:
Gen. Sheridan says:
"If the thing is pressed I think that Lee will surrender."
Let the thing be pressed.
A. LINCOLN.

NOTE ON A CARD TO SECRETARY STANTON.

April 10, 1865.

Tad wants some flags—can he be accommodated?
A. LINCOLN.

RESPONSE TO A CALL,

APRIL 10, 1865

If the company had assembled by appointment, some mistake had crept in their understanding. He had appeared before a larger audience than this one to-day, and he would repeat what he then said, namely, he supposed owing to the great, good news, there would be some demonstration. He would prefer to-morrow evening, when he should be quite willing, and he hoped ready, to say something. He desired to be particular, because every thing he said got into print. Occupying the position he did, a mistake would produce harm, and therefore he wanted to be careful not to make a mistake.

TELEGRAM TO GENERAL G. H. GORDON.

EXECUTIVE MANSION, WASHINGTON, April 11, 1865.

BRIG. GEN. G. H. GORDON, Norfolk, Va.:
Send to me at once a full statement as to the cause or causes for which, and by authority of what tribunal George W. Lane, Charles Whitlock, Ezra Baler, J. M. Renshaw, and others are restrained of their liberty. Do this promptly and fully.
A. LINCOLN.

PROCLAMATION CLOSING CERTAIN PORTS, APRIL 11, 1865.

BY THE PRESIDENT OF THE UNITED STATES OF AMERICA:

A Proclamation.
Whereas by my proclamations of the 19th and 27th days of April, A.D. 1861, the ports of the United States in the States of Virginia, North Carolina, South Carolina, Georgia, Florida, Alabama, Mississippi, Louisiana, and Texas were declared to be subject to blockade; but
Whereas the said blockade has, in consequence of actual military occupation by this Government, since been conditionally set aside or relaxed in respect to the ports of Norfolk and Alexandria, in the State of Virginia; Beaufort, in the State of North Carolina; Port Royal, in the State of South Carolina; Pensacola and Fernandina, in the State of Florida; and New Orleans, in the State of Louisiana; and
Whereas by the fourth section of the act of Congress approved on the 13th of July, 1861, entitled "An act further to provide for the collection of duties on imports, and for other purposes," the President, for the reasons therein set forth, is authorized to close certain ports of entry:
Now, therefore, be it known that I, Abraham Lincoln, President of the United States, do hereby proclaim that the ports of Richmond, Tappahannock, Cherrystone, Yorktown, and Petersburg, in Virginia; of Camden (Elizabeth City), Edenton, Plymouth, Washington, Newbern, Ocracoke, and Wilmington in North Carolina; of Charleston, Georgetown, and Beaufort, in South Carolina; of Savannah, St. Marys, and Brunswick (Darien), in Georgia; of Mobile, in Alabama; of Pearl River (Shieldsboro), Natchez and Vicksburg, in Mississippi; of St. Augustine, Key West, St. Marks (Port Leon), St. Johns (Jacksonville), and Apalachicola, in Florida; of Teche (Franklin), in Louisiana; of Galveston, La Salle, Brazos de Santiago (Point Isabel), and Brownsville, in Texas, are hereby closed, and all right of importation, warehousing, and other privileges shall, in respect to the ports aforesaid, cease until they shall have again been opened by order of the President; and if while said parts are so closed any ship or vessel from beyond the United States or having on board any articles subject to duties shall attempt to enter any such port, the same, together with its tackle, apparel, furniture, and cargo, shall be forfeited to the United States.
In witness whereof I have hereunto set my hand and caused the seal of the United States to be affixed.
Done at the city of Washington, this eleventh day of April, A.D., 1865, and of the independence of the United States of America, the eighty-ninth.
A. LINCOLN.
By the President WILLIAM H. SEWARD, Secretary of State.

PROCLAMATION OPENING THE PORT OF KEY WEST,

APRIL 11, 1865.

BY THE PRESIDENT OF THE UNITED STATES OF AMERICA:
A Proclamation.
Whereas by my proclamation of this date the port of Key West, in the State of Florida, was inadvertently included among those which are not open to commerce:
Now, therefore, be it known that I, Abraham Lincoln, President of the United States, do hereby declare and make known that the said port of Key West is and shall remain open to foreign and domestic commerce upon the same conditions by which that commerce has there hitherto been governed.
In testimony whereof I have hereunto set my hand and caused the seal of the United States to be affixed.
Done at the city of Washington, this eleventh day of April, A.D. 1865, and of the independence of the United States of America the eighty-ninth.
A. LINCOLN.
By the President: WILLIAM H. SEWARD, Secretary of State.

PROCLAMATION CLAIMING EQUALITY OF RIGHTS WITH ALL MARITIME NATIONS,

APRIL 11, 1865.

BY THE PRESIDENT OF THE UNITED STATES OF AMERICA:

A Proclamation.

Whereas for some time past vessels of war of the United States have been refused in certain foreign ports, privileges and immunities to which they were entitled by treaty, public law, or the community of nations, at the same time that vessels of war of the country wherein the said privileges and immunities have been withheld have enjoyed them fully and uninterruptedly in ports of the United States, which condition of things has not always been forcibly resisted by the United States, although, on the other hand, they have not at any time failed to protest against and declare their dissatisfaction with the same. In the view of the United States, no condition any longer exists which can be claimed to justify the denial to them by any one of such nations of customary naval rights as has heretofore been so unnecessarily persisted in........

Now, therefore, I, Abraham Lincoln, President of the United States, do hereby make known that if, after a reasonable time shall have elapsed for intelligence of this proclamation to have reached any foreign country in whose ports the said privileges and immunities shall have been refused as aforesaid, they shall continue to be so refused, then and thenceforth the same privileges and immunities shall be refused to the vessels of war of that country in the ports of the United States, and this refusal shall continue until war vessels of the United States shall have been placed upon an entire equality in the foreign ports aforesaid with similar vessels of other countries. The United States, whatever claim or pretense may have existed heretofore, are now, at least, entitled to claim and concede an entire and friendly equality of rights and hospitalities with all maritime nations.

In witness whereof, I have hereunto set my hand, and caused the seal of the United States to be affixed..................

A. LINCOLN.

By the President: WILLIAM H. SEWARD, Secretary of State.

LAST PUBLIC ADDRESS,

APRIL 11, 1865

FELLOW-CITIZENS—We meet this evening not in sorrow, but in gladness of heart. The evacuation of Petersburg and Richmond, and the surrender of the principal insurgent army, give hope of a righteous and speedy peace, whose joyous expression cannot be restrained. In the midst of this, however, He from whom blessings flow must not be forgotten.

A call for a national thanksgiving is being prepared, and will be duly promulgated. Nor must those whose harder part gives us the cause of rejoicing be overlooked. Their honors must not be parceled out with others. I myself was near the front, and had the pleasure of transmitting much of the good news to you. But no part of the honor for plan or execution is mine. To General Grant, his skillful officers, and brave men, all belongs. The gallant navy stood ready, but was not in reach to take active part. By these recent successes, the reinauguration of the national authority—reconstruction which has had a large share of thought from the first, is pressed much more closely upon our attention. It is fraught with great difficulty. Unlike a case of war between independent nations, there is no authorized organ for us to treat with—no one man has authority to give up the rebellion for any other man. We simply must begin with and mould from disorganized and discordant elements. Nor is it a small additional embarrassment that we, the loyal people, differ among ourselves as to the mode, manner, and measure of reconstruction. As a general rule, I abstain from reading the reports of attacks upon myself, Wishing not to be provoked by that to which I cannot properly offer an answer. In spite of this precaution, however, it comes to my knowledge that I am much censured for some supposed agency in setting up and seeking to sustain the new State government of Louisiana. In this I have done just so much and no more than the public knows. In the Annual Message of December, 1863, and the accompanying proclamation, I presented a plan of reconstruction, as the phrase goes, which I promised, if adopted by any State, would be acceptable to and sustained by the Executive Government of the nation. I distinctly stated that this was not the only plan that might possibly be acceptable, and I also distinctly protested that the Executive claimed no right to say when or whether members should be admitted to seats in Congress from such States. This plan was in advance submitted to the then Cabinet, and approved by every member of it. One of them suggested that I should then and in that connection apply the Emancipation Proclamation to the theretofore excepted parts of Virginia and Louisiana; that I should drop the suggestion about apprenticeship for freed people, and that I should omit the protest against my own power in regard to the admission of members of Congress. But even he approved every part and parcel of the plan which has since been employed or touched by the action of Louisiana. The new constitution of Louisiana, declaring emancipation for the whole State, practically applies the proclamation to the part previously excepted. It does not adopt apprenticeship for freed people, and is silent, as it could not well be otherwise, about the admission of members to Congress. So that, as it applied to Louisiana, every member of the Cabinet fully approved the plan. The message went to Congress, and I received many commendations of the plan, written and verbal, and not a single objection to it from any professed emancipationist came to my knowledge until after the news reached Washington that the people of Louisiana had begun to move in accordance with it. From about July, 1862, I had corresponded with different persons supposed to be interested in seeking a reconstruction of a State government for Louisiana. When the message of 1863, with the plan before mentioned, reached New Orleans, General Banks wrote me that he was confident that the people, with his military co-operation, would reconstruct substantially on that plan. I wrote to him and some of them to try it. They tried it, and the result is known. Such has been my only agency in getting up the Louisiana government. As to sustaining it my promise is out, as before stated. But, as bad promises are better broken than kept, I shall treat this as a bad promise and break it, whenever I shall be convinced that keeping it is adverse to the public interest; but I have not yet been so convinced. I have been shown a letter on this subject, supposed to be an able one, in which the writer expresses regret that my mind has not seemed to be definitely fixed upon the question whether the seceded States, so called, are in the Union or out of it. It would perhaps add astonishment to his regret were he to learn that since I have found professed Union men endeavoring to answer that question, I have purposely forborne any public expression upon it. As appears to me, that question has not been nor yet is a practically material one, and that any discussion of it, while it thus remains practically immaterial, could have no effect other than the mischievous one of dividing our friends. As yet, whatever it may become, that question is bad as the basis of a controversy, and good for nothing at all—a merely pernicious abstraction. We all agree that the seceded States, so called, are out of their proper practical relation with the Union, and that the sole object of the Government, civil and military, in regard to those States, is to again get them into their proper practical relation. I believe that it is not only possible, but in fact easier, to do this without deciding or even considering whether those States have ever been out of the Union, than with it. Finding themselves safely at home, it would be utterly immaterial whether they had been abroad. Let us all join in doing the acts necessary to restore the proper practical relations between these States and the Union, and each forever after innocently indulge his own opinion whether, in doing the acts he brought the States from without into the Union, or only gave them proper assistance, they never having been out of it. The amount of constituency, so to speak, on which the Louisiana government rests, would be more satisfactory to all if it contained fifty thousand, or thirty thousand, or even twenty thousand, instead of twelve thousand, as it does. It is also unsatisfactory to some that the elective franchise is not given to the colored man. I would myself prefer that it were now conferred on the very intelligent, and on those who serve our cause as soldiers. Still, the question is not whether the Louisiana government, as it stands, is quite all that is desirable. The question is, Will it be wiser to take it as it is and help to improve it, or to reject and disperse? Can Louisiana be brought into proper practical relation with the Union sooner by sustaining or by discarding her new State government? Some twelve thousand voters in the heretofore Slave State of Louisiana have sworn allegiance to the Union, assumed to be the rightful political power of the State, held elections, organized a State government, adopted a Free State constitution, giving the benefit of public schools equally to black and white, and empowering the Legislature to confer the elective franchise upon the colored man. This Legislature has already voted to ratify the Constitutional Amendment recently passed by Congress, abolishing slavery throughout the nation. These twelve thousand persons are thus fully committed to the Union and to perpetuate freedom in the State—committed to the very things, and nearly all things, the nation wants—and they ask the nation's recognition and its assistance to make good this committal. Now, if we reject and spurn them, we do our utmost to disorganize and disperse them. We, in fact, say to the white man: You are worthless or worse; we will neither help you nor be helped by you. To the blacks we say: This cup of liberty which these, your old masters, held to your lips, we will dash from you, and leave you to the chances of gathering the spilled and scattered contents in some vague and undefined when, where, and how. If this course, discouraging and paralyzing both white and black, has any tendency to bring Louisiana into proper practical relations with the Union, I have so far been unable to perceive it. If, on the contrary, we recognize and sustain the new government of Louisiana, the converse of all this is made true. We encourage the hearts and nerve the arms of twelve thousand to adhere to their work, and argue for it, and proselyte for it, and fight for it, and feed it, and grow it, and ripen it to a complete success. The colored man, too, in seeing all united for him, is inspired with vigilance, and energy, and daring to the same end. Grant that he desires the elective franchise, will he not attain it sooner by saving the already advanced steps towards it, than by running backward over them? Concede that the new government of Louisiana is only to what it should be as the egg is to the fowl, we shall sooner have the fowl by hatching the egg than by smashing it. Again, if we reject Louisiana, we also reject one vote in favor of the proposed amendment to the National Constitution. To meet this proposition, it has been argued that no more than three fourths of those States which have not attempted secession are necessary to validly ratify the amendment. I do not commit myself against this, further than to say that such a ratification would be questionable, and sure to be persistently questioned, while a ratification by three fourths of all the States would be unquestioned and unquestionable. I repeat the question, Can Louisiana be brought into proper practical relation with the Union sooner by sustaining or by discarding her new State government? What has been said of Louisiana will apply to other States. And yet so great peculiarities pertain to each State, and such important and sudden changes occur in the same State, and withal so new and unprecedented is the whole case, that no exclusive and inflexible plan can safely be prescribed as to details and collaterals. Such exclusive and inflexible plan would surely become a new entanglement. Important principles may and must be inflexible. In the present situation as the phrase goes, it may be my duty to make some new announcement to the people of the South. I am considering, and shall not fail to act, when satisfied that action will be proper.

TELEGRAM TO GENERAL G. WEITZEL.

WASHINGTON, D. C., April 12, 1865. MAJOR-GENERAL WEITZEL, Richmond, Va.:

I have seen your despatch to Colonel Hardie about the matter of prayers. I do not remember hearing prayers spoken of while I was in Richmond; but I have no doubt you have acted in what appeared to you to be the spirit and temper manifested by me while there. Is there any sign of the rebel legislature coming together on the understanding of my letter to you? If there is any such sign, inform me what it is; if there is no such sign, you may withdraw the offer.
A. LINCOLN.

TELEGRAM TO GENERAL G. WEITZEL. WASHINGTON, D.C., April 12, 1865.

MAJOR-GENERAL WEITZEL, Richmond, Va.:

I have just seen Judge Campbell's letter to you of the 7th. He assumes, as appears to me, that I have called the insurgent legislature of Virginia together, as the rightful legislature of the State, to settle all differences with the United States. I have done no such thing. I spoke of them, not as a legislature, but as "the gentlemen who have acted as the legislature of Virginia in support of the rebellion." I did this on purpose to exclude the assumption that I was recognizing them as a rightful body. I deal with them as men having power de facto to do a specific thing, to wit: "To withdraw the Virginia troops and other support from resistance to the General Government," for which, in the paper handed Judge Campbell, I promised a specific equivalent, to wit: a remission to the people of the State, except in certain cases, of the confiscation of their property. I meant this, and no more. Inasmuch, however, as Judge Campbell misconstrues this, and is still pressing for an armistice, contrary to the explicit statement of the paper I gave him, and particularly as General Grant has since captured the Virginia troops, so that giving a consideration for their withdrawal is no longer applicable, let my letter to you and the paper to Judge Campbell both be withdrawn, or countermanded, and he be notified of it. Do not now allow them to assemble, but if any have come, allow them safe return to their homes.
A. LINCOLN.

INTERVIEW WITH SCHUYLER COLFAX ON THE MORNING OF APRIL 14, 1865.

Mr. Colfax, I want you to take a message from me to the miners whom you visit. I have very large ideas of the mineral wealth of our nation. I believe it practically inexhaustible. It abounds all over the Western country, from the Rocky Mountains to the Pacific, and its development has scarcely commenced. During the war, when we were adding a couple of millions of dollars every day to our national debt, I did not care about encouraging the increase in the volume of our precious metals. We had the country to save first. But now that the rebellion is overthrown, and we know pretty nearly the amount of our national debt, the more gold and silver we mine, we make the payment of that debt so much the easier. "Now," said he, speaking with more emphasis, "I am going to encourage that in every possible way. We shall have hundreds of thousands of disbanded soldiers, and many have feared that their return home in such great numbers might paralyze industry, by furnishing, suddenly, a greater supply of labor than there will be demand for. I am going to try to attract them to the hidden wealth of our mountain ranges, where there is room enough for all. Immigration, which even the war has not stopped, will land upon our shores hundreds of thousands more per year from overcrowded Europe. I intend to point them to the gold and silver that wait for them in the West. Tell the miners for me, that I shall promote their interests to the utmost of my ability; because their prosperity is the prosperity of the nation; and," said he, his eye kindling with enthusiasm, "we shall prove, in a very few years, that we are indeed the treasury of the world."

TO GENERAL VAN ALLEN.

EXECUTIVE MANSION, WASHINGTON, April 14, 1865

GENERAL VAN ALLEN:
I intend to adopt the advice of my friends and use due precaution.... I thank you for the assurance you give me that I shall be supported by conservative men like yourself, in the efforts I may make to restore the Union, so as to make it, to use your language, a Union of hearts and hands as well as of States.
Yours truly,
A. LINCOLN.

LINCOLN'S LAST WRITTEN WORDS

Allow Mr. Ashmer and friend to come in at 9 A.M. to-morrow.

A. LINCOLN. April 14, 1865

Note from the Editor.

Odin's Library Classics strives to bring you unedited and unabridged works of classical literature. As such this is the complete and unabridged version of the original. The English language has evolved since the writing and some of the words appear in their original form, or at least the form most commonly used at the time. This is done to protect the original intent of the author. If at any time you are unsure of the meaning of the original meaning of a word, please do your research on that word. It is important to preserve the history of the English language.

Taylor Anderson

Printed in Great Britain
by Amazon